SHEPPARD'S BRITISH ISLES

Companion Volumes

SHEPPARD'S DIRECTORIES

Directories of Antiquarian & Secondhand Book Dealers

SHEPPARD'S BOOK DEALERS
IN EUROPE

SHEPPARD'S BOOK DEALERS
IN JAPAN

SHEPPARD'S BOOK DEALERS
IN AUSTRALIA & NEW ZEALAND

SHEPPARD'S BOOK DEALERS
IN NORTH AMERICA

SHEPPARD'S BOOK DEALERS
IN INDIA AND THE ORIENT

SHEPPARD'S BOOK DEALERS
IN LATIN AMERICA & SOUTHERN AFRICA

Other Directories

SHEPPARD'S INTERNATIONAL
DIRECTORY OF PRINT AND
MAP SELLERS

A DIRECTORY OF BUSINESSES IN THIRTY-EIGHT COUNTRIES

SHEPPARD'S INTERNATIONAL
DIRECTORY OF EPHEMERA DEALERS

A DIRECTORY OF BUSINESSES IN TWENTY-ONE COUNTRIES

Dealers in all regions can be found on our searchable website:
www.sheppardsworld.co.uk

SHEPPARD'S BRITISH ISLES

THIRTIETH EDITION

A DIRECTORY OF ANTIQUARIAN AND SECONDHAND BOOK DEALERS IN THE UNITED KINGDOM, THE CHANNEL ISLANDS, THE ISLE OF MAN AND THE REPUBLIC OF IRELAND

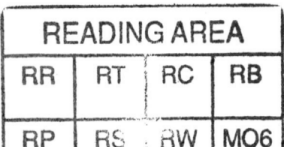

First Edition published 1951
Thirtieth published 2007

RICHARD JOSEPH PUBLISHERS LIMITED
P.O. BOX 15, TORRINGTON
DEVON EX38 8ZJ
ENGLAND
TEL: 01805 625750 FAX: 01805 625376

E-MAIL:
For book sales:
office@sheppardsworld.co.uk
For enquiries and subscription to
Sheppard's World
info@sheppardsworld.co.uk

I.S.S.N. 0950-0715
ISBN 978 1 872699 85 1

© RICHARD JOSEPH PUBLISHERS LIMITED 2007

MADE IN ENGLAND

Database and web site manager - Kevin Grimshire, www.atlanticweb.co.uk.
Printed and bound by
T J International, Padstow, Cornwall PL28 8RW

Editor's Note. Whilst every care is taken to ensure that the information given in this Directory is as accurate and complete as possible, the Publishers cannot accept any responsibility for any inaccuracies that occur or for any relevant information that was not available to the Publishers or its professional advisors at the time of going to press.

CONTENTS

SPECIALITY INDEX SUMMARY 8

INTRODUCTION 13

MISCELLANEOUS INFORMATION

Abbreviations	14
Sizes of Books	15
Metric Conversions	16
The British Book Trade	17

ANTIQUARIAN BOOKSELLERS' ASSOCIATIONS 20

PERIODICALS – Literary Magazines and Book Trade Papers 24

CURRENT REFERENCE BOOKS 26

SUPPLIES AND SERVICES

Appraisals and Valuations	32
Book Auctioneers	32
Book Display and Storage Equipment	33
Book Fair Organisers	34
Catalogue Printers	36
Craft Bookbinders	36
Packaging Materials Suppliers	39
Wholesalers and Distributors (New Book Trade)	39
Remainder Merchants	40
Suppliers of Materials & Tools for Binding and Restoring	41
Useful Websites	42

INDEX OF CITIES AND TOWNS 45

USE OF THE DIRECTORY 51

GEOGRAPHICAL DIRECTORY OF DEALERS

ENGLAND (see following pages)	53
THE CHANNEL ISLANDS	258
ISLE OF MAN	259
NORTHERN IRELAND	260
REPUBLIC OF IRELAND	262
SCOTLAND	268
WALES	283

ALPHABETICAL INDEXES

List of dealers by name of Business	295
List of dealers by name of Proprietor	311
Speciality Index (See following pages)	319
Booksearch Service	523
Large Print Books	526

DISPLAYED ADVERTISEMENT INDEX 528

CONTENTS

ENGLAND (by Counties)

BEDFORDSHIRE	53
BERKSHIRE	55
BRISTOL (incl. Unitary Authority of Bristol)	58
BUCKINGHAMSHIRE	61
CAMBRIDGESHIRE	63
CHESHIRE	68
CORNWALL	73
CUMBRIA	77
DERBYSHIRE	82
DEVON	84
DORSET	91
DURHAM (incl. Unitary Authorities of Darlington, Hartlepool & Stockton-on-Tees)	97
EAST SUSSEX	99
EAST YORKSHIRE (incl. Unitary Authorities of East Riding & Kingston-upon-Hull)	106
ESSEX	108
GLOUCESTERSHIRE (incl. Unitary Authority of South Gloucestershire)	113
GREATER MANCHESTER (incl. the Unitary Authorities of Bolton, Bury, Manchester, Oldham, Rochdale, Salford, Stockport, Tameside, Trafford & Wigan)	118
HAMPSHIRE	121
HEREFORDSHIRE	128
HERTFORDSHIRE	130
ISLE OF WIGHT	134
KENT	136
LANCASHIRE	143
LEICESTERSHIRE	147
LINCOLNSHIRE (incl. the Unitary Authorities of North East Lincolnshire & North Lincolnshire)	150
LONDON (EAST POSTAL DISTRICTS)	155
LONDON (EAST CENTRAL POSTAL DISTRICTS)	157
LONDON (NORTH POSTAL DISTRICTS)	158
LONDON (NORTH WEST POSTAL DISTRICTS)	161
LONDON (SOUTH EAST POSTAL DISTRICTS)	164
LONDON (SOUTH WEST POSTAL DISTRICTS)	167
LONDON (WEST POSTAL DISTRICTS)	172
LONDON (WEST CENTRAL POSTAL DISTRICTS)	177
LONDON (GREATER LONDON, OUTER)	181
MERSEYSIDE (incl. the Unitary Authorities of Knowsley, Liverpool, St. Helens, Sefton & Wirral)	185
NORFOLK	187
NORTH YORKSHIRE (incl. the Unitary Authorities of Cleveland, Middlesbrough, Redcar & York)	193
NORTHAMPTONSHIRE	200
NORTHUMBERLAND	202
NOTTINGHAMSHIRE	204
OXFORDSHIRE	206
RUTLAND	212
SHROPSHIRE	213
SOMERSET (incl. the Unitary Authorities of Bath & North East Somerset & North Somerset)	216
SOUTH YORKSHIRE (incl. the Unitary Authorities of Barnsley, Doncaster, Rotherham & Sheffield)	222
STAFFORDSHIRE	224
SUFFOLK	226
SURREY	231

CONTENTS

TYNE AND WEAR (incl. the Unitary Authorities of Gateshead,
Newcastle upon Tyne, North Tyneside, South Tyneside & Sunderland) 236
WARWICKSHIRE 237
WEST MIDLANDS (incl. the Unitary Authorities of Birmingham, Coventry,
Dudley, Sandwell, Solihull, Walsall & Wolverhampton) 239
WEST SUSSEX 242
WEST YORKSHIRE (incl. the Unitary Authorities of Bradford, Calderdale,
Kirklees, Leeds & Wakefield) 246
WILTSHIRE 251
WORCESTERSHIRE 255

ENGLAND (by Unitary Authorities)

To locate a dealer within a Unitary Authority, use the page references shown below in conjuction with the County Index shown above.

Barnsley 222	North Lincolnshire 150
Bath 216	North Tyneside 236
Birmingham 239	North Somerset 216
Bolton 118	Oldham 118
Bradford 246	Redcar 193
Bristol 58	Rochdale 118
Bury 118	Rotherham 222
Calderdale 246	St. Helens 185
Cleveland 193	Salford 118
Coventry 239	Sandwell 239
Darlington 97	Sefton 185
Doncaster 222	Sheffield 222
Dudley 239	Solihull 239
East Riding 106	South Gloucestershire 113
Gateshead 236	South Tyneside 236
Hartlepool 97	Stockport 118
Kingston-upon-Hull 106	Stockton-on-Tees 97
Kirklees 246	Sunderland 236
Knowsley 185	Tameside 118
Leeds 246	Trafford 118
Liverpool 185	Wakefield 246
Manchester 118	Walsall 239
Middlesbrough 193	Wigan 118
Newcastle upon Tyne 236	Wirral 185
North East Lincolnshire 150	Wolverhampton 239
North East Somerset 216	York 193

SPECIALITY INDEX

The following list has been created from the subjects provided by dealers' entry forms

Aboriginal...................... 319
Academic/Scholarly 319
Accountancy.................... 320
Acupuncture.................... 320
Adirondack Mountains, The 320
Adult............................. 320
Adventure...................... 320
Advertising..................... 321
Aeronautics 321
Aesthetic Movement 321
Aesthetics 321
African American Studies ... 321
Africana 321
Agriculture..................... 322
Aids Crisis, The................ 322
Aircraft.......................... 322
Alchemy......................... 323
Almanacs........................ 323
Alpinism/Mountaineering ... 323
Alternative Medicine 323
Amatuer Radio 323
American Indians.............. 323
American Northwet 324
American Revolution 324
Americana 324
Americana Southwest 324
Amish............................ 324
Amusements 324
Anatomy 324
Animals and Birds............ 324
Annuals 325
Anthologies 325
Anthropology 325
Anthroposophy 326
Anti-Semitism 326
Antiquarian..................... 326
Antique Paper.................. 328
Antique Stoves 328
Antiques......................... 328
Antiquitities.................... 329
Apiculture...................... 329
Applied Art..................... 329
Aquatics......................... 329
Arabica 329
Arachnology.................... 330
Archaeology 330
Archaeology
– Industrial 330
Architecture.................... 331
– Theatre 332
Archives 332
Armed Forces
– Australian Air Force....... 332
– Australian Army............ 332
– Australian Navy 332
Arms and Armour............. 332
Army, The 332

Art - General 333
– Afro-American 335
– British......................... 335
– Technique 335
– Theory........................ 335
Art Deco 336
Art History..................... 336
Art Nouveau................... 336
Art Reference.................. 337
Arthurian 337
Artists 338
Artists - Chicago 338
Arts & Crafts Era 338
Arts, The 338
Asian Studies 339
Asian-American Studies...... 339
Assassinations 339
Astrology 339
Astronautics.................... 339
Astronomy 339
Atlases 339
Auction Catalogues 340
Audio/Sound/Acoustics 340
Australiana 340
Author
– General 340
– Specific (A–Z) 340
Authors
– Australian 360
– British......................... 360
– Local........................... 360
– National....................... 360
– Women 360
Autism 361
Autobiography 361
Autographs..................... 361
Autolithography............... 361
Automata 362
Automobilia/Automotive 362
Avant-Garde 362
Aviation 362
Award Winners................ 363
Ayurveda 363

Bacteriology.................... 363
Bamboo......................... 363
Banking and Insurance....... 363
Beat Writers.................... 363
Beer.............................. 363
Bell-Ringing (Campanology) 363
Belle-Lettres.................... 363
Bibles............................ 363
Biblical Studies 364
Bibliography 364
Bibliophily...................... 364
Bindings 364
Biochemistry 365

Biography....................... 365
Biology 366
– Marine 367
Black Studies 367
Book of Hours................. 367
Bohemianism 367
Book Arts....................... 367
Book of Hours................. 367
Bookbinding.................... 367
Books about Books 367
Books in Greek 368
Botany........................... 368
Brewing 368
Braziliana 368
Bridge 368
British Art & Design......... 368
British Books.................. 368
Broadcasting................... 369
Building and Construction .. 369
Bull Fighting 369
Buses/Trams.................... 369
Bushmen 369
Business Studies............... 369
Byzantium 369

Calligraphy 369
Canadiana 370
Canals/Inland Waterways ... 370
Caricature....................... 370
Carpets 370
Carriages and Driving 370
Cartography.................... 370
Cartoons 370
Catalogues Raisonné......... 371
Catering & Hotel
Management.................. 371
Cats.............................. 371
Cattlemen 371
Celtica 371
Cemeteries 371
Censorship...................... 371
Ceramics 371
Charity 371
Chemistry....................... 371
Chess 372
Children's – General 372
– Early Titles................... 374
– Illustrated.................... 374
Christmas 375
Churchilliana 375
Cinema/Film 375
Circus............................ 376
Cities............................. 376
- City of London 376
- New York.................... 376
Civil Engineering 376
Civil Rights..................... 377

SPECIALITY INDEX

Classical Studies 377
Classics, The.................... 377
Climatology...................... 377
Coastal Defence................. 377
Cockfighting 377
Coffee............................ 377
Collectables 377
Collecting 378
Colonial 378
Colour-Plate 378
Comedy 378
Comic Books and
Annuals........................ 378
Comics........................... 379
Commerce - General 379
Commercial Vehicles 379
Communication 379
Communism 379
Company History............... 379
Computing....................... 380
Conchology 380
Conservation 380
Conspiracy 380
Cookery - Professional........ 380
Cookery/Gastronomy 380
Cosmology....................... 381
Counselling 381
Counterculture 381
Counties in England........... 381
Countries and Regions
– General........................ 381
– Specific (A–Z)................ 381
Country Houses................. 393
County - Local.................. 393
Courtesy.......................... 393
Cowboys 393
Crafts 393
Crime (True).................... 394
Criminal Law.................... 394
Criminology 394
Critical Theory.................. 394
Crochet 395
Crustacea......................... 395
Cryptography.................... 395
Cryptozoology................... 395
Cults 395
Culture
– Foreign......................... 395
– National........................ 395
– Popular......................... 395
Cuneiform Studies 395
Curiosa 395
Curiosities........................ 395
Current Affairs 395
Customs & Excise 395
Cybernetics 395

D.I.Y (Do It Yourself)........ 395
Dadaism.......................... 395
Dance............................. 395
Death & Funerals............... 396
Decorative Art 396
Deep Sea Diving................ 396
Demography..................... 396
Dentistry 396

Design 396
Diaries 396
Dictionaries...................... 396
Dinosaurs 397
Directories - General.......... 397
– British 397
Disneyana........................ 397
Divining 397
Documents - General 397
Dogs.............................. 397
Dolls and Dolls' Houses...... 397
Domesticity...................... 397
Drama 398
Drawing 398
Drugs............................. 398
Dyes............................... 398

Early Imprints................... 398
Earth Mysteries 398
Earth Sciences................... 398
Easter 398
Eastern Philosophy............. 398
Ecclesiastical History and
Architecture................... 399
Ecology 399
Economics 399
Education and School......... 400
Egyptology....................... 400
Electricty & Gas 400
Electronics 400
Emblemata 400
Embroidery 400
Enamel 400
Encaustic Art.................... 400
Encyclopaedias 401
Energy - General............... 401
– Alternative..................... 401
– Fuels............................ 401
– Power........................... 401
Engineering - General......... 401
– Electrical....................... 401
English............................ 401
Engraving 401
Entertainment 401
Entomology...................... 401
Environment, The 402
Erotica 402
Eskimos 402
Esoteric........................... 402
Espionage 402
Ethics 402
Ethnobotany..................... 403
Ethnography..................... 403
Ethnology........................ 403
Etiquette.......................... 403
European Books 403
European Studies 403
Evolution......................... 403
Ex-Libris 403
Examination Papers 403
Exhibitions....................... 403
Exotic Books 403
Expeditions 403
Exploration - General......... 403
–Polar............................. 404

Explosives 404
Expressionism 404

Fables............................. 404
Fairgrounds...................... 404
Fairy/Folk Tales 404
Family 404
Famous People (A-Z) 404
Farming & Livestock.......... 405
Farriers 405
Fashion and Costume......... 405
Feminism......................... 405
Fiction
– General......................... 406
– 18th Century 407
– Adventure...................... 407
– Crime, Detective, Spy,
Thrillers....................... 407
– Fantasy, Horror 408
– Gay Fiction.................... 409
– Historical 409
– Romantic 409
– Science Fiction................ 409
– Supernatural................... 410
– Westerns 410
– Women......................... 410
– Young Adult Mystery &
Adventure 410
Fictional Chracters 410
Finance 410
Fine and Rare 410
Fine Art 411
Fine Leather Bindings......... 412
Fine Printing..................... 412
Fire and Firefighters........... 412
Firearms/Guns 412
First Editions.................... 412
Fisheries.......................... 413
Fishes 414
Flags 414
Flora & Fauna 414
Flower Arranging............... 414
Folio Society, The 414
Folklore 415
Food and Drink................. 415
Fore-Edge Paintings........... 415
Foreign Texts.................... 415
Forestry 416
Fossils 416
Fourth Way...................... 416
Free Thought.................... 416
Freemasonry and
Anti-Masonry................. 416
French Foreign Legion 416
Freudiana 416
Fruitarianism 416
Fungi.............................. 416
Fur Trade 416
Furniture 416

Gambling......................... 416
Games 417
Gandhiana 417
Gardening - General 417
– Organic......................... 417

SPECIALITY INDEX

Gemmology..................... 418
Gender Studies 418
Genealogy...................... 418
Genetics 418
Geography 418
Geology 418
Geophysics..................... 418
Ghosts......................... 419
Glamour........................ 419
Glass........................... 419
Gnostics 419
Gold Rush 419
Goldsmiths..................... 419
Gothic Revival 419
Grand Canyon &
Colorado River, The 419
Graphic Novels 419
Graphics....................... 419
Graphology 419
Graveyards..................... 419
Guide Books.................... 419
Gynaecology.................... 420
Gypsies 420

Hairdressing 420
Halloween...................... 420
Hand Bookbinding 420
Handwriting 420
Handwritten Books............ 420
Health 420
Hebraica........................ 420
Heraldry 420
Herbalism 420
Heredity 420
Heritage 421
Hermeticism 421
Herpetology.................... 421
Himalayan Kingdoms......... 421
Hispanica 421
History
– General....................... 421
– Specific (A–Z)................ 423
History of Civilisation 429
History of Ideas................ 429
Hobbies 429
Holocaust 430
Home Improvements.......... 430
Homeopathy.................... 430
Homosexuality and
Lesbianism 430
Horizon Writers................ 430
Horology....................... 430
Horses 430
Horticulture.................... 430
Hospitals 431
Housekeeping................... 431
Hudson Bay Company........ 431
Humanism 431
Humanities..................... 431
Humour 431
Hydrography 431
Hymnology 431
Hypnotism 431

I-Ching 431

Ichthyology 431
Iconography....................432
Illuminated Manuscripts 432
Illustrated - General...........432
– 19th & 20th Century 433
Illustrators......................433
Imaginary Voyages 433
Immigration....................433
Immunology 433
Imprints 433
Incunabula 433
Industrial Design...............434
Industry........................434
Institutions.....................434
Interior Design 434
International Affairs...........434
Inventors & Inventions........434
Investments 434
Iridology.......................434
Irish Interest 434
Islands 435

Jewellery 435
Journalism......................435
Journals - General 435
– Maritime 435
Judaica.........................435
Jungiana 435
Juvenile 435

Kabbala/Cabbala/Cabala 436
Knitting........................436
Ku Klux Klan 436

Lace 436
Landscape 436
Languages
– African 436
– Ancient 436
– Foreign 436
– National......................437
– Pidgin and Creole............437
Law - General 437
– Constitutional................437
Legal Paperwork 437
Leninism.......................437
Lepidopterology................437
Lettering.......................437
Letterpress Broadsides 437
Letters 437
Libertarianism 437
Libraries - Everyman's........437
Library Science 437
Limited Editions - General...438
– Club Books 438
Linguistics.....................438
Literacy 438
Literary Criticism 438
Literary Travel 439
Literature
– General 439
– 17th Century.................442
– 19th Century.................442
– African 442
– African-American............442

– Canadian 442
– French 442
– German 442
– Irish 442
– New Zealand................. 442
– Proletariat 442
– Scottish 442
– South African................ 442
– Spanish 443
– Victorian..................... 443
– Western American 443
Literature in Translation 443
Liturgies........................ 443
Local Studies - Sussex 443
Locks and Locksmiths........ 443
Logging/Lumbering 443
Logic 443
Lost civilizations............... 443

Mafia 443
Magazines & Periodicals
– General 443
– Women's..................... 444
Magic & Conjuring 444
Magic Lanterns 444
Magick 444
Magnetism...................... 444
Malacology..................... 444
Mammals 444
Management 444
Manuals
– General 444
– Seamanship 444
Manufacturing 444
Manuscripts 444
Maori........................... 445
Maps & Mapmaking.......... 445
Marine Sciences................ 445
Maritime/Nautical
– General 445
– History....................... 446
– Log Books 446
Marque Histories
(see also motoring) 447
Marxism 447
Mathematics.................... 447
Mayflower, Voyage of 1620.. 447
Mechanical Engineering....... 447
Media 447
Medicine 447
Medicine - History of......... 448
Medieval 448
Memoirs 448
Memorabilia.................... 448
Metaphysics 448
Meteorology.................... 449
Mexicana 449
Microscopy 449
Military - General.............. 449
– History....................... 450
– Modelling.................... 451
– Uniforms 452
Mind, Body and Spirit 452
Mineralogy 452
Miniature Books............... 452

SPECIALITY INDEX

Mining.......................... 452
Minority Studies............. 452
Missionaries & Missions..... 452
Model Engineering 452
Model Railways................ 453
Model Theatre 453
Modern.......................... 453
Modern Art.................... 453
Modern First Editions 453
Monographs................... 454
Motorbikes 454
Motoring....................... 454
Mountain Men................. 455
Mountains 455
Moveable & 3D............... 455
Movie & Television Scripts . 455
Music
– General....................... 455
– Specific (A–Z)............... 456
Musical Instruments
– General...................... 459
– Guitars....................... 459
Musicians 459
Mycology 460
Mysteries....................... 460
Mysticism 460
Mythology..................... 460

National Geographic.......... 460
National Parks 460
Native American.............. 460
Native Canadian.............. 460
Natural Health 460
Natural History 460
Natural Sciences 462
Nature.......................... 463
Naturism 463
Naval........................... 463
Navigation 463
Navy, The...................... 463
Needlework 464
Neurology...................... 464
New Age 464
New Naturalist................ 464
New World 465
Newbery & Caldecott
Award Winners 465
Newspapers 465
Non-Fiction.................... 465
Nostalgia....................... 465
Novelty......................... 465
Nuclear Issues 465
Numerology 465
Numismatics................... 465
Nursery Rhymes 465
Nurses / Doctors.............. 465

Occult........................... 465
Ocean Liners 466
Oceanography 466
Odd & Unusual............... 466
Oil Industry.................... 466
Oil Lamps...................... 466

Old West 466
Ophthalmology................466
Optical..........................466
Orders, Decorations &
Medals.........................466
Organs..........................466
Oriental.........................466
Ornithology....................466
Osteopathy.....................467
Ottoman Empire..............467
Out of Print....................467
Outdoors 467
Outlaws.........................467
Oxford Movement 467

Pacifism.........................468
Paddleboats....................468
Paganism 468
Painting.........................468
Palaeography 468
Palaeontology..................468
Palmistry and Fortune
Telling.........................468
Pantomime.....................468
Paper Collectables 468
Papermaking...................468
Parapsychology................468
Parish Registers 469
Parks & Gardens...............469
Passenger Liners...............469
Patents..........................469
Pathology.......................469
Performing Arts................469
Periodicals and Magazines
– see under Magazines and
Periodicals
Petroleum Geology 469
Petroluem Technology 469
Pharmacy/Pharmacology.....469
Phenomena.....................469
Philately 469
Philology 470
Philosophy 470
Phonology......................471
Photography...................471
Phrenology.....................471
Physical Culture...............471
Physics..........................471
Physioology....................471
Pigs..............................471
Pilgrims.........................471
Pioneers.........................471
Pirates...........................471
Planning - City 472
Plant Hunting..................472
Plato 472
Plays 472
Poetry...........................472
Police Force Histories........473
Political History...............473
Politics..........................473
Pomolgy........................474
Pop-Up, 3D, Cut Out and
Movable 474

Pornography 474
Pottery & Glass............... 474
Poultry 474
Prayer Books................... 474
Pre-Raphaelite 475
Precious Metals - Silver 475
Prehistory...................... 475
Presidential 475
Printed Textiles 475
Printing
– General 475
– Nth of England Provincial. 475
– Printing and Mind of Man 475
Private Press................... 475
Proof Copies 476
Prostitution.................... 476
Provinces of Canada......... 476
Psychic 476
Physic Surgery 476
Psychoanalysis 476
Psychokiness 476
Psychology/Psychiatry 476
Psychotherapy................. 477
Public Administration 477
Public Health................... 477
Public Houses.................. 477
Public Schools 477
Public Transport.............. 477
Publishers
– General 477
– Specific (A–Z)............... 477
Publishing...................... 480
Pulps............................. 480
Punk Fazines................... 480
Puppets and Marionettes.... 480
Puzzles 480

Quakers, The.................. 480

Radar............................ 480
Radical Issues.................. 480
Radio/Wireless................ 480
Radiology....................... 480
Railways & Railroads 480
Rationalism.................... 481
Reference 481
Registers 482
Religion
– General 482
– Specific (A–Z)............... 482
Religious Texts 485
Revolutions.................... 485
Rhetoric........................ 485
Rhodesia 485
River Boats & River Men... 485
River Thames 485
Rock Art........................ 485
Romance........................ 485
Romanticism 485
Ropemaking & Knots 485
Rosicrucianism................ 485
Royalty
– General 485
– European 486

SPECIALITY INDEX

Roycroft........................ 486
Rubaiyat of Omar Khayyam 486
Rugs 486
Rupert Bear 486
Rural Life....................... 486
Russian History................ 486

Salvation Army 486
Satire............................. 486
School Registers/Rolls
of Honour.................... 487
Schools - General.............. 487
Science
– General........................ 487
– Food........................... 487
– Forensic....................... 487
– History of..................... 487
– Pure and Applied............ 488
Scientific Instruments 488
Scientists 488
Scottish Enlightenment 488
Scottish Interest................ 488
Scouts and Guides............. 489
Scrimshaw....................... 489
Sculpture 489
Sea-Faring & Shipping........ 489
Seamanship 489
Secret Societies 489
Seeds............................. 489
Self-Help 489
Self-Improvement 489
Self-Sufficiency 490
Sets of Books................... 490
Sette of Odd Volumes......... 490
Sexology......................... 490
Sheep/Shepherding 490
Shell County Guides 490
Sherlockiana 490
Ship Modelling.................. 490
Shipbuilding & Shipping...... 490
Shipwrecks 491
Shorthand....................... 491
Sigillography.................... 491
Signed Editions 491
Silversmiths 491
Sixties, The 491
Slavery........................... 491
Small Press Published Books 491
Social Economics 491
Social History 491
Social Sciences 492
Socialism 492
Sociology......................... 492
South Seas 492
South Australiana 493
South Seas 493
Southern Americana 493
Space............................. 493
Spanish Literature 493
Special Collections............. 493
Spiritism......................... 493
Spiritual 493
Spiritualism 493
Sport
– General........................ 493

– Specific (A–Z) 494
Stage 500
Stained Glass 500
States of America 500
States of Australia 500
Statistics 500
Steam Engines..................500
Statistics 500
Steam Engines..................500
Stone Masonry 500
Student Activism...............500
Suffragettes.....................500
Suffism...........................500
Sundials..........................500
Supernatural 500
Surgery...........................501
Surrealism 501
Surveying........................501
Survival..........................501
Symbolism.......................501

Tapestry 501
Taxation 501
Taxidermy.......................501
Tea 501
Teaching.........................501
Technical 501
Technology......................501
Teddy Bears.....................501
Telegraph........................502
Television........................502
Terrorism/Guerilla Warfare .. 502
Teutonic History & Culture.. 502
Texana 502
Textbooks 502
Textiles...........................502
Theatre...........................502
Theology.........................503
Theosophy......................503
Therapy – Marital & Family.. 503
Timber Technology 503
Tobacco 503
Topography
– General........................504
– Local...........................505
Topology 508
Town Planning 508
Town Plans 508
Toys..............................508
Traction Engines 508
Trade Catalogues 508
Trade Unions 508
Trades & Professions 508
Traditional Chinese Medicine . 508
Traditions 508
Transport........................508
Travel
– General........................509
– Specific (A–Z) 511
Trials.............................514
Tribal 514
Tropical Fish 514
Trotskyism 514
Typography 514

U-Boats 514
U.F.O.s 515
U.S. Presidents................. 515
Umbrellas/Parasols............ 515
Unexplained, The.............. 515
University Histories 515
University Press................. 515
University Texts 515
Urban History 515
Utopias........................... 515

Vatican and Papal
History, The.................. 515
Vegetariasm 515
Ventriloquism 515
Veterinary 515
Victorian Multi-Deckers...... 515
Victoriana 515
Vintage Cars 516
Vintage Paperbacks 516
Virology.......................... 516
Visual............................. 516
Viticulture 516
Voyages and Discovery....... 516

War
– General 517
– Specific (A–Z)................ 517
Wargames 520
Washing......................... 520
Watercolours 520
Wayside and Woodland...... 520
Weapons 520
Weird and Wonderful 520
Welsh Interest................... 520
Western Americana 520
Whaling 520
Whisky 521
Windmills and Watermills ... 521
Wine.............................. 521
Witchcraft 521
Women........................... 521
Woodland Crafts 521
Woodwork....................... 521
World Fairs & Exhibitions... 522
Wristwatches 522
Writing & Writing Rquipment 522

X-ray 522

Year Books...................... 522
Yoga.............................. 522
Youth Movements 522

Zoology 522
Zoos 522

INTRODUCTION

With each edition, we try to improve the information published and this year is no exception and included in this, the thirtieth edition, are many changes. In the preliminary pages a new section has been added listing dealers who carry out Appraisals and Valuations; in the Geographical Section, additional free text entered by dealers appears for the first time, and the Speciality Index has increased by 35% – a result of dealers listing more 'speciality subjects' on our Sheppard's World website. And Sheppard's Confidential has continued to grow too.

Our site has seen a significant increase in traffic - it attracted over 200,000 hits in the last year. Sheppard's World caters not just for dealers in the British Isles but overseas as well and as we go to press, there are well over 4,400 in 36 countries. There is a steady growth in numbers despite the removal of those dealers with whom we have lost contact and where it has not been possible to contact via the Internet or telephone.

The other feature is the surge in the number of Speciality Book Classifications stated as being a major specialisation (or that they hold a significant list of titles in that subject). This has worked successfully over the years and most organisations listing dealers and their businesses have limited these to just a few. But the Intenet has changed this - as even small groups of titles in a subject can be easily entered for searching and we have allowed this trend to continue. For users of the directory this has real advantages today and potential disadvantages in the future.

The consequence this year - is a 35% growth in the entries in the Index. There was an increase of over 200 in the last edition but 520 in this edition. Under the heading of nominated Authors, there has been an increase of over 110 - and this edition lists over 380 named authors of which dealers have many titles. As we list dealers who are not on the Internet - this must make the directory more useful than the Internet alone.

But clearly, if this growth in the index continues, the extra cost will make the cover price too high and that would be self-defeating. In the last edition of Sheppard's North America we placed this index as a PDF file on a CD and to date we have not received any criticism - so we might be forced to do this with all future editions. The result of this huge index is that it makes the directory even more important as an off-line - and conventional - source for locating dealers who have books on a particular subject.

Statistics are still not as comprehensive as we would like but this edition has 1,920 businesses listed. In quoting trade statistics, it is important to remember that they are based on information supplied to us (ie from dealers who have confirmed their entry or updated it on-line) and not a definitive total for the British Isles. As always, our database has many more dealers based in the British Isles which we will continue to refine as each month passes. Based on the information supplied for this year, there are 705 trading from shops (no change year on year), and 936 (up by 71) trading from private premises. The balance of dealers trade solely via the Internet, or from a combination of storerooms, warehouses, offices or showrooms. Most dealers are, of course, linked to the Internet and the total recorded with e-mail addresses in this edition is 1,606 an increase of 85.

For dealers who wish to register for the first time, there are two methods open. Those who are not linked to the Internet can write to us for a free dealer entry form, and those who can access our website, may register on-line. The site address is www .sheppardsworld.co.uk and the postal address is: The Editor, Richard Joseph Publishers Ltd, PO Box 15, Torrington, Devon, EX38 8ZJ.

Richard Joseph, April 2007

ABBREVIATIONS USED IN DESCRIBING BOOKS

Some booksellers and buyers use highly individualistic systems of abbreviations and others have adapted traditional terms for the Internet. The following are sufficiently well known to be generally used, but all other words should be written in full, and the whole typed if possible. Condition is described by the following scale:– Mint – Fine – Very good – Good – Fair – Poor

Abbreviation	Meaning	Abbreviation	Meaning
A.D.	Autograph document	Lea.	Leather
A.D.s.	Autograph document, signed	Ll.	Levant Morocco
A.D.*	Autograph document with seal	Ll.	Leaves
A.e.g.	All edges gilt	L.P.	Large paper
A.L.s.	Autograph letter, signed	M.	Mint
a.v.	Authorized version	Mco., mor	Morocco
B.A.R.	Book Auction Records	M.e.	Marbled edges
Bd.	Bound	M.S.(S.)	Manuscripts
Bdg.	Binding	N.d.	No date
Bds.	Boards	n.ed.	new edition
B.L.	Black letter	n.p.	no place (of publication)
C., ca.	Circa (approximately)	Ob., obl.	Oblong
C. & p.	Collated and perfect	Oct.	Octavo
Cat.	Catalogue	O.p.	Out of print
Cent.	Century	P.	Page
Cf.	Calf	P.f.	Post free
C.I.F.	Cost, insurance and freight	Pict.	Pictorial
Cl.	Cloth	Pl(s).	Plate(s)
Col(d).	Colour(ed)	Port.	Portrait
C.O.D.	Cash on delivery	P.P.	Printed privately
Cont.	Contemporary	Pp.	Pages
C.O.R.	Cash on receipt	Prelims.	Preliminary pages
Cr. 8vo.	Crown octavo	Pseud.	Pseudonym(ous)
d.e.	Deckle edges	Ptd.	Printed
Dec.	Decorated	q.v.	Quod Vide (which see)
D-j., d-w.	Dust jacket, dust wrapper	Qto.	Quarto
E.D.L.	Edition de luxe	Rev.	Revised
Edn.	Edition	Rom.	Roman letter
Endp., e.p.	Endpaper(s)	S.L.	Sine loco (without place of
Eng., engr.	Engraved, engraving		publication)
Ex-lib.	Ex-library	Sgd.	Signed
Facs.	Facsimile	Sig.	Signature
Fcp.	Foolscap	S.N.	Sine nomine (without name
F.	Fine		of printer)
F.,ff.	Folio, folios	Spr.	Sprinkled
Fo., fol.	Folio (book size)	T.e.g.	Top edge gilt
F.O.B.	Free on board	Thk.	Thick
Fp., front.	Frontispiece	T.L.s.	Typed letter, signed
Free	Post Free	T.p.	Title page
G.	Good	T.S.	Typescript
G., gt.	Gilt edges	Unbd.	Unbound
G.L.	Gothic letter	Uncut	Uncut (pages not trimmed)
Hf. bd.	Half bound	Und.	Undated
Illum.	Illuminated	V.d.	Various dates
Ill(s).	Illustrated, illustrations	V.g..	Very good
Imp.	Imperial	Vol,	Volume
Impft.	Imperfect	W.a.f.	With all faults
Inscr.	Inscribed, inscription	Wraps.	Wrappers
Ital.	Italic letter		

SIZES OF BOOKS

These are only approximate, as trimming varies and all sizes ignore the overlap of a book case.

	Octavo (8vo)		Quarto (4to)	
	Inches	*Centimetres*	*Inches*	*Centimetres*
FOOLSCAP	$6^3/4$ x $4^1/4$	17.1 x 10.8	$8^1/2$ x $6^3/4$	21.5 x 17.1
CROWN	$7^1/2$ x 5	19.0 x 12.7	10 x $7^1/2$	25.4 x 19.0
LARGE POST	$8^1/4$ x $5^1/4$	20.9 x 13.3	$10^1/2$ x $8^1/4$	26.6 x 20.9
DEMY	$8^3/8$ x $5^5/8$	22.3 x 14.2	$11^1/4$ x $8^3/4$	28.5 x 22.2
MEDIUM	9 x $5^3/4$	22.8 x 14.6	$11^1/2$ x 9	29.2 x 22.8
ROYAL	10 x $6^1/4$	25.4 x 15.8	$12^1/2$ x 10	31.7 x 25.4
SUPER ROYAL	$10^1/4$ x $6^3/4$	26.0 x 17.5	$13^3/4$ x $10^1/4$	34.9 x 26.0
IMPERIAL	11 x $7^1/2$	27.9 x 19.0	15 x 11	38.0 x 27.9
FOOLSCAP FOLIO			$13^1/2$ x $8^1/2$	34.2 x 21.5
METRIC A5	$8^1/4$ x $5^7/8$	21.0 x 14.8		
A4	$11^3/4$ x $8^1/4$	29.7 x 21.0		
'A' FORMAT PAPERBACK		17.8 X 11.1		
'B' FORMAT PAPERBACK		19 8 X 12.9		

BRITISH PAPER SIZES (untrimmed)

Sizes of Printing Papers

	Inches	*Centimetres*
Foolscap	17 x $13^1/2$	43.2 x 34.3
Double Foolscap	27 x 17	68.6 x 43.2
Crown	20 x 15	50.8 x 38.1
Double Crown	30 x 20	76.2 x 50.8
Quad Crown	40 x 30	101.6 x 76.2
Double Quad Crown	60 x 40	152.4 x 101.6
Post	$19^1/4$ x $15^1/2$	48.9 x 39.4
Double Post	$31^1/2$ x $19^1/2$	80.0 x 49.5
Double Large Post	33 x 21	83.8 x 53.3
Sheet and $^1/2$ Post	$23^1/2$ x $19^1/2$	59.7 x 49.5
Demy	$22^1/2$ x $17^1/2$	57.2 x 44.5
Double Demy	35 x $22^1/2$	88.9 x 57.2
Quad Demy	45 x 35	114.3 x 88.9
Music Demy	20 x $15^1/2$	50.8 x 39.4
Medium	23 x 18	58.4 x 45.7
Royal	25 x 20	63.5 x 50.8
Super Royal	$27^1/2$ x $20^1/2$	69.9 x 52.1
Elephant	28 x 23	71.1 x 58.4
Imperial	30 x 22	76.2 x 55.9

Available from Richard Joseph Publishers Ltd
Sheppard's Book Dealers in NORTH AMERICA
15th Edition (Royal H/b plus CD-ROM) £30.00 560pp

METRIC CONVERSIONS

SIZES

inches	m.m.		inches	m.m.
$^1/_4$	6		$7^3/_4$	197
$^1/_2$	13		8	203
$^3/_4$	19		$8^1/_4$	210
1	25		$8^1/_2$	216
$1^1/_4$	32		$8^3/_4$	222
$1^1/_2$	38		9	229
$1^3/_4$	44		$9^1/_4$	235
2	51		$9^1/_2$	241
$2^1/_4$	57		$9^3/_4$	248
$2^1/_2$	64		10	254
$2^3/_4$	70		$10^1/_4$	260
3	76		$10^1/_2$	267
$3^1/_4$	83		$10^3/_4$	273
$3^1/_2$	89		11	279
$3^3/_4$	95		$11^1/_4$	286
4	102		$11^1/_2$	292
$4^1/_4$	108		$11^3/_4$	298
$4^1/_2$	114		12	305
$4^3/_4$	121		$12^1/_4$	311
5	127		$12^1/_2$	318
$5^1/_4$	133		$12^3/_4$	324
$5^1/_2$	140		13	330
$5^3/_4$	146		$13^1/_4$	337
6	152		$13^1/_2$	343
$6^1/_4$	159		$13^3/_4$	349
$6^1/_2$	165		14	356
$6^3/_4$	171		$14^1/_4$	362
7	178		$14^1/_2$	368
$7^1/_4$	184		$14^3/_4$	375
$7^1/_2$	191		15	381

To convert inches to millimetres multiply by 25.4. Millimetres to inches may be found by multiplying by .0394.

WEIGHTS

lbs.	kgs.
1	0.45
2	0.91
3	1.36
4	1.81
5	2.27
6	2.72
7	3.18
8	3.63
9	4.08
10	4.54
11	4.99
12	5.44
13	5.90
14	6.35
15	6.80
16	7.26
17	7.71
18	8.16
19	8.62
20	9.07
21	9.53
22	9.98
23	10.43
24	10.89
25	11.34
26	11.79
27	12.25
28	12.70
56	25.40
112	50.80

To convert pounds to kilogrammes multiply by .4536. Kilogrammes to pounds may be found by multiplying by 2.205.

Looking for a dealer in the BRITISH ISLES?

Search on www.sheppardsworld.co.uk
or
reserve a copy of the next printed edition

THE BRITISH BOOK TRADE

NEW BOOKS

In the United Kingdom, marketing of new books is well organised and controlled by individual publishers. However, the British Book Trade has two highly organised trade associations, The Publishers Association and The Booksellers Association which represent a vast majority of their respective parts of the trade.

The Booksellers Association publishes an annual directory of members, listing 'over 4,400 retail outlets' in the current edition. This is an essential reference source used by all publishers. In addition, the Booksellers Association publishes an annual directory of book publishers, distributors and wholesalers.

The directory of B.A. Members includes not only general booksellers, but businesses that concentrate on specific subjects. Although, in fact, it confers no right to buy books at trade terms, entry in this directory confirms to publishers that they are eligible for trade terms.

Bibliographic information is supplied to the book trade through Nielsen BookData Ltd. Publishers supply information on the titles they have published and this is disseminated by this company to booksellers. Users of this directory will note the growing importance of this information in relation to the secondhand book trade

THE BOOKSELLERS ASSOCIATION OF THE UNITED KINGDOM AND IRELAND LIMITED, 272 Vauxhall Bridge Road, London SW1V 1BA. Tel: (020) 7802-0802. Fax: (020) 7802-0803. E-Mail: mail@booksellers.org.uk. Web Site: www.booksellers.org.uk. Est: 1895 as the Associated Booksellers of Great Britain and Ireland and changed to its present name in 1999. Chief Executive: Tim Godfray. The Association's aims are: to provide services to help members increase book sales and develop the market for new books; to assist members to reduce costs; to improve distribution between publishers, booksellers and consumers; to represent booksellers' interests; and to provide a forum for members to discuss matters of common interest. It is not concerned with the secondhand or antiquarian trade: membership is open to all those engaged in the sale of new books, some of whom also sell secondhand and antiquarian books. The Association is governed by an Annual General MeetingConference and a Council which meets four times a year, delegating much work to specialist committees and encouraging members to join groups concerned with academic bookselling, Christian bookselling, children's bookselling etc. National Book Tokens, and batch.co.uk - an electronic clearing house for the payment of accounts – are some of the services provided for members. The Association is linked with similar bodies overseas.

THE PUBLISHERS ASSOCIATION, 29B Montague Street, London WC1B 5BW. Tel: (020) 7691-9191. Fax: 7691-9199. E-Mail: mail@publishers.org.uk. Web: www.publishers.org.uk. Est: 1896. President: Stephen Page. Chief Executive: Ronnie Williams. Including the Trade Publishers Council, International Division, the Educational Publishers Council (School Books division), the Academic and Professional Publishers Division the Electronic Publishers Forum. The Association represents the interests of UK publishers of books, electronic publications and journals to governments, other bodies in the trade and the public at large. It seeks to promote the sales of British books by all suitable means, and provides members with a wide range of services and help on publishing problems and opportunities.

SECONDHAND AND ANTIQUARIAN BOOKS

Anyone who is so minded can enter this branch of the trade without any formality at all and, indeed, book lovers and collectors, buying items for their own libraries and selling duplicate or unwanted copies, have sometimes, almost unwittingly, drifted into a habit of rather casual regular dealing. This sounds easy and pleasant but, to enter seriously into business and make a profit in any way commensurate with the work involved, a great deal of expert knowledge is required.

Some dealers have large and impressive premises, but retail shops are still relatively few as most dealers now work from warehouses, storerooms, and private premises, and using the Internet as their sales platform.

THE BRITISH BOOK TRADE

In addition to these outlets, there are numerous book fairs of varying size around the country from which dealers trade. Recently, there has been a resurgence of conventional selling methods as more dealers are also issuing catalogues again.

While most dealers in second-hand and antiquarian books will try to obtain for a customer any required item which they do not have in stock, many specialists will now refer requests outside their speciality to other dealers.

The Internet has become a very useful tool to search for titles. In some respects, websites devoted to the second-hand and antiquarian book trade are better organised than those for the new book trade. Those seeking information about this aspect will find *Sheppard's World* (www.sheppardsworld.co.uk) very useful and there are others, most of which are listed on page forty-two.

The current weekly newsletter, *Sheppard's Confidential* now provides the trade with calendars of auctions, book fairs, trade events, profiles, letters, and reviews of books and catalogues. The newsletter is supplied free to all dealers listed in Sheppard's directories.

A distinctive feature of the second-hand book trade, however, is its high degree of specialisation. Almost every dealer has a particular interest, and some will be found who deal only in books on one subject, or indeed in the works of one author or group of authors. If one requires a second-hand or antiquarian book he should go or write directly to the specialist. This directory is intended to provide a handy guide that will enable the booklover to do this with the minimum of trouble, to fill its place as an essential reference book for the trade.

There are two national trade associations for antiquarian book dealers:

THE ANTIQUARIAN BOOKSELLERS' ASSOCIATION, Sackville House, 40 Piccadilly, London W1J 0DR. Tel: (020) 7439-3118. Fax: 7439-3119. E-Mail: admin@aba.org.uk. Web Site: www.aba.org.uk Est: 1906. President: Robert Frew. Vice President: Alan Shelley. Acting Treasurer: Jonathan Potter. (Officers proposed for 2007-8 are: President: Alan Shelley. Vice President: Ian Smith. Treasurer: Jonathan Potter, but not until the AGM at the end of March 2007.) Administrators: John Critchley, Marianne Harwood and Clare Pedder. The Antiquarian Booksellers' Association includes the leading dealers in antiquarian, fine and scarce secondhand books throughout Great Britain as well as in some other countries. It is the founding member of the twenty similar associations, scattered throughout Europe, the Americas, and the Far East which together form the International League of Antiquarian Booksellers.

The Association seeks to provide a comprehensive service to its members. It organises the prestigious and renowned Antiquarian Book Fair each June at Olympia, London and a more broadly-based Book Fair at Chelsea Town Hall every autumn. Branch fairs are also held in Edinburgh. All members receive an informative newsletter each month and there is a fine reference library ready to answer their bibliographical queries. Their interests are further looked after by representatives sitting on various government bodies and dealing with such subjects as the export of manuscripts, the future of the British Library, the National Book Committee, the monitoring of V.A.T. and customs regulations both here and in the Common Market. The Association organises, through the year, a series of events – sporting, social, and educational – aimed at promoting friendship and understanding among colleagues at both national and international levels. There is a Benevolent Fund upon which members may call in times of financial difficulty. Members may also benefit from advantageous rates on credit card processing, and insurance negotiated on their behalf by the Association.

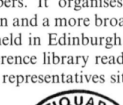

There are various ways in which the Association looks after the interest of the general public. By requiring of all its members a good experience of the trade, and high professional standards and ethics, it ensures that the public may approach with confidence any dealer displaying the A.B.A. badge. In rare cases of difficulty or dispute, the Association stands ready to arbitrate between dealer and client.

The public, especially institutions and public libraries, are further served by a sophisticated security system founded and developed by the Association and now copied throughout the world. It has already accounted for the apprehension of an impressive list of book-thieves and for the recovery and restoration to their rightful owners of many hundreds of stolen books.

From within its ranks, the Antiquarian Booksellers' Association can produce experts on most aspects of bibliography and book-collecting, and their collective expertise is available to the general public through the Association's office. A list of Members is published every two years and is available on request from the Administrators, or through the website.

PROVINCIAL BOOKSELLERS' FAIRS ASSOCIATION, The Old Coach House, 16 Melbourn Street, Royston, Hertfordshire SG8 7BZ. Tel: (01763) 248400. Fax: 248921. Fairs Information line: 249212. E-Mail: info@pbfa.org. Web: www.pbfa.org. Est: 1974. Chairman: George Newlands. Vice-Chairman: Adrian Pegg. Honorary Secretary: Roz Burmester. Honorary Treasurer: David Sedgwick. Administrator: Becky Wears.

The PBFA is the largest association of antiquarian and secondhand booksellers in Great Britain. With over 600 members it is also the largest in the world. It is non-profit making and co-operatively managed by its members through national and regional committees. The full-time administrative headquarters are in Royston.

The Association organises book fairs throughout the country – over 100 each year. Central to this programme are the monthly fairs held at the Holiday Inn Bloomsbury, Coram Street, WC1 1HT, and the international fairs held each June each year, at the Hotel Russell and Novotel London West. From January 2007, the monthly fairs will be held at the Holiday Inn Bloomsbury, Coram Street WC1 1HT

Support for members and their dependents is available at times of distress through the Association's own charity, the Richard Condon Memorial Fund. The size of the membership allows the PBFA to negotiate advantageous rates for credit card processing, postal services, insurance and bulk purchasing.

The PBFA caters for a wide range of book collecting interests and aims to promote a broader interest in antiquarian and secondhand books. The PBFA provides safeguards for the public buying from its members and is committed to maintaining the highest trading standards. In addition a newsletter is published for members and an annual Directory of Members *(£5.50 inc. p&p)* and a nationwide calendar of book fairs *(free)* are available from the Royston office.

WELSH BOOKSELLERS ASSOCIATION, c/o 44 Lion Street, Hay-on-Wye, Herefordshire HR3 5AA. Tel: (01497) 820322. Fax: 821150. Est: 1987. Chairman: Richard Booth. Secretary & Treasurer: Anna Cooper. The Association aims to encourage the development of secondhand and antiquarian bookselling in Wales. Books, maps, prints, manuscripts and ephemera all come within the scope of the Association. An annual leaflet giving details of each member is available by subscription from the Secretary, or any member.

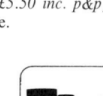

PRIVATE LIBRARIES ASSOCIATION, Ravelston, South View Road, Pinner, Middlesex HA5 3YD. Est: 1956. Web: www.plabooks.org. The Private Libraries Association is an international society of book collectors with about 500 private members (about one quarter of them in America) and about 100 institutional members. The Association publishes a quarterly journal (*The Private Library*, which contains articles, notes and other items), an annual checklist of Private Press Books, a quarterly *Newsletter and Exchange List*, a *Members' List*, and other books about various aspects of book collecting. Annual subscription £25.

SOCIETY OF BOOKBINDERS, 2 Lower Faircox, Henfield, West Sussex BN5 9UT. For all contacts, please use the web site: www.societyofbookbinders.com. Membership is open to anyone intersted in books, whether a binder or not, although most members are either binders already, or aspiring to learn the craft. Current Chairman: Gordon J. Hartley. Honorary Secretary: Mrs. J. Refern. The website includes a gallery of pictures showing the work of a number of members.

BOOK PLATE SOCIETY, 11 Nella Road, London W6 9PB. Web: www.bookplatesociety.org. President: James Wilson.

ANTIQUARIAN BOOKSELLERS' ASSOCIATIONS

Australia and New Zealand

AUSTRALIAN AND NEW ZEALAND ASSOCIATION OF ANTIQUARIAN BOOKSELLERS, (ANZAAB) 32 Maberley Crescent, Frankston, VIC 3199. Tel: (613) 5971-3230. Fax: (613) 9529-1298. E-mail: admin@anzaab.com. Web: www.anzaab.com. Est 1977. President: Peter Tinslay. Vice-Presidents: Ross Burnet. Secretary: Sam Haymes. Treasurer: Michael Sprod. 58 members.

Austria

VERBAND DER ANTIQUARE ÖSTERREICHS, Grünangergasse 4, A-1010 Wien, Austria. Tel: (01) 512 15 35. Fax: (01) 512 84 82. E-mail: sekretariat@ hvb.at. Web: www.antiquare.at. President: Norbert Donhofer. 37 members

Belgium

LA CHAMBRE PROFESSIONNELLE BELGE DE LA LIBRAIRIE ANCIENNE ET MODERNE (C.L.A.M.). DE BELGISCHE BEROEPSKAMER VAN ANTIQUAREN (B.B.A.). Secretary: Mme Dominique Basteyns, CLAM-BBA, Galerie Bortier, 12-14, B-1000 Brussels. Fax: (+32) (02) 503 24 21. E-Mail: dominique.basteyns@skynet.be. Web: www.clam-bba.be. Est: 1946. President: Henri Godts. Vice President: Jan Ceuleers. Treasurer: Alain Ferraton. Secretary: CLAM-BBA, the Belgium Antiquarian Booksellers' Association is affiliated to the International League of Antiquarian Booksellers (I.L.A.B)

Brazil

ASSOCIAÇÃO BRASILEIRA DE LIVERIROS ANTIQUÁRIOS, Rua Santos Dumont 677 25625-090 Centro Petrópolis, Brazil. Tel: (242) 42 0376. Fax: (242) 31 1695. Est: 1945 President: Mrs Ana Maria Bocayuva de Miranda Jordão. E-mail: sebofino@uol.com.br. 9 members.

Canada

ANTIQUARIAN BOOKSELLERS' ASSOCIATION OF CANADA, (A.B.A.C). c/o 783 Bank Street, Ottawa, Ontario K1S 3V5 Canada. President: Wilfrid M. de Freitas. Secretary: Charles Purpora (Tel: 604 320-0375). E-mail: info@abac.org. 70 members.

Czech Republic

SVAZ ANTIKVÁRŮ CR, Karlova 2, 110 00 Praha 1, Czech Republic. Tel: & Fax: (02) 22 22 02 86, 22 22 02 88. Est: 1922. E-mail: info@beran.ch. 5 members

Denmark

DEN DANSKE ANTIKVARBOGHANDLERFORENING, c/o Daugaard Antikvariat, Sondersognsvej 79, Tovelte, DK-4780 Stege, Denmark. E-mail: abf@antikvar.dk. Web: www.antikvar.dk. Est: 1920. President: Mr Peter Daugaard. 35 members.

PROVINCIAL BY NAME

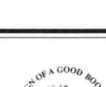

The PBFA has been running quality book fairs for more than quarter of a century. From our first event, held in London in 1972, and intended as a shop window for provincial book dealers (hence the name), to our current programme of fairs all round the country we offer the book collecting public and the secondhand book trade an unparalleled range of events to suit every taste and every pocket - large fairs, small fairs, in the North and in the South; specialist fairs, and general fairs with books on all subjects at prices ranging from £5 to £5,000. A PBFA book fair, large or small, stands out by its quality - quality of presentation, quality of organisation and quality of items offered.

Our regular monthly fairs in London have a well-deserved reputation as **the** place to buy books in town, and we will ensure that we continue to deserve this reputation at our new venue at The Holiday Inn London Bloomsbury.

Each area of the United Kingdom now boasts its own regular major event and we are delighted to be able to designate four of these as Premier Fairs in 2007 - Cambridge, Bath, Edinburgh and York will each offer an exceptional range of quality books, illustration and printed material.

Visit our website www.pbfa.org to see our full programme of fairs, lists of exhibitors, detailed information and maps for all fairs. Our published calendar is also available post free from our office address below.

All PBFA members are established bookdealers who abide by a code of practice. Their trading details are readily accessible in the Directory of Members available at £4.00 (p + p extra) and through our online directory.

The PBFA relies on volunteers to run its affairs, be it on committees, managing a fair, or helping out with putting up posters or clearing up afterwards. We could not function without these hardworking members and however large we grow, we will retain our founding principles of working co-operatively to sell quality books at quality events.

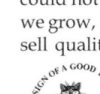

WORLDWIDE BY REPUTATION

For further information on our renowned book fairs or how to join the PBFA contact: Becky Wears, PBFA, The Old Coach House, 16 Melbourn St, Royston, Herts, SG8 7BZ. Tel: 01763 248400, Fax: 01762 248921, email: info@pbfa.org or visit our website at www.pbfa.org

ANTIQUARIAN BOOKSELLERS' ASSOCIATIONS

Finland

SUOMEN ANTIKVARIAATTIYHDISTYS. (Finnish Antiquarian Booksellers Association), P.O. Box 144, FIN-00121, Helsinki, Finland. Tel: (09) 628 004. Est: 1941. E-mail: timo.surojegin@pp.inet.fi. 23 members.

France

SYNDICAT NATIONAL DE LA LIBRAIRIE ANCIENNE ET MODERNE, 4 rue Git-le-Cœur, F-75006 Paris, France. Tel: (01) 43 29 46 38. Fax: (01) 43 25 41 63. E-mail: slam-livre@wanadoo.fr. Web: www.slam-livre.fr. Est: 1914. President: Mr Frederic Castaing. 245 members.

Germany

VERBAND DEUTSCHER ANTIQUARE e.V., Geschaftstelle, Seeblick 1, D-56459 Elbingen. Tel: (0 64 35) 90 91 47. Fax: (0 64 35) 90 91 48. E-mail: buch@antiquare.de. Web: www.antiquare.de. Est: 1949. President: Eberhard Köstler. Approximately 300 members.

Italy

ASSOCIAZIONE LIBRAI ANTIQUARI D'ITALIA, via Parione 16, 50123 Florence, Italy. Tel: (039) 055 265 8317. Fax: (039) 055 214 831. E-mail: alai@alai.it. Web: www.alai.it. Est: 1947. President: Umberto Pregliasco. Vice President: Mark Cicolini. Treasurer: Piero Crini. 120 members.

Japan

THE ANTIQUARIAN BOOKSELLERS' ASSOCIATION OF JAPAN (ABAJ), 29 San-ei-cho, Shinjuku-ku, Tokyo 160-0008, Japan. Tel: (03) 3357-1411. Fax: (03) 3351-5855. Est: 1963. President: Mr Yashio Nakao. E-mail: antiq@yushodo.co.jp. 30 members.

Korea

ANTIQUARIAN BOOKSELLERS' ASSOCIATION OF KOREA (A.B.A.K.), 1F, Eunsung Bldg, 218-9 Bongsan-dong, Jung-Gu, 700-400 Daegu. Tel: (053) 475-80 09. E-mail: ksk1262@yahoo.co.kr. Web: www.koreasa.co.kr. President: Mr Sun-Kyun Kim. 31 members.

Netherlands

NEDERLANDSCHE VEREENIGING VAN ANTIQUAREN, Prinsegracht 15, 2512 EW Den Haag. Tel: 070-3649840. Fax: 070 3643340. Web: www.nvva.nl. President: Mr. Ton Kok. E-mail: nwa@xs4all.nl. 79 Members.

Norway

NORSK ANTIKVARBOKHANDLERFORENING, Postboks 1420, Vika N-0115 Oslo, Norway. Tel: (47) 23 31 02 80. Internet: www.antikvariat.no. President: Vidar Wangsmo. E-mail: wangsmo@wangsmo.com. 20 members.

Spain

ADSCRIPTO IBERICA LIBRARIAE ANTIQUARIORUM (A.I.L.A.), San Miguel 12, E-07002 Palma de Mallorca, Spain. Tel: (971) 72 13 55. Fax: (971) 71 74 36. Internet: www.ailalibros/com. President: Mr Manuel Ripoll Billon.

ANTIQUARIAN BOOKSELLERS' ASSOCIATIONS

Sweden

SVENSKA ANTIKVARIATFÖRENINGEN, Box 22 549, SE-104 22 Stockholm, Sweden. Tel: (08) 654 80 86. Fax: (08) 654 80 06. E-Mail: main@svaf.se. Internet: www.svaf.se. President: Sten Rigselle. E-mail: antiquaria@telia.com

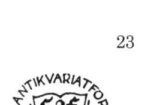

Switzerland

VEREINIGUNG DER BUCHANTIQUARE UND KUPFER-STICHHÄNDLER IN DER SCHWEIZ (V.E.B.U.K.U.) / SYNDICAT DE LA LIBRARIE ANCIENNE ET DU COMMERCE DE L'ESTAMPE EN SUISSE (S.L.A.C.E.S.), Route de Rolle, PO Box 17, CH-1162 St. prex. Tel: +41-21-806-1662. Fax: +41-21-806-3059. E-mail: f.bloch@bluewin.ch. Web: www.vebuku.ch. President: Marcus Benz.

United Kingdom

THE ANTIQUARIAN BOOKSELLERS' ASSOCIATION, Sackville House, 40 Piccadilly, London W1J 0DR. Tel: (020) 7439-3118. Fax: 7439-3119. E-Mail: admin@aba.org.uk. Web: www.aba.org. Est: 1906. President: Alan Shelley (from AGM, 24 March). Secretary: John Critchley.

PRIVATE LIBRARIES ASSOCIATION, Ravelston, South View Road, Pinner, Middlesex HA5 3YD. Est: 1956. The Private Libraries Association is an international society of book collectors with about 600 private members (about one third of them in America) and about 150 library members.

PROVINCIAL BOOKSELLERS FAIRS ASSOCIATION, The Old Coach House, 16 Melbourn Street, Royston, Hertfordshire SG8 7BZ. Tel: (01763) 248400. Fax: (01763) 248921. Fairs information line: (01763) 249212. E-Mail: info@pbfa.org. Web Site: www.pbfa.org. Est: 1974. Chairman: George Newlands. Honorary Secretary: Roz Burmester. Administrator: Becky Wears. Over 600 members.

WELSH BOOKSELLERS ASSOCIATION, c/o 44 Lion Street, Hay-on-Wye, Herefordshire HR3 5AA, Tel: (01497) 820322. Fax: 821150. E-Mail: WBA@richardbooth.demon.co.uk. Est. 1987. Chairman: Richard Booth. 29 members.

United States of America

ANTIQUARIAN BOOKSELLERS' ASSOCIATION OF AMERICA (A.B.A.A.), 20 West 44th Street, Fourth Floor, New York, N.Y. 10036-6604, U.S.A. Tel: (212) 944-8291. Fax: 944-8293. E-Mail: hq@abaa.org. Web: www.abaa.org. Est: 1949. President: David Lilburne. Over 456 members.

INTERNATIONAL LEAGUE OF ANTIQUARIAN BOOKSELLERS (I.L.A.B.) to which most national associations belong. President: Michael Steinbach, Demolistrasse 1/1, D-80638, Munchen, Germany. E-mail: michael.steinbach@steinbach.de. General Secretary: Arnoud Gerits, Prinsengracht 445, NL-1016 HN Amsterdam, Netherlands. E-mail: a.gerits@inter.nl.net.

PERIODICALS

Literary Magazines and Book Trade Papers

Please note that magazine prices and subscriptions are given as a guide only, and are liable to change.

THE AFRICAN BOOK PUBLISHING RECORD (ABPR). Covers new and forthcoming African publications, as well as publishing articles & news. Est: 1975. Quarterly. Subscription: EURO 340.00 (£244 or $435. price for 2006). Editor: Cécile Lomer. Published by: K.G. Saur Verlag GmbH, Ortlerstrasse 8, 81373 Muenchen, Germany; Postfach 70 16 20, 81316 Muenchen, Germany. Tel: +49-89-76902-0; Fax: +49-89-76902-150; E-mail: saur.info@thomson.com. Subscription enquiries to K.G. Saur Verlag.

ALMANACCO DEL BIBLIOFILO. Yearly. Publisher: Edizioni Rovello di Mario Scognamiglio, P.za Castello, 11, 20121 Milano, Italy. Tel: (02) 86464661 or (02) 866532. Fax: (02) 72022884. E-mail: edirovello@tiscali.it

ANTIQUES MAGAZINE. Fortnightly. Subscription. £52.00 – about 22 issues, plus 2 Antiques Fairs & Centres Guide (U.K.). please call for overseas rates. Published by: H.P. Publishing, 2, Hampton Court Road, Harborne, Birmingham B17 9AE. Tel: (0121) 681-8000 (General enquires); -8001 (Accounts); -8006 (Editorial). Subscriptions: Tel: (0121) 681 8003; Fax: (0121) 681-8005. E-Mail: subscriptions@antiquesmagazine.com. Website: www.antiquesmagazine.com.

ANTIQUES TRADE GAZETTE. Contains comprehensive weekly reports on antiquarian book sales worldwide plus auction calendar. Est: 1971. Weekly. Subscription: £74.00 (£133.00 North America £158.00 and rest of world, £135.00 Europe) a year. Published by: Metropress Ltd., 115 Shaftesbury Avenue, London WC2H 8AD. Tel: (020) 7420-6600. Editor: Ivan Macquisten. Antiquarian Books Editor: Ian McKay. Tel: (01795) 890475. Fax: 890014. E-mail: ianmckay1@btinternet.com

AUS DEM ANTIQUARIAT. German journal on Antiquarian booktrade by subscription. Published six times a year by MVB Marketing- und Verlagservice des Buchhandels GmbH, Grosser Hirschgraben 17-21, 60311 Frankfurt am Main (Postfach 100442, 60004 Frankfurt am Main), Germany. Tel: +49 (69) 1306 469. Fax: 1306 394. E-mail: antiquariat@mvb-online.de. Internet www.buch-antiquariat.de

BOOK AND MAGAZINE COLLECTOR. Biographies and bibliographies of collectable 19th and 20th century authors and illustrators, plus lists of books for sale and wanted. Est: 1984. Monthly. Subscription: £42.00 a year (13 issues, U.K.), £46.00 (Europe, Airmail), £53.00 (Rest of the World). Editor: Jonathan Scott. Publisher: John Dean. Published by: Diamond Publishing, Metropolis Int., Unit 101, Wales Farm Road, London W3 6UG Tel: (0870) 732-8080. Fax: (0870) 732-6060. E-mail: bmceditor@metropolis.co.uk

THE BOOK COLLECTOR. Est: 1952. Quarterly. Subscription: £48.00 (Europe & USA £52 [surface], Europe £52 and USA £60 [airmail], S E Asia & Australasia £50 [surface] and £62 [airmail]. Editor: Nicolas Barker. Published by: The Collector Ltd., 32 Swift Way, Thurlby, Nr Bourne, Lincolnshire PE10 0QA. Tel: 01778 338095. Fax: 01778 338096. Subscriptions, Advertising and Accounts: 32 Swift Way, Thurlby, Nr Bourne, Lincolnshire PE10 0QA. E-mail: info@thebookcollector.co.uk.

BOOKS FROM FINLAND English-language journal presenting Finnish literature and writers. Est. 1967. Editor-in-chief: Soila Lehtonen. Editor: Hildi Hawkins. Quarterly. Subscription: 20 euros a year (Finland and Scandinavia), 27 euros (all other countries). Published by: Finnish Literature Society, P.O. Box 259, FI-00171 Helsinki, Finland. Tel: +358 (0) 201 131345. E-mail: booksfromfinland@finlit.fi. Website: www.finlit.fi/booksfromfinland.

BOOKDEALER. First edition to be published in May 2007, published monthly by Rare Books & Berry, High Street, Porlock, Minehead, Somerset TA24 8PT. Tel: (01643) 863255. Fax: (01643) 863092. Web: www.bookdealer.org.uk. Subscription on application.

BOOKDEALER FORTNIGHTLY. Published fortnightly by John Debbage, 28 Carterford Drive, Norwich, Norfolk NR3 4DW. Subscription on application.

THE BOOKSELLER. Journal of the book trade in Great Britain. Weekly. Subscription: £179.00 a year (U.K.), £185.00 (overseas, airmail extra). Editor-in-chief: Neill Denny. Published by: VNU Entertainment Media UK Ltd., 189 Shaftesbury Avenue, London WC2H 8TJ. Tel: (020) 7420-6006. Fax: 7420-6103.

BOOK SOURCE MAGAZINE. Published since 1985, contains articles, news, reviews and information for the secondhand/antiquarian book trade in the USA. Subscription bi-monthly: $20.00 (1st class USA); $24.00 (library rate, Canada and Mexico); $48/£28.00 (overseas airmail). Editor: John C. Huckans. Published at: 2007 Syossett Drive, Cazenovia, NY 13035-9753. Tel: & Fax: (315) 655-8499. E-Mail: bsm@alltel.net. Website: www.booksourcemagazine.com.

PERIODICALS

BOOK WORLD MAGAZINE. Articles, reviews, advertisements and news of the book world in general. Monthly. Subscription: £50.00 (U.K.), $100.00 (surface mail U.S.), $140.00 (air mail U.S.). Published by: Christchurch Publishers Ltd., 2 Caversham Street, Chelsea, London SW3 4AH. Tel: & Fax: (020) 7351-4995.

CONTEMPORARY REVIEW. On politics, current affairs, theology, social questions, literature and the arts. Web: www.contemporaryreview.co.uk. Monthly. Subscription: £49.00 a year (U.K. surface mail), $195.00 (U.S.A. and Canada, airfreight), others on application. Editor: Dr. Richard Mullen. Published by: The Contemporary Review Co. Ltd., P.O. Box 1242, Oxford, OX1 4FJ, England. Tel: & Fax: (01865) 201529. E-mail: subscriptions@comtemporaryreview.co.uk. Editorial office: editorial@comtemporaryreview.co.uk.

L'ESOPO. Bibliophile magazine. Quarterly. Published at: Edizioni Rovello di Mario Scognamiglio, P.za Castello, 11, 20121 Milano, Italy. Tel: (02) 86464661 or (02) 866532. Fax: (02) 72022884. E-mail: edirovello@tiscali.it

FINE BOOKS & COLLECTIONS. Dedicated to the out-of-print, collectible, and antiquarian book world. Six full colour issues a year. US Subscription $25. Overseas $55. Published by OP Media LLC 4905 Pine Cone Drive, Suite 2, Durham NC 27707. E-mail: subscriptions@finebooksmagazine.com.

FOLIO. Produced 3-4 times a year, to members only. Editor: Kit Shepherd. Published by: The Folio Society Ltd., 44 Eagle Street, London WC1R 4FS. Web: www.foliosoc.co.uk. Tel: (020) 7400-4222.

THE LITERARY REVIEW. Covers books, arts and poetry. Est: 1978. Monthly. Subscription: £32.00 a year (U.K.), £39.00 (Europe), $75.00 (U.S.A. & Canada Airspeed), $104.00 (rest of the world Air Mail). Web: www.literaryreview.co.uk. Editor: Nancy Sladek. Published by: The Literary Review, 44 Lexington Street, London W1F 0LW. Tel: (020) 7437-9392. Fax: (020) 7734-1844.

MINIATURE BOOK NEWS. Est: 1965. Quarterly. (Now incorporated in the Miniature Book Society Newsletter – Subscription to both: $40.00 oer year, US, $45.00 Canada and $55.00 Overseas). Editor: Julian I. Edison. Published at: 8 St. Andrews Drive, St. Louis, Missouri 63124, U.S.A.

THE PRIVATE LIBRARY. Established 1957. Quarterly. Distributed free to members of the Private Libraries Association, annual subscription £25.00 ($40.00). Editors: David Chambers & Paul W. Nash. Sample copy free on request. Published by: The Private Libraries Association, Ravelston, South View Road, Pinner, Middlesex HA5 3YD.

PRIVATE PRESS BOOKS. An annual bibliography of books printed by private presses in the English speaking world. 1999 edition: 96 pp; 2000 edition 95pp; 2001 edition 64pp. £10.00 or $20.00 (£5.00 or $10.00 to PLA members) Editor: Paul W. Nash. Published by: The Private Libraries Association, Ravelston, South View Road, Pinner, Middlesex HA5 3YD.

QUILL AND QUIRE. Keeps its readers up-to-date on Canada's exciting book publishing scene and provides the earliest and most complete look at new Canadian books, with more than 500 titles reviewed each year. In addition, the Canadian Publishers Directory, which puts the book industry at your fingertips, is delivered free bi-annually. 12 issues a year for CAN$ 59.95; USA and Overseas CAN $95 (includes postage). Est: 1935. Editor: Derek Weiler. Published at: 111 Queen Street East, 3rd Floor, Toronto, Ontario M5C 1S2 Canada. Subscriptions tel: (905) 946-0406. Fax: 905 946-0410. Email: subscriptions@quillandquire.com. Web: www.quillandquire.com.

RBR (RARE BOOK REVIEW). Magazine containing articles, book reviews, auction reports and catalogue news. Est: 1974. Subscription: £34 a year (U.K.), £44.00 (Europe), £54.00 (Rest of the World). Rare Book Review, 24 Maddox Street, London W1S 1PP Tel: +44 (0) 20 7529 4220. Fax: +44 (0) 20 7409 0832. E-mail: jeff@rarebookreview.com

TRIBUNE. Books Editor. Chris McLaughlin. Published by: Tribune Publications Ltd., 9 Arkright Road, London NW3 6AN. Subscription 1 year £64.00. Tel: (020) 7433-6410. E-mail: george@tribpub.demon.co.uk. Web: www.tribunemagazine.co.uk.

INTERNET TRADE MAGAZINES

BOOK THINK. A free newsletter based in the USA. (A more comprehensive version, Gold Edition, is available on annual subscription $49.99. See at www.bookthink.com

BOOKSELLER.COM. An e-mail newsletter where the latest trade news about the new book trade can be read. Register on www.bookseller.com

PN NEWS. On-line international news service for the new book trade. To register: www.publishing news.co.uk

SHEPPARD'S CONFIDENTIAL. A free e-mail newsletter published weekly for the antiquarian and second-hand book trade: news, calendars for book fairs and auctions. Events and book reviews as well as extensive coverage of views and opinions from members of the trade. Register on www.sheppardsworld.co.uk.

CURRENT REFERENCE BOOKS

A & C BLACK COLOUR BOOKS. A collector's guide and bibliography 1900–1930. Author: Colin Inman. £30.00. Published by Werner Shaw Ltd and distributed by Veronica Daniels, Flat 1, 33 Atlantic Road, Weston-Super-Mere BS23 2DQ. Tel: 01934 628645. E-mail: vron.daniels@ukonline.co.uk. A bibliogrpahy covering 800 books in 50 series, with full historical account of this great publishing venture.

ABC OF BOOKBINDING. By Jane Greenfield. $39.95. Published by: Oak Knoll Press, 310 Delaware Street, New Castle, DE 19720, U.S.A. Tel: (302) 328-7232. Fax: 328-7274. E-Mail: oakknoll@ oakknoll.com. Sales rights: Worldwide outside of UK. Available in the UK from The Plough Press.

ABC OF LEATHER BOOKBINDING: A MANUAL FOR TRADITIONAL CRAFTSMANSHIP. Edward R. Lhotka. Illustrated manual shows the science of fine leather bindings. $19.95. Published by: Oak Knoll Press, 310 Delaware Street, New Castle, DE 19720, U.S.A. Tel: (302) 328-7232. Fax: 328-7274. E-Mail: oakknoll@oakknoll.com. Sales rights: Worldwide except in the UK; available in the UK from The British Library.

ABPC on CD-ROM. The auction season September 1975 to August 2005. $1680.76. Published by: Bancroft Parkman Inc., P.O. Box 1236, Washington, CT 06793, U.S.A. Tel: (860) 868-7408. Fax: (860) 868-0080. E-Mail: abpc@snet.net. Website: www.bookpricescurrent.com.

ALEXANDER ANDERSON: 1775–1870. Wood Engraver and Illustrator, an Annotated Bibliography. Jane R. Pomeroy. 3 vols. 2,600 pages $350. Co-published with The American Antiquarian Society, Oak Knoll Press, 310 Delaware Street, New Castle, DE 19720, U.S.A. Tel: (302) 328-7232. Fax: 328-7274. E-Mail: oakknoll@oakknoll.com.

AMERICAN BOOK TRADE DIRECTORY. Profiles retail and antiquarian book dealers plus book and magazine wholesalers, distributors and jobbers in the United States. 2006/2007: $299.00 plus $25 postage. Published by Information Today, Inc., 143 Old Marlton Pike, Medford, NJ 08055-8750. E-mail: custserv@infotoday.com. Website: www.infotoday.com.

AMERICAN TICKETED BINDINGS TO 1880. William Spawn and Thomas E. Kinsella. $85.00. First edn. Published by: Oak Knoll Press, 310 Delaware Street, New Castle, DE 19720, U.S.A. Tel: (302) 328-7232. Fax: 328-7274. E-Mail: oakknoll@ oakknoll.com.

ANTIQUARIAN BOOKS: A Companion for Booksellers, Librarians and Collectors. Edited by Philippa Bernard, leo Bernard and Angus O'Neill. £80. Published by: Ashgate Publishing Ltd., Gower House, Croft Road, Aldershot, Hampshire GU11 3HR. Website: www.ashgate.com. E-mail: info@ ashgatepublishing.com.

BE MERRY AND WISE: ORIGINS OF CHILDREN'S BOOK PUBLISHING IN ENGLAND, 1650-1850. $115.00. Co-published by Oak Knoll Press with the Pierpoint Morgan Library, The Bibliographical Society of America, and The British Library.

BOOK TALK: ESSAYS ON BOOKS, BOOKSELLERS, COLLECTING, ANS SPECIAL COLLECTIONS. Robert H. Jackson & Carol Z. Rothkopf (editors). Major ideas and controversies now current in the rare book world. $49.95. Published by: Oak Knoll Press, 310 Delaware Street, New Castle, DE 19720, U.S.A. Tel: (302) 328-7232. Fax: 328-7274. E-Mail: oakknoll@ oakknoll.com.

BOOKBINDING & CONSERVATION BY HAND: A working guide. By Laura S. Young. Hardback $35.00. Paperback $24.95. Published by: Oak Knoll Press, 310 Delaware Street, New Castle, DE 19720, U.S.A. Tel: (302) 328-7232. Fax: 328-7274. E-Mail: oakknoll@oakknoll.com.

BOOKDEALING FOR PROFIT. By Paul Minet. The philosophy behind the business as well as a look into the future and how the Internet is having a major effect on the trade. Hardback £10.00. Published by Richard Joseph Publishers Ltd, P.O. Box 15, Torrington, Devon EX38 8ZJ. UK. Tel: (01805) 625750. Fax: (01805) 625376. E-mail: office@sheppardsworld.co.uk. Website: www.sheppardsdirectories.co.uk.

BOOKWORMS. The Insect Pests of Books. Norman Hickin. Hardback £24.00. Published by Richard Joseph Publishers Ltd, P.O. Box 15, Torrington, Devon EX38 8ZJ. UK. Tel: (01805) 625750. Fax: (01805) 625376. E-mail: office@sheppardsworld.co.uk. Website: www.sheppardsdirectories.co.uk.

CHILDREN'S FICTION 1900 – 1950. John Cooper ands Jonathan Cooper. £60. Published by: Ashgate Publishing Ltd., Gower House, Croft Road, Aldershot, Hampshire GU11 3HR. Website: www.ashgate.com. E-mail: info@ashgatepublishing.com.

The Book Collector

In its fifty years of publication THE BOOK COLLECTOR has firmly established itself as the most interesting and lively current journal for collectors, bibliographers, antiquarian booksellers and custodians of rare books. Leading authorities contribute regularly on all aspects of bibliophily, from medieval manuscripts to modern first editions and each issue offers new and original insight into the world of books

Some back numbers of issues from 1956 to 1979 are available We hold complete volumes from 1980 to date.

Subscription rates and detailed list and prices from :

The Book Collector

 32 SWIFT WAY, THURLBY, NR. BOURNE
LINCOLNSHIRE PE10 0QA
Tel 01778 338095 *Fax* 01778 338096
E-mail : info@thebookcollector.co.uk
Website : www.thebookcollector.co.uk

CURRENT REFERENCE BOOKS

CILIP: the Chartered Institute of. 2006-2007. £44.95. Compilers: Kathryn Beecroft (ed.). Published by: Facet Publishing, 7 Ridgmount Street, London WC1E 7AE. Tel: (020) 7255-0590. Fax: 7255-0591. E-Mail: info@facetpublishing.co.uk. Website: www.facetpublishing.co.uk.

DETECTIVE FICTION. John Cooper and B.A. Pike. £55.00. Published by: Ashgate Publishing Ltd., Gower House, Croft Road, Aldershot, Hampshire GU11 3HR. Website: www.ashgate.com. E-mail: info@ashgatepublishing.com.

DIRECTORY OF PUBLISHING: United Kingdom & Republic of Ireland. 2007 32st Ed. 216pp £95.00. ISBN: 09780826492937. Published by Continuum, The Tower Building, 11 York Road, London SE1 7NX. ENGLAND. Tel: (020) 7922-0880. Fax: 7922-0881. Web: www.continuumbooks.com

THE DICTIONARY OF 20TH CENTURY BOOK ILLUSTRATORS. By S Alan Home. £45.00. Published by: Antique Collectors Club, Sandy Lane, Old Martlesham, Woodbridge, Suffolk IP12 4SD. Tel: (01394) 389950. Fax: 389999. E-mail: sales@antique-acc.com

DIRECTORY OF RARE BOOK AND SPECIAL COLLECTIONS IN THE UNITED KINGDOM AND REPUBLIC OF IRELAND. Editor: B.C. Bloomfield. 1997. £99.95. Published by: Facet Publishing, 7 Ridgmount Street, London WC1E 7AE. Tel: (020) 7255-0590. Fax: 7255-0591. E-Mail: info@facetpublishing.co.uk. Website: www.facetpublishing.co.uk.

EDWARD SEYMOUR AND THE FANCY PAPER COMPANY: The Story of a British Marbled Paper Manufacturer.. Sidney E. Berger. $150. Published by: Oak Knoll Press, 310 Delaware Street, New Castle, DE 19720, U.S.A. Tel: (302) 328-7232. Fax: 328-7274. E-Mail: oakknoll@oakknoll.com.

THE ENCYCLOPEDIA OF BOYS' SCHOOL STORIES. Robert J Kirkpatrick Hb. £55.00. Published by: Ashgate Publishing Ltd., Gower House, Croft Road, Aldershot, Hampshire GU11 3HR. Website: www.ashgate.com. E-mail: info@ashgatepublishing.com.

THE ENCYCLOPEDIA OF GIRLS' SCHOOL STORIES. Sue Sims and Hilary Clare Hb. £55.00. Published by: Ashgate Publishing Ltd., Gower House, Croft Road, Aldershot, Hampshire GU11 3HR. Website: www.ashgate.com. E-mail: info@ashgatepublishing.com.

THE ENCYCLOPEDIA OF PAPERMAKING AND BOOKBINDING: the definitive guide to making, embellishing and repairing paper and books by Heidi Reimer-Epp and Mary Reimer. 160 pages with 200m colour illustrations. Hardback £16.95. Published by The British Library; available from Turpin Distribution Ltd., Blackhorse Road, Letchworth, Hertfordshire SG6 1HN. E-mail turpin@tuirpinltd.com

ENCYCLOPEDIA OF THE BOOK. By: Geoffrey Ashall Glaister. Hardcover $75.00, Paperback $49.95. Published by Oak Knoll Press, 310 Delaware Street, New Castle, DE 19720, U.S.A. Tel: (302) 328-7232. Fax: 328-7274. E-Mail: oakknoll@oakknoll.com.

FIRST EDITIONS: A GUIDE TO IDENTIFICATION. 4th edition for 2001. $60.00. Editor: Edward N. Zempel. Published by: Spoon River Press, P.O. Box 3635, Peoria, IL 61612-3635, U.S.A. Tel: (309) 672-2665. Website: www.spoonriverpress.com

T.N. FOULIS: The History and Bibliography of an Edinburgh Publishing House. By Ian Elfick & Paul Harris. £30.00. Published by Werner Shaw Ltd and distributed by Veronica Daniels, Flat 1, 33 Atlantic Road, Weston-Super-Mere BS23 2DQ. Tel: 01934 628645. E-mail: vron.daniels@ukonline.co.uk.

GREATER LONDON HISTORY AND HERITAGE HANDBOOK. Next edition 2007. c. 150pp. Illus. £25 + £2p&p. Borough by borough directory and bibliographic listings with substantial London wide chapter. Editor: Peter Marcan. Published by: Peter Marcan Publications, P.O. Box 3158, London SE1 4RA. Tel: (020) 7357-0368.

A GUIDE TO CONTEMPORARY FICTION. Mandy Hicken and Ray Prytherch. £55.00. Published by: Ashgate Publishing Ltd., Gower House, Croft Road, Aldershot, Hampshire GU11 3HR. Website: www.ashgate.com. E-mail: info@ashgatepublishing.com.

A GUIDE TO WORLD LANGUAGE DICTIONAIRIES. Andrew Dalby. 1998. £74.95. Published by Facet Publishing, 7 Ridgmount Street, London WC1E 7AE. Tel: (020) 7255 0590. Fax: (0)20 7255 0591. E-mail: info@facetpublishing.co.uk. Website: www.facetpublishing.co.uk.

HEADBANDS, HOW TO WORK THEM. Jane Greenfield and Jenny Hille. $14.95. Published by: Oak Knoll Press, 310 Delaware Street, New Castle, DE 19720, U.S.A. Tel: (302) 328-7232. Fax: 328-7274. E-Mail: oakknoll@ oakknoll.com.

CURRENT REFERENCE BOOKS

HISTORY OF ENGLISH CRAFT BOOKBINDING TECHNIQUE. By Bernard C. Middleton. $55.00. Published by: Oak Knoll Press, 310 Delaware Street, New Castle, DE 19720, U.S.A. Tel: (302) 328-7232. Fax: 328-7274. E-Mail: oakknoll@oakknoll.com. Sales rights: Worldwide outside of UK. Available in the UK from The British LibraryTHE ILLUSTRATIONS OF W. HEATH ROBINSON: A COMMENTARY AND BIBLIOGRAPHY. By Geoffrey Beare. The bibliography which follows the long introduction to Heath Robinson's work as an illustrator, was compiled from primary sources. £18.95. Published by Werner Shaw Ltd and distributed by Veronica Daniels, Flat 1, 33 Atlantic Road, Weston-Super-Mere BS23 2DQ. Tel: 01934 628645. E-mail: vron.daniels@ukonline.co.uk.

INTERNATIONAL DIRECTORY OF ANTIQUARIAN BOOKSELLERS. A world list of members of organisations belonging to the International League of Antiquarian Booksellers (I.L.A.B.). Published every 2 years: 2005-6 edition £15.00 plus £2.00 p&p. 2007-2008 edition available summer 2007. Published by: I.L.A.B. Distributed in the UK by: The Antiquarian Booksellers' Association, Sackville House, 40 Piccadilly, London W1J 0DR. Tel: (020 7439-3118. Fax: (020) 7439-3119. E-mail: admin@aba.org.uk.

INTERNATIONAL MASONIC PERIODICALS 1738-2005. Larissa P. Watkins. $75.00 Published by: Oak Knoll Press, 310 Delaware Street, New Castle, DE 19720, U.S.A. Tel: (302) 328-7232. Fax: 328-7274. E-Mail: oakknoll@ oakknoll.com.

JOHN UPDIKE: A BIBLIOGRAPHY OF PRIMARY AND SECONDARY MATERIALS, 1948-2006. De Bellis and Jack & Michael Broomfield. $195.00. Published by: Oak Knoll Press, 310 Delaware Street, New Castle, DE 19720, U.S.A. Tel: (302) 328-7232. Fax: 328-7274. E Mail: oakknoll@ oakknoll.com.

LIBRARIES AND INFORMATION SERVICES IN THE UNITED KINGDOM AND REPUBLIC OF IRELAND, 2006-2007. £44.95. Published by: Facet Publishing, 7 Ridgmount Street, London WC1E 7AE. Tel: (020) 7255-0590. Fax: 7255-0591. E-mail: info@facetpublishing.co.uk. Website: www.facetpublishing.co.uk.

LITERARY MARKET PLACE. The directory of the book publishing industry for America and Canada. Published annually. 2006 edition. Priced US$299.95 plus $21.00 post and handling. Also, available online at www.infotoday.com. Fax: (01865) 730232. E-mail: info@infotoday.com.

LOCAL STUDIES LIBRARIANSHIP: A WORLD BIBLIOGRAPHY. Editor: Diana Dixon. 2001. £39.95. Published by Facet Publishing, 7 Ridgmount Street, London WC1E 7AE. Tel: (020) 7255 0590. Fax: (020) 7255 0591. E-mail: info@facetpublishing.co.uk. Website: www.facetpublishing.co.uk.

MINIATURE BOOKS. Louis Bondy. The history of miniature books up to 1981. Published by Richard Joseph Publishers Ltd, PO 15, Torrington, Devon EX38 8ZJ. E-mail: office@sheppardsworld.co.uk Website. www.sheppardsworld.co.uk. Hardback 220 pages £24.

THE MARCAN VISUAL ARTS HANDBOOK: where to go for British contacts, expertise and speciality in the fine and applied arts. vi 150pp Illus. £25 + £2.50 p&p. Almost 200 descriptive centres with many bibliogrphic listings; keywords and subject index. Published by: Peter Marcan Publications, P.O. Box 3158, London SE1 4RA. Tel: (020) 7357-0368.

NEW SCIENCE OUT OF OLD BOOKS. Studies in manuscripts and early printed books in honour of A.I. Doyle. £80.00. Edited by: Richard Beadle and A.J. Piper. Published by: Ashgate Publishing Ltd., Gower House, Croft Road, Aldershot, Hampshire GU11 3HR. Distributed by Bookpoint. Tel: (01235) 827730. Fax: 400454.

A POCKET GUIDE TO THE IDENTIFICATION OF FIRST EDITIONS. An essential guide to identifying first editions for collectors, dealers, librarians, cataloguers and auctioneers. 6th Edition $19.95 per copy plus $1 shipping 40% discount on 5 or more copies; shipping for 5 copies is $5 by Priority Mail. International orders: single copies shipping $2.50; five copies $8 by Air/Printed Matter. Published by: The Jumping Frog, McBride/Publisher, 56 Arbor Street, Hartford, CT 06106, U.S.A. Tel: (860) 523-1622. Website: www.mcbridepublisher.com.

THE PRIVATE PRESSES. Colin Franklin with new Bibliogrpahy and Indexes by John Turner. £60. Published by: Ashgate Publishing Ltd., Gower House, Croft Road, Aldershot, Hampshire GU11 3HR. Website: www.ashgate.com. E-mail: info@ashgatepublishing.com.

PROVENANCE RESEARCH IN BOOK HISTORY. By David Pearson. Hardback $45.00. Published by: Oak Knoll Press & The British Library. Information from: Oak Knoll Press, 310 Delaware Street, New Castle, DE 19720, U.S.A. Tel: (302) 328-7232. Fax: 328-7274. Sales Rights: North and South America; elsewhere, The British Library.

CURRENT REFERENCE BOOKS

RESTORATION OF LEATHER BINDINGS. By Bernard C. Middleton. $39.95. Published by: Oak Knoll Press & The British Library. Information from: Oak Knoll Press, 310 Delaware Street, New Castle, DE 19720, U.S.A. Tel: (302) 328-7232. Fax: 328-7274. Sales Rights: Worldwide except the U.K. Available in the U.K. from The British Library.

STUDIES IN THE HISTORY OF BOOKBINDING. Edited by Mirjam M. Foot. This book consists of articles on the history of bookbinding and related subjects. Grouped under seven headings ranging from general topics such as bookbinding as a subject for study and the need to preserve the book, to more detailed descriptions of individual bindings from the fifteenth to the twentieth century. £80.00. Published by: Ashgate Publishing Ltd., Gower House, Croft Road, Aldershot, Hampshire GU11 3HR. Distributed by Bookpoint. Tel: (01235) 827730. Fax: 400454.

THE TARTARUS PRESS GUIDE TO FIRST EDITION PRICES 2006/7. Edited by: R.B. Russell. £19.99 inc. p&p. Published by: Tartarus Press, Coverley House, Carlton-in-Coverdale, Leyburn, North Yorks DL8 4AY. Tel: & Fax: (01969) 640399. E-Mail: tartarus@pavilion.co.uk.

J.R.R. TOLKIEN, A DESCRIPTIVE BIBLIOGRAPHY. By Wayne G. Hammond. $94.00. Published by: Oak Knoll Press, 310 Delaware Street, New Castle, DE 19720, U.S.A. Tel: (302) 328-7232. Fax: 328-7274. E-Mail: oakknoll@oakknoll.com.

TASHA TUDOR: THE DIRECTION OF HER DREAMS. By William John & Priscilla T. Hare. $85.00. A definitive bibliography; collector's guide. Published by: Oak Knoll Press, 310 Delaware Street, New Castle, DE 19720, U.S.A. Tel: (302) 328-7232. Fax: 328-7274.

TRUE TO TYPE. By Ruari McLean. A Typographical Autobiography. £25.00. Published by Werner Shaw Ltd and distributed by Veronica Daniels, Flat 1, 33 Atlantic Road, Weston-Super-Mere BS23 2DQ. Tel: 01934 628645. E-mail: vron.daniels@ukonline.co.uk.

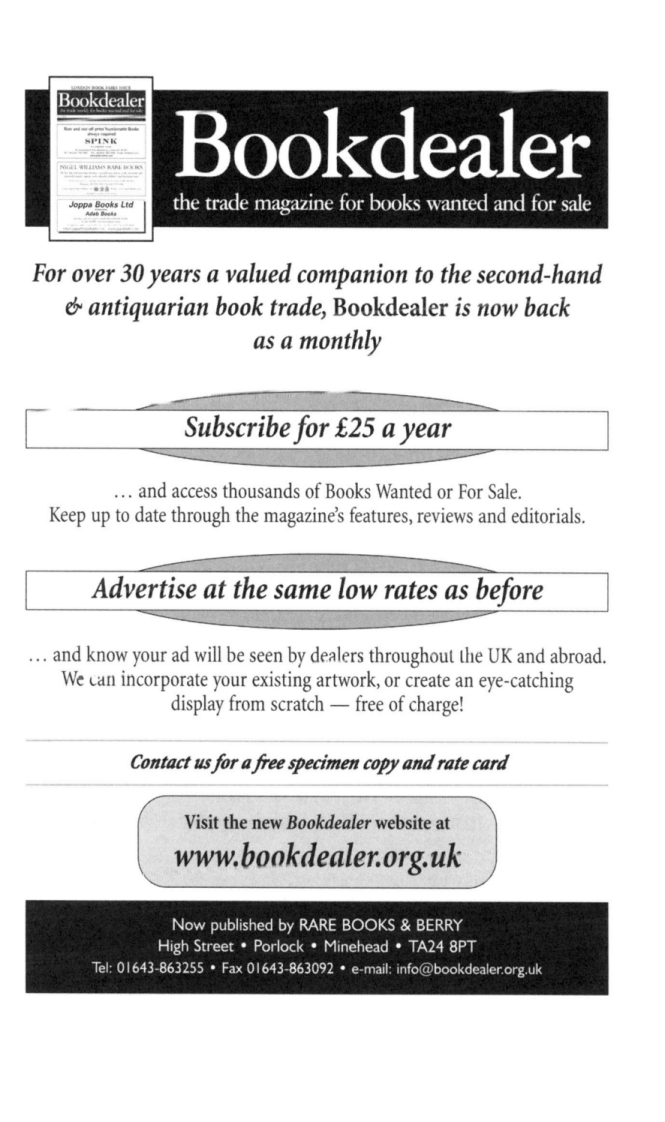

SUPPLIES AND SERVICES

APPRAISALS AND VALUATIONS

THE BOOK BUSINESS, 90 Greenford Avenue, London W7 3QS. Tel: (020) 8840 1185. E-mail: bookbusiness@homechoice.co.uk. Contact: Giles Levete.

CHURCH STREET BOOKS, 6 Church Street, Diss, Norfolk IP22 4DD. Tel: (01379) 652020. E-mail: atvidion@yahoo.co.uk. Contact: Andy Vidion.

FINE ART, 38 Tooting, London SW17 9QS. Tel: and Fax: (0208) 6961 1921. E-mail: sheppards@fineart.tm. Web: www.fineart.tm. Contact: Robert Walker.

STEVE LIDDLE, 8 Morley Square, Bishopston, Bristol BS7 9DW. Tel: (0117) 924 4846. E-mail: mail@steveliddle.co.uk. Contact: Steve Liddle.

SAX BOOKS, 4a High Street, Saxmundham, Suffolk IP17 1DF. Tel: (01728) 605775. E-mail: richard@saxbooks.co.uk. Contact: Richard W.L. smith, MVO.

BOOK AUCTIONEERS

ARMCHAIR AUCTIONS, 98 Junction Road, Andover, Hampshire SP10 3JA. Tel: and Fax: 01264 362048. Postal auction specialising in military, naval and aviation books, relics and ephemera. Monthy sales. Contact George Murdock

ANDERSON AND GARLAND, Anderson House, Crispin Court, Westerhope, Newcastle upon Tyne NE5 1BF. Tel: 0292 430 3000. Fax: 0191 430 3001. E-mail: info@andersonandgarland.com. Website: www.andersonandgarland.com.

BELLMAN'S, Newpound, Wisborough Green, Billinghurst, West Sussex RH14 0AZ. Tel: 01403 700858. E-mail: enquiries@bellmans.co.uk. *Regular sales of books, maps, autographs, ephemera and photographs.*

BLOOMSBURY AUCTIONS, Bloomsbury House, 24 Maddox Street, London W1S 1PP. Tel: (020) 7495-9494. Fax: 7495-9499. E-Mail: info@bloomsburyauctions.com. Web site: www.bloomsburyauctions.com.

BONHAMS, 101 New Bond Street, London W1S 1SR Tel: (020) 7447 7447. E-Mail: books@bonhams.com. View our catalogues on-line at www.bonhams.com. *At least 10 sales each season on books, maps, photographs, autographs and historical manuscripts.*

CAPES DUNN & CO., 38 Charles Street, Manchester M1 7DB. Tel: (0161) 273-1911. Fax: 273-3474. *Three to two sales per year. Catalogues can be accessed on* – www.ukauctioneers.com.

DOMINIC WINTER BOOK AUCTIONS, Mallard House, Broadway Lane, South Cerney, Nr Cirencester, Gloucestershire GL7 5UQ. Tel: (01285) 860006. Fax: 862461. E-Mail: info@dominicwinter.co.uk. Web: www.dominicwinter.co.uk.

FINAN & CO., The Square, Mere, Wiltshire BA12 6DJ. Tel: (01747) 861411. Fax: 861944. E-Mail: post@finanandco.co.uk. Website: www.finanandco.co.uk. 3 auctions annually, including specialist books, manuscripts, photographs and ephemera. Enquireis to Julia Finan

GEORGE KIDNER, The Saleroom, Emsworth Road, Lymington, Hampshire SO41 9BL. Tel: (01590) 670070. Fax: 675167. E-Mail: info@georgekidner.co.uk. Website: www.georgekidner.co.uk. *2 sales a year, 200-300 lots per sale. Catalogues on subscription - £20 a year.* Enquiries to: Andrew Reeves.

GOLDING YOUNG & CO, Old Wharf Road, Grantham, Lincolnshire NG31 7AA. Tel: (01476) 565118. Fax: (01476) 561475. E-mail: enquiries@goldingyoung.com. Website: www.goldingyoung.com. Contact: Colin Young. *Established in 1900, Goldings currently hold 4 Fine Art sales per annum. Each sale has a dedicated book section. For vendors a Trade Rate Card is available upon request including some 0% commissions.*

HAMPTON & LITTLEWOOD AUCTIONEERS, The Auction Rooms, Alphin Brook Road, Alphington, Exeter, Devon EX2 8TH. Tel: (01392) 413100. Fax: (01392) 413110. E-Mail: enquiries@hampton andlittlewood.co.uk. Website: www.hamptonandlittlewood.co.uk.

KEYS AUCTIONEERS, 8 Market Place, Aylsham, Norwich, Norfolk NR11 6EH. Tel: (01263) 733195. Fax: (01263) 732140. E-mail: mail@aylshamsalerooms.co.uk. Website: www.aylshamsalerooms.co.uk.

DAVID LAY, F.R.I.C.S., The Penzance Auction House, Alverton, Penzance, Cornwall TR18 4RE. Tel: (01736) 361414. Fax: 360035. E-Mail: david.lays@btopenworld.com. Website: www.davidlay.co.uk. *2 book auctions a year in March and September.* Enquiries to: Mr. John Floyd.

SUPPLIES AND SERVICES

LYON AND TURNNBULL, 33 Broughton Place, Edinburgh, EH1 3RR. Tel: (0131) 557 8844. Fax: (0131) 557 8668. Email: info@lyonandturnbull.com. Catalogues viewable at: www.lyonandturnbull.com. *Three major auctions yearly of rare books, modern first editions, photographs, autographs and historical manuscripts. Insurance, probate and sale valuations.*

MEALY'S LTD, Chatsworth Street, Castlecomer, County Kilkenny, Ireland. Tel: (056) 444-1229. Fax: (056) 444-1627. E-mail: info@mealys.com. Website: www.mealys.com. Irelands leading auctioneers of rare, interesting and valuable books. Contact: Fonsie Mealy.

OUTHWAITE & LITHERLAND, Kingsway Galleries, Fontenoy Street, Liverpool L3 2BE. Tel: (0151) 236-6561. Fax: 236-1070. E-mail: auction@lots.uk.com. Website: www.lots.uk.com.

SCARBOROUGH PERRY FINE ARTS, Unit 2, Grange Industrial Estate, Southwick, West Sussex BN42 4EN. Tel: (01273) 870371. Fax: 595706. E-Mail: info@scarboroughfinearts.co.uk.

STRIDE & SON AUCTIONEERS, Southdown House, St. John's Street, Chichester, West Sussex PO19 1XQ. Tel: (01243) 780207. Fax: 786713. E-Mail: enquiries@stridesauctions.co.uk. Website: www.stridesauctions.co.uk or www.catmaker.co.uk. Appointment necessary for consultations. Book dept open Wednesdays 9am – 12.30pm for appointments. Buyers premium 15% + VAT. *3 auctions a year covering books, documents, ephemera, stamps & postcards.* Enquiries to: Derek White (ephemera) or Adriaan Van Noorden (books).

LAWRENCES AUCTIONEERS, The Linen Yard, South Street, Crewkerne, Somerset TA18 8AB. Tel: 01460 73041. Fax: (01460) 270799. E-Mail: enquiries@lawrences.co.uk, Specialist book sales in January and July. *Also, fine art, silver and jewellery, furniture, pictures, collectables, militeria, and ceramics.*

SWORDERS INCORPORATING OLIVERS, The Salesroom, Burkitts Lane, Sudbury, Suffolk CO10 1HB. Tel: 01787 880305. E-mail: olivers@sworder.co.uk. Website: www.sworder.co.uk

TENNANTS, The Auction Centre, Leyburn, North Yorkshire DL8 5SG. Tel: 01969 623780. E-mail: enquiry@tennants-ltd.co.uk. Website: www.tennants.co.uk. 16 specialist departments; weekly sales; offices in Harrogate, North Yorkshire and Oakham, Rutland.

THOMAS MAWER & SON LTD., Dunston House, Portland Street, Lincoln, Lincolnshire LN5 7NN. Tel: 01522 524984. Fax: 01522 535600. E-mail: auctions@thosmawer.com. Web: www.thosmawer.com

THOMSON, RODDICK & MEDCALF, Coleridge House, Shaddongate, Carlisle CA2 5TU. Tel: (01228) 528939. E-mail: auctions@thomsonroddick.com. Web: www.thomsonroddick.com.

TRAFFORD BOOKS, P.O. Box 152, Salford, Manchester M17 1BP. Tel: (0161) 877 8818. E-mail: george@traffordbooks.fsnet.co.uk. *Eight sales per year at our Trafford Park premises - books, ephemera, postcards, prints, watercolours, maps and photographs.*

P.F. WINDIBANK, The Dorking Halls, Reigate Road, Dorking, Surrey RH4 1SG. Tel: (01306) 884556/ 876280. Fax: 884669. E-Mail: sjw@windibank.co.uk. Website: www.windibank.co.uk.

BOOK DISPLAY AND STORAGE EQUIPMENT, ETC

D AND M PACKAGING, 5a Knowl Road, Mirfield, West Yorkshire WF14 8DG. Tel: (01924) 495768. Fax: (01924) 491267. E-mail: packaging@dandmbooks.com. Website: www.bookcovers.co.uk. *Suppliers of all types of covers for hardbacks, paperbacks and dust jackets. Also comprehensive range of packaging and book-care materials, adhesives, book cleaners, tapes, etc. Free catalogue on request. We supply both trade and private customers and have no minimum order.*

P.B.F.A., The Old Coach House, 16 Melbourn Street, Royston, Hertfordshire SG8 7BZ. Tel: (01763) 248400. Fax: 248921. E-mail: info@pbfa.org. *Folding bookshelves in natural beech and new books on book collecting.*

POINT EIGHT LTD., Unit 14, Narrowboat Way, Blackbrook Valley Industrial Estate, Dudley, West Midlands DY2 0EZ. Tel: (01384) 238282. Free Phone 0800 731 4887. Fax: 455746. E-mail: sales@point8.co.uk. Website: www.pointeight.co.uk. *Bookshop and P.O.S. display equipment designer and manufacturer in wood, metal, plastic etc..*

SEALINE BUSINESS PRODUCTS LIMITED, Media House, 27 Postwood Green, Hertford Heath, Herts., SG13 7QJ. Tel: (01992) 558001. Fax: (01992) 304569. E-mail: sales@sealinemediastorage.com. Website: www.sealinemediastorage.com. *An attractive range of multi purpose cabinets designed to house a variety, or mix, of media types including CD, DVD, Video, Microfilm, DAT Tapes, Cassettes, Index Cards and much more. Complete with lock and anti-tilt in a choice of colour finishes. Shelving, mobile solutions and fire resistant storage compliment the range. Please visit our web site for full details.*

SUPPLIES AND SERVICES

BOOK FAIR ORGANISERS

ANTIQUARIAN BOOKSELLERS ASSOCIATION. Est: 1906. International Book Fair held annually in London, in June, also in Chelsea (UK dealers only) in Autumn and, occasional book fairs elsewhere. *For complimentary tickets or handbook of members, please contact:* Antiquarian Booksellers' Association, Sackville House, 40 Piccadilly, London W1J 0DR. Tel: (020) 7439-3118. Fax: 7439-3119. E-Mail: admin@aba.org.uk. Website: www.aba.org.uk.

BOOK COLLECTORS PARADISE. Est: 1986. *Enquiries to:* Trudy Ashford. Tel: (01442) 824440. Book fairs organiser for Wing Book Fair, 1st Sunday each month – 10–4pm.

BUXTON BOOK FAIRS, 75 Chestergate, Macclesfield, Cheshire SK11 6DG. Tel: (01625) 425352. *Enquiries to:* Sally Laithwaite. 9 fairs a year, held at Pavilion Gardens.

CIANA LTD., 24 Langroyd Road, London SW17 7PL. Tel: (020) 8682 1969. Fax: 8682 1997. E-mail: enquiries@ciana.co.uk. Organisers of remainder and promotional book fairs, held in London in September and in Brighton in January.

CLENT BOOKS OF BEWDLEY, Rose Cottage, Habberley Road, Wribbenhall, Bewdley, Worcs. DY12 1JA. Tel: + 44 (0) 1299 401090. E-mail: clent.books@btinternet.com. Website: www.clentbooks.co.uk. Co-organiser of Waverley Book Fair (Est. 1981). Third Sunday of each month at Kinver, Nr. Kidderminster. Contact: Ivor Simpson. (Member of P.B.F.A. and Francis Brett Young Soc.).

HD FAIRS LTD., 38 Fleetside, West Molesey, Surrey KT8 2NF. Tel: (020) 8224-3609. Fax: (020) 8224 3576. E-mail: admin@hdbookfairs.co.uk. Web: www.hdfairs.co.uk/books. Independent organisers for over 20 years, running the largest UK monthly Book Fairs in London – 100 plus exhibitors. Fairs in Farnham, Surrey and Kempton Park Racecourse – widest choice of books both Antiquarian and modern, as well as printed collectables. Free diary of events available on request; new exhibitors always welcome. Phone, fax, write, or e-mail HD Fairs Ltd: Wendy Collyer or Peter Sheridan.

FOREST BOOKS, 7 High Street West, Uppingham, Rutland LE15 9QB. Tel: (01572) 821173. Fax: (0870) 1326314. E-Mail: forestbooks@rutlanduk.fsnet.co.uk. Website: http://homepages.primex.co.uk/"Forest. *3 Book Fairs organised annually: 2 at Farndon Memorial Hall, near Newark, Nottinghamshire and 1 at Uppingham School, Rutland.* Please phone or e-mail for booking details. Maps & photos on our website.

GERRARDS CROSS BOOK FAIR. Est: 1974. Fairs held at the Memorial Centre, East Common, Gerrards Cross, Bucks. Dates for 2007: 13 January; 10 February; 14 April; 12 May; 8 September; 13 October; 10 November; 8 December. Enquiries to: Patty Lafferty on (01297) 21761. E-mail: patty@gxbooks.freeserve.co.uk.

LEEDS BOOK FAIR at Pudsey Civic Hall, Dawson's Corner, Pudsey. Fairs held 09:30–16:00 on first Sunday in every 2 months starting February. Refreshments. Free car parking. *Enquiries to:* Mr S. R. Cowie, Park Drive, Harrogate, N. Yorkshire HG2 9AY. Tel: (01423) 504168. Mobile: (0771) 9994728. [Updated 9.6.06]

MISSING BOOK FAIRS. Est: 1994. Book fairs Cambridge (12 a year), Peterborough (6 a year), Great Dunmow (2 a year), Knebworth House (3 a year) and Dedham (1 a year). *Enquiries to:* Chris Missing, 'Coppers', Main Road, Great Leighs, Essex CM3 1NR. Tel: (01245) 361609. E-mail: missingbooks@ madasafish.com

PROVINCIAL BOOKSELLERS' FAIRS ASSOCIATION. Est: 1974. Fairs held in Central London (monthly) and in more than 80 other towns in Great Britain. *Enquiries to:* Becky Wears, Provincial Booksellers' Fairs Association, The Old Coach House, 16 Melbourn Street, Royston, Herts, SG8 7BZ. Tel: (01763) 248400. Fax: 248921. Fairs Information Service: (24 hrs) (01763) 24921? F-Mail: info@pbfa.org. Website: www.pbfa.org. (See display advertisement).

SOUTHAMPTON BOOK FAIRS. Organiser: Bill Jackson. Tel: 023 8081 2640. E-mail: bill@ bilberry.ndo.co.uk. Venue: St Anne's School, Carlton Road, on Saturdays 10:00–16:00 21 April, 14 July, 13 October. Entrance 50p (accompanied children free).

SUFFOLK BOOK MARKETS at Long Melford. *10 Book Markets are held each year at the Village Memorial Hall with around 20+ book and ephemera dealers in attendance.* Exhibitor enquiries, dates etc. from the organiser: K. McLeod, Boxford Books and Fairs, 3 Firs Farm Cottage, Boxford, Sudbury, Suffolk CO10 5NU. Tel: (01787) 210810. Fax: (01473) 823187.

TITLE PAGE BOOK FAIRS, 176 Elmbridge Avenue, Surbiton, Surrey KT5 9HF. Tel: & Fax: (020) 8399 8168. Mobile (07966) 162758. *Fairs in Surrey: Dorking 6 a year, Cobham 4 a year, Banstead 4 a year. Fairs in Kent: Dorking open 10.00–15.30, Banstead and Cobbam open 09.15–15.30.* Contact: Keith Alexander.

Please let me take a little of your time...

Insurance is one of those matters we would all rather not think about - until something goes wrong!

Insurance is a complicated matter. It all seems so simple to begin with, pay your premium and sleep easily; that's all there is to it.

When things go wrong however - for example a burglary, missing parcel or even accidental damage by fire or flood - then anxious scrutiny of the policy can reveal that (a) you are under insured or (b) that the small print excludes your circumstances.

T.L. Dallas *(City)* **Ltd** are insurance brokers who have worked for the book trade for over 20 years, and arrange insurance cover for the PBFA and its members.

We are experienced in the needs of the antiquarian and secondhand bookseller and the particular requirements of the private collector - general house contents policies are rarely sufficient for substantial collections.

We can provide a bespoke package to suit *your* requirements. Allow us to guide you through the jargon and supply you with a policy that is right for your circumstances.

Please allow **T. L. Dallas** *(City)* **Ltd** to give you a no obligation quotation.

You may be pleasantly surprised at the cost of true peace of mind.

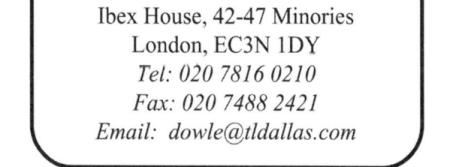

Authorised and Regulated by the Financial Services Authority

We can arrange household and book collectors insurance at favourable terms

SUPPLIES AND SERVICES

TOPAZ PROMOTIONS at Stafford 3 March, 11 August; Bristol 22 September; Reading 2 June. Also at Chiswick in January. See web site for more details: www.topaz.co.uk. E-mail: topaz@tiscali.co.uk. Tel: (020) 8274 0811.

WAVERLEY FAIRS, 9 Hayley Park Road, Halesowen B63 1EJ. Tel: (0121) 550-4123. Kinver Book Fair established 1981. 3rd Sunday of every month. Also at Powick, Malvern, Worcestershire. (2nd Sunday)

WINCHESTER BOOK FAIR. Organiser: Roly Hann. Tel: 01962 713929. Venue: Saxon Suite of Winchester Guildhall. Saturdays 10:00–16:00 17 March, 19 May, 15 September, 17 November. Entrance 50p (accompanied children free).

WORLD WAR BOOKFAIRS, Oaklands, Camden Park, Tunbridge Wells, Kent TN2 5AE. Tel: & Fax: (01892) 538465. E-Mail: wwarbooks@btinternet.com. Contact: Tim Harper. *Specialist military, aviation and naval bookfairs organised in London, Tunbridge Wells, Museum of Army Flying, Middle Wallop, Chatham and other locations from time to time.* Established in 1990, these are high quality fairs attracting some of the best specialist dealers in the UK. Held on Sundays - 22 April (Middle Wallop), 3 June (Bonnington Hotel, London), 18 November (Tonbridge Wells), 16 September (Chatham).

CATALOGUE PRINTERS

ADVANCE BOOK PRINTING, Unit 9 Northmoor Park, Church Road, Northmoor, Oxfordshire OX29 5UH. Tel: (01865) 301737. E-mail: Advancebp@aol.com. Contact: L Simister. *Catalogues, booklets and short run books.*

THE DOLPHIN PRESS, 96 Whitehill Road, Whitehill Industrial Estate, Glenrothes, Fife KY6 2RP. Tel: (01592) 771652. Fax: 630913. E-Mail: liz@dolphinpress.co.uk. Web : www.dolphinpress.co.uk *Catalogues and booklets printed.*

HOOVEY'S BOOKS, P.O. Box 27, St. Leonards-on-Sea, East Sussex TN37 6TZ. Tel & Fax: (01424) 753407. E-mail: books@hooveys.co.uk. Website: www.hooveys.co.uk. We offer a budget-priced, 24 hour turnaround Catalogue Printing Service for book dealers – ask us to quote for your next catalogue – we aim to save you money. We are also suppliers of CoverClean the Trade cleaner for cloth covers, paperbacks and dust jackets (£12.95 plus £2.00 p&p). Contact: Romney Hoovey.

JOSHUA HORGAN PRINT PARTNERSHIP, 246 Marston Road, Oxford OX3 0EL. Tel: (01865) 246762. Fax: (01865) 250555. E-mail: print@joshuahorgan.co.uk. Website: www.joshuahorgan.co.uk

PARCHMENT PRINTERS, Printworks, Crescent Road, Cowley, Oxford OX4 2PB. Tel: (01865) 747547. Fax: 747551. E-mail: print@ParchmentUK.com. Website: www.PrintUK.com. Specialist in short run production. Contact Ian Kinch.

CRAFT BOOKBINDERS

ATKINSON BOOK BINDERS, 19 Glenmore Business Park, Telford Road, Salisbury, Wiltshire SP2 7GL. Tel (01722) 329846. E-mail: atkinsonbinders@ukonline.co.uk

JOSEPHINE BACON, 197 Kings Cross Road, London WC1X 9BD. Tel: (020) 7278 9490. Fax: 7278 2447. E-mail: bacon@langservice.com. *Specialist in foreign language material, judaica and cookery and funghi.*

GEORGE BAYNTUN, incorporating Robert Riviere, Manvers Street, Bath BA1 1JW. Tel: (01225) 466000. Fax: 482122. E-mail: ebc@georgebayntun.com. Website: www.georgebayntun.com. *Fine binding in leather, restoration and case-making since 1894 (and Robert Riviere since 1829).*

CLIVE BOVILL, "Greenburn" River Lane, East Bilney, Dereham NR20 4HS. Tel: (01362) 860174. *Letterpress fine bindings, gold tooling and design. Special interest in conservation of 17th to 19th century books.*

BRADY BOOKBINDERS, Library Building, Library Avenue, Lancaster University LA1 4YH. Tel: (01524) 592512. E-mail: gerard.brady@yahoo.co.uk. Contact: Gerard Brady. *Craft binding, thesis and book restoration.*

BRISTOL BOUND BOOKBINDING, 300 North Street, Ashton Gate, Bristol BS3 1JU. Tel & Fax: (0117) 966 3300. E-mail: information@bristolbound.co.uk. Website: www.bristolbound.co.uk. Rachel and Richard James. *We are a husband and wife team first established in 1986 when Rachel gained distinctions in bookbinding from Brunel Technical College, Bristol. We aim to offer a professional, yet friendly service to our*

SUPPLIES AND SERVICES

customers, whilst maintaining a high standard of workmanship. We undertake new and restoration binding, thesis and dissertation binding, limited editions, corporate presentation binding, binding of newspapers, journals, magazines, personal memoirs, visitors books, photograph albums, wedding albums and much more.

PHILIP N. BROOK (BOOKBINDER AND BOOK RESTORER), Bell Hill Farm, Lindale in Cartmel, Grange over Sands, Cumbria LA11 6LD. Tel: (01539) 534241. *Bookbinding, book restoration and conservation. To include single volume restorations, fine binding, short run (up to 1,000) publishers. Case work. All aspects of bookbinding work considered. Serving collectors, libraries and dealers for over twenty-one years.*

FRANCIS BROWN CRAFT BOOKBINDER, 24 Camden Way, Dorchester, Dorset DT1 2RA. Tel: (01305) 266039. *Francis Brown is a journeyman bookbinder who undertakes all kinds of binding work, ranging from simple repairs to the restoration of antiquarian volumes, fine limited editions or designed bindings. He has restored books for Balliol College, Wimborne Minster chained library and the Thomas Hardy Memorial Collection in the County Museum in Dorchester.*

CHIVERS-PERIOD, Aintree Avenue, White Horse Business Park, Trowbridge, Wiltshire BA14 0XB. Tel: (01225) 752888. Fax: (01225) 752666. E-mail: info@chivers-period.co.uk. Website: www. chivers-period.co.uk. Contact: Gerry Beale. *Binding, rebinding and repairing books since 1878. Conserving paper for a quarter of a century.*

FORMBYS LTD, 19-21 Market Place, Ramsbottom, Lancashire BL0 9AJ. Tel: and Fax: (01706) 825771. E-mail: formbys@tiscali.co.uk. Website: www.artisanbooks.co.uk. *Craft Bookbinding and book restoration.*

CHRIS HICKS BOOKBINDER, 64 Merewood Avenue, Sandhills, Oxford OX3 8EF. Tel: (01865) 769346. E-Mail: chrishicksbookbinder@btinternet.com. Website: www.book-binder.co.uk. *Binding, rebinding, repairs, theses, slipcases, solander cases, fine bindings, short-run edition binding, blank books etc.*

FELICITY HUTTON, Langore House, Langore, Launceston, Cornwall PL15 8LD. Tel: (01566) 773831. E-Mail: pandfhutton@hotmail.com. *Bookbinding and restoration.*

KEW BOOKBINDING, 61a North Street, Thame, Oxfordshire OX9 3BH. Tel: and Fax: (01844) 212035. E-mail: malcolmkew@mac.com. Web: www.kewbookbinding.co.uk.. *Quality binding, short run, restoration, journals.*

KINGSWOOD BOOKS, 17 Wick Road, Milborne Port, Sherborne, Dorset DT9 5BT. Tel: & Fax: (01963) 250280. E-mail: kingswoodbooks@btinternet.com. Website: www.kingswoodbooks .btinternet.co.uk. *Bookbinding & conservation.* Enquiries to A.J. Dollery.

NEWCASTLE BOOKSHOP AT HALTWHISTLE, Market Square, Haltwhistle, Northumberland NE49 0BG. Tel: 01434 320103. Mobile: 07837 982809. E-mail: newcstlbk@aol.com. Website: www.newcastlebookshop.com. *Repair and restore books; make wedding albums, blank journals, visitors books, and custom made drop-back boxes. Also, mount artwork using archival board.*

D SANDERSON, Primrose Mill, London Road, Preston, Lancashire. Tel: (01772) 253594. Fax: (01772) 253592. E-mail: sanderson2003@aol.com. Contact: Mr J. Doherty. *Book restoration and print finishers.*

CHARLES SYMINGTON, 145 Bishopthorpe Road, York YO23 1NZ. Tel: (01904) 633995. *Bookbinding and restoration.*

JAYNE TANDY (CRAFT BOOKBINDING AND RESTORATION), Bowhayes Cross, Williton, Somerset TA4 4NL. Tel: (01984) 632293. *Bookbinding, book restoration, conservation and repair.*

COLIN TATMAN, Corner House, 121A Lairgate, Beverley, E. Yorskire HU17 8JG. Tel: (01482) 880611 (day) & 882153 (evening). *Traditional craft bookbinding; paper repair; slipcases & book boxes; restoration & conservation.*

TEASDALE BOOKBINDERS, Caxton House, Corwen, Denbighshire LL21 0AA. Tel: (01490) 412 713. 7316. E-Mail: info@teasdalebookbinders.co.uk. *Hand bookbinding and restoration. Prop: Catherine Hore.*

TEMPLE BOOKBINDERS, 10 Quarry Road, Headington, Oxford OX3 8NU. Tel: (01865) 451940. E-Mail: enquiries@templebookbinders.co.uk. Website: www.templebookbinders.co.uk. Mr. Ian Barnes. *Hand bookbinder in fine leathers, vellum, linens, cloth & buckrams. Quality restorer of antiquarian books.*

Visiting London? Think PBFA!

The monthly Holiday Inn Book Fairs are a major source of fresh material for dealers, collectors and librarians Keep ALL our London dates in mind when planning your next visit to London

HOLIDAY INN LONDON BLOOMSBURY

CORAM STREET, WC1N 1HT

Monthly one - day fairs 2007

April	Sun 8	May	Sun 13
July	Sun 8	August	Sun 12
September	Sun 9	October	Sun 14
November	Sun 11	December	Sun 9

Summer International Fairs 2007

2 Fairs in 2 locations

Fair One: Hotel Russell Sun/Mon 3 - 4 June

Fair Two: Novotel London West Shortlands, Hammersmith Fri/Sat 8 - 9 June

---

And for the specialists

Travel & Exploration Book Fair Sunday 1 April 2007, 11-5 **Royal Geographical Society, 1 Kensington Gore, SW7**

Performing Arts Book Fairs Saturday 31st March & Saturday 6th October at the **Olivier Foyer, National Theatre, South Bank**

Please note: all dates subject to change so please check our website www.pbfa.org for latest information

Organised by the PBFA, The Old Coach House, Melbourn St, Royston, Herts, Great Britain, SG8 7BZ Tel: 01763 248400, Fax: 01763 248921 email: info@pbfa.org web: www.pbfa.org

SUPPLIES AND SERVICES

JOHN TEMPLE BOOK BINDER, 5 Celia Heights, Bodmin, Cornwall PL31 1EH. Tel: 01208 76252. Mobile: 07963 199145. E-mail: john@johntemple.wanadoo.co.uk. *Hand book binding in leather, full, half and quarter; slipcases, boxes; and traditional casebinding. French marble to plain ends. Wide choice of materials, goat, calfskin and skivers, as well as cloth. Also binds PPC and paperbacks.*

TRADITIONAL BOOKCRAFTS, 28 Drayton Mill Court, Cheshire Street, Market Drayton, Shropshire TF9 1EF. Tel: (01630) 654410. *Craft bookbinder, antique and modern book repair and restoration, boxes, slipcases, gold tooling, handmade and scribed books. Established: 1983. Limited edition bindings. Prices on request. Prop: Monica Thornton.*

TUDOR BOOKBINDING LTD., 3 Lyon Close, Wigston, Leicestershire LE18 2BJ Tel: (0116) 288 3988. Fax: (0116) 288 4878. E-mail: sales@tudor-bookbinding.co.uk. Antique and modern book restoration, repair and rebinding; gold tooling; single copy restorations work undertaken.

PERIOD FINE BINDINGS, Yew Tree Farm, Stratford Road, Wootton Wawen, Warwickshire B95 6BY. Telephone: (01564) 793800. E-mail: periodfinebindings@googlemail.com. Website: http:// periodfinebindings.typepad.com/royal_bindings. *Restorer of antiquarian books using ancient formulae and hand-made materials. Fox marks, inkstains etc removed. Rare books bought, sold and valued.*

RILEY DUNN & WILSON LTD., Glasgow Road, Falkirk, Scotland FK1 4HP. Tel: 01324 621591 Fax: 01324 611508. E-mail: enquiry@rdw.co.uk. Website: www.rdw.co.uk. *Restoration of antiquarian books, fine bindings, presentation bindings and expert paper conservation.*

PACKING MATERIALS SUPPLIERS

BOOK PROTECTORS & CO., Protector House, 76 South Grove, Walthamstow, London, E17 7NU. Tel: 0181 520 0012. *Unique protective covers for paperbacks and hardbacks, adjustable sleeving and other materials.*

D AND M PACKAGING, 5a Knowl Road, Mirfield, West Yorkshire WF14 8DG. Tel: (01924) 495768. Fax: (01924) 491267. E-mail: packaging@dandmbooks.com. Website: www.bookcovers.co.uk. Contact: Daniel Hanson. *Suppliers of all types of covers for hardbacks, paperbacks and dust jackets. Also comprehensive range of packaging and book-care materials, adhesives, book cleaners, tapes, etc. Free catalogue on request. We supply both trade and private customers and have no minimum order.*

MACFARLANE GROUP PLC., **Group Head Office:** 21 Newton Place, Glasgow, Scotland G3 7PY. Tel: (0141) 333 9666. Fax: (0141) 333 1988. Website: www.macfarlanegroup.net

PACKING CASE MANUFACTURERS: **Grantham Branch:** PO Box 16, Alma Park Industrial Estate, Grantham, Lincolnshire NG31 9SF. Tel: (0870) 150 4506. Fax: (0870) 150 4507. **Westbury Branch:** Quartermaster Road, West Wilts Trading Estate, Westbury, Wiltshire BA13 4JT. Tel: (01373) 858555. Fax: (01373) 858999.

PACKAGING DISTRIBUTION: **Bristol Branch:** Unit 2 Concorde Road, Patchway Industrial estate, Bristol BS34 5TB Tel: (0870) 850 0542. Fax: (0870) 850 0543. **Exeter Branch**: Windsor Court, Manaton Close, Matford Business Park, Exeter, Devon EX2 8PF, Tel: (0870) 608 6110. Fax: (0870) 608 6111. **Coventry Branch:** Siskin Parkway East, Middlemarch Business Park, Coventry, West Midlands CV3 4PE. Tel: (0870) 608 6205. Fax: (0870) 608 6206. **Enfield Branch:** Unit 5, Delta Park, Millmarsh Lane, Enfield, EN3 7QJ. Tel: (0870) 850 0116. Fax: (0870) 850 0117 **Fareham Branch:** Unit 1, Stephenson Road, Midpoint 27, Segensworth, Fareham, Hampshire PO15 5RZ. Tel: (0870) 608 6160. Fax: (0870) 608 6161. **Glasgow Branch:** Unit 1 Linwood Industrial Estate, Burnbrae Road, Linwood, Paisley PA3 3BD. Tel: (0870) 150 4508. Fax: (0870) 150 4509. **Gloucestershire Branch:** Bloomfields Supplies Ltd., Unit 68, Quedgeley Enterprise Centre, Naas Lane, Quedgeley, Gloucester GL2 2ZZ. **Horsham Branch:** Oakhurst Business Park, Wilberforce Way, Southwater, Horsham, West Sussex RH13 9RT Tel: (0870) 608 6150. Fax: (0870) 608 6151. **Lincolnshire Branch:** Alma Park Industrial Estate, Grantham, Lincolnshire NG31 9SE. Tel: (0870) 150 4506. Fax: (0870) 150 4507. **Manchester Branch:** Empire Court, Fifth Avenue, Trafford Park, Manchester M17 1TN. Tel: (0870) 150 4500. Fax: (0870) 150 4501. **Milton Keynes Branch:** Kingston Gateway, Whitehall Avenue, Milton Keynes, Buckinghamshire MK10 0BU. Tel: (0870) 150 4502. Fax: (0870) 150 4503. **Tyne & Wear Branch:** The Waterfront, Kingfisher Boulevard, Newburn Riverside, Tyne & Wear NE15 8NZ. Tel: (0870) 608 6100. Fax: (0870) 608 6101. **Sudbury Branch:** Windham Road, Chilton Industrial Estate, Sudbury, Suffolk CO10 2XD. Tel: (0870) 608 6140. Fax: (0870) 608 6141. **Telford Branch:** Unit D2, Horton Park Industrial Estate, Hortonwood 7, Telford, Shropshire TF7 7GX. Tel: (0870) 608 6120.

Fax: (0870) 608 6121. **Wakefield Branch:** Unit H, Brunel Road, Wakefield 41 Industrial Estate, Wakefield WF2 0XG. Tel: (0870) 850 0118. Fax: (0870) 850 0119. **Wigan Branch:** Northgate Distribution Centre, Caxton Close, Wheatlea Park Industrial Estate, Wigan WN3 6XU. Tel: (0870) 150 4512. Fax: (0870) 150 4513.

Macfarlane Packaging provides a complete range of packaging materials, including New Book Pack and Super Book Pack, Postal bags and Easywrap.

PLASPAK, Piperell Way, Haverhill, Suffolk CB9 8QW (A Division of Marchant Manufacturing). Tel: (01440) 765300. Fax: 765302. E-mail: sales@marchant.co.uk. Website: www.plaspak.co.uk *Polythene manufacturer and specialist packaging.*

DISTRIBUTORS AND WHOLESALERS (NEW BOOK TRADE)

GARDNERS BOOKS LTD., 1 Whittle Drive, Willington Drove, Eastbourne, BN23 6QH. Tel: (01323) 521555. Fax: (01323) 521666. Web: www.gardners.com. Wholesalers.

GAZELLE BOOK SEVICES Ltd., White Cross Mills, High Town, Lancaster LA1 4XS. Tel: (01524) 68765. Fax: (01524) 63232. E-mail: sales@gazellebooks.co.uk. Web: www.gazellebooks.co.uk. Distributors.

REMAINDER MERCHANTS

AWARD PUBLICATIONS LTD., The Old Riding School, Welbeck Estate, Worksop, Nottinghamshire S80 3LR. Tel: (01909) 478170. Fax: (01909) 484632. *E-mail: info@awardpublications.co.uk Genuine remainders for adults and children.*

BOOKMARK REMAINDERS LTD., Rivendell, Illand, Launceston, Cornwall PL15 7LS. Tel: (01566) 782 728. Fax: (01566) 782 059. E-mail: info@book-bargains.co.uk. WebSite: www.book-bargains.co.uk. Range of genuine remainders and bargain books. Trade sales only.

BLAKETON HALL LTD., Unit 1, 26 Marsh Green Road, Marsh Barton, Exeter EX2 8PN. Tel: (01392) 210602. Fax: 421165. E-Mail: sales@blaketonhall.co.uk. *Remainders and overstocks, including scientific, technical, academic, gardening, crafts & children's.* Enquiries to: Martin Shillingford.

CONSOLIDATED BOOKS LTD., Units 3 & 4, Tyler Way, Sheffield, Yorkshire S9 1DT. Tel: (0114) 243 6323. Fax: (0114) 243 6085. E-mail: consobooks@btconnect.com. Publishers end-of lines and a cash and carry warehouse.

FANSHAW BOOKS, Unit 7, Lysnader Mews, Lysander Grove, London N19 3QP. Tel: (0845) 330 2511. Fax: (0207) 3502. E-Mail: info@roybloom.com. www.roybloom.com. *General remainders. Exhibits at all major book fairs.*

GRANGE BOOKS PLC., The Grange, Units 1–6 Kingsnorth Industrial Estate, Hoo, Nr. Rochester, Kent ME3 9ND. Tel: (01634) 256000. Fax: 255500. E-Mail: sales@grangebooks.co.uk. Website: www.grangebooks.co.uk. *Distributors of remainders, and publisher of promotional books and reprints to the adult illustrated non-fiction and children's market.*

HCB Wholesale, Unit 2, Forest Road Enterprise Park, Hay-on-Wye HR3 5DS. Tel: (01497) 820 333. Fax: (01497) 821 192. E-mail: sales@hcbwholesale.co.uk. Approx. 100,000 books on view in warehouse.

JIM OLDROYD BOOKS, 14/18 London Road, Sevenoaks, Kent TN13 1AJ. Tel: (01732) 463356. Fax: 464486. E-Mail: paula@oldroyd.co.uk. Web site: www.oldroyd.co.uk. *Adult and children's remainders.*

PUMKIN WHOLESALE. Grove Farms, Milton Hill Road, Abingdon, Oxfordshire OX14 4DP. Tel: (01235) 833450. Fax: (01235) 833490. E-mail: info@pumpkinwholesale.com. Web: www .pumpkinwholesale.com

SANDERSON BOOKS LTD, Front Street, Klondyke, Cramlington, Northumberland NE23 6RF. Tel: (01670) 735855. Fax: (01670) 730974. E-mail: sales@sandersonbooks.co.uk. Website: www. sandersonbooks.co.uk.

SANDPIPER BOOKS LTD., Offices and Showroom, 24 Langroyd Road, London SW17 7PL. Tel: (020) 8767-7421. Fax: 8682-0280. E-Mail: enquiries@sandpiper.co.uk. Website: www.sandpiper.co.uk. *Scholarly and literary remainders, academic reprints and mail order.*

SUPPLIERS OF MATERIALS AND TOOLS FOR BINDING AND RESTORING BOOKS, ETC.

FALKINER FINE PAPERS, 76 Southampton Row, London WC1B 4AR. Tel: (020) 7831-1151. E-mail: info@falkiners.com. Web: www.falkiners.com. *PAPERS. Wide selection of papers for repairs, marbled papers and coloured end papers. LEATHERS AND BOOKCLOTHS for repairs and bindings. BOOKS in print on bookbinding, calligraphy, typography, papermaking and printing history. All items can be supplied by post. Price lists available.*

FINE CUT GRAPHIC IMAGING LTD., Marlborough Road, Lancing Business Park, Lancing, West Sussex BN15 8UF. Tel: (01903) 751666. Fax: 750462. E-Mail: info@finecut.co.uk. Website: www.finecut.co.uk. *Manufacturers of bookbinders' finishing tools and accessories. Catalogue available (also available on-line) showing brass type, handle letters, hand tools and brass rolls. Special designs to order.*

HARMATAN LEATHER LTD, Westfield Avenue, Higham Ferrers, Northamptonshire NN10 8AX. Tel: (01933) 412151. Fax: (01933) 412242. E-mail: contact@harmatan.co.uk. Website: www.harmatan.co.uk.

HANDMADE PAPER COMPANY LTD., 16 Daleham Gardens, London NW3 5DA. Tel: (0207) 435 8008. *Papercrafts, and paper making, handmade paper, artists paper. Contact: David Ury.*

J. HEWIT AND SONS LIMITED, Kinauld Leather Works, Currie, Edinburgh, Scotland EH14 5RS. Tel: (0131) 449-2206. Fax: (0131) 451-5081. E-Mail: sales@hewit.com. Website: www.hewit.com. *BOOKBINDERS' TOOLS AND SUPPLIES, adhesive (paste, glue, P.V.A.), bone folders, brass type and type holders, brushes, knives, papers (marbled, etc.), presses, tapes, threads. BINDING LEATHERS, in a wide range of colours. BOOKCLOTHS, buckram, linen, cloth, mull, etc. BOOKBINDERS STARTER PACKS, basic tools to get you started.*

HOOVEY'S BOOKS, P.O. Box 27, St. Leonards-on-Sea, East Sussex TN37 6TZ. Tel & Fax: (01424) 753407. E-mail: hooveys@lineone.net. Website: www.hooveys.co.uk. *We offer a budget-priced, 24 hour turnaround Catalogue Printing Service for book dealers – ask us to quote for your next catalogue – we aim to save you money. We are also suppliers of CoverClean the Trade cleaner for cloth covers, paperbacks and dust jackets (£12.95 plus £2.00 p&p).*

ANN MUIR MARBLING, 1 St. Algar's Yard, West Woodlands, Frome, Somerset BA11 5ER. Tel: & Fax. (01985) 844786. E-mail: annmuir@marbling.freeserve.co.uk. Website: www.annmuirmarbling.co.uk. *Marbled paper in both modern and traditional patterns and colourways. Matching service for old papers in restoration work. New papers designed for individual projects. Send for catalogue of samples and price list.*

PAPERSAFE, 2 Green Bank, Adderley, Market Drayton TF9 3TH. Tel: (01630) 652217. E-Mail: philip@papersafe.demon.co.uk. Website: www.papersafe.demon.co.uk. *Suppliers of archival quality repair materials for book and paper collectors.*

PICREATOR ENTERPRISES LIMITED, 44 Park View Gardens, Hendon, London NW4 2PN. Tel: (020) 8202-8972. Fax: (020) 8202-3435. E-mail: info@picreator.co.uk. Website: www.picreator.co.uk. *Fine–art conservation and restoration materials. Manufacturers of Renaissance wax polish, Vulpex liquid soap and Groom/stick non abrasive document dry cleaner. Bookdealers are increasingly undertaking basic cleaning and restorative treatment of books and paper. Picreator Enterprises supply professional products which are simple to use and advice is given on their application. The Company has held a Royal warrant of appointment to H.M. The Queen since 1984 as suppliers of products for (fine-art) restoration and conservation.*

RUSSELL BOOKCRAFTS, Unit 1, Bluntswood Hall, Throcking, Buntingford, Hertfordshire SG9 9RN. Tel: (01763) 281430. Fax: (01763) 281431. E-Mail: office@russels.com. Website: www.russels.com. *Major supplier of very fine leathers. Range includes the world renowned, and only genuine "OASIS" goatskin, calf and sheepskin skivers – handmade bookbinders' equipment includes, specially designed work benches, nipping presses, lying presses, ploughs, sewing frames and Digby Stuart presses. We offer a fine colour range of Buckrams and bookcloths, mulls, Jaconette, tapes, threads and headbands; a large selection of specialised papers, marbled end papers, & millboards. Tools include: paring knives, bridled glue brushes, decorative hand tools and brass letters. Backing hammers, bone folders, burnishing agates and all types of bookbinders adhesives.*

SUPPLIES AND SERVICES

USEFUL WEBSITES

*Please note that in this selection the details are correct when going to press but changes and new ones may appear during the year. **Those in bold are multi-search sites.** Some trade associations also offer book searching facilities, see pages 20–23.*

FOR SEARCHING TITLES

ABooksearch	www.abooksearch.com
Addall	**www.addall.com**
Advanced Book Exchange	www.abebooks.com
Abebooks Europe GmbH	www.abebooks.co.uk
Alibris	www.alibris.com
Alibris (UK)	www.alibris.co.uk
Amazon	www.amazon.com
Antiqbook (The Netherlands)	www.antiqbook.com
Antiquarian Booksellers Association of America (ABAA)	www.abaa.org
Barnes & Noble	www.bn.com
ANZAAB (Australia & New Zealand)	www.anzaab.com.au/anzaab/search
Bibliology	www.bibliology.com
Biblion	www.biblion.co.uk
Bibliophile	www.bibliophile.net
Bibliopoly (England)	www.bibliopoly.com
BiblioQuest International (Australia)	www.biblioz.com
Books and Collectibles	www.booksandcollectibles.com.au
Bookfinder.com	**www.bookfinder.com**
Elephant Books	www.elephantbooks.com
Independent Booksellers Network (England)	www.ibooknet.co.uk
Independent OnLine Booksellers Association	www.iobabooks.com
International League of Booksellers (ILAB)	www.ilab-lila.com
The Internet Bookshop UK Ltd	www.ibuk.com
Maremagnum (Italy)	www.maremagnum.com
Powell's Books	www.powells.com
Provincial Book Fairs Association (PBFA)	www.booksatpbfa.com
Sheppard's World	www.sheppardsworld.co.uk
Strand Books (USA)	www.strandbooks.com
Tom Folio	www.tomfolio.com
UKBookWorld	www.ukbookworld.com
Used Books Central (USA)	www.usedbookcentral.com
Zentrales Verzeichnis Antiquarischer Bücher (ZVAB, Germany)	www.zvab.com

FOR SEARCHING DEALERS

Advanced Book Exchange	www.abebooks.com
Sheppard's World	www.sheppardsworld.co.uk

GENERAL SEARCH SITES

Ask Jeeves	www.askjeeves.com
EBay	www.ebay.co.uk
Google	www.google.co.uk
Dog Pile	**www.dogpile.com**
Mamma	**www.mamma.com**

BOOK SEARCH

IF YOUR SEARCHES ON ABE / ALIBRIS ET AL SHOW NO RESULTS – IT MAY NOT BE THEIR FAULT!

WHEN THIS HAPPENS – TRY A NEW METHOD FOR BOOKSEARCHES

Most book dealers do not have the time, or resources, to create records of all their stock for Internet search engines. Where dealers stock specific subjects, a substantial number of titles in those subjects will not be available to your searches.

When your search fails, Sheppard's World offers you a quick method of locating dealers who specialise in the subject of the book you seek, and provides a platform for you to rapidly send individual e-mail requests.

www.sheppardsworld.co.uk

Atlanticweb.co.uk **Websites from £200**

Bookdealer websites	▸ sell books online
	▸ secure sites
Database design	▸ online booksearches
	▸ stock control
Makeovers for existing sites	

All enquiries to: sales@atlanticweb.co.uk
Telephone: (01271) 828242

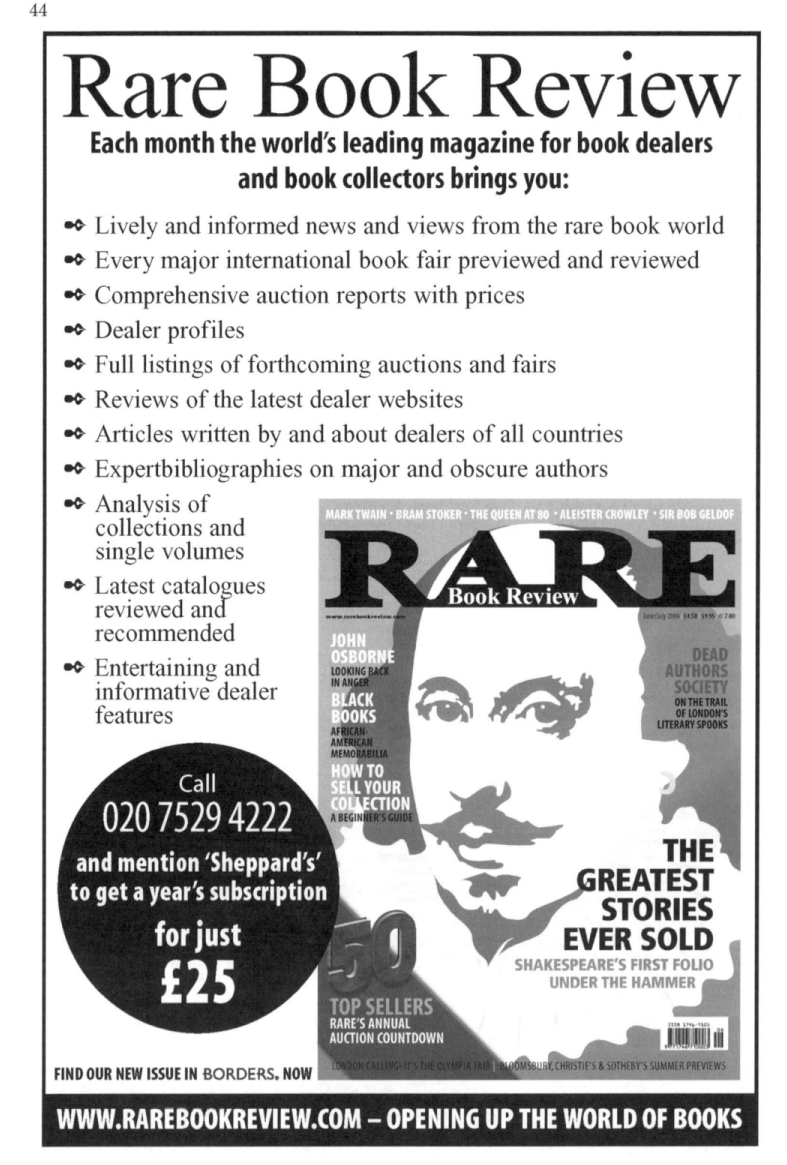

INDEX OF CITIES AND TOWNS

Dealer locations listed alphabetically by country, city, town and village, as shown in the Geographical section.

ABERDEEN................... 272
ABERFELDY.................. 281
ABERGAVENNY............ 287
ABERYSTWYTH 284
ABINGDON................... 206
ABOYNE....................... 272
ADARE 266
ADDINGHAM, ILKLEY .. 246
ADDLESTONE............... 231
AIRDRIE 279
ALCESTER.................... 237
ALFRETON.................... 82
ALFRISTON 99
ALNWICK..................... 202
ALRESFORD 121
ALSTON 77
ALTON.......................... 121
ALTRINCHAM 68, 118
ALVERSTOKE 121
AMERSHAM 61
AMMANFORD 284
ANDOVER 121
ANSTRUTHER 271
APPLEBY-IN-
-WESTMORLAND 77
ARBROATH 281
ARMAGH 260
ARUNDEL 242
ASCOT 55
ASHBURTON 84
ASHFORD...................... 136
ASHPERTON 128
ASHTEAD 231
ASHTON-UNDER-LYNE . 118
ATHERSTONE 237
AUSTWICK 193
AXMINSTER 84
AYLESBURY.................. 61
AYLSHAM 187
AYR.............................. 279
AYSGARTH 193

BAKEWELL 82
BALDERTON 204
BALLATER 273
BALLINLOUGH, ... 262
BALLINTEER 264
BALLYDEHOB............... 263
BALLYGOWAN 261
BALLYNAHINCH 261
BANBURY 206
BANBURY 207
BANGOR 261
BANGOR (WALES)......... 287
BANTRY........................ 263
BARNARD CASTLE 97
BARNSTAPLE................. 84
BARRINGTON................ 216
BARROW-IN-FURNESS.. 77
BARTON-ON-HUMBER.. 150
BASINGSTOKE 121
BATH 216
BATHEASTON 217
BATLEY 246
BATTLE 99
BEACONSFIELD 61
BEADNELL.................... 202
BEAMINSTER................. 91
BECCLES 226
BECKENHAM 136
BEDALE 193
BEDDINGTON................ 231
BEDFORD...................... 53
BEDWORTH................... 237
BELFAST 260
BERE ALSTON 84
BERKELEY 113
BERKHAMSTED............ 130
BESFORD 255
BETHESDA 287
BEULAH........................ 288
BEVERLEY 106
BEWDLEY 255
BEXHILL 99
BEXLEY 136
BICKERSTAFFE.............. 143
BIDDENDEN.................. 136
BIDEFORD 85
BIGGAR 279
BILLERICAY 108
BILLINGBOROUGH 150
BILLINGHAM 193
BILLINGHAY.................. 150
BILLINGSHURST 242
BILSTON 239
BINHAM........................ 187
BIRCH........................... 108
BIRCHWOOD 68
BIRKENHEAD................ 185
BIRMINGHAM 239
BISHOP AUCKLAND...... 97
BISHOP'S CASTLE.......... 213
BISHOP'S STORTFORD... 130
BISHOPS CLEEVE 113
BISHOPSTON.................. 58
BLACKBURN 143
BLACKHEATH 165
BLACKPOOL.................. 143
BLACKROCK 264
BLAENAU FFESTINIOG . 287
BLAENAVON 294
BLAIR ATHOLL.............. 281
BLAIRGOWRIE 281
BLANDFORD FORUM ... 91
BLEWBURY 207
BLUNTISHAM 63
BOGNOR REGIS 242
BOLTON 118
BOURNEMOUTH............ 91
BOWNESS-ON–
WINDERMERE........... 77
BOXFORD 226
BRACKLEY.................... 200
BRACKNELL................... 55
BRADFORD 246
BRADFORD ON AVON... 251
BRAINTREE................... 108
BRECON........................ 289
BRENCHLEY.................. 136
BRENTWOOD 108
BRIDGATER 217
BRIDGEND.................... 273
BRIDGEWATER 217
BRIDGNORTH 213
BRIDLINGTON............... 106
BRIDPORT 92
BRIDPORT..................... 92
BRIGHOUSE 246
BRIGHTON 99
BRINSCALL 143
BRISTOL........................ 58
BRIXHAM...................... 85
BROADWAY 136
BROCKLEY.................... 165
BROOM 53
BROUGH 77
BROUGH 77
BUCKINGHAM 61
BUDE............................ 73
BUILTH WELLS.............. 289
BULLWELL.................... 204
BUNCLODY 267
BUNGAY 226

INDEX OF CITIES AND TOWNS

BURES 226
BURFORD 207
BURTON UPON TRENT . 224
BURY............................ 143
BURY ST EDMUNDS 226
BUSHEY 130
BUXTON 82
BY DUNBLANE 269
BYFLEET 231

CAISTER-ON-SEA 187
CALLANDER 269
CALLANDER 269
CALLINGTON 73
CALNE 251
CAMBORNE................... 73
CAMBRIDGE 63
CAMBRIDGE (GLOS)...... 113
CAMPBELTOWN 279
CANTERBURY 136
CARDIFF 283
CARDIGAN.................... 284
CARLISLE...................... 78
CARLTON...................... 53
CARMARTHEN 284
CARNDONAGH.............. 263
CARNFORTH 143
CARRICK-ON-
SHANNON 266
CARSHALTON 181
CARSHALTON 181
CASTLE CAMPS 65
CASTLE CARY 217
CASTLE DOUGLAS 269
CASTLETHORPE............ 61
CASTLETON 82
CATTERICK VILLAGE ... 193
CHALFORD STROUD..... 113
CHARD 217
CHARMOUTH 92
CHATHAM 137
CHATTERIS 65
CHEADLE...................... 68
CHEADLE HULME,
CHEADLE..................... 68
CHELMSFORD 108
CHELTENHAM.............. 113
CHEPSTOW 286
CHESHAM 61
CHESHUNT................... 131
CHESTER...................... 68
CHESTER...................... 69
CHESTERFIELD 82
CHICHESTER 242
CHILBOLTON................ 122
CHIPPENHAM 251
CHIPPING CAMPDEN 114
CHIPPING NORTON 207

CHORLEY...................... 143
CIRENCESTER 114
CLACTON-ON-SEA......... 108
CLAPTON-IN-GORDANO218
CLARE 227
CLECKHEATON 246
CLEETHORPES.............. 150
CLEVEDON.................... 218
CLIFTON 60
CLIFTONWOOD 60
CLITHEROE 144
CLONTARF.................... 264
COBHAM 231
COCKERMOUTH........... 78
COLCHESTER 108
COLEFORD.................... 114
COLERNE 251
COLWYN BAY 285
COLYTON...................... 85
COMBE MARTIN 85
COOKHAM 55
COOTEHILL................... 262
CORBY GLEN 151
CORSHAM 252
COUNTESS WEAR 85
COVENTRY 240
COWES 134
COWLEY 207
CREWE 69
CREWKERNE................ 218
CRICCIETH................... 287
CROMER 187
CROMFORD 82
CROSBY 185
CROWBOROUGH 100
CROWTHORNE 55
CROYDON.................... 181
CULBOKIE.................... 274

DACRE.......................... 193
DAGENHAM 109
DARLINGTON 97
DARTMOUTH 85
DAWLISH 86
DEAL 137
DEBENHAM.................. 227
DERBY 83
DEREHAM.................... 187
DEVIZES....................... 252
DIDCOT 207
DIDSBURY 118
DINGWALL 274
DISS............................. 187
DITCHLING 101
DOLGELLAU 287
DOLLAR....................... 269
DONAGHADEE 261
DONCASTER................. 222

DOOLIN 262
DORCHESTER............... 92
DORCHESTER ON
THAMES..................... 207
DORKING 231
DOUGLAS 259
DOVER.......................... 138
DOWNHAM MARKET.... 188
DOWNPATRICK 261
DRIFFIELD.................... 106
DROITWICH 255
DUBLIN 264
DUCKLINGTON 208
DULVERTON 218
DUMFRIES 270
DUN LAOGHAIRE 265
DUNDEE 281
DUNFERMLINE 271
DUNMANWAY.............. 263
DUNSTABLE 53
DUNSTER 218
DURNESS 275

EAGLE 151
EARLSDON................... 147
EAST FINCHLEY 159
EAST GRINSTEAD 243
EAST HAGBOURNE 208
EAST HOATHLY............ 101
EAST HORSLEY 231
EAST LOOE................... 73
EAST MOLESEY 232
EAST RUDHAM 188
EASTBOURNE............... 101
EASTCOTE.................... 181
ECKINGTON.................. 222
EDGWARE.................... 181
EDINBURGH 276
EGGINGTON 54
EGHAM......................... 232
EGREMONT.................. 78
ELLESMERE 213
ELLON 274
ELSTEAD....................... 232
ELSTREE 131
ELY 65
EMSWORTH.................. 122
ENFIELD 181
ENGLEFIELD GREEN 232
ENNIS 262
EPSOM 232
EWELL 232
EXETER 86
EYE 227

FAIRFORD 115
FAKENHAM 188
FALMOUTH.................. 73

INDEX OF CITIES AND TOWNS

FAREHAM..................... 122
FARINGDON 208
FARNBOROUGH 122
FARNBOROUGH (KENT) 138
FARNHAM 233
FARNINGHAM 138
FAVERSHAM 138
FELIXSTOWE 227
FENCE 144
FERNDALE.................... 286
FINNINGHAM 228
FLAMBOROUGH 106
FLEET........................... 122
FOCHABERS 274
FOLKESTONE 138
FORDINGBRIDGE 122
FORFAR........................ 281
FORRES 274
FORT WILLIAM 275
FOWEY 73
FRAMLINGHAM 228
FRESHWATER 134
FRESHWATER BAY 134
FRISTON 102
FRODSHAM................... 69
FROGGATT 83
FROME 218

GAINSBOROUGH 151
GALWAY....................... 265
GARNANT –
AMMANFORD 283
GIGGLESWICK.............. 193
GILLINGHAM 93
GILVERSOME 246
GLASBURY.................... 128
GLASGOW 279
GLASGOW 280
GLOSSOP...................... 83
GODALMING................ 233
GODMANCHESTER 66
GORING–BY–SEA 243
GORING–ON–THAMES... 209
GORLESTON-ON-SEA..... 188
GOSPORT 123
GRANGE–OVER–SANDS. 78
GRANTHAM.................. 151
GRASMERE 79
GRAYS.......................... 109
GREAT BARROW 69
GREAT DRIFFIELD 106
GREAT DUNMOW 109
GREAT ELLINGHAM 188
GREAT LEIGHS............. 109
GREAT MALVERN 255
GREAT WALFORD 237
GREAT YARMOUTH 188
GREENFORD 181

GREENFORD 181
GREENOCK 280
GREENWICH 165
GUILDFORD.................. 233
GUISBOROUGH 194
GUNTHORPE 204

HADDENHAM 66
HADDINGTON.............. 279
HALESOWEN 240
HALESWORTH 228
HALIFAX....................... 246
HALTON 144
HAMBROOK 60
HAMPTON.................... 182
HAMPTON HILL............ 182
HARLESTON................. 188
HARPENDEN 131
HARROGATE................ 194
HARWICH 109
HASLLMERE................. 233
HASSOCKS.................... 243
HASTINGS 102
HATLWHISTLE 202
HAVANT 123
HAWARTH 247
HAY–ON–WYE 289
HAYLING ISLAND 123
HEATHFIELD................ 103
HEBDEN BRIDGE.......... 247
HELENSBURGH 280
HELMSLEY.................... 194
HELSTON 74
HENLEY ON THAMES ... 209
HENLEY–IN ARDEN 237
HEREFORD 128
HERNE BAY 139
HERTFORD 131
HERTFORD HEATH....... 131
HEXHAM 202
HIGH WYCOMBE 62
HINCKLEY 147
HINDLEY 144
HINDRINGHAM............ 189
HITCHIN 131
HOLBEACH 151
HOLLAND-ON-SEA 110
HOLMFIRTH.................. 247
HOLT 189
HOLYWOOD 261
HONITON 86
HOOK NORTON 209
HORBURY 247
HORLEY........................ 233
HORNCASTLE............... 151
HORNDEAN 123
HORSHAM.................... 243
HOVE............................ 103

HOYLAKE 69
HUDDERSFIELD 247
HUGGLESCOTE 147
HULL............................ 107
HUNSTANTON.............. 189
HUNTINGDON............... 66
HUNTLY 274
HUNTON....................... 102
HURST 55
HYDE............................. 69

ILFORD 182
ILKLEY 248
ILMINSTER.................... 219
INGLETON 194
INNERLEITHEN 268
INVERNESS 275
IPSWICH....................... 228
IRCHESTER 200
IRVINE.......................... 280
ISLE OF ARRAN............ 275
ISLE OF COLONSAY 276
ISLE OF IONA 276
ISLEWORTH 182
IVER 62

JACKFIELD 213
JEDBURGH.................... 268

KELSO 268
KEMPSFORD 115
KENDAL 79
KENILWORTH 237
KENLEY........................ 182
KESWICK 79
KEW 182
KIBWORTH HARCOURT 147
KIDDERMINSTER 255
KILLIECRANKIE 281
KILMARNOCK............... 280
KINETON 237
KING'S LYNN 189
KINGSBRIDGE............... 86
KINGSCLERE................. 55
KINGSTON 183
KINGSWINFORD........... 240
KINGTON 128
KIRKBY STEPHEN......... 79
KIRKBY–IN–ASHFIELD.. 204
KIRKCALDY.................. 271
KIRKCUDBRIGHT......... 270
KIRKELLA 107
KIRKSTALL................... 248
KIRKWALL.................... 276
KIRTON 151
KNARESBOROUGH 194
KNUTSFORD 69

INDEX OF CITIES AND TOWNS

LAMPETER 284
LANCASTER 144
LANCING 243
LANGPORT.................... 219
LARBERT 269
LAUNCESTON................ 74
LEALHOLM 194
LEAMINGTON SPA 238
LEATHERHEAD 233
LEDBURY..................... 128
LEEDS.......................... 249
LEICESTER 147
LEIGH ON SEA............... 110
LEOMINSTER................ 128
LETCHWORTH
GARDEN CITY 132
LEWES 103
LEYLAND...................... 144
LICHFIELD 224
LIMERICK 266
LINCOLN...................... 152
LIPHOOK...................... 123
LISBURN 260
LISS 124
LITTLE HALLINGBURY . 110
LITTLEBOROUGH 118
LITTLEHAMPTON 244
LITTLEOVER 83
LIVERPOOL 185
LIVERSEDGE 249
LLANDRINDOD WELLS . 291
LLANGOLLEN 286
LLANIDLOES 292
LLANRWST 285
LLANVAPLEY 288
LLANWRTYD WELLS 292
LOCHCARRON............... 275
LONDERRY 260
LONDON (E) 155
LONDON (EC) 157
LONDON (N).................. 158
LONDON (NW)............... 161
LONDON (SE)................ 164
LONDON (SW)............... 167
LONDON (W) 172
LONDON (WC) 177
LONDON (O) 181
LONDONDERRY 260
LONG BURTON.............. 93
LONG MELFORD 228
LONG PRESTON 195
LONGHOPE 276
LOOE 74
LOUGHBOROUGH......... 148
LOUTH.......................... 152
LOWER DARWEN 145
LOWESTOFT 229
LUDLOW....................... 213

LYDD........................... 139
LYME REGIS 93
LYMINGE..................... 139
LYMINGTON 124
LYMM.......................... 70
LYMPSTONE................. 87
LYNG........................... 189
LYTHAM ST. ANNES 145

MACCLESFIELD............ 70
MACHYNLLETH 292
MADELAY 214
MAIDENHEAD............... 55
MAIDSTONE 139
MALDON 110
MALMESBURY 252
MALVERN..................... 256
MANCHESTER 118
MANNINGTREE............ 110
MANSFIELD 204
MARKET DEEPING 153
MARKET
HARBOROUGH 149
MARLBOROUGH........... 252
MARPLE BRIDGE.......... 70
MATLOCK 83
MEDSTEAD 124
MELROSE 268
MELTON CONSTABLE ... 190
MELTON MOWBRAY..... 149
MERRIOTT 219
MIDHURST................... 244
MIDSOMER NORTON 219
MILBORNE PORT 94
MILLINGTON107
MILTON KEYNES.......... 62
MILVERTON 219
MINEHEAD 219
MIRFIELD 250
MITCHAM 234
MODBURY 87
MOFFAT 270
MOLD 286
MONKLEIGH 87
MONTGOMERY 292
MONTPELIER 115
MONTROSE 281
MORDEN 183
MORETON-IN-MARSH .. 115
MORETONHAMPSTEAD. 87
MORPETH 203
MOTTRAM IN
LONGDENDALE.......... 119
MOULTON SEAS END.... 153
MOYARD 266
MUCH HADHAM 132
MUCH WENLOCK 214

NAILSEA 60
NAILSWORTH............... 115
NANTWICH 70
NEATH......................... 294
NEW BARNET (HERTS) .. 132
NEW BARNET............... 183
NEW BUCKENHAM 190
NEW MALDEN............... 234
NEW MILTON 124
NEW ROSS.................... 267
NEW TREDEGAR 283
NEWARK-ON-TRENT.... 204
NEWBURY.................... 56
NEWCASTLE UPON
TYNE 236
NEWCASTLE-UNDER-
LYME......................... 224
NEWENT 115
NEWHAVEN 104
NEWMARKET................ 229
NEWNHAM ON SEVERN 115
NEWPORT (I.O.W)......... 134
NEWPORT 288
NEWPORT ON TAY 272
NEWPORT PAGNELL..... 62
NEWQUAY 74
NEWTON ABBOT........... 87
NEWTOWN 292
NORMANTON............... 250
NORTH CHERITON 219
NORTH SHIELDS........... 236
NORTH WALSHAM 190
NORTHAMPTON 200
NORTHWICH 71
NORWICH 190
NOTTINGHAM............... 204
NOTTINGHAM............... 205

OAKLEY........................ 124
OKEHAMPTON 87
OLD COLWYN 285
OLD COSTESSEY 191
OLDBURY 240
OLDHAM 120
ORPINGTON 139
OSTERLEY.................... 183
OSWESTRY 214
OTLEY 250
OTTERTON................... 87
OUNDLE 200
OVER LANE.................. 116
OVERTON..................... 124
OXFORD 209
OXTED.......................... 234

PAIGNTON 88
PATHMEAD.................. 272
PEASEDOWN ST. JOHN .. 220

INDEX OF CITIES AND TOWNS

PENN 62
PENRITH 79
PENZANCE 74
PERSHORE 256
PERTH 282
PETERBOROUGH 67
PETERSFIELD 124
PETWORTH 244
PICKERING 195
PITLOCHRY 282
PLYMOUTH 88
PONTARDAWE 294
POOLE 94
PORT ERIN 259
PORTSLADE 104
PORTSMOUTH 124
PRENTON 185
PRESCOT 186
PRESTEIGNE................. 293
PRESTON 145
PUDDLETOWN 94
PURBROOK 125

QUEEN CAMEL............. 220

RADCLIFFE 120
RADLETT 132
RAINTON 195
RAMSBURY 252
RAMSGATE 139
RAYLEIGH 111
READING 56
REDCAR 98
REDMILE 205
RHYL, SIR DDINBYCH .. 286
RICHMOND (N YORKS) . 195
RICHMOND 234
RICKMANSWORTH 132
RINGWOOD 125
RIPON 195
ROBERTSBRIDGE 104
ROCHDALE 120
ROCHE, ST. AUSTELL 75
ROCHESTER 140
ROMFORD 111
ROMSEY 125
ROSCREA 267
ROSS-ON-WYE 128
ROSSCARBERY 263
ROTHERFIELD 104
ROTHERHAM 222
ROTHLEY 149
RUGBY 238
RUISLIP MANOR........... 183
RUNCORN 71
RUSHDEN 200
RYDE 134
RYE 104

SAFFRON WALDEN 111
SALISBURY 253
SALTBURN-BY-THE-SEA 195
SALTDEAN 105
SANDIACRE 205
SANDY 54
SAXMUNDHAM 229
SCARBOROUGH 196
SEATON 88
SEATON 89
SEDBERGH 80
SELBY 196
SELKIRK 269
SETTLE 196
SEVENOAKS 140
SHAFTESBURY 94
SHARNBROOK 54
SHEFFIELD 222
SHENFIELD 111
SHENTON 149
SHERBORNE 95
SHERINGHAM 192
SHINFIELD 57
SHOREHAM-BY-SEA 244
SHREWSBURY 215
SIBLE HEDINGHAM 111
SIDCUP 140
SILVERSTONE 200
SIMONSBATH 220
SITTINGBOURNE 140
SKIPTON 197
SLEAFORD 153
SMARDEN 140
SOLIHULL 240
SOMERTON 220
SOUTH BRENT 89
SOUTH BURLINGHAM .. 192
SOUTH KELSEY 153
SOUTHAMPTON 125
SOUTHEND-ON-SEA 111
SOUTHPORT 186
SOUTHSEA 126
SOUTHWOLD 229
SPALDING 153
ST. AGNES 75
ST. ALBANS 132
ST. ANDREWS 272
ST. HELENS (I.O.W) 135
ST. HELENS 145
ST. HELIER, JERSEY 258
ST. LEONARD'S-ON-SEA . 105
ST. IVES 75
ST. JUST 75
ST. LEONARD'S-ON-SEA 105
ST. TEATH 75
STAFFORD 224
STAITHES 197
STALBRIDGE 95

STAMFORD 153
STANSTED 111
STEYNING 244
STILLORGAN 265
STOBOROUGH 95
STOCKPORT 120
STOCKSFIELD 203
STOCKTON-ON-TEES 197
STOCKTON-ON-TEES,
CLEVELAND (DURHAM) 98
STOCKTON-ON-THE-
FOREST 197
STOKE GOLDINGTON ... 62
STOKE-ON-TRENT 224
STONESFIELD 210
STOURPORT-ON-
SEVERN 256
STOW-ON-THE-WOLD... 116
STRATFORD-UPON-
AVON 238
STRATHTAY 282
STROUD 116
STUDLEY 238
STURMINSTER NEWTON 95
SUDBURY 230
SUNBURY ON THAMES . 183
SURBITON 234
SUTTON 234
SUTTON COLDFIELD 241
SUTTON IN ASHFIELD .. 205
SUTTON, SURREY 183
SWANAGE 95
SWANLAND 107
SWANSEA 293
SWANTON ABBOT 192
SWINDON 253
SYDENHAM 165

TALGARTH 293
TAMWORTH 225
TATTENHALL 71
TAUNTON 220
TAVISTOCK 89
TEDDINGTON 183
TEIGNMOUTH 89
TELFORD 215
TENBY 288
TETBURY 117
TEWKESBURY 117
THIRSK 197
THORNTON CLEVELEYS 145
THURCASTON 149
THURSO 275
TICEHURST 105
TIMPERLEY 71
TINTERN 288
TITCHFIELD 126
TIVERTON 89

INDEX OF CITIES AND TOWNS

TODMORDEN 250
TONBRIDGE 141
TOOTING 168
TORQUAY 90
TORRINGTON.............. 90
TOTNES........................ 90
TOWCESTER 201
TREFRIW 286
TREGARON 284
TRING 133
TRURO 76
TUNBRIDGE WELLS...... 141
TWICKENHAM 184

ULVERSTON 81
UPPINGHAM 212
UTTOXETER 225

VALE, GUERNSEY 258
VENTNOR 135
VICARSTOWN 266

WADEBRIDGE 76
WALDERTON 245
WALLINGFORD 211
WALLINGTON 235
WALSALL 225
WALSALL (W MIDS) 241
WALTHAMSTOW........... 156
WALTON-ON-THAMES.. 235
WANTAGE.................... 211
WARBOROUGH 211
WAREHAM.................... 95
WARFIELD 57
WARMINSTER 254
WARRINGTON.............. 71
WARSASH 126
WARWICK 238

WATERINGBURY 142
WATFORD 133
WATTON 192
WEETON....................... 146
WEIR, BACUP................ 146
WELLING 184
WELLINGBOROUGH 201
WELLINGTON 220
WELLS-NEXT-THE-SEA... 192
WELSHPOOL 293
WELTON....................... 81
WEM 215
WEOBLEY 129
WEST BROMWICH 241
WEST KINGTON 254
WEST KIRBY 186
WEST PENNARD 221
WESTBURY 254
WESTBURY-ON-SEVERN 117
WESTCLIFF-ON-SEA...... 112
WESTERHAM 142
WESTLETON 230
WESTON-SUPER-MARE . 221
WETHERBY 250
WEYBRIDGE 235
WEYMOUTH 96
WHITBY 198
WHITCHURCH 215
WHITEHAVEN............... 81
WHITHORN 270
WHITLEY BAY 236
WHITSTABLE 142
WICKFORD.................... 112
WICKHAM BISHOPS....... 112
WIGAN 120
WIGSTON 149
WIGTON 81
WIGTOWN 270

WILLESDEN GREEN 161
WILLINGTON 98
WIMBORNE.................. 96
WIMBORNE MINSTER... 96
WINCHESTER 126
WINDERMERE 81
WINDLESHAM............... 235
WINDSOR 57
WINESTEAD 107
WINSFORD................... 72
WINTERTON 154
WIRKSWORTH 83
WISBECH 67
WITNEY 211
WOKING....................... 235
WOKINGHAM 57
WOLVERHAMPTON 241
WOMBOURN 225
WOODBRIDGE.............. 230
WOODFORD GREEN 112
WOOLER....................... 203
WOOTTON BASSETT 254
WORCESTER 257
WORTHING................... 245
WYMONDHAM 192

YARKHILL.................... 129
YARM........................... 198
YARMOUTH.................. 135
YORK 198
YORK 199
YOUGHAL 263
YOXALL 225
YOXFORD..................... 230
YSTRAD MEURIG 293

ZEALS........................... 254

USE OF THE DIRECTORY

This directory is divided into four sections. The first is the *Geographical Directory of Dealers*, in which full details, where supplied, are given for each business or private dealer. These are listed alphabetically by town in which the shop or business premises are located. The details, as supplied by dealers, are presented in the following manner:

Name of business. As provided. ■ Indicates that the type of premises is a Shop.

Postal address. (*) Indicates the dealer's preference for indexing or where we have imposed current county boundaries.

Prop: Name of proprietor(s).

Website: Website address. Users should ignore the full point at the end of the entry.

Tel: Telephone number(s), together with the new codes followed by fax and/or mobile number. NOTE: If the code for the fax number is the same as for the telephone, it has sometimes been omitted.

E-Mail: Electronic mail address. Users should ignore the full point at the end of the entry.

Est: Date at which business was established.

Type of premises occupied: Shop, private, mail order/internet, market stall or storeroom.

Opening times: Of shop, or if premises are private, whether appointments to view stock may be made, or if for contacting if postal business only.

Normal level of total stock: Very small (less than 2,000), small (2,000–5,000), medium (5,000–10,000), large (10,000–20,000) or very large (more than 20,000).

Spec: Subjects of books in which the dealer specialises. NB: only the first eight are shown in the Geographical Section. All dealers' subjects are shown in the Speciality Index

PR: Price range of stock. This is intended as a guideline only.

CC: Selection of Credit & Debit Cards eg. AE – American Express, DC – Diners Club, DI – Discovery, EC – Eurocard, JCB – Japanese Credit Bureau, MC – Mastercard, SO – Solo, SW – Switch, V – VISA.

Important lines of business: Other than secondhand antiquarian books.

Cata: Approximate frequency and subject of catalogues, if issued.

Corresp: Languages, other than English, in which correspondence may be conducted.

Mem: Membership of book trade organisations, eg. A.B.A. – Antiquarian Booksellers' Association B.A. – Booksellers Association of Great Britain & Ireland P.A. – Publishers Association P.B.F.A. – Provincial Booksellers' Fairs Association

Notes These appear exactly as entered by the dealer in their Free Entry Form on Sheppard's World.

The next section is an alphabetical *Index of Businesses*, giving full name and county with the page on which their full entry is to be found.

This is followed by an alphabetical *Index of Proprietors*, giving their name and trading name followed by their page reference.

The fourth section is the *Speciality Index*. This is presented in alphabetical order by subject heading, giving the dealer's name, county and page on which their details may be found. Certain headings have extended listings - eg., Authors, History, Religion and Sport.

OLYMPIC GAMES

Jeux Olympiques – Olympische Spiele – Giochi Olimpichi

1896 – 2004

Always Buying & Selling:

Official Reports - Programs - Books - Posters - Maps - Tickets - Medals - Badges - Medallions - Collectables - etc.

Specializing in:
Olympic Games
History of Sport
Physical Education
Wrestling, Fencing
Rowing, Gymnastics
Sports & Athletics
Sport in Art
Sports Medicine
Graphic Illustrations of Sports & Athletics
Expositions & World's Fairs 1900 Paris, 1904 St. Louis

Historical research, writing & consulting services available. Catalogs by subscription – Brokerage & Private Treaty sales. Auctions – Consignments accepted – collection development.

HARVEY ABRAMS – BOOKS

P.O. Box 732 State College, P.A., U.S.A. 16804

Tel: (814) 237-8331 – Fax: (814) 237-8332
Email: Olympicbks@aol.com

BEDFORDSHIRE

BEDFORD

Books With Care, 7 Barford Road, Willington, Bedford, MK44 3QP. Prop: Gerald Ford. Tel: (01234) 831288. Fax: (01234) 831288. Web: www.bookswithcare.net. E-mail: gfbooks@bookswithcare.com. Est: 1996. Private premises. Internet and Postal. Appointment necessary. Small stock. PR: £1–200. CC: MC; V; PayPal.

Bunyan Books, 57 Purbeck Close Goldington, Bedford, MK41 9LX. Prop: R.G. Sancto. Tel: (01234) 345518. E-mail: roderick@sanctofamily.fsnet.co.uk. Est: 2002. Private premises. Internet and Postal. Appointment necessary. Large stock. Spec: Antiquarian; Religion - General. PR: £10–500. Corresp: French, German. Notes: *Advertises occasionally in Bookdealer Fortnightly & Book & Magazine Collector. Also, restoration, repair and binding. Rare and unusual items.*

The Eagle Bookshop, ■ 101 - 103 Castle Road, Bedford, MK40 3QP. Prop: Peter Budek. Tel: (01234) 269295. Fax: (01234) 290920. Web: www.eaglebookshop.co.uk. E-mail: info@eaglebookshop.co.uk. Est: 1991. Shop, Internet and Postal. Open: **M:** 10:00–17:30; **T:** 10:00–17:30; **W:** 10:00–17:30; **Th:** 10:00–17:30; **F:** 10:00–17:30; **S:** 09:30–17:00. Very large stock. Spec: Academic/Scholarly; Antiquarian; County Local; History - General; History of Ideas, Mathematics; Physics; Science - General. PR: £1–2,000. CC: MC; V; SW. Mem: PBFA. VAT No: GB 563 7690 08. Notes: *The shop expanded into adjacent premises in 2004; now has six large display rooms, covering most subjects. Emphasis on scholarly, antiquarian and collectable books.*

Kingsmere Books, 41 Haylands Way, Bedford, MK41 9BY. Prop: Brian Webb. Tel: 01234.302132. E-mail: a.webb3@ntlworld.com. Est: 1985. Private premises. Internet and Postal. Appointment necessary. Spec: Biography; Natural History; Poetry; Topography - General. Corresp: French, Spanish.

BROOM

Bolland Books, 14 The Woodlands, Broom, SG18 9NH. Prop: Les & Anne Bolland. Tel: 01767 310481. Web: www.Bollandbooks.com. E-mail: info@Bollandbooks.com. Est: 1997. Mail Order Only. Internet and Postal. Appointment necessary. Open: **M:** 0900–1700; **T:** 0900–1700; **W:** 09:00–1700; **Th:** 09:00–1700; **F:** 09:00–1700; **S:** 09:00–1700; Closed for lunch: 13:00–14:00. Spec: Crime (True); Criminology; Espionage; Famous People - Kennedy, John F; Mafia; Police Force Histories; Science - Forensic; Trials. CC: MC; V; Maestro. Cata: True Crime, Kennedy. Mem: PBFA. VAT No: GB 806 1492 42.

CARLTON

Twiggers Booksearch, 28 High Street, Carlton, MK43 7LA. Prop: Ruth Rothschild. Tel: 0123 472 0378. Web: www.twiggers.com. E-mail: booksearch@twiggers.com. Est: 1980. Private premises. Postal Only. Contactable. Open: **M:** 09:00–17:30; **T:** 09:00–17:30; **W:** 09:00–17:30; **Th:** 09:00–17:30; **F:** 09:00–17:30; **S:** 10:00–16:00. Very small stock. Spec: Booksearch. CC: AE; D; E; JCB; MC; V. VAT No: GB 726 1475 36. Notes: *a booksearch company.*

DUNSTABLE

Adrian Walker, 107 Great Northern Road, Dunstable, LU5 4BW. Prop: Adrian Walker. Tel: 01582 605824. E-mail: hawk-walker@talktalk.net. Est: 1965. Private premises. Postal Only. Open in Summer. Cata: – Falconry worldwide.

Dealers – visit your entry at least once a year. Check your details are correct. Go to:

www.sheppardsworld.co.uk

BEDFORDSHIRE

The Book Castle, ■ 12 Church St., Dunstable, LU5 4RU. Prop: Paul Bowes. Tel: (01582) 605670. Fax: (01582)662431. Web: www.book-castle.co.uk. E-mail: bc@book-castle.co.uk. Est: 1981. Shop open: **M:** 09:00–17:00; **T:** 09:00–17:00; **W:** 09:00–17:00; **Th:** 08:00–17:00; **F:** 09:00–17:00; **S:** 09:00–17:00. CC: AE; MC; V; Solo. Mem: PBFA.

Adrian Walker, 107 Great Northern Road, Dunstable, LU5 4BW. Tel: (01582) 605824. E-mail: adrianwalker@supanet.com. Est: 1965. Private premises. Postal Only. Telephone First. Very small stock. Spec: Sport - Falconry. PR: £1–250.

EGGINGTON

Robert Kirkman Ltd., Kings Cottage, Eggington, LU7 9PG. Prop: Robert Kirkman. Tel: (01525) 210647. Fax: (01525) 211184. Web: www.robertkirkman.co.uk. E-mail: robertkirkmanltd@btconnect.com. Est: 1987. Private premises. Internet and Postal. Appointment necessary. Small stock. Spec: Antiquarian; Author - Bunyan, John; - Churchill, Sir Winston; Bibles; Bindings; Cinema/Film; Famous People - Churchill, Sir Winston; Fine & Rare. PR: £20–100. CC: MC; V. Cata: 24 different subjects. Mem: ABA; PBFA; ILAB. VAT No: GB 491 0095 56. Notes: *also prints and engravings, bookbinding restoration, literary memorabilia.*

SANDY

H.J. Morgan, 47 Bedford Road, Sandy, SG19 1ES. Tel: (01767) 691383. E-mail: hedleymorgan@ ntlworld.com. Est: 1980. Private premises. Book fairs only. Appointment necessary. Small stock. Spec: Academic/Scholarly; History - General; Literature; Travel - General. Mem: PBFA. VAT No: GB 467 3823 19.

SHARNBROOK

Ouse Valley Books, 16 Home Close, Sharnbrook, Bedford, MK44 1PQ. Prop: Barrie Farnsworth. Tel: (01234) 782411. E-mail: ousevalleybooks@btconnect.com. Est: 1990. Private premises. Book fairs only. Appointment necessary. Very small stock. Spec: Academic/Scholarly; Art - British; British Art & Design; History - British; Sport - Cycling; Topography - General; Topography - Local. PR: £5–500. Mem: PBFA.

BERKSHIRE

ASCOT

Ian Cross, 83 Gainsborough Drive, Ascot, SL5 8TA. Tel: (01344) 872100. Fax: (01344) 872544. E-mail: ccross@btconnect.com. Est: 1972. Private premises. Postal Only. Appointment necessary. Small stock. Spec: Art. PR: £25–1,500. Corresp: Italian. Notes: *Books, ephemera and original art relating to Silhouettes and occassionally Portrait Minatures.*

BRACKNELL

BookzoneBracknell, 5 Flintgrove, Bracknell, RG12 2JN. Prop: John Bacon. Tel: (01344) 421770. E-mail: johnbacon@screaming.net. Est: 1990. Private premises. Internet and Postal. Appointment necessary. Small stock. Spec: Sport - General; Sport - Athletics; Boxing; Cricket; Football (Soccer); Golf; Horse Racing (inc. Riding/Breeding/Equestrian); Racing. PR: £5–50. CC: MC; V; PayPal. Notes: *Exhibits at bookfairs. Alternative Tel. No. (01344) 488825*

COOKHAM

Jean Hedger, Poultons, Cookham, SL6 9HW. Prop: Jean Hedger. Tel. 01628 523911. Fax: 01628 528217. Web: www.booksatpbfa.com. E-mail: jeanhedger@btconnect.com. Est: 1977. Private premises. Internet and Postal. Contactable. PBFA and ABA Book Fairs in UK and at Biblion, Davies Mews, London. Spec: Amusements; Art; Art - British; Artists; Author - Aesop; Ahlberg, Janet & Allan; Alcotts, The; Aldin, Cecil. CC: D; JCB; MC; V. Cata: Illustrated; Artwork; Children's; Stanley Spencer. Corresp: French; Spanish; German; Chinese (Mandarin). Mem: ABA; PBFA; ILAB. VAT No: GB 492 0257 50. Notes: *specialises in Illustrated Books and Original Artwork; Children's Books of the last three centuries; Reference Books related to these areas; Stanley Spencer. In addition stocks small selection of quality books outside these subject areas.*

CROWTHORNE

Malcolm Applin, 21 Larkswood Drive, Crowthorne, RG45 6RH. Prop: Malcolm Applin. Tel: (01344) 776881. Est: 1993. Private premises. Postal Only. Small stock. Spec: Biography; Fiction - General; Fiction - Women; Literary Criticism; Poetry. PR: £5–250.

HURST

Christopher Edwards, Hatch Gate Farmhouse Lines Road, Hurst, RG10 0SP. Prop: Christopher Edwards & Margaret Erskine. Tel: (0118) 934 0531. Web: www.christopheredwardsbooks.co.uk. E-mail: chr.edwards@which.net. Est: 1992. Private premises. Internet Only. Appointment necessary. Small stock. Spec: Early Imprints; History - General; Literature. CC: MC; V. Corresp: French. Mem: ABA; ILAB. VAT No: GB 563 0529 50.

KINGSCLERE,

Wyseby House Books, ■ Kingsclere Old Bookshop 2a George Street, Kingsclere, Nr. Newbury, RG20 5NQ. Prop: Dr. T. Oldham. Tel: (01635) 297995. Fax: (01635) 297677. Web: www.wyseby.co.uk. E-mail: info@wyseby.co.uk. Est: 1978. Internet and Postal. Shop open: **M:** 09:00–17:00; **T:** 09:00–17:00; **W:** 09:00–17:00; **Th:** 09:00–17:00; **F:** 09:00–17:00; **S:** 09:00–17:00. Very large stock. Spec: Applied Art; Architecture; Art; Art History; Art Reference; Artists; Arts, The; Biology - General. PR: £1–1,000. CC: AE; JCB; MC; V. Mem: PBFA. VAT No: GB 295 3261 54.

MAIDENHEAD

Valerie Peel, t/a Kiandra Associates 40 Culley Way, Cox Green, Maidenhead, SL6 3PX. Tel: (01628) 822439. Fax: (01628) 826118. Web: www.http://ukbookworld.com/members/valeriepeel. E-mail: valerie_peel@dogbooks.freeserve.co.uk. Est: 1985. Private premises. Internet and Postal. Contactable. Small stock. Spec: Dogs. PR: £4–750. CC: PayPal. Cata: Dog Books. Notes: *Free Booksearch*

BERKSHIRE

Eastleach Books, 3, Preston Place, Newbury, RG14 2SE. Prop: Daniel Unwin. Tel: +44 (0)1635 48444. Fax: +44 (0)1635 48444. Web: www.eastleach-book.co.uk. E-mail: dan@bookville.freeserve.co.uk. Est: 1997. Private premises. Internet and Postal. Telephone First. Open: **M:** 09:00–18:00; **T:** 09:00– 18:00; **W:** 09:00–18:00; **Th:** 09:00–18:00; **F:** 09:00–18:00; **S:** 09:00–18:00. Very large stock. Spec: Academic/Scholarly; Alpinism/Mountaineering; Antiquarian; Applied Art; Art; Biography; History - General. PR: £2–4,500. CC: E; JCB; MC; V. Corresp: little French. Mem: PBFA. Notes: *Good stocks of Academic History, and good general non fiction.*

Invicta Bookshop, ■ 8 Cromwell Place Northbrook Street, Newbury, RG14 1AF. Prop: Simon & Tina Hall. Tel: (01635) 31176. Est: 1969. Shop open: **M:** 10:30–17:30; **T:** 10:30–17:30; **Th:** 10:30–17:30; **F:** 10:30–17:30; **S:** 10:30–17:30. Large stock. Spec: Aviation; Cookery/Gastronomy; Military; Sport - Cricket; Topography - Local. PR: £1–200. CC: MC; V. Mem: PBFA. Notes: *also at Hungerford Arcade Antiquess Centre.*

Railway Book and Magazine Search, The Warren Curridge, Newbury, RG18 9DN. Prop: N.J. Bridger. Tel: (01635) 200507. Web: www.nevis-railway-bookshops.co.uk. Est: 1981. Private premises. Postal Only. Very small stock. Spec: Railways; Ephemera. PR: £1–200. Notes: *Nevis Railway Bookshop, Goring-on-Thames, Oxon (q.v.) Nevis Railway Bookshop, Marlborough, Wiltshire (q.v.).*

READING

Books for Amnesty, ■ 71 Wokingham Road, Reading, RG6 1LH. Prop: Amnesty International UK. Tel: 01189661646. E-mail: readingbookshop@btconnect.com. Est: 2003. Shop open: **M:** 10.00–17:00; **T:** 10.00–17.00; **W:** 10.00–17.00; **Th:** 10.00–17:00; **F:** 10.00–17:00; **S:** 10.00–17:00.

K.C. Brown, 11 Easington Drive Lower Earley, Reading, RG6 3XN. Tel: (0118) 966-7013. Fax: (0118) 966-7013. Est: 1991. Private premises. Appointment necessary. Small stock.

Mary Butts Books, 219 Church Road Earley, Reading, RG6 1HW. Prop: Mary Butts. Tel: (0118) 926- 1793. E-mail: mary.butts@tiscali.co.uk. Est: 1985. Private premises. Internet and Postal. Appointment necessary. Open: **M:** 09:00–17:00; **T:** 09:00–17:00; **W:** 09:00–17:00; **Th:** 09:00–17:00; **F:** 09:00–17:00; **S:** 09:00–17:00. Medium stock. Spec: Applied Art; Architecture; Art; Art - British; Art History; Art Reference; Artists; British Art & Design. PR: £2–50. Corresp: French. Notes: *specialises in children's books & modern art books.*

Footballana, 275 Overdown Road Tilehurst, Reading, RG31 6NX. Prop: Bryan Horsnell. Tel: (0118) 942 4448. Fax: (0118) 942 4448. Private premises. Postal Only. Very small stock. Spec: Sport - Football (Soccer); Collectables; Ephemera. PR: £5–100. Notes: *Also, pre-1950 football programmes, postcards and ephemera wanted. 'Wants' lists welcome.*

Forbury Fine Books, 46 Tredegar Road, Reading, RG4 8QF. Prop: Stephen Gardner. Tel: (0870) 063 8680. Fax: (0870) 286 6874. Web: www.forburyfinebooks.co.uk. E-mail: mail@forburyfinebooks .co.uk. Est: 2004. Private premises. Internet and Postal. Appointment necessary. Open: **M:** 09:00– 18:00; **T:** 09:00–18:00; **W:** 09:00–18:00; **Th:** 09:00–18:00; **F:** 09:00–18:00. Small stock. PR: £2–1,000. Notes: *Booksearch.*

J.B. Books, 3 Wenlock Edge, Charvil, Reading, RG10 9QG. Prop: John A. Baker. Tel: (0118) 934-0679. Web: www.balloonbooks.co.uk. E-mail: jb.books@btopenworld.com. Est: 1978. Private premises. Postal Only. Telephone First. Small stock. Spec: Aircraft; Aviation; Sport - Ballooning; Transport. PR: £1–250. Corresp: French.

Keegan's Bookshop, ■ Merchant's Place (off Friar Street), Reading, RG1 1DT. Prop: John & Judith Keegan. Tel: (0118) 958-7253. Web: www.keegansbookshop.com. E-mail: enquiries@ keegansbookshop.com. Est: 1979. Shop and Postal Only. Open: **M:** 09:00–17:30; **T:** 09:00–17:30; **W:** 09:00–17:30; **Th:** 09:00–17:30; **F:** 09:00–17:30; **S:** 09:00–17:30. Medium stock. Spec: Aviation; Maritime/Nautical; Military; Military History; Naval; Railroads; Railways; Topography - General. PR: £1–100. CC: MC; V; Switch. Corresp: Italian.

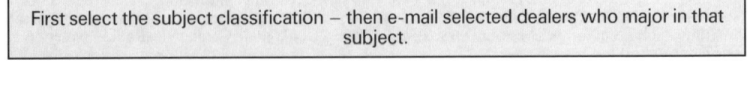

BERKSHIRE

Veronica Mayhew, Trewena, Behoes Lane Woodcote, Reading, RG8 0PP. Tel: (01491) 680743. E-mail: veronica.mayhew@virgin.net. Est: 1972. Private premises. Appointment necessary. Small stock. Spec: Animals and Birds; Apiculture; Cats; Farming & Livestock; Ornithology; Prints and Maps. PR: £1–500. VAT No: GB 537 6954 02.

SHINFIELD

Books & Bygones, 40 Hollow Lane, Shinfield, RG2 9BT. Prop: Pamela Pither and John Lilly. Tel: 0118 988 4346. Web: www.booksbygones.com. E-mail: booksbygones@btconnect.com. Est: 1990. Mail Order Only. Telephone First. Spec: Cookery - Professional; Cookery/Gastronomy; Food & Drink. CC: MC; V; Maestro. Mem: Ibooknet.

WARFIELD

Moss End Bookshop, ■ Moss End Garden Centre Moss End, Warfield, Nr. Bracknell, RG42 6EJ. Prop: K. & M.A. Precious. Tel: (01344) 422110. Est: 1981. Shop open: **T:** 10:00–17:00; **W:** 10:00–17:00; **Th:** 10:00–17:00; **F:** 10:00–17:00; **S:** 10:00–17:00; **Su:** 10:00–17:00. Spec: Antiques; Rural Life; Sport - Field Sports; Prints and Maps. PR: £2–250. CC: MC; V. Notes: *Also, prints.*

WINDSOR

Brian Billing, 28 Athlone Square Ward Royal, Windsor, SL4 1SS. Tel: (01753) 851343. Est: 1965. Private premises. Postal Only. Small stock. Spec: Economics; Natural History; Travel - General. PR: £2–250.

Eton Antique Bookshop, ■ 88 High Street Eton, Windsor, SL4 6AF. Prop: Maurice Bastians. Tel: (01753) 855534. Est. 1975. Shop open. **M:** 11:00–18:00; **T:** 11:00–18:00; **W:** 11:00–18:00; **Th:** 11:00–18:00; **F:** 11:00–18:00; **S:** 11:00–18:00; **Su:** 12:00–17:00. Medium stock. Spec: Antiquarian; Antiques; Bindings; History - General; Literature; Military; Poetry; Sets of Books. PR: £3–2,000. CC: E; MC; V; Most. Corresp: Spanish. Mem: Eton Traders Assoc. VAT No: GB 787 1877 65. Notes: *Old prints and maps, bookbinding and repairs. Often open early and late - call first.*

WOKINGHAM

John Townsend, 33 Bishop's Drive, Wokingham, RG40 1WA. Tel: (0118) 978-5463. Web: www .johntownsend.demon.co.uk. E-mail: john@johntownsend.demon.co.uk. Est: 1991. Private premises. Internet and Postal. Medium stock. Spec: Genealogy; Heraldry; History - General; Manuscripts; Parish Registers; School Registers/Rolls of Honour; Topography - General; Topography - Local. PR: £10–200. Cata: Genealogy, Heraldry, Local History, Manuscripts. Corresp: French, German. VAT No: GB 591 8061 25.

BRISTOL

BISHOPSTON

Steve Liddle, 8 Morley Square, Bishopston, BS7 9DW. Tel: (0117) 924 4846. E-mail: mail@steveliddle.co.uk. Est: 1983. Private premises. Appointment necessary. Spec: Antiquarian; Archaeology - Industrial; Architecture; Art; Author - Austen, Jane; - Rolt, L.T.C.; Bindings; General Stock. Cata: Railways, Canals, Industrial Revolution etc. Mem: ABA; PBFA; ILAB. VAT No: GB 869 4504 83. Notes: *Fine books in many subject areas. We exhibit at the major UK bookfairs and would be pleased to meet customers who remember our old bookshops (Patterson Liddle) in Bristol and Bath. Books and libraries purchased, valuations undertaken.*

BRISTOL

Lesley Aitchison, 22 West Shrubbery, Redland, Bristol, BS6 6TA. Tel: (0117) 907-6899. Fax: (0117) 974-1962. Web: www.localhistory.co.uk/la. E-mail: lesley@localhistory.co.uk. Est: 1993. Private premises. Spec: Ephemera; Genealogy; History - 19th Century; History - Family; Manuscripts; Topography - Local; Ephemera; Prints and Maps. PR: £10–1,000. CC: MC; V; Switch. Cata: maps, ephemera, manuscripts. Notes: *Also at these premises: Ambra Books. (q.v.) Also, sales particulars, prints & photographs.*

Ambra Books, 22 West Shrubbery Redland, Bristol, BS6 6TA. Prop: Ivor Cornish. Tel: (0117) 907-6899. Fax: (0117) 974-1962. Web: www.localhistory.co.uk/ambra. E-mail: ambra@localhistory.co.uk. Est: 1972. Private premises. Internet and Postal. Appointment necessary. Open: **M:** 09:00–17:00; **T:** 09:00–17:00; **W:** 09:00–17:00; **Th:** 09:00–17:00; **F:** 09:00–17::00; **S:** 09:00–12:00; **Su:** 09:00–12:00. Small stock. Spec: Counties in England; County - Local; Genealogy; History - Local; Topography - Local. PR: £10–3,000. CC: MC; V; SW. Corresp: French, Italian. Notes: *Mainly deals in books on the West Country (Bristol, Cornwall, Devon, Gloucestershire, Somerset, Wiltshire) see website:- www.localhistory.co.uk*

Arthur Hook, 54 Egerton Road, Bristol, BS7 8HL. Tel: (0117) 9144673. Web: www.hooksbooks.co.uk. E-mail: hooksbooks@blueyonder.co.uk. Est: 1997. Private premises. Internet and Postal. Appointment necessary. Spec: Atlases; Maps & Mapmaking; Topography - General; War - World War I; War - World War II. CC: PayPal. Cata: London, Railway maps & guides, World War I & II. Corresp: French. Mem: PBFA. Notes: *www.hooksbooks.co.uk has a selection of my stock on line. Many maps are not listed.*

Avon Books, ■ 4 Waterloo Street, Clifton, Bristol, BS8 4 BT. Prop: John Ray. Tel: 0117 973 9848. E-mail: sales@avonbook.co.uk. Est: 1991. Shop open: **M:** 10:00–16:00; **T:** 10:00–16:00; **W:** 10:00–16:00; **Th:** 10:00–16:00; **F:** 10:00–16:00. CC: MC; V.

Beware of the Leopard, Stalls 77 and 66 - 69 the Covered Market, Saint Nicholas Markets, Saint Nicholas Street, Bristol, BS1 1LJ. Prop: David Jackson. Tel: 01179 257277. E-mail: bewareoftheleopard@ hotmail.com. Est: 1991. Market stand/stall. Open: **M:** 10:00–17:00; **T:** 10:00–17:00; **W:** 10:00–17:00; **Th:** 10:00–17:00; **F:** 10:00–17:00; **S:** 10:00–17:00 Spec: Aircraft; Art Reference; Arts, The; Autobiography; Aviation; Cinema/Film; Classics, The; Computing. CC: MC; V.

Bishopston Books, ■ 259 Gloucester Rd, Bristol, BS7 8NY. Prop: Bill Singleton. Tel: 0117 9445303. Web: www.ibooknet.co.uk. E-mail: bishopstonbooks@btinternet.com. Est: 1993. Shop open: **T:** 10.00–17.00; **W:** 10.00–17:30; **Th:** 10.00–17:30; **F:** 10.00–17:30; **S:** 09.30–16.30. CC: MC; V; Maestro. Mem: Ibooknet.

Books for Amnesty, ■ 103 Gloucester Road Bishopston, Bristol, BS7 8AT. Prop: Amnesty International U.K. Tel: (0117) 942-2969. Est: 1998. Shop open: **M:** 10:00–16:30; **T:** 10:00–16:30; **W:** 10:00–16:30; **Th:** 10:00–16:30; **F:** 10:00–16:30; **S:** 11:00–17:00. Medium stock. PR: £1–10. Notes: *Bristol Book Fairs at BAWA.*

Batch e-mail groups of dealers with your offers or books wanted.
Use the best alternative to Internet Book Search Engines:

www.sheppardsworld.co.uk

James Burmester, Pipley Old Farm Upton Cheyney, Bristol, BS30 6NG. Prop: James & Rosamund Burmester. Tel: (0117) 932-7265. Fax: (0117) 932-7667. E-mail: james.burmester@btconnect com. Est: 1985. Private premises. Appointment necessary. Small stock. Spec: Agriculture; Author - Austen, Jane; British Books; Cookery/Gastronomy: Courtesy, Economics; Education & School; English. PR: £50–10,000. CC: MC; V. Cata: rare and unusual English books, 1600-1900. Mem: PBFA. VAT No: GB 404 6808 60.

Deverell Books, 86a Memorial Road Hanham, Bristol, BS15 3LA. Prop: Paul Deverell Hughes. Tel: (0117) 961-6234. Fax: (0117) 373-8786. E-mail: pdhbooks@hotmail.com. Est: 2001. Private premises. Appointment necessary. Very small stock. Spec: Books about Books; Children's; Children's - Illustrated; Illustrated - General. PR: £10–2,000. Cata: children's & illustrated. Mem: PBFA.

R.A. Gilbert, 4 Julius Road, Bishopston, Bristol, BS7 8EU. Tel: (0117) 924-6936. Fax: (0117) 924-4937. Est: 1963. Private premises. Appointment necessary. Small stock. Spec: Alchemy; Folklore; Freemasonry & Anti-Masonry; Gnostics / Gnosticism; Occult; Psychic; Religion - General; Theology. PR: £5 -1,000. Corresp: French. VAT No: GB 138 9728 22.

Harlequin Books, ■ 122 High Street Staple Hill, Bristol, BS16 5HH. Prop: Brian W. Ball. Tel: (0117) 970-1801. Fax: (0117) 970-1801. Web: www.harlequinbooks.co.uk. E-mail: harlequin.books@ virgin.net. Est: 1994. Shop Internet and Postal. Open: **M:** 09:30–16:30; **T:** 09:30–16:30; **W:** 09:30– 13:00; **Th:** 09:30–16:30; **F:** 09:30–16:30; **S:** 09:30- 16:30. Medium stock. Spec: Aviation; Maritime/ Nautical; Military; Military History; Motoring; Railways; Topography - Local; War - General. PR: £1–250. CC: AE; JCB; MC; V. VAT No: GB 639 7296 86.

A.R. Heath, 62 Pembroke Road, Clifton, Bristol, BS8 3DX. Tel: (0117) 974-1183. Fax: (0117) 973-2901. Web: www.heathrarebooks.co.uk. E-mail: enquiries@heathrarebooks.co.uk. Est: 1964. Spec: Fine & Rare; Manuscripts. PR: £50–10,000.

Higher Octave Books, ■ 58 Cotham Hill, Redland, Bristol, BS6 6JX. Prop: Kevin Fortey-Jones F.E.A.A. Tel: 0117 946 7772. Fax: 0117 973 0522. Web: www.higher-octave-books.co.uk. E-mail: royalfort@btconnect.com. Shop open: **M:** 10:00–18:00; **T:** 10:00–18:00; **W:** 10:00–18:00; **Th:** 10:00– 18:00; **F:** 10:00–18:00; **S:** 10:00–18:00. CC: E; MC; V. VAT No: GB 713 5195 47. Notes: *General stock bordering on the academic. Specialist subjects are Mind, Body & Spirit, Humanities, Literary Criticism, Military History and American History.*

Hinchliffe Books, Clematis Cottage 15 Castle Street, Thornbury, Bristol, BS35 1HA. Prop: Geoffrey Hinchliffe. Tel: (01454) 415177. E-mail: geoff@sumbooks.co.uk Est: 1972. Private premises. Medium stock. Spec: Homeopathy; Industry; Mathematics; Physics; Science - General; Technology; Topography - General. PR: £2–200. VAT No: GB 520 4690 69.

A.J. Kitley, 31 Perrys Lea Bradley Stoke, Bristol, BS32 0EE. Tel: (01454) 615261. Est: 1986. Private premises. Postal Only. Very small stock. Spec: Musical Instruments. PR: £1–150.

Rachel Lee Rare Books, The Old Bakery 30 Poplar Road, Warmley, Bristol, BS30 5JU. Prop: Rachel Lee. Tel: (0117) 960-6891. Fax: (0117) 960-6935. Web: www.rleerarebooks.co.uk. E-mail: rachellee.books@virgin.net. Est: 1979. Private premises. Internet and Postal. Appointment necessary. Small stock. Spec: Academic/Scholarly; Economics; History of Ideas; Humanities; Philosophy; Booksearch. PR: £30–20,000. CC: AE; MC; V. Mem: ABA; ILAB. VAT No: GB 783 5078 02. Notes: *Also, a booksearch service for philosophy only.*

M. G. Manwaring, 9 Glentworth Road, Bristol, BS6 7EG. Tel: 0117 942 2934. E-mail: malcolm@ mgmanwaring.fsnet.co.uk. Est: 1975. Private premises. Internet and Postal. Telephone First. Open: **M:** 09:00–18:00; **T:** 09:00–18:00; **W:** 09:00–18:00; **Th:** 09:00–18:00; **F:** 09:00–18:00. Spec: Applied Art; Archaeology; Architecture; Art; Art Reference; Author - 20th Century; Book Arts; Botany. CC: MC; V. Cata: All. Corresp: French.

Paperbacks Plus, ■ Regent Street Shopping Arcade 98 Regent Street, Kingswood, Bristol, BS15 8HP. Prop: Mr. T. Nicholls. Tel: (0117) 9566232. Web: www.pbplus.freeserve.co.uk. E-mail: books@ pbplus.freeserve.co.uk. Est: 1994. Internet and Postal. Shop open: **M:** 09:00–17:00; **T:** 09:00–17:00; **W:** 09:00–17:00; **Th:** 09:00–17:00; **F:** 09:00–17:00; **S:** 09:00–17:00. Spec: Biography; Children's; Fiction - General; Fiction - Crime, Detective, Spy, Thrillers; Fiction - Fantasy, Horror; Fiction - Science Fiction; Fiction - Women; Military History. PR: £1–20.

John Roberts Wine Books, 3 Weston Close, Sea Mills, Bristol, BS9 2JG. Prop: John Roberts. Tel: 0117 373 7904. E-mail: wine.books@blueyonder.co.uk. Est: 1977. Private premises. Internet and Postal. Spec: Author - Simon, Andre L.; Viticulture; Whisky; Wine. Mem: ABA; ILAB. VAT No: GB 561 9002 57.

BRISTOL

S.P.C.K., ■ 79 Park Street, Bristol, BS1 5PF. Tel: (0117) 9273461. Fax: (0117) 9293525. Web: www.spck.org.uk. E-mail: bristol@spck.org.uk. Est: 1698. Shop open: **M:** 09:00–17:30; **T:** 09:00–17:30; **W:** 09:30–17:30; **Th:** 09:00–17:30; **F:** 09:00–17:30; **S:** 09:00–17:30. Small stock. Spec: Bibles; Biblical Studies; Ecclesiastical History & Architecture; Gnostics / Gnosticism; Oxford Movement; Prayer Books; Religion - Catholic; Religion - Christian. PR: £1–250. CC: MC; V. Mem: BA. VAT No: GB 232 8071 82. Notes: *Theological Booksellers, specialising in secondhand and new Christian Theology. Also secondhand vestments and communion ware.*

Morris & Juliet Venables, 270 Henbury Road, Bristol, BS10 7QR. Prop: Morris & Juliet Venables. Tel: (0117) 950-7362. E-mail: morris.venables@ukgateway.net. Est: 1970. Private premises. Medium stock. Spec: Academic/Scholarly; Antiquarian; Art; Fine & Rare; Literary Criticism; Literature; Music - General; Music - Classical. PR: £5–1,000. CC: MC; V. Cata: Stained glass. Mem: PBFA. VAT No: GB 397 3454 11.

CLIFTON

Gerald Baker, 28 Beaconsfield Road, Clifton, BS8 2TS. Prop: Gerald Baker. Tel: (0117) 974-4319. Web: www.gwrpublicity.co.uk. E-mail: gwrpublicity@btinternet.com. Est: 1991. Private premises. Postal Only. Very small stock. Spec: Railways; Transport; Ephemera. PR: £5–200. CC: PayPal. Cata: Official publicity of British railway companies.

CLIFTONWOOD

Byass Rare Books, 22 Bellevue Crescent, Cliftonwood, BS8 4TE. Prop: Dean Byass. Tel: (0117) 9299400. E-mail: byass@bluyonder.co.uk. Est: 1994. Private premises. Internet and Postal. Telephone first. Spec: Antiquarian; Chemistry; Earth Sciences; Fine & Rare; History - Science; History of Ideas; Law - General; Literature. PR: £50–10,000. CC: AE; MC; V. VAT No: GB 799 9334 44.

HAMBROOK

Bristol Books, Champion House Moorend Farm Road, Hambrook, Bristol, BS16 1SP. Prop: Garth O'Donnell. Tel: (0117) 910 9829. Web: www.abebooks.com/home/bs6books. E-mail: bs6books@ aol.com. Est: 1985. Private premises. Internet and Postal. Appointment necessary. Medium stock. Spec: Art; Humanities; Literature; Pulps. PR: £1–50. CC: PayPal.

NAILSEA

The Old Music Master, 16 Scotch Horn Way, Nailsea, BS48 1TE. Prop: Joseph Tooley. Tel: 01275 856320. E-mail: pokefun@btinternet.com. Est: 1992. Private premises. Postal Only. Appointment necessary. Spec: Music - Illustrated Sheet Music; Music - Printed, Sheet Music & Scores. CC: PayPal. Notes: *Main stock is music sheets with illustrated covers. The music is secondary to the cover illustrations. From mid 19th century to 1960's.*

BUCKINGHAMSHIRE

AMERSHAM

Gill Bilski, 4 Sheepfold Lane, Amersham, HP7 9EL. Prop: Gill Bilski. Tel: (01494) 433895. Web: www.gillbilski.com. E-mail: gillbilski@gmail.com. Est: 1983. Private premises. Internet and Postal. Appointment necessary. Very small stock. Spec: Author - Brent-Dyer, - Elinor M.; - Fairlie–Bruce, D.; - Oxenham, Elsie; Children's. PR: £2–200. CC: via PayPal for overseas customers. Cata: Children's books with a few adult & non-fiction. Corresp: French. Notes: *Also a booksearch service.*

AYLESBURY

Great Hall Bookshop, ■ The King's Head Market Square, Aylesbury, HP20 2RW. Prop: The National Trust. Tel: 01296 381501. Fax: 10296 381502. Web: www.nationaltrust.org.uk. Est: 2004. Shop open: **M:** 10:30–16:00; **T:** 10:30–16:00; **W:** 10:30–16:00; **Th:** 10:30–16:00; **F:** 10:30–16:00; **S:** 10:30–16:00. Spec: Biography; Fiction - General; History - General; Travel - General; Collectables.

David Wilson, 95 Worlds End Lane Weston Turville, Aylesbury, HP22 5RX. Tel: (01296) 612247. Est: 1969. Private premises. Postal Only. Appointment necessary. Spec: Countries - Scotland; Natural History; Topography - Local. Notes: *Stocks major on Highlands and Islands and natural history (ornithology).*

BEACONSFIELD

Barn Books, Old Hay Barn Holtspur Top Lane, Beaconsfield, HP9 1BS. Prop: Elisabeth & Wolfgang Ansorge. Tel: (01494) 671122. Fax: (01494) 671122. E-mail: barnbooks@supanet.com. Est: 1991. Private premises. Internet and Postal. Appointment necessary. Small stock. Spec: Africana; Archaeology; Art; Churchilliana; Cinema/Film; Collecting; Countries - Africa; Countries - South Africa. PR: £5–3,000. CC: PayPal. Corresp: German. VAT No: GB 578 4204 21. Notes: *We now offer a large selection from our stock to customers in South Africa at BAOBAB BOOKS, 210 Long Street, Cape Town 8001 and also offer a search service though this shop.*

BUCKINGHAM

Corvus Books, 11 Parsons Close, Winslow, Buckingham, MK18 3BX. Prop: Chris Corbett. Tel: (01296) 713393. Fax: (01296) 713393. E-mail: corvusbooks@btinternet.com. Est: 1990. Private premises. Internet and Postal. Appointment necessary. Very small stock. Spec: Atlases; Colour-Plate; Natural History; Travel - General. PR: £50–5,000. CC: Pay Pal. Mem: PBFA. Notes: *Also attends 11 P.B.F.A. fairs a year at the Holiday Inn near Rusell Square.*

E. & J. Shelley, Quakers Orchard 12 Moreton Road, Buckingham, MK18 1LA. Prop: Jennifer Shelley. Tel: (01280) 812307. E-mail: shellbooks@btinternet.com. Est: 1996. Private premises. Postal only. Telephone First. Large stock. Spec: Children's; First Editions; Illustrated - General; Literature; Poetry. PR: £10–2,000.

CASTLETHORPE

Butler Cresswell Rare Books, Castlethorpe Lodge Hanslope Road, Castlethorpe, MK19 7HD. Prop: Stephen Butler, Peter Cresswell. Tel: 01908 511625. E-mail: stephen.finebooks@gmail.com. Est: 1979. Private premises. Appointment necessary. Open: **M:** 09:00–17:30; **T:** 09:00–17:30; **W:** 09:00–17:30; **Th:** 09:00–17:30; **F:** 09:00–17:30; **S:** 09:00–17:30; **Su:** 09:00–17:30; Closed for lunch: 13:00–14:00. Spec: Antiquarian; Bibles; Biblical Studies; Classics, The; Incunabula; Religion - Christian; Theology. CC: MC; V. Cata: Theology; Bibles. Mem: PBFA. Notes: *Antiquarian Theology; Classics; Incunabula; Bibles.*

CHESHAM

David Mundy at Nooks and Crannies, ■ 9 Market Square, Chesham, HP5 1HG. Prop: Dave Mundy. Tel: (020) 7482 7087. E-mail: dave.mundy@tiscali.co.uk. Est: 2000. Shop open: **M:** 09:30–17:30; **T:** 09:30–17:30; **W:** 09:30–17:30; **Th:** 09:30–17:30; **F:** 09:30–17:30; **S:** 09:30–17:30; **Su:** 11:00–16:30. Very small stock. Spec: Antiques; Art; History - General; Topography - General; Travel - General. PR: £1–50. CC: MC; V.

BUCKINGHAMSHIRE

HIGH WYCOMBE

Rivendale Press, PO Box 85, High Wycombe, HP14 4WZ. Prop: Steven Halliwell. Tel: 01494 562266. Fax: 01494 565533. Web: www.rivendalepress.com. E-mail: sales@rivendalepress.com. Est: 1998. Mail Order Only. Internet and Postal. Telephone First. Open: **M:** 09:00–17:30; **T:** 09:00–17:30; **W:** 09:00–17:30; **Th:** 09:00–17:30; **F:** 09:00–17:30; **S:** 09:00–17:30; **Su:** 09:00–17:30; Closed for lunch: 13:00–14:00. Spec: Academic/Scholarly; Bibliography; Biography; Books about Books; Poetry; Private Press. CC: MC; V. Mem: PBFA.

IVER

Pemberley Books, ■ 18 Bathurst Walk Richings Park, Iver, SL0 9AZ. Prop: Ian A. Johnson. Tel: (01753) 631114. Fax: (01753) 631115. Web: www.pemberleybooks.com. E-mail: info@pemberleybooks.com. Est: 1985. Internet and Postal. Shop open: **M:** 10:00–17:00; **T:** 10:00–17:00; **W:** 10:00–17:00; **Th:** 10:00–17:00; **F:** 10:00–17:00; **S:** 10:00–16:00. Medium stock. Spec: Antiquarian; Botany; Entomology; Herpetology; Lepidopterology; Natural History; New Naturalist; Ornithology. PR: £5–8,000. CC: AE; E; JCB; MC; V. Cata: Natural History, Entomology. Corresp: German. Mem: PBFA; BA. VAT No: GB 646 2266 34. Notes: *Also, new books on specialities.*

MILTON KEYNES

Daeron's Books, ■ 3 Timor Court Stony Stratford, Milton Keynes, MK11 1EJ. Prop: Angela Gardner. Tel: (01908) 568989. Fax: (01908) 266199. Web: www.daerons.co.uk. E-mail: books@daerons.co.uk. Est: 1992. Internet and Postal. Shop open: **M:** 09:30–17:15; **T:** 09:30–17:15; **W:** 09:30–17:15; **F:** 09:30–17:15; **S:** 09:30–17:15. Medium stock. Spec: Antiquarian; Arthurian; Author - Chesterton, G.K.; - Inklings, The; - Kipling, Rudyard; - Lewis, C.S.; - MacDonald, George; - Pratchett, Terry. PR: £1–500. CC: AE; D; E; JCB; MC; V. Mem: FSB SSBA. VAT No: GB 776 7066 85. Notes: *We have now expanded our range of both books and ephemera. Dragons, Daleks, fairies with a hint of Wicca are now part of our range. Still the largest collection of Tolkien and Lewis.*

Periplus Books, 160 Waterside Peartree Bridge, Milton Keynes, MK6 3DQ. Prop: John Phillips. Tel: (01908) 663579. Fax: (01908) 663579. Web: www.periplusbooks.co.uk. E-mail: john@ periplusbooks.co.uk. Est: 1997. Private premises. Postal Only. Appointment necessary. Small stock. Spec: Biology - Marine; Geology; Meteorology; Oceanography. PR: £5–200.

NEWPORT PAGNELL

Ken's Paper Collectables, ■ 29 High Street, Newport Pagnell, MK16 8AR. Prop: Ken Graham. Tel: (01908) 610003. Fax: (01908) 610003. Web: www.kens.co.uk. E-mail: ken@kens.co.uk. Est: 1983. Shop open: **M:** 09:30–17:00; **T:** 09:30–17:00; **W:** 09:30–17:00; **Th:** ; **F:** 09:30–17:00; **S:** 09:30–16:00. Large stock. Spec: Autographs; Comics; Magazines & Periodicals - General; Manuscripts; Newspapers; Paper Collectables; Collectables; Ephemera. PR: £1–400. CC: MC; V. Mem: Ephemera Society. Notes: *We sell magazines, newspapers, comics, posters, ephemera, postcards and all manner of paper collectables. No Books, stamps or currency.*

PENN

The Cottage Bookshop, ■ Elm Road, Penn, HP10 8LB. Prop: Mrs E S Tebbutt. Tel: 01494 812632. Est: 1951. Shop open: **T:** 10:00–17:00; **W:** 10:00–17:00; **Th:** 10:00–17:00; **F:** 10:00–17:00; **S:** 10:00–17:00. Mem: BA

STOKE GOLDINGTON

Fireside Books, Harebell Cottage 14 Mount Pleasant, Stoke Goldington, MK16 8LL. Prop: John Coppock. Tel: (01908) 551199. Fax: (0870) 1617621. Web: www.firesidebooks.demon.co.uk. E-mail: john@firesidebooks.demon.co.uk. Est: 1998. Private premises. Postal Only. Very small stock. Spec: Author - Morton, H.V.; History - General; Rural Life; Topography - General; Topography - Local; Travel - General; Booksearch. PR: £5–300. CC: MC; V.

CAMBRIDGESHIRE

BLUNTISHAM

Bluntisham Books, 4 East Street, Bluntisham, Huntingdon, PE28 3LS. Prop: D.W.H. & S. Walton. Tel: 01487 840449. Fax: 01487 840894. Web: www.bluntishambooks.co.uk. E-mail: contact@ bluntishambooks.co.uk. Est: 1976. Private premises. Internet and Postal. Spec: Countries - Antarctic, The; Countries - Arctic, The; Countries - Falklands, The; Countries - Greenland; Countries - Iceland; Countries - Polar; Exploration - Polar Regions; Travel - Polar. CC: MC; V. Cata: – 3 a year. VAT No: GB 344 2959 39. Notes: *Also, publishers of Antarctic book, including reprints of classics.*

CAMBRIDGE

Alister & Garon Books, Cambridge, CB4 3AQ. Prop: Paul Neeve. Tel: (07967) 227887 E-mail: p.neeve@ ntlworld.com. Est: 1980. Market stand/stall; Market Stall. Open: **M:** 09:00–17:00; **W:** 09:00–17:00; **F:** 09:00–17:00; **S:** 09:00–17:00; **Su:** 09:00–17:00. Medium stock. Spec: Art; Fiction - General; History - General, Literature; Mind, Body & Spirit; Music - General. PR: £1–25. VAT No: GB 215 8289 51.

Bookbarrow, 93 Cam Causeway, Cambridge, CB4 1TL. Prop: Frank Edwards. Tel: 01223 424 429. E-mail: bookbarrow@ntlworld.com. Est: 1988. Private premises. Internet and Postal. Appointment necessary. Spec: Africana; American Indians; Art; Astrology; Children's; Comics; Eastern Philosophy; Esoteric. Mem: PBFA. Notes: *General stock on market stall, Cambridge City Centre Market, Thursdays only 9a.m. until 4p.m. Some P.B.F.A. bookfairs attended in East Anglia.*

Books & Collectables Ltd., ■ Unit 7/8 Railway Arches Coldhams Road, Cambridge, CB1 3EW. Prop: A. Doyle, J. Cross, D.B. & M. Doyle & P. Brown. Tel: (01223) 412845. Web: www.booksandcollectables .com. E-mail: ask@booksandcollectables.com. Est: 1993. Internet and Postal. Shop open: **M:** 10:00–17:00; **T:** 10:00–17:00; **W:** 10:00–17:00; **Th:** 10:00–17:00; **F:** 10:00–17:00; **S:** 10:00–17:00; **Su:** 10:00–16:00. Very large stock. Spec: Antiques; Art; Children's; Cinema/Film; Comic Books & Annuals; Comics; Cookery/Gastronomy; Fiction - General. PR: £1–300.

Bracton Books, 25 Lode Road Lode, Cambridge, CB5 9ER. Prop: Mrs S.J. Harrison. Tel: (01223) 811976. Web. www.bractonbooks.co.uk. E-mail: bractonbooks@uk2.net. Est: 1981. Private premises. Postal Only. Appointment necessary. Large stock. Spec: Academic/Scholarly; Anthropology; Archaeology; Biology - General; Books about Books; Countries - Africa; Countries - Americas, The; Countries - Asia. PR: £2–100. CC: PayPal.

G. David, ■ 16 St. Edward's Passage, Cambridge, CB2 3PJ. Prop: D.C. Asplin, N.T. Adams & B.L. Collings. Tel: (01223) 354619. Fax: (01223) 324663. E-mail: gdavid.books@btinternet.com. Est: 1896. Shop open: **M:** 09:00–17:00; **T:** 09:00–17:00; **W:** 09:00–17:00; **Th:** 09:00–17:00; **F:** 09:00–17:00; **S:** 09:00–17:00. Medium stock. Spec: Academic/Scholarly; Antiquarian; Bindings; Children's; Early Imprints; Fine & Rare; Illustrated - General; Literature. PR: £1–1,000. CC: JCB; MC; V. Corresp: Japanese, Swedish. Mem: ABA; PBFA; BA. VAT No: GB 599 5999 44. Notes: *For any general enquiries please contact D.Asplin or N. Adams by phone or fax only. Exhibits at PBFA fair (June), York (September), ABA Chelsea (November).*

de Visser Books, 309 Milton Road, Cambridge, CB4 !XQ. Prop: Erik de Visser. Tel: (01223) 500909. Fax: (01223) 500909. E-mail: devisserbooks@hotmail.com. Est: 1988. Private premises. Internet and Postal. Appointment necessary. Small stock. Spec: Academic/Scholarly; Countries - Albania; Countries - Austria; Countries - Balkans, The; Countries - Baltic States; Countries - Bulgaria; Countries - Central East Europe; Countries - Czech Republic. PR: £10–750. CC: JCB; MC; V; Delta, Maestro, Solo. Cata: 4/5 a year on Central & East Europe only. Corresp: French, Dutch, German. VAT No: GB 493 3891 05.

Available from Richard Joseph Publishers Ltd

MINIATURE BOOKS

by Louis W. Bondy

(A5 H/b) 221pp £24.00

CAMBRIDGESHIRE

Galloway & Porter Limited, ■ 30 Sidney Street, Cambridge, CB2 3HS. Prop: Mr Porter. Tel: (01223) 367876. Fax: (01223) 360705. E-mail: galporl@aol.com. Est: 1900. Shop open: **M:** 08:45–17:00; **W:** 08:45–17:00; **Th:** 08:45–17:00; **F:** 08:45–17:00; **S:** 09:00–17:15. Large stock. Spec: Academic/Scholarly; Mythology. PR: £1–2,000. Mem: ABA; PBFA; BA; BT. VAT No: GB 213 4374 92. Notes: *Also, remainders and bargain books.*

The Haunted Bookshop, ■ 9 St. Edward's Passage, Cambridge, CB2 3PJ. Prop: Sarah Key & Phil Salin. Tel: 01223 312913. Web: www.sarahkeybooks.co.uk. E-mail: info@sarahkeybooks.co.uk. Shop open: **M:** 10:00–17:00; **T:** 10.00–17:00; **W:** 10.00–17:00; **Th:** 10.00–17.00; **F:** 10.00–17.00; **S:** 10.00–17.00. Spec: CC: JCB; MC; V. Cata: Children's & Illustrated. Corresp: French. Mem: PBFA. VAT No: GB 572 9580 04. Notes: *Specialising in children's and illustrated books 19th and 20th century, but also stocking some poetry, literature, fine bindings, East Anglian interest and some general stock. We are happy to post books, our site has secure CC facility.*

J & J Burgess Booksellers, 2 St Thomas's Road, Cambridge, CB1 3TF. Prop: John Burgess, Janet Burgess. Tel: 01223 249037. E-mail: jandjburgess2@ntlworld.com. Est: 1997. Private premises. Postal Only. Appointment necessary. Spec: Africana; Aircraft; American Revolution, The; Anatomy; Animals and Birds; Archaeology; Arctic - Antarctica; Arms & Armour.

Sarah Key, ■ The Haunted Bookshop 9 St. Edward's Passage, Cambridge, CB2 3PJ. Prop: Sarah Key & Phil Salin. Tel: (01223) 312913. Web: www.sarahkeybooks.co.uk. E-mail: info@sarahkeybooks .co.uk. Est: 1985. Shop open: **M:** 10:00–17:00; **T:** 10:00–17:00; **W:** 10:00–17:00; **Th:** 10:00–17:00; **F:** 10:00–17:00; **S:** 10:00–17:00. Medium stock. Spec: Academic/Scholarly; Aeronautics; Annuals; Author - Ardizzone, Edward; Author - Barker, Cecily M.; - Blyton, Enid; - Brent-Dyer, Elinor M.; - Buckeridge, A. PR: £1–2,000. CC: JCB; MC; V. Cata: Childrens's & Illustrated. Corresp: French. Mem: PBFA. VAT No: GB 572 9680 04. Notes: *Local interest items & a booksearch service within our specialist field.*

Paul Kunkler Books, 6 Hardwick Street, Cambridge, CB3 9JA. Tel: (01223) 321419. Fax: (01223) 321419. Private premises. Appointment necessary. Very small stock. Spec: Art History; Manuscripts.

Adam Mills Rare Books, 328 High Street, Cottenham, Cambridge, CB4 8TX. Prop: Adam Mills. Tel: (01954) 250106. Fax: (01954) 250106. Web: www.abebooks.com. E-mail: adam@heathmills .waitrose.com. Est: 1981. Private premises. Internet and Postal. Appointment necessary. Small stock. Spec: Bibliography; Books about Books; Fine Printing; Illustrated - General; Limited Editions - General; Literature; Private Press; Typography. CC: MC; V. Cata: English Literature, Private Press & Illustrated. Corresp: French, Italian. Mem: PBFA.

Peter Moore Bookseller, P.O. Box 66, Cambridge, CB1 3PD. Prop: Peter Moore. Tel: (01223) 411177. Web: www.aus-pacbooks.co.uk. E-mail: aus-pacbooks@lineone.net. Est: 1970. Office and/or bookroom. Internet and Postal. Appointment necessary. Shop at: Unit 12, The Old Maltings, 135 Ditton Walk, Cambridge. Small stock. Spec: Countries - Australia; Countries - Pacific, The; Countries - Papua New Guinea; Travel - Australasia/Australia. PR: £1–500. CC: JCB; MC; V. Mem: PBFA; BCSA. VAT No: GB 215 3610 02.

Mike Parker Books, 2 Mill Lane, Duxford, Cambridge, CB22 4PT. Tel: (01223) 835935. E-mail: mjp@lineone.net. Est: 1995. Private premises. Internet and Postal. Appointment necessary. Small stock. Spec: Adventure; Annuals; Antiquarian; Autobiography; Fiction - General; History - General; Literature; Military. PR: £5–500.

Plurabelle Books, The Grey Barn (Bldg 3) The Michael Young Centre, Purbeck Road, Cambridge, CB2 8HN. Prop: Dr. Michael Cahn. Tel: (01223) 415671. Fax: (01223) 413241. Web: www.plurabelle .co.uk. E-mail: books@plurabelle.co.uk. Est: 1993. Warehouse. Postal Only. Telephone First. Open: **M:** 09:00–16:00; **T:** 09:00–16:00; **W:** 09:00–16:00; **Th:** 09:00–16:00; **F:** 09:00–16:00. Very large stock. Spec: Academic/Scholarly; Computing; Humanities; Linguistics; Literature; Philosophy; Science - General; Science - History of. PR: £8–500. CC: E; MC; V; Switch, Maestro. Corresp: French, German, Italian. Mem: Tom Folio, IBookNnet. VAT No: GB 636 8493 00.

SEARCH on-line for dealers - and for books by speciality subject

www.sheppardsworld.co.uk

CAMBRIDGESHIRE

Quest Booksearch, 24 Hawthorne Road, Stapleford, Cambridge, CB22 5DU. Prop: Dr. Rosemary Scott. Tel: (01223) 844080. Fax: (01223) 844080. E-mail: qbs2@lineone.net. Est: 1997. Private premises. Postal Only. Spec: Literature - Victorian; Poetry.

Rupert Books, 58/59 Stonefield Bar Hill, Cambridge, CB3 8TE. Prop: Paulina M. & R. Dixon Smith. Tel: (01954) 781861. Web: www.rupert-books.co.uk. E-mail: sales@rupert-books.co.uk. Est: 1984. Private premises. Appointment necessary. Spec: Author - Conan Doyle, Sir Arthur; Crime (True); Sherlockiana. PR: £3–1,000. CC: JCB; V.

Frances Wetherell, 8 Highworth Avenue, Cambridge, CB4 2BG. Tel: (01223) 363537. E-mail: frances.wetherell@talk21.com. Est: 1988. Private premises. Postal Only. Appointment necessary. Very small stock. Spec: Art; Economics; Literature; Social History. PR: £10–100. Notes: *Also, a booksearch service.*

David White, The Old Guildhall 4 Church Lane, Linton, Cambridge, CB1 6JX. Prop: David White. Tel: (01223) 894447. Web: www.davidwhitebooks.co.uk. E-mail: david@davidwhitebooks.co.uk. Est: 1987. Private premises. Internet and Postal. Appointment necessary. Very small stock. Spec: Medicine; Medicine - History of; Pharmacy/Pharmacology. PR: £10–2,000. CC: MC; V. Cata: medicine, history of medicine, pharmacy.

Peter Wood, 51 Telegraph Street Cottenham, Cambridge, CB24 8QU. Tel: (01954) 251056. Web: www.booksatpbfa.com. E-mail: peterwoodbooks@waitrose.com. Est: 1973. Private premises. Appointment necessary. Small stock. Spec: Art; Broadcasting; Cinema/Film; Entertainment - General; Music - General; Performing Arts; Theatre; Ephemera. PR: £20–500. CC: MC; V. Mem: PBFA. VAT No: GB 214 4339 88. Notes: *Contactable Monday to Friday 08:30 – 18:00. Attends Perfoming Arts fairs at National Theatre Apr-Oct.*

CASTLE CAMPS

Harry Brett, Pepperpot Cottage Bartlow Road, Castle Camps, Cambridge, CB1 6SX. Tel: (01799) 584515. Est: 1968. Private premises. Postal Only. Small stock. PR: £2–500.

CHATTERIS

Joan Stevens, Books, ■ 3 High Street, Chatteris, PE16 6BE. Prop: Joan Stevens. Tel: (01354) 696874. Fax. (01354) 696874. E-mail: joan.stevensbooks@btinternet.com. Est: 2000. Shop. Appointment necessary. Open: **S:** 10:00–13:00. Small stock. Spec: Academic/Scholarly; Art - Afro-American; Art - Theory; Art Reference; Artists; Author - 19th Century; Authors - Women; Autographs. PR: £1–200. CC: cash/cheque. Cata: author lists. Corresp: French. Notes: *Ring the door bell between 10:00 and 17:00, other times by appointment. Stock includes 19thC women's lives.*

ELY

P.G. Bright, 11 Ravens Court, Ely, CB6 3ED. Tel: (01353) 661727. E-mail: peter.bright2@ btinternet.com. Est: 1982. Private premises. Appointment necessary. Medium stock. Spec: Children's; Illustrated - General; Literature; Sport - Cricket. PR: £1–500. Mem: PBFA. Notes: *The Bookshop, 24 Magdalene Street, Cambridge (q.v.).*

Ely Books, 24 Downham Road, Ely, CB6 1AF. Prop: Michael G. Kousah. Tel: (01353) 661824. Web: www.elybooks.com. E-mail: michael@elybooks.com. Est: 1986. Private premises. Internet Only. Very small stock. Spec: Americana - General; Antiquarian; Art; Australiana; Author - General; Author - Baring-Gould, S.; Bindings; Biography. PR: £5–2,000. Mem: PBFA. VAT No: GB 572 9042 32.

Dealers who need to update their entry should visit their page on *www.sheppardsworld.co.uk*

CAMBRIDGESHIRE

Hereward Books, ■ 17 High Street Haddenham, Ely, CB6 3XA. Prop: Roger J. Pratt. Tel: (01353) 740821. Fax: (01353) 741721. Web: www.herewardbooks.co.uk. E-mail: sales@herewardbooks.co.uk. Est: 1985. Internet and Postal. Telephone First. Shop open: **S:** 10:00–13:00. Medium stock. Spec: Bindings; Illustrated - General; Natural History; Sport - Angling/Fishing; Sport - Falconry; Sport - Field Sports; Travel - General. PR: £15–1,000. CC: JCB; MC; V; Debit. Cata: Field Sports & Angling. Mem: PBFA. VAT No: GB 382 3886 03.

Octagon Books, ■ 14 Pilgrims Way, Ely, CB6 3DL. Prop: John Williams. Tel: (01353) 610244. E-mail: octagonbooks@ntlworld.com. Est: 1982. Shop At: Cloisters Antiques, 1-1b Lynn Rd., Ely CB7 4EG. Open: **M:** 9.30–16:30; **T:** ; **W:** 9.30–16:30; **Th:** 9.30–16:30; **F:** 9.30–16:30; **S:** 9.30–16:30; **Su:** 11.00– 16:00. Small stock. Spec: Architecture; Art. CC: MC; V. Mem: PBFA. VAT No: GB 393 2186 39. Notes: *We also sell on the internet at www.abebooks.com and at Book Fairs. Interesting and scarce books on many subjects with some emphasis on art and architecture.*

GODMANCHESTER

Godmanchester Books, Staughton House 11 Post Street, Godmanchester, PE29 2BA. Prop: Doreen Lewis. Tel: (01480) 455020. Est: 1974. Private premises. Appointment necessary. Small stock. Spec: History - Local; Topography - Local; Booksearch. PR: £1–100.

HADDENHAM

John Lewcock, 6 Chewells Lane, Haddenham, Ely, CB6 3SS. Prop: John Lewcock. Tel: (01353) 741152. Fax: (01353) 741152. Web: www.abebooks.com/home/maritime. E-mail: lewcock@maritime-bookseller.com. Est: 1984. Office and/or bookroom. Internet and Postal. Telephone First. Medium stock. Spec: Academic/Scholarly; Armed Forces - Australian Navy; Canals/Inland Waterways; Deep Sea Diving; Manuals - Seamanship (see also under Seamanship); Maritime/Nautical; Naval; Navigation. PR: £5–1,500. CC: E; JCB; MC; V; Switch. Cata: maritime subjects. Mem: ABA; PBFA; ILAB; CEng/IEE. VAT No: GB 410 5334 04. Notes: *Also, insurance & probate valuations.*

HUNTINGDON

Roger Gaskell Rare Books, 17 Ramsey Road Warboys, Huntingdon, PE28 2RW. Tel: (01487) 823059. Fax: (01487) 823070. Web: www.rogergaskell.com. E-mail: roger@rogergaskell.com. Est: 1989. Private premises. Postal Only. Appointment necessary. Very small stock. Spec: Engineering; Medicine; Science - General; Technology. PR: £100–10,000. CC: AE; MC; V. Mem: ABA; ILAB. VAT No: GB 550 6050 74.

MK Book Services, 7 East Street, Huntingdon, PE29 1WZ. Prop: Melvyn R King. Tel: (01480) 353710. Fax: (01480) 431703. E-mail: mkbooks@tiscali.co.uk. Est: 1983. Private premises. Postal Only. Appointment necessary. Very small stock. Spec: Africana; Australiana; Authors - Local; Bibliography; Countries - Ascension Islands; Countries - Baltic States; Countries - Burma; Countries - South Atlantic Islands. PR: £1–50. CC: E; MC; V; UK Maestro. Mem: BA. VAT No: GB 958 0474 91.

John Robertshaw, 5 Fellowes Drive Ramsey, Huntingdon, PE26 1BE. Tel: (01487) 813330. Fax: (01487) 711901. E-mail: robertshaw.books@virgin.net. Est: 1983. Office and/or bookroom. Appointment necessary. Small stock. Spec: Antiquarian; Foreign Texts; Languages - Foreign. Cata: English and continental antiquarian books. Corresp: French, German. Mem: ABA; PBFA; ILAB. VAT No: GB 360 1311 09.

Ken Trotman, P.O.Box 505, Huntingdon, PE29 2XW. Prop: Richard & Roz Brown. Tel: (01480 454292. Fax: (01480 384651. Web: www.kentrotman.com. E-mail: rlbtrotman@aol.com. Est: 1949. Storeroom. Postal Only. Appointment necessary. Spec: History - Napoleonic; Military; Military - Modelling; Military History; Military Uniforms. PR: £5–1,500. CC: MC; V. Cata: military history & antique weapons. Corresp: French. Mem: PBFA. VAT No: GB 386 4614 23.

Available from Richard Joseph Publishers Ltd

BOOKWORMS, THE INSECT PESTS

by N. Hickin

Revised Edition (A5 H/b) 184pp £24.00

CAMBRIDGESHIRE

PETERBOROUGH

A. & H. Peasgood, 144 Broadway, Peterborough, PE1 4DG. Prop: Alan & Marion Peasgood. Tel: (01733) 565055. E-mail: marionpea@yahoo.co.uk. Est: 1997. Private premises. Book fairs only. Small stock Spec: Architecture, Art; History - General; Literature; Topography - General; Travel - General. PR: £1–25. Corresp: Spanish. Notes: *attends Cambridge Book Fair 2nd Tues each month.*

Francis Bowers Chess Suppliers, 62 Pennine Way Gunthorpe, Peterborough, PE4 7TE. Tel: (01733) 897119. E-mail: chessbower@aol.com. Est: 1991. Private premises. Spec: Chess. PR: £1–1,000.

Brian Cocks, 18 Woodgate, Helpston, Peterborough, PE6 7ED. Prop: Brian Cocks. Tel: 01733-252791. Fax: 01733-252791. Web: www.aviationbookhouse.co.uk. E-mail: brianc@uku.co.uk. Internet and Postal. Appointment necessary. Open: **M:** 09:00–17:30; **T:** 09:00–17:30; **W:** 09:00–17:30; **Th:** 09:00–17:30; **F:** 09:00–17:30; **S:** 09:00–17:30; **Su:** 09:00–17:30; Closed for lunch: 13:00–14:00. Spec: Aeronautics; Aircraft; Aviation; War - World War I; War - World War II. CC: PayPal. Cata: Aviation (all aspects). Corresp: French, Spanish, German. Mem: PBFA.

T.V. Coles, ■ 981 Lincoln Road, Peterborough, PE4 6AH. Tel: (01733) 577268. Est: 1982. Shop open: **M:** 09:30–15:30; **T:** 09:30–15:30; **W:** 09:30–15:30; **Th:** 09:30 15:30; **F:** 09:30–15:30; **S:** 09:30–15:30. Small stock. Spec: Aviation; Military; Military History; Naval; Topography - General; Collectables; Ephemera. PR: £1–200.

Paul Green, 83b London Road, Peterborough, PE? 9BS. Est: 1998 Private premises. Postal Only. Very small stock Spec: Naturism; Poetry. PR: £2–50. Notes: *Also booksearch.*

Peakirk Books, ■ Peakirk Book Shop 15 St Pegas Road, Peakirk, Peterborough, PE6 7NF. Prop: Heather & Jeff Lawrence. Tel: 01733 253182. Web: www.peakirkbooks.com. E-mail: peakirkbooks@ btinternet.com. Est: 1997. Shop open: **W:** 14:00–17:00; **Th:** 09:30–17:00; **F:** 09:30–17:00; **S:** 09:30–17:00; **Su:** 12.00–16.00. Spec: Author - Clare, John; Children's; Children's - Illustrated; General Stock; Juvenile; Topography - Local. CC: AE; MC; V. Mem: PBFA. VAT No: GB 694 8457 71. Notes: *The shop is open at other times by appointment, and internet/postal days we are available everyday except for Tuesdays. Local topography includes the fens. We specialise in childrens books & our local poet - John Clare.*

Frank T. Popeley, 27 Westbrook Park Road Woodston, Peterborough, PE2 9JG. Tel: (01333) 562386. Private premises. Postal Only. Small stock. Spec: Animals and Birds; Countries - Africa; Countries - Kenya; Countries - Tanzania; Countries - Uganda; Sport - Big Game Hunting; Tribal. PR: £1–1,000. Notes: *Books on early administration in East Africa.*

Wizard Books, 106 Church Street, Deeping St. James, Peterborough, PE6 8HB. Prop: Steve Blessctt. Tel. (01778) 343175. Fax: (01778) 380538. E-mail. wizardbooks@aol.com. Private premises. Internet and Postal. Small stock. Spec: Academic/Scholarly; Arms & Armour; Arthurian; Arts, The; Classical Studies; Cryptozoology; Divining; Ghosts. PR: £5–100. CC: JCB; MC; V.

WISBECH

Oasis Booksearch, ■ 88 Norfolk Street, Wisbech, PE13 2LF. Prop: R.G.M. & M.E. Welford. Tel: (01945) 420438. Fax: (01945) 465187. Web: www.oasisbookswisbech.co.uk. E-mail: oasiswisbech@ onetel.com. Est: 1998. Internet and Postal. Shop open: **T:** 09:00–17:00; **W:** 09:00–17:00; **Th:** 09:00–17:00; **F:** 09:00–17:00; **S:** 09:00–17:00. Small stock. Spec: Author - Ballantyne, Robert M.; - Blyton, Enid; - Bunyan, John; - Crompton, Richmal; - Goudge, Elizabeth; - Lewis, C.S.; - Morton, H.V.; - Newman, Cardinal. PR: £1–25. CC: AE; JCB; MC; V; PayPal. Cata: Christian, Theology. Mem: BA.

CHESHIRE

ALTRINCHAM (SEE ALSO UNDER GREATER MANCHESTER)

Abacus Books, ■ 24 Regent Road, Altrincham, WA14 1RP. Prop: C.D.Lawton. Tel: 0161 928 2220. E-mail: abacusbookstore@yahoo.com. Est: 1979. Shop open: **T:** 10:00–17:00; **W:** 10:00–16.00; **Th:** 10.00–17:00; **F:** 10:00–17:00; **S:** 10:00–17:00. Spec: Art; Natural History; Plant Hunting; Pottery & Glass; Watercolours; Windmills & Watermills; Woodland Crafts; Woodwork.

BIRCHWOOD

Sensawunda Books, 59 Dunnock Grove, Birchwood, Warrington, WA3 6NW. Prop: Grant Flexman-Smith. Tel: 01925 838501. E-mail: grant@sensawunda.freeserve.co.uk. Est: 1994. Private premises. Postal Only. Contactable. Spec: Fiction - Fantasy, Horror; Fiction - Science Fiction; First Editions; Signed Editions. Cata: Science Fiction, Fantasy, Horror.

CHEADLE

Geoff Booth Booksearch, 2 Hastings Close Cheadle Hulme, Cheadle, SK8 7BE. Prop: Geoff Booth. Tel: (0161) 485-4246. Web: www.boothbookmark.com. E-mail: geoff.booth131@btopenworld.com. Est: 1980. Private premises. Internet and Postal. Appointment necessary. Open: **M:** 09:00–16:00; **T:** 09:00–16:00; **W:** 09:00–16:00; **Th:** 09:00–16:00; **F:** 09:00–16:00; **S:** 09:00–12:00. Small stock. Spec: Alpinism/Mountaineering; Annuals; Antiquarian; Art; Art History; Artists; Author - Aldin, Cecil; - Ardizzone, Edward. PR: £5–400. CC: PayPal. Corresp: French, Spanish. Notes: *Out-of-Print Booksearch Service in operation - no search fee & no obligation to buy.*

Mainly Fiction, 21 Tennyson Road, Cheadle, SK8 2AR. Prop: Christopher J. Peers. Tel: (0161) 428-6836. E-mail: mainly.fiction@ntlworld.com. Est: 1986. Private premises. Book fairs only. Spec: Author - Fleming, Ian; Children's; Fiction - Crime, Detective, Spy, Thrillers; First Editions; Modern First Editions. PR: £5–200. CC: V. Mem: PBFA.

Tennis Collectables, 31 Syddall Avenue, Cheadle, SK8 3AA. Prop: Fiona & John Partington. Tel: (0161) 718-5378. Fax: (0161) 718-5378. E-mail: john@partbook.demon.co.uk. Private premises. Postal Only. Very small stock. Spec: Magazines & Periodicals - General; Sport - Tennis. PR: £2–200. CC: AE; JCB; MC; V. Cata: Tennis. VAT No: GB 748 5252 10.

CHEADLE HULME

Clifford Elmer Books Ltd., 8 Balmoral Avenue, Cheadle Hulme, Cheadle, SK8 5EQ. Prop: Clifford & Marie Elmer. Tel: 0161 485 7064. Web: www.cliffordelmerbooks.com. E-mail: sales@cliffordelmerbooks.com. Est: 1978. Private premises. Internet and Postal. Appointment necessary. Open: **M:** 09:00–17:30; **T:** 09:00–17:30; **W:** 09:00–17:30; **Th:** 09:00–17:30; **F:** 09:00–17:30; **S:** 09:00–17:30. Closed for lunch: 13:00–14:00. Spec: American Indians; Americana - General; Antiquarian; Assassinations; Biography; Crime (True); Criminology; Famous People - Kennedy, John F. CC: MC; V. Cata: Non-fiction crime and criminology. Mem: PBFA. Notes: *We specialise in rare and unusual true crime and criminology.*

CHESTER

Gildas Books, ■ 2, City Walls, Chester, CH1 2JG. Prop: Scott Lloyd and Sue Evans. Tel: 01244 311910. Web: www.gildasbooks.co.uk. E-mail: contact@gildasbooks.co.uk. Est: 2005. Shop open: **M:** 10:00–16:00; **T:** 10:00–16:00; **W:** 10.00–16.00; **Th:** 10:00–16:00; **F:** 10:00–16:00; **S:** 10:00–16:00; **Su:** 10:00–16:00. Spec: Academic/Scholarly; Alpinism/Mountaineering; Archaeology; Arthurian; Author - White, T.H.; - Wilson, Colin; British Books; Celtica. CC: MC; V. Notes: *Specialists in Arthurian Studies, Celtic Studies, Welsh History, History, Archaeology, Sci-Fi, Popular Science, Modern First editions, Topography, Folklore.*

Richard Nicholson of Chester, Stoneydale, Pepper Street Christleton, Chester, CH3 7AG. Tel: (01244) 336004. Fax: (01244) 336138. Web: www.antiquemaps.com. E-mail: richard@antiquemaps.com. Est: 1961. Private premises. Postal Only. Very small stock. Spec: Atlases; Voyages & Discovery; Prints and Maps. PR: £10–3,000. CC: MC; V. Cata: Maps, prints, atlases. VAT No: GB 159 3368 36. Notes: *See web site for stocks.*

CHESHIRE

Stothert Old Books, ■ 4 Nicholas Street, Chester, CH1 2NX. Prop: Alan Checkley. Tel: (01244) 340756. E-mail: stothertbooks@yahoo.co.uk. Est: 1970. Shop open: **M:** 10:00–17:00; **T:** 10:00–17:00; **W:** 10:00–17:00; **Th:** 10:00–17:00; **F:** 10:00–17:00; **S:** 10:00–17:00. Medium stock. Spec: Antiquarian; Antiques; Art; Children's; History - General; Illustrated - General; Sport - General; Topography - General. PR: £1–1,000. CC: E; MC; V. Corresp: French. Mem: PBFA. VAT No: GB 691 9276 88. Notes: *York and Haydock Park and other local fairs.*

CREWE

Copnal Books, ■ 18 Meredith Street, Crewe, CW1 2PW. Prop: Ruth Ollerhead. Tel: (01270) 580470. Web: www.copnalbooks.co.uk. E-mail: copnalbooks@yahoo.co.uk. Est: 1980. Shop open: **M:** 09:30–16:30; **T:** 09:30–16:30; **W:** 09:30–16:30; **Th:** 09:30–16:30; **F:** 09:30–16:30; **S:** 09:30–16:30. Large stock. Spec: Bibles; Children's; Religion - Christian; Theology; Topography - Local. PR: £1–50. Corresp: French. Notes: *Open other times by appointment.*

FRODSHAM

Cheshire Book Centre, ■ Lady Hayes Kingsley Road, Frodsham, WA6 6SU. Prop: J. R. S. Hall. Tel: 01928 788743. Fax: 01928 788743. Web: www.cheshirebookcentre.com. E-mail: enquiries@cheshirebookcentre.com. Est: 1950. Shop open: **M:** 10:00–17:00; **T:** 10:00–17:00; **W:** 10:00–17.00; **Th:** 10:00–17:00; **F:** 10:00–17:00; **S:** 10 00–17:00; **Su:** 11.00–17:00. Spec: Aeronautics; Agriculture; Alpinism/Mountaineering; Animals and Birds; Annuals; Antiquarian; Antiques; Applied Art. CC: E; MC; V. Corresp: French and German.

GREAT BARROW

Henry Wilson Books, Unit 7 Barrowmore Estate, Great Barrow, CH3 7JS. Prop: Henry Wilson. Tel: 01829 740693. Fax: 01270 219059. Web: www.henrywilsonbooks.co.uk. E-mail: hwrailwaybooks@aol.com. Est: 1983. Office and/or bookroom. Internet and Postal. Appointment necessary. Open: **M:** 09:00–17:30; **T:** 09:00–17:30; **W:** 09:00–17:30; **Th:** 09:00–17:30; **F:** 09:00–17:30; **S:** 09:00–17:30; **Su:** 09:00–17:30; Closed for lunch: 13:00–14:00. Spec: Archaeology - Industrial; Author - Rolt, L.T.C.; Canals/Inland Waterways; Countries - Antarctic, The; Exploration - Polar Regions; Fire & Fire Fighters; History - Industrial; Maritime/Nautical. CC: MC; V; Maestro. Cata: railways, canals, LTC Rolt. Corresp: French, German. Mem: PBFA; FSB. VAT No: GB 439 7672 03. Notes: *also at Dales and Lakes Book Centre, 72 Main Street, Sedbergh, Cumbria, LA10 5AD, open daily 10:00–17:00 (including Sundays) Tel. 01539 620125.*

HOYLAKE

Marine and Cannon Books, Naval & Maritime Dept., 'Nilcoptra', 3 Marine Road, Hoylake, Wirral, CH47 2AS. Prop: Michael & Vivienne Nash and Diane Churchill-Evans. Tel: (0151) 632-5365. Fax: (0151) 632-6472. E-mail: michael@marinecannon.com. Est: 1983. Private premises. Internet and Postal. Appointment necessary. Open: **M:** 09:00–18:00; **T:** 09:00–18:00; **W:** 09:00–18:00; **Th:** 09:00–18:00; **F:** 09:00–18:00; **S:** 09:00–17:00. Closed for lunch: 13:00–13:30. Medium stock. Spec: Academic/ Scholarly; Aircraft; Antiquarian; Armed Forces - Australian Air Force; Armed Forces - Australian Army; Armed Forces - Australian Navy; Army, The; Autobiography. PR: £10–20,000. CC: JCB; MC; V; Maestro. Cata: Naval & Maritime, Military & Aviation. Mem: ABA; ILAB. VAT No: GB 539 4137 32. Notes: *Military & Aviation Dept., (see separate entry) Outlets: RN Museum Portsmouth; Merseyside Maritime Museum, Albert Dock Liverpool.*

HYDE

Andrew's Books & Collectables, 38 Dowson Road, Hyde, SK14 1JS. Prop: Andrew R. Mays. Tel: 0161 351 1851. Fax: 0161 351 1851. E-mail: andrewsbooks@btinternet.com. Est: 1997. Private premises. Internet and Postal. Contactable. Spec: Theology; Topography - General; Topography - Local. CC: PayPal. Notes: *stock on Abe, Biblion, and Telephone inquiries welcome.*

J.A. Heacock, ■ 155 Market Street, Hyde, SK14 1HG. Prop: Joseph A. Heacock. Tel: 0161 3665098. E-mail: joseph@heacock.freeserve.co.uk. Est: 2000. Shop. Telephone First. Notes: *Traditional secondhand and antiquarian bookshop, interesting and better than average stock, reasonable prices, trade and public welcome, usually open but prior phone call or e-mail is very strongly advised.*

KNUTSFORD

The Arts & Antiques Centre, ■ 113 King Street, Knutsford. Shop open: **T:** 10:00–17:00; **W:** 10:00–17:00; **Th:** 10:00–17:00; **F:** 10:00–17:00; **S:** 10:00–17:00. Spec: Topography - General. Notes: *Cavern Books stock: general stock and topography. See Cavern Books, Nantwich, Cheshire (q.v.)*

CHESHIRE

BC Books, 12 Mallard Close, Knutsford, WA16 8ES. Prop: Brian Corrigan. Tel: (01565) 654014. E-mail: brian@corrigan.demon.co.uk. Est: 1993. Private premises. Postal Only. Contactable. Small stock. Spec: Collectables; Dolls & Dolls' Houses; First Editions; History - Ancient; History - British; Humour; Literature; Modern First Editions. PR: £1–250. Corresp: French. Notes: *Pre-Conquest history and literature, dolls and collectables, modern firsts.*

Fiction First, The Old Chapel Knolls Green Village, Knutsford, WA16 7BW. Tel: (01565) 872634. Web: www.abebooks.com. E-mail: richard.offer@virgin.net. Est: 1992. Private premises. Internet and Postal. Appointment necessary. Medium stock. Spec: Author - Pratchett, Terry; - Rankin, Ian; - Rice, Anne; Fiction - General; Fiction - Crime, Detective, Spy, Thrillers; Fiction - Fantasy, Horror; Fiction - Science Fiction; First Editions. PR: £10–2,000. CC: AE; MC; V.

LYMM

Jef Kay, 60 Mardale Crescent, Lymm, WA13 9PJ. Prop: Jef & Janet Kay. Tel: (01925) 755736. Web: www.ukbookworld.com/members/kbooks. E-mail: jef-kay@tiscali.co.uk. Est: 1994. Private premises. Appointment necessary. Small stock. Spec: Annuals; Astronautics; Author - Blyton, Enid; - Charteris, Leslie; - Kent, Alexander; Children's; Comic Books & Annuals; Fiction - General. PR: £1–100. Corresp: German.

MACCLESFIELD

George Longden, 71 Grimshaw Lane Bollington, Macclesfield, SK10 5LY. Prop: George Longden. Tel: (01625) 572584. E-mail: longdengeorge@hotmail.com. Est: 1998. Private premises. Postal Only. Small stock. Spec: Cartoons; Comic Books & Annuals; Comics. PR: £2–200. Notes: *Exhibits at book fairs in the North and Midlands.*

Mereside Books, ■ 75 Chestergate, Macclesfield, SK11 6DG. Prop: Sally Laithwaite & Steve Kowalski. Tel: Shop (01625) 425352. Est: 1996. Shop open: **W:** 10:00–17:00; **Th:** 10:00–17:00; **F:** 10:00–17:00; **S:** 10:00–17:00. Small stock. Spec: Illustrated - General. PR: £3–500. CC: E; JCB; MC; V. Mem: PBFA. Notes: *Organisers of Buxton Book Fairs.*

Roger J. Treglown, Sunderland House Sunderland Street, Macclesfield, SK 11 6JF. Prop: Roger Treglown. Tel: 01625 618978. E-mail: roger@rogerjtreglown.com. Est: 1980. Office and/or bookroom. Open: **M:** 09:30–17:30; **T:** 09:30–17:30; **W:** 09:30–17:30; **Th:** 09:30–17:30; **F:** 09:30–17:30; **S:** 09:30–13:00. Spec: Antiquarian; Chess; Early Imprints; Esoteric; Odd & Unusual. CC: E; MC; V. Cata: Chess. Mem: ABA; PBFA; ILAB; Macclesfield Booksellers Association. Notes: *Also, valuations for probate etc.*

MARPLE BRIDGE

Talisman Books, ■ 42 Town Street, Marple Bridge, Stockport, SK65AA. Prop: Frank Leonard and Jean Cessford. Tel: 01614499271. E-mail: frank.talismanbooks@virgin.net. Est: 1989. Shop open: **M:** 12:00–17:00; **T:** 12:00–17:00; **Th:** 11:00–17:00; **F:** 11:00–17:00; **S:** 11:00–17:00. Spec: Author - Blyton, Enid; - David, Elizabeth; - King, Stephen; - Koontz, Dean; - Pratchett, Terry; Children's - Early Titles; Cookery/Gastronomy; General Stock. CC: MC; V; Debit cards accepted. Notes: *Good general stock including childrens, collectables and literature. Specialists in Cookery and Modern 1sts especially Terry Pratchett and Stephen King.*

NANTWICH

Cavern Books, ■ Units 2-4 & 16 Dagfields Antique Centre Audlem Rd, Walgherton, Nantwich, CW5 7LG. Prop: Harry Madden. Tel: (01270) 841594. Web: www.cavernbooks.co.uk. E-mail: cavernbks@ aol.com. Est: 1997. Shop open: **M:** 11:00–17:00; **T:** 11:00–17:00; **W:** 11:00–17:00; **Th:** 11:00–17:00; **F:** 11:00–17:00; **S:** 10:00–17:00; **Su:** 10:00–17:00; Very large stock. Spec: Americana - General; Annuals; Art; Buses/Trams; Canals/Inland Waterways; Crafts; Crime (True); Egyptology. PR: £1–1,500. CC: AE; E; MC; V; SO, Maestro. VAT No: GB 823 5392 30. Notes: *Internet Bookshop, Gloucestershire (q.v.), Biblion, London W. (q.v.) & The Arts & Antiques Centre, Knutsford (qv). Also, CDs, Records (50s & 60s).*

Guildmaster Books, 81 Welsh Row, Nantwich, CW5 5ET. Prop: Guildmaster. Tel: (01270) 629982. Fax: (01270) 629982. Est: 1986. Office and/or bookroom. Internet and Postal. Appointment necessary. Very small stock. Spec: Agriculture; Antiquarian; Churchilliana; Culture - National; Firearms/Guns; Herbalism; History - British; Maritime/Nautical. PR: £10–500. CC: Most major. Cata: on request.

CHESHIRE

Leona Thomas (Books), 84 London Road, Nantwich, CW5 6LT. Prop: Leona Thomas. Tel: (01270) 627779. Web: www.leonathomas.co.uk. E-mail: books@leonathomas.co.uk. Est: 1990. Private premises. Telephone First. Small stock. Spec: Antiquarian; Antiques; Bindings, Books about Books; Folio Society, The; History - General; Poetry; Topography - Local. PR: £1–500. Corresp: French. Notes: *Brewing books at Barleycorns, Welsh Row, Nantwich.*

NORTHWICH

Forest Books of Cheshire, Northwich, CW8 2AT. Prop: E.M. Mann. Tel: 01606 882388. E-mail: info@ forest-books.co.uk. Est: 1986. Private premises. Book fairs only. Appointment necessary. Spec: Architecture; Art History; Collecting; Drama; Fashion & Costume; History - Local; Humanities; Music - General. PR: £1–600. Corresp: French, German. Notes: *The books are currently in cramped storage so the longer the time before viewing the better, plus we need to know what you particularly wish to see: many are in boxes in front of the shelves. We hope to return to a better outlet soonish.*

KSC Books, 48 Chapel Street, Castle, Northwich, CW8 1HD. Prop: Stuart Crook. Tel: 01606 79975. Fax: On request. E-mail: kscbooks@btinternet.com. Est: 1995. Private premises. Internet and Postal. Telephone First. Spec: Academic/Scholarly; Author - Laithwaite, Eric; Canals/Inland Waterways; Engineering; Geology; History - British; Music - Folk & Irish Folk; Musical Instruments. VAT No: GB 798 2130 04.

RUNCORN

Kirk Ruebotham, 16 Beaconsfield Road, Runcorn, WA7 4BX. Tel: (01928) 560540. Web: www.abebooks .com/home/kirk61. E-mail: kirk.ruebotham@ntlworld.com. Est: 1993. Private premises. Postal Only. Contactable. Small stock. Spec: Crime (True); Fiction - Crime, Detective, Spy, Thrillers; Fiction - Fantasy, Horror; Fiction - Science Fiction; Fiction - Supernatural; First Editions; Vintage Paperbacks. PR: £2–150. CC: PayPal. Cata: Fantasy, Horror, SF, Crime Fiction.

TATTENHALL

Marine & Cannon Books, Square House Farm, Tattenhall Lane, Tattenhall, CH3 9NH. Prop: Mrs Diane Churchill-Evans (Military & Aviation Dept). Tel: (01829) 771109. Fax: (01829) 771991. E-mail: diane@marinecannon.com. Est: 1983. Private premises. Internet and Postal. Open in Summer: **M:** 09:00–18:00; **T:** 09:00–18:00; **W:** 09:00–18:00; **Th:** 09:00–18:00; **F:** 09:00–18:00; **S:** 09:00–17:00. Medium stock. Spec: Academic/Scholarly; Aircraft; Antiquarian; Armed Forces - Australian Army; Armed Forces - Australian Navy; Army, The; Autographs; Aviation. PR: £10–20,000. CC: JCB; MC; V; UK Maestro. Cata: Naval & Maritime, Military & Aviation. Mem: ABA; ILAB. VAT No: GB 539 4137 32. Notes: *Occasional fairs and booksearch. We also stock manuscripts, engravings, photographs, postcards, and other items of ephemera in our fields of interest.*

TIMPERLEY

Oopalba Books, 136 Moss Lane, Timperley Altrincham, WA15 6JQ. Prop: Ann J Ferguson. Tel: 0161 973 2065. E-mail: ann@oopalbabooks.co.uk. Est: 1999. Mail Order Only. Internet Only. Appointment necessary. Spec: Academic/Scholarly; Applied Art; Architecture; Art; Art - Technique; Autobiography; Biography; Children's. CC: PayPal/Cheque/Postal Order. Cata: Children's Maths, Science, Textbooks, Literature. Corresp: French German. Notes: *Books listed on Abebooks.*

WARRINGTON

Halson Books, The Oaks Farnworth Road, Penketh, Warrington, WA5 2TT. Prop: Les Wilson. Tel: (01925) 726699. Web: www.users.zetnet.co.uk/halsongallery. E-mail: halson.gallery@zetnet.co.uk. Private premises. Internet and Postal. Appointment necessary. Large stock. Spec: Colour-Plate; Dogs; Natural History; Ephemera. CC: PayPal. Corresp: via Google language.

Dr. B.L. Shakeshaft, Springfield 15 Marlborough Crescent, Grappenhall, Warrington, WA4 2EE. Prop: Dr. B.L. Shakeshaft. Tel: (01925) 264790. E-mail: blsbooks@shakeshaft.wanadoo.co.uk. Est: 1999. Private premises. Postal Only. Very small stock. Spec: Americana - General; Animals and Birds; Annuals; Author - Watkins-Pitchford, Denys ('B.B.'); Authors - British; Biography; Children's; Children's - Illustrated. PR: £1–500. Cata: Ladybird books, Rupert annuals, New Naturalists.

CHESHIRE

Naomi Symes Books, 2 Pineways, Appleton Park, Warrington, WA4 5EJ. Prop: Naomi Symes. Tel: 44 (0)1925 602898. Fax: 44 (0)1925 602898. Web: www.naomisymes.com. E-mail: books@ naomisymes.com. Est: 1994. Private premises. Postal Only. Contactable: M: 10:00–18:00; **T:** 10:00– 18:00; **W:** 10:00–18:00; **Th:** 10:00–18:00; **F:** 10:00–18:00; **S:** 10:00–18:00; **Su:** 10:00–18:00. Medium stock. Spec: Academic/Scholarly; Authors - Women; Feminism; Fiction - Women; History - General; History - 19th Century; History - British; History - European. PR: £5–1,000. CC: AE; E; JCB; MC; V; Maestro, Solo. Cata: Women's History, Social History. Corresp: French. Mem: PBFA. Notes: *Also: History A Level tuition; booksearch service; proof reading; copy-editing and history resource centre on-line.*

The Warrington Book Loft, ■ Osnath Works Lythgoes Lane, Warrington, WA2 7XE. Prop: Mrs Pat Devlin. Tel: (01925) 633907. E-mail: WarringtonBkLoft@aol.com. Est: 1994. Shop open: **M:** 10:30– 18:00; **T:** 10:30–18:00; **W:** 10:30–18:00; **Th:** 10:30–18:00; **F:** 10:30–18:00; **S:** 10:00–17:00. Very large stock. Spec: Academic/Scholarly; Fiction - General; University Texts. PR: £1–50. CC: JCB; MC; V; Maestro. VAT No: GB 811 6681 37. Notes: *Over 40,000 books in stock, 3,000 (& rising) listed on-line. Website: http://ukbookworld.com/members/PatDevlin. Free parking outside shop; chairs for serious browsers within.*

WINSFORD

Blackman Books, 46 The Loont, Winsford, CW7 1EU. Prop: Margaret & Roger Blackman. Tel: (01606) 558527. Web: www.abebooks.com/home/rtmb. E-mail: books@blackmanbooks.freeserve.co.uk. Est: 1997. Private premises. Internet and Postal. Appointment necessary. Very small stock. PR: £10–1,000. Corresp: French.

Atlantic BookData provides a ready made site for listing books for sale.

Visit

www.atlanticbookdata.com

CORNWALL

BUDE

David Eastwood, Ardoch Poundstock, Bude, EX23 0DF. Tel: (01288) 361847. E-mail: d_eastwood37@ hotmail.com. Est: 1970. Private premises. Internet and Postal. Appointment necessary. Very small stock. Spec: Antiquarian; Children's - Illustrated; Fine & Rare; Fine leather bindings (see also Fine & Rare); First Editions; Illustrated - General; Limited Editions - General; Literature. PR: £10–1,000. Mem: PBFA. Notes: *Always interested in buying illustrated books and fine bindings. Also at PBFA bookfairs.*

CALLINGTON

Music By The Score, South Coombe, Downgate, Callington, PL17 8JZ. Prop: Eileen Hooper–Bargery. Tel: (01579) 370053. Fax: (01579) 370053. Web: www.musicbythescore.com. E-mail: musicbythescore@ kernowserve.co.uk. Est: 1993. Private premises. Internet and Postal. Appointment necessary. Open: **M:** 10:00–20:00; **T:** 10:00–20:00; **W:** 10:00–20:00; **Th:** 10:00–20:00; **F:** 10:00–20:00; **S:** 10 00–14.00. Closed for lunch: 13:00 14:00 Large stock. Spec. Music - General; Classical; - Composers; - Folk & Irish Folk; Illustrated Sheet Music; - Music Hall; - Opera; - Orchestral. PR: £4–40. CC: AE; MC; V. Notes: *Stock also available through Biblio.com and Biblio.co.uk All credit cards accepted through PayPal.*

CAMBORNE

Humanist Book Services, 15 Basset Street, Camborne, TR14 8SW. Prop: Linnea Timson. Tel: (01209) 716470. Fax: (0870) 125 8049. Web: www.cornwallhumanists.org.uk. E-mail: hbs@lsqrd.demon .co.uk. Est: 1964. Private premises. Internet and Postal. Appointment necessary. Spec: Evolution; Free Thought; Humanism; Philosophy. PR: £1–15. Mem: Rationalist Press Association. Notes: *Will issue catalogue on request.*

EAST LOOE

Bosco Books, ■ The Old Hall Bookshop Chapel Court, Shutta Road, East Looe, PL13 1BJ. Prop. Mr. & Mrs. S Hawes. Tel: (01503) 263700. Fax: (01503) 263700. E-mail: boscobooks@aol.com. Est: 1971. Shop open: **T:** 10:30–17:00; **W:** 10:30–17:00; **Th:** 10:30–17:00; **F:** 10:30–17:00; **S:** 10:30–17:00. Very large stock. Spec: Alpinism/Mountaineering; Archaeology; Architecture; Art; Art History; Art Reference; Author - Tangye, D.; Biography. PR: £1–750. CC: MC; V; Switch. Corresp: French, Italian. Notes: *We're also happy to accept PayPal. In winter please ring to confirm opening hours.*

FALMOUTH

Browsers Bookshop, ■ 13/15 St George's Arcade Church Street, Falmouth, TR11 3DH. Prop: Crispin Crofts. Tel: 01326 313464. E-mail: cemeraldisle@aol.com. Est: 1980. Shop open: **M:** 10:00–17:30; **T:** 10:00–17:30; **W:** 10:00–17:30; **Th:** 10:00–17:30; **F:** 10:00–17:30; **S:** 10:00–17:30. Spec: Archaeology - Industrial; Art; Art History; History - General; History - 20th Century; History - Local; Maritime/ Nautical; Maritime/Nautical - History. CC: MC; V; Maestro. Notes: *stock includes books on Cornish history.*

FOWEY

Bookends of Fowey, ■ 4 South Street, Fowey, PL23 1AR. Tel: (01726) 833361. Web: www.bookendsoffowey .com. E-mail: info@bookendsoffowey.com. Est: 1985. Shop open: **M:** 10:00–17:30; **T:** 10:00–17:30; **W:** 10:00–17:30; **Th:** 10:00–17:30; **F:** 10:00–17:30; **S:** 10:00–17:30; **Su:** 11:00–17:00; Large stock. Spec: Author - du Maurier, Daphne; - Quiller-Couch, Sir A.T.; Naval; Sport - Yachting; Topography - Local. CC: MC; V. VAT No: GB 813 0114 90.

Ronald C. Hicks, Ardwyn 22 Park Road, Fowey, PL23 1ED. Tel: (01726) 832739. Est: 1964. Private premises. Postal Only. Very small stock. Spec: Architecture; Art; History - Local; Maritime/Nautical - Log Books; Booksearch. PR: £1–500. Notes: *Books on Cornish history.*

Sue Moore, 37 Passage Street, Fowey, PL23 1DE. Prop: Susan M. Moore. Tel: (01726) 832397. Est: 1986. Private premises. Appointment necessary. Small stock. Spec: Modern First Editions; Booksearch. PR: £2–50.

CORNWALL

HELSTON

The Helston Bookworm, ■ 9, Church Street, Helston, TR138TA. Prop: Ann and Malcolm Summers. Tel: 01326 565079. Web: www.helstonbookworm.com. E-mail: helstonb@btopenworld.com. Est: 1994. Shop open: **M:** 10.00–17:30; **T:** 10.00–17:30; **W:** 10.00–17:30; **Th:** 10.00–17:30; **F:** 10.00–17:30; **S:** 10.00–14.00. Spec: Antiquarian; Topography - Local. CC: AE; MC; V.

J.T. & P. Lewis, 'Leaway' Tresowes Green, Ashton, Helston, TR13 9SY. Prop: John T. & Pearl Lewis. Tel: (01736) 762406. Web: www.http://ukbookworld.com/members/JTLANDPL. E-mail: JohnandPearl@aol.com. Est: 1990. Private premises. Internet and Postal. Small stock. Spec: Fiction - General; History - General; Modern First Editions; Odd & Unusual; Religion - General; Science - General; Theology; Topography - General. PR: £5–1,000. CC: PayPal. VAT No: GB 803 4711 59. Notes: *We always reply to emails promptly, so if you do not receive a reply within 24 hours please check your spam filters. Credit Card payments are welcomed via PayPal, please email for a PayPal Invoice, which makes payment quick and simple.*

Peter Clay, Heatherbank North Corner, Coverack, Helston, TR12 6TH. Prop: Peter Clay. Tel: 01326 280475. E-mail: pete.clay@virgin.net. Est: 1984. Private premises. Internet and Postal. Appointment necessary.

LAUNCESTON

Abbey Books, ■ White Hart Arcade, Launceston, PL15 8AA. Prop: Spencer Magill. Tel: 01566 779113. Web: www.abbeybookshop.co.uk. E-mail: SpencerMagill@aol.com. Est: 2003. Shop open: **M:** 09:00–17:00; **T:** 09:00–17:00; **W:** 09:00–17:00; **Th:** 09:00–17:00; **F:** 09:00–17:00; **S:** 09:00–16:00. Spec: Art Reference; Cinema/Film; Countries - Ireland; Fiction - General; Fiction - Crime, Detective, Spy, Thrillers; Fiction - Science Fiction; History - General; History - Irish.

Charles Cox Rare Books, River House, Treglasta, Launceston, PL15 8PY. Tel: (01840) 261085. Fax: (01840) 261464. Web: www.abebooks.com. E-mail: rarebooks@coxnbox.co.uk. Est: 1974. Private premises. Internet and Postal. Appointment necessary. Small stock. Spec: Aesthetic Movement; Antiquarian; Author - Browning, Robert; - Byron, Lord; - Hardy, Thomas; - Housman, A.E.; - Newman, Cardinal; - Rossetti, C. PR: £10–2,500. CC: JCB; MC; V; PayPal. Cata: Literature 1780–1920, Literary Autographs. Mem: ABA; ILAB. VAT No: GB 797 4887 40.

R & B Graham Trading, The Bookshop Church Street, Launceston, PL15 8AP. Prop: Richard & Beryl Graham. Tel: 01566 774107. Fax: 01566 777299. Web: www.cookery-books-online.com. E-mail: thebookshop@eclipse.co.uk. Est: 1999. Shop and/or gallery. Open: **M:** 09:00–17:30; **T:** 09:00–17:30; **W:** 09:00–17:30; **Th:** 09:00–17:30; **F:** 09:00–17:30; **S:** 09:00–17:30. Spec: Author - Quiller-Couch, Sir A.T.; Cookery - Professional; Cookery/Gastronomy; County - Local; Poetry. CC: AE; E; JCB; MC; V. Mem: BA. VAT No: GB 750 5071 55.

LOOE

A. & R. Booksearch, High Close, Lanreath, Looe, PL13 2PF. Prop: Avis & Robert Ronald. Tel: (01503) 220246. Web: www.musicbooksrus.com. E-mail: robert.ronald@arbooksearch.com. Est: 1984. Private premises. Postal Only. Appointment necessary. Open: **M:** 10.00–16.00; **T:** 10.00–16.00; **W:** 10.00–16.00; **Th:** 10.00–16.00; **F:** 10.00–16.00. Medium stock. Spec: Children's; Children's - Illustrated; Cookery/Gastronomy; Fiction - General; General Stock; Music - Country & Western; Music - Jazz & Blues; Music - Popular. PR: £1–500. CC: MC; V; Maestro, Electron, Delta, PayPal. Cata: Popular Music. VAT No: GB 187 4977 94. Notes: *Also sell new books.*

NEWQUAY

recollectionsbookshop.co.uk, Old Kiddlywink Cottage Tresean, Newquay, TR8 5HN. Prop: Valerie Frith & Ray Frith. Tel: (01637) 830539. Web: www.recollectionsbookshop.co.uk. E-mail: recollectionsbks@ btconnect.com. Est: 1996. Private premises. Internet and Postal. Contactable. Large stock. Spec: Railways; Topography - Local. PR: £4–100. CC: D; E; MC; V; PayPal. VAT No: GB 760 4240 56.

PENZANCE

Green Meadow Books, 2 Bellair House Bellair Road, Madron, Penzance, TR20 8SP. Prop: Sue Bell. Tel: (01736) 351708. Web: www.greenmeadowbooks.co.uk. E-mail: sue@bell83.fsnet.co.uk. Est: 1982. Private premises. Internet and Postal. Telephone First. Medium stock. Spec: Annuals; Author - Barrie, J.M.; - Blyton, Enid; - Brent-Dyer, Elinor M.; - Crompton, Richmal; - Dahl, Roald; - Durrell, Gerald; - Fairlie–Bruce, D. PR: £2–2,500. CC: MC; V; Switch. Cata: Children's & Illustrated books. Notes: *Also, a variety of toys, games, and ephemera in stock. Booksearch service if required. Always pleased to welcome visitors to the bookroom, where a warm welcome & a friendly cat await! Coffee and discounts available!*

Mount's Bay Books, Sea Glimpses 12 Garth Road, Newlyn, Penzance, TR18 5QJ. Prop: Tim Scott. Tel: 07792 797902. Web: www.seaglimpses.com. E-mail: timbook2@tiscali.co.uk. Est: 1994. Private premises. Internet and Postal. Appointment necessary. Open: **M:** 10:00–17:00; **T:** 10:00–17:00; **W:** 10:00–17:00; **Th:** 10:00–17.00; **F:** 10:00–17:00; **S:** 10:00–16:00. Very small stock. Spec: Author - Baker, Denys V.; Author - Seymour, John; Non-Fiction; Rural Life; Self-Sufficiency; Topography - Local. PR: £2–150.

Newlyn Books, ■ 9 The Old Posthouse Chapel Street, Penzance, TR18 4AJ. Prop: Kelvin Hearn. Tel: (01736) 332266. E-mail: eankelvin@yahoo.com. Est: 1992. Shop open: **M:** 10:00–17:00; **T:** 10:00–17:00; **W:** 10:00–17:00; **Th:** 10:00–17:00; **F:** 10:00–17:00; **S:** 10:00–17:00. Medium stock. Spec: Art; Arts, The; Topography - General; Topography - Local. PR: £1–350. CC: MC; V. Notes: *Try to be selective and have an interesting range of any subject that sells but always lots of art & local books.*

ROCHE

Roger Collicott Books, Beacon Cottage Belowda, Roche, St. Austell, PL26 8NQ. Prop: Roger Collicott. Tel: 01726 891885. Fax: 01726 891885. Web: www.rogercollicottbooks.com. E-mail: info@rogercollicottbooks.com. Est: 1978. Private premises. Appointment necessary. Open: **M:** 10:00 17:30; **T:** 10:00–17:30; **W:** 10:00–17:30; **Th:** 10:00 17:30; **F.** 10:00–17:30; **S:** 10:00–17:30; **Su:** 10:00–17:30. Spec. Antiquarian; Bindings; County - Local; Directories - General; Dogs; Earth Sciences; Flora & Fauna; Fossils. CC: MC; V. Cata: Antiquarian. Topography. History of Sciences. Mem: PBFA. Notes: *specialising in topographical books, maps, and prints with an emphasis on the counties of Cornwall and Devon. Always a good selection of antiquarian books, with an emphasis on the history of science, and early printed books.*

ST. AGNES

Paul Hoare, Trevaunance Point House Trevaunance Cove, St. Agnes, TR5 0RZ. Prop: Paul Hoare. Tel: 01872 553235. E-mail: pauldhoare@btinternet.com. Est: 1990. Private premises. Internet and Postal. Appointment necessary. Open: **M:** 09:00–17:30; **T:** 09:00–17:30; **W:** 09:00–17:30; **Th:** 09:00–17:30; **F:** 09:00–17:30; **S:** 09:00–17:30; **Su:** 09:00–17:30; Closed for lunch: 13:00–14:00. Spec: Publishers - Black, A. & C. Cata: A&C Black, Illustrated & Topographic. Notes: *Specialist in A&C Black publications. General illustrated items.*

ST. IVES

The Book Gallery, The Old Post Office Garage Chapel Street, St. Ives, TR26 2LR. Prop: David Wilkinson. Tel: (01736) 795616. Web: www.abebooks.com/home/tinyworld. E-mail: books@book-gallery.co.uk. Est: 1991. Private premises. Internet and Postal. Telephone First. Small stock. Spec: Archives; Art; Art - British; Art History; Art Reference; First Editions; Topography - Local; Ephemera. PR: £5–2,500. Cata: Art from Cornwall.

Tregenna Place Second Hand Books, ■ Tregenna Place, St. Ives, TR26 1AA. Prop: Linda Donaldson and Steven Macleod. Tel: 01736 799933. E-mail: tregennabooks@btinternet.com. Est: 2004. Shop open: **M:** 10:00–17:00; **T.** 10.00–17:00; **W:** 10:00–17:00; **Th:** 10:00–17:00; **F:** 10:00–17:00; **S:** 10:00–17:00. Spec: CC: MC; V. Notes: *General stock.*

ST. JUST

Bosorne Books, ■ The Cook Book 4 Cape Cornwall Street, St. Just, TR19 7JZ. Prop: David James. Tel: 01736 787266. E-mail: bosorne@hotmail.com. Est: 2003. Shop open: **T:** 10:00–17:00; **W:** 10:00–17:00; **Th:** 10:00–17:00; **F:** 10:00–17:00; **S:** 10:00–17:00; **Su:** 10:00–17:00. Spec: Alpinism/Mountaineering; Antiquarian; Archaeology; Art; Biography; Cookery/Gastronomy; County - Local; General Stock. CC: AE; MC; V; Maestro. Mem: FSB. Notes: *Cafe and bookshop.*

ST. TEATH

Christopher Holtom, Aaron's Treburgett, St. Teath, PL30 3LJ. Tel: (01208) 851062. Fax: (01208) 851062. Est: 1972. Private premises. Postal Only. Medium stock. Spec: Antiquarian; Children's; Education & School; Fables; Folklore; Juvenile; Mathematics. PR: £3–150. Corresp: French.

CORNWALL

TRURO

Bonython Bookshop, ■ 16 Kenwyn Street, Truro, TR1 3BU. Prop: R.D. Carpenter. Tel: (01872) 262886. Web: www.bonythonbookshop.co.uk. E-mail: bonythonbooks@btconnect.com. Est: 1996. Shop. open: **M:** 10:30–16:30; **T:** 10:30–16:30; **W:** 10:30–16:30; **Th:** 10:30–16:30; **F:** 10:30–16:30; **S:** 10:30– 16:30. Medium stock. Spec: Archaeology; Author - du Maurier, Daphne; - Tangye, D.; History - Local; Topography - Local; Booksearch; Ephemera. PR: £1–1,000. CC: D; E; JCB; MC; V. Corresp: French. Notes: *booksearch undertaken, specialist area - out of print books on Cornwall, i.e. mining, Cornish History, Cornish Language, Art etc.*

Just Books, ■ 9 Pydar Mews, Truro, TR1 2UX. Prop: Jennifer Wicks. Tel: (01872) 242532. E-mail: bookshopwren@yahoo.co.uk. Est: 1987. Shop open: **M:** 09:30–17:00; **T:** 09:30–17:00; **W:** 09:30–17:00; **Th:** 09:30–17:00; **F:** 09:30–17:00; **S:** 09:30–17:00. Medium stock. Spec: Antiquarian; Archaeology; Art; Art - British; Art - Technique; Art - Theory; Art History; Art Reference. PR: £1–1,000. CC: AE; E; JCB; MC; V. VAT No: GB 789 3503 84. Notes: *Small friendly bookshop, covering all subjects, and specializing in Cornwall and Art Books from America.*

Westcountry Old Books, ■ 8, St.Mary's Street, Truro, TR12AF. Prop: David Neil. Tel: (01803) 322712. Web: www.abebooks.com. E-mail: westcountryoldbooks@btopenworld.com. Est: 1988. Shop open: **M:** 09:30–17:30; **T:** 09:30–17:30; **W:** 09:30–17:30; **Th:** 09:30–17:30; **F:** 09:30–17:30; **S:** 09:30–17:30. Very small stock. Spec: Antiquarian; History - General; Literature. CC: E; JCB; MC; V. Mem: PBFA. Notes: *Also at: Top Floor, S.P.C.K. Bookshop,1-2 Catherine Street, Exeter, Devon.*

WADEBRIDGE

Polmorla Books, Hostyn Mill Burlawn, Wadebridge, PL27 7LD. Tel: (01208) 813345. Est: 2002. Private premises. Postal Only. Medium stock. Spec: History - General; History - Local; Literary Criticism; Literature; New Naturalist; Painting; Poetry; Women.

Dealers need to update their entry at least once a year. Visit your page on *www.sheppardsworld.co.uk*

CUMBRIA

ALSTON

Durham Book Centre, ■ Front Street, Alston, CA9 3HU. Prop: Mrs. A. Dumble. Tel: (01434) 381066. E-mail: ann@absolutely.fsnet.co.uk. Est: 1968. Shop open: **S:** 10:00–17:00; **Su:** 10:00–17:00. Small stock. Spec: Collectables; Ephemera. PR: £1–50. VAT No: GB 176 3861 34.

APPLEBY–IN–WESTMORLAND

Barry McKay Rare Books, Kingstone House Battlebarrow, Appleby–in–Westmorland, CA16 6XY. Prop: Barry McKay. Tel: 017683 52282. Web: www.barrymckayrarebooks.com. E-mail: barry.mckay@britishlibrary.net. Est: 1986. Shop and/or showroom. Appointment necessary. Open: **M:** 10.00–17.00; **T:** 10.00–17.00; **W:** 10.00–17.00; **Th:** 10.00–17.00; **F:** 10.00–17.00; **S:** 10.00–13.00. Spec. Advertising; Bibliography; Bindings; Book Arts; Bookbinding; Calligraphy; Early Imprints; Fine & Rare. CC: MC; V. Cata: Bibliography; rare and interesting books. Corresp: French. Mem: PBFA. VAT No: GB 448 5469 09.

BARROW–IN–FURNESS

Americanabooksuk, 72 Park Drive, Barrow–in–Furness, LA13 9BB. Prop: Alan R. Beattie. Tel: (01229) 829722. E-mail: alan.rbeattie@virgin.net. Est: 1980. Private premises. Appointment necessary. Very small stock. Spec: American Indians; Americana - General; Americana - Southwest; Art; Cattlemen; Countries - Americas, The; Countries - U.S.A.; Cowboys. PR: £3–150. CC: PayPal. Cata: Western Americana.

BOWNESS–ON–WINDERMERE

Past & Presents, ■ Crag Brow, Bowness–on–Windermere, LA23 3BX. Prop: W.F. & C.R. Johnson. Tel: (01539) 445417. E-mail: billnchris.johnson@btinternet.com. Est: 1995. Shop open: **M:** 10.00–17:30; **T:** 1000–17:30; **W:** 10.00–17:30; **Th:** 10.00–17:30; **F:** 10.00–17:30; **S:** 10.00–17:30; **Su:** 10.00–17:30. Very small stock. Spec: Author - Potter, Beatrix; - Ransome, Arthur; Collectables. PR: £2–85. CC: AE; D; MC; V. VAT No: GB 652 1595 37.

BROUGH

Summerfield Books Ltd, ■ The Arches Main Strreet, Brough, CA17 4AX. Prop: Jon & Sue Atkins. Tel: 01768341577. Fax: 01768341687. Web: www.summerfieldbooks.com. E-mail: info@summerfieldbooks .com. Est: 1986. Shop open: **M:** 09:30–16:30; **T:** 09:30–16:30; **Th:** 09:30–16:30; **F:** 09:30–16:30. Spec: Botany; Flora & Fauna; Forestry; Fungi; Gardening - General; Horticulture; Natural Sciences; Nature. CC: AE; E; JCB; MC; V. Cata: Botany, Forestry, Gardening, Horticulture. Corresp: French, German. Mem: PBFA; BA. VAT No: GB 442 8165 50. Notes: *We are specialist booksellers, selling from shop premises, by mail order and through the internet. Our stock is almost exclusively in the plant sciences, although we keep a small range of other natural history and local Cumbrian topography.*

The Book House, ■ Grand Prix Buildings Main Street, Brough, nr. Kirkby Stephen, CA17 4AY. Prop: Chris, Mary & Brigid Irwin. Tel: 017683 42748. Web: www.thebookhouse.co.uk E-mail: mail@thebookhouse.co.uk. Est: 1963. Shop open: **T:** 10:30–16.30; **W:** 10:30–16.30; **Th:** 10:30–16.30; **F:** 10:30–16.30; **S:** 10:30–16.30. Large stock. Spec: Children's; Engineering; Fiction - General; Gardening - General; History - Industrial; Industry; Languages - Foreign; Languages - National. PR: £1–750. CC: AE; E; MC; V. Cata: Industrial History & Transport, Railways, Gardening. Corresp: French, Italian. Mem: PBFA. VAT No: GB 113 8746 69. Notes: *Ample parking. If you are making a special journey please check we are open before setting out as occasionally I am away at book fairs or exhibitions. For further details please visit our website.*

Looking for ephemera? Then search Sheppard's on-line directories at:

www.sheppardsworld.co.uk

For all dealers selling ephemera

CUMBRIA

CARLISLE

Bookcase, ■ 17 - 19 Castle Street, Carlisle, CA3 8SY. Prop: S. & G. Matthews. Tel: 01228 544560. E-mail: bookcasecarlisle@aol.com. Est: 1979. Shop open: **M:** 10:00–17:00; **T:** 10:00–17:00; **W:** 10:00–17:00; **Th:** 10:00–17:00; **F:** 10:00–17:00; **S:** 10:00–17:00. Spec: Antiquarian; Antiques; Art; Bibliography; Fiction - General; Languages - Foreign; Literary Criticism; Modern First Editions. CC: AE; MC; V. Corresp: French, German. Notes: *Classical and jazz CDs(new). Also booksearch.*

Anne Fitzsimons, 3 Croft Park Wetheral, Carlisle, CA4 8JH. Tel: (01228) 562184. Fax: (01228) 562184. Est: 1978. Private premises. Postal Only. Small stock. Spec: Cinema/Film; Circus; Dance; Magic & Conjuring; Music - General; Music - Music Hall; Music - Opera; Performing Arts.

COCKERMOUTH

Alauda Books, ■ @ Market Place Books 30 Market Place, Cockermouth, CA13 9NG. Prop: Michael Green. Tel: 01900 821300. E-mail: alaudabooks@hotmail.co.uk. Est: 1986. Shop. Appointment necessary. Open: **M:** 10:00–17:00; **T:** 10:00–17:00; **W:** 10:00–17:00; **Th:** 10:00–17:00; **F:** 10:00–17:00; **S:** 10:00–17:00. Spec: Animals and Birds; Archaeology; Book Arts; Bookbinding; Botany; Cartography; Fishes; Flora & Fauna. Cata: Natural History; Angling. Mem: PBFA.

Ian Dodsworth, 1 Banks Court Market Place, Cockermouth, CA13 9NG. Prop: Ian Dodsworth. Tel: (01900) 823599. E-mail: ian@maurian.f9.co.uk. Est: 1986. Storeroom. Appointment necessary. Small stock. PR: £1–150. Notes: *Attends day fairs in Northern England.*

The Printing House, ■ 102 Main Street, Cockermouth, CA13 9LX. Prop: David Winkworth. Tel: (01900) 824984. Web: www.printinghouse.co.uk. E-mail: info@printinghouse.co.uk. Est: 1968. Shop open: **M:** 09:00–17:00; **T:** 09:00–17:00; **W:** 09:00–17:00; **Th:** 09:00–17:00; **F:** 09:00–17:00; **S:** 09:00–17:00. Large stock. PR: £1–500. CC: V. Mem: BPS, PHT, PHS, AEPM. VAT No: GB 256 8544 27. Notes: *Also art materials and picture framing.*

EGREMONT

Esoteric Dreams Bookshop, ■ 1 St Bridgets Lane, Egremont, CA22 2BB. Prop: Mrs Sue Wright. Tel: 01946 821686. Web: www.amazon.co.uk/shops/esotericdreams. E-mail: suewright2000@ btinternet.com. Est: 2004. Shop open: **T:** 10:00–16.00; **W:** 10.00–14.00; **Th:** 10.00–16.00; **F:** 10.00–16.00; **S:** 10.00–16.00. Spec: Alternative Medicine; Animals and Birds; Annuals; Art History; Author - Asimov, Isaac; - Dinesen, Isak; Authors - Local; Authors - Women. Notes: *We sell old and new books both in the shop and on the internet. We also sell cards, postcards, local maps and unusual gifts.*

GRANGE–OVER–SANDS

Rosemary Dooley, Crag House Witherslack, Grange–over–Sands, LA11 6RW. Prop: R.M.S. Dooley. Tel: (01539) 552286. Fax: (01539) 552013. Web: www.booksonmusic.co.uk. E-mail: rd@ booksonmusic.co.uk. Est: 1992. Private premises. Postal Only. Appointment necessary. Medium stock. Spec: Academic/Scholarly; Dance; Music - General; Music - Classical; Music - Composers; Music - Folk & Irish Folk; Music - Gregorian Chants; Music - Musicians. PR: £3–500. CC: AE; E; MC; V. Cata: books about music. Mem: PBFA. VAT No: GB 393 1979 09. Notes: *European distributor for Pendragon Press (USA)- scholarly books on music. Worldwide distributor for Royal Musical Association Research Chronicle and back issues of British Journal of ethnomusicology.*

Norman Kerr Booksellers, Priory Barn Cartmel, Grange–over–Sands, LA11 6PX. Prop: Hilda & John Kerr. Tel: (015395) 36247 / 32508. E-mail: enquiries@kerrbooks.co.uk. Est: 1933. Shop and/or showroom. Internet and Postal. Telephone First. Open: **S:** 13:30–16:30. Medium stock. Spec: Antiquarian; Aviation; Canals/Inland Waterways; Engineering; Fine & Rare; Illustrated - General; Maritime/Nautical; Motoring. PR: £5–1,500. Cata: General Catalogue Fine & Rare. Mem: PBFA. VAT No: GB 312 3475 89. Notes: *Alternative tel: 01772 610746. Gatehouse Bookshop, The Square, Cartmel open Saturday p.m. or other times by appointment. A wide selection of our stock is now listed online at Abebooks.com.*

Over-Sands Books, ■ The Old Waiting Room The Station, Grange–Over–Sands, LA11 6EH. Prop: Mr. S.R. Tyson. Tel: (01539) 534387. Web: www.oversandsbooks.co.uk. E-mail: over-sands.books @virgin.net. Est: 1995. Shop open: **M:** 11:00–17:00; **T:** 11:00–17:00; **W:** 11:00–17:00; **F:** 11:00–17:00; **S:** 11:00–17:00; **Su:** 13:00–17:00. Small stock. Spec: Literature; Railways; Topography - General; Topography - Local; Transport; Booksearch; Collectables; Ephemera. PR: £3–250. CC: PayPal. Cata: Various subjects. Notes: *Opening times vary between November and March, call first. Also, a booksearch service.*

CUMBRIA

GRASMERE

Yewtree Books, ■ The Lakes Crafts & Antiques Gallery 3 Oakbank Broadgate, Grasmere, LA22 9TA. Prop: Joe and Sandra Arthy. Tel: (015394) 35037. Fax: (015394) 44234. E-mail: lakescrafts@ dsl.pipex.com. Est: 1990. Shop open: **M:** 10:00–17:00; **T:** 10:00–17:00; **W:** 10:00–17:00; **Th:** 10:00–17:00; **F:** 10:00–17:00; **S:** 10:00–17:00; **Su:** 10:00–17:00. Small stock. Spec: Alpinism/Mountaineering; History - General; Railways; Sport - General; Topography - General; Topography - Local; Travel - General. PR: £1–300. CC: JCB; MC; V.

KENDAL

Kirkland Books, ■ 11 Colin Croft, Kendal, LA9 4TH. Prop: Linden Burke. Tel: 0800 0112368. Fax: 0800 0112568. Web: www.kirklandbooks.biz. E-mail: kirklandbooks@mac.com. Est: 1980. Shop open: **Th:** 10:00–17:00; **F:** 10:00–17:00; **S:** 10:00–17:00. Spec: Alpinism/Mountaineering; Author - Ransome, Arthur; - Wainwright, Arthur; Exploration; Railways; Topography - Local; Transport. CC: AE; D; E; JCB; MC; V. Cata: Alfred Wainwright, Arthur Ramsome. Notes: *Kirkland Books is an established shop offering quality new, secondhand and antiquarian books specialising in: Mountaineering, The Lake District, Alfred Wainwright, Arthur Ransome and Railways.*

Left on The Shelf, Yard 91, Highgate, Kendal, LA9 4ED. Prop: Dave Cope. Tel: (01539) 729599. Web: www.abebooks.com/home/leftontheshelf. E-mail: leftontheshelf@phonecoop.coop. Est: 1992. Storeroom. Internet and Postal. Telephone First. Very large stock. Spec: Civil Rights; Communism; Countries - Russia; Economics; Free Thought; History - Labour/ Radical Movements; History - Spanish Civil War; History - Trotskyism. PR: £2–150. CC: MC; V. Cata: Socialism. Corresp: French. Mem: PBFA.

KESWICK

Jean Altshuler, 54 St. John Street, Keswick, CA12 5AB. Tel: (01768) 775745. E-mail: books@ jopplety.demon.co.uk. Est: 1996. Private premises. Internet and Postal. Appointment necessary. Small stock. Spec: Children's; Fiction - Science Fiction. PR: £5–200.

Keswick Bookshop, ■ 4 Station Street, Keswick, CA12 5HT. Prop: Jane & John Kinnaird. Tel: (017687) 75535. E-mail: j.kinnaird22@btopenworld.co.uk. Est: 1994. Telephone First. Shop open: **M:** 10:30–17:00; **T:** 10:30–17:00; **W:** 10:30–17:00; **Th:** 10:30–17:00; **F:** 10:30–17:00; **S:** 10:30–17:00. Medium stock. Spec: Antiques; Applied Art; Architecture; Art; Children's; Decorative Art; First Editions; Illustrated - General. PR: £1–300. CC: JCB; MC; V. VAT No: GB 531 4987 33. Notes: *Winter opening: Saturday only (Nov-March) and Christmas holiday and New Year's day. Telephone first. And mail only to: Winterbourne, 18 Houghton Road, Carlisle CA3 OLA.*

KIRKBY STEPHEN

2 Ravens, ■ 2 Market Street, Kirkby Stephen, CA17 4QS. Prop: Val and Peter Harrison. Tel: 017683 71519. Est: 1997. Shop open: **W:** 10:00–16:00; **Th:** 10:00–16:00; **F:** 10:00–16:00; **S:** 10:00–16:00. Spec: New Age; Rural Life; Topography - Local. Notes: *Telephone if making a special journey.*

PENRITH

David A.H. Grayling, Verdun House Main Street, Shap, Penrith, CA10 3NG. Prop: David A H Grayling. Tel: (01931) 716746 Fax: (01931) 716746. Web: www.davidgraylingbooks.com. E-mail: admin@ davidgraylingbooks.com. Est: 1970. Private premises. Internet and Postal. Appointment necessary. Medium stock. Spec: Colour-Plate; Countries - Asia; Fine & Rare; Natural History; Scottish Interest; Sport - Angling/Fishing; Sport - Big Game Hunting; Sport - Field Sports. PR: £20–5,000. CC: AE; MC; V. Cata: Angling. Hunting. Shooting. Natural History. Corresp: French, German. Mem: PBFA. VAT No: GB 154 6592 46. Notes: *Binding & restoration. Valuation for insurance & probate etc. Cataloguing of collections and libraries. Advice on the purchase, storage and care of books. Book search.*

Dealers need to update their entry at least once a year. Visit your page on *www.sheppardsworld.co.uk*

CUMBRIA

G.K. Hadfield, Old Post Office, Great Salkeld, Penrith, CA11 9LW. Prop: G.K. & J.V. Hadfield & N.R. Hadfield–Tilly. Tel: (01768) 870111. Web: www.gkhadfield-tilly.co.uk. E-mail: gkhadfield@ dial.pipex.com. Est: 1974. Shop and/or showroom. Internet and Postal. Appointment necessary. Large stock. Spec: Antiques; Astronomy; Bell-Ringing (Campanology); Furniture; Gemmology; Horology; Mathematics; Microscopy. CC: AE; JCB; MC; V; SO, ELEC. Cata: horology, lathes, turning, music boxes sundial. Corresp: French. Mem: B.H.I. A.H.S. VAT No: GB 114 809 578. Notes: *Also, a booksearch service, quality bookbinding and restoration. Buy, sell and restore antique clocks. Mobile: 07738 546488.*

Phenotype Books Ltd, 39 Arthur Street, Penrith, CA11 7TT. Prop: J.E. Mattley. Tel: (01768) 863049. Fax: (01768) 890493. Web: www.phenotypebooks.co.uk. E-mail: phenobooks@btconnect.com. Est: 1985. Private premises. Internet and Postal. Telephone First. Small stock. Spec: Agriculture; Animals and Birds; Carriages & Driving; Cattlemen; Cockfighting; Cowboys; Farming & Livestock; Farriers. PR: £5–1,800. Cata: Agriculture Livestock Vet Farriery & related. VAT No: GB 442 8614 47. Notes: *Private premises. Visitors welcome by appointment.*

SEDBERGH

The Bookseller, ■ 77 Main Street, Sedbergh, LA10 5AB. Prop: C. J. Chambers. Tel: 015396 20991. Fax: 015396 20589. E-mail: sedberghbooks@aol.com. Est: 1994. Shop open: **M:** 10:00–17:00; **T:** 10:00– 17:00; **W:** 10:00–17:00; **Th:** 10:00–12:00; **F:** 10:00–17:00; **S:** 10:00–17:00. Spec: Children's; Children's - Illustrated. CC: AE; E; JCB; MC; V. Corresp: French. Notes: *Book repairs undertaken.*

Dales & Lakes Book Centre, ■ 72 Main Street, Sedbergh, LA10 5AD. Tel: 015396 20125. E-mail: booktown@sedbergh.org.uk. Est: 2005. Shop open: **M:** 10:00–17:00; **T:** 10:00–17:00; **W:** 10:00–17:00; **Th:** 10:00–17:00; **F:** 10:00–17:00; **S:** 10:00–17:00; **Su:** 10:00–17:00. Spec: Academic/Scholarly; Agriculture; Alpinism/Mountaineering; Alternative Medicine; Animals and Birds; Annuals; Anthologies; Antiquarian. CC: MC; V. VAT No: GB 859 4936 61. Notes: *Sedbergh - England's Booktown.*

Henry Wilson Books, Dales & Lakes Book Centre Main Street, Sedbergh, LA10 5AD. Prop: H.G.E. Wilson. Tel: (015396) 20125. Fax: 01270219059. Web: www.henrywilsonbooks.co.uk. E-mail: hwrailwaybooks @aol.com. Est: 2005. Shop and/or gallery. Shop At: Unit 7 Barrowmore Estate, Great Barrow, Chester CH3 7JS. Open: **M:** 10:00–17:00; **T:** 10:00–17:00; **W:** 10:00–17:00; **Th:** 10:00–17:00; **F:** 10:00– 17:00; **S:** 10:00–17:00; **Su:** 10:00–17:00; Very small stock. Spec: Author - Rolt, L.T.C.; Buses/Trams; Canals/Inland Waterways; History - Industrial; Model Railways; Ocean Liners; Railroads; Railways. PR: £2–500. CC: JCB; MC; V; Maestro. Cata: on railways, transport and industrial history. Corresp: French, German. Mem: PBFA; FSB. VAT No: GB 439 7672 03. Notes: *Also at Henry Wilson Books, Unit 7 Barrowmore Estate, Great Barrow, Chester CH3 7JS, telephone 01829 740693 and 0772 4114475 (q.v.) New and secondhand books & back issues of railway journals.*

R.F.G. Hollett and Son, 6 Finkle Street, Sedbergh, LA10 5BZ. Prop: C.G. & R.F.G. Hollett. Tel: (01539) 620298. Fax: (01539) 621396. Web: www.holletts-rarebooks.co.uk. E-mail: hollett@ sedbergh.demon.co.uk. Est: 1959. Shop and/or showroom. Internet and Postal. Appointment necessary. Very large stock. Spec: Alpinism/Mountaineering; Antiquarian; Antiques; Biography; Children's; Collecting; Colour-Plate; Fine Art. PR: £30–50,000. CC: AE; E; JCB; MC; V; Maestro. Mem: ABA; ILAB. VAT No: GB 343 4391 63. Notes: *Valuations.*

Orange Skies Books, ■ 46 Main Street, Sedbergh, LA10 5BL. Prop. David Johnston-Smith Tel: 0161 408 1182. Web: www.orangeskies.co.uk. E-mail: orangeskiesmusic@gmail.com. Est: 2005. Shop open: **M:** 09:00–17:30; **T:** 09:00–17:30; **W:** 09:00–17:30; **Th:** 09:00–17:30; **F:** 09:00–17:30; **S:** 09:00– 17:30; **Su:** 09:00–17:30.

Sleepy Elephant Books & Artefacts, ■ 41 Main Street, Sedbergh, LA10 5BL. Prop: Avril Whittle and Partners. Tel: 015396 21770. Fax: 015396 21770. E-mail: avrilsbooks@aol.com. Est: 2003. Shop open: **M:** 10.00–17:00; **T:** 10.00–17:00; **W:** 10.00–17:00; **Th:** 10.00–17:00; **F:** 10.00–17:00; **S:** 10.00–17:00; **Su:** 12:00–17:00. Spec: Applied Art; Art - Technique; Art History; Children's; Cinema/Film; Cookery/ Gastronomy; Crafts; Crochet. CC: MC; V. Cata: Art Craft & Design. VAT No: GB 875015816. Notes: *We specialise in the Arts, crafts and design subjects, especially textile arts. Other strong sections iclude Theatre & Drama, Food & Drink, Folio Society publications & good paperback literature.*

Westwood Books Ltd, ■ Leisure House Long Lane, Sedbergh, LA10 5AH. Tel: 015396 21233. E-mail: evelyn@markwestwood.co.uk. Est: 1987. Shop open: **M:** 10:30–17:30; **T:** 10:30–17:30; **W:** 10:30– 17:30; **Th:** 10:30–17:30; **F:** 10:30–17:30; **S:** 10:30–17:30; **Su:** 10:30–17:30. Spec: Academic/Scholarly; Alternative Medicine; Antiquarian; Archaeology; Architecture; Art; Art History; Art Reference. CC: JCB; MC; V. Corresp: French. Mem: ABA; PBFA; BA.

Avril Whittle Bookseller, ■ Whittle's Warehouse 7-9 (rear) Bainbridge Road, Sedbergh, LA10 5AU. Prop: Avril Whittle & Partners. Tel: (015396) 21770. Fax: (015396) 21770. E-mail: avrilsbooks@ aol.com. Est: 1980. Shop at: Sleepy Elephant Books & Artefacts, 41 Main Street, SEDBERGH, Cumbria 1 A10 5BL. Open: **M:** 10:00–17:00; **T:** 10:00–17:00; **W:** 10:00–17:00; **Th:** 10:00–17:00; **F:** 10:00–17:00; **S:** 10:00–17:00; **Su:** 12:00–17:00. Medium stock. Spec: Antiques; Art - Technique; Art - Theory; Art History; Calligraphy; Cinema/Film; Cookery/Gastronomy; Crafts. PR: £1–600. CC: MC; V. Cata: Arts & Crafts, Theatre & Cinema Food & Drink,. Corresp: French. Mem: Also at: Sleepy Elephant Books & Artefacts, 41 Main Street, Sedbergh, Cumbria LA10 5BL. VAT No: GB 875 0158 16. Notes: *We also sell rugs, jewellery, tassels & artefacts from Morocco; ladies' & gents' knitwear; cards & interesting gifts; textiles, yarns (inc local alpaca), needles & patterns.*

ULVERSTON

Bookfare, Lowick Hall, Ulverston, LA12 8ED. Prop: Dr. A.C.I. Naylor. Tel: (01229) 885240. Fax: (01229) 885240. Web: www.bookfare.co.uk. E-mail: ambookfare@aol.com. Est: 1977. Private premises. Postal Only. Contactable, Small stock. PR: £6–300. CC: PayPal. Corresp: French.

WELTON

The Little Bookshop, Sebergham Castle House, Welton, Near Carlisle, CA5 7HG. Prop: Frank Grant. Fax: (016974) 76079. E-mail: fjg?36@aol.com. Est 1994. Private premises. Postal Only. Appointment necessary. Small stock. Spec: Alpinism/Mountaineering; Biography; Countries - Nepal; Geology; Palaeontology; Sport - Climbing & Trekking; Topography - Local. PR: £2–500. Cata: Lake District Literature/Mountaineering/Climbing. Notes: *Also, a booksearch service.*

WHITEHAVEN

Michael Moon's Bookshop, ■ 19 Lowther Street, Whitehaven, CA28 7AL. Prop: Michael Moon. Tel: (01946) 599010. Fax: (09146) 599010. Est: 1970. Shop open: **M:** 09:30–17:00; **T:** 09:30–17:00; **W:** 09:30–17:00; **Th:** 09:30–17:00; **F:** 09:30–17:00; **S:** 09:30–17:00. Very large stock. Spec: Cinema/Film; History - Local; Topography - Local; Booksearch; Prints and Maps. PR: £1–1,000. CC: JCB; MC; V. Mem: PBFA; SBA. VAT No: GB 288 1073 42. Notes: *Closed Wed - from October to December. Publisher on Cumbrian history.*

WIGTON

Chelifer Books, Todd Close Curthwaite, Wigton, CA7 8BE. Prop: Mike Smith & Deryn Walker. Tel: (01228) 711388. Web: www military books.biz. E-mail: militbks@aol.com. Est: 1985. Private premises. Internet and Postal. Appointment necessary. Small stock. Spec: American Indians; Antiquarian; Arms & Armour; Aviation; Military; Military - Modelling; Military History; Military Uniforms. PR: £5–1,500. CC: MC; V; Maestro. Cata: on general military.

Rosley Books, Rosley Farmhouse, Rosley, Wigton, CA7 8BZ. Prop: Ian Blakemore. Tel: (016973) 49924. Fax: (016973) 45149. Web: www.rosleybooks.co.uk. E-mail: sales@rosleybooks.co.uk. Est: 2000. Private premises. Appointment necessary. Medium stock. Spec: Academic/Scholarly; Antiquarian; Author - Belloc, Hilaire; - Browning, Robert; - Bunyan, John; - Chesterton, G.K.; - Eliot, T.S.; - Inklings, The. PR: £5–5,000. CC: AE; MC; V; PayPal. Cata: Inklings, Keswick, Commentaries.

WINDERMERE

Bridge Books, 2 Sunnybrae Brook Road, Windermere. Prop: John Taylor. Tel: (01539) 445015. E-mail: jm.taylor@ic24.net. Est: 1993. Postal Only. Spec: Poetry; Topography - Local. PR: £3–750.

Fireside Bookshop, ■ 21 Victoria Street, Windermere, LA23 1AB. Prop: Mr R.D. Sheppard. Tel: (015394) 45855. Web: www.firesidebookshop.co.uk. E-mail: firesidebookshop@btconnect.com. Est: 1977. Shop open: **M:** 11:00–17:00; **T:** 11:00–17:00; **W:** 11:00–17:00; **Th:** 11:00–17:00; **F:** 11:00–17:00; **S:** 11:00–17:00; **Su:** 11:00–17:00. Large stock. Spec: Academic/Scholarly; Aeronautics; Alpinism/ Mountaineering; American Indians; Americana - General; Anthropology; Antiquarian; Art. PR: £1–1,000. CC: AE; JCB; MC; V; Maestro.

DERBYSHIRE

ALFRETON

John Titford, Yew Tree Farm Hallfieldgate, Higham, Alfreton, DE55 6AG. Tel: (01773) 520389. Fax: (01773) 833373. E-mail: J.Titford@zen.co.uk. Est: 1987. Private premises. Postal Only. Appointment necessary. Small stock. Spec: Genealogy; Heraldry; History - General; Topography - General; Booksearch. PR: £2–1,000. Cata: Genealogy & heraldry. Corresp: French. Mem: PBFA.

BAKEWELL

Country Books, Courtyard Cottage Little Longstone, Bakewell, DE45 1NN. Prop: Richard J.T. Richardson. Tel: 01629 640670. Fax: 01629 640670. E-mail: dickrichardson@country-books.co.uk. Est: 1992. Private premises. Book fairs only. Spec: Academic/Scholarly; Agriculture; Architecture; Author - Baring-Gould, S.; - Barnes, William; - Bates, H.E.; - Bell, Adrian; - Belloc, Hilaire. CC: MC; V. Cata: country writers, Gypsies, rural life, village history.

BUXTON

Birdnet Optics Ltd., ■ 5 London Road, Buxton, SK17 9PA. Prop: Paul and Sandi Flint. Tel: (01298) 71844. Fax: (01298) 27727. Web: www.birdnet.co.uk. E-mail: paulflint@birdnet.co.uk. Est: 1998. Shop open: **M:** 09:00–17:30; **T:** 09:00–17:30; **W:** 09:00–17:30; **Th:** 09:00–17:30; **F:** 09:00–17:30; **S:** 09:00–17:00. Very small stock. Spec: Natural History; New Books; New Naturalist; Ornithology; Publishers - Poysers. PR: £1–2,000. CC: MC; V.

Scrivener's Books & Bookbinding, ■ 42 High Street, Buxton, SK17 6HB. Prop: Alastar Scrivener. Tel: 01298 73100. Est: 1994. Shop open: **M:** 09:00–17:00; **T:** 09:00–17:00; **W:** 09:00–17:00; **Th:** 09:00–17:00; **F:** 09:00–17:00; **S:** 09:00–17:00; **Su:** 12:00–16:00; Closed for lunch: 13:00–14:00. Spec: Annuals; Antiquarian; Applied Art; Archaeology; Architecture; Art; Art - Technique; Art - Theory. CC: AE; D; E; JCB; MC; V. Notes: *Bookbinding, tuition, day courses, lectures.*

CASTLETON

Hawkridge Books, ■ The Cruck Barn Cross Street, Castleton, Hope Valley, S33 8WH. Prop: Dr. J. & Mrs. I. Tierney. Tel: (01433) 621999. Web: www.hawkridge.co.uk. E-mail: books@hawkridge.co.uk. Est: 1995. Shop open: **M:** 10:00–17:30; **T:** 10:00–17:30; **W:** 10:00–17:30; **Th:** 10:00–17:30; **F:** 10:00–17:30; **S:** 10:00–17:30; **Su:** 12:00–17:30. Large stock. Spec: Natural History; Ornithology. PR: £5–2,000. CC: AE; JCB; MC; V. Notes: *Also, barn bed & breakfast.*

CHESTERFIELD

Ian Broddon, Meynell Close, Chesterfield, S40 3BL. Prop: Ian Briddon. Tel: 01246 208411. E-mail: i.b@briddonbuks.ablegratis.co.uk. Est: 2004. Private premises. Internet and Postal. Contactable. Open: **M:** 09:00–17:30; **T:** 09:00–17:30; **W:** 09:00–17:30; **Th:** 09:00–17:30; **F:** 09:00–17:30; **S:** 09:00–17:30; **Su:** 09:00–17:30; Closed for lunch: 13:00–14:00. Spec: Annuals; Antiquarian; Children's - Illustrated; Fine & Rare; First Editions; Food & Drink; Homosexuality & Lesbianism; Humour.

Tilleys Vintage Magazine Shop, ■ 21 Derby Road, Chesterfield, S40 2EF. Prop: Antonius & Albertus Tilley. Tel: (01246) 563868. Web: www.tilleysvintagemagzines.com. E-mail: Tilleysoldmags@ aol.com. Est: 1978. Telephone First. Shop open: **M:** 10.00–16.30; **T:** 10.00–16.30; **W:** 10.00–16.30; **Th:** 10.00–16.30; **F:** 10.00–16.30; **S:** 10.00–16.30. Very large stock. Spec: Comic Books & Annuals; Glamour; Magazines & Periodicals - General; Magazines - Women's; Newspapers; Collectables; Ephemera. PR: £1–100. CC: MC; V; PayPal. Notes: *Other shop at 281 Shoreham Street, Sheffield (q.v.)and warehouse at Barrow Hill Roundhouse Railway Centre, Chesterfield - open for major events. Mail order,Ebay listings - 1 million + items in stock 1890s-present.*

CROMFORD

Scarthin Books, ■ The Promenade Scarthin, Cromford, DE4 3QF. Prop: Dr. D.J. Mitchell. Tel: (01629) 823272. Fax: (01629) 825094. Web: www.scarthinbooks.com. E-mail: clare@scarthinbooks.com. Est: 1974. Shop open: **M:** 09:30–18:00; **T:** 09:30–18:00; **W:** 09:30–18:00; **Th:** 09:30–18:00; **F:** 09:30–18:00; **S:** 09:30–18:00; **Su:** 12:00–18:00. Very large stock. Spec: Academic/Scholarly; Alpinism/Mountaineering; American Indians; Animals and Birds; Antiquarian; Architecture; Author - Uttley, Alison; History - Industrial. PR: £1–5,000. CC: MC; V. Corresp: French, German. Mem: BA; IPG. VAT No: GB 127 6427 64. Notes: *Also, new books, publishers of local history and walking books.*

DERBYSHIRE

DERBY

Saracen Books, 24 Kirkleys Avenue North, Spondon, Derby, DE21 7FX. Prop: Graham & Sandra Mansey. Tel: 01332 678084. Web: www.saracenbooks.com E-mail: sales@saracenbooks.com. Est: 2002. Private premises. Internet and Postal. Open in Summer. Open: **M:** 09:00–17:30; **T:** 09:00–17:30; **W:** 09:00–17:30; **Th:** 09:00–17:30; **F:** 09:00–17:30; **S:** 09:00–17:30; **Su:** 09:00–17:30; Closed for lunch: 13:00–14:00. Spec: Gardening - Organic; General Stock; History - General; History - British; History - British Empire, The; Military; Natural History; Politics. CC: PayPal. Notes: *We have a broad stock base with an emphasis on Military, History, Natural History and Politics.*

FROGGATT

Jarvis Books, Valleyside Malthouse Lane, Froggatt, Hope Valley, S32 3ZA. Prop: Grant & Valerie Jarvis. Tel: (01433) 631 951. Fax: (01433) 631 951. Web: www.mountainbooks.co.uk. E-mail: jarvis@ mountainbooks.co.uk. Est: 1979. Private premises. Internet and Postal. Telephone First. Small stock. Spec: Alpinism/Mountaineering; Expeditions; Exploration; Exploration - Polar Regions; Guide Books; Himalayan Kingdoms; Mountain Men; Mountains. CC: AE; MC; V. Cata: Mountaineering. Mem: PBFA. Notes: *Catalogues issued on mountaineering.*

GLOSSOP

George St. Books, ■ 14 - 16 George Street, Glossop, SK13 8AY. Prop: David & Emma Jones. Tel: 01457 853413. Web. www.georgestreetbooks.co.uk. E-mail: help@georgestreetbooks.co.uk. Est: 1986. Shop open: **M:** 09:00–17:00; **T:** 09:00–17:00; **W:** 09:00–17:00; **Th:** 09:00–17:00; **F:** 09:00–17:00; **S:** 09:00– 17:00; **Su:** 11:00–15:00. Spec: Alpinism/Mountaineering; Architecture; Art; Autobiography; Biography; Children's; Crafts; Fiction - General. CC: MC; V; Maestro. Mem: BA.

LITTLEOVER

Bob Mallory (Books), 14 Dean Close, Littleover, Derby, DE23 4EF. Tel: 01332 511663. E-mail: rmalloryb@aol.com. Open: **M:** 09:00–17:30; **T:** 09:00–17:30; **W:** 09:00–17:30; **Th:** 09:00–17:30; **F:** 09:00–17:30; **S:** 09:00–17:30; **Su:** 09:00–17:30; Closed for lunch: 13:00–14:00. Spec: Autobiography; Automobilia/Automotive; Biography; Cinema/Film; Horses; Humour; Journalism; Management. Notes: *Horse Racing, Gambling, Entertainment, Autobiography, Biography, Sport: Football, Cricket, Television, Cinema.*

MATLOCK

Hunter and Krageloh, Honeybee Cottage In the Dale, Wensley, Matlock, DE4 2LL. Prop: J.A. Hunter. Tel: (01629) 732845. E-mail: hunterandkrageloh@btinternet.com. Est: 1993. Telephone First. Spec: Alpinism/Mountaineering; Countries - Himalayas, The; Countries - Ladakh; Countries - Nepal; Countries - Switzerland; Countries - Tibet; Mountains; Plant Hunting. PR: £1–12,000. Mem: ABA; PBFA.

John O'Reilly - Mountain Books, Netherlea Barn Bracken Lane, Holloway, Matlock, DE4 5AS. Tel: (01629) 534559. Fax: (01629) 534773. E-mail: johnoreill@aol.com. Est: 1972. Private premises. Postal Only. Very small stock. Spec: Alpinism/Mountaineering; Sport - Climbing & Trekking; Travel - Asia; Travel - Polar; Voyages & Discovery. PR: £5–500. CC: MC; V.

WIRKSWORTH

Pastmasters, ■ 15 The Causeway, Wirksworth, DE4 4DL. Prop: Brian Jones. Tel: (01629) 823775. E-mail: brian@pastmasters.co.uk. Est: 1998. Shop open: **T:** 10:00–17:00; **F:** 10:00–17:00; **S:** 10:00–17:00. Small stock. Spec: Journalism; Music - General; Plays; Theatre. PR: £1–40. Notes: *Also, classical cds.*

DEVON

ASHBURTON

The Dartmoor Bookshop, ■ 2 Kingsbridge Lane, Ashburton, TQ13 7DX. Prop: Brenda Greysmith & Andy Collins. Tel: (01364) 653356. Web: www.thedartmoorbookshop.co.uk. E-mail: books@thedartmoorbookshop.co.uk. Est: 1981. Shop open: **W:** 10:00–17:30; **Th:** 10:00–17:30; **F:** 10:00–17:30; **S:** 10:00–17:30. Very large stock. Spec: Alpinism/Mountaineering; Antiquarian; Architecture; Art; Art History; Art Reference; Artists; Fiction - General. PR: £1–250. CC: JCB; MC; V. VAT No: GB 803 1119 82. Notes: *We have recently (Oct 2006) bought the shop from Paul & Barbara Heatley and plan to continue in the same fashion.*

Pedlar's Pack Books, ■ 2 Kingsbridge Lane, Ashburton, TQ13 7DX. Prop: Brenda Greysmith & Andy Collins. Tel: 01364 653356. E-mail: books@thepedlarspack.co.uk. Est: 2003. Internet and Postal. Shop open: **W:** 10:00–17:30; **Th:** 10:00–17:30; **F:** 10:00–17:30; **S:** 10:00–17:30. Large stock. Spec: Military; Booksearch. PR: £1–500. CC: JCB; MC; V; Switch. VAT No: GB 803 1119 82. Notes: *Pedlar's Pack Books has closed in Totnes. We are now in Ashburton where we have taken over The Dartmoor Bookshop. We are now the Dartmoor Bookshop in the real world, and Pedlar's Pack Books online on ABE.*

AXMINSTER

Bookquest, High Grange Dalwood, Axminster, EX13 7ES. Prop: E.M. Chapman. Tel: (01404) 831317. Est: 1968. Private premises. Postal Only. Spec: Booksearch.

Books Plus, ■ 1 Bristol House West Street, Axminster, EX13 5NS. Prop: Robert Starling. Tel: (01395) 578199. E-mail: books.plus@btconnect.com. Est: 1999. Shop open: **M:** 09:00–17:00; **T:** 09:00–17:00; **W:** 09:00–17:00; **Th:** 09:00–17:00; **F:** 09:00–17:00; **S:** 09:00–17:00. Small stock. Spec: Cookery/ Gastronomy; Military; Music - General; Railways; Sport - General. PR: £1–30. CC: D; E; MC; V; Solo, Switch. Notes: *Also, videos & CDs, DVDs.*

W.C. Cousens, 'The Leat' Lyme Road, Axminster, EX13 5BL. Prop: William Clifford Cousens. Tel: (01297) 32921. Est: 1988. Private premises. Appointment necessary. Small stock. Spec: Gardening - General; Topography - Local; Booksearch. PR: £1–200. Mem: PBFA.

BARNSTAPLE

Woodland Books, Woodland Books 8 St Peter's Close, West Buckland, Barnstaple, EX32 0TX. Prop: Kevin Grimshire. Tel: 01271 828242. E-mail: kevgrim@tesco.net. Est: 2004. Private premises. Internet and Postal. Spec: Adult; Aircraft; Computing. CC: PayPal. Notes: *Mainly used computer books but all with a high technical content.*

Sol Books, ■ 2 Bridge Chambers The Strand, Barnstaple, EX31 1HB. Tel: 01271327319. Fax: 01271 321640. Web: www.sol.org.uk. E-mail: books@sol.org.uk. Shop open: **M:** 10.00–16.00; **T:** 10.00–16.00; **W:** 10.00–16.00, **Th:** 10.00–16.00; **F:** 10,00–16.00; **S:** 10.00–13.00. Spec: Fiction - General; out-of-print. Notes: *Sol Books is a charity bookshop. We sell books in our shop and on the Internet to raise funds for SOL - our internaional language school.*

Tarka Books, ■ 5 Bear Street, Barnstaple, EX32 7BU. Prop: Fiona Broster. Tel: (01271) 374997. Web: www.tarkabooks.co.uk. E-mail: books@tarkabooks.co.uk. Est: 1988. Shop open: **M:** 09:45–17:00; **T:** 09:45–17:00; **W:** 09:45–17:00; **Th:** 09:45–17:00; **F:** 09:45–17:00; **S:** 09:45–17:00. Very large stock. Spec: Aircraft; Animals and Birds; Annuals; Antiques; Art; Author - Williamson, Henry; Autobiography; Aviation. PR: £1–100. CC: MC; V; Solo. Mem: BA; FSB. Notes: *Also, a booksearch service.*

BERE ALSTON

The Victoria Bookshop, ■ 9 Fore Street, Bere Alston, PL20 7AA. Prop: Peter Churcher. Tel: (01822) 841638. E-mail: victoria_bookshop@btopenworld.com. Est: 2000. Shop open: **T:** 10:30–16:30; **W:** 10:30–16:30; **Th:** 10:29–16:30; **F:** 10:30–16:30; **S:** 10:30–16:30. Very large stock. Spec: Academic/ Scholarly; Alchemy; Occult; Psychology/Psychiatry; Religion - Christian; Topography - Local. PR: £3–600. CC: AE; MC; V; SW. Notes: *Over 80,000 books in stock. In an area of outstanding natural beauty. Near Plymouth and Tavistock.*

DEVON

BIDEFORD

Allhalland Books, ■ 7 Allhalland St., Bideford, EX39 2JD. Prop: J.P. Simpson O'Gara and S. Sutherland. Tel: (01237) 479301. Est: 1997. Shop open. **M:** 09:00–17:00; **T:** 09:00–17:00; **W:** 09:00–17:00; **Th:** 09:00–17:00; **F:** 09:00–17:00; **S:** 09:00–17:00. Small stock. Spec: Natural History; Topography - General. PR: £2–500. Notes: *Also, bookbinding.*

Peter Hames, ■ Devon Cottage Churchill Way, Northam, Bideford, EX39 1NS. Prop: Peter Hames. Tel: (01237) 421065. Fax: (01237) 421065. E-mail: peterhames@hotmail.com. Est: 1980. Shop open: **M:** 09:30–17:30; **T:** 09:30–17:30; **W:** 09:30–17:30; **Th:** 09:30–17:30; **F:** 09:30–17:30; **S:** 09:30–17:30. Small stock. Spec: Motoring; Music - Jazz & Blues; Topography - Local; Ephemera. PR: £1–100. Mem: PBFA.; Notes: *Barnstaple Market: Tues, Fri, Sat and South Molton Market: Thursday and book fairs in South West. Local topography includes Exmoor, and Lundy Island.*

BRIXHAM

Kate Armitage (Booksearch), 5 Park Court, Heath Road, Brixham, TQ5 9AX. Tel: (01803) 850277. E-mail: katesbooks2003@yahoo.co.uk. Private premises. Internet and Postal. Spec: Children's; Maritime/Nautical; Military History; Modern First Editions. PR: £1–20.

COLYTON

Chandos Books, ■ London House Market Place, Colyton, EX24 6JS. Prop: George Janssen. Tel: 01297 553344. E-mail: chandosbooks@hotmail.com. Est: 1997. Shop open: **M:** 10:00–16:00; **T:** 10:00–16:00; **W:** 10:00–16:00; **Th:** 10:00–16:00; **F:** 10:00–16:00; **S:** 10:00–13:00. Spec: Animals and Birds; Antiquarian; Architecture; Art; Bibles; Bindings; Bookbinding; Books about Books. Corresp: Dutch, German. Notes: *Bookbinding and book repairs on premises.*

Island Books, Shutes Farm Northleigh, Colyton, EX24 6BL. Tel: (01843) 866999. Fax: (01843) 866999. Web: www.ukbookworld.com/members/islandbooks. E-mail: island@swauk.freeserve.co.uk. Est: 1974. Private premises. Internet and Postal. Appointment necessary. Medium stock. Spec: Academic/Scholarly; Aeronautics; Agriculture; Animals and Birds; Antiquarian; Applied Art; Archaeology; Architecture. PR: £10–10,000. CC: JCB; MC; V.

COMBE MARTIN

Golden Books Group, Blurridge Ridge Hill, Combe Martin, EX34 0NR. Tel: (01271) 883204. Fax: (01271) 883204. Web: www.abook4all.com. E-mail: ivan@abook4all.com. Est: 1991 Private premises. Internet Only. Appointment necessary. Large stock. Spec: Antiquarian; Author - Dickens, Charles; Bindings; Early Imprints; Fine & Rare; History - General; Manuscripts; Sets of Books. PR: £5–10,000. CC: MC; V; Switch, Maestro. Mem: PBFA; LAPADA, CINOA. VAT No: GB 822 1619 54. Notes: *and reated antiques.*

COUNTESS WEAR

Richard Connole, 12 Seabrook Avenue, Countess Wear, EX2 7DW. Prop: Richard Connole. Tel: O1392 201735. Web: www.yesteryearvision.co.uk. E-mail: rconnole@hotmail.com. Mail Order Only. Internet and Postal. Telephone First. Open: **M:** 09:00–17:30; **T:** 09:00–17:30; **W:** 09:00–17:30; **Th:** 09:00–17:30; **F:** 09:00–17:30; **S:** 09:00–17:30; **Su:** 09:00–17:30; Closed for lunch: 13:00–14:00. Spec: Cata: Film, T.V, Childrens, General.

DARTMOUTH

Compass Books, ■ 24 Lower Street, Dartmouth, TQ6 9AN. Prop: Emilie and Lucy Wright. Tel: 01803 835915. Fax: 01803 835915. E-mail: books@compassmarine.co.uk. Est: 2000. Shop open: **M:** 10:00–16:00; **T:** 10:00–16:00; **W:** 10:00–16:00; **Th:** 10:00–16:00; **F:** 10:00–16:00; **S:** 10:00–16:00. Spec: History - Local; Maritime/Nautical; Topography - Local. CC: MC; V; Maestro, Solo. VAT No: GB 777 3192 94.

HAVE YOUR OWN WEB SITE and BOOKS LISTED

Features include an easy to use book stock database

For more details - see
www.sheppardsworld.co.uk

DEVON

DAWLISH

Dawlish Books, ■ White Court Beach Street, Dawlish, EX7 9PN. Prop: S. French. Tel: (01626) 866882 / 01626 779500. E-mail: frenchatavalon@aol.com. Est: 2000. Shop open: **M:** 11:00–16:30; **T:** 11:00– 16:30; **Th:** 11:00–16:30; **F:** 11:00–16:30; **S:** 11:00–16:30. Medium stock. Spec: Annuals; Comic Books & Annuals; Esoteric; New Age; Occult; Psychic; Spiritualism; U.F.O.s. PR: £1–100. Notes: *Open 11:00–15:00 in winter & closed Tuesdays & Wednesdays. Trade most welcome all year round but best telephone before calling in winter.*

EXETER

- **Lisa Cox Music,** The Coach House Colleton Crescent, Exeter, EX 2 4DG. Prop: Ms. L. Cox. Tel: (01392) 490290. Fax: (01392) 277336. Web: www.lisacoxmusic.co.uk. E-mail: music@lisacoxmusic.co.uk. Est: 1984. Private premises. Internet and Postal. Appointment necessary. Open: **M:** 10:00–17:00; **T:** 10:00– 17:00; **W:** 10:00–17:00; **Th:** 10:00–17:00; **F:** 10:00–17:00; Medium stock. Spec: Aids Crisis, The; Autographs; Manuscripts; Music - Printed, Sheet Music & Scores. PR: £100–50,000. CC: MC; V. Corresp: French. Mem: ABA; BA. VAT No: GB 631 4239 64.
- **Exeter Rare Books,** ■ 13a Guildhall Shopping Centre, Exeter, EX8 5AX. Prop: R.C. Parry M.A. Tel: (01392) 436021. Est: 1977. Shop open: **M:** 10:00–17:00; **T:** 10:00–17:00; **W:** 11:00–17:00; **Th:** 10:00– 17:00; **F:** 10:00–17:00; **S:** 10:00–17:00. Closed for lunch: 13:00–14:00. Medium stock. Spec: Topography - Local. PR: £2–500. CC: MC; V. Corresp: German. Mem: ABA; PBFA. VAT No: GB 142 3267 91.
- **Exeter Traders in Collectables Ltd,** ■ The Quay, Exeter, EX2 4AP. Prop: P. Bliss, M. Desforges, and T. Hughes. Tel: 01392 493501. Est: 1986. Shop At: The Antiques Centre, The Quay, Exeter EX2 4AP. Open: **M:** 10:00–18:00; **T:** 10:00–18:00; **W:** 10:00–18:00; **Th:** 10:00–18:00; **F:** 10:00–18:00; **S:** 10:00– 18:00; **Su:** 10:00–18:00. Spec: Collectables; Ephemera; Prints and Maps. Corresp: French, Spanish. Also at: The Antiques Centre, The Quay, Exeter EX2 4AP. Notes: *NB: Winter opening times 10:00 – 17:00.*
- **John S. Hill,** 78 Pinhoe Road, Exeter, EX4 7HL. Tel: (01392) 439753. Fax: (01392) 439753. E-mail: john@hill6383.fsnet.co.uk. Est: 1988. Private premises. Internet and Postal. Appointment necessary. Small stock. Spec: Fiction - Crime, Detective, Spy, Thrillers; Fiction - Science Fiction; First Editions; Military; Booksearch. PR: £5–1,500.
- **Joel Segal Books,** 27 Fore Street, Topsham, Exeter, EX3 0HD. Tel: 01392877895. Web: www.segalbooks .com. E-mail: lily@segalbooks.com. Open: **M:** 10.30–17:00; **T:** 10.30–17.00; **W:** 10.30–17.00; **Th:** 10.30–17:00; **F:** 10.30–17:00; **S:** 10.30–17:00. Closed for lunch: 13:00–14:00. Spec: Academic/ Scholarly; Acupuncture; Adventure; Advertising; Aesthetics; Africana; Agriculture; Aircraft. CC: MC; V; Maestro/Switch. Corresp: French. Mem: Federation of Small Businesses.

HONITON

- **Ӕaenigma Designs (Books),** Whites Plot, Luppitt, Honiton, EX14 4RZ. Prop: James Dalgety. Tel: (01404) 891560. Web: www.puzzlemuseum.com. E-mail: books@puzzlemuseum.com. Est: 1973. Private premises. Internet and Postal. Appointment necessary. Spec: Puzzles. CC: PayPal. Cata: puzzles, recreational maths.
- **High Street Books,** ■ 150 High Street, Honiton, EX14 8JX. Prop: Geoff Tyson. Tel: (01404) 45570. E-mail: tysonbooks@hotmail.com. Est: 1992. Shop open: **T:** 10:00–17:00; **W:** 10:30–17:00; **Th:** 10:30– 17:00; **F:** 10:00–17:00; **S:** 10:00–17:00. Spec: Applied Art; Erotica; Maritime/Nautical; Military; Topography - General; Topography - Local; Travel - General; Ephemera. Mem: ABA; PBFA.
- **Graham York Rare Books,** ■ 225 High Street, Honiton, EX14 1LB. Tel: (01404) 41727. Fax: (01404) 44993. Web: www.gyork.co.uk. E-mail: books@gyork.co.uk. Est: 1982. Shop. Internet and Postal. Open: **M:** 09:30–17:00; **T:** 09:30–17:00; **W:** 09:30–17:00; **Th:** 09:30–17:00; **F:** 09:30–17:00; **S:** 09:30– 17:00. Large stock. Spec: Africana; Antiquarian; Art Reference; Author - Borrow, George; Countries - Europe; Countries - Portugal; Countries - Spain; County - Local. PR: £0–5,000. CC: AE; MC; V. Cata: Gypsies, George Borrow, Spain. Corresp: Spanish, French. Mem: ABA; PBFA; ILAB. VAT No: GB 429 2623 48. Notes: *Stock includes books on Devon.*

KINGSBRIDGE

Booktrace International, The Hald Kernborough, Kingsbridge, TQ7 2LL. Prop: Richard Newbold. Tel: (01548) 511366. E-mail: booktrace@aol.com. Est: 1995. Private premises. Postal Only. Spec: Booksearch.

LYMPSTONE

Reaveley Books, 1 Church Road, Lympstone, Nr Exmouth, EX8 5JU. Prop: Jane Johnson. Tel: (01395) 225462. Web: www.reaveleybooks.co.uk. E-mail: jane@johnsgrj.demon.co.uk. Est: 1998. Private premises. Internet and Postal. Small stock. Spec: Author - Murdoch, I.; Fiction - General; Fiction - Crime, Detective, Spy, Thrillers; Fiction - Historical; Fiction - Young Adult Mystery & Adventure Series; Limited Editions - General; Literature; Modern First Editions. PR: £5–500. CC: PayPal, cheque. Cata: modern literary first editions. Mem: FSB. Notes: *Monthly newsletter e-mailed on request - see www.reaveleybooks.co.uk for list of stock.*

MODBURY

Lamb's Tales Books, 63 Brownston Street, Modbury, Ivybridge, PL21 0RQ. Prop: James & Elizabeth Lamb. Tel: (01548) 830317. Web: www.lambstales.co.uk. E-mail: books@lambstales.co.uk. Est: 1988. Private premises. Internet and Postal. Contactable. Small stock. Spec: Cookery/Gastronomy; Maritime/Nautical; Military. PR: £5–150. VAT No: GB 768 6509 77.

MONKLEIGH

Catalyst Booksearch Services, Catsborough Cottage Catsborough Cross, Monkleigh, Nr Bideford, EX39 5LE. Prop: Patrick Blosse. Tel: 01805 624056. Web: www.catalystbooksearch.co.uk. E-mail: books@catalystbooksearch.co.uk. Est: 1997. Private premises. Internet and Postal. Appointment necessary. **S:** 09:00–17:30; **Su:** 09:00–17:30; Closed for lunch: 13:00–14:00. Spec: Autobiography; Biography; Children's; Drama; Fiction - General; Fiction - Crime, Detective, Spy, Thrillers; History - General; Performing Arts. CC: PayPal. Mem: PBFA. Notes: *We specialise in childrens & adult fiction, biography, performing arts & travel, with a sprinkling of history & politics. Visitors by appointment. We also provide a comprehensive, free booksearch service. Please send wants with a large S.A.E.*

MORETONHAMPSTEAD

Moreton Books, 1 The Square, Moretonhampstead, TQ13 8NF. Prop: Dave Jelfs. Tel: (01647) 441176. Web: www.moretonbooks.co.uk. E-mail: davejelfs@moretonbooks.co.uk. Est: 1994. Private premises. Telephone First. Open: **M:** 10:00–17:00; **T:** 10:00–17:00; **W:** 10:00–17:00; **Th:** 10:00–17:00; **F:** 10:00–17:00; **S:** 10:00–17:00. Medium stock. Spec: Antiquarian; Art History; Art Reference; Autobiography; Literature; Modern First Editions, Natural History; Poetry. PR: £1–500. CC: E; MC; V; SO, SW. Mem: PBFA. Notes: *Stock include Dartmoor and West Country topography.*

NEWTON ABBOT

Gerard Brookes, 68a The Square Chagford, Newton Abbot, TQ13 8AE. Prop: Gerard Brookes. Tel: (01647) 432670. Office and/or bookroom. Appointment necessary. Spec: Natural History. Mem: PBFA.

DPE Books, PO Box 5 Chudleigh, Newton Abbot, TQ130YZ. Prop: David Porteous. Tel: 01626 853310. Web: www.davidporteous.com. E-mail: porteous@eclipse.co.uk. Mail Order Only. Postal Only. Spec: Art - Technique; Art History; Crafts; Embroidery; Folklore; Hobbies; Housekeeping; Illustrated - General. VAT No: GB 441 2746 66.

OKEHAMPTON

J C Books, ■ 9 The Arcade Fore Street, Okehampton, EX20 1EX. Tel: 01837 659339. Est: 1998. Shop open: **M:** 09:00–17:00; **T:** 09:00–17:00; **W:** 09:00–17:00; **Th:** 09:00–17:00; **F:** 09:00–17:00; **S:** 09:00–17:00. Spec: History - Local; New Books; Railways; Science - General; Topography - Local; Transport.

OTTERTON

The Book Shelf, Butterfly Cottage Behind Hayes, Otterton, EX9 7JQ. Prop: Sandra George. Tel: (01395) 567565. Web: www.bookshelfuk.com. E-mail: sales@bookshelfuk.com. Est: 1994. Private premises. Internet and Postal. Telephone First. Open: **M:** 08:00–18:00; **T:** 08:00–18:00; **W:** 08:00–18:00; **Th:** 08:00–18:00; **F:** 08:00–18:00; **S:** 08:00–14:00. Medium stock. Spec: Autobiography; Biography; Illustrated - General; Modern First Editions; Poetry; Travel - General; Victoriana. PR: £5–1,200. CC: PayPal. VAT No: GB 631 2242 85. Notes: *Antiques Centre, Quayside, Topsham, Devon.*

DEVON

PAIGNTON

The Old Celtic Bookshop, ■ 43 Hyde Road, Paignton, TQ4 5BP. Prop: Michael Sutton. Tel: (01803) 558709. E-mail: michael.sutton2@virgin.net. Est: 1989. Shop open: **M:** 09:00–18:00; **T:** 09:00–18:00; **W:** 09:00–18:00; **Th:** 09:00–18:00; **F:** 09:00–18:00; **S:** 09:00–18:00; **Su:** 12:00–18:00; Medium stock. Spec: Alternative Medicine; Annuals; Author - Blyton, Enid; Author - Herbert, James; Author - King, Stephen; Author - Koontz, Dean; Author - Rice, Anne; Celtica. PR: £1–50. Notes: *Extended opening until 21:30 July to September.*

The Pocket Bookshop, ■ 159 Winner Street, Paignton, TQ3 3BP. Prop: Leon Corrall. Tel: (01803) 529804. Est: 1985. Shop open: **T:** 10:30–17:30; **W:** 10:30–17:30; **Th:** 10:30–17:30; **F:** 10:30–17:30; **S:** 10:30–17:30. PR: £1–50. Notes: *Open Mondays in from July to September.*

The Sheet Music Warehouse, Primley Mount 17 Primley Park, Paignton, TQ3 3JP. Web: www.sheetmusicwarehouse.co.uk. E-mail: pianoman@globalnet.co.uk. Est: 1991. Warehouse. Internet and Postal. Appointment necessary. Open: **M:** 09:00–17:30; **T:** 09:00–17:30; **W:** 09:00–17:30; **Th:** 09:00–17:30; **F:** 09:00–17:30; **S:** 09:00–17:30; **Su:** 09:00–17:30; Closed for lunch: 13:00–14:00. Spec: Music - General; Music - Chart Histories & Research; Music - Classical; Music - Composers; Music - Country & Western; Music - Folk & Irish Folk; Music - Gregorian Chants; Music - Illustrated Sheet Music. CC: PayPal.

PLYMOUTH

Anne Harris Books & Bags Books, 38 Burleigh Park Road, Peverell, Plymouth, PL3 4QH. Tel: (01752) 775853. E-mail: anne.harris1@virgin.net. Est: 2000. Private premises. Postal Only. Appointment necessary. Very small stock. Spec: Architecture; Art; Plant Hunting; Travel - General. PR: £1–500.

Bookcupboard, ■ Old Customs House 18 The Parade, Barbican, Plymouth, PL1 2JW. Prop: A. Donoghue. Tel: (01752) 226311. E-mail: barbbook@globalnet.co.uk. Est: 1995. Shop open: **M:** 10:30–16:30; **T:** 10:30–16:30; **W:** 10:30–16:30; **Th:** 10:30–16:30; **F:** 10:30–15:30; **S:** 10:30–16:30; **Su:** 10:30–16:30; Very large stock. Spec: CC: AE; D; E; JCB; MC; V. Mem: FSB.

books2books, 64 Glendower Road, Peverell, Plymouth, PL3 4LD. Prop: R.J.A. Paxton-Denny. Tel: 01752 510234. Web: www.abebooks/home/BOOKS2BOOKS. E-mail: rpaxtonden@blueyonder .co.uk. Est: 1984. Private premises. Internet and Postal. Contactable. Open: **M:** 07:30–23:30; **T:** 07:30–23:30; **W:** 07:30–23:30; **Th:** 07:30–23:30; **F:** 07:30–23:30; **S:** 07:30–23:30; **Su:** 07:30–23:30. Spec: Annuals; Art History; Art Reference; Author - General; Author - 20th Century; - Johns, W.E.; Autobiography; Aviation. CC: MC; V; Debit cards. Cata: Modern 1sts, Childrens, Illustrated, Biogs, Milit. Corresp: French, German. Notes: *Good quality general stock. View by arrangement, tel/email/ mail. Ship worldwide. Insurance extra.*

Cornerstone Books, ■ New Street Antiques Centre 27 New Street, The Barbican, Plymouth, PL3 4LE. Prop: Mark Treece. Tel: (01752) 661165. Web: www.abe.books.com. E-mail: mark@streece .freeserve.co.uk. Est: 1985. Shop open: **M:** 10:00–17:00; **T:** 10:00–17:00; **W:** 10:00–17:00; **Th:** 10:00–17:00; **F:** 10:00–17:00; **S:** 10:00–17:00. Large stock. PR: £1–100. Mem: ABA. Notes: *General stock*

Rods Books, ■ 20 21 Southside Street, Barbican, Plymouth, PL1 2LD. Prop: R.P. Murphy. Tel: (01752) 253546. E-mail: rmurphy980@aol.com. Est: 1996. Shop. Spec: Adventure; Alpinism/Mountaineering; Arms & Armour; Army, The; Deep Sea Diving; Fiction - Science Fiction; Fiction - Westerns; History - General. PR: £2–40. CC: AE; E; JCB; MC; V.

The Sea Chest Nautical Bookshop, ■ Queen Anne's Battery Marina Coxside, Plymouth, PL4 0LP. Prop: R.A. Dearn. Tel: (01752) 222012. Fax: (01752) 252679. Web: www.seachest.co.uk. E-mail: sales@ seachest.co.uk. Est: 1987. Shop open: **M:** 09:00–17:00; **T:** 09:00–17:00; **W:** 09:00–17:00; **Th:** 09:00–16:00; **F:** 09:00–17:00; **S:** 09:00–17:00. Small stock. Spec: Maritime/Nautical; Navigation; Seafaring & Shipping; Sport - Sailing; Sport - Yachting. PR: £2–750. CC: AE; MC; V. Mem: BA. VAT No: GB 501 5928 65. Notes: *Also, new nautical books, pilots & charts, a booksearch service & British Admiralty chart agent.*

SEATON

Hill House Books, Hill House Highcliffe Crescent, Seaton, EX12 2PS. Prop: Phil Beard. Tel: (01297) 20377. E-mail: philbeard@mac.com. Est: 1982. Private premises. Internet and Postal. Very small stock. Spec: Advertising; Art; Art History; Photography. PR: £1–500.

The End Bookshop, ■ 54 Queen Street, Seaton, EX12 2RB. Prop: Mark Elbro. Tel: 01297 20808. E-mail: maelbro@talk21.com. Est: 1993. Shop open: **M:** 09:30–16:00; **T:** 09:30–16:00; **W:** 09:30–16:00; **Th:** 09:30–13:00; **S:** 09:30–13:00.

SOUTH BRENT

Patrick Pollak Rare Books, Moorview Plymouth Road, South Brent, TQ10 9HT. Prop: Prop Patrcik & Jeanne Pollak. Tel: (01364) 73457. Fax: (01364) 649126. Web: www.rarevols.co.uk. E-mail: patrick@ rarevols.co.uk. Est: 1973. Private premises. Internet and Postal. Telephone First. Small stock. Spec: Academic/Scholarly; Economics; Medicine; Natural Sciences; Photography; Science - General; Science - History of; Scientific Instruments. PR: £50–5,000. CC: AE; JCB; MC; V. Corresp: German, French. Mem: ABA; ILAB; Linnean Society. VAT No: GB 267 5364 31.

Rosemary Stansbury, 25 Church Street, South Brent, TQ10 9AB. Tel: (01364) 72465. Est: 1985. Private premises. Appointment necessary. Small stock. Spec: Children's. PR: £1–100. Notes: *Children's titles only.*

TAVISTOCK

Bookworm Alley, 36 Brook Street, Tavistock, PI 19 0HE. Prop: Joan Williams. Tel: (01822) 617740. Web: www.bookwormalley.org.uk. E-mail: bookworm-alley@freenet.co.uk. Est: 2000. Private premises. Appointment necessary. Small stock. Spec: Religion - Christian; Religion - Salvation Army. PR: £1–50.

Lee Furneaux Books, 6 Lopes Road Dousland, Yelverton, Tavistock, PL20 6NX. Prop: Lee Furneaux. Tel: (01822) 853243. E-mail: enquiries@leefurneauxbooks.co.uk. Est: 1991. Market stand/stall. Internet and Postal. Telephone First. Shop At: Trade at Tavistock Market (Indoor Market and permanent shop). Open: **T:** 08:30–16:00; **W:** 08:30–16:00; **Th:** 08:30–16:00; **F:** 08:30–16:00; **S:** 08:30–16:00. Small stock. Spec: Art; Children's; Crafts; Gardening - General; History - General; Literature; Mind, Body & Spirit; Music - Popular. PR: £1–100. CC: PayPal & via abebooks. VAT No: GB 802 9873 14. Notes: *Open occasional Sundays - see local press.*

TEIGNMOUTH

IKON, Magnolia New Road, Teignmouth, TQ14 8UD. Prop: Dr. Nicholas & Clare Goodrick-Clarke. Tel: (01626) 776528. Fax: (01626) 776528. E-mail: ikon@globalnet.co.uk. Est: 1982. Private premises. Postal Only. Appointment necessary. Spec: Academic/Scholarly; Alchemy; Alternative Medicine; Esoteric; Gnostics / Gnosticism; Health; Herbalism; Hermeticism. PR: £10–75. Cata: History; Health; Esoteric. Corresp: German.

Milestone Books, ■ 43 Northumberland Place, Teignmouth, TQ14 8DE. Prop: V. K. Marston. Tel: 01626 775436. Fax: 01626 777023. Web: www.milestonebooks.co.uk. E-mail: admin@milestonebooks .co.uk. Est: 1996. Internet and Postal. Telephone First. Shop open: **M:** 09:30–17:30; **T:** 09:30–17:30; **W:** 09:30–17:30; **Th:** 09:30–13:30; **F:** 09:30–13:30; **S:** 09:30–17:30. Closed for lunch: 13:30–14:00. Spec: Aeronautics; Aviation; Buses/Trams; Manuals - Seamanship (see also under Seamanship); Maritime/ Nautical; Model Railways; Naval; Navigation. CC: AE; MC; V. VAT No: GB 585 7083 03. Notes: *We operate from within the Quayside Bookshop, which sells new books.*

TIVERTON

Heartland Old Books, ■ 12–14 Newport Street, Tiverton, EX16 6NL. Prop: Jeremy Whitehorn. Tel: (01884) 254488. E-mail: jeremy@whitehorn.fsworld.co.uk. Est: 2001. Shop open: **M:** 10:00–17:00; **T:** 10:00–17:00; **W:** 10:00–17:00; **Th:** 10:00–17:00; **F:** 10:00–17:00; **S:** 10:00–17:00. Medium stock. Spec: Military; Sport - Field Sports; Travel - General. PR: £1–500. Corresp: French. Notes: *Easy parking in Pannier Market opposite. Strong emphasis on uncommon military, field sports, local and railway titles. Good, broad coverage in most other subject areas.*

Kelly Books Limited, 6, Redlands, Tiverton, EX16 4DH. Prop: Props: Len & Lynda Kelly. Tel: (01884) 256170. Fax: (0871) 661 8229. Web: www.kellybooks.net. E-mail: len@kellybooks.co.uk. Est: 1972. Private premises. Internet and Postal. Appointment necessary. Open: **M:** 09:00–18:00; **T:** 09:00–18:00; **W:** 09:00–18:00; **Th:** 09:00–18:00; **F:** 09:00–18:00; **S:** 09:00–18:00. Medium stock. Spec: Advertising; Broadcasting; Cinema/Film; Journalism; Media; Radio/Wireless; Television; Ephemera. PR: £5–600. CC: AE; MC; V; SW. Cata: Broadcasting and Mass Communications. VAT No: GB 799 7192 48. Notes: *supply of back numbers of Radio Times, The Listener, and other radio books and magazines.*

DEVON

TORQUAY

Colin Baker - Books for the Collector, 66 Marldon Road, Shiphay, Torquay, TQ2 7EH. Prop: Colin and Sally Baker. Tel: (01803) 613356. E-mail: colinbakerbooks@ukonline.co.uk. Est: 1994. Private premises. Internet and Postal. Open in Summer. Small stock. Spec: Author - Betjeman, Sir John; - Buckeridge, A.; - Cook, Beryl; - Goudge, Elizabeth; - Pargeter, Edith; - Peters, Ellis; - Read, Miss; - Street, A.G. PR: £5–500. Notes: *We organise Torquay & Plymouth Book Fairs & are regular attendees at Sherborne (3rd Saturday of each Month) Wells Bristol & Lit Fests - Ways With Words, Dartington & Port Eliot St Germans each July.*

The Good Book Shop, ■ 176 Union Street, Torquay, TQ2 5NQ. Prop: Jim Goodchild. Tel: 01807 294081. Est: 2006. Shop open: **M:** 10:00–17:00; **T:** 10:00–17:00; **W:** 10:00–17:00; **Th:** 10:00–17:00; **F:** 10:00–17:00; **S:** 10:00–17:00. Spec: Music - Sheet Music; Ephemera. Notes: *Memorabilia, postcards, sheet music.*

Westcountry Oldbooks, Lilburn House 215 Babbacombe Road, Torquay, TX1 3SX. Prop: David Neil. Tel: (01803) 322712. Web: www.davidneilrarebooks.co.uk. E-mail: david-neil@btinternet.com. Est: 1988. Private premises. Appointment necessary. Open: **M:** 09:00–17:30; **T:** 09:00–17:30; **W:** 09:00– 17:30; **Th:** 09:00–17:30; **F:** 09:00–17:30; **S:** 09:00–17:30. Small stock. Spec: Antiquarian; Literature; Topography - General. Mem: PBFA.

TORRINGTON

The Archivist, Priory Cottage Frithelstock, Torrington, EX38 8JH. Tel: (01805) 625750. Fax: (01805) 625376. Web: www.thebookarchivist.co.uk. E-mail: careof@sheppardsworld.co.uk. Est: 1990. Private premises. Internet and Postal. Appointment necessary. Very small stock. Spec: Cats; Journalism; Literature; Publishers - Joseph Ltd., Michael; Reference. PR: £1–1,000. CC: PayPal.

Books Antiques & Collectables, ■ 3 Well Street, Torrington, EX38 8EP. Tel: (01805) 625624. E-mail: joannaford8@hotmail.com. Shop open: **T:** 10:30–16:00; **W:** 10:30–16:00; **Th:** 10:00–16:00; **F:** 10:00– 16:00. Closed for lunch: 13:00–14:00. Very small stock. Spec: Art; Biography; Children's; Fiction - General; History - General; Philosophy; Plays; Poetry. PR: £1–25.

Brown and Rivans Ltd, Heywood House South Street, Torrington, EX38 8HE. Prop: David Brown and Steven Rivans. Tel: 01805 623771. E-mail: david.brown78@btinternet.com. Est: 2002. Office and/or bookroom. Internet and Postal. Appointment necessary. CC: PayPal.

River Reads Bookshop, ■ 21 South Street, Torrington, EX38 8AA. Tel: (01805) 625888. Fax: (01805) 625888. Web: www.riverreads.co.uk. E-mail: keitarmshw@aol.com. Est: 2002. Shop open: **M:** 10:00– 16:00; **T:** 10:00–16:00; **W:** 10:00–13:00; **Th:** 10:00–16:00; **F:** 10:00–16:00; **S:** 10:00–16:00. Large stock. Spec: Art; Children's; Cookery/Gastronomy; Fishes; Gardening - General; Health; Hobbies; Natural History. PR: £2–200. Notes: *Also, vintage fishing tackle, fishing prints and publishers of collector's limited editions of 'BB' titles.*

TOTNES

Collards Bookshop, ■ 4 Castle Street, Totnes, TQ9 5NU. Prop: Belle Collard. Tel: (01548) 550246. E-mail: collards@freeuk.com. Est: 1970. Shop open: **M:** 10:30–17:00; **T:** 10:30–17:00; **W:** 10:30–17:00; **Th:** 10:30–17:00; **F:** 10:30–17:00; **S:** 10:30–17:00. Medium stock. PR: £1–300. Notes: *Opening varies according to season but open every weekday in summer. Closed Wednesdays in winter.*

Geoff Cox, Lower West Wing Tristford House, Harberton, Totnes, TQ9 7RZ. Tel: (01803) 866181. E-mail: geoffcox46@hotmail.com. Est. 1978. Private premises. Book fairs only. Appointment necessary. Open: **M:** 10.00–19.00; **T:** 10.00–19.00; **Th:** 10.00–19.00; **F:** 10.00–12.00; **S:** 10.00–12.00. Closed for lunch: 12.00–13.00. Medium stock. Spec: Adventure; Aeronautics; Aircraft; Archaeology - Industrial; Aviation; Buses/Trams; Canals/Inland Waterways; Civil Engineering. PR: £1–500. Cata: Transport & Indusrial Archaeology. Corresp: French, German, Dutch. Mem: PBFA. Notes: *Other interests - West Country topography, travel & exploration, history incl. military & maritime, ephemera, maps & postcards.*

Harlequin, ■ 41 High Street, Totnes, TQ9 5NP. Prop: Paul Wesley. Tel: (01803) 865794. Est: 1983. Shop open: **M:** 10:00–17:30; **T:** 09:00–17:30; **W:** 10:00–17:30; **Th:** 10:00–17:30; **F:** 10:00–17:30; **S:** 10:00– 17:30. Medium stock. PR: £1–50.

DORSET

BEAMINSTER

John E. Spooner, 18 Glebe Court Barnes Lane, Beaminster, DT8 3EZ. Tel: (01308) 862713. E-mail: johnthebookhimself@amsure.com. Est: 1975. Private premises. Postal Only. Small stock. Spec: Aviation; Military; Naval. PR: £5–100.

BLANDFORD FORUM

The Dorset Bookshop, ■ 69 East Street, Blandford Forum, DT11 7DX. Prop: Ethan Golden. Tel: (01258) 452266. Est: 1950. Shop open: **M:** 10:00–17:00; **T:** 10:00–17:00; **W:** 10:00–17:00; **Th:** 10:00–17:00; **F:** 10:00–17:00; **S:** 10:00–17:00. Small stock. PR: £1–100. Mem: BA.

BOURNEMOUTH

African Studies, 67A Muscliffe Road, Winton, Bournemouth, BH9 1GA. Prop: Alan Painter. Tel: 01202 528678. Fax: 01202 528678. E-mail: alan.painter@africanstudies.com. Est: 1998. Private premises. Appointment necessary. Open: **M:** 14:00–17:00; **T:** 08:00–17 00; **W:** 20:00–22.00; **Th:** 20:00–22:00; **F:** 20:00–?? 00. Spec: Africana. Mem: Private Libraries Association. Notes: *Deals in Africana only, in indigenous peoples, anthropology, history, ethnology and ethnographic.*

Dunstan Books, 13 Lascelles Road, Bournemouth, BH7 6NF. Prop: Steven Powrie. Tel: (01202) 246160. Fax: (01202) 246160. Web: www.abebooks.com. E-mail: dunstanbooks@aol.com. Est: 1992. Private premises. Internet and Postal. Contactable. Open: **M:** 09:00–18:00; **T:** 09:00–18:00; **W:** 09:00–18:00; **Th:** 09:00–18:00; **F:** 09:00–18:00; **S:** 09:00–17:00. Small stock. Spec: Bridge; Crime (True); Fiction - Crime, Detective, Spy, Thrillers; Medicine; Politics; Psychotherapy; Sport - Golf. PR: £5–200. CC: via abebooks or cheques. VAT No: GB 797 8711 57.

Facet Books, 18 Dolphin Avenue, Bournemouth, BH10 6DU. Prop: Mr James Allinson and Mrs Margit Allinson. Tel: (01202) 269269. Web: www.jallinson.freeserve.co.uk. E-mail: jim@jallinson .freeserve.co.uk. Est: 1982. Private premises. Internet and Postal. Telephone First. Large stock. Spec: Academic/Scholarly; Advertising; Aeronautics; - Blyton, Enid; - Cook, Beryl; - Crompton, Richmal; - Henty, G.A.; - Johns, W.E. PR: £1–2,500. Corresp: German. Mem: FSB. Notes: *Specialist in Cartoon Annuals & Books, Childrens Annuals (Beano, Dandy, Rupert etc) and British Comics (Beano, Dandy, Cowboy Picture Library, Super Detective Library etc).*

Holdenhurst Books, ■ 275 Holdenhurst Road, Bournemouth, BH8 8BZ. Prop: R.W. Reese. Tel: (01202) 397718. Est: 1985. Shop open: **M:** 10:00–17:00; **T:** 09:00–17:00; **Th:** 10:00–17:00; **F:** 10:00–17:00; **S:** 10:00–17:00. Medium stock. Spec: Aeronautics; Maritime/Nautical; Military; Motorbikes / motorcycles; Motoring. PR: £5–150.

P.F. & J.R. McInnes, 59 Richmond Park Road, Bournemouth, BH8 8TU. Tel: (01202) 394609. E-mail: jane.mcinnes@ntlworld.com. Est: 1981. Private premises. Postal Only. Very small stock. Spec: Dogs; Sport - Boxing. PR: £1–3,000. Cata: boxing and prizefighting. Notes: *Kennel Club Stud books 1949–1990.*

H. & S.J. Rowan, ■ 459 Christchurch Road Boscombe, Bournemouth, BH1 4AD. Prop: H Rowan. Tel: (01202) 398820. Est: 1969. Shop open: **M:** 09:00 17.30, **T:** 09:00–17:30; **W:** 09:00–17:30; **Th:** 09:00–17.30, **F:** 09:00–17:30; **S:** 09:00–18:00. Large stock. Spec: Antiquarian; Antiques; Art; Aviation; Topography - Local; Booksearch; Collectables; Prints and Maps. PR: £1–1,000. VAT No: GB 185 3287 39. Notes: *Also, bookearch.*

Sue Sims, 21 Warwick Road, Pokesdown, Bournemouth, BH7 6JW. Tel: (01202) 432562. E-mail: reggierhino@aol.com. Est: 1978. Private premises. Postal Only. Contactable. Very small stock. Spec: Author - Brent-Dyer, Elinor M.; - Fairlie–Bruce, D.; - Forest, A.; - Oxenham, Elsie; Children's; Religion - Catholic; Booksearch. PR: £1–500. Corresp: French, German. Notes: *Major stock of girl's books and school stories.*

Available from Richard Joseph Publishers Ltd

CLEANING, REPAIRING AND CARING FOR BOOKS

by Robert L. Shep

Revised Edition 148pp £12.00

DORSET

Yesterday Tackle & Books, Southbourne, Bournemouth. Prop: David Dobbyn. Tel: (01202) 476586. E-mail: d.dobin@ntlworld.com. Est: 1983. Private premises. Appointment necessary. Very small stock. Spec: Author - Watkins-Pitchford, Denys ('B.B.'); Sport - Angling/Fishing; Ephemera. PR: £1–100. CC: AE; PayPal. Notes: *Also, fishing tackle and related items.*

Yesterday's Books, 6 Cecil Avenue, Bournemouth, BH8 9EH. Prop: David & Jessica L. Weir. Tel: (01202) 522442. E-mail: djl.weir@btinternet.com. Est: 1974. Office and/or bookroom. Internet and Postal. Telephone First. Open: **M:** 09:00–17:00; **T:** 09:00–17:00; **W:** 09:00–17:00; **Th:** 09:00–17:00; **F:** 09:00–17:00; **S:** 09:00–13:00. Medium stock. Spec: African-American Studies; Africana; Anthropology; Antiquarian; Black Studies; Countries - Africa; Countries - East Africa; Countries - Egypt. PR: £5–500. CC: JCB; MC; V. Cata: Africa. Corresp: French, German. Mem: PBFA. Notes: *Dealers & collectors most welcome. Please telephone first. Large general stock as well as our Africa books.*

BRIDPORT

Bridport Old Bookshop, ■ 11 South Street, Bridport, DT6 3NR. Prop: Caroline Mactaggart & Rosie Young. Tel: (01308) 425689. E-mail: caroline@TextBiz.com. Est: 1981. Shop open: **M:** 10:00–17:00; **T:** 10:00–17.00; **W:** 10:00–17.00; **Th:** 10:00–17.00; **F:** 10:00–17.00; **S:** 10:00–17.00. Small stock. Spec: Children's; Children's - Illustrated. PR: £2–500. CC: MC; V. Mem: PBFA.

Caroline Mactaggart, Manor Farmhouse Swyre, Bridport, Dorchester, DT2 9DN. Tel: (01308) 898174. E-mail: caroline@textbiz.com. Est: 1984. Shop At: Bridport Old Bookshop, 11 South Street, Bridport. Open: **M:** 10.00–17.00; **T:** 10.00–17.00; **W:** 10.00–17.00; **Th:** 10.00–17.00; **F:** 10.00–17.00; **S:** 10.00–17.00. Medium stock. Spec: Scottish Interest. PR: £5–500. CC: MC; V. Mem: PBFA.

CHARMOUTH

The Lighthouse Books, ■ Langley House The Street, Charmouth, DT6 6PE. Prop: Mr Jean Vaupres. Tel: (01297) 560634. Est: 2004. Shop open: **M:** 10:00–17:00; **T:** 10:00–17:00; **Th:** 10:00–17:00; **F:** 10:00–17:00; **S:** 10:00–17:00; **Su:** 10:00–17:00; Medium stock. Spec: Architecture; Country Houses; Fashion & Costume; Folio Society, The; Irish Interest; Odd & Unusual; Sculpture; Travel - General. PR: £1–300. Corresp: French, Italian. Notes: *Outside school holidays, open 10:00 – 17:00 Friday to Monday: Easter to end October. Phone first at other times.*

DORCHESTER

The Dorchester Bookshop, ■ 3 Nappers Court Charles Street, Dorchester, DT1 1EE. Prop: Michael J. Edmonds. Tel: (01305) 269919. Est: 1993. Shop open: **T:** 10:00–17:00; **W:** 10:00–17:00; **Th:** 10:00–17:00; **F:** 10:00–17:00; **S:** 10:00–17:00. Medium stock. PR: £1–500.

Marco Polo Travel & Adventure, Marco Polo House West Bexington, Dorchester, DT2 9DE. Prop: Mark A. Culme-Seymour. Tel: (01308) 898420. Fax: (01308) 898416. Web: www.marcopolobooks.co.uk. E-mail: mark@marcopolobooks.co.uk. Est: 1977. Private premises. Internet and Postal. Appointment necessary. Very small stock. Spec: Travel - General. PR: £15–300. CC: MC; V. VAT No: GB 717 8378 00. Notes: *also booksearch.*

Judith Stinton, 21 Cattistock Road Maiden Newton, Dorchester, DT2 OAG. Tel: (01300) 320778. Web: www.abebooks.com. E-mail: judithstinton@hardycountry.fsnet.co.uk. Est: 1989. Private premises. Internet and Postal. Appointment necessary. Very small stock. Spec: Author - Hardy, Thomas; Children's; Literature; Topography - Local. PR: £1–100.

Steve Walker Fine Books, Willow Tree House 1 Sydenham Way, Dorchester, DT1 1DN. Tel: 01350 260690. E-mail: vectaphile@hotmail.com. Est: 1985. Private premises. Postal Only. Appointment necessary. Very small stock. Spec: Author - Hardy, Thomas; - Johnson, Samuel; Biblical Studies; Bookbinding; Books about Books; Folklore; History - Ancient; Languages - National. PR: £5–500. Mem: Society of Bookbinders. Notes: *Bookbinding and Restoration.*

Woolcott Books, Kingston House Higher Kingston, Dorchester, DT2 8QE. Prop: H.M. & J.R. St. Aubyn. Tel: (01305) 267773. Fax: (01305) 751899. Est: 1978. Private premises. Appointment necessary. Small stock. Spec: Colonial; Countries - Africa; Countries - India; History - National; Military; Travel - Africa; Travel - Asia; Travel - Middle East. PR: £5–500. Notes: *Also, booksearch.*

DORSET

Words Etcetera Bookshop, ■ 2, Cornhill, Dorchester, DT1 1BA. Prop: Simon Rushbrook. Tel: 01305 251919. Fax: 01305 251919. Web: www.wordsetcetera.co.uk. E-mail: info@wordsetcetera.co.uk. Est: 1974. Shop open: **M:** 10:00–17:00; **T:** 10:00–17:00; **W:** 10:00–17:00; **Th:** 10:00–17:00; **F:** 10:00–17.00, **S:** 9.30–17:00. Spec: Antiquarian; Art; Art History; Author - Hardy, Thomas; - Heaney, Seamus; - Lawrence, T.E.; - Powys Family, The; - Woolf, Virginia. CC: MC; V. Cata: Illustrated, Poetry, Mod 1sts, T. Hardy. Corresp: French. Mem: BA. Notes: *We have a few shelves rented out to other booksellers, specialising in antiquarian maps, collectable childrens, military history and Dorset topography.*

GILLINGHAM

DaSilva Puppet Books, 58 Shreen Way, Gillingham, SP8 4HT. Prop: Ray DaSilva. Tel: (01747) 835558. Web: www.puppetbooks.co.uk. E-mail: dasilva@puppetbooks.co.uk. Est: 1986. Private premises. Internet and Postal. Appointment necessary. Open: **M:** 09:00–17:30; **T:** 09:00–17:30; **W:** 09:00–17:30; **Th:** 09:00–17:30; **F:** 09:00–17:30. Closed for lunch; 12:30–02:00. Very small stock. Spec: Entertainment - General; Performing Arts; Puppets & Marionettes; Theatre; Ventriloquism; Ephemera. PR: £1–200. CC: MC; V; SW. Cata: Puppets, Toy Theatre. Corresp: French.

Lilian Modlock, Southcote Langham Lane, Wyke, Gillingham, SP8 5NT Tel: (01747) 821875. Fax: (01747) 821875 E-mail: lilianmodlock@waitrose.com. Est: 1995. Private premises. Type: Market Stall. Appointment necessary. Medium stock. Spec: Biography; Children's; Cinema/Film; Cookery/ Gastronomy; Illustrated - General; Landscape; Poetry; Topography - General. PR: £3–600. Notes: *Also, a booksearch service.*

LONG BURTON

Grahame Thornton, Bookseller, Monghyr House, Spring Lane, Long Burton, Sherborne, DT9 5NZ. Prop: Grahame Thornton. Tel: 01963 210443. Fax: 01963 210443. Web: www.grahamethornton .f9.co.uk. E-mail: grahame@grahamethornton.f9.co.uk. Est: 1995. Private premises. Internet and Postal. Contactable. Open: **M:** 09:00–17:30; **T:** 09:00–17:30; **W:** 09:00–17:30; **Th:** 09:00–17:30; **F:** 09:00–17:30; **S:** 09:00–17:30; **Su:** 09:00–17:30; Closed for lunch: 13:00–14:00. Spec: Animals and Birds; Antiquarian; Autobiography; Belle-Lettres; Biography; Children's; Churchilliana; Classical Studies. CC: E; MC; V; Maestro. Cata: Early Penguin, Antiquarian, Non Fiction, Medical. Corresp: French. VAT No: GB 608 6389 14. Notes: *Catalogues are not routinely issued, but lists can be produced on demand. Visit my website to see the subjects covered. Regular stall at the monthly Sherborne Book Market.*

LYME REGIS

Lymelight Books & Prints, 15 Haye Close, Lyme Regis, DT7 3NJ. Prop: Nigel Cozens. Tel: (01297) 443464. Fax: (01297) 443464. Web: www.lymelight-books.demon.co.uk. E-mail: nigel@lymelight-books.demon.co.uk. Est: 1994. Private premises. Appointment necessary. Open: **M:** 10:00–18:00; **T:** 10:00–18:00; **W:** 10:00–18:00; **Th:** 10:00–18:00; **F:** 10:00–18:00; **S:** 10:00–18:00; **Su:** 10:00–18:00; Medium stock. Spec: Antiquarian; Art; Atlases; Author - Darwin, Charles; - Fowles, John; - Hardy, Thomas; - Lawrence, T.E.; Children's - Illustrated. PR: £5–10,000. CC: AE; E; MC; V; Cirrus. Corresp: French. Mem: PBFA. VAT No: GB 684 4800 14. Notes: *Bookbinding and Booksearch. Print & Mapsearch and Restoration.*

The Bookshop, ■ The Old Bonded Store Marine Parade, The Cobb, Lyme Regis, DT7 3JF. Tel: (01297) 444820. Est: 2003. Shop open: **M:** 11:00–16:30; **T:** 11:00–16:30; **W:** 11:00–16:30; **Th:** 11:00–16:30; **F:** 11:00–16:30; **S:** 11:00–16:30. Medium stock. Spec: Fiction - General; Maritime/Nautical; Poetry; Psychology/Psychiatry. PR: £1–100. Notes: *Open 7 days per week in school holidays less in term time.*

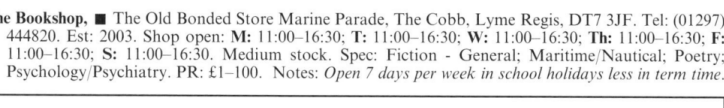

DORSET

The Sanctuary Bookshop, 65 Broad Street, Lyme Regis, DT7 3QF. Prop: Bob & Mariko Speer. Tel: 00-44-(0)1297-445815. Web: www.lyme-regis.com. E-mail: books@lyme-regis.com. Est: 1982. Shop and/ or showroom. Open: **M:** 10.30–17:30; **T:** 10.30–17:30; **W:** 10.30–17:30; **Th:** 10.30–17:30; **F:** 10.30–17:30; **S:** 10.30–17:30; **Su:** 11.00–17:30. Spec: Academic/Scholarly; Art History; Art Reference; Author - Fowles, John; - Shute, Neville; Authors - Local; Bibliography; Biography. CC: AE; E; JCB; MC; V. Corresp: Japanese, French. Notes: *General Bookshop, 2 floors + 2 floors above, each with B & B book stocked accomodation. Two doubles, with private bath. Antiques and curiosa. John Fowles, Beryl Cook, Hundertwasser & Ollie Lett stockists. Free booksearch. Japanese spoken.*

MILBORNE PORT

Kingswood Books, 17 Wick Road, Milborne Port, Sherborne, DT9 5BT. Prop: Anne Rockall & Allan Dollery. Tel: (01963) 250280. Fax: (01963) 250280. Web: www.kingswoodbooks.btinternet.co.uk. E-mail: kingswoodbooks@btinternet.com. Est: 1985. Private premises. Internet and Postal. Appointment necessary. Medium stock. Spec: Academic/Scholarly; Advertising; Anthropology; Antiquarian; Archaeology; Archaeology - Industrial; Architecture; Art History. PR: £1–2,000. CC: JCB; MC; V; Switch. Mem: PBFA. Notes: *Various book fairs listed on our web site Bookbinders & restorers. See our web site.*

POOLE

Bookstand, 53 Kings Ave., Poole, BH14 9QQ. Prop: Eleanor Smith & Wendy Marten. Tel: (01202) 716229. Fax: (01202) 734663. Web: www.abebooks.com/home/bookstand. E-mail: bookstand@ lineone.net. Est: 1997. Private premises. Internet Only. Appointment necessary. Small stock. Spec: Antiquarian; - Milne, A.A.; Author - Potter, Beatrix; - Thelwell, N; - Wheatley, Dennis; Autographs; Ephemera; Fine Printing. PR: £15–5,000. CC: MC; V.

Branksome Books, 33a Kings Avenue, Poole, BH14 9QG. Prop: P.G. Bryer–Ash. Tel: (01202) 730235. Est: 1988. Private premises. Appointment necessary. Very small stock. Spec: Author - Lawrence, T.E.; Sport - Angling/Fishing. PR: £5–200. Corresp: French, Spanish.

R.H. & P. Haskell, 64 Winston Avenue Branksome, Poole, BH12 1PG. Prop: Reg Haskell. Tel: (01202) 243608. Web: www.reghaskell.co.uk. E-mail: reg@haskell.org.uk. Est: 1973. Private premises. Postal Only. Appointment necessary. Very small stock. Spec: Architecture; Ecclesiastical History & Architecture; Gothic Revival; Interior Design; Landscape; Planning - City; Town Planning. PR: £5–1,000. CC: PayPal.

Christopher Williams, 19 Morrison Avenue Parkstone, Poole, BH12 4AD. Prop: Christopher & Pauline Williams. Tel: (01202) 743157. E-mail: cw4finebooks@lineone.net. Est: 1967. Private premises. Internet and Postal. Appointment necessary. Very small stock. Spec: Arts, The; Bibliography; Cookery/Gastronomy; Crafts; Lace; Topography - Local. PR: £5–100. CC: MC; V. Mem: PBFA. Notes: *Closing APRIL 2007 ish.*

PUDDLETOWN

The Antique Map and Bookshop, ■ 32 High Street, Puddletown, DT2 8RU. Prop: C.D. & H.M. Proctor. Tel: (01305) 848633. Fax: (01305) 848992. Web: www.puddletownbookshop.co.uk. E-mail: sales@puddletownbookshop.co.uk. Est: 1976. Internet and Postal. Shop open: **M:** 09:00–17:00; **T:** 09:00–17:00; **W:** 09:00–17:00; **Th:** 09:00–17.00; **F:** 09:00–17:00; **S:** 09:00–17:00. Medium stock. Spec: Antiquarian; Author - Barnes, William; - Conan Doyle, Sir Arthur; - Hardy, Thomas; - Henty, G.A.; - Lawrence, T.E.; - Wells, H.G.; Botany. PR: £5–3,000. CC: AE; JCB; MC; V; SW. Corresp: German. Mem: ABA; PBFA; ILAB. VAT No: GB 291 7495 21.

SHAFTESBURY

Paul Goldman, Meadow View East Orchard, Shaftesbury, SP7 0LG. Tel: (01747) 811380. Fax: (01747) 811380. Web: www.abebooks.com. E-mail: goldman@clara.net. Est: 1997. Private premises. Postal Only. Appointment necessary. Small stock. Spec: Academic/Scholarly; Art; Art History; Art Reference; Cartoons; Comedy; Humour; Illustrated - General. PR: £10–500. Cata: Illustrated books. Corresp: French, Italian, Greek. Mem: ABA; PBFA; ILAB.

Not Just Books, ■ 7a, High Street, Shaftesbury, SP7 8QZ. Prop: F. W. Barrett-Selbie. Tel: 01747 850003. E-mail: ntrevor67@supanet.com. Est: 1996. Shop. open: **W:** 10:00–16:30; **Th:** 10:00–16:30; **F:** 10:00–16:30; **S:** 10:00–16:30. Closed for lunch: 12:00–14:00. Spec: Aircraft; Army, The; Artists; Auction Catalogues; Author - Wodehouse, P.G.; Military History; Naval; Sport - Angling/Fishing. Notes: *also militaria, china, silver and coins, including hammered.*

DORSET

SHERBORNE

Chapter House Books, ■ Trendle Street, Sherborne, DT9 3NT. Prop: Claire Porter, Tudor Books Ltd. Tel: (01935) 816262. Web: www.chapterhouse-books.co.uk E-mail: chapterhousebooks@ tiscali.co.uk Est: 1988. Shop open: **M:** 10:00–17:00; **T:** 10:00–17:00; **W:** 10:00–17:00; **Th:** 10:00– 17:00; **F:** 10:00–17:00; **S:** 10:00–17:00. Large stock. Spec: Booksearch. PR: £1–500. CC: AE; MC; V. Mem: PBFA. VAT No: GB 799 9885 07. Notes: *Also, booksearch, 2nd hand CDs, videos and sheet music.*

Verandah Books, Stonegarth The Avenue, Sherborne, DT9 3AH. Prop: Michael Hougham. Tel: (01935) 815900. Fax: (01935) 815900. Web: www.verandahbooks.co.uk. E-mail: mail@verandahbooks.co.uk. Est: 1992. Private premises. Postal Only. Appointment necessary. Medium stock. Spec: Author - Kipling, Rudyard; Countries - Afganistan; Countries - Burma; Countries - Himalayas, The; Countries - India; Countries - Nepal; Countries - North West Frontier Province; Countries - Pakistan. PR: £10– 500. CC: PayPal. Cata: India and South Asia, Pakistan, Burma, Himalayas. Notes: *All our stock can be searched online by author, title, place or topic.*

STALBRIDGE

March House Books, Thornhill Road, Stalbridge, DT10 2PS. Prop: Mrs. Barbara Fisher. Tel: (01963) 364403. Fax: (01963) 364476. Web: www.http://www.marchhousebooks.com/. E-mail: books@ marchhousebooks.com. Est: 1997. Private premises. Internet and Postal. Small stock. Spec: Annuals; Children's, Children's - Early Titles; Children's - Illustrated; Illustrated - General; Collectables. PR: £5–650. CC: PayPal. Mem: ibooknet.

STOBOROUGH

Calluna Books, 54 Corfe Road, Stoborough, Wareham, BH20 5AF. Prop: Y. Gartshore. Tel: (01929) 552560 evenings. E-mail: yuki@onaga54.freeserve.co.uk. Est: 1997. Private premises. Internet Only. Appointment necessary. Small stock. Spec: Botany; Entomology; Natural History; New Naturalist; Ornithology. PR: £5–300. Notes: *Also, attends specialist bird fairs.*

STURMINSTER

Stour Bookshop, ■ Bridge Street, Sturminster Newton, DT10 1AP. Prop: Tony Butler. Tel: (01258) 473561. Est: 1982. Shop open: **M:** 10:00–18:00; **T:** 10:00–18:00; **W:** 10:00–18:00; **Th:** 10:00–18:00; **F:** 10:00–18:00; **S:** 10:00–13:00. Very small stock. Spec: Aviation; Juvenile; Motoring; Vintage Cars. PR: £5–200. CC: MC; V.

SWANAGE

Reference Works Ltd., 9 Commercial Road, Swanage, BH19 1DF. Prop: Barry Lamb. Tel: (01929) 424423. Fax: (01929) 422597. Web: www.referenceworks.co.uk. E-mail: sales@referenceworks.co.uk. Est: 1984. Office and/or bookroom. Telephone First. Small stock. Spec: Antiques; Ceramics; Decorative Art. PR: £5–800. CC: MC; V.

Norman Wright, 18 Lighthouse Road, Swanage, BH19 2JJ. Tel: (01929)426241. E-mail: wrightnorman@ hotmail.com. Est: 1989. Private premises. Postal Only. Small stock. Spec: Author - Blake, Sexton; - Blyton, Enid; - Johns, W.E.; - Richards, Frank; Cartoons; Children's; Cinema/Film; Comic Books & Annuals. PR: £5–500. Cata: children's books, British comics.

WAREHAM

Reads, Beehive Cottage East Stoke, Wareham, BH20 4JW. Prop: Reg Read & Anthony Hessey. Tel: (01929) 554971, or 5. E-mail: reginaldreads@aol.com. Est: 1998. Private premises. Postal Only. Small stock. Spec: Anthroposophy; Applied Art; Archaeology; Architecture; Art; Autobiography; Biography; Cinema/Film. PR: £5–3,000. CC: JCB; MC; V. Cata: on specialities. Corresp: French. Mem: PBFA. Notes: *Exhibits at major PBFA fairs. Stock listed on abe.com.*

Looking for a dealer in PRINTS or MAPS?

Then search Sheppard's on-line directories at:

www.sheppardsworld.co.uk

DORSET

WEYMOUTH

Books Afloat, ■ 66 Park Street, Weymouth, DT4 7DE. Prop: John Ritchie. Tel: (01305) 779774. Est: 1983. Shop open: **M:** 09:30–17:30; **T:** 09:30–17:30; **W:** 09:30–17:30; **Th:** 09:30–17:30; **F:** 09:30–17:30; **S:** 09:30–17:30. Large stock. Spec: Author - Hardy, Thomas; - Powys Family, The; Aviation; Canals/ Inland Waterways; Fiction - General; Maritime/Nautical; Military History; Navigation. PR: £1–140. Notes: *Also, maritime collectables (ship models), ephemera and postcards. Open 10:00 – 17:00 in winter (November - March).*

The Nautical Antique Centre, ■ 3 Cove Passage, Hope Square, Weymouth, DT4 8TR. Prop: Mr D.C. Warwick. Tel: (01305) 777838. Web: www.nauticalantiques.org. E-mail: info@nauticalantiques.org. Est: 1989. Internet and Postal. Telephone First. Shop open: **T:** 14:00–17:00; **W:** 10:00–17:00; **Th:** 10:00–17:00; **F:** 10:00–17:00. Closed for lunch: 13:00–14:00. Very small stock. Spec: Judaica; Manuals - Seamanship (see also under Seamanship); Maritime/Nautical; Maritime/Nautical - Log Books; Naval; Navigation; Shipbuilding and Shipping; Steam Engines. PR: £5–300.

WIMBORNE

John Graham, 52 Blandford Road Corfe Mullen, Wimborne, BH21 3HQ. Prop: John Graham. Tel: (01202) 692397. Fax: (01202) 692397. Est: 1987. Private premises. Postal Only. Small stock. Spec: Biography; History - General; History - Industrial; History - Local; History - National; Social History; Booksearch; Ephemera. PR: £1–100.

Minster Books, ■ 12, Corn Market, Wimborne Minster, BH21 1JL. Prop: John and Angela Child. Tel: 01202 883355. Web: www.minsterbooks.com. E-mail: minsterbooks@aol.com. Est: 1991. Shop open: **M:** 10:00–17:00; **T:** 10:00–17:00; **W:** 10:00–17:00; **Th:** 10:00–17:00; **F:** 10:00–17:00; **S:** 10:00–17:00. CC: MC; V. Notes: *General stock.*

DURHAM

BARNARD CASTLE

ALLTHINGSBOOKS, ■ 3 The Bank, Barnard Castle, DL12 8PH. Prop: Janet Rogers and Phil Webb. Tel: 01833 695123. Web: www.allthingsbooks.co.uk. E-mail: allthingsbooks@tiscali.co.uk. Est: 2005. Shop open: **M:** 09:00–17:00; **W:** 09:00–17:00; **Th:** 09:00–17:00; **F:** 09:00–17:00; **S:** 09:00–17:00; **Su:** 12.00–17:00; Closed for lunch: 13:00–17.00. CC: AE; MC; V.

BARNARD CASTLE

Book Aid, ■ 5 Galgate, Barnard Castle, DL12 8EQ. Prop: M J Abrahams. Tel: 01833 630209. Est: 1990. Shop open: **M:** 10:00–16:00; **T:** 10:00–16:00; **W:** 10:00–16:00; **Th:** 10:00–16:00; **F:** 10:00 16:00; **S:** 10:00–17:00. Spec: Theology.

Curlews, ■ 11 Market Place, Barnard Castle, DL12 8NF. Prop: M. J. Abrahams. Tel: 01833 630455. Est: 1984. Shop open: **M:** 09:00–17:00; **T:** 09:00–17:00; **W:** 09:00–17:00; **Th:** 09:00 17:00; **F:** 09.00–17:00; **S:** 09:00–17:00; **Su:** 12:00–16:00. Notes: *Books on theology are at Book Aid, 5 Galgate, Barnard Castle.*

Greta Books, Lodge Farm, Scargill, Barnard Castle, DL12 9SY. Prop: Gordon Thomson. Tel: (01833) 621000. Fax: (01833) 621000. E-mail: Gretabooks@xemaps.com. Private premises. Postal Only. Spec: Agriculture; Animals and Birds; Antiquarian; Architecture; Author - Baden-Powell, Lord Robert; Author - Barrie, J.M.; - Buchan, John; - Chesterton, G.K. PR: £5–50. VAT No: GB 502 3822 85.

BISHOP AUCKLAND

Vinovium Books, Wear Valley Business Centre 27 Longfield Road, Bishop Auckland, DL14 6XB. Prop: Paul Hughes. Tel: (01388) 777770. Web: www.vinoviumbooks.co.uk. E-mail: enqrj@ vinoviumbooks.co.uk. Est: 1996. Office and/or bookroom. Internet and Postal. Appointment necessary. Spec: Academic/Scholarly; Antiquarian; Firearms/Guns; Mining; Natural History; Sport - Angling/Fishing; Sport - Field Sports; Sport - Hunting. CC: JCB; MC; V; Switch. Mem: PBFA; DABA. VAT No: GB 746 9734 81.

DARLINGTON

Combat Arts Archive, 12 Berkeley Road, Darlington, DL1 5ED. Prop: Mr. J. Sparkes. Tel: (01325) 465286. Web: www.combatbooks.co.uk. E-mail: johnsparkes@ntlworld.com. Est: 1995. Private premises. Postal Only. Appointment necessary. Small stock. Spec: Physical Culture; Sport - Boxing; Sport - Duelling; Sport - Fencing; Sport - Martial Arts; Sport - Sumo; Sport - Weightlifting/ Bodybuilding; Sport - Wrestling. PR: £1–150. CC: MC; V; Maestro Delta. Cata: Martial Arts Boxing Wrestling Fencing. Notes: *Books and magazines for sale on Eastern and Western Martial Arts. Also Physical Culture.*

Tony and Gill Tiffin, 144 Coniscliffe Road, Darlington, DL3 7RW. Prop: G.A. & M.G. Tiffin. Tel: (01325) 487274. E-mail: tony.tiffin@btinternet.com. Est: 1990. Private premises. Book fairs only. Appointment necessary. Very large stock. Spec: Academic/Scholarly; Autobiography; Biography; Children's; Children's - Early Titles; Children's - Illustrated; Education & School; First Editions. PR: £1–1,000. Corresp: French. Mem: PBFA. Notes: *PBFA and local book fairs.*

Jeremiah Vokes, ■ 61 Coniscliffe Road, Darlington, DL3 7EH. Prop: Jeremiah Vokes. Tel: (01325) 469449. Est: 1979. Shop open: **M:** 09:30–17:00; **T:** 09:30–17:00; **W:** 09:30–17:00; **Th:** 09:30–17:00; **F:** 09:30–17:00; **S:** 09:30–17:00. Closed for lunch: 12:00–13:00. Medium stock. Spec: Fiction - Crime, Detective, Spy, Thrillers; Sherlockiana; Booksearch. PR: £1–1,000. Mem: PBFA. Notes: *Stocks mainly fiction (crime and detective) and Sherlockiana.*

Available from Richard Joseph Publishers Ltd

BOOK DEALING FOR PROFIT
by Paul Minet

(Quarto H/b) £10.00 144pp

DURHAM

REDCAR

Xanadu Books, 16 Kirkleatham Lane., Redcar, TS10 5BZ. Prop: Sylvia Wallace John Wallace. Tel: 01642 485516. Web: www.xanadubokks.co.uk. E-mail: sylvia@xanadubooks.co.uk. Est: 1987. Private premises. Internet Only. Appointment necessary. Spec: Annuals; Art; Children's; Children's - Illustrated; Illustrated - General; Military. CC: PayPal.

STOCKTON-ON-TEES (SEE ALSO UNDER N. YORKSHIRE)

P.R. Brown (Books), 39 Sussex Walk Norton-on-Tees, Stockton-on-Tees, Cleveland, TS20 2RG. Prop: (*) P. Robinson-Brown. Tel: (01642) 871704. Est: 1975. Private premises. Appointment necessary. Very small stock. Spec: Botany; History - Local; Ornithology; Prints and Maps. PR: £5–500.

WILLINGTON

John Turton, ■ 83 High Street, Willington. Prop: John Turton. Tel: (01388) 747600. Fax: (01388) 746741. E-mail: johnturton@turtome.co.uk. Est: 1978. Shop At: 1/2 Cochrane Terrace, Willington, Crook, DL15 0HN. Open: **F:** 12:00–17:00; **S:** 10:00–17:00. Large stock. Spec: Antiquarian; Bindings; Ecclesiastical History & Architecture; Free Thought; Genealogy; Heraldry; Journals; Military History. PR: £5–500. CC: JCB; MC; V. Cata: Topography. Mem: PBFA. (q.v.)

John Turton, ■ 1–2 Cochrane Terrace, Willington, Crook, DL15 0HN. Prop: John Turton. Tel: (01388) 745770. Fax: (01388) 746741. E-mail: johnturton@turtome.co.uk. Est: 1978. Shop open: **F:** 12.00–17:00; **S:** 10:00–17:00. Large stock. Spec: Antiquarian; Bindings; Ecclesiastical History & Architecture; Free Thought; Genealogy; Heraldry; History - Family; History - Local. PR: £50–2,000. CC: JCB; MC; V. Mem: PBFA. Notes: *Also ast 83 High Street, Willington (q.v.) credit payments only by postal sales.*

EAST SUSSEX

ALFRISTON

David Summerfield Books, 4 Wingrove The Tye, Alfriston, BN26 5TL. Tel: (01323) 870003. E-mail: summerfield1981@aol.com. Est: 1987. Private premises. Appointment necessary. Small stock. Spec: Sport - Cricket. PR: £5–500.

Much Ado Books, ■ 1 Steamer Cottage High Street, Alfriston, BN26 5TY. Prop: Nash Robbins and Cate Olson. Tel: 01323 871222. Fax: 01323 871333. Web: www.muchadobooks.com. E-mail: shop@muchadobooks.com. Est: 2003. Shop open: **M:** 10:00–17:00; **T:** 10:00–17:00; **W:** 10:00–17:00; **Th:** 10:00–17:00; **F:** 10:00–17:00; **S:** 10:00–17:00; **Su:** 11:00–17:00. Spec: Author - Bloomsbury Group, The; Children's; Cookery/Gastronomy; Fiction - General; Food & Drink. CC: MC; V. Mem: PBFA; BA. Notes: *Literary lunches and events run throughout the year. Stock also includes hand-picked new books.*

BATTLE

R.A. Whistler, The Dodo House Caldbec Hill, Battle, TN33 0JR. Prop: Mr Ralfe Whistler. Tel: (01424) 774152. Fax: (01424) 774152. Est: 1992. Private premises. Internet and Postal. Spec: Canadiana; Natural History. PR: £1–100. Notes: *Accepts US and Canadian dollars.*

BEXHILL

Raymond Elgar, 6 Blackfields Avenue, Bexhill, TN39 4JL. Prop: Raymond Elgar. Tel: (01424) 843539. Private premises. Postal Only. Very small stock. Spec: Bindings; Bookbinding; Magic & Conjuring; Music - General; Musical Instruments.

BRIGHTON

Savery Books, ■ 257 Ditchling Road, Brighton, BN1 6JH. Prop: Marianne, James, Sarah & Anne Savery. Tel: 01273 50 30 30. E-mail: saverybooks@aol.com. Est: 1992. Shop open: **W:** 10:00–16:00; **Th:** 10:00–16:00; **F:** 10:00–16:00; **S:** 10:00–16:00. Spec: Art - Theory; Art History; Art Reference; Fiction - General; Fiction - Crime, Detective, Spy, Thrillers; Military; Philosophy; Psychoanalysis.

Brighton Books, ■ 18 Kensington Gardens, Brighton, BN1 4AL. Prop: Paul Carmody & Catherine Clement. Tel: (01273) 693845. Fax: (01273) 693845. Est: 1996. Shop open: **M:** 10:00–18:00; **T:** 10:00–18:00; **W:** 10:00–18:00; **Th:** 10:00–18:00; **F:** 10:00–18:00; **S:** 10:00–18:00. Large stock. Spec: Academic/ Scholarly; Architecture; Art; Biography; Children's; Cinema/Film; Drama; Fiction - General. PR: £1–500. CC: AE; JCB; MC; V; SW.

Colin Page Books, ■ 36 Duke Street, Brighton. Prop: John Loska. Tel: 01273 325954. Est: 1969. Shop open: **M:** 09:30–17:30; **T:** 09:30–17:30; **W:** 09:30–17:30; **Th:** 09:30–17:30; **F:** 09:30–17:30; **S:** 09:30–17:30. CC: AE; D; MC; V. Mem: ABA; BA. VAT No: GB 550 5008 78. Notes: *Attends ABA Olympia and Chelsea Fairs*

Cooks Books, 34 Marine Drive Rottingdean, Brighton, BN2 7HQ. Prop: Tessa McKirdy. Tel: (01273) 302707. Fax: (01273) 301651. E-mail: tessamckirdy@hotmail.com. Est: 1975. Private premises. Appointment necessary. Medium stock. Spec: Cookery/Gastronomy; Food & Drink; Ephemera. PR: £1–500. CC: MC; V. Corresp: French. Mem: E.S. VAT No: GB 509 0878 31.

Turner Donovan Military Books, 12 Southdown Avenue, Brighton, BN1 6EG. Tel: (01273) 566230. E-mail: tom@turnerdonovan.com. Est: 1985. Private premises. Postal Only. Medium stock. Spec: Countries - India; Military; Military History; War - Napoleonic; War - World War II; Ephemera; Prints and Maps. PR: £15–2,500. CC: MC; V. Notes: *Also, soldier's diaries, trench maps, memories and regimental histories.*

Elmo Books, The Lower Floor Workshop Floor 7a Basin Road North, Brighton, BN41 1WA. Prop: Elmo. Tel: 01273 439111. Web: www.stores.ebay.co.uk/elmo-books. E-mail: elmobooks@ btconnect.com. Est: 2003. Warehouse. Internet Only. Contactable. Spec: Sport - General; Sport - Football (Soccer); Sport - Motor Racing. Notes: *Specialists in sports & motoring books.*

EAST SUSSEX

Fisher Nautical, Huntswood House, St. Helena Lane Streat, Hassocks, Brighton, BN6 8SD. Prop: (*) S. & J. Fisher. Tel: (01273) 890273. Fax: (01273) 891439. Web: www.fishernauticalbooks .co.uk. E-mail: fishernautical@seabooks.fsnet.co.uk. Est: 1969. Private premises. Postal Only. Telephone First. Open: **M:** 09:09–16:16; **T:** 09:09–16:15; **W:** 09:09–16:16; **Th:** 09:09–16:16; **F:** 09:09–15:15; **S:** 09:00– 12:00. Very large stock. Spec: Maritime/Nautical; Booksearch. PR: £10–3,000. CC: MC; V. Mem: PBFA.

Invisible Books, Unit 8 15-26 Lincoln Cottage Works Lincoln Cottages, Brighton, BN2 9UJ. Prop: Paul Holman & Bridget Penney. Tel: (01273) 694574. Web: www.invisiblebooks.co.uk. E-mail: orders@invisiblebooks.co.uk. Est: 1994. Storeroom. Internet and Postal. Appointment necessary. Medium stock. Spec: Academic/Scholarly; Counterculture; New Age. PR: £1–1,000. VAT No: GB 825 8052 27.

Kenya Books, 31 Southdown Ave., Brighton, BN1 6EH. Prop: J. McGivney. Tel: (01273) 556029. Web: www.abebooks.com/home/kenyabooks. E-mail: info@kenyabooks.com. Private premises. Internet and Postal. Open: **M:** 09:00–19:00; **W:** 09:00–19:00; **Th:** 09:00–19:00; **F:** 09:00–19:00; **S:** 09:00–19:00. Medium stock. Spec: Academic/Scholarly; Africana; Anthropology; Coffee; Countries - Africa; Countries - East Africa; Countries - France; Countries - Indian Ocean, The. PR: £1–500. Corresp: French; Swahili. Mem: PBFA.

Rainbow Books, ■ 28 Trafalgar Street, Brighton, BN1 4ED. Prop: Kevin Daly. Tel: (01273) 605101. Est: 1998. Shop open: **M:** 10:30–18:00; **T:** 10:30–18:00; **W:** 10:30–18:00; **Th:** 10:30–18:00; **F:** 10:30–18:00; **S:** 10:30–18:00. Very large stock. PR: £1–20.

BRIGHTON

Arslan Books Etc, Flat 1, Surrenden Lodge, Brighton, BN1 6QB. Prop: Mustapha Mersinoglu. Tel: 01273 559702. E-mail: m.mersinoglu@btinternet.com. Est: 2005. Private premises. Internet and postal. Small stock. Spec: Countries - Turkey; Ottoman Empire; Travel - General; Travel - Islamic World; Travel - Middle East. PR: Cheques, Postal Orders and PayPal. Cata: occasionally on Ottoman, Turkey, Travel, Mediterranean, Black Sea. Corresp: Turkish. Notes: *We have an extensive database on books, journals, and rare reports on Turkey, and will provide searches and copies of articles etc., that are not copyrighted. We also deal with maps and ephemera.*

Studio Bookshop, ■ 68 St. James's Street, Brighton, BN2 1PJ. Prop: Paul Brown. Tel: 01273-691253. Web: www.studiobookshop.co.uk. E-mail: studiobookshop@btconnect.com. Est: 1995. Shop open: **M:** 11.00–17:00; **T:** 11.00–17:00; **Th:** 11.00–17.00; **F:** 11.00–17:00; **S:** 11.00–17:00. Spec: Academic/ Scholarly; Antiques; Art; Art Reference; Artists; Auction Catalogues; Catalogues Raisonnes; Countries - Spain. CC: JCB; MC; V; Maestro, Visa Electron. Cata: Glass, Exhibition Catalogues. Corresp: French, Spanish. Notes: *Major specialities are books on Glass and Exhibition Catalogues, books on Spain, Academic and Scholarly books in the humanities.*

Trafalgar Bookshop, ■ 44 Trafalgar Street, Brighton, BN1 4ED. Prop: David Boland. Tel: (01273) 684300. Est: 1979. Shop open: **M:** 10:00–17:15; **T:** 10:00–17:15; **W:** 10:00–17:15; **Th:** 10:00–17:15; **F:** 11:00–17:15; **S:** 10:00–17:15. Medium stock. Spec: Children's; Children's - Illustrated; Cinema/Film; Literature; Mind, Body & Spirit; Philosophy; Psychic; Sport - General. PR: £1–200.

Waxfactor, ■ 24 Trafalgar Street, Brighton, BN1 4EQ. Prop: M. Driver. Tel: (01273) 673744. Est: 1985. Shop open: **M:** 10:00–17:30; **T:** 10:00–17:30; **W:** 10:00–17:30; **Th:** 10:00–17:30; **F:** 10:00–17:30; **S:** 10:00–17:30. Medium stock. Spec: Art; Astrology; Cinema/Film; Esoteric; Fiction - Science Fiction; History - General, Literature; Occult. PR: £1–25 CC: JCB; MC; V; Maestro, Solo. Notes: *Also, records & CDs, DVDs and tapes.*

CROWBOROUGH

Ray Hennessey Bookseller, Panfield House Crowborough Hill, Crowborough, TN6 2HJ. Prop: Ray & Deanna Hennessey. Tel: (01892) 653704. Fax: (0870) 0548776. Web: www.rayhennesseybookseller .co.uk. E-mail: rayhen@books4.demon.co.uk. Est: 1954. Private premises. Internet and Postal. Appointment necessary. Open: **M:** 10:00–17:00; **T:** 10:00–17:00; **W:** 10:00–17:00; **Th:** 10:00–17:00; **F:** 10:00–17:00; **S:** 10:00–17:00. Medium stock. Spec: Africana; Antiquarian; Antiques; Applied Art; Art; Art - British; Art - Technique; Art Deco. PR: £6–1,000. CC: AE; E; JCB; MC; V. Notes: *Showroom at Olinda House, Rotherfield, East Sussex. Open to Public 10-30 to 5-00 Tuesday to Saturday.*

Simply Read Books, Badgers Wood, Fielden Road, Crowborough, TN6 1TP. Prop: W.L. & W.P. Banks. Tel: 01892 664584. Web: www.abenooks.com. E-mail: Orders@simplyreadbooks.co.uk. Est: 1998. Private premises. Internet and Postal. Contactable. Open: **M:** 08:00–24.00; **T:** 08:00–24.00; **W:** 08:00– 24.00; **Th:** 08:00–24.00; **F:** 08:00–24.00; **S:** 09:00–24.00; **Su:** 09:00–24.00. Spec: Crime (True); Famous People - Monroe, Marilyn; Modern First Editions; Travel - General. CC: MC; V; PayPal. Corresp: French. Notes: *Book searches carried out.*

DITCHLING

Kenneth Ball, 7 Mulberry Lane, Ditchling, BN6 8UH. Prop: Kenneth Ball. Tel: 01273 845000. Fax: 01273 844444. E-mail: kennethball@mistral.co.uk. Est: 1947. Storeroom. Appointment necessary. Spec: Commercial Vehicles; Journals; Marque Histories (see also motoring); Motorbikes / motorcycles; Motoring; Steam Engines; Vintage Cars; Ephemera. PR: £5–1,000. Corresp: French.

EAST HOATHLY

Claras Books, 20 High Street, East Hoathly, Nr Lewes, BN8 6EB. Prop: Jane Seabrook. Tel: 01825 840263. E-mail: claras@netway.co.uk. Est: 2000. Private premises. Internet and Postal. CC: MC; V; Maestro. Notes: *Large general stock.*

EASTBOURNE

Camilla's Bookshop, ■ 57 Grove Road, Eastbourne, BN21 4TX. Prop: Camilla Francombe & Stuart Broad. Tel: (01323) 736001. E-mail: camillasbooks@tiscali.co.uk. Est: 1976. Shop open: **M:** 10:00–17:30; **T:** 10:00–17:30; **W:** 10:00–17:30; **Th:** 10:00–17:30; **F:** 10:00–17:30; **S:** 10:00–17:30. Very large stock. Spec: Aeronautics; Animals and Birds; Annuals; Arts, The; Aviation; Bindings; Botany; Children's. PR: £1–300. CC: E; MC; V; Mae, SO. VAT No: GB 583 7350 18. Notes *Closed on Bank Holidays.*

Roderick Dew, 10 Furness Road, Eastbourne, BN21 4EZ. Tel: (01323) 720239. Est: 1975. Private premises. Appointment necessary. Small stock. Spec: Applied Art; Architecture; Bibliography; Fine Art. PR: £5–500. Corresp: French, German.

Alan Gibbard Books, ■ 1 and 2 Calverley Walk, Eastbourne, BN21 4UP. Prop: Alan & Maria Tania Gibbard. Tel: (01323) 734128. Fax: (01323) 734128. Est: 1993. Shop open: **T:** 10:00–17:00; **W:** 10:00–17:00; **Th:** 10:00–17:00; **F:** 10:00–17:00; **S:** 10:00–17:00. Medium stock. Spec: Natural History; Topography - Local; Travel - General. PR: £1–1,000. CC: AE; MC; V. Corresp: Italian, Spanish. Mem: PBFA. VAT No: GB 621 5744 53.

Green Man Books, 14 Bath Road, Eastbourne, BN21 4UA. Prop: Jerry Bird. Tel: (01323) 735364. Web: www.greenman-books.co.uk. E-mail: greenmangallery@lineone.net. Est: 1999. Private premises. Appointment necessary. Spec: Antiquarian; Author - Powys Family, The; Esoteric; Fine & Rare; Folklore; Music - Folk & Irish Folk; Mythology; New Books. PR: £2–200. CC: D; E; JCB; MC; V; Maestro. Switch. Mem: NMTA. Notes: *Also, new books, music, crafts and contemporary arts.*

London & Sussex Antiquarian Books & Print Services, Southwood 15 Dittons Road, Eastbourne, BN21 1DR. Prop: Dr. G.B. Carruthers. Tel: (01323) 730857. Fax: (01323) 737550. E-mail: doctor. johnsons@virgin.net. Est: 1970. Postal Only. Spec: Alternative Medicine; Dogs; Medicine - History of; Prints and Maps. PR: £10–100.

Mellon's Books, ■ The Enterprise Centre 1 Station Parade, Eastbourne, BN21 1BD. Tel: 01323749254. Web: www.mellonsbooks.co.uk. E-mail: mellonsbooks@yahoo.co.uk. Est: 2005. Shop open: **M:** 09:30–17:00; **T:** 10:00–16:00; **W:** 09:30–17:00; **Th:** 09:30–17:00; **F:** 09:30–17:00; **S:** 09:30–17:00. Closed for lunch: 13:00–14:00. Spec: Academic/Scholarly; Author - 20th Century; Children's; Churchilliana; Cinema/Film; Cookery/Gastronomy; Drama; Famous People - Churchill, Sir Winston. CC: AE; MC; V; Maestro/Switch. Corresp: Basic French.

R. & A. Books, 4 Milton Grange, 6 Arundel Road, Eastbourne, BN21 2EL. Prop: Robert Manning and Alan Millard. Tel: (01323) 647690. Web: www.raenterprises.co.uk/. E-mail: robert.manning@ btinternet.com. Est: 2000. Private premises. Internet and Postal. Large stock. Spec: Aboriginal; Academic/Scholarly; Adult; Adventure; Advertising; Aeronautics; Aesthetic Movement; Aesthetics. PR: £1–500. CC: PayPal. Cata: All General Subjects. Notes: *Worldwide orders accepted. Payment in sterling through PayPal. UK cheques accepted.*

Dealers need to update their entry at least once a year.

Visit their page on

www.sheppardsworld.co.uk

FRISTON

Liz Seeber, 16 The Brow, Friston, BN20 0ES. Tel: (01323) 423 777. Web: www.lizseeberbooks.co.uk. E-mail: liz@lizseeber.demon.co.uk. Est: 1994. Private premises. Postal Only. Appointment necessary. Small stock. Spec: Author - David, Elizabeth; Cookery/Gastronomy; Gardening - General; Booksearch. PR: £5–3,000. CC: MC; V. Cata: cookery, food and wine. Corresp: French. VAT No: GB 629 3954 04.

HASTINGS

Anthony Sillem, 9 Tackleway, Old Town, Hastings, TN34 3DE. Prop: Anthony Sillem. Tel: 01424 446602. E-mail: tackletext@btopenworld.com. Est: 1994. Private premises. Appointment necessary. Open: **M:** 09:00–17:30; **T:** 09:00–17:30; **W:** 09:00–17:30; **Th:** 09:00–17:30; **F:** 09:00–17:30; **S:** 09:00–17:30; **Su:** 09:00–17:30; Closed for lunch: 13:00–14:00. Spec: Art - British; First Editions; Literary Travel; Literature; Literature - French. CC: MC; V; Switch. Cata: Literature, Art & Illustrated. Mem: PBFA.

Boulevard Books, ■ Boulevard Book Shop 32 George Street, Hastings, TN34 3EA. Prop: Graham Frost. Tel: 01424436521. Web: www.thehastingstrawler.co.uk. E-mail: hastingsbookshop@yahoo.co.uk. Est: 2004. Shop open: **M:** 10:30–17:30; **T:** 10:30–17:30; **W:** 10:30–17:30; **Th:** 10:30–17:30; **F:** 10:30–17:30; **S:** 10:30–17:30; **Su:** 10:30–17:30; Closed for lunch: 13:00–14:00. CC: Cash or Cheque only. Corresp: French, German, Swedish, Dutch. Notes: *Open seven days a week and we only accept cash or cheques.*

Calendula Books, 3 Amherst Garden, Hastings, TN34 1TU. Prop: Heiko Miles. Tel: (01424) 437591. Web: www.calendulabooks.com. E-mail: heiko@calendulabooks.com. Est: 1987. Private premises. Postal Only. Small stock. Spec: Author - Eliot, T.S.; - Pope, A; Flora & Fauna; Flower Arranging; Gardening - General; Herbalism; Horticulture; Landscape. PR: £5–10,000. CC: MC; V.

Chthonios Books, 7 Tamarisk Steps, Off Rock-a-Nore Road, Hastings, TN34 3DN. Prop: Stephen Ronan. Tel: (01424) 433302. Web: www.esotericism.co.uk/index.htm. E-mail: chthonios@dsl.pipex.com. Est: 1985. Private premises. Internet and Postal. Telephone First. Small stock. Spec: Acupuncture; Alchemy; Author - Crowley, Aleister; Classical Studies; Earth Mysteries; Egyptology; Gnostics / Gnosticism; Hermeticism. PR: £3–300. CC: MC; V; SW. SO. Cata: esotericism, ancient philosophy, ancient religion. Corresp: French. Notes: *Specialists in esotericism, ancient philosophy, ancient religion, occult.*

High Street Book Shop, ■ High Street Book Shop 78 High Street, Hastings, TN34 3EA. Prop: Graham Frost. Tel: 01424200833. E-mail: hastingsbookshop@yahoo.co.uk. Est: 1997. Shop open: **M:** 1030–17:30; **T:** 10:30–17:30; **W:** 10:30–17:30; **Th:** 10:30–17:30; **F:** 10:30–17:30; **S:** 10:30–17:30; **Su:** 10:30–17:30; Closed for lunch: 13:00–14:00. CC: cash or cheque only. Corresp: French, German, Italian, Spanish. Notes: *We are open seven days a week and only accept cash or cheques.*

Hoovey's Books, P.O. Box 27, St. Leonards–on–Sea, Hastings, TN37 6TZ. Prop: (*). Tel: (01424) 753407. Fax: (01424) 753407. Web: www.hooveys.co.uk. E-mail: books@hooveys.com. Est: 1968. Office and/or bookroom. Appointment necessary. Small stock. Spec: Booksearch. VAT No: GB 397 8504 94. Notes: *Catalogue printing, cleaning materials, jacket coverings.*

Howes Bookshop, ■ Trinity Hall Braybrooke Terrace, Hastings, TN34 1HQ. Prop: Miles Bartley. Tel: (01424) 423437. Fax: (01424) 460620. Web: www.howes.co.uk. E-mail: rarebooks@howes.co.uk. Est: 1921. Shop open: **M:** 09:30–17:00; **T:** 09:30–17:00; **W:** 09:30–17:00; **Th:** 09:29–17:00; **F:** 09:30–17:00. Closed for lunch: 13:00–14:00. Large stock. Spec: Antiquarian; Bibliography; Bindings; Classical Studies; History - General; Literature; Theology; Topography - Local. PR: £1–5,000. CC: E; JCB; MC; V. Mem: ABA; PBFA. Notes: *and storeroom Also, attends bookfairs.*

Jill Howell, Badgers Mount, Farley Way, Fairlight, Hastings, TN35 4AS. Prop: Jill Howell. Tel: 01424 815256. Fax: 01622 820 899. E-mail: jillphotobooks@aol.com. Est: 1993. Private premises. Postal Only. Appointment necessary. Spec: Photography. Cata: Photography. Corresp: French.

Robert's Shop, ■ 68 High Street Old Town, Hastings, TN34 3EW. Prop: Robert M. Mucci. Tel: (01424) 445340. Est: 1989. Shop open: **M:** 11:00–18:00; **T:** 11:00–18:00; **W:** 11:00–18:00; **Th:** 11:00–18:00; **F:** 11:00–18:00; **S:** 11:00–18:00; **Su:** 11:00–18:00. Very small stock. Spec: Collectables; Ephemera; Prints and Maps. PR: £1–10.

Underwater Books, 104d High Street, Hastings, TN24 3ES. Prop: J.A. Barak. Tel: (01424) 435905. Web: www.underwater-books.co.uk. E-mail: divingbooks@underwater-books.co.uk. Est: 1980. Office and/or bookroom. Internet and Postal. Appointment necessary. Very small stock. Spec: Sport - Diving/Sub-Aqua. PR: £10–150. CC: PayPal. Notes: *Books cover all aspects of diving.*

HEATHFIELD

Botting & Berry, ■ 41 High Street, Heathfield, TN21 8HU. Prop: John Botting and Dave Berry Tel: (01435) 868555. Est: 2001. Shop open. **M:** 10:00–17:00; **I:** 10:00–17:00; **W:** 10:00–17:00; **Th:** 10:00–17:00; **F:** 10:00–17:00; **S:** 10:00–17:00. Small stock. PR: £1–500. CC: MC; V. Notes: *Fairs: Royal National, Bloomsbury, London.*

HOVE

Dinnages Transport/Picture Publishing, Unit 10, Lion Mews, Hove, BN3 5RA. Prop: Mr. G. & Mrs. C. Dinnage. Fax: (0871) 433 8096. Web: www.Transport-Postcards.co.uk. E-mail: mail@dinnages .org.uk. Est: 1989. Storeroom. Internet and Postal. Appointment necessary. Shop At: Internet sales only via PO Box 2210 Brighton BN1 9WA. Otherwise visitors by prior arrangement. Very small stock. Spec: Buses/Trams; History - Local; Publishers - General; Publishers - Harding, Peter A; Publishers - Southdown Club; Railways; Transport; Collectables. PR: £1–25. CC: PayPal via internet. Cata: Some books/DVD & photo lists. Corresp: n/a. Mem: Also at: Internet sales only via PO Box 2210 Brighton BN1 9WA. Otherwise visitors by prior arrangement. Notes: *Regular stall Maidstone Collectors Fair 5x pa + others Publisher of nostalgic transport & local photographs/postcards (+ book distributor) - and publisher of 'Works Driver'.*

J.F. Holleyman, 3 Portland Avenue, Hove, BN3 5NP. Tel: (01273) 410915. Private premises. Postal Only. Appointment necessary. Small stock. Spec: Photography.

Whitehall Books, 3 Leighton Road, Hove, BN3 7AD. Prop: Peter Batten. Tel: (01273) 735252. Web: www.whitehallbooks.co.uk. E-mail: peterbatten@whitehallbooks.co.uk. Est: 1991. Private premises. Internet and Postal. Appointment necessary. Very small stock. Spec: Art; Crime (True); Criminology; Illustrated - General; Literary Criticism; Literature. PR: £1–100. Corresp: French, Russian. Notes: *Translation. Literary detective work and general literary information.*

LEWES

Richard Beaton, 24 Highdown Road, Lewes, BN7 1QD. Prop: Dr. Richard Beaton. Tel: (01273) 474147. Fax: (01273) 474147. Web: www.victorian-novels.co.uk. E-mail: richard@victorian-novels.co.uk. Est: 1996. Private premises. Internet and Postal. Appointment necessary. Small stock. Spec: Antiquarian; Fiction - General; Literature - Victorian; Publishers - Tauchnitz; Victorian multi-deckers; Victoriana. PR: £5–1,000. CC: MC; V; Maestro, also PayPal Cata: C19th & early C20th fiction. Corresp: French.

John Beck, 29 Mill Road, Lewes, BN7 2RU. Tel: (01273) 477555. Fax: (01273) 480339. Est: 1982. Office and/or bookroom. Postal Only. Appointment necessary. Open: **M:** 10:00–16:00; **T:** 10:00–16:00; **W:** 10:00–16:00; **Th:** 10:00–16:00; **F:** 10:00–16:00; **S:** 10:00–16:00; **Su:** 10:00–16:00. Small stock. Spec: Author - Blyton, Enid; Children's; Comic Books & Annuals; Comics; First Editions; Illustrated - General; Juvenile; Ephemera. PR: £1–1,000. Notes: *and market stall. Also at: The Boxroom at the Needlemarket, West Street, Lewes. Stocks 'Rupert' titles.*

Bow Windows Book Shop, ■ 175 High Street, Lewes, BN7 1YE. Prop: Alan & Jennifer Shelley. Tel: (01273) 480780. Fax: (01273) 486686. Web: www.bowwindows.com. E-mail: rarebooks@ bowwindows.com. Est: 1964. Shop open: **M:** 09:30–17:00; **T:** 09:30–17:00; **W:** 09:30–17:00; **Th:** 09:30–17:00; **F:** 09:30–17:00; **S:** 09:30–17:00. Medium stock Spec: Antiquarian; Artists, Author - Bloomsbury Group, 1he; - Rackham, Arthur; - Sackville-West, Vita; - Woolf, Virginia; Children's - Illustrated; Countries - China. PR: £1–5,000. CC: AE; MC; V. Cata: General. Corresp: German. Mem: ABA; PBFA; ILAB. VAT No: GB 370 1163 88.

Brimstones, 7f The Holdings Uckfield Road, Ringmer, Lewes, BN8 5RY. Prop: Geoff Kinderman. Tel: (01273) 814361. Web: www.brimstones.co.uk. E-mail: brimstones2@btconnect.com. Est: 1990. Storeroom. Postal Only. Appointment necessary. Open: **M:** 09:00–16:00; **T:** 09:00–16:00; **W:** 09:00–16:00; **Th:** 09:00–16:00; **F:** 09:00–16:00. Very large stock. Spec: Biography; History - General; International Affairs; Memoirs; Philosophy; Political History; Politics; Psychology/Psychiatry. PR: £1–500. CC: AE; MC; V; Mae. VAT No: GB 550 1571 71.

A. & Y. Cumming Limited, ■ 84 High Street, Lewes, BN7 1XN. Prop: A.J. Cumming. Tel: (01273) 472319. Fax: (01273) 486364. E-mail: a.y.cumming@ukgateway.net. Est: 1976. Shop open: **M:** 10:00–17:00; **T:** 10:00–17:00; **W:** 10:00–17:00; **Th:** 10:00–17:00; **F:** 10:00–17:00; **S:** 10:00–17:30. Very large stock. Spec: Art; Atlases; Bindings; Illustrated - General; Literature; Natural History; Topography - General; Travel - General. CC: AE; MC; V. Cata: Library sets, leather bindings, atlases. Mem: ABA; PBFA. VAT No: GB 412 4098 80. Notes: *Books bought, libraries, small collections or individual vloumes. Buyer will call anywhere in the UK.*

EAST SUSSEX

The Fifteenth Century Bookshop, ■ The Fifteenth Century House 99/100 High Street, Lewes, BN7 1XH. Prop: Mrs S.J. Mirabaud. Tel: 01273 474160. Web: www.oldenyoungbooks.co.uk. E-mail: sj.mirabaud@tesco.net. Est: 1936. Shop open: **M:** 10:00–1730; **T:** 10:00–1730; **W:** 10:00–1730; **Th:** 10:00–1730; **F:** 10:00–1730; **S:** 10:00–1730; **Su:** 11.00–16.00. Spec: Annuals; Arthurian; Author - 19th Century; - 20th Century; - Aesop; - Ahlberg, Janet & Allan; - Aldin, Cecil; - Ardizzone, Edward. CC: AE; MC; V. Corresp: French. Mem: PBFA. Notes: *Postal and Internet enquiries and sales welcome.*

Derek Wise, Berewood House, Barcombe, Lewes, BN8 5TW. Tel: (01273) 400559. Fax: (01273) 400559. E-mail: derekwise@pavilion.co.uk. Est: 1986. Private premises. Internet and Postal. Appointment necessary. Small stock. Spec: Author - Byron, Lord; Education & School; Literature; Maritime/ Nautical; Military; Military History; Natural History; Naval. PR: £1–1,500. Corresp: French. Mem: PBFA.

NEWHAVEN

32 Seconds, ■ 32 High Street, Newhaven, BN9 9PD. Prop: G.G.J. Haynes. Tel: 01273 611350. Est: 2000. Shop open: **T:** 10:00–16:00; **W:** 10:00–16:00; **Th:** 10:00–16:00; **F:** 10:00–16:00; **S:** 10:00–16:00. Spec: Philately; Ephemera; Prints and Maps.

PORTSLADE

Peter Scott, 14 Vale Road, Portslade, BN41 1GF. Prop: Peter Scott. Tel: (01273) 410576. Web: www. scottbooks.freeuk.com. E-mail: peter.scott45@btopenworld.com. Est: 1986. Private premises. Internet and Postal. Contactable. Small stock. Spec: Academic/Scholarly; Archaeology; Art; Books about Books; General Stock; History - General; Literature; Religion - General. PR: £1–200.

ROBERTSBRIDGE

Spearman Books, ■ The Old Saddlery Bookshop 56 High Street, Robertsbridge, TN32 5AP. Prop: John & Janet Brooman. Tel: (01580) 880631. Fax: (01580) 880631. E-mail: saddlerybooks@aol.com. Est: 1970. Shop open: **M:** 10:00–17:00; **T:** 10:00–17:00; **W:** ; **Th:** 10:00–17:00; **F:** 10:00–17:00; **S:** 10:00– 17:00. Closed for lunch: 13:00–14:15. Medium stock. Spec: Travel - General. PR: £1–1,000. Corresp: French.

ROTHERFIELD

Kennedy & Farley, 2 Brook Cottages New Road, Rotherfield, TN6 3JT. Prop: Helen Kennedy & Fran Farley. Tel: (01892) 853141. E-mail: kennedyandfarley@care4free.net. Est: 1987. Private premises. Internet and Postal. Telephone First. Small stock. Spec: Author - Francis, Dick; - Huxley, Aldous; Horses; Modern First Editions; Sport - Horse Racing (inc. Riding/Breeding/Equestrian); Sport - Hunting. PR: £4–1,000. CC: PayPal. Corresp: French. Mem: PBFA. Notes: *Current catalogue on UKBookWorld.com. Only a portion of our stock is catalogued so far, so please don't hesitate to contact us with your enquiries. 01892 853141 or kennedyandfarley@care4free.net.*

RYE

The Meads Book Service, ■ 4 & 5 Lion Street, Rye, TN31 7LB. Prop: Clive Ogden. Tel: (01797) 227057. E-mail: meadsbookservice@freenet.co.uk. Est: 1988. Shop open: **M:** 10:15–17:30; **T:** 10:15–17:30; **W:** 10:15–17:30; **Th:** 10.15–17.30; **F:** 10:15 17:30; **S·** 10·15–17:30; **Su:** 10:15–17:30. Small stock. Spec: Antiquarian; Author - Benson, A.C.; Author - Benson, E.F.; - Benson, R.H.; - Madox Ford, Ford; - Thorndike, Russell; - Wharton, Edith; Biography. PR: £1–200. Mem: PBFA. Notes: *Also, a booksearch service.*

Rye Old Books, ■ Rye Old Books 7 Lion Street, Rye, TN31 7LB. Prop: Ms Aoife Coleman. Tel: 01797 225410. Web: www.ukbookworld.com/members/ryeoldbooks. E-mail: ryeoldbooks@aol.com. Est: 1993. Shop open: **M:** 10:30–18:00; **T:** 10:30–18:00; **W:** 10:30–18:00; **Th:** 10:30–18:00; **F:** 10:30–18:00; **S:** 10:30–18:00; **Su:** 14:00–17:00. Spec: Antiquarian; Author - Austen, Jane; - Clare, John; - Dulac, Edmund; - Eliot, G.; - Rackham, Arthur; - Robinson, Heath W.; Children's. CC: AE; E; MC; V. Cata: Childrens,Illustrated Dulac Pogany Rackham,. Notes: *For Sunday opening in winter & if calling in January, phone to confirm.*

SALTDEAN

Ruth Kidson, 90 Lustrells Crescent, Saltdean, BN2 8FL. Prop: Mrs. G.R. Kidson. Tel: (01273) 307787. Web: www.ruthkidson.co.uk. E-mail: books@ruthkidson.co.uk. Est: 1992. Private premises. Internet and Postal. Appointment necessary. Small stock. PR: £5–800. CC: MC; V; Delta, Mae. Mem: ABA; Rare Books Society. VAT No: GB 777 7852 58.

N1 Books, 213 Marine Drive, Saltdean, BN2 8DA. Prop: Michael Sassen. Tel: 01273 301690. E-mail: michael@dogland.demon.co.uk. Est: 2001. Private premises. Internet and Postal. Telephone First. Open: **M:** 11:00–23:30; **T:** 11:00–23:30; **W:** 11:00–23:30; **Th:** 11:00–23:30; **F.** 11.00–23:30; **S:** 11:00–23:30. Spec: Adult; Aeronautics; Antiquarian; Antiquities; Applied Art; Archaeology; Arms & Armour; Army, The. Cata: History, Illustrated, Bindings, Arts, Oddities.

ST. LEONARD'S-ON-SEA

The Book Jungle, ■ 24 North Street, St. Leonard's–on–Sea, TN38 0EX. Prop: (*) Michael Gowen. Tel: (01424) 421187. Web: www.thebookjungle.co.uk. E-mail: mrgowen@yahoo.co.uk. Est: 1991. Shop. Internet and Postal. Open: **T:** 10:00–16:00; **Th:** 10:00–16:00; **F:** 10:00–16:00; **S:** 10:00–16:00. Large stock. PR: £1–20.

Bruce Holdsworth Books, Vale House, 9 Eversley Road, St. Leonard's-on-Sea, TN37 6QD. Prop: Bruce Holdsworth. Tel: 01424 446400. Web: www.bruceholdsworthbooks.com. E-mail: Bruce@ bruceholdsworthbooks.com. Est: 1994. Private premises. Internet and Postal. Appointment necessary. Open: **M:** 09:00–14:30; **T:** 09:00–14:30; **W:** 09:00–14:30; **Th:** 09:00–14:30; **F:** 09:00–14:30. Spec: Applied Art; Art; Art - Technique; Art - Theory; Art History; Art Reference; Artists; Arts & Crafts Era. CC: AE; E; JCB; MC, V. Cata: Art and Design and related subjects. Mem: PBFA. VAT No: GB 686 9604 74. Notes: *Stock emphasis is on British art.*

Gerald Lee Maritime Books, PO Box 7, St. Leonard's-on-Sea, TN38 8WX. Prop: Gerald Lee. Tel: 02424 853006. Web: www.leemaritimebooks.com. E-mail: enquiries@leemaritimebooks.com. Est: 1990. Private premises. Postal Only. Contactable. Open: **M:** 09:00–17:30; **T:** 09:00–17:30; **W:** 09:00–17:30; **Th:** 09:00–17:30; **F:** 09:00–17:30; **S:** 09:00–17:30; **Su:** 09:00–17:30; Closed for lunch: 13:00–14:00. Spec: Maritime/Nautical; Maritime/Nautical - History; Maritime/Nautical - Log Books; Naval; Navy, The; Ocean Liners. CC: JCB; MC; V. Cata: naval history -maritime; yachting and boating. VAT No: GB 690.48987.

John Gorton Booksearch, 22 Charles Road, St. Leonard's-on-Sea, TN38 0QH. Prop: John Gorton. Tel: (0779) 1549 745. Est: 1983. Private premises. Appointment necessary. Small stock. Spec: Art Reference; Fiction - Crime, Detective, Spy, Thrillers; Mathematics; Philosophy. PR: £1–200. Cata: on specialities.

Raymond Kilgarriff, 15 Maze Hill, St. Leonard's-on-Sea, TN38 0HN. Tel: (01424) 426146. Web: www.ilab.org. E-mail: rmkilgarriff@btinternet.com. Est: 1947. Private premises. Internet and Postal. Appointment necessary. Very small stock. Spec: Antiquarian; Fine & Rare; History - General; Literature. PR: £100–2,000. CC: MC; V. Mem: ABA; ILAB. VAT No. GB 794 2047 15.

TICEHURST

Piccadilly Rare Books, ■ Church Street, Ticehurst, TN5 7AA. Prop: Paul P.B. Minet, Robert Greenhalgh. Tel: 01580 201221. Fax: 01580 200957. Web: www.picrare.com. E-mail: minet@ btopenworld.com. Est: 1972. Shop open: **M:** 10:00–17:00; **T:** 10:00–17:00; **W:** 10:00–17:00; **Th:** 10:00–17:00; **F:** 10:00–17:00; **S:** 10:00–17:00. Large stock. Spec: Diaries; Royalty - General; Royalty - European. PR: £5–2,000. CC: AE; MC; V. Corresp: French, Greek, Spanish. Mem: ABA; PBFA. VAT No: GB 583 9618 89. Notes: *Combined coffee shop and large general bookshop. Also owns Baggins Book Bazaar in Rochester (q.v.).*

EAST YORKSHIRE

BEVERLEY

Beverley Old Bookshop, ■ 2 Dyer Lane, Beverley, HU17 8AE. Prop: Colin Tatman. Tel: (01482) 880611. Est: 1993. Shop open: **M:** 10:00–17:00; **T:** 10:00–17:00; **W:** 10:00–17:00; **Th:** 10:00–17:00; **F:** 10:00–17:00; **S:** 10:00–17:00. Medium stock. Spec: Bookbinding; Children's; History - Local; Illustrated - General. PR: £1–200. Notes: *Also, book restoration.*

Countryman Books, 42 St Matthews Court, Beverley, HU17 8JH. Prop: Christine Swift. Tel: (01482) 869710. Fax: (01482) 869710. Web: www.countryman.co.uk. E-mail: books@countryman.co.uk. Private premises. Internet and Postal. Telephone First. Open: **M:** 09:00–17:00; **T:** 09:00–17:00; **W:** 09:00–17:00; **Th:** 09:00–17:00; **F:** 09:00–17:00; **S:** 09:00–17:00; **Su:** 09:00–17:00. Spec: Author - Aldin, Cecil; Sport - Big Game Hunting; Sport - Falconry; Sport - Hunting; Sport - Polo; Sport - Shooting. PR: £5–150. CC: MC; V; Switch. Mem: PBFA.

Eastgate Bookshop, ■ 11 Eastgate, Beverley, HU17 0DR. Prop: Barry Roper. Tel: (01482) 868579. E-mail: barry@eastgatebooks.karoo.co.uk. Est: 1983. Shop open: **W:** 10:00–17:00; **Th:** 10:00–17:00; **F:** 10:00–17:00; **S:** 10:00–16:30. Large stock. Spec: Aircraft; Archaeology; Army, The; Art; Aviation; Books about Books; Calligraphy; Countries - British North Borneo. PR: £1–500. CC: JCB; MC; V; Switch. Notes: *Open Monday and Tuesday by appointment only.*

Peter Riddell, Hall Cottage Main St., Cherry Burton, Beverley, HU17 7RF. Tel: (01964) 551453. E-mail: bkscherryb@aol.com. Est: 1989. Private premises. Internet and Postal. Appointment necessary. Very small stock. Spec: Alpinism/Mountaineering; Countries - Central Asia; Countries - Polar. PR: £1–250.

Sarawak Books, ■ 11 East Close Molescroft, Beverley, HU17 7JN. Prop: Barry Roper. Tel: (01482) 868579. E-mail: eastgatebooks@eastgatebooks.caroo.co.uk. Est: 1965. Shop open: **W:** 10:00–17:00; **Th:** 10:00–17:00; **F:** 10:00–17:00; **S:** 10:00–17:00. Spec: Comedy; Countries - British North Borneo; Countries - Sarawak. CC: D; E; JCB; MC; V. Cata: on specialised subjects.

BRIDLINGTON

Family-Favourites, 51 51 First Ave, Bridlington, YO15 2JR. Prop: Shirley Jackson. Tel: 01262 6606061. Web: www.http://ukbookworld.com/members/famfav. E-mail: shirleyjackson1@talktalk.net. Est: 1989. Private premises. Postal Only. Contactable. Spec: Autobiography; Aviation; Biography; Bookbinding; Books about Books; First Editions; Large Print Books.

J.L. Book Exchange, ■ 72 Wilderthorpe Road, Bridlington, YO15 3BQ. Prop: John Ledraw. Tel: (01262) 601285. Est: 1971. Shop open in Summer: **M:** 08:30–18:00; **T:** 08:30–18:00; **W:** 08:30–18:00; **Th:** 08:30–18:00; **F:** 08:30–18:00; **S:** 08:30–18:00; **Su:** 08:30–18:00. Medium stock. PR: £1–80. Notes: *Winter opening: Mon-Sat 09.30–17.30.*

DRIFFIELD

Solaris Books, Flat 4, 13 Lockwood St., Driffield, YO25 6RU. Prop: Jim Goddard. Tel: (01377) 272022. Web: www.solaris-books.co.uk/store. E-mail: jim@solaris-books.co.uk. Private premises. Internet and Postal. Telephone First. Medium stock. Spec: Fiction - Fantasy, Horror; Fiction - Science Fiction; History - Napoleonic; Military History; Modern First Editions; Photography; Booksearch. PR: £2–1,200. CC: PayPal. Cata: sf, modern firsts.

FLAMBOROUGH

Resurgam Books, ■ The Manor House, Flamborough, Bridlington, York, YO15 1PD. Prop: Geoffrey Miller. Tel: (01262) 850943. Fax: (01262) 850943. Web: www.resurgambooks.co.uk. E-mail: gm@resurgambooks.co.uk. Est: 1998. Internet and Postal. Shop open: **M:** 09:00–17:00; **T:** 09:00–17:00; **W:** 09:00–17:00; **Th:** 09:00–17:00; **F:** 09:00–17:00; **S:** 09:00–17:00; **Su:** 10:00–16:00. Very small stock. PR: £1–400. CC: E; JCB; MC; V.

GREAT DRIFFIELD

The Driffield Bookshop, ■ 21 Middle Street North, Great Driffield, YO25 6SW. Prop: G.R. Stevens. Tel: (01377) 254210. Est: 1981. Shop open: **M:** 10:00–17:30; **T:** 10:00–17:30; **W:** 10:00–17:30; **Th:** 10:00–17:30; **F:** 10:00–17:30; **S:** 10:00–17:30. Medium stock. Spec: Fiction - Science Fiction; History - General; Literature; Military History; Modern First Editions; Travel - General. PR: £1–150. Cata: infrequent on collections.

EAST YORKSHIRE

HULL

Bowie Books & Collectables, 19 Northolt Close, Hull, HU8 0PP. Prop: James Bowie. Tel: (01482) 374609. Web: www.bowiebooks.com. E-mail: jamesbowie@bowiebooks.com. Est: 2003. Private premises. Internet and Postal. Appointment necessary. Open: **M:** 09:00–18:00; **T:** 09:00–18:00; **W:** 09:00–18:00; **Th:** 09:00–18:00; **F:** 09:00–18:00; **S:** 09:00–15:00. Small stock. Spec: Antiquarian; Fiction - General; First Editions; Literature; Modern First Editions; Religion - General; Collectables. PR: £2–150.

Harry Holmes Books, 85 Park Avenue, Hull, HU5 3EP. Prop: H.H. & P.A. Purkis. Tel: (01482) 443220. Est: 1989. Private premises. Appointment necessary. Small stock. Spec: Alpinism/Mountaineering; Biography; Countries - Scotland; Literature; Religion - Christian; Spiritualism; Topography - Local; Travel - Polar. PR: £1–100. Corresp: French and German. Notes: *Books on literary biography are also stocked.*

Hullbooks Ltd, ■ 165 Newland Avenue, Hull, HU5 2EP. Prop: Ian & Karren Barfield. Tel: 01482 444677. Web: www.hullbooks.com. E-mail: hullbooks@yahoo.co.uk. Est: 1991. Shop open: **M:** 10:00–17:00; **T:** 10:00–17:00; **W:** 10:00–17:00; **Th:** 10:00–17:00; **F:** 10:00–17:00; **S:** 10:00–17:00. Large stock. Spec: Academic/Scholarly; Authors - Local; Criminology; Education & School; Fisheries; History - General; History - 19th Century; History - 20th Century. PR: £2–200. CC: E; JCB; MC; V. Notes: *We have a large general stock with unusually high turnover. We are always looking for large collections of academic and specialist books.*

Colin Martin - Bookseller, 3 Village Road Garden Village, Hull, HU8 8QP. Prop: Colin and Jane Martin, L.L.B., B.A. Tel: (01482) 585836. Web: www.colinmartinbooks.com. E-mail: enquiries@ colinmartinbooks.com. Est: 1991. Storeroom. Internet and Postal. Appointment necessary. Open: **M:** 10:00–16:00; **T:** 10:00–16:00; **W:** 10:00–16:00; **Th:** 10:00–16:00; **F:** 10:00–16:00. Very large stock. Spec: Applied Art; Architecture; Art; Art History; Art Reference; Artists; Arts, The; Design. PR: £3– 4,000. CC: AE; D; JCB; MC; V; SW, SO. Corresp: French, German, Italian. VAT No: GB 780 4607 24.

KIRKELLA

East Riding Books, 13 Westland Road, Kirkella, HU10 7PH. Prop: Gill Carlile. Tel: (01482) 650674. Web: www.eastridingbooks.co.uk. E-mail: info@eastridingbooks.co.uk. Est: 1996. Private premises. Internet and Postal. Small stock. Spec: Music - General; Music - Classical; Music - Composers; Music - Jazz & Blues; Music - Musicians; Music - Opera; Music - Theory; Musical Instruments. PR: £1–500. CC: JCB; MC; V. Mem: PBFA; Ibooknet. VAT No: GB 747 0534 31 Notes: *Books on all aspects of Classical Music, a very small stock of scores.*

MILLINGTON

Quest Books, Harmer Hill, Millington, York, YO42 1TX. Prop: Dr. Peter Burridge. Tel: (01759) 304735. Fax: (01759) 306820. E-mail: QuestByz@aol.com. Est: 1984. Private premises. Postal Only. Appointment necessary. Very small stock. Spec: Academic/Scholarly; Archaeology; Byzantium; Classical Studies; Countries - Arabia; Countries - Asia Minor; Countries - Balkans, The; Countries - Cyprus. PR: £5–1,000. CC: JCB; MC; V. Cata: Byzantines, Near & Middle East, Early Travellers. Mem: PBFA.

SWANLAND

Cygnet Books, 86 Main Street, Swanland, HU14 3QR. Prop: Jackie Kitchen. Tel: 01482 633282. Web: www.cygnetbooks.co.uk. E-mail: jackie@cygnet.karoo.co.uk. Est: 1995. Private premises. Internet and Postal. Appointment necessary. Open: **M:** 09:00–17:30; **T:** 09:00–17:30; **W:** 09:00–17:30; **Th:** 09:00–17:30; **F:** 09:00–17:30; **S:** 09:00–13:00. Closed for lunch: 13:00–14:00. Spec: Author - Blyton, Enid; - Ransome, Arthur; - Read, Miss; Children's; Children's - Early Titles; Children's - Illustrated; Christmas; Comic Books & Annuals. CC: PayPal and cheques. Cata: Children's out of Print Books. Notes: *Booksearch for hard to find titles.*

WINESTEAD

Alex Alec–Smith Books, The Old Rectory, Winestead, Hull, HU12 0NN. Prop: Alex Alec-Smith. Tel: (01964) 630548. Fax: (01964) 631160. Web: www.alexalec-smithbooks.co.uk. E-mail: alex@ aasbooks.demon.co.uk. Est: 1985. Private premises. Appointment necessary. Small stock. Spec: Academic/Scholarly; Agriculture; Antiquarian; Author - Byron, Lord; - Coleridge, Samuel T.; - Keats, John; - Marvell, Andrew; - Shelley, Percy B. PR: £5–3,000. CC: MC; V. Cata: Byron & The Romantics, Slavery, Reference, E York. Mem: ABA; PBFA; ILAB. VAT No: GB 433 6879 22.

ESSEX

BILLERICAY

Engaging Gear Ltd., Lark Rise 14 Linkdale, Billericay, CM12 9QW. Prop: D.E. Twitchett. Tel: (01277) 624913. Est: 1965. Private premises. Postal Only. Appointment necessary. Very small stock. Spec: Author - Moore, John; Horology; Sport - Cycling. PR: £5–500. Notes: *Stock includes titles on cycling history and travel.*

BIRCH

John Cowley, Auto–in–Print, Mill Lodge Mill Lane, Birch, Colchester, CO2 0NG. Tel: (01206) 331052. Web: www.autoinprint.com. E-mail: cowley@autoinprint.freeserve.co.uk. Est: 1975. Private premises. Internet and Postal. Appointment necessary. Very large stock. Spec: Automobilia/ Automotive; Motoring; Booksearch; Ephemera.

BRAINTREE

Lawful Occasions, 68 High Garrett, Braintree, CM7 5NT. Prop: M.R. Stallion. Tel: (01376) 551819. Fax: (01376) 326073. Web: www.lawfuloccasions.co.uk. E-mail: stallion@supanet.com. Est: 1997. Private premises. Internet and Postal. Appointment necessary. Very small stock. Spec: Crime (True); Criminology; Police Force Histories; Science - Forensic; Booksearch. PR: £1–100. Cata: Police history inc forces, officers' memoirs and. Corresp: French. Notes: *Stock and booksearch on police history only. Credit/debit cards accepted via PayPal. Publisher of bibliographies on police history.*

BRENTWOOD

Book End, ■ 36–38 Kings Road, Brentwood, CM14 4DW. Prop: G.E. & M.K. Smith. Est: 1980. Shop open: **M:** 10:00–17:30; **T:** 10:00–17:30; **W:** 10:00–17:30; **Th:** 10:00–13:00; **F:** 10:00–17:30; **S:** 10:00– 17:00. Medium stock. PR: £1–100.

CHELMSFORD

Christopher Heppa, 48 Pentland Avenue, Chelmsford, CM1 4AZ. Prop: Christopher Heppa. Tel: (01245) 267679. E-mail: christopher@heppa4288.fsnet.co.uk. Est: 1982. Private premises. Internet and Postal. Appointment necessary. Medium stock. Spec: - Bates, H.E.; - Blyton, Enid; - Buchan, John; - Cornwell, Bernard; - Crofts, Freeman Wills; - Farnol, Jeffery; - Forester, C.S.; - Orwell, George. PR: £1–3,000. Cata: crime fiction; H.E. Bates; modern 1sts; childrens. Corresp: Spanish. Mem: PBFA.

CLACTON-ON-SEA

VOL:II, ■ Out of Print books 14B St. John Road, Clacton-on-Sea, CO15 4BP. Prop: Andy Durrant. Tel: 01255 470448. Web: www.bookwormshop.com. E-mail: question@bookwormshop.com. Est: 2005. Shop. Open: **M:** 09:00–17:30; **T:** 09:00–17:30; **W:** 09:00–17:30; **Th:** 09:00–17:30; **F:** 09:00–17:30; **S:** 09:00–17:30. Spec: Fiction - General. CC: AE; E; JCB; MC; V; Solo, Electron, Switch, Maestro. Notes: *Part of the 'Bookworm' Group.*

COLCHESTER

Barcombe Services, 43 Church Lane, Colchester, CO3 4AE. Prop: Dr. Stephen M Williams. Tel: (01206) 510461. Web: www.homepage.ntlworld.com/steve.williams7/book_menu. E-mail: steve.williams7@ ntlworld.com. Est: 2004. Private premises. Internet and Postal. Appointment necessary. Very small stock. Spec: Academic/Scholarly; Biography; Biology - General; Business Studies; Chemistry; Chess; Communication; Computing. PR: £1–20. Corresp: French, German. Notes: *I was a university teacher for a good number of years and the stock reflects that. I offer discounts for multiple purchases and also for particular books will be ready to negotiate a lower price.*

Available from Richard Joseph Publishers Ltd

BOOKDEALING FOR PROFIT by Paul Minet

Quarto H/b £10.00 144pp

ESSEX

Castle Bookshop, ■ 40 Osborne St., Colchester, CO2 7DB. Prop: J.R. Green. Tel: (01206) 577520. Fax: (01206) 577520. E-mail: castle40@gotadsl.co.uk. Est: 1947. Shop open: **M:** 09:00–17:00; **T:** 09:00–17:00; **W:** 09:00–17:00; **Th:** 09:00–17:00; **F:** 09:00–17:00; **S.** 09.00–17.00. Very large stock. Spec: Archaeology; Aviation; First Editions; History - Local; Military History; Modern First Editions; Topography - General; Topography - Local. PR: £1–1,500. CC: MC; V; ask about others. Mem: PBFA. VAT No: GB 360 3502 89. Notes: *Over 40,000 books in stock.*

Farringdon Books, Shrubland House 43 Mile End Road, Colchester, CO4 5BU. Prop: Alan Austin. Tel: (01206) 855 771. E-mail: alan@farringdon-books.demon.co.uk. Est: 1972. Private premises. Postal Only. Medium stock. Spec: Fiction - Crime, Detective, Spy, Thrillers; Fiction - Fantasy, Horror; Fiction - Science Fiction. PR: £1–200.

GfB: the Colchester Bookshop, ■ 92 East Hill, Colchester, CO1 2QN. Prop: Pauline & Simon Taylor. Tel: (01206) 563138. Web: www.gfb.uk.net. E-mail: books@gfb.uk.net. Est: 1983. Shop open: **M:** 10:00–17:30; **T:** 10:00–17:30; **W:** 10:00–17:30; **Th:** 10:00–17:30; **F:** 10:00–17:30; **S:** 10:00–17:30. Very large stock. Spec: Academic/Scholarly; Archaeology; Architecture; Art; Art Reference; Gardening - General; History - Ancient; History - British. PR: £2–200. Corresp: French. VAT No: GB 759 8699 37.

Quentin Books Ltd, 38 High Street Wivenhoe, Colchester, CO7 9BE. Prop: Mr. Paterson. Tel: (01206) 825433. Fax: (01206) 822990. E-mail: quentin_books@lineone.net. Est. 1990. Storeroom. Appointment necessary. Medium stock. Spec: Bibliography; Bindings; Biography; Books about Books; History - General; History - American; Maritime/Nautical; Natural History. PR: £1–1,000. Corresp: French, German. Notes: *Local topography majors on Essex.*

DAGENHAM

John Thorne, 19 Downing Road, Dagenham, RM9 6NR. Tel: (020) 8592-0259. Web: www.liquidliterature.co.uk. E-mail: liquidliterature@aol.com. Est: 1985. Private premises. Internet and Postal. Very small stock. Spec: Beer; Brewing; Burgundy; Public Houses; Viticulture; Whisky; Wine. PR: £1–300. CC: PayPal. Cata: Wines, Beers, Spirits and related subjects.

GRAYS

Phototitles.com, 50 Falcon Avenue, Grays, RM17 6SD. Prop: Steve Taylor. Tel: 07802 887319. Web: www.phototitles.com. E-mail: books@phototitles.com. Est: 2005. Mail Order Only. Internet Only. Contactable. Open: **M:** 08:00 20:00; **T:** 08:00 20:00; **W:** 08:00 20:00; **Th:** 08:00 20:00; **F:** 08:00–20:00; **S:** 08:00–20:00; **Su:** 08:00–20:00; Closed for lunch: 13:30–14:00. Spec: Photography. CC: E; JCB; MC; V. Cata: Photography. VAT No: GB 863 4039 23. Notes: *Specialising in Signed, Rare, and Out of Print Photographic Books.*

GREAT DUNMOW

Clive Smith, Brick House North Street, Great Dunmow, CM6 1BA. Tel: (01371) 873171. Fax: (01371) 873171. E-mail: clivesmith@route56.co.uk. Est: 1975. Private premises. Appointment necessary. Small stock. Spec: Antiquarian; Cookery/Gastronomy; Medicine; Military; Natural History; Topography - General; Topography - Local; Travel - General. PR: £10–1,000. Corresp: French, Indonesian. VAT No: GB 571 600 167.

GREAT LEIGHS

Missing Books, 'Coppers' Main Road, Great Leighs, CM3 1NR. Prop: Chris Missing. Tel: (01245) 361609. E-mail: missingbooks@madasafish.com. Est: 1994. Private premises. Book fairs only. Small stock. Spec: Architecture; Biography; Cities - City of London; Countries - England; History - Local; Publishers - Black, A. & C.; Rural Life; Topography - General. PR: £2–500. CC: MC; V. Mem: PBFA. Notes: *Some stock displayed at AllBooks, Maldon and some at Finchingfield antiques centre, Finchingfield.*

HARWICH

The Book Annex, 18 Church Street, Harwich, CO12 3DS. Prop: Martin Ellingham and Peter J. Hadley. Tel: 01255 551667. Web: www.thebookannex.co.uk. E-mail: victoria@thebookannex.co.uk. Est: 2004. Shop and/or showroom. Telephone First. Spec: Art; Art - Technique; Art - Theory; Art History; Arts, The; Science - General; Science - Pure & Applied; University Press. CC: MC; V. Notes: *Wide ranging stock of Academic Titles including many remainders / overstocks as well as strong sections in History, Science, Arts subjects, Literature and Media. Visitors welcome by chance or ideally by appointment.*

ESSEX

Harwich Old Books (Peter J Hadley Bookseller Ltd.), ■ 21 Market Street, Harwich, CO12 3DX. Prop: Peter J. Hadley. Tel: (01255) 551667. Web: www.hadley.co.uk. E-mail: books@hadley.co.uk. Est: 1982. Shop. Telephone First. Open: **F:** 10:00–17:00; **S:** 10:00–17:00; **Su:** 13:00–17:00. Medium stock. Spec: Academic/Scholarly; Architecture; Art Reference; Artists; Arts, The; Illustrated - General; Limited Editions - General; Literature. PR: £1–5,000. CC: MC; V; Switch. Corresp: French, Italian. Mem: ABA; ILAB. VAT No: GB 489 0588 89. Notes: *Open by chance or by appointment.*

HOLLAND-ON-SEA

Bookworm, ■ Bookworm 100 Kings Avenue, Holland-on-Sea, CO15 5EP. Tel: 01255 815984. Web: www.bookwormshop.com. E-mail: question@bookwormshop.com. Est: 1995. Shop open: **M:** 09:00–16:00; **T:** 09:00–16:00; **W:** 09:00–16:00; **Th:** 09:00–16:00; **F:** 09:00–16:00; **S:** 09:00–16:00. Spec: Children's; Military. CC: AE; E; JCB; MC; V; Maestro, Solo, Switch, Electron.

LEIGH ON SEA

Caliver Books, ■ 816-818 London Road, Leigh on Sea, SS9 3NH. Prop: Dave Ryan. Tel: 01702 473986. Fax: 01702 473986. Web: www.caliverbooks.com. E-mail: dave@caliverbooks.com. Est: 1983. Shop open: **M:** 09:00–18:00; **T:** 09:00–18:00; **W:** 09:00–18:00; **Th:** 09:00–18:00; **F:** 09:00–18:00; **S:** 09:00–18:00; Spec: Arms & Armour; Byzantium; Colonial; Fashion & Costume; Firearms/Guns; History - General; History - British Empire, The; History - Colonial. CC: E; MC; V; PayPal. Cata: 3 a year on specialities. Notes: *Mainly Military: History, Costume, Living History. Wargaming.*

Leigh Gallery Books, ■ 135–137 Leigh Road, Leigh–on–Sea, SS9 1JQ. Prop: Barrie Gretton. Tel: (01702) 715477. Fax: (01702) 715477. Web: www.abebooks.com/home/BOO/. E-mail: leighgallerybooks@bigfoot.com. Est: 1983. Shop open: **Th:** 10:00–17:00; **F:** 10:00–17:00; **S:** 10:00–17:00. Large stock. Spec: Art; Illustrated - General; Literature; Topography - Local; Ephemera; Prints and Maps. PR: £1–200. CC: AE; MC; V. Notes: *Large, reasonably priced, general stock plus ephemera, prints, records & cd's. Open 3 days, other times by appointment. Leigh is worth a visit, more bookshops, lots of charity shops, cafes, bars, pleasant walks and views. A nice day out.*

Othello's Bookshop, ■ 1376 London Road, Leigh–on–Sea, SS9 2UH. Prop: F.G. Bush & M.A. Layzell. Tel: (01702) 473334. E-mail: othellos@hotmail.com. Est: 1999. Shop open: **T:** 09:30–17:00; **W:** 09.30–17:00; **Th:** 09.30–17:00; **F:** 09.30–17.00; **S:** 09.30–17:00. Medium stock. PR: £6–200.

LITTLE HALLINGBURY

Assinder Books, Windy Walls Dell Lane, Little Hallingbury, CM22 7SH. Prop: N.M. & I. Assinder. Tel: 01279654479. Web: www.abebooks.com. E-mail: assinbooks@aol.com. Est: 1992. Private premises. Internet and Postal. Telephone First. Medium stock. Spec: Art Reference; Children's; Illustrated - General. PR: £2–300. Corresp: Norwegian.

MALDON

All Books, ■ 2 Mill Road, Maldon, CM9 5HZ. Prop: Mr. Kevin Peggs. Tel: (01621) 856214. Web: www.allbooks.demon.co.uk. E-mail: kevin@allbooks.demon.co.uk. Est: 1970. Internet and Postal. Shop open: **M:** 10:30–16.30; **T:** 10:30–16,30; **W:** 10:30–16:30; **Th:** 10:30–16.30; **F:** 10:30–16:30; **S:** 10:30–17:30; **Su:** 13:30–17:00. Very large stock. Spec: Academic/Scholarly; Advertising; Aeronautics; Africana; Arts, The; Aviation; History - General; History - Renaissance, The. PR: £1–500. CC: MC; V.

Philip Hopper, 29 Keeble Park, Maldon, CM9 6YG. Tel: 01621 850709. Est: 1985. Private premises. Internet and Postal. Spec: Curiosities; Earth Mysteries; Folklore; Gypsies; Mind, Body & Spirit; Mysteries; Mysticism; Occult. Cata: Occult, country life and angling.

MANNINGTREE

John Drury Rare Books, Strandlands Wrabness, Manningtree, CO11 2TX. Prop: David Edmunds. Tel: (01255) 886260. Fax: (01255) 880303. Web: www.johndruryrarebooks.com. E-mail: mail@ johndruryrarebooks.com. Est: 1971. Private premises. Appointment necessary. Small stock. Spec: Agriculture; Antiquarian; Banking & Insurance; Economics; Education & School; Fine & Rare; History - Dutch East India Company; History - Economic Thought. PR: £30–3,000. CC: JCB; MC; V; PayPal. Cata: economics, education, law, philosophy, social history. Corresp: French. Mem: ABA; PBFA; ILAB. VAT No: GB 325 6594 41. Notes: *We specialise in fine & rare 17th, 18th & 19th century books, pamphlets & manuscripts, on a wide range of subjects, but broadly in the social & human sciences.*

RAYLEIGH

Fantastic Literature Limited, 35 The Ramparts, Rayleigh, SS6 8PY. Prop: Simon & Laraine Gosden. Tel: (01268) 747564. Fax: (01268) 747564. Web: www.fantasticliterature.com. E-mail: sgosden@ netcomuk.co.uk. Est: 1984. Private premises. Internet and Postal. Large stock. Spec: - Blackwood, A.; - Conan Doyle, Sir Arthur; - Crichton, Michael; - King, Stephen; - Pratchett, Terry; - Wells, H.G.; Fiction - Crime, Detective, Spy, Thrillers; Fiction - Fantasy, Horror. PR: £1–900. CC: E; MC; V; Switch, PayPal. Corresp: French. Notes: *Also, booksearch and scans available of any title.*

ROMFORD

Ken Whitfield, 5 Eugene Close, Romford, RM2 6DJ. Tel: (01708) 474763. E-mail: kenkwhitfield@ aol.com. Est: 1984. Private premises. Internet and Postal. Contactable. Open: **M:** 09:00–21:00; **T:** 09:00–21:00; **W:** 09:00–21:00; **Th:** 09:00–21:00; **F:** 09:00–21:00; **S:** 09:00–17:00; **Su:** 09:00–17:00. Small stock. Spec: Art; Biography; Entertainment - General; Fiction - General; History - General; Topography - General; Transport; Travel - General. PR: £2–80.

SAFFRON WALDEN

Lankester Antiques and Books, The Old Sun Inn Church Street and Market Hill, Saffron Walden, CB10 1HQ. Prop: Paul Lankester. Tel: (01799) 522685. Est: 1964. Shop open: **M:** 10:00–17:00; **T:** 10:00–17:00; **W:** 10:00–17:00; **Th:** 10:00–17:00; **F:** 10:00–17:00. Very large stock. Spec: Collectables; Ephemera; Prints and Maps. PR: £1–50.

SHENFIELD

Booknotes, 6 York Road, Shenfield, CM15 8JT. Prop: Tony Connolly. Tel: (01277) 226130. Web: www.ascon.demon.co.uk. E-mail: booknotes@ascon.demon.co.uk. Est: 1985. Private premises. Internet and Postal. Medium stock.

SIBLE HEDINGHAM

Brad Books, The Downeys Lamb Lane, Sible Hedingham, CO 9 3 RT. Prop: Arnold Bradbury. Tel: (01787) 460405. E-mail: arnold.bradbury@ukgateway.net. Est: 1995. Private premises. Internet and Postal. Telephone First. Spec: Aircraft; Americana - General; Antiquarian; Archaeology; Architecture; Army, The; Art; Autobiography. PR: £1–250.

SOUTHEND–ON–SEA

Gage Postal Books, P.O. Box 105, Westcliff–on–Sea, Southend–on–Sea, SS0 8EQ. Prop: (*) Simon A. Routh. Tel: (01702) 715133. Fax: (01702) 715133. Web: www.gagebooks.com. E-mail: gagebooks@ clara.net. Est: 1971. Storeroom. Internet and Postal. Appointment necessary. Very large stock. Spec: Ecclesiastical History & Architecture; Religion - General; Theology. PR: £3–1,000. CC: MC; V. Cata: Theology Church History Religion. Corresp: German. Mem: PBFA.

Tony Peterson, 11 Westbury Road, Southend–on–Sea, SS2 4DW. Prop: Tony Peterson. Tel: (01702) 462757. Web: www.chessbooks.co.uk. E-mail: tony@chessbooks.co.uk. Est: 1993. Private premises. Internet and Postal. Appointment necessary. Very small stock. Spec: Chess. PR: £4–200. CC: PayPal. Cata: Chess.

STANSTED

Paul Embleton, 12 Greenfields, Stansted, CM24 8AH. Prop: Paul Embleton & Mrs. Gill Lebrun. Tel: (01279) 812627. Fax: (01279) 817576. Web: www.abebooks.com/home/embleton. E-mail: paulembleton@btconnect.com. Est: 1994. Private premises. Internet and Postal. Appointment necessary. Small stock. Spec: Antique Paper; Artists; Children's - Early Titles; Children's - Illustrated; Collecting; Illustrated - General; Maritime/Nautical; Memorabilia. PR: £5–1,000. CC: PayPal. Notes: *Also, a booksearch service. Books and ephemera for picture postcard collectors.*

Available on-line from Richard Joseph Publishers Ltd
**Sheppard's Book Dealers in
NORTH AMERICA**

WESTCLIFF-ON-SEA

Clifton Books, 34 Hamlet Court Road, Westcliff-on-Sea, SS0 7LX. Prop: John R. Hodgkins. Tel: (01702) 430101. E-mail: jhodgk9942@aol.com. Est: 1970. Private premises. Internet and Postal. Appointment necessary. Large stock. Spec: Academic/Scholarly; Agriculture; Economics; History - British; Social History; Trade Unions; Transport. CC: AE; D; E; JCB; MC; V. Mem: PBFA. Notes: *All related to West Ham.*

Marjon Books, 16 Mannering Gardens, Westcliff-on-Sea, SS0 0BQ. Prop: R.J. Cooper. Tel: (01702) 347119. Est: 1975. Private premises. Appointment necessary. Very small stock. PR: £2–120.

WICKFORD

Hugh MacFarlane Books, 40 Chaucer Walk, Wickford, SS12 9DZ. Prop: Mr H MacFarlane. Tel: (01268) 570892. Web: www.tudorblackpress.co.uk. E-mail: jmba21803@blueyonder.co.uk. Est: 1997. Private premises. Internet and Postal. Appointment necessary. Very small stock. Spec: Astronomy; Medicine; Printing; Private Press; Science - General. PR: £2–150. Cata: Scientific, Medical, Fine Press.

WICKHAM BISHOPS

Baldwin's Scientific Books, Fossilis 18 School Road, Wickham Bishops, Witham, CM8 3NU. Prop: Stuart A. Baldwin. Tel: 01621 891526. Fax: 01621 891522. Web: www.secondhandsciencebooks.com. E-mail: sbaldwin@fossilbooks.co.uk. Est: 1962. Private premises. Internet and Postal. Appointment necessary. Open: **M:** 10:00–17:30; **T:** 10:00–17:30; **W:** 10:00–17:30; **Th:** 10:00–17:30; **F:** 10:00–17:30; **S:** 10:00–17:30; **Su:** 10:00–17:30. Spec: Antiquarian; Archaeology; Astronomy; Biography; Botany; Dinosaurs; Earth Sciences; Evolution. CC: MC; V. Cata: Geology, palaeontology, science, natural history. Mem: PBFA. VAT No: GB 219 1793 51.

WOODFORD GREEN

Handsworth Books, 8 Warners Close, Woodford Green, IG8 0TF. Prop: Stephen Glover. Tel: (07976) 329042. Fax: (0870) 0520258. Web: www.handsworthbooks.co.uk. E-mail: steve@ handsworthbooks.demon.co.uk. Est: 1987. Private premises. Postal Only. Medium stock. Spec: Academic/Scholarly; Applied Art; Company History; Fine Art; History - General; History - 19th Century; History - 20th Century; History - Ancient. PR: £2–650. CC: AE; E; JCB; MC; V; PayPal. Mem: PBFA.

Salway Books, 47 Forest Approach, Woodford Green, IG8 9BP. Prop: Barry Higgs. Tel: 020 8491 7766. Web: www.salwaybooks.co.uk. E-mail: salway.books@ntlworld.com. Est: 1995. Private premises. Contactable. Spec: Aeronautics; Aircraft; Archaeology - Industrial; Buses/Trams; Canals/Inland Waterways; Company History; Engineering; History - Industrial. CC: MC; V. Cata: Industrial & Transport History. Mem: PBFA.

GLOUCESTERSHIRE

BERKELEY

Volumes of Motoring, Hertsgrove, Wanswell, Berkeley, GL13 9RR. Prop: Terry Wills. Tel: (01453) 811819. Fax: (01453) 811819. E-mail: twills@breathemail.net. Est: 1979. Private premises. Internet and Postal. Appointment necessary. Open: **M:** 08:00–22:00; **T:** 08:00–22:00; **W:** 08:00–22:00; **Th:** 08:00–22:00; **F:** 08:00–22:00; **S:** 08:00–21:00; **Su:** 09:00–22:00. Small stock. Spec: Motoring; Sport - Motor Racing. PR: £2–60. CC: MC; V. Notes: *Wide range of motoring remainders available to the trade.*

BISHOPS CLEEVE

Courtyard Books, ■ Tarlings Yard Church Road, Bishops Cleeve, Cheltenham, GL52 8RN. Tel: 01242 674335. Fax: 01242 674335. Web: www.courtyardbooks.co.uk. E-mail: post@courtyardbooks.co.uk. Est: 2000. Shop open: **M:** 09:00–17:00; **T:** 09:00–17:00; **W:** 09:00–17:00; **Th:** 09:00–17:00; **F:** 09:00–17:00; **S:** 09:00–17:00. Spec: Music - Jazz & Blues. CC: AE, MC, V. Cata: Jazz Books. Notes: *Comprehensive range of books on jazz.*

CAMBRIDGE

Internet Bookshop UK Ltd., ■ Unit 2 Wisloe Road, Cambridge, GL2 7AF. Prop: Mr. G. Cook. Tel: (01453) 890278. Fax: (0870) 442 5292. Web: www.ibuk.com. E-mail: orders@ibuk.com. Est: 1996. Internet and Postal. Telephone First. Shop open: **M:** 09:00–17:00; **T:** 09:00–17:00; **W:** 09:00–17:00; **Th:** 09:00–17:00; **F:** 09:00–17:00. Very large stock. Spec: Academic/Scholarly; Alpinism/Mountaineering; Art; Aviation; Children's; Cookery/Gastronomy; Gardening - General; Military. PR: £8–1,000. CC: AE; MC; V; Switch.

CHALFORD STROUD

Surprise Books, 14 Padin Close, Chalford Stroud, GL6 8FB. Prop: John Norman. Tel: 01453 887403. E-mail: surprisebooks@btopenworld.com. Est: 1995. Private premises. Internet and Postal. Appointment necessary. Open: **M:** 09:00–17:30; **T:** 09:00–17:30; **W:** 09.00–17.30, **Th:** 09.00–17.30, **F:** 09:00–17:30; **S:** 09:00–17:30; **Su:** 09:00–17:30; Closed for lunch: 13:00–14:00. Spec: Annuals; Author - Bainbridge, Beryl; - Blyton, Enid; - Charteris, Leslie; - Cook, Beryl; - Cornwell, Bernard; - Crompton, Richmal; - Dahl, Roald. CC: MC; V. Mem: PBFA. VAT No: GB 811 2130 94.

CHELTENHAM

David Bannister, 26 Kings Road, Cheltenham, GL52 6BG. Tel: (01242) 514287. Web: www.antiquemaps.co.uk. E-mail: db@antiquemaps.co.uk. Est: 1963. Private premises. Internet and Postal. Appointment necessary. Very small stock. Spec: Atlases; Cartography; Reference; Prints and Maps. PR: £10–5,000. CC: JCB; MC; V. VAT No: GB 391 9317 27. Notes: *Mainly maps - see under Print and Map Sellers on www.sheppardsworld.co.uk.*

Cotswold Internet Books, Unit 2 Maida Vale Business Centre Maida Vale Road, Cheltenham, GL53 7ER. Prop: John & Caro Newland. Tel: 01242-261170 or 01242-261428. Web: www. cotswoldinternetbooks.com. E-mail: john.newland@btconnect.com. Est: 1989. Warehouse. Internet and Postal. Open: **M:** 08:30–17.50; **T:** 08:30–17.50; **W:** 08:30–17.50; **Th:** 08:30–17.50; **F:** 08:30–17.50. Very large stock. Spec: Author - Johns, W.E.; Aviation; Children's; Classical Studies; Cookery/ Gastronomy; Countries - General; Fiction - Crime, Detective, Spy, Thrillers; Military. PR: £5–300. CC: AE; E; JCB; MC; V; Maestro. Mem: ibooknet. VAT No: GB 535 5039 51. Notes: *Stock of over 60,000 out-of-print books on all subjects. Particularly strong in detective fiction and children's books.*

Bruce Marshall Rare Books, Foyers, 20 Gretton Road Gotherington, Cheltenham, GL52 9QU. Tel: (01242) 672997. Fax: (01242) 675238. E-mail: marshallrarebook@aol.com. Private premises. Appointment necessary. Very small stock. Spec: Atlases; Colour-Plate; Natural History; Travel - General. Cata: Natural History, Illustrated, Atlases, Colour plates. Mem: ABA; ILAB.

Moss Books, ■ 8–9 Henrietta Street, Cheltenham, GL50 4AA. Prop: Christopher Moss. Tel: (01242) 222947. E-mail: chris.moss@virgin.net. Est: 1992. Shop open: **M:** 10:00–18:00; **T:** 10:00–18:00; **W:** 10:00–18:00; **Th:** 10:00–18:00; **F:** 10:00–18:00; **S:** 09:00–18:00. Large stock. PR: £1–100. CC: JCB; MC; V. Corresp: Japanese. VAT No: GB 618 3105 62.

GLOUCESTERSHIRE

Peter Lyons Books, ■ 11 Imperial Square, Cheltenham, GL50 1QB. Prop: Peter Lyons. Tel: (01242) 260345. Est: 2000. Shop open: **W:** 10:00–17:00; **Th:** 10:00–17:00; **F:** 10:00–17:00; **S:** 10:00–17:00. Medium stock. Spec: Art; Art - Technique; Art - Theory; Art History; Art Reference; Artists; Arts, The; Children's. PR: £2–500. Notes: *Open at other timesd by appointment. Also art catalogues.*

John Wilson Manuscripts Ltd, Painswick Lawn 7 Painswick Road, Cheltenham, GL50 2EZ. Prop: John & Gina Wilson. Tel: (01242) 580344. Fax: (01242) 580355. Web: www.manuscripts.co.uk. E-mail: mail@manuscripts.co.uk. Est: 1967. Private premises. Internet and Postal. Appointment necessary. Very large stock. Spec: Autographs; Documents - General; Manuscripts; Collectables; Ephemera. PR: £20–50,000. CC: AE; MC; V. Mem: ABA; ILAB; PADA. VAT No: GB 194 9050 39.

CHIPPING CAMPDEN

Draycott Books, ■ 2 Sheep Street, Chipping Campden, GL55 6DX. Prop: Robert & Jane McClement. Tel: Business (01386) 841392. E-mail: draycottbooks@hotmail.com. Est: 1981. Shop open: **T:** 10:00– 17:00; **W:** 10:00–17:00; **Th:** 10:00–17:00; **F:** 10:00–17:00; **S:** 10:00–17:30. Medium stock. PR: £1–1,000.

CHIPPING NORTON

Four Shire Bookshops, PO Box 231, Chipping Norton, OX7 9AP. Prop: Linda Osgood. Tel: (01608) 651451. Fax: (01608) 650827. E-mail: fourshirebooks@aol.com. Est: 1981. Private premises. Internet Only. Appointment necessary. Open: **M:** 09:30–16:00; **T:** 09:30–16:00; **W:** 09:30–16:00; **Th:** 09:30– 17:00; **F:** 09:30–17:00; **S:** 08:30–17:00. Closed for lunch: 13:00–14:00. Medium stock. Spec: Crafts; Embroidery; Needlework; Booksearch. PR: £1–100. CC: E; JCB; MC; V. Mem: FSB.

CIRENCESTER

Aviabooks, ■ 8 Swan Yard West Market Place, Cirencester, GL7 2NH. Prop: Paul Gentil. Tel: (01285) 641700. Web: www.abebooks.com. E-mail: paul@gentil.demon.co.uk. Est: 1997. Shop open: **M:** 09:30–17:00; **T:** 09:30–17:00; **W:** 09:00–12:30; **Th:** 09:30–17:00; **F:** 09:30–17:00; **S:** 09:30–18:00. Small stock. Spec: Aeronautics; Antiques; Applied Art; Architecture; Art; Art - Technique; Art History; Art Reference. PR: £1–1,000. CC: AE; MC; V; Maestro. Mem: PBFA. Notes: *Also, some book fairs & specialist events, bookbinding & repair service available.*

The Bookroom, ■ Cirencester Arcade, Market Place, Cirencester, GL7 2NX. Prop: Tetbury Old Books Ltd. Tel: (01285) 644214. Fax: (01285) 504458. E-mail: bookroom@tetbury.co.uk. Est: 1998. Shop open: **M:** 10:00–17:00; **T:** 10:00–17:00; **W:** 10:00–17:00; **Th:** 10:00–17:00; **F:** 10:00–17:00; **S:** 10:00– 17:00; **Su:** 12:00–17:00; Very small stock. Spec: Collectables; Prints & Maps. PR: £3–100. CC: MC; V.

COLEFORD

Past & Present Books, ■ 19a Gloucester Road, Coleford, GL16 8BH. Prop: Mr and Mrs J Saunders. Tel: 01594 833347. Shop open: **Th:** 16:00–17:30; **F:** 14:00–17:30; **S:** 10:00–17:30. Spec: Brewing; Industry; Mining; Topography - General; Topography - Local. Notes: *Major stockist of books on Gloucestershire and Forest of Dean - over 2,500.*

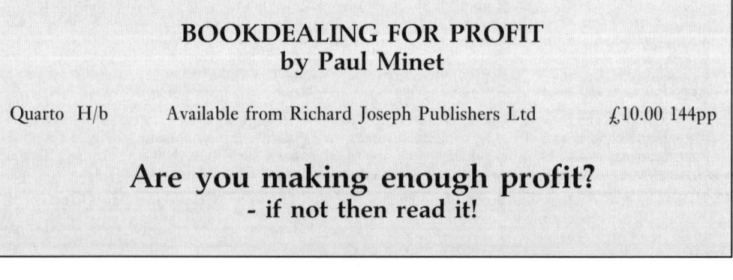

GLOUCESTERSHIRE

Simon Lewis Transport Books, PO Box 9 , Coleford, GL16 8YF. Prop: Simon Lewis. Tel: 01594 839369. Web: www.simonlewis.com. E-mail: simon@simonlewis.com. Est: 1985. Mail Order Only. Internet and Postal. Appointment necessary. Open: **M:** 09:00–16:30; **T:** 09:00–16.30, **W:** 09.00–16.30; **Th:** 09:00–16:30; **F:** 09:00–16:30; Closed for lunch: 13:00–14:00. Spec: Buses/Trams; Motorbikes / motorcycles; Motoring; Railroads; Railways; Sport - Motor Racing; Traction Engines; Transport. CC: MC; V; Solo, Electron, Maestro. Cata: Car,Motorcycle, Truck & Bus, Rail. VAT No: GB 575 9030 21. Notes: *Motor sport is our particular field. Regular bookstall run at Shelsley Walsh and Prescott speed hillclimb events & many other motor sport events during the season.*

FAIRFORD

Jacques Gander, 14 Keble Lawns, Fairford, GL7 4BQ. Tel: (01285) 712988. E-mail: jacques@jgander.fsnet.co.uk. Est: 1996. Private premises. Internet and Postal. Spec: Children's; Modern First Editions. CC: MC; V; Debit.

KEMPSFORD

Ximenes Rare Books Inc., Kempsford House, Kempsford, GL7 4FT. Prop: Stephen Weissman. Tel: (01285) 810640. Fax: (01285) 810650. E-mail: steve@ximenes.com. Est: 1965. Private premises. Appointment necessary. Small stock. Spec: Antiquarian. PR: £50–10,000. CC: MC; V. Corresp: French. Mem: ABA; PBFA; ILAB; ABAA. VAT No: GB 672 4533 30.

MONTPELIER

Cooking = The Books, ■ 2 The Courtyard, Montpelier, Cheltenham, GL50 1SR. Prop: Dr Keith R. Aris. Tel: 01242 577908. E-mail: cooking@thebooks.fslife.co.uk. Est: 1995. Shop open: **M:** 09:00– 17:00; **T:** 09:00–17:00; **W:** 09:00–17:00; **Th:** 09:00–17:00; **F:** 09:00–17:00; **S:** 09:00–17:00. Spec: Food & Drink; New Books. CC: JCB; MC; V; Mae, De. VAT No: GB 666 5230 26. Notes: *Greetings cards - many handmade. New, out of print and used cookery books only.*

MORETON–IN–MARSH

Jeffrey Formby Antiques, Orchard Cottage East Street, Moreton–in–Marsh, GL 56 0LQ. Tel: (01608) 650558. Fax: (01608) 650558. Web: www.formby-clocks.co.uk. E-mail: jeff@formby-clocks.co.uk. Est: 1993. Shop and/or gallery. Internet and Postal. Telephone First. Open: **F:** 10:00–17:00; **S:** 10:00– 17:00. Very small stock. Spec: Horology; Scientific Instruments. PR: £5–500. CC: E; JCB; MC; V. Cata: Horology. Mem: British Antique Dealers Association. Notes: *Specialists in books on horology and related subjects.*

NAILSWORTH

Keogh's Books, ■ Market St, Nailsworth, GL6 0BX. Prop: J. Keogh. Tel: (01453) 833922. Web: www.keoghsbooks.co.uk. E-mail: joekeogh@keoghbooks.fsnet.co.uk. Est: 1985. Shop. Internet and Postal. Open: **M:** 09:30–17:00; **T:** 09:30–17:00; **W:** 09:30–17:00; **Th:** 09:30–17:00; **F:** 09:30–17:00; **S:** 09:30–17:30. Small stock. Spec: Art; Art History; Art Reference; Artists; Prints and Maps. PR: £2– 200. CC: AE; MC; V; SW.

NEWENT

Oakwood Books, 37 Church Street, Newent, GL18 1AA. Prop: Jim Haslem, A.L.A. Tel: (01531) 821040. Web: www.abebooks.com/home/oakwoodbooks. E-mail: jim@haslem.fsnet.co.uk. Est: 1987. Private premises. Internet and Postal. Appointment necessary. Small stock. Spec: Topography - Local. PR: £2–450.

NEWNHAM ON SEVERN

Christopher Saunders (Orchard Books), Kingston House High Street, Newnham on Severn, GL14 1BB. Prop: Chris Saunders. Tel: (01594) 516030. Fax: (01594) 517273. Web: www.cricket-books.com. E-mail: chrisbooks@aol.com. Est: 1981. Office and/or bookroom. Appointment necessary. Open: **M:** 09:00–17:00; **T:** 09:00–17:00; **W:** 09:00–17:00; **Th:** 09:00–17:00; **F:** 09:00–17:00. Spec: Sport - Cricket. CC: MC; V; Maestro. Cata: on cricket. Mem: ABA; PBFA; ILAB.

GLOUCESTERSHIRE

OVER LANE

Michael Garbett Antiquarian Bo, 1 Over Court Mews, Over Lane, Almondsbury, BS32 4DG. Prop: Michael & Jeanne Garbett. Tel: (01454) 617376. Fax: (01454) 617376. Web: www.michaelgarbett .theanswer.co.uk. E-mail: migarb@overcourtmews.freeserve.co.uk. Est: 1965. Private premises. Appointment necessary. Small stock. Spec: Bindings; Miniature Books. Mem: ABA. VAT No: GB 358 1080 58.

STOW–ON–THE–WOLD

Bookbox, ■ Chantry House Sheep Street, Stow-on-the-Wold, GL54 1AA. Prop: Pat Brown & Connie Fisher. Tel: (01451) 831214. Est: 1987. Shop open: **M:** 11:00–16:30; **T:** 11:00–16:30; **Th:** 11:00–16:30; **F:** 11:00–16:30; **S:** 11:00–17:00. Closed for lunch: 13:00–14:15. Medium stock. Spec: Arts, The; Author - Woolf, Virginia; Cookery/Gastronomy; Drama; Folio Society, The; Gardening - General; History - General; Sport - Field Sports. PR: £2–1,000. CC: MC; V. Mem: PBFA. Notes: *In winter, telephone first.*

Paper Moon Books, 6 Durham House Antiques Centre Sheep Street, Stow–on–the–Wold, GL54 1AA. Prop: Elaine Fletcher. Tel: 01451 870404. Fax: Shop (01451) 870404. E-mail: shipston03@ yahoo.co.uk. Est: 1977. Shop and/or gallery open: **M:** 10:00–17:00; **T:** 10:00–17:00; **W:** 10:00– 17:00; **Th:** 10:00–17:00; **F:** 10:00–17:00; **S:** 10:00–17:00; **Su:** 11:00–17:00. Spec: Bibles; Bindings; Gardening - General; Literature; Poetry; Prayer Books; Topography - General. PR: £5–300. CC: D; E; JCB; MC; V; Solo, Switch.

Wychwood Books, ■ Sheep Street, Stow–on–the–Wold, GL54 1AA. Prop: Miss. Lucy Baggott & Mr. Henry Baggott. Tel: 01451 831880. Fax: 01451 870631. Web: www.wychwoodbooks.com. E-mail: info@wychwoodbooks.com. Est: 2001. Shop open: **M:** 09:30–17:30; **T:** 09:30–17:30; **W:** 09:30–17:30; **Th:** 09:30–17:30; **F:** 09:30–17:30; **S:** 09:30–17:30. Medium stock. Spec: Antiques; Antiquities; Architecture; Art; Children's; Cookery/Gastronomy; Literature; Modern First Editions. PR: £3– 4,000. CC: MC; V. Mem: PBFA.

STROUD

Anthroposophical Books, Fromehall Mill - Blk 2 Rm 9 2nd Flr Lodgemore Lane, Stroud, GL5 3EH. Prop: H. & A. Tandree. Tel: (01453) 764 932. Fax: (01453) 764 932. E-mail: herb@philosophy-books.co.uk. Est: 1988. Office and/or bookroom. Internet and Postal. Appointment necessary. Open: **M:** 09:00–18:00; **T:** 09:00–18:00; **W:** 09:00–18:00; **Th:** 09:00–18:00; **F:** 09:00–18:00. Small stock. Spec: Anthroposophy; Author - Steiner, Rudolf; Occult; Philosophy. PR: £8–50. CC: MC; V. Cata: Anthroposophy, Rudolf Steiner. Corresp: French, German. Notes: *Please call in advance for an appointment.*

The Blue Penguin, ■ Griffin Lodge Griffin Mill, London Road, Stroud, GL52AZ. Prop: Steve Pritchard. Tel: (01453) 731027. E-mail: books@bluepenguin.wanadoo.co.uk. Est: 1991. Shop open: **T:** 10:00– 16:30; **W:** 10:00–16:30; **Th:** 10:00–16:30; **F:** 10:00–16:30; **S:** 10:00–16:30. Medium stock. Spec: Booksearch; Collectables. PR: £1–300. Corresp: 'Pidgeon' French. Notes: *House clearances, antiques. Telephone first if travelling far.*

Herb Tandree Philosophy Books, Fromehall Mill - Blk 2/Rm 9 Lodgemore Lane, Stroud, GL5 3EH. Prop: Herb Tandree. Tel. (01453) 764 932. Fax. (01453) 764 932. Web: www.philosophy books.co.uk. E-mail: herb@philosophy-books.co.uk. Est: 2000. Office and/or bookroom. Internet and Postal. Appointment necessary. Open: **M:** 09:00–18:00; **T:** 09:00–18:00; **W:** 09:00–18:00; **Th:** 09:00–18:00; **F:** 09:00–18:00. Medium stock. Spec: Academic/Scholarly; Economics; History of Ideas; Philosophy; Religion - General. CC: AE; JCB; MC. Cata: philosophy. Corresp: French, German. VAT No: GB 783 4154 17. Notes: *Please call in advance for appointment.*

Ian Hodgkins and Company Limited, Upper Vatch Mill The Vatch, Slad, Stroud, GL6 7JY. Prop: G.A. Yablon, I. Hoy, Simon Weager. Tel: (01453) 764270. Fax: (01453) 755233. Web: www .ianhodgkins.com. E-mail: i.hodgkins@dial.pipex.com. Est: 1974. Private premises. Internet and Postal. Appointment necessary. Medium stock. Spec: Applied Art; Art; Art Reference; Artists; Author - Austen, Jane; - Brontes, The; - Crane, Walter; - Gaskell, E. PR: £5–5,000. CC: MC; V. Mem: ABA; PBFA; BA.

Inprint, ■ 31 High Street, Stroud, GL5 1AJ. Prop: Joy & Mike Goodenough. Tel: (01453) 759731. Fax: (01453) 759731. Web: www.inprint.co.uk. E-mail: enquiries@inprint.co.uk. Est: 1978. Internet and Postal. Shop open: **M:** 10:00–17:00; **T:** 10:00–17:00; **W:** 10:00–17:00; **Th:** 10:00–17:00; **F:** 10:00–17:00; **S:** 10:00–17:00. Medium stock. Spec: Applied Art; Architecture; Art; Art Reference; Cinema/Film; Fine Art; Gardening - General; Music - Popular. PR: £5–500. CC: AE; D; E; JCB; MC; V.

GLOUCESTERSHIRE

R & R Books, ■ Nelson Street, Stroud, GL5 2HL. Prop: Ruth Pyecroft & Ron Cree. Tel: (01453) 755788. Web: www.randrbooks.co.uk. E-mail: info@randrbooks.co.uk. Est: 1994. Shop open: **M:** 10:00–17:30; **T:** 10:00–17:30; **W:** 10:00–17:30; **Th:** 10:00–17:30; **F:** 10:00–17:30; **S:** 10:00–17:30. Medium stock. Spec: Advertising; Children's; Comic Books & Annuals; Comics; Culture - Popular; Earth Mysteries; Entertainment - General; Esoteric. PR: £1–20. CC: D; E; JCB; MC; V.

Alan & Joan Tucker The Bookshop, Epworth Lodge Field Road, Stroud, GL5 2HZ. Prop: Alan and Joan Tucker. Tel: (01453) 764738. Fax: (01453) 766899. Web: www.abebooks.com/home/SANDITON. E-mail: at80jt@globalnet.co.uk. Est: 1963. Mail Order Only. Internet and Postal. Appointment necessary. Very small stock. Spec: Arts, The; Authors - Women; Children's; Fine Printing; Limited Editions - General; Literary Criticism; Literary Travel; Literature. PR: £1–100. CC: MC; V. Cata: Humanities, children's. VAT No: GB 275 0258 60. Notes: *Now retired selling only part-time on internet, ABE and UKBookWorld. Over 40 years members of BA we have left as we no longer have a new book turnover.*

TETBURY

The Bookroom at Brown & White, 3 Tetbury Upton, Tetbury, GL8 8AA. Prop: Brian & Margaret Jarvis. Tel: 078 3789 6270. Est: 2006. Office and/or bookroom. Open: **M:** 10:00–17:00; **T:** 10:00–17:00; **W:** 10:00–17:00; **Th:** 10:00–17:00; **F:** 10:00 17:00; **S:** 10:00 17:00; **Su:** 11:00 16:00. CC: MC; V. Notes: *Bookroom within and antiques centre.*

Tetbury Old Books Limited, ■ 21, Long Street, Tetbury, GL8 8AA. Prop: Tetbury Old Books Ltd. Tel: (01666) 504330. E-mail: oldbooks@tetbury.co.uk. Est: 1994. Shop open: **M:** 09:30–18:00; **T:** 09:30–18:00; **W:** 09:30–18:00; **Th:** 09:30–18:00; **F:** 09:30–18:00; **S:** 09:30–18:00; **Su:** 12:00–17:00. Small stock. Spec: Prints and Maps. PR: £1–5,000. CC: AE; E; JCB; MC; V; PayPal. Mem: TADA. Notes: *Retail antiquarian, rare, collectable and second-hand book and print sellers prominently located in the centre of Tetbury. We have a carefully-selected general stock which varies from time to time.*

TEWKESBURY

Cornell Books, ■ The Wheatsheaf 132 High Street, Tewkesbury, GL20 5JR. Prop: Graham Cornell. Tel: (01684) 293337. E-mail: gtcornell@aol.com. Est: 1996. Internet and Postal. Shop open: **M:** 10:30–17:00; **T:** 10:30–17:00; **W:** 10:30–17:00; **Th:** 10:30–17:00; **F:** 10:30–17:00; **S:** 10:30–17:00. Large stock. Spec: Author - Moore, John; Children's; Countries - England; Countries - Scotland; Countries - Wales; Maps & Mapmaking; Prints and Maps. PR: £1–500. CC: AE; MC; V. Mem: PBFA. VAT No: GB 754 2601 43. Notes: *Stocks a range of Ordnance Survey Maps.*

WESTBURY-ON-SEVERN

Dive In Books, ■ Dive In, Lecture Hall The Village, Westbury-on-Severn, GL14 1PA. Prop: Patricia Larkham. Tel: (01452) 760124. Fax: (01452) 760590. Web: www.diveinbooks.co.uk. E-mail: mydive@globalnet.co.uk. Est: 1975. Internet and Postal. Shop open: **M:** 09:00–14:00; **T:** 09:00–14:00; **W:** 09:00–14:00; **Th:** 09:00–14:00; **F:** 09:00–14:00. Small stock. Spec: Archaeology; Calligraphy; D.I.Y. (Do It Yourself); Deep Sea Diving; Maritime/Nautical; Natural History; Pacifism; Sport - Cycling. PR: £1–150.

Order the next edition - or search www.sheppardsworld.co.uk
Sheppard's International Directory of

EPHEMERA DEALERS

GREATER MANCHESTER

ALTRINCHAM (SEE ALSO IN CHESHIRE)

Christopher Baron, 15 Crossfield Road, Hale, Altrincham, WA15 8DU. Tel: (0161) 980-1014. Fax: (0161) 980-1415. Web: www.ukbookworld.com/members/chrisbaron. E-mail: ChrisBaronBooks@aol.com. Est: 1979. Private premises. Internet and Postal. Medium stock. Spec: Games; Horology; Locks & Locksmiths; Microscopy; Natural History; Science - General; Science - History of; Scientific Instruments. CC: JCB; MC; V; Maestro. Mem: PBFA.

Edward Yarwood Rare Books, 61 Fairywell Road Timperley, Altrincham, WA15 6XB. Est: 1994. Private premises. Postal Only. Medium stock. Spec: Author - Gurdjieff, W.I.; - Wilson, Colin; Biography; Philosophy. PR: £5–250. Notes: *Also; book plates, manuscripts, booksearch and attends fairs.*

ASHTON-UNDER-LYNE

Marathon Books, 12 Lytham Close, Ashton-under-Lyne, Lancashire, OL6 9ER. Prop: Richard Bond. Tel: (0161) 343-2085. E-mail: richard.bond@jlservices.co.uk. Est: 1980. Private premises. Postal Only. Appointment necessary. Small stock. Spec: Psychology/Psychiatry; Sport - Athletics. Notes: *Also, a booksearch service.*

BOLTON

Martin Bott (Bookdealers) Ltd., ■ 6 St.Leonards Avenue, Bolton, BL6 4JE. Prop: M.L.R. & M.H. Bott. Tel: (01204) 691489. Fax: (01204) 698729. Web: www.bottbooks.com. E-mail: martin.bott@ btinternet.com. Est: 1997. Internet and Postal. Telephone First. Shop At: 28-30 Lee Lane, Horwich, Bolton, BL6 7BY. Shop open: **M:** 10:15–15:30; **T:** 10:15–15:00; **Th:** 10:15–15:00; **F:** 10:15–15:00; **S:** 10:30–16:00. Large stock. Spec: Archaeology - Industrial; Author - Rolt, L.T.C.; Aviation; Buses/Trams; Canals/Inland Waterways; Commercial Vehicles; Company History; Engineering. PR: £1–1,000. CC: AE; JCB; MC; V; Maestro, Solo. Notes: *Shop is usually closed during school holidays and some saturdays - please telephone before travelling.*

Firecatcher Books, ■ The Last Drop Village, Bromley Cross, Bolton, BL7 9PZ. Prop: Rebecca Peacock and Sam Tickner. Tel: (01204) 597511. Web: www.firecatcherbooks.co.uk. E-mail: enquiries@ firecatcherbooks.co.uk. Est: 2006. Shop open: **M:** 10:00–17:00; **T:** 10:00–17:00; **W:** 10:00–17:00; **Th:** 10:00–17:00; **F:** 10:00–17:00; **S:** 10:00–17:00; **Su:** 10:00–17:00. Small stock. Spec: Children's; Children's - Illustrated; Illustrated - General. PR: £1–1,000. CC: AE; V; Switch, Solo. Notes: *Booksearch for childhood favourites.*

DIDSBURY

Barlow Moor Books, 29 Churchwood Road, Didsbury, M20 6TZ. Prop: Dr. Roger & Dr. L.A. Finlay. Tel: (0161) 434 5073. Fax: (0161) 448 2491. E-mail: books@barlowmoorbooks.com. Est: 1990. Private premises. Postal Only. Contactable. Very small stock. Corresp; French. VAT No: GB 560 9236 38.

LITTLEBOROUGH

George Kelsall Booksellers, ■ The Bookshop 22 Church Street, Littleborough, OL15 9AA. Prop: George Kelsall and Ben Kelsall. Tel: (01706) 370244. E-mail: kelsall@bookshop22.fsnet.co.uk. Est: 1979. Shop open: **M:** 10:00–17:00; **T:** 13:00–17:00; **W:** 10:00–17:00; **Th:** 10:00–17:00; **F:** 10:00–17:00; **S:** 10:00–17:00. Large stock. Spec: Architecture; Art History; Art Reference; History - General; History - Industrial; Politics; Social History; Topography - Local. PR: £1–500. CC: AE; MC; V; Switch. Mem: PBFA. VAT No: GB 306 0657 81.

MANCHESTER

Camedia Ltd, Unit 1 Roundthorn House Floats Road, Manchester, M23 9LJ. Prop: Paul Johnson. Web: www.bookacademy.co.uk. E-mail: sales@bookacademy.co.uk. Est: 1996. Mail Order Only. Internet and Postal. Appointment necessary. Large stock. Spec: Academic/Scholarly; Black Studies; Culture - Popular; History - General; Holocaust; Homosexuality & Lesbianism; Irish Interest; Philosophy. PR: £1–50.

GREATER MANCHESTER

Browzers, 2 Buckingham Road, Prestwich, Manchester, M25 9NE. Prop: Alan Seddon. Tel: 0161 7732327. E-mail: alanseddon@tiscali.co.uk. Est: 1980. Mail Order Only. Internet and Postal. Contactable. Open: **M:** 09:00–17:30; **1:** 09:00–17:30; **W:** 09:00–17:30; **Th:** 09:00–17:30; **F:** 09:00–17:30; **S:** 09:00–17:30; **Su:** 09:00–17:30; Closed for lunch: 13:00–14:00. Spec: Antiques; Collecting; Horses; Sport - Horse Racing (inc. Riding/Breeding/Equestrian); Sport - Racing. CC: MC; V. Mem: ABA.

Classic Crime Collections, 95a Boarshaw Road Middleton, Manchester, M24 6AP. Prop: Rob Wilson. Tel: (0161) 653-4145. E-mail: Rob@mtwilson.freeserve.co.uk. Est: 1989. Private premises. Postal Only. Small stock. Spec: Author - Christie, Agatha; - Creasey, John; - Fleming, Ian; Buses/Trams; Canals/Inland Waterways; Crime (True); Fiction - Crime, Detective, Spy, Thrillers; Railways. PR: £2–400. Notes: *Also, a booksearch service.*

Franks Booksellers, Suite 33 4th Floor, St Margaret's Chambers 5 Newton Street, Piccadilly, Manchester, M1 1HL. Tel: (0161) 237-3747. Fax: (0161) 237-3747. Est: 1960. Office and/or bookroom. Open: **M:** 10:00–14:00; **T:** 10:00–14:00; **W:** 10:00–14:00; **Th:** 10:00–14:00; **F:** 10:00–14:00. Small stock. Spec: Advertising; Autographs; Children's; Cinema/Film; Comic Books & Annuals; Magazines & Periodicals - General; Magic & Conjuring; Performing Arts. PR: £1–1,000. Notes: *Also, postcards.*

Gibbs Bookshop Ltd., ■ 13 Howard Road Northenden, Manchester, M22 4EG. Tel: (0161) 998-2794. Fax: (0161) 998-2794. Web: www.gibbsbookshop.co.uk. E-mail: gibbsbookshop@beeb.net. Est: 1922. Internet and Postal. Shop open: **M:** 10:00–17:00; **1:** 10:00–17:00; **W:** 10:00–17:00; **1h:** 10:00–17:00; **F:** 10:00–17:00; **S:** 10:00–17:00. Very large stock. PR: £5–50. CC: JCB; MC; V. Mem: ABA. VAT No: GB 145 4624 68.

Tim Kendall-Carpenter, 633 Wilmslow Road, Manchester, M20 6DF. Tel: (0161) 445-6172. Web: www.timkcbooks.com. E-mail: info@timkcbooks.com. Est: 1996. Private premises. Internet and Postal. Appointment necessary. Medium stock. Spec: First Editions; Modern First Editions; Poetry; Proof Copies. PR: £5–1,000. CC: AE; MC; V; Maestro. VAT No: GB 781 2657 13.

The Little Bookshop, PO Box 134, Manchester, M8 4DJ. Prop: Valerie Clark. Tel: (0161) 740 1335. Web: www.littlebookshop.net. E-mail: info@littlebookshop.net. Est: 1989. Private premises. Internet and Postal. Medium stock. Spec: Arts, The; Autobiography; Biography; Fiction - General; History - General; Poetry; Religion - General; Travel - General. PR: £1–100. CC: PayPal. Notes: *Also sells new books under Thanatos Books.*

E.J. Morten (Booksellers), ■ 6–9 Warburton Street, Didsbury, Manchester, M20 6WA. Prop: John A. Morten. Tel: (0161) 445-7629. Fax: (0161) 448-1323. E-mail: morten.booksellers@lineone.net. Est: 1959. Shop open: **M:** 09:30–17:30; **T:** 09:30–17:30; **W:** 09:30–17:00; **Th:** 09:30–17:30; **F:** 09:30–17:30; **S:** 09:30–17:30. Large stock. Spec: Military History; Sport - General; Travel - General. CC: MC; V; Solo, Delta. Corresp: French, German. Mem: PBFA; BA; ILAB; BT; NBL.

Philip Nevitsky, P.O. Box 364, Manchester, M60 1AL. Tel: (0161) 228-2947. Fax: (0161) 236-0390. E-mail: absolutphilip@amserve.com. Est: 1974. Storeroom. Postal Only. Small stock. Spec: Cinema/ Film; Entertainment - General; Music - Popular; Collectables. Mem: Postcard Traders Assoc.

V.M. Riley Books, 3 Leyburn Avenue, Stretford, Manchester, M32 8DZ. Prop: Mrs. Valerie M. Riley. Tel: (0161) 865-6543. Web: www.ukbookworld.com/members/vmriley. E-mail: val@ rileyv.fsnet.co.uk. Est: 1989. Private premises. Postal Only. Small stock. PR: £1–50.

Star Lord Books, 72 Chester Avenue Dukinfield, Cheshire, Manchester, SK16 5BW. Prop: Steve Starlord. Tel: (0161) 338-8465. E-mail: starlord@starlord-enterprises.freeserve.co.uk. Est: 1990. Private premises. Internet and Postal. Contactable. Small stock. Spec: Anthroposophy; Astrology; Author - General; - Wilson, Colin; Crime (True); Earth Mysteries; Eastern Philosophy; Esoteric. PR: £1–100. Notes: *Esoteric. Occult, Kabbalah, QBL, Crowley, New Age, Biography, general.*

Thanatos Books, PO Box 134, Manchester, M8 4DJ. Prop: Valerie Clark. Tel: 0161 740 1335. E-mail: info@littlebookshop.net. Est: 2000. Private premises. Internet and Postal. CC: PayPal. Notes: *For other details see under entry for The Little Bookshop, Manchester.*

The Treasure Island, 4 Evesham Road, Blackley, Manchester, M9 7EH. Prop: Ray Cauwood. Tel: (0161) 795 7750. Web: www.abebooks.com/home/RAYJC2000. E-mail: ray@the-treasure-island.com. Est: 2003. Private premises. Postal Only. Appointment necessary. Small stock. Spec: Animals and Birds; Antiques; Art; Art - British; Autobiography; Autographs; Aviation; British Art & Design. PR: £1–50. CC: V.

MOTTRAM IN LONGDENDALE

Rose Books, 26 Roe Cross Green, Mottram in Longdendale, Hyde, SK14 6LP. Prop: (*) E. Alan Rose. Tel: (01457) 763485. Fax: (01457) 763485. Est: 1990. Private premises. Appointment necessary. Very small stock. Spec: History - Local; Religion - Christian; Theology. PR: £2–150.

GREATER MANCHESTER

OLDHAM

Towpath Bookshop, ■ 27 High Street Uppermill, Oldham, OL3 6HS. Prop: (*) Janet and Martin Byrom. Tel: (01457) 877078. Est: 1992. Shop open: **T:** 11:00–17:00; **W:** 10:30–17:00; **Th:** 10:30–17:00; **F:** 10:30–17:00; **S:** 10:30–17:00; **Su:** 11:00–17:00; Very small stock.

RADCLIFFE

Delph Books, 437 Bury and Bolton Road, Radcliffe, M26 4LJ. Prop: Frank Lamb. Tel: 0161 764 4488. Web: www.delphbooks.co.uk. E-mail: franklamb@delphbooks.freeserve.co.uk. Est: 1979. Private premises. Internet and Postal. Telephone First. Open: **M:** 09:00–19:30; **T:** 09:00–19:30; **W:** 09:00–19:30; **Th:** 09:00–19:30; **F:** 09:00–19:30; **S:** 09:00–19:30; **Su:** 09:00–19:30. Spec: Antiquarian; Company History; County - Local; Directories - British; Education & School; Genealogy; History - Family; History - Industrial. CC: MC; V; Maestro. Corresp: French. Mem: PBFA. Notes: *I also stand at book fairs in the North of England. I have a good stock of Lancs & Yorks Parish Registers, Co-op histories, Golf club histories, Clocks & Watches, Rolls of Honour, Lancs & Yorks Topography, Local History and Dialect.*

ROCHDALE

Rochdale Book Company, 59 Bagslate Moor Road, Rochdale, OL11 5YH. Prop: J.S. & S.M. Worthy. Tel: (01706) 658300. Fax: (01706) 713294. E-mail: worthybooks@aol.com. Est: 1971. Warehouse. Appointment necessary. Open: **S:** 10:30–17:30. Large stock. Spec: Antiquarian; Architecture; Canals/ Inland Waterways; Children's; Company History; Fine & Rare; History - Industrial; Illustrated - General. CC: MC; V. Mem: PBFA. Notes: *We have interesting books on most subjects plus a large stock of Lancashire material.*

STOCKPORT

Richard Coulthurst, 97 Green Pastures, Stockport, SK4 3RB. Tel: (0161) 431-3864. E-mail: richard .coulthurst@btinternet.com. Est: 1995. Private premises. Postal Only. Very small stock. Spec: Aviation; Buses/Trams; Canals/Inland Waterways; Energy - Alternative; Energy - Fuels; Energy - General; Energy - Power; History - Industrial. PR: £5–100.

WIGAN

R.D.M. & I.M. Price (Books), 25 Coniston Avenue Whitley, Wigan, WN1 2EY. Prop: Robert and Irene Price. Tel: (01942) 242607. Est: 1997. Private premises. Postal Only. Very small stock. Spec: Autobiography; Biography; Colonial; Fiction - General; Booksearch. PR: £1–65.

Rolling Stock Books, ■ 16 Upper Dicconson Street, Wigan, WN1 2AD. Prop: Nick Howell. Tel: (01942) 493949. E-mail: rollingstockbooks@fsmail.net. Est: 1996. Shop open: **T:** 10.00–17.00; **W:** 10.00–17:00; **Th:** 10.00–17:00; **F:** 10.00–17:00; **S:** 10.00–17:00. Medium stock. Spec: Buses/Trams; Canals/Inland Waterways; History - Industrial; Railroads; Railways; Transport; Booksearch. PR: £5–500. Cata: on transport. Mem: PBFA. VAT No: GB 692 8123 15. Notes: *Valuations booksearch some new books on transport.*

HAMPSHIRE

ALRESFORD

Bolton Books, 60 The Dean, Alresford, SO24 9BD. Prop: David Bolton. Tel: (01962) 734435. Fax: (01962) 734435. Web: www.boltonbooks.com. E-mail: david@boltonbooks.com. Est: 1997. Private premises. Internet and Postal. Appointment necessary. Very small stock. Spec: Colour-Plate; Illustrated - General; Publishers - Black, A. & C.; Publishers - Foulis, T.N.; Topography - General. PR: £5–1,250. Mem: PBFA. Notes: *Also exhibits at bookfairs.*

Laurence Oxley Ltd, ■ The Studio Bookshop 17 Broad Street, Alresford, Nr. Winchester, SO24 9AW. Prop: Anthony Oxley. Tel: (01962) 732188. E-mail: aoxley@freenet.co.uk. Est: 1950. Shop open: **M:** 09:00–17:00; **T:** 09:00–17:00; **W:** 09:00–17:00; **Th:** 09:00–17:00; **F:** 09:00–17:00; **S:** 09:00–17:00. Large stock. Spec: Countries - Far East, The; Countries - India; Topography - General; Topography - Local. PR: £1–25,000. CC: AE; D; MC; V. Mem: ABA; BA; ABA; FATG. VAT No: GB 188 5081 31. Notes: *Also, picture dealers, picture frame makers and restoration work.*

ALTON

Alton Secondhand Books, ■ 43 Normandy Street, Alton, GU34 1DQ. Prop: Mrs. J. Andrews. Tel: (01420) 89352. E-mail: joan.andrews@virgin.net. Est: 1989. Shop open: **M:** 09:30–17:30; **T:** 09:30–17:30; **W:** 09:30–17:00; **Th:** 09:30–17:30; **F:** 09:30–17:30; **S:** 09:30–17:00. Medium stock. Spec: Booksearch. PR: £1–100. VAT No: GB 631 9874 13.

Dance Books Ltd, The Old Bakery 4 Lenten Street, Alton, GU34 1HG. Prop: David Leonard. Tel: 01420 86138. Fax: 01420 86142. Web: www.dancebooks.co.uk. E-mail: dwl@dancebooks.co.uk. Est: 1960. Office and/or bookroom. Open: **M:** 10:00–16:00; **T:** 10:00–17:00; **W:** 10:00–17:00; **Th:** 10:00–17:00; **F:** 10:00–17:00. Spec: Dance. CC: AE; E; MC; V. Mem: BA. VAT No: GB 238 6405 53.

Peter White Books, Westbrooke House 76 High Street, Alton, GU34 1EN. Prop: Peter White. Tel: (01420) 86745. Fax: (01420) 86745. E-mail: pwbooks@btconnect.com. Est: 1995. Office and/or bookroom. Internet and Postal. Telephone First. Small stock. Spec: History - Local; Modern First Editions; Railways; Sport - Football (Soccer); Topography - General; Transport. PR: £4–60. CC: MC; V. Corresp: French. Notes: *Also, stocks titles on local history in most counties.*

ALVERSTOKE

R.W. Forder, 12 St Mark's Road, Alverstoke, Gosport, PO12 2DA. Prop: R.W. Forder. Tel: (023) 9252-7965. E-mail: r.w.forder@btinternet.com. Est: 1985. Private premises. Internet and Postal. Telephone First. Spec: Free Thought; Humanism; Radical Issues; Rationalism. PR: £1–200. Corresp: German. Notes: *Also, a booksearch service.*

ANDOVER

Armchair Auctions, 98 Junction Road, Andover, SP10 3JA. Prop: George Murdoch. Tel: (01264) 362048. Fax: (01264) 362048. Est: 1989. Private premises. Postal Only. Small stock. Spec: Aviation; Military; Naval; War - World War I; War - World War II; Booksearch; Prints and Maps. PR: £5–500. CC: AE; MC; V. Notes: *Main activity: postal auctions.*

BASINGSTOKE

Byblos Antiquarian & Rare Books Ltd., Broadmead 5 Worting Road, Basingstoke, RG21 8TL. Tel: (0207) 1930139. Web: www.byblos.uk.com. E-mail: books@byblos.uk.com. Est: 2005. Private premises. Internet and Postal. Very small stock. Spec: Antiquarian; Fine & Rare; Booksearch; Collectables. PR: £5–1,500. CC: AE; MC; V. Corresp: French, Italian. Mem: IOAB.

Available from Richard Joseph Publishers Ltd

BOOK DEALING FOR PROFIT

by Paul Minet

Quarto H/b £10.00 144pp

HAMPSHIRE

Squirrel Antiques, 9a New Street Joices Yard, Basingstoke, RG21 DQ. Prop: Alan Stone. Tel: (01256) 464885. Est: 1981. Office and/or bookroom. Open: **M:** 10:00–17:30; **T:** 10:00–17:30; **W:** 10:00–17:30; **Th:** 10:00–17:30; **F:** 10:00–17:30; **S:** 10:00–17:30. Small stock. PR: £1–75. Notes: *Small general stock. Also antiques, curios and jewellery.*

CHILBOLTON

Nigel Phillips, The Cart House Paddock Field, Chilbolton, SO20 6AU. Tel: 01264 861186. Fax: 01264 860269. Web: www.nigelphillips.com. E-mail: nigel@nigelphillips.com. Est: 1981. Private premises. Appointment necessary. Medium stock. Spec: Antiquarian; History of Ideas; Medicine; Science - General; Science - History of; Technology. PR: £15–50,000. CC: MC; V. Cata: Medicine, Science. Mem: ABA; ILAB. VAT No: GB 451 0394 74.

EMSWORTH

Bookends, ■ 7 High St., Emsworth, PO10 7AQ. Prop: Carol Waldron. Tel: (01243) 372154. Web: www.bookends.me.uk. E-mail: cawaldron@tinyworld.co.uk. Est: 1982. Shop open: **M:** 09:00–17:00; **T:** 09:00–17:00; **W:** 09:00–17:00; **Th:** 09:00–17:00; **F:** 09:00–17:00; **S:** 09:00–17:00; **Su:** 10:00–15:00. Large stock. Spec: Booksearch. PR: £1–300. Corresp: French. Notes: *Booksearches undertaken.*

Peter Hill, 3 Westbourne Avenue, Emsworth, PO10 7QT. Tel: (01243) 379956. Fax: (01243) 379956. E-mail: peterhill.books@btinternet.com. Est: 1986. Private premises. Book fairs only. Appointment necessary. Open: **M:** 09:00–17:00; **T:** 09:00–17:00; **W:** 09:00–17:00; **Th:** 09:00–17:00; **F:** 09:00–17:00. Small stock. Spec: Alpinism/Mountaineering; Classical Studies; Countries - Antarctic, The; Countries - Arctic, The; Topography - Local; Travel - General. PR: £10–2,000. Corresp: French. Mem: PBFA.

FAREHAM

Portus Books, 9, Union Street, Fareham, PO16 9EB. Prop: Philip Elston. Tel: 01329 220419. Web: www.portusbooks.co.uk. E-mail: enquiry@portusbooks.co.uk. Private premises. Postal Only. Telephone First. Spec: Author - Baker, Denys V.; Maritime/Nautical; Modern First Editions; Sport - Sailing; Travel - General. Corresp: German. Notes: *All books are accurately described, professionally packaged and promptly dispatched.*

FARNBOROUGH

Farnborough Gallery, 26 Guildford Road West, Farnborough, GU14 6PU. Prop: P.H. Taylor. Tel: (01252) 518033. Fax: (01252) 511503. Web: www.farnboroughgallery.co.uk. E-mail: peter-t@btconnect.com. Est: 1978. Storeroom. Internet and Postal. Appointment necessary. Open: **M:** 08:00–18:00; **T:** 08:00–18;00; **W:** 08:00–18:00; **Th:** 08:00–18;00; **F:** 08:00–18:00; **S:** 08:00–17:00. Spec: Academic/Scholarly; Aircraft; Army, The; Art; Art - British; Art - Technique; Art - Theory; Art Reference. PR: £5–1,000. CC: AE; MC; V. Mem: Fine Art Trade Guild, VAT No: GB 296 4807 13 Notes: *picture framing, mount cutting, framed artwork for sale.*

FLEET

War & Peace Books, 32 Wellington Ave., Fleet, GU51 3BF. Prop: Dr G.M. Bayliss. Tel: (01252) 677902. Fax: (01252) 677902. Web: www.abebooks.com. E-mail: gwyn.bayliss@ntlworld.com. Est: 1998. Private premises. Postal Only. Contactable. Very small stock. Spec: Army, The; Aviation; Biography; History - 20th Century; Literary Travel; Literature; Maritime/Nautical; Military. PR: £5–100.

FORDINGBRIDGE

Bristow & Garland, ■ 45–47 Salisbury Street, Fordingbridge, SP6 1AB. Prop: David Bristow & Victoria Garland. Tel: (01425) 657337. Fax: (01425) 657337. Web: www.bristowandgarland.co.uk. E-mail: mail@bristowandgarland.fsnet.co.uk. Est: 1970. Shop open: **M:** 10:00–17:00; **F:** 10:00–17:00; **S:** 10:00–17:00. Small stock. Spec: Autographs; Fine & Rare; Manuscripts. PR: £5–5,000. CC: MC; V. Cata: Manuscripts.

HAMPSHIRE

GOSPORT

Richard Martin Bookshop & Gallery, ■ 19-23 Stoke Road, Gosport, PO12 1LS. Prop: Directors - Richard and Elaine Martin. Tel: (023) 9252-0642. Web: www.richardmartingallery.co.uk. E-mail: enquiries@richardmartingallery.co.uk. Est: 1976. Shop open: **T:** 10:30–16:30; **Th:** 10:30–16:30; **F:** 10:30–16:30; **S:** 10:30–13:00. Closed for lunch: 13:00–14:15. Medium stock. Spec: Antiquarian; Illustrated - General; Maritime/Nautical; Maritime/Nautical - History; Maritime/Nautical - Log Books; Naval; Navy, The; Topography - General. PR: £10–3,000. CC: MC; V. Cata: maritime, naval, voyaging, yachting,etc. Mem: PBFA. VAT No: GB 430 6603 81. Notes: *High quality restoration of watercolours and prints. Valuations for probate, insurance,family division, etc.*

Sub Aqua Prints and Books, 3 Crescent Road Alverstoke, Gosport, PO12 2DH. Prop: Kevin F. Casey. Tel: (023) 9252 0426. Fax: (023) 9250 2428. Web: www.buyhistoryprints.com. E-mail: kevin@buyhistoryprints.com. Est: 1991. Private premises. Internet and Postal. Appointment necessary. Small stock. Spec: Conchology (see also Malacology); Deep Sea Diving; Fishes; Ichthyology; Marine Sciences; Maritime/Nautical; Maritime/Nautical - History; Naval. PR: £5– 1,000. CC: JCB; MC; V.

HAVANT

Tobo Books, 6 The Oakwood Centre Downley Road, Havant, PO9 2NP. Prop: Matthew Wingett. Tel: 02392472000. Web: www.tobo-books.com. E-mail: sheppards@tobo-books.com. Est: 2000. Office and/or bookroom. Internet Only. Appointment necessary. Open: **M:** 10–17:00; **T:** 10–17:00; **W:** 10– 17:00; **Th:** 10–17:00; **F:** 10–17:00. Small stock. Spec: Antiquarian; Architecture; - Byron, Lord; - Cruickshank, G.; - Dickens, Charles; - Fleming, Ian; - Greene, Graham; - Milne, A.A. PR: £1– 20,000. CC: JCB; MC; V. Corresp: Schoolboy French; Schoolboy Spanish. Mem: PBFA. VAT No: GB 812 1985 36.

HAYLING ISLAND

DBS Childrens Collectable Books, 43 Sea Front, Hayling Island, PO11 0AN. Prop: Dennis Cowan. Tel: 02392 637456. Fax: 02392 637456. Web: www.dbschildrenscollectablebooks.com. E-mail: dbsbooks@hotmail.com. Est: 1998. Private premises. Open: **M:** 10:30–17:30; **T:** 10:30–17:30; **W:** 10:30 17:30; **Th:** 10:30–17:30; **F:** 10:30 17:30.

HORNDEAN

Milestone Publications Goss & Crested China Club, 62 Murray Road, Horndean, PO8 9JL. Prop: Mrs. Lynda Pine. Tel: (023) 9259-7440. Fax: (023) 9259-1975. Web: www.gosschinaclub.demon.co.uk. E-mail: info@gosschinaclub.co.uk. Est: 1970. Shop and/or showroom. Open: **M:** 09:00–16:00; **T:** 09:00– 16:00; **W:** 09:00–16:00; **Th:** 09:00–16:00; **F:** 09:00–16:00. Small stock. Spec: Antiques; Author - Goss, W.H.; - Hall S.C.; - Jewett, S.O.; Ceramics; Collectables; Collecting; Collectables. PR: £1–40. CC: E; JCB; MC; V; all others. Mem: F.R.S.A. Notes: *Open at other times by appointment Also, dealers in souvenir ware china, Goss & Crested china c.1850-1940, heraldic porcelain & new books of the same topics.*

LIPHOOK

Pauline Harries Books, 4, Willow Close, Liphook, GU30 7HX. Prop: Pauline Harries. Tel: 01428 723764. Fax: 01428 722367. E-mail: pauline.harriesbooks@tiscali.co.uk. Est: 1980. Private premises. Internet and Postal. Appointment necessary. Open: **M:** 09:00–17:30; **T:** 09:00–17:30; **W:** 09:00–17:30; **Th:** 09:00–17:30; **F:** 09:00–17:30; **S:** 09:00–17:30; **Su:** 09:00–17:30; Closed for lunch: 13:00–14:00. Spec: Antiques; Architecture; Art; Biography; General Stock; Geology; History - General; Ornithology. CC: MC; V. Mem: PBFA.

Sheppard's Book Dealers in Latin America and Southern Africa

Order the next edition £24.00

HAMPSHIRE

LISS

William Duck, Highfield Farm Hatch Lane, Liss, GU33 7NH. Prop: William Duck. Tel: (01730) 895594. Fax: (01730) 894548. Est: 1963. Private premises. Appointment necessary. Very small stock. Spec: Architecture; Arms & Armour; Astronautics; Aviation; Canals/Inland Waterways; Cities - General; Civil Engineering; Decorative Art. PR: £10–5,000. Mem: ABA; PBFA.

LYMINGTON

Alastor Rare Books, 12 Wisbech Way, Hordle, Lymington, SO41 0YQ. Prop: J.A.Eaton. Tel: 01425 629756. E-mail: alastor.rarebooks@virgin.net. Private premises. Appointment necessary. Spec: Antiquarian; Illustrated - General. Cata: Early English & Continental books. Corresp: Italian, French. Mem: PBFA.

M. & B. Clapham, ■ 4 Priestmands Place, Lymington, SO41 9GA. Prop: Peter Clapham. Tel: (01590) 677019. Est: 1978. Shop open: **M:** 10:00–17:00; **T:** 10:00–17:00; **W:** 10:00–17:00; **Th:** 10:00–17:00; **F:** 10:00–17:00; **S:** 09:00–17:00. Medium stock. Spec: Music - General; Sport - Yachting. CC: MC; V.

MEDSTEAD

Soldridge Books Ltd, Soldridge House, Medstead, GU34 5JF. Prop: John & Jan Lewis. Tel: 01420 562 811. Fax: 01420 562811. Web: www.SoldridgeBooks.co.uk. E-mail: Soldridge.House@virgin.net. Est: 1991. Private premises. Internet and Postal. Appointment necessary. Open: **M:** 09:00–17:30; **T:** 09:00– 17:30; **W:** 09:00–17:30; **Th:** 09:00–17:30; **F:** 09:00–17:30; **S:** 09:00–17:30; **Su:** 09:00–17:30; Closed for lunch: 13:00–14:00. Spec: Aviation; Photography. CC: JCB; MC; V. Cata: Aviation. Photography. Corresp: French. Mem: PBFA. VAT No: GB 799 6939 25.

NEW MILTON

J.H. Day, 33 Ashley Common Road, New Milton, BH25 5AL. Tel: 01425 619406. E-mail: JAMESJday @aol.com. Est: 1988. Private premises. Internet and Postal. Open: **M:** 09:00–17:30; **T:** 09:00–17:30; **W:** 09:00–17:30; **Th:** 09:00–17:30; **F:** 09:00–17:30; **S:** 09:00–17:30; **Su:** 09:00–17:30. Spec: General; General Stock; Sport - Horse Racing (inc. Riding/Breeding/Equestrian). CC: PayPal.

OAKLEY

David Flint, 30 Barn Lane, Oakley, Basingstoke, RG23 7HT. Prop: David Flint. Tel: 01256 781413. E-mail: davidaflint@aol.com. Est: 1985. Private premises. Postal Only. Contactable. Spec: Art; Artists; Children's; Children's - Early Titles; Design; Ephemera. Cata: Children's & Illustrated.

OVERTON

David Esplin, 30 High Street, Overton, RG25 3HA. Tel: (01256) 771108. E-mail: books@esplin.fsworld .co.uk. Est: 1978. Private premises. Postal Only. Small stock. Spec: Astronomy; Mathematics; Medicine - History of; Natural Sciences; Physics; Science - History of; Technology. PR: £5–1,000. CC: MC; V; SW, So. Cata: History of Science, Medicine and Technology. Corresp: French.

PETERSFIELD

The Petersfield Bookshop, ■ 16a Chapel Street, Petersfield, GU32 3DS. Prop: Frank, Ann, John & David Westwood. Tel: (01730) 263438. Fax: (01730) 269426. Web: www.petersfieldbookshop.com. E-mail: sales@petersfieldbookshop.com. Est: 1918. Shop open: **M:** 09:00–17:30; **T:** 09:00–17:30; **W:** 09:00–17:30; **Th:** 09:00–17:30; **F:** 09:00–17:30; **S:** 09:00–17:30. Spec: Sport - Angling/Fishing; Travel - General; Booksearch; Prints and Maps. PR: £1–2,000. CC: AE; D; MC; V. Mem: ABA; PBFA; BA; ILAB. VAT No: GB 192 6013 72. Notes: *Also, maps, prints, new books, art materials, picture framing & a booksearch service.*

David Schutte, 'Waterside' 119 Sussex Road, Petersfield, GU31 4LB. Tel: (01730) 269115. Fax: (01730) 231177. Web: www.http://davidschutte.co.uk. E-mail: david.schutte@virgin.net. Est: 1980. Private premises. Internet and Postal. Appointment necessary. Spec: Author - Blyton, Enid; - Buckeridge, A.; - Crompton, Richmal; - Johns, W.E.; - Ransome, Arthur; - Richards, Frank; - Saville, M.; Children's. PR: £3–1,500. CC: MC; V. Cata: Children's and original artwork. Mem: PBFA.

Alexander Books, ■ 62 Castle Road, Southsea, Portsmouth, PO5 3AZ. Prop: Michael Wilson. Tel: 023 927 53207. Web: www.alexanderbooks.com. E-mail: michael@alexanderbooks.com. Est: 2003. Shop. **S:** 10:00–17:00.

PORTSMOUTH

Art Reference Books, 3 Portswood Road, Portsmouth, PO2 9QX. Prop: Andy Ralph. Tel: (02392) 790861. Fax: (02392) 650756. Web: www.artreferencebooks.com. E-mail: artreferencebooks@ hotmail.com. Est: 1999. Private premises. Internet and Postal. Appointment necessary. Medium stock. Spec: Antiquarian; Antiques; Applied Art; Architecture; Art; Art History; Art Reference; Artists. PR: £2–1,000. CC: E; MC; V.

PURBROOK

Hobgoblin Books, 66 Privett Road, Purbrook, PO7 5JW. Prop: Jacqueline & Philip Barrett. Tel: (023) 9271-3129. E-mail: goblinbook@aol.com. Est: 1988. Private premises. Appointment necessary. Medium stock. Spec: Authors - Women; Countries - China; Countries - Japan; Folklore; Medieval; Women. PR: £5–500. CC: PayPal.

RINGWOOD

E. Chalmers Hallam, Trees, 9 Post Office Lane St. Ives, Ringwood, BH24 2PG. Prop. Laura Hiscock. Tel: (01425) 470060, Fax: (01425) 470060. Web: www.hallam-books.co.uk. E-mail: laura@hallam-books.co.uk. Est: 1946. Private premises. Internet and Postal. Appointment necessary. Large stock. Spec: Africana; Anthropology; Arms & Armour; Author - Baden-Powell, Lord Robert; - Chapman, Abel; - Dinesen, Isak; - Jefferies, R.; - Niall, Ian. PR: £5–5,000. CC: MC; V; Debit card. Cata: Angling, Africa, Travel, Field Sports, BB, Guns. Mem: PBFA.

ROMSEY

Bufo Books, 32 Tadfield Road, Romsey, SO51 5AJ. Prop: Ruth Allen & Peter Hubbard. Tel: (01794) 517149. Fax: (08700) 516786. Web: www.bufobooks.demon.co.uk. E-mail: bufo@ bufobooks .demon.co.uk. Est: 1979. Private premises. Internet and Postal. Appointment necessary. Medium stock. Spec: Award Winners; Children's; Military; Newbery & Caldecott Award-Winners; War - General. PR: £1–200. CC: JCB; MC; V; Maestro/Switch; Bartercard. Cata: Military; Children's Literature. Corresp: French. Mem: PBFA; Bartercard; Cardsave. VAT No: GB 522 4988 32. Notes: *Mainly internet & postal but we also still exhibit at a few bookfairs each year.*

SOUTHAMPTON

Vincent G. Barlow, 24 Howerts Close Warsash, Southampton, SO31 9JR. Tel: (01489) 582431. E-mail: vg.books@ntlworld.com. Est: 1981. Storeroom. Book fairs only. Appointment necessary. Small stock. Spec: Art Reference; Catalogues Raisonnes; Children's - Illustrated; Decorative Art; Fine Printing; Graphics; Illustrated - General; Illustrated - 19th & 20th Century. PR: £3–2,000. Mem: PLA; IBIS. Notes: *Attends monthly fairs at Royal National. Also prints.*

Broadwater Books, 62 Britannia Gardens, Hedge End, Southampton, SO30 2RP. Prop: J.E. Dancy. Tel: (01489) 786035. E-mail: john@jdancy.fsnet.co.uk. Est: 1988. Private premises. Postal Only. Large stock. Spec: Author - Wheatley, Dennis; Countries - England; Countries - Great Britain; Countries - Melanesia; Countries - Scotland; History - General; History - European; Religion - General. PR: £1–400. Notes: *Also, wants lists welcomed.*

W.E. Jackson, 6 Shepherds Close, Bartley, Southampton, SO40 2LJ. Prop: Bill Jackson. Tel: (02380) 812640. E-mail: bill@bilberry.ndo.co.uk. Est: 1988. Private premises. Postal Only. Telephone First. Small stock. PR: £1–100. Notes: *Also organiser of Southampton and Winchester Book Fairs - and attends other fairs.*

Morley Case, 24 Wildburn Close Calmore, Southampton, SO40 2SG. Prop: David Case. Tel: (023) 8086-4264. Web: www.abebooks.com/home/case. E-mail: morleycase@aol.com. Est: 1973. Private premises. Internet and Postal. Appointment necessary. Small stock. Spec: Art; Aviation; Military; Sport - Golf. PR: £5–200. CC: Pay Pal.

Available from Richard Joseph Publishers Ltd

Sheppard's Book Dealers in NORTH AMERICA

15th Edition (Royal H/b, plus CD-ROM) £30.00 560pp

HAMPSHIRE

Peter Rhodes, Bookseller, ■ 21 Portswood Road, Southampton, SO17 2ES. Tel: (02380) 399003. E-mail: peterrhodes.books@virgin.net. Est: 1996. Shop open: **T:** 10:00–17:00; **W:** 10:00–17:00; **Th:** 10:00–17:00; **F:** 10:00–17:00; **S:** 10:00–17:00. Large stock. Spec: Anthropology; Author - 20th Century; Children's - Illustrated; Countries - India; Photography; Theatre. Notes: *insurance and probate valuation. Also coffee shop.*

SOUTHSEA

Palladour Books, 23 Eldon Street, Southsea, PO5 4BS. Prop: Jeremy & Anne Powell. Tel: (02392) 826935. Fax: (02392) 826935. E-mail: jeremy.powell@ntlworld.com. Est: 1985. Private premises. Internet and Postal. Appointment necessary. Very small stock. Spec: First Editions; Literature; Magazines & Periodicals - General; Military; Poetry; School Registers/Rolls of Honour; War - General; War - World War I. PR: £1–500.

Jade Mountain Bookshop, ■ 17-19 Highland Road, Southsea, Portsmouth, PO4. 9AD. Prop: Mr. Ian Stemp. Tel: 02392732951. E-mail: ianstemp@btinternet.com. Est: 1990. Shop open: **M:** 09:30–17:30; **W:** 09:30–17:30; **F:** 09:30–17:30; **S:** 09:30–17:30. Spec: Accountancy; Agriculture; Aircraft; Animals and Birds; Antiquarian; Antiques; Archaeology; Architecture.

TITCHFIELD

Ardis Books, 3, Mill Street, Titchfield, Fareham, PO14 4AB. Prop: Robert Newbury. Tel: 01329 517724. Web: www.ardis.co.uk. E-mail: RNewbury@ardis.co.uk. Est: 1989. Mail Order Only. Internet Only. Telephone First. Open: **M:** 09:00–17:30; **T:** 09:00–17:30; **W:** 09:00–17:30; **Th:** 09:00–17:30; **F:** 09:00–17:30; **S:** 09:00–17:30; **Su:** 09:00–17:30; Closed for lunch: 13:00–14:00. Spec: Antiquarian; Author - Johns, W.E.; - Saville, M.; Bibles; Business Studies; Comics; Commerce - General; Computing. VAT No: GB 522 2143 96.

WARSASH

Warsash Nautical Bookshop, ■ 6 Dibles Road, Warsash, Southampton, SO31 9HZ. Prop: Mr. Andrew Marshall. Tel: (01489) 572384. Fax: (01489) 885756. Web: www.nauticalbooks.co.uk. E-mail: orders@nauticalbooks.co.uk. Est: 1973. Internet and Postal. Shop open: **M:** 09:00–17:30; **T:** 09:00–17:30; **W:** 09:00–17:30; **Th:** 09:00–17:30; **F:** 09:00–17:30; **S:** 09:30–17:00. Small stock. Spec: Academic/Scholarly; Maritime/Nautical; Maritime/Nautical - Log Books; Navigation; Booksearch; Prints and Maps. PR: £5–500. CC: AE; D; E; JCB; MC; V. Mem: BA. VAT No: GB 108 3293 82.

WINCHESTER

Boris Books, Winnall Manor Farm Wales Street, Winchester, SO23 0HA. Prop: Pam Stevenson. Tel: (01962) 890355. Web: www.borisbooks.co.uk. E-mail: pam@borisbooks.wanadoo.co.uk. Est: 1995. Office and/or bookroom. Internet and Postal. Appointment necessary. Open: **M:** 09:30–16:30; **T:** 09:30–16:30; **W:** 09:30–16:30; **Th:** 09:30–16:30; **F:** 09:30–16:30. Closed for lunch: 13:15–14:15. Small stock. Spec: Author - Heyer, Georgette; Children's; Fiction - General; Fiction - Historical; First Editions; Illustrated - General; Literature; Music - General. PR: £1–200. CC: MC; V. VAT No: GB 717 6806 15.

H.M. Gilbert & Son, 5 Rooks Down, Winchester, SO22 4QN. Prop: Richard Gilbert. Tel: (023) 8022-6420. Est: 1859. Private premises. Appointment necessary. Small stock. Spec: Antiquarian; Literature; Topography - General; Topography - Local. PR: £1–500. CC: MC; V. Mem: PBFA.

John Barton, 84 Old Kennels Lane, Winchester, SO22 4JT. Tel: 01962 866543. E-mail: jg.barton@virgin.net. Est: 1966. Private premises. Postal Only. Appointment necessary. Spec: Archaeology; History - Local; Topography - Local.

Kingsgate Books & Prints, ■ Kingsgate Arch, Winchester, SO23 9PD. Prop: Michael Fowkes. Tel: (01962) 864710. Fax: (01962) 864710. Est: 1992. Shop open: **T:** 12:30–17:00; **W:** 12:30–17:00; **Th:** 12:30–17:00; **F:** 12:30–17:00; **S:** 10:30–17:00. Very small stock. Spec: Art History; Art Reference; History - Local; Literary Criticism; Literature; Natural History; Poetry; Prints and Maps. PR: £1–150. CC: AE; MC; V; Any.

Oxfam Books and Music, ■ 74 Parchment St., Winchester, SO23 8AT. Prop: Oxfam. Tel: (01962) 841627. Web: www.oxfam.org.uk/shops. E-mail: oxfamshopf4034@btconnect.com. Est: 1989. Shop open: **M:** 09:30–17:00; **T:** 09:30–17:00; **W:** 09:30–17:00; **Th:** 09:30–17:00; **F:** 09:30–17:00; **S:** 09:30–17:00. Small stock. Spec: Academic/Scholarly; Art; Children's; Collectables; Fiction - General; Fiction - Crime, Detective, Spy, Thrillers; Health; History - General. PR: £1–150. CC: MC; V. Cata: all.

HAMPSHIRE

Peter M Daly, Ronald Bowker Court Greenhill Road, Winchester, SO22 5EA. Prop: Peter Daly. Tel: 01962 867732. Fax: 01962 867732. E-mail: petermdaly@rarebooks.fsnet.co.uk. Est: 1978. Office and/ or bookroom. Book fairs only Appointment necessary. Open: **M:** 10:00 17:00; **T:** 10.00–17.00, **W:** 10:00–17:00; **Th:** 10:00–17:00; **F:** 10:00–17:00; **S:** 10:30–16:30. Closed for lunch: 13:00–14:00. Spec: Africana; Alpinism/Mountaineering; Animals and Birds; Antiquarian; Applied Art; Architecture; Art; Colour-Plate. CC: JCB; MC; V; Solo.Maestro.Switch. Mem: PBFA. VAT No: GB 411 8630 76. Notes: *Books are listed online at ABE.Biblion.Biblio & Antiqbook*.

S.P.C.K., ■ 24 The Square, Winchester, SO23 9EX. Tel: (01962) 866617. Fax: (01962) 890312. E-mail: winchester@spck.org.uk. Est: 1698. Shop open: **M:** 09:00–16:30; **T:** 08:00–17:30; **W:** 09:00–17:30; **Th:** 09:00–17:30; **F:** 09:00–17:30; **S:** 08:00–17:30. Large stock. Spec: Religion - Christian; Theology; Booksearch. PR: £1–300. CC: MC; V. Mem: BA. VAT No: GB 232 8071 82. Notes: *Also, wide Christian booksearch service.*

Sen Books, 3 Long Barrow Close South Wonston, Winchester, SO21 3ED. Prop: Andrew Duckworth. Tel: (01962) 884405. Fax: (01962) 884405. E-mail: andrew.duckworth_senbooks@btopenworld.com. Est: 1975. Private premises. Appointment necessary. Small stock. Spec: Author - Trollope, Anthony; - White, Gilbert; Booksearch; Collectables; Ephemera; Prints and Maps. PR: £1 – 200.

The Winchester Bookshop, ■ 10a St George's Street, Winchester, SO23 8BG. Prop: Messrs Barnes & Brown. Tel: 01962855630. E-mail: winchester books@btinternet.com. Est: 1991. Shop open **M:** 10.00–1700; **T:** 10:00–17:00; **W:** 10:00–17:00; **Th:** 10:00–17:00; **F:** 10:00–17:00; **S:** 10:00–17:00. Spec: Academic/Scholarly; Antiquarian; Archaeology; Architecture; Army, The; Art; Canals/Inland Waterways; Civil Engineering. CC: MC; V; Most debit cards. Corresp: German. Notes: *A general bookshop, with particular strengths in Winchester local history, fishing and literature. Some good antiquarian and modern firsts are stocked.*

HEREFORDSHIRE

ASHPERTON

Books for Content, Spring Grove Farm Wood End, Ashperton, Ledbury, HR8 2RS. Prop: H.M. Jones. Tel: (01432) 890279. E-mail: hettie.jones@btopenworld.com. Est: 1989. Private premises. Postal Only. Small stock. Spec: Agriculture; Author - Street, A.G.; Cookery/Gastronomy; Crafts; Farming & Livestock; Gardening - General; Horticulture; Rural Life. PR: £3–100. Notes: *Booksearch service incorporating the Hilary Rittner Booksearch which is now closed.*

GLASBURY

babelog books, Victoria House , Glasbury, Hereford, HR3 5NR. Prop: Simon Cartwright. Tel: (01497) 847190. Web: www.ukbookworld.com/members/mason. E-mail: simon.cartwright1@virgin.net. Est: 2000. Private premises. Postal Only. Appointment necessary. Very small stock. Spec: Drama; English; Fiction - General; Literature; Literature - 19th C; Literature in Translation; Modern First Editions; Plays. PR: £5–1,000.

HEREFORD

The New Strand Bookshop, ■ Eardisley, Hereford, HR3 6PW. Prop: R. & A. Cardwell. Tel: (01544) 327285. Shop open: **W:** 09:30–18:00; **Th:** 09:30–18:00; **F:** 09:30–18:00; **S:** 09:30–18:00; **Su:** 09:30–18:00; Very large stock. Spec: Children's; Fiction - General; Fiction - Crime, Detective, Spy, Thrillers; Fiction - Science Fiction; Natural History. PR: £1–250.

B.A. & C.W.M. Pratt, Huntington House Huntington Lane, Hereford, HR4 7RA. Tel: (01432) 350927. Fax: (01432) 350927. Est: 1967. Private premises. Postal Only. Spec: Medicine.

KINGTON

Castle Hill Books, ■ 12 Church Street, Kington, HR5 3AZ. Prop: Peter Newman. Tel: (01544) 231195/ 231161. Fax: (01544) 231161. Web: www.castlehillbooks.co.uk. E-mail: sales@castlehillbooks.co.uk. Est: 1987. Shop open: **M:** 10:30–13:00; **T:** 10:30–13:00; **W:** 10:30–13:00; **Th:** 10:30–13:00; **F:** 10:30–13:00; **S:** 10:30–16:00. Very large stock. Spec: Agriculture; Antiquarian; Archaeology; History - General; History - Local; Natural History; Topography - General; Topography - Local. PR: £3–15,000. CC: MC; V. VAT No: GB 489 2054 19. Notes: *Also, new books, and maps in stock.*

LEDBURY

Keith Smith Books, ■ 78b The Homend, Ledbury, HR8 1BX. Prop: Keith Smith. Tel: Day (01531) 635336. E-mail: keith@ksbooks.demon.co.uk. Est: 1986. Shop open: **T:** 10:00–17:00; **W:** 10:00–17:00; **Th:** 10:00–17:00; **F:** 10:00–17:00; **S:** 10:00–17:00. Medium stock. Spec: Author - Brooke, Rupert; - Dymock Poets, The; - Frost, Robert; - Masefield, John; - Thomas, Edward; Crafts; Embroidery; History - General. PR: £1–250. CC: E; JCB; MC; V; Switch, Delta. Cata: Needlecrafts, Textiles and Rugmaking.

LEOMINSTER

Hummingbird Books, ■ 16 South Street, Leominster, HR6 8JB. Prop: Jill Gibbs. Tel: (01568) 616471. E-mail: hummingbirdbooks@btinternet.com. Est: 2001. Shop open: **M:** 10:00–17:30; **T:** 10:00–17:30; **Th:** 10:00–17:30; **F:** 10:00–17:30; **S:** 09:00–16:00. Medium stock. Spec: Illustrated - General; Military History; Sport - General; Topography - General. CC: AE; MC; V. Notes: *Concession at 6 Broad Street, Hay-on-Wye specialising in maritime, military and sport.*

ROSS–ON–WYE

Ross Old Books, ■ 51 & 52 High Street, Ross–on–Wye, HR9 5HH. Prop: Phil Thredder. Tel: +44 (0)1989 567458. Web: www.rossoldbooks.co.uk. E-mail: enquiries@rossoldbooks.co.uk. Est: 1986. Shop open: **W:** 10:00–17:00; **Th:** 10:00–17:00; **F:** 10:00–17:00; **S:** 10:00–17:00. Medium stock. Spec: Folio Society, The; History - Local; Topography - General; Prints and Maps. PR: £1–1,000. CC: AE; MC; V; SW, SO. Mem: PBFA. VAT No: GB 435 3892 33. Notes: *High turnover bookshop, competitive prices, with small internet stock stored upstairs and offered for sale on our website. Also antique maps.*

HEREFORDSHIRE

WEOBLEY

Hereford Booksearch (John Trevitt), Rose Cottage Church Road, Weobley, HR4 8SD. Tel: 01544 318388. E-mail: john@trevitt.freeserve.co.uk. Est: 2004. Private premises. Postal Only. Appointment necessary. Very small stock.

Weobley Bookshop, ■ Broad Street, Weobley, HR4 8SA. Prop: Karen Stout. Tel: 01544 319292. Web: www.weobleybookshop.co.uk. E-mail: sales@weobleybookshop.co.uk. Est: 1999. Shop open: **M:** 10.00–17.00; **T:** 10.00–17.00; **W:** 10.00–17.00; **Th:** 10.00–17.00; **F:** 10.00–17.00; **S:** 10.00–17.00. Closed for lunch: 13.15–14:00. Spec: New Books; Ephemera. CC: MC; V. Mem: BA. Notes: *New and secondhand books, CDs and greetings cards.*

YARKHILL

David Warnes Books, One Pound Cottage, Yarkhill, HR1 3TA. Tel: 01432 890275. E-mail: davidwarnesbooks@talktalk.net. Private premises. Book fairs only. Telephone First. Open: **M:** 09:00–17:30; **T:** 09:00–17:30; **W:** 09:00–17:30; **Th:** 09:00–17:30; **F:** 09:00–17:30; **S:** 09:00 17:30, **Su:** 09:00–17:30; Closed for lunch: 13:00–14:00. Spec: Alpinism/Mountaineering; Anthropology; Countries - Afganistan; Countries - Alaska; Countries - Arabia; Countries - Armenia; Countries - Asia; Countries - Balkans, The. Mem: PBFA.

Available from Richard Joseph Publishers Ltd

Sheppard's Book Dealers in AUSTRALIA & NEW ZEALAND

Order the next edition now — £30.00

HERTFORDSHIRE

BERKHAMSTED

Richard Frost Books, Sunhaven Northchurch Common, Berkhamsted, HP4 1LR. Prop: Richard Frost. Tel: 01442 862011. E-mail: richardfrost4@btinternet.com. Est: 1988. Private premises. Book fairs only. Appointment necessary. Open: **M:** 09:00–17:30; **T:** 09:00–17:30; **W:** 09:00–17:30; **Th:** 09:00–17:30; **F:** 09:00–17:30; **S:** 09:00–17:30; **Su:** 09:00–17:30; Closed for lunch: 13:00–14:00. Spec: Biography; First Editions; History - General; Literary Criticism; Philately; Topography - General; Travel - General. Cata: General books. Notes: *Organiser of the Berkhamsted Book Fair.See my books at Jordans Antiques Centre, 63 Old High Street, Hemel Hempstead, Herts HP1 3AF. Open daily 10.00am - 5.00pm. Graham Green Specialist.*

David Mundy at Heritage Antiques, ■ 24 Castle Street, Berkhamsted, HP4 2DD. Prop: David Mundy. Tel: (020) 7482 7087. E-mail: dave.mundy@tiscali.co.uk. Est: 1994. Shop open: **M:** 10:00–17:30; **T:** 10:00–17:30; **W:** 10:00–17:30; **Th:** 10:00–17:30; **F:** 10:00–17:30; **S:** 10:00–17:30; **Su:** 10:00–17:30. Small stock. Spec: Art; Fiction - General; History - General; Military; Sport - General; Topography - General; Topography - Local. PR: £1–50. CC: MC; V. Notes: *Nooks & Crannies, Chesham, Bucks HP5 1HG (q.v.)*

Red Star Books, 4 Hamilton Road, Berkhamsted, HP4 3EF. Prop: Conor Pattenden. Tel: (01442) 870775. Web: www.http://ukbookworld.com/members/redstarbooks. E-mail: redstarbooks@ btopenworld.com. Est: 2001. Private premises. Internet and Postal. Appointment necessary. Medium stock. Spec: Academic/Scholarly; Antiquarian; Bindings; Communism; Countries - Ireland; Feminism; Fine leather bindings (see also Fine & Rare); History - Anarchism. PR: £2–1,000.

James Wilson, 22 Castle Street, Berkhamsted, HP4 2DW. Tel: (01442) 873396. Est: 1975. Private premises. Appointment necessary. Spec: Books about Books; Colour-Plate. PR: £2–500. Mem: Pres: Book Plate Society. Notes: *Mainly book plates in stock.*

BISHOP'S STORTFORD

Sheila Rainford, White Pine Cottage High St., Henham, Bishop's Stortford, CM22 6AS. Tel: (01279) 851129. Fax: (01279) 851129. E-mail: sheilarainford@talk21.com. Est: 1983. Private premises. Internet and Postal. Small stock. Spec: Banking & Insurance; Cookery/Gastronomy; Economics; History - Industrial; Industry; Literature. PR: £5–1,000. CC: V. Corresp: French and German. Mem: PBFA. VAT No: GB 632 2122 89.

Ray Smith, 'Lynwood', 111 Parsonage Lane, Bishop's Stortford, CM23 5BA. Tel: (01279) 324780. Fax: (01279) 324780. E-mail: raymond.smith63@ntlworld.com. Est: 1994. Private premises. Postal Only. Very small stock. Spec: Countries - South Africa; Travel - Africa. PR: £5–250. Notes: *Also, Cecil Rhodes, Rhodesiana and Southern Africa.*

Edwin Trevorrow, 5 Pryors Close, Bishop's Stortford, CM23 5JX. Tel: (01279) 652902. Est: 1994. Private premises. Appointment necessary. Small stock. Spec: Biography; Fiction - General; Fiction - Historical; Fiction - Science Fiction; First Editions; Literature; Modern First Editions; Vintage Paperbacks. PR: £1–200.

www.AntiqueWatchStore.com, Grooms Cottage Elsenham Hall, Bishop's Stortford, CM22 6DP. Tel: 01279-814 946. Fax: 01279-814 962. Web: www.antiquewatchstore.com. E-mail: info@ davidpenney.co.uk. Est: 1994. Private premises. Internet and Postal. Appointment necessary. Very small stock. Spec: Antiques. PR: £1–20,000. CC: AE; MC; V. Mem: FBHI. VAT No: GB 354 3041 82.

BUSHEY

Aviation Book Supply, ■ 10 Pasture Close, Bushey, WD23 4HP. Prop: R.K. Tomlinson. Tel: (020) 8386 1880. Web: www.aero-shop.co.uk. Est: 1996. Shop. Appointment necessary. Medium stock. Spec: Aviation. PR: £5–250.

G. & R. Leapman Ltd., 37 Hogarth Court Steeplands, Bushey, WD23 1BT. Prop: Gillian Leapman. Tel: (020) 8950-2995. E-mail: gleapman1@compuserve.com. Est: 1970. Private premises. Appointment necessary. Very small stock. Spec: Countries - Bermuda; Countries - Caribbean, The; Travel - Americas; Booksearch; Prints and Maps. PR: £10–1,000. Corresp: French. VAT No: GB 197 6103 41. Notes: *West Indies material.*

CHESHUNT

Denis W. Amos, 10 Mill Lane, Cheshunt, Waltham Cross, EN8 0JH. Tel: (01992) 630486. Est: 1948. Private premises. Postal Only. Large stock. Spec: Gambling; Sport - General; Sport - Football (Soccer); Sport - Horse Racing (inc. Riding/Breeding/Equestrian); Sport - Tennis. Notes: *majors on horse racing only.*

ELSTREE

Elstree Books, 12 West View Gardens, Elstree, WD6 3DD. Prop: Shirley Herbert. Tel: 0208 953 2999. Fax: 0208 953 2999. E-mail: elstreebooks@hotmail.com. Est: 1991. Private premises. Postal Only. Appointment necessary. Open: **M:** 09:00–17:30; **T:** 09:00–17:30; **W:** 09:00–17:30; **Th:** 09:00–17:30; **F:** 09:00–17:30; **S:** 09:00–17:30. Closed for lunch: 13:00–14:00. Spec: Classics, The; Illustrated - General; Private Press; Topography - General; Topography - Local; Woodcut novels; Booksearch. CC: through ABE only. Cata: Illustrated; New Additions.

HARPENDEN

Mavis Eggle, 34 Cowper Road, Harpenden, AL5 5NG. Prop: Mavis Eggle. Tel: (01582) 762603. Fax: (01582) 762603. E-mail: mavis_eggle@yahoo.co.uk. Est: 1979 Private premises. Book fairs only. Appointment necessary. Small stock. Spec: Antiquarian; Social History; Sport - Angling/Fishing; Technology; Ephemera. PR: £1–500. Mem: PBFA.

HERTFORD

Gillmark Gallery, 25 Parliament Square, Hertford, SG14 1EX. Prop: Mark Pretlove & Gill Woodhouse. Tel: (01992) 534444. Web: www.gillmark.com. E-mail: gillmark@btinternet.com. Est: 1997. Shop and/or gallery. Open: **T:** 10:00–17:00; **W:** 10:00–17:00; **Th:** 10:00–14:00; **F:** 10:00–17:00; **S:** 10:00–17:00. Medium stock. Spec: Antiquarian; Atlases; Natural History; Topography; Topography - General; Topography - Local; Booksearch; Prints and Maps. PR: £1–3,000. CC: AE; JCB; MC; V. VAT No: GB 740 8541 36.

HERTFORD HEATH

G Collins Bookdealers, 18 Postwood Green, Hertford Heath, SG13 7QJ, Tel: 01992 509928. Fax: 01992 584190. E-mail: hadnbrowne@aol.com. Postal Only. Open: **M:** 09:00–17:30; **T:** 09:00–17:30; **W:** 09:00–17:30; **Th:** 09:00–17:30; **F:** 09:00–17:30; **S:** 09:00–17:30; **Su:** 09:00–17:30; Closed for lunch: 13:00–14:00. Spec: Sport - Yachting; Topography - Local. Cata: Hertfordshire topography sailing history. Notes: *Specialist in Hertfordshire books.*

HITCHIN

Adrem Books, 7 Bury End, Pirton, Hitchin, SG5 3QB. Prop: David Braybrooke. Tel: 01462712668. Fax: 01462712668. E-mail: braybrooke35@AOL.com. Est: 1992. Private premises. Internet and Postal. Appointment necessary. Open: **M:** 06:00–24:00; **T:** 06:00–24:00; **W:** 06:00–24:00; **Th:** 06:00–24:00; **F:** 06:00–24:00; **S:** 06:00–24:00; **Su:** 06:00–24:00; Closed for lunch: 06:00–24:00. Spec: Academic/ Scholarly; Adult; Aeronautics; Publishers General, Puzzles; Railroads; Reference; Religion - General. CC: AE; E; MC; V.

Eric T. Moore Books, ■ 24 Bridge Street, Hitchin, SG5 2DF. Prop: John Leeson. Tel: (01462) 450497. Web: www.erictmoore.co.uk. E-mail: booksales@erictmoore.co.uk. Est: 1965. Internet and Postal. Shop open: **M:** 09:30–17:30; **T:** 09:30–17:30; **W:** 09:30–17:30; **Th:** 09:30–17:30; **F:** 09:30–17:30; **S:** 09:30–17:30; **Su:** 11:00–16:00. Very large stock. CC: MC; V. Mem: Ibooknet. VAT No: GB 759 7801 77. Notes: *Eric T. Moore Books was established in 1965 and sells secondhand, rare and antiquarian books, maps and prints. Housed in two converted cottages, the shop contains approximately 35,000 books.*

Phillips of Hitchin (Antiques), ■ The Manor House 26 Baycroft, Hitchin, SG5 1JW. Prop: Jerome Phillips. Tel: (01462) 432067. Fax: (01462) 441368. E-mail: phillips.of.hitchin@talk21.com. Est: 1884. Shop open: **M:** 09:00–17:30; **T:** 09:00–17:30; **W:** 09:00–17:30; **Th:** 09:00–17:30; **F:** 09:00–17:30. Medium stock. Spec: Antiques; Applied Art; Architecture; Furniture; Interior Design; Woodwork; Booksearch. PR: £5–3,000. CC: AE; E; MC; V. Corresp: French, German, Italian, Spanish, Russian, Portuguese. Mem: PBFA; British Antique Dealers Association. VAT No: GB 197 1842 28. Notes: *Open Saturdays by appointment. Also, antique furniture.*

HERTFORDSHIRE

LETCHWORTH

Gallimaufry Books, ■ 50 Leys Avenue, Letchworth Garden City, SG6 3EQ. Prop: Barry Meaden. Tel: 01462 686129. Web: www.ukbookworld.com/members/spitfire. E-mail: barrymeaden@waitrose.com. Est: 2005. Shop open: **M:** 10:00–17:00; **T:** 10:00–17:00; **Th:** 10:00–17:00; **F:** 10:00–17:00; **S:** 10:00–17:00. Spec: Aviation; Military; Military - Modelling; Naval; Textiles; War - General; Prints and Maps. Cata: aviation. Notes: *Attends Wing Book Fair.*

MUCH HADHAM

H.M. Fletcher, Wynches Barn, Much Hadham, SG10 6BA. Prop: Marina & Keith R. Fletcher. Tel: (01279) 843883. Fax: (01279) 842830. E-mail: keith@hmfletcher.co.uk. Est: 1902. Private premises. Appointment necessary. Spec: Antiquarian; Bindings; Fine & Rare; Illustrated - General; Incunabula. PR: £50–20,000. CC: MC; V. Cata: General antiquarian. Corresp: French. Mem: ABA; PBFA; ILAB. VAT No: GB 626 2128 60.

NEW BARNET

ForensicSearch, 17 Greenacres, Glyn Avenue, New Barnet, EN4 9PJ. Prop: Nick Danks and Samantha Sproates. Tel: (020) 8440-8896. E-mail: forensicsearch@hotmail.com. Est: 1999. Private premises. Postal Only. Very small stock. Spec: Crime (True); Science - Forensic; Booksearch. PR: £2–200.

RADLETT

G.L. Green Ltd., 18 Aldenham Avenue, Radlett, WD7 8HX. Prop: G. L. Grenn. Tel: (01923) 857077. Fax: (01923) 857077. Web: www.glgreen.co.uk. E-mail: orders@glgreen.co.uk. Est: 1972. Storeroom. Internet and Postal. Appointment necessary. Small stock. Spec: Deep Sea Diving; History - Napoleonic; Maritime/Nautical; Naval; Navy, The; Passenger Liners; Shipbuilding and Shipping; Transport. PR: £1–1,000. CC: AE; JCB; MC; V; PayPal. Cata: Naval and Maritime. Mem: PBFA. Notes: *Booksearch service.*

RICKMANSWORTH

Clive A. Burden Ltd., Elmcote House, The Green Croxley Green, Rickmansworth, WD3 3HN. Tel: (01923) 778097. Fax: (01923) 896520. Web: www.caburden.com. E-mail: pburden@caburden.com. Est: 1966. Private premises. Appointment necessary. Very large stock. Spec: Atlases; Botany; Cartography; Illustrated - General; Natural History; Topography - General; Topography - Local; Town Plans. PR: £5–10,000. Mem: ABA; ILAB; IMCoS. VAT No: GB 196 7570 11. Notes: *Also, decorative books.*

ST. ALBANS

L.M.S. Books, 52 Westminster Court, St. Albans, AL1 2DX. Prop: Chris Fruin. Tel: (01727) 855312. Web: www.lmsbooks.co.uk. E-mail: lmsbooks@hotmail.com. Est: 1994. Office and/or bookroom. Appointment necessary. Medium stock. Spec: Author - Pratchett, Terry; Countries - Mexico; Fiction - General; First Editions, Literature; Modern First Editions; Mysteries; Signed Editions. PR: £10–350. CC: MC; V; SW. Notes: *Also, a selection of stock at: Biblion, London W1. Publishers of Booker Prize 1969-2006 catalogue. 290 books listed. Stocks first editions of Booker Prize titles.*

Paton Books, ■ 34 Holywell Hill, St. Albans, AL1 1DE. Prop: Richard & Josie Child. Tel: (01727) 853984. Fax: (01727) 865764. Web: www.patonbooks.co.uk. E-mail: patonbooks@aol.com. Est: 1962. Shop open: **M:** 09:00–18:00; **T:** 09:00–18:00; **W:** 09:00–18:00; **Th:** 09:00–18:00; **F:** 09:00–18:00; **S:** 09:00–18:00; **Su:** 10:30–18:00. Very large stock. Spec: Art; Fiction - General; First Editions; History - General; History - Local; Maritime/Nautical; Military; Railways. PR: £1–400. CC: D; JCB; MC; V; Switch, SO. Corresp: French. Mem: BA; Notes: *This long established bookshop is situated in 18th century buildings a stone's throw from St Albans Cathedral. We specialise in very good quality secondhand books, including modern, out of print and collectable books.*

RM Books, 18 Cornwall Road, St. Albans, AL1 1SH. Prop: Robert Moore. Tel: (01727) 830058. Web: www.rmbooks.co.uk. E-mail: rmbooks@verulamium94.freeserve.co.uk. Est: 1988. Private premises. Postal Only. Very small stock. Spec: Anatomy; Bacteriology; Biochemistry; Biology - General; Crime (True); Criminology; Entomology; Evolution. PR: £10–100. Cata: medicine & related sciences. Mem: PBFA.

Reg & Philip Remington, 23 Homewood Road, St. Albans, AL1 4BG. Tel: 01727 893531. Fax: 01727 893532. Web: www.remingtonbooks.com. E-mail: philip@remingtonbooks.com. Est: 1979. Private premises. Appointment necessary. Spec: American Indians; Colour-Plate; Countries - Afghanistan; Countries - Africa; Countries - Alaska; Countries - Albania; Countries - Algeria; Countries - Americas, The. PR: £5–5,000. CC: MC; V. Cata: on specialised subjects. Mem: ABA; BA; ILAB.

TRING

David Ford Books, Midwood, Shire Lane Cholesbury, Tring, HP23 6NA. Tel: (01494) 758663. E-mail: dford.books@ukgateway.net. Est: 1985. Private premises. Internet and Postal. Telephone First. Large stock. Spec: Animals and Birds; Archaeology; Art; Art History; Children's; Cinema/Film; Egyptology; Fiction - General. PR: £1–500. CC: JCB; MC; V. Mem: PBFA. Notes: *Also 2 floors of books at The Gillmark Gallery, Parliament Square, Hertford. Tues - Sat 10am - 5pm, early closing Thursday.*

WATFORD

medievalbookshop, PO Box 2082, Watford, WD18 0AD. Prop: Nick Gorman. Tel: 01923 227323. Fax: 01923 227323. Web: www.medievalbookshop.co.uk. E-mail: admin@medievalbookshop.co.uk. Est: 2001. Private premises. Internet and Postal. Small stock. Spec: Academic/Scholarly; Archaeology; History - European; History - Middle Ages; History - Reformation; History - Renaissance, The; Medieval, Religion - General. PR: £1–200. CC: PayPal.

Peter Taylor & Son, 1 Ganders Ash Leavesden, Watford, WD25 7HE. Prop: Peter Taylor. Tel: (01923) 663325. E-mail: taylorbooks@clara.co.uk. Est: 1973. Storeroom. Postal Only. Contactable. Medium stock. Spec: Academic/Scholarly; Antiquarian; Archaeology; Art History; Bibliography; Biography; Ecclesiastical History & Architecture; Fine & Rare. PR: £15–1,000. CC: MC; V. Corresp: French.

Westons Booksellers Ltd., 44 Stratford Road, Watford, WD17 4NZ. Prop: Jeremy Weston. Tel: (01923) 229081. Fax: (01923) 243343. Web: www.westons.co.uk. E-mail: books@westons.co.uk. Est: 1977. Private premises. Internet and Postal. Appointment necessary. Medium stock. Spec: Aeronautics; Agriculture; Aids Crisis, The; Alchemy; Architecture; Astronautics; Astronomy; Autism. PR: £3–300. CC: E; MC; V. Cata: Science, Medicine, Technology. VAT No: GB 225 0259 93. Notes: *Very recently published scientific, medical & technical books, all in new condition offered at substantial discounts.*

ISLE OF WIGHT

COWES

The Bookroom, ■ 37 Goss Street, Cowes, PO31 7TA. Prop: M.C. & V.F. Edmondson. Tel: 01983 873897. E-mail: mothergoose4books@btinternet.com. Shop open: **M:** 10:30–17:00; **T:** 10:30–17:00; **W:** 10:30–17:00; **Th:** 10:30–17:00; **F:** 10:30–17:00; **S:** 10:30–17:00. Notes: *Also at Mothergoose Bookshop, St Helens, and The Bookroom, Yarmouth.*

Curtle Mead Books, 105 Curtle Mead, Baring Road, Cowes, PO31 8DS. Prop: John Lucas. Tel: (01983) 294312. E-mail: lucas@curtlemead.demon.co.uk. Est: 1999. Private premises. Telephone First. Medium stock. Spec: Maritime/Nautical; Natural History; Naval; Navigation; Ornithology; Ship Modelling; Shipbuilding and Shipping; Sport - Yachting. PR: £1–500. CC: PayPal. Corresp: German. Mem: PBFA.

FRESHWATER

David G. Bancroft, Little Orchard Court Road, Freshwater, PO40 9NU. Tel: (01983) 759069. Est: 1995. Private premises. Postal Only. Small stock. Spec: Aviation; Ephemera. PR: £3–150. Notes: *Catalogues also include gliding and technical aspects of aviation.*

Cameron House Books, ■ Dimbola Lodge Terrace Lane, Freshwater Bay, PO40 9QE. Prop: L.J. Sklaroff. Tel: 01983 754960. Web: www.cameronhousebooks.com. E-mail: ljs@cambooks-dimbola.freeserve.co.uk. Est: 1994. Shop open: **T:** 10:00–16:00; **W:** 10:00–16:00; **Th:** 10:00–16:00; **F:** 10:00–16:00; **S:** 10:00–16:00; **Su:** 10:00–16:00. Spec: Art; Artists; Author - Ardizzone, Edward; - Cameron, Julia Margaret; - Clarke, Arthur C.; - Darwin, Charles; - Dickens, Charles; - Durrell, Lawrence. CC: via PayPal. Cata: Modern firsts, illustrated, photography. Corresp: German, Spanish, French. Mem: PLA. Notes: *Specialist in Mervyn Peake, Charles Keeping, Julia Margaret Cameron & her circle (Darwin, Tennyson et al.), 20th century illustrated books, early photography, modern first editions, Isle of Wight writers.*

NEWPORT

Firsts in Print, 95 St. John's Road, Newport, PO30 1LS. Prop: Peter Elliston. Tel: (01983) 521748. Web: www.firsts-in-print.co.uk. E-mail: peter@firsts-in-print.co.uk. Est: 1984. Private premises. Internet and Postal. Appointment necessary. Open: **M:** 09:00–17:00; **T:** 09:00–17:00; **W:** 09:00–17:00; **Th:** 09:00–17:00; **F:** 09:00–17:00. Medium stock. Spec: Children's; Fiction - Crime, Detective, Spy, Thrillers; Fiction - Fantasy, Horror; Literature; Modern First Editions; Proof Copies; Signed Editions. PR: £3–1,000. CC: MC; V; Switch/Maestro. VAT No: GB 768 9507 66. Notes: *Corner House, 68-70 Lugley St, Newport, Isle of Wight.*

Marcus Niner, Willow Cottage Marks Corner, Newport, PO30 5UD. Tel: (01983) 209473. E-mail: mail@ninerbooks.co.uk. Private premises. Book fairs only. Telephone First. Very small stock. Spec: Art; General; History - British; Literature; Topography - Local; Travel - General. PR: £10–2,000. CC: MC; V. Mem: PBFA.

RYDE

Heritage Books, ■ 7 Cross Street, Ryde, PO33 2AD. Prop: Rev. D.H. Nearn. Tel: (01983) 562933. Fax: (01983) 812634. E-mail: heritagebooksryde@btconnect.com. Est: 1978. Shop open: **M:** 10:00–17:00; **T:** 10:00–17:00; **W:** 10:00–17:00; **Th:** ; **F:** 10:00–17:00; **S:** 10:00–17:00. Large stock. Spec: Countries - Africa; Countries - Isle of Wight; Theology. PR: £1–500. CC: MC; V. Corresp: French, Portuguese. VAT No: GB 339 0615 58.

Kalligraphia, 66 Bettesworth Road, Ryde, PO33 3EJ. Prop: Louisa Mamakou. Tel: 00 44 (0) 1983 562702. Web: www.kalligraphia.com. E-mail: books@kalligraphia.com. Est: 2003. Private premises. Internet and Postal. Contactable. Spec: Archaeology; Art; Astronomy; Biography; Books in Greek; Botany; Children's; Countries - Cyprus. CC: MC; V; PayPal. Cata: Most subjects. Corresp: Greek; French. Notes: *Free Booksearch Service. Email Catalogues issued. See us at Isle of Wight Book Fairs and mainland fossil fairs.*

The Ryde Bookshop, ■ 135 High Street, Ryde, PO33 2RJ. Prop: M.D. Sames. Tel: (01983) 565227. E-mail: rydebookshop@yahoo.co.uk. Est: 1988. Shop open: **M:** 09:00–17:00; **T:** 09:00–17:00; **W:** 09:00–17:00; **Th:** 09:00–17:00; **F:** 09:00–17:00; **S:** 09:00–17:00. Very large stock. PR: £1–200. CC: E; JCB; MC; V. Mem: BA. Notes: *Also, new books.*

ISLE OF WIGHT

ST. HELENS

Mothergoose Bookshop, ■ West Green House Upper Green Road, St. Helens, PO33 1XB. Prop: M.C. and V.F. Edmondson. Tel: 01983 874063 E-mail: mothergoose4books@btinternet.com. Est: 1980. Shop At: Mothergoose Bookshop Lower Green Road St Helens I O W. Open: **M:** 10:30–17:00; **T:** 10:30–17:00; **W:** 10:30–17:00; **Th:** 10:30–17:00; **F:** 10:30–17:00; **S:** 10:30–17:00; **Su:** 10.30–16.30. Spec: Maritime/Nautical; Military; Prints and Maps. Mem: Also at: Mothergoose Bookshop Lower Green Road St Helens I O W. Notes: *Also at The Bookroom, Cross Street Cowes I O W and The Bookroom, Jirah Place Yarmouth I O W and stocks cover most subjects.*

VENTNOR

Shirley Lane Books, St. Lawrence Dene Undercliff Drive, Ventnor, PO38 1XJ. Prop: Shirley Lane. Tel: (01983) 852309. Web: www.abebook.co.uk. E-mail: shirleylane@talk21.com. Est: 1976. Private premises. Internet and Postal. Appointment necessary. Small stock. Spec: Authors - Women; Feminism; Women. PR: £1–500. Corresp: French.

Ventnor Rare Books, ■ 32 Pier Street, Ventnor, PO38 1SX. Prop: Nigel & Teresa Traylen. Tel: (01983) 853706. Fax: (01983) 854706. E-mail: vrb@andytron.demon.co.uk. Est: 1989. Shop open: **M:** 10:00–17:00; **T:** 10:00–17:00; **Th:** 10:00–17:00; **F:** 10:00–17:00; **S:** 10:00–17:00. Medium stock. Spec: Academic/Scholarly; Antiquarian; Antiques; Art Reference; Bibliography; Bindings; Fiction - General; Literature. PR: £1 500. CC: MC, V; UK Switch. Corresp: French. Mem: ABA; PBFA; ILAB. VAT No: GB 566 5246 19.

YARMOUTH

Alan Argent, Two Ways, Sconce Road Norton, Yarmouth, PO41 0RT. Prop: Alan Argent. Tel: (01983) 760851. E-mail: alanthebook@aol.com. Storeroom. Appointment necessary. Very small stock. Spec: Maritime/Nautical; Seamanship; Sport - Sailing. PR: £3–100. Notes: *Also, attends the occasional bookfair.*

Available from Richard Joseph Publishers Ltd

BOOKDEALING FOR PROFIT

by Paul Minet

Quarto H/b £10.00 144pp

KENT

ASHFORD

Stephen Dadd, 18 Dunkery Rise, Ashford, TN24 8QX. Prop: Stephen Dadd. Tel: 01233-638682. Fax: 01233-638682. E-mail: books@orchidserve.com. Est: 2001. Private premises. Internet and Postal. Contactable. Open: **M:** 09:00–17:30; **T:** 09:00–17:30; **W:** 09:00–17:30; **Th:** 09:00–17:30; **F:** 09:00–17:30; **S:** 09:00–17:30; **Su:** 09:00–17:30; Spec: CC: PayPal. Notes: *General stock covering all topics. No personal callers as no books on display. Mail-order only. Always seeking Kent & SE London street directories for my personal collection. (Kelly's etc.)*

Woodside Books, 1 Woodside Cottages Westwell Lane, Ashford, TN26 1JB. Prop: Ann Gipps. Tel: (01233) 624495. E-mail: ann.gipps@btinternet.com. Est: 1991. Private premises. Internet and Postal. Appointment necessary. Very small stock. Spec: Botany; Entomology; Natural History; Ornithology. PR: £1–500. Cata: Botany, Entomology, Ornithology, Natural History. Notes: *Payment by cheque only.*

BECKENHAM

Julia Sesemann, 10 Kemerton Road, Beckenham, BR3 6NJ. Prop: Julia Sesemann. Tel: (020) 8658-6123. Est: 1977. Private premises. Postal Only. Appointment necessary. Open: **M:** 09:30–18:00; **T:** 09:30–18:00; **W:** 09:30–18:00; **Th:** 09:30–18:00; **F:** 09:30–18:00. Very small stock. Spec: Author - Blyton, Enid; Children's; Comic Books & Annuals; Illustrated - General; Juvenile. PR: £2–250.

BEXLEY

Ruskin Books, 42 Red Lodge Road Joydens Wood, Bexley, DA5 2JP. Prop: Frederick W. Lidyard. Tel: 01322 558291. E-mail: fwlidyard@aol.com. Est: 2000. Private premises. Postal Only. Telephone First. Spec: Booksearch. Notes: *Mainly a booksearch service.*

BIDDENDEN

P.R. & V. Sabin t/a Printed Works, Saxton House The Nightingales, Biddenden, TN27 8HN. Prop: Paul and Vivien Sabin. Tel: (01580) 715603. E-mail: paulsabin@btopenworld.com. Est: 1995. Private premises. Book fairs only. Appointment necessary. Medium stock. Spec: Illustrated - General; Limited Editions - General; Private Press. Mem: PBFA. Notes: *Private press specialist.*

BRENCHLEY

Anthony Whittaker, Four Seasons Chill Mill Green, Brenchley, Tonbridge, TN12 7AL. Prop: Anthony Whittaker. Tel: 01892 723494. E-mail: bookant@hotmail.com. Est: 1980. Private premises. Telephone First. Open: **M:** 09:00–17:30; **T:** 09:00–17:30; **W:** 09:00–17:30; **Th:** 09:00–17:30; **F:** 09:00–17:30; **S:** 09:00–17:30; **Su:** 09:00–17:30; Closed for lunch: 13:00–14:00. Spec: Applied Art; Children's; Illustrated - General; Natural History; Topography - Local. CC: MC; V.

BROADWAY

Albion Bookshop, ■ Albion Street, Broadway, CT10 1LX. Prop: Alan Kemp. Tel: 01843 862877. Fax: 01843 860084. E-mail: albionbooks@hotmail.com. Est: 1956. Shop open: **M:** 09:00–17:30; **T:** 09:00–17:30; **W:** 09:00–17:30; **Th:** 09:00–17:30; **F:** 09:00–17:30; **S:** 09:00–17:30; **Su:** 10:30–16:30. Spec: CC: MC; V.

CANTERBURY

The Canterbury Bookshop, ■ 37 Northgate, Canterbury, CT1 1BL. Prop: David Miles. Tel: (01227) 464773. Fax: (01227) 780073. E-mail: canterburybookshop@btconnect.com. Est: 1980. Shop open: **M:** 10:00–17:00; **T:** 10:00–17:00; **W:** 10:00–17:00; **Th:** 10:00–17:00; **F:** 10:00–17:00; **S:** 10:00–17:00. Small stock. Spec: Children's; Illustrated - General; Juvenile; Typography; Prints and Maps. PR: £1–2,000. CC: MC; V. Mem: ABA; PBFA; BA; ILAB. Notes: *Fairs attended: all London, ABA, Olympia, Chelsea and in USA.*

Chaucer Bookshop, ■ 6-7 Beer Cart Lane, Canterbury, CT1 2NY. Prop: Sir Robert Sherston-Baker, Bt. Tel: 01227 453912. Fax: 01227 451893. Web: www.chaucer-bookshop.co.uk. E-mail: chaucerbooks@ btconnect.com. Est: 1956. Shop open: **M:** 10:00–17:00; **T:** 10:00–17:00; **W:** 10:00–17:00; **Th:** 10:00–17:00; **F:** 10:00–17:00; **S:** 10:00–17:00. Spec: Antiques; Art; Art History; Arts, The; Autobiography; Biography; Fiction - General; Gardening - General. CC: AE; E; JCB; MC; V; Switch / Solo. Mem: ABA; PBFA; BA; ILAB. Notes: *Within the city walls, less than 5 minutes walk from the Cathedral.*

Little Stour Books, North Court House, West Stourmouth, Nr Preston, Canterbury, CT3 1HT. Prop: Colin Button. Tel: (01227) 722371. Fax: (01227) 722021. Web: www.littlestourbooks.com. E-mail: sales@littlestourbooks.com. Est: 1996. Warehouse. Internet and Postal. Appointment necessary. Shop At. Book Depository Grove Road, Preston, Canterbury, Kent KEN CT3 1EF. Open: **M:** 10.00–18.00; **T:** 10.00–18.00; **W:** 10.00–18.00; **Th:** 10.00–18.00; **F:** 10.00–18.00; **S:** 10.00–18.00; **Su:** 10.00–16.00. Very large stock. Spec: Author - Blyton, Enid; - Brent-Dyer, Elinor M.; - Buckeridge, A.; - Carroll, Lewis; - Crompton, Richmal; - Henty, G.A.; - Johns, W.E.; - Oxenham, Elsie. PR: £6–500. CC: E; JCB; MC; V; SW, SO. Cata: W. E. Johns, Spike Milligan, Kent, Military. Mem: PBFA. Also at: Book Depository Grove Road, Preston, Canterbury, Kent KEN CT3 1EF. VAT No: GB 878 4455 69.

Oast Books, 1 Denstead Oast, Chartham Hatch, Canterbury, CT4 7SH. Prop: Bill & Jennie Reading. Tel: (01227) 730808. Web: www.http://members.aol.com/oastbooks/home.htm. E-mail: oastbooks@aol.com. Est: 1997. Market stand/stall; Postal Only. Small stock. Spec: Counselling; Psychoanalysis; Psychology/Psychiatry; Psychotherapy. PR: £2–40. CC: PayPal.

Tiger Books, Yew Tree Cottage Westbere, Canterbury, CT2 0HH. Prop: Dr. Bryan & Mrs. Sylvia Harlow. Tel: (01227) 710030. Fax: (01227) 712066. Web: www.tigerbooks-online.com. E-mail: tiger@sharlow.fsbusiness.co.uk. Est: 1988. Private premises. Internet and Postal. Appointment necessary. Large stock. Spec: Antiquarian; Author - Dickens, Charles; Authors - Women; Fiction - 18th Century; Fiction - Women; Literary Travel; Literature; Literature - Victorian. PR: £10–5,500. CC: E; JCB; MC; V. Cata: literature. Mem: ABA; PBFA; ILAB. Notes: *Also, a booksearch service*

CHATHAM

Roadmaster Books, P.O. Box 176, Chatham, ME5 9AQ. Prop: Malcolm & Sue Wright. Tel: (01634) 862843. Fax: (01634) 201555. E-mail: info@roadmasterbooks.co.uk. Est: 1976. Private premises. Postal Only. Spec: Canals/Inland Waterways; Company History; Conservation; Dolls & Dolls' Houses; Flower Arranging; Geography; Geology; Maritime/Nautical. PR: £1–350. Cata: transport & topography. Corresp: French. VAT No: GB 619 3009 52. Notes: *To contact publishing business info@roadmasterpublishing.co.uk*

Sandstone Books, 14 Seymour Road, Chatham, ME5 7AE. Prop: Verne Sanderson. Tel: 01634 306437. Web: www.sandstonebooks.co.uk. E-mail: verne@sandstonebooks.co.uk. Est: 1989. Private premises. Internet and Postal. Appointment necessary. Open: **M:** 09:00–17:30; **T:** 09:00–17:30; **W:** 09:00–17:30; **Th:** 09:00–17:30; **F:** 09:00–17:30; **S:** 09:00–17:30; **Su:** 09:00 17:30; Closed for lunch: 13:00–14:00. Spec: Cata: modern first editions.

DEAL

Books, ■ 168 High Street, Deal, CT14 6BQ. Prop: Peter Ritchie. Tel: (01304) 368662. Shop open: **M:** 10:00–17:00; **W:** 10:00–17:00; **Th:** 10:00–17:00; **F:** 10:00–17:00; **S:** 10:00–17:00. Medium stock. Spec: Antiques; Architecture; Art; Collecting. PR: £2–300.

Books, ■ 168 High Street, Deal, CT14 6BQ. Prop: Peter Ritchie. Tel: 01304 368662. Est: 1970. Shop open: **T:** 09:00–17:30; **W:** 10:00–17:00; **Th:** 10:00–17:00; **F:** 10:00–17:00; **S:** 10:00–17:00. Spec: Architecture; Art Reference; Transport.

J. Clarke–Hall Limited, 75 Middle Street, Deal, CT14 6HN. Prop: S.M. Edgecombe. Tel: (01304) 375467. Est: 1934. Private premises. Appointment necessary. Very small stock. Spec: Author - Carroll, Lewis; - Johnson, Samuel. PR: £5–750. Cata: on Samuel Johnson and his world. Notes: *Attends Bonnington Fair in June.*

Inch's Books, 7 Western Road, Deal, CY14 6RX. Prop: Peter & Eleanor Inch. Tel: 01304 371752. Fax: 01304 375154. Web: www.inchsbooks.co.uk. E-mail: inchs.books@dial.pipex.com. Est: 1986. Office and/or bookroom. Telephone First. Open: **M:** 09:00–17:00; **T:** 09:00–17:00; **W:** 09:00–17:00; **Th:** 09:00–17:00; **F:** 09:00–17:00; **S:** . Medium stock. Spec: Architecture; Building & Construction; Cities - General; Design; History - Design; Landscape; Town Planning; Urban History. PR: £10–2,000. CC: MC; V; SW. Corresp: French. Mem: ABA; PBFA; ILAB. VAT No: GB 412 1286 94. Notes: *Also, books on international exhibitions.*

McConnell Fine Books, ■ The Golden Hind 85 Beach Street, Deal, CT14 6JB. Prop: Nick McConnell. Tel: (01304) 375086. Web: www.abebooks.com/home/sandwichfinebooks. E-mail: mcconnellbooks@aol.com. Est: 1972. Shop. Telephone First. Open: **W:** 10:30–17:00; **Th:** 10:30–17:00; **F:** 10:30–17:00; **S:** 10:30–17:00. Medium stock. Spec: Antiquarian; Bindings; Maritime/Nautical. PR: £2–1,000. CC: MC; V. Corresp: French, Russian. Mem: ABA; PBFA; ILAB.

DOVER

Pat Castleton Books, 26 Kearsney Avenue, Dover, CT16 3BU. Prop: Pat Castleton. Tel: 01304 330371. E-mail: patriciacastleton@hotmail.com. Est: 2002. Private premises. Internet and Postal. Telephone First. Open: **M:** 09:00–17:30; **T:** 09:00–17:30; **W:** 09:00–17:30; **Th:** 09:00–17:30; **F:** 09:00–17:30; **S:** 09:00–17:30; **Su:** 09:00–17:30; Closed for lunch: 13:00–14:00. Spec: Agriculture; Aircraft; Animals and Birds; Art Reference; Autobiography; Aviation; Biography; Botany. CC: PayPal, Cheque. Cata: General non-fiction, Childrens. Corresp: French. Notes: *Homepage on Abebooks.com - www.abebooks.com/home/PATCASTLETON.*

FARNBOROUGH

Lewis First Editions, 9 Ferndale Way, Farnborough, BR6 7EL. Prop: David Fordyce. Tel: (01689) 854261. Web: www.abebooks.com/home/davidfordyce/. Est: 2000. Internet and Postal. Small stock. Spec: Author - Lewis, C.S.; - Saville, M.; - Shute, Neville; Modern First Editions. PR: £5–2,000. Notes: *lewisfirsteditions@hotmail.com.*

FARNINGHAM

Wadard Books, ■ 6 High Street, Farningham, DA4 0DG. Tel: (01322) 863151. E-mail: wadardbooks@ btinternet.com. Est: 2001. Shop. open: **M:** 10.00–13.00; **T:** 10:00–18:00; **W:** 10.00–13.00; **Th:** 10:00– 18:00; **F:** 10:00–18:00; **S:** 10:00–18:00. Medium stock. Spec: Antiquarian; Art; Aviation; Children's; Children's - Early Titles; Children's - Illustrated; Churchilliana; Cookery/Gastronomy. PR: £1–5,000. CC: AE; JCB; MC; V. VAT No: GB 586 5906 86.

FAVERSHAM

Faversham Books, 49 South Road, Faversham, ME13 7LS. Prop: Mr. & Mrs. C.M. Ardley. Tel: (01795) 532873. E-mail: max.a@virgin.net. Est: 1979. Private premises. Postal Only. Spec: Author - Kipling, Rudyard. PR: £5–1,000. Cata: Rudyard Kipling; writings and critical works. Corresp: French. Notes: *Some stock on sale at the National Trust Shop at 'Bateman's', Burwash, East Sussex.*

John O'Kill, 'Coulthorn Lodge' 9 Ospringe Road, Faversham, ME13 7LJ. Tel: (01795) 534510. E-mail: john.okill@virgin.net. Est: 1990. Private premises. Postal Only. Small stock. Spec: Antiquarian; Illustrated - General. PR: £1–500.

Past Sentence, ■ 119 West Street, Faversham, ME13 7JB. Prop: Adrian and Kate Rowland. Tel: 01795 590000. Web: www.pastsentences.com. E-mail: p@stsentence.com. Est: 1996. Shop open: **T:** 10:00– 17:00; **W:** 10:00–17:00; **Th:** 10:00–17:00; **F:** 10:00–17:00; **S:** 10:00–17:00. Spec: CC: MC; V; Maestro, Switch. VAT No: GB 781 8038 11.

FOLKESTONE

Jenny Hurst, The Old Coach House Rectory Lane, Lyminge, Folkestone, CT18 8EG. Prop: Jenny Hurst. Tel: (01303) 862693. Web: www.abebooks.com. E-mail: intabooks@btopenworld.com. Est: 1996. Private premises. Internet and Postal. Medium stock. Spec: Academic/Scholarly; Alternative Medicine; Autobiography; Biography; Children's; Fiction - General; Food & Drink; Health. PR: £5–100. Notes: *Many books not listed on internet.*

Marrin's Bookshop, ■ 149 Sandgate Road, Folkestone, CT20 2DA. Prop: Patrick Marrin. Tel: 01303 253016. Fax: 01303 850956. Web: www.marrinbook.co.uk. E-mail: patrick@marrinbook.co.uk. Est: 1945. Shop open: **T:** 09.30–17.30; **W:** 09:30 17:30; **Th:** 09·30–17·30; **F:** 09;30–17:30; **S:** 09:30–17:30. Spec: Antiquarian; Topography - Local. CC: MC; V; Debit. Cata: Kent Topography. Corresp: French, Italian. Mem: ABA; PBFA; BA; ILAB. VAT No: GB 316 6132 80. Notes: *We specialize in Kent Books, Prints, Maps and Ephemera and have in addition, a good selection of Antiquarian and secondhand books.*

MilitaryHistoryBooks.com, PO Box 590, Folkestone, CT20 2WX. Prop: Ian H. & Gillian M. Knight. Tel: (01303) 246500. Fax: (01303) 245133. Web: www.militaryhistorybooks.com. E-mail: info@ militaryhistorybooks.com. Est: 1970. Private premises. Internet and Postal. Appointment necessary. Open: **M:** 10:00–17:00; **T:** 10:00–17:00; **W:** 10:00–17:00; **Th:** 10:00–17:00; **F:** 10:00–17:00; **S:** 09:00– 14:00. Spec: Aeronautics; Aircraft; Armed Forces - Australian Army; Arms & Armour; Army, The; Autobiography; Aviation; Coastal Defence. CC: AE; D; E; JCB; MC; V; SW. VAT No: GB 770 7124 36.

Nick Spurrier, 27 Plain Road, Folkestone, CT20 2QF. Tel: (01303) 246100. Fax: (01303) 245800. Web: www.nick-spurrier.co.uk. E-mail: spurrier@btconnect.com. Est: 1977. Private premises. Internet and Postal. Appointment necessary. Medium stock. Spec: Black Studies; Company History; Economics; Feminism; History - General; Marxism; Pacifism; Philosophy. PR: £1–50. CC: JCB; MC. VAT No: GB 362 1931 64.

HERNE BAY

Herne Bay Books, 22 Western Esplanade, Herne Bay, CT6 8RW. Prop: Mr. R.J.C. Eburne (Dick). Tel: (01227) 743201. E-mail: dickeburne@yahoo.co.uk. Est: 1995. Private premises. Postal Only. Appointment necessary. Small stock. Spec: Genealogy; General Stock. PR: £1–20. Corresp: French, German. Notes: *Trading infrequently.*

LYDD

Anthony Neville, New Hall High Street, Lydd, TN29 9AJ. Tel: 01797 320180. Fax: 01797 320140. E-mail: neville.anthony@talk21.com. Est: 1985. Private premises. Appointment necessary. Spec: Art; Author - James, Henry; Foreign Texts; Illustrated - General; Private Press. CC: MC; V. Cata: 10 a year on specialities. Corresp: French, German and Russian. Mem: ABA; PBFA; BA. VAT No: GB 515 9087 34.

LYMINGE

Scott Brinded, 17 Greenbanks, Lyminge, CT18 8HG. Tel: (01303) 862258. Fax: (01303) 862660. Est: 1991. Private premises. Internet and Postal. Small stock. Spec: Antiquarian; Bibliography; Books about Books; Literature; Palaeography; Papermaking; Printing; Topography - General. PR: £1–5,000. CC: MC; V. Mem: ABA; PBFA. VAT No: GB 624 9115 38. Notes: *Also, UK distributors for Martin Publishing, Oak Knoll Press.*

Periwinkle Press, ■ 2 Rose Cottages Woodland Road, Lyminge, Folkstone, CT18 8DR. Prop: (*) Antony & Clare Swain. Tel: (01303) 863595. Fax: Mobile (07709) 918361. E-mail: cswain1805@aol.com. Est: 1968. Internet and Postal. Shop open: **M:** 10:00–17:00; **T:** 10:00–17:00; **W:** 10:00–14:00; **Th:** 10:00–17:00; **F:** 10:00–17:00; **S:** 10:00–17:00. Medium stock. Spec: Author - Ardizzone, Edward; Rural Life; Topography - Local; Transport; Prints and Maps. PR: £1–100. CC: AE; JCB; V; PayPal. Mem: PBFA. Notes: *Also, trade & retail print and picture framers, colourists, restoration.*

MAIDSTONE

Peter Blest, Little Canon Cottage Wateringbury, Maidstone, ME18 5PJ. Prop: Peter & Jan Blest. Tel: (01622) 812940. E-mail: pmblest@aol.com. Est: 1974. Private premises. Postal Only. Very large stock. Spec: Agriculture; Animals and Birds; Botany; Cockfighting; Entomology; Flower Arranging; Gardening - General; Herbalism. PR: £5–5,000. CC: AE; JCB; MC; V. Cata: Natural History, Gardening & Botanical, Sporting. Corresp: French. Mem: PBFA.

Wealden Books, 39 Adisham Drive, Maidstone, ME16 0NP. Prop: Alfred & C.A. King. Tel: (01622) 762581. E-mail: wealdenbooks@talk21.com. Est: 1980. Private premises. Appointment necessary. Large stock. Spec: Fiction - General; History - Local; Topography - General; Topography - Local. PR: £2–1,000. VAT No: GB 304 1457 96. Notes: *Main stream subjects are on and about Kent, Surrey and Sussex.*

ORPINGTON

Roland Books, 60 Birchwood Road, Petts Wood, Orpington, BR5 1NZ. Prop: A.R. Hughes. Tel: (01689) 838872. Fax: (01689) 838872. E-mail: py32@dial.pipex.com. Private premises. Internet and Postal. Appointment necessary. Open: **M;** 09:00–17:00; **T:** 09:00 17:00; **W.** 09.00–17:00; **1h:** 09:00–17:00; **F:** 09:00–1/:00. Medium stock. Spec: Advertising; Animals and Birds; Annuals; Antiques; Archaeology; Architecture; Art; Autobiography. PR: £1–75.

RAMSGATE

michaelsbookshop.com, ■ 72 King St., Ramsgate, CT11 8NY. Prop: Michael Child. Tel: (01843) 589500. Web: www.michaelsbookshop.com. E-mail: michaelsbookshop@aol.com. Est: 1984. Shop open: **M:** 09:30–17:30; **T:** 09:30–17:30; **W:** 09:30–17:30; **F:** 09:30–17:30; **S:** 09:30–17:30; **Su:** 00.00–00.00. Very large stock. PR: £1–100. CC: MC; V. Cata: East Kent. Notes: *Mostly general modern secondhand with some remainders we are also specialist publishers and stockists of books about southeast England.*

Yesteryear Railwayana, Stablings Cottage Goodwin Road, Ramsgate, CT11 0JJ. Prop: Patrick & Mary Mullen. Tel: 01843 587283. Fax: 01843 587283. Web: www.yesrail.com. E-mail: mullen@yesrail.com. Est: 1978. Private premises. Internet and Postal. Large stock. Spec: Buses/Trams; Model Engineering; Model Railways; Paddle Boats; Public Transport; Railroads; Railways; Steam Engines. PR: £1–500. CC: AE; MC; V. Cata: Railways, all aspects. Notes: *Yesteryear Railwayana are also known as YesRail, we are trading in scarce out of print railway books and printed material of every kind that relates to some aspect of railway history worldwide, and in any language.*

ROCHESTER

Baggins Book Bazaar, ■ 19 High Street, Rochester, ME1 1PY. Prop: Paul Minet, Godfrey & Bee George. Tel: 01634 811651. Fax: 01634 840591. Web: www.bagginsbooks.co.uk. E-mail: godfreygeorge@ btinternet.com. Est: 1986. Shop open: **M:** 10:00–18:00; **T:** 10:00–18:00; **W:** 10:00–18:00; **Th:** 10:00– 18:00; **F:** 10:00–18:00; **S:** 10:00–18:00; **Su:** 10:00–18:00. CC: AE; E; JCB; MC; V; plus all major debit cards. Cata: most subjects.

Baggins Book Bazaar Ltd., ■ 19 High Street, Rochester, ME1 1PY. Prop: Manager: Godfrey George. Tel: (01634) 811651. Fax: (01634) 840591. Web: www.bagginsbooks.co.uk. E-mail: godfreygeorge@ btconnect.com. Est: 1986. Shop open: **M:** 10:00–18:00; **T:** 10:00–18:00; **W:** 10:00–18:00; **Th:** 10:00– 18:00; **F:** 10:00–18:00; **S:** 10:00–18:00; **Su:** 10:00–18:00; Very large stock. Spec: Booksearch. PR: £1– 200. CC: AE; E; JCB; MC; V; Maestro, Electron. VAT No: GB 472 9061 36. Notes: *Other services: Booksearch, new book ordering, local interest new titles always in stock. The Largest Secondhand Bookshop in England.*

Stained Glass Books, 13 Parkfields, Rochester, ME2 2TW. Prop: K.R. & S.J. Hill. Tel: (01634)719050. Web: www.glassconservation.com. E-mail: bookmail@glassconservation.com. Est: 1987. Private premises. Postal Only. Contactable. Very small stock. Spec: Glass; Stained Glass. PR: £5–500.

SEVENOAKS

Roderick M. Barron, P.O. Box 67, Sevenoaks, TN13 3WW. Tel: (01732) 742558. Fax: (01732) 742558. Web: www.barron.co.uk. E-mail: rod@barron.co.uk. Est: 1989. Private premises. Internet and Postal. Spec: Atlases; Prints and Maps. PR: £100–10,000. CC: AE; MC; V. Corresp: French, German. Mem: ABA; IMCoS. VAT No: GB 602 6465 60.

Garwood & Voigt, 55 Bayham Road, Sevenoaks, TN13 3XE. Prop: Nigel Garwood & Rainer G. Voigt. Tel: (01732) 460025. Fax: (01732) 460026. Web: www.garwood-voigt.com. E-mail: gv@garwood-voigt.com. Est: 1977. Office and/or bookroom. Appointment necessary. Small stock. Spec: Atlases; Cookery/Gastronomy; Gambling; Games; Maps & Mapmaking; Music - Opera; Performing Arts; Sport - General. CC: AE; E; MC; V. Cata: Antique Maps, Atlases, Prints, Cookery Books. Corresp: German, French. Mem: ABA; PBFA; ILAB; IMCoS. Notes: *Antique Maps, Atlases, Panoramas, Views, Decorative Prints & Engravings, Cookery & Gastronomy Books.*

Geophysical Books, 82 Granville Rd., Sevenoaks, TN13 1HA. Prop: Miss Bobbie Smith. Tel: 01732 456018. Web: www.geophysicalbooks.com. E-mail: geo.books@which.net. Est: 1986. Private premises. Telephone First. Open: **M:** 09:00–17:30; **T:** 09:00–17:30; **W:** 09:00–17:30; **Th:** 09:00–17:30; **F:** 09:00–17:30; **S:** 09:00–17:30. Closed for lunch: 13:00–14:00. Spec: Geology; Geophysics; Petroleum Geology; Petroleum Technology. CC: MC; V. Corresp: French.

Martin Wood Cricket Books, 1c Wickenden Road, Sevenoaks, TN13 3PJ. Tel: (01732) 457205. Fax: (01732) 457205. Web: www.martinwoodcricketbooks.co.uk. Est: 1970. Private premises. Appointment necessary. Small stock. Spec: Sport - Cricket; Ephemera. PR: £1–500.

SIDCUP

Mark W. Corder, 9 Townshend Close, Sidcup, DA14 5HY. Prop: Mark Corder. Tel: (020) 8309-5665. Web: www.mark.corder btinternet.co.uk. E-mail: mark.corder@btinternet.com. Est: 1988. Private premises. Internet and Postal. Appointment necessary. Small stock. Spec: Academic/Scholarly; History - British; Reference; Theology; Topography - Local. PR: £10–500.

SITTINGBOURNE

J. & J. Fox Books, 48 Woodstock Road, Sittingbourne, ME10 4HN. Prop: M.V. Fox. Tel: (01795) 470310. Fax: (01795) 470310. Est: 1981. Storeroom. Appointment necessary. Small stock. Spec: Antiquarian; Cookery/Gastronomy; Maritime/Nautical; Military; Typography; Ephemera. PR: £10– 1,500. Corresp: French, Portugese, Spanish. Mem: PBFA.

Underwater Antiques, 12 West Lane, Sittingbourne, ME10 3AA. Tel: (01795) 472664. E-mail: philsidey@aol.com. Est: 1980. Private premises. Postal Only. Very small stock. Spec: Military; Sport - Diving/Sub-Aqua. PR: £3–500. CC: AE; D; E; MC; V; PayPal, Sw. Notes: *Attends book fairs.*

SMARDEN

Mrs Janet Cameron, The Meeting House, Smarden, TN27 8NR. Tel: (01233) 770552. Est: 1992. Private premises. Postal Only. Small stock.

TONBRIDGE

C. & A.J. Barmby, 140 Lavender Hill, Tonbridge, TN9 2AY. Prop: Chris & Angela Barmby. Tel: 01732 356479. E-mail: bookpilot@aol.com Est: 1981. Storeroom. Internet and Postal. Appointment necessary. Large stock. Spec: Antiquarian; Antiques; Applied Art; Archaeology; Architecture; Art; Art Reference; Author - 20th Century. PR: £5–4,000. CC: MC; V; SW, DE. VAT No: GB 367 4200 58.

Chas J. Sawyer, 46, The Haydens, Tonbridge, TN9 1NS. Prop: Richard Sawyer. Tel: 01732 353183. Fax: 01732 353183. E-mail: cjsbks@btinternet.com. Est: 1894. Private premises. Internet and Postal. Appointment necessary. Open: **M:** 09:00–17:30; **T:** 09:00–17:30; **W:** 09:00–17:30; **Th:** 09:00–17:30; **F:** 09:00–17:30. Closed for lunch: 13:00–14:00. Spec: Africana; Author - Burton, R.F.; - Carroll, Lewis; - Chapman, Abel; - Churchill, Sir Winston; Autographs; Bibliography; Bindings. CC: MC; V; PayPal. Cata: Churchilliana, Africana, inc Ephemera. Notes: *Insurance and Consultancy work undertaken based on 40 years experience of antiquarian booktrade. UK Representative and agent for auctionexplorerbooks.com - dedicated auction website for bookdealers and collectors.*

Grant Demar Books, 15 White Cottage Road, Tonbridge, TN10 4PX. Prop: Grant Demar. Tel: (01732) 360208. Web: www.garntdemarbooks.co.uk. E-mail: grantdemar@tiscali.co.uk. Est: 1974. Private premises. Appointment necessary. Small stock. Spec: Animals and Birds; Conservation; Entomology; Natural History; Nature; New Naturalist; Ornithology; Zoology PR. £1–1,000. Cata. Birds and Natural History.

Mr. Books Bookshop, ■ 2 Bank Street, Tonbridge, TN9 1BL. Prop: Mark Richardson. Tel: 01732 363000. Web: www.mrbooks.co.uk. E-mail: mrbooks@btinternet.com. Est: 2004. Shop open: **T:** 10:00–18:00; **W:** 10:00–15:00; **Th:** 10:00–18:00; **F:** 10:00–15:00; **S:** 10:00–18:00. CC: AE; D; E; JCB; MC; V. Notes: *Organiser of West Kent Book Fair at Tonbridge School, High Street, Tonbridge. 2007 fair dates are Sunday April 1st; Sunday October 28th. Events include Poetry at the Fair; Poetry at the Shop; Poetry at the Pub. See web site for details.*

Tony Skelton, The Old School House, Shipbourne, Tonbridge, TN11 9PB. Prop: D.A.L. Skelton. Tel: (01732) 810481. E-mail: tskelt@waitrose.com. Est: 1992. Private premises. Internet and Postal. Contactable. Open: **M:** 08:00–20:00; **T:** 08:00–20:00; **W:** 08:00–20:00; **Th:** 08:00–20:00; **F:** 08:00–20:00; **S:** 09:00–20:00; **Su:** 09:00–20:00. Small stock. Spec: Author - Heaney, Seamus; Countries - Ireland; First Editions; Literature; Literature - Irish; Modern First Editions; Plays; Poetry. PR: £5–500. Cata: Irish interest. Corresp: French, German. Mem: PBFA. VAT No: GB 796 5067 79.

P. & F. Whelan, 68 The Drive, Tonbridge, TN9 2LR. Prop: Tony & Mary Whelan. Tel: (01732) 354882. Fax: (01732) 354882. E-mail: whelanirishbooks@lineone.net. Est: 1986. Private premises. Postal Only. Small stock. Spec: Countries - Ireland; History - National; Irish Interest. PR: £5–250. Cata: Irish interest.

TUNBRIDGE WELLS

Hall's Bookshop, ■ 20–22 Chapel Place, Tunbridge Wells, TN1 1YQ. Prop: Sabrina Izzard. Tel: (01892) 527842. Fax: (01892) 527842. Web: www.hallsbookshop.com. E-mail: sabizzard@waitrose.com. Est: 1898. Shop open: **M:** 09:30–17:00; **T:** 09:30–17:00; **W:** 09:30–17:00; **Th:** 09:30–17:00; **F:** 09:30–17:00; **S:** 09:30–17:00. Large stock. Spec: Archaeology; Architecture; Art; Art History; Aviation; Bindings; Biography; Books in Greek. Mem: PBFA.

Pantiles Bookshop, ■ The Corn Exchange The Pantiles, Tunbridge Wells, TN2 5TE. Prop: Steve and Val Marshall. Tel: 01892 618191. Web: www.pantilesbooksop.co.uk. E-mail: pantiles@btconnect.com. Est: 2004. Shop open: **M:** 09:00–17:30; **T:** 09:00–17:30; **W:** 09:00–17:30; **Th:** 09:00–17:30; **F:** 09:00–17:30; **S:** 09:00–17:30; **Su:** 10:00–17:00. CC: AE; MC; V. Notes: *A well stocked mainly non-fiction bookshop specialising in Sport, Railway, Military, Cinema, Mind, Body, Spirit and books on Kent.*

The Secondhand Bookshop, ■ 13 Nevill Street, Tunbridge Wells, TN2 5RU. Prop: David Neal. Tel: (01892) 547005. Est: 1992. Shop open: **M:** 10:00–16:30; **T:** 10:00–16:30; **Th:** 10:00–16:30; **F:** 10:00–16:30; **S:** 10:00–16:30. Medium stock. Spec: Brewing. PR: £1–500. VAT No: GB 725 4573 27. Notes: *Attends Titlepage and HD Fairs.*

World War Books, Oaklands Camden Park, Tunbridge Wells, TN2 5AE. Prop: Tim Harper. Tel: (01892) 538465. Fax: (01892) 538465. Web: www.worldwarbooks.com. E-mail: wwarbooks@btinternet.com. Est: 1993. Private premises. Internet and Postal. Contactable. Medium stock. Spec: Aviation; Holocaust; Maritime/Nautical; Military; Military - Modelling; Naval; School Registers/Rolls of Honour; War - General. PR: £10–5,000. CC: MC; V. Cata: Military and manuscripts/photograph albums. Mem: PBFA; OMRS. Notes: *We specialize in hard to find and rare Military, Aviation and Naval books, manuscripts and photograph albums etc. We also organise specialist Military,Naval and Aviation bookfairs at Tunbridge Wells, Chatham, London and Middle Wallop.*

KENT

WATERINGBURY

Cobnar Books, 567 Red Hill, Wateringbury, Maidstone, ME18 5BE. Prop: Lawrence Ilott. Tel: 01622 813230. Web: www.cobnarbooks.com. E-mail: info@cobnarbooks.co.uk. Est: 1995. Office and/or bookroom. Internet and Postal. Appointment necessary. Spec: Academic/Scholarly; Agriculture; Antiquarian; Bibles; Bindings; Cookery/Gastronomy; County - Local; Early Imprints. CC: JCB; MC; V. Cata: Antiquarian, bindings, Provincial Printing, Topography. Mem: PBFA. VAT No: GB 874 3008 26.

WESTERHAM

Barely Read Books, ■ 18 The Green, Westerham, TN16 1AX. Prop: Ross Williams. Tel: 01959 565854. Web: www.barelyreadbooks.co.uk. E-mail: barelyreadbooks@yahoo.ie. Est: 2001. Shop. Open: **T:** 10:00–18:00; **W:** 10:00–18:00; **Th:** 10:00–18:00; **F:** 10:00–18:00; **S:** 10:00–18:00; **Su:** 10:00–18:00. Spec: Author - Johns, W.E.; Aviation; Children's; Children's - Illustrated; Churchilliana.

Derek Stirling Bookseller, 1 Quebec Avenue, Westerham, TN16 1BJ. Tel: (01959) 561 822. Fax: (01959) 561 822. E-mail: derekfs@dialstart.net. Est: 1999. Private premises. Internet and Postal. Appointment necessary. Very small stock. Spec: Academic/Scholarly; Advertising; Antiquarian; Author - Dickens, Charles; - Hardy, Thomas; - Pope, A; Bibles; Ex-Libris. PR: £10–2,000. Notes: *Purchases bound volumes, runs or quantities of newspapers and periodicals published pre-1850.*

The Design Gallery 1850-1950, ■ 5 The Green, Westerham, TN16 1AS. Prop: Chrissie Painell. Tel: (01959 561234. Web: www.designgallery.co.uk. E-mail: sales@designgallery.co.uk. Est: 2002. Shop open: **M:** 10:00–17:30; **T:** 10:00–17:30; **W:** 10:00–17:30; **Th:** 10:00–17:30; **F:** 10:00–17:30; **S:** 10:00– 17:30; **Su:** 13:00–17:00. Spec: Aesthetic Movement; Art Deco; Art Nouveau; Arts & Crafts Era; Bindings; Crafts; Gothic Revival; Jewellery. CC: AE; MC; V. Mem: LAPADA. Notes: *Also, Victorian fine bindings, and original illustrations. Call in advance to see all stock. Also 19th & 20th C designer jewellery.*

WHITSTABLE

Alan & Margaret Edwards, 10 Meteor Avenue, Whitstable, CT5 4DH. Tel: (01227) 262276. Fax: (01227) 261158. E-mail: a.m.books@lineone.net. Est: 1988. Private premises. Appointment necessary. Small stock. Spec: Ecclesiastical History & Architecture; Theology; Topography - General. PR: £1–500. Corresp: French, German.

Sheppard's Book Dealers in JAPAN

Order the next printed edition – or search on www.sheppardsworld.co.uk

LANCASHIRE

BICKERSTAFFE

Michael S Kemp Bookseller, The Barn, Barrow Nook Hall Sineacre Lane, Bickerstaffe, L39 0HR. Prop: Mike Kemp. Tel: 07711 856075. Web: www.kempbooksellers.co.uk. E-mail: mike@ kempbooksellers.co.uk. Est: 1979. Private premises. Appointment necessary. Spec: Author - Peake, Mervyn; History - General; Topography - General; Topography - Local. CC: MC; V; Maestro. Cata: British Topography. Corresp: French. Mem: PBFA.

BLACKBURN

Neil Summersgill, Pigeon Hall Abbott Brow, Mellor, Blackburn, DD2 7HT. Prop. Neil Summersgill. Tel: (01254) 813559. E-mail: summersgillbooks@btinternet.com. Est: 1984. Private premises. Internet and Postal. Appointment necessary. Very small stock. Spec: Antiquarian; Atlases; Autographs; Bindings; Letters; Manuscripts; Natural History; Sport - Field Sports. PR: £10–5,000. CC: MC; V. Mem: PBFA.

BLACKPOOL

Book Mad, ■ 151 Church Street, Blackpool, FY1 3NX. Prop: Nick Street. Tel: 01253 291969. E-mail: bookmad151@hotmail.com. Est: 1991. Shop open: **M:** 10:00–17:30; **T:** 10:00–17:30; **W:** 10:00–17:30; **Th:** 10:00–17:30; **F:** 10:00–17:30; **S:** 10:00–17:30; **Su:** 10:00–16:00; Closed for lunch: 10:00–16:00. Spec: out-of-print; Prints and Maps.

Bob Dobson, 3 Staining Rise, Staining, Blackpool, FY3 0BU. Tel: (01253) 895678. Fax: (01253) 895678. E-mail: peggie@peggiedobson.wanadoo.co.uk. Est: 1969. Private premises. Appointment necessary. Large stock. Spec: History - Local; Topography - Local. PR: £1–100. VAT No: GB 534 3982 30. Notes: *Incl: books on Lancashire, Yorkshire and Cheshire. Also publishes as Landy Publishing.*

John McGlynn, 173 Newton Drive, Blackpool, FY3 8ND. Tel: (01253) 300100. Fax: (01253) 300020. Web: www.vintagetechnology.org. E-mail: johnmcglynn@blueyonder.co.uk. Est: 1996. Private premises. Postal Only. Medium stock. Spec: Motoring; Transport. PR: £10–200. Notes: *Rolls-Royce and Bentley Motor Cars material only.*

BRINSCALL

Modern Firsts Etc., Hilltops Windsor Drive, Brinscall, PR6 8PX. Prop: R.J. Leek. Tel: (01254) 830861. Est: 1985. Private premises. Postal Only. Very small stock. Spec: Autographs; First Editions; Painting. PR: £1–500.

BURY

Richard Byrom Textile Bookroom, 3 Hawkshaw Lane, Bury, BL8 4JZ. Prop: Richard Byrom. Tel: (01204) 883110 Fax: (01204) 880155. Est: 1984. Private premises. Appointment necessary. Large stock. Spec: Carpets; Company History; Crochet; Embroidery; Fashion & Costume; Industry; Knitting; Lace. PR: £1–500.

CARNFORTH

The Carnforth Bookshop, ■ 38–42 Market Street, Carnforth, LA5 9JX. Prop: P. & G. Seward. Tel: (01524) 734588. Fax: (01524) 735893. Web: www.carnforthbooks.co.uk. E-mail: carnforthbkshop@ aol.com. Est: 1977. Internet and Postal. Shop open: **M:** 09:00–17:30; **T:** 09:00–17:30; **W:** 09:00–17:30; **Th:** 09:00–17:30; **F:** 09:00–17:30; **S:** 09:00–17:30. Very large stock. Spec: Alpinism/Mountaineering; Art; Art History; Biography; Classical Studies; Fiction - General; Fine & Rare; History - General. PR: £1–500. CC: AE; E; JCB; MC; V. Mem: BA. VAT No: GB 306 8293 93.

CHORLEY

Bowland Bookfinders, 88 Bury Lane, Withnell, Chorley, PR6 8SD. Prop: D.S. Suttie. Tel: (01254) 830619. E-mail: david@bookfind.freeserve.co.uk. Est: 1987. Private premises. Internet and Postal. Appointment necessary. Spec: Academic/Scholarly; Advertising; War - General; Booksearch.

LANCASHIRE

CLITHEROE

Bowdon Books, ■ 33 Lowergate, Clitheroe, BB7 1AD. Prop: Gordon & Gillian Hill. Tel: (01200) 425333. E-mail: bowdonbooks-hill@tiscali.co.uk. Est: 1987. Shop open: **Th:** 10:00–16:30; **F:** 10:00–16:30; **S:** 10:00–16:30. Medium stock. Spec: Topography - Local. PR: £5–500. CC: JCB; MC; V; Switch. Notes: *May close earlier without prior notice. Telephone call advised if planning a visit from afar.*

Moorside Books Ltd, ■ Moorside Cottage Whalley Old Road, Billington, Clitheroe, BB7 9JF. Prop: David Sedgwick. Tel: (01254) 824104. Web: www.abebooks.com/home/DFSBOOKS/. E-mail: dsbooks@easynet.co.uk. Est: 1985. Internet and Postal. Shop open: **T:** 10:00–17:00; **Th:** 10:00–17:00; **F:** 10:00–17:00; **S:** 10:00–17:00. Small stock. Spec: Astronomy; Author - Lawrence, T.E.; Bindings; Cosmology; Countries - Arabian Peninsula; Maps & Mapmaking; Mathematics; Natural Sciences. PR: £5–10,000. CC: MC; V; Maestro. Cata: T E Lawrence. Mem: PBFA. VAT No: GB 787 8011 92. Notes: *29 Moor Lane, Clitheroe, Lancashire.*

Roundstone Books, ■ 29 Moor Lane, Clitheroe, BB7 1BE. Prop: Jo Harding. Tel: (01200) 444242. Web: www.roundstonebooks.co.uk. E-mail: joharbooks@aol.com. Est: 1995. Shop open: **T:** 09:00–17:00; **Th:** 09:00–17:00; **F:** 09:00–17:00; **S:** 09:00–17:00. Spec: Alternative Medicine; Biography; Children's; County - Local; Drama; Fiction - General; Health; History - General. PR: £1–100. CC: JCB; MC; V; Debit cards. Notes: *Free booksearch service.*

FENCE

Pendleside Books, 359 Wheatley Lane Road, Fence, Nr. Burnley, BB12 9QA. Prop: E. & B. Sutcliffe. Tel: (01282) 615617. Est: 1974. Private premises. Appointment necessary. Very small stock. Spec: Entomology; Mycology; Topography - Local. PR: £5–500. Corresp: French, Italian.

HALTON

Mark Towers, 45 Beech Road, Halton, LA2 6QQ. Tel: (01524) 811556. Web: www.royoftherovers.com. E-mail: mark@royoftherovers.com. Est: 1999. Private premises. Postal Only. Contactable. Spec: Comic Books & Annuals; Comics. PR: £2–50.

HINDLEY

Wiend Books, Unit 1 Hindley Business Centre Platt Lane, Hindley, Wigan, WN2 3PA. Prop: Paul Morris. Tel: (07976) 604203. Web: www.wiendbooks.co.uk. E-mail: wiendbooks@lycos.co.uk. Est: 1997. Office and/or bookroom. Appointment necessary. Open: **M:** 09:00–17:30; **W:** 09:00–17:30; **Th:** 09:00–17:30; **F:** 09:00–17:30; **S:** 09:00–13.00. Spec: Africana; Annuals; Archaeology - Industrial; Architecture; Art; Arthurian; Astronomy; Autobiography. Notes: *We used to be located in The Wiend and now operate only from the address above. During 2007 we will be clearing a whole warehouse at bargain prices as well as operating as normal. Always a discount for a personal visit – just quote Sheppards.*

LANCASTER

Hardback Hotel, 68 Windermere Road, Lancaster, LA1 3EZ. Prop: Jonathan Bean. Tel: 07763 814587. Web: www.hardbackhotel.co.uk. E-mail: mail@hardbackhotel.co.uk. Est: 2001. Private premises. Internet Only. Open: **M:** 09:00–17:30; **T:** 09.00–17.30, **W:** 09:00 17:30; **Th:** 09:00–17:30; **F:** 09:00–17:30; **S:** 09:00–17:30; **Su:** 09:00–17:30; Closed for lunch: 13:00–14:00. Spec: Fiction - General; Fiction - Crime, Detective, Spy, Thrillers; Fiction - Science Fiction; First Editions. CC: PayPal. Notes: *Modern fiction first editions and proof copies.*

Interstellar Master Traders, ■ 33 North Road, Lancaster, LA1-1NS. Prop: P. Pinto. Tel: +44-1524-382181. Web: www.i-m-t.demon.co.uk/. E-mail: ppshepp@i-m-t.demon.co.uk. Est: 1985. Internet and Postal. Shop open: **M:** 10:00–19:00; **T:** 10:00–19:00; **W:** 10:00–19:00; **Th:** 10:00–19:00; **F:** 10:00–19:00; **S:** 10:00–19:00. Large stock. Spec: Fiction - Fantasy, Horror; Fiction - Science Fiction. PR: £0–750. Notes: *Titles want-listed 'til found | deleted by customer.*

LEYLAND

Browse Books, 10 Silverdale Close Worden Park, Leyland, Leyland, PR25 3BY. Prop: T.B. Bowe. Tel: (01772) 431608. E-mail: b_bowe@hotmail.com. Est: 1989. Display/stand. Internet and Postal. Telephone First. Open: **M:** 10:00–17:00; **T:** 10:00–17:00; **W:** 10:00–20:00; **Th:** 10:00–15:00; **F:** 10:00–17:00; **S:** 10:00–16:00; **Su:** 10:00–17:00. Spec: Antiques; Buses/Trams; Crafts; Crochet; Embroidery; Gardening - General; General; Humour. PR: £2–50. Notes: *Extensive Sheet Music Stock.*

LANCASHIRE

Great Grandfather's, ■ 82 Towngate, Leyland, PR25 2LR. Prop: Greg D. Smith. Tel: (01772) 422268. E-mail: books@greatgrandfathers.fsnet.co.uk. Est: 1985. Shop open: **T:** 10:00–17:30; **Th:** 10:00–17:30; **F:** 10:00–17:30; **S:** 10:00–17:30. Large stock. Spec: General Stock. PR: £1–200. CC: pending. Corresp: French, German. Mem: PBFA. Notes: *Open other times by appointment. Large general stock. 5 mins from M6, Junction 28. Easy parking.*

LOWER DARWEN

Red Rose Books, Brook Mill Complex Branch Road, Lower Darwen, BB3 0PR. Prop: K.M. Tebay. Tel: (01254) 290029. Web: www.redrosebooks.co.uk. E-mail: info@redrosebooks.co.uk. Est: 1993. Office and/or bookroom. Internet and Postal. Appointment necessary. Small stock. Spec: Sport - Cricket. PR: £1–1,000. CC: MC; V; PayPal. Cata: cricket. VAT No: GB 693 2135 32. Notes: *Specialist cricket booksellers and publishers.*

LYTHAM ST. ANNES

Robert F. Butterworth, 33 Eldon Court Glen Eldon Road, Lytham St. Annes, FY8 2BH. Prop: Robert F Butterworth. Tel: (01253) 729031. Fax: (01253) 729031. E-mail: rfbutters@compuserve.com. Est: 1982. Private premises. Internet and Postal. Appointment necessary. Small stock. Spec: Maritime/ Nautical; Ephemera. PR: £1–750. Notes: *Antique Centre, St.George's Road, St.Annes.*

PRESTON

B D McManmon, 6 SeaView, Walmer Bridge, Preston, PR4 5GH. Prop: Barry McManmon. Tel: 01772 612727. E-mail: barry@mcmanmon.fsbusiness.co.uk. Est: 1982. Private premises. Appointment necessary. Spec: Academic/Scholarly; Archaeology; Military; Travel - General. CC: AE; D; E; JCB; MC; V; Debit cards. Mem: ABA; PBFA; ILAB. Notes: *Stock includes books on academic history, travel and military history.*

Halewood & Sons, ■ 37 Friargate, Preston, PR1 2AT. Tel: (01772) 252603. E-mail: halewoodandsons@aol.com. Est: 1867. Shop open: **M:** 09:30–17:30; **T:** 09:30–17:30; **W:** 09:30– 17:30; **Th:** 09:30–17:30; **F:** 09:30–17:30; **S:** 09:30–17:30. Very large stock. Spec: Countries - Africa; Countries - Americas, The; Countries - Australia; Booksearch; Prints and Maps. CC: AE; MC; V; Solo, Maestro. Corresp: French, German, Spanish. Mem: ABA; PBFA; BA. Notes: *Open Sunday by appointment.*

O'Connor Fine Books, 9 Garrison Road, Fulwood, Preston, PR2 8AL. Prop: John and Evelyn O'Connor. Tel: 01297 32431. E-mail: oconnorfinebooks@hotmail.com. Est: 2002. Private premises. Appointment necessary. Very small stock. Spec: Bibliography; Folio Society, The; Printing. Corresp: French.

Pamona Books, Canberra Road, Preston, PR25 3JH. Prop: Mr. D. W. Heald. Tel: 01772 452198. E-mail: pamonabooks@aol.com. Private premises. Postal Only. Contactable. Spec: Fiction - General; First Editions; General Stock. Notes: *Free booksearch service*

Preston Book Company, ■ 68 Friargate, Preston, PR1 2ED. Prop: M. Halewood. Tel: (01772) 252613. E-mail: prestonrarebooks@halewood221b.freeserve.co.uk. Est: 1960. Shop open: **M:** 10:00–17:00; **T:** 10:00–17:00; **W:** 10:00–17:00; **Th:** 10:00–17:00; **F:** 10:00–17:00; **S:** 10:00–17:00. Large stock. Spec: Africana; Americana - General; Anthropology; Antiquarian; Atlases; Australiana; Author - Conan Doyle, Sir Arthur; Author - Dickens, Charles. PR: £10–1,000. CC: JCB; MC; V.

ST. HELENS

Harvest Books, 25 Thickwood Moss Lane, Rainford, St. Helens, WA11 8QL. Prop: Mrs. Janet Christie. Tel: (01744) 885747. E-mail: harvestbooks@btinternet.com. Est: 1998. Private premises. Internet and Postal. Appointment necessary. Spec: Authors - British; Children's; Fairy/Folk Tales; Folklore; Illustrated - General; Literature; Rural Life; Social History. CC: PayPal. Mem: PBFA. Notes: *Attendance at Book Fairs, mainly in North West. Also selection of stock at Dales & Lakes Book Centre, Sedbergh, Cumbria.*

THORNTON CLEVELEYS

Seabreeze Books, 39 Woodfield Road, Thornton Cleveleys, FY5 4EQ. Prop: Martin L. Johnson. Tel: (01253) 850075. Est: 1994. Private premises. Appointment necessary. Medium stock. Spec: Antiquarian; Art; Books about Books; Children's; Churchilliana; Fiction - General; Limited Editions - General; Literature - Victorian. PR: £1–5,000. Notes: *Skipton Antiques Centre, Skipton (q.v.)*

LANCASHIRE

WEETON

Fylde Books, 31 Knowsley Crescent, Weeton, Preston, PR4 3ND. Prop: Richard Eaves. Tel: 07984 701728. Web: www.ukbookworld.com/members/fyldebooks. E-mail: richard@fyldebooks.co.uk. Est: 1997. Private premises. Postal Only. Appointment necessary. Spec: Aviation; Dogs; General Stock; Marque Histories (see also motoring); Motoring; Sport - Angling/Fishing; Sport - Field Sports; Sport - Shooting. CC: PayPal. Mem: PBFA. Notes: *General stock with an emphasis on Northern Topography, Fishing, Shooting, Transport,Dogs & Technical. Books always wanted.*

WEIR

Neville Chapman, 3, Rochester Close, Weir, Bacup, OL13 8RN. Tel: 01706 879778. Web: www.abebooks.com/home/chapbooks. E-mail: chapbooks@btinternet.com. Est: 1992. Private premises. Internet and Postal. Appointment necessary. Small stock. Spec: Academic/Scholarly; Advertising; Author - du Maurier, Daphne; Countries - England; History - Local; Topography - Local. PR: £1–100.

LEICESTERSHIRE

EARLSDON

Armstrong's Books & Collectables, ■ 178 Albany Street, Earlsdon, Coventry, CV5 6NG. Prop: Colin Rowe Armstrong. Tel: 02476 714344. Est: 1983. Shop open: **T:** 10:00–17:00; **W:** 10:00–17:00; **Th:** 10:00–17:00; **F:** 10:00–17:00; **S:** 10:00–17:00. Spec: Annuals; Cinema/Film; Comics; Cookery/ Gastronomy; Fiction - Crime, Detective, Spy, Thrillers; Fiction - Fantasy, Horror; Fiction - Science Fiction; Law - General.

HINCKLEY

Caduceus Books, 28 Darley Road, Burbage, Hinckley, LE10 2RL. Prop: Ben Fernee. Tel: (01455) 250542. Fax: (0870) 055-2982. Web: www.caduceusbooks.com. E-mail: ben@caduceusbooks.com. Est: 1989. Private premises. Appointment necessary. Very small stock. Spec: Alchemy; Astrology; Esoteric; Occult; Supernatural; Witchcraft. PR: £1–1,000. CC: MC; V; Switch. Notes: *Also, manuscripts, associated items.*

HUGGLESCOTE

Aucott & Thomas, 46 Dennis Street, Hugglescote, LE67 2FP. Prop: Roger Thomas. Tel: 01530 831604. Fax: 01530 831604. Web: www.aucott.com. E-mail: info@aucott.co.uk. Est: 1996. Office and/or bookroom. Internet Only. Appointment necessary. Open: **M:** 09:00–18:00; **T:** 09:00–18:00; **W:** 09:00–18:00; **Th:** 09:00–18:00; **F:** 09:00–18:00; **S:** 09:00–18:00. Small stock. Spec: Author - Bell, Adrian; - Moore, John; Children's; Fiction - Crime, Detective, Spy, Thrillers; Music - Folk & Irish Folk; Music - Rock & Roll; Sport - Angling/Fishing; Sport - Horse Racing (inc. Riding/Breeding/Equestrian). PR: £5–25. CC: AE; JCB; MC; V; Maestro. Mem: Ibooknet. VAT No: GB 800 2360 90.

KIBWORTH HARCOURT

The Countryman Gallery, The Croft 14 Leicester Road, Kibworth Harcourt, LE8 0NN. Prop: Pamela M. Turnbull. Tel: (0116) 279-3211. Fax: Null. E-mail: pamturnbull@countrymansgallery.fsnet.co.uk. Est: 1980. Private premises. Appointment necessary. Small stock. Spec: Children's; Dogs; Ornithology; Poultry; Sport - Angling/Fishing; Sport - Field Sports; Sport - Hunting; Sport - Shooting. PR: £1–500. CC: MC; V. Notes: *Shop also at above premises but appointment necessary.*

LEICESTER

Black Cat Bookshop, ■ 90 Charles St., Leicester, LE1 1GE. Prop: Philip & Karen Woolley. Tel: (0116) 251-2756. Fax: (0116) 281-3545. Web: www.blackcatbookshop.com. E-mail: blackcatuk@aol.com. Est: 1987. Shop open: **M:** 09:30–17:00; **T:** 09:30–17:00; **Th:** 09:30–17:00; **F:** 09:30–17:00; **S:** 09:30–17:00. Large stock. Spec: Author - Conan Doyle, Sir Arthur; - Crompton, Richmal; - Fleming, Ian; - Johns, W.E.; Children's; Comic Books & Annuals; Comics; Counterculture. PR: £1–500. CC: E; JCB; MC; V; SW, De. Cata: Crime, Sherlock Holmes James Bond, British Comics. Mem: PBFA. Notes: *Attends book fairs - Mostly Midlands and North. Worldwide mail order service, selling also on ABE, AMAZON, BIBLION, and EBAY.*

Clarendon Books, ■ 144 Clarendon Park Road, Leicester, LE2 3AE. Prop: Julian Smith. Tel: (0116) 270-1856. E-mail: clarendonbooks@aol.com. Est: 1985. Shop open: **M:** 10:00–17:00; **T:** 10:00–17:00; **W:** 10:00–17:00; **Th:** 10:00–17:00; **F:** 10:00–17:00; **S:** 10:00–17:00. Medium stock. Spec: History - General; History - Local; Literary Criticism; Literature. PR: £1–1,000. CC: AE; E; JCB; MC; V. Mem: PBFA. VAT No: GB 890 0309 37.

Cottage Books, The Cottage, Rempstne Rd Gelsmoor, Coleorton, Leicester, LE67 8HR. Prop: Jennifer M. Boyd-Cropley. Tel: None. E-mail: Jenny@friendlyweb.co.uk. Est: 1970. Private premises. Postal Only. Medium stock. Spec: Agriculture; Architecture; Canals/Inland Waterways; Crafts; Fairgrounds; Folklore; Gypsies; History - Local. PR: £1–2,000. Cata: Rural Life Past & Present. Gypsies. Mem: PBFA.

Rebecca Dearman Rare Books, 66 Gartree Road Stonygate, Leicester, LE2 2FW. Prop: Rebecca Dearman. Tel: (0116) 270-0469. Est: 1967. Private premises. Postal Only. Open: **M:** 09:00–17:00; **T:** 09:00–17:00; **W:** 09:00–17:00; **Th:** 09:00–17:00; **F:** 09:00–17:00; **S:** 09:00–17:00. Medium stock. PR: £1–1,000. Cata: on various subjects. Notes: *Catalogues and occasional fairs. General stock.*

Alfred Lenton, ■ 27 Saint Nicholas Place, Leicester, LE1 4LD. Prop: Philip Lenton. Tel: (0116) 262-7827. Est: 1942. Shop. Telephone First. Small stock. Spec: Art; Arts, The; Illustrated - General; Literature; Natural History; Science - General; Prints and Maps. PR: £1–100.

LEICESTERSHIRE

Bruce Main–Smith & Co. Ltd., 5 Lincoln Drive Wigston, Leicester, LE18 4XU. Prop: (*) D.R. & M.E. Mitchell (Directors). Tel: (0116) 277-7669. Fax: (0116) 277-7669. Web: www.brucemainsmith.com. E-mail: sales@brucemainsmith.com. Est: 1972. Mail Order Only. Open: **M:** 08.00–17.00; **T:** 08.00–17:00; **W:** 08:00–17:00; **Th:** 08:00–17:00; **F:** 08:00–17:00; **S:** 08:00–17:00; **Su:** 08:00–17:00. Spec: Motorbikes / motorcycles. PR: £4–100. CC: MC; V; Switch. Cata: Motor Cycle Literature. Corresp: none. Notes: *Also, virtually a complete stock of all new motor cycle books, plus 4,000 photocopied manuals, spares lists & brochures.*

Maynard & Bradley, ■ 1 Royal Arcade, Silver Street, Leicester, LE1 5YW. Prop: David Maynard & Stephen Bradley. Tel: (0116) 253-2712. Web: www.maynardandbradley.com. E-mail: orders@ maynardandbradley.com. Est: 1971. Shop open: **M:** 09:15–17:15; **T:** 09:15–17:15; **W:** 09:15–17:15; **Th:** 09:15–17:15; **F:** 09:15–17:15; **S:** 09:00–17:00. Medium stock. Spec: Bindings; Colour-Plate; Cookery/ Gastronomy; Illustrated - General; Private Press; Sport - Cricket; Sport - Field Sports; Topography - General. PR: £1–3,000. CC: E; MC; V; Solo, Maestro. Mem: PBFA. VAT No: GB 416 3807 58. Notes: *Also, booksearch, pictures, picture-framing, conservation services, print colouring & decorative mount cutting service (trade)*

Pooks Motor Books, ■ Unit 4 Victoria Road, Fowke Street, Rothley, Leicester, LE7 7PJ. Prop: (*) Barrie Pook & John Pook. Tel: (0116) 237-6222. Fax: (0116) 237-6491. Web: www.abebooks.com. E-mail: pooks.motorbooks@virgin.net. Shop open: **M:** 09:00–17:00; **T:** 09:00–17:00; **W:** 09:00–17:00; **Th:** 09:00–17:00; **F:** 09:00–17:00. Very large stock. Spec: Biography; Marque Histories (see also motoring); Motorbikes / motorcycles; Motoring; Transport; Vintage Cars; Collectables; Ephemera. PR: £3–1,000. CC: MC; V. Mem: FSB. Notes: *Also, sales catalogues for cars & motorcycles. Open at other times by appointment.*

Rosanda Books, 11 Whiteoaks Road Oadby, Leicester, LE2 5YL. Prop: David Baldwin BA, M. Phil, & Joyce Baldwin. Tel: (0116) 2713880. E-mail: d.baldwin@talktalk.net. Est: 1994. Private premises. Appointment necessary. Spec: History - Ancient; History - British; History - European; History - Middle Ages. PR: £2–50.

Tin Drum Books, ■ 68 Narborough Road, Leicester, LE3 0BR. Prop: Valerie & Ian Smalley. Tel: (0116) 224-8409. E-mail: tindrum@ntlworld.com. Est: 1986. Shop open: **M:** 10:00–18:00; **T:** 10:00–18:00; **W:** 10:00–18:00; **Th:** 10:00–18:00; **F:** 10:00–18:00; **S:** 10:00–18:00. Medium stock. PR: £1–10. Notes: *Also, bookbinding.*

Treasure Trove Books, ■ 21 Mayfield Road, Leicester, LE2 1LR. Prop: Linda Sharman. Tel: (0116) 2755933. E-mail: sales@treasuretrovebks.plus.com. Est: 1993. Shop open: **M:** 09:30–16:30; **T:** 09:30– 16:30; **Th:** 09:30–16:30; **F:** 09:30–16:30; **S:** 09:30–16:30. Very large stock. Spec: Annuals; Author - Bellaires, George; - Blyton, Enid; - Brent-Dyer, Elinor M.; - Buckeridge, A.; - Christie, Agatha; - Johns, W.E.; - Potter, Beatrix. PR: £1–500. CC: PayPal.

Tony Yates Antiquarian Books, 3 Melton Avenue, Leicester, LE4 7SE. Prop: Tony and June Yates. Tel: (0116) 266-1891. E-mail: tonyyatesbooks@btopenworld.com. Est: 1989. Private premises. Appointment necessary. Small stock. Spec: Academic/Scholarly; Almanacs; Antiquarian; Atlases; Bindings; Books about Books; Chess; Children's - Early Titles. PR: £5–1,000. Cata: On specialist areas. Mem: PBFA. Notes: *We attend bookfairs in the Midlands and North of England. As well as issuing the occasional catalogue we shall also be dealing on the Internet. Our specialisms include books on Leicestershire, and the work of Thomas & John Bewick.*

LOUGHBOROUGH

Booklore, 6, The Green, East Leake, Loughborough, LE12 6LD. Prop: (*) Ralph & Simon Corbett. Tel: (01509) 820614. E-mail: Ralphcorbett@aol.com. Est: 1994. Private premises. Internet and Postal. Appointment necessary. Open: **M:** 09:30–17:30; **T:** 09:30–17:30; **W:** 09:30–17:30; **Th:** 09:30–17:30; **F:** 09:30–17:30; **S:** 09:00–16:00. Large stock. Spec: Antiquarian; Bindings; Fine leather bindings (see also Fine & Rare). PR: £10–1,000. CC: MC; V; Maestro. Mem: PBFA; Society of Bookbinders. VAT No: GB 815 6907 13. Notes: *We are always keen to buy and sell quality books. We deal with honesty and integrity.*

Eric Goodyer, Natural History, Hathern, Loughborough, LE12 5LE. Prop: Sue Duerdoth & Eric Goodyer. Tel: (01509) 844473. Fax: (01509) 844473. Web: www.abebooks.com/home/ ERICGOODYER/. E-mail: eric.goodyer@btinternet.com. Est: 1992. Private premises. Postal Only. Telephone First. Very small stock. Spec: Antiquarian; Natural History. PR: £5–300. CC: PayPal. VAT No: GB 6165 474 433.

Magis Books, 64 Leopold Street, Loughborough, LE11 5DN. Prop: Tom Clarke. Tel: 01509210626. Fax: 01509 238034. Web: www.magis.co.uk. E-mail: enquiries@magis.co.uk. Est: 1975. Private premises. Internet and Postal. Telephone First. Open. **M:** 09.00–18.30; **T:** 09:00–18:30; **W:** 09:00–18:30; **Th:** 09:00–18.30; **F:** 09:00–18:30; **S:** 09:00–18:30; **Su:** 09:00–17:30; Closed for lunch: 13:00–14:00. Spec: Alchemy; Divining; Esoteric; Folklore; Ghosts; Graphology; Hermeticism; Homeopathy. CC: MC; V. Cata: Esoteric, occult, Eastern & Western philosophies,. Mem: PBFA.

MARKET HARBOROUGH

Bowden Books, 14 Station Road Great Bowden, Market Harborough, LE16 7HN. Prop: Terry Bull. Tel: (01858) 466832. Est: 1986. Private premises. Postal Only. Very small stock. Spec: Architecture; Art; Colour-Plate; Publishers - Black, A. & C.; Topography - General; Travel - General. PR: £5–750. Corresp: French, Italian. Mem: PBFA. Notes: *book fairs.*

Christine's Book Cabin, ■ 7 Coventry Road, Market Harborough, LE16 9BX. Prop: Malcolm & Christine Noble. Tel: (01858) 433233 Web: www.bookcabin.co.uk. E-mail: malcolm@ bookcabin.co.uk. Est: 1992. Shop open: **M:** 10:00–16:30; **T:** 10:00–16:30; **W:** ; **Th:** 10:00–16:30; **F:** 10:00–16:30; **S:** 10:00–16:30. Small stock. Spec: Booksearch; Ephemera. PR: £1–400. CC: AE; JCB; MC; V. Notes: *General stock*

MELTON MOWBRAY

Witmeha Productions, The Orchard Wymondham, Melton Mowbray, LE14 2AZ.

ROTHLEY

Whig Books Ltd., 11 Grangefields Drive, Rothley. Prop: Dr. J. Pollock & Mrs. A. Hinchliffe. Tel: (0116) 237-4420. Est: 1985. Private premises. Appointment necessary. Very small stock. Spec: Art; History - General; Literature. PR: £1–500.

SHENTON

Michael D. Raftery (Books), Whitemoors Antique Centre Mill Lane, Shenton, CV13 0LA. Prop: Mike Raftery. Tel: Home (01455) 611017. E-mail: mdraftery@supanet.com. Est: 1976. Office and/or bookroom. Open: **M:** 11:00–16:00; **T:** 11:00–16:00; **W:** 11:00–16:00; **Th:** 11:00–16:00; **F:** 11:00–16:00; **S:** 11:00–16:00; **Su:** 11:00–16:00. Small stock. Spec: Booksearch. PR: £1–30. CC: AE; D; E; JCB; MC; V. Corresp: French, German. Notes: *Tea Rooms, gardens visitor attractions (at Whitemoor only). Also at Leicester Antiques Warehouse, Leicester (q.v.).*

THURCASTON

Ian Kilgour (Sporting Books), 3 Hall Farm Road, Thurcaston, LE7 7JF. Prop: Ian Kilgour. Tel: (0116) 235-0025. E-mail: sportingbooks@ntlworld.com. Est: 1972. Private premises. Internet and Postal. Appointment necessary. Small stock. Spec: Cockfighting; Dogs; Farming & Livestock; Firearms/ Guns; Rural Life; Sport - Angling/Fishing; Sport - Big Game Hunting; Sport - Coursing. PR: £2–500. Cata: fishing shooting hunting falconry.

WIGSTON

Michael D. Raftery (Books), Leicester Antiques Warehouse Clarkes Road, Wigston, Leicester, LE18 2DG. Prop: Mike Raftery. Display/stand. Notes: *Also at: Whitemoors Antique Centre, Shenton, Leicestershire (q.v.)*

LINCOLNSHIRE

BARTON–ON–HUMBER

Humber Books, Rozel House 4 St. Mary's Lane, Barton–on–Humber, DN18 5EX. Prop: Peter M. Cresswell. Tel: (01652) 634958. Fax: (01652) 634965. Web: www.humberbooks.co.uk. E-mail: pmc@ humberbooks.co.uk. Est: 1972. Private premises. Contactable. Spec: Antiquarian; Bibles; Hymnology; Manuscripts; Religion - Christian; Religion - Methodism; Religion - Non conformity; Religion - Protestantism. PR: £20–2,000. CC: AE; D; E; JCB; MC; V.

BILLINGBOROUGH

Brockwells Booksellers, Unit 1C White Leather Square, Billingborough, NG34 0QP. Prop: Matthew & Richard Peace. Tel: (01529)241222. Fax: (01529)455890. Web: www.brockwells.co.uk. E-mail: books@brockwells.co.uk. Est: 1997. Warehouse. Internet and Postal. Telephone First. Open: **M:** 09:00–12:00; **T:** 09:00–12:00; **W:** 09:00–12:00; **Th:** 09:00–12:00; **F:** 09:00–12:00. Large stock. Spec: Academic/Scholarly; Antiquarian; Business Studies; Engineering; History - General; Military History; Politics; Travel - General. PR: £7–2,250. CC: AE; MC; V; Maestro. Mem: Bibliographical Society. Notes: *Prints and maps selling. New Boook Sales, Secure Credit Card Facility on web site.*

Alan Redmond Books, 25 High Street, Billingborough, Sleaford, NG34 0QB. Prop: Mrs R. Redmond. Tel: 01529 240215. Est: 1981. Storeroom. Open: **S:** 10:00–17:00; **Su:** 10:00–17:00. Spec: Notes: *Also open on Bank Holidays but closed between 1 November and 1 March. Appointment may be possible outside these times.*

BILLINGHAY

Maggy Browne, 27-29 High Street, Billinghay, Lincoln, LN4 4AU. Prop: Maggy Browne. Tel: (01526) 860294. Fax: (0870) 7059623. Web: www.njbonline.com. E-mail: books@notjustbooks.f9.co.uk. Est: 1981. Private premises. Internet and Postal. Appointment necessary. Medium stock. Spec: Biography; Crime (True); Fiction - General; Fire & Fire Fighters; History - General; Police Force Histories; Politics; Publishers - Chambers. PR: £5–50. CC: AE; JCB; MC; V; Switch. Mem: FSB. Notes: *Props for Theatre/Film/TV. Mailroom supplies, DJ sleeving , PB covers etc. Maps, Prints, Engravings, Vintage Adverts. Ephemera. Original Paintings. Largest stock Guinness titles in the WORLD!Audio Books + Tape Drops - solves tangled tapes.*

CLEETHORPES

Soccer Books Limited, 72 St Peter's Avenue, Cleethorpes, DN35 8HU. Prop: John, Michael & Glenys Robinson. Tel: 01472-696226. Fax: 01472-698546. Web: www.soccer-books.co.uk. E-mail: info@ soccer-books.co.uk. Est: 1982. Office and/or bookroom. Postal Only. Contactable. Open: **M:** 09:00– 17:00; **T:** 09:00–17:00; **W:** 09:00–17:00; **Th:** 09:00–17:00; **F:** 09:00–12.00. Closed for lunch: 13:00– 14:00. Spec: New Books; Railways; Sport - Football (Soccer). CC: AE; E; JCB; MC; V; Maestro. Cata: soccer. Corresp: none. Mem: PBFA. VAT No: GB 546 5008 49. Notes: *Publishers of 15 to 20 titles each year and mailorder suppliers of other publishers new and used football books throughout the world.*

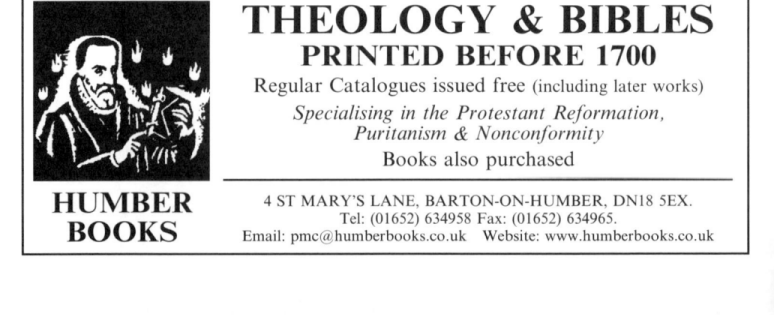

CORBY GLEN

Anchor Books, 20 Walsingham Drive, Corby Glen, NG33 4TA. Prop: Mr. C.R. Dunn. Tel: 01476 550103. Web: www.abebooks.com/colindunn/home. E-mail: c.r.dunn@btinternet.com. Est: 1990. Private premises. Postal Only. Appointment necessary. Medium stock. Spec: Aeronautics; Aircraft; Aviation; Canals/Inland Waterways; History - General; Maritime/Nautical; Maritime/Nautical - History; Maritime/Nautical - Log Books. CC: JCB; MC; V; Switch. Corresp: German. Notes: *We specialise in Maritime (particularly shipping company histories), Regimental History, Boer War, Naval, Combat Aeronautical, Canals.*

EAGLE

J. & J. Books, Holly Cottage, 14 Scarle Lane, Eagle, LN6 9EJ. Prop: Jim & Jan Rayner. Tel: (01522) 869597. Fax: (01522) 869597. Web: www.jandjbooks.com. E-mail: jimandjanrayner@btinternet.com. Est: 1994. Private premises. Internet and Postal. Appointment necessary. Small stock. Spec: Fiction - Crime, Detective, Spy, Thrillers; Natural History; New Naturalist; Publishers - Penguin; Publishers - Shell Guides; Topography - Local; Vintage Paperbacks. PR: £4–500. CC: MC; V; Switch. Corresp: German and French. Mem: PBFA. Notes: *We offer a booksearch service.*

GAINSBOROUGH

Hemswell Antique Centre, Caenby Corner Estate Hemswell Cliff, Gainsborough, DN21 5TJ. Prop: Mr. R. Miller. Tel: (01427) 668389. Fax: 668935. E-mail: info@Hemswell-Antiques.com. Est: 1986. Shop and/or gallery. Open: **M:** 10:00–17:00; **T:** 10:00–17:00; **W:** 10:00–17:00; **Th:** 10:00–17:00; **F:** 10:00– 17:00; **S:** 10:00–17:00; **Su:** 10:00–17:00. CC: AE; D; E; JCB; MC; V.

GRANTHAM

Gravity Books, 110 Harrowby Road, Grantham, NG31 9DS. Prop: Philip Emery. Tel: 01476 575682. E-mail: gravitybks@aol.com. Est: 1999. Private premises. Internet Only. Spec: Architecture; Art; General; Music - Rock & Roll; Sport - General. CC: MC; V; Maestro, PayPal.

HOLBEACH

Bookshop at the Plain, 55 Fleet Street, Holbeach, PE12 7AU. Prop: M.D. Watts. Tel: (01406) 422 942. E-mail: wattsmc@aol.com. Est: 1987. Private premises. Internet Only. Appointment necessary. Medium stock. Spec: Academic/Scholarly; Children's; History - General; History - Middle Ages; History - Modern; Literature; Religion - General; Religion - Christian. PR: £3–250. CC: MC; V.

HORNCASTLE

Good for Books, ■ Good for Books 23 North Street, Horncastle, LN9 5DX. Prop: Richard & Sarah Ingram-Hill. Tel: 01507 525021. Fax: 01507 524415. Web: www.goodforbooks.co.uk. E-mail: books @goodforbooks.co.uk. Est: 2004. Shop open: **M:** 10.00–16:30; **T:** 10.00–16:30; **W:** 10:00–16:30; **Th:** 10:00–16:30; **F:** 10:00–16:30; **S:** 10:00–16:30. Spec: Animals and Birds; Antiquarian; Architecture; Art; Author 20th Century, Aviation; Biography; Children's. Notes: *Shop divided into 3 rooms - Good for Books - eclectic mix! Books Two - All books £2.00 or under. Book 3 - All books 3 for £1.00. A coke burning stove adds to an ambient browsing atmosphere during the winter months!*

Jabberwock Books, ■ 14 - 16 St Lawrence Street, Horncastle, LN9 5BJ. Prop: Robert Flanagan and Pauline Flanagan. Tel: 01507 522112. Web: www.jabberwockbooks.co.uk. E-mail: info@ jabberwockbooks.co.uk. Est: 1986. Shop open: **M:** 10:30–16.30; **T:** 10:30–16.30; **W:** 10.30–16.30; **Th:** 10:30–16.30; **F:** 10:30–16.30; **S:** 10:30–16.30.

Roger Lucas Booksellers, 44 Queen Street, Horncastle, LN9 6BG. Prop: Roger Lucas. Tel: 01507 522261. Web: www.rogerlucasbooks.com. E-mail: Rogerbks@aol.com. Est: 1984. Private premises. Internet and Postal. Appointment necessary. Spec: General. CC: PayPal.

KIRTON

D.C. Books, 11 Hemington Way, Kirton, Boston, PE20 1EA. Prop: D.J. & C. Lidgett. Tel: (01205) 724507. Fax: (01205) 724507. E-mail: dave.lidgett@fsmail.net. Est: 1984. Private premises. Internet and Postal. Very small stock. Spec: Travel - General; Booksearch. PR: £3–5.

LINCOLNSHIRE

LINCOLN

Aardvark Cricket Books, 19 Vanwell Drive, Waddington, Lincoln, LN6 9LT. Prop: Peter & Elizabeth Taylor. Tel: 01522 722671. E-mail: pete@aardvarkcricketbooks.co.uk. Est: 1998. Private premises. Appointment necessary. Open: **M:** 09:00–17:00; **T:** 09:00–17:00; **W:** 09:00–17:00; **Th:** 09:00–17:00; **F:** 09:00–17:00; **S:** 09:00–17:00. Spec: Annuals; Sport - Cricket. Cata: Wisden Cricketers Almanacks. Mem: FSB. Notes: *A major dealer in Wisden Cricketers Almanacks. Also, book restoration.*

Autumn Leaves, ■ 19 The Green, Nettleham, Lincoln, LN2 2NR. Prop: Ian & Sue Young. Tel: (01522) 750779. E-mail: leaves@onetel.com. Est: 1997. Shop open: **T:** 09:15–16:30; **W:** 09:15–16:30; **Th:** 09:15–16:30; **F:** 09:15–17:00; **S:** 09:15–12:30. Medium stock. Spec: Antiques; Art; Cookery/ Gastronomy; Drama; Entertainment - General; Fiction - General; Health; History - General. PR: £2–100. CC: AE; JCB; MC; V; Maestro. Corresp: French, German, Swedish. VAT No: GB 737 8648 80.

Begging Bowl Books, 25 Queens Crescent, Lincoln, LN1 1LR. Prop: Rob Bradley. Tel: (01522) 801132 (home). Web: www.abebooks.com. E-mail: robt.bradley@gmail.com. Est: 1998. Spec: Academic/ Scholarly; Author - Graves, Robert; - Powys Family, The; Ecclesiastical History & Architecture; Esoteric; Fiction - General; Fiction - Crime, Detective, Spy, Thrillers; First Editions. PR: £1–1,000. CC: MC; V; credit cards via abebooks, PayPal. Notes: *Many titles not listed – please enquire for specific wants.*

Chapter & Verse, 17 Queensway, Lincoln, LN2 4AJ. Prop: Roy Fines. Tel: (01522) 523202. E-mail: roy@fines18.freeserve.co.uk. Est: 1977. Private premises. Internet and Postal. Appointment necessary. Open: **M:** 09:00–18:00; **T:** 09:00–18:00; **W:** 09:00–18:00; **Th:** 09:00–18:00; **F:** 09:00–18:00; **S:** 09:00–18:00; **Su:** 09:00–18:00. Very small stock. Spec: Antiquarian; Architecture; Bindings; Books about Books; Directories - British; Engraving; Humour; Limited Editions - General. PR: £1–5,000. Cata: Lincolnshire Topography. Corresp: German. Notes: *Payment accepted by cheque, Postal order, cash or via PayPal.*

Gladstone Books, ■ The Shambles 4 Westgate, Lincoln, LN1 3AS. Prop: Prof. Ben Mepham. Tel: 01636 813601. E-mail: ben.mepham@btopenworld.com. Est: 2005. Shop open: **Th:** 11:00–17:00; **F:** 11:00– 17:00; **S:** 11:00–17:00; **Su:** 13:00–16:00. Notes: *Exhibits at fairs.*

Golden Goose Books, ■ 20–21 Steep Hill, Lincoln, LN2 1LT. Prop: Mrs Anna Cockram & Richard West–Skinn. Tel: (01522) 522589. E-mail: harlequin@acockram.fsbusiness.co.uk. Est: 1984. Internet Only. Shop open: **M:** 11:00–17:00; **T:** 11:00–17:00; **Th:** 11:00–17:00; **F:** 11:00–17:00; **S:** 11:00–17:15. Spec: Antiques; Art; Illustrated - General. Notes: *Harlequin Gallery, 20–22, Steep Hill, Lincoln (q.v.).*

Harlequin Gallery, ■ 22 Steep Hill, Lincoln, LN2 1LT. Prop: Richard West–Skinn. Tel: (01522) 522589. E-mail: harlequin@acockram.fsbusiness.co.uk. Est: 1964. Shop open: **M:** 11:00–17:30; **T:** 11:00– 17:30; **W:** 12:00–16:00; **Th:** 11:00–17:30; **F:** 11:00–17:30; **S:** 11:00–17:00. Very large stock. Spec: Art; Maps & Mapmaking; Prints and Maps. PR: £1–20,000. Notes: *Antiquarian & secondhand books, antique maps & prints. Very wide general stock. Also at Golden Goose Books, 20–21, Steep Hill, Lincoln (R.W. West-Skinn & Anna Cockram) Internet sellers. Also, Golden Goose Globe Restorers.*

Orlando Booksellers, 1 Rasen Lane, Lincoln, LN1 3EZ. Prop: Alison Smith & Christopher McKee. Tel: (01522) 510828. Web: www.abebooks.com/home/ORLAN_DO/. E-mail: orlando@booksellers .fsworld.co.uk. Est: 1994. Private premises. Internet and Postal. Contactable. Small stock. Spec: Beat Writers; Fine & Rare; Literature; Modern First Editions; Photography; Poetry; Publishers - Hogarth Press; Publishers - Pan. PR: £20–1,000. CC: PayPal. Cata: Modern Firsts. VAT No: GB 629 3707 21.

Readers Rest, ■ 13–14 Steep Hill, Lincoln, LN2 1LT. Prop: Nick Warwick. Tel: (01522) 543217. Est: 1982. Shop open: **M:** 11:00–15:00; **T:** 11:00–15:00; **W:** 11:00–15:00; **Th:** 11:00–15:00; **F:** 11:00–15:00; **S:** 09:30–16:00. Very large stock. PR: £1–50. Notes: *Readers Rest Hall of Books, Steep Hill, Lincoln.*

LOUTH

Mostly Mysteries Bookstore, 64 Legbourne Road, Louth, LN11 8ER. Prop: Victor H. Brown & Mary Brown. Tel: 01507 354990. E-mail: victro3@operamail.com. Est: 1985. Storeroom. Appointment necessary. Spec: Mysteries.

MARKET DEEPING

Cornucopia Books, 2 Godsey Crescent, Market Deeping, PE6 8HX. Prop: Roy Dennis. Web: www.cornucopiabooks.co.uk. E-mail: mycornucopia@btinternet.com. Est. 1986. Mail Order Only. Internet and Postal. Contactable. Spec: Academic/Scholarly; Advertising; Aeronautics; Aircraft; American Indians; Animals and Birds; Anthologies; Antiques. CC: PayPal. Notes: *I am disabled and deal by Internet Only. Most major credit cards can be accepted from my website using PayPal. Alternatively you may like to visit my eBay shop http://stores.ebay.co.uk/Cornucopia-Internet-Book-Shop.*

MOULTON SEAS END

P. Cassidy (Bookseller), Warren Lodge Common Road, Moulton Seas End, PE12 6LF. Prop: Patrick Cassidy. Tel: (01406) 370990. Web: www.cassidysbooks.co.nr. E-mail: bookscass@aol.com. Est: 1974. Mail Order Only. Postal Only. Medium stock. Spec: Agriculture; Art; General; Military; Military History; Topography - Local; Prints and Maps. PR: £1–250. CC: AE; MC; V; PayPal. Notes: *Postal business only. Enquiries and orders by telephone, e-mail or via my web site.*

SLEAFORD

Phillip Austen, 50 Main Street Ewerby, Sleaford, NG34 9PJ. Tel: (01529) 461074. E-mail: phillip.austen@militarybooks.19.co.uk. Est: 1989. Private premises. Postal Only. Medium stock. Spec: Military. CC: D; E; JCB; MC; V. Mem: PBFA.

Mark Evans, 34 Northgate, Sleaford, NG34 7DA. Prop: Mark Evans. Tel: (0798) 1938165. Est: 1985. Private premises. Postal Only. Very small stock. Spec: Cinema/Film; Music - General; Sport - General; Television; Theatre; Booksearch. PR: £3–100.

Julian Roberts Fine Books, Hill House Braceby, Sleaford, NG34 0TA. Tel: (01529) 497271. Fax: (01529) 497271. Web: www.jrfinebooks.com. E-mail: jrfinebooks@aol.com. Est: 1997. Private premises. Appointment necessary. Small stock. Spec: Antiquarian; Children's; Children's - Early Titles; Children's - Illustrated; Cookery/Gastronomy; Fiction - General; Literature; Modern First Editions. PR: £10–5,000. CC: MC; V. Mem: PBFA. Notes: *General stock including First Editions, Childrens & Antiquarian*

Westgate Bookshop, ■ 45 Westgate, Sleaford, NG34 7PU. Prop: Geoffrey Almond. Tel: (01529) 304276. Web: www.abebooks.com/home/WESTGATEBOOKSHOP/. E-mail: geoff.almond@btinternet.com. Est: 1986. Shop open: **M:** 10:00–16.30; **T:** 10:00–16.30; **W:** 10:00–16.30; **F:** 10:00–16.30; **S:** 10:00–16.00. Small stock. PR: £1–15. CC: MC; V.

SOUTH KELSEY

Winghale Books Ltd., Grassmere Cottage Brigg Road, South Kelsey, LN7 6PH. Prop: Directors: Irwin & Hilary Johnston. Tel: (01652) 678752. E-mail: winghale@btinternet.com. Est: 1984. Private premises. Internet and Postal. Appointment necessary. Medium stock. Spec: Academic/Scholarly; Americana - General; Archaeology; Christianity – Syrian Orthodox; Classical Studies; Colonial; Ecclesiastical History & Architecture; European Studies. PR: £10–200. CC: AE; MC; V. Cata: academic history. Mem: PBFA. VAT No: GB 365 1833 46.

SPALDING

Robin Peake, 26 Balmoral Avenue, Spalding, PE11 2RN. Tel: (01775) 724050. E-mail: robin.peake@ btinternet.com. Est: 1989. Postal Only. Spec: Motorbikes / motorcycles; Motoring; Vintage Cars. PR: £2–250. CC: MC; V.

Michael Prior, 34 Fen End Lane, Spalding, PE12 6AD. Prop: Michael Prior. Tel: (01775) 761851. E-mail: mikevprior1@msn.com. Est: 1970. Private premises. Internet and Postal. Appointment necessary. Medium stock. Spec: Advertising; Author - Churchill, Sir Winston; - Forester, C.S.; - Masefield, John; Aviation; Maritime/Nautical; Military; Military History. PR: £10–250. Cata: infrequent on maritime. Corresp: French. Notes: *Dealer in cigarette and other trade cards, continental chromo cards, postcards & printed maritime ephemera.*

STAMFORD

Andrew Burroughs Books, 3 Empingham Road, Stamford, PE9 2RH. Tel: (01780) 751363. Fax: (01780) 765140. E-mail: militarybooks@andrewburroughs.co.uk. Est: 1983. Private premises. Postal Only. Spec: Armed Forces - Australian Army; Armed Forces - Australian Navy; Arms & Armour; Automobilia/Automotive; Espionage; French Foreign Legion, The; History - 20th Century; History - British Empire, The. PR: £5–500. Cata: Naval and military.

LINCOLNSHIRE

Robert Humm & Co, ■ Station House Gresley Drive, Stamford, PE9 2JN. Prop: Robert Humm and Clare Humm. Tel: 01780 766266. Fax: 01780 757929. Web: www.roberthumm.co.uk. E-mail: books@roberthumm.co.uk. Est: 1974. Alternative web: www.rhbooks.co.uk. Shop open: **M:** 09:30–17:00; **T:** 09:30–17:00; **W:** 09:30–17:00; **Th:** 09:30–17:00; **F:** 09:30–17:00; **S:** 09:30–17:00. Spec: Aeronautics; Aircraft; Archaeology - Industrial; Author - Rolt, L.T.C.; Aviation; Buses/Trams; Canals/Inland Waterways; Commerce - General. CC: JCB; MC; V. Cata: Railways and trams; industrial history. Corresp: French at a pinch. VAT No: GB 226 1728 73. Notes: *Specialists in railway, tramway, aviation, shipping, waterway, industrial and commercial history; no road transport or non-transport subjects stocked. We ship worldwide and welcome phone and email enquiries. Occasionally shut for lunch.*

St. Mary's Books & Prints, ■ 9 St. Mary's Hill, Stamford, PE9 2DP. Prop: N.A.M., M.G.D. P.A. Tyers. Tel: (01780) 763033. Fax: (01780) 763033. Web: www.stmarysbooks.com. E-mail: orders@stmarysbooks.com. Est: 1971. Internet and shop open: **M:** 08:00–18:00; **T:** 08:00–18:00; **W:** 08:00–18:00; **Th:** 08:00–18:00; **F:** 08:00–18:00; **S:** 08:00–18:00; **Su:** 09:00–18:00. Large stock. Spec: Academic/Scholarly; Archaeology; Architecture; Author - Aldin, Cecil; - Fleming, Ian; - Rackham, Arthur; -Rowling, J.K.; - Watkins-Pitchford, Denys ('B.B.'). PR: £10–50,000. CC: AE; D; E; JCB; MC; V. Corresp: German, Latin, French, Spanish, Italian. Notes: *Open Sundays. Bookbinding, Valuations, Book Search & major stock of Wisdens.*

St. Paul's Street Bookshop, ■ 7, St. Paul's Street, Stamford, PE9 2BE. Prop: James Blessett. Tel: (01780) 482748. Fax: (01778) 380538. E-mail: stpaulsbookshop@aol.com. Est: 1986. Shop open: **M:** 10:00–17:00; **T:** 10:00–17:00; **W:** ; **Th:** 10:00–17:00; **F:** 10:00–17:00; **S:** 10:00–17:00. Medium stock. Spec: Motoring; Sport - Motor Racing; Topography - Local. PR: £1–500. CC: E; MC; V. Corresp: French, German. Mem: PBFA. VAT No: GB 551 0471 74. Notes: *Also, catalogues on motorsport.*

Staniland (Booksellers), ■ 4/5 St. George's Street, Stamford, PE9 2BJ. Prop: V.A. & B.J. Valentine Ketchum. Tel: (01780) 755800. Fax: (01780) 755800. E-mail: stanilandbooksellers@btinternet.com. Est: 1972. Internet and shop open: **M:** 10:00–17:00; **T:** 10:00–17:00; **W:** 10:00–17:00; **Th:** ; **F:** 10:00–17:00; **S:** 10:00–17:00. Closed for lunch: 13:00–14:00. Large stock. Spec: Academic/Scholarly; Antiquarian; Applied Art; Archaeology; Architecture; Art; Art History; Art Reference. PR: £1–3,000. CC: MC; V. Mem: PBFA. VAT No: GB 200 8434 08.

Undercover Books, ■ 30 Scotgate, Stamford, PE9 2YQ. Prop: Tony Dodson. Tel: 01780 480989. Fax: 01780 763963. Web: www.usedbooknews.com. E-mail: undercoverbooks@btinternet.com. Est: 1990. Internet and Postal. Shop open: **M:** 10:00–16:00; **T:** 10:00–16:00; **W:** 10:00–16:00; **Th:** 10:00–16:00; **F:** 10:00–16:00; **S:** 10:00–16:00. Very large stock. Spec: Crime (True); Criminology; Espionage; Law -General; Police Force Histories; Travel - Europe; Booksearch. CC: AE; D; E; JCB; MC; V; SW, De. Cata: Criminology and Police. Corresp: Any. Mem: Police History Ass. VAT No: GB 797 0827 78. Notes: *All titles available to be viewed through www.usedbooknews.com. Booksearch undertaken for rare and out-of-print titles on the following specialities including Police, True Crime, Espionage, Terrorism, Criminology, Court and Prison History.*

WINTERTON

Richard Williams (Bookdealer), 4-A Enterprise Way Roxby Road, Winterton, DN15 9SU. Prop: Richard Williams. Tel: (01724) 733011. Web: www.http://rwilliamsbookdealer.mysite.wanadoo-members/. E-mail: rich@rahwilliams.freeserve.co.uk. Est: 1975. Private premises. Internet and Postal. Appointment necessary. Very large stock. Spec: Academic/Scholarly; Annuals; - Simenon, Georges; Author - Wallace, Edgar; Bibliography; Books about Books, Cinema/Film; Cowboys. PR: £2–200. CC: MC; V. Corresp: French, German. Notes: *We are also the Dragonby Press publishers of bibliographies and checklists.*

LONDON

EAST POSTAL DISTRICTS

Antique City Bookshop, ■ 2 - 3 Antique City Market 98 Wood Street, Walthamstow, London, E17 3HX. Prop: Alan Stone. Tel: 020 8520 8300. Est: 1994. Shop open: **M:** 10:30–16:30; **T:** 10:30–17:30; **F:** 10:30–17:30; **S:** 10:30–16:30.

Bibliophile Books, Unit 5 Industrial Estate Thomas Road, London, E14 7BN. Prop: A. Quigley. Tel: (0207) 515-9222. Fax: (0207) 538-4115. Web: www.bibliophilebooks.com. E-mail: customercare@ bibliophilebooks.co.uk. Est: 1978. Storeroom. Open: **M:** 08:30–17:00; **T:** 08:30–17:00; **W:** 08:30–17:00; **Th:** 08:30–17:00; **F:** 08:30–17:00. Medium stock. Spec: First Editions; Signed Editions; Social History. PR: £1–30. CC: AE; MC; V. Cata: All. Corresp: French, Spanish. Mem: BA VAT No: GB 242 6934 55. Notes: *Upmarket half price remainders and re-prints selected from publishers backlists and carefully reviewed in-house by dedicated Bibliophiles. Full customer service and despatch from Docklands warehouse and only £3 flat rate p&p UK mainland.*

Birchden Books, 3 Edith Road East Ham, London, F1 1DE. Prop: Michael Vetterlein. Tel: (020) 8472-3651. E-mail: mike@mvetterlein.freeserve.co.uk. Est: 2001. Private premises. Postal Only. Appointment necessary. Very small stock. Spec: Architecture; Art Reference; Bell-Ringing (Campanology); Cemeteries; Ecclesiastical History & Architecture; Illuminated Manuscripts; Music - Gregorian Chants; Needlework. PR: £2–500.

Brian Troath Books, 106 Graham Road, London, E8 1BX. Prop: Brian Troath. Tel: 020 7254 2912. E-mail: briantroathbooks@onetel.com. Est: 1970. Private premises. Internet and Postal. Appointment necessary. Open: **M:** 10:00–16.00; **T:** 10:00–16.00; **W:** 10:00–16.00; **Th:** 10.00–16.00; **F:** 10.00–16.00. Spec: Academic/Scholarly; Aesthetic Movement; Aesthetics; Arts, The; Author - Spark, Muriel; Belle-Lettres; Books about Books; Cinema/Film. Cata: English literature - first and limited editions.

Crimes Ink, 35 Moreton Close Upper Clapton, London, E5 9EP. Prop: Leigh.M.Piercy. Tel: (020) 8806-1895. E-mail: crimesink@q-serve.com. Est: 1987. Private premises. Internet and Postal. Appointment necessary. Medium stock. Spec: Assassinations; Crime (True); Criminology; Espionage; Fiction - General; Fiction - Crime, Detective, Spy, Thrillers; Fiction - Fantasy, Horror; Fiction - Science Fiction. PR: £1–150. CC: Via www.abe.com.

David Houston - Bookseller, 26 North Birkbeck Road, London, E11 4JG. Prop: David Houston. Tel: 020 8556 9048. Fax: 020 8556 9048. Web: www.abebooks.com/home/dghbooks. E-mail: scotsbooks@ aol.com. Est: 1997. Private premises. Internet and Postal. Open: **M:** 09:00–17:30; **T:** 09:00–17:30; **W:** 09:00–17:30; **Th:** 09:00–17:30; **F:** 09:00–17:30; **S:** 09:00–17:30; **Su:** 09:00–17:30; Closed for lunch: 13:00–14:00. Spec: Countries - Scotland; Literature - Scottish. CC: MC; V. Cata: Scottish Books, Scottish Literature. Notes: *Postal business only.*

I.D. Edrich, 17 Selsdon Road Wanstead, London, E11 2QF. Prop: I. D. & S. Edrich. Tel: (020) 8989-9541. Fax: 020 8989 9541. Web: www.idedrich.co.uk. E-mail: idedrich@idedrich.co.uk. Est: 1966. Private premises. Postal Only. Contactable. Open: **M:** 09:00–17:00; **T:** 09:00–17:00; **W:** 09:00–17:00; **Th:** 09:00–17:00; **F:** 09:00–17:00. Large stock. Spec: Literature; Poetry. PR: £3–1,000. CC: PayPal. Cata: Modern First Editions, Literary Periodicals, Illu. Corresp: French/german. VAT No: GB 410 1439 10. Notes: *On our web site we itemise, in detail, issues of numerous literary periodicals. We are prepared to search, through our stock of periodicals, for individual authors.*

Keith Langford, Tredegar House 97-99 Bow Road, London, E3 2AN. Prop: Keith Langford. Tel: 02089804326. E-mail: keith@dannibill.fsnet.co.uk. Est: 1977. Private premises. Internet and Postal. Contactable. Open: **M:** 09:00–17:30; **T:** 09:00–17:30; **W:** 09:00–17:30; **Th:** 09:00–17:30; **F:** 09:00–17:30; **S:** 09:00–17:30; **Su:** 09:00–17:30; Closed for lunch: 13:00–14:00. Spec: Adventure; Antiquities; Applied Art; Canals/Inland Waterways; Caricature; Cities - General; Furniture; History - General. Cata: travel, mountaineering, antiquarian. Corresp: French. Notes: *Specialist in collectable books on all subjects.*

M.A. Stroh, Riverside House Leaside Road, Upper Clapton, London, E5 9LU. Prop: M.A. Stroh. Tel: (0208) 806 3690. Fax: (0208) 806 3690. Web: www.webspawner.com/users/Buttonbook/. E-mail: patent@stroh.demon.co.uk. Est: 1956. Storeroom. Internet and Postal. Appointment necessary. Open: **M:** 10:00–17:30; **T:** 10:00–17:30; **W:** 10:00–17:30; **Th:** 10:00–17:30; **F:** 10:00–12:00. Very large stock. Spec: Aeronautics; Aircraft; Antique Stoves; Archives; Arms & Armour; Astronautics; Astronomy; Auction Catalogues. PR: £10–1,000. Cata: science technology patents.

LONDON EAST POSTAL DISTRICTS

Dr Jeremy Parrott, 31A Beacontree Avenue, Walthamstow, E17 4BU. Tel: (0208) 5274315. Web: www.abebooks.com. E-mail: jeremy@invitel.hu. Est: 1985. Private premises. Internet and Postal. Appointment necessary. Large stock. Spec: Author - Beckett, S.; - Benson, E.F.; - Conrad, Joseph; - Orczy, Baroness; - Stevenson, Robert Louis; - Twain, Mark; Author - Verne, Jules; Bibliography. PR: £5–1,000. Corresp: French, German, Spanish, Hungarian. Notes: *Book search for any book in Hungarian.*

LONDON EAST CENTRAL POSTAL DISTRICTS

Amwell Book Company, ■ 53 Amwell Street , London, EC1R 1UR. Prop: Charlotte Robinson. Tel: 020 7837 4891. Web: www.amwellbookcompany.co.uk. E-mail: sixrobins@aol.com. Est: 1981. Shop open: **M:** 11.00–18.00; **T:** 11:00–18:00; **W:** 11:00–18.00; **Th:** 11:00–18.00; **F:** 11.00–18.00; **S:** 11.00–18.00. Spec: Applied Art; Architecture; Art; Art - Theory; Art History; Art Reference; Artists; Arts, The. CC: AE; MC; V. Cata: Architecture, Modern Firsts, childrens & Illustrated. Corresp: French, Italian. Mem: PBFA; FSB.

Elizabeth Crawford, 5 Owen's Row, London, EC1V 4NP. Prop: Elizabeth Crawford. Tel: (020) 7278-9479. Fax: (020) 7278-9479. E-mail: E.Crawford@sphere20.freeserve.co.uk. Est: 1984. Private premises. Postal Only. Appointment necessary. Very small stock. Spec: Authors Women, Women, Ephemera. PR: £5–5,000. Cata: Books and ephemera by and about women. Mem: PBFA.

Andrew Sclanders (Beatbooks), Apt. 32 St Paul's View 15 Amwell Street, London, EC1R 1UP. Prop: Andrew Sclanders. Tel: (020) 7278-5034. Fax: (020) 7278-5034. Web: www.beatbooks.com. E-mail: sclanders@beatbooks.com. Est: 1990. Private premises. Internet and Postal. Appointment necessary. Small stock. Spec: Art; Author - Burroughs, William; - Kerouac, Jack; Avant-Garde; Beat Writers; Counterculture; Music - Rock & Roll. PR: £5–2,500. CC: AE; E; JCB; MC; V.

LONDON NORTH POSTAL DISTRICTS

Alpha Books, 60 Langdon Park Road, London, N6 5QG. Prop: Tony Maddock. Tel: (020) 8348-2831. Fax: (020) 8348-2831. Web: www.abebooks.com/home/alphabks. E-mail: alpha.books@virgin.net. Est: 1983. Private premises. Appointment necessary. Medium stock. Spec: Academic/Scholarly; Alchemy; Astrology; Egyptology; Esoteric; Folklore; Freemasonry & Anti-Masonry; Hermeticism. PR: £1–500. CC: MC; V.

G.W. Andron, 162a Brunswick Park Road, London, N11 1HA. Tel: (020) 8361-2409. Est: 1972. Private premises. Postal Only. Medium stock. Spec: Aeronautics; Aviation; Bibliography; Bookbinding; Books about Books; Maritime/Nautical; Military; Military History. PR: £1–100.

Antique Prints of the World, 6 Livingstone Road Palmers Green, London, N13 4SD. Prop: Mr Mel Menelaou. Tel: (020) 8292-0622. Fax: (020) 8292-0622. Web: www.antique19thcenturyprints.com. E-mail: mel@worldprints.freeserve.co.uk. Est: 1994. Private premises. Appointment necessary. Spec: Countries - Cyprus; Countries - Greece; Collectables; Ephemera; Prints and Maps. CC: PayPal. Corresp: Greek.

Atlas, 17 Pitfield Street, London, N1 6HB. Prop: Alastair Brotchie. Tel: 07770 784 185. Fax: (020) 7490-8742none. E-mail: atlaspress@compuserve.com. Est: 1996. Private premises. Postal Only. Contactable. Spec: Art Reference; Counterculture; Foreign Texts; Literature in Translation; Surrealism. PR: £40–500. Cata: Surrealism/ Pataphysics. Notes: *Also, a publishers.*

Bannatyne Books, 6 Bedford Road, London, N8 8HL. Prop: Mr. & Mrs. Court. Tel: (020) 8340-1953. Est: 1980. Private premises. Postal Only. Spec: Author - Buchan, John. PR: £2–300.

Cavendish Rare Books, 19 Chesthunte Road, London, N17 7PU. Prop: Barbara Grigor-Taylor. Tel: 0208 808 4595. Fax: 0208 808 4595. E-mail: Grigorbooks@aol.com. Est: 1976. Private premises. Postal Only. Appointment necessary. Open: **M:** 09:00–17:30; **T:** 09:00–17:30; **W:** 09:00–17:30; **Th:** 09:00–17:30; **F:** 09:00–17:30; **S:** 09:00–17:30; **Su:** 09:00–17:30; Closed for lunch: 13:00–14:00. Spec: Alpinism/Mountaineering; Asian Studies; Countries - Alaska; Countries - Antarctic, The; Countries - Arctic, The; Countries - Asia; Countries - Australasia; Countries - Central Asia. Cata: Travel, Exploration, Alpine, Polar, Asia. Corresp: French. Spanish. Mem: ABA; PBFA; ILAB.

Church Street Bookshop, ■ 142 Stoke Newington Church Street, London, N16 0JU. Prop: Tim Watson. Tel: 0207 241 5411. Web: www.abebooks.com. E-mail: churchstreetbookshopn16@btopenworld.com. Est: 1984. Shop open: **M:** 11:30–18:00; **T:** 11:30–18:00; **W:** 11:30–18:00; **Th:** 11:30–18:00; **F:** 11:30–18:00; **S:** 11:00–18:00; **Su:** 11:30–18:00. Spec: Academic/Scholarly. CC: MC; V.

Decorum Books, 24 Cloudesley Square, London, N1 0HN. Prop: David Soames. Tel: 020 7278 1838. Web: www.decorunbooks.co.uk. E-mail: decorumbooks@lineone.net. Est: 1971. Office and/or bookroom. Internet and Postal. Contactable. Spec: Applied Art; Architecture; Architecture - Theatre; Art; Art - Afro-American; Art - British; Art - Technique; Art - Theory. CC: MC; V; Maestro. VAT No: GB 230 3437 06. Notes: *For Music Biographies, Historical & Subject Studies, Technica + Scores & Sheet Music - Classical, Light, Pop, Film, TV, Theatre Subject Studies, Directors & Actors Biographies. Art, Design, Architecture Subject Studies, Biographies,*

Erian Books, 24 Woodside Avenue Highgate, London, N6 4SS. Prop: Dr. Eric Nieman. Tel: (020) 8444-9851. E-mail: eric@enieman.fsnet.co.uk. Est: 1992. Internet and Postal. Spec: Bridge; Illustrated - General; Medicine; Medicine - History of; Neurology; Poetry; Psychology/Psychiatry; Science - History of. PR: £15–750. Corresp: French.

Fantasy Centre, ■ 157 Holloway Road, London, N7 8LX. Prop: Ted Ball & Erik Arthur. Tel: (020) 7607-9433. Fax: (020) 7607-9433. Web: www.fantasycentre.biz. E-mail: books@fantasycentre.biz. Est: 1972. Shop open: **M:** 10:00–18:00; **T:** 10:00–18:00; **W:** 10:00–18:00; **Th:** 10:00–18:00; **F:** 10:00–18:00; **S:** 10:00–18:00. Medium stock. Spec: Fiction - Fantasy, Horror; Fiction - Science Fiction. CC: E; MC; V. Cata: Science Fiction, Fantasy & Horror. VAT No: GB 227 3306 83. Notes: *We are the oldest science fiction book shop in the world.*

Fisher & Sperr, ■ 46 Highgate High Street, London, N6 5JB. Tel: (020) 8340-7244. Fax: (020) 8348-4293. Est: 1939. Shop open: **M:** 10:30–17:00; **T:** 10:30–17:00; **W:** 10:30–17:00; **Th:** 10:30–17:00; **F:** 10:30–17:00; **S:** 10:00–17:30. Very large stock. Spec: Art; Art History; Folio Society, The; Literary Criticism; Philosophy; Sets of Books; Topography - General; Collectables. PR: £1–100. CC: AE; D; E; JCB; MC; V. Corresp: French. Mem: ABA; ILAB. VAT No: GB 229 2603 70. Notes: *Bookbinding.*

LONDON NORTH POSTAL DISTRICTS

Nicholas Goodyer, 8 Framfield Road Highbury Fields, London, N5 1UU. Tel: (020) 7226-5682. Fax: (020) 7354-4716. Web: www.nicholasgoodyer.com. E-mail: email@nicholasgoodyer.com. Private premises. Internet and Postal. Telephone First. Open: **M:** 10:00–17:00; **T:** 10:00–17:00; **W:** 10:00 17:00; **Th:** 10:00–17:00; **F:** 10:00–17:00. Very small stock. Spec: Animals and Birds; Architecture; Art; Botany; Colour-Plate; Decorative Art; Fashion & Costume; Gardening - General. CC: MC; V. Cata: General. Corresp: French, German, Italian, Spanish, Portuguese. Mem: ABA; PBFA; ILAB. VAT No: GB 629 6750 05. Notes: *Business operates by appointment or by chance, weekdays. Specialising in Antiquarian Illustrated Books, Natural History, Arts and Architecture, Rare and Unusual Books.*

F. & J. Hogan, 31 Tranmere Road Edmonton, London, N9 9EJ. Prop: Frederick & Joan Hogan. Tel: (020) 8360-6146. Est: 1969. Private premises. Postal Only. Small stock. Spec: Atlases; Caricature; Cartography; Prints and Maps. PR: £5–1,000.

Idle Genius Books, 115 Cluse Court St. Peter Street, London, N1 8PE. Prop: Philip Obeney. Tel: (020) 7704-3193. E-mail: p.obeney@btopenworld.com. Est: 2000. Storeroom. Book fairs only. Appointment necessary. Small stock. Spec: Archaeology; - Christie, Agatha; - Wolfe, Thomas; Fiction - Science Fiction; Literature; Modern First Editions; Topography - Local. PR: £5–400. Notes: *Attends HD Book Fairs. Also, ephemera on London in wartime.*

InterCol London, 43 Templars Crescent, London, N3 3QR. Prop: Yasha Beresiner. Tel: (020) 8349-2207. Fax: (020) 8346-9539 Web: www.intercol.co.uk. E-mail yasha@intercol.co.uk. Est: 1981. Private premises. Internet and Postal. Small stock. Spec: Cartography; Erotica; Freemasonry & Anti-Masonry; Gambling; Games; Numismatics; Topography - General. PR: £5–500. CC: AE; E; JCB; MC; V; PayPal. Corresp: French, Italian, Spanish, Turkish, Hebrew. Mem: ANA; IBNS; IMCoS; IPCS. VAT No: GB 350 6069 69.

M. Eric Korn, 32 North Grove, London, N15 5QP. Prop: Eric Korn. Tel: 0208 800 1302. Fax: 0208 800 1302. E-mail: korn.eric@googlemail.com. Office and/or bookroom. Appointment necessary. Spec: Antiquarian; Author - Darwin, Charles; Juvenile; Languages - Foreign; Natural History. Cata: languages, Darwin, medicine, juvenile, biology. Corresp: French, Russian, Spanish. Mem: ABA; PBFA.

Barrie Marks Limited, 24 Church Vale Fortis Green, London, N2 9PA. Tel: (020) 8883-1919. Spec: Fine & Rare; Illustrated - General; Limited Editions - General; Literature; Private Press.

Ian McKelvie Bookseller, 45 Hertford Road, East Finchley, N2 9BX. Prop: Ian McKelvie. Tel: 020-8444-0567. Fax: 020-8444-0567. Web: www.http://ukbookworld.com/members/Dudley1. E-mail: ianmckelvie@supanet.com Est: 1969. Private premises. Postal Only. Contactable. Spec: Fiction - General; Fiction - Crime, Detective, Spy, Thrillers; Fine & Rare; First Editions; Literary Criticism; Literary Travel; Literature; Literature - Irish. CC: AE; MC; V; Maestro. Cata: British, American & World Literature.

Mountaineering Books, 6 Bedford Road, London, N8 8HL. Prop: Mr. R. & Mrs. A. Court. Tel: (020) 8340-1953. Est: 1990. Private premises. Appointment necessary. Very small stock. Spec: Alpinism/ Mountaineering. PR: £10–500.

Nicolas - Antiquarian Bookseller, 59 Fallowcourt Avenue, London, N12 0BE. Tel: (020) 8445-9835. Fax: (020) 8446-9615. Web: www.nicolasrarebooks.com. E-mail: nicolas@nicolasbooks.demon.co.uk. Est: 1971. Private premises. Internet and Postal. Spec: Canals/Inland Waterways; Countries - Cyprus; Countries - Greece; Countries - Malta; Countries - Turkey; History - General; Topography - General, Travel - General. Mem: ABA; PBFA; BA; ILAB. Notes: *Also, pictures.*

Pendleburys Bookshop, ■ Church House Portland Avenue, Stamford Hill, London, N16 6HJ. Prop: Jonathan Pendlebury. Tel: +44 (0)20 8809-4922. Web: www.pendleburys.com. E-mail: books@ pendleburys.com. Est: 1984. Shop. Telephone First. Open: **M:** 10:00–17:00; **T:** 10:00–17:00; **Th:** 10:00– 17:00; **F:** 10:00–17:00; **S:** 10:00–17:00. Very large stock. Spec: Bibles; Biblical Studies; Ecclesiastical History & Architecture; History - Reformation; History of Ideas; Missionaries & Missions; Mysticism; Philosophy. PR: £1–300. CC: MC; V; PayPal, Cheque, Cash. Cata: All aspects of the Christian faith. Corresp: English Afrikaans. Mem: PBFA; IOBA.

John Price, 8 Cloudesley Square, London, N1 0HT. Tel: (020) 7837-8008. Fax: (020) 7278-4733. Web: www.johnpriceantiquarianbooks.com. E-mail: books@jvprice.com. Est: 1988. Private premises. Internet and Postal. Appointment necessary. Very small stock. Spec: Antiquarian; Cookery/ Gastronomy; History of Ideas; Literature; Music - Composers; Music - Musicians; Music - Opera; Music - Theory. PR: £45–4,500. CC: AE; E; MC; V. Cata: Philosophy, literature, musicology, aethetics. Corresp: French, German. Mem: ABA; PBFA; BA; ILAB. Notes: *I specialize in books printed in the hand-press era (i.e., before c. 1820) on philosophy, literature, history, musicology, classics, theology, etc.*

LONDON NORTH POSTAL DISTRICTS

Richard Thornton Books, 25 Beechdale, Winchmore Hill, London, N21 3QE. Prop: Richard Thornton. Tel: 020 8886 8202. Web: www.richardthorntonbooks.co.uk. E-mail: richard.thorntonbooks@ btinternet.com. Est: 1997. Office and/or bookroom. Telephone First. Open: **M:** 09:30–21:30; **T:** 09:30–21:30; **W:** 09:30–21:30; **Th:** 09:30–21:30; **F:** 09:30–21:30; **S:** 09:30–21:30; **Su:** 09:30–21:30. Spec: Arts, The; Autobiography; Bindings; Children's; History - General; History - Local; Literature; Military. CC: AE; D; E; JCB; MC; V. Mem: PBFA. Notes: *We now have open 2 Large bookrooms to view with over 12,000 Books in many subjects incl. Modern 1st's,Childrens, Antiquarian, Military & Sporting Books. Impromptu callers are welcome, but it's best to ring Richard or Theresa on 020 8886 8202.*

Ripping Yarns, ■ 355 Archway Road, London, N6 4EJ. Prop: Celia Mitchell. Tel: (020) 8341-6111. Fax: (020) 7482-5056. Web: www.rippingyarns.co.uk. E-mail: yarns@rippingyarns.co.uk. Est: 1984. Internet and Postal. Shop open: **T:** 11:00–17:00; **W:** 11:00–17:00; **Th:** 11:00–17:00; **F:** 11:00–17:00; **S:** 10:00–17:00; **Su:** 11:00–16:00. Very large stock. Spec: Children's; Illustrated - General; Literature. PR: £1–500. CC: MC; V. Corresp: French Spanish. Mem: PBFA.

Robert Temple, 65 Mildmay Road, London, N1 4PU. Prop: P.J. Allen. Tel: (020) 7254-3674. Web: www.telinco.co.uk/RobertTemple/. E-mail: roberttemple@telinco.co.uk. Est: 1977. Warehouse. Internet and Postal. Appointment necessary. Medium stock. Spec: Academic/Scholarly; Anthologies; Antiquarian; Drama; Fiction - General; Fiction - Crime, Detective, Spy, Thrillers; Fiction - Fantasy, Horror; Fiction - Historical. PR: £5–15,000. CC: PayPal. Cata: Recent acquisitions (e-mail only). Corresp: French. Mem: ABA; ILAB. VAT No: GB 292 2648 41. Notes: *Credit and Debit cards taken via the PayPal secure server only (VISA, non-corporate AmEx, MasterCard, Discover, Switch, Solo).*

Susanne Schulz-Falster Rare Books, 22 Compton Terrace, London, N1 2UN. Prop: Susanne Schulz-Falster. Tel: 020 7704 9845. Fax: 020 7354 4202. Web: www.schulz-falster.com. E-mail: sfalster@ btinternet.com. Est: 1998. Private premises. Internet and Postal. Appointment necessary. Spec: Accountancy; Alchemy; Antiquarian; Arts, The; Auction Catalogues; Authors - Women; Banking & Insurance; Bibliography. CC: AE; MC; V. Cata: Economics, History of Ideas. Corresp: French, German, Italian. Mem: ABA; ILAB. VAT No: GB 714420079. Notes: *Continental Books (17th & 18th century), especially Italian, German and French imprints, Economics, History of Ideas, Law, Philosophy, Social Sciences, Language, History of the Book, History of Printing.*

John Trotter Books, 80 East End Road, London, N3 2SY. Prop: John Trotter. Tel: (020) 8349-9484. Web: www.bibliophile.net/John-Trotter-Books.htm. E-mail: jtrotter@freenetname.co.uk. Est: 1973. Office and/or bookroom. Internet and Postal. Open: **M:** 09:00–17:00; **T:** 09:09–17:00; **W:** 09:00–17:00; **Th:** 09:00–17:00; **Su:** 10:00–13:00. Large stock. Spec: Countries - Middle East, The; History - Ancient; Religion - Jewish; Travel - Middle East; Booksearch; Prints and Maps. PR: £5–1,500. CC: MC; V. Corresp: French, German, Italian. Mem: PBFA.

Tyger Press, 41 Cheverton Road, London, N19 3BA. Prop: Alaric Bamping. Tel: (020) 7272-3234. Web: www.tygerpress.com. E-mail: tygerpress@clara.net. Est: 1984. Private premises. Internet and Postal. Appointment necessary. Spec: Genealogy; Guide Books; History - General; History - Family; History - Industrial; History - Local; Manuscripts; Maritime/Nautical - Log Books. PR: £1–750. CC: MC; V; Maestro/Switch. Delta. Cata: Topography. Mem: PBFA. VAT No: GB 646 2440 44.

Graham Weiner, 78 Rosebery Road, London, N10 2LA. Tel: (020) 8883-8424. Fax: (020) 8444-6505. E-mail: graham weiner@btopenworld.com. Est: 1973. Private premises. Internet and Postal. Appointment necessary. Medium stock. Spec: Academic/Scholarly; Aeronautics, Aircraft; Alchemy; Almanacs; Anatomy; Antiquarian; Aviation. PR: £20–2,500. CC: MC; V. Cata: Science, Technology, Medicine. Corresp: French. Mem: ABA; ILAB; IEE. VAT No: GB 230 6110 23.

Woburn Books, 5 Caledonian Road, London, N1 9DX. Prop: Andrew Burgin. Tel: (020) 7263 5196. Fax: (020) 7263 5196. Web: www.abebooks/home/woburnbooks. E-mail: woburn@burgin.freeserve.co.uk. Est: 1991. Office and/or bookroom. Internet and Postal. Medium stock. Spec: Academic/Scholarly; Africana; Anthropology; Antiquarian; Architecture; Art; Arts, The; Avant-Garde. PR: £1–5,000. CC: JCB; MC; V; SW. Mem: PBFA.

Ripping Yarns (Celia Mitchell)	355 Archway Road London N6 4EJ Tel: 020 8341 6111 Fax: 020 7482 5056
Antiquarian & secondhand stock bought and sold All subjects but especially **CHILDREN'S** Highgate Tube. Free car parking (1 hour) just north of shop in Archway Road Email: yarns@rippingyarns.co.uk. Web site: www.rippingyarns.co.uk	Tuesday-Friday 12.00-17.00 Saturdays 10.00-17.00 Sundays 12.00-16.00 Closed Mondays

LONDON

NORTH WEST POSTAL DISTRICTS

Aurelian Books, 31 Llanvanor Road, London, NW2 2AR. Prop: David Dunbar. Tel: (020) 8455 9612. E-mail: dgldunbar@aol.com. Est: 1970. Private premises. Appointment necessary. Small stock. Spec: Colour-Plate; Conservation; Entomology; Lepidopterology; Natural History. PR: £5–5,000. CC: MC; V; SW. Mem: PBFA.

H. Baron, 121 Chatsworth Road, London, NW2 4BH. Prop: Christel Wallbaum. Tel: (020) 8459-2035. Fax: (020) 8459-2035. Est: 1949. Private premises. Postal Only. Spec: Autographs; Iconography; Letters; Music - General. CC: E; MC; V. Corresp: French, German. Mem: ABA; ILAB. VAT No: GB 227 1452 82.

Biblipola, ■ 25 Church Street, London, NW8 8D7. Prop: Joseph Delgrosso. Tel: 020 7724 7231. Web: www.alfiesantiques.com. E-mail: info@alfiesantiques.com. Est: 1986. Shop at: Alfie's Antique Market, 25 Church Street, Marylebone, London NW8 8D7. Open: **T:** 10:00–17:30; **W:** 10:00–17:30; **Th:** 10:00–17:30; **F:** 10:00–17:30; **S:** 10:00–17:30. Spec: Antiquarian; Children's; Children's - Early Titles; Children's - Illustrated; First Editions; Modern First Editions; Natural History; Pop-Up, Movable & Cut Out. Also at: Alfie's Antique Market, 25 Church Street, Marylebone, London NW8 8D7. Notes: *Alternative e-mail address: delgro.bks@aol.com*

The Book Depot, 111 Woodcote Avenue Mill Hill, London, NW7 2PD. Prop: Conrad Wiberg. Tel: (020) 8906-3708. E-mail: conrad@adword.fsnet.co.uk. Est: 1980. Postal Only. Spec: Booksearch. PR: £5–10.

Cranhurst Books, 20 Cranhurst Road, Willesden Green, NW2 4LN. Prop: Heidi Stransky. Tel: 02084527845. E-mail: HStransky@aol.com. Est: 1996. Private premises. Internet and Postal. Appointment necessary. Open: **M:** 09:00–17:30; **T:** 09:00–17:30; **W:** 09:00–17:30; **Th:** 09:00–17:30; **F:** 09:00–17:30; **S:** 09:00–17:30; **Su:** 09:00–17:30; Closed for lunch: 13:00–14:00. Spec: Author - Ahlberg, Janet & Allan; - Aldin, Cecil; - Ardizzone, Edward; - Asimov, Isaac; - Bainbridge, Beryl; - Barrie, J.M.; - Burgess, A.; - Carroll, Lewis. CC: MC; V. Notes: *A mixture of old and new out of print children's books as well as a selection of modern firsts including, Rankin, Cornwall, Le Carre etc.*

Keith Fawkes, ■ 1–3 Flask Walk Hampstead, London, NW3 1HJ. Prop: Keith Fawkes. Tel: (020) 7435-0614. Est: 1970. Shop open: **M:** 10:00–18:00; **T:** 09:00–18:00; **W:** 10:00–18:00; **Th:** 09:00–18:00; **F:** 10:00–18:00; **S:** 10:00–18:00; **Su:** 13:00–18:00. Large stock. PR: £1–100. VAT No: GB 232 0644 04. Notes: *Also, bric a brac.*

Fishburn Books, 43 Ridge Hill, London, NW11 8PR. Prop: Jonathan Fishburn. Tel: (0208) 455-9139. Fax: (0208) 922-5008. Web: www.fishburnbooks.com. E-mail: fishburnbooks@yahoo.co.uk. Est: 2000. Private premises. Appointment necessary. Spec: Bibles; Biblical Studies; Countries - Israel; Countries - Middle East, The; Holocaust; Immigration; Judaica; Religion - Hebraica. PR: £15–5,000. CC: AE; MC; V. Mem: ABA; PBFA; ILAB. VAT No: GD 805 4963 16. Notes: *Specialists in Judaica, Hebraica and all items of Jewish interest, including Zionism, Holocaust, Jewish History, Synagogues etc.*

Fortune Green Books, 74 Fortune Green Road, London, NW6 1DS. Prop: Eric Stevens & Jane Bell. Tel: (020) 7435-7545. E-mail: belleric@dircon.co.uk. Est: 1992. Office and/or bookroom. Internet and Postal. Appointment necessary. Medium stock. Spec: Academic/Scholarly; Art; Belle-Lettres; Bibliography; Feminism; Fiction - General; Fiction - Women; Literary Criticism. PR: £1–50. CC: MC; V. Mem: PBFA. Notes: *regular catalogues issued on 19th & early 20th century literature, women writers & women's history including academic books in these fields.*

Stephen Foster, ■ 95 Bell Street, London, NW1 6TL. Prop: Stephen Foster. Tel: (020) 7724-0876. Fax: (020) 7724-0927. Web: www.95bellstreet.com. E-mail: stephen.foster@sfbooks.co.uk. Est: 1987. Shop open: **M:** 10:30–18:00; **T:** 10:30–18:00; **W:** 10:30–18:00; **Th:** 10:30–18:00; **F:** 10:30–18:00; **S:** 10:30–18:00. Medium stock. Spec: Antiquarian; Antiques; Architecture; Art History; Art Reference; Artists; Arts, The; Decorative Art. PR: £1–1,000. CC: AE; JCB; MC; V; Switch/ Maestro. Mem: ABA; PBFA; ILAB; ibooknet. VAT No: GB 521 5504 81. Notes: *During July and August, the shop is closed Monday to Wednesday. Stock at Biblion, Davies Mews. Booksearch service; new books at a discount. See also Foster's Bookshop, London W4. (q.v.)*

LONDON NORTH WEST POSTAL DISTRICTS

Hellenic Bookservices, ■ 91 Fortess Road Kentish Town, London, NW5 1AG. Prop: M. Williams & Andrew Stoddart. Tel: (020) 7267-9499. Fax: (020) 7267-9498. Web: www.hellenicbooks.com. E-mail: info@hellenicbookservice.com. Est: 1966. Shop open: **M:** 09:30–18:00; **T:** 09:30–18:00; **W:** 09:30–18:00; **Th:** 09:30–18:00; **F:** 09:30–18:00; **S:** 10:00–17:00. Large stock. Spec: Academic/Scholarly; Books in Greek; Byzantium; Classical Studies; Countries - Cyprus; Countries - Greece; Foreign Texts; Guide Books. PR: £1–500. CC: AE; JCB; MC; V. Corresp: Modern Greek. Mem: PBFA. Notes: *Also, a booksearch service, school supplies – all subjects.*

Hosains Books, 12 Honeybourne Road West Hampstead, London, NW6 1JJ. Prop: Mrs. Y. Hosain and Mr. K.S. Hosain. Tel: (020) 7794-7127. Web: www.indoislamica.com. Est: 1979. Private premises. Appointment necessary. Spec: Oriental; Ottoman Empire; Travel - Africa; Voyages & Discovery; Prints and Maps. PR: £100–5,000. CC: MC; V.

C.R. Johnson Rare Books, 4, Keats Grove, Hampstead, London, NW3 2RT. Prop: C.R. Johnson & C.A. Forster. Tel: (020) 7794-7940. Fax: (020) 7433-3303. Web: www.crjohnson.com. E-mail: mail@crjohnson.com. Est: 1970. Private premises. Internet and Postal. Appointment necessary. Very large stock. Spec: Authors - Women; Fiction - 18th Century; Fine & Rare; Literature; Social Economics. PR: £50–5,000. CC: MC; V. Cata: English Literature and Social Economics. Mem: PBFA; CERL.

Terence Kaye - Bookseller, 52 Neeld Crescent, London, NW4 3RR. Prop: H Terence Kaye. Tel: (020) 8202-8188. Fax: (020) 8202-8188. E-mail: kforbook@onetel.com. Est: 1996. Office and/or bookroom. Appointment necessary. Open: **M:** 09:00–20:00; **T:** 09:00–20:00; **W:** 09:00–20:00; **Th:** 09:00–20:00; **F:** 09:00–18:00; **S:** 10:00–20:00; **Su:** 10:00–20:00. Spec: Cinema/Film; Circus; Drama; Entertainment - General; Fairgrounds; Music - Music Hall; Performing Arts; Television. Corresp: Hebrew. Notes: *Also, a booksearch service (specialist subjects only), and library/collection development.*

Loretta Lay Books, 24 Grampian Gardens, London, NW2 1JG. Prop: Loretta Lay. Tel: 020 8455 3069. Web: www.laybooks.com. E-mail: lorettalay@hotmail.com. Est: 2001. Mail Order Only. Internet and Postal. Telephone First. Open: **M:** 09:00–17:30; **T:** 09:00–17:30; **W:** 09:00–17:30; **Th:** 09:00–17:30; **F:** 09:00–17:30; **S:** 09:00–17:30; **Su:** 09:00–17:30. Spec: Author - Tully, Jim; - Upfield, Arthur; - Wilson, Colin; Crime (True); Criminology; Espionage; Fiction - Crime, Detective, Spy, Thrillers; Ghosts. CC: JCB; MC; V; Delta, Switch, Solo. Cata: all true crime. Notes: *A comprehensive stock of true crime including Notable British Trials and specialising in Jack the Ripper.*

Richard Lucas, 114 Fellows Road, London, NW3 3JH. Prop: Richard Lucas. Tel: (020) 7449-9431. Est: 1975. Private premises. Appointment necessary. Medium stock. Spec: Brewing; Cookery/ Gastronomy; Etiquette; Food & Drink; Herbalism; Public Houses; Travel - General; Viticulture. PR: £10–1,000.

Moss Books, 14 Manor Park Gardens Edgware, London, HA8 7NA. * Tel: (020) 8386-2707. Fax: (020) 8958-6731. E-mail: moss.books@ntlworld.com. Est: 2002. Market stand/stall; Internet and Postal. Appointment necessary. Medium stock. Spec: Antiquarian; Archaeology; Architecture; Ceramics; Ecclesiastical History & Architecture; General Stock; Lepidopterology; Odd & Unusual. PR: £5–800. CC: PayPal. VAT No: GB 805 4666 26.

Neil's Books, 151 Fordwych Road, London, NW2 3NG. Prop: Neil Aptaker. Tel: (020) 8452–0933. Fax: (02082) 2082434. E-mail: neilsbooks@lineone.net. Est: 1990. Internet and Postal. Open: **M:** 10:00–18:45; **Th:** 10:00–18:45. Medium stock. Spec: Fiction - General; Modern First Editions. PR: £2–200.

Primrose Hill Books, 134 Regents Park Road, London, NW1 8XL. Tel: (0207) 586 2027. Fax: (0207) 722 9653. E-mail: phbooks@btconnect.com. Est: 1987. Storeroom. Internet and Postal. Appointment necessary. Medium stock. Spec: Biography; First Editions; Poetry; Theatre. PR: £4–1,000. CC: AE; JCB; MC; V. VAT No: GB 523 4672 53.

Paul Rassam, Flat 5 18 East Heath Road, London, NW3 1AJ. Tel: (020) 7794-9316. E-mail: paul@ rassam.demon.co.uk. Est: 1972. Private premises. Internet and Postal. Appointment necessary. Very small stock. Spec: Autographs; First Editions; Literature; Manuscripts. CC: MC; V. Cata: Late19th & 20th Century Literature. Mem: ABA.

Robert G Sawers Ltd, No.5 Inglewood Road, London, NW6 1qT. Tel: (0207) 794 9618. Fax: (0207) 794 9571. Web: www.bobsawers.clara.net. E-mail: bobsawers@clara.net. Est: 1970. Private premises. Internet and Postal. Appointment necessary. Very small stock. Spec: Countries - Far East, The; Countries - Japan. Corresp: French, Spanish, Japanese. Mem: ABA. VAT No: GB 233 701 02.

Sevin Seydi Rare Books, 13 Shirlock Road, London, NW3 2HR. Prop: Sevin Seydi & Maurice Whitby. Tel: (020) 7485 9801. E-mail: sevin@seydi.fsnet.co.uk. Est: 1970. Private premises. Internet and Postal. Appointment necessary. Large stock. Spec: Antiquarian; Antiquities; Architecture; Architecture - Theatre; Art History; Art Reference; Bibliography; Bindings. CC: MC; V. Cata: antiquarian English and European. Corresp: French, Turkish. Mem: PBFA.

LONDON NORTH WEST POSTAL DISTRICTS

Unsworth's Booksellers, ■ 101 Euston Road, London, NW1 2RA. Prop: (*) Charlie Unsworth. Tel: (020) 7383 5507. Fax: (020) 7383 7557. Web: www.unsworths.com. E-mail: books@unsworths.com. Est: 1986. Shop open: **M:** 10:00–18:30; **T:** 10:00–18:30; **W:** 10:00–18:30; **Th:** 10:00 18:30; **F:** 10.00– 18:30; **S:** 10:00–18.30, **Su:** 12:00–17:00; Very large stock. Spec: Academic/Scholarly; Archaeology; Art History; Bibliography; Books about Books; Byzantium; Classical Studies; Dictionaries. PR: £3–5,000. CC: AE; D; E; JCB; MC; V. Corresp: Latin, French, Portuguese. Mem: ABA; ILAB. VAT No: GB 480 1145 75.

Walden Books, ■ 38 Harmood Street, London, NW1 8DP. Prop: David Tobin. Tel: 020 7267 8146. Fax: 020 7267 8147. Web: www.ukbookworld.com/members/waldenbooks. E-mail: waldenbooks@ lineone.net. Est: 1979. Shop. Open: **Th:** 10.30–18.30; **F:** 10.30–18.30; **S:** 10.30–18.30; **Su:** 10.30– 18.30; Spec: Academic/Scholarly; Art; Art - Technique; Art History; Literature; Literature - 19th C; Modern First Editions; Monographs. CC: AE; MC; V. Mem: PBFA.

Eva M. Weininger, Antiquarian Bookseller 79 Greenhill, London, NW3 5TZ. Tel: (020) 7435-2334. Est: 1979. Private premises. Appointment necessary. Very small stock. Spec: Courtesy; Culture - Foreign; Culture - National; Etiquette; History of Ideas; Social History. PR: £10–150.

J. & S. Wilbraham, 1 Wise Lane Mill Hill, London, NW7 2RL. Prop: John and Shahin Wilbraham Tel: (0208) 9593709. Web: www.wilbraham.demon.co.uk. E-mail: john@wilbraham.demon.co.uk. Est: 1981. Private premises. Postal Only. Contactable. Very small stock. Spec: Antiquarian; Children's, Literature. PR: £10–1,000. CC: AE; MC; V. Cata: Antiquarian and Foreign Litrature. Corresp: French.

LONDON

SOUTH EAST POSTAL DISTRICTS

Bermondsey Basement Bookstore, PO Box 3158, London, SE1 4RA. Prop: Peter Marcan. Tel: 020 7357 0368. Est: 2006. Office and/or bookroom. Appointment necessary. Open: **M:** 10:00–19:00; **T:** 10:00–19:00; **W:** 10:00–19:00; **Th:** 10:00–19:00; **F:** 10:00–19:00; **S:** 10:00–19:00. Spec: Architecture; Art - British; History - Sports; Illustrated - General; Music - Classical; Parks and gardens; Photography; Social History. Notes: *Also publishers 'Peter Marcan Publications' London SE. Issues up to 3 catalogues a year. (q.v.)*

The Book Palace, Jubilee House Bedwardine Road, Crystal Palace, London, SE19 3AP. Prop: G West. Tel: 020 8768 0022. Fax: 020 8768 0563. Web: www.bookpalace.com. E-mail: books@ bookpalace.com. Est: 1997. Warehouse. Internet and Postal. Appointment necessary. Open: **M:** 10:00–18:00; **T:** 10:00–18:00; **W:** 10:00–18:00; **Th:** 10:00–18:00; **F:** 10:00–18:00. Spec: Annuals; Art; Art - Theory; Art History; Art Reference; Artists; Arts, The; Author - Burroughs, Edgar R. CC: AE; MC; V; Maestro. Cata: Popular culture. Corresp: Dutch, French. VAT No: GB 756 4588 84. Notes: *Wholesale on many titles.*

The Bookshop on the Heath Ltd, ■ 74 Tranquil Vale Blackheath, London, SE3 0BW. Prop: Richard Platt. Tel: (020) 88524786. Fax: (020) 83189875. Web: www.bookshopontheheath.co.uk. E-mail: orders@bookshopontheheath.co.uk. Est: 2003. Shop open: **M:** 12:00–18:00; **T:** 10:00–18:00; **W:** 10:00–18:00; **F:** 10:00–18:00; **S:** 10:00–18:00; **Su:** 12:00–18:00. Medium stock. Spec: Art; Astronomy; Auction Catalogues; Author - Bates, H.E.; - Bennett, (Enoch) Arnol; - Blyton, Enid; - Churchill, Sir Winston; - Fleming, Ian. PR: £1–5,000. CC: MC; V; Switch, Maestro. Corresp: German, Mandarin. Mem: BA. VAT No: GB 831 1125 78. Notes: *Our best crime and detective fiction first editions are on sale at our Mayfair outlet, Biblion, 1-7 Davies Mews, London W1. Tel. 0207 6291374. Also many posters, incl. original James Bonds. Many Marilyn Monroe & Beatles items too.*

Fiona Campbell, 158 Lambeth Road, London, SE1 7DF. Tel: (020) 7928-1633. Fax: (020) 7928-1633. E-mail: fcampbell@britishlibrary.net. Est: 1970. Private premises. Appointment necessary. Small stock. Spec: Countries - Italy; Travel - General; Travel - Europe. Corresp: French, German and Italian. Mem: ABA; PBFA; ILAB.

Marcus Campbell Art Books, ■ 43 Holland Street, Bankside, London, SE1 9JR. Prop: Marcus Campbell. Tel: (020) 7261-0111. Fax: (020) 7261-0129. Web: www.marcuscampbell.co.uk. E-mail: info@marcuscampbell.co.uk. Est: 1998. Internet and Postal. Shop open: **M:** 10:30–18:00; **T:** 10:30–18:00; **W:** 10:30–18:00; **Th:** 10:30–18:00; **F:** 10:30–18:00; **S:** 10:30–18:00; **Su:** 12:00–18:00. Very large stock. Spec: Art; Art Reference; Artists; Monographs; Ephemera. PR: £2–2,000. CC: AE; E; MC; V; Switch. Corresp: French. Mem: PBFA. VAT No: GB 605 8695 15.

Chapter Two, Fountain House Conduit Mews, Woolwich, London, SE18 7AP. Prop: Manager: Miss P. Brachotte. Tel: (020) 8316-5389. Fax: (020) 8854-5963. Web: www.chaptertwobooks.org.uk. E-mail: chapter2uk@aol.com. Est: 1976. Office and/or bookroom. Internet and Postal. Telephone First. Open: **M:** 09:00–17:00; **T:** 09:00–17:00; **W:** 09:00–17:00; **Th:** 09:00–17:00; **F:** 06:00–17:00. Closed for lunch: 13:00–14:30. Medium stock. Spec: Author - Baring-Gould, S.; - Blyton, Enid; - Bunyan, John; - Johns, W.E.; Bibles; Children's; Countries - Africa; Countries - Asia. PR: £2–3,500. CC: AE; MC; V. Corresp: Afrikaans, French, German, Dutch, Spanish, Norwegian. Notes: *Chapter Two Christian Bookshop, 199 Plumstead Common Rd, Plumstead Common, London SE18 2UJ. Also, publisher/retailer of new books & foreign language Christian literature, Bible distributor, archive & booksearch service.*

BOOKDEALING FOR PROFIT

by Paul Minet

Quarto H/b   Available from Richard Joseph Publishers Ltd   £10.00 144pp

LONDON SOUTH EAST POSTAL DISTRICTS

Nigel A. Clark, 28 Ulundi Road, Blackheath, SE3 7UG. Prop: Sole Propreietor. Tel: (020) 8858-4020. E-mail: nigel.a.clark@btinternet.com. Est: 1975. Private premises. Postal Only. Appointment necessary. Very small stock. Spec: Antiques; Art History; Art Reference; Artists; Auction Catalogues; Ceramics; Collectables; Collecting. PR: £1–100. Cata: Numismatic Publications. VAT No: GB 311 6080 06. Notes: *Also, British coins & Tokens*

Collectable Books, 15 West Park, London, SE9 4RZ. Prop: Partners: Tom & Sue Biro. Tel: (020) 8851-8487. Web: www.collectablebooks.co.uk. E-mail: biro@collectablebooks.co.uk. Est: 1992. Private premises. Appointment necessary. Very small stock. Spec: Antiquarian; Architecture; Architecture - Theatre; Arts, The; Food & Drink; Health; Medicine; Natural History. PR: £10–20,000. CC: E; JCB; MC; V; SO, SW. Corresp: French, German, Italian, Hungarian, Portuguese. Mem: ABA; PBFA; ILAB. VAT No: GB 299 3282 10.

Eclectica, 48 Rosendale Road West Dulwich, London, SE21 8DP. Prop: Michael Coupe. Tel: (0208) 761-4138. E-mail: coupleplanning@btinternet.com. Office and/or bookroom. Appointment necessary. Very small stock. Spec: Antiquarian; Bindings; Illustrated - General; Ephemera. PR: £1–2,000. Mem: PBFA. Notes: *General antiquarian, decorated/pictorial cloth bindings (especially Victorian and Edwardian children's), illustrated books and ephemera.*

Enscot Books, 17 Crantock Road, Catford, London, SE6 2QS. Prop: Michael Enscot and Philip Enscot. Tel: (020) 8698 1976. Fax: (020) 8698 1976. E-mail: smith.pipe@virgin.net. Est 1998. Private premises. Small stock. Spec: Fiction - Historical; Modern First Editions. PR: £2–50. Corresp: French, German.

Jane Gibberd, ■ 20 Lower Marsh, London, SE1 7RJ. Tel: (020) 7633-9562. Est: 1968. Shop open: **W:** 11:00–19:00; **Th:** 11:00–19:00; **F:** 11:00–19:00. Small stock. PR: £1–25.

Hava Books, 110 Aspinall Road, Brockley, SE4 2EG. Prop: J. Havercroft. Tel: (0207) 6398339. E-mail: salesmailbox-hava@yahoo.co.uk. Est: 1998. Private premises. Internet Only. Appointment necessary. Medium stock. Spec: Antiquarian; Atlases; Author - Dickens, Charles; Countries - Italy; Dictionaries; European Books; Fine & Rare; Fine leather bindings (see also Fine & Rare). PR: £5–5,000. CC: PayPpal. Corresp: French, Spanish. Mem: PBFA. VAT No: GB 782 4918 92. Notes: *We specialise in rare, out of print and collectible books. Only part of our stock is on the net- the books we sell at fairs are not yet catalogued and are not for sale elsewhere.*

James Hawkes, Flat One 63 East Dulwich Road, London, SE22 9AP. Tel: (0208) 299 2995. Web: www.abebooks.com/home/JAMESHAWKES/. E-mail: jameshawkes1977@yahoo.com. Private premises. Internet and Postal. Appointment necessary. Small stock. Spec: Academic/Scholarly; Antiquarian, Literary Criticism; Literature. PR: £20–1,500. CC: AE; MC; V; Maestro (Switch), Solo.

Junk & Spread Eagle, ■ 9 Greenwich South Street Greenwich, London, SE10 8NW. Prop: Tobias Moy. Tel: (020) 8305-1666. Est: 1960. Shop open: **M:** 10:00–18:00; **T:** 10:00–18:00; **W:** 10:00–18:00; **Th:** 10:00–18:00; **F:** 10:00–18:00; **S:** 10:00–18:00; **Su:** 10:00–18:00; Closed for lunch: 13:00–14:00. Medium stock. Spec: Advertising; Animals and Birds; Antiquarian; Arts, The; Author - Churchill, Sir Winston; Bindings; Children's; Children's - Illustrated. PR: £3–100. CC: D; E; JCB; MC; V; SW. Notes: *Also, ephemera, collectables and antiques.*

Kirkdale Bookshop, ■ 272 Kirkdale, Sydenham, SE26 4RS. Prop: Ms. Geraldine A. Cox. Tel: (020) 8778-4701. Fax: (020) 8776-6293. E-mail: kirkdalebookshop@hotmail.com. Est: 1966. Shop open: **M:** 09:00–17:30; **T:** 09:00–17:30; **W:** 09:00–17:30; **Th:** 09:00–17:30; **F:** 09:00–17:30; **S:** 09:00–17:30. Medium stock. CC: MC; V. Mem: BA. Notes: *Also, new books, greetings cards, selected gift items and a small art gallery showing work by local artists.*

Peter Marcan, Bookseller, P.O. Box 3158, London, SE1 4RA. Prop: Peter Marcan. Tel: (020) 7357 0368. Est: 2000. Private premises. Appointment necessary. Open: **M:** 10:00–19:00; **T:** 10:00–19:00; **W:** 10:00–19:00; **Th:** 10:00–19:00; **F:** 10:00–19:00; **S:** 10:00–19:00. Very small stock. Spec: Music - Classical; Social History; Topography - General; Topography - Local. PR: £3–50. Notes: *Small stock of books on 18th - 20th C British art, Greater London and S. East England topography. Publishing (est 1978) - reprints, handbooks, catalogues and Art - British. Also trades as Bermondsey Basement Bookstore.*

Marcet Books, ■ The Bookshop 4a Nelson Road, Greenwich, SE10 9JB. Prop: Martin Kemp. Tel: 020 8853 5408. Web: www.marcetbooks.co.uk. E-mail: info@marcetbooks.co.uk. Est: 1980. Shop open: **M:** 10:00–17:30; **T:** 10:00–17:30; **W:** 10:00–17:30; **Th:** 10:00–17:30; **F:** 10:00–17:30; **S:** 09:00–17:30; **Su:** 10:00–17:30. Spec: Africana; Aircraft; Arabica; Art History; Canals/Inland Waterways; Cartography; Cities - City of London; Cookery - Professional. CC: AE; MC; V; PayPal. Cata: Foreign Travel.

Military Bookworm, P.O. Box 235, London, SE23 1NS. Prop: David W. Collett. Tel: (020) 8291-1435. Fax: (020) 8291-1435. Web: www.militarybookworm.co.uk. E-mail: info@militarybookworm.co.uk. Est: 1975. Storeroom. Internet Only. Contactable. Medium stock. Spec: Military; Military History; School Registers/Rolls of Honour; Collectables. PR: £5–300. CC: MC; V.

LONDON SOUTH EAST POSTAL DISTRICTS

Herbert Murch Booksend, 258/260 Creek Road, Greenwich, London, SE10 9SW. Prop: D. Herbert. Tel: (020) 8858 2414. E-mail: herbertmurch@btinternet.com. Est: 1974. Private premises. Postal Only. Spec: Arts, The; Biography; Literature; Media. PR: £8–25. Cata: Poetry, Sex & Gender, Biography. Notes: *Has large stock of biographies, especially first half 20th Century.*

Print Matters, 23 Phoenix Road, London, SE20 7BT. Prop: Paul Tanner. Tel: 020 8778 8580. Fax: 020 8776 8476. Web: www.printmatters.com (being reconstructed!). E-mail: paul@printmatters.com. Est: 1997. Office and/or bookroom. Internet and Postal. Telephone First. Open: **M:** 10:30–17:30; **T:** 10:30–17:30; **W:** 10:30–17:30; **Th:** 10:30–17:30; **F:** 10:30–17:30; **S:** 10:30–17:30. Closed for lunch: 13:00–14:00. Spec: Art; Art - Technique; Art Deco; Art Nouveau; Art Reference; Artists; Arts, The; Calligraphy. CC: AE; MC; V; PayPal. Cata: visual arts; graphic novels; illustration. Corresp: French, Spanish.

Rogers Turner Books, 87 Breakspears Road, London, SE4 1TX. Prop: P.J.Turner. Tel: (0208) 692-2472. Fax: (0208) 692-2472. E-mail: rogersturner@compuserve.com. Est: 1976. Private premises. Appointment necessary. Open: **Th:** 10:00–18:00; **F:** 10:00–18:00. Small stock. Spec: Horology; Science - General; Science - History of; Scientific Instruments; Technology. CC: AE; D; JCB; MC; V. Corresp: French, German, Spanish. Mem: ABA; PBFA.

Hillary Rittner Booksearch, Greenwich, London SE10 8ER. Business transferred. See under Books For Content, Ashperton, Herefordshire (q.v.)

John Rolfe, 39 Combe Avenue, Blackheath, London, SE3 7PZ. Prop: John Rolfe. Tel: (020) 8858-3349. Web: www.abebooks.com/home/johnrolfe. E-mail: rolfebooks@btinternet.com. Est: 1990. Private premises. Internet and Postal. Appointment necessary. Very small stock. Spec: Dogs. PR: £5–500. Cata: Dogs.

Michael Silverman, P.O. Box 350, London, SE3 0LZ. Tel: (020) 8319-4452. Fax: (020) 8856-6006. Web: www.michael-silverman.com. E-mail: ms@michael-silverman.com. Est: 1989. Private premises. Internet and Postal. Appointment necessary. Medium stock. Spec: Art; Autographs; Documents - General; History - General; Letters; Literature; Manuscripts. CC: AE; MC; V. Cata: Literary & historical autographs & manuscripts. Mem: ABA; ILAB. VAT No: GB 532 9017 59.

Anthony J. Simmonds, ■ 66 Royal Hill Greenwich, London, SE10 8RT. Prop: Anthony & Setitia Simmonds. Tel: (020) 8692 1794. E-mail: anthony@anthonysimmonds.demon.co.uk. Shop open: **T:** 10:00–18:00; **W:** 10:00–18:00; **Th:** 10:00–18:00; **F:** 10:00–18:00; **S:** 10:00–18:00; **Su:** 10:00–18:00. Spec: Maritime/Nautical; Naval; Booksearch. PR: £1–5,000. CC: MC; V. Cata: on specialities, naval and maritime history. Mem: PBFA.

Stephen E. Tilston, 7 Dartmouth House Dartmouth Row, Greenwich, SE10 8BF. Prop: Steve & Frances Tilston. Tel: (020) 8691 3108. Web: www.ukbookworld.com/members/tilston. E-mail: tilston@attglobal.net. Est: 1985. Private premises. Internet and Postal. Appointment necessary. Medium stock. Spec: Architecture; Art; Author - Lawrence, D.H.; Biography; Cookery/Gastronomy; Fiction - General; History - General; Maritime/Nautical. PR: £5–1,000. CC: AE; MC; V; Maestro. VAT No: GB 626 4185 35.

Warwick Leadlay Gallery, 5 Nelson Road Greenwich, London, SE10 9JB. Tel: (020) 8858-0317. Web: www.warwickleadlay.com. E-mail: info@warwickleadlay.com. Est: 1974. Shop and/or gallery. Open: **M:** 09:30–17:30; **T:** 09:30–17:30; **W:** 09:30–17:30; **Th:** 09:30–17:30; **F:** 09:30–17:30; **S:** 09:30–17:30; **Su:** 11:00–17:30. Very small stock. Spec: Naval. PR: £5–500. CC: AE; D; JCB; MC; V.

LONDON

SOUTH WEST POSTAL DISTRICTS

Allsworth Rare Books, P.O.Box 134 235 Earls Court Road, London, SW5 9FE. Tel: (020) 7377-0552. Fax: (020) 7377-0552. Web: www.allsworthbooks.com. E-mail: jenny@allsworthbooks.com. Est: 2002. Office and/or bookroom. Appointment necessary. Spec: Africana; Countries - Africa; Countries - Arabia; Countries - Asia; Countries - Caribbean, The; Countries - Central Asia; Countries - China; Countries - Hong Kong. PR: £50–50,000. CC: MC; V; Maestro. Cata: Travel & Exploration. Mem: ABA; PBFA; ILAB. VAT No: GB 798 7327 57. Notes: *Stock may be viewed (by appt.) at central London office. Valuation service.*

Ancient Art Books (and at Biblion), 34 East Sheen Ave., East Sheen, London, SW14 8AS. Prop: D.G. Giles. Tel: (020) 8878-8951. Fax: (020) 8878-9201. Web: www.gilesancientart.com. E-mail: Ancientartbooks@aol.com. Est: 1999. Shop and/or gallery. Internet and Postal. Appointment necessary. Shop At: Biblion, 1-7 Davies Mews, London W1K 5AB (near Bond St Station). Small stock. Spec: Antiques; Applied Art; Archaeology; Collecting, Glass; Pottery & Glass. PR: £10–15,000. CC: AE; D; MC; V. Cata: ancient, old and antique glass. Mem: PBFA. Notes: *Also at Biblion, London. Biblion gallery open Monday to Friday and appointment not required, freely open.*

Ash Rare Books, 43 Huron Road, London, SW17 8RE. Prop: Laurence Worms. Tel: (020) 8672-2263. Web: www.ashrare.com. E-mail: books@ashrare.com. Est: 1946. Private premises. Internet and Postal. Appointment necessary. Open: **M:** 10:00–17:00; **T:** 10:00–17:00; **W:** 10:00–17:00; **Th:** 10:00–17:00; **F:** 10:00–17:00 . Medium stock. Spec: Author - 20th Century; - Bennett, (Enoch) Arnol; - Dickens, Charles; - Trollope, Anthony; Bibliography; Cities - City of London; First Editions; Poetry. PR: £20–5,000. CC: AE; D; E; JCB; MC; V. Cata: Literary First Editions; Modern Poetry; London. Mem: ABA; ILAB. VAT No: GB 244 2896 45.

Book Mongers, ■ 439 Coldharbour Lane, London, SW9 8LN. Prop: Patrick Kelly. Tel: (020) 7738-4225. Fax: (020) 7738-4225. Web: www.freespace.virgin.net/book.mongers. E-mail: book.mongers@ virgin.net. Est: 1992. Shop open: **M:** 10:30–18:30; **T:** 10:30–18:30; **W:** 10:30–18:30; **Th:** 10:30–18:30; **F:** 10:30–18:30; **S:** 10:30–18:30. Very large stock. PR: £1–10. CC: D; E; JCB; MC; V; Mae. So.

Classic Bindings Ltd, ■ 61 Cambridge Street, Pimlico, London, SW1V 4PS. Prop: Mr. Sasha Poklewski-Koziell. Tel: (020) 7834-5554. Fax: (020) 7630-6632. Web: www.classicbindings.net. E-mail: info@ classicbindings.net. Est: 1988. Shop open: **M:** 09:30–17:30; **T:** 09:30–17:30; **W:** 09:30–17:30; **Th:** 09:30–17:30; **F:** 09:30–17:30. Large stock. Spec: Architecture; Art; Bindings; Biography; Foreign Texts; History - General; Poetry; Religion - Christian. PR: £10–5,000. CC: E; MC; V. VAT No: GB 562 2080 66.

Robin de Beaumont, 25 Park Walk, Chelsea, London, SW10 0AJ. Tel: (0207) 352-3440. Fax: (0207) 352-1260. Web: www.abebooks.com/home/RDEBOOKS. E-mail: rdebooks@aol.com. Est: 1980. Private premises. Internet and Postal. Telephone First. Small stock. Spec: Art; Bindings; Illustrated - General; Victoriana. PR: £20–3,000. CC: MC; V. Corresp: French. Mem: ABA; BA; ILAB.

Earlsfield Bookshop, ■ 513 Garratt Lane Wandsworth, London, SW18 4SW. Prop: Charles Dixon. Tel: (020) 8946-3744. Est: 1995. Shop open: **M:** 16:00–18:00; **T:** 16:00–18:00; **W:** 16:00–18:00; **Th:** 16:00–18:00; **F:** 11:00–18:00; **S:** 10:00–17:00. Small stock. PR: £1–50.

Harfield Books of London, 1 Engadine Street Southfields, London, SW18 5BJ. Prop: P.H. Eastman. Tel: (020) 8871-0880. Fax: (020) 8871-0880. Web: www.harfieldbooks.com. E-mail: internet@ harfieldbooks.com. Est: 1989. Warehouse. Internet and Postal. Appointment necessary. Very large stock. Spec: Academic/Scholarly. CC: AE; E; MC; V; PayPal. Notes: *Also, a booksearch service & academic publishing.*

Edmund Pollinger Rare Books, Flat D 27 Bramham Gardens, London, SW5 0JE. Prop: Edmund Pollinger. Tel: 07834 601432. Fax: 0207 244 8498. Web: www.etpollinger.com. E-mail: etpollinger@ hotmail.com. Est: 2004. Office and/or bookroom. Contactable. Open: **M:** 10:00–17:30; **T:** 10:00–17:30; **W:** 10:00–17:30; **Th:** 10:00–17:30; **F:** 10:00–17:30. Closed for lunch: 12:00–14:00. Spec: Adventure; Africana; Animals and Birds; Apiculture; - Selous, Frederick; Curiosa; Entomology; Erotica. CC: MC; V. Cata: natural history, game hunting, fishing,food,drink. Corresp: French. Mem: PBFA. Notes: *Usually somebody here all the time, but call first to be sure.*

LONDON SOUTH WEST POSTAL DISTRICTS

Fine Art, 38, Tooting, London, SW17 9QS. Prop: Robert Walker. Tel: 0208 6961921. Fax: 0208 6961921. Web: www.fineart.tm. E-mail: sheppards@fineart.tm. Est: 1991. Private premises. Internet and Postal. Appointment necessary. Open: **M:** 10:00–17:00; **T:** 10:00–17:00; **W:** 10:00–17:00; **Th:** 10:00– 17:00; **F:** 10:00–17:00. Small stock. Spec: Antiquarian; Arts, The; Colour-Plate; Natural History; Topography - General; Topography - Local; ppraisals & Valuations; Collectables. PR: £100–1,000. CC: AE; MC; V. Corresp: French. Mem: PBFA. Notes: *Please contact by e-mail, or telephone. Internet expert for the trade.*

Folios Limited, Flat 5 193/195 Brompton Road, London, SW3 1LZ. Prop: Mr. Badr El–Hage. Tel: (020) 7581-2706. Fax: (020) 7581-2563. E-mail: folios@folios.demon.co.uk. Est: 1990. Private premises. Appointment necessary. Spec: Countries - Africa; Countries - Arabia; Religion - Islam; Prints and Maps. PR: £5–1,000. CC: MC; V. Corresp: Arabic, French.

Paul Foster Books, 49 Clifford Avenue, London, SW14 7BW. Tel: (020) 8876-7424. Fax: (020) 8876 7424. Web: www.paulfosterbooks.com. E-mail: paulfosterbooks@btinternet.com. Est: 1990. Office and/or bookroom. Internet and Postal. Appointment necessary. Open: **M:** 10:00–18:00; **T:** 10:00–18:00; **W:** 10:00–18:00; **Th:** 10:00–18:00; **F:** 10:00–18:00; **S:** 10:00–18:00. Medium stock. Spec: Antiquarian; Art; Author - 20th Century; Author - Austen, Jane; - Carroll, Lewis; - Churchill, Sir Winston; - Dickens, Charles; - Fleming, Ian. PR: £5–10,000. CC: JCB; MC; V. Mem: ABA; PBFA; ILAB.

Gardener & Cook, 90 Clancarty Road, London, SW6 3AA. Prop: Jonathan Tootell & Simon Cobley. Tel: 020 7751 3377. Fax: 020 7731 8400. Web: www.gardenerandcook.com. E-mail: info@ gardenerandcook.com. Est: 2005. Office and/or bookroom. Appointment necessary. Open: **M:** 09:00–17:30; **T:** 09:00–17:30; **W:** 09:00–17:30; **Th:** 09:00–17:30; **F:** 09:00–17:30; **S:** 09:00–17:30. Spec: Antiquarian; Catering & Hotel Management; Cookery - Professional; Cookery/Gastronomy; Fine & Rare; Food & Drink; Fungi; Gardening - General. CC: MC; V. Cata: Gardening & Cookery.

Geneva Books, 58 Elms Road, London, SW4 9EW. Tel: (020) 7627-4070. Est: 1985. Private premises. Appointment necessary. Spec: Religion - General. PR: £1–350.

Gloucester Road Bookshop, ■ 123 Gloucester Road, London, SW7 4TE. Prop: Nick Dennys. Tel: (020) 7370-3503. Fax: (020) 7373-0610. E-mail: manager@gloucesterbooks.co.uk. Est: 1983. Shop open: **M:** 09:30–22:30; **T:** 09:30–22:30; **W:** 09:30–22:30; **Th:** 09:30–22:30; **F:** 09:30–22:30; **S:** 10:30–18:30; **Su:** 10:30–18:30; Large stock. Spec: Antiques; Architecture; Art; - Greene, Graham; Children's; Fiction - General; History - General; Literature. PR: £0–5,000. CC: E; MC; V.

Grays of Westminster, ■ 40 Churton Street Pimlico, London, SW1V 2LP. Prop: Gray Levett & Nick Wynne. Tel: (020) 7828-4925. Fax: (020) 7976-5783. Web: www.graysofwestminster.co.uk. E-mail: info@graysofwestminster.co.uk. Est: 1985. Internet and Postal. Shop open: **M:** 10:00–17:29; **T:** 10:00– 17:30; **W:** 10:00–17:30; **Th:** 10:00–17:30; **F:** 10:00–17:30; **S:** 10:00–13:00. Spec: Photography. PR: £10– 200. CC: AE; D; E; MC; V; Maestro. Corresp: Japanese, Italian, Polish, German. VAT No: GB 503 1317 05. Notes: *Also, new, secondhand and vintage Nikon cameras.*

Robin Greer, 434 Fulham Palace Road, London, SW6 6HX. Prop: Robin Greer. Tel: (020) 7381-9113. Web: www.rarerobin.com. E-mail: rarities@rarerobin.com. Est: 1966. Private premises. Appointment necessary. Small stock. Spec: Arthurian; Author - Lang, Andrew; Children's; Children's - Illustrated; Illustrated - 19th & 20th Century, Illustrators. PR: £1 5,000. CC: MC; V. Cata: Children's & Illustrated Book. Corresp: Spanish. Mem: ABA; PBFA; ILAB.

Hanshan Tang Books, Unit 3 Ashburton Centre, 276 Cortis Road, London, SW15 3AY. Prop: John Cayley, John Constable, Myrna Chua. Tel: 0208 788 4464. Fax: 02087801565. Web: www. hanshan.com. E-mail: hst@hanshan.com. Est: 1973. Office and/or bookroom. Internet and Postal. Appointment necessary. Open: **M:** 10:00–17:00; **T:** 10:00–17:00; **W:** 10:00–17:00; **Th:** 10:00–17:00; **F:** 10:00–17:00. Spec: Antiquarian; Antiques; Antiquities; Archaeology; Architecture; Art; Art History; Art Reference. CC: AE; MC; V. Cata: East Asian Art and Archaeology. Mem: ABA; BA. VAT No: GB 749 5193 91.

Available from Richard Joseph Publishers Ltd

Sheppard's International Directory of EPHEMERA DEALERS

Order the next printed edition – or search on www.sheppardsworld.co.uk

LONDON SOUTH WEST POSTAL DISTRICTS

Peter Harrington Antiquarian Bookseller, ■ 100 Fulham Road, London, SW3 6HS. Prop: Peter Harrington. Tel: 020 7591 0220. Fax: 020 7225 7054. Web: www.peter-harrington-books.com. E-mail: mail@peter-harrington-books.com. Est: 1969. Shop open: **M:** 10:00–18:00; **T:** 10:00 18:00; **W:** 10:00–18:00; **Th:** 10:00–18:00; **F:** 10:00–18:00; **S:** 10:00–18:00. Very large stock. Spec: Aeronautics; Antiquarian; Architecture; Atlases; Autographs; Bibles; Bindings; Botany. PR: £10–100,000. CC: AE; E; JCB; MC; V. Cata: General, Literature, Travel, Children's. Corresp: Spanish, Polish. Mem: ABA; PBFA; ILAB. VAT No: GB701 5578 50.

Thomas Heneage Art Books, ■ 42 Duke Street, St. James's, London, SW1Y 6DJ. Tel: (020) 7930-9223. Fax: (020) 7839-9223. Web: www.heneage.com. E-mail: artbooks@heneage.com. Est: 1977. Shop open: **M:** 09:30–18:00; **T:** 09:30–18:00; **W:** 09:30–18:00; **Th:** 09:30–18:00; **F:** 09:30–18:00. Medium stock. Spec: Antiques; Applied Art; Arms & Armour; Art; Art History; Carpets; Catalogues Raisonnes; Ceramics. PR: £2–30,000. CC: MC; V. Mem: ABA; ILAB; LAPADA. VAT No: GB 242 1045 14. Notes: *Also, a booksearch service and publishers of Art Book Survey. Open at other times by appointment.*

Hesketh & Ward Ltd., 31 Britannia Road, London, SW6 2HJ. Prop: Viscount Bangor. Tel: (020) 7736-5705. Fax: (020) 7736-1089. E-mail: heskward@bradford44.plus.com. Est: 1985. Private premises. Appointment necessary. Very small stock. Spec: Foreign Texts. PR: £80–5,000. CC: MC; V. Cata: early continental. Corresp: French, Italian. Mem: ABA. VAT No: GB 394 8008 27. Notes: *Stock is mainly 16th century Continental, especially Italian.*

Hünersdorff Rare Books, P.O. Box 582, London, SW10 9RP. Prop: Richard von Hünersdorff. Tel: (020) 7373-3899. Fax: (020) 7370-1244. Web: www.abebooks.com/hunersdorff/home. E-mail: rarebooks@hunersdorff.com. Est: 1969. Private premises. Appointment necessary. Spec: Architecture; Countries - Latin America; Countries - South America; Gardening - General; Horses; Horticulture; Landscape; Languages - Foreign. PR: £25–500,000. CC: MC; V. Corresp: German, Spanish, French. Mem: ABA; ILAB.

Andrew Hunter–Rare Books, Box 9 34 Buckingham Palace Road, London, SW1W 0RH. Tel: (020) 7834-4924. Fax: (020) 7834-4924. Web: www.rarebookhunter.com. E-mail: andrew@rarebookhunter.com. Est: 2001. Private premises. Appointment necessary. Very small stock. Spec: Earth Sciences; Incunabula; Literature; Manuscripts; Mathematics; Medicine; Medicine - History of; Pharmacy/ Pharmacology. PR: £200–25,000. Cata: Science, medicine, literature, the Scot abroad. Corresp: French, Spanish. Mem: ABA; ILAB. VAT No: GB 782 2863 04.

J.C. Deyong Books, 17 Cadogan Court Draycott Avenue, London, SW3 3BX. Prop: J.C. Deyong (Previously of Snowden Smith Books) Tel: 020 7581 8665. Fax: 020 7581 0031. Web: www.jcdeyong .co.uk. E-mail: snowsmithbooks@hotmail.com. Est: 1973. Private premises. Internet and Postal. Contactable. Spec: Aboriginal; Anthropology; Countries - Africa; Countries - Arabia; Countries - Arabian Peninsula; Countries - Asia; Countries - Australasia; Countries - Central Asia. CC: MC; V. Cata: Travel & Related Subjects. Corresp: French. Mem: PBFA. Notes: *Selection of stock can be seen at Biblion, 1-7 Davies Mews,London W1K5AB. Open Monday to Friday. Telephone: +44 (0)20 7629 1374. website: www.biblion.com.*

Romilly Leeper, 12 Bolton Garden Mews, London, SW10 9LW. Prop: Romilly Leeper. Tel: (020) 7373-8370. Fax: (020) 7370-3226. Est: 1986. Private premises. Appointment necessary. Small stock. Spec: Sport - Horse Racing (inc. Riding/Breeding/Equestrian); Travel - Asia, South East. PR: £6–100. Corresp: French, German, Portuguese.

Mandalay Bookshop, 36c Sisters Avenue, London, SW11 5SQ. Prop: Nicholas Greenwood. Web: www.mandalaybookshop.com. E-mail: mandalaybookshop@mousehut.com. Est: 1994. Private premises. Internet and Postal. Small stock. Spec: Animals and Birds; Anthropology; Antiquarian; Architecture; Army, The; Art; Asian Studies; Author - Orwell, George. PR: £5–1,500. Corresp: French, German, Burmese, Thai. Notes: *WWII includes the Burma Campaign.*

Michael Graves-Johnston, 54 Stockwell Park Road, London, SW9 0DA. Prop: Michael Graves-Johnston. Tel: +4420-7274-2069. Fax: +4420-7738-3747. Web: www.Graves-Johnston.com. E-mail: Books@gravesjohnston.demon.co.uk. Est: 1978. Private premises. Postal Only. Appointment necessary. Large stock. Spec: Aboriginal; African-American Studies; Africana; American Indians; Anthropology; Archaeology; Art - Afro-American; Australiana. PR: £5–25,000. CC: AE; E; MC; V. Cata: Africa, Oceania, Ancient World, Archaeology. Mem: ABA; BA; ILAB. VAT No: GB 238 2333 72.

My Back Pages, ■ 8-10 Balham Station Road, London, SW16 6RT. Prop: Douglas Jeffers. Tel: 0208 675 9346. Fax: 0208 769 9741. E-mail: douglasjeffers@aol.com. Est: 1990. Shop open: **M:** 10:10–20:00; **T:** 10:00–20:00; **W:** 10:00–20:00; **Th:** 10:00–20:00; **F:** 10:00–20:00; **S:** 10:00–19:00; **Su:** 11:00–18:00. Very large stock. Spec: Academic/Scholarly; Architecture; Art; Art - British; Art Reference; Cinema/Film; Countries - India; Egyptology. CC: AE; JCB; MC; V. VAT No: GB 5620 221 84.

LONDON SOUTH WEST POSTAL DISTRICTS

Nibris Books, 14 Ryfold Road Wimbledon Park, London, SW19 8BZ. Prop: Nigel Israel. Tel: (020) 8946-7207. Fax: (020) 8946-7207. E-mail: nibris_books@yahoo.com. Est: 1980. Private premises. Postal Only. Appointment necessary. Small stock. Spec: Antiquarian; Antiques; Gemmology; Horology; Jewellery; Mineralogy; Precious Metals - Silver; Silversmiths. PR: £10–500. Cata: As per classifications. VAT No: GB 446 2021 80. Notes: *Included in clasifications: Jewellery, gem stones, engraved gems, crown jewels, regalia & ceremony, silver, horology.*

Paul Orssich, 2 St. Stephen's Terrace South Lambeth, London, SW8 1DH. Tel: (020) 7787-0030. Fax: (020) 7735-9612. Web: www.orssich.com. E-mail: paulo@orssich.com. Est: 1980. Private premises. Internet and Postal. Telephone First. Very large stock. Spec: Author - Cervantes Saavedra, Miguel de; Braziliana; Bull Fighting; Countries - Andorra; Countries - Central America; Countries - Gibraltar; Countries - Guatemala; Countries - Madeira. PR: £25–5,000. CC: MC; V. Cata: Hispanic Studies in general. Corresp: Spanish, Catalan, French, German, Italian. Mem: PBFA. VAT No: GB 442 4102 94. Notes: *Open any time by appointment.*

Hugh Pagan Limited, P.O. Box 4325, London, SW7 1DD. Tel: (020) 7589-6292. Fax: (020) 7589-6303. Web: www.hughpagan.com. E-mail: enquiries@hughpagan.com. Est: 1987. Appointment necessary. Spec: Antiquarian; Applied Art; Architecture; Architecture - Theatre; Art History; Art Reference; Arts & Crafts Era; British Art & Design. CC: MC; V. Cata: Architecture and the Allied Arts 16th to 20th cen. Mem: ABA; ILAB. VAT No: GB 468 6672 90.

Pimpernel Booksearch, 90 Clencarty Road, London, SW6 3AA. Prop: Jonathan Tootell. Tel: (020) 7731-8500. Fax: (020) 7731-8400. Web: www.pimpernelbooks.co.uk. E-mail: jt@pimpernelbooks.co.uk. Est: 1999. Private premises. Postal Only. Contactable. Open: **M:** 09:00–18:00; **T:** 09:00–18:00; **W:** 09:00–18:00; **Th:** 09:00–18:00; **F:** 09:00–18:00; **S:** 09:00–14:00. Very small stock. Spec: Booksearch. CC: MC; V. Corresp: French.

Russell Rare Books, ■ 239A Fulham Road Chelsea, London, SW3 6HY. Tel: (020) 7351-5119. Fax: (020) 7376-7227. Web: www.russellrarebooks.com. E-mail: c.russell@russellrarebooks.com. Est: 1977. Shop open: **M:** 14:00–18:00; **T:** 14:00–18:00; **W:** 14:00–18:00; **Th:** 14:00–18:00; **F:** 14:00–18:00. Very small stock. Spec: Atlases; Bindings; Natural History; Social History; Travel - General; Prints and Maps. PR: £200–10,000. CC: V. Mem: ABA; PBFA; ILAB. Notes: *When closed telephone 07768 004152 usually open but appointment advisable.*

SaBeRo Books, 27 Cavendish Road, Colliers Wood, London, SW19 2ET. Prop: Ron, Bethani and Sarah Travis. Tel: 44 (0) 20 85 40 60 2. E-mail: saberobooks@blueyonder.co.uk. Est: 2002. Private premises. Internet and Postal. Contactable. Open: **M:** 09:00–17:00; **T:** 09:00–17:00; **W:** 09:00–17:00; **Th:** 09:00–17:00; **F:** 09:00–17:00; **S:** 09:00–17:00. Medium stock. PR: £2–500. CC: PayPal. Cata: Various, as requested. Mem: Biblion.

Sandpiper Books Ltd., 24 Langroyd Road, London, SW17 7PL. Prop: Robert Collie. Tel: (020) 8767-7421. Fax: (020) 8682-0280. Web: www.sandpiper.co.uk. E-mail: enquiries@sandpiper.co.uk. Est: 1983. Office and/or bookroom. Internet and Postal. Appointment necessary. Open: **M:** 09:00–17:00; **T:** 09:00–17:00; **W:** 09:00–17:00; **Th:** 09:00–17:00; **F:** 09:00–17:00. Medium stock. Spec: Academic/ Scholarly; Classical Studies; Medieval. PR: £1–100. CC: MC; V. Mem: BA. Notes: *Trade and scholarly remainders from general history, religion and reference to classical studies. Visit our wholesale website at www.sandpiper.co.uk or our mail order Postscript selling to individuals at www.psbooks.co.uk*

Sims Reed Limited, ■ 43a Duke Street, London, SW1Y 6DD. Prop: John Sims Tel: 020 7493 5660. Fax: 020 7493 8468. Web: www.simsreed.com. E-mail: info@simsreed.com. Est: 1978. Shop open: **M:** 10:00–18:00; **T:** 10:00–18:00; **W:** 10:00–18:00; **Th:** 10:00–18:00; **F:** 10:00–18:00. Spec: Antiquarian; Art; Artists; Illustrated - General; Prints and Maps. CC: AE; E; MC; V; Maestro. Mem: ILAB. VAT No: GB 242 9715 52. Notes: *Open at other times by appointment.*

Tsbbooks, 214 Ferndale Road, London, SW9 8AG. Tel: (0207) 7330965. E-mail: tsbbooks@ hotmail.com. Est: 1989. Mail Order Only. Internet and Postal. Small stock. Spec: Adult; Author - Benson, E.F.; - Isherwood, Christopher; - Paul Bowles; - Williams, Tennessee; Comics; Erotica; Fiction - Gay Fiction. PR: £4–450.

Mary Wells, 24 Minehead Road, London, SW16 2AW. Prop: Mary Wells. Tel: (020) 8769-0778. Fax: (020) 8769-0778. Est: 1980. Private premises. Book fairs only. Small stock. Spec: Booksearch. PR: £1–500. Notes: *Attends Bloomsbury Fair, Royal National.*

Whistler's Books, 11 Ashbourne Terrace Wimbledon, London, SW19 1QX. Prop: Ronald H. Ashworth. Tel: (020) 8540-7370. Est: 1993. Private premises. Appointment necessary. Very small stock. Spec: Building & Construction; Chess; Company History; Electronics; Engineering; Industry; Mathematics; Music - Composers. PR: £5–50.

Worlds End Bookshop, ■ 357 Kings Road, London, SW3 5ES. Prop: Stephen Dickson. Tel: 020 7352 9376. E-mail: stevdcksn@btinternet.com. Est: 1990. Shop open: **M:** 10:00–18:30; **T:** 10:00–18:30; **W:** 10:00–18:30; **Th:** 10:00–18:30; **F:** 10:00–18:30; **S:** 10:00 18:30; **Su:** 10:00–18:30. Spec. Antiquarian; Antiques; Architecture; Art; Avant-Garde; Beat Writers; Biography; Children's - Illustrated. CC: AE; JCB; MC; V; Switch. Notes: *20% discounts every Saturday, Sunday & Monday. 40% discounts every Bank Holiday.*

Wykeham Books, 64 Ridgway, Wimbledon, London, SW19 4RA. Prop: H.S.G. Mather. Tel: (020) 8879-3721. Web: www.bibliographies.co.uk. E-mail: wykbooks@msn.com. Est: 1976. Private premises. Internet and Postal. Medium stock. Spec: Author - Kipling, Rudyard; Bibliography; Book Arts; Bookbinding; Books about Books. PR: £5–15,000. Mem: PBFA.

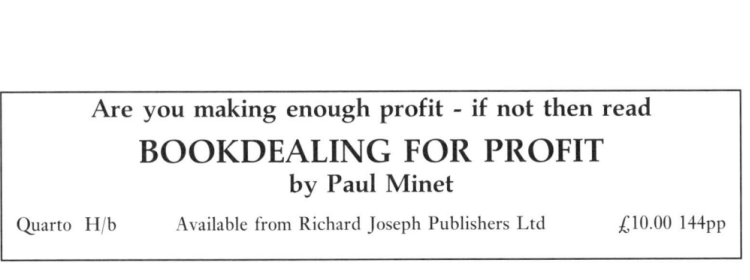

LONDON
WEST POSTAL DISTRICTS

Al Saqi Books, ■ 26 Westbourne Grove, London, W2 5RH. Prop: Arab Books Ltd. Tel: (020) 7229-8543. Fax: (020) 7229-7492. E-mail: alsaqibooks@aol.com. Est: 1978. Shop open: **M:** 10:00–18:00; **T:** 10:00–18:00; **W:** 10:00–18:00; **Th:** 10:00–18:00; **F:** 10:00–18:00; **S:** 10:00–18:00. Medium stock. Spec: Academic/Scholarly; Antiquarian; Arabica; Architecture; Art; Authors - Women; Canals/Inland Waterways; Cookery/Gastronomy. PR: £5–800. CC: AE; D; E; JCB; MC; V. Cata: Middle East. Corresp: French, Arabic. Mem: BA. VAT No: GB 242 6953 51. Notes: *Also, important stock of Arabic books, also new books.*

Altea Gallery, 35 Saint George St., London, W1S 2FN. Prop: Mr. Massimo De Martini. Tel: (020) 7491 0010. Fax: (020) 7491 0015. Web: www.alteagallery.com. E-mail: info@alteagallery.com. Est: 1993. Shop and/or gallery. Internet and Postal. Open: **M:** 10:00–18:00; **T:** 10:00–18:00; **W:** 10:00–18:00; **Th:** 10:00–18:00; **F:** 10:00–18:00; **S:** 11:00–16:00. Medium stock. Spec: Antiquarian; Astronomy; Atlases; Geography; Maps & Mapmaking; Maritime/Nautical; Topography - General; Topography - Local. PR: £50–10,000. CC: AE; E; JCB; MC; V. Cata: Antiquarian Maps & Atlases. Corresp: Italian. Mem: ABA; PBFA; ILAB; IMCoS. VAT No: GB 649 5809 86. Notes: *Also, map search, colouring & restoration.*

David Batterham, 36 Alexander Street, London, W2 5NU. Tel: (020) 7229-3845. E-mail: david.batterham@virgin.net. Est: 1966. Private premises. Appointment necessary. Small stock. Spec: Applied Art; Architecture; Caricature; Fashion & Costume; Illustrated - General; Journals; Technology; Typography. PR: £5–5,000. CC: MC; V. Corresp: French. Mem: PBFA.

Nicholas Bernstein, 2 Vaughan Avenue, London, W6 0XS. Prop: Nicholas Bernstein. Tel: (020) 874 17140. Est: 1986. Private premises. Appointment necessary. Medium stock. Spec: Antiquarian; Bibles; Bindings; Curiosities; Dictionaries; Economics; Fiction - General; History of Ideas. PR: £25–5,000. Corresp: French. Mem: PBFA. Notes: *Appointments: 7 days a week. Exhibits at monthly PBFA fairs at Holiday Inn Bloomsbury.*

Biblion Ltd, ■ 1–7 Davies Mews, London, W1K 5AB. Prop: Director: Leo Harrison. Manager: Ben Houston. Tel: (020) 7629-1374. Fax: (020) 7493-7158. Web: www.biblion.co.uk. E-mail: info@ biblion.co.uk. Est: 1999. Internet and Postal. Shop open: **M:** 10:00–18:00; **T:** 10:00–18:00; **W:** 10:00–18:00; **Th:** 10:00–18:00; **F:** 10:00–18:00. Large stock. Spec: Alpinism/Mountaineering; Antiquarian; Applied Art; Architecture; Art; Bibles; Bibliography; Bindings. PR: £10–50,000. CC: E; JCB; MC; V.

J. & S.L. Bonham, Flat 14 84 Westbourne Terrace, London, W2 6QE. Prop: John & Suzanne Bonham. Tel: (020) 7402-7064. Fax: (020) 7402-0955. Web: www.bonbooks.dial.pipex.com. E-mail: bonbooks@dial.pipex.com. Est: 1976. Private premises. Internet and Postal. Appointment necessary. Medium stock. Spec: Africana; Alpinism/Mountaineering; Australiana; Countries - Africa; Countries - Arabia; Countries - Asia; Countries - Australasia; Countries - Australia. PR: £10–2,000. CC: MC; V; SW, SO. Corresp: German. Mem: ABA; PBFA; ILAB. VAT No: GB 362 1962 53. Notes: *Valuations.*

The Book Business, 90 Greenford Avenue, London, W7 3QS. Prop: Giles Levete. Tel: (020) 8840-1185. E-mail: bookbusiness@homechoice.co.uk. Est. 1990. Private premises. Internet and Postal Appointment necessary. Very small stock. Spec: Academic/Scholarly; Antiquarian; Architecture; Arts, The; Autographs; Children's; Fiction - Crime, Detective, Spy, Thrillers; First Editions. PR: £10–2,000. Mem: PBFA.

Books & Things, P.O. Box 17768, London, W8 6ZD. Prop: M.M. Steenson. Tel: (020) 7370-5593. Fax: (020) 7370-5593. Web: www.booksandthings.co.uk. E-mail: martin@booksandthings.co.uk. Est: 1972. Warehouse. Internet and Postal. Small stock. Spec: Advertising; Applied Art; Art Reference; Children's - Illustrated; Decorative Art; Illustrated - General; Magazines & Periodicals - General; Modern First Editions. PR: £20–1,000. CC: E; JCB; MC. Mem: ABA; PBFA; ILAB. Notes: *Also, a booksearch service.*

Don Kelly Books, Admiral Vernon L16-20 141-149 Portobello Rd, London, W11. Prop: Don Kelly. Tel: 020 7731 0482. Fax: 020 7731 0482. E-mail: donkellybooks@btinternet.com. Est: 1978. Market stand/ stall. Shop At: P.O.Box 44132, London SW6 2RP. Open: **S:** 07.30 15.30. Spec: Antiques; Antiquities; Art Deco; Art History; Art Nouveau; Art Reference; Arts, The; Carpets. CC: MC; V. Cata: Reference books for the Art & Antique trade. VAT No: GB 563 2239 49. Notes: *I also exhibit at The Olympia Fine Art and Antique Fair three times a year. Although I am only open on Saturdays, a selection of my stock can be viewed by appointment throughout the week.*

LONDON WEST POSTAL DISTRICTS

Marc-Antoine du Ry Medieval Art, 13 New Burlington Street, London, W1S 3BG. Prop: Marc du Ry. Tel: 0044 (0) 207 287 905. Fax: (cell) 0044 (0) 777 0888 116. Web: www.earlyart.net. E-mail: info@marcdury.com. Est: 1997. Office and/or bookroom. Telephone First. Spec: Bibles; Book of Hours; Illuminated Manuscripts; Medieval. PR: £100–100,000. Corresp: French, Italian. VAT No: GB 735 7640 16. Notes: *Also contactable in Belgium on 0032 (0) 475 866073.*

Elton Engineering Books, 32 Fairfax Road, London, W4 1EW. Prop: Julia Elton. Tel: (0208) 747 0967. E-mail: elton_engineering_books@compuserve.com. Est: 1985. Private premises. Internet and Postal. Appointment necessary. Very small stock. Spec: Architecture; Building & Construction; Electricity & Gas; Engineering; Industry; Inventors & Inventions; Maritime/Nautical; Mechanical Engineering. PR: £30–8,000. CC: MC; V. Corresp: French, German. Mem: ABA; ILAB. VAT No: GB 429 7966 90.

Simon Finch Rare Books Ltd., ■ 53 Maddox Street, London, W1S 2PN. Tel: (020) 7499-0974. Fax: (020) 7499-0799. Web: www.simonfinch.com. E-mail: rarebooks@simonfinch.com. Est: 1981. Shop open: **M:** 11:00–18:00; **T:** 11:00–18:00; **W:** 11:00–18:00; **Th:** 11:00–18:00; **F:** 11:00 18:00. Spec: Antiquarian; Art; Autographs; Bindings; Design; Early Imprints; Literature; Manuscripts. PR: £1–500,000. CC: AE; MC; V; SW.

First State Books, 15 Talbot Road, London, W2 5JG. Prop: Euan Stuart. Tel: (020) 7792-2672. Fax: (020) 7792-2672. Web: www.firststatebooks.com. E-mail: info@firststatebooks.com. Est: 2001. Private premises. Internet and Postal. Spec: Children's; Fiction - General; First Editions; Modern First Editions. PR: £15–100. CC: AE; D; E; JCB; MC; V; Maestro, Solo.

Sam Fogg Ltd, ■ 15d Clifford Street, London, W1S 4JZ. Tel: (020) 7534-2100. Fax: (020) 7534-2122. Web: www.samfogg.com. E-mail: info@samfogg.com. Est: 1978. Shop. Appointment necessary. Open: **M:** 09:30–17:30; **T:** 09:30–17:30; **W:** 09:30–17:30; **Th:** 09:30–17:30; **F:** 09:30–17:30. Small stock. Spec: Manuscripts. CC: MC; V. Corresp: French, German. Mem: ABA. VAT No: GB 467 6893 80.

Richard Ford, 70 Chaucer Road, London, W3 6DP. Tel: (020) 8993-1235. Fax: (020) 8752-1431. E-mail: richard.rmford@btopenworld.com. Est: 1982. Private premises. Internet and Postal. Appointment necessary. Very small stock. Spec: Autographs; Bibliography; Bibliophily; Book Arts; Books about Books; Documents - General; Manuscripts; Publishers; Publishers - General. PR: £10–1,000. Cata: Bookselling & Publishing. Corresp: French, Italian. Mem: ABA; ILAB. Notes: *Printed ephemera, manuscripts, autograph letters. Any subject.*

Fosters Bookshop, ■ 183 Chiswick High Road, London, W4 2DR. Prop: Stephen Foster. Tel: (020) 8995-2768. Web: www.fostersbookshop.co.uk. E-mail: stephen@fostersbookshop.co.uk. Est: 1968. Shop open: **Th:** 10:30–17:00; **F:** 10:30–17:00; **S:** 10:30–17:00. Medium stock. Spec: Antiquarian; Applied Art; Architecture; Art; Bindings; Children's; Children's - Illustrated; Fine & Rare. PR: £2–1,000. CC: AE; MC; V. Mem: ABA; PBFA; ILAB; ibooknet. Notes: *Family run bookshop, now with the 2nd generation. See also Stephen Foster, London NW (q.v.).*

Robert Frew Ltd, ■ 31 Maddox Street, London, W1S 2PB. Tel: (020) 7290 3800. Fax: (020) 72903801. Web: www.robertfrew.com. E-mail: shop@robertfrew.com. Est: 1993. Shop open: **M:** 10:00–18:00; **T:** 10:00–18:00; **W:** 10:00–18:00; **Th:** 10:00–18:00; **F:** 10:00–18:00; **S:** 11.00–15.00. Spec: Antiquarian; Atlases; Author - Churchill, Sir Winston; Bindings; Cartography; Colour-Plate; Encyclopaedias; History - General. PR: £10–30,000. CC: AE; D; E; JCB; MC; V. Mem: ABA; PBFA; ILAB. VAT No: GB 625 8877 92. Notes: *Book packing and shipping service.*

Fuller D'Arch Smith, 37b New Cavendish Street, London, W1G 8JR. Prop: Jean Overton Fuller & Timothy D'Arch Smith. Tel: (020) 7722-0063. Fax: (020) 7722-0063. E-mail: mustardpot@ hotmail.com. Est: 1969. Private premises. Appointment necessary. Very small stock. PR: £5–500. Corresp: French, German, Italian, Russian.

Hab Books, 35 Wellington Road Ealing, London, W5 4UJ. Prop: T. Habraszewski. Tel: (020) 8932-5058. Fax: (020) 8932-5058. E-mail: tomhab@ntlworld.com. Est: 1981. Private premises. Postal Only. Spec: Annuals; Autobiography; Biography; Communism; Countries - East Europe; Countries - Russia; Fiction - General; Folio Society, The. Notes: *Stock includes books in Polish.*

Adrian Harrington, 64a Kensington Church Street Kensington, London, W8 4DB. Tel: (020) 7937-1465. Fax: (020) 7368-0912. Web: www.harringtonbooks.co.uk. E-mail: rare@harringtonbooks.co.uk. Est: 1971. Spec: Aesthetic Movement; Antiquarian; Art; Author - General; - Aickman, R.; - Churchill, Sir Winston; - Conan Doyle, Sir Arthur; - Cornwell, Bernard. PR: £10–50,000. CC: AE; MC; V. Mem: ABA; PBFA; ILAB. Notes: *Also, bookbinding, library sets, decorative bindings.*

LONDON WEST POSTAL DISTRICTS

G. Heywood Hill Limited, ■ 10 Curzon Street, London, W1J 5HH. Tel: (020) 7629-0647. Fax: (020) 7408-0286. Web: www.heywoodhill.com. E-mail: anthony@heywoodhill.com. Est: 1936. Shop open: **M:** 09:00–17:30; **T:** 09:00–17:30; **W:** 09:00–17:30; **Th:** 09:00–17:30; **F:** 09:00–17:30; **S:** 09:00–12:30. Medium stock. Spec: Architecture; Children's; History - General; Illustrated - General; Literature; Natural History; Booksearch. PR: £5–10,000. CC: MC; V; Switch. Corresp: French, German, Spanish, Italian. Mem: ABA; BA. VAT No: GB 239 4090 56. Notes: *Also, new books & a booksearch service.*

P.J. Hilton (Books), ■ 12 Cecil Court Charing Cross Road, London, WC2N 4HE. Prop: Paul John Hilton. Tel: (020) 7379-9825. E-mail: paul.hilton@britishlibrary.net. Est: 1988. Shop open: **M:** 1100–1730; **T:** 1100–1730; **W:** 1100–1730; **Th:** 1100–1730; **F:** 1100–1730; **S:** 1100–1730. Spec: Antiquarian; Bibles; Bibliophily; Biography; Fiction - General; Prayer Books; Religion - Catholic; Religion - Christian. PR: £1–1,000. CC: MC; V. Cata: Antiquarian, Literature, Religion. Notes: *We are always pleased to deal with enquiries by telephone or email and to make a note of your interests if we may be able to help. We can also provide larger quantities of books if required.*

Judith Hodgson, 11 Stanwick Road, London, W14 8TL. Tel: (020) 7603-7414. Fax: (020) 7602-1431. E-mail: judith.hodgson@btinternet.com. Est: 1986. Private premises. Internet and Postal. Appointment necessary. Small stock. Spec: Antiquarian; Braziliana; Countries - Argentina; Countries - Azores, The; Countries - Bolivia; Countries - Brazil; Countries - Cuba; Countries - Latin America. Cata: Spain, Portugal, Latin America. Corresp: French, Spanish, Portuguese. Mem: ABA; ILAB. VAT No: GB 446 0649 44.

James Fergusson Books & Manuscripts, 39 Melrose Gardens, London, W6 7RN. Tel: 020 7602 3536. Fax: 020 7602 0502. E-mail: jamesfergusson@btinternet.com. Est: 1986. Private premises. Postal Only. Appointment necessary. Closed for lunch: 13:00–14:00. Spec: Letters; Manuscripts. Notes: *Also, 19th & 20th century literary association copies, autographs and photographs.*

Kay Books, Roger's Arcade 65 Portobello Road, London, W11 2QB. Prop: Peter Degnan. Tel: (020) 8640-7779. Fax: (Mobile) 07940 833870. E-mail: peter@pdegnan.fsnet.co.uk. Est: 1968. Private premises. Telephone First. Spec: Bindings; Topography - General; Travel - General.

Robert J. Kirkpatrick, 6 Osterley Park View Road, London, W7 2HH. Tel: (020) 8567-4521. E-mail: rkirkpatrick.molesworth@virgin.net. Est: 1986. Private premises. Postal Only. Appointment necessary. Very small stock. Spec: Children's; Education & School; Juvenile; Memoirs; Public Schools; Schools - General. PR: £1–100. Cata: Boys school fiction, school memoirs & histories.

Maggs Brothers Limited, ■ 50 Berkeley Square, London, W1J 5BA. Tel: (020) 7493-7160. Fax: (020) 7499-2007. Web: www.maggs.com. E-mail: postmaster@maggs.com. Est: 1853. Shop open: **M:** 09:30–17:00; **T:** 09:30–17:00; **W:** 09:30–17:00; **Th:** 09:30–17:00; **F:** 09:30–17:00. Very large stock. Spec: Autographs; Bibliography; Bindings; Cookery/Gastronomy; Early Imprints; Fine Printing; Geology; Illuminated Manuscripts. PR: £5–5,000,000. CC: MC; V. Corresp: Japanese, Mandarin, German, French, Italian, Spanish. Mem: ABA; PBFA; BA; ILAB; BADA.

Marlborough Rare Books Ltd, ■ 144/146 New Bond Street, London, W1S 2TR. Prop: Jonathan Gestetner. Tel: (020) 7493-6993. Fax: (020) 7499-2479. E-mail: sales@mrb-books.co.uk. Est: 1948. Shop open: **M:** 09:30–17:30; **T:** 09:30–17:30; **W:** 09:30–17:30; **Th:** 09:30–17:30; **F:** 09:30–17:30. Medium stock. Spec: Architecture; Bibliography; Bindings; Cities - City of London; Cities - General; Colour-Plate; Country Houses; Fine Art. PR: £50–50,000. CC: E; MC; V. Cata: Art, Architecture, London, Travel, Topography. Corresp: French, German. Mem: ABA; ILAB. VAT No: GB 341 2642 86.

Melvin Tenner, 51 Gayford Road, London, W12 9BY. Prop: Melvin Tenner. Tel: 020 8740 6677. Fax: 010 8740 6960. E-mail: tenner@abelgratis.com. Est: 1980. Private premises. Appointment necessary. Spec: International Affairs; Booksearch. Notes: *Also, a booksearch service.*

DOES YOUR WEBSITE NEED A MAKE-OVER?

Features now include an easy-to-use book stock database

For more details - see

www.sheppardsworld.co.uk

LONDON WEST POSTAL DISTRICTS

Orbis Books (London) Ltd., 206 Blythe Road, London, W14 0HH. Prop: Dir: Mr. Jerzy Kulczycki & Dr. Aleksandra Kulczycka. Fax: (020) 8742-7686. E-mail: bookshop@orbis-books.co.uk. Est: 1944. Spec: Countries - East Europe; Countries - Poland; Countries - Russia; Foreign Texts; Booksearch. PR: £2–20,000. Notes: *Also, new books, booksearch, large print books, CDs & cassettes of Polish music.*

Diana Parikian, Rare Books, 3 Caithness Road, London, W14 0JB. Tel: (020) 7603-8375. Fax: (020) 7602-1178. E-mail: dparikian@mac.com. Est: 1960. Private premises. Appointment necessary. Spec: Emblemata; Fine & Rare; Foreign Texts; Iconography. PR: £200–10,000. Corresp: French, Italian. Mem: ABA. VAT No: GB 194 5853 21.

Pickering & Chatto, ■ 36 St. George Street, London, W!S 2FA. Tel: (020) 7491-2656. Fax: (020) 7491-9161. Web: www.pickering-chatto.com. E-mail: j.hudson@pickering-chatto.com. Est: 1820. Shop open: **M:** 09:30–17:30; **T:** 09:30–17:30; **W:** 09:30–17:30; **Th:** 09:30–17:30; **F:** 09:30–17:30. Small stock. Spec: Chemistry; Early Imprints; Economics; Education & School; Health; Humanities; Incunabula; Literature. PR: £100–10,000. CC: MC; V. Corresp: French. Mem: ABA; PBFA; ILAB. VAT No: GB 691 3252 35.

William Poole, 97 New Bond Street, London, W1S 1SL. Tel: (020) 7629-8738. Est: 1979. Private premises. Appointment necessary. Small stock. Spec: Academic/Scholarly; Classical Studies; Fine & Rare; Foreign Texts; Humanism; Publishers - General. Notes: *Also books by Foulis Press.*

Portobello Books, ■ 328 Portobello Road, London, W10 5RU. Prop: Lawrence Thompson. Tel: 020 8964 3166. Fax: 020 8964 3166. Web: www.portobello-books.com. E-mail: sales@portobello-books.com. Est: 1985. Shop open: **T:** 11:00–17:00; **W:** 11:00–17:00; **Th:** 11:00–17:00; **F:** 11:00–17:00; **S:** 09:00–17:00. Spec: Anthropology; Architecture; Art - Technique; Art History; Astronomy; Biography; Children's - Illustrated; Cinema/Film. CC: AE; D; E; JCB; MC; V. Cata: Various. Notes: *We are a second hand book shop, specialising in out of print books. Not open on Mondays or Sundays.*

Bernard Quaritch Ltd., ■ 8 Lower John Street Golden Square, London, W1F 9AU. Prop: John Koh. Tel: (020) 7734-2983. Fax: (020) 7437-0967. Web: www.quaritch.com. E-mail: rarebooks@quaritch.com. Est: 1847. Shop open: **M:** 09:00–1800; **T:** 0900–1800; **W:** 0900–1800; **Th:** 0900–1800; **F:** 0900–1800. Large stock. Spec: Alchemy; Antiquarian; Architecture; Art; Bibliography; Cookery/Gastronomy; Early Imprints; Economics. PR: £100–500,000. CC: AE; MC; V; SW. Cata: rare books and manuscripts in most fields. Corresp: French, German, Italian, Spanish, Russian. Mem: ABA; PBFA; ILAB; SLAM, VDA, BADA. VAT No: GB 840 1358 54.

Leslie Robert, t/a Hyde Park Books, 74 Devonport 23 Southwick Street, London, W2 2QH. Tel: (020) 7402-9567. E-mail: hydeparkbooks@dsl.pipex.com. Est: 1978. Private premises. Internet and Postal. Appointment necessary. Spec: Fiction - General; Fiction - Crime, Detective, Spy, Thrillers; Fiction - Young Adult Mystery & Adventure Series; First Editions; Modern First Editions. PR: £20–500. CC: Cheques in sterling. Notes: *We specialise in modern first editions of which many are signed by the author. We are situated near to Paddington station so it is easy to call in by appointment only. Most of our books are in fine condition.*

St. Swithin's Illustrated & Children's Books, 87 Portobello Road, London, W11 2QB. Prop: Mrs. Margaret Davies. Tel: (020) 8573-8556. Shop and/or showroom. Appointment necessary. Spec: Advertising; Artists; Cats; Children's; Children's - Illustrated; Christmas; Circus; Decorative Art. Notes: *None of the stock is shown on the Internet*

A.F. Sephton, 16 Bloemfontein Avenue Shepherds Bush, London, W12 7BL. Prop: A.F. Sephton. Tel: (020) 8749-1454. E-mail: albertsephton@onetel.com. Est: 1966. Private premises. Appointment necessary. Very small stock. Spec: Artists; Colour-Plate; Illustrated - General; Social History; Prints and Maps. PR: £10–100. Notes: *Work by W Hogart included.*

Bernard J. Shapero Rare Books, ■ 32 St. George Street, London, W1S 2EA. Tel: (020) 7493-0876. Fax: (020) 7229-7860. Web: www.shapero.com. E-mail: rarebooks@shapero.com. Est: 1979. Internet and Postal. Shop open: **M:** 09:30–18:30; **T:** 09:30–18:30; **W:** 09:30–18:30; **Th:** 09:30–18:30; **F:** 09:30–18:30; **S:** 11:00–17:00. Large stock. Spec: Atlases; Cartography; Colour-Plate; Guide Books; Modern First Editions; Travel - General; Travel - Africa; Voyages & Discovery. PR: £50–100,000. CC: AE; D; E; MC; V. Cata: travel, colour-plate, cartography, baedekers, mod. Corresp: French, German. Mem: ABA; PBFA; ILAB; BADA; IMCOS; VDA. VAT No: GB 466 5294 16.

Sokol Books Ltd, P.O. Box 2409, London, W1A 2SH. Prop: C.J. Sokol. Tel: (020) 7499-5571. Fax: (020) 7629-6536. Web: www.sokol.co.uk. E-mail: books@sokol.co.uk. Est: 1977. Appointment necessary. Spec: Antiquarian; Classical Studies; Early Imprints; Fine & Rare; History of Ideas; Incunabula; Literature; Science - History of. PR: £100–100,000. Mem: ABA; ILAB.

LONDON WEST POSTAL DISTRICTS

Henry Sotheran Limited, ■ 2–5 Sackville Street Piccadilly, London, W1S 3DP. Tel: (020) 7439-6151. Fax: (020) 7434-2019. Web: www.sotherans.co.uk. E-mail: sotherans@sotherans.co.uk. Est: 1761. Shop open: **M:** 09:30–18:00; **T:** 09:30–18:00; **W:** 09:30–18:00; **Th:** 09:30–18:00; **F:** 09:30–18:00; **S:** 10:00–16:00. Very large stock. Spec: Architecture; Art; Bindings; Children's; Churchilliana; Illustrated - General; Literature; Natural History. PR: £20–100,000. CC: AE; D; MC; V. Mem: ABA; PBFA; ILAB. VAT No: GB 689 7172.

Sue Lowell Natural History Books, 101 Cambridge Gardens, London, W10 6JE. Prop: Sue Lowell. Tel: (020) 8960-4382. Web: www.abebooks.com. E-mail: sue4382@aol.com. Est: 1972. Private premises. Internet and Postal. Appointment necessary. Open: **M:** 10.00–17.00; **T:** 10.00–17.00; **W:** 10.00–17.00; **Th:** 10.00–17.00; **F:** 10.00–18.00; **S:** 10.00–13.00; **Su:** 10.00–12.00. Medium stock. Spec: Academic/ Scholarly; Animals and Birds; Art Reference; Artists; Bibliography; Bookbinding; Botany; Egyptology. PR: £10–4,000. CC: MC; V. Corresp: French. Notes: *Callers are asked to telephone first just to make sure we are available. Also, booksearch.*

The Travel Bookshop, 13-15 Blenheim Crescent Notting Hill, London, W11 2EE. Prop: Sarah Anderson. Tel: (020) 7229-5260. Fax: (020) 7243-1552. Web: www.thetravelbookshop.co.uk. E-mail: post@thetravelbookshop.co.uk. Est: 1979. Spec: New Books; Travel - General. PR: £1–200. Notes: *Also, new books on travel.*

Valentine Rare Books, 20 Fitzroy Square, London, W1T 6EJ. Prop: Gaston Chappell. Tel: 020 7387 5454. E-mail: vrb@easynet.co.uk. Est: 1983. Office and/or bookroom. Appointment necessary. Spec: Author - Austen, Jane; - Dickens, Charles; - Hardy, Thomas; - James, Henry; Authors - British; Fiction - 18th Century; Fine & Rare; Literature. PR: £20–10,000. Cata: Fiction (mostly 19th century). Mem: ABA; ILAB. VAT No: GB 504 6399 43.

C.R. White, 22 Denbigh Terrace, London, W11 2QJ. Tel: (020) 7228-7317. Fax: (020) 7598-1248. E-mail: chris.white@breezynet.co.uk. Postal Only. Very small stock. Spec: Travel - Africa; Travel - Polar. Notes: *Travel stock is mainly East Africa.*

Mrs. Teresa White, Flat 4 79 St. Helen's Gardens, London, W10 6LJ. Prop: Mrs. Teresa White. Private premises. Postal Only. Small stock. Spec: Ephemera. PR: £1–100. Notes: *General non-fiction.*

LONDON

WEST CENTRAL POSTAL DISTRICTS

Any Amount of Books, ■ 56 Charing Cross Road, London, WC2H 0QA. Prop: Nigel Burwood. Tel: (020) 7836-3697. Fax: (020) 7240-1769. Web: www.anyamountofbooks.com. E-mail: charingx@ anyamountofbooks.com. Est: 1975. Shop open: **M:** 10:30–21:30; **T:** 10:30–21:30; **W:** 10:29–21:30; **Th:** 10:30–21:30; **F:** 10:30–21:30; **S:** 10:30–21:30; **Su:** 11:30–20:30. Spec: Academic/Scholarly; Antiquarian; Art Reference; General Stock; Collectables; Ephemera. PR: £1–25,000. CC: AE; JCB; MC; PayPal. Cata: Literature. Mem: ABA; PBFA; ILAB. VAT No: GB 662 6656 11. Notes: *Also, books by the yard, i.e. for furnishing, film sets etc. & we offer valuations/appraisals for probate, insurance etc.,*

The Atlantis Bookshop, ■ 49a Museum Street, London, WC1A 1LY. Prop: Bali Beskin & Geraldine Beskin. Tel: (020) 7405-2120. Web: www.theatlantisbookshop.com. E-mail: atlantis@ theatlantisbookshop.com. Est: 1922. Shop open: **M:** 10:30–18:00; **T:** 10:30–18:00; **W:** 10:30–18:00; **Th:** 10:30–18:00; **F:** 10:30–18:00; **S:** 10:30–18:00. Small stock. Spec: Alchemy; Archaeology; Author - Crowley, Aleister; - Spare, Austin Osman; Celtica; Countries Egypt; Cryptozoology, Faith Mysteries. PR: £4–40. CC: AE; E; MC; V; SW. Notes: *Crowley, Spare, Grant, Alchemy, Qabalah,Witchcraft, Druidism, Mystery History, all the Esoteric Sciences. New and Secondhand. Please send your wants lists or phone.*

Josephine Bacon, 197 Kings Cross Road, London, WC1X 9DB. Tel: (020) 7278 9490. Fax: (020) 7278 2447. E-mail: bacon@americanization.com. Private premises. Spec: Cookery/Gastronomy; Judaica; Languages - Foreign.

Bertram Rota Ltd., ■ 31 Long Acre Covent Garden, London, WC2E 9LT. Tel: (020) 7836-0723. Fax: (020) 7497 9058. Web: www.bertramrota.co.uk. E-mail: bertramrota@compuserve.com. Est: 1923. Contactable. Shop open: **M:** 09:30–17:30; **T:** 09:30–17:30; **W:** 09:30–17:30; **Th:** 09:30–17:30; **F:** 09:30– 17:30. Medium stock. Spec: Antiquarian; Autographs; Book Arts; First Editions; Literature; Manuscripts; Modern First Editions; Private Press. CC: E; JCB; MC; V. Mem: ABA; ILAB. VAT No: GB 239 6020 67. Notes: *Also, a booksearch service, valuations.*

Steve Burak, ■ 18 Leigh Street off Judd Street, London, WC1H 9EW. Prop: Steve Burak. Tel: (020) 7388-1153. E-mail: SteveBurakLondon@yahoo.com. Est: 2002. Shop. Telephone First. Open: **M:** 11:00–19:00; **T:** 11:00–19:00; **W:** 11:00–19:00; **Th:** 11:00–19:00; **F:** 11:00–19:00; **S:** 11:00–19:00. Large stock. Spec: Academic/Scholarly; Antiquarian; Ephemera; Prints and Maps. PR: £5–1,000. Corresp: French. Notes: *Also, ephemera artwork and various eclectica.*

Collinge & Clark, ■ The Bookshop 13 Leigh Street, London, WC1H 9EW. Prop: Michael Collinge & Oliver Clark. Tel: 0207 387 7105. Fax: 0207 388 1315. E-mail: collingeandclark@aol.com. Est: 1987. Shop open: **M:** 11:00–18:30; **T:** 11:00–18:30; **W:** 11:00–18:30; **Th:** 11:00–18:30; **F:** 11:00–18:30. Spec: Book Arts; Books about Books; Engraving; Fine Printing; Limited Editions - General; Printing; Private Press; Typography. CC: AE; MC; V. Cata: Private Press & Typography. Corresp: Francais, Deutsch. Mem: PBFA. VAT No: GB 523 1738 64.

Delectus Books, 27 Old Gloucester Street, London, WC1N 3XX. Prop: Michael R. Goss. Tel: (020) 8963-0979. Fax: (020) 8963-0502. Web: www.delectusbooks.co.uk. E-mail: mgdelectus@aol.com. Est: 1987. Private premises. Internet and Postal. Very large stock. Spec: Academic/Scholarly; Adult; Aesthetic Movement; Animals and Birds; Anthropology; Antiques; Art Reference; Astrology. PR: £20–5,000. CC: E; JCB; MC; V; Switch, Solo, Delta. Corresp: French, German, Spanish, Dutch. VAT No: GB 532 3080 82.

David Drummond at Pleasures of Past Times, 11 Cecil Court Charing Cross Road, London, WC2N 4EZ. Prop: David Drummond. Tel: (020) 7836-1142. Fax: (020) 7836-1142. E-mail: drummond@ popt.fsnet.co.uk. Est: 1967. Open: **M:** 11:00–17:45; **S:** 11:00–14:30. Closed for lunch: 02:30–15:30. Spec: Children's; Circus; Illustrated - General; Magic & Conjuring; Performing Arts. PR: £10–500. Notes: *Also, juvenile illustrated.*

Francis Edwards (London) Limit, ■ 13 Great Newport Street Charing Cross Road, London, WC2H 7JA. Tel: (020) 7240 7279. Fax: (020) 7836-5977. Web: www.francisedwards.co.uk. E-mail: sales@femilitary.demon.co.uk. Shop open: **M:** 10:00–19:00; **T:** 10:00–19:00; **W:** 10:00–19:00; **Th:** 10:00–19:00; **F:** 10:00–19:00; **S:** 10:00–19:00. Small stock. Spec: Architecture; Art; Aviation; Bindings; Economics; Folklore; History - General; Law - General. PR: £15–5,000. CC: AE; D; E; JCB; MC; V. Corresp: Spanish. Mem: ABA; PBFA; ILAB. VAT No: GB 594 2720 23.

LONDON WEST CENTRAL POSTAL DISTRICTS

Peter Ellis, Bookseller, ■ 18 Cecil Court, London, WC2N 4HE. Tel: (020) 7836 8880. Fax: (020) 8318-4748. Web: www.peter-ellis.co.uk. E-mail: ellisbooks@lineone.net. Est: 1999. Shop open: **M:** 10:30–19:00; **T:** 10:30–19:00; **W:** 10:30–19:00; **Th:** 10:30–19:00; **F:** 10:30–19:00; **S:** 10:30–17:30. Medium stock. Spec: Academic/Scholarly; Art; Artists; Arts, The; - Betjeman, Sir John; - Brooke, Rupert; -Buchan, John; - Burgess, A. PR: £10–1,000. CC: AE; MC; V. Cata: modern firsts, illustrated, literature. Corresp: French, German. Mem: ABA; ILAB. VAT No: GB 751 8751 12.

Fine Books Oriental Ltd., ■ 38 Museum Street, London, WC1A 1LP. Prop: Jeffrey Somers. Tel: (020) 7242-5288. Fax: (020) 7242-5344. Web: www.finebooks.demon.co.uk. E-mail: oriental@ finebooks.demon.co.uk. Est: 1977. Shop open: **M:** 09:30–18:00; **T:** 09:30–18:00; **W:** 09:30–18:00; **Th:** 09:30–18:00; **F:** 09:30–18:00; **S:** 11:00–18:00. Medium stock. Spec: Aviation; Canals/Inland Waterways; Cartoons; Countries - Asia; Countries - India; Countries - Japan; Psychic; Religion -Oriental. PR: £3–15,000. CC: AE; JCB; MC; V; Switch, Solo. Corresp: Japanese. Mem: PBFA.

Gay's The Word, ■ 66 Marchmont Street, London, WC1N 1AB. Prop: Noncyp Ltd. Tel: (020) 7278-7654. Web: www.gaystheword.co.uk. E-mail: sales@gaystheword.co.uk. Est: 1979. Shop open: **M:** 10:00–18:30; **T:** 10:00–18:30; **W:** 10:00–18:30; **Th:** 10:00–18:30; **F:** 10:00–18:30; **S:** 10:00–18:30; **Su:** 14:00–18:30. Spec: Homosexuality & Lesbianism; New Books. PR: £1–60. CC: AE; D; E; JCB; MC; V; Switch. Notes: *Also, new books.*

Gekoski Booksellers, ■ Pied Bull Yard 15a Bloomsbury Square, London, WC1A 2LP. Prop: R.A. Gekoski & P.A. Grogan. Tel: (020) 7404-6676. Fax: (020) 7404-6595. Web: www.gekoski.com. E-mail: rick@gekoski.com. Est: 1982. Shop open: **M:** 10:00–17:30; **T:** 10:00–17:30; **W:** 10:00–17:30; **Th:** 10:00–17:30; **F:** 10:00–17:30. Small stock. Spec: First Editions; Letters; Manuscripts. PR: £100–1,000. CC: MC; V. Mem: ABA. VAT No: GB 418 5464 40.

Grosvenor Prints, 19 Shelton Street, London, WC2H 9JN. Prop: Nigel Talbot. Tel: 020 7836 1979. Fax: 020 7379 6695. Web: www.grosvenorprints.com. E-mail: grosvenorprints@btinternet.com. Est: 1979. Shop and/or gallery. Open: **M:** 10:00–18:00; **T:** 10:00–18:00; **W:** 10:00–18:00; **Th:** 10:00–18:00; **F:** 10:00–18:00; **S:** 11:00–16:00. Spec: Animals and Birds; Art Reference; Fine Art; Painting; Printing. CC: AE; MC; V; Maestro/Switch. Mem: ABA; BA; ILAB. VAT No: GB 217 6907 49.

Jarndyce Antiquarian Bookselle, 46 Great Russell Street (opp. British Museum), London, WC1B 3PA. Prop: Brian Lake & Janet Nassau. Tel: (020) 7631-4220. Fax: (020) 7631-1882. Web: www.jarndyce.co.uk. E-mail: books@jarndyce.co.uk. Est: 1969. Shop and/or showroom. Internet and Postal. Open: **M:** 10:30–17:30; **T:** 10:30–17:30; **W:** 10:30–17:30; **Th:** 10:30–17:30; **F:** 10:30–17:30. Large stock. Spec: Antiquarian; Author - Austen, Jane; - Byron, Lord; - Dickens, Charles; Economics; Education & School; First Editions; Literature. PR: £5–5,000. CC: AE; MC; V. Corresp: French. Mem: ABA; PBFA; ILAB; BBA. VAT No: GB 524 0890 57. Notes: *Valuations and book search within our specialist areas.*

Judd Books, ■ 82 Marchmont Street, London, WC1N 1AG. Prop: Nigel Kemp & A. Donaldson. Tel: (020) 7387-5333. E-mail: hb@juddbooks.demon.co.uk. Est: 1995. Shop open: **M:** 11:00–19:00; **T:** 11:00–19:00; **W:** 11:00–19:00; **Th:** 11:00–19:00; **F:** 11:00–19:00; **S:** 11:00–19:00; **Su:** 12.00–18:00. Large stock. Spec: Architecture; Art; Cinema/Film; Drama; Feminism; History - General; Homosexuality & Lesbianism; Interior Design. PR: £1–100. CC: AE; E; MC; V. Corresp: French, Spanish.

The Maghreb Bookshop, ■ 45 Burton Street, London, WC1H 9AL. Prop: Mohamed Ben Madani. Tel: (020) 7388-1840. Fax: (020) 7388-1840. Web: www.maghreview.com. E-mail: maghreb@ maghrebreview.com. Est: 1981. Shop. Appointment necessary. Open: **M:** 09:00–18:00; **T:** 09:00–18:00; **W:** 08:00–18:00; **Th:** 09:00–18:00; **F:** 09:00–18:00; **S:** 09:00–18:00. Spec: Academic/Scholarly; Anthropology; Archaeology; Architecture; Authors - Women; Colonial; Countries - Middle East, The; Countries - North Africa. Cata: Maghreb, Middle East, Africa and Islam. Corresp: Arabic, French. VAT No: GB 735 8794 81.

Marchpane, ■ 16 Cecil Court Charing Cross Road, London, WC2N 4HE. Prop: Kenneth R. Fuller. Tel: (020) 7836-8661. Fax: (020) 7497-0567. Web: www.marchpane.com. E-mail: K_Fuller@btclick.com. Est: 1989. Shop open: **M:** 11:00–18:00; **T:** 11:00–18:00; **W:** 11:00–18:00; **Th:** 11:00–18:00; **F:** 11:00–18:00; **S:** 11:00–18:00. Spec: Author - Carroll, Lewis; Children's; Illustrated - General; Punk Fanzines; War - WWII Home Front UK (1939-45). PR: £1–2,000. CC: AE; E; JCB; MC; V; Debit. Mem: ABA; PBFA; ILAB.

Tim Bryars Ltd, ■ 8 Cecil Court, London, WC2N 4HE. Prop: Tim Bryars. Tel: (020) 7836-1901. Fax: (020) 7836-1910. Web: www.timbryars.co.uk. E-mail: tim@timbryars.co.uk. Est: 2004. Shop open: **M:** 11:00–18:00; **T:** 11:00–18:00; **W:** 11:00–18:00; **Th:** 11:00–18:00; **F:** 11:00–18:00; **S:** 12:00–17:00. Very large stock. Spec: Antiquarian; Atlases; Cartography; Classical Studies; Early Imprints; Fine & Rare; Natural History; Topography - General. PR: £10–30,000. CC: MC; V. Mem: ABA; ILAB; IAMA. VAT No: GB 839 6884 58.

Pholiota Books, 197 Kings Cross Road, London, WC1X 9DB. Prop: Josephine Bacon. Tel: (020) 7278-9490. Fax: (020) 7278-2447. Web: www.pholiota.cc. E-mail: bacon@pholiota.cc. Est: 1996. Office and/or bookroom. Internet and Postal. Telephone First. Open: **M:** 09:00–17.30; **T:** 09:00–17:00; **W:** 09:00–17:00; **Th:** 09:00–17:00; **F:** 09:00–17:00; **S:** 09:00–17:00; **Su:** 09:00–17:00. Medium stock. Spec: Academic/Scholarly; Botany; Cookery/Gastronomy; Countries - Europe; Countries - Israel; Food & Drink; Fungi; Languages - Foreign. PR: £1–60. Corresp: French, Hebrew, Russian, German, Italian, Spanish, Portuguese. Mem: ATA, ITI. VAT No: GB 778 0611 12. Notes: *Translations to and from any language.*

Photo Books International, ■ 99 Judd Street, London, WC1H 9NE. Prop: Bill Herbert & Jasper Howard. Tel: (020) 7813-7363. Web: www.pbi-books.com. E-mail: pbi@britishlibrary.net. Est: 1998. Shop open: **M:** ; **T:** ; **W:** 11:00–18:00; **Th:** 11:00–18:00; **F:** 11:00–18:00; **S:** 11:00–18:00. Medium stock. Spec: Fashion & Costume; Photography. PR: £5–200. CC: AE; MC; V. Notes: *With more than 5,000 different photography books in stock at any time we are able to offer a wide selection of new & used books from around the world.*

Henry Pordes Books Ltd., ■ 58-60 Charing Cross Road, London, WC2H 0BB. Prop: Gino Della-Ragione. Tel: (020) 7836 9031. Fax: (020) 7240 4232. Web: www.henrypordesbooks.com. E-mail: info@henrypordesbooks.com. Est: 1980. Shop open: **M:** 10:00–19:00; **T:** 10:00–19:00; **W:** 10:00–19:00; **Th:** 10:00–19:00; **F:** 10:00 19:00; **S:** 10:00 23:00; **Su:** 13:00–18:00. Spec: Academic/Scholarly, Advertising; Aeronautics; Africana; Antiques; Archaeology; Architecture; Art. PR: £1–2,000. CC: AE; MC; V. Mem: PBFA.

Arthur Probsthain, ■ 41 Great Russell Street, London, WC1B 3PE. Prop: Arthur Probsthain. Tel: (020) 7636-1096. Fax: (020) 7636-1096. E-mail: ap@oriental-african-books.com. Est: 1902. Shop open: **M:** 09:30–17:30; **T:** 09:30–17:30; **W:** 09:30–17:30; **Th:** 09:30–17:30; **F:** 09:30–17:30; **S:** 11:00–16:00. Spec: Countries - Africa; Oriental. CC: AE; D; E; JCB; MC; V. Cata: on specialised subjects.

Quinto of Charing Cross Road, ■ 48a Charing Cross Road, London, WC2H 0BB. Prop: Hay Cinema Bookshop Ltd. Tel: (0207) 379 7669. Fax: (0207) 836-5977. Web: www.haycinemabookshop.co.uk. E-mail: sales@femilitary.demon.co.uk. Est: 1905. Shop open: **M:** 09:00–21:00; **T:** 09:00–21:00; **W:** 09:00–21:00; **Th:** 09:00–21:00; **F:** 09:00–21:00; **S:** 09:00–21:00; **Su:** 12:00–08:00. Very large stock. Spec: Art; Fiction - General; History - General; Literature; Medicine; Military History; Music - General; Philosophy. PR: £1–100. CC: AE; D; E; JCB; MC; V. Corresp: Spanish. VAT No: GB 594 2720 23.

Quinto of Great Russell Street, ■ 63 Great Russell Street, London, WC1B 3BF. Tel: (0207) 430 2535. Fax: (0207) 430 2566. Web: www.haycinemabookshop.co.uk. E-mail: sales@quintogrs.co.uk. Est: 2002. Shop open: **M:** 10:00–19:00; **T:** 10:00–19:00; **W:** 10:00–19:00; **Th:** 10:00–19:00; **F:** 10:00–19:00; **S:** 10:00–19:00; **Su:** 10:00–19:00. Very large stock. Spec: Art; Fiction - General; History - General; Literature; Medicine; Military; Music - General; Natural History. PR: £5–1,000. CC: AE; D; E; JCB; MC; V. Corresp: Spanish. VAT No: GB 594 2720 23.

Omega Bookshop, 30 Charing Cross Road, London, WC2H 0DB. Prop: Angus O'Neill. Tel: (020) 7836-3336. Web: www.omegabookshop.com. E-mail: angus@omegabookshop.com. Est: 1984. Mail Order Only. Internet and Postal. Appointment necessary. Spec: Antiques; Applied Art; Architecture; Art; Illustrated - General; Literature; Modern First Editions. CC: E; MC; V. Mem: ABA; ILAB. Notes: *Valuations, consultancy, logistics.*

Roe and Moore, ■ 29 Museum Street, London, WC1A 1LH. Prop: Anthony and Deana Roe. Tel: (020) 7636 4787. E-mail: roeandmoore@fsbdial.co.uk. Est: 1992. Shop open: **M:** 10:30–18:00; **T:** 10:30–18:00; **W:** 10:30–18:00; **Th:** 10:30–18:00; **F:** 10:30–18:00; **S:** 10:30–18:00. Medium stock. Spec: Art; Art Reference; Artists; Children's; Design; Fine Art; Illustrated - General; Juvenile. PR: £1–3,000. CC: MC; V.

Spink, Southampton Row, London, WC1B 4ET. Prop: Olivier Stocker. Tel: 020 7563 4000. Fax: 020 7563 4066. Web: www.spink.com. E-mail: info@spink.com. Est: 1666. Shop and/or gallery open: **M:** 09:00–17:30; **T:** 09:00–17:30; **W:** 09:00–17:30; **Th:** 09:00–17:30; **F:** 09:00–17:30. Spec: Collectables; Collecting; Military; Numismatics. CC: AE; MC; V. Cata: Numismatics. Corresp: Any. Mem: BNTA. VAT No: GB 791 6271 08. Notes: *Specialists in books relating to coins, medals, tokens, banknotes, commemorative medals.*

Tindley & Chapman, ■ 4 Cecil Court, London, WC2N 4HE. Prop: James Tindley, Ron Chapman. Tel: (0207) 240-2161. Fax: (0207) 379-1062. Est: 1975. Shop open: **M:** 10:00–17:30; **T:** 10:00–17:30; **W:** 10:00–17:30; **Th:** 10:00–17:30; **F:** 10:00–17:30; **S:** 11:00–17:00. Medium stock. Spec: Fiction - General; Fiction - Crime, Detective, Spy, Thrillers; Fiction - Women; First Editions; Literature; Poetry. PR: £10–5,000. CC: MC; V. Mem: PBFA. Notes: *Ron Chapman, London SW10 9LW. (q.v.)*

LONDON WEST CENTRAL POSTAL DISTRICTS

Travis & Emery Music Bookshop, ■ 17 Cecil Court off Charing Cross Road, London, WC2N 4EZ. Tel: (020) 7240-2129. Fax: (020) 7497-0790. Web: www.travis-and-emery.com. E-mail: shepenq@travis-and-emery.com. Est: 1960. Shop open: **M:** 10:15–18:45; **T:** 10:15–18:45; **W:** 10:15–18:45; **Th:** 10:15–18:45; **F:** 10:15–18:45; **S:** 10:15–18:45; **Su:** 11:30–17:30; Closed for lunch: 14:00–14:45. Spec: Drama; Hymnology; Music - General; Music - Chart Histories & Research; Music - Classical; Music - Composers; Music - Country & Western; Music - Folk & Irish Folk. CC: AE; MC; V. Cata: Music, Books on music. Mem: ABA; PBFA; ILAB. VAT No: GB 239 5258 39. Notes: *Also, secondhand sheet music & new music books, plus prints.*

Treadwell's Books, ■ 34 Tavistock Street, Covent Garden, London, WC2E 7PB. Prop: Christina Harrington. Tel: 0207 240 8906. Web: www.treadwells-london.com. E-mail: info@treadwells-london.com. Est: 2003. Shop open: **M:** 12:00–19:00; **T:** 12:00–19:00; **W:** 12:00–19:00; **Th:** 12:00–19:00; **F:** 12:00–19:00; **S:** 12:00–19:00; **Su:** 12:00–19:00. Spec: History of Civilisation; History of Ideas; Mythology; Occult; Travel - General. CC: AE; MC; V; Switch. Cata: esoterica, cultural history. VAT No: GB 810 3399 51.

Ulysses, ■ 40 Museum Street, London, WC1A 1LU. Prop: Peter Jolliffe. Tel: (020) 7831-1600. E-mail: ulyssesbooks@fsbdial.co.uk. Est: 1990. Shop open: **M:** 10:30–18:00; **T:** 10:30–18:00; **W:** 10:30–18:00; **Th:** 12:00–18:00; **F:** 10:30–18:00; **S:** 12:00–18:00. Large stock. Spec: Illustrated - General; Modern First Editions. PR: £5–1,000. CC: AE; MC; V. Cata: Modern First Editions. Mem: PBFA.

Unsworth's Antiquarian Books, ■ at Foyles 113-119 Charing Cross Road, London, WC2H 0EB. Prop: Charlie Unsworth. Tel: 020 7494 9820. Fax: 020 7494 9830. Web: www.unsworths.com. E-mail: books@unsworths.com. Est: 1986. Shop open: **M:** 09:30–21:00; **T:** 09:30–21:00; **W:** 09:30–21:00; **Th:** 09:30–21:00; **F:** 09:30–21:00; **S:** 09:30–21:00; **Su:** 12:00–18:00. Spec: Academic/Scholarly; Antiquarian; Bibliography; Books about Books; Byzantium; Classical Studies; Early Imprints; Fine & Rare. CC: AE; D; E; JCB; MC; V. Corresp: Latin, French. Mem: ABA; ILAB. VAT No: GB 480 1145 75. Notes: *See also under London, NW. (q.v.)*

Waterstone's, ■ 82 Gower Street, London, WC1E 6EQ. Prop: HMV Media Group. Tel: (020) 7636-1577. Fax: (020) 7580-7680. Web: www.waterstones.com/. E-mail: secondhand@gowerst .waterstones.co.uk. Est: 1936. Shop open: **M:** 09:30–20:00; **T:** 10:00–20:00; **W:** 09:30–20:00; **Th:** 09:30–20:00; **F:** 09:30–20:00; **S:** 09:30–19:00; **Su:** 12:00–18:00. Medium stock. Spec: Academic/ Scholarly. CC: AE; D; JCB; MC; V. Notes: *Dept. also sells academic remainders and is situated within large, well-known bookshop.*

Watkins Books Ltd., ■ 19–21 Cecil Court off Charing Cross Road, London, WC2N 4EZ. Tel: (020) 7836-2182. Fax: (020) 7836-6700. Web: www.watkinsbooks.com. E-mail: service@watkinsbooks.com. Est: 1894. Shop open: **M:** 11:00–19:00; **T:** 11:00–19:00; **W:** 11:00–19:00; **Th:** 11:00–19:00; **F:** 11:00–19:00; **S:** 11:00–19:00. Large stock. Spec: Aboriginal; Academic/Scholarly; Acupuncture; African-American Studies; Alchemy; Almanacs; Alternative Medicine; American Indians. PR: £50–500. CC: MC; V; Switch.

Wildy & Sons Ltd, ■ Lincoln's Inn Archway Carey Street, London, WC2A 2JD. Prop: John Sinkins. Tel: 02072425778. Fax: 02074300897. Web: www.wildy.co.uk. E-mail: info@wildy.co.uk. Est: 1830. Shop open: **M:** 09:00–18:00; **T:** 09:00–18:00; **W:** 09:00–18:00; **Th:** 09:00–18:00; **F:** 09:00–18:00. Spec: Law - General; Law - Constitutional. CC: AE; D; MC; V. Cata: Law. VAT No: GB 233 5262 84. Notes: *Exclusively sell law books and sets, new and secondhand (including antiquarian).*

Nigel Williams Rare Books, ■ 25 Cecil Court Charing Cross Road, London, WC2N 4EZ. Tel: (020) 7836-7757. Fax: (020) 7379-3918. Web. www.nigelwilliams.com. E-mail: sales@nigelwilliams.com. Est: 1989. Shop open: **M:** 10:00–18:00; **T:** 10:00–18:00; **W:** 10:00–18:00; **Th:** 10:00–18:00; **F:** 10:00–18:00; **S:** 10:00–18:00. Large stock. Spec: Author - Christie, Agatha; - Fleming, Ian; - Greene, Graham; - Joyce, James; - Wodehouse, P.G.; Fables; Fiction - General; Fiction - Historical. PR: £5–10,000. CC: AE; D; E; JCB; MC; V. Cata: First editions, P.G. Wodehouse. Mem: ABA; PBFA; ILAB. VAT No: GB 574 3776 05.

LONDON GREATER LONDON OUTER

CARSHALTON

Croydon Bookshop, ■ 304 Carshalton Road, Carshalton, SM5 3QB. Prop: Mrs. P.F. Reding & P.J. Rogers. Tel: (020) 8643-6857. Est: 1954. Shop open: **M:** ; **T:** 10:30–17:30; **W:** 10:30–17:30; **Th:** 10:30–17:30; **F:** 10:30–17:30; **S:** 10:30–17:30. Medium stock. PR: £2–100. Corresp: French, German, Spanish.

Crosby Nethercott Books, 16 Kings Avenue, Carshalton, Surrey, SM5 4NX. Prop: (*) D.W. Beer. Tel: (020) 8643 4124. E-mail: crosbybooks@cwcom.net. Est: 1991. Private premises. Internet and Postal. Appointment necessary. Small stock. Spec: Author - Rolt, L.T.C.; Canals/Inland Waterways; Company History; History - Industrial; Railways; Transport. PR: £5–100. Corresp: French, German. Notes: *Also, a booksearch service.*

CROYDON

Steve Archer, 11 Bedford Place, Croydon, Surrey, CR0 2BS. Prop: (*). Tel: (020) 8686 3736. Web: www.ukbookworld.com/members/stevearcher. E-mail: stevearcher2000@yahoo.co.uk. Est: 2000. Private premises. Internet and Postal. Small stock. Spec: Autobiography; Biography; Canals/Inland Waterways; Literary Travel; Literature; Modern First Editions; Booksearch. PR: £2–200. CC: PayPal.

EASTCOTE

The Eastcote Bookshop, ■ 156/160 Field End Road, Eastcote, Middlesex, HA5 1RH. Prop: Eileen & David May. Tel: (020) 8866-9888. Fax: (020) 8905-9387. Est: 1993. Shop open: **T:** 12:00–16:00; **Th:** 12:00–16:00; **F:** 12:00–16:00; **S:** 10:00–17:00. Very large stock. Spec: Alpinism/Mountaineering; American Indians; Annuals; Antiques; Art; Canals/Inland Waterways; Children's; Cinema/Film. PR: £2–500. CC: MC; V. Mem: **PBFA.** Notes: *Occasional fairs.*

EDGWARE

Two Jays Bookshop, ■ 119 High Street, Edgware, HA8 7DB. Prop: Joyce and Mark Matthews. Tel: (020) 8952-1349. Est: 1977. Shop open: **T:** 09:00–17:00; **W:** 09:00–17:00; **Th:** 09:00–17:00; **F:** 09:00–17:00; **S:** 09:00–17:00. Large stock. PR: £2–100.

ENFIELD

Terence J. McGee, 20 Slades Close, Enfield, Middlesex, EN2 7EB. Prop: T.J. & J.I. McGee. Tel: (020) 8366-5727. E-mail: tmcgee@globalnet.co.uk. Est: 1972. Private premises. Appointment necessary. Open: **S:** 09:00–19:00; **Su:** 09:00–19:00. Small stock. Spec: Author - Betjeman, Sir John; Cinema/Film; Comedy; Comics; Counterculture; Countries - Italy; Education & School; Inventors & Inventions. PR: £1–500. Corresp: French, German, Italian, Spanish. Mem: Brit. Ephemera Society. Notes: *Also, sound and video recordings & record tapes (inc. 16s, 33s, 45s, 78s, CDs and DVDs).*

Felicity J. Warnes, ■ 82 Merryhills Drive, Enfield, Middlesex, EN2 7PD. Prop: F. J. Warnes. Tel: (020) 8367-1661. Fax: (020) 8372-1035. E-mail: felicity@fjwarnes.u-net.com. Est: 1978. Shop. Appointment necessary. Large stock. Spec: Embroidery; Fashion & Costume; Jewellery; Knitting; Lace; Military; Social History; Textiles. PR: £5–200. CC: MC; V. Mem: **PBFA;** ES.

GREENFORD

Jack Ben–Nathan, 22 Teignmouth Gardens Perivale, Greenford, UB6 8BX. Prop: (*). Tel: (020) 8997-6574. E-mail: jack.ben-nathan@the-sun.co.uk. Est: 1980. Private premises. Appointment necessary. Very small stock. Spec: Sport - Billiards/Snooker/Pool; Booksearch. PR: £3–300. Cata: 8.

Books B.C., 58 Elton Avenue, Greenford, Middlesex, UB6 0PP. Prop: Martin McCrory. Tel: (020) 8864-0580. Est: 1987. Private premises. Postal Only. Appointment necessary. Very small stock. Spec: Archaeology; Egyptology; Fiction - Fantasy, Horror; Fiction - Science Fiction; History - Ancient. PR: £1–500.

HAMPTON HILL

Bates Books, 95 High Street, Hampton Hill, Middlesex, TW12 1NH. Prop: Garry and Jackie Bates. Tel: (020) 8941-6782. E-mail: gbates@dsl.pipex.com. Est: 2002. Private premises. Postal Only. Telephone First. Small stock. Spec: Books about Books; Children's; Children's - Illustrated; Comic Books & Annuals; First Editions; Illustrated - General; Linguistics. PR: £2–30.

HAMPTON

R. W. Clements, 114 High Street, Hampton, Middlesex, TW12 2ST. Prop: R. W. Clements. Tel: (020) 8979-3069. Est: 1992. Private premises. Appointment necessary. Large stock. Spec: Archaeology; Art; Autobiography; Biography; Children's; Drama; Fiction - General; History - General. PR: £5–1,000. Notes: *All speciality subjects shown relate to Ireland. Also, ephemera and prints related to Ireland.*

R. S. & P. A. Scowen, 9 Birchwood Grove, Hampton, TW12 3DU. Prop: Roger Scowen. Tel: +44 (0) 20 8979 7429. E-mail: patscowen@waitrose.com. Est: 1987. Private premises. Internet and Postal. Appointment necessary. Open: **M:** 09:00–17:30; **T:** 09:00–17:30; **W:** 09:00–17:30; **Th:** 09:00–17:30; **F:** 09:00–17:30; **S:** 09:00–17:30; **Su:** 09:00–17:30; Closed for lunch: 13:00–14:00. Spec: Bridge; Chess; Games; Sport - Billiards/Snooker/Pool. Notes: *We specialise in indoor games of skill, for example: chess, bridge, draughts, checkers, snooker, billiards.*

ILFORD

Bloomsbury Bookshop, 41 Eton Road, Ilford, IG1 2UD. Prop: Mike Thompson. Tel: 0208-262-5729. E-mail: Dullbooks@AOL.com. Est: 1989. Private premises. Postal Only. Telephone First. Open: **M:** 09:00–17:30; **T:** 09:00–17:30; **W:** 09:00–17:30; **Th:** 09:00–17:30; **F:** 09:00–17:30. Spec: Academic/ Scholarly; Africana; Economics; History - Ancient; History - European; History - Irish; History - Labour/ Radical Movements; History - Middle Ages. CC: JCB; MC; V. Cata: history. Corresp: French.

Porcupine Books, 37 Coventry Road, Ilford, Essex, IG1 4QR. Prop: (*) Brian Ameringen. Tel: 020 8554-3799. Web: www.porcupine.demon.co.uk. E-mail: brian@porcupine.demon.co.uk. Est: 1998. Private premises. Internet and Postal. Appointment necessary. Open: **M:** 08:00–21:00; **T:** 08:00–21:00; **W:** 18:00–21:00; **Th:** 18:00–21:00; **F:** 20:00–21:00; **S:** 18:00–21:00; **Su:** 08:00–21:00. Medium stock. Spec: Children's; Fiction - Crime, Detective, Spy, Thrillers; Fiction - Fantasy, Horror; Fiction - Science Fiction; Fiction - Supernatural; Fiction - Young Adult Mystery & Adventure Series. PR: £1–2,500. CC: MC; V. Cata: Science Fiction, Fantasy, Horror, Young Adult.

ISLEWORTH

Chaters Motoring Booksellers, ■ 8 South Street, Isleworth, Middlesex, TW7 7DH. Prop: C. Stroud. Tel: (020) 8568-9750. Fax: (020) 8569-8273. Web: www.chaters.co.uk. E-mail: books@chaters.co.uk. Est: 1957. Shop open: **M:** 09:00–17:30; **T:** 09:00–17:30; **W:** 09:00–17:30; **Th:** 09:00–17:30; **F:** 09:00–17:30; **S:** 10:00–17:00. Spec: Motorbikes / motorcycles; Motoring; New Books; Booksearch. PR: £1–500. CC: JCB; MC; V; plus Debit cards. Mem: BA; Notes: *Also, new books in specialities & a booksearch service.*

Patrick Tuft, 68 Worple Road, London, TW7 7HU. Prop: Patrick Tuft. Tel: (withheld). Private premises. Postal Only. Very small stock. Spec: Bibles; Bibliography; History - General; Religion - Christian; Vatican and Papal History, The.

KENLEY

David & Lynn Smith, The Hermitage 21 Uplands Road, Kenley, Surrey, CR8 5EE. Prop: David & Lynn Smith. Tel: (020) 8660-9908. E-mail: smithbookskenley@tiscali.co.uk. Est: 1980. Storeroom. Appointment necessary. Small stock. Spec: Biology - General; Medicine; Medicine - History of; Pharmacy/Pharmacology; Science - General; Science - History of; Scientific Instruments. PR: £10–500. CC: JCB; MC; V. Cata: Medicine and its history. Mem: PBFA.

KEW

Criterion Books, 6 Nylands Avenue, Kew, Richmond, TW9 4HH. Prop: (*) Terence Crimmings. Tel: (020) 8876-1773. Fax: (020) 8876-1773. E-mail: terry.crimmings@tinyworld.co.uk. Est: 1992. Private premises. Postal Only. Contactable. Very small stock. Spec: Art Reference; - Ardizzone, Edward; - Barrie, J.M.; - Bloomsbury Group, The; - Bowles, Paul; - Durrell, Lawrence; - Forester, C.S.; - Isherwood, Christopher. PR: £10–350.

KINGSTON

Modern First Editions, 32 Woodlands Avenue New Malden, Surrey, Kingston, KT3 3UQ. Prop: (*) Nicholas & Helen Burrows. Tel: (020) 8942-2677. E-mail: nick@burrbook.demon.co.uk. Est: 1993. Private premises. Internet and Postal. Appointment necessary. Small stock. Spec: Countries - Melanesia; Countries - Mexico; Fiction - General; Fiction - Fantasy, Horror; Fiction - Science Fiction; First Editions; Limited Editions - General; Modern First Editions. PR: £5–500. CC: AE; MC; V. Notes: *Email lists of new signed First editions provided monthly upon request to nick@ burrbook.demon.co.uk*

MORDEN

A. Burton–Garbett, 35 The Green, Morden, Surrey, SM4 4HJ. Tel: (020) 8540-2367. Fax: (020) 8540-4594. Est: 1959. Private premises. Appointment necessary. Small stock. Spec: Countries - Caribbean, The; Countries - Central America; Countries - Mexico; Countries - South America. PR: £5–1,000.

NEW BARNET

Chandos Books, 111 Park Road, New Barnet, Hertfordshire, EN4 9QR. Prop: Stan Brett. Tel: (020) 8449-9457. E-mail: stanbrett@f2s.com. Est: 1970. Private premises. Internet and Postal. Appointment necessary. Small stock. Spec: Bibliography; Humanities. PR. £10–300. Mem: PBFA.

OSTERLEY

Osterley Bookshop, ■ 168a Thornbury Road, Osterley, Middlesex, TW7 4QE. Prop: Pennie Smith & Tony Vesely. Tel: (020) 8560-6206. E-mail: avesely@lineone.net. Est: 1973. Shop. Internet and Postal open: **M:** 09:30–17:30; **T:** 09:30–17:30; **W:** 09:30–17:30; **Th:** 09:30–17:30; **F:** 09:30–17:30; **S:** 09:30–17:30; **Su:** 09:30–17:30. Medium stock. PR: £3–150. CC: AE; JCB; MC; V; Maestro. Notes: *Large general stock.*

RUISLIP MANOR

Dr Bernard Dixon and Kath Adams, 130 Cornwall Rd, Ruislip Manor, HA4 6AW. Prop: Dr Bernard Dixon and Kath Adams. Tel: 01895 632390. Fax: 01895 678645. E-mail: kathadams@ blueyonder.co.uk. Est: 2000. Private premises. Postal Only. Telephone First. Open: **M:** 09:00–17:30; **T:** 09:00–17:30; **W:** 09:00–17:30; **Th:** 09:00–17:30; **F:** 09:00–17:30; **S:** 09:00–17:30; **Su:** 09:00–17:30; Closed for lunch: 13:00–14:00 Spec: Bacteriology; Biochemistry; Biology - General, Botany; Brewing; Chemistry; Drugs; Ecology. Cata: medicine, science, biology, biography, history. Notes: *We deal in all biomedical sciences, especially microbiology and infectious diseases. As well as offering catalogues at least annually, we retain details of customers' specific wants. We are also interested in buying books.*

SUNBURY ON THAMES

Cecilia Marsden, 98 Manor Lane, Sunbury on Thames, TW16 6JB. Prop: Cecilia Marsden. Tel: 01932 785705. Fax: 01932 785705. E-mail: mairob@tiscali.co.uk. Est: 1993. Private premises. Postal Only. Appointment necessary. Open: **M:** 09:00–17:30; **T:** 09:00–17:30; **W:** 09:00–17:30; **Th:** 09:00–17:30; **F:** 09:00–17:30; **S:** 09:00–17:30; **Su:** 09:00–17:30; Closed for lunch: 13:00–14:00. Spec: Fiction - Crime, Detective, Spy, Thrillers; Fiction - Science Fiction; Irish Interest.

SUTTON

Mike Park, 351 Sutton Common Road, Sutton, Surrey, SM3 9HZ. Prop: Mike Park & William To. Tel: (020) 8641-7796. Fax: (020) 8641-3330. E-mail: mikeparkbooks@aol.com. Est: 1974. Private premises. Appointment necessary. Open: **M:** 09:00–17:00; **T:** 09:00–17:00; **W:** 09:00–17:00; **Th:** 09:00–17:00; **F:** 09:00–17:00. Small stock. Spec: Agriculture; Bamboo; Botany; Countries - British North Borneo; Countries - Indonesia; Ethnobotany; Flower Arranging; Forestry. PR: £1–1,000. CC: E; MC; V. Cata: Gardening. Botany. Natural History. Mem: PBFA. Notes: *Search service available for books within our speciality. Catalogues are available by email as well as by post.*

TEDDINGTON

Chris Hollingshead Horticulture, 10 Linden Grove, Teddington, TW11 8LT. Tel: (0208) 977 6051. E-mail: c.hollingshead@btinternet.com. Est: 1995. Private premises. Small stock. Spec: Agriculture; Botany; Gardening - General; Herbalism; Horticulture; Landscape; Mycology; Natural History. PR: £5–3,000. CC: MC; V. Notes: – *& garden history, design landscape and architecture; farming, botanical academic & antiquarian.*

GREATER LONDON OUTER

TWICKENHAM

Books on Spain, P.O. Box 207, Twickenham, TW2 5BQ. Prop: (*) Keith Harris. Tel: (020) 8898-7789. Fax: (020) 8898-7789 (24 hours). E-mail: booksonspainplus@aol.com. Est: 1993. Private premises. Internet and Postal. Contactable. Large stock. Spec: Antiquarian; Bull Fighting; Countries - Andorra; Countries - Central America; Countries - Cuba; Countries - Gibraltar; Countries - Latin America; Countries - Mexico. PR: £5–1,000. CC: AE; JCB; MC; V; Switch. Corresp: Spanish, Portuguese, French. Mem: PBFA. VAT No: GB 720 5623 63.

Anthony C. Hall, Antiquarian Bookseller, ■ 30 Staines Road, Twickenham, TW2 5AH. Prop: Anthony C. Hall. Tel: (020) 8898-2638. Fax: (020) 8893-8855. Web: www.hallbooks.co.uk. E-mail: ahall@hallbooks.co.uk. Est: 1966. Shop open: **M:** 10:00–17:00; **Th:** 10:00–17:00; **F:** 10:00–17:00. Closed for lunch: 12:30–01:30. Small stock. Spec: Countries - Africa; Countries - Asia; Countries - East Europe; Countries - Middle East, The; Countries - Russia; History - Industrial; Travel - Africa; Travel - Asia. PR: £10–1,000. CC: MC; V. Cata: Russian & East European Studies. Corresp: French, German, Russian, Spanish. Mem: ABA; PBFA. VAT No: GB 224 2699 61. Notes: *Large specialist stock on Russian & East European Studies (including scarce books in Russian) the Middle East, Africa, Asia, Business & Industrial History, seen by appointment.*

John Ives Bookseller, 5 Normanhurst Drive St. Margarets, Twickenham, TW1 1NA. Prop: (*)John Ives. Tel: (020) 8892-6265. Fax: (020) 8744-3944. Web: www.ukbookworld.com/members/johnives. E-mail: jives@btconnect.com. Est: 1978. Private premises. Internet and Postal. Appointment necessary. Small stock. Spec: Antiques; Architecture; Art Reference; Ceramics; Collecting; Fashion & Costume; Jewellery; Needlework. PR: £5–500. CC: MC; V. Mem: PBFA. VAT No: GB 409 8526 30.

Marble Hill Books, 35 Napoleon Road, St Margarets Twickenham, TW1 3EW. Prop: Philip Dawson. Tel: 020 8892 0511. Fax: n/a. Web: www.marblehillbooks.com. E-mail: info@marblehillbooks.com. Est: 1999. Mail Order Only. Internet and Postal. Telephone First. Spec: American Indians; Antiquarian; Architecture; Author - 20th Century; Countries - Africa; Countries - Antarctic, The; Countries - Far East, The; Countries - Latin America. CC: AE; JCB; MC; V; Maestro/Switch. Cata: Modern First Editions; Antiquarian; General. Corresp: French; German. Mem: Title Page Book Fairs.

John Prescott - The Bookseller, ■ Paul Hoffmann House 57 York Street, Twickenham, TW1 3LP. Prop: John Prescott. Tel: (020) 8940-3066. E-mail: johnprescott@avdv.demon.co.uk. Est: 1998. Shop open: **F:** 10:30–18:00; **S:** 10:30–18:00. Medium stock. Spec: Antiques; Archaeology; Architecture; Art; Art History; Cinema/Film; Countries - South America; Fables. PR: £1–100. Corresp: German, French, Spanish, Dutch. Notes: *Shop sales only.*

Stephen Miller, 19 Clifden Road, Twickenham, Middlesex, TW1 4LU. Tel: (020) 8892-0331. Est: 1981. Private premises. Very small stock. Spec: Antiquarian. PR: £1–500. Corresp: French.

WELLING

Falconwood Transport & Military Bookshop, ■ 5 Falconwood Parade The Green, Welling, DA16 2PL. Prop: (*) A.M. Doran. Tel: (020) 8303-8291. Fax: (020) 8303-8291. E-mail: falconw@globalnet.co.uk. Est: 1985. Shop open: **Th:** 09:30–17:30; **F:** 09:30–17:30; **S:** 09:30–17:30. Medium stock. Spec: Automobilia/Automotive; Aviation; Buses/Trams; Engineering; Maritime/Nautical; Maritime/ Nautical - History; Marque Histories (see also motoring); Military. PR: £5–50. CC: E; JCB; MC; V. VAT No: GB 427 0309 76. Notes: *Easy parking. No yellow lines. Falconwood Station 10 minute walk away or from Falconwood Station B16 bus passes door. No general stock.*

MERSEYSIDE

BIRKENHEAD

Grange Old Bookshop, ■ 32 Oxton Road, Birkenhead, Wirral, CH41 2QT. Prop: Paul A. Dearden. Tel: 0151 653 3090. E-mail: deardenpaul@hotmail.co.uk. Est: 1992. Shop open: **T:** 11:30–17:30; **W:** 11:30–17:30; **Th:** 11:30–17:30; **F:** 11:30–17:30; **S:** 11:30–17:30. Spec: Children's; Children's - Early Titles. Notes: *Also sells postcards and old childrens' books.*

CROSBY

Ahbooks, 12 College Green Road, Crosby, Crosby, L23 3DR. Prop: Andrew Harty. Tel: 0151 284 4446 (M. 0785 1128145). Web: www.ahbooks.co.uk. E-mail: ah_books@yahoo.co.uk. Est: 2000. Storeroom. Internet and Postal. Appointment necessary. Shop At: Unit 5 Parrs Corner, Marsh Lane/Stanley Rd, Bootle, L20. Spec: Fiction - General; Modern First Editions. CC: PayPal. VAT No: GB 867 1615 04.

LIVERPOOL

Black Voices, 2, Saville Road, Liverpool, L13 4DP. Prop: T. Aitman. Tel: (0151) 475 2936. E-mail: tonyaitman@blackvoices.freeserve.co.uk. Est: 1992. Private premises. Internet and Postal. Appointment necessary. Very small stock. Spec: African-American Studies; Africana; Author - Baldwin, James; Black Studies; Literature - African-American; Literature - South African; Booksearch. PR: £3–2,000. Notes: *Also booksearches in specialist subjects*

Hylton Booksearch, 23 Chelsea Court West Derby, Liverpool, L12 6RS. Prop: Mr. R.A. Hylton. Tel: (0151) 259-5163. Web: www.rahylton@btinternet.com. E-mail: hylton.booksearch@btinternet.com. Est: 1992. Private premises. Postal Only. Appointment necessary. Very small stock. Spec: Author - General; Black Studies; Books about Books; Children's; Collectables; Communism; Countries - Central East Europe; Countries - East Europe. PR: £5–500. CC: V; PayPal. Notes: *Also trade as "liverpoolbooqshop" on Amazon Internet Site.*

Modern Welsh Publications Ltd., 32 Garth Drive, Liverpool, L18 6HW. Prop: Professor D. Ben Rees. Tel: (0151) 724 1989. Fax: (0151) 724-5691. E-mail: ben@garthdrive.fsnet co uk Est: 1962. Private premises. Postal Only. Medium stock. Spec: Countries - Wales; History - General; Literature in Translation; Politics; Theology; Ephemera. Corresp: Welsh.

Reid of Liverpool, ■ 105 Mount Pleasant, Liverpool, L3 5TB. Prop: Gerard Fitzpatrick. Tel: (0151) 709-2312. E-mail: liverpoolbooks@btconnet.com. Est: 1980. Shop open: **M:** 10:30–17:30; **T:** 10:30–17:30; **W:** 10:30–17:30; **Th:** 10:30–17:30; **F:** 10:30–17:30; **S:** 10:30–17:30. Spec: Academic/Scholarly; Culture - Popular; Esoteric; Fiction - Science Fiction; Finance - General; Mysticism; Odd & Unusual; Psychology/Psychiatry. CC: PayPal.

PRENTON

Thin Read Line, 11 St. Andrews Road, Prenton, CH43 1TB. Tel: 0151 652 4483. E-mail: richmond_dutton@hotmail.com. Est: 1995. Private premises. Postal Only. Contactable. Open: **M:** 09:00–17:30; **T:** 09:00–17:30; **W:** 09:00–17:30; **Th:** 09:00–17:30; **F:** 09:00–17:30; **S:** 09:00–17:30; **Su:** 09:00–17:30; Closed for lunch: 13:00–14:00. Spec: Aeronautics; Africana; Agriculture; Aircraft; Animals and Birds; Antiques; Arms & Armour; Army, The. Corresp: Dutch. Notes: *We are principally dealers in oop military collectibles reference books (guns, swords, badges medals uniforms etc., but also stock a wide range of military history titles too with special emphasis on colonial wars, WW1 & WW2.*

Searching for a title - and cannot find it on any Internet database?

Then try searching for a dealer specialising in the subject on www.sheppardsworld.co.uk

Select the subject classification – then chose the dealer to send your request to.

PRESCOT

Nostalgia Unlimited, 19 Dunbeath Avenue Rainhill, Prescot, L35 0QH. Tel: (0151) 426-2046. Est: 1988. Private premises. Postal Only. Small stock. Spec: Christmas; Collecting; Comic Books & Annuals; Comics; Magazines & Periodicals - General; Newspapers; Nostalgia. PR: £1–35.

SOUTHPORT

Broadhurst of Southport Ltd., ■ 5 & 7 Market Street, Southport, PR8 1HD. Prop: Laurens R. Hardman. Tel: (01704) 532064 & 534. Fax: (01704) 542009. Web: www.ckbroadhurst.com. E-mail: litereria@ aol.com. Est: 1926. Shop open: **M:** 09:00–17:30; **T:** 09:00–17:30; **W:** 09:00–17:30; **Th:** 09:00–17:30; **F:** 09:00–17:30; **S:** 09:00–17:30. Very large stock. Spec: Aircraft; Architecture; Art; Aviation; Bibliography; Biography; Buses/Trams; Children's. PR: £5–10. CC: MC; V. Corresp: French. Mem: ABA; PBFA; BA; ILAB. Notes: *Also, bookbinding & restoration service, new books on all subjects & a booksearch service.*

Cover to Cover, 252 Balmoral Drive, Southport, PR9 8QA. Prop: Arthur Reeve. Tel: (01704) 231443. Web: www.covers.freeuk.com. E-mail: covers@freeuk.com. Est: 1996. Private premises. Internet and Postal. Telephone First. Open: **M:** 09.00–17.00; **W:** 09.00–17.00; **Th:** 09.00–17.00; **F:** 09.00–17.00. Spec: Applied Art; Architecture; Art; Art - Technique; Art - Theory; Art Reference; Arts, The; Ceramics. PR: £1–300.

Kernaghans, ■ 57–65 Wayfarers Arcade Lord Street, Southport, PR8 1NT. Prop: Alwyn & Bryan Kernaghan. Tel: (01704) 546329. Fax: (01704) 546329. E-mail: kernaghanbooks@hotmail.com. Est: 1972. Shop open: **M:** 10:00–17:00; **T:** 10:00–17:00; **W:** 10:00–17:00; **Th:** 10:00–17:00; **F:** 10:00–17:00; **S:** 10:00–17:00. Very large stock. Spec: Children's - Illustrated; Countries - Ireland; Countries - Isle of Man; Fine & Rare; Irish Interest; Natural History; Pop-Up, Movable & Cut Out; Religion - Christian. PR: £5–5,000. CC: AE; MC; V. Mem: PBFA.

Parkinsons Books, ■ In Parkinson's Ginnel between Monsoon & Lakeland 359-363 Lord Street, Southport, PR8 1NH. Prop: K.A. & J. Parkinson. Tel: 01704-547016. Web: www.parki.com. E-mail: sheppards@parki.com. Shop open: **M:** 10:00–17:00; **T:** 10:00–17:00; **W:** 10:00–17:00; **Th:** 10:00–17:00; **F:** 10:00–17:00; **S:** 10:00–17:00; **Su:** 13:00–17:00. Spec: Aesthetics; Agriculture; Alchemy; Animals and Birds; Antiquarian; Antiquities; Aquatics; Arachnology. CC: AE; JCB; MC; V; most major cards. Notes: *We occupy three floors on the main shopping street, between Monsoon & Lakeland. The stock is is well classified, with a leaning towards the academic. We also sell coins, antiquities, tropical shells, fossils, mineral specimens & crystals.*

WEST KIRBY

Don Mulyan, 5 Redhouse Lane, West Kirby, CH48 5ED. Prop: Don Mulyan. Tel: 0151 625 7525. E-mail: donmulyan@onetel.com. Est: 1970. Private premises. Internet and Postal. Appointment necessary. Open: **M:** 10:00–20:00; **T:** 10:00–20:00; **W:** 10:00–20:00; **Th:** 10:00–20:00; **F:** 10:00–20:00; **S:** 10:00– 20:00. Very small stock. Spec: Adventure; Archaeology; Architecture; Art; Bibliography; Countries - Isle of Man; Countries - Norway; Engraving. Notes: *Specialist in Norway pre 1940, Isle of Man, Liverpool. Wirral, Merseyside.*

NORFOLK

AYLSHAM

Burebank Books, ■ 44 Red Lion Street, Aylsham, NR11 6ER. Prop: Roger M Crouch. Tel: 01263 735710. Fax: 01263 735703. E-mail: roger.crouch@freenet.co.uk. Est: 1993. Shop open: **M:** 10:00–17:00; **T:** 10:00–17:00; **W:** 10:00–13:00; **Th:** 10:00–17:00; **F:** 10:00–17:00; **S:** 09:00–17:00. Closed for lunch: 13:00–14:00. Spec: Archaeology; Countries - Japan; History - Local; Landscape; Maritime/ Nautical. CC: MC; V; Solo, Switch. Corresp: Italian, Japanese.

BINHAM

John Hart, Doc Barn Front Street, Binham, NR21 0AL. Tel: 01328 830877. Fax: 01328 830266. E-mail: johnhartbks@btopenworld.com. Est: 1987. Private premises. Appointment necessary. Small stock. Spec: Literature. PR: £20–2,000. CC: MC; V. Cata: English Literature. Corresp: French. Mem: ABA; PBFA. VAT No: GB 529 2455 28.

CAISTER–ON–SEA

Brian Beighton, Garfield Villa Garfield Terrace, Caister–on–Sea, NR30 5DQ. Tel: 01493 728114. Private premises. Postal Only. Appointment necessary. Small stock. Spec: Almanacs; Sport - Cricket.

CROMER

Bookworms, ■ 9 New Street, Cromer, NR27 9HP. Prop: Susan & Ted Liddell & I.R. Petrie. Tel: (01263) 515078. Fax: (01263) 519008. Web: www.susanlid.freeserve.co.uk. E-mail: bookworms@ susanlid.freeserve.co.uk. Est: 1987. Shop open: **M:** 10:00–17:00; **T:** 10:00–17:00; **W:** 10:00–17:00; **Th:** 10:00–17:00; **F:** 10:00–17:00; **S:** 10:00–17:00; **Su:** 10:00–17:00; Large stock. Spec: Art; Aviation; Biography; Children's; History - General; Literature; Music - General; Natural History. PR: £1–100. CC: AE.

DEREHAM

Village Books, ■ 20a High Street, Dereham, NR19 1DR. Prop: Mr Jack James. Tel: (01362) 853066. Fax: (01362) 853066. E-mail: villagebkdereham@aol.com. Est: 1996. Shop open: **M:** 09:30–16:30; **T:** 09:30–16:30; **W:** ; **Th:** 09:30–16:30; **F:** 09:30–16:30; **S:** 09:00–16:00. Very large stock. Spec: Art; History - General; Medicine; Military History. PR: £1–100. CC: PayPal.

DISS

Catmax Books, ■ 9 Market Hill, Diss, IP22 4JZ. Prop: Stephen Besley. Tel: 01379 650280. Fax: 0870 1347008. Web: www.catmaxbooks.com. E-mail: stephen@catmaxbooks.com. Est: 2006. Shop open: **M:** 10:00–17:30; **T:** 10:00–17:30; **W:** 10:00–17:30; **Th:** 10:00–17:30; **F:** 10:00–17:30; **S:** 09:30–17:00. Spec: Architecture; Art; Non-Fiction. CC: MC; V. VAT No: GB 871 5998 68. Notes: *The shop has a good general stock over two floors. Primarily non-fiction, the stock is particularly strong in Art and Architecture, together with some Antiquarian.*

Church Street Books, ■ 6 Church Street, Diss, IP22 4DD. Prop: Andy Vidion. Tel: 01379 652020. E-mail: atvidion@yahoo.co.uk. Est: 2005. Shop open: **M:** 10:00–17:30; **T:** 10:00–17:30; **Th:** 10:00–17:30; **F:** 10:00–17:30; **S:** 10:00–17:30. Spec: Alpinism/Mountaineering; Autobiography; Aviation; Biography; Counterculture; Dictionaries; Fiction - General; Free Thought.

Riderless Horse Books, Oakfields Redgrave Road, Blo Norton, Diss, IP22 2JA. Prop: (*) Richard B. Hamburger. Tel: (01379) 898481. Fax: +44 (0)870 912 1193. E-mail: riderlesshorse@clara.co.uk. Est: 1991. Private premises. Internet and Postal. Appointment necessary. Small stock. Spec: Author - Paul Bowles; First Editions; Literary Criticism; Literature; Literature in Translation; Magazines & Periodicals - General; Poetry. PR: £2–1,000. CC: MC; V. Cata: Literature, Modern Poetry, First Editions. Corresp: French. Mem: PBFA.

Michael Taylor Rare Books, Hoblins, One Eyed Lane Weybread, Diss, IP21 5TT. Tel: (01379) 853889. Fax: (01379) 853889. E-mail: michael@hoblins.demon.co.uk. Est: 1984. Private premises. Appointment necessary. Small stock. Spec: Bibliography; Calligraphy; Illustrated - General; Private Press; Typography. PR: £5–1,000. CC: MC; V. Cata: Private, Illustrated Books, Typography. Mem: PBFA.

DOWNHAM MARKET

Richard Everett, Sandfield House 58 Lynn Road, Downham Market, PE38 9NN. Prop: Richard & Jenny Everett. Tel: (01366) 382074. Est: 1983. Office and/or bookroom. Appointment necessary. Large stock. Spec: Children's; Illustrated - General; Publishers - Warnes; Topography - Local; Collectables. PR: £2–400. Mem: PBFA. Notes: *Also at: Southwold Antiques Centre, Suffolk (q.v.)*

EAST RUDHAM

Victor Sutcliffe, Mulberry Coach House, East Rudham, PE31 8RD. Prop: Victor Sutcliffe. Tel: (01485) 528463. Web: www.victorsutcliffe.demon.co.uk. E-mail: vhs@victorsutcliffe.demon.co.uk. Est: 1970. Private premises. Internet and Postal. Appointment necessary. Very small stock. Spec: Military; Military History. PR: £15–5,000. CC: MC; V.

FAKENHAM

The Dancing Goat Bookshop, ■ 5 Oak Street, Fakenham, NR21 9DX. Prop: Michael Goss. Tel: (01328) 855757. E-mail: dancinggoatbooks@talk21.com. Est: 1998. Shop open: **M:** 10:00–16:00; **T:** 10:00– 16:00; **W:** 10:00–16:00; **Th:** 10:00–16:00; **F:** 10:00–16:00; **S:** 10:00–16:00. Medium stock. Spec: American Indians; Americana - General; Folklore; Music - Folk & Irish Folk; Music - Popular; Music - Rock & Roll; Ornithology; Poetry. PR: £1–100. Notes: *Also a coffee shop (coffee, tea, home made cakes & light lunches).*

GORLESTON-ON-SEA

C. & J. Read - Gorleston Books, Unit 10 Longs Industrial Estate, Englands Lane, Gorleston-on-Sea, NR31 6NE. Prop: Cynthia & John Read. Tel: (01493) 656511. E-mail: jc@bookshop1 .fsbusiness.co.uk. Est: 1993. Storeroom. Internet and Postal. Telephone First. Medium stock. Spec: Aeronautics; Architecture; Artists; Arts, The; Collectables; Collecting; Countries - England; Countries - Scotland. PR: £1–1,000. CC: AE; MC; V; Maestro, PayPal. Notes: *We welcome visitors and are here most days between about 10.30 and 5.00, but please ring first as we are sometimes out buying.*

GREAT ELLINGHAM

John Knowles, Brick Kiln Farm Hingham Road, Great Ellingham, Nr. Attleborough, NR17 1JE. Prop: John Knowles. Tel: (01953) 452257. Fax: (01953) 452733. E-mail: enquire@johnknowlesbooks.com. Est: 1985. Private premises. Internet and Postal. Appointment necessary. Open: **M:** 09:00–19:00; **T:** 09:00–19:00; **W:** 09:00–19:00; **Th:** 09:00–19:00; **F:** 09:00–19:00; **S:** 09:00–19:00; **Su:** 09:00–19:00. Small stock. Spec: Buses/Trams; Marque Histories (see also motoring); Motorbikes / motorcycles; Motoring; Sport - Motor Racing; Transport; Vintage Cars. PR: £5–1,000. CC: E; JCB; MC; V; SW. Cata: Motoring, Motor Sport and other road transport. Corresp: French, German.

GREAT YARMOUTH

R.F. & C. Ward, 27, Great Yarmouth, NR30 2EX. Prop: Frank & Carol Ward. Tel: (01493) 856280. Fax: (01493) 853909. Web: www.ashbook.co.uk. E-mail: wardf@dsl.pipex.com. Est: 1985. Private premises. Postal Only. Very large stock. Spec: Fiction - General; Fiction - Crime, Detective, Spy, Thrillers; Fiction - Science Fiction; Fiction - Westerns; First Editions; War - General. PR: £1–500. CC: AE; JCB; MC; V. Cata: all. Notes: *We have a stock of 25,000 plus titles priced from 50 pence to £500.00. If we do not have it we can normally get it. We have sold books world wide since 1985. Try our web site at www.ashbook.co.uk there you will fine over 30 catalogues.*

HARLESTON

Black Cat Books, Meadow Cottage High Road, Wortwell, Harleston, IP20 OEN. Prop: Ann Morgan– Hughes. Tel: (01986) 788826. Fax: (01986) 788826. Web: www.blackcatbooks.co.uk. E-mail: ann@blackcatbooks.co.uk. Est: 1984. Office and/or bookroom. Telephone First. Small stock. Spec: Colour-Plate; Cookery/Gastronomy; Courtesy; Embroidery; Etiquette; Fashion & Costume; Food & Drink; Hairdressing. PR: £10–2,000. CC: MC; V; PayPal. Corresp: French, German, Greek. Mem: ABA; PBFA; ILAB. VAT No: GB 446 3847 25. Notes: *Visitors are most welcome, but please telephone first to make sure I am at home and to ask for directions.*

Riviera Books, ■ 9 Market Place, Harleston, IP20 9AD. Prop: David Chatten. Tel: (01379) 855123. Web: www.rivierabooks.co.uk. E-mail: rivierabooks@yahoo.co.uk. Est: 1999. Shop open: **T:** 10:00–16:30; **W:** 10:00–16:30; **Th:** 10:00–13:00; **F:** 10:00–16:30; **S:** 10:00–16:30. Large stock. PR: £2–200. CC: MC; V. Corresp: French.

HINDRINGHAM

Fullerton's Booksearch, The Dukes House 1 Moorgate Road, Hindringham Fakenham, NR21 0PT. Prop. Humphrey Boon. Tel: 01328 87 87 81. Web: www.glavenvalley.co.uk/fullertons. E-mail: fullertons.books@virgin.net. Est: 1991. Mail Order Only. Telephone First. Open: **M:** 09:00–17:00; **T:** 09:00–17:00; **W:** 09:00–17:00; **Th:** 09:00–17:00; **F:** 09:00–17:00. Spec: Booksearch. PR: £18–2,000. CC: JCB; MC; V; Debit cards. VAT No: GB 631 8838 22. Notes: *Fullerton's Book search are leading booksearchers within the U.K; looking for around 12,000 titles for 10,000 customers per annum. We will look for almost any book, published in the English language, on any subject, anywhere in the world!*

HOLT

Simon Finch Norfolk, ■ 3-5 Fish Hill, Holt, NR25 6BD. Prop: Simon Finch Rare Books Limited. Tel: 01263 712650. Fax: 01263 711153. Web: www.simonfinchnorfolk.com/. E-mail: simonfinch.norfolk@ virgin.net. Est: 1980. Shop open: **M:** 10:00–17:00; **T:** 10:00–17:00; **W:** 10:00–17:00; **Th:** 10:00–17:00; **F:** 10:00–17:00; **S:** 10:00–17:00. Spec: CC: AE; JCB; MC; V. Cata: General. VAT No: GB 867 8126 81.

Jackdaw Books, 10 New Street, Holt, NR25 6JJ. Prop: Eleanor and Mick Finn. Tel: 01263 711658. Fax: 01263 710056. Web: www.jackdawbooks.co.uk. E-mail: eleanor.finn@btopenworld.com. Est: 1997. Private premises. Internet and Postal. Appointment necessary. Spec: Academic/Scholarly; Architecture; Book Arts; Countries - Great Britain; History - 19th Century; History - Local; History - Middle Ages; Irish Interest. CC: MC; V; PayPal. VAT No: GB 700 1936 76. Notes: *Specialists in Norfolk history and topography.*

HUNSTANTON

Musicalania, 8B Melton Drive, Hunstanton, PE36 5DD. Prop: David Burkett. Tel: (01485) 534282. E-mail: musicalania@btinternet.com. Est: 1973. Private premises. Internet and Postal. Telephone First. Small stock. Spec: Music - Classical; Music - Composers; Music - Gilbert & Sullivan; Music - Opera; Music - Popular; Music - Printed, Sheet Music & Scores; Music - Songs & Ballads. PR: £1–50. Cata: Piano solo; organ; songs; wind, brass & strings. Corresp: French and German. Notes: *Secondhand music bought and sold. We also sell secondhand classical compact discs and concert programmes. Music by British composers our speciality.*

KING'S LYNN

Bookends, ■ 4 King Street, King's Lynn, PE30 1ES. Prop: Iain Dempster. Tel: 01553 774374. E-mail: bookendskingslynn@hotmail.co.uk. Est: 2002. Shop open: **M:** 10:00–16:00; **T:** 10:00–16:00; **Th:** 10:00–16:00; **F:** 10:00–16:00; **S:** 10:00–16:00. Spec: CC: AE; MC; V; Meastro. Notes: *Also, prints and fine art cards.*

Brazenhead Ltd., The Brazen Head Bookshop Market Place Burnham Market, King's Lynn, PE31 8HD. Prop: H.S. Kenyon. Tel: (01328) 730700. Web: www.brazenhead.co.uk. E-mail: brazenheadbook@ aol.com. Est: 1996. Shop and/or gallery. Internet and Postal open: **M:** 09:30–17:00; **T:** 09:30–17:00; **W:** 09:30–17:00; **Th:** 09:30–17:00; **F:** 09:30–17:00; **S:** 09:30–17:00. Very large stock. Spec: Architecture; Art; Children's; History - Local; Military; Collectables; Ephemera. PR: £1–10,000. CC: MC; V; Maestro.

John Lowe, 7 Orchard Grove West Lynn, King's Lynn, PE34 3LE. Tel: (01553) 661271. E-mail: john@lowebooks.fsnet.co.uk. Est: 1982. Spec: Academic/Scholarly; Advertising; Aeronautics; Alternative Medicine; Archaeology; Folklore; History - British; Topography - General. PR: £2–200. Mem: PBFA.

Torc Books, ■ 9 Hall Road, Snettisham, King's Lynn, PE31 7LU. Prop: Heather Shepperd. Tel: (01485) 541188 and 5. Est: 1977. Shop open: **F:** 10:00–16:00; **S:** 10:00–16:00. Medium stock. PR: £1–100. Notes: *Open other times by appointment.*

LYNG

Lyngheath Books, 51 Pightle Way, Lyng, Norwich, NR9 5RL. Prop: Tim Holt. Tel: 01603 879037. Web: www.lyngheathbooks.co.uk. E-mail: lyngheathbooks@hotmail.com. Est: 1999. Private premises. Internet and Postal. Appointment necessary. Open: **M:** 09:00–17:30; **T:** 09:00–17:30; **W:** 09:00–17:30; **Th:** 09:00–17:30; **F:** 09:00–17:30; **S:** 09:00–17:30; **Su:** 09:00–17:30; Closed for lunch: 13:00–14:00. Spec: Autobiography; Biography; Sport - General. CC: UK Bank sterling cheque. Corresp: French. Notes: *The main focus of LyngHeath Books is book searching. Only a small stock of books is held - mainly biography and autobiography. Web site being updated.*

MELTON CONSTABLE

Enigma Books, Stow House, 3 Thornton Close Briston, Melton Constable, NR24 2LZ. Prop: A.E.R.M. Stevens. Tel: (01263) 861609. E-mail: stevens@stowhouse3060.fsnet.co.uk. Est: 1976. Private premises. Postal Only. Appointment necessary. Very small stock. Spec: Fiction - Crime, Detective, Spy, Thrillers; Fiction - Fantasy, Horror; Fiction - Supernatural; First Editions; Ghosts; Literature - Victorian; Occult; Supernatural. PR: £5–1,000. Cata: 19th Century fiction, Ghost Stories.

NEW BUCKENHAM

John Underwood Antiquarian Books, Hill House Chapel Street, New Buckenham, NR16 2BB. Prop: John Underwood. Tel: 01953 860746. Web: www.abebooks.com. E-mail: mrjunder@aol.com. Est: 1991. Office and/or bookroom. Telephone First. Open: **Th:** 1400–17:30; **F:** 09:00–17:30; **S:** 09:00–17:30; **Su:** 09:00–17:30. Spec: Antiquarian; Author - Norton, Mary; - White, T.H.; Book of Hours; Calligraphy; Children's; Children's - Illustrated; Crime (True). CC: Cheques /Cash. Mem: PBFA. Notes: *Book Fairs with PBFA. London Fair most months.Bookroom open by appointment, telephone, leave message, or e-mail. Small quality stock of Antiquarian, Children's, Newspapers, Manuscripts, Medieval leaves,True Crime,some Modern Firsts.*

NORTH WALSHAM

C.J. Murphy, 5 Burton Avenue, North Walsham, NR28 0EW. Tel: (01692) 402831. Web: www.abebooks.com/home/Chrismurphy/home. E-mail: chris@cmurphy6.fsnet.co.uk. Est: 1999. Private premises. Postal Only. Telephone First. Medium stock. Spec: Academic/Scholarly; Annuals; Antiquarian; Art Reference; Atlases; Author - General; Autobiography; Children's. PR: £1–1,000. Corresp: English only. Notes: *Also, a booksearch service.*

NORWICH

Carlton Books, 44 Langley Road Chedgrave, Norwich, NR14 6HD. Prop: A.P. Goodfellow. Tel: (01508) 520124. Est: 1974. Private premises. Postal Only. Appointment necessary. Small stock. Spec: History - Local; Natural History; Ornithology; Topography - Local. PR: £1–500. Mem: PBFA. Notes: *also attends book fairs.*

J. & D. Clarke, The Elms 19 Heigham Grove, Norwich, NR2 3DQ. Tel: (01603) 619226. E-mail: janddclarke@norwichnorfolk.freeserve.co.uk. Est: 2004. Private premises. Postal Only. Very small stock. Spec: Topography - General; Topography - Local. PR: £1–500. Mem: PBFA. Notes: *Attends local PBFA fairs.*

John Debbage, 28 Carterford Drive, Norwich, NR3 4DW. Tel: (01603) 488015. Fax: (01603) 788933. E-mail: norvicsales@btopenworld.com. Est: 1954. Private premises. Internet and Postal. Telephone First. Spec: Antiquarian; Author - Bell, Adrian; - Borrow, George; - Cobbett, William; - Haggard, Sir Henry Rider; Dogs; Farming & Livestock; History - General. Cata: Norfolk history.

The Dormouse Bookshop, ■ 29 Elm Hill, Norwich, NR3 1HG. Prop: Philip Goodbody. Tel: 01603 621021. E-mail: dormouse1@btopenworld.com. Est: 1985. Shop open: **M:** 10:00–16:00; **T:** 10:00– 16:00; **W:** 10:00–16:00; **Th:** 10:00–16:00; **F:** 10:00–16:00; **S:** 10:00–17:00. Spec: Author - Blyton, Enid; - Johns, W.E.; Children's; Fiction - General; History - General; History - Local; Military History; Modern First Editions. CC: MC; V. Notes: *Book lovers welcomed.*

J.R. & R.K. Ellis, ■ 53 St. Giles Street, Norwich, NR2 1JR. Prop: John Ellis and Robert Ellis. Tel: (01603) 623679. Est. 1960. Shop open. **M.** 08:30–18:00; **T:** 08:30 18:00; **W:** 08:30 18:00; **Th** 08:30 18:00; **F:** 08:30–18:00; **S:** 08:30–18:00. Large stock. PR: £1–100. Notes: *also, Market Stalls. 25,000 books in stock.*

firstpagebooks, Oakdale House Church Road Bergh Apton, Norwich, NR15 1BP. Prop: Mr Kim Sergeant. Tel: 01508 558484. Fax: 01508 558484. Web: www.firstpagebooks.com. E-mail: kim@firstpagebooks.com. Est: 2002. Mail Order Only. Internet and Postal. Contactable. Open: **M:** 09.30–17:00; **T:** 09:30–17:00; **W:** 09.30–17:00; **Th:** 09:30–17:00; **F:** 09:30–17:00; **S:** 09:30–17:00; **Su:** 09:30–17:00. Spec: Annuals; Author - Francis, Dick; - Greene, Graham; Autobiography; Autographs; Children's; Cinema/Film; Comedy. Cata: Modern First Editions, Giles, Rupert, Cricket. Corresp: Japanese. Notes: *General booksellers, specialising in Modern First Editions, Rock/Pop music, Cricket, Rupert, Football, Giles, Military as well as stockists in Sport & Pop memorabilia.*

Tombland Bookshop, ■ 8 Tombland, Norwich, NR3 1HF. Prop: J.G. & A.H. Freeman. Tel: 01603 490000. Fax: 01603 760610. E-mail: sales@tomblandbookshop.co.uk. Est: 1973. Shop open: **M:** 09:30–17:00; **T:** 09:30–17:00; **W:** 09:30–17:00; **Th:** 09:30–17:00; **F:** 09:30–17:00; **S:** 09:30–16:30. Spec: Antiquarian; Archaeology; Architecture; Art; Books about Books; Countries - General; Fiction - General; Fine leather bindings (see also Fine & Rare). CC: MC; V. Corresp: Italian, Spanish, German and French. Notes: *short term parking is available directly outside the shop on the double yellow lines!*

NORFOLK

Freya Books & Antiques, St. Mary's Farm Cheney's Lane, Tacolneston, Norwich, NR16 1DB. Prop: Colin Lewsey. Tel: (01508) 489252. Web: www.freyaantiques.co.uk. E-mail: freyaantiques@ yahoo.co.uk. Est: 1971. Storeroom. Telephone First. Medium stock. Spec: Children's; Fiction - General; Juvenile; Booksearch; Collectables; Ephemera. PR: £1–50. CC: MC; V. Corresp: French, Danish. Notes: *Also, 3,000sq ft antique furniture. Organiser of book fairs.*

Hawes Books, 8 Keswick Road Cringleford, Norwich, NR4 6UG. Prop: T.L.M. & H.J. Hawes. Tel: (01603) 452043. Est: 1980. Private premises. Postal Only. Appointment necessary. Large stock. Spec: Genealogy; History - Local; History - National; Topography - General. PR: £2–200. VAT No: GB 342 4870 57.

Katnap Arts, 1 Whitefields Norwich Road, Saxlingham Nethergate, Norwich, NR15 1TP. Prop: Margaret Blake. Tel: 01508 498323. Fax: 01508 498323. Web: www.katnap.co.uk. E-mail: mail@ katnap.co.uk. Est: 1999. Private premises. Internet and Postal. Contactable. Open: **M:** 09:00–17:30; **T:** 09:00–17:30; **W:** 09:00–17:30; **Th:** 09:00–17:30; **F:** 09:00–17:30; **S:** 09:00–17:30; **Su:** 09:00–17:30; Closed for lunch: 13:00 14:00. Spec: Annuals; Architecture, Art, Art History; Art Reference; Children's; Entertainment - General; First Editions. CC: MC; V.

David Lake, 36 Colney Lane, Cringleford, Norwich, NR4 7RE. Tel: 07909 896 809. Web: www. ukbookworld.com/members/davidlake. E-mail: djl@netcom.co.uk. Est: 1990. Private premises. Postal Only. Small stock. Spec: Antiquarian; Children's; Children's - Early Titles; Children's - Illustrated; Colour-Plate; Nursery Rhymes; Publishers - Nister; Topography - Local. PR: £5–500. CC: PayPal.

Steven Simpson Books, 5 Hardingham Road, Hingham, Norwich, NR9 4LX. Prop: S.J. Simpson. Tel: 01953-850-471. Fax: 01953-850-471. Web: www.stevensimpsonbooks.com. E-mail: info@ stevensimpsonbooks.com. Est: 1986. Warehouse. Internet and Postal. Open: **M:** 09:00–17:30; **T:** 09:00–17:30; **W:** 09:00–17:30; **Th:** 09:00–17:30; **F:** 09:00–17:30; **S:** 09:00–17:30; **Su:** 09:00–17:30; Closed for lunch: 13:00–14:00. Spec: Botany; Fishes; Herpetology; Zoology. CC: E; MC; V. Corresp: German, French, Spanish, Portuguese. VAT No: GB 711 6055 70. Notes: *Exclusive UK book trade distributors for Aqualog Verlag A.C.S. GmbH., Hans A Baensch/Mergus Verlag, NTV & Verlag Eugen Ulmer KG. Main Sales Agent for FAO (Food and Agriculture Organisation of the United Nations).*

Tasburgh Books, 20 Henry Preston Road, Tasburgh, Norwich, NR15 1NU. Prop: Janet Lamb & David Newton. Tel: (01508) 471921. E-mail: tasburgh@btinternet.com. Est: 1995. Private premises. Internet and Postal. Telephone First. Small stock. Spec: Applied Art; Architecture; Art; Art - British; Art History; Art Reference; Decorative Art; Fine Art. CC: AE; MC; V. Cata: Architectuure, Art. Folio Society. Mem: PBFA.

Tombland Bookshop, ■ 8, Tombland, Norwich, NR3 1HF. Prop: J.G. & A.H. Freeman. Tel: 01603 490000. Fax: 01603 760610. E-mail: sales@tomblandbookshop.co.uk. Est: 1973. Shop open: **M:** 09.30–17.00; **T:** 09.30–17.00; **W:** 09.30–17.00; **Th:** 09.30–17.00; **F:** 09.30–17.00; **S:** 09.30–16.30. Spec: Academic/Scholarly; Antiquarian; Archaeology; Architecture; Art; Biography; Literary Criticism; Military. CC: E; MC; V; PayPal. VAT No: GB 366 6678 01. Notes: *short term parking is available on double yellow lines directly outside shop.*

OLD COSTESSEY

Wensumbooks, 113 The Street, Old Costessey, NR8 5DF. Prop: Elke Katherina McKinlay. Tel: 01603 742957. Web: www.abebooks.com. E-mail: mckinlay@wensumbooks.wanadoo.co.uk. Est: 2005. Private premises open: **T:** 10:00–17:00; **W:** 10:00–17:00; **Th:** 10:00–17:00; **F:** 10:00–17:00; **S:** 10:00– 17:00. Closed for lunch: 13:00–14:00. Spec: Ornithology; Ephemera; Prints and Maps. CC: PayPal. Corresp: German.

Searching for a title - and cannot find it on any Internet database?

Then try www.sheppardsworld.co.uk

Select the subject classification – requests and offers can be made to selected specialist dealers

NORFOLK

SHERINGHAM

Peter Pan Bookshop, ■ 5 The Courtyard Station Road, Sheringham, NR26 8RF. Prop: Peter Cox. Tel: (01263) 824411. Est: 1994. Shop open: **M:** 10:30–17:00; **T:** 10:30–17:00; **W:** 10:30–17:00; **Th:** 10:30–17:00; **F:** 10:30–17:00; **S:** 10:30–17:00; **Su:** 12:00–16:00. Small stock. PR: £1–20. Notes: *Peter's Bookshop, 19 St Peter's Road (q.v.) Secondhand books published after 1990.*

Peter's Bookshop, ■ 19 St. Peter's Road, Sheringham, NR26 8QY. Prop: Peter Cox. Tel: (01263) 823008. Est: 1984. Shop open: **M:** 10:00–17:30; **T:** 10:00–17:30; **W:** 10:00–17:30; **Th:** 10:00–17:30; **F:** 10:00–17:30; **S:** 10:00–17:30; **Su:** 13:00–17:00. Very large stock. Spec: Children's; Fiction - General; Literature; Ephemera; Large Print Books. PR: £1–100. Notes: *The Peter Pan Bookshop, Sheringham, Norfolk (q.v.) Winter hours: (Nov. to Mar.) Mon./Tue. & Thurs. to Sat. 10:30–16:30.*

SOUTH BURLINGHAM

Mermaid Books (Burlingham), Old Hall Norwich Road, South Burlingham, NR13 4EY. Prop: (*) Peter Scupham. Tel: (01493) 750804. Fax: (01493) 750804. Est: 1991. Private premises. Appointment necessary. Spec: Antiquarian; Literature; Poetry. PR: £5–500. Mem: PBFA.

SWANTON ABBOT

Hamish Riley-Smith, Swanton Abbot Hall , Swanton Abbot, NR10 5DJ. Prop: Hamish Riley-Smith. Tel: 01692538244. Web: www.riley-smith.com. E-mail: hamish@riley-smith.com. Est: 1974. Private premises. Internet and Postal. Appointment necessary. Open: **M:** 09:00–17:30; **T:** 09:00–17:30; **W:** 09:00–17:30; **Th:** 09:00–17:30; **F:** 09:00–17:30; **S:** 09:00–17:30; **Su:** 09:00–17:30; Closed for lunch: 13:00–14:00. Spec: Antiquarian; Arabica; Economics; History - Economic Thought; Philosophy; Printing and Mind of Man; Science - History of; Scottish Enlightenment. Cata: Economics, Philosophy, PMM, Sciences, Arithmetic.

WATTON

J.C. Books, ■ 55 High Street, Watton, IP25 6AB. Prop: C.F. & J.A. Ball & T.F. Robinson. Tel: (01953) 883488. E-mail: j_c_books@lineone.net. Est: 1992. Shop open: **M:** 10:00–16:30; **T:** 10:00–16:30; **W:** 10:00–16:30; **F:** 10:00–16:30; **S:** 10:00–16:30. Medium stock. Spec: Theatre. PR: £1–1,000. CC: MC; V. Mem: PBFA. Notes: *Exhibits at PBFA fairs.*

WELLS-NEXT-THE-SEA

The Old Station Pottery & Bookshop, The Old Station, Wells-next-the-Sea, NR23 1LY. Prop: Thom Borthwick. Tel: 01328 710847. E-mail: oldstation.books@btinternet.com. Est: 1975. Shop and/or gallery open: **M:** 09:00–17:30; **T:** 14.00–17:30; **W:** 09:00–17:30; **F:** 09:00–17:30; **S:** 09:00–17:30; **Su:** 09:00–17:30; Closed for lunch: 12.30–13.30. Large stock. Spec: Annuals; Archaeology; Art; Cats; Children's; Esoteric; Famous People - Nelson & Lady Hamilton, Lord; Farming & Livestock. PR: £1–50. CC: Cash & Cheques only. Notes: *General stock including a large range of children's, Edwardian / Victorian 'ripping yarns' and penguins.*

WYMONDHAM

The Bookshop, ■ 1 Town Green, Wymondham, NR18 OPN. Prop: M. & A.C. Thompson. Tel: (01953) 602244. Web: www.abebooks.com/home/MANDACTHOMPSON. E-mail: mac.thompson@btopenworld.com. Est: 1975. Shop open: **M:** 10:45–16:45; **T:** 10:30–16:45; **W:** ; **Th:** 10:30–16:45; **F:** 10:30–16:45; **S:** 10:00–17:00. Medium stock. Spec: Autographs; Aviation; Cinema/Film; Comics; Entertainment - General; Literature; Music - General; Music - Folk & Irish Folk. PR: £1–300.

Turret House, ■ 27 Middleton Street, Wymondham, NR18 0AB. Prop: Dr. D.H. & R.A. Morgan. Tel: (01953) 603462. E-mail: hughmorgan@turrethouse.demon.co.uk. Est: 1972. Shop open: **M:** 10.00–17.00; **T:** 10.00–17.00; **W:** 00.00–00.00; **Th:** 10.00–17.00; **F:** 10.00–17.00; **S:** 10:00–17:00. Very small stock. Spec: Astronomy; Bacteriology; Biochemistry; Biology - General; Chemistry; Evolution; Genetics; History - Science. PR: £1–1,000. Cata: lists of science & medicine. Mem: PBFA. Notes: *Usually open Monday – Saturday 09:00–17:00 but telephone first to save a wasted journey. Please ring the bell even if apparently closed.*

NORTH YORKSHIRE

AUSTWICK

Austwick Hall Books, Austwick Hall Town Head, Austwick, Lancaster, LA2 8BS. Prop: Michael Pearson. Tel: 015242 51794. E-mail: Austwickhall@btinternet.com. Est: 2000. Private premises. Internet Only. Appointment necessary. Open: **M:** 09:00–17:30; **T:** 09:00–17:30; **W:** 09:00–17:30; **Th:** 09:00–17:30; **F:** 09:00–17:30; **S:** 09:00–17:30; **Su:** 09:00–17:30; Closed for lunch: 13:00–14:00. Spec: Academic/Scholarly; Antiquarian; Biology - General; Botany; Evolution; Exploration; Farriers; Geology. CC: PayPal.

AYSGARTH

Richard Axe Rare & Out of Print Books, The Old Youth Hostel, Aysgarth, DL8 3SR. Prop: Richard Axe. Tel: . Est: 2006. Office and/or bookroom. Appointment necessary. Open: **M:** 09:00–17:30; **T:** 09:00–17:30; **W:** 09:00–17:30; **Th:** 09:00–17:30; **F:** 09:00–17:30; **S:** 09:00–17:30; **Su:** 09:00–17:30; Closed for lunch: 13:00–14:00. Spec: CC: AF; D; F; ICR; MC; V. Notes: *35 rooms of books to be developed over next two years. Open strictly by appointment. Also at 12 Cheltenham Crescent, Harrogate North Yorkshire (q.v.)*

BEDALE

Sugen & Co., Southwood House Well, Bedale, DL8 2RL. Prop: Mark. Tel: (01677) 470079. Web: www.film-tvtieins.com. E-mail: sugenbooks@ukf.net. Est: 1993. Private premises. Internet and Postal. Medium stock. PR: £3–100. CC: PayPal. Mem: IOBA.

BILLINGHAM

Spike's Books, 23 Roseberry Flats The Causeway, Billingham, TS23 2LD. Prop: Stephen Phelps. Tel: 01642 643651. Web: www.stores.ebay.co.uk/Shop-of-Things-to-Come. E-mail: stephen.phelps@ ntlworld.com. Est: 2003. Private premises. Internet Only. Spec: Adult; Fiction - Adventure; Fiction - Crime, Detective, Spy, Thrillers; Fiction - Fantasy, Horror; Fiction - Historical; Fiction - Romantic; Fiction - Science Fiction; Fiction - Westerns. CC: PayPal, Nochex, Moneybookers. Notes. *Credit Card payments accepted through PayPal, Nochex, Moneybookers*

CATTERICK VILLAGE

Brock Books, 43 High Street, Catterick Village, DL10 7LL. Prop: Jude Haslam. Tel: (01748) 818729. Web: www.brockbooks.com. E-mail: judehaslam@btopenworld.com. Est: 2002. Private premises. Internet and Postal. Appointment necessary. Open: **M:** 09:00–18.00; **T:** 09:00–15.00; **W:** 09:00–17.00; **Th:** 09:00–18.00; **F:** 19:00–18.00; **S:** 09:00–17:00; **Su:** 10:00–15:00. Very small stock. Spec: Animals and Birds; Annuals; Antiquarian; Archaeology; Art; Art - British; Art History; Art Reference. PR: £5–500. CC: PayPal. Corresp: Espanol. Notes: *Illustrations, Book Restoration.*

DACRE

Theatreshire Books, Dacre Hall, Dacre, HG3 4ET. Prop: Catherine Shire. Tel: (01423) 780497. Fax: (01423) 781957. E-mail: theatreshire@theatresearch.co.uk. Est: 2000. Private premises. Internet and Postal. Telephone First. Small stock. Spec: Architecture; Cinema/Film; Drama; Engineering; Fire & Fire Fighters; Music - Gilbert & Sullivan; Performing Arts; Theatre. PR: £1–5,000. CC: PayPal. Cata: Theatre. Notes: *Specialising in theatre, performing arts, cinema, theatre prints and engravings, theatre postcards.*

GIGGLESWICK

Post Horn Books, ■ Belle Hill, Giggleswick, BD24 0BA. Prop: Patricia & Edward Saunders. Tel: (01729) 823438. Web: www.abebooks.com/home/posthorn. E-mail: posthornbooks@btinternet.com. Est: 1979. Shop open: **T:** 10:30–17:30; **W:** 10:30–17:30; **Th:** 10:30–17:30; **F:** 10:30–17:30; **S:** 10:30–17:30. Closed for lunch: 12:00–13:00. Medium stock. Spec: Alpinism/Mountaineering; Countries - Africa; Countries - Asia; County - Local; Environment, The; Religion - Quakers; Sport - Caving (Spelaeology); Topography - Local. PR: £1–200. Notes: *A second-hand bookshop with wide ranging general stock specialising in caving, mountaineering and local history (Yorkshire/ Lancashire).*

NORTH YORKSHIRE

GUISBOROUGH

The Guisborough Bookshop, 4 Chaloner Street, Guisborough, TS14 6QD. Tel: (01287) 639018. E-mail: books@guisboroughbookshop.com.

K.A. McCaughtrie, 7 Grosvenor Square, Guisborough, TS14 6PB. Tel: (01287) 633663. Est: 1986. Private premises. Postal Only. Appointment necessary. Very small stock. Spec: Biography; Crime (True); Fiction - Crime, Detective, Spy, Thrillers. PR: £1–50.

HARROGATE

Richard Axe Rare & Out of Print Books, ■ 12 Cheltenham Crescent, Harrogate, HG1 1DH. Prop: Richard Axe. Tel: (01423) 561867. Fax: (01423) 561837. E-mail: rja@tiscali.co.uk. Est: 1981. Shop. at: The Old Youth Hostel, Aysgarth, Nth Yorkshire DL8 3SR. Open: **T:** 10:00–17:30; **W:** 10:00–17:30; **Th:** 10:00–17:30; **F:** 10:00–17:30; **S:** 10:00–17:30. Very large stock. Spec: Antiquarian; Antiques; Art History; Ceramics; Cookery/Gastronomy; History - General; Literary Criticism; Literature. PR: £2–1,000. CC: AE; D; E; JCB; MC; V. Mem: PBFA. Also at: The Old Youth Hostel, Aysgarth, Nth Yorkshire DL8 3SR. Notes: *Libraries purchased throughout UK and worldwide. Open at other times by appointment. 100,000 books in stock. Viewing at alternateive premises by appointment only (q.v.)*

Books (For All), ■ 23a Commercial Street, Harrogate, HG1 1UB. Prop: Jenny Todd. Tel: (01423) 561982. E-mail: booksforall@amserve.net. Est: 1998. Shop open: **M:** 10:30–17:00; **T:** 10:30–17:00; **W:** 10:30–17:00; **Th:** 10:30–17:00; **F:** 10:30–17:00; **S:** 10:30–17:00. Large stock. Spec: Art History; Biography; Children's; Cookery/Gastronomy; Esoteric; Fiction - Science Fiction; History - General; Horticulture. PR: £1–100. CC: MC; V; SW.

Books For All, ■ 23a Commercial Street, Harrogate, HG1 1UB. Prop: Jenny Todd. Tel: 01423 561982. Est: 1997. Shop open: **M:** 09:00–17:30; **T:** 09:00–17:30; **W:** 09:00–17:30; **Th:** 09:00–17:30; **F:** 09:00–17:30; **S:** 09:00–17:30; **Su:** 09:00–17:30; Closed for lunch: 13:00–14:00. Spec: Architecture; Art; Biography; Children's; Children's - Early Titles; Children's - Illustrated; Cinema/Film; Cookery/ Gastronomy. Notes: *Telephone to check opening times before visiting.*

Macbuiks, 7 Leadhall Crescent, Harrogate, HG2 9NG. Prop: Sally Mackenzie. Tel: 01423870978. E-mail: macbuiks@ntlworld.com. Est: 1997. Private premises. Internet and Postal. Appointment necessary. Open: **M:** 09:00–17:30; **T:** 09:00–17:30; **W:** 09:00–17:30; **Th:** 09:00–17:30; **F:** 09:00–17:30; **S:** 09:00–17:30; **Su:** 09:00–17:30. Spec: Author - Kipling, Rudyard; Children's; Children's - Illustrated; Crafts; Gardening - General; Wine. CC: PayPal. Mem: Ibooknet.

HELMSLEY

Helmsley Antiquarian & Secondhand Books, ■ The Old Fire Station Borogate, Helmsley, YO62 5BN. Prop: Myles Moorby. Tel: (01439) 770014. Est: 1985. Shop. Open: **M:** 10:00–17:00; **T:** 10:00–17:00; **W:** 09:00–17:00; **Th:** 10:00–17:00; **F:** 10:00–17:00; **S:** 10:00–17:00; **Su:** 12:00–17:00. Medium stock. Spec: Architecture; Art; Topography - Local. PR: £1–100. CC: MC; V. VAT No: GB 390 4976 18.

INGLETON

John Killeen, Pendragon 16 Main Street, Ingleton, LA6 3HF. Prop: John Killeen. Tel: (015242) 41021. Est: 1974. Private premises open: **M:** 09:00–17:00; **T:** 09:00–17:00; **W:** 09:00–17:00; **Th:** 09:00–17:00; **F:** 09:00–17:00 Medium stock. Spec: Literature; Marxism; Philosophy; Religion - Catholic; Topography - Local; Travel - General. PR: £4–1,000. Corresp: French. Mem: PBFA. Notes: *Attends fairs in Northern England. Irregular opening hours.*

KNARESBOROUGH

Pennymead Books, 1 Brewerton Street, Knaresborough, HG5 8AZ. Prop: David Druett. Tel: (01423) 865962. Fax: (01423) 547057. Web: www.pennymead.com. E-mail: pennymead@aol.com. Est: 1984. Private premises. Internet and Postal. Telephone First. Small stock. Spec: Carriages & Driving; Colonial; Countries - Bahamas, The; Countries - Bermuda; Countries - Caribbean, The; Countries - Cuba, Countries - Dominican Republic; Countries - Haiti. PR: £5–5,000. CC: JCB; MC; V. Mem: PBFA. VAT No: GB 387 9262 94. Notes: *Also, postage stamp auctioneer.*

LEALHOLM

Stepping Stones Bookshop, ■ Stepping Stones, Lealholm, near Whitby, YO21 2AJ. Prop: Judith & Lawrence Davies. Tel: (01947) 897382. E-mail: info@steppingstonesantiques.co.uk. Est: 1970. Shop open: **M:** 10:00–17:00; **T:** 10:00–17:00; **W:** 10:00–17:00; **Th:** 09:00–17:00; **F:** 10:00–17:00; **S:** 10:00–17:00; **Su:** 10:00–17:00. Medium stock. Spec: Children's; Children's - Illustrated. PR: £1–100.

LONG PRESTON

Jo Lunt, Barn Cottage Church Street, Long Preston, BD23 4NJ. Prop: Jo Lunt. Tel: (01729) 840152. E-mail: jo.lunt3@tiscali.co.uk. Est: 1993. Private premises. Postal Only. Appointment necessary. Medium stock. Spec: Publishers - Penguin; Publishers - Puffin; Ephemera. PR: £1–100. Cata: Penguin Books, all series. Corresp: French, German.

PICKERING

Alan Avery, 15 Middleton Road, Pickering, YO18 8AL. Prop: Alan Avery. Tel: (01751) 476863. Web: www.abebooks.com/home/avery. E-mail: avery_uk@yahoo.com. Est: 1988. Private premises. Postal Only. Appointment necessary. Open: **M:** 09:00–17:00; **T:** 09:09–17:17; **W:** 09:00–17:00; **Th:** 09:00–17:00; **F:** 09:00–17:00; **S:** 09:00–13:00. Small stock. Spec: Folio Society, The. PR: £5–60. CC: AE; MC; V. Notes: *Specialist in Folio Society books. Issues 'Avery's Folio Society Catalogue, 1947 - 2007' which lists all known Folio Society books and their used values. Available via the web site or direct from the dealer. £5-50 in the UK, including P&P.*

Sybil Buckley, ■ Pickering Antique Centre Southgate, Pickering, YO18 8BN. Tel: (01751) 477210. E-mail: buckleysbooks@lineone.net. Est: 1998. Shop open: **M:** 10:00–17:00; **T:** 10:00–17:00; **W:** 10:00–17.00, **Th:** 10.00–17:00; **F:** 10:00–17:00; **S:** 10:00–17:00; **Su:** 10:00–17:00. Small stock. PR: £1–200. CC: MC; V; Delta.

Cobweb Books, ■ Ye Olde Corner Shoppe 1 Pickering Road, Thornton-Le-Dale, Pickering, YO18 7LG. Prop: Robin & Sue Buckler. Tel: (01751) 476638. Web: www.cobwebbooks.co.uk. E-mail: robin@cobweb-books-yorks.fsnet.co.uk. Est: 17. Shop open: **M:** 10:00–17:00; **T:** 10:00–17:00; **W:** 10:00–17:00; **Th:** 10:00–17:00; **F:** 10:00–17:00; **S:** 10:00–17:00; **Su:** 10:00–17:00. Very large stock. Spec: Antiquarian; Art; Aviation; Biography; Children's; Children's - Illustrated; Fine & Rare; First Editions. PR: £1–1,000. CC: AE; E; JCB; MC; V; SW.

RAINTON

Pandion Books, 10 Carr Close, Rainton, Thirsk, YO7 3QE. Prop: Les Wray. Tel: 01845 578224. E-mail: pandionbks@aol.com. Est: 1980. Private premises. Internet and Postal. Appointment necessary. Spec: Natural History; Ornithology. Mem: PBFA.

RICHMOND

Richmond Books, ■ 20 Trinity Church Square, Richmond, DL10 4QN. Prop: Bob & Gail Ions. Tel: (01325) 377332. E-mail: richmondbooks@ions.ndo.co.uk. Est: 1995. Shop. Internet and Postal open: **M:** 09:30–16:30; **T:** 09:30–16:30; **W:** 09:30–16:30; **Th:** 09:30–16:30; **F:** 09:30–16:30; **S:** 09:30–16:30; **Su:** 10:00–16:30. Medium stock. Spec: Art; Aviation; Biography; Fiction - General; Fiction - Crime, Detective, Spy, Thrillers; History - General; Literature; Maritime/Nautical. PR: £1–200. Cata: 8.

J.P. Vokes, Linton House 43 Bargate, Richmond. Prop: Jonathan Peter Vokes. Tel: (01748) 824946. Fax: (01748) 824946. Est: 1972. Private premises. Postal Only. Small stock. Spec: Fiction - General; Gardening - General; Horticulture; Military History; Natural History; Topography - General; Travel - General; Booksearch. PR: £1–500. Notes: *Also, a booksearch service.*

RIPON

Hornseys' of Ripon, ■ 3 Kirkgate, Ripon, HG4 1PA. Prop: Bruce, Susan & Daniel Hornsey. Tel: (01765) 602878. E-mail: dan@hornseys.com. Est: 1976. Shop open: **M:** 09:00–17:30; **T:** 09:00–17:30; **W:** 09:00–17:30; **Th:** 09:00–17:30; **F:** 09:00–17:30; **S:** 09:00–17:30. Very large stock. Spec: Alpinism/Mountaineering; Architecture; Aviation; Children's; Fashion & Costume; History - General; Military History; Motoring. PR: £1–8,000. CC: MC; V; Switch.

SALTBURN-BY-THE-SEA

Saltburn Bookshop, ■ 3 Amber Street, Saltburn-by-the-Sea, TS12 1DT. Prop: Jösef Thompson. Tel: (01287) 623335. E-mail: aflaj@tiscali.co.uk. Est: 1978. Shop open: **M:** 11:00–17:00; **T:** 11:00–17:00; **W:** 11:00–17:00; **Th:** 11:00–17:00; **F:** 11:00–17:00; **S:** 11:00–17:00. Closed for lunch: 13:00–14:00. Medium stock. Spec: Booksearch. PR: £1–100. Notes: *Winter opening hours: Wed to Sat 11-4 (Closed for lunch 1-2).*

SCARBOROUGH

Antiquary Ltd., (Bar Bookstore), ■ 4 Swanhill Road, Scarborough, YO11 1BW. Prop: Michael Chaddock. Tel: (01723) 500141. Web: www.ukbookworld.com/members/Barbooks. E-mail: antiquary@tiscali.co.uk. Est: 1976. Shop open: **T:** 10:30–17:00; **W:** 10:30–17:00; **Th:** 10:30–17:00; **F:** 10:30–17:00; **S:** 10:30–17:00. Medium stock. Spec: Academic/Scholarly; Antiquarian; Archaeology; Architecture; Art; Author - Housman, A.E.; Biography; History - General. PR: £1–450. Mem: PBFA. Notes: *Booksearch.*

The Bookshelf, ■ 6 Victoria Road, Scarborough, YO11 1SD. Prop: Mrs. Leslie Anne Stones. Tel: (01723) 381677. Web: www.bookshelf.scarborough.co.uk. E-mail: internet@worldaccess.co.uk. Est: 2000. Shop open: **M:** 10:00–17:00; **T:** 10:00–17:00; **W:** 10:00–17:00; **Th:** 10:00–17:00; **F:** 10:00–17:00; **S:** 10:00–17:00. Small stock. PR: £1–100. Corresp: Some French.

Richard Dalby, 4 Westbourne Park, Scarborough, YO12 4AT. Tel: (01723) 377049. Est: 1976. Private premises. Postal Only. Very small stock. Spec: Fiction - Fantasy, Horror; Fiction - Supernatural; Ghosts; Literature. Mem: PBFA.

Doodles Bookshop, ■ 45 Newborough, Scarborough, YO11 1NF. Prop: Nicholas Paul Ironside. Tel: 01723 379079. E-mail: doodlebooks@fsmail.net. Est: 2004. Shop open: **M:** 10:00–17:00; **T:** 10:00–17:00; **W:** 10:00–17:00; **Th:** 10:00–17:00; **F:** 10:00–17:00; **S:** 10:00–17:00; **Su:** 10:00–17:00. Spec: CC: AE; MC; V. Notes: *Open in winter: 11:00 – 16:00.*

Reeves Technical Books, San Marino Limestone Road, Burniston, Scarborough, YO13 0DG. Prop: W.H. & L.I. Reeves. Tel: 01723 870267. Fax: 01723 870267 (Ring First). Web: www. reevestechnicalbooks.co.uk. E-mail: busterjut@yahoo.co.uk. Est: 1975. Private premises. Telephone First. Open: **M:** 09:00–17:30; **T:** 09:00–17:30; **W:** 09:00–17:30; **Th:** 09:00–17:30; **F:** 09:00–17:30; **S:** 09:00–17:30; **Su:** 09:00–17:30; Closed for lunch: 13:00–14:00. Spec: Academic/Scholarly; Annuals; Architecture; Botany; Bridge; Building & Construction; Catalogues Raisonnes; Civil Engineering. CC: PayPal. Cata: Carpentry, Wood Machining, Furniture, Building Co. Notes: *I specialise in Books mainly for the Building Industry (Woodworking in all its forms). With a few exceptions all my Books are of a technical nature with no fiction.*

Book Emporium, ■ 2, Queen Street, Scarborough, YP11 1HA. Prop: Shaun Lofthouse. Tel: 01723 506057. Fax: 01723 506057. E-mail: shaunlofthouse@netscape.net. Est: 1989. Shop open: **M:** 10:00–17:00; **T:** 10:00–17:00; **W:** 10:00–17:00; **Th:** 10:00–17:00; **F:** 10:00–17:00; **S:** 10:00–17:00; **Su:** 10:00–17:00. Spec: CC: MC; V. Notes: *We believe that each customer is important.*

SELBY

Anthony Vickers Books, 23 Baffam Gardens, Selby, Y08 9AY. Prop: Anthony Vickers. Tel: 01757 705949. E-mail: books@anthonyvickers.com. Est: 1994. Private premises. Internet and Postal. Telephone First. Spec: Aeronautics; Alpinism/Mountaineering; Antiques; Archaeology - Industrial; Architecture; Author - Raistrick, Arthur; - Rolt, L.T.C.; - Wainwright, Alfred. Mem: PBFA.

Anthony Vickers, 23 Baffam Gardens, Selby, YO8 9AY. Tel: (01757) 705949. E-mail: books@ anthonyvickers.com. Est: 1993. Private premises. Internet and Postal. Telephone First. Small stock. Spec: Aeronautics; Alpinism/Mountaineering; Antiques; Archaeology; Archaeology - Industrial; Architecture; Author - Raistrick, Arthur; - Rolt, L.T.C. PR: £5–500. Mem: PBFA. Notes: *Specialist Subjects:- Alfred Wainwright, Northern Topography and Local History, Mountaineering, Architecture, Industrial History (Mining, Textiles, Transport).*

SETTLE

Peter M. Thornber, 3 School Hill, Settle, BD24 9HB. Tel: (01729) 824067. E-mail: hastathaas@ hotmail.com. Est: 1997. Private premises. Appointment necessary. Small stock. Spec: Agriculture; Antiquarian; Archives; Auction Catalogues; Bibliography; Bibliophily; Books about Books; Ecclesiastical History & Architecture. PR: £5–500. Corresp: French. Notes: *Also, valuations, consultancy and researcher, commissions at auctions, bookhunting, talks and masterclasses on all aspects of bookmanship.*

SKIPTON

Grove Rare Books, ■ The Old Post Office Bolton Abbey, Skipton, BD23 6EX. Prop: Andrew & Janet Sharpe. Tel: (01756) 710717. Fax: (01756) 711098. Web: www.grovebookshop.co.uk. E-mail: antiquarian@groverarebooks.co.uk. Est: 1984. Shop open: **T:** 10:00–17:00; **W:** 10:00–17:00; **Th:** 10:00–17:00; **F:** 10:00–17:00; **S:** 10:00–17:00. Closed for lunch: 13:00–14:00. Medium stock. Spec: Antiquarian; Architecture; Author - Brontes, The; - Raistrick, Arthur; - Ratcliffe, Dorothy Una; - Williamson, Henry; Bindings; Countries - England. PR: £10–3,000. CC: JCB; MC; V; SW, SO. Cata: Sporting, Yorkshire Topography. Mem: ABA; PBFA; ILAB. VAT No: GB 756 1269 18. Notes: *Charming 18th Century building on The Duke of Devonshire's estate in the Yorkshire Dales National Park. Specialising in Yorkshire Topography, Hunting, Shooting, Fishing, Fine Bindings and Library sets. Trade callers welcome.*

C. L. Hawley, 26 Belgrave Street, Skipton, BD23 1QB. Prop: Catherine Hawley. Tel: (01756) 792380. Web: www.clhawley.co.uk. E-mail: clh@clhawley.co.uk. Est: 2000. Private premises. Postal Only. Contactable. Small stock. Spec: Academic/Scholarly; Arts, The; Biography; Children's; Ecology; English; Ethics; History - General. PR: £2–250. CC: JCB; MC; V; debit cards. Cata: Literary criticism of children's works. Mem: Ibooknet. Notes: *Academic books especially literary criticism, literary and cultural theory, as well as history, psychology, etc. Small selection of Yorkshire local history. Some children's books including Fidra reprints. No-obligation booksearch service.*

Skipton Antiques Centre, ■ Cavendish Square, Skipton, BD23 2AB. Tel: (01756) 797667. Shop open: **M:** 11:00–16:30; **T:** 11:00–16:30; **W:** 11:00–16:30; **Th:** 11:00–16:30; **F:** 11:00–16:30; **S:** 11:00–16:30; **Su:** 11:00–16:30. PR: £1–5,000. Notes: *Display stock from Seabreeze, for details see under Thornton Cleveleys, Lancs. (q.v.)*

STAITHES

John L Capes (Books Maps & Prints), Church Street, Staithes, TS13 5DB. Prop: John Capes. Tel: 01947 840790. Web: www.johncapes.com. E-mail: capes@staithes.fsbusiness.co.uk. Est: 1969. Private premises. Internet and Postal. Appointment necessary. Spec: History - Industrial; Topography - General; Topography - Local. Mem: PBFA. Notes: *specialising Yorkshire Topograpy. Sheffield Local & Industrial History, Fishing Industry. Staithes Group Painters.*

STOCKTON–ON–TEES (SEE ALSO UNDER DURHAM)

Norton Books, 18 Wolviston Road Billingham, Stockton-on-Tees, Cleveland, TS22 5AA. Prop: C. Casson. Tel: (01642) 553965. Fax: (01642) 553965. E-mail: sales@ricardmarketing.com. Est: 1981. Private premises. Internet and Postal. Appointment necessary. Spec: Antiquarian; Author - Beckett, S.; - Cocteau, Jean; - Crane, Hall; - Crosby, Harry & Caresse; - Cunard, Nancy; - Durrell, Lawrence; - Eliot, T.S. PR: £10–2,000. CC: PayPal. Cata: Ex-patriate literature 1920-1940.

STOCKTON-ON-THE-FOREST

York Modern Books, 14 The Bull Centre, Stockton-on-the-Forest, York. Prop: Philip Barraclough. Tel: 01904 400 331. Fax: 01904 400 331. Web: www.yorkbooks.com. E-mail: yorkbooks@btconnect.com. Est: 2005. Storeroom. Appointment necessary. Open: **T:** 10:00–18:00; **W:** 10:00–18:00; **Th:** 10:00–18:00; **F:** 10:00–18:00; **S:** 10:00–18:00. Spec: History - 20th Century; History - British; Illustrated - General; Literary Travel; Modern First Editions; Private Press. CC: AE; MC; V; PayPal. Cata: on modern firsts, private press, illustrated. VAT No. GB 859 9635 50.

THIRSK

Hambleton Books, ■ 43 Market Place, Thirsk, YO7 1HA. Prop: Terry & Vicki Parr. Tel: 01845 522343. Est: 1997. Shop. Open: **M:** 09:00–17:00; **T:** 09:00–17:00; **W:** 09:00–17:00; **Th:** 09:00–17:00; **F:** 09:00–17:00; **S:** 09:00–17:00; **Su:** 10:30–16:30. Spec: Annuals; Children's; Cinema/Film; Comic Books & Annuals; Fiction - General; First Editions; History - General; Politics. CC: MC; V; Maestro. Mem: BA. Notes: *Also at The Pickering Bookshop, Thirsk (q.v.)*

Pickering Bookshop, ■ 43 Market Place, Thirsk, YO7 1HA. Prop: Terry & Vicki Parr. Tel: 01845 522343. Est: 1997. Shop open: **M:** 09:00–17:00; **T:** 09:00–17:00; **W:** 09:00–17:00; **Th:** 09:00–17:00; **F:** 09:00–17:00; **S:** 09:00–17:00. Spec: Annuals; Children's; Cinema/Film; Comic Books & Annuals; Fiction - General; First Editions; History - General. CC: MC; V; Maestro. Mem: BA. Notes: *See also Hambleton Books (q.v.).*

Potterton Books, The Old Rectory Sessay, Thirsk, YO7 3LZ. Prop: Clare Jameson. Tel: (01845) 501218. Fax: (01845) 501439. Web: www.pottertonbooks.co.uk. E-mail: sales@pottertonbooks.co.uk. Est: 1982. Spec: Antiquarian; Antiques; Applied Art; Architecture; Art Reference; Carpets; Ceramics; Decorative Art. PR: £5–5,000. CC: AE; D; MC; V. Notes: *Also, booksearch.*

NORTH YORKSHIRE

WHITBY

Clewlow Books of Whitby, ■ Sandringham House 6 & 8 Skinner Street, Whitby, YO21 3AJ. Prop: Allan Clewlow. Tel: (01947) 821655. E-mail: allan.clewlow@ntlworld.com. Est: 1979. Shop open: **F:** 11.00– 17.00; **S:** 11.00–17.00. PR: £5–500. CC: MC; V. Corresp: French. Mem: PBFA. Notes: *Often open at other times than those specified, but perhaps ring first before calling.*

Endeavour Books, ■ 1 Grape Lane, Whitby, YO22 4BA. Tel: (01947) 821331. Web: www.enbooks.co.uk. E-mail: linda@enbooks.co.uk. Est: 1989. Shop. Internet and Postal open: **M:** 10:30–17:00; **T:** 10:30– 17:00; **W:** 10:30–17:00; **Th:** 10:30–17:00; **F:** 10:30–17:00; **S:** 10:30–17:00; **Su:** 10:30–17:00. Large stock. PR: £3–50. CC: MC; V.

John R. Hoggarth, Thorneywaite House Glaisdale, Whitby, YO21 2QU. Prop: John R. Hoggarth. Tel: 01947 897338. Web: www.johnrhoggarth.co.uk. E-mail: john@johnrhoggarth.co.uk. Est: 1979. Private premises. Internet and Postal. Telephone First. Open: **M:** 09:00–17:30; **T:** 09:00–17:30; **W:** 09:00–17:30; **Th:** 09:00–17:30; **F:** 09:00–17:30; **S:** 09:00–17:30; **Su:** 09:00–17:30; Closed for lunch: 13:00–14:00. Spec: Annuals; Antiques; Author - Baden-Powell, Lord Robert; - Milligan, Spike; Collecting; Famous People - Baden Powell, Lord & Lady R.S.S.; Juvenile; Music - Classical. CC: PayPal.

YARM

Richard J. Hodgson (Books), Manor Farm Kirklevington, Yarm, TS15 9PY. Prop: Richard Hodgson. Tel: (01642) 780445. E-mail: rjhodgsonbooks@clara.co.uk. Est: 1989. Private premises. Book fairs only. Appointment necessary. Medium stock. Spec: Agriculture; Author - Baedeker, Karl Travel - Antiquarian; - Darwin, Charles; Cattlemen; Colour-Plate; Ex-Libris; Farming & Livestock; Guide Books. PR: £1–1,000. Mem: PBFA. Notes: *Visitors are welcome, by appointment, to view items specific to their previous requests.*

YORK

Barbican Bookshop, ■ 24 Fossgate, York, YO1 9TA. Prop: Christian Literature Stalls Ltd. Tel: (01904) 653643. Fax: (01904) 653643. Web: www.barbicanbookshop.co.uk. E-mail: mail@ barbicanbookshop.co.uk. Est: 1960. Shop open: **M:** 09:00–17:30; **T:** 09:15–17:30; **W:** 09:00–17:30; **Th:** 09:00–17:30; **F:** 09:15–17:30; **S:** 09:00–17:30. Large stock. Spec: Aeronautics; Aviation; Bibles; Buses/Trams; Canals/Inland Waterways; Ecclesiastical History & Architecture; Folio Society, The; History - General. PR: £1–500. CC: E; JCB; MC; V. Mem: PBFA; BA; York Tourism Bureau. VAT No: GB 169 3696 12. Notes: *Also, new books, remainders, cards & videos/dvds.*

Boer War Books, 8 Mill Lane, Heworth, York, YO31 7TE. Prop: E. A. Hackett. Tel: 01904 415829. Fax: 01904 415829. E-mail: ahackett9@aol.com. Est: 1969. Private premises. Postal Only. Appointment necessary. Spec: Countries - South Africa; Military; War - Boer, The.

Courtney & Hoff, Hutton Hall Farm Hutton Wendasley, York, YO26 7LZ. Prop: Gerrit van Hoff. Tel: (01904) 738885. Fax: Mob: 07762 378540. E-mail: frankievanhoff@hotmail.com. Est: 1986. Storeroom. Appointment necessary. Small stock. Spec: Antiquarian; Architecture; Bindings; Ecclesiastical History & Architecture; Stone Masonry. PR: £1–900. Corresp: Dutch. Mem: PBFA. Notes: *Abstract & figurative sculpture; also vellum and leather.*

Empire Books, 12 Queens Staith Mews, York, YO1 6HH. Prop: Colin Hinchcliffe. Tel: (01904) 610679. Fax: (01904) 641664. Web: www.empirebooks.org.uk. E-mail: colin@empirebooks.org.uk. Est: 1990. Private premises. Internet and Postal. Appointment necessary. Large stock. Spec: Academic/ Scholarly; Aeronautics; Africana; Agriculture; Almanacs; Alternative Medicine; Architecture; Australiana. PR: £3–1,000. CC: AE; MC; V; PayPal. Cata: Pacific Islands. VAT No: GB 647 2977 92.

Fossgate Books, ■ 36 Fossgate, York, YO1 9TF. Prop: Alex Helstrip. Tel: (01904) 641389. E-mail: alexhelstrip@hotmail.com. Est: 1992. Shop open: **M:** 10:00–17:30; **T:** 10:00–17:30; **W:** 10:00–17:30; **Th:** 10:00–17:30; **F:** 10:00–17:30; **S:** 10:00–17:30. Very large stock. Spec: Academic/Scholarly; Antiquarian; Arts, The; Cinema/Film; Fiction - General; Folio Society, The; History - General; Literature. PR: £2–300. CC: MC; V. Cata: Folio Society. Corresp: Spanish.

Knapton Bookbarn, Back Lane Knapton, York, YO26 6QJ. Tel: (01904) 339493. Est: 1996. Postal Only. Spec: Natural History; Topography - General; Travel - General. PR: £5–100.

NORTH YORKSHIRE

Lucius Bookshop & Gallery, ■ 50 Fossgate, York, YO1 9TF. Prop: James Hallgate & Georgina Harris. Tel: 01904 640111. Fax: 01904 640444. Web: www.luciusbooks.com. E-mail: info@luciusbooks.com. Est: 1993. Shop open: **T:** 10:00 18:00; **W:** 10:00 18:00; **Th:** 10:00 18:00; **F:** 10:00 18:00; **S:** 10:00– 18:00. Very small stock. Spec: Author - Aldin, Cecil; - Barker, Cecily M.; - Blyton, Enid; - Bramah, Ernest; - Brent-Dyer, Elinor M.; - Burroughs, William; - Carr, John Dickson; - Chandler, Raymond. PR: £30–20,000. CC: D; E; JCB; MC; V; Debit. Corresp: French. Mem: ABA; PBFA; ILAB. VAT No: GB 766 9110 08.

Philip Martin Music Books, ■ 22 Huntington Road (Office), York, YO31 8RL. Prop: Martin & Eleanor Dreyer. Tel: (01904) 636111. Fax: (01904) 658889. E-mail: musicbooks@philipmartin.demon.co.uk. Est: 1975. Shop. Shop At: 38 Fossgate, York YO1 9TF. Open: **T:** 10:00–17:30; **W:** 10:00–17:30; **Th:** 10:00–17:30; **F:** 10:00–17:30; **S:** 10:00–17:30. Closed for lunch: 13:00–14:00. Spec: Music - General; Music - Composers; Music - Gilbert & Sullivan; Music - Jazz & Blues; Music - Opera; Music - Printed, Sheet Music & Scores; Musical Instruments; Musicians. PR: £1–75. CC: AE; MC; V; most debit and credit cards. Cata: 3 per year. Corresp: French. Mem: Also at: 38 Fossgate, York YO1 9TF. VAT No: GB 332 3786 58. Notes: *As well as secondhand books, we have a comprehensive display of new books about music. We also stock secondhand music for most instruments and orchestral scores.*

Minster Gate Bookshop, ■ 8 Minster Gates, York, YO1 7HL. Prop: Nigel Wallace. Tel: (01904) 621812. Fax: (01904) 622960. Web: www.minstergratebooks.co.uk. E-mail: rarebooks@minstergatebooks .co.uk. Est: 1970. Shop open: **M:** 10:00–17:30; **T:** 10:00–17:30; **W:** 10:00–17:30; **Th:** 10:00–17:30; **F:** 10:00–17:30; **S:** 10:00–17:30; **Su:** 11:00–17:00; Large stock. Spec: Antiquarian; Arthurian; Children's; Children's - Early Titles; Children's - Illustrated; Folklore; History - British; Illustrated - General. PR: £1–500. CC: MC; V. Cata: Folklore, Illustrated & Children's books. Corresp: French. Mem: PBFA. VAT No: GB 450 7122 78.

O'Flynn Books, Dalguise Green Heworth Green, York, YO31 7SY. Prop: D. Francis O'Flynn. Tel: 01904-414925. Web: www.oflynnbooks.com. E-mail: oflynnbooks@tiscali.co.uk. Est: 1969. Private premises. Internet and Postal. Appointment necessary. Shop At: Red House Antique Centre, Duncombe Place, York. Spec: Animals and Birds; Antiquities; Art Reference; Atlases; British Books; Cartography; Cities - General; Classical Studies. CC: MC; V. Cata: Miscellaneous Antiquarian, Topography, etc. Notes: *We have a large stock of maps and prints of the UK and the rest of the World.*

Janette Ray Rare and Out of Print Books, ■ 8 Bootham, York, YO30 7BL. Prop: Janette Ray. Tel: (01904) 623088. Fax: (01904) 620814. Web: www.janetteray.co.uk. E-mail: books@janetteray.co.uk. Est: 1995. Internet and Postal. Shop open: **W:** 09:30–17:30; **Th:** 09:30–1730; **F:** 09:30–17:30; **S:** 09:30– 17:30. Medium stock. Spec: Applied Art; Architecture; Artists; Arts, The; Design; Fine Art; Interior Design; Landscape. PR: £20–8,000. CC: E; MC; V. Cata: Architecture, Design, Gardens, Art, Photography. Corresp: French, Spanish. Mem: ABA; PBFA; ILAB. VAT No: GB 698 7195 56. Notes: *We also sell original drawings & photographic material. Valuations undertaken.*

Ken Spelman, ■ 70 Micklegate, York, YO1 6LF. Prop: Peter Miller & Tony Fothergill. Tel: (01904) 624414. Fax: (01904) 626276. Web: www.kenspelman.com. E-mail: ask@kenspelman.com. Est: 1948. Shop open: **M:** 09:00–17:30; **T:** 09:00–17:30; **W:** 09:00–17:30; **Th:** 09:00–17:30; **F:** 09:00–17:30; **S:** 09:00–17:30. Very large stock. Spec: Academic/Scholarly; Antiquarian; Applied Art; Architecture; Art; Author - Sterne, L; Countries - Italy; Fine Art. PR: £1–10,000. CC: E; MC; V; PayPal. Cata: Art, Arch, Lit, Manuscripts, Italy, 18th century. Mem: ABA; PBFA; BA; ILAB. Notes: *Books bought in all quantities, major items handled on commission if required. Insurance valuations. Full on-line ordering via our web site.*

Jeffrey Stern Antiquarian Book, Little Hall, Heslington, York, YO10 5EB. Tel: (01904) 413711. Fax: (01904) 412761. Web: www.abebooks.com/home/STARLIN. E-mail: jeffrey@sternj.demon.co.uk. Est: 1971. Internet and Postal. Spec: Academic/Scholarly; Anthropology; Antiquarian; Architecture; Art; Biography; Business Studies; Computing. PR: £25–2,000. CC: MC; V.

Stone Trough Books, ■ 38 Fossgate, York, YO1 9TF. Prop: George Ramsden. Tel: (01904) 670323. Fax: (01944) 768465. E-mail: george@stonetrough.demon.co.uk. Est: 1981. Shop open: **T:** 10:00–17:30; **W:** 10:00–17:30; **Th:** 10:00–17:30; **F:** 10:00–17:30; **S:** 10:00–17:30. Small stock. Spec: Art; Literature. PR: £2–200. CC: MC; V. Corresp: French, German. Mem: PBFA. VAT No: GB 237 5500 70.

Westfield Books, 28 Easthorpe Drive, York, YO26 6NR. Prop: A E Cunningham. Tel: 01904 794711. E-mail: westfieldbooks@btopenworld.com. Est: 1992. Mail Order Only. Internet and Postal. Contactable. Spec: Antiquarian; Law - General. CC: PayPal. Mem: PBFA. VAT No: GB 827 4126 32. Notes: *General antiquarian booksellers.*

York Fine Books, B10 Parkside Commercial Centre Terry Avenue, York, YO23 1JP. Prop: Helen Mackfall. Tel: 0190 4644277. Web: www.ukbookworld.com/members/hemackfall. E-mail: yorkfinebooks@hotmail.co.uk. Est: 2006. Office and/or bookroom. Internet and Postal. Appointment necessary. Spec: Cata: Music Biography. VAT No: GB 874 8963 54.

NORTHAMPTONSHIRE

BRACKLEY

The Old Hall Bookshop, ■ 32 Market Place, Brackley, NN13 7DP. Prop: John & Lady Juliet Townsend. Tel: 01280 704146. Web: www.oldhallbooks.com. E-mail: books@oldhallbooks.com. Est: 1977. Shop open: **M:** 09:30–17:30; **T:** 09:30–17:30; **W:** 09:30–17:30; **Th:** 09:30–17:30; **F:** 09:30–17:30; **S:** 09:30–17:30. Medium stock. Spec: Children's; Topography - Local; Travel - General. PR: £1–10,000. CC: AE; JCB; MC; V; Maestro. Mem: ABA; PBFA; BA; ILAB. Notes: *New books, Ordnance Survey Mapping & Data Centre, fast order service, Book Tokens, book search etc.*

IRCHESTER

Jane Badger Books, Manor House Farm High St, Irchester, Wellingborough, NN29 7AA. Prop: Jane Badger. Tel: (01933) 410943. Web: www.janebadgerbooks.co.uk. E-mail: janebadger.books@ btinternet.com. Est: 2002. Mail Order Only. Internet and Postal. Appointment necessary. Open: **M:** 09:00–17:00; **T:** 09:00–17:00; **W:** ; **Th:** 09:00–17:00; **F:** 09:00–17:00. Spec: Children's; Horses; Sport - Horse Racing (inc. Riding/Breeding/Equestrian); Sport - Hunting. CC: PayPal. Cata: Pony Books and Equine Non-Fiction. Mem: Ibooknet.

NORTHAMPTON

Occultique, 30 St. Michael's Avenue, Northampton, NN1 4JQ. Prop: Michael John Lovett. Tel: (01604) 627727. Fax: (01604) 603860. Web: www.occultique.co.uk. E-mail: enquiries@occultique.co.uk. Est: 1973. Private premises. Internet and Postal. Appointment necessary. Medium stock. Spec: Acupuncture; Alchemy; Alternative Medicine; American Indians; Astrology; Author - Crowley, Aleister; - Spare, Austin Osman; Countries - Egypt. PR: £1–1,000. CC: PayPal. Notes: *Also, new books, essential oils, herbs & occult paraphernalia.*

Roosterbooks, 7 Elysium Terrace, Northampton, NN2 6EN. Tel: 01604 720983. Fax: 01604 720983. E-mail: roosterbooks@aol.com. Est: 1997. Private premises. Internet and Postal. Telephone First. Large stock. Spec: Mind, Body & Spirit; Philosophy. PR: £3–3,000. CC: MC; V. VAT No: GB 655 1461 40. Notes: *Free booksearch service.*

Ryeland Books, 18 St. George's Place, Northampton, NN2 6EP. Prop: Alan & Joy Riley. Tel: (01604) 716901. E-mail: amriley@ryeland.demon.co.uk. Est: 1998. Private premises. Appointment necessary. Small stock. Spec: Architecture; Art History; Children's; Countries - Middle East, The; Natural History. PR: £3–1,000. Mem: PBFA.

OUNDLE

Geraldine Waddington Books & Prints, ■ 3 West Street, Oundle, PE8 4EJ. Tel: (01832) 275028. Fax: (01832) 275028. Web: www.geraldinewaddington.com. E-mail: g.waddington@dial.pipex.com. Est: 1984. Internet and Postal. Shop open: **M:** 10:00–17:00; **T:** 10:00–17:00; **W:** ; **Th:** 10:00–17:00; **F:** 10:00–17:00; **S:** 10:00–17:00. Medium stock. Spec: Art Reference; Engraving; Ex-Libris; Folio Society, The; Illustrated - General; Private Press; Prints and Maps. PR: £2–500. CC: MC; V. Mem: PBFA. VAT No: GB 745 9396 81.

RUSHDEN

Booksmart, 4 Manning Rise, Rushden, NN10 0LY. Prop: Andy Wagstaff. Tel: (01933) 357416. Web: www.booksmart.co.uk. E-mail: wagstaa@hotmail.com. Est: 1990. Postal Only. Spec: Ephemera. PR: £1–10.

SILVERSTONE

Collectors Carbooks, ■ 2210 Silverstone Technolgy Park Silverstone Circuit, Silverstone, NN12 8TN. Prop: Chris Knapman. Tel: (01327) 855888. Fax: (01327) 855999. Web: www.collectorscarbooks.com. E-mail: info@collectorscarbooks.com. Est: 1993. Shop. Internet and Postal open: **M:** 10:00–17:00; **T:** 10:00–17:00; **W:** 10:00–17:00; **Th:** 10:00–17:00; **F:** 10:00–17:00. Large stock. Spec: Collectables; History - Sports; Maritime/Nautical; Marque Histories (see also motoring); Memorabilia; Motorbikes / motorcycles; Motoring; Sport - Motor Racing. PR: £1–1,200. CC: MC; V. VAT No: GB 649 2588 91. Notes: *Open certain race Saturdays 08:30–14:30. Also, a free booksearch service.*

NORTHAMPTONSHIRE

TOWCESTER

Mr. Pickwick of Towcester, Lavender Cottage Shutlanger, Towcester, NN12 7RR. Prop: William Mayes. Tel: (01604) 862006. Fax: (01604) 862006. Web: www.yell.co.uk.sites/pickwickbookfinders. Est: 1963. Private premises. Internet and Postal. Very large stock. Spec: Author - Dickens, Charles; Biography; Books about Books; Fiction - General; Literature; Magazines & Periodicals - General; Memoirs; Newspapers. PR: £3–300.

WELLINGBOROUGH

Lost Books, 103 Leyland Trading Estate, Wellingborough, NN8 1RT. Prop: Meisterco Limited. Tel: 01933 228828. Fax: 01933 228828. Web: www.lostbooks.net. E-mail: sales@lostbooks.net. Est: 2000. Warehouse. Internet and Postal. Telephone First. Open: **M:** 09:30–17:00; **T:** 09:30–17:00; **W:** 09:30–17:00; **Th:** 09:30–17:00; **F:** 09:30–17:00. Spec: Aeronautics; Aircraft; Arms & Armour; Army, The; Author - Churchill, Sir Winston; Aviation; Deep Sea Diving; Espionage. CC: AE; MC; V; Debit Cards. Cata: Over 100 military, history & exploation subjects. Corresp: Basic French & German. VAT No: GB 818 7468 87. Notes: *We specialise in the sale of books covering military, history and exploration.*

The Park Gallery & Bookshop, ■ 16 Cannon Street, Wellingborough, NN8 4DJ. Prop: J.A. Foster. Tel: (01933) 222592. Web: www.ukbookworld.com/members/parkbookshop. E mail: judy@ parkbookshop.freeserve.co.uk. Est: 1979. Shop. Internet and Postal open: **M:** 10:00–17:30; **T:** 10:00–17:30; **W:** 10:00–17:30; **Th:** 10:00–14:30; **F:** 10:00–17:30; **S:** 10:00–18:00. Medium stock. Spec: Antiquarian; Antiques; Author - Bates, H.E.; - Blyton, Enid; - Clare, John; - Dickens, Charles; - Pasternak, Boris; Autobiography. PR: £1–500. Notes: *Also, a booksearch service, collectables, ephemera, prints & maps, plus picture framing.*

NORTHUMBERLAND

ALNWICK

Barter Books, ■ Alnwick Station, Alnwick, NE66 2NP. Prop: Stuart & Mary Manley. Tel: (01665) 604888. Fax: (01665) 604444. Web: www.barterbooks.co.uk. E-mail: bb@barterbooks.co.uk. Est: 1991. Shop open: **M:** 09:00–19:00; **T:** 09:00–19:00; **W:** 09:00–19:00; **Th:** 09:00–19:00; **F:** 09:00–19:00; **S:** 09:00–19:00; **Su:** 09:00–19:00. Very large stock. Spec: Agriculture; Antiquities; Author - Blyton, Enid; - Henty, G.A.; - Tolkien, J.R.R.; Children's; Children's - Early Titles; County - Local. PR: £1–13,000. CC: AE; JCB; MC; V. Corresp: French. Mem: IOBA; IBookNet. VAT No: GB 414 3504 88. Notes: *One of the largest secondhand bookshops in Britain. Branch: Barter Books, 67 Main Street, Seahouses, Northumberland.*

BEADNELL

Shearwater Books, Shearwater 78 Harbour Road, Beadnell, NE67 5BE. Prop: John Lumby. Tel: 01665 720654. Web: www.shearwaterbooks.co.uk. E-mail: shearwaterbooks@yahoo.co.uk. Est: 1964. Private premises. Internet and Postal. Open: **M:** 09:00–20:00; **T:** 09:00–20:00; **W:** 09:00–20:00; **Th:** 09:00–20:00; **F:** 09:00–20:00; **S:** 09:00–20:00; **Su:** 09:00–20:00; Closed for lunch: 13:00–14:00. Spec: Ecology; Entomology; Flora & Fauna; Hand bookbinding; Natural History; New Naturalist; Ornithology; Publishers - Collins (Crime Clb, The). Cata: ornithology, new naturalist, poyser, wayside. Notes: *E-mail for Catalogues on New Naturalist, Poysers, Wayside & Woodland,Bird art & artists,Pre-1955. Website opens in January/Febuary 2007. Bookbinding/repair service & booksearch. Also B&B. Small stock of other branches of natural history.*

HALTWHISTLE

Newcastle Bookshop At Haltwhistle, ■ Market Square, Haltwhistle, NE49 0BG. Prop: Valerie Levitt. Tel: 01434 320103. Web: www.Newcastlebookshop.com. E-mail: Newcstlbk@aol.com. Est: 1973. Shop. Spec: Architecture. CC: AE; MC; V. Notes: *We now have a fully equipped bindery in the bookshop. Opening times are Thurs, Fri & Sat 11-4 April to October. Other times browsers are welcome any day when I am working in the bindery, bell on the door. Mobile 07837982809.*

HEXHAM

Alex Fotheringham, East Chesterhope West Woodburn, Hexham, NE48 2RQ. Tel: (01434) 270046. Fax: (01434) 632931. Est: 1975. Private premises. Appointment necessary. Very small stock. Spec: Antiquarian; Architecture; Art; Bibliography; Literature; Theology. PR: £20–2,500. Mem: ABA; PBFA. VAT No: GB 646 1882 17.

Hencotes Books & Prints, ■ 8 Hencotes, Hexham, NE46 2EJ. Prop: Penny Pearce. Tel: (01434) 605971. Web: www.hencotes.com. E-mail: enquiries@hencotesbooks.onyxnet.co.uk. Est: 1981. Shop open: **M:** 10:30–17:00; **T:** 10:30–17:00; **W:** 10:30–17:00; **Th:** ; **F:** 10:30–17:00; **S:** 10:30–17:00. Medium stock. Spec: Booksearch. PR: £1–1,000. CC: JCB; MC; V; SW. Mem: PBFA. VAT No: GB 796 9893 26. Notes: *Also, booksearch service & attends P.B.F.A. and local fairs.*

Newgate Books and Translations, 3 Quatre Bras, Hexham, NE46 3JY. Prop: Davina and John Dwyer. Tel: (01434) 607650. Fax: (01434) 607650. E-mail: newgate.books@btinternet.com. Est: 1987. Private premises. Postal Only. Contactable. Open: **M:** 09:00–18:00; **T:** 09:00–18:00; **W:** 09:00–17:00; **Th:** 09:00–18:00; **F:** 09:00–18:00; **S:** 09:00–12:00. Closed for lunch: 12:45–14:15. Small stock. Spec: Conservation; Environment, The; Fiction - Crime, Detective, Spy, Thrillers; Music - General; Music - Classical. PR: £5–300. Corresp: French, German. Notes: *Booksearch. French - English Translation. Also small stock of books available to purchase online through ABE.*

Priestpopple Books, ■ 9b Priestpopple, Hexham, NE46 1PF. Prop: John B. Patterson. Tel: (01434) 607773. E-mail: priestpopple.books@tinyworld.co.uk. Est: 1997. Shop open: **M:** 09:00–17:00; **T:** 09:00–17:00; **W:** 09:00–17:00; **Th:** 09:00–17:00; **F:** 09:00–17:00; **S:** 09:00–17:00. Very large stock. Spec: Academic/Scholarly; Art Reference; Author - General; Author - Carlyle, Thomas; Children's; Cinema/Film; Crafts; Dogs. PR: £1–500. Notes: *Also, sheet music and used LPs.*

MORPETH

Intech Books, 14 Bracken Ridge, Morpeth, NE61 3SY. Prop: Mr. D. J. Wilkinson. Tel: (01670) 519102. Fax: (01670) 515815. E-mail: djw.intech@virgin.net. Est: 1981. Private premises. Internet and Postal. Appointment necessary. Small stock. Spec: American Indians; Annuals; Author - Ahlberg, Janet & Allan; - Bainbridge, Beryl; - Barker, Cecily M.; - Bates, H.E.; - Beardsley, Aubrey; - Belloc, Hilaire. PR: £1–100. Notes: *We also trade at many independent book fairs, including Pudsey, Keswick, Tynemouth Station, Bedale and Ingleton. A booksearch service is also offered.*

STOCKSFIELD

Leaf Ends, Leaf End Ridley Mill, Stocksfield, NE43 7QU. Prop: Moira Tait. Tel: 01661 844261. Fax: 01661 844261. Web: www.abebooks.com. E-mail: alexander.tait@virgin.net. Est: 1995. Mail Order Only. Internet and Postal. Appointment necessary. Spec: Children's. CC: MC; V. VAT No: GB 747 2468 08. Notes: *No set opening hours but contactable at any time, mixed general stock, including over 5,000 childrens' books, stock listed on abebooks.com and viewable by appointment*

WOOLER

Hamish Dunn Antiques & Books, ■ 17 High Street, Wooler, NE71 6BU. Tel: (01668) 281341. Est: 1986. Shop open: **M:** 09:00–16:00; **T:** 09.00–16 00. **W:** 09:00–16:00; **F:** 09:00 16:00; **S:** 09:00–16:00. Small stock. Spec: Collectables; Ephemera; Prints and Maps. PR: £1–100. CC: D; JCB; MC; V.

NOTTINGHAMSHIRE

BALDERTON

Anthony W. Laywood, Kercheval House 79 Main Street, Balderton, Newark, NG24 3NN. Prop: Anthony Laywood. Tel: (01636) 659031. Fax: (01636) 659219. E-mail: books@ anthonylaywood.co.uk. Est: 1965. Private premises. Internet and Postal. Appointment necessary. Open: **M:** 09:00–17:30; **T:** 09:00–17:30; **W:** 09:00–17:30; **Th:** 09:00–17:30; **F:** 09:00–17:30. Medium stock. Spec: Antiquarian. PR: £25–3,000. CC: MC; V. Cata: Books in English before 1850.

BULLWELL

A Holmes Books, 82 Highbury Avenue, Bullwell, Nottingham, NG6 9DB. Prop: Andrew Holmes. Tel: 0115 9795603. Web: www.amazon.co.uk/shops/aholmesbooks. E-mail: aholmesbooks@ ntlworld.com. Est: 1989. Private premises. Internet and Postal. Contactable. Open: **M:** 09:00–17:30; **T:** 09:00–17:30; **W:** 09:00–17:30; **Th:** 09:00–17:30; **F:** 09:00–17:30; **S:** 09:00–17:30; **Su:** 09:00–17:30; Closed for lunch: 13:00–14:00. Spec: General Stock; Gypsies. Notes: *General stock most subjects.*

GUNTHORPE

Letterbox Books, The Coach House, Gunthorpe, NG14 7ES. Prop: Bob Dakin. Tel: (0115) 966-4349. E-mail: enquiries@letterboxbooks.plus.com. Est: 1993. Private premises. Internet and Postal. Very small stock. Spec: Alpinism/Mountaineering; History - Local; Sport - Caving (Spelaeology); Sport - Potholing; Topography - General; Topography - Local; Booksearch; Ephemera. PR: £1–200.

KIRKBY–IN–ASHFIELD

Kyrios Books, ■ 11 Kingsway, Kirkby–in–Ashfield, NG17 7BB. Prop: Keith Parr. Tel: (01623) 452556 answerphone. Web: www.kyriosbooks.co.uk. E-mail: keith@kyriosbooks.co.uk. Est: 1989. Shop. Internet and Postal. Telephone First. Open: **M:** 09:00–16:30; **T:** 09:00–16:30; **W:** 09:00–16:00; **Th:** 09:00–16:30; **F:** 09:00–16:30; **S:** 09:00–16:30. Closed for lunch: 12:00–13:00. Large stock. Spec: Autobiography; Ecclesiastical History & Architecture; Philosophy; Prayer Books; Religion - General; Religion - Christian; Theology. PR: £1–100. Mem: FSB.

MANSFIELD

Fiona Edwards, 33 Crompton Road, Mansfield, NG19 7RG. Tel: 07710 410325. E-mail: fionaedwardsbks@aol.com. Est: 1994. Private premises. Appointment necessary. Spec: Art; Cookery/Gastronomy; Music - General; Sport - General; Booksearch; Ephemera. CC: AE; JCB; MC; V. Mem: PBFA. Notes: *Also, ephemera and exhibits at PBFA fairs*

R. W. Price, 19 Park Avenue, Mansfield, NG18 2AU. Prop: Mr G.D. Price. Tel: (01623) 629858. Web: www.gdprice.com. E-mail: gdp@gdprice.freeserve.co.uk. Est: 1986. Private premises. Internet and Postal. Very large stock. Spec: Beat Writers; Children's; Comedy; Erotica; Espionage; Fiction - General; Fiction - Crime, Detective, Spy, Thrillers; Fiction - Fantasy, Horror. PR: £0–100.

NEWARK ON TRENT

Lawrence Books, Newark Antiques Centre Lombard Street, Newark–on–Trent, NG24 1XP. Prop: Arthur Lawrence. Tel: (01636) 605865. E-mail: acklawrence@btinternet.com. Est: 1987. Warehouse. Open: **M:** 09:30–17:00; **T:** 09:30–17:00; **W:** 09:30–17:00; **Th:** 09:30–17:00; **F:** 09:30–17:00; **S:** 09:30–17:00; **Su:** 11:00–16:00. Small stock. Spec: Aviation; Diaries; History - General; Letters; Maritime/Nautical; Military; Poetry; Topography - Local. PR: £1–200. Mem: Bookbinding Society. Notes: *Exhibits at book fairs; bookbinding. Trades from bookroom/warehouse. Alternative tel: (01636) 701619.*

NOTTINGHAM

Artco, 6 Grantham Road Radcliffe on Trent, Nottingham, NG12 2HD. Prop: Mr. H. Boehm. Tel: (0115) 933-3530. Fax: (0115) 911-9746. Est: 1970. Private premises. Appointment necessary. Small stock. Spec: Applied Art; Art; Art Reference; Artists; Arts, The; Colour-Plate; Foreign Texts; Illustrated - General. PR: £10–1,000. CC: MC; V. Corresp: German.

Geoffrey Blore's Bookshop, ■ 484 Mansfield Road Sherwood, Nottingham, NG5 2BF. Tel: (0115) 969-1441. Est: 1987. Shop open: **M:** 10:30–17:00; **T:** 10:30–17:00; **W:** 10:30–17:00; **Th:** 10:30–17:00; **F:** 10:30–17:00; **S:** 10:30–17:00. Very large stock. Spec: History - Local; Topography - Local. Notes: *Stock includes books on Nottinghamshire history and topography.*

NOTTINGHAMSHIRE

Guy Davis, Antiquarian Books, 61 Bakerdale Road Bakersfield, Nottingham, NG3 7GJ. Tel: (0115) 940-3835. Fax: (0115) 940-0093. Est: 1970. Spec: Bindings; Fore-Edge Paintings; Prints and Maps. PR: £50–5,000.

Jermy & Westerman, ■ 203 Mansfield Road, Nottingham, NG1 3FS. Prop: G.T. Blore. Tel: (0115) 947-4522. Est: 1977. Shop open: **M:** 11:00–17:00; **T:** 11:00–17:00; **W:** 11:00–17:00; **Th:** 11:00–17:00; **F:** 11:00–17:00; **S:** 11:00–17:00. Medium stock. Spec: Illustrated - General; Literature; Topography - Local. Notes: *Geoffrey Blore's Bookshop, Nottingham. Stocks books on Nottingham history and topography.*

Frances Wakeman Books, 103 Austin Street , Nottingham, NG6 9HE. Prop: Frances & Paul Wakeman. Tel: (0115) 875 3944. Fax: none. Web: www.fwbooks.com. E-mail: info@fwbooks.com. Est: 1970. Private premises. Internet and Postal. Appointment necessary. Very small stock. Spec: Bibliography; Books about Books; Papermaking; Printing; Private Press; Publishing; Typography. PR: £100–6,000. CC: AE; E; JCB; MC; V. Mem: PBFA. VAT No: GB 685 4226 14. Notes: *Also, publishing books about books.*

REDMILE

Forest Books, Overfields 1, Belvoir Road, Redmile, NG13 OGL. Prop: William Laywood. Tel: (01949) 842360 Fax: (01949) 844196. Web: www.forestbooks.co.uk. E mail: bib@forestbooks.co.uk. Est: 1979. Private premises. Internet and Postal. Appointment necessary. Medium stock. Spec: Bibliography; Bindings; Bookbinding; Books about Books; Papermaking; Printing; Typography. PR: £5–5,000. CC: MC; V. Mem: PBFA.

SANDIACRE

A.E. Beardsley, 14 York Avenue, Sandiacre, NG10 5HB. Prop: Tony and Irene Beardsley. Tel: (0115) 917-0082. Web: www.ukbookworld.com/members/aebbooks. E-mail: aebbooks@ntlworld.com. Est: 1991. Private premises. Appointment necessary. Small stock. Spec: Countries - Malaysia; Topography - General; Travel - General; Booksearch. PR: £4–400. Notes: *Exhibits at Buxton Book Fair - 1,000 books on www.abebooks.com*

SUTTON IN ASHFIELD

Fackley Services, 6 Ash Grove Skegby, Sutton in Ashfield, NG17 3FH. Prop: Malcolm Walters. Tel: (01623) 552530. Fax: (01623) 552530. Web: www.kingfisher-books.co.uk. E-mail: searcher@ fackley.co.uk. Est: 1991. Private premises. Postal Only. Very small stock. Spec: Children's, Fiction - General; History - Local; Military; Military History; Non-Fiction; out-of-print; Royalty - European. PR: £3–100. CC: AE; E; JCB; MC; V. Notes: *Specialising mainly on Booksearch, Observer's Pocket Series, Military and General stock.*

OXFORDSHIRE

ABINGDON

Bennett & Kerr Books, Millhill Warehouse Church Lane, Steventon, Abingdon, OX13 6SW. Prop: (*) Edmund Bennett & Andrew Kerr. Tel: (01235) 820604. Fax: (01235) 821047. Web: www. abebooks.com/home/bennettkerr. E-mail: bennettkerr@aol.com. Est: 1982. Office and/or bookroom. Internet and Postal. Telephone First. Open: **M:** 09:30–17:30; **T:** 09:30–17:30; **W:** 09:30– 17:30; **Th:** 09:30–17:30; **F:** 09:30–17:30; **S:** 10:00–13:00. Closed for lunch: 13:15–14:15. Medium stock. Spec: Academic/Scholarly; Architecture; Art History; Arthurian; Author - James, M.R.; - Shakespeare, William; Byzantium; Ecclesiastical History & Architecture. PR: £5–1,000. CC: MC; V; Switch. Cata: Medieval & Renascence studies. Corresp: French, Italian. Mem: ABA; PBFA; ILAB. VAT No: GB 348 7058 28. Notes: *We specialise in books on the European Middle Ages, from late antiquity to the renascence,including art, architecture, history & literature.*

Courtenay Bookroom, Appleford, Abingdon, OX14 4PB. Prop: G. Duffield. Tel: (01235) 848319. Est: 1960. Spec: Academic/Scholarly; Antiquarian; Bibles; Dictionaries; History - General; Theology; Ephemera; Prints and Maps. PR: £1–10,000.

B. & N. Kentish, Old Farmhouse Longworth, Abingdon, OX13 5ET. Tel: (01865) 820711. E-mail: briankentish@yahoo.co.uk. Private premises. Postal Only. Spec: Atlases. Notes: *Also see under Prints & Map Sellers.*

Mary Mason, 55 Winterborne Road, Abingdon, OX14 1AL. Prop: Mary Mason. Tel: (01235) 559929. Web: www.masonpeett.co.uk. E-mail: marymason@mmbooks.freeserve.co.uk. Est: 1988. Private premises. Internet and Postal. Appointment necessary. Medium stock. Spec: Art; Author - Ardizzone, Edward; Children's; Illustrated - General; Juvenile. PR: £1–1,000. CC: PayPal. Corresp: French. Notes: *Booksearch*

PsychoBabel Books & Journals, 56b Milton Park, Abingdon, OX14 4RX. Prop: Chris Edwards. Tel: 01235 861411. Fax: 01235 861422. Web: www.psychobabel.co.uk. E-mail: psychobabel@ btconnect.com. Est: 2003. Warehouse. Internet and Postal. Contactable. Open: **M:** 08:30–18:00; **T:** 08:30–18:00; **W:** 08:30–18:00; **Th:** 08:30–18:00; **F:** 08:30–18:00; **S:** 10:00–14:00; **Su:** 10:00–14:00. Spec: Academic/Scholarly; Biblical Studies; Celtica; Communism; Eastern Philosophy; Ecclesiastical History & Architecture; Economics; Encyclopaedias. CC: AE; MC; V; PayPal, £ or $ cheques. Corresp: German, French, Spanish. VAT No: GB 824 8827 00. Notes: *PsychoBabel specialises in academic texts, although we maintain a stock of general literature and non-fiction titles. More stock added daily. Sameday despatch. You can browse/buy from our homepage or http://ukbookworld.com/ members/PsychoBab.*

BANBURY

Books, The Old Forge Upper Brailes, Banbury, OX15 5AT. Prop: Mrs E.M. Pogmore. Tel: (01608) 685260. Web: www.pogmore@marg3.freeserve.co.uk. E-mail: pogmore@marg3.freeserve.co.uk. Est: 1985. Private premises. Postal Only. Contactable. Small stock. Spec: Author - Fleming, Ian; Autobiography; Cookery/Gastronomy, Modern First Editions, Poetry; Tapestry. PR: £1 200.

PROJECT PORTMANTEAUX - EVERY MAN A DEBTOR

Give thought - Virtue can be fun

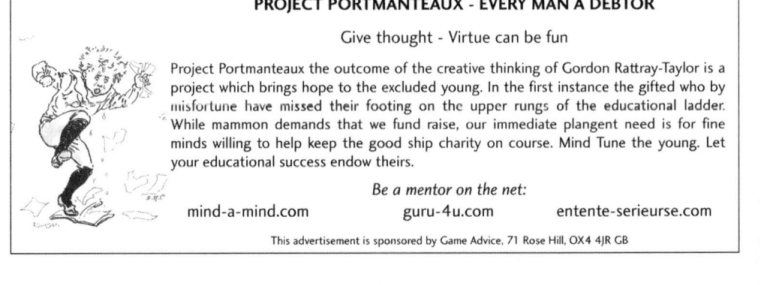

Project Portmanteaux the outcome of the creative thinking of Gordon Rattray-Taylor is a project which brings hope to the excluded young. In the first instance the gifted who by misfortune have missed their footing on the upper rungs of the educational ladder. While mammon demands that we fund raise, our immediate plangent need is for fine minds willing to help keep the good ship charity on course. Mind Tune the young. Let your educational success endow theirs.

Be a mentor on the net:
mind-a-mind.com   guru-4u.com   entente-serieurse.com

This advertisement is sponsored by Game Advice, 71 Rose Hill, OX4 4JR GB

OXFORDSHIRE

Books & Ink, ■ 4 White Lion Street, Banbury, OX16 5UD. Prop: Sheryl Root and Samantha Barnes. Tel: 01295 709769. Web: www.booksandink.co.uk. E-mail: books@booksandink.co.uk. Est: 2005. Shop open: **M:** 09:00–17:30; **T:** 09:00–17:30; **W:** 09:00–17:30; **Th:** 09:00–17:30; **F:** 09:00–17:30; **S:** 09:00–17:30. Spec: Prints and Maps. CC: MC; V. Mem: BA; Ibooknet. VAT No: GB 868 2729 75. Notes: *We also stock a range of gifts, cards and prints.*

BLEWBURY

Blewbury Antiques, ■ London Road, Blewbury, OX11 9NX. Prop: Eric Richardson. Tel: (01235) 850366. Est: 1971. Shop open: **M:** 10:00–18:00; **Th:** 10:00–18:00; **F:** 10:00–18:00; **S:** 10:00–18:00; **Su:** 10:00–18:00. Very small stock. Spec: Notes: *Also, collectables, garden ornaments.*

BURFORD

The Classics Bookshop, Greyhounds 23 Sheep Street, Burford, OX18 4LS. Prop: Anne and Philip Powell-Jones. Tel: 01993 822969. Fax: 01993 822969. Web: www.classicsbookshop.com. E-mail: sales@ classicsbookshop.com. Est: 1975. Office and/or bookroom open: **W:** 10:00–17:00; **S:** 10.00–17:00. Closed for lunch: 13:00–14:00. Spec: Archaeology; Art; Classical Studies; English; History - Ancient, Sport - Angling/Fishing. CC: AE; MC; V. Cata: Latin and Greek Classics. Mem: PBFA. VAT No: GB 298 2963 94.

CHIPPING NORTON

Greensleeves, P.O. Box 156, Chipping Norton, OX7 3XT. Prop: P.R. & C. Seers. Tel: 01993 832423. Fax: 01993 832423. Web: www.greensleevesbooks.co.uk. E-mail: greensleeves.books@virgin.net. Est: 1982. Private premises. Internet and Postal. Medium stock. Spec: Alternative Medicine; Anthroposophy; Astrology; Esoteric; Health; Herbalism; Homeopathy; Metaphysics. PR: £1–500. CC: MC; V; Switch. Cata: on specialised subjects. Mem: BA. VAT No: GB 596 3357 96. Notes: *Also, new books and booksearch service.*

Kellow Books, ■ 6 Market Place, Chipping Norton, OX7 5NA. Prop: Peter & Jan Combellack. Tel: (01608) 644293. E-mail: kellowbooks@yahoo.co.uk. Est: 1998. Shop open: **M:** 10:00–16:30; **T:** 10:00–16:30; **W:** 10:00–16:30; **Th:** 10:00–16:30; **F:** 10:00–16:30; **S:** 10:00–16:30. Medium stock. Spec: Children's; Company History; Fiction - General; Maritime/Nautical; Military History; Natural History; Ornithology; Topography - General. PR: £2–800. CC: D; E; JCB; MC; V; All cards.

COWLEY

Thornton's Bookshop, 65 St Luke's Road, Cowley, Oxford, OX4 3JE. Prop: W.A. Meeuws. Tel: (01865) 779832. Fax: (01865) 321126. Web: www.thorntonsbooks.co.uk. E-mail: thorntons@ booknews.demon.co.uk. Est: 1835. Private premises. Internet and Postal. Contactable. Medium stock. Spec: Academic/Scholarly; Africana; Antiquarian; Antiquities; Arabica; Archaeology; Author - Tolkien, J.R.R.; Bindings. PR: £15–1,000. CC: E; MC; V; Maestro. Corresp: French, Dutch, German, Spanish, Italian. Mem: ABA; BA; ILAB; BASEES. VAT No: GB 194 4663 31. Notes: *Oxford's oldest university bookshop closed to the public at the end of 2002 after 167 years. Business now only via the internet.*

DIDCOT

The Parlour Bookshop, ■ 30 Wantage Road, Didcot, OX11 0BT. Prop: Roy Burton. Tel: (01235) 818989. Fax: (01235) 814494. Est: 1995. Shop open: **W:** 10:00–16:00; **Th:** 10:00–16:00; **F:** 10:00–16:00. Closed for lunch: 12:45–13:45. Small stock. Spec: Military; Railways; Topography - General. PR: £1–50. Notes: *Closed Bank Holidays, Good Friday, Easter Monday, Christmas Eve to 4 January.*

Wayside Books & Cards, Wayside Wellshead Harwell, Didcot, OX11 0HD. Prop: J.A.B. & J.L. Gibson. Tel: (01235) 835256. E-mail: gibsonjab@aol.com. Est: 1985. Private premises. Postal Only. Open in Summer. Medium stock. Spec: Astronomy; Author - Asimov, Isaac; Author - Cecil, H.; - Clarke, Arthur C.; - Cornwell, Bernard; - Greene, Graham; - Le Carre, John; - MacDonald, George. PR: £1–100.

DORCHESTER ON THAMES

Pablo Butcher, Overy Mill, Dorchester on Thames, OX10 7JU. Tel: (01865) 341445. Fax: (01865) 340180. Est: 1974. Private premises. Appointment necessary. Small stock. Spec: Art; Ethnography; Photography; Travel - Africa; Travel - Americas; Travel - Asia, South East; Travel - India; Travel - Islamic World. Mem: ABA; PBFA; ILAB.

OXFORDSHIRE

DUCKLINGTON

Demetzy Books, Manor House 29 Standlake Road, Ducklington, OX29 7UX. Prop: Paul & Marie Hutchinson. Tel: 01993 702209. Fax: 01993 702209. E-mail: demetzybooks@tiscali.co.uk. Est: 1971. Prem: Market stand/stall; Shop At: 113 Portobello Road, London W.11. Open: **S:** 07:00–15.00. Spec: Antiquarian; Juvenile; Miniature Books; Natural Sciences; Surgery; Travel - General. CC: JCB; MC; V. Mem: ABA; PBFA; ILAB.

EAST HAGBOURNE

E.M. Lawson & Company, Kingsholm Main Street, East Hagbourne, OX11 9LN. Prop: W.J. & K.M. Lawson. Tel: (01235) 812033. Est: 1921. Private premises. Appointment necessary. Very small stock. Spec: Antiquarian; Countries - Africa; Countries - Americas, The; Countries - Australasia; Economics; Literature; Medicine; Science - General. Cata: on general subjects. Mem: ABA; ILAB;

FARINGDON

Evergreen Livres, Westland House Westland Road, Faringdon, SN7 7EY. Prop: N.S. O'Keeffe. Tel: (01367) 244773. Fax: (01367) 244773. E-mail: ocker@oxfree.com. Est: 1984. Display/stand. Telephone First. Very small stock. Spec: Dogs; Farming & Livestock; First Editions; Gardening - General; Horticulture; Natural History. PR: £2–500.

N.W. Jobson, 8 Weston Cottages Buscot Wick, Faringdon, SN7 8DN. Prop: Nigel Jobson. Tel: (01367) 252240. E-mail: jobbobookfinder@tiscali.co.uk. Est: 1981. Private premises. Internet and Postal. Small stock. Spec: Booksearch. PR: £1–100. Mem: National Fedreration of Market Traders. Notes: *Also, a booksearch service. Secondhand Bookstall, Shambles Market, Every Tuesday,7.30am - 3pm.*

Bed and Books   Birds and Beauty

The High Road to the islands lined with literature

book-lined.com

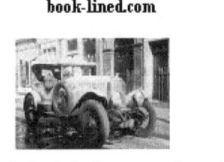

If you like to see and feel before you buy the books you will love you will buy from and stay with one of the partners who support the entente-serieuse.com who you will find listed near a scenic route at not-the-M40.com which will brings you to-

Game-Advice

A Mecca for "medics-beyond-medicine.com"

On the ground @ 71 Rose Hill OX4 4JR +44 1865 777 317

GORING–ON–THAMES

Nevis Railway Books, ■ Barbara's The Orchard, Goring–on–Thames, RG8 9HB. Prop: N.J. Bridger. Tel: 01635 200507 and 01635 200507. Web: www.nevis-railway-bookshops.co.uk. Est: 1992. Shop open: **M:** 10:00–17:00; **T:** 10:00–17:00; **W:** 10:00–17:00; **Th:** 10:00–17:00; **F:** 10:00–17:00; **S:** 10:00–17:00. Closed for lunch: 13:00–14:15. Very small stock. Spec: Railways (GWR). PR: £1–50. Notes: *Railway Book & Magazine Search, Newbury, Berks. (qv.) Nevis railway Bookshops, Marlborough, Wilts (q.v).*

HENLEY ON THAMES

Jonkers Rare Books, 24 Hart Street, Henley on Thames, RG9 2AU. Tel: (01491) 576427. Web: www.jonkers.co.uk. E-mail: info@jonkers.co.uk. Est: 1990. Shop and/or showroom open: **M:** 10:00– 17:30; **T:** 10:00–17:30; **W:** 10:00–17:30; **Th:** 10:00–17:30; **F:** 10:00–17:30; **S:** 10:00–17:30. Small stock. Spec: Arthurian; Author - 19th Century; - 20th Century; - Betjeman, Sir John; - Blyton, Enid; - Brontes, The; - Christie, Agatha; - Eliot, T.S. PR: £25–1,000,000. CC: AE; E; MC; V. Cata: on specialist subjects. Corresp: Italian, French, Spanish. Mem: ABA; PBFA; BA; ILAB.

Way's Bookshop, ■ 54B Friday Street, Henley on Thames, RG9 1AH. Prop: Diana Cooks and Richard Way. Tel: 01491 576663. Fax: 01491 576663. E-mail: waybooks@btconnect.com. Est: 1978. Shop open: **M:** 10:00–17:00; **T:** 10:00–17:00; **W:** 10:00–17:00; **Th:** 10:00–17:00; **F:** 10:00–17:00; **S:** 10:00– 17:00. Spec: CC: MC; V. Mem: ABA; Notes: *Parking at rear of shop.*

HOOK NORTON

Orangeberry Books, Rowan House Queens Street, Hook Norton, Banbury, OX15 5PH. Prop: Paul Tranter. Tel: (01608) 737928. Fax: (01608) 730810. Web: www.orangeberry.co.uk. E-mail: books@orangeberry.co.uk. Est: 1995. Private premises. Internet and Postal. Telephone First. Medium stock. Spec: Literature; Poetry; Science - General; Technology; Travel - General. PR: £5– 1,000. CC: E; MC; V; Maestro/Switch. Corresp: French. Mem: IBN. VAT No: GB 800 0734 85. Notes: *Vistors welcomed - it is advisable to phone first.*

OXFORD

Antiques on High, ■ 85 High Street, Oxford, OX1 4BG. Prop: Tony Sloggett and Joan Lee. Tel: (01865) 251075. Web: www.antiquesonhigh.co.uk. E-mail: enquiries@antiquesonhigh.co.uk. Est: 1997. Shop open: **M:** 10:00–17:00; **T:** 10:00–17:00; **W:** 10:00–17:00; **Th:** 10:00–17:00; **F:** 10:00–17:00; **S:** 10:00– 17:00; **Su:** 11:00–17:00; Medium stock. Spec: Antiques; Architecture; Art; Art History; Autobiography; Biography; Children's; Collecting. PR: £1–200. CC: AE; E; MC; V. Mem: TVADA. Notes: *Has stock for 'Books on High' and 'Music Bookshop'.*

Arcadia, ■ 4 St. Michael's Street, Oxford, OX1 2DU. Tel: (01865) 241757. Est: 1975. Shop open: **M:** 10:00–17:30; **T:** 10:00–17:30; **W:** 10:00–17:30; **Th:** 10:00–17:30; **F:** 10:00–17:30; **S:** 10:00–18:00. Very small stock. Spec: Publishers - Penguin; Ephemera; Prints and Maps. PR: £1–50. CC: AE; D; E; JCB; MC; V. Mem: PBFA. Notes: *Mainly prints and postcards.*

Ars Artis, 31 Abberbury Road, Oxford, OX4 4ET. Prop: G.B. & H.J. Lowe. Tel: 01865 770714. Est: 1976. Private premises. Appointment necessary. Spec: Applied Art; Architecture; Art History; Art Reference; Artists; Catalogues Raisonnes; Fine Art; Photography. VAT No: GB 119 1785 58.

Blackwell's Music Shop, ■ 23-25 Broad Street, Oxford, OX1 3AX. Tel: (01865) 333580. Fax: (01865) 728020. Web: www.blackwell.co.uk/printedmusic. E-mail: books.music@blackwell.co.uk. Est: 1955. Shop. Internet and Postal open: **M:** 09:00–18:00; **T:** 09:30–18:00; **W:** 09:00–18:00; **Th:** 09:00–18:00; **F:** 09:00–18:00; **S:** 09:00–18:00; **Su:** 11:00 17:00, Very large stock. Spec: Music - General; Music - Classical; Music - Composers; Music - Musicians; Music - Opera. PR: £2–175. CC: MC; V.

Blackwell's Rare Books, ■ 48 - 51 Broad Street, Oxford, OX1 3BQ. Tel: (01865) 333555. Fax: (01865) 794143. Web: www.rarebooks.blackwell.co.uk. E-mail: rarebooks@blackwell.co.uk. Est: 1879. Shop. Internet and Postal open: **M:** 09:00–18:00; **T:** 09:30–18:00; **W:** 09:00–18:00; **Th:** 09:00–18:00; **F:** 09:00– 18:00; **S:** 09:00–18:00. Small stock. Spec: Antiquarian; British Books; Children's - Early Titles; Children's - Illustrated; Countries - General; County - Local; Early Imprints; Fiction - General. PR: £20–20,000. CC: MC; V. Cata: Wide range of subjects. Corresp: French, German. Mem: ABA; PBFA; BA; ILAB. Notes: *Blackwell's Rare Books is situated within the famous Blackwell's Bookshop, which houses a huge range of new books,often in great depth, particularly in academic subjects. There is also a large secondhand books section in the same building.*

Roy Davids Ltd., The Old Forge Rectory Road, Great Haseley, Oxford, OX44 7JG. Prop: Roy Davids. Tel: (01844) 279154. Fax: (01844) 278221. Web: www.roydavids.com. E-mail: manuscripts@ roydavids.com. Est: 1994. Private premises. Spec: Autographs; History - General; Letters; Manuscripts; Music - General; Collectables; Ephemera. PR: £50–100,000. CC: MC; V. Mem: ABA; ILAB. Notes: *Also, portraits and related artefacts.*

OXFORDSHIRE

Game Advice, 71 Rose Hill, Oxford, OX4 4JR. Prop: Alick Elithorn & Karen Stevenson. Tel: (01865) 777317. Fax: (01865) 433050. Web: www.game-advice.com. E-mail: a.elithorn@ntlworld.com. Est: 1975. Private premises. Internet and Postal. Telephone First. Large stock. Spec: Academic/Scholarly; Alternative Medicine; Anthropology; Children's; Computing; Education & School; Feminism; Fore-Edge Paintings. PR: £3–9,000. Corresp: French. Notes: *Also, chess sets, antique games & puzzles, chess prints, educational software, computer & personal consultancy, booksearch & loan.*

Hanborough Books, The Foundry Church Hanborough, Nr. Witney, Oxford, OX29 8AB. Prop: Dennis Hall. Tel: (01993) 881260. Fax: (01993) 883080. Web: www.parrotpress.co.uk. E-mail: dennis@ parrotpress.co.uk. Est: 1970. Private premises. Telephone First. Small stock. Spec: Antiquarian; Illustrated - General; Limited Editions - General; Private Press; Typography. PR: £5–650. CC: MC; V. VAT No: GB 490 6827 17.

The Inner Bookshop, ■ 111 Magdalen Road, Oxford, OX4 1RQ. Prop: R.E. Ashcroft & A.S. Cheke. Tel: (01865) 245301. Fax: (01865) 245521. Web: www.innerbookshop.com. E-mail: mail@ innerbookshop.com. Est: 1982. Shop. Internet and Postal open: **M:** 10:00–17:45; **T:** 10:00–17:45; **W:** 10:00–17:45; **Th:** 10:00–17:45; **F:** 10:00–17:45; **S:** 10:00–17:45. Large stock. Spec: Aboriginal; Academic/Scholarly; Acupuncture; Alchemy; Alternative Medicine; American Indians; Animals and Birds; Anthroposophy. PR: £1–1,000. CC: MC; V; SW, SO. Corresp: French. Mem: BA; FSB. Notes: *Also, new books on specialities & tarot cards, New Age music, bargain books and a passive booksearch service.*

Leabeck Books, Meadowbrook Farm Sheepwash Lane, Steventon, Oxford, OX13 6SD. Prop: Tony Sloggett. Tel: (01235) 820914. E-mail: tony.sloggett@btinternet.com. Est: 1993. Private premises. Internet and Postal. Appointment necessary. Small stock. Spec: Antiques; Art; Children's; First Editions; History - General; Illustrated - General; Literature; Travel - General. PR: £5–200. Corresp: French, German. Notes: *Antiques on High, 85 High Street, Oxford, OX1 4BG.*

Chris Morris Secondhand & Antiquarian Books, 67 Home Close Wolvercote, Oxford, OX2 8PT. Tel: (01865) 557806. E-mail: chrisandbarbara@yahoo.com. Est: 1992. Private premises. Internet and Postal. Small stock. Spec: Automobilia/Automotive; Broadcasting; Cinema/Film; Countries - Greece; Media; Memorabilia; Motoring; Music - Chart Histories & Research. PR: £1–75. Notes: *Also, a booksearch service*

Oxfam Bookshop, St Giles, ■ 56 St Giles, Oxford, OX1 3LU. Prop: Manager: Jen Elford. Tel: 01865 310145. Web: www.oxfamstgiles.co.uk. E-mail: stgiles56@yahoo.co.uk. Est: 1987. Shop open: **M:** 10:00–17:30; **T:** 10:00–17:30; **W:** 10:00–17:30; **Th:** 10:00–17:30; **F:** 10:00–17:30; **S:** 10:00–17:30. CC: E; JCB; MC; V; Switch, Maestro. Cata: but on-line only. Corresp: French, German, Italian.

St Philip's Books, ■ 82 St. Aldates, Oxford, OX1 1RA. Prop: Christopher James Zealley. Tel: (01865) 202182. Fax: (01865) 202184. Web: www.stphilipsbooks.co.uk. E-mail: sales@stphilipsbooks.co.uk. Est: 1995. Internet and Postal. Shop open: **M:** 10:00–17:00; **T:** 10:00–17:00; **W:** 10:00–17:00; **Th:** 10:00–17:00; **F:** 10:00–17:00; **S:** 10:00–17:00. Large stock. Spec: Academic/Scholarly; Antiquarian; Art History; Author - Belloc, Hilaire; - Benson, R.H.; - Chesterton, G.K.; - Inklings, The; - Lewis, C.S. PR: £1–2,000. CC: MC; V; SO, SW, Maestro. Cata: Theology, Church History. Mem: PBFA; BA. VAT No: GB 717 925 021. Notes: *Religious books bought nationwide. Our special interests include Roman Catholicism, Eastern Christianity, Newman and Oxford Movement, C.S.Lewis and Inklings, Biblical studies, Patristics, Chesterton and Distributism, Latin liturgy & chant.*

Waterfield's, ■ 52 High Street, Oxford, OX1 4AS. Prop: Robin Waterfield Ltd. Tel: (01865) 721809. Est. 1973. Shop open: **M:** 09:45–17:45; **T:** 09:45–17:45; **W:** 09:45–17:44; **Th:** 08:45–17:45; **F:** 09:45–17:45; **S:** 09:45–17:45. Large stock. Spec: Academic/Scholarly; Antiquarian; Arts, The; First Editions; History - General; Humanities; Literary Criticism; Literature. PR: £1–5,000. CC: MC; V. Corresp: French. Mem: ABA; PBFA. VAT No: GB 195 8007 39. Notes: *Catalogues also on 17th and 18thC books.*

STONESFIELD

Austin Sherlaw-Johnson, Woodland View Churchfields, Stonesfield, OX29 8PP. Tel: (01993) 898223. E-mail: austin.sherlaw-johnson@virgin.net. Est: 2001. Private premises. Appointment necessary. Open. **M:** 09:00–17:00; **T:** 09:00–17:00; **W:** 09:00–17:00; **Th:** 09:00–17:00; **F:** 09:00–17:00. Medium stock. Spec: Music - General; Music - Classical; Music - Composers; Music - Folk & Irish Folk; Music - Gilbert & Sullivan; Music - Gregorian Chants; Music - Illustrated Sheet Music; Music - Jazz & Blues. PR: £1–500. Notes: *Malvern Bookshop, Malvern, Worcestershire (q.v.) Antiques on High, 85 High Street, Oxford.*

WALLINGFORD

Toby English, ■ 10 St. Mary's Street, Wallingford, OX10 0EL. Tel: (01491) 836389. Fax: (01491) 836389. Web: www.tobyenglish.com. E-mail: toby@tobyenglish.com. Est: 1981. Shop open: **M:** 09:30 17:00, **T:** 09:30–17:00; **W:** 09:30–17:00; **Th:** 09:30–16:45; **F:** 09:30–16:45; **S:** 09:30–17:00. Large stock. Spec: Academic/Scholarly, Architecture; Art; Art Reference; Author - Inklings, The; First Editions; Private Press; Topography - Local. PR: £1–500. CC: AE; JCB; MC; V; SW. Mem: PBFA. Notes: *General stock, specialities art and architecture, Thames books, also provide a booksearch service.*

Tooley, Adams & Co, PO Box 174, Wallingford D.O., OX10 0RB. Prop: Steve Luck. Tel: 01491 838298. Fax: 01491834616. Web: www.tooleys.co.uk. E-mail: steve@tooleys.co.uk. Est: 1979. Private premises. Internet and Postal. Telephone First. Open: **M:** 09:00–17:00; **T:** 09:00–17:00; **W:** 09:00– 17:00; **Th:** 09:00–17:00; **F:** 09:00–17:00. Spec: Antiquarian; Caricature; Cartography; Geography; River Thames. CC: AE; D; E; MC; V. Cata: Maps, Atlases, Views, Cartobibliographies. Corresp: French, Spanish. Mem: ABA; ILAB; International Antiquarian Mapdealers Assoc. VAT No: GB 371 2110 01.

WANTAGE

Parrott Books, ■ Regent Mall Town Centre, Wantage, OX12 8BU. Tel: (01367) 820251. Fax: (01367) 820210. E-mail: parrottbooks@aol.com. Est: 1997. Shop open: **M:** 08:30–17:30; **T:** 08:30–17:30; **W:** 08:30–17:30; **Th:** 08:30–17:30; **F:** 08:30–17:30; **S:** 08:30–17:00. Very large stock. Spec: Aircraft; Alpinism/Mountaineering; Animals and Birds, Archaeology; Architecture; Art Reference; Biography; Children's. PR: £2–50. Notes: *Parrott Books try to offer an eclectic mix of secondhand and antiquarian books.*

Regent Furniture, ■ Regent Shopping Mall Newbury Street, Wantage, OX12 8BU. Prop: W.O. & S. Mudway. Tel: 01235 766625. Est: 1995. Shop open: **M:** 08:30–17:00; **T:** 08:30–17:00; **W:** 08:30–17:00; **Th:** 08:30–17:00; **F:** 08:30–17:00; **S:** 08:30–17:00. VAT No: GB 685 6589 65.

WARBOROUGH

Nineteenth Century Books, St. Mary's Cottage 61 Thame Road, Warborough, Wallingford, OX10 7EA. Prop: Dr. Ann M. Ridler. Tel: (01865) 858379. Fax: (01865) 858575. Web: www.ukbookworld.com/ members/papageno. E-mail: annridlersoutter@warboro.fsnet.co.uk. Est: 1984. Private premises. Internet and Postal. Small stock. Spec: Author - Borrow, George; Biography; Books about Books; History - General; Literary Criticism; Literary Travel; Literature; Natural History. PR: £5–500. CC: MC; V. Cata: Nineteenth Century. Corresp: French, Spanish. Mem: PBFA.

WITNEY

Brian Carter, 8 Swan Court, Corn Street, Witney, OX28 6EA. Prop: Brian Carter. Tel: (01993) 866627. E-mail: carterbe@btinternet.com. Est: 1974. Private premises. Postal Only. Contactable. Small stock. Spec: Ecclesiastical History & Architecture; Oxford Movement; Philosophy; Theology. PR: £5–500. CC: MC; V. Cata: Theology/Church History. Notes: *We take telephone calls from 09:00 to 21:00 all week.*

Church Green Books, ■ 46 Market Square, Witney, OX28 6AL. Prop: Roger & Margaret Barnes. Tel: (01993) 700822. Web: www.churchgreen.co.uk. E-mail: books@churchgreen.co.uk. Est: 1992. Shop open: **M:** 10:00–16:00; **T:** 10:00–16:00; **W:** 10:00–16:00; **Th:** 10:00–16:00; **F:** 10:00–16:00. Medium stock. Spec: Bell-Ringing (Campanology); Music - Folk & Irish Folk; Rural Life; Topography - Local; Booksearch. PR: £1–300. CC: MC; V. Mem: PBFA. Notes: *Valuations of Bell-ringing books.*

RUTLAND

UPPINGHAM

The Rutland Bookshop, ■ 13 High Street West, Uppingham, LE15 9QB. Prop: Mr & Mrs Edward Baines. Tel: 01572 823450 (24 hr answerphone). Est: 1979. Shop open: **M:** ; **T:** 11:00–17:00; **W:** 11:00–17:00; **Th:** 11:00–17:00; **F:** 11:00–17:00; **S:** 11:00–17:00. Medium stock. Spec: Education & School; Farming & Livestock; Farriers; Fiction - General; Fine & Rare; Gardening - General; Literary Criticism; Natural History. PR: £1–500. Corresp: French, German. Mem: PBFA. Notes: *Attends: Burghley Horse Trials, Rutland Water Bird Fair and Rutland & Leicester Agricultural Show. Lists on request.*

Forest Books, ■ 7 High Street West, Uppingham, Rutland, LE15 9QB. Prop: David Siddons. Tel: (01572) 821173. Fax: (0870) 1326314. Web: www.homepages.primex.co.uk/forest. E-mail: forestbooks@rutlanduk.fsnet.co.uk. Est: 1986. Shop open: **M:** 10:30–17:00; **T:** 10:30–17:00; **W:** 10:30–17:00; **Th:** 10:30–17:00; **F:** 10:30–17:00; **S:** 10:30–17:00; **Su:** 13:30–16:30. Very large stock. Spec: Music - Sheet Music; Booksearch; Ephemera. PR: £1–500. CC: JCB; MC; V; Solo Maestro. Corresp: French. VAT No: GB 424 4691 51. Notes: *We also organise book fairs - 2 a year in Farndon, Nottinghamshire, and one a year in Uppingham. Also, full copying service in the shop (including A3 colour copying). Secondhand sheet music, postcards. We also sell local new OS maps.*

SHROPSHIRE

BISHOP'S CASTLE

Autolycus, ■ 10 Market Square, Bishop's Castle, SY9 5BN. Prop: David & Jay Wilkinson. Tel: (01588) 630078. Fax: (01588) 630078. Web: www.booksonline.uk.com. E-mail: autolycusbc@aol.com. Est: 1996. Shop. Internet and Postal open: **M:** 11:00–16:30; **T:** 11:00–16:30; **W:** 11:00–16:30; **Th:** 11:00–16:30; **F:** 11:00–17:00; **S:** 10:30–17:00. Medium stock. Spec: Antiquarian; Children's; Children's - Early Titles; Children's - Illustrated; First Editions; Illustrated - General; Literature; Modern First Editions. PR: £1–1,500. CC: MC; V; Maestro, also PayPal. Cata: Lists on request. Corresp: French, German. VAT No: GB 771 9717 90. Notes: *Please telephone if travelling from afar as opening hours may vary.*

Yarborough House Bookshop, ■ Yarborough House The Square, Bishop's Castle, SY9 5BN. Prop: Carol Wright. Tel: (01588) 638318. E-mail: mail@yarboroughhouse.com. Est: 1980. Shop open: **T:** 10:00–17:30; **Th:** 10:00–17:30; **F:** 10:00–17:30; **S:** 09:00–17:30; **Su:** 10:00–17:30. Medium stock. Spec: Fiction - General; Collectables. PR: £1–20. CC: AE; D; E; JCB; MC; V Notes: *Also, 4,000 secondhand classic records 4,000 classic CDs and coffee house home made cakes coffees and teas.*

BRIDGNORTH

The Bookpassage, ■ 57a High Street, Bridgnorth, WV16 4DX. Prop: David Lamont. Tel: (01746) 768767. Web: www.thebookpassage.co.uk. E-mail: bookman@btconnect.com. Est: 1990. Shop open: **M:** 09:00–17:15; **T:** 09:00–17:15; **W:** 08:00–17:15; **Th:** 09:00–17:15; **F:** 09:00–17:15; **S:** 09:00–17:15. Large stock. Spec: Author - General; - 20th Century; - Saville, M.; Authors - Local; County - Local; Fiction - General; Fiction - Adventure; Fiction - Crime, Detective, Spy, Thrillers. PR: £1–500. Notes: *Open occasionally on Sundays, specialists in local history and local authors.*

ELLESMERE

Glyn's Books, 6 The Avenue, Lyneal, Ellesmere, SY12 0QJ. Prop: Glyn Watson. Tel: (01948) 710591. Fax: (01948) 710442. Web: www.glynsbooks.com. E-mail: glyn@glynsbooks.com. Est: 1986. Private premises. Internet and Postal. Spec: Astrology; First Editions; History - General; Literature; Booksearch. CC: AE; D; E; JCB; MC; V. Notes: *Also, a major international booksearch service.*

JACKFIELD

The Boox-Box, 10 Chapel View Chapel Road, Jackfield, TF8 7LU. Tel: 07976 579848. E-mail: johnjones3@btinternet.com. Private premises. Internet Only. Telephone First. Open: **M:** 09:00–17:30; **T:** 09:00–17:30; **W:** 09:00–17:30; **Th:** 09:00–17:30; **F:** 09:00–17:30. Closed for lunch: 13:00–14:00. Spec: Author - Rolt, L.T.C.; Steam Engines.

LUDLOW

Ampersand Books, Ludford Mill, Ludlow, SY8 1PR. Prop: Michael Dawson. Tel: (01584) 877813. Fax: (01584) 877519. Web: www.ampersandbooks.co.uk. E-mail: poppingup@ampersandbooks.co.uk. Est: 1982. Private premises. Appointment necessary. Small stock. Spec: Children's; Children's - Illustrated; Pop-Up, Movable & Cut Out; Collectables; Ephemera. PR: £5–1,000. Notes: *Also, repairing of pop-ups & moveables.*

New dealers in the British Isles can register their business on

www.sheppardsworld.co.uk

SHROPSHIRE

Lyndon Barnes - Books, 3 Mortimer Drive, Ludlow, SY8 4JW. Prop: Lyndon Barnes. Tel: (01568) 780641. Web: www.abebooks.co.uk. E-mail: lyndonbarnes@lyndonbarnes51.wanadoo.co.uk. Est: 1988. Private premises. Internet and Postal. Contactable. Open: **M:** 09:00–20:00; **T:** 09:00–20:00; **W:** 09:00–20:00; **Th:** 09:00–20:00; **F:** 09:00–20:00; **S:** 09:00–20:00; **Su:** 09:00–20:00. Very small stock. Spec: Music - Classical; Music - Country & Western; Music - Jazz & Blues; Music - Popular; Music - Rock & Roll. PR: £2–100. CC: PayPal. Notes: *All stock on abebooks.*

Innes Books, 22 Julian Road, Ludlow, SY8 1HA. Prop: Pat Innes. Tel: (01584) 878146. Web: www.innesbooks.co.uk. E-mail: patricia@innesbooks.fsnet.co.uk. Est: 1997. Private premises. Internet and Postal. Appointment necessary. Open: **M:** 09:00–10:00; **T:** 09:00–10:00; **W:** 09:00–10:00; **Th:** 09:00–10:00; **F:** 09:00–10:00; **S:** 10:00–06:00; **Su:** 10:00–05:00. Small stock. Spec: Academic/ Scholarly; Children's; Fiction - General; Fiction - Crime, Detective, Spy, Thrillers; General Stock; Illustrated - General; Literary Criticism; Literature. PR: £3–600. CC: PayPal. VAT No: GB 812 5174 53.

Offa's Dyke Books, Old School House Downton-on-the Rock, Ludlow, SY8 2HX. Prop: S.R. Bainbridge. Tel: (01584) 856212. Fax: (01584) 856757. E-mail: books@offas-dyke.fsnet.co.uk. Est: 1974. Private premises. Telephone First. Spec: Academic/Scholarly; Advertising; Antiquarian; Antiques; Art; Bindings; Fine & Rare; Literature. CC: PayPal. VAT No: GB 393 9270 15.

Olynthiacs, 19 Castle View Terrace, Ludlow, SY8 2NG. Prop: Neil MacGregor. Tel: (01584) 872671. Web: www.ukbookworld.com/members/olynthiacs. E-mail: juvenal@martial.fsnet.co.uk. Est: 1735. Private premises. Postal Only. Contactable. Open: **M:** 09:00–18:00; **T:** 09:00–18:00; **W:** 09:00–18:00; **Th:** 09:00–18:00; **F:** 09:00–18:00; **S:** 09:00–18:00. Closed for lunch: 13:00–14:00. Medium stock. Spec: Author - Burgess, A.; - Stevenson, Robert Louis; - Wodehouse, P.G.; Biography; Classical Studies; Ecclesiastical History & Architecture; English; Fiction - General. PR: £5–500. Cata: English Language,History, Eton, Oxford, Theology.

MADELAY

C. R. Moore, Park House, Park Lane, Madelay, TF7 5HF. Prop: C. R. Moore. Tel: 01952 585231. Est: 1995. Private premises. Appointment necessary. Spec: Antiquarian; Bindings; Genealogy; Heraldry; Printing; Sport - General; Sport - Football (Soccer); Topography - Local. Notes: *Exhibits at bookfairs.*

MUCH WENLOCK

Good Books, Hill Top Farm Hill Top, Much Wenlock, TF13 6DJ. Prop: Judith Goodman. Tel: (01746) 785250. Web: www.abebooks.com. E-mail: jude_good@btinternet.com. Est: 1996. Private premises. Appointment necessary. Spec: Children's; Private Press; Railways; Sport - Angling/Fishing; Sport - Field Sports. PR: £1–200.

P.J. Mead, 6 Blakeway Hollow, Much Wenlock, TF13 6AR. Tel: (01952) 727591. E-mail: meadbooks@yahoo.com. Est: 1976. Private premises. Postal Only. Spec: Antiquarian; Bibliography; Bindings; Books about Books; Juvenile; Miniature Books; Sport - General. PR: £10–1,000. Mem: PBFA. VAT No: GB 349 3412 50.

Wenlock Books, ■ 12 High Street, Much Wenlock, TF13 6AA. Prop: Anna Dreda. Tel: (01952) 727877. Fax: (01952) 727877. Web: www.wenlockbooks.co.uk. E-mail: info@wenlockbooks.co.uk. Est: 1985. Shop open: **M:** 10:00–17:00; **T:** 10:00–17:00; **W:** 10:00–17:00; **Th:** 10:00–17:00; **F:** 10:00–17:00; **S:** 10:00–17:00. Medium stock. PR: £10–25. CC: MC; V. Mem: BA. VAT No: GB 823 8745 08. Notes: *March to December 09:00 to 17:30 Sundays 11:00 - 17:00. British Book Trade Award awarded Wenlock Books the 'Independent Bookseller of the Year 2006'.*

NEWPORT

Newport Book Shop, ■ 16 Upper Bar, Newport TF10 7EJ. Prop: Mike Barwell. Tel: (01952) 813900. E-mail: michaelmikebar1@aol.com Open: **Th:** 11:30–17:30; **F:** 11:30–17:30; **S:** 11:30–17:30. Medium stock. PR: £1 – 60.

OSWESTRY

Bookworld, ■ 32 Beatrice Street, Oswestry, SY11 1QG. Prop: John Cranwell. Tel: (01691) 657112. Fax: (01691) 657112. Web: www.tgal.co.uk/bookworld. E-mail: jc.bookworld@arrowweb.co.uk. Est: 1993. Shop open: **M:** 09:00–17:00; **T:** 09:00–17:00; **W:** 09:00–17:00; **Th:** 09:00–17:00; **F:** 09:00–17:00; **S:** 09:00–17:00. Medium stock. Spec: Booksearch. PR: £1–1,500. CC: E, JCB; MC; V.

John Read Antiques, 59 Church Street, Oswestry, SY11 2SZ. Prop: John Read. Tel: (01691) 672914. Est: 1964. Open: **T:** 10:00–17:00; **W:** 10:00–17:00; **F:** 10:00–17:00; **S:** 10:00–17:00. PR: £1–150. Notes: *Also antiques. Mobile No: 07802 844891.*

SHREWSBURY

Candle Lane Books, ■ 28 & 29 Princess Street, Shrewsbury, SY1 1LW. Prop: John & Margaret Thornhill. Tel: (01743) 365301. Est: 1974. Shop open: **M:** 09:30–17:00; **T:** 09:00–17:00; **W:** 09:00–17:00; **Th:** 09:00–17:00; **F:** 09:00–17:00; **S:** 09:00–17:00. Very large stock. Spec: Booksearch. PR: £1–3,000. CC: MC; V.

Gemini–Books, The Old Post Office Main Road, Pontesbury, Shrewsbury, SY5 0PS. Prop: Geoff and Rosalie Davies. Tel: 01743 790999. E-mail: gemini-books@uwclub.net. Est: 2000. Storeroom. Appointment necessary. Open: **M:** 10:00–16:00; **T:** 10:00–16:00; **W:** 10:00–16:00; **Th:** 10:00–16:00; **F:** 10:00–16:00; **S:** 10:00–16:00; **Su:** 10:00–16:00; Medium stock. Spec: Children's; Fiction - General. PR: £4–300. CC: AE; JCB; MC; V; Maestro. Notes: *Exhibits at Kinver Book Fair in Staffordshire (3rd Sunday every month).*

Roundwood Books, ■ 24 Claremont Hill, Shrewsbury, SY1 1RD. Prop: Andrew Cork. Tel: (01743) 244833. Web: www.roundwoodbooks.com. E-mail: roundwoodbooks@btconnect.com. Est: 1995. Shop open: **T:** 10:00–16:00; **W:** 10:00–16:00; **Th:** 10:00–16:00; **F:** 10:00–16:00; **S:** 10:00–16:00. Medium stock. PR: £1–50. CC: MC; V. Mem: DTMFC.

The Victorian Gallery, ■ 40 St. John's Hill, Shrewsbury, SY1 1JQ. Prop: R.D. Vernon. Tel: (01743) 356351. Fax: (01743) 356351. E-mail: victoriangallery@xln.co.uk. Est: 1987. Shop open: **M:** 09:00–17:00; **T:** 09:00–17:00; **W:** 09:00–17:00; **Th:** 09:00–17:00; **F:** 09:00–17:00. Very large stock PR · £6–600. CC: accepted.

TELFORD

Andrew Cox, 16 Garbett Road Aqueduct, Telford, TF4 3RX. Prop: Andrew Cox. Tel: (01952) 590630. E-mail: andyaituk@aol.com. Est: 2000. Private premises. Postal Only. Telephone First. Small stock. Spec: Antiquarian; Author - Austen, Jane; - Verne, Jules; - Wells, H.G.; Children's - Illustrated; Fairy/Folk Tales; Fiction - Historical; Fiction - Science Fiction. PR: £10–10.

WEM

Black 5 Books, ■ 54 High Street, Wem, SY4 5DW. Prop: Ken Simpson. Tel: 0845 166 4084. Web: www.black5books.com. E-mail: info@black5books.com. Est: 1984. Shop. Internet and Postal open: **M:** 10:30–17:00; **T:** 10:30–17:00; **W:** ; **Th:** 10:30–17:00; **F:** 10:30–17:00; **S:** 10:30–13.30. Closed for lunch: 13:30–15:00. Very large stock. Spec: Army, The; Autobiography; Aviation; Biography; Children's; Education & School; Fiction - General; Fiction - Historical. PR: £1–200. CC: MC; V; Maestro. Mem: BA. VAT No: GB 701 2786 58. Notes: *If travelling any distance, you are advised to check availability first, as other priorities could lead to temporary closure or early closing.*

Booksets.com Ltd, Unit 5 & 6 Wem Business Park, New Street, Wem, SY4 5JX. Tel: (01948) 710345. Fax: 0870 0521838. Web: www.booksets.com. E-mail: sales@booksets.com. Est: 1974. Warehouse. Internet Only. Contactable. Very large stock. Spec: Academic/Scholarly; Computing; Magazines & Periodicals - General; Reference; Special Collections; University Texts; Ephemera. PR: £5–5,000. CC: AE; MC; V; Maestro. VAT No: GB 696 1311 25.

Kabristan Archives, 19 Foxleigh Grove, Wem, SY4 5BS. Prop: Eileen Hewson FRGS. Tel: (01939) 234061. Web: www.kabristan.org.uk. E-mail: info@kabristan.org.uk. Est: 2004. Private premises. Internet and Postal. Very small stock. Spec: Countries - Himalayas, The; Countries - India; Countries - Ireland; Countries - Ladakh; Genealogy; Geography; Graveyards; Himalayan Kingdoms. PR: £5–100. CC: MC; V. Cata: Irish & Indian graveyards. Notes: *Stock include books on Indian and Irish graveyards. Irish genealogy search engine on web site.*

WHITCHURCH

Barn Books, ■ Pear Tree Farm Norbury, Whitchurch, SY13 4HZ. Prop: Mary Perry. Tel: (01948) 663742. Fax: (01948) 663742. Web: www.barnbooks.co.uk. E-mail: barnbooks@barnbooks.co.uk. Est: 1985. Shop. Internet and Postal open: **F:** 10:00–17:30; **S:** 10:00–17:30; **Su:** 10:00–17:30. Spec: Agriculture; Countries - England, County - Local; Farming & Livestock; Gardening - General; History - Local; Horticulture; Rural Life. PR: £1–500. CC: MC; V. Cata: Gardening, & Local History. Notes: *Also, open on Bank Holidays.*

SOMERSET

BARRINGTON

R.G. Watkins, Books and Prints 7 Water Street, Barrington, Ilminster, TA19 0JR. Prop: Richard Watkins. Tel: (01460) 54188. Web: www.rgwatkins.co.uk. E-mail: inquiries@rgwatkins.co.uk. Est: 1985. Mail Order Only. Contactable. Small stock. Spec: Arts, The; Author - Lawrence, T.E.; Collecting; History - General; Booksearch; Prints and Maps. PR: £1–500. CC: AE; MC; V. Cata: Lawrence of Arabia, Engraved Portraits. Corresp: French. Notes: *Also, a booksearch service.*

BATH

Bath Book Exchange, ■ 35 Broad Street, Bath, BA1 5LP. Tel: (01225) 466214. Est: 1959. Shop open: **M:** 09:30–17:00; **T:** 09:30–17:00; **W:** 09:30–17:00; **Th:** 09:30–17:00; **F:** 09:30–17:00; **S:** 09:30–17:00. Closed for lunch: 13:00–14:00. Medium stock. Spec: Booksearch. PR: £1–10.

Bath Old Books, ■ 9c Margarets Buildings, Bath, BA1 2LP. Prop: Chris Crook, Steven Ferdinando, Chris Phillips, Richard Selby, John Williams. Tel: (01225) 422244. Fax: 0870 8312098. E-mail: batholdbooks@yahoo.co.uk. Est: 1990. Shop. Open in Summer. Open: **M:** 10:00–17:00; **T:** 10:00–17:00; **W:** 10:00–17:00; **Th:** 10:00–17:00; **F:** 10:00–17:00; **S:** 10:00–17:00. Large stock. Spec: Antiquarian; Art; Children's - Illustrated; County - Local; First Editions; Folio Society, The; General Stock; History - General. CC: JCB; MC; V; All Major cards. Corresp: French. Mem: PBFA. Notes: *Booksearch service, Valuations for probate and Insurance purposes.*

George Bayntun, ■ Manvers Street, Bath, BA1 1JW. Prop: E.W.G. Bayntun–Coward. Tel: (01225) 466000. Fax: (01225) 482122. Web: www.georgebayntun.com. E-mail: ebc@georgebayntun.com. Est: 1894. Shop open: **M:** 09:00–17:30; **T:** 09:00–17:30; **W:** 09:00–17:30; **Th:** 09:00–17:30; **F:** 09:00–17:30; **S:** 09:30–13:00. Closed for lunch: 13:00–14:00. Small stock. Spec: Bindings; Children's; Children's - Illustrated; Classics, The; Fine leather bindings (see also Fine & Rare); First Editions; Illustrated - General; Literature. PR: £10–5,000. CC: MC; V; SW, SO. Corresp: French. Mem: ABA; PBFA; ILAB. VAT No: GB 137 5073 71. Notes: *Also, bindery incorporating the famous binding firm of Robert Riviere & Son, est. 1829.*

Camden Books, Bath, BA15JD. Prop: Victor Suchar. Tel: (01225) 337026. Web: www.camdenbooks.com. E-mail: suchcam@msn.com. Est: 1984. Private premises. Internet and Postal. Small stock. Spec: Academic/Scholarly; Antiquarian; Architecture; Art History; Civil Engineering; Classical Studies; Economics; Fine & Rare. PR: £10–2,000. CC: Cheque. Mem: **PBFA**. Notes: *Online business only.*

Janet Clarke, 3 Woodside Cottages Freshford, Bath, BA2 7WJ. Prop: Janet Clarke. Tel: (01225) 723186. Fax: (01225) 722063. Web: www.janetclarke.com. E-mail: janetclarke@ukgateway.net. Est: 1973. Private premises. Postal Only. Small stock. Spec: Author - David, Elizabeth; Cookery/Gastronomy; Food & Drink; Wine; Ephemera. PR. £5–3,000. CC: PayPal. Cata: on specialities. Mem: ABA; BA; ILAB.

Peter Goodden Books Ltd, 7 Clarendon Villas, Widcombe Hill, Bath, BA2 6AG. Prop: Peter Goodden. Tel: (01225) 310986. E-mail: peter.goodden@ukonline.co.uk. Est: 1976. Mail Order Only. Internet and Postal. Open: **M:** 09:00–18:00; **T:** 09:00–18:00; **W:** 09:00–18:00; **Th:** 0900–1800; **F:** 09:00–18:00; **S:** 09:00–18:00; **Su:** 09:00–18:00. Small stock. Spec: Music - General; Music - Classical; Music - Composers; Music - Gilbert & Sullivan; Music - Gregorian Chants; Music - Musicians; Music - Theory; Musical Instruments. PR: £5–1,500. CC: JCB; MC; V. Cata: Music ; some general. Corresp: Simple French. Mem: PBFA. VAT No: GB 195 9854 90. Notes: *Please, no casual callers : much of the stock is not easily viewed.*

George Gregory, Manvers Street, Bath, BA1 1JW. Prop: Charlotte Bayntun-Coward. Tel: (01225) 466000. Fax: (01225) 482122. E-mail: julie@georgebayntun.com. Est: 1846. Shop and/or gallery open: **M:** 09:00–17:30; **T:** 09:00–17:30; **W:** 09:00–17:30; **Th:** 09:00–17:30; **F:** 09:00–17:30; **S:** 09:30–13:00. Closed for lunch: 13:00–14:00. Large stock. Spec: Literature; Prints and Maps. PR: £1–200. CC: MC; V. Notes: *Engraved portraits and views.*

SOMERSET

Hugh Ashley Rayner, 4 Malvern Buildings Fairfield Park, Bath, BA1 6JX. Prop: Hugh A. Rayner. Tel: (01225) 463552. Fax: (01225) 463552. Web: www.indiabooks.co.uk. E-mail: hughrayner@ indiabooks.co.uk. Est: 1986. Private premises. Telephone First. Open: **M:** 10:00–19:00; **T:** 10:00– 19:00; **W:** 10:00–19:00; **Th:** 10:00 19:00; **F:** 10:00–19.00, **S:** 10:00–19:00; **Su:** 12:00–18:00. Small stock. Spec: Antiquarian; Asian Studies; Countries - Asia; Countries - Burma; Countries - Central Asia; Countries - Himalayas, The; Countries - India; Countries - Ladakh. PR: £35–500. CC: AE; D; JCB; MC; V. Cata: India and South Asia. Corresp: German. Mem: PBFA. Notes: *Valuations, Library Cataloguing.*

Solitaire Books, Holly Lawn Prospect Place, Beechen Cliff, Bath, BA2 4QP. Prop: Martyn Thomas. Tel: (01225) 469441. Fax: 0870 135 8843. Web: www.solitairebooks.co.uk. E-mail: sales@ solitairebooks.co.uk. Est: 1994. Private premises. Postal Only. Spec: Author - Ruskin, John; Bibliography; Book Arts; Books about Books; Fine & Rare; Fine Printing; Printing; Private Press. CC: PayPal. Cata: Fine Press & Books about Books. Corresp: Dutch, French, Spanish. Notes: *Solitaire Books specialises in UK private presses, fine printing and related bibliography. We have an excellent selection of books from these presses, although many others are stocked: Alembic, Daniel, Fleece, Old School, Whittington.*

The Traveller's Bookshelf, Canal House 64 Murhill, Limpley Stoke, Bath, BA2 7FQ. Prop: Jenny Steadman. Tel: (01225) 777589 E-mail: jenny@travellersbookshelf.co.uk. Est 1991 Private premises. Internet and Postal. Spec: Countries - Afganistan; Countries - Albania; Countries - Arabia; Countries - Armenia; Countries - Asia Minor; Countries - Balkans, The; Countries - Central Asia; Countries - China. PR: £20–5,000. CC: MC; V; Switch. Cata: Travel & Exploration. Mem: PBFA. VAT No: GB 779 2193 85. Notes: *We specialise in books of travel, exploration and scholarship on the Balkans, North Africa, the Middle East, Central Asia, the Himalayan region, South East Asia and the Far East.*

BATHEASTON

Libris (Weston) Books, 68 London Road West, Batheaston, BA1 7DA. Tel: (01225) 858809. E-mail: libriswestonbooks@hotmail.com. Private premises. Book fairs only. Spec: Aviation; Countries - Antarctic, The; History - General; Performing Arts; Poetry; Topography - General. Mem: PBFA.

BRIDGATER

R.W. Millard, 112 Wembdon Hill, Bridgater, TA6 7QA.

Wembdon Books, 112 Wembdon Hill, Bridgewater, TA6 7QA. Prop: Ray Millard. Tel: (01278) 424060. Est: 1987. Private premises. Internet and Postal. Very small stock. Spec: Antiquarian; Diaries; Military; Topography - Local; Travel - General; War - World War II; Booksearch. PR: £3–150.

CASTLE CARY

Avedikian Rare Books, Bank House, Castle Carey, BA7 7AW. Prop: Stephen James Avedikian. Tel: 01963 359680. Web: www.militarybookshop.com. Open: **M:** 09:00–17:30; **T:** 09:00–17:30; **W:** 09:00– 17:30; **Th:** 09:00–17:30; **F:** 09:00–17:30; **S:** 09:00–17:30; **Su:** 09:00–17:30; Closed for lunch: 13:00– 14:00. Spec: Author - Lawrence, T.E.; Aviation; Military History; Voyages & Discovery; War - World War I. Mem: ABA.

militarybookshop.com, 'Bank House' High Street, Castle Cary, BA7 7AW. Prop: Stephen Avedikian. Tel: 01963-359680. Web: www.militarybookshop.com. E-mail: books@militarybookshop.com. Est: 1989. Private premises. Internet and Postal. Appointment necessary. Open: **M:** 09:00–17:30; **T:** 09:00–17:30; **W:** 09:00–17:30; **Th:** 09:00–17:30; **F:** 09:00–17:30; **S:** 09:00–17:30; **Su:** 09:00–17:30; Closed for lunch: 13:00–14:00. Spec: CC: MC; V. Mem: ABA; ILAB.

CHARD

P.J. Baron - Scientific Book Sales, Lakewood, Chard, TA20 4AJ. Prop: Dr. P. Baron. Tel: (01460) 66319. Fax: (01460) 66319. Web: www.books.free-online.co.uk. E-mail: pb@sciencebaron .demon.co.uk. Est: 1975. Private premises. Internet and Postal. Small stock. Spec: Academic/Scholarly; Biology - General; Botany; Chemistry; Ecology; Engineering; Mathematics; Medicine. PR: £5–150. CC: MC; V; SW, Delta, PayPal. Cata: all science, engineering, medicine. Corresp: French. VAT No: GB 549 4779 82.

SOMERSET

CLAPTON–IN–GORDANO

Avonworld Books, 1 Swancombe, Clapton–in–Gordano, BS20 7RR. Prop: Michael C. Ross. Tel: (01275) 842531. Fax: (01275) 849221. Web: www.avonworld-booksource.co.uk. E-mail: books@ avonworld.demon.co.uk. Est: 1984. Office and/or bookroom. Internet and Postal. Appointment necessary. Open: **M:** 09:00–18:00; **T:** 09:00–18:00; **W:** 09:00–18:00; **Th:** 09:00–18:00; **F:** 09:00–18:00. Closed for lunch: 13:00–14:00. Small stock. Spec: Art; Author - Buchan, John; - Coward, Noel; - Graves, Robert; - Kipling, Rudyard; - Sayers, Dorothy; Literature; Modern First Editions. PR: £1– 500. CC: MC; V. Corresp: German (post only, not e-mail). Mem: PBFA. VAT No: GB 496 6867 66. Notes: *Valuations for insurance or probate of private collections in our author specialities.*

CLEVEDON

Clevedon Books, Canbourne Cottage 6 Seavale Road, Clevedon, BS21 7QB. Prop: George & Wendy Douthwaite. Tel: (01275) 872304. Fax: (01275) 342817. E-mail: wecd@uwclub.net. Est: 1970. Private premises. Internet and Postal. Appointment necessary. Open: **Th:** 11:00–16:30; **F:** 11:00–16:30; **S:** 11:05–16:30. Closed for lunch: 13:00–14:15. Very large stock. Spec: Architecture; Art History; Geology; History - Industrial; History of Ideas; Science - History of; Transport; Travel - General. PR: £10–3,000. CC: JCB; MC; V; Debit. Mem: PBFA. Notes: *Also at: 27 Copse Road, Clevedon. (q.v.) Also, colouring & mounting service.*

K.W. Cowley, Bookdealer, Trinity Cottage 153 Old Church Road, Clevedon, BS21 7TU. Prop: Ken Cowley. Tel: (01275) 872247. E-mail: kencowley@blueyonder.co.uk. Est: 1987. Private premises. Postal Only. Telephone First. Small stock. Spec: Anthologies; Books about Books; Cinema/Film; Fiction - Crime, Detective, Spy, Thrillers; Fiction - Fantasy, Horror; Fiction - Science Fiction; Ghosts; Pulps. PR: £1–100. Cata: S/F, Fantasy, Horror, Crime, Supernatural. Notes: *Small presses a speciality.*

CREWKERNE

Gresham Books, ■ 31 Market Street, Crewkerne, TA18 7JU. Prop: James Hine. Tel: (01460) 77726. Fax: (01460) 52479. Web: www.greshambooks.co.uk. E-mail: jameshine@btconnect.com. Est: 1972. Shop open: **M:** 10:00–17:00; **T:** 10:00–17:00; **W:** 10:00–17:00; **Th:** 10:00–17:00; **F:** 10:00–17:00; **S:** 10:00– 17:00. Medium stock. Spec: Antiquarian; Antiques; Architecture; Cookery/Gastronomy; Fashion & Costume; Food & Drink; Needlework; Sport - Golf. PR: £1–1,000. CC: AE; MC; V; Switch. Mem: PBFA.

Anne Hine / Gresham Books, ■ 31 Market Street, Crewkerne, TA18 7JU. Tel: (01460) 77726. Fax: (01460) 52479. E-mail: annehine@gresham-books.demon.co.uk. Est: 1994. Shop open: **M:** 10:00– 17:00; **T:** 10:00–17:00; **W:** 10:00–17:00; **Th:** 10:00–17:00; **F:** 10:00–17:00; **S:** 10:00–17:00. Very small stock. Spec: Publishers - Warnes. CC: AE; MC; V. Notes: *Also, provides a booksearach service for all plant related books, and Japanese gardening.*

DULVERTON

Rothwell & Dunworth, ■ 2 Bridge Street, Dulverton, TA22 9HJ. Tel: 01398 323169. E-mail: rothwellm@ aol.com. Est: 1975. Shop open: **M:** 10:30–17:15; **T:** 10:30–17:15; **W:** 10:30–17:15; **Th:** 10:30–17:15; **F:** 10:30–17:15; **S:** 10:30–17:15; **Su:** 11:00–16:00. Spec: Aircraft; Antiquarian; Architecture; Army, The; Art History; Author - Aldin, Cecil; Autobiography; History - General. CC: MC; V; Debit. Mem: ABA;

DUNSTER

Cobbles Books, ■ 14 - 16 Church Street, Dunster, TA24 6SH. Prop: Adrian Corley. Tel: 01643 821305. Fax: 01643 821305. E-mail: books@cobbles1416.fsnet.co.uk. Est: 2003. Shop open: **M:** 10:30–17:00; **T:** 10:30–17:00; **W:** 10:30–17:00; **F:** 10:30–17:00; **S:** 10:30–17:00; **Su:** 10:30–17:00. Spec: Antiques; Art; Aviation; Biography; Fiction - General; Folio Society, The; History - General; History - British. CC: MC; V. Notes: *Opening times may vary between November and March. Please telephone for details.*

FROME

Upper–Room Books, ■ Above Antiques & Country Living 43 - 44 Vallis Way, Babcox, Frome, BA11 3BA. Prop: Victor Adams. Tel: (01373) 467125. Fax: (01373) 467125. Web: www.vabooks.co.uk. E-mail: victoradams@vabooks.co.uk. Est: 1990. Shop. Internet and Postal open: **M:** 09:30–17:30; **T:** 09:30–17:30; **W:** 09:30–17:30; **Th:** 09:30–17:30; **F:** 09:30–17:30; **S:** 09:30–17:30. Medium stock. Spec: Art; Artists; Author - Morris, William; Crafts; Furniture; Woodwork. PR: £5–1,000. CC: JCB; MC; V. Mem: PBFA. Notes: *2 hours free parking 30 yards from shop.*

ILMINSTER

David Clarke Books, P.O. Box 24, Ilminster, TA19 0YU. Prop: David Clarke. Tel: (01460) 242330. E-mail: dclarke@lineone.net. Est: 1999. Private premises. Internet and Postal. Appointment necessary. Medium stock. Spec: Aeronautics; Agriculture; Countries - Great Britain; Farming & Livestock; Fiction - General; Gardening - General; History - British; Horticulture. PR: £4–300. Corresp: French.

Ile Valley Bookshop, ■ 10 Silver Street, Ilminster, TA19 0DJ. Prop: Chris Chapman. Tel: (01460) 57663. Fax: (01460) 57188. E-mail: ilevalley@aol.com. Est: 1985. Shop open. Very small stock.

LANGPORT

Keeble Antiques, ■ Cheapside, Langport, TA10 9PW. Prop: Clive Keeble. Tel: (01458) 259627. Fax: (01458) 259627. Web: www.keebleantbks.co.uk. E-mail: clive@keebleantiques.com. Est: 1998. Internet and Postal. Shop open: **M:** 09:00–18:00; **T:** 09:00–18:00; **W:** 09:00–18:00; **Th:** 09:00–18:00; **F:** 09:00–18:00; **S:** 09:00–18:00; **Su:** 10:00–16:30; Medium stock. Spec: Antiques; Art; Carriages & Driving; Natural History; Private Press; Rural Life; Topography - Local; Travel - General. PR: £1–1,000.

MERRIOTT

Richard Budd, The Coach House Glebelands, Merriott, TA16 5RE. Prop: Richard Budd. Tel: (01460) 78297. E-mail: richard@buddbooks.co.uk. Est: 1972. Private premises. Postal Only. Appointment necessary. Small stock. Spec: Author - Beckett, S.; Bibliography; Bibliophily; First Editions; Limited Editions - General; Literary Criticism; Literature; Literature - 19th C. PR: £10–5,000. CC: E; MC; V. Cata: English, French and American Literature only. Corresp: French. Mem: ABA; PBFA; ILAB. Notes: *Also, attends 50 bookfairs a year.*

MIDSOMER NORTON

Tom Randall, Welton Hill Cottage Welton Grove, Midsomer Norton, Radstock, BA3 2TS. Prop: Tom Randall. Tel: (01761) 418926. Web: www.ukbookworld.com/members/folklorist. E-mail: tom.randal@dsl.pipex.com. Est: 1987. Private premises. Internet and Postal. Contactable. Spec: Agriculture; Antique Stoves; Archaeology - Industrial; Arthurian; Author - Baring-Gould, S.; - Lang, Andrew; - Rolt, L.T.C.; Automata. PR: £2–500. Cata: folklore & folkmusic. Notes: *Also, a booksearch service.*

MILVERTON

Cat Lit, Loundshay Manor Cottage Preston Bowyer, Milverton, TA4 1QF. Tel: (01823) 401527. Fax: (01823) 401527. E-mail: amolibros@aol.com. Est: 2002. Private premises. Postal Only. Appointment necessary. Spec: Cats; Dogs; Sport - Field Sports.

MINEHEAD

Rare Books & Berry, ■ 11 owerbourne House High Street, Porlock, Minehead, TA24 8PT. Prop: Helen & Michael Berry. Tel: (01643) 863255. Fax: (01643) 863092. Web: www.rarebooksandberry.co.uk. E-mail: search@rarebooksandberry.co.uk. Est: 1992. Shop open: **M:** 09:30–17:00; **T:** 09:30–17:00; **W:** 09:30–17:00; **Th:** 09:30–17:00; **F:** 09:30–17:00; **S:** 09:30–17:00. Closed for lunch: 13:00–14:00. Medium stock. Spec: Author - Edwards, Lionel; Sport - Angling/Fishing; Sport - Hunting; Topography - Local. PR: £1–1,000. CC: MC; V; S, SW. VAT No: GB 801 1222 04. Notes: *Also trading in New Books from our website www.rarebooksandberry.co.uk with a choice of over 500,000 titles all at competitive discounted prices.*

NORTH CHERITON

Paper Pleasures, Holt Farm, North Cheriton, BA8 OAQ. Prop: Lesley Tyson. Tel: (01963) 33718. Web: www.paperpleasures.com. E-mail: books@paperpleasures.com. Est: 1998. Private premises. Postal Only. Appointment necessary. Small stock. Spec: Art; Erotica; Ex-Libris; Glamour; Homosexuality & Lesbianism; Literature; Magazines & Periodicals - General; Photography. PR: £5–2,000. CC: MC; V; Switch. Cata: Erotica. Mem: PBFA. Notes: *To receive the Erotica catalogue just phone, email or write to go on the confidential mailing list.*

SOMERSET

PEASEDOWN ST. JOHN

BookLovers.co.uk, ■ The Post Office 12 Bath Road, Peasedown St. John, BA2 8DH. Prop: David Gower-Spence. Tel: 0845 009 4455. Fax: 0845 009 1786. Web: www.booklovers.co.uk. E-mail: dgs@booklovers.co.uk. Est: 1994. Shop. Internet and Postal open: **M:** 09:00–17:30; **T:** 09:00–17:30; **W:** 09:00–13.00; **Th:** 09:00–17:30; **F:** 09:00–17:30; **S:** 09:00–12.30. Closed for lunch: 13:00–14:00. Spec: CC: AE; D; JCB; MC; V. Notes: *A small eclectic selection of 500+ books in the shop only - majority of stock is available mail order only.*

QUEEN CAMEL

Steven Ferdinando, The Old Vicarage, Queen Camel, Nr. Yeovil, BA22 7NG. Tel: (01935) 850210. E-mail: stevenferdinando@onetel.com. Est: 1977. Office and/or bookroom. Telephone First. Medium stock. Spec: Agriculture; Author - Hardy, Thomas; Author - Powys Family, The; Illustrated - General; Irish Interest; Literature; Topography - Local; Travel - General. PR: £10–800. CC: MC; V. Mem: PBFA. Notes: *Bath Old Books, Bath. (q.v.).*

SIMONSBATH

Spooner & Co, Mead Cottage Honeymead, Simonsbath, TA24 7JX. Prop: Brian John Spooner. Tel: (01643) 831562. E-mail: spoonerb@supanet.com. Est: 1985. Private premises. Internet and Postal. Appointment necessary. Small stock. Spec: Antiquarian; Archaeology; Architecture; Bibles; Biblical Studies; Bibliography; Bookbinding; Books about Books. PR: £3–230. Notes: *Also, booksearch, bookbinding and repairs.*

SOMERTON

Simon's Books, ■ Broad Street, Somerton, . Prop: Bryan Ives. Tel: (01458) 272313. Est: 1978. Shop open: **M:** 10:00–16:30; **T:** 10:00–16:30; **W:** 09:00–16:30; **Th:** 09:00–16:30; **F:** 10:00–16:30; **S:** 10:00–16:30. Large stock. PR: £1–100.

TAUNTON

Badger Books, 2 The Orchard, Dowell Close, Taunton, TA2 6BN. Prop: Janet & Nic Tall. Tel: (01823) 323180. Web: www.badgerbooks.co.uk. E-mail: janetnic@badgerbooks.co.uk. Est: 2002. Private premises. Internet and Postal. Appointment necessary. Small stock. Spec: Author - Brent-Dyer, Elinor M.; - Forest, A.; - Hill, Lorna; - Oxenham, Elsie; Children's. PR: £1–200. Corresp: German.

Boxwood Books & Prints, Ashbrook House Winsford, Minehead, Taunton, TA24 7HN. Prop: (*) Peter & Catherine Nicholls. Tel: (01643) 851588. Fax: (01643) 851588. E-mail: boxwood.books@virgin.net. Est: 1995. Private premises. Appointment necessary. Very small stock. Spec: Art Reference; Illustrated - General; Printing; Private Press; Prints and Maps. PR: £50–1,500. CC: MC; V. Mem: PBFA. Notes: *Attends Oxford Fine Press Fair only.*

Dene Barn Books & Prints, Brackenbury Ash Priors, Taunton, TA4 3NF. Prop: Derek Cundy. Tel: (01823) 433103. Est: 1990. Private premises. Appointment necessary. Very small stock. Spec: Botany; Natural History; Topography - Local; Prints and Maps. PR: £10–500. Notes: *Picture Framing and mounting.*

The Eastern Traveller, 52 Mountway Road Bishops Hull, Taunton, TA1 5LS. Prop: Anna Mullett. Tel: (01823) 327012. E-mail: books@gamullett.fsnet.co.uk. Est: 1979. Private premises. Book fairs only. Spec: Adventure; Asian Studies; Countries - Arabia; Countries - Asia; History - General; Military; Military History; Travel - General. PR: £5–50. Cata: Travel esp. Eastern. Corresp: French. Mem: PBFA.

Russell Needham Books, 5 Silver St., Milverton, Taunton, TA4 1LA. Prop: (*). Tel: (01823) 400470. Fax: (0870) 0561167. Web: www.needhambooks.demon.co.uk. E-mail: russell@needhambooks.demon.co.uk. Private premises. Internet and Postal. Very small stock. Spec: Academic/Scholarly; Alchemy; Author - Bennett, J.G.; Foreign Texts; Fourth Way; Literature; Modern First Editions; Mysticism. PR: £5–300. Corresp: French Francais.

WELLINGTON

Peter J. Ayre, Greenham Hall Greenham, Wellington, TA21 0JJ. Tel: (01823) 672603. Fax: (01823) 672307. E-mail: peterjayre@aol.com. Est: 1980. Private premises. Internet and Postal. Appointment necessary. Small stock. Spec: Africana; Countries - Africa; Countries - Kenya; Countries - Tanzania; Natural History; Sport - Big Game Hunting; Travel - Africa; Booksearch. PR: £10–5,000. CC: JCB; MC; V. Cata: East Africa. Mem: PBFA.

SOMERSET

Mary Sharpe, 55 Twitchen Holcombe Rogus, Wellington, TA21 0PS. Tel: (01823) 672304. Est: 1995. Private premises. Postal Only. Small stock. Spec: Author - Austen, Jane; - Brontes, The; - Burney, Fanny; - Eliot, G.; - Gaskell, E.; - Hardy, Thomas; Children's; Illustrated - General. PR: £5–200. Notes: *Exhibits at bookfairs.*

WEST PENNARD

Eddie Baxter - Books, The Old Mill House, West Pennard, BA6 8ND. Prop: Josie Matthews. Tel: (01749) 890369. Fax: (01749) 890369. Est: 1956. Private premises. Postal Only. Very small stock. Spec: Dance; Music - General; Music - Jazz & Blues; Booksearch.

WESTON–SUPER–MARE

Manna Bookshop, ■ 30 Orchard Street, Weston–Super–Mare, BS23 1RQ. Prop: Peter Fairnington. Tel: (01934) 636228. Est: 1981. Shop open: **M:** 10:00–17:00; **T:** 10:00–17:00; **W:** 10:00–17:00; **Th:** 10:00–17:00; **F:** 10:00–17:00; **S:** 10:00–17:00. Large stock. PR: £1–100. Notes: *(Notice on door: sometimes closed on Thursday).*

Sterling Books, ■ 43a Locking Road, Weston–Super–Mare, BS23 3DG. Prop: David Nisbet. Tel: (01934) 625056. Web: www.abe.com. E-mail: sterling.books@talk21.com. Est: 1966. Shop open: **M:** ; **T:** 10:00–17:30; **W:** 10:00–17:30; **Th:** 10:00–13:00; **F:** 10:00–17:30; **S:** 10:00–17:30. Very large stock. Spec: Academic/Scholarly; Advertising; Aeronautics; Antiquarian; Art; Bindings; Crafts; History - General. PR: £1–1,500. CC: AE; D; E; JCB; MC; V. Mem: ABA; PBFA; ILAB. Notes: *Also, bookbinding & restoration, picture-framing & a booksearch service.*

SOUTH YORKSHIRE

DONCASTER

Hedgerow Books, 10 Whitbeck Close Wadworth, Doncaster, DN11 9DZ. Prop: Peter & Elizabeth Hedge. Tel: (01302) 856311. Web: www.hedgerowbooks.com. E-mail: info@hedgerowbooks.com. Est: 1988. Private premises. Internet and Postal. Appointment necessary. Open: **M:** 09:00–21:00; **T:** 09:00–21:00; **W:** 09:00–21:00; **Th:** 09:00–21:00; **F:** 09:00–21:00; **S:** 09:00–12:30. Closed for lunch: 12:30–14:00. Small stock. Spec: Architecture; Ecclesiastical History & Architecture; History - Industrial; Sport - Boxing; Sport - Football (Soccer). PR: £1–500. CC: MC; V; Switch. Cata: Boxing. Mem: PBFA. VAT No: GB 657 8581 80.

Saxton Books Ltd, 18 Saxton Avenue, Doncaster, DN4 7AX. Tel: 01302 371600. Fax: 01302 371071. Web: www.saxtonbooks.com. E-mail: becky@capitalbooks.co.uk. Est: 1997. Private premises. Internet and Postal. Very small stock. Spec: Author - Austen, Jane; - Bates, H.E.; - Bramah, Ernest; - Flint, William Russell; - Rand, Ayn; - Shute, Neville; Economics; Engraving. PR: £10–1,000.

ECKINGTON

The Bibliophile, 42 Fern Close, Eckington, S21 4 HE. Prop: (*) Michael P. Russell. Tel: (01246) 434025. Fax: (01246) 434025. E-mail: mpr@supanet.com. Est: 1997. Spec: Freemasonry & Anti-Masonry; Medicine; Printing; Collectables; Ephemera. PR: £1–50.

ROTHERHAM

Anthony Singleton, 6 Birkwood Terrace, Braithwell, Rotherham, S66 7AE. Tel: (01709) 813396. E-mail: ajsingleton.books@virgin.net. Est: 1996. Private premises. Postal Only. Very small stock. Spec: History - General; Rural Life; Theology; Topography - General; Travel - General.

SHEFFIELD

Annie's Books, 28 Blackbrook Drive, Sheffield, S10 4LS. Prop: Chris Wren. Tel: (0114) 2306494. Web: www.anniesbooks.co.uk. E-mail: wrentrading@talk21.com. Est: 1999. Private premises. Internet and Postal. Appointment necessary. Open: **M:** 09:00–17:00; **T:** 09:00–17:00; **W:** 09:00–17:00; **Th:** 09:00–17:00; **F:** 09:00–17:00. Small stock. Spec: Adult; Adventure; Animals and Birds; Author - Blyton, Enid; - Cornwell, Bernard; - Durrell, Gerald; - Read, Miss; - Tangye, D. PR: £1–200. Notes: *Booksearch - free, no obligation.*

Baedekers & Murray Guides, 11 St. Quentin Drive, Sheffield, S17 4PN. Prop: Dr. R.H. Hickley. Tel: (0114) 236-6306. Web: www.roger_hickley@dial.Pipex.com. E-mail: roger_hickley@dial.pipex.com. Est: 1991. Private premises. Appointment necessary. Very small stock. Spec: Guide Books; Travel - General. PR: £10–500. Cata: travel and topography. Corresp: French, German, Swedish, Finnish.

Chantrey Books, 24 Cobnar Road, Sheffield, S8 8QB. Prop: Clare Brightman. Tel: (0114) 274-8958. E-mail: chantrey.24@btinternet.com. Est: 1981. Private premises. Spec: Agriculture; Botany; Cookery/ Gastronomy; Food & Drink; Gardening - General; Herbalism; Illustrated - General; Plant Hunting. PR: £5–500. CC: MC; V. Cata: gardening, rural life. Mem: PBFA.

Alan Hill Books, Unit 4, Meersbrook Works Valley Road, Sheffield, S8 9FT. Prop: Alan Hill. Tel: (01142) 556242. E-mail: alanhillbooks@supanet.com. Est: 1980. Shop and/or showroom. Internet and Postal. Telephone First. Open: **M:** 10:30–13:30; **T:** 10:30–13:30; **W:** 10:30–13:30; **Th:** 10:30–13:30; **F:** 10:30–13:30. Large stock. Spec: Academic/Scholarly; Genealogy; Topography - Local. PR: £5–500. CC: MC; V. VAT No: GB 533 9950 19.

Howard Loftus Rail Books, 11 Collier Road Kiverton Park, Sheffield, S26 6LR. Prop: Howard Loftus. Tel: 01909 771408. Private premises. Postal Only. Open: **M:** 09:00–17:30; **T:** 09:00–17:30; **W:** 09:00–17:30; **Th:** 09:00–17:30; **F:** 09:00–17:30; **S:** 09:00–17:30; **Su:** 09:00–17:30; Closed for lunch: 13:00–14:00. Spec: Railways. Notes: *Specialist in British Modern Traction Railway Books.*

The Porter Bookshop, ■ 227 Sharrowvale Road, Sheffield, S11 8ZE. Prop: Margot Armitage. Tel: (0114) 266-7762. Est: 1988. Shop. Telephone First. Medium stock. Spec: Academic/Scholarly; Crime (1rue); Humanities; Literature.

Rare & Racy, ■ 164–166 Devonshire Street, Sheffield, S3 7SG. Prop: Allen Capes & Joseph Mhlongo. Tel: (0114) 270-1916. Web: www.rareandracy.co.uk. E-mail: shop@rareandracy.fsnet.co.uk. Est: 1969. Shop open: **M:** 10:00–18:00; **T:** 10:00–18:00; **W:** 10:00–18:00; **Th:** 10:00–18:00; **F:** 10:00–18:00; **S:** 10:00–18:00. Spec: Gardening - General; History - Local; Topography - Local. PR: £1–250. CC: MC; V; Solo, Maestro. Mem: PBFA. VAT No: GB 173 1507 80.

SOUTH YORKSHIRE

Tilleys Vintage Magazine Shop, ■ 281 Shoreham Street, Sheffield, S1 4SS. Prop: Antonius & Albertus Tilley. Tel: (0114) 275-2442. Web: www.tilleysmagazines.com. E-mail: antoniusttilley@yahoo.co.uk. Est: 1978. Shop open: **T:** 10:00–16:30; **W:** 10:00–16:30; **Th:** 10:00–16:30; **F:** 10:00–16:30; **S:** 10:00–16:30. Very large stock. Spec: Comic Books & Annuals; Comics; Magazines & Periodicals - General; Spiritualism; Ephemera; Prints and Maps. PR: £1–200. CC: AE; MC; V. Notes: *Also at: 21 Derby Road, Chesterfield (q.v.)*.

Need a website? Need to have your books listed?
Basic web sites from £220
for details visit
www.sheppardsworld.co.uk

STAFFORDSHIRE

BURTON UPON TRENT

Ian J. Sherratt, Rhoslyn Victoria St. Yoxall, Burton upon Trent, DE13 8NG. Est: 1989. Private premises. Postal Only. Small stock. PR: £1–20. Notes: *Also attends book fairs.*

LICHFIELD

Mike Abrahams, 14 Meadowbrook Road, Lichfield, WS13 7RN. Tel: (01543) 256200. Est: 1979. Private premises. Appointment necessary. Spec: Antiques; Banking & Insurance; Canals/Inland Waterways; Children's; Collecting; Comic Books & Annuals; Cookery/Gastronomy; Crime (True). PR: £1–500.

Steve Brown (Books), 2 Curborough Cottages Watery Lane, Lichfield, WS13 8ER. Prop: Steve Brown. Tel: (01543) 264498. Web: www.abebooks.com/servlet/StoreFrontDisplay?cid=621. E-mail: steve.brown26@virgin.net. Est: 1992. Private premises. Internet and Postal. Appointment necessary. Small stock. Spec: Sport - Horse Racing (inc. Riding/Breeding/Equestrian). PR: £5–500. Cata: Horse Racing. Corresp: French. Notes: *Small general stock at Curborough Hall Antiques Centre, Watery Lane, Lichfield also at Brownhills Books, The Old Sorting Office, Main Street, Brownhills.*

David Clegg, 6 Longbridge Road, Lichfield, WS14 9EL. Prop: David Clegg. Tel: (01543) 252117. Est: 1984. Private premises. Postal Only. Very small stock. Spec: Author - Dickens, Charles; Occult; Religion - General; Travel - General. PR: £5–20.

Terry W. Coupland, 15 Harwood Road, Lichfield, WS13 7PP. Tel: (01543) 256599. E-mail: tcfortypo@btinternet.com. Est: 1980. Private premises. Appointment necessary. Small stock. Spec: Bookbinding; Children's; Illustrated - General; Juvenile; Papermaking; Printing; Private Press; Publishing. PR: £5–1,500. Mem: PBFA. Notes: *Attends PBFA fairs.*

Colin Shakespeare Books, 3 Chestnut Drive Shenstone, Lichfield, WS14 OJH. Prop: Colin & Lilian Shakespeare. Tel: (01543) 480978. Est: 1991. Private premises. Postal Only. Contactable. Open: **M:** 09:00–21:00; **T:** 09:00–21:00; **W:** 09:00–21:00; **Th:** 09:00–21:00; **F:** 09:00–21:00. Small stock. Spec: Literature; Topography - General. PR: £3–1,500.

The Staffs Bookshop, 4 and 6 Dam Street, Lichfield, WS13 6AA. Prop: Miss Hawkins. Tel: (01543) 264093. Fax: (01543) 264093. Web: www.staffsbookshop.co.uk. E-mail: contact@ staffsbookshop.co.uk. Est: 1938. Shop and/or gallery. Internet and Postal open: **M:** 10:00–17:00; **T:** 10:00–17:00; **W:** 10:00–17:00; **Th:** 10:00–17:00; **F:** 10:00–17:00; **S:** 10:00–17:00. Very large stock. Spec: Author - Johnson, Samuel; Children's; Dolls & Dolls' Houses; General; History - General; Literature; Railways; Theology. PR: £1–1,000. CC: MC; V; Maestro. VAT No: GB 784 5011 28. Notes: *Prints, Sheet Music, Ephemera*

NEWCASTLE–UNDER–LYME

Pomes Penyeach, 25 Curzon Street, Basford, Newcastle–under–Lyme, ST5 0PD. Prop: Paul Robinson. Tel: (01782) 630729. Web: www.abebooks.com. E-mail: books@pomes-penyeach.co.uk. Est: 1985. Private premises. Appointment necessary. Small stock. Spec: Academic/Scholarly; Children's; First Editions; History - General; Literary Criticism; Literature; Modern First Editions; Philosophy. PR: £1–500. CC: AE; MC; V; Delta. Notes: *Also, a booksearch service.*

Keith Twigg Toy Books, 27 Lansdell Avenue, Porthill, Newcastle-under-Lyme, ST5 8E1. Tel: (01782) 642932. Est: 1970. Postal Only. Spec: Dolls & Dolls' Houses; Toys. PR: £20–200.

STAFFORD

Ray Roberts (Booksellers), Whiston Hall Mews, Whiston Hall Whiston, Nr. Penkridge, Stafford, ST19 5QH. Tel: (01785) 712232. Fax: (01785) 712232. Est: 1980. Private premises. Appointment necessary. Small stock. Spec: Motoring; Traction Engines; Travel - General; Vintage Cars; Collectables. PR: £1– 500. CC: AE; MC; V. Notes: *Also: author and publisher – Bentley Specials & Special Bentleys.*

STOKE-ON-TRENT

Abacas Books & Cards, ■ 56–60 Millrise Road Milton, Stoke-on-Trent, ST2 7BW. Prop: Dave & Margaret Mycock. Tel: (01782) 543005. E-mail: margaret.mycock@byinternet.com. Est: 1980. Shop open: **M:** 09:00–17:00; **T:** 09:00–17:00; **W:** 09:00–17:00; **Th:** 09:00–17:00; **F:** 09:00–17:00; **S:** 09:00– 13:00. Medium stock. Spec: Art; Autobiography; Bindings; Biography; Ceramics; Cookery/ Gastronomy; Fiction - General; Gardening - General. PR: £1–200. VAT No: GB 478 7684 71. Notes: *Attends Buxton Book Fairs.*

STAFFORDSHIRE

Acumen Books, Rushton House 167 Nantwich Road, Audley, Stoke-on-Trent, ST7 8DL. Prop: Managing Director: C.B. Pearson. Tel: (01782) 720753. Fax: (01782) 720798. Web: www. acumenbooks.co.uk. E-mail: shep@acumenbooks.co.uk. Est: 1978. Private premises. Internet and Postal. Appointment necessary. Open: **M:** 10:00–15:00; **T:** ; **W:** ; **Th:** 10:00–15:00; **F:** ; **S:** . Spec: Sport - Cricket. PR: £1–20. CC: MC; V. Mem: ACU&S MCIArb. VAT No: GB 319 300 584. Notes: *We specialise in books for cricket umpires, scorers, coaches and other officials, both new and secondhand also players and spectators interested in Laws of Cricket - we also supply equipment.*

TAMWORTH

G. & J. Chesters, ■ 14 Market Street Polesworth, Tamworth, B78 1HW. Prop: Geoff & Jean Chesters. Tel: (01827) 894743. Web: www.abebooks.com/home/geoffchesters. E-mail: gandjchesters@ tiscali.co.uk. Est: 1970. Shop open: **M:** 9.30–17:30; **T:** 9.30–17:30; **W:** 9.30–21:00; **Th:** 9.30–17:30; **F:** 9.30–17:30; **S:** 9.30–17:30. Very large stock. Spec: Academic/Scholarly; Anthropology; Criminology; Economics; Geography; Geology; History - General; Linguistics. PR: £1–1,000. CC: AE; MC; V; Maestro. VAT No: GB 112 6448 93. Notes: *Large stocks of academic subjects, enthusiasts' books, and original antique maps and prints. There are some 7 other bookshops within close range of Polesworth.*

UTTOXETER

J.O. Goodwin, Woodcrofts Farm Highwood, Uttoxeter, ST14 8PS. Prop: J.O. Goodwin. Tel: (01889) 562792. Est: 1965. Private premises. Appointment necessary. Small stock. Spec: Prints and Maps. PR: £1–200. VAT No: GB 125 9041 83.

WALSALL (SEE ALSO UNDER W. MIDLANDS)

SETI Books, 3C Kingswood Drive, Walsall, WS6 6NX. Prop: David J Ward. Tel: 01922 413277. Fax: 01922 413277. Web: www.ukbookworld.com/members/setibooks. E-mail: davidjward@ setibooks.freeserve.co.uk. Est: 2002. Private premises. Internet and Postal. Telephone First. Very small stock. Spec: Autobiography; Conspiracy; Countries - England; Cryptozoology; Earth Mysteries; Esoteric; Famous People - Entertainers; Famous People - Kennedy, John F. PR: £1– 175. Notes: *PayPal accepted.*

WOMBOURN

Rookery Bookery, 39 Rookery Road, Wombourn, WV5 0JH. Prop: Colin Hardwick. Tel: (01902) 895983. Est: 1987. Private premises. Appointment necessary. Very small stock. PR: £1–250. Corresp: French.

YOXALL

Ray Sparkes (Books), The Hollies Bond End, Yoxall, DE13 8NH. Tel: (01543) 472274. Est: 1987. Private premises. Appointment necessary. Small stock. Spec: Directories - General; Directories - British. PR: £2–3,000. Mem: PBFA. VAT No: GB 478 2190 24.

SUFFOLK

BECCLES

Besleys Books, ■ 4 Blyburgate, Beccles, NR34 9TA. Prop: Piers & Gabby Besley. Tel: (01502) 715762. Fax: {01502) 675649. Web: www.besleysbooks.demon.co.uk. E-mail: piers@ besleysbooks .demon.co.uk. Shop open: **M:** 09:30–17:00; **T:** 09:30–17:00; **W:** 09:30–17:00; **Th:** 09:30–17:00; **F:** 09:30–17:00; **S:** 09:30–17:00. Large stock. Spec: Agriculture; Animals and Birds; Art; Art Reference; Author - Bell, Adrian; Books about Books; Botany; Colour-Plate. PR: £1–1,000. CC: JCB; MC; V. Cata: gardening, natural history, literature, private press. Mem: ABA; PBFA. Notes: *Traditional general antiquarian and secondhand bookshop.*

BOXFORD

Dolphin Books, Old Coach House Broad Street, Boxford, CO10 5DX. Prop: Mrs. Rita Watts. Tel: (01787) 211630. Web: www.ukbookworld.com/members/DOLPHINBOOKS. E-mail: Rwdolphinbooks@ aol.com. Est: 1988. Private premises. Internet and Postal. Telephone First. Small stock. Spec: Academic/Scholarly; Adventure; Agriculture; Animals and Birds; Anthologies; Art; Art - British; Art Deco. PR: £5–50. CC: PayPal. Notes: *Selected Stock also listed on Alibris.uk.com. Booksearch service.*

BUNGAY

Bardsley's Books, ■ 22 Upper Olland Street, Bungay, NR35 1BH. Prop: W.N.A. & D.H. Bardsley. Tel: (01986) 892077. Web: www.bardsleysbooks.co.uk. E-mail: antonybardsley@easynet.co.uk. Est: 1998. Shop open: **M:** 10:00–17:30; **T:** 10:00–17:30; **W:** ; **Th:** 10:00–17:30; **F:** 10:00–17:30; **S:** 10:00–17:30. Very large stock. Spec: Antiquarian; Art; Bibles; Books about Books; Cinema/Film; Countries - Mexico; Countries - Poland; Ecclesiastical History & Architecture. PR: £1–250. Notes: *Also, cards, O.S. Maps, CDs & new books to order.*

Beaver Booksearch, 33 Hillside Road East, Bungay, NR35 1JU. Prop: Sarah Coulthurst & Nicholas Watts. Tel: (01986) 896698. Fax: (01986) 896698. Web: www.www.beaverbooksearch.co.uk. E-mail: nick@beaverbooksearch.co.uk. Est: 1995. Private premises. Postal Only. Small stock. Spec: Bridge; Booksearch. PR: £1–50. CC: AE; MC; V; SW. VAT No: GB 638 1296 25. Notes: *Professional Out-of-print Booksearch service. Office hours weekdays 9am-1pm.*

Scorpio Books, Autumn Cottage Low Street, Ilketshall St Margaret, Bungay, NR35 1QZ. Prop: Lorna & Patrick Quorn. Tel: 01986 781721. Web: www.scorpiobooks.co.uk. E-mail: scorpiobooks .suffolk@virgin.net. Est: 1987. Private premises. Postal Only. Appointment necessary. Spec: Aircraft; History - Women; Military History; Music - Jazz & Blues; Performing Arts; Women. CC: JCB; MC; V. Cata: Jazz, Military History, Aviation, Womens' Studies. Mem: PBFA.

BURES

Major Iain Grahame, Daws Hall Lamarsh, Bures, CO8 5EX. Prop: Iain Grahame. Tel: (01787) 269213. Fax: (01787) 269634. Web: www.iaingrahamerarebooks.com. E-mail: majorbooks@compuserve.com. Est: 1979. Private premises. Internet and Postal. Appointment necessary. Medium stock. Spec: Africana; Fine & Rare; Natural History; Sport - Field Sports; Booksearch; Prints and Maps. PR: £5– 50,000. CC: AE; MC; V. Corresp: French, Italian. Mem: ABA. VAT No: GB 341 7566 51. Notes: *Also, John Gould original lithographs.*

BURY ST EDMUNDS

Bury Bookshop, ■ 28A Hatter Street, Bury St Edmunds, IP33 1NE. Prop: Joe and Sheila Wakerley. Tel: (01284) 703107. Fax: 01284 755936. E-mail: burybooks@btconnect.com. Est: 1980. Shop open: **M:** 09:00–17:00; **T:** 09:00–17:00; **W:** 09:00–17:00; **Th:** 09:00–1700; **F:** 09:00–17:00; **S:** 09:00–17:30. Spec: County - Local; History - Local; Topography - Local. CC: AE; E; MC; V. Notes: *Major stock of books on and about Suffolk.*

Janet Carters, 40 Church Lane Barton Mills, Bury St. Edmunds, IP28 6AY. Prop: Janet Carters. Tel: (01638) 717619. Fax: (01638) 717619. Web: www.http://ukbookworld.com/members/janetcarters. E-mail: cartersbooks@aol.com. Est: 1978. Private premises. Internet and Postal. Appointment necessary. Small stock. Spec: Sport - Horse Racing (inc. Riding/Breeding/Equestrian). PR: £2–500. Cata: Horseracing.

SUFFOLK

Churchgate Books, ■ 47 Churchgate Street, Bury St. Edmunds, IP33 1RG. Prop: Stephen Cook. Tel: 01284 704604. E-mail: thebookman@btinternet.com. Est: 2006. Shop open: **M:** 09:30–17:00; **T:** 09:30–17:00; **W:** 09:30–15:30; **Th:** 09:30–17:00; **F:** 09:30–17:00; **S:** 09:30–17:00. Spec: Children's; County - Local; Military History. Corresp: French. VAT No: GB pending. Notes: *Two roomed shop with general stock. Spec: East Anglia, Military History, Children's Collectables. Bookbinding and booksearch offered.*

Sally Smith Books, 13 Manor Garth, Pakenham, Bury St. Edmunds, IP31 2LB. Tel: (01359) 230431. Web: www.sallysmithbooks.co.uk. E-mail: sally@sallysmithbooks.co.uk. Est: 1989. Private premises. Internet Only. Appointment necessary. Medium stock. Spec: Antiques; Art; Art Reference; Bibliography; Biography; Children's; Children's - Early Titles; Crafts. PR: £1–1,000. Corresp: French.

CLARE

Trinders' Fine Tools, ■ Malting Lane, Clare, Sudbury, CO10 8NW. Prop: Peter and Rosemary Trinder Tel: (01787) 277130. Web: www.trindersfinetools.co.uk. E-mail: peter@trindersfinetools.co.uk. Est: 1975. Shop open: **W:** 10:00–17:30; **Th:** 10:00–17:30; **F:** 10:00–17:30; **S:** 10:00–17:30. Closed for lunch: 13:00–14:00. Small stock. Spec: Antiques; Applied Art; Architecture; Art; Art Reference; Artists; Arts, The; Building & Construction. PR: £2–500. CC: AE; JCB; MC; V. Mem: PBFA. VAT No: GB 299 6375 77. Notes: *NB. Please phone before travelling lest we be closed! In addition to our books, we also trade from our Malting Lane shop as '20th Century Fashion', selling nearly new designer clothes and accessories.*

DEBENHAM

David Shacklock (Books), ■ Cheese Hill House 27 High St., Debenham, IP14 6QN. Prop: David Shacklock. Tel: (01728) 861286. E-mail: riley01@globalnet.co.uk. Est: 1986. Shop open: **T:** 10:00– 17:00; **F:** 14:00–20:00; **S:** 10:00–16:00. Medium stock. Spec: Annuals; Anthologies; Author - Baring-Gould, S.; - Conan Doyle, Sir Arthur; - Henty, G.A.; - Ruskin, John; Biography; Churchilliana. PR: £1–150. Notes: *Shop closed Tuesday 13:00–14:00. Stands at Halstead (Townsford Mill); Harwich (The Old Bank);Long Melford (Antiques Warehouse). Also at bookfairs (Cambridge/Missing; Dedham; Clare)*

EYE

Elizabeth Nelson, Owl Cottage 153 The Street, Stoke Ash, Eye, IP23 7EW. Tel: (01379) 678481. Fax: (01379) 678481. E-mail: eliznelson@owlcot.demon.co.uk. Est: 1982. Private premises. Appointment necessary. Small stock. Spec: Antiques; Applied Art; Architecture; Art; Art History; Art Reference; Aviation; British Art & Design. PR: £5–1,500. CC: MC; V. Cata: Fine and Applied Arts, Antiques. Mem: PBFA. VAT No: GB 428 0755 47.

Thomas Rare Books, Valley Farm House, Yaxley, Eye, IP23 8BX. Prop: G.L. Thomas. Tel: (01379) 783288. Fax: (01379) 783288. Web: www.abebooks.com. E-mail: thomasrarebooks@btinternet.com. Est: 1978. Private premises. Postal Only. Spec: Antiquarian; Prints and Maps. PR: £10–10,000. CC: JCB; V. Mem: PBFA.

FELIXSTOWE

Books Only, 84 Garrison Lane, Felixstowe, IP11 7RQ. Prop: Colin E. Sharman. Tel: (01394) 285546. Web: www.booksonly.co.uk. E-mail: colin.sharman@btopenworld.com. Est: 1980. Private premises. Internet and Postal. Telephone First. Open: **M:** 10:10–17:17; **T:** 10:10–17:17; **W:** 10:10–17:17; **Th:** 10:10–17:17; **F:** 10:10–17:17; **S:** 10:00–17:00. Spec: Antiquarian; Comedy; Cookery/Gastronomy; First Editions; General Stock; Humanism; Humour; Marxism.

Poor Richard's Books, ■ 17 Orwell Road, Felixstowe, IP11 7EP. Prop: Dick Moffat. Tel: 01394 283138. E-mail: moffatsfx@aol.com. Est: 1997. Shop open: **M:** 09:30–17:00; **T:** 09:30–17:00; **W:** 09:30–17:00; **Th:** 09:30–17:00; **F:** 09:30–17:00; **S:** 09:30–17:00; **Su:** 09:30–17:00. Spec: Fiction - General; Fiction - Women; Literature; New Naturalist; Ornithology; Performing Arts; Poetry; Sport - Cricket. CC: MC; V; SO, SW. Corresp: French. Mem: PBFA. Notes: *Booksearch*

Treasure Chest Books, ■ Null 61 Cobbold Road, Felixstowe, IP11 7BH. Prop: R. & R. Green. Tel: (01394) 270717. Est: 1982. Shop open: **M:** 09:30–17:30; **T:** 09:30–17:30; **W:** 09:30–17:30; **Th:** 09:30– 17:30; **F:** 09:30–17:30; **S:** 09:30–17:30. Very large stock. Spec: Art; Aviation; Cinema/Film; Occult; Topography - Local; Transport; Collectables; Ephemera. CC: E; JCB; MC. Mem: PBFA. Notes: *None of our stock is on the Internet.*

SUFFOLK

FINNINGHAM

Abington Bookshop, Primrose Cottage Westhorpe Road, Finningham, IP14 4TW. Prop: J. Haldane. Tel: (01449) 780303. Fax: (01449) 780202. E-mail: abington-books@btconnect.com. Est: 1971. Private premises. Appointment necessary. Small stock. Spec: Carpets; Tapestry; Textiles; Travel - Asia. PR: £1–5,000. Corresp: French, German. VAT No: GB 213 3817 89. Notes: *Also, new books.*

FRAMLINGHAM

Mrs. V.S. Bell (Books), ■ 19 Market Hill, Framlingham, Nr. Woodbridge, IP13 9BB. Tel: (01728) 723046. E-mail: rvbell@breathe.com. Est: 1974. Shop open: **M:** 10:00–16:00; **T:** 10:00–16:00; **W:** 10:00–13:00; **Th:** 10:00–16:00; **F:** 10:00–16:00; **S:** 09:00–16:00. Medium stock. Spec: Fiction - Crime, Detective, Spy, Thrillers; Booksearch. PR: £2–200.

Mrs. A. Kent (Books), ■ 19 Market Hill, Framlingham, Nr. Woodbridge, IP13 9BB. Tel: (01728) 723046. Est: 1974. Shop open: **M:** 10:00–16:00; **T:** 10:00–16:00; **W:** 10:00–13:00; **Th:** 10:00–16:00; **F:** 10:00–16:00; **S:** 09:00–16:00. Closed for lunch: 13:00–14:00. Medium stock. Spec: Fiction - Crime, Detective, Spy, Thrillers; Booksearch. PR: £1–100.

HALESWORTH

Andrew Jones, 25 Rectory Street, Halesworth, IP19 8AE. Tel: (01986) 835944. E-mail: andrewjones.history@dsl.pipex.com. Est: 1977. Private premises. Postal Only. Very small stock. Spec: Academic/Scholarly; Fine & Rare; History - General. PR: £5–1,000. Cata: History.

IPSWICH

Roy Arnold, 77 High Street Needham Market, Ipswich, IP6 8AN. Tel: (01449) 720110. Fax: (01449) 722498. Web: www.royarnold.com. E-mail: books@royarnold.com. Est: 1976. Office and/or bookroom. Internet and Postal open: **M:** 10:00–17:30; **T:** 10:00–17:30; **W:** 10:00–17:30; **Th:** 10:00–17:30; **F:** 10:00–17:30; **S:** 10:00–17:30. Medium stock. Spec: Antiquarian; Antiques; Applied Art; Rural Life; Scientific Instruments; Windmills & Watermills; Woodwork. PR: £4–3,000. CC: JCB; MC; V. Mem: PBFA; TATHS, EAIA, MWTCA. VAT No: GB 334 0169 85. Notes: *Also, new books on specialities & a booksearch service.*

The Art Book Company, 35 Belstead Road, Ipswich, IP2 8AU. Prop: Priscilla Pilkington. Tel: (01473) 602133. Fax: (01473) 602133. E-mail: artbookco@hotmail.co.uk. Est: 1974. Private premises. Postal Only. Appointment necessary. Open: **M:** 09.30–18.30; **T:** 09:30–18:30; **W:** 09:30–18:30; **Th:** 09:30–18:30; **F:** 09:30–12:30. Closed for lunch: 13:30–16:30. Small stock. Spec: Annuals; Architecture; Art Deco; Art History; Art Nouveau; Art Reference; Artists; Arts, The. PR: £15–1,000. Cata: artists,design & graphics, architecture, textiles. VAT No: GB 728 7258 02.

Claude Cox Old & Rare Books, ■ College Gateway Bookshop 3 & 5 Silent Street, Ipswich, IP1 1TF. Prop: Anthony Brian Cox. Tel: (01473) 254776. Fax: (01473) 254776. Web: www.claudecox.co.uk. E-mail: books@claudecox.co.uk. Est: 1944. Shop open: **W:** 10:00–17:00; **Th:** 10:00–17:00; **F:** 10:00–17:00; **S:** 10:00–17:00. Medium stock. Spec: Antiquarian; Art Reference; Bibliography; Bibliophily; Bindings; Bookbinding; Books about Books; Children's - Early Titles. CC: E; JCB; MC; V; SW. Cata: General Antiquarian; Fine Printing; Suffolk. Corresp: French. Mem: ABA; PBFA; ILAB; PLA, PHS. VAT No: GB 304 7952 56. Notes: *We issue regular catalogues of General Antiquarian, Private Press & Typography, William Pickering Publications, Suffolk & East Anglia, which may also be viewed at our website. Binding Repairs Suffolk Prints & Maps.*

Footrope Knots, 501 Wherstead Road, Ipswich, IP2 8LL. Prop: Des & Liz Pawson. Tel: (01473) 690090. E-mail: knots@footrope.fsnet.co.uk. Est: 1981. Private premises. Postal Only. Appointment necessary. Very small stock. Spec: Crafts; Manuals - Seamanship (see also under Seamanship); Maritime/Nautical; Ropemaking & Knots; Seamanship; Sport - Yachting. PR: £1–100.

The Idler, ■ 37 High Street Hadleigh, Ipswich, IP7 5AF. Prop: Bryan & Jane Haylock. Tel: (01473) 827752. Est: 1980. Shop open: **M:** 09:30–17:00; **T:** 09:30–17:00; **W:** 09:30–12:00; **Th:** 09:30–17:00; **F:** 09:30–17:00; **S:** 09:30–17:00. Medium stock. Spec: Art; New Books; Booksearch. PR: £1–100. VAT No: GB 410 6933 74. Notes: *Also, new books, publisher's remainders, art materials, greetings cards.*

LONG MELFORD

Lime Tree Books, ■ Hall Street, Long Melford, CO10 9JF. Prop: Bryan Marsh. Tel: (01787) 311532. E-mail: limetreebooks@tiscali.co.uk. Est: 1992. Shop open: **M:** 10:00–17:00; **T:** 10:00–17:00; **W:** 10:00–17:00; **Th:** 10:00–17:00; **F:** 10:00–17:00; **S:** 10:00–17:00; **Su:** 10:00–17:00. Medium stock. PR: £1–200. CC: MC; V. VAT No: GB 623 0516 79.

LOWESTOFT

A Book For All Reasons, Rockville House 6 Pakefield Road, Lowestoft, NR33 0HS. Prop: G. A. Michael Sims. Tel: 01502 581011. Fax: 01502 574891. Web: www.abfar.co.uk E-mail: books@abfar.co.uk. Est: 1984. Private premises. Internet and Postal. Appointment necessary. Open: **M:** 09:00–18:00; **T:** 09:00–18:00; **W:** 09:00–18:00; **Th:** 09:00–18:00; **F:** 09:00–18:00; **S:** 09:00–18:00. Closed for lunch: 13:00–16:00. Spec: Author - Heyer, Georgette; - Yates, Dornford; Fiction - General; Fiction - Historical; Fiction - Romantic; History - Local; Naval; Topography - Local. CC: JCB; MC; V; Switch, Maestro. Mem: PBFA; Ibooknet. VAT No: GB 770 1056 57. Notes: *Also on www.ibooknet.com*

R. W. Lamb, Talbot House 158 Denmark Road, Lowestoft, NR32 2EL. Tel: (01502) 564306. Fax: (01502) 564306. E-mail: talbot@rwlamb.co.uk. Est: 1972. Private premises. Internet and Postal. Appointment necessary. Spec: Classical Studies.

NEWMARKET

Miles Apart, 5 Harraton House Exning, Newmarket, CB8 7HF. Prop: Ian Mathieson. Tel: 01638 577627. Fax: 01638 577874. Web: www.sthelena.se. E-mail: imathieson2000@yahoo.co.uk. Est: 1994. Private premises. Appointment necessary. Open: **M:** 09:00–21:00; **T:** 09:00–21:00; **W:** 09:00–21:00; **Th:** 09:00–21:00; **F:** 09:00–21:00; **S:** 09:00–21:00; **Su:** 09:00–21:00. Spec: Countries - Falklands, The; Countries - South Atlantic Islands; Islands; Travel - General; Travel - Polar; War - Napoleonic. CC: MC; V. Cata: South Atlantic Islands, Antarctic and Travel. Mem: PBFA. Notes: *Specialising in islands of South Atlantic - St Helena, Ascension, Tristan, Falklands also the Antarctic and general travel.*

David Paramor, 25 St. Mary's Square, Newmarket, CB8 0HZ. Tel: (01638) 664416. Web: www.http:// ukbookworld.com/members/Paramor. E-mail: cdparamor@btopenworld.com. Est: 1974. Private premises. Appointment necessary. Medium stock. Spec: Cinema/Film; Dance; Entertainment - General; Music - General; Music - Music Hall; Music - Printed, Sheet Music & Scores; Music - Songs & Ballads; Performing Arts. PR: £1–350. Notes: *I specialise in books and ephemera on all the performing arts, including musical theatre, Gilbert and Sullivan, original cast vinyl discs, The Spoken Word, picture postcards, and plays ancient and modern, etc. Stock searches undertaken.*

R.E. & G.B. Way, Brettons Burrough Green, Newmarket, CB8 9NA. Prop: Greg Way. Tel: 01638 507217. Fax: 01638 508058. Web: www.way-books.co.uk. E-mail: waybks@msn.com. Est: 1958. Private premises. Telephone First. Open: **M:** 08:30–17:30; **T:** 08:30–17:30; **W:** 08:30–17:30; **Th:** 08:30–17:30; **F:** 08:30–17:30; **S:** 08:30–17:30. Spec: Animals and Birds; Natural History; Private Press; Sport - Big Game Hunting; Sport - Field Sports. CC: MC; V. Cata: Horses,Hunting and Field sports. Mem: PBFA. VAT No: GB 103 4378 02.

SAXMUNDHAM

Roger Ballantyne–Way, Kiln House Benhall Low Street, Saxmundham, IP17 1JQ. Prop: Roger Ballantyne-Way. Tel: (01728) 604711. E-mail: ballantyne.way@virgin.net. Est: 1979. Private premises. Internet and Postal. Appointment necessary. Medium stock. Spec: Architecture; Art; Art History; Art Reference; Artists; Arts, The; Author - Durrell, Lawrence; Countries - Greece. PR: £5–1,000. CC: MC; V; PayPal. Cata: Art. Mem: PBFA. Notes: *British Art, Illustrated, Private Press, Typography, Fine Printing, Design Domestic and Industrial, Architecture.*

Keith A. Savage, ■ 35 High Street, Saxmundham, IP17 1AJ. Prop: Keith Savage. Tel: 01728 604538. Fax: 01986 872231 (answerphone). Est: 1992. Shop open: **M:** 10:30–13:00; **T:** 10:30–17:00; **W:** 10:30–17:00; **F:** 10:30–17:00; **S:** 10:30–13:00. Small stock. Spec: Children's; Comic Books & Annuals; Comics; Ephemera; Prints and Maps. PR: £1–150.

Sax Books, ■ 4a High Street, Saxmundham, IP17 1DF. Prop: Richard W.L. Smith, MVO. Tel: (01728) 605775. E-mail: richard@saxbooks.co.uk. Est: 2000. Shop open: **W:** 10:00–16:00; **Th:** 10:00–16:00; **F:** 10:00–16:00; **S:** 10:00–16:00. Medium stock. Spec: Animals and Birds; Antiques; Architecture; Army, The; Art History; Art Reference; Author - Churchill, Sir Winston; Autobiography. PR: £1–250. Notes: *Also open on Tuesdays 10-4 in Summer and near to Christmas, as well as on Bank Holiday Mondays.*

SOUTHWOLD

Richard Everett, ■ Southwold Antiques Centre, Buckenham Mews 83 High Street, Southwold, IP18 6DS. Tel: (01502) 723060. Shop open: **M:** 10:00–17:00; **T:** 10:00–17:00; **W:** 10:00–17:00; **Th:** 10:00–17:00; **F:** 10:00–17:00; **S:** 10:00–17:00; **Su:** 11:00–17:00. Small stock. Spec: Children's; Publishers - Warnes; Topography - Local. PR: £2–50. Mem: PBFA. Notes: *Richard Everett at Downham Market, Norfolk. Local topography includes Adrian Bell.*

SUFFOLK

SUDBURY

Beckham Books Ltd., Chilton Mount Newton Road, Sudbury, CO10 2RS. Prop: Mr A.M. Beckham. Tel: (01787) 373683. Fax: (01787) 375441. Web: www.beckhambooks.com. E-mail: beckhambooks1@ btconnect.com. Est: 1998. Office and/or bookroom. Internet and Postal. Telephone First. Open: **M:** 09.00–17.00; **T:** 09.00–17.00; **W:** 09.00–17.00; **Th:** 09.00–17.00; **F:** 09.00–17.00; **S:** 10.00–17.00; Closed for lunch: 12.00–13.00. Very large stock. Spec: Antiquarian; Bibles; Biblical Studies; Ecclesiastical History & Architecture; General Stock; Hebraica; History - Local; Liturgics. PR: £1–2,000. CC: AE; D; E; JCB; MC; V. Mem: PBFA. VAT No: GB 750 9305 36. Notes: *We specialize in theology and religious books including bibles and prayer books, but we also stock a wide range of other subjects. We now have over 17,000 books online, with thousands of additional books on our shelves.*

Parade Bookshop, ■ 10 North Street Parade, Sudbury, CO10 1GL. Prop: Mrs. G. Cawthorn. Tel: 01787 881626. Est: 1975. Shop open: **M:** 10:00–16:30; **T:** 10:00–16:30; **Th:** 10:00–16:30; **F:** 10:00–16:30; **S:** 10:00–16:30.

Suffolk Rare Books, 7 New Street, Sudbury, CO10 1JB. Prop: T.M. Cawthorn. Tel: (01787) 372075. Web: www.abebooks.com. E-mail: morrisbooks@hotmail.com. Est: 1975. Private premises. Telephone First. Open: **M:** ; **T:** 10:30–16:30; **W:** ; **Th:** 10:30–16:30; **F:** 10:30–16:30; **S:** 10:30–16:30. Medium stock. Spec: Aviation; History - Local; Maritime/Nautical; Military; Railways; Topography - General; Topography - Local; Transport. PR: £1–40. CC: PayPal.

Derek Vanstone - Aviation Book, Tymperley Farm Great Henny, Sudbury, CO10 7LX. Tel: (01787) 269291. Fax: (01787) 269291. Web: www.aircraftbooks.com. E-mail: derek.vanstone@lineone.net. Est: 1996. Private premises. Internet and Postal. Contactable. Open: **M:** 09:00–18:00; **T:** 09:00–18:00; **W:** 09:00–18:00; **Th:** 09:00–18:00; **F:** 09:00–18:00; **S:** 09:00–13:00. Small stock. Spec: Aeronautics; Aircraft; Aviation; Maritime/Nautical; Military. PR: £1–200. CC: AE; MC; V. Cata: Aviation. Mem: PBFA. VAT No: GB 711 3364 72.

WESTLETON

Chapel Books, ■ The Chapel , Westleton, Saxmundham, IP17 3AA. Prop: Robert Jackson. Tel: 01728 648616. Web: www.chapelbooks.com. E-mail: bob.thechapel@virgin.net. Est: 1982. Shop open: **M:** 12.00–17:0; **T:** 12.00–17:0; **W:** 12.00–17:0; **Th:** 12.00–17:0; **F:** 12.00–17:0; **S:** 12.00–17:0; **Su:** 12.00–17:0; Closed for lunch: 12.00–17:00. CC: AE; MC; V; Maestro.

WOODBRIDGE

W.H. Collectables, 24 Ipswich Road, Woodbridge, IP12 4BU. Prop: Michael Wheeler. Tel: (01394) 385021. Fax: (01394) 385021. Est: 1981. Storeroom. Appointment necessary. Open: **M:** 09:00–20:00; **T:** 09:00–20:00; **W:** 09:00–20:00; **Th:** 09:00–20:00; **F:** 09:00–20:00. Large stock. Spec: Aeronautics; Alpinism/Mountaineering; Americana - General; Banking & Insurance; Children's; Colonial; Comics; Documents - General. PR: £10–500. CC: D; MC; V. Corresp: German. Mem: ES. Notes: *Stock also covers Australia, Canada and New Zealand.*

YOXFORD

Skoob Russell Square, Woodhill Farm Willow Marsh Lane, Yoxford, IP17 3JR. Prop: Chris Edwards. Tel: 07816 027 642. Web: www.skoob.com. E-mail: skoobrussellsquare@hotmail.com. Est: 1979. Private premises. Internet and Postal. Appointment necessary. Very large stock. Spec: Academic/ Scholarly; Anthropology; Architecture; Art; Art Reference; Biography; Cinema/Film; Classical Studies. PR: £1–500. CC: AE; E; MC; V. VAT No: GB 824 8827 00. Notes: *Skoob are intending to open a new shop premises, near the previous shop in The Brunswick Centre, near Russell Square tube in central London, early in 2007. Further details on dates and address etc will be forthcoming.*

SURREY

ADDLESTONE

Corfe Books, ■ 163 Station Road, Addlestone, KT15 2BA. Prop: Mark Hayhoe. Tel: (01932) 850674. Fax: (01932) 850674. Est: 2001. Shop open: **W:** 10:00–15:00; **Th:** 10:00–15:00; **F:** 10:00–17:00; **S:** 10:00–17:00. Large stock. Spec: Aeronautics; Animals and Birds; Antiques; Archaeology; Architecture; Espionage; Fiction - General; History - General. PR: £1–300. Notes: *Nearly new stock from postal and airline lost property.*

ASHTEAD

Bagot Books, 2 Bagot Close, Ashtead, KT21 1NS. Prop: Nigel Smith. Tel: (01372) 430034. Web: www.bagotbooks.com. E-mail: info@bagotbooks.com. Est: 1999. Private premises. Internet and Postal. Medium stock. PR: £2–300. CC: PayPal. Mem: ibooknet.

BEDDINGTON

Mrs. Patricia Clear, 33 Cedars Road, Beddington, CR0 4PU. Prop: Mrs Patricia Clear. Tel: (020) 8681-0251. Web: www.patriciasbooks.co.uk. E-mail: patricia@mybooks.freeserve.co.uk. Est: 1990. Private premises. Postal Only. Telephone First. Small stock. Spec: Children's. PR: £1–120. Cata: Childrens Books.

BYFLEET

Joppa Books Ltd., ■ 68 High Road, Byfleet, KT14 7QL. Prop: Nadeem M. Elissa. Tel: (01932) 336777. Fax: (01932) 348881. Web: www.joppabooks.com. E-mail: joppa@joppabooks.com. Est: 1989. Shop. Internet and Postal open: **M:** 10:00–14:00; **T:** 10:00–16:00; **W:** 10:00–16:00; **Th:** 10:00–16:00; **F:** 10:00–16:00; Closed for lunch: 12:00–14:00. Large stock. Spec: Antiquarian; Arabica; Archaeology; Asian Studies; Author - Bell, Gertrude; Author - Lawrence, T.E.; Countries - Albania; Countries - Arabian Peninsula. PR: £5–5,000. CC: AE; MC; V; SW. Cata: Middle East and related areas. Corresp: Arabic, French. Mem: PBFA. VAT No: GB 493 7403 24. Notes: *Usual opening times as above, but advisable to make an appointment.*

COBHAM

Nectar Books, P.O. Box 263, Cobham, KT11 2YZ. Prop: T.G. Kent. Tel: (01932) 868863. E-mail: sales@nectarbooks.co.uk. Est: 1976. Private premises. Postal Only. Appointment necessary. Very small stock. Spec: Broadcasting; Cinema/Film; Drama; Entertainment - General; Genealogy; Memorabilia; Music - General; Music - Popular. PR: £5–200. CC: PayPal. Notes: *Also a booksearch service. We accept payments via PayPal.*

DORKING

A.J. Coombes, 24 Horsham Road, Dorking, RH4 2JA. Prop: John Coombes. Tel: (01306) 880736. Fax: (01306) 743641. E-mail: john.coombes@ukgateway.net. Est: 1967. Private premises. Appointment necessary. Small stock. Spec: Architecture; History - General; History - British; History - Local; Topography - General; Topography - Local. Cata: British Topography & Local History. Corresp: German. Mem: ABA. VAT No: GB 210 5273 14.

C.C. Kohler, The Gatehouse, Harrow Road West, Dorking, RH4 3BH. Tel: 01306 886407. Fax: 01306 741988. E-mail: cornflwr@cornflwr.demon.co.uk. Est: 1963. Storeroom. Appointment necessary. Medium stock. Spec: Special Collections. Corresp: German. Mem: ABA; ILAB. VAT No: GB 293 7862 08.

EAST HORSLEY

Emjay Books, Ashdene High Park Avenue, East Horsley, KT24 5DF. Prop: M. Gardner. Tel: (01483) 283373. E-mail: emjaybooks@lineone.net. Est: 1990. Private premises. Internet and Postal. Appointment necessary. Large stock. Spec: American Indians; Author - Bates, H.E.; - Byron, Lord; - Christie, Agatha; - Francis, Dick; - Tangye, D.; Motoring; Private Press. PR: £5–3,000. Notes: *Also, a booksearch service.*

SURREY

EAST HORSLEY

Rowan House Books, Rowans Norrels Ride, East Horsley, KT24 5EH. Prop: George Spranklins. Tel: (01483) 282482. Fax: (01483) 285924. Web: www.abebooks.com. E-mail: gsprankling@aol.com. Est: 1995. Private premises. Internet and Postal. Appointment necessary. Medium stock. Spec: Children's; First Editions; Illustrated - General. PR: £10–500. CC: MC; V.

EAST MOLESEY

Books Bought & Sold, ■ 68 Walton Road, East Molesey, KT8 ODL. Prop: P.J. Sheridan & W.J. Collyer. Tel: (020) 8224-3609. Fax: (020) 8224-3576. Web: www.booksinstore.co.uk. E-mail: sheridan@ books.keyuk.com. Est: 1985. Shop open: **T:** 10:00–17:00; **W:** 10:00–17:00; **Th:** 10:00–17:00; **F:** 10:00– 17:00; **S:** 10:00–17:00. Medium stock. Spec: Aeronautics; Aviation; Children's; History - General; Illustrated - General; Military; Motoring; Railways. PR: £1–900. CC: D; E; JCB; MC; V. VAT No: GB 644 1831 46. Notes: *Organisers of HD Book Fairs.*

Londinium Books, 10 Summer Avenue, East Molesey, KT8 9LU. Prop: Eric & Jean Mahoney. Tel: (020) 8398-7165. Web: www.abebooks.com. E-mail: j.jm.mahoney@talk21.com. Prem: Market stand/stall; Open: **M:** 11:00–18:30; **S:** 11:00–18:30; **Su:** 11:00–18:30.

EGHAM

Blacklock's, ■ 8 Victoria Street Englefield Green, Egham, TW20 0QY. Prop: Graham Dennis. Tel: (01784) 438025. Web: www.blacklockspoloart.com. Est: 1988. Shop open: **M:** 09:00–17:00; **W:** 09:00– 17:00; **Th:** 09:00–17:00; **F:** 09:00–17:00; **S:** 09:00–13:00. Closed for lunch: 13:00–14:00. Small stock. Spec: Sport - Polo; Prints and Maps. PR: £2–250. CC: MC; V. Notes: *Prints on Venice. General bookshop and polo expert.*

ELSTEAD

Brian P. Martin (Books and Pictures), ■ Honeypot Antiques Milford Road, Elstead, Nr. Godalming, GU8 6HP. Prop: Brian P. Martin. Tel: Shop (01252) 703614. Web: www.honeypotantiques.co.uk. E-mail: brianphilipmartin@yahoo.co.uk. Est: 2000. Shop. Open: **M:** 10:00–17:00; **T:** 10:00–17:00; **W:** 10:00–17:00; **Th:** 10:00–17:00; **F:** 10:00–17:00; **S:** 10:00–17:00; **Su:** 11:00–17:00. Spec: Antiques; Arts, The; Collecting; Natural History; Ornithology; Rural Life; Topography - General; Topography - Local. PR: £1–500. CC: AE; MC; V. Corresp: French, Spanish. Notes: *Home tel: (01428) 682567. Also at Biblion, London W1K 5AB.*

ENGLEFIELD GREEN

Glasheen-Books, 57 Alexandra Road, Englefield Green, TW20 0RR. Prop: Patric Glasheen. Tel: 01784 479766. E-mail: orders@glasheens-books.co.uk. Est: 1996. Private premises. Internet and Postal. Spec: Authors - British; Books about Books; Countries - General; County - Local; Fiction - General; Fiction - Science Fiction; Gardening - General; General. CC: MC; V. VAT No: GB 666 2692 03.

EPSOM

Ewell Bookshop Ltd, ■ 9a High Street Ewell Village, Epsom, KT17 1SG. Prop: Stephen Fordham. Tel: 02083931283. E-mail: ewellbookshop@aol.com. Est: 2003. Shop open: **T:** 10:00–17.00; **W:** 10:00– 17:00; **Th:** 10:00–17:00; **F:** 10:00–18:00; **S:** 10:00–17:00. Spec: Art; Art - Technique; Author - General; Autobiography; Aviation; Children's; Children's - Illustrated; Cities - City of London. VAT No: GB 876 1724 95. Notes: *A continuous supply of new stock every month. Large collection of aviation and railway. Most subjects in stock.*

Vandeleur Antiquarian Books, 6 Seaforth Gardens Stoneleigh, Epsom, KT19 0NR. Prop: E.H. Bryant. Tel: (020) 8393-7752 (24h. Fax: (020) 8393-7752 (24hrs). Est: 1971. Private premises. Appointment necessary. Small stock. Spec: Alpinism/Mountaineering; Antiquarian; Bindings; Sport - Big Game Hunting; Sport - Rowing; Travel - Africa; Travel - Americas; Travel - Asia. PR: £5–2,000. Mem: PBFA Notes: *Exhibits at bookfairs. Also, rowing prints and Indian Mogul-style paintings. Maps.*

EWELL

J.W. McKenzie Ltd, ■ 12 Stoneleigh Park Road, Ewell, Epsom, KT19 0QT. Tel: (0208) 393 7700. Fax: (0208) 393 1694. Web: www.mckenzie-cricket.co.uk. E-mail: mckenziecricket@btconnect.com. Est: 1971. Shop. Internet and Postal open: **M:** 09:00–17:00; **T:** 09:00–17:00; **W:** 09:00–17:00; **Th:** 09:00– 17:00; **F:** 09:00–17:00; **S:** 10:00–13:00. Closed for lunch: 13:00–14:00. Medium stock. Spec: Sport - Cricket. CC: E; JCB; MC; V.

FARNHAM

Bodyline Books, The Oast House Park Row, off Castle Street, Farnham, GU9 7JH. Prop: Giles Lyon and Mike Scott. Tel: 01252 727222. Web: www.bodylinebooks.co.uk. E-mail: info@bodylinebooks.com. Est: 1996. Private premises. Internet and Postal. Appointment necessary. Open: **M:** 09:00–17:30; **T:** 09:00– 17:30; **W:** 09:00–17:30; **Th:** 09:00–17:30; **F:** 09:00–17:30; **S:** 09:00–17:30; **Su:** 09:00–17:30; Closed for lunch: 13:00–14:00. Spec: Sport - General; Sport - American Football; Sport - Angling/Fishing; Sport - Archery; Sport - Athletics; Sport - Badminton; Sport - Ballooning; Sport - Baseball. CC: E; MC; V; Maestro, Solo. Cata: Football, Cricket, Rugby, Tennis, Golf, Boxing. Notes: *We hold the largest selection of Wisden's Cricketers Almanack in the world, with well over 1000 issues on our shelves at any one time.*

Derek Burden, 1 Boundstone Road Wrecclesham, Farnham, GU10 4TH. Prop: Derek Burden. Tel: (01252) 793615. Fax: (01252) 794789. E-mail: dweburden@aol.com. Est: 1967. Private premises. Internet and Postal. Appointment necessary. Large stock. Spec: Graphics; Illustrated - General; Prints and Maps. PR: £0–1,000.

GODALMING

Crouch Rare Books, Syringa Tuesley Lane, Godalming, GU7 1SB. Prop: A.S. Crouch. Tel: (01483) 420390. Fax: (01483) 421371. Web: www.crbooks.co.uk. E-mail: tony.crouch@crbooks.co.uk. Est: 1970. Storeroom. Internet and Postal. Telephone First. Open: **M:** 09:00–17:30; **T:** 09:00–17:30; **W:** 09:00–17:30; **F:** 09:00–17:30; **S:** 09:00–17:30. Closed for lunch: 13:00–14:00. Medium stock. Spec: Academic/Scholarly; Antiquarian; Archaeology; Classical Studies; Countries - Cyprus; Countries - Greece; Crafts; Ecclesiastical History & Architecture. PR: £2–1,000. CC: AE; JCB; MC; V; Switch. Corresp: French, Greek, Latin. VAT No: GB 417 6129 55. Notes: *Also, publishers.*

GUILDFORD

Apocalypse, 51 Woking Road, Guildford, GU1 1QD. Prop: Richard Grenville Clark. Tel: 01483 841550. Fax: 01483 841550. E-mail: richardg.clark1000@ntlworld.com. Est: 1996. Mail Order Only. Internet and Postal. Appointment necessary. Spec: Academic/Scholarly; Adult; Aesthetic Movement; Aesthetics; Aircraft; Alchemy; Almanacs; Amish. CC: PayPal. Cata: Non-Fiction and Fiction of all kinds. Corresp: Some French. Notes: *We also publish books on art, education, poetry and fiction [see: www.apocalypsepress.co.uk]*

HASLEMERE

Anglo-American Rare Books, Galleons Lap P.O. Box 71, Haslemere, GU27 1YT. Prop: Jack Laurence. Tel: 01428 606462. E-mail: anglobooks@aol.com. Private premises. Postal Only. Spec: Americana - General; Author - Eliot, T.S.; - Greene, Graham; - Hemingway, Ernest; - James, Henry; - Mailer, Norman; - Sassoon, Siegfried; Fiction - General. Mem: PBFA.

G. Bickford-Smith (formerly Snowden Smith Books), Linden Holdfast Lane, Haslemere, GU27 2EY. Prop: Gillian Bickford-Smith. Tel: 01428 641363. Fax: 01428 641363. E-mail: g.bickfordsmith@ virgin.net. Est: 1975. Private premises. Internet and Postal. Spec: Colonial; Ethnography; International Affairs; Travel - Africa; Travel - Asia; Travel - Balkans; Travel - Islamic World; Travel - Middle East. Cata: on specialities listed.

HORLEY

Reigate Galleries, Cedar Cottage Haroldslea Drive, Horley, RH6 9PH. Prop: K. & J. Morrish. Tel: (01293) 773426. Est: 1960. Private premises. Postal Only. Appointment necessary. Small stock. PR: £5–300. CC: MC; V. Mem: PBFA.

LEATHERHEAD

Dandy Lion Editions, ■ 63 High Street, Leatherhead, KT22 8AQ. Prop: Angela McCarthy. Tel: (01372) 377785. Web: www.dandylioneditions.co.uk. E-mail: angela@dandylioneditions.co.uk. Est: 1995. Shop open: **T:** 10:00–16:30; **W:** 10:00–16:30; **Th:** 10:00–16:30; **F:** 10:00–16:30; **S:** 09:00–17:00. Medium stock. Spec: Academic/Scholarly; Art; Biography; Children's; Children's - Illustrated; Folio Society, The; General Stock; History - General. PR: £1–100. CC: AE; MC; V. Notes: *Retail shop plus internet & postal sales. General stock including Children's, Transport, History, Natural History, Local & topography & much more. Please visit our website www.dandylioneditions.co.uk*

SURREY

MITCHAM

J.G. Natural History Books, 149 Sherwood Park Road, Mitcham, CR4 1NJ. Prop: J. Greatwood. Tel: (020) 8764-4669. Fax: (020) 8764-4669. Web: www.reptilebooks.com. E-mail: jgbooks@ btinternet.com. Est: 1969. Private premises. Internet and Postal. Appointment necessary. Spec: Gemmology; Herpetology; New Books. PR: £10–500. CC: MC; V; PayPal. Cata: herpetology gemmology. Notes: *Also, new books.*

NEW MALDEN

Steve Baxter, 13 Westbury Road, New Malden, KT3 5BE. Tel: (020) 8942-4431. Web: www. baxterfinebooks.com. E-mail: baxterfinebooks@aol.com. Private premises. Postal Only. Small stock. Spec: Antiquarian; Author - Churchill, Sir Winston; Bindings; Churchilliana; Fine & Rare; First Editions; History - General; Literature. CC: AE; JCB; MC; V. Mem: ABA; PBFA; ILAB. VAT No: GB 711 1425 88.

OXTED

Postings, P.O. Box 1, Oxted, RH8 0FD. Prop: R.N. Haffner. Tel: (01883) 722646. Fax: (01883) 722646. E-mail: postingsauctions@yahoo.co.uk. Est: 1992. Private premises. Postal Only. Very small stock. Spec: Aviation; History - Postal; Philately; Railways; Sport - Ballooning; Topography - Local; Transport; Ephemera. PR: £5–300. CC: E; JCB; MC; V. Mem: PTS. Notes: *Also, postcards.*

Secondhand Bookshop, ■ 56 Station Road West, Oxted, RH8 9EE. Prop: David Neal. Tel: (01883) 715755. Est: 1992. Shop open: **M:** 10:00–17:00; **T:** 10:00–17:00; **W:** 10:00–17:00; **Th:** 10:00–17:00; **F:** 10:00–17:00; **S:** 10:00–17:00. Medium stock. PR: £1–400. VAT No: GB 725 4573 27.

RICHMOND

W & A Houben, ■ 2, Church Court, Richmond, TW9 1JL. Prop: C.J.W. & A.K.D. Dunlop. Tel: 020 8940 1055. E-mail: houbens@tiscali.co.uk. Est: 1963. Shop open: **M:** 10:00–18:00; **T:** 10:00–18:00; **W:** 10:00–18:00; **Th:** 10:00–18:00; **F:** 10:00–18;00; **S:** 10:00–18:00. Spec: CC: MC; V. VAT No: GB 215 9473 53.

SURBITON

Tony Hutchinson, 44 Raeburn Ave, Surbiton, KT5 9DP. Prop: Tony Hutchinson. Tel: . Web: www.flyingant.co.uk. E-mail: argh@onetel.com. Est: 1997. Private premises. Postal Only. Appointment necessary. Open: **M:** 09:00–17:30; **T:** 09:00–17:30; **W:** 09:00–17:30; **Th:** 09:00–17:30; **F:** 09:00–17:30; **S:** 09:00–17:30; **Su:** 09:00–17:30; Closed for lunch: 13:00–14:00. Spec: Magazines & Periodicals - General; Science - General; Scientific Instruments; Ephemera; Prints and Maps. CC: PayPal. Notes: *Also trade out of Hampton Court Emporium, Surrey.*

The Bookroom, ■ 146 Chiltern Drive, Surbiton, KT5 8LS. Prop: Keith Alexander. Tel: 020 8404 6644. Web: www.abebooks.com/home/keithalexander. E-mail: kmabooks@aol.com. Est: 2002. Shop open: **W:** 11:00–18.00; **Th:** 11:00–18.00; **F:** 11:00–18.00; **S:** 10:00–18.00. Spec: Architecture; Art; Art History; Art Reference; Artists; Autobiography; Biography; Ceramics. CC: JCB; MC; V; Solo, Maestro. Notes: *I accept PayPal.*

Caissa Books, 5 Pembroke Avenue, Berrylands, Surbiton, KT5 8HN. Prop: Mike Sheehan. Tel: (020) 8399 6591. E-mail: caissa.book1@googlemail.com. Est: 1980. Private premises. Postal Only. Contactable. Open: **M:** 14:00–1700; **T:** 14:00–1700; **W:** 14:00–1700; **Th:** 14:00–1700; **F:** 14:00–1700. Small stock. Spec: Chess; Collectables; Ephemera; Prints and Maps. PR: £3–3,000. CC: MC; V. Cata: Chess. Corresp: French and German. Notes: *Also deal in chess pictures, prints, ephemera, stamps, cancels, cigarette cards and postcards and collectables but not sets, only books on sets.*

SUTTON

Nonsuch Books, 176 Mulgrave Road, Cheam, Sutton, SM2 6JS. Prop: Robert and Lynette Gleeson. Tel: (020) 8770 7875. E-mail: nonsuch.books@virgin.net. Est: 1990. Private premises. Postal Only. Appointment necessary. Open: **M:** 09:00–17:00; **T:** 09:00–17:00; **W:** 09:00–17:00; **Th:** 09:00–17:00; **F:** 09:00–17:00; **S:** 09:00–17:00. Small stock. Spec: Archaeology; Architecture; Art; Art History; Art Reference; History - General; Illustrated - General; Literature. PR: £5–200.

WALLINGTON

RGS Books, 3 Dower Avenue, Wallington, SM6 0RG. Tel: (0208) 647 2003. Fax: (0208) 647 2003. E-mail: rgsbooks@btinternet.com. Est: 1960. Private premises. Internet and Postal. Large stock. Spec: Art; Author - Wells, H.G.; Bibliography; Books about Books; Ex-Libris; Fiction - General; Heraldry; History - General. PR: £2–500. Mem: PLA; SB; RSA; CILIP. Notes: *Stocks titles on history of London.*

WALTON–ON–THAMES

Fred Lake, 104 Kings Road, Walton–on–Thames, KT12 2RE. Tel: (01932) 227824. Private premises. Postal Only. Very small stock. Spec: Sport - Archery. PR: £1–150.

WEYBRIDGE

Fun in Books, P.O. Box 608, Weybridge, KT13 3BL. Prop: Michael J. White. Tel: (01932) 852625. E-mail: mail@melitzer.freeserve.co.uk. Est: 1994. Storeroom. Postal Only. Spec: Freemasonry & Anti-Masonry; Glamour; Humour; Collectables; Ephemera. PR: £5–1,000. CC: MC; V.

WEYBRIDGE

Mrs. D.M. Green, 7 Tower Grove, Weybridge, KT13 9LX. Tel: (01932) 241105. Est: 1974. Private premises. Appointment necessary. Very small stock. Spec: Atlases; Topography - General; Prints and Maps. PR: £1–3,500. Mem: IMCos.

WINDLESHAM

Cold Tonnage Books, 22 Kings Lane, Windlesham, GU20 6JQ. Prop: Andy Richards. Tel: (01276) 475388. E-mail: andy@coldtonnage.com. Est: 1989. Private premises. Internet and Postal. Appointment necessary. Medium stock. Spec: Fiction - Science Fiction. PR: £5–500. CC: MC; V. VAT No: GB 530 1816 81.

WOKING

Glenwood Books, Highlands Cedar Road, Woking, GU22 0JJ. Prop: Lesleyanne Woolvett. Tel: 01483 725628. Fax: 01483 725628. E-mail: lawoolvett@hotmail.com. Est: 1994. Private premises. Book fairs only. Contactable. Spec: Author - Austen, Jane; History - Local; Literature - 19th C. Cata: 19th Century Literature. Notes: *Small stock of local topography/history.*

Goldsworth Books & Prints Ltd, 16 Beacon Hill, Woking, GU21 7QR. Prop: Brian & Joyce Hartles. Tel: (01483) 767670. Fax: (01483) 767670. Web: www.goldsworthbooks.com. E-mail: brian@ goldsworthbooks.com. Est: 1986. Private premises. Internet and Postal. Appointment necessary. Very large stock. Spec: Booksearch; Prints and Maps. PR: £1–5,000. CC: JCB; MC; V. Mem: PBFA. VAT No: GB 641 2513 73.

Peter Kennedy, 2 Shirley Place Knaphill, Woking, GU21 2PL. Tel: (01483) 797293. Web: www. peterkennedy.com. E-mail: peter@peterkennedy.com. Est: 1972. Private premises. Internet and Postal. Appointment necessary. Open: **S:** 08:00–16:00. Spec: Antiques; Atlases; Botany; Illustrated - General; Natural History; Prints and Maps. CC: MC; V. Mem: ABA; Notes: *Also, antique prints. Callers welcome Mon-Friday by prior appointment only.*

World War II Books, P.O. Box 55, Woking, GU22 8HP. Prop: C.G. Palmer. Tel: (01483) 722880. Fax: (01483) 721348. Web: www.worldwarbooks.co.uk. E-mail: ww2books@churchill.net.uk. Est: 1982. Postal Only. Spec: Armed Forces - Australian Air Force; Armed Forces - Australian Army; Author - Rackham, Arthur; Military History; Naval; Navy, The; Shell County Guides (UK only); War - Australian.

TYNE AND WEAR

NEWCASTLE UPON TYNE

Christopher Handley, 38 Beacon Drive, Wideopen, Newcastle Upon Tyne, NE13 7HB. Tel: (0191) 2367759. Web: www.DiarySearch.co.uk. E-mail: christopherhandley@cdsh2.fsnet.co.uk. Est: 1990. Private premises. Postal Only. Very small stock. Spec: Diaries; Journals. PR: £3–200. Cata: diaries and letters. Notes: *My website includes a bibliography of diaries printed in English.*

Frank Smith Maritime Aviation, ■ 92 Heaton Road, Newcastle upon Tyne, NE6 5HL. Prop: Alan Parker. Tel: (0191) 265-6333. Fax: (0191) 224-2620. E-mail: alan.parker4@btconnect.com. Est: 1981. Internet and Postal. Shop open: **M:** 10:00–16:00; **T:** 10:00–16:00; **W:** 10:00–16:00; **Th:** 10:00–16:00; **F:** 09:00–16:00. Large stock. Spec: Aviation; Maritime/Nautical; Motoring; Shipbuilding and Shipping; Sport - Yachting. PR: £4–1,000. CC: AE; E; JCB; MC; V. Corresp: German, French, Dutch. Mem: PBFA. VAT No: GB 297 9302 12.

Stalagluft Books, 73 Titan House Berry Close, Newcastle Upon Tyne, NE63DQ. Prop: Richard Cartwright. Tel: 0191 209 1720. Web: www.stores.ebay.co.uk/STALAGLUFT. E-mail: ric59@ blueyonder.co.uk. Est: 2002. Private premises. Internet and Postal. Telephone First. Open: **M:** 09:00– 20.00; **T:** 09:00–20.00; **W:** 09:00–20.00; **Th:** 09:00–20.00; **F:** 09:00–20.00; **S:** 09:00–22.00; **Su:** 09:00– 22.00. Spec: Academic/Scholarly; Agriculture; Archaeology; Architecture; Autobiography; Bibliophily; Biography; Cartography. CC: MC; V. Notes: *Specialise in obscure, out of print titles & wide selection of Ex-Reference library material. Local interest including Northumberland, Durham, art, indexes, london interest, reference, topography, British history & many other titles.*

Robert D. Steedman, ■ 9 Grey Street, Newcastle upon Tyne, NE1 6EE. Prop: D.J. Steedman. Tel: (0191) 232-6561. Est: 1907. Shop open: **M:** 09:00–17:00; **T:** 09:00–17:00; **W:** 09:00–17:00; **Th:** 09:00–17:00; **F:** 09:00–17:00; **S:** 09:00–12:30. Large stock. PR: £1–5,000. CC: JCB; MC; V; S, SW. Mem: ABA; BA. VAT No: GB 177 1638 41.

NORTH SHIELDS

Keel Row Bookshop, ■ 11 Fenwick Terrace, North Shields, NE29 OLU. Prop: Anthony J Smithson. Tel: 01912960664. Web: www.keelrowbookshop.co.uk. E-mail: anthony.books@wildmail.com. Est: 1980. Shop. Open: **M:** 10:00–17:30; **T:** 10:00–17:30; **W:** 10:00–17:30; **Th:** 10:00–1730; **F:** 10:00–17:30; **S:** 10:00–17:30; **Su:** 10:00–17:30. Spec: Antiquarian; Art Reference; Aviation; Children's; Fiction - Historical; History - General; Industry; Maritime/Nautical - History. CC: MC; V. Cata: Antiquarian, Modern Firsts, Childrens. Mem: ABA. Notes: *The shop is located a mile from the coast on the north bank of the tyne, a large eight-roomed Victorian townhouse with a well arranged good quality stock, in excess of 40,000 titles.*

WHITLEY BAY

The Rider Haggard Society, 27 Deneholm, Monkseaton, Whitley Bay, NE25 9AU. Prop: Roger Allen. Tel: (0191) 252-4516. Fax: (0191) 252-4516. Web: www.riderhaggardsociety.org.uk. E-mail: rb27allen@blueyonder.co.uk. Very small stock. Spec: Author - Haggard, Sir Henry Rider; Author - Heyer, Georgette; Author - Stoker, B. PR: £2–300. Corresp: French, Spanish. Notes: *Also, a booksearch service and Editor for the Rider Haggard Society*

WARWICKSHIRE

ALCESTER

Home Farm Books, 44 Evesham Road Cookhill, Alcester, B49 5LJ. Prop: Tony Read. Tel: (01789) 763115. Fax: (01789) 766086. E-mail: readbk@globalnet.co.uk. Est: 1979. Private premises. Postal Only. Small stock. Spec: Cockfighting; Dogs; Firearms/Guns; Natural History; Rural Life; Sport - Angling/Fishing; Sport - Big Game Hunting; Sport - Falconry. PR: £2–400. CC: E; MC; V. Cata: dogs, fieldsports, natural history. Notes: *Also, a booksearch service.*

ATHERSTONE

The Sit-a-While Bookshop and Tea Room, ■ 18-20 Church Street, Atherstone, CV9 1HA. Prop: Lisa Dundas. Tel: 01827 722593 Web: www.atherstonebooktown.com. E-mail: thesit-a-while@fsmail.net. Est: 2006. Shop open: **M:** 09:00–17:00; **T:** 09:00–17:00; **Th:** 09:00–17:00; **F:** 09:00–17:00; **S:** 09:00– 17:00.

Throckmorton's Bookshop, ■ 16 Market Place, Atherstone, CV9 1EX. Prop: Peter Playdon and Molly Rogers. Tel: 01827 717570 Web: www.atherstonebooktown.com/throckmortons.htm. E mail: throckmortons@gmail.com. Est: 2005. Shop open: **M:** 10:00–17:00; **T:** 10:00–17:00; **W:** 10:00– 17:00; **Th:** 10.00–17.00; **F:** 10:00–17:00; **S:** 10:00–17:00. Spec: CC: MC; V. Corresp: French, Spanish.

BEDWORTH

Astley Book Farm, ■ Astley Lane, Bedworth, CV12 0NE. Prop: Vivienne Mills and Sarah Exley. Tel: 02476 490235. Web: www.astleybookfarm.com. E-mail: astleybookfarm@yahoo.co.uk. Est: 2004. Shop open: **M:** 10:00–17:00; **T:** 10:00–17:00; **W:** 10:00–17:00; **Th:** 10:00–17:00; **F:** 10:00–17:00; **S:** 10:00–17:00; **Su:** 10:00–17:00. CC: AE; MC; V. VAT No: GB 831 8247 29. Notes: *Approximately 50,000 titles in stock.*

GREAT WALFORD

NV Books, 4 Carters Leaze, Great Walford, CV36 5NS. Prop: Tom Verrall. Tel: 0800 0830281. Web: www.nvrarebooks.co.uk. E-mail: nvbooks@nvmanagement.co.uk. Est: 2005. Private premises. Internet Only. Appointment necessary. Open: **M:** 09:00–18:00; **T:** 09:00–18:00; **W:** 09:00–18:00; **Th:** 09:00–18:00; **F:** 09:00–18:00; **S:** 09:00–18:00; **Su:** 09:00–18:00. Spec: Antiquarian; Author - Wodehouse, P.G.; Fine & Rare; First Editions; Limited Editions - General; Memoirs; Modern First Editions; Signed Editions. CC: MC; V; Solo, Maestro, Visa Electron. Cata: latest acquisitions by e-mail. VAT No: GB 783 9189 70. Notes: *Specialising in PG Wodehouse and Douglas Adams.*

HENLEY–IN–ARDEN

Arden Books & Cosmographia, 11 Pound Field, Wootton Wawen, Henley–in–Arden, B95 6AQ. Prop: David Daymond. Tel: (01564) 793476. Est: 1998. Private premises. Postal Only. Small stock. Spec: Antiques; Art; Biography; Canals/Inland Waterways; Children's; Crafts; Food & Drink; Gardening - General. PR: £1–50. Corresp: French, German.

KENILWORTH

Frank & Stella Allinson, 25 Brooke Road, Kenilworth, CV8 2BD. Tel: (01926) 854662. Web: www.booksatpbfa.com. E-mail: fandsallinson@onetel.net. Est: 1989. Private premises. Internet and Postal. Appointment necessary. Spec: Academic/Scholarly; Aeronautics; Alpinism/Mountaineering; Archaeology - Industrial; Author - Ardizzone, Edward; - Brent-Dyer, Elinor M.; - Pratchett, Terry; - Searle, Ronald. PR: £3–40. CC: D; E; JCB; MC; V; Solo, Switch, PayPal. Mem: PBFA. VAT No: GB 776 6995 47. Notes: *We sell at book fairs and on the Internet, preferably would like orders through www.booksatpbfa.com to avoid ABE's exhorbitant charges. All orders through booksatpbfa over 10 will be post free in UK, reduced rates to the rest of the world.*

KINETON

Kineton Books, ■ Bookshop Southam Street, Kineton, CV35 0LP. Prop: J Neal. Tel: (01926) 640700. Web: www.kinetonbooks.co.uk. E-mail: josie@kinetonbooks.co.uk. Est: 1998. Shop open: **W:** 10:00– 17:00; **Th:** 10:00–17:00; **F:** 10:00–17:00; **S:** 10:00–16:00. Medium stock. Spec: Annuals; Author - Milligan, Spike; Children's; Children's - Illustrated; Expeditions; Exploration - Polar Regions; Famous People - Churchill, Sir Winston; First Editions. PR: £1–200. Cata: 8.

WARWICKSHIRE

LEAMINGTON SPA

Alexander's Books, 58 Greatheed Road, Leamington Spa, CV32 6ET. Prop: Andrew Parkes. Tel: (01926) 314508. E-mail: agmparkes@btinternet.com. Est: 1987. Private premises. Appointment necessary. Spec: Biography; Children's; History - General; Illustrated - General; Literature; Medieval; Topography - General; Booksearch. PR: £2–500. Corresp: French, Italian.

RUGBY

Central Bookshop, ■ 4 Central Buildings Railway Terrace, Rugby, CV21 3EL. Prop: J. & A. Sewell. Tel: 01788 577853. Web: www.central-bookshop.com. E-mail: centralbookshop@aol.com. Est: 1996. Shop open: **M:** 09:30–17:00; **T:** 09:30–13.00; **W:** 00.00–00.00; **Th:** 09:30–17:00; **F:** 09:30–17.00; **S:** 09.30–17.00. Spec: Art; Esoteric; Fine Art; Folio Society, The; History - General; Military; Military History; Modern First Editions. CC: AE; E; JCB; MC; V; Switch, Solo.

STRATFORD-UPON-AVON

- **Chaucer Head Bookshop,** ■ 21, Chapel Street, Stratford-upon-Avon, CV37 6EP. Prop: Richard and Vanessa James. Tel: 01789 415691. Web: www.stratford-upon-avonbooks.co.uk. E-mail: richard@ chaucerhead.co.uk. Shop open: **M:** 10.00–17:30; **T:** 10.00–17:30; **W:** 10.00–17:30; **Th:** 10.00–17:30; **F:** 10.00–17:30; **S:** 10.00–17:30. Spec: Author - Shakespeare, William; Drama; Topography - Local. CC: MC; V; Switch, Visa Debit. Corresp: French, German.
- **Paul Meekins Books,** Valentines Long Marston, Stratford-upon-Avon, CV37 8RG. Prop: Paul Meekins. Tel: (01789) 722434. Fax: (01789) 722434. Web: www.paulmeekins.co.uk. E-mail: paul@ paulmeekins.co.uk. Est: 1989. Private premises. Internet and Postal. Appointment necessary. Large stock. Spec: Arms & Armour; Aviation; Fashion & Costume; Firearms/Guns; History - General; History - Ancient; History - British; History - Middle Ages. PR: £2–200. CC: MC; V; Meastro.
- **The Stratford Bookshop,** ■ 45a Rother Street, Stratford-upon-Avon, CV37 6LT. Prop: Sue and John Hill. Tel: 01789 298362. Web: www.thestratfordbookshop.co.uk. E-mail: thestratfordbookshop@ btinternet.com. Shop open: **M:** 10:00–18:00; **T:** 10:00–18:00; **W:** 10:00–18:00; **Th:** 10:00–18:00; **F:** 10:00–18:00; **S:** 10:00–18:00. Spec: General. CC: MC; V; Switch; Maestro. VAT No: GB 785 7543 76.

STUDLEY

Brewin Books Ltd., Doric House 56 Alcester Road, Studley, B80 7NP. Prop: Director: K.A.F. Brewin. Tel: (01527) 854228. Fax: (01527) 852746. Web: www.brewinbooks.com. E-mail: admin@ brewinbooks.com. Est: 1973. Office and/or bookroom. Internet and Postal. Telephone First. Open: **M:** 09:00–17:00; **T:** 09:00–17:00; **W:** 09:00–17:00; **Th:** 09:00–17:00; **F:** 09:00–17:00. Closed for lunch: 13:00–13:30. Medium stock. Spec: Aviation; Genealogy; Motoring; New Books; Railways; Steam Engines; Topography - Local; Transport. Mem: BA. VAT No: GB 705 0077 73. Notes: *Also, publishers of local history books.*

WARWICK

- **Duncan M. & V. Allsop,** ■ 68 Smith Street, Warwick, CV34 4HU. Tel: (01926) 493266. Fax: (01926) 493266. Web: www.abe.com/ukbookworld.commembers/allsop. E-mail: duncan.allsop@ btopenworld.com. Est: 1966. Book fairs only. Shop open: **M:** 11:00–16:30; **T:** 10:00–17:00; **W:** 10:00–17:00; **Th:** 10:00–17:00; **F:** 10:00–17:00; **S:** 10:00–17:00. Large stock. Spec: Antiquarian; Bindings; Fine & Rare. PR: £5–3,000. CC: MC; V; SW, SO. Mem: ABA; BA; Notes: *We stock a good selection of books in all subjects.*
- **Eastgate Bookshop,** ■ 11 Smith Street, Warwick, CV34 4JA. Prop: Robert Allsop. Tel: 01926 490607. E-mail: eastgatebookshop@tiscali.co.uk. Est: 1996. Shop open: **M:** 09:30–17:30; **T:** 09:30–17:30; **W:** 09:30–17:30; **Th:** 09:30–17:30; **F:** 09:30–17:30; **S:** 09:30–17:30. Spec: CC: JCB; MC; V. Mem: PBFA. VAT No: GB 670 3384 38.
- **Phillip Robbins,** 3 Normandy Close Hampton Magna, Warwick, CV35 8UB. Prop: Phillip John Robbins. Tel: (01926) 494368. E-mail: phillrobbins@yahoo.co.uk. Est: 1990. Private premises. Internet and Postal. Contactable. Small stock. Spec: Author - Moore, John; Conservation; Entomology; Magic & Conjuring; Manuals; Manuals - Seamanship (see also under Seamanship); Manuscripts; Marine Sciences. PR: £3–50. Mem: PBFA. Notes: *Secretary the John Moore Society.*

WEST MIDLANDS

BILSTON

Christine M. Chalk (Old & Out of Print Books), Conway House 17 Regent Street, Bilston, WV14 6AP. Prop: Mrs Christine Chalk. Tel: (01902) 403978. E-mail: ChristineMChalk@aol.com. Est: 1996. Private premises. Postal Only. Very small stock. Spec: Art; Art Reference; Artists; Book Arts; Children's - Illustrated; Collectables; Collecting; Decorative Art. PR: £1–200. Cata: Art, Illustrated, Fiction, Biographies.

BIRMINGHAM

Afar Books International, 11 Church Place 135 Edward Road, Balsall Heath, Birmingham, B12 9JQ. Prop: Alf Richardson. Tel: (0121) 440-3918. Est: 1990. Private premises. Postal Only. Medium stock. Spec: Anthropology; Black Studies; Colonial; Countries - Africa; Countries - Caribbean, The; Countries - Egypt; Egyptology; Voyages & Discovery. PR: £1–300. Notes: *Only telephone evenings or Sunday.*

Albion Books, Beechcroft 15 Woodlands Road, Saltley, Birmingham, B8 3AG. Prop: John Bentley. Tel: (0121) 328 2878. Est: 1984. Private premises. Postal Only. Small stock. Spec: Military; Military History; War - General; War - World War I. PR: £1–150. Notes: *Also has stock on the 'origins of the Great War'. Open at irregular times. Also, booksearch.*

Birmingham Books, 202 Witton Lodge Road, Birmingham, B23 5BW. Prop: Mike Attree. Tel: (0121) 3845318. E-mail: mike.attree@blueyonder.co.uk. Est: 2004. Private premises. Internet and Postal. Appointment necessary. Spec: Alpinism/Mountaineering; Author - Fleming, Ian; - Greene, Graham; Children's - Illustrated; Fiction - Crime, Detective, Spy, Thrillers; Fiction - Fantasy, Horror; Fiction - Science Fiction; Folio Society, The.

Elmfield Books, 24 Elmfield Crescent Moseley, Birmingham, B13 9TN. Prop: Liz Palmer. Tel: (0121) 689-6246. Web: www.elmfieldbooks.co.uk. E-mail: elmfieldbooks@blueyonder.co.uk. Est: 1999. Private premises. Internet and Postal. Appointment necessary. Small stock. Spec: Cookery/Gastronomy; Food & Drink; Illustrated - General; Natural History; Topography - General; Topography - Local. PR: £5–500. Notes: *Attend bookfairs and other events.*

Heritage, P.O. Box 3075 Edgbaston, Birmingham, B15 2EW. Prop: Gill & Jem Wilyman. Tel: 0121 455 0093. E-mail: Heritagebook@aol.com. Est: 1985. Private premises. Postal Only. Telephone First. Spec: Antiquarian; Atlases; Bindings; Cartography; Directories - General; Engraving; Ex-Libris; Fine & Rare. Cata: Ex-Libris, Heraldry, Maps, Private Press,. Mem: PBFA. Notes: *We also exhibit at PBFA Book Fairs.*

Robin Doughty - Fine Books, 100a Frederick Road Stechford, Birmingham, B33 8AE. Prop: Robin Doughty. Tel: 01210 783 7289. E-mail: robin.doughty@btinternet.com. Est: 1994. Private premises. Postal Only. Small stock. Spec: Antiquarian; Art; Art - British; Art Reference; Engraving; Illustrated - General: Illustrated - 19th & 20th Century; Literature. PR: £10–2,500. CC: PayPal. Cata: East Anglia, Art & Illustrated, Private Press,. Corresp: French. Mem: PBFA. Notes: *Deals from home and occasionally at Book Fairs.*

David Temperley, 19 Rotton Park Road Edgbaston, Birmingham, B16 9JH. Prop: David Temperley. Tel: (0121) 454 0135. Fax: (0121) 454 1124. Est: 1969. Private premises. Appointment necessary. Medium stock. Spec: Atlases; Autolithography; Bindings; Colour-Plate; Decorative Art; Fine & Rare; Illustrated - General; Miniature Books.

Stephen Wycherley, ■ 508 Bristol Road Selly Oak, Birmingham, B29 6BD. Prop: Stephen & Elizabeth Wycherley. Tel: (0121) 471-1006. E-mail: wycherley@btopenworld.com. Est: 1971. Shop open: **M:** 10:00–17:00; **T:** 10:00–17:00; **W:** ; **Th:** 10:00–17:00; **F:** 10:00–17:00; **S:** 10:00–17:00. Large stock. PR: £1–500. Corresp: French, Dutch. Mem: PBFA. Notes: *Summer (July-August) open on Thursdays, Fridays and Saturdays only.*

Readers World, ■ 137 Digbeth, Birningham, B5 6DR. Prop: G.M. Eastwood. Tel: 0121 643 8664. E-mail: readers@btinternet.com. Est: 1966. Shop. Open: **T:** 10:00–17:30; **W:** 10:00–17:30; **Th:** 10:00–17:30; **F:** 10:00–17:30; **S:** 10:00–17:30. Spec: Comic Books & Annuals; Military; Philosophy; Theatre; Vintage Paperbacks; Booksearch.

WEST MIDLANDS

COVENTRY

Silver Trees Books, Silver Trees Farm Balsall St., Balsall Common, Coventry, CV7 7AR. Prop: Brian and Elaine Hitchens. Tel: (01676) 533143. Fax: (01676) 533143. Web: www.abebooks.com. E-mail: brian.hitchens@tesco.net. Est: 1999. Private premises. Postal Only. Telephone First. Medium stock. Spec: Author - Crompton, Richmal; Ceramics; Children's; Gardening - General; General; Military; Modern First Editions. PR: £3–1,500. CC: AE; JCB; MC; V; Switch. Corresp: French.

Uncle Phil's Books, Wit's End 10, Mary Slessor Street, Coventry, CV3 3BY. Prop: Phil and Susie James. Tel: 02476 639989. Web: www.unclephilsbooks.co.uk. E-mail: pjames@unclephilsbooks.co.uk. Est: 1962. Mail Order Only. Internet and Postal. Appointment necessary. Open: **M:** 09:00–17:30; **T:** 09:00–17:30; **W:** 09:00–17:30; **Th:** 09:00–17:30; **F:** 09:00–17:30; **S:** 09:00–17:30; **Su:** 09:00–17:30; Closed for lunch: 13:00–14:00. Spec: Antiques; Archaeology; Art; Art - Technique; Art - Theory; Art History; Artists; Arts, The. CC: MC; V; Switch, Maestro, PayPal. Cata: general stock. Mem: ibooknet. Notes: *We are an on-line or mail order business only.*

HALESOWEN

Anvil Books, ■ 52 Summer Hill, Halesowen, B63 3BU. Prop: J.K. Maddison and C.J.Murtagh. Tel: (0121) 550-0600. E-mail: jkm@anvilbookshalesowen.co.uk. Est: 1997. Shop. Internet and Postal open: **T:** 10:00–17:00; **Th:** 10:00–17:00; **S:** 10:00–17:00. Medium stock. Spec: Buses/Trams; Canals/ Inland Waterways; History - Industrial; Industry; Maritime/Nautical; Navigation; Railways; Shipbuilding and Shipping. PR: £1–200.

Janus Books / Waverley Fairs, Newlands 9 Hayley Park, Hayley Green, Halesowen, B63 1EJ. Prop: Royston Thomas Slim. Tel: (0121) 550-4123. Est: 1968. Private premises. Postal Only. Small stock. Spec: Motoring; Topography - General; Topography - Local; War - General; Collectables; Ephemera; Prints and Maps. PR: £1–500. Notes: *(Incl: books on Black Country & Midland Local History) Also, book fair organiser – see prelims: Kinver (est 1981), Powick (Malvern) and Bromsgrove Antique Fairs.*

KINGSWINFORD

Wright Trace Books, 70 Ash Crescent, Kingswinford, DY6 8DH. Prop: Colin Micklewright and Pam Wright. Tel: (01384) 341211. E-mail: bandogge-books@blueyonder.co.uk. Est: 2001. Private premises. Postal Only. Very small stock. Spec: Animals and Birds; Annuals; Dogs; Modern First Editions; Booksearch. PR: £5–1,000. CC: AE; D; E; JCB; MC; V; PayPal. Cata: Dogs, Specific interest Bull Breeds. Notes: *We can accept credit cards through our payment proccesor PayPal but you will need an internet access to allow this.*

OLDBURY

Anthony Dyson, 57 St John's Road, Oldbury, B68 9SA. Tel: (0121) 544-5386. Est: 1973. Private premises. Appointment necessary. Small stock. Spec: Fashion & Costume; Fiction - Crime, Detective, Spy, Thrillers; Literary Criticism; Literature.

SOLIHULL

Court Hay Books, 1563 Warwick Road, Knowle, Solihull, B93 9LF. Prop: Howard and Gilian Walters. Tel: 01564 732 380. Web: www.courthaybooks.co.uk. E-mail: courthaybooks@btconnect.com. Est: 1990. Private premises. Internet and Postal. Appointment necessary. Small stock. Spec: Botany; Flower Arranging; Forestry; Fungi; Gardening - General; Gardening - Organic; Horticulture. PR: £10–2,000. CC: AE; JCB; MC; V; Maestro. Cata: Yes. Notes: *Specialist Dealers in Books on The Garden, Garden History, Garden Design, Trees,Botany, Floras and Flower Arranging.*

Fifth Element, 15 St. Lawrence Close, Knowle, Solihull, B93 0EU. Prop: Michael Rogers. Tel: (01564) 773106. E-mail: fifthelement@postmaster.co.uk. Est: 1996. Private premises. Postal Only. Spec: Author - Wilson, Colin; Beat Writers; Counterculture. Corresp: German.

Helion & Company Ltd, 26 Willow Road, Solihull, B91 1UE. Prop: D. Rogers. Tel: (0121) 705-3393. Fax: (0121) 711-4075. Web: www.helion.co.uk. E-mail: books@helion.co.uk. Est: 1992. Private premises. Postal Only. Very large stock. Spec: Academic/Scholarly; Archaeology; Arms & Armour; Aviation; Countries - Germany; Firearms/Guns; History - General; History - 19th Century. PR: £1–3,500. CC: AE; E; JCB; MC; V; Switch. Cata: on military history. Corresp: German, French, Spanish. Mem: IPG. VAT No: GB 797 4185 72. Notes: *Also, a free booksearch service.*

WEST MIDLANDS

SUTTON COLDFIELD

Patrick Walcot, 60 Sunnybank Road, Sutton Coldfield, B73 5RJ. Prop: Patrick Walcot. Tel: (0121) 382-6381. Fax: 0870 0511 418. Web: www.walcot.demon.co.uk. E-mail: patrick@walcot.demon.co.uk. Est: 1980. Private premises. Internet and Postal. Appointment necessary. Very small stock. Spec: Travel - Polar. PR: £10–5,000.

WALSALL (SEE ALSO UNDER STAFFORDSHIRE)

Brownhills Books, ■ Old Sorting Office 43c High Street, Brownhills, Walsall, W58 6SD. Prop: Jon Eadon. Tel: 01543 377660. E-mail: j.ead@tiscali.co.uk. Est: 2006. Shop open: **T:** 10:00–17:00; **W:** 10:00–17:00; **Th:** 10:00–17:00; **F:** 10:00–17:00; **S:** 10:00–17:00. Spec: Notes: *Fairs attended – Lichfield and Kinver.*

A.J. Mobbs, 65 Broadstone Avenue, Walsall, WS3 1JA. Tel: (01922) 477281. Web: www. mobbs.birdbooks.btinternet.co.uk. E-mail: mobbs.birdbooks@btinternet.com. Est: 1982. Private premises. Internet and Postal. Appointment necessary. Small stock. Spec: Academic/Scholarly; Entomology; General Stock; Herpetology; Horticulture; Mammals; Natural History; Natural Sciences. PR: £1–200. Notes: *Payment via PayPal accepted.*

J. & M.A. Worrallo, 5 Allington Close Orchard Hills, Walsall, WS5 3DS. Prop: John & Mark Anthony Worrallo. Tel: (01922) 724519. Web: www.ukbookworld.com/members/worras. E-mail: jworrallo@aol.com. Est: 1980. Private premises. Postal Only. Appointment necessary. Small stock. Spec: Booksearch. PR: £1–100.

WEST BROMWICH

Books at Star Dot Star, Flat 23 Salisbury House Lily Street, West Bromwich, B71 1QD. Prop: Bruce Tober. Tel: (0121) 553-4284. Web: www.star-dot-star.net. E-mail: books@star-dot-star.net. Est: 2003. Private premises. Internet and Postal. Appointment necessary. Small stock. Spec: Antiquarian; British Books; Buses/Trams; Cookery - Professional; Cookery/Gastronomy; Fine & Rare; Food & Drink; History - General. PR: £5–1,000. CC: AE; JCB; MC; V; PayPal. Cata: various. Mem: IOBA.

WOLVERHAMPTON

Books & Bygones (Pam Taylor), ■ 19 Hollybush Lane Penn, Wolverhampton, WV4 4JJ. Prop: Pam Taylor. Tel: (01902) 334020. Fax: (01902) 334747. Est: 1987. Shop open: **S:** 08:30–17:00; **Su:** 08:30–17:00; Medium stock. Spec: Authors - Women; Autographs; Dictionaries; Fiction - Science Fiction; History - General; History - Industrial; Magic & Conjuring; Performing Arts. PR: £1–10. Notes: *On Saturday and Sunday - telephone before travelling. Open other varied times or by appointment.*

R. & S. Crombie, 73 Griffiths Drive, Wednesfield, Wolverhampton, WV11 2JN. Tel: (01902) 733462. E-mail: royandsheila@rcrombie.freeserve.co.uk. Est: 1995. Private premises. Book fairs only. Telephone First. PR: £1–100.

GS Cricket Books / The Old Book Shop, ■ 53 Bath Road, Chapel Ash, Wolverhampton, WV1 4EL. Prop: Gerry Stack. Tel: 01902 421055. Fax: 01902 569597. E-mail: gscricketbooks@hotmail.co.uk. Est: 2005. Shop open: **T:** 10.00–16.30; **W:** 10.00–16.30; **Th:** 10.00–16.30; **F:** 09.00–16.30; **S:** 11.00–16.30. Spec: Sport - Cricket.

Mogul Diamonds, ■ 17 High Street, Albrighton, Wolverhampton, WV7 3JT. Prop: Gerald Leach. Tel: (01902) 372288. Web: www.ukbookworld.com/members/moguld. E-mail: moguldiamonds@btopenworld.com. Est: 1999. Shop open: **M:** 09:00–17.30; **T:** 09.00–17.30, **W:** 09.30–17.30; **F:** 09.00–17.30; **S:** 09.00–13.00. Spec: Biography; Biology - General; History - Local; Music - General; Music - Classical; Music - Composers; Music - Sheet Music; Science - General. PR: £1–200. CC: PayPal. Corresp: French. Notes: *Specialises in books about Shropshire. Also sheet music - catalogues available printed, by e-mail or at website www.moguldiamonds.co.uk*

The Old Bookshop, ■ 53 Bath Road, Wolverhampton, WV1 4EL. Prop: Jerry Stack. Tel: 01902 421055. E-mail: gscricketbooks@hotmail.co.uk. Est: 1967. Shop open: **T:** 10:00–16:30; **W:** 10:00–16:30; **Th:** 10:00–16:30; **F:** 09:00–16:30; **S:** 10.00–16:30. Spec: Art; Embroidery; History - General; History - 20th Century; History - Local; History - Sports; Literature; Needlework. Cata: cricket.

WEST SUSSEX

ARUNDEL

Baynton–Williams Gallery, ■ 37a High Street, Arundel, BN18 9AG. Prop: Sarah & Roger Baynton–Williams. Tel: (01903) 883588. Fax: (01903) 883588. Web: www.baynton-williams.com. E-mail: gallery@baynton-williams.freeserve.co.uk. Est: 1946. Shop open: **M:** 10:00–18:00; **T:** 10:00–18:00; **W:** 10:00–18:00; **Th:** 10:00–18:00; **F:** 10:00–18:00; **S:** 10:00–18:00. Very small stock. Spec: Antiquarian; Art Reference; Atlases; Maps & Mapmaking; Maritime/Nautical - History; Naval; Printing; Sport - Hunting. PR: £100–15,000. CC: MC; V. Cata: antiquarian maps and prints. Corresp: French. VAT No: GB 587-7418-83. Notes: *We undertake valuations for insurance and probate and are more than happy to advise on any aspect of collecting antiquarian maps and prints.*

Kim's Bookshop, ■ 10 High Street, Arundel, BN18 9AB. Prop: Mrs L Flowers. Tel: (01903) 882680. E-mail: kimsbookshoparundel@yahoo.co.uk. Est: 2003. Shop open: **M:** 10:00–17:00; **T:** 10:00–17:00; **W:** 10:00–17:00; **Th:** 10:00–17:00; **F:** 10:00–17:00; **S:** 9.:30–17:30; **Su:** 10:30–17:00. Large stock. Spec: Antiquarian; Arts, The; Fiction - General; History - General; Music - General; Natural History; Topography - General; Topography - Local. CC: MC; V. Corresp: Spanish. Notes: *Also at 19 Crescent Road, Worthing, West Sussex, BN11 1RL, and at 28 South Street, Chichester, West Sussex, PO19 1EL. Open on Bank Holidays 10:30–17:00*

BILLINGSHURST

Bianco Library, Oaklands West Chiltington Lane, Broadford Bridge, Billingshurst, RH13 9EA. Prop: Anthony Bianco. Tel: 01403 741038. Fax: 01403 741038. Web: www.biancolibrary.com. E-mail: sales@biancolibrary.com. Est: 1999. Private premises. Internet Only. Spec: Architecture; Art; Bibliography; Biography; Botany; Canals/Inland Waterways; Collecting; Colour-Plate. CC: PayPal. Notes: *Web site has advanced search facility & multiple picture gallery. We have 70 book categories - see website.*

BOGNOR REGIS

Bookshelf – Aviation Books, 26 Westingway, Bognor Regis, PO21 2XX. Prop: Roger Billings. Tel: (01243) 866817. E-mail: airbooks@gmail.com. Est: 1996. Private premises. Internet and Postal. Telephone First. Spec: Aviation; Booksearch. PR: £1–300. CC: MC; V; PayPal. Cata: Aviation. Mem: PBFA. VAT No: GB 728 5963 88.

mcbooks, 21 upper bognor road, Bognor Regis, PO21 1JA. Prop: Emma Laing. Tel: 01243 868614. Web: www.meadowcroftbooks.demon.co.uk. E-mail: emma@meadowcroftbooks.demon.co.uk. Est: 1996. Private premises. Internet and Postal. Telephone First. Open: **M:** 09:00–17:30; **T:** 09:00–17:30; **W:** 09:00–17:30; **Th:** 09:00–17:30; **F:** 09:00–17:30; **S:** 09:00–17:30; **Su:** 09:00–17:30; Closed for lunch: 13:00–14:00. Spec: CC: MC; V; Maestro. VAT No: GB 699 0227 01. Notes: *Primarily booksearch.*

Meadowcroft Books, 21 Upper Bognor Road, Bognor Regis, PO21 1JA. Prop: Emma Laing & Anthony Parry. Tel: (01243) 868614 (24hr. Fax: (01243) 868714 (24hr). Web: www.meadowcroftbooks .demon.co.uk. E-mail: quotes@meadowcroftbooks.demon.co.uk. Est: 1996. Private premises. Appointment necessary. Very small stock. Spec: Booksearch. PR: £1–50. CC: MC; V; SW. VAT No: GB 699 0227 01. Notes: *Primarily a booksearch service.*

CHICHESTER

back2books.tv, Dorvic House Quarry Lane, Chichester, PO19 8RR. Prop: David Combes. Tel: 01243 533536. Web: www.back2book.tv. E-mail: info@back2books.tv. Est: 2005. Mail Order Only. Internet and Postal. Contactable. Open: **M:** 09:00–17:30; **T:** 09:00–17:30; **W:** 09:00–17:30; **Th:** 09:00–17:30; **F:** 09:00–17:30; **S:** 09:00–17:30; **Su:** 09:00–17:30; Closed for lunch: 13:00–14:00. CC: AE; D; E; JCB; MC; V.

The Chichester Bookshop, ■ 39 Southgate, Chichester, PO19 1DP. Prop: Chris & Carol Lowndes. Tel: (01243) 785473. Web: www.chichesterbookshop.co.uk. E-mail: redbooks@fsmail.net. Est: 1994. Shop open: **T:** 10:30–17:30; **W:** 10:30–17:30; **Th:** 10:30–17:30; **F:** 10:30–17:30; **S:** 10:30–17:30. Very large stock. Spec: Politics; Topography - Local. PR: £1–1,000. VAT No: GB 860 5568 09. Notes: *Five rooms on two floors full of books, sheet music, collectable postcards and all sorts of ephemera. If you can't see what you're looking for please ask, as we carry a large reserve stock on the premises.*

WEST SUSSEX

Peter Hancock Antiques, ■ 40–41 West Street, Chichester, PO19 1RP. Tel: (01243) 786173. Fax: (01243) 778865. Est: 1965. Shop open: **M:** ; **T:** 10:00–17:30; **W:** 10:00–17:30; **Th:** 10:00–17:30; **F:** 10:00–17:30; **S:** 10:30–17:30. Small stock. Spec: Aeronautics; Alpinism/Mountaineering; Americana - General; Antiquarian; Children's; Classics, The; Military; Mysticism. PR: £5–500. CC: AE; E; JCB; MC; V. VAT No: GB 192 8554 28. Notes: *Also, antiques.*

Kim's Bookshop, ■ 28 South Street, Chichester, PO19 1EL. Prop: Mrs L Flowers. Tel: (01243) 778477. E-mail: kimsbookshopchichester@yahoo.co.uk. Est: 2004. Shop open: **M:** 10:00–17:00; **T:** 10:00–17:00; **W:** 10:00–17:00; **Th:** 10:00–17:00; **F:** 10:00–17:00; **S:** 10:00–17:00. Large stock. Spec: Academic/ Scholarly; Antiquarian; Art; Art - Technique; Arts, The; Fiction - General; History - General; Music - General. PR: £1–1,000. CC: MC; V. Corresp: Spanish. VAT No: GB 825 9120 31. Notes: *Also, 19 Crescent Road, Worthing, West Sussex, BN11 1RL and at 10 High Street, Arundel, West Sussex, BN18 9AB.*

EAST GRINSTEAD

The Bookshop, ■ Tudor House 22 High Street, East Grinstead, RH19 3AW. Prop: J. & H. Pye. Tel: (01342) 322669. Shop open: **M:** 09:00–17:30; **T:** 09:00–17:30; **W:** 09:00–17:30; **Th:** 09:00–17:30; **F:** 09:00–17:30; **S:** 09:00–17:30. Medium stock. Spec: History - General; Booksearch. CC: AE; MC; V. Mem: BA. VAT No: GB 472 9663 08

GORING–BY–SEA

Barry Jones, Daymer Cottage 28 Marine Crescent, Goring–by–Sea, BN12 4JF. Prop: Barry Jones. Tel: (01903) 244655. Fax: (01903) 244655. Est: 1990. Private premises. Appointment necessary. Medium stock. Spec: Railways; Traction Engines; Transport; Ephemera. PR: £1–500. Notes: *Appointments only between 09:00 and 21:00. Railway Collectors Fairs Organiser.*

HASSOCKS

Post Mortem Books Ltd, 58 Stanford Ave, Hassocks, BN6 8JH. Prop: Ralph Spurrier. Tel: (01273) 843066. Fax: (0870) 161-7332. Web: www.postmortembooks.com. E-mail: ralph@ pmbooks.demon.co.uk. Est: 1979. Private premises. Internet and Postal. Appointment necessary. Open: **M:** 08:15–18:00; **T:** 08:15–18:00; **W:** 08:15–18.00; **Th:** 08:15–18:00; **F:** 10:00–18:00; **S:** 10.00–12.00. Medium stock. Spec: Fiction - Crime, Detective, Spy, Thrillers; Sherlockiana. PR: £5–1,000. CC: AE; MC; V; Maestro. Cata: crime fiction.

HORSHAM

Horsham Rare Books, P.O. Box 770, Horsham, RH12 9BA. Tel: 01403 252187. Web: www. horshamrarebooks.com. Private premises. Internet and Postal. Contactable. Open: **M:** 09:00–17:30; **T:** 09:00–17:30; **W:** 09:00–17:30; **Th:** 09:00–17:30; **F:** 09:00–17:30; **S:** 09:00–17:30; **Su:** 09:00–17:30; Closed for lunch: 13:00–14:00. Spec: Antiquarian; Art; Aviation; Bindings; Biography; History - General; History - Local; Motoring. CC: AE; MC; V; Maestro. Mem: PBFA.

Merlin Books, P.O. Box 153, Horsham, RH12 2YG. Prop: Mike Husband. Tel: (01403) 257626. Fax: (01403) 257626. Web: www.merlinbooks.com. E-mail: info@merlinbooks.com. Est: 1990. Private premises. Internet and Postal. Telephone First. Very small stock. Spec: Motorbikes / motorcycles; Booksearch. PR: £2–60. CC: E; JCB; MC; V. Cata: Motorcycle. Notes: *New motorcycle books & manuals sold, Secondhand Motoring & Motorcycle books always wanted.*

Michael Phelps, Felled Oaks Brighton Road, Horsham, RH13 6ER. Prop: Michael Phelps. Tel: (01403) 754222. E-mail: phelobooks@tiscali.co.uk. Est: 1974. Private premises. Appointment necessary. Spec: Acupuncture; Aeronautics; Alchemy; Anatomy; Anthropology; Antiquarian; Astronomy; Aviation. PR: £10–100. CC: E; MC; V. Cata: Science & Technol; Medicine, Nat His. Mem: ABA; ILAB. Notes: *Broad coverage of books the subjects stated above, but also associated ephemera engravings, etc. A surprisingly wide range. Buying on commission & valuations.*

LANCING

Paul Evans Books, 13 Berriedale Drive Sompting, Lancing, BN15 0LE. Tel: (01903) 764655. Fax: (01903) 764655. Web: www.paulevansbooks.com. E-mail: paulevans@paulevansbooks.com. Est: 1991. Private premises. Postal Only. Appointment necessary. Small stock. Spec: Art; Author - Bloomsbury Group, The; - Sackville-West, Vita; - Strachey, Lytton; - Woolf, Leonard; - Woolf, Virginia; Publishers - Hogarth Press. PR: £5–30,000. CC: MC; V. Notes: *Also, art by members of the Bloomsbury Group.*

LITTLEHAMPTON

Chris Adam Smith Modern First Editions, 9, Western Road, Littlehampton, BN17 5NP. Prop: Chris Adam Smith. Tel: 01903 722392. Web: www.adamsmithbooks.com. E-mail: chrisadamsmith@ btinternet.com. Est: 1993. Mail Order Only. Internet Only. Appointment necessary. Open: **T:** 09:00– 17:30; **W:** 09:00–17:30; **Th:** 09:00–17:30; **F:** 09:00–17:30. Spec: Modern First Editions. CC: AE; D; MC; V; Switch; Maestro. Cata: Crime, Maritime, Children's, Science Fiction. Notes: *We cover most modern fiction in fine first edition and signed copies are a speciality.*

JB Books & Collectables, 14 Kingsmead Thornlea Park, Lyminster, Littlehampton, BN17 7QS. Prop: Mrs J. Brittain. Tel: (01903) 725819. Fax: (01903) 725819. Web: www.jbbooks.co.uk. E-mail: jan@jbbooks.co.uk. Est: 1997. Private premises. Internet and Postal. Telephone First. Open: **M:** 09:00–17:30; **T:** 09:00–17:30; **W:** 09:00–17:30; **Th:** 09:00–17:30; **F:** 09:00–17:30; **S:** 09:00–17:00. Closed for lunch: 13:00–14:00. Small stock. Spec: Antiquarian; Art - British; Art - Technique; Art History; Art Reference; Artists; Auction Catalogues; Children's. PR: £1–500. CC: PayPal. Mem: PBFA.

South Downs Book Service, Garden Cottage 39c Arundel Road, Littlehampton, BN17 7BY. Prop: Ms. J.A. Bristow. Tel: (01903) 723401. Fax: (01903) 726318. Est: 1994. Private premises. Appointment necessary. Open: **M:** 08:00–20:00; **T:** 08:00–20:00; **W:** 08:00–20:00; **Th:** 08:00–20:00; **F:** 08:00–20:00; **S:** 08:00–20:00; **Su:** 08:00–20:00. Very small stock. Spec: Academic/Scholarly; Antiquarian; Ecclesiastical History & Architecture; Literature - Victorian; Social History; Ephemera; Prints and Maps. PR: £4– 600. Notes: *accredited valuers and cataloguers to libraries and leading private libraries.*

MIDHURST

Canon Gate Books, 2 The Common off Carron Lane, Midhurst, GU29 9LF. Prop: Philip & Wendy Pegler. Tel: 01730 815962. Web: www.canongate-thoughtful-books.com. E-mail: member@ canongate.fsbusiness.co.uk. Est: 1980. Private premises. Internet and Postal. Very small stock. Spec: Oriental; Religion - General; Religion - Christian; Booksearch. PR: £5–1,000. VAT No: GB 543 8777 05.

Wheeler's Bookshop, ■ Red Lion Street, Midhurst, GU29 9PB. Tel: 01730 817666. Web: www.wheelersbookshop.co.uk. E-mail: simon@wheelersbookshop.co.uk. Shop open: **M:** 10:00–17:00; **T:** 10:00–17:00; **W:** 10:00–17:00; **Th:** 10:00–17:00; **F:** 10:00–17:00; **S:** 10:00–17:00. Spec: General Stock; New Books. CC: MC; V. Notes: *Thousands of secondhand books on many and varied subjects, plus a wide range of in-print titles. The shop has recently expanded upstairs, to accommodate even more books. Please call in if you are in the area.*

PETWORTH

Tim Boss, North Street, Petworth, GU28 0DD. Prop: Tim Boss. Tel: (01798) 343170. Est: 1993. Private premises. Postal Only. Small stock. Spec: Ephemera; Prints and Maps. PR: £1–350. Notes: *Also, 10,000 inexpensive prints; some maps. Exhibits at bookfairs*

Muttonchop Manuscripts, ■ The Playhouse Gallery Lombard Street, Petworth, GU28 0AG. Prop: Roger Clarke. Tel: (01798) 344471. Fax: (01798) 344471. E-mail: rogmutton@aol.com. Est: 1992. Shop open: **W:** 10:00–16:00; **S:** 10:00–16:00. Medium stock. Spec: Agriculture; Antiquarian; Bibliography; Bindings; Books about Books; Fables; Farming & Livestock; Firearms/Guns. PR: £5–5,000. Corresp: French. VAT No: GB 704 6864 26. Notes: *Our lease expires 30 June 2007. After then the shop will be closed and we will be selling via ebay only.*

Petworth Antique Market (Bookroom), East Street, Petworth, GU28 0AB. Prop: Doris Rayment. Tel: (01798) 342073. Web: www.petworthantiquecentre.co.uk. E-mail: info@ petworthantiquecentre.co.uk. Est: 1965. Shop and/or gallery open: **M:** 10:00–17:00; **T:** 10:00–17:00; **W:** 10:00–17:00; **Th:** 10:00–17:00; **F:** 10:00–17:00; **S:** 10:00–17:30. Spec: Antiques; Art; Bindings; Rural Life; Sport - Angling/Fishing; Sport - Field Sports. PR: £1–400. CC: MC; V; Maestro, Solo.

SHOREHAM–BY–SEA

Sansovino Books, 9 Mill Lane, Shoreham–By–Sea, BN43 5AG. Prop: Q. & R. Barry. Tel: (01273) 455753. Est: 1991. Storeroom. Appointment necessary. Medium stock. Spec: First Editions; Literature; Maritime/Nautical; Military; Private Press; Booksearch. PR: £5–200. Notes: *Also at: Sansovino, Stokelsy, Cleveland.*

STEYNING

dgbbooks, 15 Ingram Road, Steyning, BN44 3PF. Prop: Denise Bennett. Tel: (01903) 814895. Web: www.ukbookworld.com/members/dgbbooks. E-mail: dgbbooks@talk21.com. Est: 1999. Mail Order Only. Internet Only. Contactable. Spec: Authors - Women; Biography; Fiction - General. PR: £5–50. Cata: Fiction, Biography.

WALDERTON

John Henly, 1 Brooklands, Walderton, Chichester, PO18 9EE. Tel: (023) 9263-1426. Fax: (023) 9263-1514. E mail: johnhenly@tiscali.co.uk. Est: 1986. Private premises Postal Only. Appointment necessary. Small stock. Spec: Geology; Mineralogy; Natural History; Palaeontology. CC: MC; V. Cata: Earth Sciences & Natural History. Mem: PBFA. VAT No: GB 582 5689 92.

WORTHING

Badgers Books, ■ 8–10 Gratwicke Road, Worthing, BN11 4BH. Prop: Ray Potter & Meriel Cocks. Tel: (01903) 211816. E-mail: ray@badgersbooks.freeserve.co.uk. Est: 1982. Shop open: **M:** 09:00–17:30; **T:** 09:00–17:30; **W:** 09:00–17:30; **Th:** 09:00–17:30; **F:** 09:00–17:30; **S:** 09:00–18:00. Large stock. Spec: CC: E; JCB; MC; V; SW, EL, SO. VAT No: GB 587 5552 89.

Kim's Bookshop, ■ 19 Crescent Road, Worthing, BN11 1RL. Prop: Mrs L Flowers. Tel: (01903) 206282. E-mail: kimsbookshop@yahoo.co.uk. Est: 1971. Shop open: **M:** 09:00–17:30; **T:** 09:00–17:30; **W:** 09:00–17:30; **Th:** 09:00–17:30; **F:** 09:00–17:30; **S:** 09:00–17:30. Very large stock. Spec: Antiquarian; Arts, The; Fiction - General; History - General; Music - General; Natural History; Topography - General; Topography - Local. PR: £1–1,000. CC: E; MC; V. VAT No: GB 717 5863 08. Notes: *10 High Street, Arundel, West Sussex, BN18 9AB 28 South Street, Chichester, West Sussex, PO19 1EL. Over 40,000 titles in stock.*

Optimus Books Ltd, ■ 8 Ann Street, Worthing, BN11 1NX. Tel: (01903) 205895. Fax: (01903) 213438. E-mail: optimusbooks@easynet.co.uk. Est: 1975. Internet and Postal. Contactable. Shop open: **M:** 09:00–13.00; **W:** 09:00–13.00; **F:** 09:00–13.00. Medium stock. Spec: Gardening - General; Native American. CC: MC; V. Mem: BA. VAT No: GB 193 7839 11. Notes: *Shop likely to close in April but intend to remain a book dealer.*

WEST YORKSHIRE

ADDINGHAM

TP Children's Bookshop, ■ 71 Main Street, Addingham, Ilkley, LS29 0PS. Prop: Louise Harrison. Tel: 01943 830095. E-mail: tpbooks@btinternet.com. Est: 2005. Shop open: **F:** 10:00–16:00; **S:** 10:00–16:00. Spec: Annuals; Author - Brent-Dyer, Elinor M.; - Fairlie–Bruce, D.; - Hill, Lorna; - Johns, W.E.; - Oxenham, Elsie; - Saville, M.; Children's. CC: MC; V. Mem: PBFA. Notes: *Have traded for 5 years from private premises. Also, attends book fairs at least once a month. Open at other times by appointment.*

BATLEY

Vintage Motorshop, ■ 749 Bradford Road, Batley, WF17 8HZ. Prop: R. & C. Hunt. Tel: (01924) 470773. Fax: (01924) 470773. Web: www.vintagemotorshop.co.uk. E-mail: books@vintagemotorshop.co.uk. Est: 1976. Telephone First. Shop open: **Th:** 11:00–17:00; **F:** 11:00–17:00; **S:** 11:00–17:00. Medium stock. Spec: Buses/Trams; Motorbikes / motorcycles; Motoring; Sport - Motor Racing; Steam Engines; Traction Engines; Transport; Vintage Cars. PR: £1–30. CC: MC; V.

BRADFORD

Idle Booksellers (The), 7 Town Lane, Idle, Bradford, BD10 8PR. Prop: Ros Stinton & Michael Compton. Tel: (01274) 613737. E-mail: idlebooks@bd108pr.freeserve.co.uk. Est: 1990. Private premises. Telephone First. Small stock. Spec: Author - Brontes, The; - Gissing, George; Genealogy; Topography - Local. PR: £1–600. CC: PayPal. Cata: George Gissing. Mem: PBFA.

Woodbine Books, 15 Stone Street, Bradford, BD15 9JR. Prop: Colin Neville. Tel: (01274) 824759. Web: www.abebooks.com/home/woodbine. E-mail: woodbine@blueyonder.co.uk. Private premises. Internet and Postal. Appointment necessary. Very small stock. Spec: Art - British; Art Deco; Art History; Art Reference; Artists; Arts & Crafts Era; Author - Webb, Mary; Bindings. PR: £5–1,300. Mem: PBFA; FPBA, PLA.

BRIGHOUSE

Northern Herald Books, 5 Close Lea Rastrick, Brighouse, HD6 3AR. Prop: R.W. Jones. Tel: (01484) 721845. E-mail: bobjones_nhb@talk21.com. Est: 1985. Private premises. Postal Only. Large stock. Spec: Academic/Scholarly; Communism; Economics; Free Thought; History - Anarchism; History - Economic Thought; History - Labour/ Radical Movements; History - Trotskyism. PR: £1–100. CC: AE; MC; V. Corresp: French, Spanish. Mem: PBFA.

CLECKHEATON

Sparrow Books, 10 Peaseland Close, Cleckheaton, BD19 3HA. Tel: (01274) 876995. Fax: (01274) 876995. E-mail: aplnnock@clx.co.uk. Est: 1992. Private premises. Internet and Postal. Medium stock. Spec: Academic/Scholarly; Architecture; Geography; Geology; Politics; Topography - General; Topography - Local; Booksearch. PR: £1–80. Notes: *Exhibits at Leeds Book Fairs.*

GILVERSOME

Moorhead Books, Suffield Cottage Gildersome Lane, Gilversome, Gilversome, LS27 7BA. Prop: Frank Spicer. Tel: 0113 285 2264. Web: www.moorheadbooks.co.uk. E-mail: frank@moorheadbooks.co.uk. Est: 1964. Private premises. Internet and Postal. Appointment necessary. Spec: Annuals; Art; Bibliography; Bindings; Children's; Colour-Plate; Cookery/Gastronomy; Miniature Books. Notes: *Also, attends Pudsey Book Fair.*

HALIFAX

M.R. Clark, 18 Balmoral Place, Halifax, HX1 2BG. Tel: (01422) 357475. Web: www.abebooks.com. Est: 1980. Private premises. Appointment necessary. Medium stock. Spec: Gardening - General; Natural History; Booksearch. Notes: *Also, booksearch and stock also on www.books@pbfa.co.uk*

HAWORTH

Yorkshire Relics, ■ 11 Main Street, Haworth, BD21 8DA. Prop: Colin and Jacqueline Ruff. Tel: 01535 642218. Est: 1999. Shop open: **M:** 12:00–17:00; **T:** 12:00–17:00; **W:** 12:00–17:00; **Th:** 12:00–17:00; **F:** 12:00–17:00; **S:** 12:00–17:00; **Su:** 12:00–17:00. Spec: Annuals; Children's; Comic Books & Annuals; Comics; Magazines & Periodicals - General; Music - Popular; Music - Rock & Roll; Vintage Paperbacks.

Hatchard & Daughters, ■ 91 Main Street, Haworth, BD22 8DA. Prop: Mary Hatchard. Tel: (01535) 648720. E-mail: mary@maryhatchard.fsnet.co.uk. Est: 1989. Shop open: **F:** 12:00–17:00; **S:** 11.00– 17:00; **Su:** 11.00–17:00. Spec: Author - Brontes, The; Illustrated - General; Railways; Sport - General. PR: £5–200. CC: MC; V. Mem: PBFA.

HEBDEN BRIDGE

Christopher I. Browne, Hawdon Hall, Hebden Bridge, HX7 7AW. Prop: C.I.Browne. Tel: (01422) 844744. Fax: (01422) 844744. Web: www.gilbertandsullivanonline.com. E-mail: sales@ gilbertandsullivanonline.com. Est: 1998. Private premises. Internet and Postal. Telephone First. Medium stock. Spec: Music - General; Music - Classical; Music - Composers; Music - Gilbert & Sullivan; Music - Gregorian Chants; Music - Illustrated Sheet Music; Music - Music Hall; Music - Musicians. CC: AE; MC; V. Mem: SASS/G&S Society.

The Glass Key, Old Town Mill Wadsworth, Hebden Bridge, HX7 8SW. Prop: James Fraser. Tel: 01422 842786. Web: www.ibooknet.co.uk. E-mail: glasskey@3-c.coop. Est: 1990. Mail Order Only. Postal Only. Contactable. Open: **Th:** 09:00–17:30; **F:** 09:00–17:30; **S:** 09:00–17:30; **Su:** 09:00–17:30; Closed for lunch: 13:00–14:00. Spec: Antiques; Author - 20th Century; Fiction - Crime, Detective, Spy, Thrillers; Fiction - Fantasy, Horror; Fiction - Science Fiction; Fiction - Supernatural; First Editions; Food & Drink. CC: AE; JCB; MC; V. Corresp: French. Mem: Ibooknet. Notes: *Retail premises recently closed. Currently trading via the internet only.*

HOLMFIRTH

Beardsell Books, ■ Toll House Bookshop 32–34 Huddersfield Road, Holmfirth, HD9 2JS. Prop: Elaine V. Beardsell. Tel: (01484) 686541. Fax: (01484) 688406. Web: www.toll-house.co.uk. E-mail: tollhouse.bookshop@virgin.net. Est: 1977. Internet and Postal. Shop open: **M:** 09:00 17:00; **T:** 09:00–17:00; **W:** 09:00–17:00; **Th:** 09:00–17:00; **F:** 09:00–17:00; **S:** 09:00–17:30; **Su:** 13:00–16:30. Very large stock. Spec: Antiquarian; History - General; History - Local. PR: £1–1,000. CC: MC; V. Mem: ABA; PBFA; BA. VAT No: GB 333 4195 70.

Daisy Lane Books, ■ 15 Towngate, Holmfirth, HD9 1HA. Prop: J. & B. Townsend–Cardew. Tel: (01484) 688409. Est: 1990. Shop open: **M:** 09:30–17:00; **T:** 09:30–17:00; **W:** 09:30–17:00; **Th:** 09:30– 17:00; **F:** 09:30–17:00; **S:** 09:30–17:00; **Su:** 09:30–17:00. Large stock.

Madalyn S. Jones, Horsegate Hill House 3 Town End Road, Wooldale, Holmfirth, HD9 1AH. Prop: Madalyn S. Jones. Tel: (01484) 681580. Fax: (01484) 681580. Web: www.madalynjonesbooks.co.uk. E-mail: madalynjonesbooks@yahoo.co.uk. Est: 1978. Private premises. Internet and Postal. Appointment necessary. Spec: Sculpture; Booksearch. Mem: PBFA. Notes: *General stock and a booksearch service Specialising in books on sculpture and related arts.*

HORBURY

Rickaro Books, ■ 17 High Street, Horbury, Wakefield, WF4 5AB. Prop: Richard Knowles and Carole Heaton. Tel: 01924 278811. Fax: 01924 278811. Web: www.rickarobooks.co.uk. E-mail: info@rickarobooks.co.uk. Est: 2001. Shop open: **M:** 08:30–17:30; **T:** 08:30–17:30; **W:** 08:30–17:30; **Th:** 08:30–17:30; **F:** 08:30–17:30; **S:** 08:30–17:30; **Su:** 09:00–17:30; Closed for lunch: 13:00–14:00. Spec: Author - Lawrence, T.E.; Children's; History - Local; Military. CC: E; MC; V. Cata: military, T.E. Lawrence, children's, local history. Mem: PBFA; BA. Notes: *Also exhibits at book fairs.*

HUDDERSFIELD

Aphra Books, See under 'Susan Taylor Books', Huddersfield, HD4 6XZ. Prop: Susan Taylor. Tel: 01484 662120. Open: **M:** 09:00–17:30; **T:** 09:00–17:30; **W:** 09:00–17:30; **Th:** 09:00–17:30; **F:** 09:00–17:30; **S:** 09:00–17:30; **Su:** 09:00–17:30; Closed for lunch: 13:00–14:00.

WEST YORKSHIRE

Children's Bookshop, ■ 37/39 Lidget Street Lindley, Huddersfield, HD3 3JF. Prop: Sonia & Barry Benster. Tel: (01484) 658013. Fax: (01484) 460020. E-mail: barry@hudbooks.demon.co.uk. Est: 1975. Shop open: **M:** 09:00–17:30; **T:** 09:00–17:30; **W:** 09:00–17:30; **Th:** 09:00–17:30; **F:** 09:00–17:30; **S:** 09:00–17:00. Small stock. Spec: Author - Dickens, Charles; - Kipling, Rudyard; - Lawrence, D.H.; Autobiography; Bibliography; Biography; Children's; Christmas. CC: MC; V. Cata: Childrens on Biblion. Mem: BA. VAT No: GB 185 0068 66. Notes: *Mainly new childrens books with a small antiquarian and second hand section.*

Elaine Lonsdale Books, 4 Scar Top Golcar, Huddersfield, HD7 4DT. Prop: Elaine Lonsdale. Tel: 01484 644193. Fax: 01484 644193. E-mail: Lainelonsdale@yahoo.co.uk. Est: 1990. Private premises. Appointment necessary. Spec: Antiquarian; Art - British; Author - 20th Century; Author - Alcotts, The; Authors - Women; Biography; Fiction - General; Fiction - Women. PR: £1–100. CC: MC; V. Mem: PBFA; Society of Bookbinders. Notes: *Also, bookbinder.*

Susan Taylor Books, 2 Top of the Hill Thurstonland, Huddersfield, HD4 6XZ. Prop: Susan Taylor. Tel: 01484 662120. E-mail: susan@mosleyr.freeserve.co.uk. Est: 1987. Mail Order Only. Internet and Postal. Telephone First. Spec: Domesticity; Feminism; Fiction - Women; Housekeeping; Spiritual; Textiles; Women. Cata: Women.

Nick Tozer Railway Books, 159 Church Street, Paddock, Huddersfield, HD1 4UJ. Prop: Nick Tozer. Tel: (01484) 518159. Web: www.railwaybook.com. E-mail: nick@railwaybook.com. Est: 1997. Office and/ or bookroom. Internet and Postal. Appointment necessary. Medium stock. Spec: Railways; Booksearch. PR: £0–50. CC: MC; V; Maestro, PayPal.

William H. Roberts, The Crease, 113 Hill Grove Salendine Nook, Huddersfield, HD3 3TL. Tel: (01484) 654463. Fax: (01484) 654463. Web: www.williamroberts-cricket.com. E-mail: william.roberts2@ virgin.net. Est: 1997. Private premises. Internet and Postal. Telephone First. Spec: Sport - Cricket. CC: V. Mem: PBFA.

ILKLEY

Fine Books at Ilkley, 41 Manley Road, Ilkley, LS29 8QP. Prop: Dr. F.P. Williams. Tel: (01943) 600168. Fax: (01943) 603828. E-mail: finebooksilkley@dialstart.net. Est: 1979. Private premises. Appointment necessary. Spec: Alpinism/Mountaineering; Antiquarian; Bindings; Children's - Illustrated; Natural History; Technical; Travel - Africa; Travel - Americas. PR: £10–1,000. Mem: ABA; PBFA; ILAB. VAT No: GB 427 7108 51.

Greenroom Books, 9 St. James Road, Ilkley, LS29 9PY. Prop: Geoff Oldham. Tel: (01943) 607662. Web: www.www.ukbookworld.com/members/greenroom. E-mail: greenroombooks@blueyonder.co.uk. Est: 1991. Private premises. Internet and Postal. Appointment necessary. Open: **M:** 09:00–18:00; **T:** 09:00–18:00; **W:** 09:00–18:00; **Th:** 09:00–18:00; **F:** 09:00–18:00; **S:** 09:00–18:00. Small stock. Spec: Academic/Scholarly; Broadcasting; Cinema/Film; Comedy; Dance; Design; Drama; Entertainment - General. PR: £8–50. CC: PayPal. Corresp: French. Notes: *Specialises in the Performing Arts. Booksearch.*

Skyrack Books, ■ 20 Skipton Road, Ilkley, LS29 9EJ. Prop: Steven Dyke. Tel: (01943) 601598. Fax: (01943) 601598. Est: 2000. Shop open: **T:** 10:00–17:00; **W:** 10:00–17:00; **Th:** 10:00–17:00; **F:** 10:00– 17:00; **S:** 10:00–17:00. Closed for lunch: 13:00–14:00. Medium stock. Spec: Canals/Inland Waterways; History - Industrial; History - Local; New Books; Railways; Topography - Local; Booksearch. PR: £1–100. Mem: BA. Notes: *Also stocks on Yorkshire, new books, book tokens.*

Mark Sutcliffe, 14 St. John's Avenue, Addingham, Ilkley, LS29 0QB. Tel: (01943) 830117. Fax: (01943) 830117. Web: www.marksutcliffebooks.com. E-mail: msfe@btinternet.com. Est: 1996. Private premises. Internet and Postal. Appointment necessary. Very small stock. Spec: Author - Blake, N.; - Carr, John Dickson; - Chandler, Raymond; - Crofts, Freeman Wills; - Fleming, Ian; - Hammett, Dashiell; Fiction - Crime, Detective, Spy, Thrillers; First Editions. PR: £5–3,000. CC: E; JCB; MC; V. Cata: Detective Fiction, Modern Firsts, Children's. Mem: PBFA. Notes: *Specializing in Detective Fiction, especially, Dashiell Hammett, Raymond Chandler, The Crime Club and the Golden Age 1920- 1943.*

KIRKSTALL

The Bookshop, Kirkstall, ■ 10 Commercial Road, Kirkstall, Leeds, LS5 3AQ. Prop: R.A. & P.P. Brook. Tel: (0113) 278-0937. Fax: (0113) 278-0937. E-mail: book.shop@btinternet.com. Est: 1982. Shop open: **M:** 10:15–17:30; **T:** 10:15–17:30; **W:** 10:15–16:30; **Th:** 10:15–16:30; **F:** 10:15–17:30; **S:** 10:15– 17:30. Large stock. Spec: Antiquarian. PR: £1–2,000. CC: MC; V.

LEEDS

Bates & Hindmarch, 2 Cumberland Road Headingley, Leeds, LS6 2EF. Prop: Jeffery Bates. Tel: (0113) 278-3306. Web: www.abcbooks.com. E mail: jefferybates@aol.com Est: 1987 Private premises. Appointment necessary. Small stock. Spec: Almanacs; Antiquarian; Bindings; Countries - Afganistan; Countries - Asia; Countries - Central Asia; Countries - India; Countries - Iran. PR: £20–1,000. CC: AE; JCB; MC; V; Maestro, Delta, Switch. Mem: PBFA. VAT No: GB 417 9947 06. Notes: *Very specialist stock. India and the East India Company, books on India published before 1948, Delhi Durbars, Central Asia. Folding maps and city plans outside UK.*

John Blanchfield, 5 Stanmore Place, Leeds, LS4 2RR. Prop: John Blanchfield. Tel: (0113) 274-2406. E-mail: john@blanchfield.demon.co.uk. Est: 1984. Private premises. Internet and Postal. Appointment necessary. Medium stock. Spec: Academic/Scholarly; History - Industrial; Industry. PR: £5–500. CC: JCB; V. Mem: PBFA. VAT No: GB 405 5743 61. Notes: *and PBFA book fairs.*

John Bonner, 82a Allerton Grange Rise Moortown, Leeds, LS17 6LH. Tel: (0113) 2695012. E-mail: johnbonner@btinternet.com. Est: 1990. Private premises. Postal Only. Small stock. Spec: Aviation; Biography; Military. PR: £1–250.

Bryony Books, 11 Woodhall Avenue, Leeds, LS5 3LH. Prop: Joan & Bill Martin. Tel: (0113) 258-7283. Est: 1976. Private premises. Appointment necessary. Very small stock. Spec: Children's. PR: £2–100. Notes: *Please note: limited trading only.*

Draca Books, 22 Templenewsam Road, Leeds, LS15 0DX. Prop: Dr. & Mrs Michael Dickenson. Tel: 0113 294 7188. Web: www.dracabooks.co.uk. E-mail: books@dracabooks.co.uk. Est: 2004. Private premises. Internet and Postal. Spec: Children's; Collectables. CC: PayPal. Corresp: French, German. Notes: *Entry also appears on www.yorkbooksellers.co.uk*

Elephant Books, ■ off Midland Road Nr. Hyde Park Corner, Leeds, LS6 1BQ. Prop: Neil Whitworth. Tel: (0113) 274-4021. Est: 1987. Shop open: **M:** 10:00–18:00; **T:** 10:00–18:00; **W:** 10:00–18:00; **Th:** 10:00–18:00; **F:** 10:00–18:00; **S:** 10:00–18:00. Large stock. Spec: Arts, The; Beat Writers; Literature; Philosophy; Psychology/Psychiatry. PR: £1–100. CC: AE; D; E; JCB; MC; V; Solo. Corresp: German, French, Spanish.

Find That Book, 74 Oxford Avenue Guiseley, Leeds, LS20 9BX. Prop: David Herries. Tel: (01943) 872699. Web: www.findthatbook.demon.co.uk. E-mail: david@findthatbook.demon.co.uk. Est: 1991. Private premises. Internet and Postal. Spec: Booksearch.

Leeds Bookseller, 3 Wedgewood Drive Roundhay, Leeds, LS8 1EF. Prop: J.B. Wilkinson. Tel: (0113) 266-7183 Est: 1980 Private premises. Postal Only. Contactable. Very small stock. Spec: Academic/ Scholarly; Palaeography. PR: £1–8.

Peregrine Books (Leeds), 27 Hunger Hills Avenue Horsforth, Leeds, LS18 5JS. Prop: J. & M.A. Whitaker. Tel: (0113) 258-5495. Est: 1986. Private premises. Appointment necessary. Small stock. Spec: Natural History; Travel - General. PR: £5–3,000. Notes: *Also publishers of books on natural history.*

David Spenceley Books, 75 Harley Drive, Leeds, LS13 4QY. Prop: David Spenceley. Tel: (0113) 257-0715 (24h). Web: www.abebooks.com/home/davidspenceleybooks. E-mail: davidspenceley@email.com. Est: 1990. Private premises. Internet and Postal. Contactable. Open: **M:** 09:00–21:00; **T:** 09:00–21:00; **W:** 09:00–21:00; **Th:** 09:00–21:00; **F:** 09:00–21:00; **S:** 09:00–17:00; **Su:** 09:00–19:00; Closed for lunch: 12:00–14:00. Medium stock. Spec: Academic/Scholarly; Arms & Armour; Country Houses; Ecclesiastical History & Architecture; History British; History - Middle Ages; History - Renaissance, The; History - Women. PR: £1–200. CC: PayPal. Notes: *Outside quoted opening times - contactable at all reasonable times.*

Graham Sykes, 81 Gledhow Park Grove, Leeds, LS7 4JW. Tel: (0113) 262-1547. Est: 1985. Private premises. Postal Only. Small stock. Spec: Fine Art; First Editions; History - General; Natural History; Palaeontology; Photography; Topography - General; Travel - General. Mem: PBFA.

Woodlands Books, 65 Gledhow Wood Road, Leeds, LS8 4DG. Prop: Bill & Valerie Astbury. Tel: (0113) 266-7834. Est: 1986. Private premises. Postal Only. Small stock. Spec: Music - General; Music - Musicians. PR: £2–150.

LIVERSEDGE

Heckmondwike Book Shop, ■ 66 Union Road, Liversedge, WF15 7JF. Prop: David Sheard. Tel: (01924) 505666. E-mail: david.sheard@ntlworld.com. Est: 1984. Shop. Internet and Postal. Telephone First. Open: **S:** 10:00–16.00. Large stock. Spec: Author - Charteris, Leslie; - Christie, Agatha; - Creasey, John; - Wheatley, Dennis; Fiction - General; Fiction - Crime, Detective, Spy, Thrillers; Fiction - Science Fiction; Publishers - Pan. PR: £1–500. VAT No: GB 427 5900 45. Notes: *Will open shop at other times by arrangement or email requirements for listing on eBay.*

MIRFIELD

D. & M. Books, 5a Knowl Road, Mirfield, WF14 8DQ. Prop: Daniel J. Hanson. Tel: (01924) 495768. Fax: (01924) 491267. Web: www.dandmbooks.com. E-mail: daniel@dandmbooks.com. Est: 1989. Warehouse. Internet and Postal. Telephone First. Small stock. Spec: Annuals; Author - Blake, Sexton; - Blyton, Enid; - Brent-Dyer, Elinor M.; - Crompton, Richmal; - Johns, W.E.; - Oxenham, Elsie; - Richards, Frank. PR: £10–1,000. CC: JCB; MC; V. Cata: Children's books, annuals, comics. Mem: PBFA. VAT No: GB 686 8348 71. Notes: *Also suppliers and manufacturers of book jacket covers and mailing supplies. We are the official UK distributor for Brodart. Catalogue available upon request.*

NORMANTON

Andrew Warrender, 4 West Street, Normanton, WF6 2AP. Tel: (01924) 892117. Fax: (01924) 215327. Web: www.warrender.demon.co.uk. E-mail: andrew@4yourprinting.co.uk. Est: 1995. Private premises. Postal Only. Small stock. Spec: Author - Fleming, Ian; Modern First Editions. PR: £1–150.

OTLEY

- **Books Upstairs,** ■ 9 Newmarket [Street], Otley, LS21 3AE. Prop: John Hepworth. E-mail: buxupstairs@onetel.com. Est: 2002. Shop open: **T:** 11:00–16:00; **F:** 11:00–16:00; **S:** 11:00–16:00.
- **Chevin Books,** 19 Manor Square, Otley, LS21 3AP. Prop: Simon Michael. Tel: (01943) 466599. E-mail: chevinbooks@yahoo.co.uk. Est: 1996. Private premises open: **Th:** 10:00–17:00; **F:** 10:00–17:00; **S:** 10:00–17:00. Medium stock. Spec: Architecture; Art History; Aviation; Folio Society, The; Literature; Military; Military History; Motoring. PR: £1–1,000. CC: MC; V.

TODMORDEN

- **Border Bookshop,** ■ 61a & 63 Halifax Road, Todmorden, OL14 5BB. Prop: Victor H. Collinge. Tel: (01706) 814721. Web: www.borderbookshop.co.uk. E-mail: collinge@borderbookshop.fsnet.co.uk. Est: 1980. Shop open: **M:** 10:00–17:00; **T:** ; **W:** 10:00–17:00; **Th:** 10:00–17:00; **F:** 10:00–17:00; **S:** 10:00– 17:00. Closed for lunch: 13:00–14:00. Large stock. Spec: Children's; Comic Books & Annuals; Comics; Magazines & Periodicals - General; Nostalgia; Sport - Cricket; Sport - Football (Soccer); Ephemera. CC: AE; E; JCB; MC; V. Cata: british comics & storypapers. Corresp: French. Mem: BA; Notes: *Also, new books, book tokens & book ordering service.*
- **John Eggeling Books,** Claremont South 56 Burnley Road, Todmorden, OL14 5LH. Prop: John Eggeling. Tel: (01706) 816487. Fax: (01706) 816487. Web: www.abebooks.com/home/TODBOOKS/. E-mail: todmordenbooks@ndirect.co.uk. Est: 1972. Private premises. Internet and Postal. Appointment necessary. Medium stock. Spec: Adventure; Africana; Anthologies; Australiana; Author - General; Author - 20th Century; Authors - Australian; Authors - British. PR: £2–1,000. CC: MC; V; Switch. Cata: Fiction by Minor Authors. Notes: *Also, a booksearch service.*
- **Judith Mansfield,** Claremont South, Claremont Road, Todmorden, OL14 5LH. Prop: Judith Mansfield. Tel: (01706) 816487. Fax: (01706) 816487. Web: www.abebooks.com/home/TODBOOKS/. E-mail: todmordenbooks@ndirect.co.uk. Est: 1983. Private premises. Internet and Postal. Appointment necessary. Spec: Applied Art; Carpets; Crafts; Crochet; Decorative Art; Dyes; Embroidery; Hairdressing. CC: MC; V; PayPal. Cata: Needlework, textiles, costume and fashion. Mem: PBFA; Textile Society.
- **Magpie Books,** Mellor Barn Farm Peel Cottage Road, Walsden, Todmorden, OL14 7QJ. Prop: Graeme Roberts. Tel: (01706) 815005. Web: www.magpie books.co.uk. E mail: magpie@mellorbarn.co.uk. Private premises. Internet and Postal. Appointment necessary. Medium stock. PR: £5–2,000. CC: AE; JCB; MC; V. Mem: Ibooknet. Notes: *Large general stock.*

WETHERBY

Steve Schofield Golf Books, 29 Nichols Way, Wetherby, LS22 6AD. Tel: (01937) 581276. Fax: (01937) 581276. E-mail: golfbooks@steveschofield.com. Est: 1993. Private premises. Postal Only. Contactable. Open: **M:** 09:00–17:00; **T:** 09:00–17:00; **W:** 09:00–17:00; **Th:** 09:00–17:00; **F:** 09:00– 17:00. Very small stock. Spec: Sport - Golf. PR: £10–1,500. CC: MC; V.

WILTSHIRE

BRADFORD ON AVON

Ex Libris, ■ 1 The Shambles, Bradford on Avon, BA15 1JS. Prop: Roger Jones. Tel: (01225) 863595. Fax: (01225) 863595. Web: www.ex-librisbooks.co.uk. E-mail: roger.jones@ex-librisbooks.co.uk. Est: 1980. Internet and Postal. Shop open: **M:** 09:00–17:30; **T:** 09:00–17:30; **W:** 09:00–17:30; **Th:** 09:00–17:30; **F:** 09:00–17:30; **S:** 09:00–17:30. PR: £1–10. CC: AE; JCB; MC. Notes: *Also, new books publishing as Ex Libris Press.*

CALNE

Clive Farahar & Sophie Dupre, Horsebrook House XV The Green, Calne, SN11 8DQ. Tel: (01249) 821121. Fax: (01249) 821202. Web: www.farahardupre.co.uk. E-mail: sophie@farahardupre.co.uk. Est: 1978. Private premises. Internet and Postal. Appointment necessary. Open: **M:** 09:00–17:00; **T:** 09:00–17:00; **W:** 09:00 17:00; **Th:** 09:00–17:00; **F:** 09:00–17:00; **S:** 10:00–13:00. Closed for lunch: 13:00–14:00. Large stock. Spec: Antiquarian; Autographs; Documents - General; Letters; Literature; Manuscripts; Photography; Royalty - General. PR: £10–10,000. CC: AF, ICB, MC; V. Corresp: French. Mem: ABA; ILAB; PADA, Manuscript Society. VAT No: GB 341 0770 87.

CHIPPENHAM

Vernon Askew Books, Preston East Farm Nr. Lyneham, Chippenham, SN15 4DX. Prop: Vernon Askew. Tel: (01249) 892177 and 890846. Fax: (01249) 892177. E-mail: vernonaskewbooks@tiscali.co.uk. Est: 1997. Storeroom. Appointment necessary. Very large stock. Spec: Alpinism/Mountaineering; Aviation; Bibliography; Biography; Bull Fighting; Byzantium; Churchilliana; Countries - Cyprus. PR: £3–75. Corresp: Swedish. Notes: *Contactable all week but by appointment.*

Ben Bass, Greyne House Marshfield, Chippenham, SN14 8LU. Tel: (01225) 891279. E-mail: benbassbooks@hotmail.com. Est: 1689. Storeroom. Internet and Postal. Telephone First. Open: **M:** 08:00–20:00; **T:** 08:00–20:00; **W:** 08:00–20:00; **Th:** 08:00–20:00; **F:** 08:00–20:00. Large stock. Spec: Author - Bates, H.E.; - Chesterton, G.K.; - Cunningham-Grahame, R.B.; - Durrell, Gerald; - Machen, Arthur; - Morris, William; - Simenon, Georges; - Tangye, D. PR: £2–20. CC: PayPal. Corresp: French, German, Italian, Spanish. Notes: *Street car parking is still reasonably easy.*

Granny's Attic, ■ The Old Citadel, Attic Rooms Bath Road, Chippenham, SN15 2AA. Tel: 01249 715327. Est: 2005. Shop open: **M:** 09:45–16:00; **T:** 09:45–16:00; **W:** 09:45–16:00; **Th:** 09:45–16:00; **F:** 09:45–16:00; **S:** 09:45–16:00. Notes: *General stock.*

Tony Pollastrone Railway Books, 4, Wells Close, Chippenham, SN14 0QD. Prop: Tony Pollastrone. Tel: 01249 444298. Web: www.tp-railbooks.co.uk. E-mail: sales@tp-railbooks.co.uk. Est: 2000. Private premises. Internet and Postal. Appointment necessary. Open: **M:** 09:00–17:30; **T:** 09:00–17:30; **W:** 09:00–17:30; **Th:** 09:00–17:30; **F:** 09:00–17:30; **S:** 09:00–17:30; **Su:** 09:00–17:30; Closed for lunch: 13:00–14:00. Spec: Canals/Inland Waterways; History - Industrial; Public Transport; Railroads. CC: MC; V; Switch; Maestro. Cata: Railways, Canals, and General Interest. VAT No: GB 840 9362 23.

COLERNE

Chris Phillips, 28 Roundbarrow Close, Colerne, Chippenham, SN14 8EF. Prop: Chris Phillips. Tel: (01225) 742755. Fax: 0870 8312098. E-mail: batholdbooks@yahoo.co.uk. Est: 1997. Private premises. Book fairs only. Small stock. Spec: Antiquarian; Antiques; Archaeology - Industrial; Architecture; Art; Children's - Illustrated; Illustrated - General; Literature. PR: £1–500. CC: JCB; MC; V; most Major Cards. Corresp: French. Mem: PBFA. Notes: *Booksearch, Valuations for Insurance or Probate.*

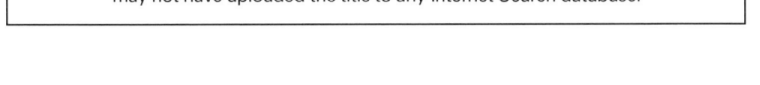

CORSHAM

Ashwell Books, Lower Leaze House Bath Road, Box, Corsham, SN13 8DU. Prop: J. De Normann. Tel: (01225) 742786. Est: 1960. Postal Only. Spec: Botany; Gardening - General. PR: £5–100. Corresp: French, Italian, Spanish.

DEVIZES

D'Arcy Books, ■ The Chequers High Street, Devizes, SN10 1AT. Prop: Colin & Jenifer MacGregor. Tel: Shop (01380) 726922. E-mail: darcybooks@btclick.com. Est: 1974. Shop open: **M:** 10:00–17:30; **T:** 10:00–17:30; **W:** 10:00–17:30; **Th:** 10:00–17:30; **F:** 10:00–17:30; **S:** 10:00–17:30. Large stock. Spec: Archaeology; Architecture; Arts, The; Aviation; Children's; Cookery/Gastronomy; Fiction - General; Gardening - General. VAT No: GB 196 1414 55. Notes: *Also, a booksearch, bookbinding & repair service.*

MALMESBURY

Earth Science Books, Old Swan House Swan Barton, Sherston, Malmesbury, SN16 0LJ. Prop: Geoff Carss. Tel: (01666) 840995. Web: www.earthsciencebooks.com. E-mail: geoff@ earthsciencebooks.com. Est: 2002. Private premises. Internet and Postal. Contactable. Very small stock. Spec: Academic/Scholarly; Animals and Birds; Antiquarian; Archaeology; Coastal Defence; Conchology (see also Malacology); Conservation; Evolution. PR: £3–10,000.

MARLBOROUGH

Anthony Spranger, 67 London Road, Marlborough, SN8 2AJ. Prop: Anthony Spranger. Tel: 01672 516338. E-mail: sprangerbooks@hotmail.com. Private premises. Appointment necessary. Spec: Alpinism/Mountaineering; Army, The; Art - British; Art Reference; Autobiography; Biography; General Stock; History - British. CC: AE; JCB; MC; V; Switch. Corresp: French. Mem: PBFA. VAT No: GB 639 6193 04.

John Bevan Catholic Bookseller, Romans Halt Mildenhall, Marlborough, SN8 2LX. Tel: (01672) 519817. Web: www.catholic-books.co.uk. E-mail: johnbevan@catholicbooks.co.uk. Est: 1978. Storeroom. Internet and Postal. Appointment necessary. Medium stock. Spec: Religion - Christian. PR: £1–500. CC: AE; MC; V. Corresp: French, German. Mem: PBFA.

Katharine House Gallery, ■ Katharine House The Parade, Marlborough, SN8 1NE. Prop: Christopher Gange. Tel: (01672) 514040. Web: www.katharinehousegallery.co.uk. E-mail: chrisgange@fsmail.net. Est: 1983. Shop open: **T:** 10:00–17:30; **W:** 10:00–17:30; **Th:** 10:00–17:30; **F:** 10:00–17:30; **S:** 10:00–17:30. Medium stock. Spec: Antiques; Art; Illustrated - General; Modern First Editions. PR: £3–300. CC: MC; V. Notes: *Also, 20thC British art and antiques.*

Military Parade Bookshop, The Parade, Marlborough, SN8 1NE. Prop: Graham & Peter Kent. Tel: (01672) 515470. Fax: (01980) 630150. Web: www.militaryparadebooks.com. E-mail: enquiry@ militaryparadebooks.com. Est: 1988. Spec: Aviation; Maritime/Nautical; Military History. PR: £2–150.

Nevis Railway Bookshops, ■ Katharine House Gallery The Parade, Marlborough, SN8 1NE. Prop: N.J. Bridger. Tel: Shop (01672) 514040. Web: www.nevis-railway-bookshops.co.uk. Est: 1988. Shop open: **T:** 10:00–17:30; **W:** 10:00–17:30; **Th:** 10:00–17:30; **F:** 10:00–17:30; **S:** 10:00–17:30. Closed for lunch: 13:00–14:15. Medium stock. Spec: Archaeology; Canals/Inland Waterways; Railways. PR: £1–75. Notes: *Alt. tel no: 01635 200507. Stock includes 50,000 photos. Railway Book and Magazine Search, Newbury, Berks (q.v.) Nevis Railway Bookshop, Goring-on-Thames, Oxon (q.v.) Mainly industrial archeology.*

RAMSBURY

Heraldry Today, ■ Parliament Piece, Ramsbury, Nr. Marlborough, SN8 2QH. Prop: Rosemary Pinches. Tel: (01672) 520617. Fax: (01672) 520183. Web: www.heraldrytoday.co.uk. E-mail: heraldry@ heraldrytoday.co.uk. Est: 1954. Shop open: **M:** 10.00–16:00; **T:** 10.00–16:00; **W:** 10.00–16:00; **Th:** 10.00–16:00; **F:** 10.00–16:00. Large stock. Spec: Biography; Ex-Libris; Genealogy; Heraldry; History - General; Royalty - General; School Registers/Rolls of Honour; Booksearch. PR: £1–5,000. CC: E; MC; V; Maestro. Cata: heraldry, genealogy and peerage. Corresp: French. Mem: ABA; ILAB. VAT No: GB 238 8244 41. Notes: *Also, back-numbers of journals, new books, periodicals & a booksearch service.*

SALISBURY

Badger, Boxwood Broadchalke, Salisbury, SP5 5EP. Prop: Peter Bletsoe. Tel: (01722) 326033. Est: 1987. Prem: Market stand/stall. Open: **M:** 10:00–17:00; **T:** 10:00–17:00; **W:** 10:00–17:00; **Th:** 10:00–17:00; **F:** 10:00–17:00; **S:** 10:00–17:00. Small stock. Spec: Prints and Maps. PR: £5–200. CC: AE; D; E; JCB; MC; V.

Ellwood Books, ■ 38 Winchester Street, Salisbury, SP1 1HG. Prop: Mark Harrison and Helen Ford. Tel: (01722) 322975. Web: www.ellwoodbooks.com. E-mail: info@ellwoodbooks.com. Est: 2001. Shop open: **M:** 10:00–17:00; **T:** 10:00–17:00; **W:** 10:00–17:00; **Th:** 10:00–17:00; **F:** 10:00–17:00; **S:** 10:00–17:00; **Su:** 10:00–16:00; Medium stock. Spec: Alternative Medicine; Antiquarian; Archaeology; Art - British; Celtica; Fiction - General; Fine & Rare; Folio Society, The. PR: £1–50. CC: AE; D; E; JCB; MC; V; Switch; Solo. Mem: PBFA. VAT No: GB 832 0693 40. Notes: *Also attends London HD bookfairs, some PBFA fairs & Internet trading.*

John & Judith Head, ■ The Barn Book Supply 88 Crane Street, Salisbury, SP1 2QD. Prop: John and Judith Head. Tel: (01722) 327767. Fax: (01722) 339888. Web: www.johnandjudithhead.co.uk. E-mail: info@johnandjudithhead.co.uk. Est: 1958. Shop. Appointment necessary. Open: **M:** 10.00–17.00; **T:** 10.00–17.00; **W:** 10.00–17.00; **Th:** 10.00–17.00; **F:** 10.00–17.00. Closed for lunch: 13.00–14.00. Medium stock. Spec: Author - Edwards, Lionel; Dogs; Fisheries; Fishes; Sport - Angling/Fishing; Sport - Archery; Sport - Big Game Hunting; Sport - Coursing. PR: £1–18,000. CC: AE; D; E; JCB; MC; V; Maestro, So. Cata: angling and field sports. Mem: ABA; ILAB. VAT No: GB 188 9664 84. Notes. *Open on Saturday by appointment.*

Rosemary Pugh Books, 59b Old Sarum Airfield, Salisbury, SP4 6DZ. Prop: Mrs. R M Pugh, Mr J M Pugh, Mr A.E. Pugh. Tel: 01722 330132. Fax: 01722 330132. Web: www.rosemarypughbooks.co.uk. E-mail: rosemarypugh@btopenworld.com. Est: 1990. Storeroom. Internet and Postal. Telephone First. Open: **M:** 08:00–16:00; **T:** 08:00–16:00; **W:** 08:00–16:00; **Th:** 08:00–16:00. Spec: Bibles; Ecclesiastical History & Architecture; Ecology; Feminism; Gnostics / Gnosticism; Holocaust; Hymnology; Iconography. CC: JCB; MC; V; Delta, Maestro, Solo, Fortoak. Cata: Areas within Theology. Mem: FSB. VAT No: GB 699 1250 01.

Water Lane Bookshop, ■ 24 Water Lane, Salisbury, SP2 7TE. Prop: Peter Shouler. Tel: 01722 337929. Web: www.dorsetrarebooks.co.uk. E-mail: peter@dorsetrarebooks.co.uk. Est: 2000. Shop open: **M:** 10:00–17:00; **T:** 10:00–17:00; **W:** 10:00–17:00; **Th:** 10:00–17:00; **F:** 10:00–17:00; **S:** 10:00–17:00. Spec: Antiquarian; Antiques; Art; Art - Technique; Art - Theory; Art History; Art Reference; Artists. CC: MC; V. Mem: PBFA. VAT No: GB 723 3951 38.

SWINDON

Peter Barnes, 138 Ermin Street Stratton St Margaret, Swindon, SN3 4NQ. Prop: Peter Barnes. Tel: (01793) 821327. Est: 2001. Private premises. Postal Only. Small stock. Spec: Aviation; History - General; Magazines & Periodicals - General; Military; Military History; Naval; Topography - General; Topography - Local. PR: £1–50. Notes: *Exhibits at book fairs.*

Bookmark (Children's Books), Fortnight, Wick Down Broad Hinton, Swindon, SN4 9NR. Prop: Anne & Leonora Excell. Tel: (01793) 731693. Fax: (01793) 731782. E-mail: leonora-excell@btconnect.com. Est: 1973. Private premises. Postal Only. Appointment necessary. Open: **M:** 09:00–18:00; **T:** 09:00–18:00; **W:** 09:00–18:00; **Th:** 09:00–18:00; **F:** 09:00–18:00; **S:** 10:00–18:00. Medium stock. Spec: Annuals; Antiquarian; Author - Aesop; - Ahlberg, Janet & Allan; - Aldin, Cecil; - Ardizzone, Edward; - Ballantyne, Robert M.; - Barker, Cecily M PR: £5–2,000 CC: F; JCB; MC; V; Maestro; Delta. Cata: Childrens Books and related juvenilia. Mem: PBFA. Notes: *Main PBFA bookfairs. Also, a specialist booksearch service leonora-excell@btconnect.com.*

Collectors Corner, ■ 227 Kingshill, Swindon, SN1 4NG. Prop: Fred Stevens. Tel: (01793) 521545. Est: 1986. Shop. Postal Only open: **M:** 10:30–16:45; **T:** 10:30–16:45; **Th:** 10:30–16:45; **F:** 10:30–16:45; **S:** 10:30–16:45. Closed for lunch: 12:00–12:30. Very small stock. Spec: Collecting; Military; Railways; Topography - Local; Transport; Collectables; Ephemera; Prints and Maps. PR: £1–100. Notes: *Stock includes: postcards, cigarette cards, coins, medals, badges, toys, and ephemera.*

Ice House Books, Hard Crag Foxhill, Swindon, SN4 0DR. Prop: Mr Simon Miles. Tel: 01793 791975. Web: www.icehousebooks.co.uk. E-mail: shop@icehousebooks.co.uk. Est: 2000. Warehouse. Internet and Postal. Appointment necessary. Shop At: Unit A Pigeon House Lane, Stratton St. Margaret, Swindon, SN3 4QH. Open: **M:** 09:00–18:00; **T:** 09:00–18:00; **W:** 09:00–18:00; **Th:** 09:00–18:00; **F:** 09:00–18:00; **S:** 09:00–18:00; **Su:** 09:00–18:00; Closed for lunch: 13:00–14:00. Spec: Academic/ Scholarly; Arts, The; Evolution; History - General; Natural History; Philology; Politics; Science - General. CC: MC; V; SW. Cata: website updates. Notes: *Spec. Acadameic and professional non-fiction; sciences; arts; social sciences; equestrian; classics; politics; humanities. Relocated under new ownership from Leicester.*

WILTSHIRE

WARMINSTER

Sturford Books, Landfall, 35 Corton, Warminster, BA12 0SY. Prop: Robert Mayall. Tel: (01985) 850478/ 85058. E-mail: maria@booksfortravel.org.uk. Est: 1993. Private premises. Postal Only. Appointment necessary. Small stock. Spec: Archaeology - Industrial; Art; Autobiography; Biography; Fiction - General; Fiction - Historical; Foreign Texts; History - General. PR: £5–800. CC: JCB; MC; V. Cata: History, Literature and Travel.

WEST KINGTON

Peter Barnitt, Latimer's Yard, West Kington, Chippenham, SN14 7JJ. Tel: (01249) 782099. E-mail: barnitt.latlo@virgin.net. Private premises. Appointment necessary. Very small stock. Spec: Fine Printing; Private Press. PR: £20–3,000.

WESTBURY

Aardvark Books, 50 Bratton Road, Westbury, BA13 3EP. Prop: Clive & Caroline Williams. Tel: (01225) 867723. Fax: (01225) 867723. Web: www.aardvarkmilitarybooks.com. E-mail: aardvarkbooks@ blueyonder.co.uk. Est: 1998. Private premises. Internet and Postal. Telephone First. Open: **M:** 09:00– 19:00; **T:** 09:00–19:00; **W:** 09:00–19:00; **Th:** 09:00–19:00; **F:** 09:00–19:00; **S:** 09:00–19:00; **Su:** 09:00– 19:00. Large stock. Spec: Aircraft; Armed Forces - Australian Air Force; Armed Forces - Australian Army; Armed Forces - Australian Navy; Arms & Armour; Army, The; Company History; Heraldry. PR: £5–250. CC: MC; V; Switch. Notes: *We are a family run, military history dealership. We have a wide range of stock but specialise in WWI and WWII.*

Zardoz Books, 20 Whitecroft Dilton Marsh, Westbury, BA13 4DJ. Prop: M Flanagan. Tel: (01373) 865371. Web: www.zardozbooks.co.uk. E-mail: zardoz@blueyonder.co.uk. Est: 1990. Warehouse. Internet and Postal. Appointment necessary. Very large stock. Spec: Author - Lovecraft, H.P.; - Rohmer, Sax; - Wallace, Edgar; Beat Writers; Books about Books; Cinema/Film; Crime (True); Erotica. PR: £2–100. CC: MC; V. Notes: *50000 plus paperback and hardcover mainly fiction plus collectors books and magazines. Areas SF, Horror, Crime, Western, Adventure etc.*

WOOTTON BASSETT

G. Jackson, 10 Dryden Place, Wootton Bassett, SN4 8JP. Prop: Geoffrey Jackson. Tel: (01793) 849660. Fax: (01793) 849660. E-mail: geoff.jackson.bookseller@ntlworld.com. Est: 2001. Private premises. Appointment necessary. Open: **M:** 09:30–17:30; **T:** 09:30–17:30; **W:** 09:30–17:30; **Th:** 09:30–17:30; **F:** 09:30–17:30. Small stock. Spec: Antiquarian; Antiques; Art Reference; Author - Graves, Robert; Bibliography; Children's; Children's - Illustrated; Countries - India. PR: £25–9,000. CC: MC; V; PayPal.

ZEALS

Hurly Burly Books, ■ 47 Zeals Rise, Zeals, BA12 6PL. Prop: Moira Lord. Tel: (01747) 840691. E-mail: hurlyburly@fsmail.net. Est: 1995. Shop At: Within, Words Etcetera Bookshop, 2 Cornhill, Dorchester, Dorset. Open: **M:** 10.00–17.00; **T:** 10.00–17.00; **W:** 10.00–17.00; **Th:** 10.00–17.00; **F:** 10.00–17.00; **S:** 10.00–17.00. Small stock. Spec: Children's; Children's - Illustrated; Illustrated - General. CC: JCB; MC; V. Notes: *We rent space on the ground floor within 'Words Etcetera Bookshop'.*

WORCESTERSHIRE

BESFORD

Louise Ross Books, 28 Besford Court, Besford, Nr. Worcester, WR8 9LZ. Tel: (01368) 550461. E-mail: louise.ross@btclick.com. Est: 1977. Private premises. Postal Only. Contactable. Very small stock. Spec: Children's; Illustrated - General; Literature. PR: £25–5,000.

BEWDLEY

Clent Books of Bewdley, Rose Cottage Habberley Road, Bewdley, DY12 1JA. Prop: Ivor Simpson. Tel: (01299) 401090. Web: www.clentbooks.co.uk. E-mail: clent.books@btinternet.com. Est: 1977. Private premises. Internet and Postal. Medium stock. Spec: Antiquarian; Author - Read, Miss; - Young, Francis Brett; Autobiography; Biography; Fiction - General; General; History - General. PR: £20–200.

DROITWICH

Grant Books, The Coach House New Road, Cutnall Green, Droitwich, WR9 0PQ. Prop: Bob & Shirley Grant. Tel: (01299) 851588. Fax: (01299) 851446 Web: www.grantbooks-memorabilia.com. E-mail: golt@grantbooks.co.uk. Est: 1972. Office and/or bookroom open: **M:** 09:00–17:00; **T:** 09:00–17:00; **W:** 09:00–17:00; **Th:** 09:00–17:00; **F:** 09:00–17:00. Small stock. Spec: Antiquarian; Sport - Golf. PR: £10–2,500. CC: AE; D; MC; V; US dollars. Cata: Golf and related books and ephemera. Mem: PBFA; BGCS; GCS(USA). VAT No: GB 275 8638 10. Notes: *Open at other times by appointment.*

DROITWICH SPA

M. & D. Books, ■ 16 High Street, Droitwich Spa, WR9 8EW. Prop: Mike Hebden. Tel: (01905) 775814. E-mail: michael@hebdendroitwich.wanadoo.co.uk. Est: 1996. Internet and Postal. Shop open: **T:** 10:00–17:00; **W:** 10:00–17:00; **Th:** 10:00–17:00; **F:** 10:00–17:00; **S:** 09:30–17:00. Medium stock. Spec: Topography - Local. PR: £1–250. CC: AE; JCB; MC; V; Maestro, Solo.

GREAT MALVERN

The Malvern Bookshop, ■ 7 Abbey Road, Great Malvern, WR14 3ES. Prop: Howard and Julie Hudson. Tel: (01684) 575915. Fax: (01684) 575915. E-mail: browse@malvernbookshop.co.uk Est: 1955. Shop open: **M:** 10:00–17:00; **T:** 10:00 17:00; **W.** 10.00–17:00; **F:** 10:00–17:00; **S:** 10:00–17:00. Large stock. Spec: Antiques; Architecture; Art; Aviation; Bindings; Biography; Books about Books; Children's. PR: £1–1,000. Notes: *Also, a booksearch service.*

Wildside Books, Rectory House 26 Priory Road, Great Malvern, WR14 3DR. Prop: Chris & Christine Johnson. Tel: (01684) 562818. Fax: (01684) 566491. Web: www.wildsidebooks.co.uk. E-mail: enquire@wildsidebooks.co.uk. Est: 1982. Private premises. Internet and Postal. Appointment necessary. Small stock. Spec: Art; Natural History; New Naturalist; Ornithology; Zoology. PR: £20–20,000. CC: MC; V; SW, Mae. Cata: Ornithology; Natural History; Naturalists' Travel. Notes: *We are biased towards ornithology where we aim to source the best available copies for the collector. We sell many books to clients via their 'wants' list, and recommend you lodge your list with us. The New Naturalists is another speciality.*

Wildside Books, Rectory House 26 Priory Road, Great Malvern, WR14 3DR. Prop: Chris & Christine Johnson. Tel: (01684) 562 818. Fax: (01684) 566 491. Web: www.wildsidebooks.co.uk. E-mail: enquire@wildsidebooks.co.uk. Est: 1982. Private premises. Internet and Postal. Appointment necessary. Small stock. Spec: Animals and Birds; Ecology; Fine & Rare; Natural History; Natural Sciences; New Naturalist; Ornithology; Rural Life. PR: £15–10,000. CC: E; MC; V; Maestro. Cata: Ornithology; Natural History; Naturalists' Travel. VAT No: GB 162 5737 56. Notes: *Gallery: original works of art in ornithology from the 18th-21st Centuries.*

KIDDERMINSTER

M. & M. Baldwin, ■ 24 High St, Cleobury Mortimer, Kidderminster, DY14 8BY. Prop: Mark & Myfanwy Baldwin. Tel: (01299) 270110. Web: www.www.enigmatixuk.com. E-mail: mb@ mbaldwin.free-online.co.uk. Est: 1978. Shop open: **W:** 14:00–18:00; **S:** 10:00–18:00. Closed for lunch: 13:00–14:00. Medium stock. Spec: Author - Rolt, L.T.C.; Aviation; Canals/Inland Waterways; Crafts; Cryptography; Espionage; History - Industrial; Maritime/Nautical. PR: £1–500. CC: MC; V. Corresp: French. Mem: Fed. of Small Businesses. VAT No: GB 547 6638 05. Notes: *Also, publisher of books, and lecturer on WW2 Codebreaking.*

WORCESTERSHIRE

Lion Books, ■ 52, Blackwell St, Kidderminster, DY10 2EE. Prop: Colin Raxter. Tel: (0156) 745060. Web: www.lionbooks.co.uk. E-mail: info@lionbooks.co.uk. Est: 1987. Shop open: **T:** 10:30–17:00; **Th:** 10:30–17:00; **F:** 10:30–17:00; **S:** 10:30–14:00. Closed for lunch: 13:00–14:00. Medium stock. Spec: Sport - Angling/Fishing; Sport - Cricket; Sport - Football (Soccer); Sport - Motor Racing; Sport - Rugby. PR: £1–1,000. CC: E; JCB; MC; V; PayPal. Mem: PBFA. Notes: *Telephone commitments and not all stock available in shop.*

Salsus Books, Elderfield Gardens 42 Coventry Street, Kidderminster, DY10 2BT. Prop: Dr. D.T. Salt. Tel: (01562) 742081. Fax: (01562) 824583. E-mail: salsus@books93.freeserve.co.uk. Est: 1991. Private premises. Internet and Postal. Appointment necessary. Medium stock. Spec: Academic/Scholarly; Advertising; Aeronautics; Ecclesiastical History & Architecture; Religion - General; Religion - Christian; Religion - Muslim; Theology. PR: £1–250. CC: JCB; MC; V; SW. Mem: PBFA.

MALVERN

Jonathan Gibbs Books, The Lakes Cottages Drake Street, Welland, Malvern, WR13 6LN. Prop: Jonathan and Angela Gibbs. Tel: (01684) 593169. Web: www.jgibbsbooks.co.uk. E-mail: info@jgibbsbooks.co.uk. Est: 2001. Private premises. Internet and Postal. Appointment necessary. Small stock. Spec: Academic/Scholarly; Antiquarian; Literature; Music - General; Music - Classical; Music - Illustrated Sheet Music; Music - Printed, Sheet Music & Scores; Performing Arts. PR: £10– 1,000. CC: AE; MC; V. Cata: music. Mem: PBFA.

Golden Age Books, PO Box 45, Malvern, WR14 1XT. Prop: Tony Byatt, Adrian and Gillian Ainge. Tel: (01684) 578419. Web: www.ukbookworld.com/members/goldenage. E-mail: enquiries@ goldenagebooks.co.uk. Est: 1981. Private premises. Internet and Postal. Appointment necessary. Small stock. Spec: Academic/Scholarly; Archaeology; Bibles; Biblical Studies; History - Ancient; Judaica; Religion - General; Religion - Christian. PR: £1–500. CC: E; JCB; MC; V; Maestro, Switch. Cata: English Bibles, translations and texts, & related. Notes: *We also sell new Bibles and books on the Bible, and Bible study aids including study of Hebrew and Greek. 3 printed catalogues a year, plus online/ email catalogues available on request.*

PERSHORE

Coach House Books, ■ 17a Bridge Street, Pershore, WR10 1AJ. Prop: Michael & Sue Ellingworth. Tel: (01386) 554633. Fax: (01386) 554633. E-mail: sue.chb@virgin.net. Est: 1982. Shop. Telephone First. Open: **W:** 09:00–05:00. Medium stock. Spec: Architecture; Art Reference; Author - Lawrence, T.E.; Folio Society, The; Horticulture; Limited Editions - General; Military; Ornithology. PR: £5–2,000. CC: AE; D; MC; V. Corresp: French. Mem: BA. VAT No: GB 396 2460 27.

Ian K. Pugh Books, ■ 40 Bridge Street, Pershore, WR10 1AT. Tel: (01386) 552681. Mob: 07968 429112. E-mail: iankpugh.books@virgin.net. Est: 1974. Shop. Open: **M:** 10:30–15:30; **T:** 10:30–15:30; **W:** 10:30–15:30; **Th:** 10:30–15:30; **F:** 10:30–15:30; **S:** 09:30–17:00. Medium stock. Spec: Fine Art; Horticulture; Illustrated - General; Collectables. PR: £1–7,000. Notes: *My opening times are dictated to a large extent by school picking up times so in the school holidays I try to open longer till 5pm if possible. Ringing first before a special trip is advisable.*

Sedgeberrow Books, ■ Retail Market Cherry Orchard, Pershore, WR10 1EY. Prop: Mrs. Jayne Winter. Tel: (01386) 751830. Web: www.sedgeberrowbooks.co.uk. E-mail: sales@sedgeberrowbooks.co.uk. Est: 1985. Shop open: **W:** 09:00–17:00; **Th:** 09:00–17:00; **F:** 09:00–17:00; **S:** 09:00–17:00. Large stock. Spec: Author - Moore, John; - Young, Francis Brett; Aviation; History - Local; Military; Mind, Body & Spirit; Railways; Topography - General. PR: £1–300. CC: MC; V; Switch.

STOURPORT-ON-SEVERN

P. and P. Books, Dairy Cottage Yarhampton, Stourport, Stourport-on-Severn, DY13 0UY. Prop: J.S. Pizey. Tel: (01299) 896996. Fax: (01299) 896996. E-mail: pandpbooks_jim@compuserve.com. Est: 1982. Private premises. Telephone First. Very small stock. Spec: Archaeology; Countries - Arabia; Countries - Arabian Peninsula; Countries - Egypt; Countries - Holy Land, The; Countries - Middle East, The; Countries - Sudan, The; Egyptology. PR: £5–2,000. Cata: Egyptology and archaeology of the Middle East. Corresp: French. Mem: ABA. VAT No: GB 441 7426 59. Notes: *Early (19-18th C.) travel in Egypt and the Middle East.*

WORCESTER

Ann & Mike Conry, 14 St George's Square, Worcester, WR1 1HX. Tel: 01905 25330. Web: www.abe.com. E-mail: irishallsorts@aol.com. Est: 1998. Private premises. Internet and Postal. Spec: History - Irish; Irish Interest; Literary Criticism; Literary Travel; Literature; Literature - Irish; Modern First Editions; Politics. Notes: *For sale through Abe but direct contact available. Specialists in football, irish interest and modern firsts.*

Bookworms of Evesham, ■ 81 Port Street Evesham, Worcester, WR11 3LF. Prop: T.J. Sims. Tel: (01386) 45509. E-mail: terry_bookworms@hotmail.co.uk. Est: 1971. Shop open: **T:** 10:00–17:00; **W:** 10:00– 17:00; **Th:** 10:00–17:00; **F:** 10:00–17:00; **S:** 10:00–17:00. Medium stock. Spec: Art; History - General; Literature; Military; Topography - Local; Transport; Travel - General. Mem: PBFA. Notes: *Fairs attended: Cheltenham, Bath, Cirencester; and Churchdown Book Fair (organiser).*

Davies Fine Books, 21 Droitwich Road, Worcester, WR3 7LG. Prop: Richard Davies. Tel: (01905) 23919. E-mail: daviesfinebooks@yahoo.co.uk. Est: 2002. Private premises. Internet and Postal. Contactable. Small stock. Spec: Antiquarian; Gardening - General; Illustrated - General; Natural History; Travel - General. CC: AE; JCB; MC; V. Mem: PBFA. VAT No: GB 823 3339 44.

Restormel Books, 1 East Corner St. John's, Worcester, WR2 6BF. Prop. Roy Slade. Tel: (01905) 422290. Est: 1978. Display/stand. Open: **M:** 10:00–17:00; **T:** 10:00–17:00; **W:** 10:00–17:00; **Th:** 10:00–17:00; **F:** 10:00–17:00; **S:** 10:00–17:00. Small stock. Spec: Collecting; Topography - Local; Collectables. PR: £1– 50. Corresp. French, Spanish.

Worcester Rare Books, c/o 22 Oakland Close Upton Upon Severn, Worcester, WR8 0ES. Prop: D.I. Lloyd. Tel: (01905) 28780. E-mail: rarebooks@worcester74.freeserve.co.uk. Est: 1972. Private premises. Internet and Postal. Appointment necessary. Very small stock. Spec: Academic/Scholarly; Antiquarian; Architecture; Medicine; Philosophy; Religion - General; Science - General; Science - History of. PR: £10–200. CC: MC; V. Corresp: French, German. Mem: PBFA.

CHANNEL ISLANDS

GUERNSEY

VALE

Galleries Limited, ■ Les Clospains Rue de L'Ecole, Vale, Guernsey, GY3 5LL. Prop: Geoffrey P. & Christine M. Gavey. Tel: Shop (01481) 247337. Fax: (01481) 243538. E-mail: geoff.gavey@ cigalleries.f9.co.uk. Est: 1967. Postal Only. Shop open: **M:** 10:00–17:00; **T:** 10:00–17:00; **W:** 10:00– 17:00; **Th:** 10:00–13:00; **F:** 10:00–17:00; **S:** 10:00–13:00. Small stock. Spec: Antiquarian; Atlases; History - General; Natural History; Topography - General; Topography - Local; Prints and Maps. PR: £5–4,000. CC: E; MC; V. Corresp: French, German. Notes: *Also, antique maps, prints, watercolours and paintings - featuring The Channel Islands, coins & CI bank notes.*

JERSEY

ST. HELIER

Books and Things Limited, ■ First Tower, St. Helier, Jersey, JE2 3LN. Prop: Sarah Burrow. Tel: 01534 759949. Fax: n/a. Web: www.newnats.com. E-mail: bob@newnats.com. Est: 1998. Shop open: **M:** 10.00–16.00; **T:** 10.00–16.00; **W:** 10.00–16.00; **Th:** 10.00–16.00; **F:** 10.00–16.00; **S:** 10.00–16.00; **Su:** 10:00–16.00; Medium stock. Spec: Countries - Channel Islands, The; Natural History; New Naturalist. PR: £1–5,000. Corresp: English.

ISLE OF MAN

DOUGLAS

Garretts Antiquarian Books, 4 Summerhill, Douglas, IM2 4PJ. Prop: Mr. Jonathon Hall. Tel: (01624) 675065. Web: www.isleofmanbooks.com. E-mail: garrettsbooks_iom@yahoo.co.uk. Est: 1987. Private premises. Internet and Postal. Telephone First. Small stock. Spec: Countries - Isle of Man; History - Local; Topography - Local. PR: £1–1,000. Mem: PBFA.

PORT ERIN

Bridge Bookshop Ltd, Shore Road, Port Erin, IM9 6HL. Tel: 01624 833376. Fax: 01624 835381. E-mail: bbs@manx.net.

NORTHERN IRELAND

CO. ANTRIM

BELFAST

P. & B. Rowan, Carleton House 92 Malone Road, Belfast, BT9 5HP. Prop: Peter & Briad Rowan. Tel: (028) 9066-6448. Fax: (028) 9066-3725. E-mail: peter@pbrowan.thegap.com. Est: 1973. Private premises. Appointment necessary. Large stock. Spec: Academic/Scholarly; Antiquarian; Archives; Countries - Ireland; Economics; Fine & Rare; History - General; History - Irish. PR: £25–25. CC: MC; V. Cata: Irish History, Literature, & Antiquarian. Corresp: French. Mem: PBFA; IADA.

The Bell Gallery, 13 Adelaide Park, Belfast, BT9 6FX. Prop: James Nelson Bell. Tel: 02890 662998. Fax: 02890 381524. Web: www.bellgallery.com. E-mail: bellgallery@btinternet.com. Est: 1965. Shop and/ or gallery. Spec: Countries - Ireland; Irish Interest. PR: £10–100. Notes: *Also, Irish paintings & sculpture.*

LISBURN

JIRI Books, 11 Mill Road, Lisburn, BT27 5TT. Prop: Jim & Rita Swindall. Tel: (028) 9082-6443. Fax: (028) 9082-6443. Web: www.abebooks.com/home/WJS/. E-mail: jiri.books@dnet.co.uk. Est: 1978. Private premises. Postal Only. Appointment necessary. Medium stock. Spec: Antiquarian; Author - Heaney, Seamus; Countries - Ireland; Irish Interest; Literature; Poetry; Topography - Local; Travel - General. CC: MC; V. Notes: *Organise Annual Belfast Book Fair. Next fair the 25th is on 10th November 2007.*

CO. ARMAGH

ARMAGH

Craobh Rua Books, 12 Woodford Gardens, Armagh, BT60 2AZ. Prop: James Vallely. Tel: (028) 3752- 6938. E-mail: craobh@btinternet.com. Est: 1990. Private premises. Internet and Postal. Appointment necessary. Medium stock. Spec: Antiquarian; Author - James, Henry; - Machen, Arthur; - Yeats, W.B.; Bull Fighting; Churchilliana; Countries - Antarctic, The; Countries - Arctic, The. PR: £1–400. CC: MC; V. Cata: Irish Related. Corresp: French. Notes: *Also, a booksearch service.*

CO. DERRY

LONDERRY

George Harris, 163 Legavallon Road Dungiven, Londerry, BT47 4QN. Prop: George Harris. Tel: (02877) 740012. Est: 1976. Private premises. Appointment necessary. Medium stock. Spec: Aeronautics; Arms & Armour; Aviation; Irish Interest; Military; Military History; Naval; War - General. PR: £5–500. Corresp: French. Mem: PBFA. Notes: *Attends PBFA fairs.*

Foyle Books, ■ 12 Magazine Street, Londonderry, BT48 6HH. Prop: Ken Thatcher & Art Byrne. Tel: (028) 7137-2530. E-mail: foylebookshopni@btconnect.com. Est: 1984. Shop open: **M:** 11:00–17:00; **T:** 11:00–17:00; **W:** 11:00–17:00; **Th:** 11:00–17:00; **F:** 11:00–17:00; **S:** 10:00–17:00. Very large stock. Spec: Academic/Scholarly; Countries - Ireland; Foreign Texts; History - Local; History - National; Irish Interest; Literature - French; Religion - Christian. PR: £1–200. Corresp: French. Gaelic. Notes: *Stock includes titles on Derry and Donegal. Also, a booksearch service.*

CO. DOWN

BALLYGOWAN

Saintfield Antiques & Fine Books, Vestry Hall 49 Vestry Road, Ballygowan, BT23 6HQ. Prop: (*) Joseph Leckey. Tel: (028) 97528428. Fax: (028) 97528428. Web: www.antiquesireland.com. E-mail: home@ antiquesireland.com. Est: 1988. Private premises. Internet and Postal. Appointment necessary. Medium stock. Spec: Academic/Scholarly; Aircraft; Art; Broadcasting; Children's; Cinema/Film; Company History; Exploration. PR: £1–500. Notes: *Our preferred method of payment is by PayPal, although we accept Sterling cheques and money orders. On www.antiquesireland.com, under how to order and pay, there is a Buy Now icon. This is a direct link to PayPal.*

BALLYNAHINCH

Davidson Books, 34 Broomhill Road, Ballynahinch, BT24 8QD. Prop: Arthur Davidson. Tel: (028) 9756-2502. Fax: (028) 9756-2502. Est: 1958. Private premises. Postal Only. Appointment necessary. Medium stock. Spec: History - National; Irish Interest; Literature; Topography - Local; Ephemera; Prints and Maps.

BANGOR

Books Ulster, 12 Bayview Road, Bangor, BT19 6AL. Prop: D.A. Rowlinson. Tel. (028) 914-70310. Web: www.booksulster.com. E-mail: orders@booksulster.com. Est: 1995. Private premises. Postal Only. Large stock. Spec: Irish Interest. PR: £1–500. CC: JCB; MC; V.

DONAGHADEE

Prospect House Books, Prospect House 4 Millisle Road, Donaghadee, BT21 0HY. Web: www. antiquarianbooksellers.co.uk. E-mail: rarebooks.phb@btopenworld.com. Est: 1983. Private premises. Internet and Postal. Appointment necessary. Spec: Africana; Agriculture; Animals and Birds; Archaeology; Architecture; Art; Asian Studies; Banking & Insurance. CC: MC; V. Cata: Irish related, ornithology, medicine, religion. Notes: *Smaller subjects: philosophy, philology, Scotland.*

DOWNPATRICK

Bookline, 35 Farranfad Road, Downpatrick, BT30 8NH. Prop: Lady Faulkner. Tel: (028) 4481-1712. Web: www.abebooks.com/home/bookline. E-mail: BooklineUK@aol.com. Est: 1988. Spec: Animals and Birds; Cats; Children's; Dogs; History - Irish; Illustrated - General; Private Press; Sport - Field Sports. PR: £5–500. Notes: *Also, a booksearch service.*

HOLYWOOD

The Old Abbey Bookshop, ■ Audley Court 118 High Street, Holywood, BT18 9HW. Prop: Harold Mitchell. Tel: BT18 9HW. Est: 1996. Shop open: **T:** 09:00–17:00; **Th:** 09:00–17:00; **S:** 09:00–17:00. Spec: Antiquarian; Children's; Irish Interest; Natural History; Poetry.

REPUBLIC OF IRELAND

CO. CAVAN

COOTEHILL

Sillan Books, Richelieu Drumgreen, Cootehill. Prop: Patricia H. Smyth. Tel: 0044 49 5552343. Fax: 00444 49 5552343. Web: www.abebooks.com. E-mail: greenaway@eircom.net. Est: 1990. Mail Order Only. Postal Only. Telephone First. Spec: Antiquarian; Children's; History - General; Illustrated - General; Irish Interest; Literature - 19th C; Modern First Editions; New Books. CC: MC; V. Cata: Irish/Childrens/Religion/History/Biography/General.

CO. CLARE

DOOLIN

Doolin Dinghy Books, ■ Fisher Street, Doolin. Prop: Cynthia Sinnott Griffin. Tel: (065) 70 74449. E-mail: csgriffindoolindinghy@yahoo.ie. Est: 1982. Shop open: **M:** 10:00–20:00; **T:** 10:00–20:00; **W:** 10:00–20:00; **Th:** 10:00–20:00; **F:** 10:00–20:00; **S:** 10:00–20:00; **Su:** 12:00–15:00. Small stock. Spec: Art; Biography; Children's; Fiction - General; Folklore; History - National; Languages - National; Literature. PR: £1–150. Corresp: French. Mem: ASBI. Notes: *Between November to February, short hours or by appointment. Stock includes Irish, British and American fiction. Alternate tel. No. 065 7075980.*

ENNIS

Orchid Book Distributors, Unit 2 Fitzpatrick Centre Tulla Road, Ennis. Tel: 00 353 65 6842 862. Fax: 00 353 65 6842 862. Web: www.orchidbooks.org. E-mail: info@orchidbooks.org. Est: 2002. Shop and/or showroom. Internet and Postal, open: **T:** 10.00–18.00; **W:** 10.00–18.00; **Th:** 10.00–18.00; **F:** 10.00–18.00; **S:** 10.00–18.00. Closed for lunch: 13:00–14:00. Spec: Acupuncture; American Indians; Anatomy; Art - Theory; Biology - General; Botany; Earth Sciences; Eastern Philosophy. CC: MC; V. Corresp: Dutch, French, German. VAT No: IE 5333275R.

CO. CORK

BALLINLOUGH

Royal Carbery Books Ltd., Lissadell 36 Beechwood Park, Ballinlough. Prop: G. & M. Feehan. Tel: (021) 4294191. Fax: (021) 4294191. Est: 1976. Private premises Appointment necessary. Medium stock. Spec: Folklore; Guide Books; History - General; History - Local; Irish Interest; Literary Travel; Military; Music - Folk & Irish Folk.

Are you making enough profit? If in doubt then read

BOOKDEALING FOR PROFIT by Paul Minet

Quarto H/b £10.00 144pp

BALLYDEHOB

Barbara and Jack O'Connell (t/a Schull Books), The Bookshop Main Street, Ballydehob, . Prop: Barbara & Jack O'Connell. Tel: (+353) [0]28 37317. Fax: (+353) [0]28 37317. Web: www.schullbooks.com. E-mail: schullbooks@eircom.net. Est: 1981. Private premises. Telephone First. Open: **M:** 10:00–19:00; **T:** 10:00–19:00; **W:** 10:00–19:00; **Th:** 10:00–19:00; **F:** 10:00–19:00; **S:** 10:00–19:00. Medium stock. Spec: Countries - Ireland; General Stock; History Irish; Irish Interest; Military History; Booksearch. PR: £10–500. CC: MC; V. Cata: Irish interest, military history. Corresp: French, German, Irish. Notes: *Also summer shop, Ballydehob village, June - Sept, and book fairs throughout Ireland.*

BANTRY

Karen Millward, Coorycommane Coomhola, Bantry, . Prop: Karen Millward. Tel: 00353-27-53898. Web: www.ukbookworld.com/members/irishmaid. E-mail: karenmillward@eircom.net. Est: 2001. Private premises. Internet and Postal. Telephone First. Open: **M:** 09:00–17:30; **T:** 09:00–17:30; **W:** 09:00–17:30; **Th:** 09:00–17:30; **F:** 09:00–17:30; **S:** 09:00–17:30; **Su:** 09:00–17:30; Closed for lunch: 13:00–14:00. Spec: Animals and Birds; Author - Frost, Robert; Author - Joyce, James; - Russell, W; - Thomas, Edward; - Wilde, Oscar; Autobiography; Biography. CC: MC; V; Sterling or Euro Cheques. Mem: The Independent Booksellers' Network Limited. Notes: *Irish Books A Speciality, I also carry a large comprehensive general stock of quality books.*

BANTRY

Michael J Carroll, Sunville House Wolfe Tone Square, Bantry Prop: Michael J Carroll. Tel: +353 (0) 27 50064. Fax: + 353 (0) 27 52042. Web: www.abebooks.com. E-mail: bantrydesigns@iol.ie. Private premises. Internet and Postal. Appointment necessary. Spec: Antiquarian; Biography; Celtica; Countries - Ireland, Ecclesiastical History & Architecture; Folklore; Guide Books; History - Local. Notes: *Specialising in Irish History.*

DUNMANWAY

Darkwood Books, Darkwood, Dunmanway. Prop: Annette Sheehan. Tel: (023) 55470. Fax: (023) 55224. Web: www.darkwoodbooks.com. E-mail: darkwood@indigo.ie. Est: 2000. Private premises. Internet and Postal. Medium stock. Spec: Architecture; Art; Art History; Art Reference; Artists; Arts, The; Author - Somerville & Ross; Author - Walsh, M. PR: £1–500. CC: MC; V. Cata: Irish Interest.

ROSSCARBERY

C.P. Hyland, 4, Closheen Lane, Rosscarbery, Prop: Cal & Joan Hyland. Tel: (023) 48063. Web: www.cphyland.com. E-mail: calbux@iol.ie. Est: 1966. Private premises. Internet and Postal. Telephone First. Open: **M:** 10:00–22.00; **T:** 10:00–22.00; **W:** 10:00–22.00; **Th:** 10:00–22.00; **F:** 10:00–22.00; **S:** 10:00–22.00; **Su:** 12:00–27.00. Large stock. Spec: Celtica; Countries - Ireland; Irish Interest; Languages - National. PR: £1–10,000. Cata: Relating to Ireland. Corresp: Gaelic. VAT No: IE 9/T/ 09940R.

YOUGHAL

Alan Prim, ■ 6 South Main Street, Youghal. Prop: Alan Prim. Tel: 003532492781. E-mail: waprim@ hotmail.com. Est: 1998. Shop open: **M:** 10.00–17.30; **T:** 10.00–17.30; **W:** 10.00–17.30; **Th:** 10:00–17.30; **F:** 10:00–17.30; **S:** 09:00–17.30; Closed for lunch: 13:00–14:00. Spec: CC: AE; MC; V. Corresp: French & Spanish. Notes: *Open Sunday 2-5 June to October.*

CO. DONEGAL

CARNDONAGH

The Bookshop, ■ Court Place, Carndonagh. Prop: Michael Herron. Tel: 07493 74389. Fax: 07493 74935. E-mail: info@visitinishowen.com. Est: 1989. Shop At: Churchtown, Carndonagh, Co Donegal. Open: **M:** 14:00–18:00; **T:** 14:00–18:00; **Th:** 14:00–18:00; **F:** 14:00–18:00; **S:** 14:00–18:00; **Su:** 14:00–18:00; Very large stock. Spec: Antiquarian; First Editions; History - Local; Irish Interest; Medicine; Philosophy; Religion - Christian; Science - General. PR: £1–100. Mem: Also at: Churchtown, Carndonagh, Co Donegal. Notes: *Also, half price sales in August, December and Easter.*

CO. DUBLIN

BALLINTEER

Taney Books, 13 The Close Woodpark, Ballinteer. Prop: Morrough Lacy. Tel: 2157880. E-mail: maplacy@eircom.net. Est: 1982. Private premises. Type: Market Stall. Telephone First. Open: **S:** 11:00–18:00; **Su:** 11:00–18:00. Spec: Antiquarian; Cartography; Countries - Ireland; Geography; Prints and Maps. Cata: Irish Interest. Notes: *Attends Temple Bar Book Market Temple Bar Square Dublin 2 Phone 186 1902892 11:00-18:00 Saturday and Sunday.*

BLACKROCK

Carraig Books Ltd., ■ 73 Main Street, Blackrock. Prop: Sean L. Day. Tel: (01) 2882575. Fax: (01) 2834209. E-mail: carraigb@indigo.ie. Est: 1968. Shop open: **M:** 09:30–17:00; **T:** 09:30–17:00; **W:** 09:30–17:00; **Th:** 09:30–17:00; **F:** 09:30–17:00; **S:** 10.00–17:00. Closed for lunch: 13:00–14:00. Spec: Irish Interest; Religion - Catholic. PR: £2–100. CC: AE; MC; V. Cata: Irish, General Interests & Catholic. Notes: *Also, back-numbers of Irish journals.*

Samovar Books, 63 Ardagh Park, Blackrock. Prop: Louis Hemmings. Tel: 00-353-1-2104990. Web: www.samovarbooks.com. E-mail: louis@samovarbooks.com. Est: 1993. Private premises. Internet Only. Contactable. Open: **M:** 09:00–17:30; **T:** 09:00–17:30; **W:** 09:00–17:30; **Th:** 09:00–17:30; **F:** 09:00–17:30; **S:** 09:00–17:30; **Su:** 09:00–17:30; Closed for lunch: 13:00–14:00. Spec: Africana; Archaeology; Architecture; Author - Inklings, The; Autobiography; Bibles; Biblical Studies; Biography. CC: MC; V. Cata: Theology, Topography, Politics, History, Irish. Mem: Librarians Christian Fellowship. Notes: *Ireland's only online used theology book dealer.*

CLONTARF

Read Ireland, 392 Clontarf Road, Clontarf, 3. Prop: Gregory Carr. Tel: 35318532063. Fax: 35318532063. Web: www.readireland.ie. E-mail: gregcarr@readireland.ie. Est: 1995. Private premises. Internet Only. Appointment necessary. Open: **M:** 09:00–17:30; **T:** 09:00–17:30; **W:** 09:00–17:30; **Th:** 09:00–17:30; **F:** 09:00–17:30; **S:** 09:00–17:30; **Su:** 09:00–17:30; Closed for lunch: 13:00–14:00. Spec: Author - Beckett, S.; - Heaney, Seamus; - Yeats, W.B.; Countries - Ireland; History - Irish; Irish Interest. CC: MC; V. Cata: Irish Interest only. VAT No: IE 5093937G. Notes: *Ireland's Irish Interest Specialist Internet Booksellers.*

DUBLIN

Cathach Books Ltd, ■ Cathach Books Ltd 10 Duke Street, Dublin, 2. Prop: David Cunningham. Tel: +353 16718676. Fax: +353 1675120. Web: www.rarebooks.ie. E-mail: info@rarebooks.ie. Est: 1988. Shop open: **M:** 09:30–17:45; **T:** 09:30–17:45; **W:** 09:30–17:45; **Th:** 09:30–17:45; **F:** 09:30–17:45; **S:** 09:30–17:45. CC: AE; JCB; V; Laser. Cata: Literature, History (mostly Irish interest). Mem: ABA; BA; ILAB. Notes: *Together with our general stock, we offer an excellent selection of rare and first edition books by Oscar Wilde, James Joyce and William Butler Yeats. In addition, we stock a wide variety of Books on Irish History.*

Chapters Bookstore, ■ Ivy Exchange Parnell Street, Dublin, Dublin 1. Prop: William Kinsella. Manager John Gannon. Tel: 00 353 1 8723297. Fax: 00 353 1 8723044. Web: www.chapters.ie. E-mail: info@chapters.ie Est: 1982. Shop open: **M:** 09:30–18:30; **T:** 09:30–18:30; **W:** 09:30–18:30; **Th:** 09:30–20:00; **F:** 09:30–18:30; **S:** 09:30–18:30; **Su:** 12:00–18:30; Very large stock. Spec: Booksearch. PR: £1–1,000. CC: AE; MC; V. Mem: BA. VAT No: IE 643 9260 D. Notes: *(Alternate Tel: (01) 872-0773, 872-3024)*

De Burca Rare Books, 'Cloonagashel' 27 Priory Drive, Blackrock, Dublin. Prop: Famonn & Vivien de Burca. Tel: (01) 288-2159. Fax: (01) 283-4080. Web: www.deburcararebooks.com. E-mail: deburca@ indigo.ie. Est: 1979. Private premises. Internet and Postal. Telephone First. Large stock. Spec: Bindings; Countries - Ireland; Culture - National; Genealogy; History - National; Incunabula; Irish Interest; Literature. PR: £5–30,000. CC: JCB; MC. Corresp: French, German, Italian. Mem: ABA; PBFA; ILAB. VAT No: IE 16193333M. Notes: *Also, manuscripts of Irish interest, a worldwide mail order service & publishers of fine historical books.*

James Fenning, Antiquarian Books, 12 Glenview Rochestown Avenue, Dun Laoghaire, Dublin. Prop: Jim & Chris Fenning. Tel: (01) 2857855. Fax: (01) 2857919. E-mail: fenning@indigo.ie. Est: 1969. Private premises. Internet and Postal. Appointment necessary. Open: **M:** 08:00–16:00; **T:** 08:00–16:00; **W:** 08:00–16:00; **F:** 08:00–17:00. Small stock. Spec: Antiquarian. PR: £20–15,000. CC: MC; V. Mem: ABA. VAT No: IE 9T56885O.

REPUBLIC OF IRELAND

Glenbower Books, 46 Howth Road Clontarf, Dublin, Dublin 3. Prop: Martin Walsh. Tel: (01) 833-5305. Web: www.abebooks.com/home/GLENBOWERBOOKS. E-mail: glenbower@iol.ie. Private premises. Postal Only. Medium stock. Spec: Academic/Scholarly; Antiquarian; Bridge; Chemistry; Chess; Children's - Early Titles; Economics; Fiction - General. PR: £3–340. CC: MC, V; PayPal.

Greene's Bookshop Ltd, ■ 16, Clare St., Dublin 2. Tel. 00-353-1-6762554. Fax: 00-353-1-6789091. Web: www.greenesbookshop.com. E-mail: info@greenesbookshop.com. Est: 1843. Shop. Internet and Postal open. **M:** 09:00–17:30; **T:** 09:00–17:30; **W:** 09:00–17:30; **Th:** 09:09–17:30; **F:** 09:00–17:30; **S:** 09:00–17:00. Medium stock. Spec: Countries - Ireland; Irish Interest. CC: AE; D; MC; V. VAT No: IE 4810086O.

Obscurebooks, 17 St. Peters Crescent Walkinstown, Dublin. Prop: Tom Murray. Tel: +353-1-4567830. Web: www.obscurebooks.co.uk. E-mail: obscurebooks@yahoo.co.uk. Est: 2005. Mail Order Only. Internet Only. Appointment necessary. Open: **M:** 09:00–17:30; **T:** 09:00–17:30; **W:** 09:00–17:30; **Th:** 09:00–17:30; **F:** 09:00–17:30; **S:** 09:00–17:30; **Su:** 09:00–17:30; Closed for lunch: 13:00–14:00. CC: PayPal.

Phelan Books, 7 May Street Drumcondra, Dublin 3, Dublin. Prop: Brian J. Phelan. Tel: (01) 874-7316. E-mail: brianp@esatclear.ie. Est: 1995. Spec: Antiques; Architecture; Decorative Art; Fine Art; Booksearch. PR: £5–200. Notes: *Also, a booksearch service.*

Stokes Books, ■ 19 Market Arcade South Great George's Street, Dublin, Dublin 2. Prop: Stephen Stokes. Tel: (01) 671-3584. Fax: (01) 671-3181. Web: www.usedbooksirleand.ie. E-mail: stokesbooks@eircom.net. Est: 1982. Shop open: **M:** 11:00–18:00; **T:** 11:00–18:00; **W:** 11:00–18:00; **Th:** 11:00–18:00; **F:** 11:00–18:00; **S:** 11:00–18:00. Spec: Culture - National; History - Irish; Irish; Irish Interest; Languages - Foreign; Literature; Literature - Irish; Philosophy; Theology. PR: £5–50. CC: AE; MC; V. Cata: Irish History and Literature. Corresp: German.

DUN LAOGHAIRE

Naughton Booksellers, ■ 8 Marine Terrace, Dun Laoghaire. Prop: Susan Naughton. Tel: +353 1 280 4392. Web: www.naughtonsbooks.com. E-mail: sales@naughtonsbooks.com. Est: 1976. Shop open: **M:** 10:00–17:00; **T:** 10:00–17:00; **W:** 10:00–17:00; **Th:** 10:00–17:00; **F:** 10:00–17:00; **S:** 10:00–17:00. Spec: Academic/Scholarly; Anthologies; Antiquarian; Art History; Arts, The; Author - General; Author - 20th Century; Biography. CC: AE; MC; V. VAT No: IE 8495489V.

STILLORGAN

Dublin Bookbrowsers, 12 Weirview Drive, Stillorgan, None. Prop: Dave Downes. Tel: (00353) 872636347. Fax: (00353) 1210300. Web: www.abebooks.com. E-mail: dave@dubbookbrowsers.com. Est: 1996. Private premises. Appointment necessary. Large stock. Spec: Antiquarian; Irish Interest; Sport - General; Sport - Boxing; Sport - Golf. PR: £1–20,000. CC: MC; V. Cata: Ireland, Irish literature, Irish sport, general. Corresp: Some French. Mem: PBFA.

CO. GALWAY

GALWAY

Charlie Byrne's Bookshop, ■ Middle Street, Galway. Prop: Charlie Byrne. Tel: (0035) 391 561766. Fax: (0035) 391 561766. Web: www.charliebyrne.com. E-mail: info@charliebyrne.com. Internet and Postal. Shop open: **M:** 09:00–18:00; **T:** 09:00–18:00; **W:** 09:00–18:00; **Th:** 09:00–18:00; **F:** 09:00–20:00; **S:** 09:00–18:00; **Su:** 12:00–18:00. CC: AE; MC; V.

Kenny's Book Export Co., Kilkerrin Park Liosban, Tuam Road, Galway. Tel: (091) 709350. Fax: (091) 709351. E-mail: conor@kennys.ie. Est: 1999. Office and/or bookroom open: **M:** 09:00–17:00; **T:** 09:00–17:00; **W:** 09:00–17:00; **Th:** 09:00–17:00; **F:** 09:00–17:00. Very large stock. PR: £2–16,000. CC: AE; D; JCB; MC; V. Mem: ABA; BA. VAT No: IE 6328356V. Notes: *Kenny's Bookshop & Art Gallery, Galway (q.v).*

Kennys Bookshops and Art Galleries Limited, ■ Art Galleries Ltd High Street, Galway. Prop: Managing Director: Mr. Conor Kenny. Tel: (091) 562739 and 534760. Fax: (091) 568544. Web: www.kennys.ie. E-mail: conor@kennys.ie. Est: 1940. Shop open: **M:** 09:00–18:00; **T:** 09:00–18:00; **W:** 09:00–18:00; **Th:** 09:00–18:00; **F:** 09:00–18:00; **S:** 09:00–18:00. Very large stock. Spec: Americana - General; Anthropology; Archaeology; Architecture; Art Reference; Author - 20th Century; Authors - Women; Bindings. PR: £1–5,000. CC: AE; D; E; JCB; MC; V; Laser. Cata: 99 per year. Corresp: French, Italian. Mem: ABA; BA; ILAB. VAT No: IE 2238521A. Notes: *Additional web site: www.kennyscollections.com. Kennys Export Book Co., Galway (q.v) Also, a booksearch service, in-house fine bindings & large comtemporary Irish Art Gallery.*

MOYARD

The House of Figgis Ltd, Ross House, Moyard. Prop: Neville Figgis. Tel: (095) 41092. Fax: (095) 41261. E-mail: figgisbooks@eircom.net. Private premises. Appointment necessary. Small stock. Spec: Early Imprints; Irish Interest; Literature; Modern First Editions. CC: MC; V. VAT No: IE 9 N 543 415.

CO. LAOIS

VICARSTOWN

Courtwood Books, Vicarstown, Stradbally, Vicarstown. Prop: PJ Tynan. Tel: (0507) 8626384. E-mail: LBLOOM@EIRCOM.NET. Est: 1984. Private premises. Internet and Postal. Appointment necessary. Medium stock. Spec: Academic/Scholarly; Advertising; Author - Beckett, S.; - Joyce, James; - Wilde, Oscar; Countries - Ireland; Engineering; History - Local. PR: £1–500. CC: MC; V. Cata: Mostly Irish interest.

CO. LEITRIM

CARRICK–ON–SHANNON

Trinity Rare Books, ■ Bridge Street, Carrick–on–Shannon. Prop: Nick Kaszuk. Tel: 00353 71 9622144. Web: www.trinityrarebooks.com. E-mail: nickk@iol.ie. Est: 1999. Shop open: **M:** 09:30–18:00; **T:** 09:30–18:00; **W:** 09:30–18:00; **Th:** 09:30–18:00; **F:** 09:30–18:00; **S:** 09:30–18:00; **Su:** 13:00–17:00. Large stock. Spec: Agriculture; American Indians; Animals and Birds; Antiquarian; Antiquities; Archaeology; Architecture; Art. PR: £3–150. Cata: Irish books. Corresp: French, German.

CO. LIMERICK

ADARE

George Stacpoole, ■ Main Street, Adare. Prop: George Stacpoole. Tel: (061) 396409. Fax: (061) 396733. Web: www.georgestacpooleantiques.com. E-mail: stacpoole@iol.ie. Shop open: **M:** 10:00–17:30; **T:** 10:00–17:30; **W:** 10:00–17:30; **Th.** 10:00–17:30; **F:** 10:00–17:30; **S:** 10:00–17:30. Spec: History - Local; Sport - Field Sports; Prints and Maps. PR: £5–2,000. CC: AF; E; JCB; MC; V. Mem: IADA. Notes: *Also, a booksearch service.*

LIMERICK

The Celtic Bookshop, ■ 2 Rutland Street, Limerick. Prop: Caroline O'Brien. Tel: (061) 401155. E-mail: celticbk@iol.ie. Est: 1982. Shop. Internet and Postal. Telephone First. Open: **M:** 10:00–17:00; **T:** 10:00–17:00; **W:** 10:00–17:00; **Th:** 10:00–17:00; **F:** 10:00–17:00; **S:** 10:00–17:00. Medium stock. Spec: Academic/Scholarly; Antiquarian; Countries - Ireland; Fiction - General; History - General; History - Irish; Literature - Irish. PR: £3–1,000. CC: MC; V. Cata: Ireland. Corresp: Irish. VAT No: IE 3229665i.

O'Brien Books & Photo Gallery, ■ 26 High Street, Limerick. Prop: John O'Brien. Tel: (061) 412833. E-mail: ob.books@oceanfree.net. Est: 1988. Shop open: **T:** 10:30–17:30; **W:** 10:30–00:17; **Th:** 10:30–17:30; **F:** 10:30–17:30; **S:** 10:00–17:30. Closed for lunch: 13:00–13:30. Medium stock. Spec: Art; Art History; Biography; Cinema/Film; Fiction - General; Folio Society, The; History - General; Irish Interest. PR: £1–400. CC: D; E; JCB; MC; V. VAT No: IE 192 620 9a.

CO. TIPPERARY

ROSCREA

Roscrea Bookshop & Newsagents, ■ Roscrea Bookshop & Newsagents Rosemary Square, Roscrea, N/A. Prop: Tom and Pauline Deegan. Tel: 00-353-505-22894. Fax: 00-353-505-22894. Web: www. roscreabookshop.com. E-mail: info@roscreabookshop.com. Est: 1997. Telephone First. Shop open: **M:** 07:30–19:00; **T:** 07:30–19:00; **W:** 07:30–00:20; **Th:** 07:30–19:00; **F:** 07:30–19:00; **S:** 07:30–20:00; **Su:** 07:30–14:00. Large stock. Spec: Academic/Scholarly; Africana; Agriculture; American Indians; Bibles; Children's; Children's - Illustrated; Christmas. PR: £3–50. CC: MC; V. Corresp: French and Irish. Mem: BA; LAI. VAT No: IE 327613 4P.

CO. WEXFORD

BUNCLODY

Fuchsia Books, Ballyprecacus, Bunclody. Prop: Mary Mackey. Tel: 054 75577. E-mail: marymackey@ ercom.net. Est: 1988. Private premises. Internet and Postal. Contactable. Small stock. Spec: History - National; Irish Interest; Booksearch; Prints and Maps. PR: £10–500.

NEW ROSS

Britons Catholic Library, Riverview Arthurstown, New Ross. Prop: Mr. N.M. Gwynne. Tel: (51) 389111. E-mail: riverview@esatclear.ie. Est: 1976. Private premises. Appointment necessary. Small stock. Spec: Religion - Catholic. PR: £2–100. Notes: *Stock majors on traditional Catholic titles.*

SCOTLAND

Including the Unitary Authorities of Aberdeenshire, Angus, Argyll & Bute, Borders, Clackmannan, Dumfries & Galloway, Dumbarton & Clydebank, Dundee, East Ayrshire, East Dunbartonshire, East Lothian, East Renfrewshire, Edinburgh, Falkirk, Fife, Glasgow, Highland, Inverclyde, Mid Lothian, Moray, North Ayrshire, North Lanarkshire, Orkney Islands, Perthshire & Kinross, Renfrewshire, Shetland Islands, South Ayrshire, South Lanarkshire, Stirling, Western Isles and West Lothian

---

BORDERS

INNERLEITHEN

Spike Hughes Rare Books, Willow Bank, Damside, Innerleithen, EH44 6HR. Tel: (01896) 830019. Fax: (01896) 831499. E-mail: spike@buik.demon.co.uk. Est: 1981. Private premises. Internet and Postal. Appointment necessary. Small stock. Spec: Countries - Scotland; Fine & Rare; History - General; History - Local; History - National; Literature; Philosophy; Social History. PR: £10–5,000. CC: MC; V. Mem: ABA. VAT No: GB 345 4470 55.

Last Century Books, ■ 34 High Street, Innerleithen, EH44 6HF. Prop: Keith & Gillian Miller. Tel: 01896 831759. Web: www.lastcenturybooks.com. E-mail: last.century@btinternet.com. Est: 1998. Shop open: **M:** 11:00–17:00; **T:** 11:00–17:00; **W:** 11:00–17:00; **Th:** 11:00–17:00; **F:** 11:00–17:00; **S:** 11:00– 17:00. Spec: Art; Countries - Scotland; Fiction - General; Military; Religion - General. CC: E; JCB; MC; V; Maestro.

JEDBURGH

G. & R. Stone, Hap House 5 Allerton Court, Jedburgh, Roxburghshire, TD8 6RT. Prop: Gillian & Ralph Stone. Tel: (01835) 864147. Fax: (01835) 864147. Est: 1972. Private premises. Appointment necessary. Spec: Agriculture; Antiquarian; Natural History; Poetry; Women. PR: £5–100. CC: MC; V. Mem: PBFA.

KELSO

Border Books, ■ The Bookshop 47–51 Horsemarket, Kelso, TD5 7AA. Prop: Ronald C. Hodges. Tel: (01573) 225861. Fax: (01573) 224390. Est: 1981. Shop open: **M:** 10:30–16:00; **T:** 10:30–16:00; **W:** 10:30–16:00; **Th:** 10:30–16:00; **F:** 10:30–16:00; **S:** 10:30–16:00. Spec: Countries - Scotland; History - Local; Journals; Military; Sport - Field Sports; Topography - Local; Transport; Travel - General. PR: £1 500 Notes: *Closed Wednesdays in winter.*

MELROSE

Stroma Books, Charlesfield, St. Boswells, Melrose, TD6 0HH. Tel: (01835) 824169. Web: www. stromabooks.co.uk. E-mail: kenny@stromabooks.fsnet.co.uk. Est: 2000. Private premises. Internet and Postal. Appointment necessary. Medium stock. Spec: Academic/Scholarly; Art; Biography; Children's; Children's - Illustrated; Cinema/Film; Cookery/Gastronomy; Countries - Scotland. PR: £1–500. CC: AE; JCB; MC; V; M, SW, SO.

Searching for a title - and cannot find it on any Internet database?

Try www.sheppardsworld.co.uk

SELKIRK

Wheen O'Books, Glyndwr, Mill Street, Selkirk, TD7 5AE. Prop: Margaret Tierney. Tel: (01750) 721009. Web: www.wheenobooks.com. E-mail: megtie@aol.com. Est: 1997. Private premises. Internet Only. Telephone First. Large stock. Spec: Adventure; Animals and Birds; Annuals; Army, The; Art; Author - General; Autobiography; Aviation. PR. £2–1,500. CC: PayPal. Notes: *General stock. You can browse our books at http://www.wheenobooks.com for hard to find, out of print, used, and rare books at decent prices with first-class personal service.*

CENTRAL

BY DUNBLANE

Sheriffmuir Books, Glentye Sheriffmuir, by Dunblane, FK15 OLN. Tel: 01786 822269. E-mail: sheriffmuirbooks@hotmail.com. Private premises. Postal Only

CALLANDER

HP Bookfinders, Mosslaird Brig O'Turk, Callander, FK17 8HT. Tel: (01877) 376177. Fax: (01877) 376377. Web: www.hp-bookfinders.co.uk. E-mail: martin@hp-bookfinders.co.uk. Est: 1986. Private premises Internet and Postal. Contactable. Very small stock. Spec: Booksearch. CC: E; JCB; MC; V; Switch.

Kings Bookshop Callander, ■ 91–93 Main Street, Callander, Trossachs, FK17 8BQ. Prop: Ian King & Sally Evans. Tel: (01877) 339 449. E-mail: sally.king4@btinternet.com. Est: 1987. Shop open: **M:** 09:00–19:00; **T:** 09:00–19:00; **W:** 09:00–19:00; **Th:** 09:00–19:00; **F:** 09:00–19:00; **S:** 09:00–19:00; **Su:** 09:00–19:00. Spec: Bindings; Classical Studies; Poetry; Scottish Interest. PR: £1–1,000. CC: cheques or cash only. Notes: *Shop open Monday through to Sunday. NB When sending e-mails - add 'bookshop' to subject field. Good bookbindings for sale.*

DOLLAR

Volume Three, 4 The Glebe, Dollar, FK14 7AN. Prop: Helen Prior. Tel: 01259 742168. Web: www. ukbookworld.com/members/volumethree. E-mail: hespri@btinternet.com. Est: 2002. Mail Order Only. Internet and Postal. Contactable. Spec: out-of-print.

LARBERT

Dave Simpson, Lorne Villa 161 Main Street, Larbert, FK5 4AL. Tel: (01324) 558628. Fax: (01324) 558628. E-mail: dave.simpson3@btinternet.com. Est: 2000. Private premises. Internet and Postal. Contactable. Small stock. Spec: Author - General; Author - 20th Century; Children's; Fiction - General; Fiction - Adventure; Fiction - Crime, Detective, Spy, Thrillers; Fiction - Fantasy, Horror; Fiction - Historical. PR: £10–300. CC: E; JCB; MC; V; Switch. Notes: *Sells through Abebooks.com, The Book and Magazine Collector and long standing contacts.*

DUMFRIES & GALLOWAY

CASTLE DOUGLAS

Benny Gillies Books Ltd, ■ 33 Victoria Street, Kirkpatrick Durham, Castle Douglas, DG7 3HQ. Prop: Benny Gillies. Tel: 01556 650412. Web: www.bennygillies.co.uk. E-mail: benny@bennygillies.co.uk. Est: 1979. Shop. Telephone First. Open: **M:** 10:00–17:00; **T:** 10:00–17:00; **W:** 10:00–17:00; **Th:** 10:00–17:00; **F:** 10:00–17:00; **S:** 10:00–17:00. Spec: Countries - Scotland; County - Local; Scottish Interest; Topography - Local; Prints and Maps. CC: AE; MC; V. Cata: Scotland. Corresp: French. Mem: PBFA. VAT No: GB 499 0638 93. Notes: *Specialist dealer in Scottish material only (Books maps and prints) Kirkpatrick Durham is situated 6 miles from Castle Douglas. Please telephone before making a special journey especially in winter.*

Douglas Books, ■ 207 King Street, Castle Douglas, Kirkcudbrightshire, DG7 1DT. Prop: Martin Close. Tel: (01556) 504006. E-mail: crescent.books@virgin.net. Est: 1995. Shop open: **M:** 10.00–17.00; **T:** 10.00–17.00; **W:** 10.00–17.00; **F:** 10.00–17.00; **S:** 10.00–17.00. PR: £1–100. CC: MC; V.

SCOTLAND

DUMFRIES

Anwoth Books, ■ Mill on the Fleet Gatehouse of Fleet, Dumfries, DG7 2HS. Prop: R. Munro. Tel: 01557814774. E-mail: AnwothBooks@aol.com. Est: 1992. Open in Summer. Shop open: **M:** 10.30–17:00; **T:** 10:30–1700; **W:** 1030–1700; **Th:** 1030–1700; **F:** 1030–1700; **S:** 1030–1700; **Su:** 1030–1700; Closed for lunch: 13:00–14:00. Spec: Children's; Ethnology; Ornithology; Poetry; Rural Life; Scottish Interest. CC: JCB; MC; V. Corresp: German. Notes: *Open weekends throughout the winter.*

KIRKCUDBRIGHT

Solway Books, ■ 14 St. Cuthbert's Street, Kirkcudbright, DG6 4DU. Prop: Mrs Beverley Chadband. Tel: 01557 330635. E-mail: beverley.chadband@btinternet.com. Est: 2003. Shop open: **M:** 09:00–17:00; **T:** 09:00–17:00; **W:** 09:00–17:00; **Th:** 09:00–17:00; **F:** 09:00–17:00; **S:** 10:00–17:00. Spec: Ephemera; Prints and Maps. PR: £1–300. CC: JCB; MC; V; Switch. Mem: BA.

Vailima Books, ■ 61 High Street, Kirkcudbright, DG6 4JZ. Prop: Elizabeth Kirby. Tel: (01557) 330583. E-mail: vailimabooks@supanet.com. Est: 1988. Shop open: **M:** 10:00–17:00; **T:** 10:00–17:00; **Th:** 10:00–17:00; **F:** 10:00–17:00; **S:** 10:00–17:00. Small stock. Spec: Railways; Transport. PR: £1–20. Notes: *Large stock of railways and other transport.*

MOFFAT

Moffat Book Exchange, ■ 5 Well Street, Moffat, DF10 9DP. Prop: Andy Armstrong. Tel: (01683) 220059. E-mail: dandrewarmstrong@aol.com. Est: 1998. Shop open: **M:** 10:00–16:30; **W:** 10:00–16:30; **Th:** 10:00–16:30; **F:** 10:00–16:30; **S:** 10:00–17:00; **Su:** 13:00–16:00; Closed for lunch: 13:00–14:00. Spec: Fiction - General. PR: £1–25. Notes: *Stock includes large selection of paperback fiction, and large selection of general non-fiction.*

WHITHORN

Pend Books, ■ 55 George Street, Whithorn, Newton Stewart, DG8 8NU. Prop: Julia M. Watt. Tel: 01988 500469. Fax: 01988 500469. Est: 2000. Shop. Appointment necessary. Open: **M:** 09:00–17:30; **T:** 09:00–17:30; **W:** 09:00–17:30; **Th:** 09:00–17:30; **F:** 09:00–17:30; **S:** 09:00–17:30; **Su:** 09:00–17:30; Closed for lunch: 13:00–14:00. Spec: CC: AE; JCB; MC; V. Corresp: French, German. VAT No: GB 817 1312 57.

WIGTOWN

AA1 Books at Windy Hill, ■ Unit 3 Duncan Park, Wigtown, DG8 9JD. Prop: Marion Richmond. Tel: (01988) 402653. Web: www.bookavenue/hosted/AA1. E-mail: AA1books@supanet.com. Est: 2001. Shop open: **M:** 10:00–17:00; **T:** 10:00–17:00; **W:** 10:00–17:00; **Th:** 10:00–17:00; **F:** 10:00–17:00; **S:** 08:00–17:00; **Su:** 11:00–15:00; Very large stock. Spec: Children's; Espionage; Fiction - Crime, Detective, Spy, Thrillers; Fiction - Fantasy, Horror; Fiction - Science Fiction; Fiction - Westerns; Ghosts; History - General. PR: £1–150. CC: AE; MC; V. Corresp: French, German. Notes: *Also, new books. In association with Ming Books.*

A.P. & R. Baker Limited, The Laigh House Church Lane, Wigtown, DG8 9HT. Prop: Anthony P. & Rosemary Baker. Tel: (01988) 403348. Fax: (01988) 403443. Web: www.apandrbaker.co.uk. E-mail: rosemaryapandrb@yahoo.co.uk. Est: 1974. Private premises. Postal Only. Telephone First. Spec: Archaeology; History - General. PR: £2–500. CC: JCB; MC; V; Delta Solo Electron Train (SW & U). Cata: Archaeology & History. Mem: Wigtown Chamber of Commerce.

The BookShop, ■ 17 North Main Street, Wigtown, DG8 9HL. Prop: Shaun Bythell. Tel: 01988 402499. Web: www.the-bookshop.com. E-mail: mail@the-bookshop.com. Est: 1984. Shop open: **M:** 09:00–17:00; **T:** 09:00–17:00; **W:** 09:00–17:00; **Th:** 09:00–17:00; **F:** 09:00–17:00; **S:** 09:00–17:00. Spec: Aircraft; Antiquarian; Antiques; Art - British; Aviation; Canals/Inland Waterways; Churchilliana; Cinema/Film. CC: MC; V. Notes: *Scotland's largest second-hand book shop, 9 large rooms with books on all subjects. Take advantage of our free coffee, or relax in one of the armchairs in front of the woodburning stove.*

Byre Books, ■ 24 South Main St., Wigtown, DG8 9EH. Prop: Laura Mustian, Shani Mustian and Chris Ballance. Tel: (01988) 402133. Web: www.byrebooks.co.uk. E-mail: info@byrebooks.co.uk. Est: 2000. Internet and Postal. Shop open: **M:** 10:00–17:30; **T:** 10:00–17:30; **W:** 10:00–17.30; **Th:** 10:00–17:30; **F:** 10:00–17:30; **S:** 10:00–17:30; **Su:** 11:00–16:30. Small stock. Spec: Aboriginal; American Indians; Anthropology; Anthroposophy; Arthurian; Author - Aesop; - Shakespeare, William; Celtica. PR: £3–100. CC: E; JCB; MC; V; Switch, Delta. Corresp: French, Spanish. Mem: Wigtown Book Trades Ass. VAT No: GB 789 1742 76. Notes: *During the winter we are usually closed on a Wednesday, and our opening hours are 10:00-16:00. Please call before visiting for exact times during your stay.*

G. C. Books Ltd., Unit 10 Book Warehouse Bladnoch Bridge Estate, Wigtown, DG8 9AB. Prop: Beverley and Keith Chadband. Tel: 01988 402 688. Fax: 01988 402 688. E-mail: sales@gcbooks.demon.co.uk. Est: 2005. Warehouse. Internet and Postal open: **M:** 10.00–17.00; **T:** 10.00–17.00; **W:** 10.00–17.00; **Th:** 10.00–17.00; **F:** 10.00–17.00; **S:** 10.00–17.00. Spec: Academic/ Scholarly; Africana; Aircraft; Antiquarian; Archaeology; Architecture; Atlases; Autobiography. CC: MC; V. Cata: as required. Mem. FSB. Notes: *Visitors, Trade Overseas Enquiries Welcome - Free Booksearch Service - International Shipping.*

M.E. McCarty, Bookseller, ■ 13 North Main St., Wigtown, DG8 9HL. Tel: (01988) 402062. E-mail: moi@orkneybooks.co.uk. Est: 1980. Shop open: **M:** 10:00–17:00; **T:** 10:00–17:00; **W:** 10:00–17:00; **Th:** 10:00–17:00; **F:** 10:00–17:00; **S:** 10:00–17:00; **Su:** 10:00–17:00. Spec: Literature; Maritime/Nautical; Travel - General. PR: £1–100. CC: AE; JCB; MC; V; Maestro, Solo. Corresp: French, German, Norwegian. Notes: *Also at: 54 Junction Road, Kirkwall Orkney. 01856 870860.*

Ming Books, Beechwood House Acre Place, Wigtown, DG8 9DU. Prop: Mrs Marion Richmond. Tel: (01988) 403241. Web: www.alibris.com/bookstore/GALLOWAY. E-mail: mingbooks@yahoo.com. Est: 1982. Office and/or bookroom. Internet and Postal. Appointment necessary. Open: **M:** 10:00– 18:00; **T:** 10:00–18:00; **W:** 10:00–18:00; **Th:** 10:00–18:00, **F:** 10:00–18:00; **S:** 10:00–18:00. Closed for lunch: 12:00–13:00. Very large stock. Spec: Cats; Crime (True); Espionage; Fiction - Crime, Detective, Spy, Thrillers; Fiction - Fantasy, Horror; Fiction - Historical; Fiction - Science Fiction; Fiction - Westerns. PR: £4–1,000. CC: AE; MC; V; PayPal;. Cata: crime fiction; Penguins Corresp. German and French. Mem: IOBA. VAT No: GB 432 9993 15. Notes: *AA1 Books at Windy Hill, Unit 3 Duncan Park Wigtown is the retail outlet. Open Monday to Saturday in Summer otherwise by appointment or chance.*

Reading Lasses, ■ 17 South Main Street, Wigtown, DG8 9EH. Prop: Angela Everitt. Tel: 00 (44) 1988 403266. Web: www.reading-lasses.com. E-mail: books@reading-lasses.com. Est: 1997. Shop open: **M:** 10:00–17:00; **T:** 10:00–17:00; **W:** 10:00–17:00; **Th:** 10:00–17:00; **F:** 10:00–17:00; **S:** 10:00–17:00; **Su:** 12:00–17:00. Spec: Academic/Scholarly; Adult; African-American Studies; Africana; Alternative Medicine; Anthropology; Art; Asian Studies. CC: MC; V. Mem: PBFA. Notes: *The bookshop hosts an award-winning cafe specialising in home-made and local produce.*

Transformer, ■ 26 Bladnoch, Wigtown, DG8 9AB. Prop: C.A. Weaver. Tel: 0044 (0) 1988-403455. Web: www.abebooks.com/home/TRANSFORMER/home.htm. E-mail: transformer@tesco.net. Est: 1998. Shop. Internet and Postal. Open in Summer. Very large stock. Spec: Academic/Scholarly; Astronomy; Biology - General; Chemistry; Children's; Countries - China; Countries - Japan; Countries - Korea. PR: £1–400. Corresp: French. Notes: *Open also by appointment.*

FIFE

ANSTRUTHER

Rising Tide Books, 51 John Street, Cellardyke, Anstruther, KY10 3BA. Prop: Stephen Checkland. Tel: (01333) 310948. Fax: (01333) 310948. E-mail: stevecheckland@risingtidebooks.com. Est: 1997. Private premises. Book fairs only. Appointment necessary. Very small stock. Spec: Illustrated - General; Modern First Editions; Scottish Interest. PR: £5–500. Mem: PBFA.

DUNFERMLINE

Larry Hutchison (Books), 27 Albany Street, Dunfermline, KY12 0QZ. Tel: (01383) 725566. Fax: (01383) 620394. Web: www.larryhutchisobooks.com. E-mail: larry@larryhutchisonbooks.com. Est: 1987. Private premises. Appointment necessary. Medium stock. Spec: Antiquarian; Countries - Scotland; Fine & Rare; Folklore; Genealogy; History - General; History - Industrial; Literature. PR: £5–5,000. CC: AE; MC; V. Cata: Scottish. Corresp: most major European. Mem: PBFA. VAT No: GB 716 9500 30. Notes: *Also, a booksearch service.*

Gary Walker, Swallowdrum Cottage Milesmark, Dunfermline, KY12 9BB. Prop: Gary Walker. Tel: (01383) 737977. Private premises. Small stock. PR: £2–500. Notes: *Open daily.*

KIRKCALDY

R. Campbell Hewson Books, 6 West Albert Road, Kirkcaldy, KY1 1DL. Tel: (01592) 262051. Est: 1996. Private premises. Appointment necessary. Small stock. Spec: Author - Burton, R.F.; Ethnography; Rural Life; Sport - Big Game Hunting; Travel - Africa; Voyages & Discovery. PR: £10–3,500.

SCOTLAND

NEWPORT ON TAY

Gordon Bettridge, 4 Myrtle Terrace, Newport on Tay, DD6 8DN. Tel: (01382) 542377. Est: 1984. Private premises. Postal Only. Spec: Advertising; Bibliography; Books about Books; Calligraphy; Illustrated - General; Journals; Papermaking; Printing. PR: £1–75.

Mair Wilkes Books, 3 St. Mary's Lane, Newport on Tay, DD6 8AH. Tel: (01382) 542260. E-mail: mairwilkes.books@zoom.co.uk. Est: 1969. Storeroom. Open: **T:** 10:00–16:30; **W:** 10:00–16:30; **Th:** 10:10–16:30; **F:** 10:00–16:30; **S:** 10:00–17:00. Closed for lunch: 12:30–14:00. Spec: Academic/ Scholarly; Bindings; Fine & Rare; History of Ideas; Medicine - History of; Modern First Editions; Neurology; Psychology/Psychiatry. PR: £2–1,000. CC: AE; MC; V; PayPal. Cata: on Scottish Interests. Mem: PBFA. VAT No: GB 397 9923 69. Notes: *Scottish Antiques Ctre, Abernyte, Inchture, Perthshire.*

PATHMEAD

Midnight Oil Books, ■ 120 Commercial Street, Pathmead, Kirkcaldy, KY1 2NX. Prop: David P McHutchon. Tel: 01592 260818. Web: www.midoil.co.uk. E-mail: enquiries@midoil.co.uk. Est: 2006. Shop open: **M:** 09:00–17:00; **T:** 09:00–17:00; **W:** 09:00–17:00; **Th:** 09:00–20:00; **F:** 09:00–17:00; **S:** 09:00–17:00. Spec: Languages - Foreign; Linguistics; Philology. Corresp: French, German, Polish, Russian.

ST. ANDREWS

The Bouquiniste Bookshop, ■ 31 Market Street, St. Andrews, KY16 9NS. Prop: E Anne Anderson. Tel: 01334 467724. Est: 1982. Shop open: **M:** 11:00–17:00; **T:** 11:00–17:00; **W:** 11:00–17:00; **Th:** 11:00– 17:00; **F:** 11:00–17:00; **S:** 10:00–17:00. Spec: Scottish Interest. Corresp: French.

GRAMPIAN

ABERDEEN

Aberdeen Antique and Art Centre, 24 South College Street, Aberdeen. Tel: 01224 575075. E-mail: aberdeenantiques@btconnect.com. Shop and/or gallery open: **M:** 10:00–17:00; **T:** 10:00–17:00; **W:** 10:00–17:00; **Th:** 10:00–17:00; **F:** 10:00–17:00; **S:** 10:00–17:00; **Su:** 12:00–16:00.

Books and Beans, ■ 22 Belmont Street, Aberdeen, AB10 1JH. Prop: Craig Willox. Tel: 01224 646438. Fax: 01224 646483. Web: www.booksandbeans.co.uk. E-mail: sales@booksandbeans.co.uk. Est: 2003. Shop open: **M:** 09:30–16:30; **T:** 09:30–16:30; **W:** 09:30–16:30; **Th:** 09:30–16:30; **F:** 09:30–16:30; **S:** 09:00–16:00; **Su:** 11:00–15:30. Spec: Fiction - Fantasy, Horror. CC: AE; E; JCB; MC; V; Switch. VAT No: GB 827 2519 23.

Clifford Milne Books, 6 Hill Crest Place, Aberdeen, AB2 7BP. Tel: (01224) 697654. Est: 1994. Private premises. Postal Only. Spec: Art; Countries - Scotland; Modern First Editions; Sport - Golf. CC: PayPal. Mem: PBFA.

Elizabeth Ferguson, 34 Woodburn Avenue, Aberdeen, AB15 8JQ. Tel: (01224) 315949. Fax: (01224) 315949. E-mail: efergusonbooks@aol.com. Est: 2000. Postal Only. Small stock. Spec: Children's; Children's - Early Titles; Children's - Illustrated; Countries - Scotland; Illustrated - General; Music - Illustrated Sheet Music; Music - Sheet Music; Pop-Up, Movable & Cut Out. PR: £5–500. Corresp: French, German. Notes: *Very small stock at Aberdeen Antique and Art Centre, 24 South College Street, Aberdeen Telephone 01224 575075(q.v.).*

Old Aberdeen Bookshop, ■ 140 Spital, Aberdeen, AB24 3TU. Tel: 01224 658355. E-mail: cscottpaul@ btinternet.com. Est: 1996. Shop open: **M:** 11:30–17:00; **T:** 11:30–17:00; **W:** 11:30–17:00; **Th:** 11:30– 17:00; **F:** 11:30–17:00; **S:** 11:30–17:00. Medium stock. Spec: Academic/Scholarly; Art; Esoteric; Literature; Military; Theology. PR: £1–20. CC: D; MC; V.

ABOYNE

Jane Jones Books, ■ The Old Shop Dinnet, Aboyne, AB34 5JY. Prop: Jane Jones. Tel: 013398 85662. Fax: 013398 85662. E-mail: jjbooks@tiscali.co.uk. Est: 2003. Shop open: **M:** 11.00–18.00; **T:** 11.00– 18.00; **Th:** 11.00–18.00; **F:** 11.00–18.00; **S:** 10.30–18.00; **Su:** 11.30–17.30; Spec: Adventure; Agriculture; Animals and Birds; Antiquarian; Authors - National; Children's; Children's - Illustrated; Dogs. Cata: General stock . Corresp: French. Mem: PBFA. Notes: *My stock is general with an emphasis on Natural History , Scottish , Illustrated and childrens. I do have a booksearch facility. Not all of my stock is on show at the shop.*

SCOTLAND

BALLATER

Deeside Books, ■ 18-20 Bridge Street, Ballater, AB35 5QP. Prop: Bryn Wayte. Tel: 01339 754080. Fax: 01339 754080. E-mail: deesidebk@aol.com. Est: 1998. Shop open: **M:** 10:00–17:00, **T:** 10:00–17:00; **W:** 10:00–17:00; **Th:** 10:00–17:00; **F:** 10:00–17:00; **S:** 10:00–17:00; **Su:** 12:00–17:00. Spec: Arms & Armour; Army, The; Cookery/Gastronomy; Countries - Africa; Countries - Arctic, The; First Editions; History - General; Maritime/Nautical - History. CC: AE; JCB; MC; V. Mem: PBFA. VAT No: GB 716 9705 12.

McEwan Fine Books, Glengarden, Ballater, AB35 5UB. Prop: Dr. Peter McEwan. Tel: (01339) 755429. Fax: (01339) 755995. E-mail: pjmm@easynet.co.uk. Est: 1968. Private premises. Postal Only. Appointment necessary. Medium stock. Spec: Animals and Birds; Art - British; Art History; Art Reference; Artists; Author - Watkins-Pitchford, Denys ('B.B.'); Canadiana; Ceramics. PR: £5–5,000. CC: E; MC; V; LAPADA. Cata: Scottish (non-fiction); family histories; polar. Corresp: German. Mem: LAPADA. Notes: *Rhod McEwan Golf Books (q.v.) Also, works of art.*

Rhod McEwan Golf Books, Glengarden, Ballater, AB35 5UB. Tel: (013397) 55429. Fax: (013397) 55995. Web: www.rhodmcewan.com. E-mail: teeoff@rhodmcewan.com. Est: 1985. Private premises. Appointment necessary. Medium stock. Spec: Sport - Golf. PR: £3–5,000. CC: F; MC; V, PayPal, Debit. Corresp: German, Hungarian, Russian. Mem: ABA; PBFA; ILAB. VAT No: GB 605 2115 89. Notes: *At same premises: McEwan Fine Books. (q.v.) Also, golf posters, paintings and memorabilia.*

BRIDGEND

Kevin S. Ogilvie Modern First, Tolquhon, Bridgend, Ellon, AB41 8LX. Tel: 07841 289308. E-mail: kevinsogilvie@boltblue.com. Est: 1991. Private premises. Postal Only. Spec: Children's; Fiction - Crime, Detective, Spy, Thrillers; First Editions; Modern First Editions; Signed Editions. PR: £7–100.

RHOD McEWAN GOLF

Specialist dealer in antiquarian, out-of-print and elusive books on golf

Annuals
Architecture
Biographies
Cigarette Cards
Club Histories
Ephemera
Essays
Fiction
Handbooks

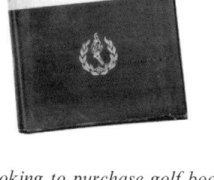

Histories
Humour
Instructionals
Magazines
Rules
Tournament Histories
Turf Management
Upkeep
Women's Golf

I am always looking to purchase golf books in any quantity

Ballater, Royal Deeside, Aberdeenshire AB35 5UB
Telephone: (013397) 55429 Fax: (013397) 55995
E-mail: teeoff@rhodmcewan.com www.rhodmcewan.com

SCOTLAND

ELLON

Grampian Books, South Ardo Methlick, Ellon, AB41 7HP. Prop: David Fleming. Tel: 01651806165. E-mail: grampianbooks@btinternet.com. Est: 1990. Private premises. Internet and Postal. Appointment necessary. Spec: Almanacs; Antiquarian; Architecture; Bibliography; Countries - Scotland; Ecclesiastical History & Architecture; Folklore; Genealogy. CC: MC; V. Cata: Scottish books ; Books by Scottish authors. Corresp: French Spanish. Mem: PBFA. VAT No: GB 553 1059 63. Notes: *We purchase good-quality Scottish books of all kinds, particularly non-fiction, from single items to libraries.*

FOCHABERS

Alba Books, Maxwell Street, Fochabers, IV32 7DE. Prop: Mike Seton. Tel: (01343) 820575. Fax: (01343) 820780. Web: www.albabooks.com. E-mail: Albabooks@dial.pipex.com. Est: 1997. Warehouse. Internet and Postal. Appointment necessary. Very large stock. Spec: Alternative Medicine; Art; Biology - General; Countries - Scotland; Education & School; Gynaecology; Literature; Maritime/ Nautical. PR: £2–200. CC: AE; E; MC; V; Switch. Corresp: French, German. Mem: IBooknet. VAT No: GB 751 3324 56.

Marianne Simpson, ■ 61/63 High Street, Fochabers, IV32 7DU. Tel: (01343) 821192. Est: 1990. Shop open: **M:** 10:00–16:00; **T:** 10:00–16:00; **W:** 10:00–16:00; **Th:** 10:00–16:00; **F:** 10:00–16:00; **S:** 10:00–16:00. Closed for lunch: 13:00–14:00. Small stock. PR: £1–100. Corresp: French. Notes: *Winter opening: Oct to Easter - Tues, Thurs & Sat 10:00-16:00. Closed lunch.*

FORRES

Logie Steading Bookshop, ■ Dunphail, Forres, IV36 2QN. Prop: Helen Trussell. Tel: 01309 611373. E-mail: helen.trussell@btinternet.com. Est: 1999. Shop open: **M:** 11:00–17:00; **T:** 11:00–17:00; **W:** 11:00–17:00; **Th:** 11:00–17:00; **F:** 11:00–17:00; **S:** 11:00–17:00; **Su:** 11:00–17:00. Spec: History - Local; Collectables; Ephemera; Prints and Maps. CC: JCB; MC; V. Cata: one general, one local history. VAT No: GB 890 438 501.

HUNTLY

Orb's Bookshop, ■ 33a Deveron Street, Huntly, AB54 8BY. Prop: Anne Lamb. Tel: (01466) 793765. E-mail: info@orb.demon.co.uk. Est: 2001. Shop open: **M:** 09:15–17:00; **T:** 09:15–17:00; **W:** 09:15–17:00; **Th:** 09:15–17:00; **F:** 09:15–17:00; **S:** 09:15–17:00. Closed for lunch: 13:00–14:00. Spec: Animals and Birds; Author - Barrie, J.M.; - Borrow, George; - Buchan, John; - Burns, Robert; - Francis, Dick; - Heyer, Georgette; - Kipling, Rudyard. CC: MC; V; Maestro. Corresp: French. Mem: BA; FSB. Notes: *Also, new books. Open Saturdays 9:15 to 16:00 (no lunch break).*

HIGHLAND

CULBOKIE

Tom Coleman, 2 Schoolcroft, Culbokie, IV7 8LB. Prop: Tom Coleman. Tel: (01349) 877502. Fax: (01349) 877502. E-mail: tomcoleman@mailsaq.net. Private premises. Postal Only. Appointment necessary. Medium stock. Spec: General Stock; Scottish Interest. PR: £10–1,000. CC: PayPal.

DINGWALL

Mercat Books, ■ 6 Church Street, Dingwall, IV15 9HP. Tel: 01349 865593. Fax: 01349 865593. Web: www.mercatbooks.com. E-mail: mercat.books@zetnet.co.uk. Est: 1994. Shop. Open in Summer. Open: **M:** 10.00–17.00; **T:** 10.00–17.00; **W:** 10.00–16.00; **Th:** 10.00–17.00; **F:** 09:00–17:30; **S:** 09:00–17:30; **Su:** 09:00–17:30; Closed for lunch: 13:00–14:00. Spec: Alpinism/Mountaineering; Animals and Birds; Art; Art Reference; Author - Blyton, Enid; - Brent-Dyer, Elinor M.; - Burns, Robert; - Oxenham, Elsie. CC: AE; JCB; V. Notes: *Shop premises now up for sale but trading still via internet, please ring 01349 865593/867535 for up to date information, specialising in Scottish, topography and natural history.*

DURNESS

Loch Croispol Bookshop & Restaurant, ■ 2, Balnakeil, Durness, IV27 4PT. Prop: Kevin Crowe. Tel: 01971-511777. Web: www.scottish-books.net. E-mail: lochcroispol@btopenworld.com. Est: 1999. Shop open: **M:** 10.00–17.00; **T:** 10.00–17:00; **W:** 10:00 17:00, **Th:** 10:00–17:00; **F:** 10:00–17:00; **S:** 10:00–17:00; **Su:** 10:00 16.00. Spec: Countries - Scotland; History - Scottish; Literature - Scottish; Poetry; Scottish Enlightenment; Scottish Interest; Seafaring & Shipping. CC: MC; V; Maestro, PayPal. VAT No: GB 734 9262 18. Notes: *We specialise in Scottish titles. We have a large stock of poetry. We also stock general adult and children's titles. Members of the international cooperative of independent booksellers:* www.worldbookmarket.com.

FORT WILLIAM

Creaking Shelves, Arkaig Cottage Achintore Road, Fort William, PH33 6RN. Prop: Chris Robinson. Tel: (01397) 702886. Web: www.abebooks.com. E-mail: creakingshelves@btinternet.com. Est: 1998. Private premises. Postal Only. Appointment necessary. Very small stock. Spec: Alpinism/ Mountaineering; Countries - Scotland; Mountains; Natural History; New Naturalist; Topography - Local. PR: £5–500.

INVERNESS

Leakey's Bookshop Ltd, ■ Church Street, Inverness, IV1 1EY. Prop: Charles Leakey. Tel: (01463) 239947. Est: 1979. Shop open: **M:** 10:00–17:30; **T:** 10:00–17:30; **W:** 10:00–17:30; **Th:** 10:00–17:30; **F:** 10:00–17:30; **S:** 10:00–17:30. Very large stock. Spec: Countries - Scotland; Culture - National; Scottish Enlightenment; Scottish Interest; Topography - Local; Prints and Maps. CC: E; JCB; MC; V. Notes: *Stock level - 80,000.*

LOCHCARRON

Blythswood Charity Shop, ■ Main Street, Lochcarron, IV54 8YD. Prop: Blythswood Trading Ltd. Tel: (01520) 722337. Fax: (01520) 722264. Web: www.blythswood.org. E-mail: a.stewart@ blythswood.org. Est: 1984. Shop. Internet and Postal open: **Th:** 10:00–16:00; **F:** 10:00–16:00; **S:** 10:00–16:00. Medium stock. Spec: Biography; First Editions; Religion - General; Religion - Christian; Theology; Booksearch; Collectables. PR: £2–200. CC: MC; V. Mem: BA. VAT No: GB 742 9279 06. Notes: *Also at: Portree, Isle of Skye. Dingwell, Ross-shire. Stornoway, Isle of Lewis, and Cromer, Norfolk. Also, new books.*

THURSO

Tall Tales Bookshop, ■ 1 Princes Street, Thurso, KW14 7HF. Prop: Stanley J. Morrison. Tel: 07900 284488. E-mail: stanmorrison@lineone.net. Est: 1995. Shop open: **M:** 09:00–17:30; **T:** 09:00–17:30; **W:** 09:00–17:30; **Th:** 09:00–17:30; **F:** 09:00–17:30; **S:** 09:00–17:30.

ISLES OF SCOTLAND

ISLE OF ARRAN

Barnhill Books, Old Schoolhouse, Kilmory, Isle of Arran, KA27 8PQ. Prop: John Rhead. Tel: (01770) 870368. E-mail: rheadz@btinternet.com. Est: 1985. Private premises. Postal Only. Spec: Alpinism/ Mountaineering; Gardening - General; Natural History; Ornithology; Plant Hunting; Sport - Big Game Hunting; Sport - Falconry; Sport - Field Sports. PR: £5–2,000. Cata: ornithology, fieldsports, natural history big game.

Audrey McCrone, Windyridge, Whiting Bay, Isle of Arran, North Ayrshire, KA27 8QT. Tel: (01770) 700564. Web: www.ukbookworld.com/members/finora. E-mail: a.mccrone@btinternet.com. Est: 1980. Private premises. Internet and Postal. Telephone First. Small stock. Spec: Alpinism/ Mountaineering; Animals and Birds; Anthologies; Antiquarian; Antiquities; Archaeology; Architecture; Art - Technique. PR: £5–200. Cata: Scottish, War, Biography, Poetry, Mysteries.

SCOTLAND

ISLE OF COLONSAY

Colonsay Bookshop, ■ Isle of Colonsay Argyll, Isle of Colonsay, PA61 7YR. Prop: Kevin & Christa Byrne. Tel: (01951) 200232. Fax: (01951) 200232. Web: www.colonsay.org.uk. E-mail: colonsaybookshop@zetnet.co.uk. Est: 1988. Open in Summer. Shop open: **M:** 14.00–17.00; **T:** 14:00–17:00; **W:** 12:00–17:00; **Th:** 14:00–17:00; **F:** 14:00–17:00; **S:** 12:00–17:00. Very small stock. Spec: Archaeology; Authors - Local; Celtica; Conservation; Countries - Scotland; History - Irish; History - Local; History - Scottish. PR: £1–300. CC: MC; V; Switch. Notes: *Also, new books & publisher specialising in West Highland and other Scottish history. new relevant books in natural history etc and maps and guide books.*

ISLE OF IONA

The Iona Bookshop, ■ The Old Printing Press Building, Isle of Iona, Argyll, PA76 6SL. Prop: Angus L. & Alison Johnston. Tel: (01681) 700699. Est: 1978. Shop open: **M:** 10:30–16:30; **T:** 10:30–16:30; **W:** 10:30–16:30; **Th:** 10:30–16:30; **F:** 10:30–16:30; **S:** 10:30–16:30; **Su:** 10:30–16:30. Small stock. Spec: Countries - Scotland; History - Local; Topography - Local. PR: £1–500. Notes: *Winter: open by appointment only. Also, Celtic tapestry kits.*

ORKNEY ISLANDS

Bygone Books, Chuccaby Farm, Longhope, KW16 3PQ. Prop: Isaac Lipkowitz. Tel: (01856) 701443. E-mail: lipkowitz@hotmail.com. Est: 1987. Private premises. Postal Only. Appointment necessary. Very small stock. Spec: Illustrated - General; Kabbala/Cabbala/Cabala; Kabbalah; Magick; Mysticism; Occult; Paganism. PR: £1–200.

WESTERN ISLES

M.E.McCarty, Bookseller, ■ 54 Junction Road, Kirkwall, KW15 1AG. Prop: Moi McCarty. Tel: 01856 870860. E-mail: jim@scapabooks.co.uk. Est: 1986. Shop open: **M:** 10:30–17:00; **T:** 10:30–17:00; **W:** 10:30–17:00; **Th:** 10:30–17:00; **F:** 10:30–17:00; **S:** 10:30–17:00. Closed for lunch: 13:00–1:00. Medium stock. Spec: Literature; Maritime/Nautical; Travel - General. PR: £1–100. CC: AE; JCB; MC; V; Maestro, Solo. Notes: *13 North Main Street ,Wigtown, Scotland (q.v.).*

LOTHIAN

EDINBURGH

Archways Sports Books, P.O. Box 13018, Edinburgh, EH14 2YA. Prop: Iain C. Murray. Web: www.archwaysbooks.com. E-mail: archways@blueyonder.co.uk. Est: 1992. Mail Order Only. Internet and Postal. Appointment necessary. Spec: Sport - General; Sport - American Football; Sport - Athletics; Sport - Basketball; Sport - Boxing; Sport - Cricket; Sport - Cycling; Sport - Football (Soccer). CC: AE; JCB; MC; V. Cata: Sports.

Armchair Books, ■ 72-74 West Port, Edinburgh, EH1 2LE. Prop: David Govan. Tel: (0131) 229-5927. Web: www.armchairbooks.co.uk. E-mail: armchairbooks@hotmail.com. Est: 1989. Shop open: **M:** 10:00–19:00; **T:** 10:00–19:00; **W:** 10:00–19:00; **Th:** 10:00–19:00; **F:** 10:00–18:00; **S:** 10:00–18:00; **Su:** 10:00–18:00. Large stock. Spec: Africana; Annuals; Art; Author - Belloc, Hilaire; - Buchan, John; - Chesterton, G.K.; - Conan Doyle, Sir Arthur; - Kipling, Rudyard. PR: £1–1,000. CC: MC; V.

Aurora Books Ltd, ■ 6, Tanfield, Edinburgh, EH3 5DA. Prop: Tom and Annabel Chambers. Tel: 00 44 (0)131 557 8466. Fax: 00 44 (0)131 557 8466. Web: www.aurorabooks.co.uk. E-mail: aurorabooks@ btconnect.com. Est: 2003. Shop open: **M:** 10:00–18:00; **T:** 10:00–18:00; **W:** 10:00–18:00; **Th:** 10:00– 18:00; **F:** 10:00–18:00; **S:** 10:00–18:00. Spec: Art; Artists; Arts, The; Author - General; Author - 20th Century; Biography; Children's; Countries - General. CC: AE; JCB; MC; V; Maestro, Solo, Visa Electron. VAT No: GB 808 8104 30.

Peter Bell, ■ 68 West Port, Edinburgh, EH1 2LD. Tel: (0131) 556-2198. Fax: (0131) 229-0562. Web: www.peterbell.net. E-mail: books@peterbell.net. Est: 1980. Shop open: **T:** 10:00–17:00; **W:** 10:00– 17:00; **Th:** 10:00–17:00; **F:** 10:00–17:00; **S:** 10:00–17:00. Medium stock. Spec: Academic/Scholarly; Antiquarian; Autobiography; Biography; Company History; Countries - England; Countries - Scotland; Ecclesiastical History & Architecture. PR: £1–500. CC: MC; V. Cata: miscellanies of new stock. Mem: ABA; PBFA. VAT No: GB 416 0959 50.

SCOTLAND

Blacket Books, 1 Leadervale Terrace, Edinburgh, EH16 6NX. Prop: Elizabeth and Ian Laing. Tel: (0131) 666-1542. Web: www.blacketbooks.co.uk. E-mail: liz@blacketbooks.co.uk. Est: 1985. Private premises. Internet and Postal. Telephone First. Small stock. Spec: Children's; Military; Scottish Interest. PR: £10–1,500. CC: JCB; MC; V. Mem: PBFA.

Bookworm, ■ 210 Dalkeith Road, Edinburgh, EH16 5DT. Prop: Peter Ritchie. Tel: (0131) 662-4357. Web: www.scottishbookworm.com. E-mail: peterthebook@btinternet.com. Est: 1986. Shop open: **M:** 09:30–17:30; **T:** 09:30–17:30; **W:** 09:30–17:30; **Th:** 09:30–17:30; **F:** 09:30–17:30; **S:** 09:30–17:15. Medium stock. Spec: Aircraft; Arms & Armour; Art; Art History; Author - Rankin, Ian; Countries - Scotland; Egyptology; Fiction - General. CC: AE; D; JCB; MC; V; SW.

The Bookworm, ■ 210 Dalkeith Road, Edinburgh, EH16 5DT. Prop: Peter Ritchie. Tel: 0131 662 4357. Web: www.scottishbookworm.com. E-mail: peterthebook@btinternet.com. Est: 1989. Shop open: **M:** 09:30–17:30; **T:** 09:30–17:30; **W:** 09:30–17:30; **Th:** 09:30–17:30; **F:** 09:30–17:30; **S:** 09:30–17:00. Spec: Art Reference; Fiction - General; Fiction - Crime, Detective, Spy, Thrillers; Fiction - Fantasy, Horror; Fiction - Science Fiction; Firearms/Guns; History - General; Military. CC: AE; D; JCB; MC; V.

D Robertson (Booksellers & Booksearch Services), 48 Caiystane Avenue, Edinburgh, EH10 6SH. Prop: D Robertson. Tel: 0131 445 1221. Web: www.ukbookworld.com/members/david1955. E-mail: david .robertson@nativeweb.net. Lst. 2006. Mail Order Only. Internet and Postal open: **M:** 09:00–17:30; **T:** 09:00–17:30; **W:** 09:00–17:30; **Th:** 09:00–17:30; **F:** 09:00–17:30; **S:** 09:00–17:30; **Su:** 09:00–17:30; Closed for lunch: 13:00–14:00. Spec: Booksearch. CC: Cash,Cheque, Postal Order, PayPal.

Duncan & Reid, ■ 5 Tanfield, Edinburgh, EH3 5DA. Prop: Maraget Duncan. Tel: 0131 556 4591. Est: 1978. Shop open: **T:** 11:00–17:00; **W:** 11:00–17:00; **Th:** 11:00–17:00; **F:** 11:00–17:00; **S:** 11:00–17:00. Spec: Antiquarian; Antiques; Art; Fashion & Costume; Literature; Scottish Interest. CC: MC; V. Corresp: French and German.

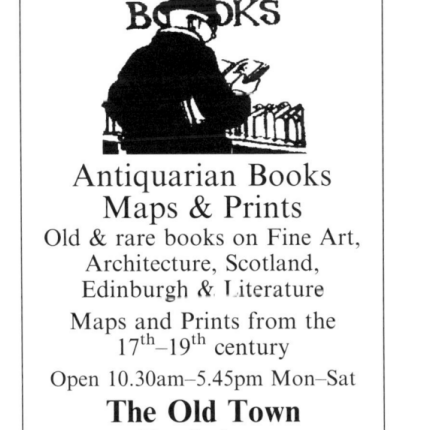

Grant, 14 Winton Drive, Edinburgh, EH10 7ES. Tel: 0131 477 0922. E-mail: bgsc25096@ blueyonder.co.uk. Private premises. Internet and Postal. Open: **S:** 09:00–17:30; **Su:** 09:00–17:30. Spec: Aviation; Military History. Cata: Military, Aviation, 2nd World War. Mem: PBFA.

Grant & Shaw Ltd., 10 Leslie Place, Edinburgh, EH4 1NH. Prop: A.S. Grant. Tel: (0131) 332 8088. Fax: (0131) 332 9080. E-mail: grantshaw@btconnect.com. Est: 1989. Private premises. Appointment necessary. Spec: Antiquarian. PR: £20–10,000. CC: MC; V. Mem: ABA.

Jay Books, Rowll House Roull Grove, Edinburgh, EH12 7JP. Prop: David Brayford. Tel: 0131 316 4034. Web: www.jaybooks.demon.co.uk. E-mail: djb@jaybooks.demon.co.uk. Est: 1977. Private premises. Telephone First. Open: **M:** 09:00–21.00; **T:** 09:00–21.00; **W:** 09:00–21.00; **Th:** 09:00–21.00; **F:** 09:00– 21.00; **S:** 09:00–21.00; **Su:** 09:00–21.00. Spec: Animals and Birds; Antiquarian; Earth Sciences; Flora & Fauna; Natural History; New Naturalist; Ornithology; Science - General. CC: MC; V. Corresp: Spanish German French. Mem: ABA; PBFA; ILAB. Notes: *Valuations for probate and insurance.*

Main Point Books, ■ 8 Lauriston Street, Edinburgh, EH3 9DJ. Prop: Richard Browne. Tel: (0131) 228 4837. Fax: (0131) 228 4837. Est: 2001. Shop open: **T:** 11:00–17:00; **W:** 11:00–17:00; **Th:** 11:00–17:00; **F:** 11:00–17:00; **S:** 11:00–17:00. Medium stock. Spec: Alpinism/Mountaineering; Esoteric; Fiction - General; Literature; Poetry; Scottish Interest; Sport - Climbing & Trekking; Theology.

McNaughtan's Bookshop, ■ 3a and 4a Haddington Place Leith Walk, Edinburgh, EH7 4AE. Prop: Elizabeth A. Strong. Tel: (0131) 556-5897. Fax: (0131) 556 8220. Web: www.mcnaughtansbookshop .com. E-mail: mcnbooks@btconnect.com. Est: 1957. Shop open: **M:** ; **T:** 09:30–17:30; **W:** 09:30–17:30; **Th:** 09:30–17:30; **F:** 09:30–17:30; **S:** 09:30–17:30. Very large stock. Spec: Antiquarian; Applied Art; Architecture; Art; Children's; Cookery/Gastronomy; Countries - Scotland; History - General. PR: £1–3,500. CC: JCB; MC; V; Maestro. Mem: ABA; ILAB. VAT No: GB 327 3505 69.

The Old Town Bookshop, ■ 8 Victoria Street, Edinburgh, EH1 2HG. Prop: Ronald Wilson. Tel: (0131) 225-9237. Fax: (0131) 229-1503. Web: www.oldtownbookshop.co.uk. Est: 1992. Shop open: **M:** 10:30–17:45; **T:** 10:30–17:45; **W:** 10:30–17:45; **Th:** 10:30–17:45; **F:** 10:30–17:45; **S:** 10:00–17:45. Medium stock. Spec: Architecture; Art; Art Reference; Bindings; Botany; Catalogues Raisonnés; Children's; Country Houses. PR: £1–3,000. CC: JCB; MC; V; SW. Mem: PBFA. Notes: *Exhibits at 18 book fairs around the country.*

David Page, 47 Spottiswoode Road, Edinburgh, EH9 1DA. Tel: (0131) 447-4553. Fax: (0131) 447-4553. E-mail: dcampbellpage@blueyonder.co.uk. Private premises. Telephone First. Small stock. Spec: Alpinism/Mountaineering; Mountains; Natural History; Plant Hunting; Travel - General; Travel - Africa; Travel - Asia; Travel - Middle East. Corresp: French, German.

Pinnacle Books, 13 Westgarth Avenue, Edinburgh, EH13 0BB. Tel: 0131 441 3870. Web: www. pinnaclebooks.net. E-mail: pinnaclebooks@blueyonder.co.uk. Private premises. Internet and Postal. Appointment necessary. Spec: Alpinism/Mountaineering; Exploration; Mountain Men; Mountains; Scottish Interest; Sport - Skiing; Travel - Americas; Travel - Asia. Cata: Mountaineering. Mem: PBFA. Notes: *Pinnacle Books is a specialist antiquarian bookshop with a large selection of rare and interesting secondhand books in the following areas - Mountaineering, Central Asia, Polar Exploration, Skiing, Scottish Topography and Travel.*

Andrew Pringle Booksellers, ■ 62 West Port, Edinburgh, EH1 2LD. Tel: (0131) 228-8880. Web: www. pringlebooks.co.uk. E-mail: pringlebooks@yahoo.co.uk. Est: 1988. Shop. Medium stock. Spec: Antiquarian; Art; Biography; History - National; Literature; Modern First Editions; Scottish Interest; Prints and Maps. PR: £3–500. CC: JCB; V; Switch. Corresp: French. Mem: PBFA.

Robertson Books, 60 Craigcrook Road, Edinburgh, EH4 3PJ. Prop. Vanessa Robertson Tel: 0131 343 3118. Web: www.robertsonbooks.co.uk. E-mail: vanessa@robertsonbooks.co.uk. Est: 2003. Private premises. Internet and Postal. Spec: Children's. CC: cheque. Cata: children's books. Mem: Ibooknet. Notes: *Specialists in children's literature.*

Second Edition, ■ 9 Howard Street, Edinburgh, EH3 5JP. Prop: Mrs. Maureen E. and W.A. Smith. Tel: (0131) 556-9403. Web: www.secondeditionbookshop.co.uk. E-mail: secondedition@tiscali.co.uk. Est: 1978. Market Stall. Shop open: **M:** 10:30–17:30; **T:** 10:30–17:30; **W:** 10:30–17:30; **Th:** 10:30–17:30; **F:** 10:30–17:30; **S:** 09:30–17:30. Large stock. Spec: Architecture; Art; Children's; Fine Art; Illustrated - General; Literature; Medicine; Military History. PR: £10–500. Corresp: Spanish.

The Old Children's Bookshelf, ■ 175 Canongate, Edinburgh, EH8 8BN. Prop: Shirley Neilson. Tel: 0131 558 3411. E-mail: shirleyOCB@aol.com. Shop open: **M:** 10:30–17:00; **T:** 10:30–17:00; **W:** 10:30– 17:00; **Th:** 10:30–17:00; **F:** 10:30–17:00; **S:** 10:00–17:00; **Su:** 11:00–16:30. Spec: Annuals; Children's; Children's - Illustrated; Comics; Education & School; Juvenile; Pop-Up, Movable & Cut Out; Scouts & Guides. CC: AE; MC; V. Cata: on children's books only. Mem: PBFA. Notes: *Exhibits at PBFA fairs.*

Till's Bookshop, ■ 1 Hope Park Crescent (Buccleugh Street), Edinburgh, EH8 9NA. Tel: (0131) 667-0895. Web: www.tillsbookshop.co.uk. E-mail: tillsbookshop@btconnect.com. Est: 1986. Shop. Internet and Postal open: **M:** 12:00–19:30; **T:** 12:00–19:30; **W:** 12:00–19:30; **Th:** 12:00–19:30; **F:** 12:00–19:30; **S:** 11:00–18:00; **Su:** 12:00–17:30; Large stock. Spec: Alternative Medicine; Annuals; Arts, The; Children's; Cinema/Film; Classics, The; Comic Books & Annuals; Drama. PR: £2–100. CC: E; MC; V; De, SW, SO. Notes: *We also sell cinema posters, LP's, comics etc. A wide range of subjects, not solely books.*

John Updike Rare Books, 7 St. Bernard's Row, Edinburgh, EH4 1HW. Prop: John S. Watson & Edward G. Nairn. Tel: (0131) 332-1650. Fax: (0131) 332-1347. Est: 1965. Private premises. Appointment necessary. Medium stock. Spec: Books about Books; Children's; Churchilliana; Drama; Fine & Rare; Fine Printing; First Editions; Illustrated - General. Mem: ABA.

HADDINGTON

Yeoman Books, 37 Hope Park Crescent, Haddington, East Lothian, EH41 3AN. Prop: D.A. Hyslop. Tel: (01620) 822307. E-mail: yeomanbooks@talk21.com. Est: 1924. Private premises. Appointment necessary. Very small stock. Spec: Aviation; Military; Military History; Motorbikes / motorcycles; Motoring; War - General. PR: £5–150. Mem: PBFA. Notes: *Also attends PBFA book fairs.*

STRATHCLYDE

AIRDRIE

Brown-Studies, Woodside Cottage Longriggend, Airdrie, ML6 7RU. Prop: (*) Mr. M.G. & Mrs. B.J. Brown. Tel: (01236) 843826. Fax: (01236) 842545. Web: www.brown-studies-books.co.uk. E-mail: brendajbrown@btconnect.com. Est: 1990. Private premises. Internet and Postal. Appointment necessary. Open: **M:** 09:00–20:00; **T:** 09:00–20:00; **W:** 09:00–20:00; **Th:** 09:00–20:00; **F:** 09:00–20:00; **S:** 09:00–20:00; **Su:** 09:00–20:00; Very large stock. Spec: Artists; Author - Read, Miss; Building & Construction; Cookery/Gastronomy; D.I.Y. (Do It Yourself); Ecology; Gardening - General; Herbalism. PR: £3–300. CC: E; JCB; MC; V; Switch. VAT No: GB 556 6923 05. Notes: *Illustrators - J S Goodall.*

AYR

Ainslie Books, ■ 1 Glendoune St., Girvan, Ayr, KA26 0AA. Prop. Gordon Clark. Tel: (01465) 715453. Fax: (01465) 715453. Web: www.ainsliebooks.co.uk. E-mail: sales@ainsliebooks.co.uk. Shop. Internet and Postal open: **M:** 10:00–17:00; **T:** 10:00–17:00; **W:** 10:00–17:00; **Th:** 10:00–17:00; **F:** 10:00–17:00; **S:** 10:00–17:00. Large stock. Spec: Academic/Scholarly; Advertising; Aeronautics; Africana; Shorthand; Booksearch. PR: £1–200. CC: MC; V. Notes: *Free booksearch.*

BIGGAR

Karen Thomson, South Lindsaylands, Biggar, ML12 6NR. Tel: 01899 221991. Fax: 01899 221955. E-mail: kthomson@dircon.co.uk. Est: 1987. Private premises. Postal Only. Open: **W:** 09:00–17:30; **Th:** 09:00–17:30; **F:** 09:00–17:30; **S:** 09:00–17:30; **Su:** 09:00–17:30; Closed for lunch: 13:00–14:00. CC: MC; V.

CAMPBELTOWN

The Old Bookshelf, ■ 8 Cross Street, Campbeltown, PA28 6HU. Prop: Cynthia Byrne. Tel: (01586) 551114. Web: www.theoldbookshelf.co.uk. E-mail: theoldbookshelf@aol.com. Est: 2001. Shop. Internet and Postal open: **M:** 10:00–17:00; **T:** 10:00–17:00; **W:** 10:00–17:00; **Th:** 10:00–17:00; **F:** 10:00–17:00; **S:** 10:00–15:00. Large stock. Spec: History - Local; Scottish Interest; Topography - Local. PR: £2–3,000. CC: AE; E; JCB; MC; V; Maestro. Corresp: Spanish. Mem: ibooknet. VAT No: GB 808 8668 81. Notes: *Books about and on Kintyre.*

GLASGOW

Alba Secondhand Music, ■ 55 Otago Street, Glasgow, G12 8PQ. Prop: Robert Lay. Tel: (0141) 357 1795. Web: www.albamusick.co.uk. E-mail: robert@albamusick.co.uk. Est: 1994. Shop open: **M:** 11:00–17:30; **T:** 11:00–17:30; **W:** 11:00–17:30; **Th:** 11:00–17:30; **F:** 11:00–17:30; **S:** 11:00–17:30. Large stock. Spec: Music - General; Music - Classical; Music - Composers; Music - Folk & Irish Folk; Music - Gilbert & Sullivan; Music - Gregorian Chants; Music - Illustrated Sheet Music; Music - Musicians. PR: £1–100. CC: MC; V. Notes: *Shop located behind Otago cafe & open at other times by appointment.*

SCOTLAND

Jack Baldwin, 34 Hamilton Park Avenue, Glasgow, G12 8DT. Prop: Jack Baldwin. Tel: (0141) 334-8684. Fax: (0141) 334-8684. Web: www.jackbaldwin.dial.pipex.com. E-mail: jackbaldwin@dial.pipex.com. Est: 1985. Private premises. Internet and Postal. Appointment necessary. Small stock. Spec: Antiquarian; Countries - Baltic States; Countries - Latin America; Countries - Mexico; Countries - Portugal; Countries - Russia; Countries - South America; Countries - Spain. PR: £5–1,000. CC: JCB; MC; V. Corresp: French, German, Italian, Spanish, Portuguese.

Caledonia Books, ■ 483 Great Western Road Kelvinbridge, Glasgow, G12 8HL. Prop: Maureen Smillie & Charles McBride. Tel: (0141) 334-9663. Fax: (0141) 334-9663. Web: www.caledoniabooks.co.uk. E-mail: caledoniabooks@aol.com. Est: 1984. Shop open: **M:** 10:00–18:00; **T:** 10:00–18:00; **W:** 10:00–18:00; **Th:** 10:00–18:00; **F:** 10:00–18:00; **S:** 10:00–18:00. Spec: Art; Art History; Bibliography; Biography; Cinema/Film; Countries - Poland; Drama; Fiction - General. PR: £2–200. CC: MC; V.

Cooper Hay Rare Books, ■ 182 Bath Street, Glasgow, G2 4HG. Prop: Cooper Hay and Marianne Hay. Tel: (0141) 333-1992. Fax: (0141) 333-1992. E-mail: chayrbooks@aol.com. Est: 1985. Shop open: **M:** 10:00–17:30; **T:** 10:00–17:30; **W:** 10:00–17:30; **Th:** 10:00–17:30; **F:** 10:00–17:30; **S:** 10:00–13:00. Closed for lunch: 13:00–14:15. Medium stock. Spec: Antiquarian; Art; Art - British; Art Reference; Bibliography; Bindings; Books about Books; Children's - Illustrated. PR: £5–5,000. CC: MC; V. Mem: ABA. VAT No: GB 402 9241 83. Notes: *Attends ABA fairs in Edinburgh and Chelsea.*

The Studio, ■ De Courcy's Arcade 5-21 Cresswell Lane, Glasgow, G12 8AA. Prop: Liz McKelvie. Tel: (0141) 334 8211. Web: www.wglasgowwestend.co.uk/shopping/antiques/studio. E-mail: lizthestudio@aol.com. Est: 1997. Shop open: **M:** ; **T:** 10:00–17:30; **W:** 10:00–17:30; **Th:** 10:00–17:30; **F:** 10:00–17:30; **S:** 10:00–17:30; **Su:** 12:00–17:00. Small stock. Spec: Bindings; Children's - Illustrated; Decorative Art; History - Local; Publishers - Blackie. PR: £5–1,000. CC: D; E; JCB; MC; V; SW, MAE. Notes: *Also, books about Glasgow and Glasgow style antiques, furnishings, metalware, textiles, ceramics - circa 1900.*

Thistle Books, 61 Otago Street, Glasgow, G12 8PQ. Prop: Robert Dibble. Tel: (0141) 334 8777. Est: 1997. Open: **M:** 11:00–17:30; **T:** 11:00–17:30; **W:** 11:00–17:30; **Th:** 11:00–17:30; **F:** 11:00–17:30; **S:** 11:00–17:30. Large stock. Spec: Fiction - General; History - General; History - National; History - Scottish; Literature - Scottish; Modern First Editions; Scottish Interest. PR: £1–100.

GREENOCK

Westwords, ■ 14 Newton Street, Greenock, PA16 8UJ. Tel: (01475) 892467. Est: 1982. Shop. PR: £1–50.

HELENSBURGH

McLaren Books, 22 John Street, Helensburgh, G84 8BA. Tel: (01436) 676453. Fax: (01436) 673747. Web: www.mclarenbooks.co.uk. E-mail: george@mclarenbooks.demon.co.uk. Est: 1976. Office and/or bookroom open: **F:** 10:00–17:00; **S:** 10:00–17:00. Medium stock. Spec: Manuals - Seamanship (see also under Seamanship); Maritime/Nautical; Maritime/Nautical - Log Books; Naval; Navigation; Ship Modelling; Shipbuilding and Shipping; Sport - Canoeing/Kayaks. PR: £5–2,000. CC: MC; V; Switch. Mem: ABA; PBFA; ILAB. VAT No: GB 293 0008 81. Notes: *Open at other times by appointment.*

IRVINE

D. Webster, 43 West Road, Irvine, KA12 8RE. Tel: (01294) 272257. Fax: (01294) 276322. Est: 1958. Private premises. Appointment necessary. Small stock. Spec: Circus; Physical Culture; Sport - Highland Games; Sport - Weightlifting/Bodybuilding; Sport - Wrestling; Booksearch; Collectables; Ephemera. PR: £5–40. Notes: *Also, booksearch. davidpwebster@hotmail com.*

KILMARNOCK

Roberts Books, 8, Main Road, Waterside, Kilmarnock, KA3 6JB. Prop: Richard Roberts. Tel: (01560) 600349. Fax: (01560) 600349. Web: www.ukbookworld.com/members/roberts. E-mail: books@clanroberts.net. Est: 1976. Private premises. Internet and Postal. Appointment necessary. Small stock. Spec: Academic/Scholarly; British Books; Building & Construction; Countries - England; Countries - Japan; Countries - Scotland; Earth Sciences; Engineering. PR: £5–450. Corresp: French, German.

TAYSIDE

ABERFELDY

Freader's Books, ■ 8 Dunkeld Street, Aberfeldy, PH15 2DA. Prop: Christopher Rowley. Tel: (01887) 829519. Fax: (01887) 829519. E-mail: Rowley@freaders.freeserve.co.uk. Est: 1991. Shop open: **M:** 10:00–16:00; **T:** 10:00–16:00; **W:** ; **Th:** 10:00–16:00; **F:** 10:00–16:00; **S:** 10:00–16:00. Closed for lunch: 13:00–14:00. Very small stock. Spec: Countries - Scotland; General; Natural History; Physics; Scottish Interest; Topography - General; Topography - Local. PR: £4–200. Mem: BA.

ARBROATH

A Jolly Good Read, 94 Brechin Road, Arbroath, DD11 1SX. Tel: (01241) 877552. Web: www. ajollygoodread.co.uk. E-mail: books@ajollygoodread.co.uk. Est: 2004. Private premises. Internet and Postal. Contactable. Small stock. Spec: Children's. PR: £5–500. CC: PayPal. Cata: Childrens Books.

BLAIR ATHOLL

Atholl Browse, ■ by the Station, Blair Atholl, PH18 5SG. Prop: John and Mary Herdman. Tel: 01796 481530. Web: www.athollbrowse.co.uk. E-mail: mary@athollbrowse.co.uk. Est: 1989. Shop open: **M:** 11.00–17:00; **T.** 11.00–17:00; **W:** 11.00–17:00; **Th:** 11.00–17:00; **F:** 11.00–17:00; **S:** 11.00–17:00; **Su:** 12:00–17:00. Spec: Scottish Interest. Notes: *Open March-November.*

BLAIRGOWRIE

Blairgowrie Books, ■ 3 Meadow Place, Blairgowrie, PH10 6NG. Prop: Marlene Hill. Tel: 01250 875855. E-mail: marlene.hill@tiscali.co.uk. Est: 1981. Shop open: **M:** 09:00–17:30; **T:** 09:00–17:30; **W:** 09:00– 17:30; **Th:** 09:00–17:30; **F:** 09:00–17:30; **S:** 09:00–17:30; **Su:** 09:00–17:30; Closed for lunch: 13:00– 14:00. Spec: Ephemera; Prints and Maps.

DUNDEE

Big Bairn Books, ■ 17 Exchange Street, Dundee, DD1 3DJ. Prop: Douglas Hill. Tel: 01382 220225. E-mail: bigbairn@btconnect.com. Est: 1998. Shop open: **M:** 10:30–17:00; **T:** 10:30–17:00; **W:** 10:30– 17:00; **Th:** 10:30–17:00; **F:** 10:30–17:00; **S:** 10:30–17:00. Spec: Annuals; Art; Military; Poetry; Scottish Interest; Sport - Angling/Fishing; Sport - Football (Soccer); Sport - Golf. Notes: *Also, postcards and greetings cards.*

FORFAR

Hilary Farquharson, Deuchar Farm, Fern, Forfar, DD8 3QZ. Prop: H. Farquharson. Tel: (01356) 650278. Fax: (01356) 650417. E-mail: deucharfarm@btopenworld.com. Est: 1992. Private premises. Book fairs only. Appointment necessary. Open: **M:** 09:00–21:00; **T:** 09:00–21:00; **W:** 09:00–21:00; **Th:** 09:00–21:00; **F:** 09:00–21:00; **S:** 09:00–21:00; **Su:** 09:00–21:00. Medium stock. Spec: Agriculture; Antiquarian; Architecture; Authors - Local; Countries - Scotland; Farming & Livestock; Fine & Rare; Genealogy. PR: £5–1,000. CC: JCB; MC; V. Mem: PBFA.

KILLIECRANKIE

Atholl Fine Books, Clunemore, Killiecrankie, Pitlochry, PH16 5LS. Prop: Nancy Foy Cameron. Tel: 01796 473470. E-mail: nancy.foy@btinternet.com. Est: 1988. Private premises. Internet and Postal. Appointment necessary. Open: **M:** 09:00–17:30; **T:** 09:00–17:30; **W:** 09:00–17:30; **Th:** 09:00–17:30; **F:** 09:00–17:30; **S:** 09:00–17:30; **Su:** 09:00–17:30; Closed for lunch: 13:00–14:00. Spec: Antiquarian, Author - Pennant, Thomas; Authors - Local; Bindings; Countries - Scotland; Fine & Rare; Fine leather bindings (see also Fine & Rare); Fishes. CC: MC; V. Corresp: French. Notes: *Very happy to deal over the phone, 01796 473 470.*

MONTROSE

Devanha Military Books, 4 Castle Terrace, Inverbervie, Montrose, DD10 0RE. Prop: Nick Ducat. Tel: (01561) 361387. E-mail: nickducat@devbooks.fsnet.co.uk. Est: 2001. Private premises. Postal Only. Small stock. Spec: Military; Military History. PR: £5–350.

SCOTLAND

PERTH

Bookseeker, P O Box 7535, Perth, PH2 1AF. Prop: Paul Thompson. Tel: (01738) 620688. Web: www. bookseeker.myby.co.uk. E-mail: Bookseeker@blueyonder.co.uk. Private premises. Postal Only. Spec: Quakers, The; Religion - Quakers; Booksearch. Notes: *Booksearch only. Specialise in Quakerism, but will look for anything.*

PITLOCHRY

Glacier Books, Ard-Darach Strathview Terrace, Pitlochry, PH16 5AT. Prop: Chris Bartle. Tel: (01796) 470056. Fax: (01796) 470056. Web: www.glacierbooks.com. E-mail: sales@glacierbooks.com. Est: 1999. Private premises. Internet and Postal. Telephone First. Open: **M:** 10:00–15:00; **W:** 10:00–15:00; **F:** 10:00–15:00. Medium stock. Spec: Alpinism/Mountaineering; Calligraphy; Countries - Antarctic, The; Countries - Canada; Countries - France; Countries - Greenland; Countries - Himalayas, The; Countries - Iceland. PR: £1–3,000. CC: MC; V. Cata: Mountaineering, Polar.

STRATHTAY

Strathtay Antiquarian - Secondhand Books, Upper Derculich, Pitlochry, Strathtay, PH9 0LR. Prop: Alistair and Pamela Robinson. Tel: 01887 840373. Fax: 01887 840777. E-mail: airr@aol.com. Est: 2006. Private premises. Internet and Postal. Open: **M:** 09:00–17:30; **T:** 09:00–17:30; **W:** 09:00–17:30; **Th:** 09:00–17:30; **F:** 09:00–17:30; **S:** 09:00–17:30; **Su:** 09:00–17:30; Closed for lunch: 13:00–14:00. Spec: Antiques; Biography; Children's; Fiction - General; Modern First Editions; Scottish Interest; Sport - Field Sports; Sport - Golf.

WALES

The Unitary Authorities of Caerphilly, Cardiff, Carmarthenshire, Ceredigion, Conwy, Denbighshire, Dyfed, Flintshire, Gwynedd, Monmouthshire, Neath Port Talbot, Newport, Powys, Rhondda Cynon Taff, Swansea and Wrexham.

CAERPHILLY

NEW TREDEGAR

Tom Saunders, 9 Woodland Terrace, New Tredegar, NP24 6LL. Tel: (01443) 836946. Fax: (02920) 371921. E-mail: saunderstgc@tiscali.co.uk. Est: 1989. Private premises. Postal Only. Telephone First. Small stock. Spec: Academic/Scholarly; Biography; Chess; Children's; Education & School; Politics; Religion - General; Sport - American Football. PR: £3–50.

CARDIFF

CARDIFF

Bear Island Books, ■ Cardiff Central Market St. Mary Street, Cardiff, CF10 1AU. Tel: (029) 2038 8631. E-mail: bearislandbooks@talk21.com. Shop open: **M:** 10:00–17:00; **T:** 10:00–17:00; **W:** 10:00–17:00; **Th:** 10:00–17:00; **F:** 10:00–17:00; **S:** 10:00–17:00. Spec: History - Local; Topography - Local; Welsh Interest. CC: PayPal.

Capital Bookshop, ■ 27 Morgan Arcade, Cardiff, CF10 1AF. Prop: A.G. Mitchell. Tel: (029) 2038-8423. E-mail: capitalbooks@cardiffwales.fsnet.co.uk. Est: 1981. Shop open: **M:** 10:00–17:30; **T:** 10:00– 17:30; **W:** 10:00–17:30; **Th:** 10:00–17:30; **F:** 10:00–17:30; **S:** 10:00–17:30. Large stock. Spec: Antiquarian; Countries - Wales; Booksearch; Prints and Maps. PR: £1–500. CC: E; MC; V; Maestro, Solo. Mem: PBFA.

Len Foulkes, 28 St. Augustine Road Heath, Cardiff, CF14 4RE. Tel: (029) 2062-7703. Est: 1971. Private premises. Postal Only. Very large stock. PR: £5–100. Notes: *Now semi-retired.*

Whitchurch Books Ltd., ■ 67 Merthyr Road, Whitchurch, Cardiff, CF14 1DD. Prop: Mr. G.L. Canvin. Tel: (029) 2052-1956. Fax: (029) 2062-3599. E-mail: whitchurchbooks@btopenworld.com. Est: 1994. Shop open: **T:** 10:00–17:30; **W:** 10:00–17:30; **Th:** 10:00–17:30; **F:** 10:00–17:30; **S:** 10:00–17:30. Very large stock. Spec: Anthropology; Archaeology; Art History; Arthurian; Byzantium; Cookery/ Gastronomy; Countries - Wales; Ecclesiastical History & Architecture. PR: £1–100. CC: AE; D; E; JCB; MC; V; SW; S; EL. Mem: WBA. VAT No: GB 648 3263 23. Notes: *Also, a booksearch service.*

Nicholas Willmott Bookseller, 97 Romilly Road, Canton, Cardiff, CF5 1FN. Prop: Nicholas Willmott & Judith Wayne. Tel: (029) 2037-7268. Fax: (029) 2037-7268. Web: www.members.lycos.co.uk/ nicholaswillmott/id17.htm. E-mail: willmott_wayne@hotmail.com. Est: 1982. Private premises. Postal Only. Contactable. Large stock. Spec: Authors - Women; Autobiography; Biography; Drama; Feminism; Fiction - General; History - General; Humour. PR: £2–500. Corresp: French. VAT No: GB 368 3564 19. Notes: *Freelance tenor.*

CARMARTHENSHIRE

AMMANFORD

Discovery Bookshop, 52 Cwmamman Road, Garnant, Ammanford, SA18 1LT. Prop: George & Kate Stent. Tel: 01269 823839. Web: www.discoverybookshop.co.uk. E-mail: discovery@ garnant.fsworld.co.uk. Est: 2002. Shop and/or showroom open: **M:** 10:00–17:00; **T:** 10:00–17:00; **W:** 10:00–17:00; **Th:** 10:00–17:00; **F:** 10:00–17:00. Spec: Aircraft; Americana - General; Art; Autobiography; Biblical Studies; Biography; Cookery/Gastronomy; Crafts. CC: PayPal. Notes: *Retail/trade sales through the shop premises. Direct sales over the phone and internet sales through three internet sites.*

WALES

Stobart Davies Limited, Stobart House, Pontyclerc, Penybanc Road, Ammanford, SA18 3HP. Tel: (01269) 593100. Fax: (01269) 596116. Web: www.stobartdavies.com. E-mail: sales@ stobartdavies.com. Est: 1989. Office and/or bookroom. Internet and Postal open: **M:** 09:00–17:00; **T:** 09:00–17:00; **W:** 09:00–17:00; **Th:** 09:00–17:00; **F:** 09:00–17:00; **S:** . Very large stock. Spec: Building & Construction; Crafts; D.I.Y. (Do It Yourself); Forestry; Woodwork. PR: £3–60. CC: AE; D; MC; V. Mem: BA;

CARMARTHEN

Sue Lloyd-Davies, 94 St. Catherine Street, Carmarthen, SA31 1RF. Prop: Sue Lloyd-Davies. Tel: (01267) 235462. Fax: (01267) 235462. E-mail: sue@lloyd-davies.fsnet.co.uk. Est: 1979. Private premises. Internet and Postal. Telephone First. Open: **M:** 10:00–20.00; **T:** 10:00–20.00; **W:** 10:00–20.00; **Th:** 10:00–20.00; **F:** 10:00–20.00; **S:** 10:00–20.00; **Su:** 11:0–20.00; Closed for lunch: odd–times. Medium stock. Spec: Annuals; Children's; Children's - Illustrated; First Editions; General Stock; Illustrated - General; Literature; Travel - General. PR: £5–2,000. CC: E; JCB; MC; V; Switch etc. Corresp: French Japanese Welsh. Mem: PBFA; WBA. Notes: *Traded for 27+ years, to date, now mainly selling online and exhibiting at Major London Bookfairs only. View by Appointment. Happy to see customers but they must be able to squeeze through the book aisles/piles! Regret no wheelchair access.*

CEREDIGION

ABERYSTWYTH

Colin Hancock, Ty'n Y Llechwedd Hall, Llandre, Aberystwyth, SY24 5BX. Prop: Colin Hancock. Tel: 01970 828709. Fax: 01970 828709. E-mail: colin-hancock@wales-books.demon.co.uk. Est: 1998. Private premises. Appointment necessary. Shop At: Colin Hancock, Ty'n Y Llechwedd Hall, Llandre, Aberystwyth, Ceredigion. SY24 5BX. Spec: Antiquarian; Archaeology; Celtica; Countries - Wales; Culture - National; Fine & Rare; Fine Printing; History - Local. Corresp: French, Welsh. Mem: Welsh Booksellers Association.

Ystwyth Books, ■ 7 Princess Street, Aberystwyth, SY23 1DX. Prop: Mrs. H.M. Hinde. Tel: (01970) 639479. Est: 1976. Shop open: **M:** 09:30–17:15; **T:** 09:30–17:15; **W:** 09:30–17:15; **Th:** 09:30–17:15; **F:** 09:30–17:15; **S:** 09:30–17:15. Medium stock. Spec: Countries - Wales; History - Industrial; Technology; Topography - Local. PR: £2–100. CC: MC; V. Mem: BA. VAT No: GB 124 7218 86.

CARDIGAN

Books in Cardigan, ■ 2, Pwllhai, Cardigan, SA43 1BZ. Prop: Mary Sinclair. Tel: (012 39) 682517. Web: www.http://cardiganbooks.hypermart.net/. E-mail: csinclair@lineone.net. Est: 1986. Shop. Internet and Postal open: **M:** 09:00–17:00; **T:** 09:00–17:00; **W:** 09:00–17:00; **Th:** 09:00–17:00; **F:** 09:00–17:00; **S:** 09:00–17:00. Large stock. Spec: Travel - General; Welsh Interest. Corresp: French, Spanish, Portuguese. Notes: *Cardigan Market Stall open 6 days a week.*

LAMPETER

Barry Thomas Poultry Books, The Vicarage, Felinfach, Lampeter, SA48 8AE. Tel: (01570) 470944. Fax: (01570) 471557. E-mail: barry.thomas3@tiscali.co.uk. Est: 1976. Private premises. Internet and Postal. Contactable. Open: **M:** 09:00–21:00; **T:** 09:00–21:00; **W:** 09:00–21:00; **Th:** 09:00–21:00; **F:** 09:00–21:00. Very small stock. Spec: Cockfighting; Poultry; Ephemera; Prints and Maps. PR: £1– 1,000. Corresp: French, German, Welsh.

TREGARON

Nigel Bird (Books), Bryn Hir Llwynygroes, Tregaron, SY25 6PY. Prop: Nigel & Sue Bird. Tel: (01974) 821281. Fax: (01974) 821548. Web: www.nigelbirdbooks.co.uk. E-mail: nigelbird.books@virgin.net. Est: 1985. Private premises. Internet and Postal. Telephone First. Medium stock. Spec: Author - Rolt, L.T.C.; Canals/Inland Waterways; Railways; Transport. PR: £1–200. CC: E; JCB; MC; V. Cata: Railways. VAT No: GB 549 6927 83. Notes: *I offer a booksearch service for railway titles only.*

CONWY

COLWYN BAY

Bay Bookshop, ■ 14 Seaview Road, Colwyn Bay, LL29 8DG. Prop: A.P. Morley. Tel: (01492) 531642. Web: www.baybookshop.co.uk. E-mail: andy@baybookshop.fsnet.co.uk. Est: 1971. Shop open: **M:** 09:30–17:30; **T:** 09:30–17:30; **W:** 09:30–17:30; **Th:** 09:30–17:30; **F:** 09:30–17:30; **S:** 09:30–17:30. Spec: Collectables; Ephemera; Prints and Maps. PR: £1–500. CC: E; MC; V.

Colwyn Books, ■ 66 Abergele Road, Colwyn Bay, LL29 7PP. Prop: John & Linda Beagan. Tel: (01492) 530683. E-mail: colwynbooks@waitrose.com. Est: 1989. Shop open: **M:** 09:30–17:00; **T:** 09:30–17:00; **W:** 09:30–13:00; **Th:** 09:30–17:00; **F:** 09:30–17:00; **S:** 09:30–17:00. Closed for lunch: 13:00–13:30. Medium stock. Spec: Countries - France; Fiction - General; Foreign Texts; New Books; Publishers - Haynes Publishing; Religion - General; Theology; Booksearch. PR: £1–15. Cata: Religion and theology. Corresp: Welsh. Mem: Welsh Booksellers Assoc. Notes: *Also selling new books published by Gwasg Carreg Gwalch, and hand-made bookmarks and greetings cards.*

D. Gathern, 42a Seaview Road, Colwyn Bay, LL29 8DG. Prop: David Gathern. Tel: 01492 532569. E-mail: deagathern@btinternet.com. Private premises. Appointment necessary. Open. **M:** 09:30–17.30; **T:** 09:30–17.30; **W:** 09:30–17.30; **Th:** 09:30–17.30; **F:** 09:30–17.30; **S:** 09:30–17.30; **Su:** 10.00–17.30; Medium stock. Spec: Sport - General; Sport - Baseball; Sport - Cricket; Sport - Football (Soccer); Sport - Golf. CC: PayPal.

owenbooks65, 13 Wynn Drive, Old Colwyn, Colwyn Bay, LL29 9DE. Prop: Jack Owen. Tel: (01492) 516600. E-mail: owenbooks65@hotmail.com. Est: 1989. Private premises. Internet Only. Appointment necessary. Small stock. Spec: Countries - Europe; Countries - France; Foreign Texts; Languages - African; Languages - Foreign; Languages - National. CC: PayPal. Cata: Foreign languages. Corresp: French, Italian, German, Spanish. Mem: WBA. Notes: *on Amazon and Biblio.*

Rhos Point Books, ■ 85 The Promenade Rhos–on–Sea, Colwyn Bay, LL28 4PR. Prop: Gwyn & Beryl Morris. Tel: (01492) 545236. Fax: (01492) 540862. Web: www.ukbookworld.com/members/brynglas. E-mail: rhos.point@btinternet.com. Est: 1986. Shop. Internet and Postal open: **M:** 10:00–17:30; **T:** 10:00–17:30; **W:** 10:00–17:30; **Th:** 10:00–17:30; **F:** 10:00–17:30; **S:** 10:00–17:30; **Su:** 11:00–17:30; Medium stock. Spec: Antiquarian; Welsh Interest. PR: £1–300. CC: AE; MC; V Corresp: Welsh.

Yesterday's News, 43 Dundonald Road, Colwyn Bay, LL29 7RE. Prop: Elfed Jones. Tel: (01492) 531195. Web: www.giftnewspapers.co.uk/. E-mail: elfedjones@btinternet.com. Est: 1967. Private premises open: **M:** 09:00–21:00; **T:** 09:00–21:00; **W:** 09:00–21:00; **Th:** 09:00–21:00; **F:** 09:00–21:00; **S:** 09:00–21:00. Very large stock. Spec: Broadcasting; Canadiana; Churchilliana; Cinema/Film; Comic Books & Annuals; Comics; Crime (True); Entertainment - General. PR: £5–50. Corresp: German, Welsh. Notes: *Majors in newspapers, periodicals and paper ephemera.*

CONWY

Prospect Books, 10 Trem Arfon, Llanrwst, LL26 0BP. Prop: M. R. Dingle. Tel: 01492 640111. Web: www.gunbooks.co.uk. E-mail: prospectbooks@aol.com. Est: 1982. Private premises. Appointment necessary. Open: **M:** 09:00–15:30; **T:** 09:00–15:30; **W:** 09:00–15:30; **Th:** 09:00–15:30; **F:** 09:00–15:30. Spec: Arms & Armour; Firearms/Guns; Weapons. CC: JCB; MC; V; Maestro/Switch. Cata: weapons. Notes: *Specialist books on weaponry.*

OLD COLWYN

J V Owen, 13 Wynn Drive, Old Colwyn, LL29 9DE. Tel: (01492) 516600. Fax: (01492) 516600. E-mail: owenbooks65@hotmail.com. Est: 2002. Private premises. Postal Only. Appointment necessary. Small stock. Spec: Countries - France; Foreign Texts; Languages - Foreign. PR: £1–100. CC: PayPal. Cata: Foreign languages. Corresp: French, German, Italian. Mem: WBA.

E. Wyn Thomas, Old Quarry 9 Miners Lane, Old Colwyn, LL29 9HG. Prop: E. Wyn Thomas. Tel: (01492) 515336. Est: 1947. Private premises. Postal Only. Appointment necessary. Small stock. Spec: Countries - Wales; Fiction - General; History - General; Natural History; Topography - Local; Prints and Maps. PR: £1–1,000. Corresp: Welsh.

WALES

TREFRIW

Roz Hulse, Llanrwst Road, Trefriw, LL27 0JR. Prop: Roz Hulse. Tel: (01492) 640963. Web: www.rozhulse.com. E-mail: roz@rozhulse.com. Est: 2004. Private premises. Internet and Postal. Appointment necessary. Small stock. Spec: Academic/Scholarly; Alpinism/Mountaineering; American Northwest; Animals and Birds; Antiquarian; Atlases; Author - Barrie, J.M.; Author - Beardsley, Aubrey. PR: £40–5,000. CC: MC; V. Notes: *Very good International Customer Support offered. Response to all contact within 8 hours. Beautiful Books and Maps.*

DENBIGHSHIRE

LLANGOLLEN

Books, ■ 17 Castle Street, Llangollen, LL20 8NY. Prop: Mr. Thor Sever. Tel: (01978) 860334. Web: www.llangollen.org.uk/pages/books.htm. E-mail: books@easynet.co.uk. Est: 1983. Shop open: **M:** 10:00–17:00; **T:** 10:00–17:00; **W:** 10:00–17:00; **Th:** 10:00–17:00; **F:** 10:00–17:00; **S:** 10:00–17:00; **Su:** 10:00–17:00. Spec: Alpinism/Mountaineering; American Indians; Art; Astrology; Cinema/Film; Countries - Melanesia; Folklore; Gardening - General. PR: £3–50. CC: JCB; MC; V.

RHYL

Siop y Morfa, ■ 109 Stryd Fawr, Rhyl, Sir Ddinbych, LL18 1TR. Prop: Dafydd Timothy. Tel: (01745) 339197. Web: www.siopymorfa.com. E-mail: dafydd@siopymorfa.com. Est: 1980. Shop. Internet and Postal open: **M:** 09:30–17:30; **T:** 09:30–17:30; **W:** 09:30–17:30; **Th:** 09:30–17:30; **F:** 09:30–16:30; **S:** 09:30–17:30. Closed for lunch: 13:00–14:00. Medium stock. Spec: History - National; Literature; Welsh Interest. PR: £5–200. CC: AE; JCB; MC; V; Solo. Corresp: French, Cymraeg/Welsh. Mem: PBFA. VAT No: GB 771 0696 20.

FLINTSHIRE

MOLD

BOOKS4U, 7 The Firs, Mold, CH7 1JX. Prop: Norman MacDonald. Tel: (01352) 751121. Web: www.http://ukbookworld.com/members/bks4u. E-mail: norman_macdonald@btinternet.com. Est: 1997. Private premises. Internet and Postal. Appointment necessary. Spec: Academic/Scholarly; Aeronautics; Agriculture; Aircraft; Animals and Birds; Annuals; Antiquarian; Antiquities. PR: £4– 1,500. CC: PayPal.

GLAMORGAN

FERNDALE

Norman F. Hight, 149 North Road, Ferndale, CF43 4RA. Tel: (01443 756552. E-mail: norman.f.hight@ care4free.net. Est: 1998. Private premises. Internet and Postal. Appointment necessary. Open: **M:** 10:00–19:00; **T:** 10:00–18:00; **W:** 10:00–19:00; **Th:** 10:00–19:00; **F:** 10:00–18:00; **S:** 10:00–14:00. Small stock. Spec: Fiction - Crime, Detective, Spy, Thrillers; Fiction - Fantasy, Horror; Fiction - Science Fiction; Modern First Editions. PR: £1–200. CC: PayPal.

GWENT

CHEPSTOW

Glance Back Books, 17 Upper Church Street, Chepstow, NP6 5EX. Prop: Greg Lance–Watkins. Tel: (01291) 626562. Fax: (01291) 626562. Web: www.glanceback.co.uk. E-mail: greg@glanceback .demon.co.uk. Est: 1981. Private premises. Internet and Postal. PR: £1–2,000. CC: PayPal. Notes: *Large general stock.*

GWYNED

BANGOR

The Muse Bookshop, ■ 43 Holyhead Road, Bangor, LL57 2EU. Prop: Huw Jones. Tel: (01248) 362072. Fax: (01248) 362072. E-mail: themusebookshop@yahoo.co.uk. Est: 1992. Shop open: **M:** 09:00–17:30; **T:** 09:00–17:30; **W:** 09:00–17:30; **Th:** 09:00–18:30; **F:** 09:00–17:30; **S:** 10:00–16:30. Medium stock. Spec: Aboriginal; Academic/Scholarly; Accountancy; Adirondack Mountains, The; Adult; Alpinism/Mountaineering; Natural History; New Naturalist. PR: £1–500. CC: MC; V. Mem: BA; Notes: *Also, new books.*

BETHESDA

A.E. Morris, ■ 40 High Street, Bethesda, LL57 3AN. Tel: (01248) 602533. Est: 1987. Shop open: **M:** 10:00–17:00; **T:** 10:00–17:00; **W:** 10:00–17:00; **Th:** 10:00–17:00; **F:** 10:00–17:00; **S:** 10:00–17:00. Spec: Prints and Maps. PR: £1–100.

BLAENAU FFESTINIOG

P. & D. Doorbar, Min-y-ffordd Bethania, Blaenau Ffestiniog, LL41 3LZ. Prop: Mr. K.P. & Mr. D.L. Doorbar. Tel: (01766) 831995. Fax: (01766) 831995. Web: www.doorbar.co.uk/books/. E-mail: books@doorbar.co.uk. Est: 1991. Shop and/or showroom. Internet and Postal. Contactable. Shop At: Llyfrau Llanbedr Books, Wenallt, Llanbedr, Gwynedd LL45 2LD. Open: **M:** ; **T:** 13:30–17:00; **S:** 10:30–17:00. Small stock. Spec: Art; Art - Technique; Art History; Art Reference; Children's; Children's - Illustrated; Dogs; Gypsies. PR: £5–500. Mem: PBFA.

Siop Lyfrau'r Hen Bost, ■ 45 High Street, Blaenau Ffestiniog, LL41 3AA. Prop: Elin Angharad Jones. Tel: (01766) 831802. E-mail: henbost.blaenau@virgin.net. Est: 1988. Shop open: **M:** 10:00–16.30; **T:** 10:00–16.30; **W:** 10:00–16.30; **Th:** 10:00–16.30; **F:** 10:00–16.30; **S:** 10:00–16.30. Medium stock. Spec: Countries - Wales; History - Local; Journals; Literature; New Books; Welsh Interest; Ephemera. PR: £1–200. Corresp: Welsh. Mem: BA; WBA. Notes: *Large stock of out of print Welsh books.*

CRICCIETH

Capel Mawr Collectors Centre, ■ 21 High Street, Criccieth, LL52 0BS. Prop: Alun & Dee Turner. Tel: (01766) 523600. E-mail: capelmawr@aol.com. Est: 1998. Shop open: **M:** 11:00–17:00; **T:** 11:00–17:00; **W:** 11:00–17:00; **Th:** 11:00–17:00; **F:** 11:00–17:00; **S:** 11:00–17:00; **Su:** 11:00–16:00. Very large stock. Spec: Cinema/Film; Comics; Cookery/Gastronomy; Counterculture; Fiction - General; Food & Drink; Sport - General; Theology. PR: £1–100. CC: AE; E; JCB; MC; V. Notes: *Winter opening Thursday, Friday, Saturday 10:00–17:00. Also, collectables & ephemera.*

DOLGELLAU

Cader Idris Bookshop, ■ 2 Maldwyn House Finsbury Square, Dolgellau, LL40 1TR. Prop: Barbara Beeby & Son. Tel: 07743378300. Web: www.dyfivalleybookshop.com. E-mail: bceb@ dvbookshop.fsnet.co.uk. Shop. Telephone First. Spec: Mem: WBA. Notes: *Sister shop to The Dyfi Valley Bookshop. Machynlleth.*

MONMOUTHSHIRE

ABERGAVENNY

Books for Writers, 'Avondale' 13 Lansdown Drive, Abergavenny, NP7 6AW. Prop: Ms. Sonia A. Hughes. Tel: (01873) 853967. Est: 1999. Private premises. Postal Only. Very small stock. Spec: Biography; Fiction - General; Reference; Booksearch. PR: £2–50.

Skirrid Books, 58 Poplars Road Mardy, Abergavenny, NP7 6LX. Prop: Mrs. G.M. Parry. Tel: (01873) 857004. E-mail: skirbook@skirbook.freeserve.co.uk. Est: 1995. Private premises. Appointment necessary. Small stock. Spec: Fiction - Supernatural. PR: £5–200. CC: E; JCB; MC; V; PayPal.

WALES

LLANVAPLEY

Monmouth House Books, Monmouth House, Llanvapley, Abergavenny, NP7 8SN. Prop: Richard Sidwell. Tel: (01600) 780236. Fax: (01600) 780532. Web: www.monmouthhousebooks.co.uk. E-mail: monmouthhousebooks@compuserve.com. Est: 1985. Private premises. Postal Only. Small stock. Spec: Architecture. PR: £5–1,000. Cata: Architecture & related subjects. VAT No: GB 615 8003 63. Notes: *Booksearch & stock lists on architecture only. Publishes facsimile reprints of early architectural books.*

TINTERN

Stella Books, ■ Monmouth Road, Tintern, NP16 6SE. Prop: Chris Tomaszewski. Tel: (01291) 689755. Fax: (01291) 689998. Web: www.stellabooks.com. E-mail: enquiry@stellabooks.com. Est: 1990. Shop open: **M:** 09:30–17:30; **T:** 09:30–17:30; **W:** 09:30–17:30; **Th:** 09:30–17:30; **F:** 09:30–17:30; **S:** 09:30–17:30; **Su:** 09:30–17:30. Very large stock. Spec: Agriculture; Aircraft; Animals and Birds; Annuals; Antiquarian; Antiques; Army, The; Author - Blyton, Enid. PR: £1–3,000. CC: AE; JCB; MC; V. Cata: all. Corresp: French. Mem: PBFA; Ibooknet.co.uk. VAT No: GB 667 0422 36. Notes: *Wants matching. Let us know your interests and books you are seeking. Over 4,000 different catalogues issued quarterly by email and post. Partner shop: Rose's Books., 14 Broad Street, Hay-On-Wye, HR3 5DB.*

PEMBROKESHIRE

NEWPORT

Carningli Centre, ■ East St, Newport, SA42 0SY. Prop: Ann Gent. Tel: 01239 820724. Web: www.carningli.co.uk. E-mail: info@carningli.co.uk. Est: 1982. Shop open: **M:** 10:00–17:30; **T:** 10:00–17:30; **W:** 10:00–17:30; **Th:** 10:00–17:30; **F:** 10:00–17:30; **S:** 10:00–17:30. Spec: Agriculture; Animals and Birds; Anthologies; Antiques; Art; Cookery/Gastronomy; Countries - Wales; D.I.Y. (Do It Yourself). CC: AE; MC; V; Maestro. VAT No: GB 491 0134 72.

TENBY

Cofion Books, ■ Bridge Street, Tenby, SA70 7BU. Prop: Albie Smosarski. Tel: (01834) 845741. Fax: (01834) 843864. Web: www.cofion.com. E-mail: albie@cofion.com. Est: 1994. Shop open: **M:** 10:30–17:30; **T:** 10:30–17:30; **W:** 10:30–17:30; **Th:** 10:30–17:30; **F:** 10:30–17:30; **S:** 10:30–17:30; **Su:** 11:30–17:30. Very large stock. Spec: Animals and Birds; Art; Art Reference; Arthurian; Astrology; Author - Thomas, Dylan; Autobiography; Biography. PR: £1–500. Notes: *Stock includes illustrated titles covering Pembrokeshire.*

POWYS

BEULAH

Myra Dean Illustrated Books, Crossways, Beulah, LD5 4UB. Prop: Myra Dean. Tel: (01591) 620647. Web: www.myradean-illustatedbooks.co.uk. E-mail: myra.dean@hotmail.co.uk. Est: 1984. Private premises. Internet and Postal. Telephone First. Very small stock. Spec: Children's; Fine & Rare; Fine Printing; Illustrated - General; Limited Editions - General; Limited Editions - Club Books; Printing; Private Press. PR: £5–2,000. CC: MC; V; Maestro.

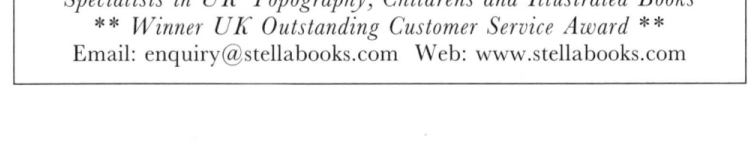

BRECON

Andrew Morton Books, ■ 11 Lion Yard, Brecon, LD3 7BA. Tel: (01874) 620086. E-mail: sales@morton-books.co.uk. Est: 1999. Shop open: **M:** 09:30–17:30; **T:** 09:30–17:30; **W:** 09:30–17:30; **Th:** 09:30–17:30; **F:** 09:30–17:30; **S:** 09·30–17:30. Very large stock. Spec. Art; Children's; Crafts; History - General; Literature; Military. PR: £2–30. CC: MC; V; SW, SO. Notes: *Also at: 7 Lion Street, Brecon. Also, open on Sundays in season.*

BUILTH WELLS

Louise Boer, Arthurian Books, The Rectory, Rhosgoch, Builth Wells, LD2 3JU. Prop: Louise Boer. Tel: (01497) 851260. Fax: (01497) 851260. E-mail: louise.boer@btinternet.com. Est: 1996. Private premises. Internet and Postal. Contactable. Medium stock. Spec: Academic/Scholarly; Arthurian; Business Studies; Literary Criticism. PR: £2–150. CC: MC; V. Corresp: Dutch.

HAY–ON–WYE

The Addyman Annexe, ■ 27 Castle Street, Hay–on–Wye, HR3 5DF. Prop: Derek Addyman and Anne Brichto. Tel: 01497 821600. Web: www.hay-on-wyebooks.com. E-mail: madder@hay-on-wyebooks.com. Shop open: **M:** 10:00–17:30; **T:** 10:00–17:30; **W:** 10:00–17:30; **Th:** 10:00–17:30; **F:** 10:00–17:30; **S:** 10:00–17:30. **Su:** 10:00–17:30. Spec: Bindings, Literature; Military; Modern First Editions. CC: MC; V; Maestro.

Addyman Books, ■ 39 Lion Street, Hay–on–Wye, HR3 5AA. Prop: Derek Addyman & Anne Brichto. Tel: (01497) 821136. Fax: (01497) 821732. Web: www.hay-on-wyebooks.com. E-mail: madness@hay-on-wyebooks.com. Est: 1987. Internet and Postal. Shop open: **M:** 10:00–17:30; **T:** 10:00–17:30; **W:** 10:00–17:30; **Th:** 10:00–17:30; **F:** 10:00–17:30; **S:** 10:00–17:30; **Su:** 10:30–17:30. Large stock. Spec: Adult; Aeronautics; Africana; Agriculture; Aircraft; Americana - General; Anthologies; Antiquarian. PR: £1–20,000. CC: MC; V; De, SW, Maestro, Solo. Notes: *Murder & Mayhem, 5 Lion St., Hay-on-Wye (q.v) The Addyman Annexe, 27 Castle St., Hay-on-Wye, (q.v.) NB: add 'via Hereford' after Hay-on-Wye when sending by post.*

C. Arden, Bookseller, ■ 'Radnor House' Church Street, Hay–on–Wye, HR3 5DQ. Prop: Chris & Catherine Arden. Tel: (01497) 820471. Fax: (01497) 820498. Web: www.ardenbooks.co.uk. E-mail: c.arden@virgin.net. Est: 1993. Internet and Postal. Shop open: **M:** 10.30–17.30; **T:** 10.30–17.30; **W:** 10.30–17.30; **Th:** 10.30–17.30; **F:** 10:30–17:30; **S:** 10:30–17:30; **Su:** 11:00–16:00. Medium stock. Spec: Antiquarian; Biology - General, Botany; Conservation; Ecology; Entomology; Evolution; Fine & Rare. PR: £3–10,000. CC: JCB; MC; V. Cata: Natural History, Gardening, Zoology, Botany. Mem: PBFA.

B. and K. Books of Hay-on-Wye, Riverside Newport Street, Hay–on–Wye, HR3 5BG. Prop: Betty & Karl Showler. Tel: (01497) 820386. Web: www.hay-on-wye.co.uk/bkbooks. Est: 1966. Private premises. Appointment necessary. Very small stock. Spec: Apiculture. PR: £6–600. Notes: *Also at storeroom.*

Richard Booth's Bookshop Ltd, ■ 44 Lion Street, Hay–on–Wye, HR3 5AA. Prop: Director: Mr. Richard Booth. Tel: (01497) 820322. Fax: (01497) 821150. Web: www.richardbooth.demon.co.uk. E-mail: postmaster@richardbooth.demon.co.uk. Est: 1961. Shop open: **M:** 09:00–17:30; **T:** 09:00–17:30; **W:** 09:00–17:30; **Th:** 09:00–17:30; **F:** 09:00–19:00; **S:** 09:00–19:00; **Su:** 11:00–17:30. Very large stock. Spec: Agriculture; Archaeology; Atlases; Children's; Cookery/Gastronomy; Countries - Mexico; Economics; Fiction - Science Fiction. PR: £1–1,000. CC: AE; D; JCB; MC; V. Mem: WBA. VAT No: GB 412 7744 60. Notes: *Hay Castle, Hay-on-Wye. (q.v.) Also, paperbacks & magazines. NB:add 'via Hereford' after Hay-on-Wye when sending by post.*

Boz Books, ■ 13a Castle Street, Hay–on–Wye, HR3 5DF. Prop: Peter Harries. Tel: (01497) 821277. Fax: (01497) 821277. Web: www.bozbooks.co.uk. E-mail: peter@bozbooks.co.uk. Est: 1987. Internet and Postal. Shop open: **M:** 10:00–17:00; **T:** 10:00–17:00; **W:** 10:00–17:00; **Th:** 10:00–17:00; **F:** 10:00–17:00; **S:** 10:00–17:00. Closed for lunch: 13:00–14:00. Medium stock. Spec: Author - Dickens, Charles; Fiction - General; Literature; Literature - 19th C. PR: £5–10,000. CC: JCB; MC; V. Mem: ABA. VAT No: GB 489 1240 27. Notes: *Opening times vary in winter.*

The Children's Bookshop, ■ Toll Cottage Pontvaen, Hay–on–Wye, HR3 5EW. Prop: Judith M Gardner. Tel: (01497) 821083. Web: www.childrensbookshop.com. E-mail: judith@childrensbookshop.com. Est: 1980. Internet and Postal. Shop open: **M:** 09:30–17:30; **T:** 09:30–13.00; **W:** 09:30–17:30; **Th:** 09:30–00:30; **F:** 09:31–17:30; **S:** 09:30–17:30. Medium stock. Spec: Children's; Children's - Early Titles; Children's - Illustrated; Fairy/Folk Tales; Booksearch. PR: £5–500. CC: JCB; MC; V. Corresp: French, German. Notes: *Hay-on-Wye (q.v.) Also, a booksearch service.*

WALES

davidleesbooks.com, ■ Marches Gallery 2 Lion Street, Hay-on-Wye, HR3 5AA. Prop: David Lees. Tel: (01497) 822969. Web: www.davidleesbooks.com. E-mail: julie@davidleesbooks.com. Est: 1985. Internet and Shop open: **M:** 11:00–17:00; **T:** 11:00–17:00; **W:** 11:00–17:00; **Th:** 11:00–17:00; **F:** 11:00–17:00; **S:** 11:00–17:00; **Su:** 11:00–17:00. Medium stock. PR: £0–1,000. CC: MC; V; Debit Card. VAT No: GB 488 7008 07.

Francis Edwards in Hay-on-Wy, ■ The Old Cinema Castle Street, Hay-on-Wye, via Hereford, HR3 5DF. Prop: Hay Cinema Bookshop Ltd. Tel: (01497) 820071. Fax: (01497) 821900. Web: www.francisedwards.co.uk. E-mail: sales@francisedwards.demon.co.uk. Est: 1855. Shop open: **M:** 09:00–19:00; **T:** 09:00–19:00; **W:** 09:00–19:00; **Th:** 09:00–19:00; **F:** 09:00–19:00; **S:** 09:00–19:00; **Su:** 11:30–17:30. Medium stock. Spec: Architecture; Art; Economics; Folklore; History - General; Law - General; Literature; Medicine. PR: £20–10,000. CC: AE; D; E; JCB; MC; V; Switch. Cata: Voyages, Naval, Military, Art, Literature, Scienc. Mem: ABA; PBFA; ILAB. VAT No: GB 594 2720 23.

Hancock & Monks Music Emporium, ■ 6 Broad Street, Hay-on-Wye, HR3 5DB. Prop: Eric Hancock & Jerry Monks. Tel: (01591) 610555. Fax: (01591) 610555. Web: www.hancockandmonks.co.uk. E-mail: jerry@hancockandmonks.co.uk. Est: 1974. Shop open: **M:** 10:00–17:00; **T:** 10:00–17:00; **W:** 10:00–17:00; **Th:** 10:00–17:00; **F:** 10:00–17:00; **S:** 10:00–17:00; **Su:** 10:00–17:00; Medium stock. Spec: Cinema/Film; Music - General; Music - Classical; Music - Composers; Music - Gilbert & Sullivan; Music - Gregorian Chants; Music - Illustrated Sheet Music; Music - Jazz & Blues. PR: £1–250. CC: AE; MC; V; Maestro. Cata: CDs, Scores & Books on Music. VAT No: GB 139 8108 51. Notes: *Long established classical music retailer selling CDs, DVDs, Sheet Music, Scores and Books on Music. Worldwide mail order. Extensive on-line catalogue.*

Hay Castle (Booth Books), ■ Hay Castle Oxford Road, Hay-on-Wye, HR3 5DQ. Prop: Hope Booth (Richard Booth Bookshops Ltd.). Tel: (01497) 820503. Fax: (01497) 821314. Web: www.boothbooks .co.uk. E-mail: books@haycastle.freeserve.co.uk. Est: 1987. Shop open: **M:** 10:00–17:30; **T:** 10:00–17:30; **W:** 10:00–17:30; **Th:** 10:00–17:30; **F:** 10:00–17:30; **S:** 10:00–17:30; **Su:** 10:00–17:30. Very large stock. Spec: American Indians; Architecture; Art; Cinema/Film; Crafts; Humour; Photography; Railways. PR: £1–2,500. CC: AE; D; MC; V. Corresp: French. Mem: WBA. Notes: *44 Lion Street, Hay-on-Wye (q.v.) Also, photographic images from 1850s onwards. NB:add 'via Hereford' after Hay-on-Wye when sending by post.*

Hay Cinema Bookshop Ltd., ■ Castle Street, Hay-on-Wye, HR3 5DF. Tel: (01497) 820071. Fax: (01497) 821900. Web: www.haycinemabookshop.co.uk. E-mail: sales@haycinemabookshop.co.uk. Est: 1982. Shop open: **M:** 09:00–19:00; **T:** 09:00–19:00; **W:** 09:00–19:00; **Th:** 09:00–19:00; **F:** 09:00–19:00; **S:** 09:00–19:00; **Su:** 11:30–17:30. Very large stock. Spec: Academic/Scholarly; Aeronautics; Applied Art; Art; Calligraphy; Cinema/Film; Cookery/Gastronomy; Economics. PR: £1–25. CC: AE; D; JCB; MC; V. Mem: ABA; PBFA. VAT No: GB 594 2720 23. Notes: *Quinto, 48a Charing Cross Road, London WC2H 0BB (q.v.) Quinto, 63 Great Russell Street, London WC1B 3BF Fine and Antiquarian books in all subjects via our sister business Francis Edwards.*

HCB Wholesale, Unit 2 Forest Road Enterprise Park, Hay-on-Wye, HR3 5DS. Prop: (A Division of Hay Cinema Bookshop Ltd.). Tel: (01497) 820333. Fax: (01497) 821192. Web: www.hcbwholesale .co.uk. E-mail: sales@hcbwholesale.co.uk. Est: 2002. Warehouse. Open: **M:** 09:00–18:00; **T:** 09:00–18:00; **W:** 09:00–18:00; **Th:** 09:00–18:00; **F:** 09:00–18:00. Very large stock. Spec: Art; Children's; Cinema/Film; Cookery/Gastronomy; Crime (True); Fiction - Crime, Detective, Spy, Thrillers; Fiction - Fantasy, Horror; Gardening - General. Notes: *Main stock: publishers' returns, academic overstocks, and remainders. NB: add 'via Hereford' after Hay-on-Wye when sending by post.*

Kestrel Books, 6 De Breos Court, Hay on Wye, HR3 5DL. Prop: David Rees. Tel: 01497 822890. Fax: 01497 822891. Web: www.hay-kestrel.com. E-mail: david@hay-kestrel.com. Est: 2005. Private premises. Appointment necessary. Open: **M:** 09:00–17:30; **T:** 09:00–17:30; **W:** 09:00–17:30; **Th:** 09:00–17:30; **F:** 09:00–17:30; **S:** 09:00–17:30; **Su:** 09:00–17:30. Closed for lunch: 13:00–14:00. Spec: Modern First Editions. CC: MC; V. VAT No: GB 863 5090 18. Notes: *Specialist in Modern First Editions.*

Marijana Dworski Books, ■ Backfold, Hay-on-Wye, HR3 5EQ. Prop: Marijana Dworski. Tel: (01497) 820200. Fax: (01497) 820200. Web: www.dworskibooks.com. E-mail: sales@dworskibooks.com. Est: 1991. Shop open: **M:** 10:30–17:00; **T:** 10:30–17:00; **W:** 10:30–17:00; **Th:** 10:30–17:00; **F:** 10:30–17:00; **S:** 10:30–17:30. Closed for lunch: 13:00–14:00. Spec: Art; Countries - Balkans, The; History - General; History - Russian Imperial; Languages - African; Languages - Ancient; Languages - Foreign; Languages - National. CC: D; JCB; MC; V; debit. Cata: Balkans, Russian, Central/Eastern Europe. Corresp: French, German, Croatian. VAT No: GB 794 1222 28. Notes: *U.K's premier specialists in language books: Dictionaries and Grammars in 350 languages from Akkadian to Zulu. Also a large selection of books on the Balkans, Central and Southeastern Europe, Russia & Central Asia.*

Murder & Mayhem, ■ 5 Lion Street, Hay-on-Wye, HR3 5AA. Prop: Derek Addyman & Anne Brichto. Tel: (01497) 821613. Fax: (01497) 821732. Web: www.hay-on-wyebooks.com. E-mail: madness@hay-on-wyebooks.com. Est: 1997. Shop open: **M:** 10:30–17:30; **T:** 10:30–17:30; **W:** 10:30–17:30; **Th:** 10:30–17:30; **F:** 10:30–17:30; **S:** 10:30–17:30. Medium stock. Spec: Crime (True); Criminology; Fiction - Crime, Detective, Spy, Thrillers, Fiction - Fantasy, Horror; Sherlockiana. PR: £1–1,000. CC: MC; V; Switch, Maestro, Solo. Notes: *Addyman Books, 39 Lion Street, Hay-on-Wye (q.v.).*

O'Donoghue Books, PO Box 162, Hay-on-Wye, HR3 5WZ. Prop: Sean O'Donoghue. Tel: 01497 822831. Web: www.intertextuality.com. E-mail: odonoghue.books@zen.co.uk. Est: 1994. Private premises. Internet Only. Large stock. Spec: Academic/Scholarly; Biography; Philosophy; Politics; Psychology/Psychiatry; Social Sciences; Sociology. PR: £10–50. CC: MC; V; Switch Maestro. Mem: Ibooknet. VAT No: GB 751 8509 19.

Oxford House Books, ■ Montpelier 21 Broad Street, Hay-on-Wye, HR3 5DB. Prop: Paul Harris. Tel: (01497) 820191. Web: www.oxfordhousebooks.com. E-mail: oxfordbook@aol.com. Est: 2003. Shop open: **M:** 10.30–17.30; **T:** 10:30–17:30; **W:** 10:30 17:30, **Th:** 10:30–17:30; **F:** 10:30–17:30; **S:** 10:30–17:30; **Su:** 10:30–17:30. Spec: CC: MC; V; Electron, Maestro, Solo, Delta, Switch. Notes: *Shop hours are for Spring/Summer/Autumn. Some variations possible during Winter. A call ahead is advised. We are always keen to purchase good collections of Philosophy, Theology, History, Art, and related subjects. Will travel if necessary.*

Outcast Books, ■ 15a Broad St., Hay-on-Wye, HR3 5DB. Prop: David Howard. Tel: (01497) 821292. Web: www.ukbookworld.com/members/outcastbooks. E-mail: outcastbooks@supanet.com. Est: 1993. Shop open: **M:** 10:30–17:00; **T:** 10:30–17:00; **W:** 10:30–17:00; **Th:** 10:30–17:00; **F:** 10:30–17:00; **S:** 11:30–17:00; **Su:** 12:00–14:00. Small stock. Spec: Academic/Scholarly; Alternative Medicine; Medicine; Psychoanalysis; Psychology/Psychiatry; Psychotherapy; Social Sciences. PR: £1–150. CC: AE; E; JCB; MC; V. Mem: Welsh Booksellers Assoc. Notes: *NB:add 'via Hereford' after Hay-on-Wye when sending by post.*

The Poetry Bookshop, ■ Ice House Brook Street, Hay-on-Wye, HR3 5BQ. Prop: Christopher & Melanie Prince. Tel: (01497) 821812. Fax: (01497) 821812. Web: www.poetrybookshop.co.uk. E-mail: info@poetrybookshop.co.uk. Est: 1998. Shop open: **M:** 10:00–18:00; **T:** 10:00–18:00; **W:** 10:00–18:00; **Th:** 10:00–18:00; **F:** 10:00–18:00; **S:** 10:00–18:00; **Su:** 11:00–17:00; Large stock. Spec: Academic/Scholarly; Anthologies; Antiquarian; Autobiography; Beat Writers; Bindings; Biography; Counterculture PR: £1–10,000. CC: MC, V, Maestro. VAT No: GB 831 777 901. Notes: *All subjects that relate to poets and poetry inc criticism, biography, readers guides, work in translation and anthologies.*

Rose's Books, ■ 14 Broad Street, Hay-on-Wye, HR3 5DB. Tel: (01497) 820013. Fax: (01497) 820031. Web: www.rosesbooks.com. E-mail: enquiry@rosesbooks.com. Est: 1982. Internet and Postal. Shop open: **M:** 09:30–17:30; **T:** 09:30–17:30; **W:** 09:30–17:30; **Th:** 09:30–17:30; **F:** 09:30–17:30; **S:** 09:30–17:30; **Su:** 09:30–17:30. Large stock. Spec: Children's; Children's - Illustrated; Illustrated - General; Publishers - Ladybird Books; Publishers - Ladybird Books. PR: £1–2,000. CC: AE; JCB; MC: V; SW. Cata: childrens. Mem: PBFA; www.ibooknet.co.uk. VAT No: GB 667 0422 36. Notes: *bookmatch service - we can let you know when a book comes into stock.*

Mark Westwood Books, ■ High Town, Hay-on-Wye, HR3 5AE. Tel: (01497) 820068. Fax: (01497) 821641. E-mail: books@markwestwood.co.uk. Est: 1987. Shop open: **M:** 10:30–17:30; **T:** 10:30–17:30; **W:** 10:30–17:30; **Th:** 10:30–17:30; **F:** 10:30–17:30; **S:** 10:30–17:30; **Su:** 10:30–17:30. Very large stock. Spec: Folio Society, The; History - General; Mathematics; Medicine; Medicine - History of; New Naturalist; Philosophy; Psychology/Psychiatry. PR: £5–1,000. CC: E; JCB; MC; V. Corresp: French. Mem: ABA; PBFA. VAT No: GB 315 3343 88.

LLANDRINDOD WELLS

Udo K.H. Polczynski, Rose & Crown Llanbadarn Fynydd, Llandrindod Wells, LD1 6YH. Prop: Udo K.H. Polczynski. Tel: 01597 840569. Fax: 01597 840569. Est: 1984. Private premises. Internet and Postal. Appointment necessary. Medium stock. Spec: Anthropology; Archaeology; History - Science; Philology; Philosophy. PR: £10–5,000. Cata: on special collections. Corresp: French, German, Malay, Polish, Russian, Spanish.

LLANIDLOES

Trade Priced Old Books, Neuadd Ddu Llangurig, Llanidloes, SY18 6RX. Prop: Sally Winston-Smith. Tel: (01686) 440730 m077 477 88 429. Web: www.DeadMensMinds.co.uk. E-mail: TPOBooks@ aol.com. Est: 2000. Private premises. Internet and Postal. Very small stock. Spec: Antiquarian; Arts, The; Philosophy; Taxidermy; Theology; Collectables. PR: £10–2,000. CC: MC; V; Switch, PayPal. Cata: Art, Philosophy, Theology, all pre 1830. Notes: *All our books are 16th - 19th century and many are not previously listed. Mostly leatherbound and part of treasured stock, a number of our odd volumes have helped happy searchers worldwide to complete their collections since the Millennium!*

Dusty Books, The Old Woollen Mill, Shortbridge Street, Llanidloes, SY18 6AD. Prop: Bernard Conwell. Tel: (01686) 411247. Fax: (01442) 270808. Web: www.dustybooks.co.uk. E-mail: alex@ dustybooks.co.uk. Postal Only. Spec: Author - Farnol, Jeffery; - Forester, C.S.; - Heyer, Georgette; - Sabatini, R.; - Shute, Neville; Cookery/Gastronomy; Crafts; Food & Drink. PR: £5–250.

The Great Oak Bookshop, ■ Great Oak Street, Llanidloes, SY18 6BW. Prop: B. Boswell. Tel: (01686) 412959. Web: www.midwales.com/gob. E-mail: greatoak@europe.com. Est: 1988. Internet and Postal. Shop open: **M:** 09:32–17:30; **T:** 09:31–17:30; **W:** 09:29–17:30; **Th:** 09:31–17:30; **F:** 09:30–17:30; **S:** 09:31–16:30. Very large stock. Spec: Autobiography; Biography; Countries - Wales; Welsh Interest. PR: £1–50. CC: AE; E; JCB; MC; V. Corresp: German, French. Mem: BA; WBA. Notes: *Also, new books, greetings cards & a resident parrot.*

LLANWRTYD WELLS

Andrew Dally, Berthllwyd Beulah, Llanwrtyd Wells, Powys, LD5 4UN. Prop: Andrew Dally. Tel: (01591) 610892. E-mail: andrew@thedallys.fsnet.co.uk. Est: 2001. Private premises. Internet and Postal. Contactable. Small stock. Spec: History - Photography; Memorabilia; Military; Military History; Photography; Royalty - General; War - General; War - World War I. PR: £1–200.

MACHYNLLETH

Dyfi Valley Bookshop, ■ 6 Doll Street, Machynlleth, SY20 8BQ. Prop: Barbara Beeby & Son. Tel: (01654) 703849. Web: www.dyfivalleybookshop.com. E-mail: beeb@dvbookshop.fsnet.co.uk. Est: 1988. Shop open: **M:** 09:30–17:00; **T:** 09:30–17:00; **W:** 09:30–17:00; **Th:** 09:30–17:00; **F:** 09:30–17:00; **S:** 09:30–17:00; Closed for lunch: 12:00–12:30. Medium stock. Spec: Arms & Armour; Firearms/Guns; Military; Sport - Archery; Welsh Interest. PR: £1–500. CC: AE; JCB; MC; V. Cata: Archery. Corresp: French. Mem: WBA.

Coch-y-Bonddu Books Ltd., ■ Papyrus Pentrerhedyn Street, Machynlleth, SY20 8DJ. Prop: Paul Morgan. Tel: (01654) 702837. Fax: (01654) 702857. Web: www.anglebooks.com. E-mail: paul@ anglebooks.com. Est: 1982. Internet and Postal. Shop open: **M:** 09:00–17:00; **T:** 09:00–17:00; **W:** 09:00–17:00; **Th:** 09:00–17:00; **F:** 09:00–17:00; **S:** 09:00–17:00. Large stock. Spec: Africana; Agriculture; Animals and Birds; Antiquarian; Author - Buchan, John; - Dinesen, Isak; - Jefferies, R.; - Seymour, John. PR: £1–2,000. CC: AE; D; E; JCB; MC; V. Corresp: French, German, Spanish, Portuguese, Welsh. Mem: PBFA; BA. Notes: *We stock new books in our fields, as well as remainders, s/hand and antiquarian.*

Martin's Books, Zion Chapel, Llanwrin, Machynlleth, SY20 8QH. Prop: Martin Ashby. Tel: (01650) 511595. E-mail: martin.ashby@martin-ashby.demon.co.uk. Est: 2000. Storeroom. Internet and Postal. Appointment necessary. Spec: Animals and Birds; Biography; Botany; Fiction - General; First Editions; Natural History; Ornithology; Poetry. PR: £6–500. Mem: PBFA.

MONTGOMERY

Castle Bookshop, The Old Rectory Llandyssil, Montgomery, SY15 6LQ. Prop: C.N., E.J. & S.J. Moore. Tel: (01686) 668484. Fax: (01686) 668842. Web: www.archaeologybooks.co.uk. E-mail: castlebooks@ dial.pipex.com. Est: 1987. Office and/or bookroom. Telephone First. Large stock. Spec: Archaeology; Archaeology - Industrial; Architecture; Countries - Wales; Welsh Interest. PR: £5–1,000. CC: JCB; MC; V; Switch/Maestro. Cata: Archaeology, Architecture, Wales, Celtic Studies. Corresp: French, German, Welsh. Mem: ABA; PBFA; ILAB. VAT No: GB 482 4054 51.

NEWTOWN

David Archer, The Pentre, Kerry, Newtown, SY16 4PD. Prop: David Archer & Alison Brown. Tel: (01686) 670382. Web: www.david-archer-maps.co.uk. E-mail: david@david-archer-maps.co.uk. Est: 1985. Private premises. Internet and Postal. Telephone First. Open: **M:** 08:30–20:00; **T:** 08:30–20:00; **W:** 08:30–20:00; **Th:** 08:30–20:00; **F:** 08:30–20:00; **S:** 09:00–13:00. Very large stock. Spec: Cartography; Geography; Geology; Transport; Prints and Maps. PR: £1–150. Mem: Welsh Booksellers Assoc.

Carta Regis Ltd, Agriculture House Old Kerry Road, Newtown, SY16 4LE. Prop: David Pugh. Tel: (01686) 624274. Web: www.davidp@cartaregis.com. E-mail: davidp@cartaregis.com. Est: 1997. Office and/or bookroom. Internet and Postal. Telephone First. Open: **M:** 10:00–17:00; **T:** 10:00–17:00; **W:** 10:00–17:00; **Th:** 10:00–17:00; **F:** 10:00–17:00; **S:** 10:00 17:00. Large stock. Spec: Academic/ Scholarly; Agriculture; Alpinism/Mountaineering; Animals and Birds; Antiques; Arts, The; First Editions; Fore-Edge Paintings. PR: £5–300. CC: MC; V; PayPal. VAT No: GB 850 5402 50. Notes: *New Books. Altenative web site: www.cartaregisbooks.co.uk Booksearch.*

D.M. Newband, Drefor Cottage,Kerry, Newtown, SY16 4PQ. Prop: D.M. Newband. Tel: (01686) 670205. Fax: please ask. Web: www.davidnewbandbooks.co.uk. E-mail: enquiries@ davidnewbandbooks.co.uk. Est: 1983. Office and/or bookroom. Internet and Postal. Appointment necessary. Open: **M:** 09:00–19:00; **T:** 09:00–19:00; **W:** 09:00–19:00; **Th:** 09:00–19:00; **F:** 09:00–19:00; **S:** 09:00–19:00; **Su:** 10:00–18:00. Small stock. Spec: Railways; Steam Engines; Transport; Booksearch. PR: £1–200. CC: PayPal. Notes: *Also, valuation service railways only.*

Tant Yn Ellen Books, Draenllwynellen Sarn, Newtown, SY16 4ET. Prop: Jim and June Crundwell. Tel: 01686 668475. Est: 2002. Private premises. Appointment necessary. Open: **M:** 09:00–17:30; **T:** 09:00 17:30; **W:** 09:00–17:30; **Th:** 09:00–17:30; **F:** 09:00–17:30; **S:** 09:00–17:30; **Su:** 09:00–17:30; Closed for lunch: 13:00–14:00. Spec: Botany; Children's; Children's - Illustrated; Cookery/Gastronomy; Entomology; Gardening - General; Natural History; Poetry. Notes: *Exhibits at book fairs.*

PRESTEIGNE

Antique & Book Shop, ■ 2 Hereford Street, Presteigne, LD8 2AW. Prop: A. L. Bird. Tel: (01544) 260316. Est: 1988. Shop open: **M:** 10:00–17:00; **T:** 10:00–17:00; **W:** 10:00–17:00; **Th:** 10:00–17:00; **F:** 10:00– 17:00; **S:** 10:00–17:00. Large stock. Spec: Topography - Local. PR: £1–200. Notes: *Open on Sundays by appointment.*

Kingshead Books, ■ 45 High St., Presteigne, Powys. Prop: Ivan Monckton. Tel: (01547) 560100. Est: 1983. Shop open: **M:** 10:00–17:00; **T:** 10:00–17:00; **W:** 09:00–17:00; **Th:** 10:00–17:00; **F:** 10:00–17:00; **S:** 10:00–17:00. Medium stock. Spec: Natural History; Welsh Interest; Collectables. PR: £1–250. Notes: *Open as above in summer. Winter: Saturdays & various others. Phone first.*

Tony Bird, 2 Hereford Street, Presteigne, LD8 2AW. Tel: (01544) 260316. Private premises. Spec: Topography - Local.

TALGARTH

The Strand Bookshop, ■ Regent Street, Talgarth, LD3 0DB. Prop: Ms Kate Cardwell. Tel: (01874) 711195. Shop open: **M:** 10:00–15:30; **Th:** 10:00–15:30; **F:** 10:00 15:30; **S:** 10:00 17:00; **Su:** 09:00– 17:00; Medium stock. PR: £1–50.

WELSHPOOL

D. & J. Young, Fairview Cottage, Groes Llwyd, Welshpool, SY21 9BZ. Prop: David & Joy Young. Tel: (01938) 553149. Web: www.abebooks.com. E-mail: joy_young@lineone.net. Est: 20. Private premises. Postal Only. Appointment necessary. Small stock. Spec: Calligraphy; Embroidery; Fashion & Costume; Knitting; Lace; Textiles. PR: £1–300.

YSTRAD MEURIG

Garfi Books, ■ Bron y Graig Pontrhydygroes, Ystrad Meurig, SY25 6DN. Prop: Barbara & Salvatore Garfi. Tel: 01974 282684. E-mail: garfibooks@btinternet.com. Est: 2000. Shop At: The Book Unit, Brecon Antiques Centre, 22a High St., Brecon, Powys LD3 7LA. Open: **M:** 10:00–17:00; **T:** 10.00– 17:00; **W:** 10.00–17:00; **Th:** 10.00–17.00; **F:** 10:00–17:00; **S:** 10:00–17:00. Spec: Alpinism/ Mountaineering; Anthropology; Archaeology; Art; Art History; Author - Aldin, Cecil; - Armour, G. D.; - Churchill, Sir Winston. CC: MC; V; Maestro & Switch. Notes: *Open Sundays from Easter to Christmas. 11:00-16:00*

SWANSEA

SWANSEA

J.M. Farringdon, Ariel Cottage 8 Hadland Terrace, West Cross, Swansea, SA3 5TT. Prop: M.G. Farringdon. Tel: (01792) 405267. Fax: (01792) 405267. E-mail: bellbooks@aol.com. Est: 1970. Private premises. Internet and Postal. Appointment necessary. Very small stock. Spec: Antiquarian; Author - Masefield, John; - Ransome, Arthur; Bell-Ringing (Campanology); Booksearch. PR: £20–1,000. Cata: Bells and Bell-Ringing. VAT No: GB 558 2330 40. Notes: *Also publishing as 'Ariel House Publications'.*

WALES

PONTARDAWE

Mollie's Loft Books, 31 Cilmaengwyn, Pontardawe, SA8 4QL. Prop: M.J.P. Evans. Tel: (01792) 863556. Web: www.Molliesloft.com. E-mail: books@mollies.freeserve.co.uk. Est: 1998. Private premises. Internet and Postal. Appointment necessary. Small stock. Spec: Science - General; Technology; Welsh Interest. PR: £5–150. CC: MC; V; Switch. Corresp: French.

SWANSEA

Dylans Bookstore, ■ Salubrious House 23 King Edward Road, Swansea, SA1 4LL. Prop: Jeff and Elizabeth Towns. Tel: 01792 655255. Fax: 01792 655255. Web: www.dylans.com. E-mail: jefftowns@ dylans.com. Est: 1970. Internet and Postal. Shop open: **M:** 10:00–16:00; **T:** 10.00–16:00; **W:** 10.00– 16.00; **Th:** 10.00–16.00; **F:** 10.00–16.00; **S:** 10.00–13.00. Spec: Academic/Scholarly; African-American Studies; Antiquarian; Arthurian; Author - Steadman, Ralph; - Thomas, Dylan; - Thomas, Edward; - Watkins, Vernon. CC: JCB; MC; V. Cata: Dylan Thomas, Wales, women. Corresp: French. Mem: ABA; BA; ILAB; Welsh Booksellers Association. Notes: *We have two open shops in Swansea - the other is in the Dylan Thomas Centre. We exhibit at bookfairs and sell on the internet.*

TORFAEN

BLAENAVON

Broadleaf Books, ■ 12 Broad Street, Blaenavon, NP4 9ND. Prop: Joanna Chambers and Latagrifrith-Unny. Tel: (01495) 792852. E-mail: broadleaf12@aol.com. Est: 2003. Shop open: **T:** 10:00–17:00; **W:** 10:00–17:00; **Th:** 10.00–17:00; **F:** 10:00–17:00; **S:** 10:00–17:00. Medium stock. Spec: Children's; Design; Natural History; Photography. PR: £1–50. CC: V. Notes: *Good collection of photography and natural history with broad range of other subjects.*

Blaenavon Books, ■ 71 Broad Street, Blaenavon, NP4 9NH. Prop: James Hanna. Tel: (01495) 793093. E-mail: blaenavonbooks@yahoo.co.uk. Est: 2003. Shop open: **M:** 10:00–17:00; **T:** 10:00–17:00; **W:** 10:00–17:00; **Th:** 10:00–17:00; **F:** 10:00–17:00; **S:** 09:00–17:00; **Su:** 10:00–17:00. Medium stock. Spec: Art; Design; Photography. PR: £1–100. CC: MC; V; SW, SO. Notes: *Only open Sundays in summer. Large general stock.*

Browning Books, ■ 33 Broad Street, Blaenavon, NP4 9NF. Prop: Stephanie and Andrew Nummelin. Tel: (01495) 790089. Web: www.browningbooks.co.uk. E-mail: info@browningbooks.co.uk. Est: 2001. Internet and Postal. Shop open: **T:** 10:00–17:00; **W:** 10:00–17:00; **Th:** 10:00–17:00; **F:** 10:00– 17:00; **S:** 10:00–17:00. Medium stock. Spec: Children's; Children's - Illustrated; Countries - Wales; History - Local; Languages - National; Mining; New Books; Railways. PR: £1–150. CC: AE; E; JCB; MC; V; MAE, ELEC. Mem: BA.

Queen Victoria PH, Prince Street, Blaenavon, NP4 9BD. Prop: Kim Winstone. Tel: 01495 791652. Web: www.webster.uk.net/queenvictoriainn. E-mail: queenvictoriainn@webster.uk.net. Est: 2003. Storeroom. Open: **M:** 11:00–23:00; **T:** 11:00–23:00; **W:** 11:00–23:00; **Th:** 11:00–23:00; **F:** 11:00– 23:00; **S:** 11:00–23:00; **Su:** 12:00–20:30. Spec: Cookery/Gastronomy; Gardening - General; Military; Military History. Notes: *Accommodation available. In Good Beer Guide.*

The Railway Shop, ■ 13a Broad Street, Blaenavon, NP4 9ND. Prop. Peter Hunt. Tel: (01495) 792263. Web: www.railwaymodelshop.co.uk. E-mail: shop@railwaymodelshop.co.uk. Est: 1998. Shop open: **M:** 11:00–17:30; **T:** 11:00–17:30; **W:** 11:00–17:30; **Th:** 11:00–17:30; **F:** 11:00–17:30; **S:** 11:00–16:00. Large stock. Spec: Railways; Shipbuilding and Shipping; Transport. PR: £1–20. CC: MC; V.

WEST GLAMORGAN

NEATH

www.rugbyrelics.com, 61 Leonard Street, Neath, SA11 3HW. Prop: Dave Richards. Tel: (01639) 646725. Fax: (01639) 638142. Web: www.rugbyrelics.com. E-mail: sales@rugbyrelics.com. Est: 1991. Private premises. Postal Only. Appointment necessary. Very small stock. Spec: Sport - Athletics; Sport - Boxing; Sport - Cricket; Sport - Cycling; Sport - Football (Soccer); Sport - Golf; Sport - Rugby; Sport - Swimming. PR: £2–2,000. CC: MC; V.

ALPHABETICAL INDEX BY NAME OF BUSINESS

(Business name followed by county, some of which have been abbreviated)

2 Ravens, Cumbria 79
32 Seconds, East Sussex 104
A Holmes Books, Nottinghamshire................. 204
AÆnigma Designs (Books), Devon................. 86
A. & H. Peasgood, Cambridgeshire 67
A. & R. Booksearch, Cornwall...................... 74
AA1 Books, Dumfries & Galloway................. 270
Aardvark Books, Wiltshire 254
Aardvark Books, Lincolnshire...................... 152
Abacus Books, Cheshire.............................. 68
Abacus Gallery, Staffordshire....................... 224
Abbey Books, Cornwall 74
Aberdeen Antique and Art Centre, Grampian... 272
Abington Bookshop, Suffolk........................ 228
Abrahams (Mike), Staffordshire 224
Acumen Books, Staffordshire....................... 225
Addyman Annexe (The), Powys.................... 289
Addyman Books, Powys.............................. 289
Adrem Books, Hertfordshire......................... 131
Adrian Walker, Bedfordshire 53
Afar Books International, West Midlands........ 239
African Studies, Dorset 91
ahbooks, Merseyside 185
Ainslie Books, Strathclyde........................... 279
Aitchison (Lesley), Bristol 58
Al Saqi Books, London W........................... 172
Alan Prim, Co. Cork.................................. 263
Alan Redmond Books, Lincolnshire............... 150
Alastor Rare Books, Hampshire 124
Alauda Books, Cumbria.............................. 78
Alba Books, Grampian 274
Alba Secondhand Music, Strathclyde.............. 279
Albion Books, West Midlands....................... 239
Albion Bookshop, Kent 136
Alec-Smith Books (Alex), East Yorkshire 107
Alexander Books, Hampshire........................ 124
Alexander's Books, Warwickshire.................. 238
All Books, Essex....................................... 110
Allhalland Books, Devon............................. 85
Allinson (Frank & Stella), Warwickshire 237
Allsop (Duncan M.), Warwickshire................ 238
Allsworth Rare Books Ltd., London SW.......... 167
ALLTHINGSBOOKS, Durham 97
Alpha Books, London N 158
Altea Antique Maps & Books, London W....... 172
Alton Secondhand Books, Hampshire............. 121
Altshuler (Jean), Cumbria 79
Ambra Books, Bristol................................. 58
Americanabooksuk, Cumbria........................ 77
Amnesty International UK, Berkshire.............. 56
Amos (Denis W.), Hertfordshire 131
Ampersand Books, Shropshire...................... 213
Amwell Book Company, London EC.............. 157
Anchor Books, Lincolnshire 151
Ancient Art Books, London SW.................... 167
Andrew Morton (Books), Powys.................... 289
Andrews Books & Collectables, Cheshire......... 69
Andron (G.W.), London N 158
Anglo-American Rare Books, Surrey.............. 233

Ann & Mike Conry, Worcestershire............... 257
Anne Harris Books & Bags Booksearch, Devon . 88
Annie's Books, South Yorkshire 222
Anthony Neville, Kent................................ 139
Anthony Sillem, East Sussex........................ 102
Anthony Spranger, Wiltshire........................ 252
Anthony Vickers Books, North Yorkshire 196
Anthony Whittaker, Kent 136
Anthroposophical Books, Gloucestershire 116
Antiquary Ltd., (Bar Bookstore)
North Yorkshire 196
Antique & Book Shop, Powys...................... 293
Antique City Bookshop, London E 155
Antique Map and Bookshop (The), Dorset 94
Antique Prints of the World, London N.......... 158
Antiques on High, Oxfordshire..................... 209
Anvil Books, West Midlands 240
Anwoth Books Ltd, Dumfries & Galloway 270
Any Amount of Books, London WC 177
Aphra Books, West Yorkshire....................... 247
Apocalypse, Surrey 233
Applin (Malcolm), Berkshire........................ 55
Arcadia, Oxfordshire................................. 209
Archer (David), Powys............................... 292
Archer (Steve), London Outer...................... 181
Archivist (The), Devon............................... 90
Archways Sports Books, Lothian 276
Arden Books & Cosmographia, Warwickshire... 237
Arden, Bookseller (C.), Powys..................... 289
Ardis Books, Hampshire 126
Argent (Alan), Isle of Wight 135
Armchair Auctions, Hampshire 121
Armchair Books, Lothian 276
Armitage (Booksearch), (Kate), Devon 85
Armstrong's Books & Collectables
Leicestershire 147
Arnold (Roy), Suffolk................................. 228
Ars Artis, Oxfordshire 209
Art Book Company, (The), Suffolk................. 228
Art Reference Books, Hampshire 125
Artco, Nottinghamshire.............................. 204
Arthur Husk, Bristol.................................. 58
Arts & Antiques Centre (The), Cheshire.......... 69
Ash Rare Books, London SW....................... 167
Ashwell Books, Wiltshire............................ 252
Askew Books (Vernon), Wiltshire.................. 251
Assinder Books, Essex 110
Astley Book Farm, Warwickshire................... 237
Atholl Browse, Perthshire 281
Atholl Fine Books, Tayside 281
Atlantis Bookshop, London WC................... 177
Atlas, London N....................................... 158
Aucott & Thomas, Leicestershire................... 147
Aurelian Books, London NW 161
Aurora Books Ltd, Lothian.......................... 276
Austen (Phillip), Lincolnshire 153
Austwick Hall Books, North Yorkshire............ 193
Autolycus, Shropshire................................ 213
Autumn Leaves, Lincolnshire....................... 152

ALPHABETICAL INDEX: Business (A – B)

Avedikian Rare Books, Somerset 217
Avery (Alan), North Yorkshire...................... 195
Aviabooks, Gloucestershire 114
Aviation Book Supply, Hertfordshire 130
Avon Books, Bristol.................................... 58
Avonworld Books, Somerset......................... 218
Axe Rare & Out of Print Books (Richard)
North Yorkshire 194
Ayre (Peter J.), Somerset 220
B D McManmon, Lancashire 145
B. and K. Books, Powys 289
babelog.books, Herefordshire 128
back2books.tv, West Sussex......................... 242
Bacon (Josephine), London WC 177
Badger, Wiltshire 253
Badger Books, Somerset.............................. 220
Badgers Books, West Sussex 245
Baedekers & Murray Guides, South Yorkshire.. 222
Baggins Book Bazaar, Kent.......................... 140
Baker (Gerald), Bristol................................. 60
Baker - Books for the Collector (Colin), Devon.. 90
Baker Limited (A.P. & R.)
Dumfries & Galloway............................... 270
Baldwin (Jack), Strathclyde 280
Baldwin (M. & M.), Worcestershire 255
Baldwin's Scientific Books, Essex 112
Ballantyne-Way (Roger), Suffolk 229
Bancroft (David G.), Isle of Wight 134
Bannatyne Books, London N........................ 158
Bannister (David), Gloucestershire................. 113
Barbican Bookshop, North Yorkshire............. 198
Barcombe Services, Essex............................ 108
Bardsley's Books, Suffolk............................. 226
Barely Read Books, Kent 142
Barlow (Vincent G.), Hampshire.................... 125
Barlow Moor Books, Greater Manchester........ 118
Barmby (C. & A.J.), Kent............................ 141
Barn Books, Shropshire............................... 215
Barn Books, Buckinghamshire....................... 61
Barnes (Peter), Wiltshire 253
Barnes - Books (Lyndon), Shropshire 214
Barnhill Books, Isle of Arran 275
Barnitt (Peter), Wiltshire............................. 254
Baron (Christopher), Greater Manchester 118
Baron (H.), London NW............................. 161
Baron - Scientific Book Sales (P.J.), Somerset ... 217
Barron (Robert M.), Kent............................ 140
Barry McKay Rare Books, Cumbria............... 77
Barter Books, Northumberland 202
Bass (Ben), Wiltshire 251
Bates & Hindmarch, West Yorkshire.............. 249
Bates Books, London Outer 182
Bath Book Exchange, Somerset 216
Bath Old Books, Somerset 216
Batterham (David), London W...................... 172
Baxter (Steve), Surrey 234
Baxter - Books (Eddie), Somerset 221
Bay Bookshop, Conwy 285
Baynton-Williams Gallery, West Sussex 242
Bayntun (George), Somerset 216
BC Books, Cheshire.................................... 70
Bear Island Books, Cardiff........................... 283
Beardsell Books, West Yorkshire.................... 247
Beardsley (A.E.), Nottinghamshire................. 205
Beaton (Richard), East Sussex....................... 103

Beaver Booksearch, Suffolk 226
Beck (John), East Sussex 103
Beckham Books Ltd., Suffolk 230
Beighton (Brian), Norfolk 187
Bell (Books) (Mrs. V.S.), Suffolk.................... 228
Bell (Peter), Lothian................................... 276
Bell Gallery (The), Co. Antrim 260
Ben-Nathan (Jack), London Outer 181
Bennett & Kerr Books, Oxfordshire................ 206
Benny Gillies Books Ltd
Dumfries & Galloway............................... 269
Bermondsey Basement Bookstore, London SE .. 164
Bernard Dixon and Kath Adams, Middlesex 183
Bernstein (Nicholas), London W.................... 172
Bertram Rota Ltd., London WC 177
Berwick Books, Lincolnshire......................... 152
Besleys Books, Suffolk 226
Bettridge (Gordon), Fife.............................. 272
Bevan (John), Wiltshire............................... 252
Beverley Old Bookshop, East Yorkshire 106
Beware of the Leopard, Bristol...................... 58
Bianco Library, West Sussex......................... 242
Biblion, London W..................................... 172
Bibliophile (The), South Yorkshire 222
Bibliophile Books, London E 155
Biblipola, London NW 161
Bickford-Smith (G.) Surrey 233
Big Bairn Books, Tayside 281
Billing (Brian), Berkshire 57
Bilski (Gill), Buckinghamshire 61
Birchden Books, London E 155
Bird (Tony), Powys.................................... 293
Bird Books (Nigel), Ceredigion...................... 284
Birdnet Optics Ltd., Derbyshire 82
Birmingham Books, West Midlands 239
Bishopston Books, Bristol 58
Black Cat Books, Norfolk............................. 188
Black Cat Bookshop, Leicestershire 147
Black Five Books, Shropshire 215
Black Voices, Merseyside............................. 185
Blacket Books, Lothian................................ 277
Blacklock's, Surrey 232
Blackman Books, Cheshire........................... 72
Blackwell's Music Shop, Oxfordshire.............. 209
Blackwell's Rare Books, Oxfordshire.............. 209
Blaenavon Books, Torfaen 294
Blairgowrie Books, ... 281
Blanchfield (John), West Yorkshire................. 249
Blest (Peter), Kent 139
Blewbury Antiques, Oxfordshire 207
Bloomsbury Bookshop, London Outer............ 182
Blore's Bookshop (Geoffrey), Nottinghamshire.. 204
Blue Penguin (The), Gloucestershire 116
Bluntisham Books, Cambridgeshire................. 63
Blythswood Bookshop, Highland 275
Bob Mallory (Books), Derbyshire................... 83
Bodyline Books, Surrey 233
Boer (Louise), Arthurian Books, Powys 289
Boer War Books, North Yorkshire 198
Bolland Books, Bedfordshire......................... 53
Bolton Books, Hampshire............................. 121
Bonham (J. & S.L.), London W 172
Bonner (John), West Yorkshire 249
Bonython Bookshop, Cornwall...................... 76
Book Aid, Durham..................................... 97

ALPHABETICAL INDEX: Business (B – B)

Book Annex (The), Essex 109
Book Business (The), London W 172
Book Castle, (The), Bedfordshire.................... 54
Book Depot (The), London NW.................... 161
Book End, Essex.. 108
Book For All Reasons (A.), Suffolk 229
Book Gallery (The), Cornwall 75
Book House (The), Cumbria......................... 77
Book Jungle (The), East Sussex 105
Book Mad, Lancashire................................ 143
Book Mongers, London SW......................... 167
Book Palace (The), London SE 164
Book Shelf (The), Devon 87
Bookbarrow, Cambridgeshire........................ 63
Bookbox, Gloucestershire 116
Bookcase, Cumbria.................................... 78
Bookcupboard, Devon................................ 88
Bookends, Hampshire................................. 122
Bookends, Norfolk 189
Bookends of Fowey, Cornwall 73
Bookfare, Cumbria 81
Bookline, Co. Down 261
Booklore, Leicestershire.............................. 148
BookLovers.co.uk, Somerset......................... 220
Bookmark (Children's Books), Wiltshire.......... 253
Booknotes, Essex 111
Bookpassage (The), Shropshire...................... 213
Bookquest, Devon...................................... 84
Bookroom (The), Surrey.............................. 234
Bookroom (The), Gloucestershire................... 114
Bookroom (The), Isle of Wight...................... 134
Bookroom at Brown & White, The
Gloucestershire 117
Books, Kent 137
Books, Oxfordshire.................................... 206
Books, Denbighshire 286
Books, Kent 137
Books & Bygones, Berkshire......................... 57
Books & Bygones (Pam Taylor)
West Midlands 241
Books & Collectables Ltd., Cambridgeshire 63
Books & Ink, Oxfordshire............................ 207
Books & Things, London W......................... 172
Books (For All), North Yorkshire................... 194
Books Afloat, Dorset.................................. 96
Books and Beans, Grampian 272
Books and Things, Channel Islands 258
Books Antiques & Collectables, Devon 90
Books at Star Dot Star, West Midlands 241
Books at the Warehouse, North Yorkshire....... 195
Books B.C., London Outer 181
Books Bought & Sold, Surrey 232
Books For All, North Yorkshire..................... 194
Books for Amnesty, Bristol 58
Books for Content, Herefordshire................... 128
Books for Writers, Monmouthshire................. 287
Books in Cardigan, Ceredigion 284
Books on Spain, London Outer..................... 184
Books Only, Suffolk................................... 227
Books Plus, Devon 84
Books Ulster, Co. Down 261
Books Upstairs, West Yorkshire 250
Books With Care, Bedfordshire 53
books2books, Devon.................................. 88
BOOKS4U, Flintshire................................. 286

Bookseeker, Tayside................................... 282
Bookseller (The), Cumbria 80
Bookshelf (The), North Yorkshire 196
Bookshelf – Aviation Books, West Sussex........ 242
Bookshop (The), Greater Manchester.............. 118
Bookshop (The), Co. Donegal....................... 263
Bookshop (The), West Sussex 243
Bookshop (The), Norfolk 192
Bookshop at the Plain, Lincolnshire............... 151
Bookshop on the Heath, The, London SE 164
Bookshop, Kirkstall (The), West Yorkshire 248
BookShop, The, Dumfries & Galloway............ 270
Booksmart, Northamptonshire 200
Bookstand, Dorset..................................... 94
Booktrace International, Devon..................... 86
Bookworld, Shropshire............................... 214
Bookworm, Lothian................................... 277
Bookworm, Essex...................................... 110
Bookworm (The), Lothian 277
Bookworm Alley, Devon............................. 89
Bookworms, Norfolk.................................. 187
Bookworms of Evesham, Worcestershire 257
Bookzone, Berkshire 55
Booth (Booksearch Service), (Geoff), Cheshire... 68
Booth Books, Powys.................................. 289
Boox-Box (The), Shropshire 213
Border Books, Borders................................ 268
Border Bookshop, West Yorkshire 250
Boris Books, Hampshire.............................. 126
Bosco Books, Cornwall 73
Bosorne Books, Cornwall 75
Boss (Tim), West Sussex.............................. 244
Bott, (Bookdealers) Ltd., (Martin), Greater
Manchester 118
Botting & Berry, East Sussex 103
Boulevard Books, East Sussex....................... 102
Bouquiniste Bookshop, Fife......................... 272
Bow Windows Book Shop, East Sussex 103
Bowden Books, Leicestershire 149
Bowdon Books, Lancashire 144
Bowers Chess Suppliers (Francis)
Cambridgeshire...................................... 67
Bowie Books & Collectables, East Yorkshire 107
Bowland Bookfinders, Lancashire................... 143
Boxwood Books & Prints, Somerset................ 220
Boz Books, Powys..................................... 289
Bracton Books, Cambridgeshire..................... 63
Brad Books, Essex 111
Branksome Books, Dorset............................ 94
Brazenhead Ltd., Norfolk 189
Brett (Harry), Cambridgeshire....................... 65
Brewin Books Ltd., Warwickshire 238
Brian Troath Books, London E...................... 155
Bridge Books, Cumbria............................... 81
Bridge Bookshop Ltd, Isle of Man 259
Bridport Old Books, Dorset 92
Bright (P.G.), Cambridgeshire 65
Brighton Books, East Sussex......................... 99
Brimstones, East Sussex 103
Brinded (Scott), Kent 139
Bristol Books, Bristol 60
Bristow & Garland, Hampshire 122
Britons Catholic Library, Co. Wexford 267
Broadhurst of Southport Ltd., Merseyside 186
Broadleaf Books, Torfaen 294

ALPHABETICAL INDEX: Business (B – C)

Broadwater Books, Hampshire 125
Brock Books, North Yorkshire...................... 193
Brockwells Booksellers, Lincolnshire 150
Brookes (Gerard), Devon............................. 87
Brown (Books) (P.R.), Durham 98
Brown (Books) (Steve), Staffordshire 224
Brown (K.C.), Berkshire.............................. 56
Brown and Rivans Ltd, Devon....................... 90
Brown-Studies, Strathclyde........................... 279
Browne (Christopher I.), West Yorkshire......... 247
Brownhills Books, West Midlands 241
Browning Books, Torfaen 294
Browse Books, Lancashire 144
Browsers Bookshop, Cornwall....................... 73
Browzers, Greater Manchester....................... 119
Bruce Holdsworth Books, East Sussex 105
Bryony Books, West Yorkshire...................... 249
Buckley (Sybil), North Yorkshire 195
Budd (Richard), Somerset............................ 219
Bufo Books, Hampshire 125
Bunyan Books, Bedfordshire......................... 53
Burak (Steve), London WC 177
Burden (Derek), Surrey 233
Burden Ltd., (Clive A.), Hertfordshire 132
Burebank Books, Norfolk 187
Burmester (James), Bristol........................... 59
Burroughs (Andrew), Lincolnshire 153
Burton-Garbett (A.), London Outer 183
Bury Bookshop, Suffolk 226
Butcher (Pablo), Oxfordshire 207
Butler Cresswell Rare Books, Buckinghamshire . 61
Butterworth (Robert F.), Lancashire 145
Butts Books (Mary), Berkshire 56
Byblos Antiquarian & Rare Book, Hampshire .. 121
Bygone Books, Orkney 276
Byre Books, Dumfries & Galloway 270
Byrom Textile Bookroom (Richard)
Lancashire 143
Cader Idris Books, Powys............................ 292
Cader Idris Bookshop, Gwynedd 287
Caduceus Books, Leicestershire..................... 147
Caissa Books, Surrey.................................. 234
Caledonia Books, Strathclyde....................... 280
Calendula Horticultural Books, East Sussex 102
Caliver Books, Essex 110
Calluna Books, Dorset................................ 95
Camden Books, Somerset 216
Cameron (Mrs Janet), Kent.......................... 140
Cameron House Books, Isle of Wight.............. 134
Camilla's Bookshop, East Sussex 101
Campbell (Fiona), London SE 164
Campbell Art Books (Marcus), London SE...... 164
Campbell Hewson Books (R.), Fife................. 271
Candle Lane Books, Shropshire 215
Canon Gate Books, West Sussex.................... 244
Canterbury Bookshop (The), Kent 136
Capel Mawr Collectors Centre, Gwynedd 287
Capital Bookshop, Cardiff 283
Carlton Books, Norfolk 190
Carnforth Bookshop (The), Lancashire 143
Carningli Centre, Pembrokeshire 288
Carraig Books Ltd., Co. Dublin 264
Carta Regis, Powys.................................... 293
Carter, (Brian), Oxfordshire.......................... 211
Carters (Janet), Suffolk 226

Cassidy (Bookseller) (P.), Lincolnshire 153
Castle Bookshop, Powys.............................. 292
Castle Bookshop, Essex............................... 109
Castle Hill Books, Herefordshire 128
Castleton (Pat), Kent.................................. 138
Cat Lit, Somerset 219
Catalyst Booksearch Services, Devon.............. 87
Cathach Books Ltd, Co. Dublin 264
Catmax Books, Norfolk 187
Cavendish Rare Books, London N 158
Cavern Books, Cheshire 70
Cecilia Marsden, Middlesex 183
Celtic Bookshop (The), Co. Limerick 266
Central Bookshop, Warwickshire 238
Chalk (Old & Out of Print Books)
(Christine M.), West Midlands 239
Chalmers Hallam (E.), Hampshire.................. 125
Chandos Books, Devon................................ 85
Chandos Books, London Outer 183
Channel Islands Galleries Limited
Channel Islands 258
Chantrey Books, South Yorkshire 222
Chapel Books, Suffolk 230
Chapman (Neville), Lancashire...................... 146
Chapter & Verse, Lincolnshire...................... 152
Chapter House Books, Dorset....................... 95
Chapter Two, London SE............................. 164
Chapters Bookstore, Co. Dublin 264
Charlie Byrne's Bookshop, Co. Galway........... 265
Chas J. Sawyer, Kent 141
Chaters Motoring Booksellers, London Outer ... 182
Chaucer Bookshop, Kent............................. 136
Chaucer Head Bookshop, Warwickshire.......... 238
Chelifer Books, Cumbria 81
Cheshire Book Centre, Cheshire.................... 69
Chesters (G. & J.), Staffordshire 225
Chevin Books, West Yorkshire....................... 250
Chichester Bookshop (The), West Sussex 242
Children's Bookshop (The), Powys 289
Childrens Bookshop, West Yorkshire 248
Chris Adam Smith Modern First Editions
West Sussex.. 244
Chris Phillips, Wiltshire............................... 251
Christine's Book Cabin, Leicestershire 149
Christopher Saunders (Orchard Books),
Gloucestershire 115
Chthonios Books, East Sussex....................... 102
Church Green Books, Oxfordshire.................. 211
Church Street Books, Norfolk 187
Church Street Bookshop, London N............... 158
Churchgate Books, Suffolk........................... 227
Clapham (M. & B.), Hampshire..................... 124
Claras Books, East Sussex............................ 101
Clarendon Books, Leicestershire.................... 147
Clark (M.R.), West Yorkshire 246
Clark (Nigel A.), London SE 165
Clarke (J.&D), Norfolk 190
Clarke (Janet), Somerset 216
Clarke Books (David), Somerset 219
Clarke-Hall (J.) Limited, Kent 137
Classic Bindings Ltd, London SW 167
Classic Crime Collections, Greater Manchester .. 119
Classics Bookshop (The), Oxfordshire............. 207
Clear (Mrs. Patricia), Surrey 231
Clegg (David), Staffordshire......................... 224

ALPHABETICAL INDEX: Business (C – D)

Clements (R.W.), London Outer 182
Clent Books, Worcestershire 255
Clevedon Books, Somerset 218
Clewlow Books of Whitby, North Yorkshire 198
Clitford Elmer Books Ltd., Cheshire 68
Clifford Milne Books, Grampian.................... 272
Clifton Books, Essex 112
Coach House Books, Worcestershire 256
Cobbles Books, Somerset............................. 218
Cobnar Books, Kent 142
Cobweb Books, North Yorkshire 195
Coch-y-Bonddu Books, Powys 292
Cocks (Brian), Cambridgeshire 67
Cofion Books, Pembrokeshire 288
Cold Tonnage Books, Surrey 235
Coleman (Tom), Highland 274
Coles (T.V.), Cambridgeshire 67
Colin Hancock, Ceredigion 284
Colin Page Books, East Sussex 99
Collards Bookshop, Devon 90
Collectable Books, London SE 165
Collectables (W.H.), Suffolk 230
Collectors Carbooks, Northamptonshire.......... 200
Collectors Corner, Wiltshire......................... 253
Collinge & Clark, London WC...................... 177
Colonsay Bookshop, Isle of Colonsay............. 276
Colwyn Books, Conwy 285
Combat Arts Archive, Durham 97
Compass Books, Devon 85
Cooking = The Books, Gloucestershire 115
Cooks Books, East Sussex 99
Coombes (A.J.), Surrey 231
Cooper Hay Rare Books, Strathclyde 280
Copnal Books, Cheshire 69
Corder (Mark W.), Kent 140
Corfe Books, Surrey................................... 231
Cornell Books, Gloucestershire 117
Cornerstone Books, Devon 88
Cornucopia Books, Lincolnshire 153
Corvus Books, Buckinghamshire.................... 61
Cotswold Internet Books, Gloucestershire 113
Cottage Books, Leicestershire........................ 147
Cottage Bookshop (The), Buckinghamshire 62
Coulthurst (Richard), Greater Manchester 120
Country Books, Derbyshire 82
Countryman Books, East Yorkshire................ 106
Countrymans Gallery (The), Leicestershire 147
Coupland (Terry W.), Staffordshire................ 224
Court Hay Books, West Midlands.................. 240
Courtenay Bookroom, Oxfordshire 206
Courtney & Hoff, North Yorkshire................ 198
Courtwood Books, Co. Laois........................ 266
Courtyard Books, Gloucestershire 113
Cousens (W.C.), Devon............................... 84
Cover to Cover, Merseyside.......................... 186
Cowley, Auto-in-Print (John), Essex............... 108
Cowley, Bookdealer (K.W.), Somerset 218
Cox (Geoff), Devon 90
Cox Music (Lisa), Devon............................. 86
Cox Old & Rare Books (Claude), Suffolk 228
Cox Rare Books (Charles), Cornwall............... 74
Cox, Andrew, Shropshire............................. 215
Cranhurst Books, London 161
Craobh Rua Books, Co. Armagh................... 260
Crawford (Elizabeth), London EC.................. 157

Creaking Shelves, Inverness-shire................... 275
Crimes Ink, London E................................ 155
Criterion Books, London Outer..................... 182
Crombie (R. & S.), West Midlands................. 241
Crosby Nethercott Books, London Outer 181
Cross (Ian), Berkshire 55
Crouch Rare Books, Surrey.......................... 233
Croydon Bookshop, London Outer 181
Cumming Limited (A. & Y.), East Sussex........ 104
Curlews, Durham 97
Curtle Mead Books, Isle of Wight 134
Cygnet Books, East Yorkshire....................... 107
D Robertson (Booksellers & Booksearch Services), Lothian 277
D'Arcy Books, Wiltshire............................. 252
D. & M. Books, West Yorkshire 250
D.C. Books, Lincolnshire............................ 151
Dadd, Stephen, Kent.................................. 136
Daeron's Books, Buckinghamshire................. 62
Daisy Lane Books, West Yorkshire 247
Dalby (Richard), North Yorkshire.................. 196
Dales & Lakes Book Centre, Cumbria............ 80
Dally Books & Collectables, Powys................ 292
Dance Books Ltd, Hampshire 121
Dancing Goat Bookshop (The), Norfolk 188
Dandy Lion Editions, Surrey 233
Darkwood Books, Co. Cork......................... 263
Dartmoor Bookshop (The), Devon 84
DaSilva Puppet Books, Dorset 93
David (G.), Cambridgeshire......................... 63
David Flint, Hampshire 124
David Houston - Bookseller, London E 155
David Summerfield Books, East Sussex........... 99
David Warnes Books, Herefordshire 129
davidleesbooks.com, Powys 290
Davids Ltd., (Roy), Oxfordshire 209
Davidson Books, Co. Down 261
Davies Fine Books, Worcestershire 257
Davis, Antiquarian Books (Guy)
Nottinghamshire 205
Dawlish Books, Devon 86
DBS Childrens Collectable Books, Hampshire... 123
de Beaumont (Robin), London SW 167
De Burca Rare Books, Co. Dublin 264
de Visser Books, Cambridgeshire................... 63
Dead Mens Minds.co.uk, Powys 292
Dean Byass, Bristol.................................... 60
Dean Illustrated Books (Myra), Powys 288
Dearman Rare Books (Rebecca), Leicestershire . 147
Debbage (John), Norfolk 190
Decorum Books, London N 158
Deeside Books, Grampian............................ 273
Delectus Books, London WC........................ 177
Delph Books, Greater Manchester.................. 120
Demar Books (Grant), Kent......................... 141
Demetzy Books, Oxfordshire 208
Dene Barn Books & Prints, Somerset 220
Derek Stirling Bookseller, Kent 142
Design Gallery 1850-1950 (The), Kent 142
Devanha Military Books, Tayside 281
Deverell Books, Bristol 59
Dew (Roderick), East Sussex 101
dgbbooks, West Sussex 244
Dinnages Transport Publishing, East Sussex 103
Discovery Bookshop, Carmarthenshire............ 283

ALPHABETICAL INDEX: Business (D – F)

Dobson (Bob), Lancashire 143
Dodsworth (Ian), Cumbria........................... 78
Dolphin Books, Suffolk............................... 226
Don Kelly Books, London W 172
Donovan Military Books (Tom), East Sussex.... 99
Doodles Bookshop, North Yorkshire 196
Dooley (Rosemary), Cumbria 78
Doolin Dinghy Books, Co. Clare 262
Doorbar (P. & D.), Gwyned 287
Dorchester Bookshop (The), Dorset 92
Dormouse Bookshop (The), Norfolk 190
Dorset Bookshop (The), Dorset 91
Douglas Books, Dumfries & Galloway 269
Downie Fine Books Ltd., (Robert), Shropshire.. 215
DPE Books, Devon 87
Draca Books, West Yorkshire 249
Draycott Books, Gloucestershire 114
Driffield Bookshop (The), East Yorkshire 106
Drummond Pleasures of Past Times (David),
London WC 177
Drury Rare Books (John), Essex................... 110
Du Ry Medieval Manuscripts (Marc-Antoine),
London W 173
Dublin Bookbrowsers, Co. Dublin................. 265
Duck (William), Hampshire......................... 124
Duncan & Reid, Lothian 277
Dunn Antiques & Books (Hamish),
Northumberland 203
Dunstan Books, Dorset............................... 91
Durham Book Centre, Cumbria.................... 77
Dusty Books, Powys 292
Dylans Bookstore, Swansea 294
Dyson (Anthony), West Midlands 240
Eagle Bookshop (The), Bedfordshire 53
Earlsfield Bookshop, London SW................. 167
Earth Science Books, Wiltshire 252
East Riding Books, East Yorkshire 107
Eastcote Bookshop (The), London Outer......... 181
Eastern Books of London, London SW 167
Eastern Traveller (The), Somerset 220
Eastgate Bookshop, East Yorkshire 106
Eastgate Bookshop, Warwickshire 238
Eastleach Books, Berkshire.......................... 56
Eastwood Books (David), Cornwall 73
Eclectica, London SE 165
Edmund Pollinger Rare Books, London SW..... 167
Edrich (I.D.), London E.............................. 155
Edwards (Alan & Margaret), Kent 142
Edwards (Christopher), Berkshire 55
Edwards (London) Limited (Francis)
London WC 177
Edwards in Hay-on-Wye (Francis), Powys 290
Eggeling Books (John), West Yorkshire 250
Eggle (Mavis), Hertfordshire 131
Elaine Lonsdale Books, West Yorkshire 248
Elephant Books, West Yorkshire................... 249
Elgar (Raymond), East Sussex...................... 99
Ellis (J.R. & R.K.), Norfolk 190
Ellis, Bookseller (Peter), London WC 178
Ellwood Editions, Wiltshire 253
Elmbury Books, Warwickshire 238
Elmfield Books, West Midlands 239
Elmo Books, East Sussex............................ 99
Elstree Books, Hertfordshire 131
Elton Engineering Books, London W 173

Ely Books, Cambridgeshire 65
Embleton (Paul), Essex 111
Emjay Books, Surrey................................. 231
Empire Books, North Yorkshire 198
Endeavour Books, North Yorkshire............... 198
Engaging Gear Ltd., Essex 108
English (Toby), Oxfordshire......................... 211
Enigma Books, Norfolk 190
Enscot Books, London SE 165
Erian Books, London N.............................. 158
Esoteric Dreams Bookshop, Cumbria 78
Esplin (David), Hampshire 124
Eton Antique Bookshop, Berkshire................ 57
Evans (Mark), Lincolnshire 153
Evans Books (Paul), West Sussex 243
Everett (Richard), Norfolk 188
Everett (Richard, at the Southwold
Antiques Centre, Suffolk........................... 229
Evergreen Livres, Oxfordshire 208
Ewell Bookshop Ltd, Surrey 232
Ex Libris, Wiltshire................................... 251
Exeter Rare Books, Devon.......................... 86
Exeter Traders in Collectables Ltd, Devon 86
Facet Books, Dorset.................................. 91
Fackley Services, Nottinghamshire 205
Falconwood Transport & Military Bookshop,
London Outer 184
Family-Favourites, East Yorkshire................. 106
Fantastic Literature, Essex 111
Fantasy Centre, London N 158
Farahar & Dupre (Clive & Sophie), Wiltshire ... 251
Farnborough Gallery, Hampshire.................. 122
Farquharson, (Hilary), Tayside 281
Farringdon (J.M.), Swansea 293
Farringdon Books, Essex 109
Faversham Books, Kent 138
Fawkes (Keith), London NW 161
Fenning (James), Co. Dublin 264
Ferdinando (Steven), Somerset 220
Ferguson (Elizabeth), Grampian 272
Fiction First, Cheshire 70
Fifteenth Century Bookshop (The), East Sussex. 104
Fifth Element, West Midlands...................... 240
Finch Rare Books Ltd. (Simon), London W..... 173
Find That Book, West Yorkshire 249
Fine Art, London SW 168
Fine Books at Ilkley, West Yorkshire 248
Fine Books Oriental Ltd., London WC........... 178
Fiona Edwards, Nottinghamshire 204
Firecatcher Books, Greater Manchester........... 118
Fireside Books, Buckinghamshire 62
Fireside Bookshop, Cumbria....................... 81
First State Books, London W 173
firstpagebooks, Norfolk.............................. 190
Firsts in Print, Isle of Wight 134
Fishburn Books, London NW...................... 161
Fisher & Sperr, London N 158
Fisher Nautical, East Sussex 100
Fitzsimons (Anne), Cumbria 78
Fletcher (H.M.), Hertfordshire 132
Fogg Rare Books & Manuscripts (Sam)
London W 173
Folios Limited, London SW 168
Footballana, Berkshire 56
Footrope Knots, Suffolk............................. 228

ALPHABETICAL INDEX: Business (F – H)

Forbury Fine Books, Berkshire...................... 56
Ford (Richard), London W 173
Ford Books (David), Hertfordshire................. 133
Forder (R.W.), Hampshire 121
ForensicSearch, Hertfordshire 132
Forest Books, Nottinghamshire 205
Forest Books, Rutland................................ 212
Forest Books of Manchester, Cheshire 71
Formby Antiques (Jeffrey), Gloucestershire 115
Fortune Green Books, London NW................ 161
Fossgate Books, North Yorkshire 198
Foster (Stephen), London NW 161
Foster Bookshop (Paul), London SW 168
Fosters Bookshop, London W 173
Fotheringham (Alex), Northumberland 202
Foulkes (Len), Cardiff 283
Four Shire Bookshops, Gloucestershire 114
Fox Books (J. & J.), Kent............................ 140
Foyle Books, Co. Derry 260
Franks Booksellers, Greater Manchester.......... 119
Freader's Books, Tayside............................. 281
Freeman's Corner Shop, Norfolk 190
Frew Limited (Robert), London W................. 173
Freya Books & Antiques, Norfolk.................. 191
Fuchsia Books, Co. Wexford 267
Fuller D'Arch Smith, London W 173
Fullerton's Booksearch, Norfolk 189
Fun in Books, Surrey 235
Furneaux Books (Lee), Devon....................... 89
Fylde Books, Lancashire 146
G Collins Bookdealers, Hertfordshire 131
G. C. Books Ltd., Dumfries & Galloway......... 271
Gage Postal Books, Essex 111
Gallimaufry Books, Hertfordshire................... 132
Galloway & Porter Limited
Cambridgeshire...................................... 64
Game Advice, Oxfordshire 210
Gander, (Jacques), Gloucestershire................. 115
Garbett Antiquarian Books (Michael),
Gloucestershire 116
Gardener & Cook, London SW..................... 168
Garfi Books, Powys 293
Garretts Antiquarian Books, Isle of Man......... 259
Garwood & Voigt, Kent.............................. 140
Gaskell Rare Books (Roger), Cambridgeshire ... 66
Gathern (D.), Conwy 285
Gaullifmaufry Books, Hertfordshire 132
Gay's The Word, London WC 178
Gekoski (R.A.), London WC 178
Gemini–Books, Shropshire 215
Geneva Books, London SW 168
Geophysical Books, Kent............................. 140
George St. Books, Derbyshire 83
Gerald Lee Maritime Books, East Sussex......... 105
GfB: the Colchester Bookshop, Essex 109
Gibbard (A. & T.), East Sussex 101
Gibberd (Jane), London SE.......................... 165
Gibbs Books, (Jonathan), Worcestershire......... 256
Gibbs Bookshop Ltd., Greater Manchester 119
Gilbert (R.A.), Bristol................................. 59
Gilbert and Son (H.M.), Hampshire............... 126
Gildas Books, Cheshire 68
Gillmark Gallery, Hertfordshire..................... 131
Glacier Books, Tayside 282
Gladstone Books, Lincolnshire 152

Glance Back Books, Gwent.......................... 286
Glasheen-Books, Surrey 232
Glenbower Books, Co. Dublin 265
Glenwood Books, Surrey............................. 235
Gloucester Road Bookshop, London SW 168
Glyn's Books, Shropshire............................ 213
Godmanchester Books, Cambridgeshire 66
Golden Age Books, Worcestershire................. 256
Golden Books Group, Devon 85
Golden Goose Books, Lincolnshire................. 152
Goldman (Paul), Dorset 94
Goldsworth Books, Surrey 235
Good Book Shop, The, Devon...................... 90
Good Books, Shropshire 214
Good for Books, Lincolnshire 151
Goodden (Peter), Somerset.......................... 216
Goodwin (J.O.), Staffordshire....................... 225
Goodyer (Nicholas), London N 159
Goodyer, Natural History Books (Eric),
Leicestershire 148
Graham (John), Dorset 96
Grahame (Major Iain), Suffolk 226
Grahame Thornton, Bookseller, Dorset........... 93
Grampian Books, Grampian......................... 274
Grange Old Bookshop, Merseyside 185
Granny's Attic, Wiltshire 251
Grant, Lothian 278
Grant & Shaw Ltd., Lothian 278
Grant Books, Worcestershire 255
Gravity Books, Lincolnshire 151
Grayling (David A.H.), Cumbria 79
Grays of Westminster, London SW 168
Great Grandfather's, Lancashire 145
Great Hall Bookshop, Buckinghamshire.......... 61
Great Oak Bookshop (The), Powys 292
Green (Mrs. D.M.), Surrey.......................... 235
Green (Paul), Cambridgeshire 67
Green Ltd. (G.L.), Hertfordshire................... 132
Green Man Books, East Sussex 101
Green Meadow Books, Cornwall 74
Greene's Bookshop Ltd, Co. Dublin 265
Greenroom Books, West Yorkshire 248
Greensleeves, Oxfordshire 207
Greer (Robin), London SW.......................... 168
Gregory (George), Somerset 216
Gresham Books, Somerset 218
Greta Books, Durham 97
Grosvenor Prints, London WC 178
Grove Bookshop (The), North Yorkshire 197
GS Cricket Books / The Old Book Shop
West Midlands 241
Guildmaster Books, Cheshire 70
Guisborough Bookshop (The)
North Yorkshire 194
Hab Books, London W............................... 173
Hadfield (G.K.), Cumbria 80
Halewood & Sons, Lancashire...................... 145
Hall's Bookshop, Kent................................ 141
Hall, (Anthony C.) Antiquarian Bookseller
London Outer 184
Halson Books, Cheshire 71
Hambleton Books, North Yorkshire 197
Hames (Peter), Devon................................. 85
Hamish Riley-Smith, Norfolk........................ 192
Hanborough Books, Oxfordshire.................... 210

ALPHABETICAL INDEX: Business (H – J)

Hancock & Monks, Powys........................... 290
Hancock (Peter), West Sussex 243
Handley (Christopher), Tyne and Wear........... 236
Handsworth Books, Essex........................... 112
Hanshan Tang Books, London SW 168
Hardback Hotel, Lancashire 144
Harlequin, Devon..................................... 90
Harlequin Books, Bristol 59
Harlequin Gallery, Lincolnshire 152
Harrington (Adrian), London W.................... 173
Harrington Antiquarian Bookseller (Peter)
London SW... 169
Harris (George J.), Co. Derry 260
Hart (John), Norfolk................................. 187
Harvest Books, Lancashire.......................... 145
Harwich Old Books, Essex.......................... 110
Haskell (R.H. & P.), Dorset 94
Hatchard & Daughters, West Yorkshire.......... 247
Haunted Bookshop (The), Cambridgeshire....... 64
Hava Books, London SE............................. 165
Hawes Books, Norfolk............................... 191
Hawkes (James), London SE 165
Hawkridge Books, Derbyshire...................... 82
Hawley (C.L.), North Yorkshire 197
Hay Castle, Powys................................... 290
Hay Cinema Bookshop Ltd., Powys............... 290
HCB Wholesale, Powys............................. 290
Head (John & Judith), Wiltshire 253
Heartland Old Books, Devon....................... 89
Heath (A.R.), Bristol................................. 59
Heckmondwike Book Shop, West Yorkshire 249
Hedgerow Books, South Yorkshire................ 222
Helion & Company, West Midlands 240
Hellenic Bookservices, London NW............... 162
Helmsley Antiquarian & Secondhand Books
North Yorkshire 194
Helston Bookworm, The, Cornwall................ 74
Hemswell Antique Centre, Lincolnshire........... 151
Hencotes Books & Prints, Northumberland...... 202
Heneage Art Books (Thomas), London SW 169
Henly (John), West Sussex 245
Hennessey Bookseller (Ray), East Sussex......... 100
Henry Wilson Books, Cheshire..................... 69
Heppa (Christopher), Essex 108
Heraldry Today, Wiltshire.......................... 252
Herb Tandree Philosophy Books, Glos............ 116
Hereford Booksearch (John Trevitt)
Herefordshire 129
Hereward Books, Cambridgeshire.................. 66
Heritage, West Midlands 239
Heritage Books, Isle of Wight 134
Herne Bay Books, Kent 139
Hesketh & Ward Ltd., London SW 169
Heywood Hill Limited (G.), London W 174
Hicks (Ronald C.), Cornwall 73
High Street Book Shop, East Sussex 102
High Street Books, Devon 86
Higher Octave Books, Bristol....................... 59
Hight (Norman F.), Glamorgan.................... 286
Hill (John S.), Devon 86
Hill (Peter), Hampshire 122
Hill Books (Alan), South Yorkshire 222
Hill House Books, Devon 88
Hilton (Books) (P.J.), London W 174
Hinchliffe Books, Bristol............................ 59

Hine (Anne), Somerset.............................. 218
Hobgoblin Books, Hampshire 125
Hodgkins and Company Limited (Ian),
Gloucestershire 116
Hodgson (Books) (Richard J.)
North Yorkshire 198
Hodgson (Judith), London W 174
Hogan (F. & J.), London N 159
Holdenhurst Books, Dorset 91
Hollett and Son (R.F.G.), Cumbria 80
Holleyman (J.F.), East Sussex 103
Hollingshead (Chris), London Outer 183
Holmes Books (Harry), East Yorkshire............ 107
Holtom (Christopher), Cornwall 75
Home Farm Books, Warwickshire.................. 237
Hoovey's Books, East Sussex 102
Hornsey's, North Yorkshire......................... 195
Horsham Rare Books, West Sussex 243
Hosains Books, London NW........................ 162
House of Figgis Ltd (The), Co. Galway 266
Howard Loftus Rail Books, South Yorkshire.... 222
Howes Bookshop, East Sussex 102
HP Bookfinders, Central 269
Hünersdorff Rare Books, London SW............ 169
Hughes Rare Books (Spike), Borders.............. 268
hullbooks.com, East Yorkshire 107
Humanist Book Services, Cornwall 73
Humber Books, Lincolnshire 150
Hummingbird Books, Herefordshire............... 128
Hunter and Krageloh, Derbyshire 83
Hunter-Rare Books (Andrew), London SW 169
Hurly Burly Books, Wiltshire....................... 254
Hurst (Jenny), Kent 138
Hutchison (Books) (Larry), Fife.................... 271
Hyland (C.P.), Co. Cork 263
Hylton Booksearch, Merseyside 185
Ian Briddon, Derbyshire............................. 82
Ian McKelvie Bookseller, London N............... 159
Ice House Books, Wiltshire 253
Idle Booksellers (The), West Yorkshire 246
Idle Genius Books, London N 159
Idler (The), Suffolk 228
IKON, Devon.. 89
Inch's Books, Kent 137
Inner Bookshop (The), Oxfordshire................ 210
Innes Books, Shropshire............................. 214
Inprint, Gloucestershire 116
Intech Books, Northumberland 203
InterCol London, London N 159
Internet Bookshop UK Ltd., Gloucestershire.... 113
Interstellar Master Traders, Lancashire 144
Invicta Bookshop, Berkshire 56
Invisible Books, East Sussex 100
Iona Bookshop (The), Isle of Iona................. 276
Island Books, Devon................................. 85
Ives Bookseller (John), London Outer 184
J & J Burgess Booksellers, Cambridgeshire....... 64
J. & J. Books, Lincolnshire 151
J.A. Heacock, Cheshire 69
J.B. Books, Berkshire 56
J.C. Books, Devon.................................... 87
J.C. Books, Norfolk 192
J.C. Deyong Books, London SW 169
J.G. Natural History Books, Surrey 234
J.H. Day, Hampshire 124

ALPHABETICAL INDEX: Business (J – L)

J.L. Book Exchange, East Yorkshire 106
Jabberwock Books, Lincolnshire 151
Jackdaw Books, Norfolk 189
Jackson (M.W.), Wiltshire........................... 254
Jackson (W.E.), Hampshire 125
Jade Mountain Bookshop, Hampshire 126
James Fergusson Books & Manuscripts
London W 174
Jane Badger Books, Northamptonshire 200
Jane Jones Books, Grampian 272
Janus Books, West Midlands 240
Jarndyce Antiquarian Booksellers, London WC.. 178
Jarvis Books, Derbyshire 83
Jay Books, Lothian................................... 278
JB Books & Collectables, West Sussex 244
Jean Hedger, Berkshire 55
Jermy & Westerman, Nottinghamshire............ 205
Jill Howell, Kent 102
Jiri Books, Co. Antrim 260
Jobson (N.W.), Oxfordshire.......................... 208
Joel Segal Books, Devon 86
John Barton, Hampshire 126
John Gorton Booksearch, East Sussex 105
John L Capes (Books Maps & Prints)
Cleveland 197
John R. Hoggarth, North Yorkshire 198
John Read Antiques, Shropshire 214
John Underwood Antiquarian Books, Norfolk .. 190
Johnson Rare Book Collections (C.R.)
London NW 162
Jolly Good Read (A.), Tayside 281
Jones (Andrew), Suffolk 228
Jones (Barry), West Sussex.......................... 243
Jonkers Rare Books, Oxfordshire 209
Joppa Books Ltd., Surrey 231
Judd Books, London WC 178
Judith Mansfield, West Yorkshire.................. 250
Junk & Spread Eagle, London SE 165
Just Books, Cornwall 76
K Books, Cheshire.................................... 70
K.S.C. Books, Cheshire.............................. 71
Kabristan Archives, Shropshire..................... 215
Kalligraphia, Isle of Wight 134
Karen Millward, Co. Cork 263
Karen Thomson, Strathclyde 279
Katharine House Gallery, Wiltshire 252
Katnap Arts, Norfolk 191
Kay Books, London W 174
Keeble Antiques, Somerset 219
Keegan's Bookshop, Berkshire 56
Keel Row Bookshop, Tyne and Wear 236
Keith Langford, London E 155
Kellow Books, Oxfordshire 207
Kelly Books, Devon 89
Kelsall (George), Greater Manchester 118
Kemp Booksellers, Lancashire 143
Ken's Paper Collectables, Buckinghamshire 62
Kendall–Carpenter (Tim), Greater Manchester .. 119
Kennedy & Farley, East Sussex 104
Kennedy (Peter), Surrey 235
Kenneth Ball, East Sussex........................... 101
Kenny's Book Export Co., Co. Galway 265
Kenny's Bookshops and Art Galleries Ltd,
Co. Galway 266
Kent (Books) (Mrs. A.), Suffolk 228

Kent T. G., Surrey 231
Kentish (B. & N.), Oxfordshire..................... 206
Kenya Books, East Sussex 100
Keogh's Books, Gloucestershire 115
Kernaghans, Merseyside 186
Kerr (Norman), Cumbria 78
Kestrel Books, Hereford 290
Keswick Bookshop, Cumbria 79
Kevin S. Ogilvie Modern First Editions,
Grampian 273
Key Books (Sarah), Cambridgeshire............... 64
Kidson (Ruth), East Sussex 105
Kilgarriff (Raymond), East Sussex 105
Kilgour (Sporting Books) (Ian), Leicestershire ... 149
Killeen (John), North Yorkshire 194
Kim's Bookshop, West Sussex................. 242, 245
Kineton Nooks, Warwickshire....................... 237
Kings Bookshop Callander, Central 269
Kingsgate Books & Prints, Hampshire............ 126
Kingshead Books, Wales 293
Kingsmere Books, Bedfordshire 53
Kingswood Books, Dorset 94
Kirkcudbright Books, Dumfries & Galloway 270
Kirkdale Bookshop, London SE 165
Kirkland Books, Cumbria............................ 79
Kirkman Ltd., (Robert), Bedfordshire............. 54
Kirkpatrick (Robert J.), London W 174
Kitley (A.J.), Bristol 59
Knapton Bookbarn, North Yorkshire.............. 198
Knowles (John), Norfolk 188
Kohler (C.C.), Surrey 231
Korn (M. Eric), London N 159
Kunkler Books (Paul), Cambridgeshire 64
Kyrios Books, Nottinghamshire 204
L.M.S. Books, Hertfordshire........................ 132
Lake (David), Norfolk 191
Lake (Fred), Surrey 235
Lamb (R.W.), Suffolk 229
Lamb's Tales Books, Devon 87
Lane Books (Shirley), Isle of Wight 135
Lankester Antiques and Books, Essex............. 111
Larkham Books (Patricia), Gloucestershire....... 117
Last Century Books, Borders 268
Lawful Occasions, Essex 108
Lawrence Books, Nottinghamshire 204
Lawson & Company (E.M.), Oxfordshire 208
Laywood (Anthony W.), Nottinghamshire 204
Leabeck Books, Oxfordshire 210
Leaf Ends, Northumberland 203
Leakey's Bookshop, Highland 275
Leapman Ltd. (G. & R.), Hertfordshire 130
Lee Rare Books (Rachel), Bristol 59
Leeds Bookseller, West Yorkshire 249
Leeper (Romilly), London SW 169
Left on The Shelf, Cumbria......................... 79
Leigh Gallery Books, Essex 110
Lenton (Alfred), Leicestershire..................... 147
Letterbox Books, Nottinghamshire 204
Lewcock (John), Cambridgeshire................... 66
Lewis (J.T. & P.), Cornwall 74
Lewis First Editions, Kent 138
Libris (Weston) Books, Somerset 217
Liddle (Steve), Bristol 58
Lighthouse Books (The), Dorset 92
Lime Tree Books, Suffolk 228

ALPHABETICAL INDEX: Business (L – M)

Lion Books, Worcestershire 256
Little Bookshop (The), Greater Manchester 119
Little Bookshop (The), Cumbria 81
Little Stour Books, Kent 137
Lloyd-Davies (Sue), Carmarthenshire 284
Loch Croispol Bookshop & Restaurant
Highland 275
Logie Steading Bookshop, Grampian 274
Londinium Books, Surrey 232
London & Sussex Antiquarian Book &
Print Services, East Sussex 101
Longden (George), Cheshire 70
Loretta Lay Books, London NW 162
Lost Books, Northamptonshire...................... 201
Lowe (John), Norfolk 189
Lucas (Richard), London NW....................... 162
Lucius Books, North Yorkshire 199
Lymelight Books & Prints, Dorset 93
Lyngheath Books, Norfolk 189
M. & D. Books, Worcestershire 255
Macbuiks, North Yorkshire.......................... 194
Macfarlane (Mr. H.), Essex 112
Mactaggart (Caroline), Dorset 92
Madalyn S. Jones, West Yorkshire 247
Maggs Brothers Limited, London W 174
Maggy Browne, Lincolnshire 150
Maghreb Bookshop (The), London WC 178
Magis Books, Leicestershire......................... 149
Magpie Books, West Yorkshire 250
Main Point Books, Lothian 278
Main–Smith & Co. Ltd. (Bruce), Leicestershire.. 148
Mainly Fiction, Cheshire 68
Mair Wilkes Books, Fife 272
Malvern Bookshop (The), Worcestershire 255
Mandalay Bookshop, London SW 169
Manna Bookshop, Somerset 221
Mannwaring (M.G.), Bristol 59
Marathon Books, Greater Manchester 118
Marble Hill Books, Middlesex 184
Marcan, Bookseller (Peter), London SE 165
Marcet Books, London SE........................... 165
March House Books, Dorset 95
Marchpane, London WC............................. 178
Marco Polo Travel & Adventure Books, Dorset 92
Marijana Dworski Books, via Hereford........... 290
Marine & Cannon Books, Cheshire 71
Marine and Cannon Books, Cheshire 69
Marine Workshop Bookshop, Dorset 93
Marjon Books, Essex.................................. 112
Marks Limited (Barrie), London N................. 159
Marlborough Rare Books Ltd., London W 174
Marrin's Bookshop, Kent 138
Marshall Rare Books (Bruce), Gloucestershire... 113
Martin (Books and Pictures), (Brian P)., Surrey. 232
Martin - Bookseller (Colin), East Yorkshire 107
Martin Bookshop & Gallery (Richard), Hants... 123
Martin Music Books (Philip), North Yorkshire . 199
Martin's Books, Powys 292
Mason (Mary), Oxfordshire.......................... 206
Mayhew (Veronica), Berkshire....................... 57
Maynard & Bradley, Leicestershire 148
mcbooks, West Sussex 242
McCarty, Bookseller (M.E.), Western Isles 276
McCarty, Bookseller (M.E.)
Dumfries & Galloway............................... 271

McCaughtrie (K.A.), North Yorkshire 194
McConnell Fine Books, Kent........................ 137
McCrone (Audrey), Isle of Arran 275
McEwan Fine Books, Grampian.................... 273
McEwan Golf Books (Rhod), Grampian 273
McGee (Terence J.), London Outer 181
McGlynn (John), Lancashire........................ 143
McInnes (P.F. & J.R.), Dorset 91
McKenzie (J.W.), Surrey 232
McLaren Books, Strathclyde........................ 280
McNaughtan's Bookshop, Lothian 278
Mead (P.J.), Shropshire.............................. 214
Meadowcroft Books, West Sussex 242
Meads Book Service (The), East Sussex........... 104
medievalbookshop, Hertfordshire 133
Meekins Books (Paul), Warwickshire.............. 238
Mellon's Books, East Sussex 101
Melvin Tenner, London W........................... 174
Mercat Books, Highland 274
Mereside Books, Cheshire 70
Merlin Books, West Sussex 243
Mermaid Books (Burlingham), Norfolk........... 192
Michael D. Raftery (Books), Leicestershire....... 149
Michael Graves-Johnston, London SW 169
Michael J Carroll, Co. Cork 263
michaelsbookshop.com, Kent 139
Midnight Oil Books, Fife............................. 272
Miles Apart, Suffolk................................... 229
Milestone Books, Devon 89
Milestone Publications Goss &
Crested China, Hampshire 123
Military Bookworm, London SE.................... 165
Military Parade Bookshop, Wiltshire.............. 252
militarybookshop.com, Somerset 217
MilitaryHistoryBooks.com, Kent.................... 138
Millard (R.W.), Somerset............................ 217
Miller (Stephen), London Outer.................... 184
Mills Rare Books (Adam), Cambridgeshire 64
Ming Books, Dumfries & Galloway 271
Minster Books, Dorset 96
Minster Gate Bookshop, North Yorkshire 199
Missing Books, Essex 109
MK Book Services, Cambridgeshire 66
Mobbs (A.J.), West Midlands 241
Modern First Editions, London Outer 183
Modern Firsts Etc, Lancashire 143
Modern Welsh Publications Ltd., Merseyside 185
Modlock (Lilian), Dorset 93
Moffat Book Exchange, Dumfries & Galloway.. 270
Mogul Diamonds, West Midlands 241
Mollie's Loft, Swansea 294
Monmouth House Books, Monmouthshire 288
Moon's Bookshop (Michael), Cumbria 81
Moore (C.R.), Shropshire 214
Moore (Eric T.), Hertfordshire 131
Moore (Peter), Cambridgeshire 64
Moore (Sue), Cornwall 73
Moorhead Books, West Yorkshire.................. 246
Moorside Books, Lancashire......................... 144
Moreton Books, Devon............................... 87
Morgan (H.J.), Bedfordshire 54
Morley Case, Hampshire 125
Morris (A.E.), Gwynedd.............................. 287
Morris Secondhand & Antiquarian
Books (Chris), Oxfordshire 210

ALPHABETICAL INDEX: Business (M – P)

Morten (Booksellers) (E.J.) Greater Manchester .... 119 Moss Books, Gloucestershire .... 113 Moss Books, London NW .... 162 Moss End Bookshop, Berkshire .... 57 Mostly Mysteries Bookstore, Lincolnshire .... 152 Mothergoose Bookshop, Isle of Wight .... 135 Mount's Bay Books, Cornwall .... 75 Mountaineering Books, London N .... 159 Mr Books Bookshop, Kent .... 141 Mr. Pickwick of Towcester, Northamptonshire .. 201 Much Ado Books, East Sussex .... 99 Mulyan (Don), Merseyside .... 186 Mundy (David), Hertfordshire....................... 130 Mundy (David), Buckinghamshire .... 61 Murch Booksend, (Herbert), London SE .... 166 Murder & Mayhem, Powys .... 291 Murphy (C.J.), Norfolk .... 190 Muse Bookshop (The), Gwynedd .... 287 Music By The Score, Cornwall .... 73 Musicalania, Norfolk.................................. 189 Muttonchop Manuscripts, West Sussex .... 244 My Back Pages, London SW .... 169 N V Books, Warwickshire............................ 237 N1 Books, East Sussex .... 105 Naughton Booksellers, Co. Dublin .... 265 Nautical Antique Centre (The), Dorset .... 96 Needham Books, (Russell), Somerset .... 220 Neeve (P.), Cambridgeshire .... 63 Neil Summersgill, Lancashire .... 143 Neil's Books, London NW............................ 162 Nelson (Elizabeth), Suffolk .... 227 Nevis Railway Books, Oxfordshire .... 209 Nevis Railway Bookshops (The Antique & Book Collector), Wiltshire........................ 252 Nevitsky (Philip), Greater Manchester .... 119 New Strand Bookshop (The), Herefordshire ..... 128 Newband (D.M.), Powys .... 293 Newcastle Bookshop At Haltwhistle, Northumberland .... 202 Newgate Books and Translations Northumberland .... 202 Newlyn & New Street Books, Cornwall .... 75 Newport Book Shop .... 214 Nibris Books, London SW .... 170 Nicholson of Chester (Richard), Cheshire ....68 Nicolas - Antiquarian Booksellers & Art Dealers, London N .... 159 Niner (Marcus), Isle of Wight .... 134 Nineteenth Century Books, Oxfordshire .... 211 Nonsuch Books, Surrey............................... 234 Northern Herald Books, West Yorkshire .... 246 Norton Books, North Yorkshire .... 197 Nostalgia Unlimited, Merseyside .... 186 Not Just Books, Dorset............................... 94 O'Brien Books & Photo Gallery, Co. Limerick .. 266 O'Connor Fine Books, Lancashire.................. 145 O'Donoghue Books, Powys .... 291 O'Flynn Books, North Yorkshire .... 199 O'Kill (John), Kent .... 138 O'Reilly - Mountain Books (John), Derbyshire.. 83 Oakwood Books, Gloucestershire .... 115 Oasis Booksearch, Cambridgeshire................. 67 Oast Books, Kent .... 137 Obscurebooks, Co. Dublin 265

Occultique, Northamptonshire....................... 200 Octagon Books, Cambridgeshire .... 66 Offa's Dyke Books, Shropshire .... 214 Old Aberdeen Bookshop, Grampian .... 272 Old Bookshelf (The), Strathclyde................... 279 Old Bookshop (The), West Midlands .... 241 Old Celtic Bookshop (The), Devon .... 88 Old Hall Bookshop (The), Northamptonshire ... 200 Old Station Pottery & Bookshop (The) Norfolk .... 192 Old Town Bookshop (The), Lothian .... 278 Olynthiacs, Shropshire .... 214 Onepoundpaperbacks, North Yorkshire .... 193 Oopalba Books, Cheshire............................. 71 Optimus Books Ltd, West Sussex .... 245 Orange Skies Books, Cumbria....................... 80 Orangeberry Books, Oxfordshire .... 209 Orb's Bookshop, Grampian.......................... 274 Orbis Books (London) Ltd., London W .... 175 Orchid Book Distributors, Co. Clare............... 262 Orlando Booksellers, Lincolnshire .... 152 Orssich (Paul), London SW .... 170 Osterley Bookshop, London Outer .... 183 Othello's Bookshop, Essex .... 110 Ouse Valley Books, Bedfordshire .... 54 Outcast Books, Powys .... 291 Over-Sands Books, Cumbria .... 78 Owen (J.V.), Conwy .... 285 owenbooks65, Conwy.................................. 285 Oxfam Books and Music, Hampshire .... 126 Oxfam Bookshop St Giles, Oxfordshire........... 210 Oxford House Books, Powys .... 291 Oxley (Laurence), Hampshire....................... 121 P. and P. Books, Worcestershire .... 256 Pagan Limited (Hugh), London SW................ 170 Page (David), Lothian .... 278 Palladour Books, Hampshire .... 126 Pamona Books, Lancashire .... 145 Pandion Books, North Yorkshire .... 195 Pantiles Bookshop, Kent .... 141 Paper Moon Books, Gloucestershire .... 116 Paper Pleasures, Somerset .... 219 Paperbacks Plus, Bristol .... 59 Parade Bookshop, Suffolk............................ 230 Paragon Books, Somerset .... 219 Paralos Ltd., London WC .... 178 Paramor (C.D.), Suffolk .... 229 Parikian, Rare Books (Diana), London W ..... 175 Park (Mike), London Outer.......................... 183 Park Gallery & Bookshop (The) Northamptonshire .... 201 Parker Books (Mike), Cambridgeshire .... 64 Parkinsons Books, Merseyside....................... 186 Parlour Bookshop (The), Oxfordshire .... 207 Parrott (Jeremy), London E.......................... 156 Parrott Books, Oxfordshire .... 211 Past & Present Books, Gloucestershire .... 114 Past & Presents, Cumbria .... 77 Past Sentence, Kent .... 138 Pastmasters, Derbyshire.............................. 83 Paton Books, Hertfordshire .... 132 Paul Hoare, Cornwall .... 75 Pauline Harries Books, Hampshire .... 123 Peake (Robin), Lincolnshire.......................... 153 Peakirk Books, Cambridgeshire 67

ALPHABETICAL INDEX: Business (P – R)

Pedlar's Pack Books, Devon 84
Peel (Valerie), Berkshire 55
Pemberley Books, Buckinghamshire 62
Pend Books, Dumfries & Galloway 270
Pendleburys Bookshop, London N 159
Pendleside Books, Lancashire........................ 144
Pennymead Books, North Yorkshire 194
Peregrine Books (Leeds), West Yorkshire......... 249
Periplus Books, Buckinghamshire.................... 62
Periwinkle Press, Kent 139
Peter Clay, Cornwall 74
Peter Lyons Books, Gloucestershire 114
Peter M Daly, Hampshire............................. 127
Peter Pan Bookshop, Norfolk 192
Peter White, Hampshire............................... 121
Peter's Bookshop, Norfolk 192
Petersfield Bookshop (The), Hampshire........... 124
Peterson (Tony), Essex................................ 111
Petworth Antique Market (Bookroom)
West Sussex... 244
Phelan Books, Co. Dublin 265
Phelps (Michael), West Sussex...................... 243
Phenotype Books, Cumbria 80
Philip Hopper, Essex 110
Phillips (Nigel), Hampshire.......................... 122
Phillips of Hitchin (Antiques) Ltd.
Hertfordshire 131
Pholiota Books, London WC......................... 179
Photo Books International, London WC 179
Phototitles.com, Essex................................. 109
Piccadilly Rare Books, East Sussex 105
Pickering & Chatto, London W..................... 175
Pickering Bookshop, North Yorkshire 197
Pimpernel Booksearch, London SW................ 170
Pinnacle Books, Lothian............................... 278
Plurabelle Books, Cambridgeshire................... 64
Pocket Bookshop (The), Devon 88
Poetry Bookshop (The), Powys...................... 291
Polczynski (Udo K.H.), Powys 291
Pollak (P.M.), Devon 89
Polmorla Books, Cornwall 76
Pomes Penyeach, Staffordshire 224
Pooks Motor Books, Leicestershire................. 148
Poole (William), London W 175
Poor Richard's Books, Suffolk 227
Popeley (Frank T.), Cambridgeshire................ 67
Porcupine Books, London Outer.................... 182
Pordes Books Ltd., (Henry), London WC......... 179
Porter Bookshop (The), South Yorkshire......... 222
Portobello Books, London W 175
Portus Books, Hampshire............................. 122
Post Mortem Books, West Sussex 243
Post–Horn Books, North Yorkshire................. 193
Postings, Surrey 234
Potterton Books, North Yorkshire.................. 197
Pratt (B.A. & C.W.M.), Herefordshire 128
Prescott - The Bookseller (John)
London Outer 184
Preston Book Company, Lancashire 145
Price (John), London N 159
Price (R.D.M. & I.M.) (Books) Gr Man 120
Price (R.W.), Nottinghamshire 204
Priestpopple Books, Northumberland 202
Primrose Hill Books, London NW 162
Pringle Booksellers (Andrew), Lothian 278

Print Matters, London SE............................. 166
Printing House (The), Cumbria 78
Prior (Michael), Lincolnshire 153
Probsthain (Arthur), London WC 179
Prospect Books, Conwy 285
Prospect House Books, Co. Down.................. 261
PsychoBabel Books & Journals, Oxfordshire..... 206
Pugh Books (Ian K.), Worcestershire.............. 256
Pyecroft (Ruth), Gloucestershire 117
Quaritch Ltd., (Bernard), London W.............. 175
Queen Victoria PH, Torfaen 294
Quentin Books Ltd, Essex............................ 109
Quest Books, East Yorkshire 107
Quest Booksearch, Cambridgeshire 65
Quinto of Charing Cross Road, London WC ... 179
Quinto of Great Russell Street, London WC 179
R M Books, Hertfordshire 132
R & B Graham Trading, Cornwall.................. 74
R. & A. Books, East Sussex 102
R. S. & P. A. Scowen, Middlesex 182
R.E. & G.B. Way, Suffolk 229
Raftery Books (Michael D.), Leicestershire....... 149
Railway Book and Magazine Search, Berkshire . 56
Railway Shop (The), Torfaen........................ 294
Rainbow Books, East Sussex 100
Rainford (Sheila), Hertfordshire..................... 130
Randall (Tom), Somerset............................. 219
Rare & Racy, South Yorkshire...................... 222
Rare Books & Berry, Somerset...................... 219
Rassam (Paul), London NW 162
Ray Rare and Out of Print Books (Janette)
North Yorkshire 199
Rayner (Hugh Ashley), Somerset 217
Read Ireland, Co. Dublin 264
Read - Gorleston Books, (C. & J.), Norfolk 188
Readers Rest, Lincolnshire 152
Readers World, West Midlands 239
Reading Lasses, Dumfries & Galloway 271
Reads, Dorset 95
Reaveley Books, Devon 87
recollectionsbookshop.co.uk, Cornwall............. 74
Red Rose Books, Lancashire 145
Red Star Books, Hertfordshire 130
Rees & O'Neill Rare Books, London WC......... 179
Reeves Technical Books, North Yorkshire 196
Reference Works Ltd., Dorset....................... 95
Regent Furniture, Oxfordshire....................... 211
Reid of Liverpool, Merseyside....................... 185
Reigate Galleries, Surrey 233
Remington (Reg & Philip), Hertfordshire......... 133
Restormel Books, Worcestershire 257
Resurgam Books, East Yorkshire.................... 106
RGS Books, Surrey 235
Rhodes, Bookseller (Peter), Hampshire 126
Rhos Point Books, Conwy............................ 285
Richard Axe Rare & Out of Print Books
North Yorkshire 193
Richard Connole, Devon 85
Richard Thornton Books, London N 160
Richmond Books, North Yorkshire 195
Rickaro Books, West Yorkshire...................... 247
Riddell (Peter), East Yorkshire 106
Rider Haggard Society (The), Tyne and Wear... 236
Riderless Horse Books, Norfolk...................... 187
Riley Books (V.M.), Greater Manchester......... 119

ALPHABETICAL INDEX: Business (R – S)

Ripping Yarns, London N 160
Rising Tide Books, Fife.............................. 271
Rivendale Press, Buckinghamshire 62
River Reads Bookshop, Devon...................... 90
Riviera Books, Norfolk 188
Roadmaster Books, Kent............................. 137
Robert (Leslie), London W 175
Robert G Sawers Ltd, London NW................ 162
Robert Humm & Co, Lincolnshire 154
Robert Temple, London N........................... 160
Robert's Shop, East Sussex 102
Roberts (Booksellers), (Ray), Staffordshire 224
Roberts Books, Ayrshire 280
Roberts Fine Books (Julian), Lincolnshire........ 153
Roberts Wine Books (John), Bristol 59
Robertshaw (John), Cambridgeshire 66
Robertson Books, Lothian 278
Robin Doughty - Fine Books, W Midlands...... 239
Rochdale Book Company, Gr Man 120
Rods Books, Devon 88
Roe and Moore, London WC 179
Roger Collicott Books, Cornwall 75
Roger Lucas Booksellers, Lincolnshire 151
Roger Treglown, Cheshire........................... 70
Rogers Turner Books, London SE.................. 166
Roland Books, Kent 139
Rolfe (John), London SE............................ 166
Rolling Stock Books, Greater Manchester........ 120
Rookery Bookery, Staffordshire.................... 225
Roosterbooks, Northamptonshire................... 200
Rosanda Books, Leicestershire 148
Roscrea Bookshop, Co. Tipperary................. 267
Rose Books, Greater Manchester 119
Rose's Books, Powys................................. 291
Rosemary Pugh Books, Wiltshire 253
Rosley Books, Cumbria 81
Ross & Company Ltd, (Louise), Worcs.......... 255
Ross Old Books & Prints, Herefordshire 128
Rothwell & Dunworth, Somerset 218
Roundstone Books, Lancashire...................... 144
Roundwood Books, Shropshire 215
Rowan (H. & S.J.), Dorset.......................... 91
Rowan (P. & B.), Co. Antrim 260
Rowan House Books, Surrey 232
Royal Carbery Books Ltd., Co. Cork 262
Roz Hulse, Conwy 286
Ruebotham (Kirk), Cheshire........................ 71
Rugby Relics, West Glamorgan 294
Rupert Books, Cambridgeshire 65
Ruskin Books, Kent................................... 136
Russell (Charles), London SW...................... 170
Rutland Bookshop (The), Rutland 212
Ryde Bookshop (The), Isle of Wight 134
Rye Old Books, East Sussex 104
Ryeland Books, Northamptonshire 200
S.P.C.K., Bristol 60
S.P.C.K., Hampshire 127
SaBeRo Books, London SW........................ 170
Sabin (Printed Works) (P.R. & V.), Kent......... 136
St Ann's Books, Worcestershire 255
St Mary's Books & Prints, Lincolnshire 154
St Paul's Street Bookshop, Lincolnshire 154
St Philip's Books, Oxfordshire...................... 210
St Swithin's Illustrated & Children's
Books, London W................................... 175

Saintfield Antiques & Fine Books, Co. Down ... 261
Salsus Books, Worcestershire 256
Saltburn Bookshop, North Yorkshire 195
Salway Books, Essex 112
Samovar Books, Co. Dublin 264
Sandpiper Books Ltd., London SW 170
Sandstone Books, Kent 137
Sansovino Books, West Sussex 244
Saracen Books, Derbyshire.......................... 83
Sarawak Books, East Yorkshire.................... 106
Saunders (Tom), Caerphilly 283
Savage (Keith A.), Suffolk 229
Sax Books, Suffolk 229
Scarthin Books, Derbyshire 82
Schofield Golf Books (Steve), West Yorks 250
Schull Books, Co. Cork 263
Schutte (David), Hampshire......................... 124
Sclanders (Beatbooks), (Andrew), London EC... 157
Scorpio Books, Suffolk 226
Scott (Peter), East Sussex............................ 104
Scrivener's Books & Bookbinding, Derbyshire... 82
Sea Chest Nautical Bookshop (The), Devon 88
Seabreeze Books, Lancashire........................ 145
Second Edition, Lothian 278
Secondhand Bookshop, Surrey 234
Secondhand Bookshop, The, Kent................. 141
Sedgeberrow Books & Framing, Worcs........... 256
Seeber (Liz), East Sussex 102
Sen Books, Hampshire............................... 127
Sensawunda Books, Cheshire 68
Sephton (A.F.), London W 175
Sesemann (Julia), Kent............................... 136
SETI Books, Staffordshire........................... 225
Seydi Rare Books (Sevin), London NW 162
Shacklock Books (David), Suffolk 227
Shakeshaft (Dr. B.), Cheshire....................... 71
Shakespeare Books (Colin), Staffordshire 224
Shapero Rare Books (Bernard J.), London W... 175
Sharpe (Mary), Somerset 221
Shaun Lofthouse, North Yorkshire................. 196
Shearwater Books, Northumberland............... 202
Sheet Music Warehouse (The), Devon 88
Shelley (E. & J.), Buckinghamshire 61
Sheriffmuir Books, Central 269
Sherlaw-Johnson (Austin), Oxfordshire 210
Sherratt (Ian J.), Staffordshire 224
Sidey, Bookdealer (Philip), Kent 140
Sillan Books, Co. Cavan............................. 262
Silver Trees Books, West Midlands................ 240
Silverman (Michael), ... 166
Simmonds (Anthony J.), London SE............... 166
Simon Lewis Transport Books, Glos 115
Simon's Books, Somerset............................ 220
Simply Read Books, East Sussex................... 101
Simpson (Dave), Stirlingshire 269
Simpson (Marianne), Grampian.................... 274
Sims (Sue), Dorset.................................... 91
Sims Reed Limited, London SW................... 170
Singleton (Anthony), South Yorkshire 222
Siop Lyfrau'r Hen Bost, Gwynedd 287
Siop y Morfa, Denbighshire 286
Sit-a-While Bookshop and Tea Room, The,
Warwickshire 237
Skelton (Tony), Kent................................. 141
Skipton Antiques Centre, North Yorkshire....... 197

ALPHABETICAL INDEX: Business (S – T)

Skirrid Books, Monmouthshire..................... 287
Skoob Russell Square, Suffolk...................... 230
Skyrack Books, West Yorkshire.................... 248
Sleepy Elephant Books & Artefacts, Cumbria ... 80
Smith (Clive), Essex 109
Smith (David & Lynn), London Outer............ 182
Smith (Ray), Hertfordshire........................... 130
Smith Books (Keith), Herefordshire 128
Smith Books, (Nigel), Surrey 231
Smith Books, (Sally), Suffolk 227
Smith Maritime Aviation Books (Frank)
Tyne and Wear....................................... 236
Soccor Books Limited, Lincolnshire 150
Sokol Books Ltd., London W....................... 175
Solaris Books, East Yorkshire 106
Soldridge Books Ltd, Hampshire 124
Solitaire Books, Somerset............................ 217
Sotheran Limited (Henry), London W 176
South Downs Book Service, West Sussex......... 244
Sparkes (Books) (Ray), Staffordshire 225
Sparrow Books, West Yorkshire 246
Spearman Books, East Sussex 104
Spelman (Ken), North Yorkshire 199
Spenceley Books (David), West Yorkshire........ 249
Spink, London WC 179
Spooner & Co, Somerset 220
Spooner (John E.), Dorset 91
Spurrier (Nick), Kent 138
Squirrel Antiques, Hampshire 122
Stackpoole (George), Co. Limerick.................. 266
Staffs Bookshop (The), Staffordshire 224
Stained Glass Books, Kent........................... 140
Stalagluft Books, Tyne and Wear................... 236
Staniland (Booksellers), Lincolnshire 154
Stansbury (Rosemary), Devon....................... 89
Star Lord Books, Greater Manchester 119
Steedman (Robert D.), Tyne and Wear........... 236
Stella Books, Monmouthshire 288
Stepping Stones Bookshop, North Yorkshire 194
Sterling Books, Somerset 221
Stern Antiquarian Bookseller (Jeffrey), N Yorks 199
Steven Simpson Books, Norfolk 191
Stevens (Joan), Cambridgeshire..................... 65
Stinton (Judith), Dorset.............................. 92
Stobart Davies Limited, Carmarthernshire 284
Stokes Books, Co. Dublin............................ 265
Stone Trough Books, North Yorkshire 199
Stone, (G.& R.), Borders 268
Stothert Old Books, Cheshire........................ 69
Stour Bookshop, Dorset.............................. 95
Strand Bookshop (The), Powys 293
Strathtay Antiquarian - Secondhand Books
Tayside 282
Stroh (M.A.), London E 155
Stroma Books, Borders 268
Studio (The), Strathclyde 280
Studio Bookshop, East Sussex....................... 100
Sturford Books, Wiltshire 254
Sub Aqua Prints and Books, Hampshire 123
Sue Lowell Natural History Books, London W. 176
Suffolk Rare Books, Suffolk 230
Sugen & Co., North Yorkshire...................... 193
Summerfield Books Ltd, Cumbria 77
Surprise Books, Gloucestershire 113
Susan Taylor Books, West Yorkshire 248

Susanne Schulz-Falster Rare Books, London N. 160
Sutcliffe (Mark), West Yorkshire.................... 248
Sutcliffe (Victor), Norfolk 188
Sykes (Graham), West Yorkshire 249
Symes Books (Naomi), Cheshire 72
Talisman Books, Cheshire............................ 70
Tall Tales Bookshop, Highland 275
Taney Books, Co. Dublin 264
Tant Yn Ellen Books, Powys 293
Tarka Books, Devon 84
Tasburgh Books, Norfolk 191
Taylor & Son (Peter), Hertfordshire................ 133
Taylor Rare Books (Michael), Norfolk 187
Temperley (David), West Midlands................. 239
Tennis Collectables, Cheshire 68
Tetbury Old Books, Gloucestershire................ 117
Thanatos Books, Greater Manchester.............. 119
The End Bookshop, Devon 89
The Glass Key, West Yorkshire...................... 247
The Old Abbey Bookshop, Co. Down 261
The Old Children's Bookshelf, Lothian 278
The Old Music Master, Bristol 60
The Sanctuary Bookshop, Dorset................... 94
The Stratford Bookshop, Warwickshire........... 238
Theatreshire Books, North Yorkshire 193
Thin Read Line, Merseyside 185
Thistle Books, Strathclyde............................ 280
Thomas (Barry), Ceredigion 284
Thomas (Books) (Leona), Cheshire................. 71
Thomas (E. Wyn), Conwy 285
Thomas Rare Books, Suffolk 227
Thornber (Peter M.), North Yorkshire............. 196
Thorne (John), Essex.................................. 109
Thorntons of Oxford Ltd., Oxfordshire............ 207
Throckmorten's Bookshop, Warwickshire 237
Tiffin (Tony and Gill), Durham..................... 97
Tiger Books, Kent..................................... 137
Till's Bookshop, Lothian 279
Tilleys Vintage Magazine Shop
South Yorkshire...................................... 223
Tilleys Vintage Magazine Shop, Derbyshire...... 82
Tilston (Stephen E.), London SE.................... 166
Tin Drum Books, Leicestershire..................... 148
Tindley & Chapman, London WC 179
Titford (John), Derbyshire 82
Tobo Books, Hampshire.............................. 123
Tombland Bookshop, Norfolk 191
Tony Pollastrone Railway Books, Wiltshire...... 251
Tooley, Adams & Co, Oxfordshire 211
Torc Books, Norfolk 189
Towers (Mark), Lancashire 144
Townsend (John), Berkshire 57
Towpath Bookshop, Greater Manchester......... 120
Tozer Railway Books (Nick), West Yorkshire ... 248
TP Children's Bookshop, West Yorkshire 246
Trafalgar Bookshop, East Sussex 100
Transformer, Dumfries & Galloway 271
Travel Bookshop (The), London W 176
Traveller's Bookshelf (The), Somerset 217
Travis & Emery Music Bookshop
London WC 180
Treadwell's Books, London WC 180
Treasure Chest Books, Suffolk 227
Treasure Island (The), Greater Manchester....... 119
Treasure Trove Books, Leicestershire.............. 148

ALPHABETICAL INDEX: Business (T – W)

Tregenna Place Second Hand Books, Cornwall . 75
Trevorrow (Edwin), Hertfordshire 130
Trinders' Fine Tools, Suffolk 227
Trinity Rare Books, Co. Leitrim 266
Trotman (Ken), Cambridgeshire 66
Trotter Books (John), London N 160
Tsbbooks, London SW 170
Tucker (Alan & Joan), Gloucestershire 117
Tuft (Patrick), London Outer........................ 182
Turret House, Norfolk................................ 192
Turton (John), Durham 98
Twigg (Keith), Staffordshire......................... 224
Twiggers Booksearch, Bedfordshire................. 53
Two Jays Bookshop, London Outer................ 181
Tyger Press, London N............................... 160
Ulysses, London WC................................. 180
Uncle Phil's Books, West Midlands 240
Undercover Books, Lincolnshire 154
Underwater Books, East Sussex..................... 103
Unsworth's Booksellers, London WC 180
Unsworths Booksellers, London WC.... ... 180
Updike Rare Books (John), Lothian 279
Upper-Room Books, Somerset....................... 218
Vailima Books, Dumfries & Galloway 270
Valentine Rare Books, London W.................. 176
Vandeleur Antiquarian Books, Surrey............. 232
Vanstone - Aviation Books, (Derek), Suffolk 230
Venables (Morris & Juliet), Bristol.................. 60
Ventnor Rare Books, Isle of Wight................. 135
Verandah Books, Dorset 95
Vickers (Anthony), North Yorkshire 196
Victoria Bookshop (The), Devon.................... 84
Victorian Gallery (The), Shropshire................. 215
Village Books, Norfolk 187
Vinovium Books, Durham 97
Vintage Motorshop, West Yorkshire 246
Vokes (Jeremiah), Durham.................. 97
Vokes Books Ltd., North Yorkshire................ 195
VOL:II, Essex 108
Volume Three, Clackmannanshire 269
Volumes of Motoring, Gloucestershire 113
W & A Houben, Surrey 234
Wadard Books, Kent 138
Waddington Books & Prints (Geraldine),
Northamptonshire 200
Wakeman Books (Frances), Nottinghamshire.... 205
Walcot (Patrick), West Midlands.................... 241
Walden Books, London NW 163
Walker (Adrian) Bedfordshire 54
Walker (Gary), Fife 271
Walker Fine Books (Steve), Dorset 92
War & Peace Books, Hampshire.................... 122
Ward (R.F. & C.), Norfolk 188
Warnes (Felicity J.), London Outer................. 181
Warrender (Andrew), West Yorkshire.............. 250
Warrington Book Loft (The), Cheshire 72
Warsash Nautical Bookshop, Hampshire......... 126
Warwick Leadley Gallery, London SE............. 166
Water Lane Bookshop, Wiltshire 253
Waterfield's, Oxfordshire 210
Waterstone's, London WC........................... 180
Watkins (R.G.), Somerset 216
Watkins Books Ltd., London WC.................. 180
Waxfactor, East Sussex 100
Way's Bookshop, Oxfordshire....................... 209

Wayside Books and Cards, Oxfordshire 207
Wealden Books, Kent................................. 139
Webb Books (John), South Yorkshire.............. 222
Webster (D.), Strathclyde............................ 280
Weiner (Graham), London N 160
Weininger Antiquarian Books (Eva M.)
London NW.. 163
Wells (Mary), London SW........................... 170
Wembdon Books, Somerset......................... 217
Wenlock Books, Shropshire.......................... 214
Wensum Books, Norfolk 191
Weobley Bookshop, Herefordshire................. 129
Westcountry Old Books, Cornwall.................. 76
Westcountry Oldbooks, Devon...................... 90
Westfield Books, North Yorkshire.................. 199
Westgate Bookshop, Lincolnshire.................. 153
Westons, Hertfordshire 133
Westwood Books (Mark), Powys 291
Westwood Books Ltd, Cumbria..................... 80
Westwords, Strathclyde 280
Wetherell (Frances), Cambridgeshire 65
Wheeler's Bookshop, West Sussex 244
Wheen O'Books, Scottish Borders 269
Whelan (P. & F.), Kent............................... 141
Whig Books Ltd., Leicestershire.................... 149
Whistler (R.A.), East Sussex 99
Whistler's Books, London SW 170
Whitchurch Books Ltd., Cardiff..................... 283
White (C.R.), London W............................. 176
White (David), Cambridgeshire..................... 65
White (Mrs. Teresa), London W 176
Whitehall Books, East Sussex........................ 103
Whitfield (Ken), Essex 111
Whittle, Bookseller (Avril), Cumbria 81
Wiend Books, Lancashire 144
Wilbraham (J. & S.), London NW 163
Wildside Books, Worcestershire 255
Wildy & Sons Ltd, London WC 180
William H. Roberts, West Yorkshire............... 248
Williams (Bookdealer), (Richard)
North Lincolnshire 154
Williams (Christopher), Dorset 94
Williams Rare Books (Nigel), London WC 180
Willmott Bookseller (Nicholas), Cardiff........... 283
Wilson (David), Buckinghamshire 61
Wilson (James), Hertfordshire 130
Wilson (Manuscripts) Ltd., (John)
Gloucestershire 114
Winchester Bookshop (The), Hampshire.......... 127
Winghale Books, Lincolnshire 153
Wise (Derek), East Sussex............................ 104
Witmehaé Productions, Leicestershire 149
Wizard Books, Cambridgeshire...................... 67
Woburn Books, London N 160
Wood (Peter), Cambridgeshire...................... 65
Wood Cricket Books (Martin), Kent............... 140
Woodbine Books, West Yorkshire.................. 246
Woodlands Books, West Yorkshire................. 249
Woodside Books, Kent 136
Woolcott Books, Dorset.............................. 92
Worcester Rare Books, Worcestershire............ 257
Words Etcetera Bookshop, Dorset.................. 93
World War Books, Kent 141
World War II Books, Surrey 235
Worlds End Bookshop, London SW............... 171

ALPHABETICAL INDEX: Business (W – Z)

Worrallo (J. & M.A.), West Midlands 241
Wright (Norman), Dorset 95
Wright Trace Books, West Midlands............... 240
www.AntiqueWatchStore.com, Hertfordshire 130
Wycherley (Stephen), West Midlands.............. 239
Wychwood Books, Gloucestershire 116
Wykeham Books, London SW 171
Wyseby House Books, Berkshire................... 55
Xanadu Books, Cleveland 98
Ximenes Rare Books Inc., Gloucestershire 115
Yarborough House Bookshop, Shropshire 213
Yarwood Rare Books (Edward), Gr Man........ 118
Yates Antiquarian Books (Tony), Leicestershire. 148
Yeoman Books, Lothian 279
Yesterday Tackle & Books, Dorset 92
Yesterday's Books, Dorset 92
Yesterday's News, Conwy........................... 285
Yesteryear Railwayana, Kent....................... 139
Yewtree Books, Cumbria............................ 79
York (Graham), Devon.............................. 86
York Fine Books, North Yorkshire 199
York Modern Books, North Yorkshire............ 197
Yorkshire Relics, West Yorkshire................... 247
Young (D. & J.), Powys............................. 293
Ystwyth Books, Ceredigion 284
Zardoz Books, Wiltshire............................. 254

ALPHABETICAL INDEX BY NAME OF PROPRIETOR

Adams (N.T.) = G. David 63
Adams (V.) = Upper–Room Books 218
Addyman (D.) = Addyman Books 289
Addyman (D.) = Murder & Mayhem 291
Ainge (G.) = Golden Age Books..................... 256
Aitman (T.) = Black Voices.......................... 185
Allcoat (K.) = Tarka Books 84
Allen (P.J.) = Robert Temple 160
Allen (R.) = Bufo Books 125
Allinson (J. & M.) = Facet Books 91
Allsop (D.) = Duncan M. Allsop 238
Almond (G.) = Westgate Bookshop 153
Altshuler (J.) = Jean Altshuler....................... 79
Ameringen (B.) = Porcupine Books 182
Anderson (S.) = The Travel Bookshop Ltd 176
Andrews (Mrs. J.) – Alton Secondhand Books... 121
Ansorge (E. & W.) = Barn Books 61
Applin (M.) = Malcolm Applin 55
Aptaker (N.) = Neil's Books.......................... 162
Archer (D.) = David Archer 292
Ardley (C.M.) = Faversham Books.................. 138
Armishaw (K.& S.) = River Reads Bookshop 90
Armitage (M.) = The Porter Bookshop 222
Armstrong (A.) = Moffat Book Exchange 270
Arthur (E.J.L.) = Fantasy Centre 158
Ashby (M.) = Martin's Books........................ 292
Ashcroft (R.E.) = The Inner Bookshop............ 210
Ashworth (R.H.) = Whistler's Books............... 170
Askew Books (V.) = Vernon Askew Books 251
Asplin (D.C.) = G. David 63
Astbury (B. & V.) = Woodlands Books 249
Attree (M.) = Birmgham Books...................... 239
Austen (P.) = Phillip Austen 153
Austin (A.) = Farringdon Books..................... 109
Bacon (J) = Bookzone 55
Bacon (J.) = Pholiota Books......................... 179
Baggott (L. & H.) = Wychwood Books 116
Bainbridge (S.R.) = Offa's Dyke Books........... 214
Baine (Mr & Mrs) = The Rutland Bookshop..... 212
Baker (J.A.) = J.B. Books............................. 56
Baldwin (D. & J.) = Rosanda Books................ 148
Ball (B.W.) = Harlequin Books 59
Ball (C.F. & I A.) = J.C. Books...................... 192
Ball (E.W.) = Fantasy Centre 158
Ballance (C.) = Byre Books.......................... 270
Bamping (A.) = Tyger Press 160
Bangor (Viscount) = Hesketh & Ward Ltd........ 169
Barfield (I.&K.) = hullbooks.com 107
Barnes (R. & M.) = Church Green Books 211
Baron (Dr. P.J.) = P.J. Baron -
Scientific Book Sales................................. 217
Barrett (J. & P.) = Hobgoblin Books 125
Barry (Q. & R.) = Sansovino Books 244
Bartle (C.) = Glacier Books........................... 282
Bartley (M.) = Howes Bookshop 102
Barwell(M.) = Newport Book Shop 214
Bastians(M) = Eton Antique Bookshop 57
Bates (G. & J.) = Bates Books 182
Bates (J.) = Bates & Hindmarch 249

Batten (P.) = Whitehall Books 103
Bayliss (Dr G.M) = War & Peace Books.......... 122
Bayntun-Coward (C.) = George Gregory.......... 216
Bayntun–Coward (G.) = George Bayntun......... 216
Beard (P.) = Hill House Books....................... 88
Beardsell (E.V.) = Beardsell Books 247
Beattie (A.) = Americanabooksuk 77
Beckham (J.E.) = Beckham Books Ltd............. 230
Beeby (B. & Son) = Cader Idris Books 292
Beer (D.W.) = Crosby Nethercott Books 181
Bell (J.) = Fortune Green Books..................... 161
Bell (S.) = Green Meadow Books.................... 74
Bennett (D.) = dgbbooks.............................. 244
Benster (S. & B.) = Childrens Bookshop 248
Bentley (J.) = Albion Books 239
Beresiner (Y.) = InterCol London 159
Bertsein (N.) = Nicholas Bernstein.................. 172
Berry (D.) = Botting & Berry......................... 103
Berry (M.) = Rare Books & Berry................... 219
Besley (P.& G.) = Besleys Books.................... 226
Biro (T. & S.) = Collectable Books 165
Blackman (M. & R.) = Blackman Books.......... 72
Blakemore (I.) = Rosley Books 81
Blessett (J.) = St. Paul's Street Bookshop......... 154
Blessett (S.) = Wizard Books 67
Bletsoe (P.) = Badger 253
Blore (G.T.) = Jermy & Westerman 205
Boehm (H.) = Artco 204
Boland (D.) = Trafalgar Bookshop 100
Bond (R.) = Marathon Books......................... 118
Boon (H.) – Fullerton's Booksearch 189
Borthwick (T.) = The Old Station Pottery &
Bookshop 192
Boss (T.) = Tim Boss 244
Boswell (B.) = The Great Oak Bookshop 292
Botting (J.) = Botting & Berry 103
Bowe (T.B.) = Browse Books........................ 144
Bowie (J.) = Bowie Books & Collectables 107
Boyd-Cropley (J.M.) = Cottage Books 147
Brachotte (P.) = Chapter Two........................ 164
Bradbury (A.) = Brad Books, ... 111
Bradley (S.) = Maynard & Bradley 148
Brett (S.) = Chandos Books 183
Brewin (K.A.F.) = Brewin Books Ltd.............. 238
Brichto (A.) = Addyman Books...................... 289
Brichto (A.) = Murder & Mayhem 291
Bridger (N.J.) = Railway Book and
Magazine Search 56
Bridger (N.J.) = Nevis Railway
Bookshops 209, 252
Brightman (C.) = Chantrey Books................... 222
Bristow (J.A.) = South Downs Book Service 244
Brittain (J.) = JB Books & Collectables............ 244
Broad (S.) = Camilla's Bookshop 101
Brook (R.A. & P.P.) = The Bookshop,
Kirkstall 248
Brooman (J. & J.) = Spearman Books 104
Brotchie (A.) = Atlas................................... 158
Brown (A.) = David Archer 292

ALPHABETICAL INDEX: Proprietor (B – D)

Brown (M.G. & B.J.) = Brown-Studies 279
Brown (P.) = Bookbox 116
Brown (R. & R.) = Ken Trotman 66
Browne (M.) = Maggy Browne 150
Browne (R.) = Main Point Books 278
Bryant (E.H.) = Vandeleur Antiquarian Books... 232
Bryer-Ash (P.G.) = Branksome Books 94
Bryers (T.) = Tim Bryers Ltd......................... 178
Buck (J.) = Polmorla Books 76
Buckler (R. & S.) = Cobweb Books 195
Budek (P.M. & M.M.) = The Eagle Bookshop... 53
Bull (T.) = Bowden Books 149
Burca (E.) and (V.) = De Burca Rare Books 264
Burden (C.) = Clive A. Burden Ltd.................. 132
Burden (D.) = Derek Burden 233
Burgin (A.) = Woburn Books 160
Burkett (D.) = Musicalania 189
Burmester (J.R.) = James Burmester 59
Burridge (Dr. Peter) = Quest Books................. 107
Burrow (b.) = Books and Things 258
Burrows (N. & H.) = Modern First Editions 183
Burton (R.F.) = The Parlour Bookshop 207
Burwood (N.) = Any Amount of Books............ 177
Bush (F.) = Othello's Bookshop 110
Butler (T.) = Stour Bookshop 95
Button (C.) = Little Stour Books 137
Byatt (T.) = Golden Age Books....................... 256
Byrne (A.) = Foyle Books.............................. 260
Byrne (C.) = The Old Bookshelf 279
Byrne (C.) = Charlie Byrne's Bookshop 265
Byrne (K. & C.) = Colonsay Bookshop 276
Byrom (J.) = Towpath Bookshop.................... 120
Byrom (R.) = Richard Byrom
Textile Bookroom................................... 143
Cahn (M.) = Plurabelle Books 64
Canvin (G.L.) = Whitchurch Books Ltd............ 283
Cardwell (R. & A.) = The New Strand
Bookshop 128
Carlile (G.) = East Riding Books 107
Carmody (P.) = Brighton Books 99
Carpenter (R.D.) = Bonython Bookshop.......... 76
Carruthers (Dr. G.B.) = London & Sussex
Ant. Books & Print Sevices 101
Carss (G.) = Earth Science Books 252
Cartwright (S.) = babelog.books 128
Case (D.) = Morley Case............................... 125
Casey (K.F.) = Sub Aqua Prints and Books 123
Casson (C.) = Norton Books 197
Cauwood (R.) = The Treasure Island 119
Cawthorn (T.M.) = Suffolk Rare Books............ 230
Chadband (Mrs. B.) = Solway Books 270
Chaddock (M.) = Antiquary Ltd.(Bar Bookstore) 196
Chambers (J.) = Broadleaf Books.................... 294
Chapman (C.) = Paragon Books...................... 219
Chapman (E.M.) = Bookquest 84
Chapman (R.) = Tindley & Chapman 179
Chappell (G.) = Valentine Rare Books 233
Chatten (D.) = Riviera Books 188
Checkland (S.) = Rising Tide Books 271
Checkley (A.) = Stothert Old Books 69
Cheke (A.S.) = The Inner Bookshop 210
Child (M.) = michaelsbookshop.com 139
Child (R. & J.) = Paton Books........................ 132
Christian Literature Stalls = Barbican
Bookshop 198

Churcher (P.R.) = The Victoria Bookshop 84
Churchill–Evans (D.) = Marine and
Cannon Books 69, 71
Clark (A. & G.) = Ainslie Books 279
Clarke (J.) = Janet Clarke.............................. 216
Clarke (R.) = Muttonchop Manuscripts 244
Clarke (V.) = The Little Bookshop 119
Clegg (D.) = David Clegg 224
Clement (C.) = Brighton Books 99
Cockram (A.) = Golden Goose Books.............. 152
Cocks (M.) = Badgers Books......................... 245
Collard (B.) = Collards Bookshop 90
Collett (D.W.) = Military Bookworm 165
Collie (R.) = Sandpiper Books Ltd. 170
Collinge (V.H.) = The Border Bookshop 250
Collins (A.) = Pedlar's Pack Books.................. 84
Collyer (W.J.) = Books Bought & Sold 232
Combellack (P. & J.) = Kellow Books 207
Compton (M.) = The Idle Booksellers 246
Connolly (T.) = Booknotes 111
Conway (Ms. S.A.) = Books for Writers 287
Conwell (B.) = Dusty Books.......................... 292
Cook (M.) = Internet Bookshop UK Ltd. 113
Cooper (R.J.) = Marjon Books 112
Cope (D.) = Left on The Shelf 79
Coppock (C.) and (J.) = Fireside Books 62
Corbett (C.) = Corvus Books.......................... 61
Corbett (R.) and (S.) = Booklore 148
Cork (A.) = Roundwood Books 215
Cornell (G.) = Cornell Books.......................... 117
Cornish (I.) = Ambra Books 58
Corrall (L.) = The Pocket Bookshop 88
Coulthurst (S.) = Beaver Booksearch............... 226
Coupe (M.) = Eclectica 165
Court (Mr. & Mrs.) = Bannatyne Books 158
Court (R. & A.) = Mountaineering Books 159
Cox (G.A.) = Kirkdale Bookshop 165
Cox (A.B.) = Claude Cox Old & Rare Books 228
Cox (L.) = Lisa Cox Music............................ 86
Cox (P.) = Peter's Bookshop 192
Cox (P.) = Peter Pan Bookshop...................... 192
Cozens (N.) = Lymelight Books & Prints 93
Cranwell (J.) = Bookworld............................. 214
Cresswell (P.M.) = Humber Books 150
Crimmings (T.) = Criterion Books................... 182
Crook (C.) = Bath Old Books......................... 216
Cross (J.) = Books & Collectables Ltd. 63
Crouch (A.S.) = Crouch Rare Books 233
Culme-Seymour (M.A.) = Marco Polo
Travel & Adventure Books,........................ 92
Cundy (D.) = Dene Barn Books & Prints 220
Dakin (B.) = Letterbox Books 204
Daly (K.) = Rainbow Books 100
Dancy (J.E. & A.B.) = Broadwater Books 125
Danks (N.) = ForensicSearch.......................... 132
D'Arch Smith (T.) = Fuller D'Arch Smith 173
Davies (G.&R.) = Gemini–Books.................... 215
Davies (J. & L.) = Stepping Stones Bookshop.... 194
Davies (R.) = Davies Fine Books..................... 257
Dawson (M.) = Ampersand Books 213
Daymond (D.) = Arden Books &
Cosmographia 237
de Visser (E.) = de Visser Books 63
Dearn (R.A.) = The Sea Chest Nautical
Bookshop 88

ALPHABETICAL INDEX: Proprietor (D – G)

Degnan (P.) = Kay Books 174
Della–Ragione (G.) = Henry Pordes Books Ltd.. 179
Demar (G.) = Grant Demar Books 141
De Martini (M.) = Altea Antique Maps & Books . 172
Dennis (G.) = Blacklock's.............................. 232
Dennys (N.) = Gloucester Road Bookshop 168
Devlin (Mrs P.) = The Warrington Book Loft ... 72
Dibble (R.) = Thistle Books 280
Dinnage (Mr G. & C.) = Dinnages
Transport/Picture Publishing...................... 103
Dixon (C.) = Earlsfield Bookshop 167
Bobbyn (D. & A.) = Yesterday Tackle and
Books 92
Dollery (A.) = Kingswood Books.................... 94
Donaldson (A.) = Judd Books 178
Doran (A.) = Falconwood Transport &
Military Bookshop.................................. 184
Douthwaite (G. & W.) = Clevedon Books 218
Downes (D.) = Dublin Bookbrowsers............... 265
Doyle (A.) = Books & Collectables Ltd............ 63
Dreda (A.) = Wenlock Books 214
Dreyer (M. & L.) = Philip Martin Music Books . 199
Driver (M.) = Waxfactor 100
Druett (D.) = Pennymead Books 194
Ducat (N.) = Devanha Military Books 281
Duckworth (A.) = Sen Books 127
Duerdoth (S.) = Eric Goodyer, Natural History
Books 148
Dumble (Mrs. A.) = Durham Book Centre 77
Dunbar (D.) = Aurelian Books 161
Dunn (C.R.) = Anchor Books........................ 151
Dwyer (D.&J.) = Newgate Books and
Translations.. 202
Dyke (S.) = Skyrack Books........................... 248
Eastman (P.V.) = Eastern Books of London...... 167
Edgecombe (S.M.) = J. Clarke–Hall Limited 137
Edmonds (M.J.) = The Dorchester Bookshop .. 92
Edmunds (D.R.D.) = John Drury Rare Books ... 110
Edwards (C.) = Christopher Edwards............... 55
Elgar (R.) = Raymond Elgar 99
Elissa (N.M.) = Joppa Books Ltd.................... 231
Elithorn (A.) = Game Advice 210
Ellingworth (M. & S.) = Coach House Books 256
Elliston (P.) = Firsts in Print,......................... 134
Erskine (M.) = Christopher Edwards............... 55
Evans (M.) = Mark Evans 153
Evans (M.) = Mollie's Loft 294
Evans (S.) = Kings Bookshop Callander,........... 269
Excell (A. & L.F.) = Bookmark
(Children's Books) 253
Fairnington (P.) = Manna Bookshop 221
Farley (F.) = Kennedy & Farley 104
Farnsworth (B.) = Ouse Valley Books 54
Faulkner (Lady) = Bookline 261
Feehan (G. & M.) = Royal Carbery Books Ltd.. 262
Fenning (J. & C.) = James Fenning,
Antiquarian Books 264
Fernee (B.) = Caduceus Books 147
Figgis (N.) = The House of Figgis Ltd 266
Fines (R.) = Chapter & Verse 152
Finlay (Dr. R. & Dr L.A.) = Barlow Moor Books. 118
Fishburn (J.) = Fishburn Books...................... 161
Fisher (B.) = March House Books................... 95
Fisher (C.) = Bookbox................................. 116
Flanagan (M. & L.) = Zardoz Books 254

Flint (P.) = Birdnet Optics Ltd. 82
Flowers (L.) = Kim's Bookshop 242, 243, 245
Ford (G.) = Books With Care......................... 53
Ford (J.) = Books Antiques & Collectables 90
Fordyce (D.) = Lewis First Editions................. 138
Forster (C.A.) = C.R. Johnson Rare
Book Collections..................................... 162
Foster (J.A.) = The Park Gallery & Bookshop ... 201
Foster (P.) = Paul Foster Bookshop................. 168
Foster (W.A.&M.A.) = Fosters Bookshop 173
Fothergill (T.) = Ken Spelman 199
Fowkes (M.) = Kingsgate Books & Prints 126
Francombe (C.) = Camilla's Bookshop 101
French (S.) = Dawlish Books.......................... 86
Frith (V. & R.) = recollectionsbookshop.co.uk .. 74
Fruin (C.) = L.M.S. Books 132
Gange (C.) = Katharine House Gallery............. 252
Gardner (A.) = Daeron's Books 62
Gardner (J. & M.) = The Children's Bookshop . 289
Gardner (M.) = Emjay Books........................ 231
Gardner (R.) – Forbury Fine Books................. 56
Gartshore (Y.) = Calluna Books 95
Garwood (N.) = Garwood & Voigt 140
Gavey (G.P.& C.M.) = Channel Islands
Galleries Ltd. 258
Gentil (P.) = Aviabooks 114
George (G.) = Baggins Book Bazaar Ltd.......... 140
George (S.) = The Book Shelf 87
Gestetner (J.) = Marlborough Rare Books Ltd... 174
Gibbs (J.) = Hummingbird Books 128
Gibson (J.A.B. & J.L.) = Wayside Books
& Cards 207
Gilbert (R.A.) = R.A. Gilbert 59
Giles (D. G.) = Ancient Art Books.................. 167
Gipps (A.) = Woodside Books 136
Gleeson (L.) = Nonsuch Books 234
Gleeson (R.) – Nonsuch Books....................... 234
Glover (S.) = Handsworth Books.................... 112
Goddard (J.) = Solaris Books 106
Goddard (M.) = Rose's Books 291
Golden (E.) = Dorset Bookshop, The............... 91
Goodenough (M.) = Inprint 116
Goodfellow (A.P.) = Carlton Books................. 190
Goodrick–Clarke (Dr. N. & C.) = IKON 89
Goodwin (J.O.) = J.O. Goodwin..................... 225
Goodyer (E.) = Eric Goodyer, Natural
History Books 148
Gorman (N.) = medievalbookshop 133
Gorton (J.) = John Gorton Booksearch 105
Gosden (S.G.) = Fantastic Literature 111
Goss (M.) = The Dancing Goat Bookshop 188
Goss (M.R.) = Delectus Books....................... 177
Goulding (J.) = Optimus Books Ltd 245
Govan (D.) = Armchair Books........................ 276
Gowen (M.) = The Book Jungle 105
Graham (K. & J.) = Ken's Paper Collectables.... 62
Grant (B.& S.) = Grant Books 255
Grant (F.) = The Little Bookshop 81
Graves-Johnston (M.) = Michael
Graves-Johnston 169
Greatwood (J.) = J.G. (Natural History Books).. 234
Green (J.R.) = Castle Bookshop 109
Green (R.&R.) = Treasure Chest Books............ 227
Greenhalgh (R.) = Piccadilly Rare Books 105
Greenwood (N.) = Right Now Books (Burma)... 169

ALPHABETICAL INDEX: Proprietor (G – K)

Gretton (B.) = Leigh Gallery Books................. 110
Greysmith (B.) = Pedlar's Pack Books.............. 84
Grogan (P.) = R.A. Gekoski 178
Gwynne (Mr. N.M.) = Britons Catholic Library.. 267
Habraszewski (T.) = Hab Books..................... 173
Hadfield (G.K. & J.V.) = G.K. Hadfield 80
Hadfield–Tilly (N.R.) = G.K. Hadfield 80
Hadley (P.J.) = Harwich Old Books................. 110
Haffner (R.N.) = Postings............................. 234
Haldane (J.) = Abington Bookshop 228
Halewood (M.) = Preston Book Company........ 145
Hall (D.) = Hanborough Books...................... 210
Hall (J.) = Garretts Antiquarian Books............. 259
Hall (S.&T.) = Invicta Bookshop 56
Hallgate (J.) = Lucius Books 199
Hamburger (R.B.) = Riderless Horse Books...... 187
Hancock (E.) = Hancock & Monks 290
Hanna (J.) = Blaenavon Books...................... 294
Hanson (D. & M.) = D. & M. Books 250
Harding (J.) = Roundstone Books.................. 144
Hardman (L.R.) = Broadhurst of
Southport Ltd. 186
Hardwick (C.) = Rookery Bookery.................. 225
Harlow (Dr. B.J. & S.) = Tiger Books.............. 137
Harper (T.) = World War Books 141
Harries (P.) = Boz Books 289
Harris (K.) = Books on Spain........................ 184
Harrison (L.) = Biblion................................ 172
Harrison (S.J.) = Bracton Books.................... 63
Hartles (D.B. & J.) = Goldsworth Books.......... 235
Haslam (J.) = Brock Books.......................... 193
Haslem (J.) = Oakwood Books...................... 115
Havercroft (J.) = Hava Books....................... 165
Hawes (S. & J.) = Bosco Books..................... 73
Hawkin (S.) = The Staffs Bookshop................ 224
Hay Cinema Bookshop Ltd = Francis
Edwards in Hay–on–Wye 290
Hayhoe (M.) = Corfe Books......................... 231
Haylock (B. & J.) = The Idler....................... 228
Hearn (K.) = Newlyn & New Street Books 75
Heatley (Mr. & Mrs. P.R.) = The Dartmoor
Bookshop 84
Hebden (M.) = M. & D. Books...................... 255
Hedge (P. & E.) = Hedgerow Books 222
Helstrip (A.) = Fossgate Books 198
Herbert (W.) = Photo Books International........ 179
Herries (D.) = Find That Book 249
Herron (M.) = The Bookshop........................ 263
Hessey (A.) = Reads 95
Hewson (E.) = Kabristan Archives 215
Hickley (Dr. R.H.) = Baedekers &
Murray Guides...................................... 222
Hill (A.) = Alan Hill Books........................... 222
Hill (G. & G.) = Bowdon Books 144
Hill (K.R.) and (S.J.) = Stained Glass Books 140
Hinchcliffe (C.) = Empire Books.................... 198
Hinchliffe (Mrs. A.) = Whig Books Ltd............ 149
Hinde (H.M.) = Ystwyth Books 284
Hine (J.) = Gresham Books.......................... 218
Hiscock (L.) = E. Chalmers Hallam................ 125
Hitchens (B. & E.) = Silver Trees Books 240
HMV Media Group = Waterstone's 180
Hinchliffe (G.) = Hinchliffe Books.................. 59
Hodgkins (J.R.) = Clifton Books 112
Holman (P.) = Invisible Books...................... 100

Holtom (C.) = Christopher Holtom 75
Hooper–Bargery (E.) = Music By The Score 73
Hornseys' (B.,S., &D.) = Hornseys' of Rippon... 195
Horsnell (B.) = Footballana 56
Hougham (M.) = Verandah Books.................. 95
Howard (D.) = Outcast Books 291
Howard (J.) = Photo Books International......... 179
Howell (N.) = Rolling Stock Books 120
Hoy (I.) = Ian Hodgkins and Company Limited. 116
Hubbard (P.) = Bufo Books 125
Hudson (H.G.) = The Malvern Bookshop 255
Hughes (A.R.) = Roland Books 139
Hughes (P.D.) = Deverell Books.................... 59
Hulse (R.) = Roz Hulse............................... 286
Hunt (P.) = The Railway Shop 294
Hunt (R. & C.) = Vintage Motorshop.............. 246
Hunter (J.A.) = Hunter and Krageloh 83
Husband (M.) = Merlin Books....................... 243
Hutchison (C. & R.) = Chapter House Books.... 95
Hyslop (D.A.) = Yeoman Books.................... 279
Inch (P.&E.) = Inch's Books......................... 137
Innes (P.) = Innes Books 214
Ions (B. & G.) = Richmond Books.................. 195
Irvine (J.A.M.) = R.A. Gekoski..................... 178
Irwin (C. & M.) = The Book House 77
Israel (N.) = Nibris Books 170
Ives (B.) = Simon's Books 220
Izzard (S.) = Hall's Bookshop....................... 141
James (J.A.R.) = Village Books 187
Jameson (C.) = Potterton Books.................... 197
Jeffers (D.) = My Back Pages 169
Jelfs (D.) = Moreton Books 87
Johnson (C. & C.) = On the Wild Side 255
Johnson (C.R.) = C.R. Johnson Rare Book
Collections 162
Johnson (I.A.) = Pembury Books................... 62
Johnson (J.) = Reaveley Books...................... 87
Johnson (M.L.) = Seabreeze Books................ 145
Johnson (P.) = The Bookshop....................... 118
Johnson (W.F. & C.R.) = Past & Presents 77
Johnston (A.L. & A.) = The Iona Bookshop 276
Johnston (I. & H.) = Winghale Books 153
Jolliffe (P.) = Ulysses................................. 180
Jones (B.) = Barry Jones 243
Jones (B.) = Pastmasters.............................. 83
Jones (E.) = Yesterday's News 285
Jones (E.A.) = Siop Lyfrau'r Hen Bost 287
Jones (H.M.) = Books for Content.................. 128
Jones (N.) = Musebookshop.......................... 287
Jones (R.) = Ex Libris 251
Jones (R.W.) = Northern Herald Books........... 246
Karlou (P.G.) = Crouch Rare Books 233
Kaszuk (N.) = Trinity Rare Books 266
Kay (J. & J.) = K Books............................... 70
Keegan (J.&J.) = Keegan's Bookshop.............. 56
Kelly (L.&L.) = Kelly Books Limited............... 89
Kelly (P.) = Book Mongers 167
Kemp (N.) = Judd Books 178
Kennedy (H.) = Kennedy & Farley 104
Kenny (C.) = Kennys Bookshop and Art Galleries
Ltd 266
Kent (G. & P.) = Military Parade Bookshop 252
Kenyon (H.S.) = Brazenhead Ltd................... 189
Kernaghan (A.&B.) = Kernaghans 186
Key (S.) = Sarah Key Books 64

ALPHABETICAL INDEX: Proprietor (K – N)

Kaindra Associates Ltd = Valerie Peel 55
Kinderman (G.) = Brimstones 103
King (A. & C.A.) = Wealden Books 139
King (I. W.) = Kings Bookshop Callander, ... 269
Kinnaird (J. & J.) = Keswick Bookshop 79
Kinsella (W.) = Chapters Bookstore................. 264
Kirby (E.) = Vailima Books 270
Kitley (A.J.) = A.J. Kitley............................. 59
Knapman (C.) = Collectors Carbooks 200
Koh (J.) = Bernard Quaritch Ltd. 175
Kousah (M.G.) = Ely Books 65
Kowalski (S.) = Mereside Books...................... 70
Kunkler (P.) = Paul Kunkler Books.................. 64
Laing (E.) = Blacket Books............................ 277
Laing (E.) = Meadowcroft Books.................... 242
Laithwaite (S.) = Mereside Books 70
Lake (B.) = Barndyce Antiquarian Booksellers.... 178
Lamb (J.) = Tasburgh Books.......................... 191
Lamb (J. & E.) = Lamb's Tales....................... 87
Lamont (D.) = The Bookpassage 213
Larkham (P.) = Dive In Books 117
Lawrence (A.) = Lawrence Books 204
Lay (R.) = Alba Secondhand Music................. 279
Layzell (M.) = Othello's Bookshop 110
Leach (G.) = Mogul Diamonds 241
Leckey (J.) = Saintfield Antiques and Fine Books.. 261
Ledraw (J.) = J.L. Book Exchange 106
Lee (R.) = Rachel Lee Rare Books................... 59
Leek (R.J.) = Modern Firsts Etc. 143
Leeper (R.) = Romilly Leeper 169
Leeson (J.) = Eric T. Moore Books 131
Levete (G.) = The Book Business.................... 172
Levett (G.) = Grays of Westminster................. 168
Lewis (D. & J.) = Bookshop (Godmanchester) ... 66
Lewsey (C.) = Freya Books & Antiques 191
Liddell (S. & E.) = Bookworms 187
Liddle (S.) = Steve Liddle 58
Lidgett (D.J. & C.) = D.C. Books 151
Lidyard (F.W.) = Ruskin Books 136
Lipson (P.) = Antiques on High 209
Lloyd (D.I.) = Worcester Rare Books 257
Loh (C.Y.) = Skoob Russell Square................. 230
Lord (M.) = Hurly Burly Books 254
Lovett (M. J.) = Occultique........................... 200
Lowndes (C.) = The Chichester Bookshop 242
Lucas (R.) = Richard Lucas 162
Lunt (J.) = Books at the Warehouse 195
McBride (C.) = Caledonia Books 280
McCarthy (A.) = Dandy Lion Editions 233
McClement (R.H. & J.M.) = Draycott Books 114
McConnell (N.) = McConnell Fine Books 137
McCrory (M.) = Books B.C. 181
MacDonald (N.) = BOOKS4U 286
MacGregor (C. & J.) = D'Arcy Books.............. 252
MacGregor (N.) = Olynthiacs 214
McKee (C.) = Orlando Booksellers.................. 152
Mackey (M.) = Fuchsia Books........................ 267
McKirdy (T.) = Cooks Books......................... 99
MacTaggart (C.) = Bridport Old Books 92
Madani (M.B.) = The Maghreb Bookshop........ 178
Madden (H.) = Cavern Books......................... 70
Maddison (J.K.) = Anvil Books...................... 240
Maddock (T.) = Alpha Books......................... 158
Maggs (E.) = Maggs Brothers Limited.............. 174

Mair (J.) = Mair Wilkes Books 272
Manley (S. & M.) = Barter Books................... 202
Manning (R.) = R. & A. Books 102
Marcan (P.) = Peter Marcan........................... 165
Marsh (B.) = Lime Tree Books 228
Marshall (A.) = Warsash Nautical Bookshop..... 126
Marten (W.) = Bookstand 94
Martin (J. & B.) = Bryony Books 249
Martin (R. & E.) = Richard Martin Bookshop & Gallery.. 123
Mather (H.S.G) = Wykeham Books 171
Matthews (J. & M.) = Two Jays Bookshop....... 181
Matthews (J.) = Eddie Baxter - Books.............. 221
Mattley (J.E.) = Phenotype Books................... 80
May (E. & D.) = The Eastcote Bookshop.......... 181
Mayall (M. & R.) = Sturford Books 254
Mayes (W.) = Mr. Pickwick of Towcester......... 201
Maynard (D.) = Maynard & Bradley 148
McGivney (J.) = Kenya Books........................ 100
McKelvie (L.) = The Studio 280
Mcaden (B.) = Gullifmaufry Books 132
Meeuws (W.A.) = Thorntons of Oxford Ltd...... 207
Menelaou (M.) = Antique Prints of the World ... 158
Michael (S.) = Chevin Books......................... 250
Micklewright (C.) = Wright Trace Books 240
Miles (D.) = The Canterbury Bookshop 136
Miles (H.) = Calendula Horticultural Books 102
Millard (A.) = R. & A. Books 102
Millard (R.) = Wembdon Books..................... 217
Miller (G.) = Resurgam Books....................... 106
Miller (P.) = Ken Spelman............................ 199
Minet (P.P.B.) = Piccadilly Rare Books 105
Missing (C.) = Missing Books........................ 109
Mitchell (A.G.) = Capital Bookshop 283
Mitchell (C.) = Ripping Yarns 160
Mitchell (Dr. D.J.) = Scarthin Books 82
Mitchell (D.R. & M.E.) = Bruce Main-Smith & Co. Ltd. 148
Monckton (I.) = Kingshead Books 293
Monks (J.) = Hancock & Monks 290
Moore (C.N., E.J. & S.J.) = Castle Bookshop.... 292
Moore (R.) = R M Books 132
Morgan (Dr. D.H. & R.A.) = Turret House...... 192
Morgan (P.) = Coch-y-Bonddu Books 292
Morgan-Hughes (A.) = Black Cat Books 188
Morley (A.P.) = Bay Bookshop 285
Morris (G. & B.) = Rhos Point Books.............. 285
Morrish (K. & J.) = Reigate Galleries 233
Morton (A.) = Andrew Morton Books 289
Moy (R.F.) = Spread Eagle Bookshop............. 165
Mucci (R. M.) = Robert's Shop...................... 102
Mullen (P. & M.) = Yesteryear Railwayana 139
Mullett (G.&A.) = The Eastern Traveller.......... 220
Mundy (D.) = David Mundy at Heritage Antiques.. 130
Mundy (D.) = David Mundy at Nooks and Crannies.. 61
Murdoch (G.) = Armchair Auctions 121
Murphy (R.P.) = Rods Books......................... 88
Murtagh (C.J.) = Anvil Books 240
Mustin (L.) = Byre Books............................. 270
Mycock (D. & M.) = Abacus Books and Cards . 224
Nairn (E.G.) = John Updike Rare Books 279
Nash (M. & V.) = Marine and Cannon Books... 69
Nassau (J.) = Jarndyce Antiquarian Booksellers . 178

ALPHABETICAL INDEX: Proprietor (N – R)

Naylor (Dr. A.C.I.) = Bookfare 81
Neal (D.) = The Secondhand Bookshop 141
Neal (D.) = Secondhand Bookshop 234
Neal (j.) = Kineton Books 237
Nearn (Rev. D.H.) = Heritage Books 134
Neil (D.) = Westcountry Oldbooks 76, 90
Neville (C.) = Woodbine Books 246
Newbold (R.) = Booktrace International 86
Newland (J.& C.) = Cotswold Internet Books 113
Newlands (G.M.D.) = McLaren Books 280
Newman (P.) = Castle Hill Books 128
Newton (D.) = Tasburgh Books 191
Nicholls (P. & C.) = Boxwood Books & Prints... 220
Nicholls (T.) = Paperbacks Plus 59
Nisbet (D.) = Sterling Books 221
Noble (C. & M.) = Christine's Book Cabin 149
Nummelin (S.&A.) = Browning Books 294
O'Brien (C.) = The Celtic Bookshop 266
Obeney (P.) = Idle Genius Books 159
O'Connell (B. & J.) = Schull Books 263
O'Connor (J.&E.) = O'Connor Fine Books 145
O'Donnell (G.) = Bristol Books 60
Ogden (C.) = The Meads Book Service 104
O'Keeffe (N.S.) = Evergreen Livres 208
Oldham (G.) = Greenroom Books 248
Oldham (Dr. T.) = Wyseby House Books 55
Ollerhead (P.E.) = Copnal Books 69
Ondaatje (C.) = Rare Books & Berry 219
O'Neill (A.) = Rees & O'Neill Rare Books 179
Osgood (L.) = Four Shire Bookshops 114
Overton Fuller (J.) = Fuller D'Arch Smith 173
Owen (J.V.) = Colwyn Books 285
Owen (J.) = owenbooks65 285
Painell (C.) = The Design Gallery 1850-1950 142
Palmer (E.) = Elmfield Books,........................ 239
Papworth (M.J.) = Hunter and Krageloh 83
Park (M.) = Mike Park 183
Parker (A.) = Frank Smith Maritime Aviation ... 236
Parker (M.) = Mike Parker Books 64
Parr (K.) = Kyrios Books 204
Parry (A.) = Meadowcroft Books 242
Parry (G.M.) = Skirrid Books 287
Parry (R.C.) = Exeter Rare Books 86
Partington (F. & J.) = Tennis Collectables 68
Pattenden (C.) = Red Star Books 130
Patterson (J.B.) = Priestpopple Books 202
Pawson (D. & L.) = Footrope Knots 228
Peace (R.) = Brockwells Booksellers 150
Peacock (R.) = Firecatcher Books 118
Pearce (P.) = Hencotes Books & Prints 202
Peers (C.J.) = Mainly Fiction 68
Peggs (K.) = All Books 110
Pegler (P. & W.) = Canon Gate Bookshop 244
Penney (B.) = Invisible Books 100
Perry (I.) = The Strand Bookshop 293
Perry (M.) = Barn Books 215
Petrie (I.R.) = Bookworms 187
Phil (M.) = Rosanda Books 148
Phillips (C.) = Bath Old Books 216
Phillips (C.) = Chris Phillips 251
Phillips (J.) = Periplus Books 62
Phillips (J.) = Phillips of Hitchin 131
Phillips (S.D.) = Bygone Books 276
Piercy (N.S.) = Crimes Ink 155
Pilkington (P.) = The Art Book Company 228
Pinches (R.) = Heraldry Today 252
Pine (L.) = Milestone Publications Goss &
Crested China 123
Pinto (P.) = Interstellar Master Traders 144
Pipe (M.) = Enscot Books 165
Pizey (J.S.) = P. and P. Books 256
Platt (R.) = Bookshop on the Heath, The 164
Pogmore (Mrs. E.M.) = Books 206
Poklewski-Koziell (S.) = Classic Bindings 167
Pollock (Dr. J.) = Whig Books Ltd 149
Pook (B.&J.) = ... 148
Poole (S.) = Biblion 172
Potter (R.) = Badgers Books 245
Powell (J. & A.) = Palladour Books 126
Pratt (R.J.) = Hereward Books 66
Pretlove (M.) = Gillmark Gallery 131
Prince (C.) = The Poetry Bookshop 291
Pritchard (S.) = The Blue Penguin 116
Proctor (C.D. & H.M.) = The Antique Map
& Bookshop 94
Pugh (D.) = Carta Regis 293
Purkis (H.H. & P.A.) = Harry Holmes Books 107
Pye (J. & H.) = The Bookshop 243
Quigley (A.) = Bibliophile Books 155
Ralph (A.) = Art Reference Books 125
Ramsden (G.) = Stone Trough Books 199
Raxter (C.) = Lion Books 256
Rayner (J. & J.) = J. & J. Books 151
Read (C. & J.) = Gorleston Books 188
Read (T.) = Home Farm Books 237
Reading (B. & J.) = Oast Books 137
Reding (Mrs. P.F.) = Croydon Bookshop 181
Reese (R.W.) = Holdenhurst Books 91
Reeve (A.) = Cover to Cover 186
Rhead (J.) = Barnhill Books 275
Richards (A.) = Cold Tonnage Books 235
Richards (D.) = Rugby Relics 294
Richardson (A.) = Afar Books International 239
Richardson (E.) = Blewbury Antiques 207
Richmond (M.) = AA1 Books 270
Richmond (M.) = Ming Books 271
Ridler (Dr. A.M.) = Nineteenth Century Books.. 211
Riley (A. & J.) = Ryeland Books, ... 200
Riley (V.M.) = V.M. Riley Books 119
Ritchie (J.) = Books Afloat 96
Ritchie (P.) = Books 137
Ritchie (P.) = Bookworm 277
Robbins (P.J.) = Elmbury Books 238
Roberts (G.) = Magpie Books 250
Robinson (C.) = Creaking Shelves 275
Robinson (P. & S.) = Pomes Penyeach 224
Robinson (T.F.) = J.C. Books 192
Robinson-Brown (P.) = P.R. Brown (Books) 98
Rockall (A.) = Kingswood Books 94
Roe (A.&D.) = Roe and Moore 179
Rogers (D.) = Helion & Company 240
Rogers (M.) = Fifth Element 240
Rogers (P.J.) = Croydon Bookshop 181
Rogers (P.J.) = Rogers Turner Books 166
Rowan (H.) = H. & S.J. Rowan 91
Ronald (A.) = A. & R. Booksearch 74
Ronald (R.) = A. & R. Booksearch 74
Ronan (S.) = Chthonios Books 102
Roper (B.) = Eastgate Bookshop 106
Ross (M.C.) = Avonworld Books 218

ALPHABETICAL INDEX: Proprietor (R – T)

Rothschild (R.) = Twiggers Booksearch 53
Routh (S.A.) = Gage Postal Books.................. 111
Rowley (F.) = Freader's Books 281
Rowlinson (D.A.) = Books Ulster 261
Russell (M.P.) = The Bibliophile..................... 222
St. Aubyn (H.M. & J.R.) = Woolcott Books 92
Salin (P.) = Sarah Key Books 64
Salt (D.T.) = Salsus Books............................ 256
Sames (M.D.) = The Ryde Bookshop............... 134
Sancto (R.G.) = Bunyan Books...................... 53
Saunders (P. & E.) = Post-Horn Books 193
Savage (K.) = Keith Savage 229
Scott (T.) = Mount's Bay Books..................... 75
Sedgwick (D.) = Moorside Books.................... 144
Seers (P.R. & C.) = Greensleeves 207
Sephton (A.F.) = A.F Sephton 175
Sesemann (J.) = Luia Sesemann..................... 136
Seton (M.) = Alba Books 274
Sever (T.P.) = Books................................... 286
Seward (P.& G.) = The Carnforth Bookshop..... 143
Seydi (S) = Sevin Seydi Rare Books 162
Shakeshaft (B.L.) = Dr. B. Shakeshaft............. 71
Shakespeare (C. & L.) = Colin Shakespeare 224
Sharman (L.) = Treasure Trove Books 148
Sharpe (A.&J.) = Grove Rare Books................ 197
Sheard (D.) = Heckmondwike Book Shop 249
Sheehan (A.) = Darkwood Books 263
Sheehan (M.) = Caissa Books 234
Sheffield (R.) = Roosterbooks 200
Shelley (A. & J.) = Bow Windows Book Shop ... 103
Shelly (E.& J.) = E.J. Shelly 61
Sheppard (R.D.) = Fireside Bookshop 81
Shepperd (H.) = Torc Books 189
Sheridan (P.J.) = Books Bought & Sold 232
Shire (C.) = Theatreshire Books..................... 193
Showler (B. & K.) = B. and K. Books.............. 289
Siddons (D) = Forest Books 212
Sidwell (R.) = Monmouth House Books 288
Simpson (I.) = Clent Books........................... 255
Simpson (K.M.L.) = Black Five Books............ 215
Simpson O'Gara (J.P.) = Allhalland Books 85
Sims (T.J.) = Bookworms of Evesham 257
Sinclair (M.) = Books in Cardigan 284
Slade (R.) = Restormel Books........................ 257
Slim (R.T.) = Janus Books & Antiques 240
Sloggett (T.) = Leabeck Books 210
Smillie (M.) = Caledonia Books...................... 280
Smith (A.) = Orlando Booksellers 152
Smith (E.) = Bookstand 94
Smith (G.E. & M.K.) = Book End 108
Smith (G.D.) = Great Grandfather's 145
Smith (J.) = Clarendon Books........................ 147
Smith (K.) = Keith Smith Books 128
Smith (M.) = Enscot Books........................... 165
Smith (M.E & W.A.) = Second Edition 278
Smith (M.) = Chelifer Books 81
Smith (N.) = Nigel Smith Books..................... 231
Smith (P.M. & R.D.) = Rupert Books.............. 65
Smith (R.W.L.) = Sax Books......................... 229
Smosarki (A.) = Cofion Books 288
Somers (J.) = Fine Books Oriental Ltd. 178
Sparkes (J.) = Combat Arts Archive 97
Spranklins (G.) = Rowan House Books 232
Sproates (S.) = ForensicSearch 132
Spurrier (R.) = Post Mortem Books................. 243

Stallion (M.R.) = Lawful Occasions 108
Starling (R.) = Books Plus 84
Steadman (J.) = The Traveller's Bookshelf 217
Steenson (M.M.) = Books & Things 172
Stevens (A.E.R.M.) = Enigma Books 190
Stevens (E.) = Fortune Green Books................ 161
Stevens (F.) = Collectors Corner 253
Stevens (G.R.) = The Driffield Bookshop 106
Stevens (J.) = Joan Stevens 65
Stevenson (K.) = Game Advice 210
Stevenson (P.A.) = Boris Books...................... 126
Stinton (R.) = The Idle Booksellers................. 246
Stoddart (A.) = Hellenic Bookservices 162
Stone (A.) = Squirrel Antiques 122
Stones (L. A.) = The Bookshelf 196
Strong (E.A.) = McNaughtan's Bookshop 278
Stroud (F.P.A.) = Chaters Motoring
Booksellers 182
Stuart (E.) = First State Books....................... 173
Suchar (V. & E.) = Camden Books 216
Sutcliffe (T.) = Pendleside Books.................... 144
Sutherland (S.) = Allhalland Books 85
Suttie (D.S.) = Bowland Bookfinders............... 143
Sutton (M.) = The Old Celtic Bookshop 88
Swain (A. & C.) = Periwinkle Press 139
Swift (H. & C.) = Countryman Books.............. 106
Swindall (J. & R.) = Jiri Books 260
Tall (J. & N.) = Badger Books 220
Tandree (H. & A.) = Anthroposophical Books... 116
Tandree (H.) = Rachel Lee Rare Books 59
Tatam (J.) = Cat Lit 219
Tatman (C.) = Beverley Old Bookshop 106
Taylor (P. & S.) = Greyfriars Books 109
Taylor (P.H.) = Farnborough Bookshop
& Gallery.. 122
Taylor (P.) = Books & Bygones...................... 241
Tcbay (K.M.) – Red Rose Books 145
Thatcher (K.) = Foyle Books......................... 260
Thompson (J.) = Saltburn Bookshop 195
Thompson (M. & A.C.) = The Bookshop......... 192
Thompson (P.) = Bookseeker......................... 282
Thomson (G.) = Greta Books........................ 97
Thornhill (J. & M.) = Candle Lane Books 215
Thredder (P.) = Ross Old Books & Prints 128
Tickner (S.) = Firecatcher Books 118
Tierney (Dr. J. & Mrs. I.) = Hawkridge Books .. 82
Tierney (M.) = Wheen O'Books,.................... 269
Tilley (A. & A.) = Tilleys Vintage Magazine
Shop 82
Timothy (D.) = Siop y Morfa 286
Timson (L.) = Humanist Book Services 73
Tindley (J.) = Tindley & Chapman 179
To (W.) = Mike Park 183
Tober (B.) = Bruce Tober 241
Todd (J.) = Books (For All) 194
Tomaszewski (C.) = Stella Books 288
Tomlinson (R.K.) = Aviation Book Supply....... 130
Tootell (J.) = Pimpernel Booksearch 170
Townsend (J. & J.) = The Old Hall Bookshop ... 200
Townsend-Cardew (J. & B.) = Daisy Lane
Books 247
Tozer (N.) = Roscrea Bookshop 248
Tranter (P.) = Orangeberry Books................... 209
Travis (R., B., and S.) = SaBeRo Books 170
Traylen (N. & T.) = Ventnor Rare Books......... 135

ALPHABETICAL INDEX: Proprietor (T – Z)

Treece (M.) = Cornerstone Books 88
Trevitt (J.) = Hereford Booksearch 129
Trinder (R.) = Trinders' Fine Tools 227
Tuft (P.) = Patrick Tuft 182
Turnbull (P.M.) = The Countryman's Gallery 147
Turner (A. & D.) = Capel Mawr Collectors Centre 287
Turner (A.J.) = Rogers Turner Books 166
Turner (L.M.) = Bath Book Exchange 216
Twitchett (D.E.) = Engaging Gear Ltd.............. 108
Tyers (N.A.M., M.G.D. & P.A.) = St. Mary's Books & Prints 154
Tynan (P.) = Courtwood Books 266
Tyson (L.) = Paper Pleasures 219
Tyson (S.R.) = Over-Sands Books 78
Unny (L.) = Broadleaf Books 294
Unsworth (C.) = Unsworth's Booksellers 180
Unwin (D.) = Eastleach Books 56
Valentine Ketchum (V.A. & B.J.) = Staniland (Booksellers) 154
Vallely (J.) = Craobh Rua Books 260
Vaupres (J.) = The Lighthouse Books 92
Vetterlein (M.) = Birchden Books 155
Voigt (R.G.) = Garwood & Voigt 140
Wagstaff (A.) = Booksmart 200
Wakeman (P. & F.) = Frances Wakeman Books 205
Waldron (C.) = Bookends 122
Walker (D.) = Chelifer Books 81
Walker (G.) = Gary Walker 271
Walker (R.) = Fine Art 168
Wallace (N.) = Minster Gate Bookshop 199
Wallbaum (C.) = H. Baron 161
Walsh (M.) = Glenbower Books 265
Walters (H. & G.) = Court Hay Books 240
Walters (M.) = Fackley Services 205
Ward (D.J.) = SETI Books 225
Warwick (D.C.) = The Nautical Antique Centre . 96
Warwick (N.) = Readers Rest 152
Watson (J.S.) = John Updike Rare Books 279
Watts (M.D.) = Bookshop at the Plain 151
Watts (N.) = Beaver Booksearch 226
Watts (R.) = Dolphin Books 226
Wayne (J.) = Nicholas Willmott Bookseller 283
Weaver (C.A.) = Transformer 271
Weir (D. & J.L.) = Yesterday's Books 92
Weissman (S.) = Ximenes Rare Books Inc. 115
Welford (R.G.M.& M.E.) = Oasis Booksearch ... 67
Wells (M.) = Mary Wells 170
Wesley (P.) = Harlequin 90
Weston (J.) = Westons Booksellers Ltd 133
West-Skinn (R.) = Golden Goose Books 152
West-Skinn (R.) = Harlequin Gallery 152
Westwood (F.) = The Petersfield Bookshop 124
Wheeler (M.A.) = W.H. Collectables 230
Whitaker (J. & M.A.) = Peregrine Books (Leeds) 249
Whitby (M.) = Sevin Seydi Rare Books 162
White (M.J.) = Fun in Books 235
Whitehorn (J.) = Heartland Old Books 89
Whitworth (N.) = Elephant Books 249
Wiberg (C.) = The Book Depot 161
Wicks (J.) = Just Books 76
Wilkes (A.) = Mair Wilkes Books 272
Wilkinson (D. & T.) = The Book Gallery 75

Wilkinson (D.J.) = Intech Books 203
Wilkinson (D.&J.) = Autolycus 213
Wilkinson (J.B.) = Leeds Bookseller 249
Williams (C. & C.) = Aardvark Books 254
Williams (J. & J.) = Octagon Books 66
Williams (J.) = Bookworm Alley 89
Williams (M.) = Hellenic Bookservices 162
Williams (Dr. S.M.) = Barcombe Services 108
Willmott (N.) = Nicholas Willmott Bookseller ... 283
Wills (T.) = Volumes of Motoring 113
Wilson (H.G.E.) = Dales and Lakes Book Centre 80
Wilson (J.) = John Wilson (Manuscripts) Ltd. 114
Wilson (L.) = Halson Books 71
Wilson (R.) = The Old Town Bookshop 278
Wilson (R.) = Classic Crime Collections 119
Winkworth (D.) = The Printing House 78
Winston-Smith (M. & S.) = Dead Mens Minds.co.uk 292
Winter (Mrs.J.) = Sedgeberrow Books & Framing 256
Wise (C.) = Atlantis Bookshop 177
Woodhouse (G.) = Gillmark Gallery 131
Woolley (P. & K.) = Black Cat Bookshop 147
Worms (L.) = Ash Rare Books 167
Worthy (J.S. & S.) = Rochdale Book Company . 120
Wren (C.) = Annie's Books 222
Wright (C.) = Yarborough House Bookshop 213
Wright (M. & S.) = Roadmaster Books 137
Wright (P.) = Wright Trace Books 240
Wynne (N.) = Grays of Westminster 168
Yablon (G.A.) = Ian Hodgkins and Company Limited 116
Young (I. & S.) = Autumn Leaves 152
Young (R.) = Bridport Old Books 92
Young (S.) = Antiques on High 209
Zealley (C.J.) = St. Philip's Books 210

SPECIALITY INDEX

Index of dealers by stock speciality followed by county

ABORIGINAL

Byre Books, Dumfries & Galloway 270
Gaullifmaufry Books, Hertfordshire 132
Inner Bookshop (The), Oxfordshire................. 210
J.C. Deyong Books, London SW 169
Michael Graves-Johnston, London SW 169
Muse Bookshop (The), Gwynedd 287
R. & A. Books, East Sussex 102
Watkins Books Ltd., London WC 180

ACADEMIC/SCHOLARLY

Adrem Books, Hertfordshire......................... 131
Ainslie Books, Strathclyde............................ 279
Al Saqi Books, London W 172
Alec-Smith Books (Alex), East Yorkshire 107
All Books, Essex 110
Allinson (Frank & Stella), Warwickshire 237
Alpha Books, London N 158
Antiquary Ltd., (Bar Bookstore), N Yorks....... 196
Any Amount of Books, London WC 177
Apocalypse, Surrey 233
Austwick Hall Books, N Yorks 193
B D McManmon, Lancashire 145
Barcombe Services, Essex............................ 108
Baron - Scientific Book Sales (P.J.), Somerset ... 217
Bell (Peter), Lothian................................... 276
Bennett & Kerr Books, Oxfordshire 206
Berwick Books, Lincolnshire 152
Blanchfield (John), W Yorks........................ 249
Bloomsbury Bookshop, London Outer............. 182
Boer (Louise), Arthurian Books, Powys 289
Book Business (The), London W 172
BOOKS4U, Flintshire................................. 286
Bookshop (The), Gr Man 118
Bookshop at the Plain, Lincolnshire 151
Bowland Bookfinders, Lancashire................... 143
Bracton Books, Cambridgeshire 63
Brian Troath Books, London E 155
Brighton Books, East Sussex......................... 99
Brockwells Booksellers, Lincolnshire 150
Burak (Steve), London WC 177
Camden Books, Somerset 216
Carta Regis, Powys.................................... 293
Celtic Bookshop (The), Co. Limerick 266
Chapman (Neville), Lancashire 146
Chesters (G. & J.), Staffordshire 225
Church Street Bookshop, London N 158
Clifton Books, Essex 112
Cobnar Books, Kent 142
Corder (Mark W.), Kent 140
Cornucopia Books, Lincolnshire 153
Country Books, Derbyshire 82
Courtenay Bookroom, Oxfordshire 206
Courtwood Books, Co. Laois........................ 266
Crouch Rare Books, Surrey.......................... 233
Dales & Lakes Book Centre, Cumbria 80
Dandy Lion Editions, Surrey 233
David (G.), Cambridgeshire.......................... 63
de Visser Books, Cambridgeshire.................... 63

Delectus Books, London WC........................ 177
Derek Stirling Bookseller, Kent 142
Dolphin Books, Suffolk............................... 226
Dooley (Rosemary), Cumbria 78
Downie Fine Books Ltd., (Robert), Shropshire.. 215
Dylans Bookstore, Swansea 294
Eagle Bookshop (The), Bedfordshire 53
Earth Science Books, Wiltshire 252
Eastern Books of London, London SW 167
Eastleach Books, Berkshire........................... 56
Ellis, Bookseller (Peter), London WC 178
Empire Books, N Yorks.............................. 198
English (Toby), Oxfordshire......................... 211
Facet Books, Dorset................................... 91
Farnborough Gallery, Hampshire 122
Fireside Bookshop, Cumbria......................... 81
Fortune Green Books, London NW................ 161
Fossgate Books, N Yorks 198
Foyle Books, Co. Derry 260
G. C. Books Ltd., Dumfries & Galloway......... 271
Galloway & Porter Limited, Cambridgeshire..... 64
Game Advice, Oxfordshire 210
Gaullifmaufry Books, Hertfordshire 132
GfB: the Colchester Bookshop, Essex 109
Gibbs Books, (Jonathan), Worcestershire......... 256
Gildas Books, Cheshire 68
Glenbower Books, Co. Dublin 265
Golden Age Books, Worcestershire................. 256
Goldman (Paul), Dorset 94
Greenroom Books, W Yorks 248
Handsworth Books, Essex............................ 112
Harwich Old Books, Essex 110
Hawkes (James), London SE 165
Hawley (C.L.), N Yorks.............................. 197
Hay Cinema Bookshop Ltd., Powys............... 290
Helion & Company, West Midlands 240
Hellenic Bookservices, London NW 162
Herb Tandree Philosophy Books, Glos 116
Hill Books (Alan), South Yorkshire 222
hullbooks.com, East Yorkshire 107
Hurst (Jenny), Kent 138
Ice House Books, Wiltshire 253
IKON, Devon 89
Inner Bookshop (The), Oxfordshire................. 210
Innes Books, Shropshire 214
Internet Bookshop UK Ltd., Glos.................. 113
Invisible Books, East Sussex 100
Island Books, Devon 85
Jackdaw Books, Norfolk 189
Joel Segal Books, Devon 86
Jones (Andrew), Suffolk 228
K.S.C. Books, Cheshire............................... 71
Kenya Books, East Sussex 100
Key Books (Sarah), Cambridgeshire................ 64
Kim's Bookshop, West Sussex....................... 243
Kingswood Books, Dorset 94
Lee Rare Books (Rachel), Bristol 59
Leeds Bookseller, W Yorks 249
Lewcock (John), Cambridgeshire.................... 66

SPECIALITY INDEX

Lowe (John), Norfolk................................. 189
Maghreb Bookshop (The), London WC......... 178
Mair Wilkes Books, Fife 272
Marine & Cannon Books, Cheshire 71
Marine and Cannon Books, Cheshire 69
medievalbookshop, Hertfordshire 133
Mellon's Books, East Sussex......................... 101
Mobbs (A.J.), West Midlands 241
Morgan (H.J.), Bedfordshire.......................... 54
Murphy (C.J.), Norfolk................................ 190
Muse Bookshop (The), Gwynedd 287
My Back Pages, London SW........................ 169
Naughton Booksellers, Co. Dublin 265
Needham Books, (Russell), Somerset.............. 220
Northern Herald Books, W Yorks.................. 246
O'Donoghue Books, Powys.......................... 291
Offa's Dyke Books, Shropshire..................... 214
Old Aberdeen Bookshop, Grampian 272
Oopalba Books, Cheshire.............................. 71
Ouse Valley Books, Bedfordshire 54
Outcast Books, Powys 291
Oxfam Books and Music, Hampshire 126
Pholiota Books, London WC........................ 179
Plurabelle Books, Cambridgeshire.................. 64
Poetry Bookshop (The), Powys..................... 291
Pollak (P.M.), Devon 89
Pomes Penyeach, Staffordshire 224
Poole (William), London W 175
Pordes Books Ltd., (Henry), London WC....... 179
Porter Bookshop (The), South Yorkshire......... 222
Priestpopple Books, Northumberland 202
PsychoBabel Books & Journals, Oxfordshire..... 206
Quest Books, East Yorkshire 107
R. & A. Books, East Sussex 102
Reading Lasses, Dumfries & Galloway 271
Red Star Books, Hertfordshire 130
Reeves Technical Books, N Yorks.................. 196
Reid of Liverpool, Merseyside....................... 185
Rivendale Press, Buckinghamshire 62
Robert Temple, London N............................ 160
Roberts Books, Ayrshire 280
Roscrea Bookshop, Co. Tipperary.................. 267
Rosley Books, Cumbria 81
Rowan (P. & B.), Co. Antrim 260
Roz Hulse, Conwy 286
St Mary's Books & Prints, Lincolnshire 154
St Philip's Books, Oxfordshire....................... 210
Saintfield Antiques & Fine Books, Co. Down ... 261
Salsus Books, Worcestershire 256
Sandpiper Books Ltd., London SW 170
Saunders (Tom), Caerphilly.......................... 283
Scarthin Books, Derbyshire 82
Scott (Peter), East Sussex............................. 104
Skoob Russell Square, Suffolk....................... 230
South Downs Book Service, West Sussex......... 244
Sparrow Books, W Yorks............................. 246
Spelman (Ken), N Yorks.............................. 199
Spenceley Books (David), W Yorks 249
Stalagluft Books, Tyne and Wear................... 236
Staniland (Booksellers), Lincolnshire 154
Sterling Books, Somerset 221
Stern Antiquarian Bookseller (Jeffrey), N Yorks 199
Stevens (Joan), Cambridgeshire..................... 65
Stroma Books, Borders 268
Studio Bookshop, East Sussex....................... 100

Sue Lowell Natural History Books, London W . 176
Symes Books (Naomi), Cheshire 72
Taylor & Son (Peter), Hertfordshire............... 133
The Sanctuary Bookshop, Dorset................... 94
Thorntons of Oxford Ltd., Oxfordshire........... 207
Tiffin (Tony and Gill), Durham 97
Tombland Bookshop, Norfolk 191
Transformer, Dumfries & Galloway................ 271
Unsworth's Booksellers, London WC 163, 180
Venables (Morris & Juliet), Bristol.................. 60
Ventnor Rare Books, Isle of Wight................. 135
Victoria Bookshop (The), Devon.................... 84
Vinovium Books, Durham 97
Walden Books, London NW 163
Warrington Book Loft (The), Cheshire 72
Warsash Nautical Bookshop, Hampshire......... 126
Waterfield's, Oxfordshire 210
Waterstone's, London WC............................ 180
Watkins Books Ltd., London WC................... 180
Weiner (Graham), London N 160
Westwood Books Ltd, Cumbria..................... 80
Williams (Bookdealer), (Richard), N Lincs....... 154
Winchester Bookshop (The), Hampshire.......... 127
Winghale Books, Lincolnshire 153
Wizard Books, Cambridgeshire...................... 67
Woburn Books, London N 160
Worcester Rare Books, Worcestershire............ 257
Yates Antiquarian Books (Tony), Leicestershire. 148

ACCOUNTANCY

Jade Mountain Bookshop, Hampshire 126
Muse Bookshop (The), Gwynedd 287
Susanne Schulz-Falster Rare Books, London N. 160

ACUPUNCTURE

Chthonios Books, East Sussex....................... 102
Inner Bookshop (The), Oxfordshire................ 210
Joel Segal Books, Devon 86
Occultique, Northamptonshire....................... 200
Orchid Book Distributors, Co. Clare............... 262
Phelps (Michael), West Sussex....................... 243
Watkins Books Ltd., London WC................... 180

ADIRONDACK MOUNTAINS, THE

Muse Bookshop (The), Gwynedd 287

ADULT

Addyman Books, Powys............................... 289
Adrem Books, Hertfordshire.......................... 131
Annie's Books, South Yorkshire 222
Apocalypse, Surrey 233
Delectus Books, London WC........................ 177
Muse Bookshop (The), Gwynedd 287
N1 Books, East Sussex 105
Onepoundpaperbacks, N Yorks..................... 193
R. & A. Books, East Sussex 102
Reading Lasses, Dumfries & Galloway 271
Tsbbooks, London SW 170
Woodland Books, Devon.............................. 84

ADVENTURE

Annie's Books, South Yorkshire 222
Cox (Geoff), Devon 90
Dolphin Books, Suffolk................................ 226
Eastern Traveller (The), Somerset.................. 220

SPECIALITY INDEX

Edmund Pollinger Rare Books, London SW..... 167
Eggeling Books (John), W Yorks 250
Jane Jones Books, Grampian 272
Joel Segal Books, Devon 86
Keith Langford, London E 155
Mulyan (Don), Merseyside........................... 186
Parker Books (Mike), Cambridgeshire 64
R. & A. Books, East Sussex 102
Rods Books, Devon 88
Wheen O'Books, Scottish Borders 269

ADVERTISING

Ainslie Books, Strathclyde............................ 279
All Books, Essex 110
Barry McKay Rare Books, Cumbria............... 77
Bettridge (Gordon), Fife.............................. 272
Books & Things, London W......................... 172
Bowland Bookfinders, Lancashire.................. 143
Chapman (Neville), Lancashire...................... 146
Cornucopia Books, Lincolnshire 153
Courtwood Books, Co Laois......................... 266
Derek Stirling Bookseller, Kent 142
Facet Books, Dorset.................................... 91
Franks Booksellers, Gr Man......................... 119
Hill House Books, Devon 88
Joel Segal Books, Devon 86
Junk & Spread Eagle, London SE.................. 165
Kelly Books, Devon.................................... 89
Kingswood Books, Dorset 94
Lowe (John), Norfolk................................. 189
Offa's Dyke Books, Shropshire..................... 214
Pordes Books Ltd., (Henry), London WC........ 179
Prior (Michael), Lincolnshire 153
Pyecroft (Ruth), Glos 117
R. & A. Books, East Sussex 102
Roland Books, Kent 139
St Swithin's Illustrated & Children's Books,
London W 175
Salsus Books, Worcestershire 256
Sterling Books, Somerset 221

AERONAUTICS

Addyman Books, Powys.............................. 289
Adrem Books, Hertfordshire......................... 131
Ainslie Books, Strathclyde........................... 279
All Books, Essex 110
Allinson (Frank & Stella), Warwickshire 237
Anchor Books, Lincolnshire 151
Andron (G.W.), London N 158
Anthony Vickers Books, N Yorks 196
Aviabooks, Glos 114
Barbican Bookshop, N Yorks 198
Books Bought & Sold, Surrey 232
BOOKS4U, Flintshire.................................. 286
Camilla's Bookshop, East Sussex 101
Cheshire Book Centre, Cheshire.................... 69
Clarke Books (David), Somerset 219
Cocks (Brian), Cambridgeshire 67
Collectables (W.H.), Suffolk 230
Corfe Books, Surrey................................... 231
Cornucopia Books, Lincolnshire 153
Cox (Geoff), Devon 90
Empire Books, N Yorks............................... 198
Facet Books, Dorset.................................... 91
Fireside Bookshop, Cumbria......................... 81

Gaullifmaufry Books, Hertfordshire 132
Hancock (Peter), West Sussex 243
Harrington Antiquarian Bookseller (Peter),
London SW... 169
Harris (George J.), Co. Derry 260
Hay Cinema Bookshop Ltd., Powys............... 290
Holdenhurst Books, Dorset 91
Island Books, Devon................................... 85
Key Books (Sarah), Cambridgeshire............... 64
Lost Books, Northamptonshire...................... 201
Lowe (John), Norfolk................................. 189
Milestone Books, Devon 89
MilitaryHistoryBooks.com, Kent................... 138
N1 Books, East Sussex 105
Phelps (Michael), West Sussex...................... 243
Pordes Books Ltd., (Henry), London WC........ 179
R. & A. Books, East Sussex 102
Read (C.&J.), Gorleston Books, Norfolk......... 188
Robert Humm & Co, Lincolnshire 154
Salsus Books, Worcestershire 256
Salway Books, Essex 112
Sterling Books, Somerset 221
Stroh (M.A.), London E 155
Thin Read Line, Merseyside 185
Vanstone - Aviation Books, (Derek), Suffolk 230
Vickers (Anthony), N Yorks......................... 196
Weiner (Graham), London N 160
Westons, Hertfordshire 133

AESTHETIC MOVEMENT

Apocalypse, Surrey 233
Brian Troath Books, London E...................... 155
Cox Rare Books (Charles), Cornwall............... 74
Delectus Books, London WC........................ 177
Design Gallery 1850-1950 (The), Kent 142
Harrington (Adrian), London W.................... 173
R. & A. Books, East Sussex 102

AESTHETICS

Apocalypse, Surrey 233
Brian Troath Books, London E...................... 155
Joel Segal Books, Devon 86
Parkinsons Books, Merseyside....................... 186
R. & A. Books, East Sussex 102

AFRICAN-AMERICAN STUDIES

Black Voices, Merseyside 185
Dylans Bookstore, Swansea.......................... 294
Michael Graves-Johnston, London SW 169
Reading Lasses, Dumfries & Galloway 271
Watkins Books Ltd., London WC.................. 180
Yesterday's Books, Dorset 92

AFRICANA

Addyman Books, Powys.............................. 289
African Studies, Dorset 91
Ainslie Books, Strathclyde........................... 279
All Books, Essex 110
Allsworth Rare Books Ltd., London SW......... 167
Armchair Books, Lothian 276
Ayre (Peter J.), Somerset 220
Barn Books, Buckinghamshire....................... 61
Black Voices, Merseyside 185
Bloomsbury Bookshop, London Outer............ 182
Bonham (J. & S.L.), London W 172

SPECIALITY INDEX

Bookbarrow, Cambridgeshire 63
Chalmers Hallam (E.), Hampshire 125
Chas J. Sawyer, Kent 141
Coch-y-Bonddu Books, Powys 292
Edmund Pollinger Rare Books, London SW 167
Eggeling Books (John), W Yorks 250
Empire Books, N Yorks 198
G. C. Books Ltd., Dumfries & Galloway 271
Grahame (Major Iain), Suffolk 226
Hennessey Bookseller (Ray), East Sussex 100
J & J Burgess Booksellers, Cambridgeshire 64
Joel Segal Books, Devon 86
Kenya Books, East Sussex 100
Marcet Books, London SE 165
Michael Graves-Johnston, London SW 169
MK Book Services, Cambridgeshire 66
Peter M Daly, Hampshire 127
Pordes Books Ltd., (Henry), London WC 179
Preston Book Company, Lancashire 145
Prospect House Books, Co. Down 261
R. & A. Books, East Sussex 102
Reading Lasses, Dumfries & Galloway 271
Roscrea Bookshop, Co. Tipperary 267
Samovar Books, Co. Dublin 264
Thin Read Line, Merseyside 185
Thorntons of Oxford Ltd., Oxfordshire 207
Wiend Books, Lancashire 144
Woburn Books, London N 160
Yesterday's Books, Dorset 92
York (Graham), Devon 86

AGRICULTURE

Addyman Books, Powys 289
Alec-Smith Books (Alex), East Yorkshire 107
Barn Books, Shropshire 215
Barter Books, Northumberland 202
Besleys Books, Suffolk 226
Blest (Peter), Kent 139
Books for Content, Herefordshire 128
BOOKS4U, Flintshire 286
Booth Books, Powys 289
Burmester (James), Bristol 59
Carningli Centre, Pembrokeshire 288
Carta Regis, Powys 293
Cassidy (Bookseller) (P.), Lincolnshire 153
Castle Hill Books, Herefordshire 128
Castleton (Pat), Kent 138
Chantrev Books, South Yorkshire 222
Cheshire Book Centre, Cheshire 69
Clarke Books (David), Somerset 219
Clifton Books, Essex 112
Cobnar Books, Kent 142
Coch-y-Bonddu Books, Powys 292
Cottage Books, Leicestershire 147
Country Books, Derbyshire 82
Dales & Lakes Book Centre, Cumbria 80
Dolphin Books, Suffolk 226
Drury Rare Books (John), Essex 110
Empire Books, N Yorks 198
Farquharson, (Hilary), Tayside 281
Ferdinando (Steven), Somerset 220
Greta Books, Durham 97
Guildmaster Books, Cheshire 70
Hodgson (Books) (Richard J.), N Yorks 198
Hollingshead (Chris), London Outer 183

Island Books, Devon 85
Jade Mountain Bookshop, Hampshire 126
Jane Jones Books, Grampian 272
Joel Segal Books, Devon 86
Muttonchop Manuscripts, West Sussex 244
Park (Mike), London Outer 183
Parkinsons Books, Merseyside 186
Phenotype Books, Cumbria 80
Prospect House Books, Co. Down 261
R. & A. Books, East Sussex 102
Randall (Tom), Somerset 219
Roscrea Bookshop, Co. Tipperary 267
Stalagluft Books, Tyne and Wear 236
Stella Books, Monmouthshire 288
Stone, (G.& R.), Borders 268
Thin Read Line, Merseyside 185
Thornber (Peter M.), N Yorks 196
Trinity Rare Books, Co. Leitrim 266
Westons, Hertfordshire 133

AIDS CRISIS, THE

Cox Music (Lisa), Devon 86
R. & A. Books, East Sussex 102
Westons, Hertfordshire 133

AIRCRAFT

Aardvark Books, Wiltshire 254
Addyman Books, Powys 289
Anchor Books, Lincolnshire 151
Apocalypse, Surrey 233
Beware of the Leopard, Bristol 58
BOOKS4U, Flintshire 286
BookShop, The, Dumfries & Galloway 270
Bookworm, Lothian 277
Brad Books, Essex 111
Broadhurst of Southport Ltd., Merseyside 186
Castleton (Pat), Kent 138
Cocks (Brian), Cambridgeshire 67
Cornucopia Books, Lincolnshire 153
Cox (Geoff), Devon 90
Discovery Bookshop, Carmarthenshire 283
Eastgate Bookshop, East Yorkshire 106
Farnborough Gallery, Hampshire 122
G. C. Books Ltd., Dumfries & Galloway 271
J & J Burgess Booksellers, Cambridgeshire 64
J.B. Books, Berkshire 56
Jade Mountain Bookshop, Hampshire 126
Joel Segal Books, Devon 86
Lost Books, Northamptonshire 201
Marcet Books, London SE 165
Marine & Cannon Books, Cheshire 71
Marine and Cannon Books, Cheshire 69
MilitaryHistoryBooks.com, Kent 138
Not Just Books, Dorset 94
Parrott Books, Oxfordshire 211
R. & A. Books, East Sussex 102
Robert Humm & Co, Lincolnshire 154
Rothwell & Dunworth, Somerset 218
Saintfield Antiques & Fine Books, Co. Down ... 261
Salway Books, Essex 112
Scorpio Books, Suffolk 226
Stella Books, Monmouthshire 288
Stroh (M.A.), London E 155
Tarka Books, Devon 84
Thin Read Line, Merseyside 185

SPECIALITY INDEX

Vanstone - Aviation Books, (Derek), Suffolk 230
Weiner (Graham), London N 160
Woodland Books, Devon............................ 84

ALCHEMY

Alpha Books, London N 158
Apocalypse, Surrey 233
Atlantis Bookshop, London WC................... 177
Caduceus Books, Leicestershire..................... 147
Chthonios Books, East Sussex...................... 102
Gilbert (R.A.), Bristol................................ 59
IKON, Devon... 89
Inner Bookshop (The), Oxfordshire................ 210
Joel Segal Books, Devon 86
Magis Books, Leicestershire......................... 149
Needham Books, (Russell), Somerset.............. 220
Occultique, Northamptonshire...................... 200
Parkinsons Books, Merseyside...................... 186
Phelps (Michael), West Sussex...................... 243
Quaritch Ltd., (Bernard), London W.............. 175
Susanne Schulz-Falster Rare Books, London N. 160
Victoria Bookshop (The), Devon................... 84
Watkins Books Ltd., London WC.................. 180
Weiner (Graham), London N 160
Westons, Hertfordshire 133

ALMANACS

Apocalypse, Surrey 233
Bates & Hindmarch, W Yorks 249
Beighton (Brian), Norfolk 187
Empire Books, N Yorks............................. 198
Grampian Books, Grampian........................ 274
R. & A. Books, East Sussex 102
Watkins Books Ltd., London WC.................. 180
Weiner (Graham), London N 160
Yates Antiquarian Books (Tony), Leicestershire. 148

ALPINISM/MOUNTAINEERING

Allinson (Frank & Stella), Warwickshire 237
Anthony Spranger, Wiltshire........................ 252
Anthony Vickers Books, N Yorks 196
Askew Books (Vernon), Wiltshire.................. 251
Barnhill Books, Isle of Arran 275
Biblion, London W................................... 172
Birmingham Books, West Midlands................ 239
Bonham (J. & S.L.), London W 172
Books, Denbighshire 286
Booth (Booksearch Service), (Geoff), Cheshire... 68
Bosco Books, Cornwall.............................. 73
Bosorne Books, Cornwall 75
Carnforth Bookshop (The), Lancashire 143
Carta Regis, Powys.................................. 293
Cavendish Rare Books, London N 158
Cheshire Book Centre, Cheshire.................... 69
Church Street Books, Norfolk 187
Collectables (W.H.), Suffolk 230
Creaking Shelves, Inverness-shire.................. 275
Dales & Lakes Book Centre, Cumbria............ 80
Dartmoor Bookshop (The), Devon 84
David Warnes Books, Herefordshire 129
Eastcote Bookshop (The), London Outer......... 181
Eastleach Books, Berkshire.......................... 56
Fine Books at Ilkley, W Yorks..................... 248
Fireside Bookshop, Cumbria........................ 81
Garfi Books, Powys 293

George St. Books, Derbyshire 83
Gildas Books, Cheshire.............................. 68
Glacier Books, Tayside 282
Hancock (Peter), West Sussex 243
Hill (Peter), Hampshire 122
Hollett and Son (R.F.G.), Cumbria 80
Holmes Books (Harry), East Yorkshire............ 107
Hornsey's, N Yorks.................................. 195
Hunter and Krageloh, Derbyshire 83
Internet Bookshop UK Ltd., Glos.................. 113
Jarvis Books, Derbyshire 83
Joel Segal Books, Devon 86
Kirkland Books, Cumbria........................... 79
Letterbox Books, Nottinghamshire 204
Little Bookshop (The), Cumbria 81
Main Point Books, Lothian......................... 278
McCrone (Audrey), Isle of Arran.................. 275
Mercat Books, Highland 274
Mountaineering Books, London N 159
Muse Bookshop (The), Gwynedd.................. 287
O'Reilly - Mountain Books (John), Derbyshire.. 83
Page (David), Lothian 278
Parrott Books, Oxfordshire 211
Peter M Daly, Hampshire........................... 127
Pinnacle Books, Lothian............................. 278
Post-Horn Books, N Yorks 193
R. & A. Books, East Sussex 102
Riddell (Peter), East Yorkshire..................... 106
Rods Books, Devon.................................. 88
Roz Hulse, Conwy 286
Scarthin Books, Derbyshire 82
Vandeleur Antiquarian Books, Surrey............. 232
Vickers (Anthony), N Yorks........................ 196
Yewtree Books, Cumbria............................ 79

ALTERNATIVE MEDICINE

Alba Books, Grampian 274
Dales & Lakes Book Centre, Cumbria............ 80
Ellwood Editions, Wiltshire......................... 253
Empire Books, N Yorks............................. 198
Esoteric Dreams Bookshop, Cumbria 78
Game Advice, Oxfordshire.......................... 210
Greensleeves, Oxfordshire 207
Hurst (Jenny), Kent 138
IKON, Devon... 89
Inner Bookshop (The), Oxfordshire................ 210
Joel Segal Books, Devon 86
London & Sussex Antiquarian Book &
Print Services, East Sussex 101
Lowe (John), Norfolk................................ 189
Occultique, Northamptonshire...................... 200
Old Celtic Bookshop (The), Devon................ 88
Outcast Books, Powys 291
R. & A. Books, East Sussex 102
Reading Lasses, Dumfries & Galloway 271
Roundstone Books, Lancashire..................... 144
Till's Bookshop, Lothian 279
Watkins Books Ltd., London WC.................. 180
Westwood Books Ltd, Cumbria.................... 80

AMATEUR RADIO [HAM RADIO]

R. & A. Books, East Sussex 102

AMERICAN INDIANS

Americanabooksuk, Cumbria....................... 77

SPECIALITY INDEX

Bookbarrow, Cambridgeshire........................ 63
Books, Denbighshire................................. 286
Byre Books, Dumfries & Galloway................. 270
Chelifer Books, Cumbria............................. 81
Clifford Elmer Books Ltd., Cheshire.............. 68
Cornucopia Books, Lincolnshire................... 153
Dancing Goat Bookshop (The), Norfolk......... 188
Eastcote Bookshop (The), London Outer......... 181
Emjay Books, Surrey................................. 231
Fireside Bookshop, Cumbria........................ 81
Hay Castle, Powys.................................... 290
Inner Bookshop (The), Oxfordshire................ 210
Intech Books, Northumberland..................... 203
Joel Segal Books, Devon............................. 86
Marble Hill Books, Middlesex...................... 184
Michael Graves-Johnston, London SW........... 169
Occultique, Northamptonshire...................... 200
Orchid Book Distributors, Co. Clare.............. 262
R. & A. Books, East Sussex......................... 102
Remington (Reg & Philip), Hertfordshire......... 133
Roscrea Bookshop, Co. Tipperary................. 267
Scarthin Books, Derbyshire.......................... 82
Trinity Rare Books, Co. Leitrim.................... 266
Watkins Books Ltd., London WC.................. 180

AMERICAN NORTHWEST

Joel Segal Books, Devon............................. 86
Roz Hulse, Conwy.................................... 286

AMERICAN REVOLUTION, THE

J & J Burgess Booksellers, Cambridgeshire....... 64
Joel Segal Books, Devon............................. 86
R. & A. Books, East Sussex......................... 102

AMERICANA - GENERAL

Addyman Books, Powys.............................. 289
Americanabooksuk, Cumbria........................ 77
Anglo-American Rare Books, Surrey.............. 233
Brad Books, Essex..................................... 111
Cavern Books, Cheshire.............................. 70
Clifford Elmer Books Ltd., Cheshire.............. 68
Collectables (W.H.), Suffolk........................ 230
Dancing Goat Bookshop (The), Norfolk......... 188
Discovery Bookshop, Carmarthenshire............ 283
Ely Books, Cambridgeshire.......................... 65
Fireside Bookshop, Cumbria........................ 81
Hancock (Peter), West Sussex...................... 243
Joel Segal Books, Devon............................. 86
Kenny's Bookshops and Art Galleries Ltd,
Co. Galway.. 266
Preston Book Company, Lancashire............... 145
Shakeshaft (Dr. B.), Cheshire....................... 71
Winghale Books, Lincolnshire...................... 153

AMERICANA - SOUTHWEST

Americanabooksuk, Cumbria........................ 77
Joel Segal Books, Devon............................. 86

AMISH

Apocalypse, Surrey.................................... 233
Joel Segal Books, Devon............................. 86

AMUSEMENTS

Jean Hedger, Berkshire............................... 55
Joel Segal Books, Devon............................. 86

R. & A. Books, East Sussex......................... 102

ANATOMY

J & J Burgess Booksellers, Cambridgeshire....... 64
Joel Segal Books, Devon............................. 86
Orchid Book Distributors, Co. Clare.............. 262
Phelps (Michael), West Sussex..................... 243
R M Books, Hertfordshire........................... 132
R. & A. Books, East Sussex......................... 102
Watkins Books Ltd., London WC.................. 180
Weiner (Graham), London N....................... 160

ANIMALS AND BIRDS

Alauda Books, Cumbria.............................. 78
Annie's Books, South Yorkshire.................... 222
Apocalypse, Surrey.................................... 233
Besleys Books, Suffolk................................ 226
Blest (Peter), Kent.................................... 139
Bookline, Co. Down.................................. 261
BOOKS4U, Flintshire................................. 286
Brock Books, N Yorks............................... 193
Camilla's Bookshop, East Sussex.................. 101
Carningli Centre, Pembrokeshire................... 288
Carta Regis, Powys................................... 293
Castleton (Pat), Kent................................. 138
Chandos Books, Devon............................... 85
Cheshire Book Centre, Cheshire.................... 69
Coch-y-Bonddu Books, Powys..................... 292
Cofion Books, Pembrokeshire...................... 288
Corfe Books, Surrey.................................. 231
Cornucopia Books, Lincolnshire................... 153
Dales & Lakes Book Centre, Cumbria............ 80
Delectus Books, London WC....................... 177
Demar Books (Grant), Kent......................... 141
Dolphin Books, Suffolk............................... 226
Earth Science Books, Wiltshire..................... 252
Edmund Pollinger Rare Books, London SW..... 167
Esoteric Dreams Bookshop, Cumbria............. 78
Ford Books (David), Hertfordshire................ 133
Good for Books, Lincolnshire...................... 151
Goodyer (Nicholas), London N.................... 159
Grahame Thornton, Bookseller, Dorset........... 93
Greta Books, Durham................................ 97
Grosvenor Prints, London WC..................... 178
Inner Bookshop (The), Oxfordshire................ 210
Island Books, Devon.................................. 85
J & J Burgess Booksellers, Cambridgeshire....... 64
Jade Mountain Bookshop, Hampshire............ 126
Jane Jones Books, Grampian........................ 272
Jay Books, Lothian.................................... 278
Joel Segal Books, Devon............................. 86
Junk & Spread Eagle, London SE.................. 165
Karen Millward, Co. Cork........................... 263
Mandalay Bookshop, London SW................. 169
Martin's Books, Powys............................... 292
Mayhew (Veronica), Berkshire...................... 57
McCrone (Audrey), Isle of Arran................... 275
McEwan Fine Books, Grampian.................... 273
Mercat Books, Highland............................. 274
O'Flynn Books, N Yorks............................. 199
Orb's Bookshop, Grampian......................... 274
Parkinsons Books, Merseyside...................... 186
Parrott Books, Oxfordshire.......................... 211
Peter M Daly, Hampshire............................ 127
Phenotype Books, Cumbria.......................... 80

SPECIALITY INDEX

Popeley (Frank T.), Cambridgeshire 67
Prospect House Books, Co. Down.................. 261
R. & A. Books, East Sussex 102
R.E. & G.B. Way, Suffolk 229
Roland Books, Kent 139
Roz Hulse, Conwy 286
Sax Books, Suffolk 229
Scarthin Books, Derbyshire 82
Shakeshaft (Dr. B.), Cheshire 71
Stella Books, Monmouthshire 288
Sue Lowell Natural History Books, London W. 176
Tarka Books, Devon 84
Thin Read Line, Merseyside 185
Treasure Island (The), Gr Man...................... 119
Trinity Rare Books, Co. Leitrim 266
Wheen O'Books, Scottish Borders 269
Wildside Books, Worcestershire 255
Wright Trace Books, West Midlands................ 240

ANNUALS

Aardvark Books, Lincolnshire 152
Armchair Books, Lothian 276
Armstrong's Books & Collectables, Leics 147
Art Book Company, (The), Suffolk.................. 228
Big Bairn Books, Tayside 281
Book Palace (The), London SE 164
Bookmark (Children's Books), Wiltshire........... 253
books2books, Devon 88
BOOKS4U, Flintshire................................. 286
Booth (Booksearch Service), (Geoff), Cheshire... 68
Brock Books, N Yorks 193
Camilla's Bookshop, East Sussex 101
Cavern Books, Cheshire 70
Cheshire Book Centre, Cheshire..................... 69
D. & M. Books, W Yorks 250
Dales & Lakes Book Centre, Cumbria.............. 80
Dawlish Books, Devon 86
Eastcote Bookshop (The), London Outer......... 181
Esoteric Dreams Bookshop, Cumbria 78
Fifteenth Century Bookshop (The), East Sussex. 104
firstpagebooks, Norfolk............................... 190
Green Meadow Books, Cornwall 74
Hab Books, London W............................... 173
Hambleton Books, N Yorks 197
Ian Briddon, Derbyshire.............................. 82
Intech Books, Northumberland 203
Joel Segal Books, Devon 86
John R. Hoggarth, N Yorks......................... 198
K Books, Cheshire..................................... 70
Katnap Arts, Norfolk 191
Key Books (Sarah), Cambridgeshire................ 64
Kineton Nooks, Warwickshire....................... 237
Lloyd-Davies (Sue), Carmarthenshire 284
March House Books, Dorset 95
Moorhead Books, W Yorks 246
Murphy (C.J.), Norfolk............................... 190
Old Celtic Bookshop (The), Devon 88
Old Station Pottery & Bookshop (The), Norfolk 192
Parker Books (Mike), Cambridgeshire 64
Pickering Bookshop, N Yorks....................... 197
R. & A. Books, East Sussex 102
Reeves Technical Books, N Yorks.................. 196
Roland Books, Kent 139
Scrivener's Books & Bookbinding, Derbyshire... 82
Shacklock Books (David), Suffolk 227

Shakeshaft (Dr. B.), Cheshire........................ 71
Stella Books, Monmouthshire 288
Surprise Books, Glos.................................. 113
Tarka Books, Devon 84
The Old Children's Bookshelf, Lothian 278
Till's Bookshop, Lothian 279
TP Children's Bookshop, W Yorks................. 246
Treasure Trove Books, Leics......................... 148
Wheen O'Books, Scottish Borders 269
Wiend Books, Lancashire 144
Williams (Bookdealer), (Richard), N Lincs 154
Wright Trace Books, West Midlands............... 240
Xanadu Books, Cleveland 98
Yorkshire Relics, W Yorks........................... 247

ANTHOLOGIES

Addyman Books, Powys.............................. 289
Carningli Centre, Pembrokeshire 288
Cornucopia Books, Lincolnshire 153
Cowley, Bookdealer (K.W.), Somerset 218
Dales & Lakes Book Centre, Cumbria.............. 80
Dolphin Books, Suffolk............................... 226
Eggeling Books (John), W Yorks 250
McCrone (Audrey), Isle of Arran 275
Naughton Booksellers, Co. Dublin 265
Poetry Bookshop (The), Powys..................... 291
R. & A. Books, East Sussex 102
Robert Temple, London N........................... 160
Shacklock Books (David), Suffolk 227

ANTHROPOLOGY

Afar Books International, West Midlands 239
Apocalypse, Surrey 233
Bracton Books, Cambridgeshire 63
Byre Books, Dumfries & Galloway.................. 270
Chalmers Hallam (E.), Hampshire 125
Chesters (G. & J.), Staffordshire 225
David Warnes Books, Herefordshire 129
Delectus Books, London WC........................ 177
Fireside Bookshop, Cumbria......................... 81
Game Advice, Oxfordshire 210
Garfi Books, Powys 293
J.C. Deyong Books, London SW 169
Joel Segal Books, Devon 86
Kenny's Bookshops and Art Galleries Ltd,
Co. Galway 266
Kenya Books, East Sussex 100
Kingswood Books, Dorset 94
Maghreb Bookshop (The), London WC 178
Mandalay Bookshop, London SW 169
Michael Graves-Johnston, London SW 169
Phelps (Michael), West Sussex 243
Polczynski (Udo K.H.), Powys 291
Portobello Books, London W 175
Preston Book Company, Lancashire 145
R. & A. Books, East Sussex 102
Reading Lasses, Dumfries & Galloway 271
Rhodes, Bookseller (Peter), Hampshire 126
Skoob Russell Square, Suffolk....................... 230
Stern Antiquarian Bookseller (Jeffrey), N Yorks 199
Watkins Books Ltd., London WC.................. 180
Whitchurch Books Ltd., Cardiff..................... 283
Woburn Books, London N 160
Yesterday's Books, Dorset 92

SPECIALITY INDEX

ANTHROPOSOPHY

Anthroposophical Books, Glos 116
Byre Books, Dumfries & Galloway 270
Greensleeves, Oxfordshire 207
Inner Bookshop (The), Oxfordshire................ 210
Joel Segal Books, Devon 86
Reads, Dorset 95
Star Lord Books, Gr Man 119
Watkins Books Ltd., London WC 180

ANTI-SEMITISM

Joel Segal Books, Devon 86

ANTIQUARIAN

Addyman Books, Powys............................... 289
Al Saqi Books, London W 172
Alastor Rare Books, Hampshire 124
Alec-Smith Books (Alex), East Yorkshire 107
Allsop (Duncan M.), Warwickshire................. 238
Altea Antique Maps & Books, London W 172
Antiquary Ltd., (Bar Bookstore), N Yorks....... 196
Antique Map and Bookshop (The), Dorset 94
Any Amount of Books, London WC 177
Apocalypse, Surrey 233
Arden, Bookseller (C.), Powys...................... 289
Ardis Books, Hampshire 126
Arnold (Roy), Suffolk.................................. 228
Art Reference Books, Hampshire 125
Atholl Fine Books, Tayside 281
Austwick Hall Books, N Yorks 193
Autolycus, Shropshire................................. 213
Axe Rare & Out of Print Books (Richard),
N Yorks.. 194
Baldwin (Jack), Strathclyde 280
Baldwin's Scientific Books, Essex 112
Bardsley's Books, Suffolk............................. 226
Barmby (C. & A.J.), Kent............................ 141
Bates & Hindmarch, W Yorks 249
Bath Old Books, Somerset 216
Baxter (Steve), Surrey 234
Baynton-Williams Gallery, West Sussex 242
Beardsell Books, W Yorks 247
Beaton (Richard), East Sussex....................... 103
Beckham Books Ltd., Suffolk 230
Bell (Peter), Lothian................................... 276
Bernstein (Nicholas), London W 172
Bertram Rota Ltd., London WC 177
Biblion, London W..................................... 172
Biblipola, London NW 161
Blackwell's Rare Books, Oxfordshire 209
Book Business (The), London W 172
Bookcase, Cumbria.................................... 78
Booklore, Leics... 148
Bookmark (Children's Books), Wiltshire.......... 253
Books at Star Dot Star, West Midlands 241
Books on Spain, London Outer..................... 184
Books Only, Suffolk.................................... 227
BOOKS4U, Flintshire................................. 286
Bookshop (The), Co. Donegal....................... 263
Bookshop, Kirkstall (The), W Yorks.............. 248
BookShop, The, Dumfries & Galloway............ 270
Bookstand, Dorset...................................... 94
Booth (Booksearch Service), (Geoff), Cheshire... 68
Bosorne Books, Cornwall 75
Bow Windows Book Shop, East Sussex 103
Bowie Books & Collectables, East Yorkshire 107
Brad Books, Essex...................................... 111
Brinded (Scott), Kent 139
Brock Books, N Yorks 193
Brockwells Booksellers, Lincolnshire 150
Bunyan Books, Bedfordshire......................... 53
Burak (Steve), London WC.......................... 177
Butler Cresswell Rare Books, Buckinghamshire . 61
Byblos Antiquarian & Rare Book, Hampshire .. 121
Camden Books, Somerset 216
Capital Bookshop, Cardiff 283
Castle Hill Books, Herefordshire.................... 128
Celtic Bookshop (The), Co. Limerick 266
Chandos Books, Devon................................ 85
CI Galleries Limited, CI 258
Chapter & Verse, Lincolnshire...................... 152
Chelifer Books, Cumbria 81
Cheshire Book Centre, Cheshire.................... 69
Chris Phillips, Wiltshire.............................. 251
Clent Books, Worcestershire 255
Clifford Elmer Books Ltd., Cheshire 68
Cobnar Books, Kent................................... 142
Cobweb Books, N Yorks............................. 195
Coch-y-Bonddu Books, Powys 292
Colin Hancock, Ceredigion 284
Collectable Books, London SE 165
Cooper Hay Rare Books, Strathclyde 280
Courtenay Bookroom, Oxfordshire................. 206
Courtney & Hoff, N Yorks 198
Cox Old & Rare Books (Claude), Suffolk 228
Cox Rare Books (Charles), Cornwall............... 74
Cox, Andrew, Shropshire............................. 215
Craobh Rua Books, Co. Armagh 260
Crouch Rare Books, Surrey.......................... 233
Daeron's Books, Buckinghamshire.................. 62
Dales & Lakes Book Centre, Cumbria............ 80
Dartmoor Bookshop (The), Devon 84
David (G.), Cambridgeshire.......................... 63
Davies Fine Books, Worcestershire 257
Dead Mens Minds.co.uk, Powys 292
Dean Byass, Bristol.................................... 60
Debbage (John), Norfolk.............................. 190
Delph Books, Gr Man................................. 120
Demetzy Books, Oxfordshire 208
Derek Stirling Bookseller, Kent 142
Drury Rare Books (John), Essex.................... 110
Dublin Bookbrowsers, Co. Dublin.................. 265
Duncan & Reid, Lothian.............................. 277
Dylans Bookstore, Swansea 294
Eagle Bookshop (The), Bedfordshire 53
Earth Science Books, Wiltshire 252
Eastleach Books, Berkshire........................... 56
Eastwood Books (David), Cornwall 73
Eclectica, London SE 165
Eggle (Mavis), Hertfordshire........................ 131
Elaine Lonsdale Books, W Yorks.................. 248
Ellwood Editions, Wiltshire 253
Ely Books, Cambridgeshire 65
Eton Antique Bookshop, Berkshire................. 57
Farahar & Dupre (Clive & Sophie), Wiltshire ... 251
Farquharson, (Hilary), Tayside..................... 281
Farringdon (J.M.), Swansea......................... 293
Fenning (James), Co. Dublin 264
Finch Rare Books Ltd. (Simon), London W..... 173
Fine Art, London SW 168

SPECIALITY INDEX

Fine Books at Ilkley, W Yorks..................... 248
Fireside Bookshop, Cumbria......................... 81
Fletcher (H.M.), Hertfordshire 132
Fossgate Books, N Yorks 198
Foster (Stephen), London NW 161
Foster Bookshop (Paul), London SW.............. 168
Fosters Bookshop, London W 173
Fotheringham (Alex), Northumberland 202
Fox Books (J. & J.), Kent............................ 140
Freeman's Corner Shop, Norfolk 190
Frew Limited (Robert), London W................. 173
G. C. Books Ltd., Dumfries & Galloway......... 271
Gardener & Cook, London SW...................... 168
Gibbs Books, (Jonathan), Worcestershire......... 256
Gilbert and Son (H.M.), Hampshire............... 126
Gillmark Gallery, Hertfordshire 131
Glenbower Books, Co. Dublin 265
Golden Books Group, Devon 85
Good for Books, Lincolnshire 151
Goodyer, Natural History Books (Eric), Leics... 148
Grahame Thornton, Bookseller, Dorset........... 93
Grampian Books, Grampian.......................... 274
Grant & Shaw Ltd., Lothian 278
Grant Books, Worcestershire 255
Green Man Books, East Sussex 101
Gresham Books, Somerset 218
Greta Books, Durham 97
Grove Bookshop (The), N Yorks................... 197
Guildmaster Books, Cheshire 70
Hamish Riley-Smith, Norfolk........................ 192
Hanborough Books, Oxfordshire.................... 210
Hancock (Peter), West Sussex 243
Hanshan Tang Books, London SW 168
Harrington (Adrian), London W.................... 173
Harrington Antiquarian Bookseller (Peter), London SW... 169
Hava Books, London SE.............................. 165
Hawkes (James), London SE 165
Helston Bookworm, The, Cornwall................. 74
Hennessey Bookseller (Ray), East Sussex......... 100
Heritage, West Midlands 239
Hilton (Books) (P.J.), London W 174
Hodgson (Judith), London W 174
Hollett and Son (R.F.G.), Cumbria 80
Holtom (Christopher), Cornwall 75
Horsham Rare Books, West Sussex 243
Howes Bookshop, East Sussex 102
Humber Books, Lincolnshire 150
Hutchison (Books) (Larry), Fife..................... 271
Ian Briddon, Derbyshire.............................. 82
Island Books, Devon 85
Jackson (M.W.), Wiltshire........................... 254
Jade Mountain Bookshop, Hampshire............. 126
Jane Jones Books, Grampian 272
Jarndyce Antiquarian Booksellers, London WC. 178
Jay Books, Lothian..................................... 278
JB Books & Collectables, West Sussex............ 244
Jiri Books, Co. Antrim 260
Joel Segal Books, Devon 86
John Underwood Antiquarian Books, Norfolk .. 190
Joppa Books Ltd., Surrey 231
Junk & Spread Eagle, London SE.................. 165
Just Books, Cornwall 76
Keel Row Bookshop, Tyne and Wear 236
Kerr (Norman), Cumbria 78

Kilgarriff (Raymond), East Sussex.................. 105
Kim's Bookshop, West Sussex...........242, 243, 245
Kingswood Books, Dorset 94
Kirkman Ltd., (Robert), Bedfordshire............. 54
Korn (M. Eric), London N 159
Lake (David), Norfolk 191
Lawson & Company (E.M.), Oxfordshire 208
Laywood (Anthony W.), Nottinghamshire 204
Liddle (Steve), Bristol 58
Lymelight Books & Prints, Dorset.................. 93
Mandalay Bookshop, London SW 169
Marble Hill Books, Middlesex....................... 184
Marine & Cannon Books, Cheshire 71
Marine and Cannon Books, Cheshire 69
Marrin's Bookshop, Kent 138
Martin Bookshop & Gallery (Richard), Hampshire 123
McConnell Fine Books, Kent........................ 137
McCrone (Audrey), Isle of Arran................... 275
McNaughtan's Bookshop, Lothian 278
Mead (P.J.), Shropshire.............................. 214
Meads Book Service (The), East Sussex........... 104
Mermaid Books (Burlingham), Norfolk........... 192
Michael J Carroll, Co. Cork 263
Miller (Stephen), London Outer.................... 184
Minster Gate Bookshop, N Yorks.................. 199
Moore (C.R.), Shropshire 214
Moreton Books, Devon................................ 87
Moss Books, London NW 162
Murphy (C.J.), Norfolk............................... 190
Muttonchop Manuscripts, West Sussex 244
N V Books, Warwickshire............................ 237
N1 Books, East Sussex 105
Naughton Booksellers, Co. Dublin 265
Neil Summersgill, Lancashire 143
Nibris Books, London SW........................... 170
Norton Books, N Yorks............................... 197
O'Kill (John), Kent.................................... 138
Offa's Dyke Books, Shropshire..................... 214
Pagan Limited (Hugh), London SW............... 170
Paralos Ltd., London WC 178
Park Gallery & Bookshop (The), Northants 201
Parker Books (Mike), Cambridgeshire 64
Parkinsons Books, Merseyside....................... 186
Pemberley Books, Buckinghamshire 62
Peter M Daly, Hampshire............................ 127
Phelps (Michael), West Sussex...................... 243
Phillips (Nigel), Hampshire.......................... 122
Poetry Bookshop (The), Powys..................... 291
Potterton Books, N Yorks 197
Preston Book Company, Lancashire 145
Price (John), London N 159
Pringle Booksellers (Andrew), Lothian............ 278
Quaritch Ltd., (Bernard), London W.............. 175
R. & A. Books, East Sussex 102
Rayner (Hugh Ashley), Somerset 217
Red Star Books, Hertfordshire 130
Rhos Point Books, Conwy........................... 285
Robert Temple, London N........................... 160
Roberts Fine Books (Julian), Lincolnshire........ 153
Robertshaw (John), Cambridgeshire............... 66
Robin Doughty - Fine Books, West Midlands... 239
Rochdale Book Company, Gr Man 120
Roger Collicott Books, Cornwall 75
Roger Treglown, Cheshire........................... 70

SPECIALITY INDEX

Rosley Books, Cumbria 81
Rothwell & Dunworth, Somerset 218
Rowan (H. & S.J.), Dorset.......................... 91
Rowan (P. & B.), Co. Antrim 260
Roz Hulse, Conwy 286
Rye Old Books, East Sussex 104
St Philip's Books, Oxfordshire...................... 210
Scarthin Books, Derbyshire 82
Scrivener's Books & Bookbinding, Derbyshire... 82
Seabreeze Books, Lancashire........................ 145
Seydi Rare Books (Sevin), London NW 162
Sillan Books, Co. Cavan............................. 262
Sims Reed Limited, London SW 170
Smith (Clive), Essex 109
Sokol Books Ltd., London W 175
South Downs Book Service, West Sussex......... 244
Spelman (Ken), N Yorks 199
Spooner & Co, Somerset 220
Staniland (Booksellers), Lincolnshire 154
Stella Books, Monmouthshire 288
Sterling Books, Somerset 221
Stern Antiquarian Bookseller (Jeffrey), N Yorks 199
Stone, (G.& R.), Borders 268
Stothert Old Books, Cheshire....................... 69
Susanne Schulz-Falster Rare Books, London N . 160
Taney Books, Co. Dublin 264
Taylor & Son (Peter), Hertfordshire 133
The Old Abbey Bookshop, Co. Down 261
Thomas (Books) (Leona), Cheshire 71
Thomas Rare Books, Suffolk 227
Thornber (Peter M.), N Yorks 196
Thorntons of Oxford Ltd., Oxfordshire 207
Tiger Books, Kent 137
Tobo Books, Hampshire............................. 123
Tombland Bookshop, Norfolk 191
Tooley, Adams & Co, Oxfordshire 211
Trinity Rare Books, Co. Leitrim 266
Turton (John), Durham 98
Unsworth's Booksellers, London WC 180
Vandeleur Antiquarian Books, Surrey............. 232
Venables (Morris & Juliet), Bristol................. 60
Ventnor Rare Books, Isle of Wight................ 135
Vinovium Books, Durham 97
Wadard Books, Kent 138
Water Lane Bookshop, Wiltshire 253
Waterfield's, Oxfordshire 210
Watkins Books Ltd., London WC.................. 180
Weiner (Graham), London N 160
Wembdon Books, Somerset......................... 217
Westcountry Old Books, Cornwall................. 76
Westcountry Oldbooks, Devon 90
Westfield Books, N Yorks........................... 199
Westwood Books Ltd, Cumbria.................... 80
Wilbraham (J. & S.), London NW 163
Winchester Bookshop (The), Hampshire.......... 127
Woburn Books, London N 160
Worcester Rare Books, Worcestershire............ 257
Words Etcetera Bookshop, Dorset................. 93
Worlds End Bookshop, London SW 171
Ximenes Rare Books Inc., Glos 115
Yates Antiquarian Books (Tony), Leics........... 148
Yesterday's Books, Dorset 92
York (Graham), Devon............................... 86

ANTIQUE PAPER

Embleton (Paul), Essex 111

ANTIQUE STOVES

Randall (Tom), Somerset............................ 219
Stroh (M.A.), London E 155

ANTIQUES

Abrahams (Mike), Staffordshire.................... 224
Addyman Books, Powys............................. 289
Ancient Art Books, London SW 167
Anthony Vickers Books, N Yorks 196
Antiques on High, Oxfordshire..................... 209
Apocalypse, Surrey 233
Arden Books & Cosmographia, Warwickshire... 237
Arnold (Roy), Suffolk................................ 228
Art Reference Books, Hampshire 125
Autumn Leaves, Lincolnshire....................... 152
Aviabooks, Glos 114
Axe Rare & Out of Print Books (Richard),
N Yorks.. 194
Barnby (C. & A.J.), Kent........................... 141
Bookcase, Cumbria................................... 78
Books, Kent 137
Books & Collectables Ltd., Cambridgeshire...... 63
BookShop, The, Dumfries & Galloway 270
Browse Books, Lancashire 144
Browzers, Gr Man.................................... 119
Carningli Centre, Pembrokeshire 288
Carta Regis, Powys................................... 293
Chaucer Bookshop, Kent........................... 136
Cheshire Book Centre, Cheshire.................... 69
Chris Phillips, Wiltshire............................. 251
Clark (Nigel A.), London SE 165
Cobbles Books, Somerset............................ 218
Corfe Books, Surrey.................................. 231
Cornucopia Books, Lincolnshire 153
Delectus Books, London WC....................... 177
Don Kelly Books, London W 172
Duncan & Reid, Lothian 277
Eastcote Bookshop (The), London Outer......... 181
Eton Antique Bookshop, Berkshire 57
Foster (Stephen), London NW 161
Gloucester Road Bookshop, London SW 168
Golden Goose Books, Lincolnshire................ 152
Gresham Books, Somerset 218
Hadfield (G.K.), Cumbria 80
Hanshan Tang Books, London SW 168
Heneage Art Books (Thomas), London SW 169
Hennessey Bookseller (Ray), East Sussex 100
Hollett and Son (R.F.G.), Cumbria 80
Ives Bookseller (John), London Outer 184
Jackson (M.W.), Wiltshire.......................... 254
Jade Mountain Bookshop, Hampshire 126
Joel Segal Books, Devon 86
John R. Hoggarth, N Yorks........................ 198
Katharine House Gallery, Wiltshire 252
Keeble Antiques, Somerset 219
Kennedy (Peter), Surrey 235
Keswick Bookshop, Cumbria 79
Leabeck Books, Oxfordshire 210
Malvern Bookshop (The), Worcestershire 255
Martin (Books and Pictures), (Brian P)., Surrey . 232
Milestone Publications Goss &
Crested China, Hampshire 123

Moss End Bookshop, Berkshire 57
Mundy (David), Buckinghamshire 61
Nelson (Elizabeth), Suffolk 227
Nibris Books, London SW 170
Offa's Dyke Books, Shropshire 214
Park Gallery & Bookshop (The), Northants 201
Pauline Harries Books, Hampshire 123
Petworth Antique Market (Bookroom),
W Sussex 244
Phelan Books, Co. Dublin 265
Phillips of Hitchin (Antiques) Ltd., Hertfordshire 131
Pordes Books Ltd., (Henry), London WC 179
Potterton Books, N Yorks 197
Prescott - The Bookseller (John), London Outer 184
R. & A. Books, East Sussex 102
Rees & O'Neill Rare Books, London WC 179
Reference Works Ltd., Dorset 95
Roland Books, Kent 139
Rowan (H. & S.J.), Dorset 91
Sax Books, Suffolk 229
Smith Books, (Sally), Suffolk 227
Stella Books, Monmouthshire 288
Stothert Old Books, Cheshire 69
Strathtay Antiquarian - Secondhand Books,
Tayside 282
Studio Bookshop, East Sussex 100
Tarka Books, Devon 84
The Glass Key, W Yorks 247
Thin Read Line, Merseyside 185
Thomas (Books) (Leona), Cheshire 71
Treasure Island (The), Gr Man 119
Trinders' Fine Tools, Suffolk 227
Uncle Phil's Books, West Midlands 240
Ventnor Rare Books, Isle of Wight 135
Vickers (Anthony), N Yorks 196
Water Lane Bookshop, Wiltshire 253
Whittle, Bookseller (Avril), Cumbria 81
Worlds End Bookshop, London SW 171
www.AntiqueWatchStore.com, Hertfordshire 130
Wychwood Books, Glos 116

ANTIQUITIES

Apocalypse, Surrey 233
Barter Books, Northumberland 202
BOOKS4U, Flintshire 286
Don Kelly Books, London W 172
Hanshan Tang Books, London SW 168
Joel Segal Books, Devon 86
Keith Langford, London E 155
McCrone (Audrey), Isle of Arran 275
N1 Books, East Sussex 105
O'Flynn Books, N Yorks 199
Parkinsons Books, Merseyside 186
R. & A. Books, East Sussex 102
Seydi Rare Books (Sevin), London NW 162
Thorntons of Oxford Ltd., Oxfordshire 207
Trinity Rare Books, Co. Leitrim 266
Wychwood Books, Glos 116

APICULTURE

B. and K. Books, Powys 289
Edmund Pollinger Rare Books, London SW 167
Joel Segal Books, Devon 86
Mayhew (Veronica), Berkshire 57

APPLIED ART

Amwell Book Company, London EC 157
Ancient Art Books, London SW 167
Anthony Whittaker, Kent 136
Arnold (Roy), Suffolk 228
Ars Artis, Oxfordshire 209
Art Reference Books, Hampshire 125
Artco, Nottinghamshire 204
Aviabooks, Glos 114
Barmby (C. & A.J.), Kent 141
Batterham (David), London W 172
Biblion, London W 172
Books & Things, London W 172
Bruce Holdsworth Books, East Sussex 105
Butts Books (Mary), Berkshire 56
Cheshire Book Centre, Cheshire 69
Cornucopia Books, Lincolnshire 153
Cover to Cover, Merseyside 186
Decorum Books, London N 158
Dew (Roderick), East Sussex 101
Eastleach Books, Berkshire 56
Fosters Bookshop, London W 173
Handsworth Books, Essex 112
Hay Cinema Bookshop Ltd., Powys 290
Heneage Art Books (Thomas), London SW 169
Hennessey Bookseller (Ray), East Sussex 100
High Street Books, Devon 86
Hodgkins and Company Limited (Ian), Glos 116
Inprint, Glos 116
Island Books, Devon 85
Joel Segal Books, Devon 86
Judith Mansfield, W Yorks 250
Keith Langford, London E 155
Keswick Bookshop, Cumbria 79
Mannwaring (M.G.), Bristol 59
Martin - Bookseller (Colin), East Yorkshire 107
McNaughtan's Bookshop, Lothian 278
N1 Books, East Sussex 105
Nelson (Elizabeth), Suffolk 227
Oopalba Books, Cheshire 71
Pagan Limited (Hugh), London SW 170
Peter M Daly, Hampshire 127
Phillips of Hitchin (Antiques) Ltd., Herts 131
Potterton Books, N Yorks 197
R. & A. Books, East Sussex 102
Ray Rare and Out of Print Books (Janette),
N Yorks 199
Reads, Dorset 95
Rees & O'Neill Rare Books, London WC 179
Scrivener's Books & Bookbinding, Derbyshire ... 82
Sleepy Elephant Books & Artefacts, Cumbria ... 80
Spelman (Ken), N Yorks 199
Staniland (Booksellers), Lincolnshire 154
Tasburgh Books, Norfolk 191
Trinders' Fine Tools, Suffolk 227
Wyseby House Books, Berkshire 55

AQUATICS

Parkinsons Books, Merseyside 186
R. & A. Books, East Sussex 102

ARABICA

Al Saqi Books, London W 172
Apocalypse, Surrey 233
Hamish Riley-Smith, Norfolk 192

SPECIALITY INDEX

Joppa Books Ltd., Surrey 231
Marcet Books, London SE........................... 165
R. & A. Books, East Sussex 102
Thorntons of Oxford Ltd., Oxfordshire 207
Watkins Books Ltd., London WC.................. 180

ARACHNOLOGY

Parkinsons Books, Merseyside...................... 186

ARCHAEOLOGY

Addyman Books, Powys.............................. 289
Alauda Books, Cumbria.............................. 78
Ancient Art Books, London SW.................... 167
Antiquary Ltd., (Bar Bookstore), N Yorks....... 196
Atlantis Bookshop, London WC................... 177
B D McManmon, Lancashire 145
Baker Limited (A.P. & R.), D&G, Scotland 270
Baldwin's Scientific Books, Essex 112
Barmby (C. & A.J.), Kent........................... 141
Barn Books, Buckinghamshire...................... 61
Bonython Bookshop, Cornwall..................... 76
Books B.C., London Outer 181
Booth Books, Powys 289
Bosco Books, Cornwall 73
Bosorne Books, Cornwall 75
Bracton Books, Cambridgeshire.................... 63
Brad Books, Essex..................................... 111
Brock Books, N Yorks 193
Burebank Books, Norfolk............................ 187
Castle Bookshop, Powys............................. 292
Castle Bookshop, Essex.............................. 109
Castle Hill Books, Herefordshire................... 128
Cheshire Book Centre, Cheshire.................... 69
Classics Bookshop (The), Oxfordshire............. 207
Clements (R.W.), London Outer 182
Colin Hancock, Ceredigion 284
Colonsay Bookshop, Isle of Colonsay............. 276
Corfe Books, Surrey.................................. 231
Cornucopia Books, Lincolnshire 153
Crouch Rare Books, Surrey......................... 233
D'Arcy Books, Wiltshire............................. 252
Earth Science Books, Wiltshire 252
Eastgate Bookshop, East Yorkshire 106
Ellwood Editions, Wiltshire 253
Ford Books (David), Herts 133
Freeman's Corner Shop, Norfolk 190
G. C. Books Ltd., Dumfries & Galloway......... 271
Garfi Books, Powys 293
GfB: the Colchester Bookshop, Essex 109
Gildas Books, Cheshire 68
Golden Age Books, Worcestershire................ 256
Hall's Bookshop, Kent............................... 141
Hanshan Tang Books, London SW 168
Helion & Company, West Midlands 240
Idle Genius Books, London N 159
Island Books, Devon 85
J & J Burgess Booksellers, Cambridgeshire....... 64
Jade Mountain Bookshop, Hampshire 126
Joel Segal Books, Devon 86
John Barton, Hampshire 126
Joppa Books Ltd., Surrey 231
Just Books, Cornwall 76
Kalligraphia, Isle of Wight 134
Kenny's Bookshops and Art Galleries Ltd, Co.
Galway 266

Kingswood Books, Dorset 94
Larkham Books (Patricia), Glos.................... 117
Lowe (John), Norfolk 189
Maghreb Bookshop (The), London WC.......... 178
Mannwaring (M.G.), Bristol 59
McCrone (Audrey), Isle of Arran 275
medievalbookshop, Herts............................ 133
Michael Graves-Johnston, London SW 169
Moss Books, London NW........................... 162
Mulyan (Don), Merseyside.......................... 186
N1 Books, East Sussex 105
Nevis Railway Bookshops (The Antique &
Book Collector), Wiltshire........................ 252
Nonsuch Books, Surrey.............................. 234
Old Station Pottery & Bookshop (The), Norfolk 192
P. and P. Books, Worcestershire 256
Parkinsons Books, Merseyside...................... 186
Parrott Books, Oxfordshire 211
Polczynski (Udo K.H.), Powys 291
Pordes Books Ltd., (Henry), London WC........ 179
Prescott - The Bookseller (John), London Outer 184
Prospect House Books, Co. Down................. 261
Quest Books, East Yorkshire 107
R. & A. Books, East Sussex 102
Reads, Dorset 95
Roland Books, Kent 139
St Mary's Books & Prints, Lincolnshire 154
Samovar Books, Co. Dublin........................ 264
Scott (Peter), East Sussex........................... 104
Scrivener's Books & Bookbinding, Derbyshire.... 82
Spooner & Co, Somerset 220
Stalagluft Books, Tyne and Wear.................. 236
Staniland (Booksellers), Lincolnshire 154
Taylor & Son (Peter), Herts........................ 133
Thorntons of Oxford Ltd., Oxfordshire........... 207
Tombland Bookshop, Norfolk 191
Trinity Rare Books, Co. Leitrim 266
Uncle Phil's Books, West Midlands 240
Unsworths Booksellers, London WC.............. 163
Vickers (Anthony), N Yorks........................ 196
Westwood Books Ltd, Cumbria.................... 80
Whitchurch Books Ltd., Cardiff.................... 283
Winchester Bookshop (The), Hampshire.......... 127
Winghale Books, Lincolnshire 153

ARCHAEOLOGY - INDUSTRIAL

Allinson (Frank & Stella), Warwickshire 237
Anthony Vickers Books, N Yorks 196
Bott, (Bookdealers) Ltd., (Martin), Gr Man 118
Browsers Bookshop, Cornwall...................... 73
Castle Bookshop, Powys............................. 292
Chris Phillips, Wiltshire............................. 251
Cornucopia Books, Lincolnshire 153
Cox (Geoff), Devon 90
Henry Wilson Books, Cheshire..................... 69
Joel Segal Books, Devon 86
Kingswood Books, Dorset 94
Liddle (Steve), Bristol 58
Randall (Tom), Somerset............................ 219
Robert Humm & Co, Lincolnshire 154
Salway Books, Essex 112
Sturford Books, Wiltshire 254
Vickers (Anthony), N Yorks........................ 196
Wiend Books, Lancashire 144

SPECIALITY INDEX

ARCHITECTURE - GENERAL

A. & H. Peasgood, Cambridgeshire 67
Addyman Books, Powys.............................. 289
Al Saqi Books, London W........................... 172
Amwell Book Company, London EC............. 157
Anne Harris Books & Bags Booksearch, Devon 88
Anthony Vickers Books, N Yorks 196
Antiquary Ltd., (Bar Bookstore), N Yorks....... 196
Antiques on High, Oxfordshire...................... 209
Apocalypse, Surrey 233
Ars Artis, Oxfordshire 209
Art Book Company, (The), Suffolk................. 228
Art Reference Books, Hampshire 125
Aviabooks, Glos 114
Ballantyne–Way (Roger), Suffolk 229
Barmby (C. & A.J.), Kent............................ 141
Batterham (David), London W...................... 172
Bennett & Kerr Books, Oxfordshire................ 206
Bermondsey Basement Bookstore, London SE .. 164
Bianco Library, W Sussex............................ 242
Biblion, London W.................................... 172
Birchden Books, London E 155
Book Business (The), London W 172
Bookroom (The), Surrey.............................. 234
Books, Kent 137
Books, Kent 137
Books For All, N Yorks 194
Bosco Books, Cornwall............................... 73
Bowden Books, Leics 149
Brad Books, Essex..................................... 111
Brazenhead Ltd., Norfolk 189
Brighton Books, East Sussex......................... 99
Broadhurst of Southport Ltd., Merseyside 186
Butts Books (Mary), Berkshire 56
Camden Books, Somerset 216
Castle Bookshop, Powys............................. 292
Catmax Books, Norfolk 187
Chandos Books, Devon............................... 85
Chapter & Verse, Lincolnshire...................... 152
Chevin Books, W Yorks.............................. 250
Chris Phillips, Wiltshire.............................. 251
Classic Bindings Ltd, London SW 167
Clevedon Books, Somerset 218
Coach House Books, Worcestershire 256
Collectable Books, London SE 165
Coombes (A.J.), Surrey 231
Corfe Books, Surrey................................... 231
Cornucopia Books, Lincolnshire 153
Cottage Books, Leics.................................. 147
Country Books, Derbyshire 82
Courtney & Hoff, N Yorks 198
Cover to Cover, Merseyside.......................... 186
D'Arcy Books, Wiltshire............................. 252
Darkwood Books, Co. Cork.......................... 263
Dartmoor Bookshop (The), Devon 84
Decorum Books, London N 158
Dew (Roderick), East Sussex 101
Duck (William), Hampshire.......................... 124
Edwards (London) Limited (Francis),
London WC 177
Edwards in Hay–on–Wye (Francis), Powys 290
Elton Engineering Books, London W 173
Empire Books, N Yorks.............................. 198
English (Toby), Oxfordshire......................... 211
Farquharson, (Hilary), Tayside...................... 281

Forest Books of Manchester, Cheshire............ 71
Foster (Stephen), London NW 161
Fosters Bookshop, London W 173
Fotheringham (Alex), Northumberland 202
Freeman's Corner Shop, Norfolk 190
G. C. Books Ltd., Dumfries & Galloway......... 271
George St. Books, Derbyshire 83
GfB: the Colchester Bookshop, Essex 109
Gloucester Road Bookshop, London SW 168
Good for Books, Lincolnshire 151
Goodyer (Nicholas), London N..................... 159
Grampian Books, Grampian......................... 274
Gravity Books, Lincolnshire 151
Gresham Books, Somerset 218
Greta Books, Durham 97
Grove Bookshop (The), N Yorks 197
Hall's Bookshop, Kent................................ 141
Hanshan Tang Books, London SW 168
Harrington Antiquarian Bookseller (Peter),
London SW... 169
Harwich Old Books, Essex........................... 110
Haskell (R.H. & P.), Dorset 94
Hay Castle, Powys..................................... 290
Hedgerow Books, South Yorkshire................. 222
Helmsley Antiquarian & Secondhand Books,
N Yorks... 194
Heywood Hill Limited (G.), London W 174
Hicks (Ronald C.), Cornwall 73
Hornsey's, N Yorks 195
Hünersdorff Rare Books, London SW............ 169
Inch's Books, Kent 137
Inprint, Glos.. 116
Island Books, Devon 85
Ives Bookseller (John), London Outer 184
Jackdaw Books, Norfolk 189
Jade Mountain Bookshop, Hampshire 126
Joel Segal Books, Devon 86
Judd Books, London WC............................ 178
Katnap Arts, Norfolk................................. 191
Kelsall (George), Gr Man............................ 118
Kenny's Bookshops and Art Galleries Ltd,
Co. Galway 266
Keswick Bookshop, Cumbria........................ 79
Kingswood Books, Dorset 94
Liddle (Steve), Bristol 58
Lighthouse Books (The), Dorset 92
Maghreb Bookshop (The), London WC.......... 178
Malvern Bookshop (The), Worcestershire 255
Mandalay Bookshop, London SW 169
Mannwaring (M.G.), Bristol 59
Marble Hill Books, Middlesex...................... 184
Marlborough Rare Books Ltd., London W...... 174
Martin - Bookseller (Colin), East Yorkshire 107
McCrone (Audrey), Isle of Arran................... 275
McNaughtan's Bookshop, Lothian 278
Missing Books, Essex 109
Monmouth House Books, Monmouthshire 288
Moss Books, London NW........................... 162
Mulyan (Don), Merseyside........................... 186
My Back Pages, London SW 169
Nelson (Elizabeth), Suffolk 227
Newcastle Bookshop At Haltwhistle,
Northumberland 202
Nonsuch Books, Surrey............................... 234
Octagon Books, Cambridgeshire 66

SPECIALITY INDEX

Old Town Bookshop (The), Lothian 278
Oopalba Books, Cheshire............................. 71
Pagan Limited (Hugh), London SW................ 170
Parkinsons Books, Merseyside...................... 186
Parrott Books, Oxfordshire 211
Pauline Harries Books, Hampshire 123
Peter M Daly, Hampshire............................ 127
Phelan Books, Co. Dublin 265
Phillips of Hitchin (Antiques) Ltd., Herts......... 131
Pordes Books Ltd., (Henry), London WC........ 179
Portobello Books, London W....................... 175
Potterton Books, N Yorks 197
Prescott - The Bookseller (John), London Outer 184
Prospect House Books, Co. Down................. 261
Quaritch Ltd., (Bernard), London W............... 175
R. & A. Books, East Sussex 102
Ray Rare and Out of Print Books (Janette),
N Yorks... 199
Read (C.&J.), Gorleston Books, Norfolk......... 188
Reads, Dorset 95
Rees & O'Neill Rare Books, London WC........ 179
Reeves Technical Books, N Yorks.................. 196
Rochdale Book Company, Gr Man................ 120
Roland Books, Kent 139
Rothwell & Dunworth, Somerset 218
Ryeland Books, Northants........................... 200
St Mary's Books & Prints, Lincolnshire 154
Samovar Books, Co. Dublin 264
Sax Books, Suffolk.................................... 229
Scarthin Books, Derbyshire 82
Scrivener's Books & Bookbinding, Derbyshire... 82
Second Edition, Lothian.............................. 278
Seydi Rare Books (Sevin), London NW.......... 162
Skoob Russell Square, Suffolk...................... 230
Sotheran Limited (Henry), London W............ 176
Sparrow Books, W Yorks............................ 246
Spelman (Ken), N Yorks............................. 199
Spooner & Co, Somerset 220
Stalagluft Books, Tyne and Wear.................. 236
Staniland (Booksellers), Lincolnshire 154
Stern Antiquarian Bookseller (Jeffrey), N Yorks 199
Tasburgh Books, Norfolk 191
Theatreshire Books, N Yorks........................ 193
Tilston (Stephen E.), London SE................... 166
Tobo Books, Hampshire.............................. 123
Tombland Bookshop, Norfolk 191
Trinders' Fine Tools, Suffolk 227
Trinity Rare Books, Co. Leitrim 266
Vickers (Anthony), N Yorks......................... 196
Westons, Herts 133
Westwood Books Ltd, Cumbria..................... 80
Wiend Books, Lancashire 144
Winchester Bookshop (The), Hampshire.......... 127
Woburn Books, London N 160
Worcester Rare Books, Worcestershire............ 257
Worlds End Bookshop, London SW 171
Wychwood Books, Glos.............................. 116
Wyseby House Books, Berkshire.................... 55

- THEATRE

Collectable Books, London SE...................... 165
Decorum Books, London N 158
Pagan Limited (Hugh), London SW................ 170
R. & A. Books, East Sussex 102
Seydi Rare Books (Sevin), London NW.......... 162

ARCHIVES

Book Gallery (The), Cornwall....................... 75
Joel Segal Books, Devon 86
R. & A. Books, East Sussex 102
Rowan (P. & B.), Co. Antrim 260
Stroh (M.A.), London E 155
Thornber (Peter M.), N Yorks 196

ARMED FORCES

- AUSTRALIAN AIR FORCE

Aardvark Books, Wiltshire........................... 254
Marine and Cannon Books, Cheshire 69
R. & A. Books, East Sussex 102
World War II Books, Surrey 235

- AUSTRALIAN ARMY

Aardvark Books, Wiltshire........................... 254
Burroughs (Andrew), Lincolnshire................. 153
Marine & Cannon Books, Cheshire 71
Marine and Cannon Books, Cheshire 69
MilitaryHistoryBooks.com, Kent.................... 138
World War II Books, Surrey 235

- AUSTRALIAN NAVY

Aardvark Books, Wiltshire........................... 254
Burroughs (Andrew), Lincolnshire................. 153
Lewcock (John), Cambridgeshire................... 66
Marine & Cannon Books, Cheshire 71
Marine and Cannon Books, Cheshire 69
R. & A. Books, East Sussex 102

ARMS & ARMOUR

Aardvark Books, Wiltshire........................... 254
Bookworm, Lothian................................... 277
Burroughs (Andrew), Lincolnshire................. 153
Cader Idris Books, Powys........................... 292
Caliver Books, Essex 110
Chalmers Hallam (E.), Hampshire................. 125
Chelifer Books, Cumbria 81
Deeside Books, Grampian............................ 273
Duck (William), Hampshire.......................... 124
Harris (George J.), Co. Derry 260
Helion & Company, West Midlands 240
Heneage Art Books (Thomas), London SW 169
J & J Burgess Booksellers, Cambridgeshire....... 64
Lost Books, Northants................................ 201
Meekins Books (Paul), Warwickshire.............. 238
MilitaryHistoryBooks.com, Kent.................... 138
N1 Books, East Sussex 105
Prospect Books, Conwy 285
R. & A. Books, East Sussex 102
Rods Books, Devon................................... 88
Spenceley Books (David), W Yorks 249
Stroh (M.A.), London E 155
Thin Read Line, Merseyside 185
Wizard Books, Cambridgeshire..................... 67

ARMY, THE

Aardvark Books, Wiltshire........................... 254
Addyman Books, Powys.............................. 289
Anthony Spranger, Wiltshire........................ 252
Apocalypse, Surrey 233
Black Five Books, Shropshire 215
Brad Books, Essex..................................... 111

SPECIALITY INDEX

Cornucopia Books, Lincolnshire 153
Deeside Books, Grampian............................ 273
Eastgate Bookshop, East Yorkshire 106
Farnborough Gallery, Hampshire................... 122
Gaullifmaufry Books, Herts......................... 132
Jade Mountain Bookshop, Hampshire 126
Joel Segal Books, Devon 86
Lost Books, Northants................................ 201
Mandalay Bookshop, London SW 169
Marine & Cannon Books, Cheshire 69, 71
MilitaryHistoryBooks.com, Kent................... 138
N1 Books, East Sussex 105
Not Just Books, Dorset............................... 94
R. & A. Books, East Sussex 102
Rods Books, Devon................................... 88
Rothwell & Dunworth, Somerset 218
Sax Books, Suffolk 229
Stella Books, Monmouthshire 288
Thin Read Line, Merseyside 185
War & Peace Books, Hampshire................... 122
Wheen O'Books, Scottish Borders 269
Winchester Bookshop (The), Hampshire.......... 127

ART - GENERAL

A. & H. Peasgood, Cambridgeshire 67
Abacus Books, Cheshire.............................. 68
Abacus Gallery, Staffordshire....................... 224
Addyman Books, Powys.............................. 289
Al Saqi Books, London W........................... 172
Alba Books, Grampian 274
Americanabooksuk, Cumbria........................ 77
Amwell Book Company, London EC.............. 157
Andrew Morton (Books), Powys.................... 289
Anne Harris Books & Bags Booksearch, Devon 88
Anthony Neville, Kent................................ 139
Antiquary Ltd., (Bar Bookstore), N Yorks....... 196
Antiques on High, Oxfordshire..................... 209
Apocalypse, Surrey 233
Arden Books & Cosmographia, Warwickshire... 237
Armchair Books, Lothian 276
Art Reference Books, Hampshire 125
Artco, Nottinghamshire............................... 204
Aurora Books Ltd, Lothian........................... 276
Autumn Leaves, Lincolnshire....................... 152
Aviabooks, Glos 114
Avonworld Books, Somerset........................ 218
Ballantyne-Way (Roger), Suffolk 229
Bardsley's Books, Suffolk 226
Barmby (C. & A.J.), Kent........................... 141
Barn Books, Buckinghamshire...................... 61
Bath Old Books, Somerset 216
Besleys Books, Suffolk 226
Bianco Library, W Sussex........................... 242
Biblion, London W.................................... 172
Big Bairn Books, Tayside 281
Blaenavon Books, Torfaen 294
Book Annex (The), Essex 109
Book Gallery (The), Cornwall....................... 75
Book Palace (The), London SE 164
Bookbarrow, Cambridgeshire....................... 63
Bookcase, Cumbria.................................... 78
Bookroom (The), Surrey............................. 234
Books, Denbighshire 286
Books, Kent 137
Books & Collectables Ltd., Cambridgeshire...... 63

Books Antiques & Collectables, Devon 90
Books For All, N Yorks 194
BOOKS4U, Flintshire................................. 286
Bookshop on the Heath, The, London SE 164
Bookworm, Lothian................................... 277
Bookworms, Norfolk.................................. 187
Bookworms of Evesham, Worcestershire 257
Booth (Booksearch Service), (Geoff), Cheshire... 68
Bosco Books, Cornwall............................... 73
Bosorne Books, Cornwall 75
Bowden Books, Leics 149
Brad Books, Essex..................................... 111
Brazenhead Ltd., Norfolk 189
Brighton Books, East Sussex........................ 99
Bristol Books, Bristol 60
Broadhurst of Southport Ltd., Merseyside 186
Brock Books, N Yorks 193
Browsers Bookshop, Cornwall...................... 73
Bruce Holdsworth Books, East Sussex 105
Butcher (Pablo), Oxfordshire 207
Butts Books (Mary), Berkshire 56
Caledonia Books, Strathclyde....................... 280
Cameron House Books, Isle of Wight............. 134
Campbell Art Books (Marcus), London SE...... 164
Carnforth Bookshop (The), Lancashire 143
Carningli Centre, Pembrokeshire 288
Cassidy (Bookseller) (P.), Lincolnshire 153
Catmax Books, Norfolk 187
Cavern Books, Cheshire 70
Central Bookshop, Warwickshire 238
Chalk (Old & Out of Print Books)
(Christine M.), West Midlands 239
Chandos Books, Devon............................... 85
Chaucer Bookshop, Kent............................ 136
Cheshire Book Centre, Cheshire.................... 69
Chris Phillips, Wiltshire.............................. 251
Classic Bindings Ltd, London SW 167
Classics Bookshop (The), Oxfordshire............ 207
Clements (R.W.), London Outer 182
Clifford Milne Books, Grampian................... 272
Cobbles Books, Somerset............................ 218
Cobweb Books, N Yorks............................. 195
Cofion Books, Pembrokeshire 288
Cooper Hay Rare Books, Strathclyde 280
Cover to Cover, Merseyside......................... 186
Cross (Ian), Berkshire................................ 55
Cumming Limited (A. & Y.), East Sussex........ 104
Dales & Lakes Book Centre, Cumbria 80
Dandy Lion Editions, Surrey 233
Darkwood Books, Co. Cork......................... 263
Dartmoor Bookshop (The), Devon 84
David Flint, Hampshire 124
de Beaumont (Robin), London SW 167
Decorum Books, London N 158
Discovery Bookshop, Carmarthenshire............ 283
Dolphin Books, Suffolk............................... 226
Doolin Dinghy Books, Co. Clare 262
Doorbar (P. & D.), Gwyned 287
Duncan & Reid, Lothian............................. 277
Eastcote Bookshop (The), London Outer......... 181
Eastgate Bookshop, East Yorkshire 106
Eastleach Books, Berkshire.......................... 56
Edwards (London) Limited (Francis),
London WC 177
Edwards in Hay-on-Wye (Francis), Powys 290

SPECIALITY INDEX

Ellis, Bookseller (Peter), London WC 178
Ely Books, Cambridgeshire 65
English (Toby), Oxfordshire......................... 211
Evans Books (Paul), W Sussex 243
Ewell Bookshop Ltd, Surrey........................ 232
Farnborough Gallery, Hampshire................... 122
Finch Rare Books Ltd. (Simon), London W 173
Fiona Edwards, Nottinghamshire 204
Fireside Bookshop, Cumbria........................ 81
Fisher & Sperr, London N.......................... 158
Ford Books (David), Herts 133
Fortune Green Books, London NW................ 161
Foster Bookshop (Paul), London SW............. 168
Fosters Bookshop, London W 173
Fotheringham (Alex), Northumberland 202
Freeman's Corner Shop, Norfolk 190
Furneaux Books (Lee), Devon...................... 89
Garfi Books, Powys 293
George St. Books, Derbyshire 83
GfB: the Colchester Bookshop, Essex 109
Gloucester Road Bookshop, London SW 168
Golden Goose Books, Lincolnshire 152
Goldman (Paul), Dorset 94
Good for Books, Lincolnshire 151
Goodyer (Nicholas), London N 159
Gravity Books, Lincolnshire 151
Hall's Bookshop, Kent............................... 141
Hanshan Tang Books, London SW 168
Harlequin Gallery, Lincolnshire 152
Harrington (Adrian), London W................... 173
Hay Castle, Powys................................... 290
Hay Cinema Bookshop Ltd., Powys............... 290
HCB Wholesale, Powys............................. 290
Helmsley Antiquarian & Secondhand Books,
N Yorks 194
Heneage Art Books (Thomas), London SW 169
Hennessey Bookseller (Ray), East Sussex......... 100
Hicks (Ronald C.), Cornwall 73
Hill House Books, Devon 88
Hodgkins and Company Limited (Ian), Glos 116
Horsham Rare Books, W Sussex................... 243
Idler (The), Suffolk 228
Inprint, Glos.. 116
Internet Bookshop UK Ltd., Glos................. 113
Jade Mountain Bookshop, Hampshire 126
Jean Hedger, Berkshire 55
Joel Segal Books, Devon 86
Judd Books, London WC 178
Just Books, Cornwall 76
Kalligraphia, Isle of Wight.......................... 134
Katharine House Gallery, Wiltshire 252
Katnap Arts, Norfolk................................ 191
Keeble Antiques, Somerset 219
Keogh's Books, Glos................................. 115
Keswick Bookshop, Cumbria 79
Kim's Bookshop, W Sussex......................... 243
Last Century Books, Borders 268
Leabeck Books, Oxfordshire 210
Leigh Gallery Books, Essex 110
Lenton (Alfred), Leics............................... 147
Liddle (Steve), Bristol 58
Lymelight Books & Prints, Dorset 93
Malvern Bookshop (The), Worcestershire 255
Mandalay Bookshop, London SW 169
Mannwaring (M.G.), Bristol 59

Marijana Dworski Books, via Hereford........... 290
Martin - Bookseller (Colin), East Yorkshire 107
Mason (Mary), Oxfordshire......................... 206
McNaughtan's Bookshop, Lothian 278
Mercat Books, Highland 274
Moorhead Books, W Yorks 246
Morley Case, Hampshire 125
Mulyan (Don), Merseyside.......................... 186
Mundy (David), Herts 130
Mundy (David), Buckinghamshire................. 61
My Back Pages, London SW 169
Nl Books, East Sussex 105
Neeve (P.), Cambridgeshire 63
Nelson (Elizabeth), Suffolk.......................... 227
Newlyn & New Street Books, Cornwall 75
Niner (Marcus), Isle of Wight 134
Nonsuch Books, Surrey.............................. 234
O'Brien Books & Photo Gallery, Co. Limerick .. 266
Octagon Books, Cambridgeshire 66
Offa's Dyke Books, Shropshire..................... 214
Old Aberdeen Bookshop, Grampian 272
Old Bookshop (The), West Midlands 241
Old Station Pottery & Bookshop (The), Norfolk 192
Old Town Bookshop (The), Lothian 278
Oopalba Books, Cheshire............................ 71
Oxfam Books and Music, Hampshire 126
Paper Pleasures, Somerset 219
Paton Books, Herts................................... 132
Pauline Harries Books, Hampshire 123
Peter Lyons Books, Glos 114
Peter M Daly, Hampshire........................... 127
Petworth Antique Market (Bookroom),
W Sussex 244
Pordes Books Ltd., (Henry), London WC........ 179
Prescott - The Bookseller (John), London Outer 184
Pringle Booksellers (Andrew), Lothian 278
Print Matters, London SE........................... 166
Prospect House Books, Co. Down................. 261
Quaritch Ltd., (Bernard), London W.............. 175
Quinto of Charing Cross Road, London WC ... 179
Quinto of Great Russell Street, London WC 179
R. & A. Books, East Sussex 102
Reading Lasses, Dumfries & Galloway 271
Reads, Dorset 95
Rees & O'Neill Rare Books, London WC........ 179
RGS Books, Surrey 235
Richmond Books, N Yorks.......................... 195
River Reads Bookshop, Devon..................... 90
Robin Doughty - Fine Books, West Midlands... 239
Roe and Moore, London WC....................... 179
Roland Books, Kent 139
Rowan (H. & S.J.), Dorset.......................... 91
Saint Ann's Books, Worcestershire 255
Saintfield Antiques & Fine Books, Co. Down ... 261
Sclanders (Beatbooks), (Andrew), London EC... 157
Scott (Peter), East Sussex........................... 104
Scrivener's Books & Bookbinding, Derbyshire... 82
Seabreeze Books, Lancashire........................ 145
Second Edition, Lothian............................. 278
Silverman (Michael), ... 166
Sims Reed Limited, London SW................... 170
Skoob Russell Square, Suffolk...................... 230
Smith Books, (Sally), Suffolk 227
Sotheran Limited (Henry), London W 176
Spelman (Ken), N Yorks............................ 199

SPECIALITY INDEX

Staniland (Booksellers), Lincolnshire 154
Sterling Books, Somerset 221
Stern Antiquarian Bookseller (Jeffrey), N Yorks 199
Stone Trough Books, N Yorks...................... 199
Stothert Old Books, Cheshire........................ 69
Stroma Books, Borders 268
Studio Bookshop, East Sussex....................... 100
Sturford Books, Wiltshire 254
Tarka Books, Devon 84
Tasburgh Books, Norfolk 191
Tilston (Stephen E.), London SE.................... 166
Tombland Bookshop, Norfolk 191
Treasure Chest Books, Suffolk 227
Treasure Island (The), Gr Man...................... 119
Trinders' Fine Tools, Suffolk 227
Trinity Rare Books, Co. Leitrim 266
Uncle Phil's Books, West Midlands 240
Upper–Room Books, Somerset...................... 218
Venables (Morris & Juliet), Bristol.................. 60
Village Books, Norfolk 187
Wadard Books, Kent 138
Walden Books, London NW 163
Water Lane Bookshop, Wiltshire 253
Watkins Books Ltd., London WC.................. 180
Waxfactor, East Sussex 100
Westwood Books Ltd, Cumbria..................... 80
Wetherell (Frances), Cambridgeshire 65
Wheen O'Books, Scottish Borders 269
Whig Books Ltd., Leics............................... 149
Whitehall Books, East Sussex........................ 103
Whitfield (Ken), Essex 111
Wiend Books, Lancashire 144
Winchester Bookshop (The), Hampshire.......... 127
Woburn Books, London N 160
Wood (Peter), Cambridgeshire....................... 65
Words Etcetera Bookshop, Dorset.................. 93
Worlds End Bookshop, London SW 171
Wychwood Books, Glos 116
Wyseby House Books, Berkshire 55
Xanadu Books, Cleveland 98

- AFRO-AMERICAN

Apocalypse, Surrey 233
Decorum Books, London N 158
Michael Graves-Johnston, London SW 169
R. & A. Books, East Sussex 102
Stevens (Joan), Cambridgeshire...................... 65
Watkins Books Ltd., London WC 180

- BRITISH

Addyman Books, Powys.............................. 289
Anthony Sillem, East Sussex......................... 102
Anthony Spranger, Wiltshire......................... 252
Bermondsey Basement Bookstore, London SE .. 164
Book Gallery (The), Cornwall 75
BookShop, The, Dumfries & Galloway 270
Brock Books, N Yorks 193
Butts Books (Mary), Berkshire 56
Cooper Hay Rare Books, Strathclyde 280
Decorum Books, London N 158
Dolphin Books, Suffolk............................... 226
Elaine Lonsdale Books, W Yorks................... 248
Ellwood Editions, Wiltshire 253
Farnborough Gallery, Hampshire................... 122
Hennessey Bookseller (Ray), East Sussex 100

JB Books & Collectables, W Sussex 244
Jean Hedger, Berkshire 55
Joel Segal Books, Devon 86
Just Books, Cornwall 76
McEwan Fine Books, Grampian.................... 273
My Back Pages, London SW 169
Ouse Valley Books, Bedfordshire 54
R. & A. Books, East Sussex 102
Robin Doughty - Fine Books, West Midlands... 239
Tasburgh Books, Norfolk 191
Treasure Island (The), Gr Man...................... 119
Woodbine Books, W Yorks.......................... 246

- TECHNIQUE

Addyman Books, Powys.............................. 289
Apocalypse, Surrey 233
Aviabooks, Glos 114
Book Annex (The), Essex 109
Bruce Holdsworth Books, East Sussex 105
Cheshire Book Centre, Cheshire.................... 69
Cornucopia Books, Lincolnshire 153
Cover to Cover, Merseyside.......................... 186
Decorum Books, London N 158
Doorbar (P. & D.), Gwyned 287
DPE Books, Devon 87
Ewell Bookshop Ltd, Surrey 232
Farnborough Gallery, Hampshire................... 122
Hennessey Bookseller (Ray), East Sussex 100
Jade Mountain Bookshop, Hampshire 126
JB Books & Collectables, W Sussex 244
Joel Segal Books, Devon 86
Just Books, Cornwall 76
Kim's Bookshop, W Sussex.......................... 243
McCrone (Audrey), Isle of Arran 275
N1 Books, East Sussex 105
Oopalba Books, Cheshire............................. 71
Peter Lyons Books, Glos 114
Portobello Books, London W 175
Print Matters, London SE............................ 166
R. & A. Books, East Sussex 102
Scrivener's Books & Bookbinding, Derbyshire... 82
Sleepy Elephant Books & Artefacts, Cumbria ... 80
Uncle Phil's Books, West Midlands 240
Walden Books, London NW 163
Water Lane Bookshop, Wiltshire 253
Whittle, Bookseller (Avril), Cumbria 81

- THEORY

Addyman Books, Powys.............................. 289
Amwell Book Company, London EC 157
Apocalypse, Surrey 233
Book Annex (The), Essex 109
Book Palace (The), London SE 164
Bruce Holdsworth Books, East Sussex 105
Cheshire Book Centre, Cheshire.................... 69
Cover to Cover, Merseyside.......................... 186
Decorum Books, London N 158
Farnborough Gallery, Hampshire................... 122
Jade Mountain Bookshop, Hampshire 126
Joel Segal Books, Devon 86
Just Books, Cornwall 76
Orchid Book Distributors, Co. Clare 262
Peter Lyons Books, Glos 114
R. & A. Books, East Sussex 102
Savery Books, East Sussex 99

SPECIALITY INDEX

Scrivener's Books & Bookbinding, Derbyshire... 82
Stevens (Joan), Cambridgeshire..................... 65
Uncle Phil's Books, West Midlands 240
Water Lane Bookshop, Wiltshire 253
Whittle, Bookseller (Avril), Cumbria 81

ART DECO

Art Book Company, (The), Suffolk................. 228
Cheshire Book Centre, Cheshire.................... 69
Cornucopia Books, Lincolnshire 153
Decorum Books, London N 158
Design Gallery 1850-1950 (The), Kent 142
Dolphin Books, Suffolk.............................. 226
Don Kelly Books, London W 172
Hennessey Bookseller (Ray), East Sussex......... 100
Joel Segal Books, Devon 86
N1 Books, East Sussex 105
Print Matters, London SE........................... 166
R. & A. Books, East Sussex 102
Scrivener's Books & Bookbinding, Derbyshire... 82
Woodbine Books, W Yorks.......................... 246

ART HISTORY

Addyman Books, Powys.............................. 289
Amwell Book Company, London EC.............. 157
Antiques on High, Oxfordshire..................... 209
Apocalypse, Surrey 233
Ars Artis, Oxfordshire 209
Art Book Company, (The), Suffolk................. 228
Art Reference Books, Hampshire 125
Aviabooks, Glos 114
Axe Rare & Out of Print Books (Richard),
N Yorks... 194
Ballantyne-Way (Roger), Suffolk 229
Bennett & Kerr Books, Oxfordshire............... 206
Book Annex (The), Essex 109
Book Gallery (The), Cornwall....................... 75
Book Palace (The), London SE 164
Bookroom (The), Surrey............................. 234
Books (For All), N Yorks............................ 194
books2books, Devon.................................. 88
Bookworm, Lothian................................... 277
Booth (Booksearch Service), (Geoff), Cheshire... 68
Bosco Books, Cornwall 73
Brock Books, N Yorks 193
Browsers Bookshop, Cornwall....................... 73
Bruce Holdsworth Books, East Sussex 105
Butts Books (Mary), Berkshire 56
Caledonia Books, Strathclyde....................... 280
Camden Books, Somerset 216
Carnforth Bookshop (The), Lancashire 143
Chaucer Bookshop, Kent............................ 136
Cheshire Book Centre, Cheshire.................... 69
Chevin Books, W Yorks.............................. 250
Clark (Nigel A.), London SE 165
Clevedon Books, Somerset 218
Cornucopia Books, Lincolnshire 153
Darkwood Books, Co. Cork......................... 263
Dartmoor Bookshop (The), Devon 84
Decorum Books, London N 158
Dolphin Books, Suffolk............................... 226
Don Kelly Books, London W 172
Doorbar (P. & D.), Gwyned........................ 287
DPE Books, Devon 87
Esoteric Dreams Bookshop, Cumbria 78

Fisher & Sperr, London N.......................... 158
Ford Books (David), Herts 133
Forest Books of Manchester, Cheshire............ 71
Foster (Stephen), London NW 161
Garfi Books, Powys 293
Goldman (Paul), Dorset 94
Hall's Bookshop, Kent............................... 141
Hanshan Tang Books, London SW 168
Heneage Art Books (Thomas), London SW 169
Hill House Books, Devon 88
JB Books & Collectables, W Sussex 244
Joel Segal Books, Devon 86
Just Books, Cornwall 76
Katnap Arts, Norfolk................................. 191
Kelsall (George), Gr Man........................... 118
Keogh's Books, Glos................................. 115
Kingsgate Books & Prints, Hampshire............ 126
Kingswood Books, Dorset 94
Kunkler Books (Paul), Cambridgeshire 64
Marcet Books, London SE........................... 165
Martin - Bookseller (Colin), East Yorkshire 107
McCrone (Audrey), Isle of Arran................... 275
McEwan Fine Books, Grampian.................... 273
Moreton Books, Devon............................... 87
Naughton Booksellers, Co. Dublin 265
Nelson (Elizabeth), Suffolk.......................... 227
Nonsuch Books, Surrey.............................. 234
O'Brien Books & Photo Gallery, Co. Limerick.. 266
Pagan Limited (Hugh), London SW............... 170
Peter Lyons Books, Glos 114
Pordes Books Ltd., (Henry), London WC........ 179
Portobello Books, London W 175
Prescott - The Bookseller (John), London Outer 184
R. & A. Books, East Sussex 102
Rothwell & Dunworth, Somerset 218
Ryeland Books, Northants........................... 200
St Philip's Books, Oxfordshire...................... 210
Savery Books, East Sussex 99
Sax Books, Suffolk 229
Scrivener's Books & Bookbinding, Derbyshire... 82
Seydi Rare Books (Sevin), London NW 162
Sleepy Elephant Books & Artefacts, Cumbria ... 80
Staniland (Booksellers), Lincolnshire 154
Tasburgh Books, Norfolk 191
Taylor & Son (Peter), Herts......................... 133
The Sanctuary Bookshop, Dorset.................. 94
Uncle Phil's Books, West Midlands 240
Unsworths Booksellers, London WC.............. 163
Walden Books, London NW 163
Water Lane Bookshop, Wiltshire 253
Westwood Books Ltd, Cumbria..................... 80
Whitchurch Books Ltd., Cardiff.................... 283
Whittle, Bookseller (Avril), Cumbria 81
Woodbine Books, W Yorks.......................... 246
Words Etcetera Bookshop, Dorset................. 93
Wyseby House Books, Berkshire.................... 55

ART NOUVEAU

Apocalypse, Surrey 233
Art Book Company, (The), Suffolk................. 228
Cornucopia Books, Lincolnshire 153
Decorum Books, London N 158
Design Gallery 1850-1950 (The), Kent 142
Don Kelly Books, London W 172
Joel Segal Books, Devon 86

SPECIALITY INDEX

N1 Books, East Sussex 105
Print Matters, London SE........................... 166
R. & A. Books, East Sussex 102

ART REFERENCE

Abbey Books, Cornwall 74
Amwell Book Company, London EC.............. 157
Anthony Spranger, Wiltshire........................ 252
Any Amount of Books, London WC 177
Ars Artis, Oxfordshire 209
Art Book Company, (The), Suffolk................. 228
Art Reference Books, Hampshire 125
Artco, Nottinghamshire.............................. 204
Assinder Books, Essex 110
Atlas, London N....................................... 158
Aviabooks, Glos 114
Ballantyne–Way (Roger), Suffolk 229
Barlow (Vincent G.), Hampshire................... 125
Barmby (C. & A.J.), Kent........................... 141
Baynton–Williams Gallery, W Sussex 242
Bealeys Books, Suffolk 226
Beware of the Leopard, Bristol..................... 58
Birchden Books, London E 155
Book Gallery (The), Cornwall...................... 75
Book Palace (The), London SE 164
Bookroom (The), Surrey............................. 234
Books, Kent 137
Books & Things, London W........................ 172
books2books, Devon................................. 88
Bookworm (The), Lothian 277
Bosco Books, Cornwall.............................. 73
Boxwood Books & Prints, Somerset............... 220
Brock Books, N Yorks 193
Bruce Holdsworth Books, East Sussex 105
Butts Books (Mary), Berkshire 56
Campbell Art Books (Marcus), London SE...... 164
Castleton (Pat), Kent................................. 138
Chalk (Old & Out of Print Books)
(Christine M.), West Midlands 239
Cheshire Book Centre, Cheshire.................... 69
Clark (Nigel A.), London SE 165
Coach House Books, Worcestershire 256
Cofion Books, Pembrokeshire 288
Cooper Hay Rare Books, Strathclyde............. 280
Cover to Cover, Merseyside......................... 186
Cox Old & Rare Books (Claude), Suffolk 228
Criterion Books, London Outer.................... 182
Darkwood Books, Co. Cork......................... 263
Dartmoor Bookshop (The), Devon 84
Decorum Books, London N 158
Delectus Books, London WC....................... 177
Don Kelly Books, London W 172
Doorbar (P. & D.), Gwyned 287
English (Toby), Oxfordshire......................... 211
Farnborough Gallery, Hampshire.................. 122
Foster (Stephen), London NW 161
GfB: the Colchester Bookshop, Essex 109
Goldman (Paul), Dorset 94
Grosvenor Prints, London WC..................... 178
Hanshan Tang Books, London SW 168
Harwich Old Books, Essex 110
Hennessey Bookseller (Ray), East Sussex 100
Hodgkins and Company Limited (Ian), Glos 116
Inprint, Glos... 116
Ives Bookseller (John), London Outer 184

Jackson (M.W.), Wiltshire........................... 254
JB Books & Collectables, W Sussex 244
Joel Segal Books, Devon 86
John Gorton Booksearch, East Sussex 105
Just Books, Cornwall 76
Katnap Arts, Norfolk 191
Keel Row Bookshop, Tyne and Wear 236
Kelsall (George), Gr Man........................... 118
Kenny's Bookshops and Art Galleries Ltd,
Co. Galway 266
Keogh's Books, Glos................................. 115
Kingsgate Books & Prints, Hampshire............ 126
Mannwaring (M.G.), Bristol 59
Martin - Bookseller (Colin), East Yorkshire 107
McEwan Fine Books, Grampian................... 273
Mercat Books, Highland 274
Moreton Books, Devon.............................. 87
Murphy (C.J.), Norfolk.............................. 190
My Back Pages, London SW 169
N1 Books, East Sussex 105
Nelson (Elizabeth), Suffolk 227
Nonsuch Books, Surrey.............................. 234
O'Flynn Books, N Yorks............................ 199
Old Town Bookshop (The), Lothian 278
Pagan Limited (Hugh), London SW............... 170
Parrott Books, Oxfordshire 211
Peter Lyons Books, Glos 114
Potterton Books, N Yorks 197
Priestpopple Books, Northumberland 202
Print Matters, London SE........................... 166
R. & A. Books, East Sussex 102
Robin Doughty - Fine Books, West Midlands... 239
Roe and Moore, London WC....................... 179
Savery Books, East Sussex 99
Sax Books, Suffolk 229
Scrivener's Books & Bookbinding, Derbyshire... 82
Seydi Rare Books (Sevin), London NW 162
Skoob Russell Square, Suffolk...................... 230
Smith Books, (Sally), Suffolk 227
Staniland (Booksellers), Lincolnshire 154
Stevens (Joan), Cambridgeshire..................... 65
Studio Bookshop, East Sussex...................... 100
Sue Lowell Natural History Books, London W . 176
Tasburgh Books, Norfolk 191
The Sanctuary Bookshop, Dorset 94
Trinders' Fine Tools, Suffolk 227
Ventnor Rare Books, Isle of Wight................ 135
Waddington Books & Prints (Geraldine),
Northants 200
Water Lane Bookshop, Wiltshire 253
Westwood Books Ltd, Cumbria.................... 80
Woodbine Books, W Yorks......................... 246
Wyseby House Books, Berkshire................... 55
York (Graham), Devon.............................. 86

ARTHURIAN

Addyman Books, Powys............................. 289
Apocalypse, Surrey 233
Bennett & Kerr Books, Oxfordshire............... 206
Boer (Louise), Arthurian Books, Powys 289
Byre Books, Dumfries & Galloway................ 270
Cheshire Book Centre, Cheshire.................... 69
Cofion Books, Pembrokeshire 288
Daeron's Books, Buckinghamshire................. 62
Dolphin Books, Suffolk.............................. 226

SPECIALITY INDEX

Dylans Bookstore, Swansea 294
Fifteenth Century Bookshop (The), East Sussex . 104
Gildas Books, Cheshire 68
Greer (Robin), London SW......................... 168
Inner Bookshop (The), Oxfordshire................ 210
Joel Segal Books, Devon 86
Jonkers Rare Books, Oxfordshire 209
Minster Gate Bookshop, N Yorks.................. 199
R. & A. Books, East Sussex 102
Randall (Tom), Somerset............................ 219
Whitchurch Books Ltd., Cardiff.................... 283
Wiend Books, Lancashire 144
Wizard Books, Cambridgeshire..................... 67

ARTISTS

Addyman Books, Powys............................. 289
Amwell Book Company, London EC.............. 157
Apocalypse, Surrey 233
Ars Artis, Oxfordshire 209
Art Book Company, (The), Suffolk................. 228
Art Reference Books, Hampshire 125
Artco, Nottinghamshire.............................. 204
Aurora Books Ltd, Lothian.......................... 276
Aviabooks, Glos 114
Ballantyne-Way (Roger), Suffolk 229
Book Palace (The), London SE 164
Bookroom (The), Surrey............................. 234
Booth (Booksearch Service), (Geoff), Cheshire... 68
Bow Windows Book Shop, East Sussex 103
Brock Books, N Yorks 193
Brown-Studies, Strathclyde.......................... 279
Bruce Holdsworth Books, East Sussex 105
Butts Books (Mary), Berkshire 56
Cameron House Books, Isle of Wight............. 134
Campbell Art Books (Marcus), London SE...... 164
Chalk (Old & Out of Print Books)
  (Christine M.), West Midlands 239
Cheshire Book Centre, Cheshire.................... 69
Clark (Nigel A.), London SE 165
Cornucopia Books, Lincolnshire 153
Darkwood Books, Co. Cork 263
Dartmoor Bookshop (The), Devon 84
David Flint, Hampshire 124
Decorum Books, London N 158
Ellis, Bookseller (Peter), London WC 178
Embleton (Paul), Essex 111
Foster (Stephen), London NW 161
Harwich Old Books, Essex.......................... 110
Hodgkins and Company Limited (Ian), Glos 116
Jade Mountain Bookshop, Hampshire 126
JB Books & Collectables, W Sussex 244
Jean Hedger, Berkshire 55
Joel Segal Books, Devon 86
Just Books, Cornwall 76
Keogh's Books, Glos................................. 115
Martin - Bookseller (Colin), East Yorkshire 107
McEwan Fine Books, Grampian.................... 273
Not Just Books, Dorset.............................. 94
Peter Lyons Books, Glos 114
Print Matters, London SE........................... 166
R. & A. Books, East Sussex 102
Ray Rare and Out of Print Books (Janette),
  N Yorks... 199
Read (C.&J.), Gorleston Books, Norfolk 188
Roe and Moore, London WC....................... 179

St Swithin's Illustrated & Children's Books,
  London W 175
Sephton (A.F.), London W 175
Sims Reed Limited, London SW................... 170
Stevens (Joan), Cambridgeshire.................... 65
Studio Bookshop, East Sussex...................... 100
Sue Lowell Natural History Books, London W . 176
Trinders' Fine Tools, Suffolk 227
Uncle Phil's Books, West Midlands 240
Upper-Room Books, Somerset...................... 218
Water Lane Bookshop, Wiltshire 253
Westwood Books Ltd, Cumbria.................... 80
Woodbine Books, W Yorks......................... 246
Wyseby House Books, Berkshire................... 55

ARTISTS - CHICAGO

Decorum Books, London N 158
R. & A. Books, East Sussex 102

ARTS & CRAFTS ERA

Addyman Books, Powys............................. 289
Bruce Holdsworth Books, East Sussex 105
Decorum Books, London N 158
Design Gallery 1850-1950 (The), Kent 142
Dolphin Books, Suffolk.............................. 226
Jade Mountain Bookshop, Hampshire 126
Joel Segal Books, Devon 86
Pagan Limited (Hugh), London SW............... 170
R. & A. Books, East Sussex 102
Woodbine Books, W Yorks......................... 246

ARTS, THE

Addyman Books, Powys............................. 289
All Books, Essex 110
Amwell Book Company, London EC.............. 157
Apocalypse, Surrey 233
Art Book Company, (The), Suffolk................. 228
Artco, Nottinghamshire.............................. 204
Aurora Books Ltd, Lothian.......................... 276
Ballantyne-Way (Roger), Suffolk 229
Beware of the Leopard, Bristol..................... 58
Book Annex (The), Essex 109
Book Business (The), London W 172
Book Palace (The), London SE 164
Bookbox, Glos 116
Brian Troath Books, London E..................... 155
Bruce Holdsworth Books, East Sussex 105
Camilla's Bookshop, East Sussex 101
Carta Regis, Powys................................... 293
Chaucer Bookshop, Kent............................ 136
Collectable Books, London SE...................... 165
Cornucopia Books, Lincolnshire 153
Cover to Cover, Merseyside......................... 186
D'Arcy Books, Wiltshire............................. 252
Darkwood Books, Co. Cork 263
Dead Mens Minds.co.uk, Powys 292
Decorum Books, London N 158
Dolphin Books, Suffolk.............................. 226
Don Kelly Books, London W 172
Elephant Books, W Yorks 249
Ellis, Bookseller (Peter), London WC 178
Farnborough Gallery, Hampshire.................. 122
Fine Art, London SW 168
Fossgate Books, N Yorks 198
Foster (Stephen), London NW 161

SPECIALITY INDEX

Harwich Old Books, Essex 110
Hawley (C.L.), N Yorks 197
Ice House Books, Wiltshire 253
Joel Segal Books, Devon 86
Junk & Spread Eagle, London SE 165
Just Books, Cornwall 76
Kim's Bookshop, W Sussex 242, 243, 245
Lenton (Alfred), Leics................................ 147
Little Bookshop (The), Gr Man..................... 119
Martin (Books and Pictures), (Brian P)., Surrey. 232
Martin - Bookseller (Colin), East Yorkshire 107
Murch Booksend, (Herbert), London SE 166
N1 Books, East Sussex 105
Naughton Booksellers, Co. Dublin 265
Newlyn & New Street Books, Cornwall 75
Peter Lyons Books, Glos 114
Pordes Books Ltd., (Henry), London WC........ 179
Print Matters, London SE............................ 166
R. & A. Books, East Sussex 102
Ray Rare and Out of Print Books (Janette),
N Yorks 199
Read (C.&J.), Gorleston Books, Norfolk 188
Richard Thornton Books, London N 160
Susanne Schulz-Falster Rare Books,
London N... 160
Till's Bookshop, Lothian 279
Trinders' Fine Tools, Suffolk 227
Trinity Rare Books, Co. Leitrim 266
Tucker (Alan & Joan), Glos 117
Uncle Phil's Books, West Midlands 240
Waterfield's, Oxfordshire 210
Watkins (R.G.), Somerset 216
Williams (Christopher), Dorset 94
Wizard Books, Cambridgeshire..................... 67
Woburn Books, London N 160
Wyseby House Books, Berkshire.................... 55

ASIAN STUDIES

Cavendish Rare Books, London N 158
Eastern Traveller (The), Somerset.................. 220
Hanshan Tang Books, London SW 168
Joel Segal Books, Devon 86
Joppa Books Ltd., Surrey 231
Mandalay Bookshop, London SW 169
Prospect House Books, Co. Down.................. 261
R. & A. Books, East Sussex 102
Rayner (Hugh Ashley), Somerset 217
Reading Lasses, Dumfries & Galloway 271

ASIAN-AMERICAN STUDIES

R. & A. Books, East Sussex 102
Watkins Books Ltd., London WC.................. 180

ASSASSINATIONS

Clifford Elmer Books Ltd., Cheshire 68
Crimes Ink, London E................................ 155
R. & A. Books, East Sussex 102

ASTROLOGY

Alpha Books, London N 158
Bookbarrow, Cambridgeshire........................ 63
Books, Denbighshire 286
Caduceus Books, Leics............................... 147
Cheshire Book Centre, Cheshire.................... 69
Cofion Books, Pembrokeshire 288

Delectus Books, London WC........................ 177
Glyn's Books, Shropshire............................ 213
Greensleeves, Oxfordshire 207
Inner Bookshop (The), Oxfordshire................ 210
Jade Mountain Bookshop, Hampshire 126
Joel Segal Books, Devon 86
Occultique, Northants................................. 200
R. & A. Books, East Sussex 102
Star Lord Books, Gr Man 119
Watkins Books Ltd., London WC.................. 180
Waxfactor, East Sussex 100

ASTRONAUTICS

Duck (William), Hampshire......................... 124
K Books, Cheshire..................................... 70
R. & A. Books, East Sussex 102
Stroh (M.A.), London E 155
Westons, Herts 133
Westwood Books Ltd, Cumbria..................... 80

ASTRONOMY

Addyman Books, Powys.............................. 289
Altea Antique Maps & Books, London W 172
Apocalypse, Surrey 233
Aviabooks, Glos 114
Baldwin's Scientific Books, Essex 112
Bookshop on the Heath, The, London SE 164
Cheshire Book Centre, Cheshire.................... 69
Esplin (David), Hampshire 124
Hadfield (G.K.), Cumbria 80
Jade Mountain Bookshop, Hampshire 126
Just Books, Cornwall 76
Kalligraphia, Isle of Wight 134
Macfarlane (Mr. H.), Essex 112
Moorside Books, Lancashire......................... 144
N1 Books, East Sussex 105
Phelps (Michael), W Sussex 243
Portobello Books, London W 175
R. & A. Books, East Sussex 102
Stroh (M.A.), London E 155
Transformer, Dumfries & Galloway................ 271
Turret House, Norfolk 192
Wayside Books and Cards, Oxfordshire 207
Westons, Herts 133
Westwood Books Ltd, Cumbria..................... 80
Wiend Books, Lancashire 144

ATLASES

Altea Antique Maps & Books, London W 172
Apocalypse, Surrey 233
Arthur Hook, Bristol................................... 58
Bannister (David), Glos.............................. 113
Barron (Robert M.), Kent............................ 140
Baynton-Williams Gallery, W Sussex 242
Booth Books, Powys 289
Burden Ltd., (Clive A.), Herts...................... 132
CI Galleries Limited, CI 258
Cheshire Book Centre, Cheshire.................... 69
Corvus Books, Buckinghamshire.................... 61
Cumming Limited (A. & Y.), East Sussex........ 104
Frew Limited (Robert), London W................. 173
G. C. Books Ltd., Dumfries & Galloway......... 271
Garwood & Voigt, Kent.............................. 140
Gillmark Gallery, Herts.............................. 131
Green (Mrs. D.M.), Surrey.......................... 235

SPECIALITY INDEX

Harrington Antiquarian Bookseller (Peter), London SW... 169 Hava Books, London SE............................. 165 Heritage, West Midlands .... 239 Hogan (F. & J.), London N .... 159 Kennedy (Peter), Surrey .... 235 Kentish (B. & N.), Oxfordshire...................... 206 Lymelight Books & Prints, Dorset .... 93 Marshall Rare Books (Bruce), Glos .... 113 Murphy (C.J.), Norfolk.............................. 190 Neil Summersgill, Lancashire .... 143 Nicholson of Chester (Richard), Cheshire .... 68 O'Flynn Books, N Yorks............................. 199 Paralos Ltd., London WC .... 178 Preston Book Company, Lancashire .... 145 R. & A. Books, East Sussex .... 102 Roz Hulse, Conwy .... 286 Russell (Charles), London SW...................... 170 Shapero Rare Books (Bernard J.), London W ... 175 Temperley (David), West Midlands................. 239 Yates Antiquarian Books (Tony), Leics........... 148

AUCTION CATALOGUES

Bookshop on the Heath, The, London SE .... 164 Clark (Nigel A.), London SE .... 165 JB Books & Collectables, W Sussex .... 244 Not Just Books, Dorset.............................. 94 R. & A. Books, East Sussex .... 102 Stroh (M.A.), London E .... 155 Studio Bookshop, East Sussex...................... 100 Susanne Schulz-Falster Rare Books, London N . 160 Thornber (Peter M.), N Yorks 196

AUDIO/SOUND/ACOUSTICS

Watkins Books Ltd., London WC.................. 180

AUSTRALIANA

Bonham (J. & S.L.), London W .... 172 Eggeling Books (John), W Yorks .... 250 Ely Books, Cambridgeshire .... 65 Empire Books, North Yorkshire .... 198 Joel Segal Books, Devon .... 86 Michael Graves-Johnston, London SW .... 169 MK Book Services, Cambridgeshire .... 66 Preston Book Company, Lancashire .... 145 Watkins Books Ltd., London WC.................. 180

AUTHOR - GENERAL

Aurora Books Ltd, Lothian.......................... 276 Bookpassage (The), Shropshire..................... 213 books2books, Devon................................. 88 Cornucopia Books, Lincolnshire .... 153 Eggeling Books (John), W Yorks .... 250 Ely Books, Cambridgeshire .... 65 Ewell Bookshop Ltd, Surrey........................ 232 Harrington (Adrian), London W................... 173 Hylton Booksearch, Merseyside .... 185 J & J Burgess Booksellers, Cambridgeshire....... 64 Jade Mountain Bookshop, Hampshire .... 126 Joel Segal Books, Devon .... 86 Murphy (C.J.), Norfolk.............................. 190 Naughton Booksellers, Co. Dublin .... 265 Priestpopple Books, Northumberland .... 202 R. & A. Books, East Sussex .... 102 Reading Lasses, Dumfries & Galloway 271

Simpson (Dave), Stirlingshire .... 269 Star Lord Books, Gr Man .... 119 Watkins Books Ltd., London WC.................. 180 Wheen O'Books, Scottish Borders 269

- 19TH CENTURY

Fifteenth Century Bookshop (The), East Sussex. 104 Jonkers Rare Books, Oxfordshire .... 209 Stevens (Joan), Cambridgeshire..................... 65

- 20TH CENTURY

Apocalypse, Surrey .... 233 Ash Rare Books, London SW....................... 167 Aurora Books Ltd, Lothian.......................... 276 Barmby (C. & A.J.), Kent........................... 141 Bookpassage (The), Shropshire..................... 213 books2books, Devon................................. 88 Cornucopia Books, Lincolnshire .... 153 Dolphin Books, Suffolk.............................. 226 Eggeling Books (John), W Yorks .... 250 Elaine Lonsdale Books, W Yorks.................. 248 Fifteenth Century Bookshop (The), East Sussex. 104 Foster Bookshop (Paul), London SW............. 168 Good for Books, Lincolnshire .... 151 Island Books, Devon................................. 85 Joel Segal Books, Devon .... 86 Jonkers Rare Books, Oxfordshire .... 209 Kenny's Bookshops and Art Galleries Ltd, Co. Galway .... 266 Mannwaring (M.G.), Bristol .... 59 Marble Hill Books, Middlesex...................... 184 Mellon's Books, East Sussex........................ 101 Naughton Booksellers, Co. Dublin .... 265 R. & A. Books, East Sussex .... 102 Rhodes, Bookseller (Peter), Hampshire .... 126 Simpson (Dave), Stirlingshire .... 269 The Glass Key, W Yorks............................ 247

- ABBEY, EDWIN

Trinity Rare Books, Co. Leitrim 266

- AESOP

Bookmark (Children's Books), Wiltshire.......... 253 Byre Books, Dumfries & Galloway................. 270 Fifteenth Century Bookshop (The), East Sussex. 104 Jean Hedger, Berkshire .... 55 R. & A. Books, East Sussex 102

- AHLBERG, JANET & ALLAN

Bookmark (Children's Books), Wiltshire.......... 253 Cranhurst Books, London .... 161 Fifteenth Century Bookshop (The), East Sussex. 104 Intech Books, Northumberland .... 203 Jean Hedger, Berkshire 55

- AICKMAN, R.

Harrington (Adrian), London W................... 173 R. & A. Books, East Sussex .... 102 Trinity Rare Books, Co. Leitrim 266

- ALCOTTS, THE

Elaine Lonsdale Books, W Yorks.................. 248 Jean Hedger, Berkshire 55

SPECIALITY INDEX

- ALDIN, CECIL
Bookmark (Children's Books), Wiltshire.......... 253
Booth (Booksearch Service), (Geoff), Cheshire... 68
Countryman Books, East Yorkshire............... 106
Cranhurst Books, London 161
Fifteenth Century Bookshop (The), East Sussex. 104
Garfi Books, Powys 293
Jean Hedger, Berkshire 55
Lucius Books, North Yorkshire.................... 199
R. & A. Books, East Sussex 102
Rothwell & Dunworth, Somerset 218
St Mary's Books & Prints, Lincolnshire 154

- AMICIS, EDMONDO DE
Trinity Rare Books, Co. Leitrim 266

- ARDIZZONE, EDWARD
Allinson (Frank & Stella), Warwickshire 237
Bookmark (Children's Books), Wiltshire.......... 253
Booth (Booksearch Service), (Geoff), Cheshire... 68
Cameron House Books, Isle of Wight 134
Cranhurst Books, London 161
Criterion Books, London Outer.................... 182
Fifteenth Century Bookshop (The), East Sussex. 104
Jean Hedger, Berkshire 55
Key Books (Sarah), Cambridgeshire............... 64
Mason (Mary), Oxfordshire......................... 206
Periwinkle Press, Kent 139
R. & A. Books, East Sussex 102

- ARMOUR, G. D.
Garfi Books, Powys 293
Jean Hedger, Berkshire 55
Trinity Rare Books, Co. Leitrim 266

- ASIMOV, ISAAC
Apocalypse, Surrey 233
Cranhurst Books, London 161
Esoteric Dreams Bookshop, Cumbria 78
Wayside Books and Cards, Oxfordshire 207

- AUSTEN, JANE
Apocalypse, Surrey 233
Booth (Booksearch Service), (Geoff), Cheshire... 68
Burmester (James), Bristol.......................... 59
Cox, Andrew, Shropshire............................ 215
Dolphin Books, Suffolk.............................. 226
Foster Bookshop (Paul), London SW............. 168
Glenwood Books, Surrey............................ 235
Hodgkins and Company Limited (Ian), Glos 116
Island Books, Devon................................. 85
Jarndyce Antiquarian Booksellers, London WC. 178
Liddle (Steve), Bristol 58
R. & A. Books, East Sussex 102
Rye Old Books, East Sussex........................ 104
Sharpe (Mary), Somerset............................ 221
Trinity Rare Books, Co. Leitrim 266
Valentine Rare Books, London W.................. 176
Webb Books (John), South Yorkshire.............. 222

- BADEN-POWELL, LORD ROBERT
Chalmers Hallam (E.), Hampshire................. 125
Greta Books, Durham 97
John R. Hoggarth, North Yorkshire 198
R. & A. Books, East Sussex 102

- BAEDEKER, KARL
Hodgson (Books) (Richard J.), North Yorkshire 198

- BAINBRIDGE, BERYL
Apocalypse, Surrey 233
Booth (Booksearch Service), (Geoff), Cheshire... 68
Cranhurst Books, London 161
Dolphin Books, Suffolk.............................. 226
Intech Books, Northumberland 203
R. & A. Books, East Sussex 102
Surprise Books, Glos................................. 113
Trinity Rare Books, Co. Leitrim 266

- BAKER, DENYS V.
Mount's Bay Books, Cornwall 75
Portus Books, Hampshire 122

- BALDWIN, JAMES
Black Voices, Merseyside............................ 185

- BALLANTYNE, ROBERT M.
Bookmark (Children's Books), Wiltshire.......... 253
Booth (Booksearch Service), (Geoff), Cheshire... 68
Dolphin Books, Suffolk.............................. 226
Fifteenth Century Bookshop (The), East Sussex. 104
Oasis Booksearch, Cambridgeshire................. 67
R. & A. Books, East Sussex 102
Trinity Rare Books, Co. Leitrim 266

- BARING-GOULD, S.
Chapter Two, London SE........................... 164
Country Books, Derbyshire......................... 82
Ely Books, Cambridgeshire 65
Island Books, Devon................................. 85
Randall (Tom), Somerset............................ 219
Shacklock Books (David), Suffolk 227

- BARKER, CECILY M.
Bookmark (Children's Books), Wiltshire.......... 253
Dolphin Books, Suffolk.............................. 226
Fifteenth Century Bookshop (The), East Sussex. 104
Intech Books, Northumberland 203
Jean Hedger, Berkshire 55
Key Books (Sarah), Cambridgeshire............... 64
Lucius Books, North Yorkshire.................... 199

- BARKER, CLIVE
Apocalypse, Surrey 233
Trinity Rare Books, Co. Leitrim 266

- BARNES, WILLIAM
Antique Map and Bookshop (The), Dorset 94
Country Books, Derbyshire......................... 82

- BARRIE, J.M.
Bookmark (Children's Books), Wiltshire.......... 253
Cranhurst Books, London 161
Criterion Books, London Outer.................... 182
Fifteenth Century Bookshop (The), East Sussex. 104
Green Meadow Books, Cornwall 74
Greta Books, Durham 97
Jean Hedger, Berkshire 55
Orb's Bookshop, Grampian......................... 274
R. & A. Books, East Sussex 102
Roz Hulse, Conwy 286

SPECIALITY INDEX

- BATES, H.E.
Bass (Ben), Wiltshire 251
Bookshop on the Heath, The, London SE 164
Country Books, Derbyshire 82
Emjay Books, Surrey.................................. 231
Heppa (Christopher), Essex 108
Intech Books, Northumberland 203
Park Gallery & Bookshop (The), Northants 201
R. & A. Books, East Sussex 102
Webb Books (John), South Yorkshire............. 222

- BAUM, FRANK
Bookmark (Children's Books), Wiltshire.......... 253
R. & A. Books, East Sussex 102

- BEARDSLEY, AUBREY
Apocalypse, Surrey 233
Intech Books, Northumberland 203
Jean Hedger, Berkshire 55
R. & A. Books, East Sussex 102
Roz Hulse, Conwy 286

- BEATON, CECIL
Apocalypse, Surrey 233
R. & A. Books, East Sussex 102

- BECKETT, S.
Apocalypse, Surrey 233
Budd (Richard), Somerset 219
Courtwood Books, Co. Laois........................ 266
Norton Books, North Yorkshire 197
Parrott (Jeremy), London E.......................... 156
R. & A. Books, East Sussex 102
Read Ireland, Co. Dublin 264

- BELL, ADRIAN
Aucott & Thomas, Leics.............................. 147
Besleys Books, Suffolk 226
Country Books, Derbyshire 82
Debbage (John), Norfolk 190
Dolphin Books, Suffolk................................ 226

- BELL, GERTRUDE
Joppa Books Ltd., Surrey 231

- BELLAIRES, GEORGE
Treasure Trove Books, Leics........................ 148

- BELLOC, HILAIRE
Armchair Books, Lothian 276
Bookmark (Children's Books), Wiltshire.......... 253
Country Books, Derbyshire 82
Dolphin Books, Suffolk................................ 226
Fifteenth Century Bookshop (The), East Sussex. 104
Intech Books, Northumberland 203
Island Books, Devon 85
R. & A. Books, East Sussex 102
Rosley Books, Cumbria 81
St Philip's Books, Oxfordshire 210

- BENNETT, (ENOCH) ARNOL
Ash Rare Books, London SW 167
Bookshop on the Heath, The, London SE 164

- BENNETT, J.G.
Needham Books, (Russell), Somerset.............. 220
R. & A. Books, East Sussex 102
Watkins Books Ltd., London WC.................. 180

- BENSON, A.C.
Meads Book Service (The), East Sussex........... 104

- BENSON, E.F.
Meads Book Service (The), East Sussex........... 104
Parrott (Jeremy), London E.......................... 156
Tsbbooks, London SW 170

- BENSON, R.H.
Meads Book Service (The), East Sussex........... 104
St Philip's Books, Oxfordshire 210

- BETJEMAN, SIR JOHN
Baker - Books for the Collector (Colin), Devon. 90
Booth (Booksearch Service), (Geoff), Cheshire... 68
Ellis, Bookseller (Peter), London WC............. 178
Fifteenth Century Bookshop (The), East Sussex. 104
Intech Books, Northumberland 203
Island Books, Devon 85
Jonkers Rare Books, Oxfordshire 209
McGee (Terence J.), London Outer 181

- BLACKWOOD, A.
Delectus Books, London WC........................ 177
Fantastic Literature, Essex 111

- BLAKE, N.
Sutcliffe (Mark), W Yorks 248

- BLAKE, SEXTON
D. & M. Books, W Yorks 250
Wright (Norman), Dorset 95

- BLOOMSBURY GROUP, THE
Bow Windows Book Shop, East Sussex 103
Bruce Holdsworth Books, East Sussex 105
Criterion Books, London Outer 182
Evans Books (Paul), W Sussex 243
Fifteenth Century Bookshop (The), East Sussex. 104
Much Ado Books, East Sussex 99
R. & A. Books, East Sussex 102

- BLYTON, ENID
Annie's Books, South Yorkshire 222
Apocalypse, Surrey 233
Barter Books, Northumberland 202
Beck (John), East Sussex 103
Bookmark (Children's Books), Wiltshire.......... 253
Bookshop on the Heath, The, London SE 164
Chapter Two, London SE............................ 164
Cygnet Books, East Yorkshire....................... 107
D. & M. Books, W Yorks 250
Dormouse Bookshop (The), Norfolk 190
Facet Books, Dorset................................... 91
Fifteenth Century Bookshop (The), East Sussex. 104
Green Meadow Books, Cornwall 74
Heppa (Christopher), Essex 108
Jonkers Rare Books, Oxfordshire 209
K Books, Cheshire..................................... 70
Key Books (Sarah), Cambridgeshire............... 64

SPECIALITY INDEX

Little Stour Books, Kent 137
Lucius Books, North Yorkshire 199
Mercat Books, Highland 274
Oasis Booksearch, Cambridgeshire.................. 67
Old Celtic Bookshop (1he), Devon 88
Park Gallery & Bookshop (The), Northants 201
R. & A. Books, East Sussex 102
Schutte (David), Hampshire......................... 124
Sesemann (Julia), Kent................................ 136
Stella Books, Monmouthshire 288
Surprise Books, Glos 113
Talisman Books, Cheshire 70
Treasure Trove Books, Leics......................... 148
Wright (Norman), Dorset 95

- BORROW, GEORGE
Country Books, Derbyshire 82
Debbage (John), Norfolk 190
Nineteenth Century Books, Oxfordshire 211
Orb's Bookshop, Grampian.......................... 274
York (Graham), Devon................................ 86

- BOSWELL, JAMES
Island Books, Devon 85

- BOWEN, M.
Dolphin Books, Suffolk................................ 226

- BOWLES, PAUL
Criterion Books, London Outer 182

- BRAMAH, ERNEST
Dolphin Books, Suffolk................................ 226
Lucius Books, North Yorkshire 199
Webb Books (John), South Yorkshire............. 222

- BRENT-DYER, ELINOR M.
Allinson (Frank & Stella), Warwickshire 237
Badger Books, Somerset 220
Bilski (Gill), Buckinghamshire 61
Bookmark (Children's Books), Wiltshire.......... 253
D. & M. Books, W Yorks 250
Fifteenth Century Bookshop (The), East Sussex. 104
Green Meadow Books, Cornwall 74
Intech Books, Northumberland 203
Key Books (Sarah), Cambridgeshire................ 64
Little Stour Books, Kent 137
Lucius Books, North Yorkshire 199
Mercat Books, Highland 274
Sims (Sue), Dorset 91
TP Children's Bookshop, W Yorks................ 246
Treasure Trove Books, Leics......................... 148

- BROMFIELD, LOUIS
Dolphin Books, Suffolk................................ 226

- BRONTES, THE
Dolphin Books, Suffolk................................ 226
Grove Bookshop (The), North Yorkshire 197
Hatchard & Daughters, W Yorks................... 247
Hodgkins and Company Limited (Ian), Glos 116
Idle Booksellers (The), W Yorks 246
Jonkers Rare Books, Oxfordshire 209
R. & A. Books, East Sussex 102
Sharpe (Mary), Somerset 221

- BROOKE, RUPERT
Apocalypse, Surrey 233
Ellis, Bookseller (Peter), London WC 178
R. & A. Books, East Sussex 102
Smith Books (Keith), Herefordshire 128

- BROWNING, ROBERT
Cox Rare Books (Charles), Cornwall............... 74
R. & A. Books, East Sussex 102
Rosley Books, Cumbria 81

- BRUCE, MARY GRANT
Fifteenth Century Bookshop (The), East Sussex. 104

- BUCHAN, JOHN
Armchair Books, Lothian 276
Avonworld Books, Somerset 218
Bannatyne Books, London N......................... 158
Booth (Booksearch Service), (Geoff), Cheshire... 68
Coch-y-Bonddu Books, Powys 292
Ellis, Bookseller (Peter), London WC 178
Greta Books, Durham 97
Heppa (Christopher), Essex 108
Orb's Bookshop, Grampian.......................... 274

- BUCKERIDGE, A.
Baker - Books for the Collector (Colin), Devon . 90
Bookmark (Children's Books), Wiltshire.......... 253
Booth (Booksearch Service), (Geoff), Cheshire... 68
Fifteenth Century Bookshop (The), East Sussex. 104
Key Books (Sarah), Cambridgeshire................ 64
Little Stour Books, Kent 137
R. & A. Books, East Sussex 102
Schutte (David), Hampshire.......................... 124
Stella Books, Monmouthshire 288
Treasure Trove Books, Leics......................... 148

- BUKOWSKI, CHARLES
Apocalypse, Surrey 233

- BUNYAN, JOHN
Chapter Two, London SE............................. 164
Kirkman Ltd., (Robert), Bedfordshire.............. 54
Oasis Booksearch, Cambridgeshire................. 67
Rosley Books, Cumbria 81

- BURGESS, A.
Cranhurst Books, London 161
Ellis, Bookseller (Peter), London WC 178
Olynthiacs, Shropshire 214

- BURNEY, FANNY
Dolphin Books, Suffolk................................ 226
Sharpe (Mary), Somerset 221

- BURNS, ROBERT
Mercat Books, Highland 274
Orb's Bookshop, Grampian.......................... 274

- BURROUGHS, EDGAR R.
Book Palace (The), London SE 164

- BURROUGHS, WILLIAM
Apocalypse, Surrey 233

SPECIALITY INDEX

Lucius Books, North Yorkshire 199
Sclanders (Beatbooks), (Andrew), London EC... 157
Watkins Books Ltd., London WC.................. 180

- BURTON, R.F.
Campbell Hewson Books (R.), Fife................. 271
Chas J. Sawyer, Kent 141

- BYRON, LORD
Alec-Smith Books (Alex), East Yorkshire 107
Cox Rare Books (Charles), Cornwall............... 74
Emjay Books, Surrey.................................. 231
Jarndyce Antiquarian Booksellers, London WC. 178
R. & A. Books, East Sussex 102
Roz Hulse, Conwy 286
Tobo Books, Hampshire.............................. 123
Wise (Derek), East Sussex........................... 104

- CALDICOTT, R.
Bookmark (Children's Books), Wiltshire.......... 253
Fifteenth Century Bookshop (The), East Sussex. 104
Jean Hedger, Berkshire 55
R. & A. Books, East Sussex 102

- CAMERON, JULIA MARGARET
Cameron House Books, Isle of Wight.............. 134
Dolphin Books, Suffolk............................... 226

- CARLYLE, THOMAS
Priestpopple Books, Northumberland 202

- CARR, JOHN DICKSON
Booth (Booksearch Service), (Geoff), Cheshire... 68
Lucius Books, North Yorkshire 199
Sutcliffe (Mark), W Yorks 248

- CARROLL, LEWIS
Apocalypse, Surrey 233
Bookmark (Children's Books), Wiltshire.......... 253
Chas J. Sawyer, Kent 141
Clarke-Hall (J.) Limited, Kent 137
Cranhurst Books, London 161
Fifteenth Century Bookshop (The), East Sussex. 104
Foster Bookshop (Paul), London SW............. 168
Jean Hedger, Berkshire 55
Key Books (Sarah), Cambridgeshire............... 64
Little Stour Books, Kent 137
Marchpane, London WC............................. 178
R. & A. Books, East Sussex 102

- CARTER, FREDERICK
Apocalypse, Surrey 233

- CECIL, H.
Booth (Booksearch Service), (Geoff), Cheshire... 68
Wayside Books and Cards, Oxfordshire 207

- CERVANTES SAAVEDRA, MIGUEL DE
Apocalypse, Surrey 233
Orssich (Paul), London SW......................... 170

- CHANDLER, RAYMOND
Cranhurst Books, London 161
Dolphin Books, Suffolk............................... 226
Lucius Books, North Yorkshire 199

R. & A. Books, East Sussex 102
Sutcliffe (Mark), W Yorks 248

- CHAPMAN, ABEL
Chalmers Hallam (E.), Hampshire................. 125
Chas J. Sawyer, Kent 141

- CHARTERIS, LESLIE
Cranhurst Books, London 161
Heckmondwike Book Shop, W Yorks 249
K Books, Cheshire..................................... 70
Lucius Books, North Yorkshire 199
Surprise Books, Glos.................................. 113

- CHESTERTON, G.K.
Armchair Books, Lothian 276
Bass (Ben), Wiltshire 251
Booth (Booksearch Service), (Geoff), Cheshire... 68
Daeron's Books, Buckinghamshire................. 62
Dolphin Books, Suffolk............................... 226
Fifteenth Century Bookshop (The), East Sussex. 104
Greta Books, Durham 97
R. & A. Books, East Sussex 102
Rosley Books, Cumbria 81
St Philip's Books, Oxfordshire...................... 210

- CHRISTIE, AGATHA
Apocalypse, Surrey 233
Classic Crime Collections, Gr Man................. 119
Cranhurst Books, London 161
Emjay Books, Surrey.................................. 231
Heckmondwike Book Shop, W Yorks 249
Idle Genius Books, London N 159
Intech Books, Northumberland 203
Jonkers Rare Books, Oxfordshire.................. 209
Lucius Books, North Yorkshire 199
R. & A. Books, East Sussex 102
Treasure Trove Books, Leics........................ 148
Williams Rare Books (Nigel), London WC 180

- CHURCHILL, SIR WINSTON
Apocalypse, Surrey 233
Baxter (Steve), Surrey 234
Bookshop on the Heath, The, London SE 164
Booth (Booksearch Service), (Geoff), Cheshire... 68
Chas J. Sawyer, Kent 141
Dolphin Books, Suffolk............................... 226
Fifteenth Century Bookshop (The), East Sussex. 104
Foster Bookshop (Paul), London SW............. 168
Frew Limited (Robert), London W................. 173
Garfi Books, Powys 293
Harrington (Adrian), London W................... 173
Island Books, Devon.................................. 85
Junk & Spread Eagle, London SE 165
Kirkman Ltd., (Robert), Bedfordshire............. 54
Lost Books, Northants................................ 201
Prior (Michael), Lincolnshire 153
R. & A. Books, East Sussex 102
Sax Books, Suffolk 229

- CLARE, JOHN
Country Books, Derbyshire 82
Park Gallery & Bookshop (The), Northants 201
Peakirk Books, Cambridgeshire 7
R. & A. Books, East Sussex 102

SPECIALITY INDEX

Rye Old Books, East Sussex 104

- CLARKE, ARTHUR C.
Apocalypse, Surrey 233
Cameron House Books, Isle of Wight............. 134
Cranhurst Books, London 161
Wayside Books and Cards, Oxfordshire 207

- COBBETT, WILLIAM
Country Books, Derbyshire 82
Debbage (John), Norfolk 190
Greta Books, Durham 97
Island Books, Devon 85

- COCTEAU, JEAN
Norton Books, North Yorkshire 197
R. & A. Books, East Sussex 102

- COLERIDGE, SAMUEL T.
Alec-Smith Books (Alex), East Yorkshire 107
R. & A. Books, East Sussex 102
Roz Hulse, Conwy 286

- CONAN DOYLE, SIR ARTHUR
Antique Map and Bookshop (The), Dorset 94
Apocalypse, Surrey 233
Armchair Books, Lothian 276
Black Cat Bookshop, Leics 147
Fantastic Literature, Essex 111
Fifteenth Century Bookshop (The), East Sussex. 104
Harrington (Adrian), London W.................... 173
Island Books, Devon 85
Lucius Books, North Yorkshire 199
Preston Book Company, Lancashire 145
R. & A. Books, East Sussex 102
Rupert Books, Cambridgeshire 65
Shacklock Books (David), Suffolk 227

- CONRAD, JOSEPH
Booth (Booksearch Service), (Geoff), Cheshire... 68
Greta Books, Durham 97
Parrott (Jeremy), London E......................... 156

- COOK, BERYL
Apocalypse, Surrey 233
Baker - Books for the Collector (Colin), Devon. 90
Facet Books, Dorset................................... 91
Intech Books, Northumberland 203
Jean Hedger, Berkshire 55
R. & A. Books, East Sussex 102
Surprise Books, Glos.................................. 113

- CORELLI, MARIE
Inner Bookshop (The), Oxfordshire................ 210

- CORNWELL, BERNARD
Annie's Books, South Yorkshire 222
Apocalypse, Surrey 233
Harrington (Adrian), London W.................... 173
Heppa (Christopher), Essex 108
Intech Books, Northumberland 203
Surprise Books, Glos.................................. 113
Wayside Books and Cards, Oxfordshire 207

- COWARD, NOEL
Avonworld Books, Somerset......................... 218
R. & A. Books, East Sussex 102

- CRANE, HALL
Norton Books, North Yorkshire 197

- CRANE, WALTER
Bookmark (Children's Books), Wiltshire.......... 253
Fifteenth Century Bookshop (The), East Sussex. 104
Hodgkins and Company Limited (Ian), Glos 116
Jean Hedger, Berkshire 55

- CREASEY, JOHN
Classic Crime Collections, Gr Man 119
Heckmondwike Book Shop, W Yorks 249

- CRICHTON, MICHAEL
Booth (Booksearch Service), (Geoff), Cheshire... 68
Dolphin Books, Suffolk............................... 226
Fantastic Literature, Essex 111
R. & A. Books, East Sussex 102

- CROFTS, FREEMAN WILLS
Ellis, Bookseller (Peter), London WC 178
Heppa (Christopher), Essex 108
Lucius Books, North Yorkshire 199
Sutcliffe (Mark), W Yorks 248

- CROMPTON, RICHMAL
Black Cat Bookshop, Leics 147
Bookmark (Children's Books), Wiltshire.......... 253
D. & M. Books, W Yorks 250
Facet Books, Dorset................................... 91
Fifteenth Century Bookshop (The), East Sussex. 104
Green Meadow Books, Cornwall 74
Intech Books, Northumberland 203
Key Books (Sarah), Cambridgeshire............... 64
Little Stour Books, Kent 137
Lucius Books, North Yorkshire 199
Oasis Booksearch, Cambridgeshire................. 67
R. & A. Books, East Sussex 102
Schutte (David), Hampshire......................... 124
Silver Trees Books, West Midlands................ 240
Surprise Books, Glos.................................. 113

- CROSBY, HARRY & CARESSE
Norton Books, North Yorkshire 197

- CROWLEY, ALEISTER
Atlantis Bookshop, London WC.................... 177
Chthonios Books, East Sussex...................... 102
Inner Bookshop (The), Oxfordshire................ 210
Lucius Books, North Yorkshire 199
Occultique, Northants................................ 200

- CRUICKSHANK, G.
Bookmark (Children's Books), Wiltshire.......... 253
Jean Hedger, Berkshire 55
R. & A. Books, East Sussex 102
Tobo Books, Hampshire.............................. 123

- CUNARD, NANCY
Norton Books, North Yorkshire 197

SPECIALITY INDEX

- CUNNINGHAM-GRAHAME, R.B.
Bass (Ben), Wiltshire 251

- DAHL, ROALD
Bookmark (Children's Books), Wiltshire.......... 253
Fifteenth Century Bookshop (The), E Sussex 104
Green Meadow Books, Cornwall 74
Intech Books, Northumberland 203
Jean Hedger, Berkshire 55
Key Books (Sarah), Cambridgeshire.............. 64
Lucius Books, N Yorks............................... 199
R. & A. Books, E Sussex............................. 102
Surprise Books, Glos.................................. 113

- DARWIN, CHARLES
Cameron House Books, Isle of Wight............. 134
Hodgson (Books) (Richard J.), N Yorks 198
Island Books, Devon 85
Korn (M. Eric), London N 159
Lymelight Books & Prints, Dorset................. 93
R. & A. Books, E Sussex............................. 102

- DAVID, ELIZABETH
Clarke (Janet), Somerset 216
Seeber (Liz), E Sussex................................ 102
Talisman Books, Cheshire........................... 70

- DE SADE, MARQUIS
Booth (Booksearch Service), (Geoff), Cheshire... 68
Watkins Books Ltd., London WC.................. 180

- DICK, PHILIP K
Surprise Books, Glos.................................. 113

- DICKENS, CHARLES
Apocalypse, Surrey 233
Ash Rare Books, London SW....................... 167
Boz Books, Powys..................................... 289
Brock Books, N Yorks 193
Cameron House Books, Isle of Wight............. 134
Childrens Bookshop, W Yorks..................... 248
Clegg (David), Staffordshire......................... 224
Derek Stirling Bookseller, Kent 142
Fifteenth Century Bookshop (The), E Sussex 104
Foster Bookshop (Paul), London SW 168
Golden Books Group, Devon 85
Harrington (Adrian), London W.................... 173
Hava Books, London SE............................. 165
Jarndyce Antiquarian Booksellers, London WC. 178
Mr. Pickwick of Towcester, Northants............ 201
Park Gallery & Bookshop (The), Northants 201
Preston Book Company, Lancashire 145
R. & A. Books, E Sussex............................. 102
Tiger Books, Kent 137
Tobo Books, Hampshire.............................. 123
Valentine Rare Books, London W 176

- DINESEN, ISAK
Booth (Booksearch Service), (Geoff), Cheshire... 68
Chalmers Hallam (E.), Hampshire 125
Coch-y-Bonddu Books, Powys 292
Esoteric Dreams Bookshop, Cumbria 78

- DR. ZEUSS
Jean Hedger, Berkshire 55

- DU MAURIER, DAPHNE
Apocalypse, Surrey 233
Bonython Bookshop, Cornwall..................... 76
Bookends of Fowey, Cornwall 73
Booth (Booksearch Service), (Geoff), Cheshire... 68
Chapman (Neville), Lancashire..................... 146
Dolphin Books, Suffolk............................... 226
Fifteenth Century Bookshop (The), E Sussex 104

- DULAC, EDMUND
Bookmark (Children's Books), Wiltshire.......... 253
Cranhurst Books, London 161
Fifteenth Century Bookshop (The), E Sussex 104
Jean Hedger, Berkshire 55
Lucius Books, N Yorks............................... 199
R. & A. Books, E Sussex............................. 102
Rye Old Books, E Sussex 104

- DUMAS, ALEXANDRE
R. & A. Books, E Sussex............................. 102

- DUNSANY, LORD
Roz Hulse, Conwy 286

- DURRELL, GERALD
Annie's Books, South Yorkshire 222
Apocalypse, Surrey 233
Bass (Ben), Wiltshire 251
Bookmark (Children's Books), Wiltshire.......... 253
Booth (Booksearch Service), (Geoff), Cheshire... 68
Dolphin Books, Suffolk............................... 226
Fifteenth Century Bookshop (The), E Sussex 104
Green Meadow Books, Cornwall 74
R. & A. Books, E Sussex............................. 102

- DURRELL, LAWRENCE
Apocalypse, Surrey 233
Ballantyne-Way (Roger), Suffolk 229
Barmby (C. & A.J.), Kent........................... 141
Booth (Booksearch Service), (Geoff), Cheshire... 68
Cameron House Books, Isle of Wight............. 134
Criterion Books, London Outer.................... 182
Fifteenth Century Bookshop (The), E Sussex 104
Island Books, Devon 85
Norton Books, N Yorks.............................. 197
R. & A. Books, E Sussex............................. 102

- DYMOCK POETS, THE
Ellis, Bookseller (Peter), London WC 178
Smith Books (Keith), Herefordshire 128

- EDWARDS, LIONEL
Booth (Booksearch Service), (Geoff), Cheshire... 68
Head (John & Judith), Wiltshire 253
Jean Hedger, Berkshire 55
Rare Books & Berry, Somerset..................... 219
Surprise Books, Glos.................................. 113

- ELIOT, G.
Booth (Booksearch Service), (Geoff), Cheshire... 68
Dolphin Books, Suffolk............................... 226
Rye Old Books, E Sussex 104
Sharpe (Mary), Somerset 221

SPECIALITY INDEX

- ELIOT, T.S.
Anglo-American Rare Books, Surrey............... 233
Apocalypse, Surrey.................................... 233
Booth (Booksearch Service), (Geoff), Cheshire... 68
Calendula Horticultural Books, E Sussex......... 102
Ellis, Bookseller (Peter), London WC 178
Jonkers Rare Books, Oxfordshire.................. 209
Lucius Books, N Yorks............................... 199
Norton Books, N Yorks............................... 197
R. & A. Books, E Sussex............................. 102
Rosley Books, Cumbria 81

- FAIRLIE-BRUCE, D.
Bilski (Gill), Buckinghamshire....................... 61
Bookmark (Children's Books), Wiltshire........... 253
Fifteenth Century Bookshop (The), E Sussex 104
Green Meadow Books, Cornwall 74
Intech Books, Northumberland 203
Key Books (Sarah), Cambridgeshire............... 64
Sims (Sue), Dorset..................................... 91
TP Children's Bookshop, W Yorks................. 246

- FARNOL, JEFFERY
Dusty Books, Powys 292
Fifteenth Century Bookshop (The), E Sussex 104
Heppa (Christopher), Essex 108

- FARRELL, JAMES T.
Fifteenth Century Bookshop (The), E Sussex 104

- FAULKNER, WILLIAM
Booth (Booksearch Service), (Geoff), Cheshire... 68
Ellis, Bookseller (Peter), London WC 178
R. & A. Books, E Sussex............................. 102

- FIELDING, HENRY
R. & A. Books, E Sussex............................. 102

- FITZGERALD, F.S.
R. & A. Books, E Sussex............................. 102

- FLEMING, IAN
Apocalypse, Surrey.................................... 233
Birmingham Books, West Midlands................ 239
Black Cat Bookshop, Leics 147
Books, Oxfordshire.................................... 206
Bookshop on the Heath, The, London SE 164
Booth (Booksearch Service), (Geoff), Cheshire... 68
Classic Crime Collections, Gr Man................. 119
Cranhurst Books, London 161
Ellis, Bookseller (Peter), London WC 178
Foster Bookshop (Paul), London SW.............. 168
Harrington (Adrian), London W.................... 173
Intech Books, Northumberland 203
Jonkers Rare Books, Oxfordshire.................. 209
Lucius Books, N Yorks............................... 199
Mainly Fiction, Cheshire 68
R. & A. Books, E Sussex............................. 102
St Mary's Books & Prints, Lincolnshire 154
Sutcliffe (Mark), W Yorks 248
Tobo Books, Hampshire.............................. 123
Warrender (Andrew), W Yorks 250
Williams Rare Books (Nigel), London WC 180

- FLINT, WILLIAM RUSSELL
Booth (Booksearch Service), (Geoff), Cheshire... 68
R. & A. Books, E Sussex............................. 102
Webb Books (John), South Yorkshire.............. ???

- FOREST, A.
Badger Books, Somerset 220
Fifteenth Century Bookshop (The), E Sussex 104
Key Books (Sarah), Cambridgeshire............... 64
Sims (Sue), Dorset..................................... 91

- FORESTER, C.S.
Booth (Booksearch Service), (Geoff), Cheshire... 68
Criterion Books, London Outer..................... 182
Dusty Books, Powys 292
Fifteenth Century Bookshop (The), E Sussex 104
Greta Books, Durham 97
Heppa (Christopher), Essex 108
Prior (Michael), Lincolnshire 153
R. & A. Books, E Sussex............................. 102
Surprise Books, Glos.................................. 113

- FOWLES, JOHN
Apocalypse, Surrey.................................... 233
Barmby (C. & A.J.), Kent........................... 141
Booth (Booksearch Service), (Geoff), Cheshire... 68
Dolphin Books, Suffolk............................... 226
Lymelight Books & Prints, Dorset................. 93
The Sanctuary Bookshop, Dorset................... 94

- FRANCIS, DICK
Apocalypse, Surrey.................................... 233
Booth (Booksearch Service), (Geoff), Cheshire... 68
Emjay Books, Surrey.................................. 231
firstpagebooks, Norfolk............................... 190
Greta Books, Durham 97
Intech Books, Northumberland 203
Kennedy & Farley, E Sussex......................... 104
Lucius Books, N Yorks............................... 199
Orb's Bookshop, Grampian......................... 274
R. & A. Books, E Sussex............................. 102

- FREEMAN, R. AUSTIN
Lucius Books, N Yorks............................... 199

- FREUD, SIGMUND
Apocalypse, Surrey.................................... 233
Watkins Books Ltd., London WC.................. 180

- FROST, ROBERT
Karen Millward, Co. Cork........................... 263
Smith Books (Keith), Herefordshire 128

- GASKELL, E.
Dolphin Books, Suffolk............................... 226
Fifteenth Century Bookshop (The), E Sussex 104
Hodgkins and Company Limited (Ian), Glos 116
Sharpe (Mary), Somerset 221

- GILBERT, MICHAEL
Lucius Books, N Yorks............................... 199
R. & A. Books, E Sussex............................. 102

- GILL, ERIC
Booth (Booksearch Service), (Geoff), Cheshire... 68

SPECIALITY INDEX

- GISSING, GEORGE
Dolphin Books, Suffolk................................. 226
Idle Booksellers (The), W Yorks 246

- GOREY, EDWARD
Cranhurst Books, London 161
Jean Hedger, Berkshire 55

- GOSS, W.H.
Milestone Publications Goss & C. China, Hants 123
R. & A. Books, E Sussex............................. 102

- GOUDGE, ELIZABETH
Baker - Books for the Collector (Colin), Devon. 90
Bookmark (Children's Books), Wiltshire.......... 253
Booth (Booksearch Service), (Geoff), Cheshire... 68
Dolphin Books, Suffolk............................... 226
Fifteenth Century Bookshop (The), E Sussex 104
Oasis Booksearch, Cambridgeshire................. 67
R. & A. Books, E Sussex............................. 102

- GRAVES, ROBERT
Apocalypse, Surrey 233
Avonworld Books, Somerset......................... 218
Barmby (C. & A.J.), Kent............................ 141
Berwick Books, Lincolnshire......................... 152
Fifteenth Century Bookshop (The), E Sussex 104
Island Books, Devon.................................. 85
Jackson (M.W.), Wiltshire............................ 254
R. & A. Books, E Sussex............................. 102

- GREENE, GRAHAM
Anglo-American Rare Books, Surrey.............. 233
Apocalypse, Surrey 233
Birmingham Books, West Midlands................ 239
Booth (Booksearch Service), (Geoff), Cheshire... 68
Cranhurst Books, London 161
Dolphin Books, Suffolk............................... 226
Ellis, Bookseller (Peter), London WC 178
Fifteenth Century Bookshop (The), E Sussex 104
firstpagebooks, Norfolk............................... 190
Gloucester Road Bookshop, London SW 168
Harrington (Adrian), London W.................... 173
Intech Books, Northumberland 203
Jonkers Rare Books, Oxfordshire................... 209
Lucius Books, N Yorks............................... 199
R. & A. Books, E Sussex............................. 102
Tobo Books, Hampshire 123
Wayside Books and Cards, Oxfordshire 207
Williams Rare Books (Nigel), London WC 180

- GURDJIEFF, W.I.
Inner Bookshop (The), Oxfordshire................. 210
Watkins Books Ltd., London WC.................. 180
Yarwood Rare Books (Edward), Gr Man........ 118

- HAGGARD, SIR HENRY RIDER
Debbage (John), Norfolk............................. 190
Fifteenth Century Bookshop (The), E Sussex 104
Lucius Books, N Yorks............................... 199
Rider Haggard Society (The), Tyne and Wear... 236

- HALL S.C.
Milestone Publications Goss & C. China, Hants 123

- HAMMETT, DASHIELL
Booth (Booksearch Service), (Geoff), Cheshire... 68
Lucius Books, N Yorks............................... 199
Sutcliffe (Mark), W Yorks 248

- HARDY, THOMAS
Antique Map and Bookshop (The), Dorset 94
Apocalypse, Surrey 233
Books Afloat, Dorset.................................. 96
Booth (Booksearch Service), (Geoff), Cheshire... 68
Country Books, Derbyshire 82
Cox Rare Books (Charles), Cornwall.............. 74
Derek Stirling Bookseller, Kent 142
Dolphin Books, Suffolk............................... 226
Ferdinando (Steven), Somerset 220
Fifteenth Century Bookshop (The), E Sussex 104
Island Books, Devon.................................. 85
Lymelight Books & Prints, Dorset................. 93
Sharpe (Mary), Somerset 221
Stinton (Judith), Dorset.............................. 92
Valentine Rare Books, London W.................. 176
Walker Fine Books (Steve), Dorset 92
Words Etcetera Bookshop, Dorset................. 93

- HEANEY, SEAMUS
Apocalypse, Surrey 233
Jiri Books, Co. Antrim 260
Read Ireland, Co. Dublin 264
Skelton (Tony), Kent.................................. 141
Words Etcetera Bookshop, Dorset................. 93

- HEINE, HEINRICH
Apocalypse, Surrey 233

- HEINLEIN, ROBERT A.
Booth (Booksearch Service), (Geoff), Cheshire... 68
Cranhurst Books, London 161

- HEMINGWAY, ERNEST
Anglo-American Rare Books, Surrey.............. 233
Apocalypse, Surrey 233
Cranhurst Books, London 161
Dolphin Books, Suffolk............................... 226
Foster Bookshop (Paul), London SW............. 168
Norton Books, N Yorks.............................. 197
R. & A. Books, E Sussex............................. 102

- HENTY, G.A.
Antique Map and Bookshop (The), Dorset 94
Barter Books, Northumberland 202
Bookmark (Children's Books), Wiltshire.......... 253
Booth (Booksearch Service), (Geoff), Cheshire... 68
Facet Books, Dorset................................... 91
Fifteenth Century Bookshop (The), E Sussex 104
Greta Books, Durham 97
Little Stour Books, Kent 137
R. & A. Books, E Sussex............................. 102
Shacklock Books (David), Suffolk 227

- HERBERT, JAMES
Booth (Booksearch Service), (Geoff), Cheshire... 68
Old Celtic Bookshop (The), Devon 88
R. & A. Books, E Sussex............................. 102
Surprise Books, Glos.................................. 113

SPECIALITY INDEX

- HEYER, GEORGETTE
Apocalypse, Surrey 233
Book For All Reasons (A.), Suffolk 229
Booth (Booksearch Service), (Geoff), Cheshire... 68
Boris Books, Hampshire.............................. 126
Dusty Books, Powys 292
Fifteenth Century Bookshop (The), E Sussex 104
Intech Books, Northumberland 203
Orb's Bookshop, Grampian.......................... 274
R. & A. Books, E Sussex............................. 102
Rider Haggard Society (The), Tyne and Wear... 236

- HILL, LORNA
Badger Books, Somerset 220
Bookmark (Children's Books), Wiltshire.......... 253
Fifteenth Century Bookshop (The), E Sussex 104
Green Meadow Books, Cornwall 74
Intech Books, Northumberland 203
TP Children's Bookshop, W Yorks................ 246

- HODGSON, W.H.
Booth (Booksearch Service), (Geoff), Cheshire... 68
R. & A. Books, E Sussex............................. 102

- HOOD, THOMAS
R. & A. Books, E Sussex............................. 102

- HOUSMAN, A.E.
Antiquary Ltd., (Bar Bookstore), N Yorks....... 196
Cox Rare Books (Charles), Cornwall............... 74
Dolphin Books, Suffolk............................... 226
Island Books, Devon 85
R. & A. Books, E Sussex............................. 102

- HUBBARD, L. RON
Watkins Books Ltd., London WC 180

- HUDSON, W.H.
Country Books, Derbyshire 82
Dolphin Books, Suffolk............................... 226

- HUXLEY, ALDOUS
Booth (Booksearch Service), (Geoff), Cheshire... 68
Cranhurst Books, London 161
Dolphin Books, Suffolk............................... 226
Kennedy & Farley, E Sussex......................... 104
R. & A. Books, E Sussex............................. 102
Watkins Books Ltd., London WC 180

- HUYSMANS, J.K.
Delectus Books, London WC........................ 177

- INKLINGS, THE
Daeron's Books, Buckinghamshire.................. 62
English (Toby), Oxfordshire......................... 211
Rosley Books, Cumbria 81
St Philip's Books, Oxfordshire...................... 210
Samovar Books, Co. Dublin 264

- INNES, HAMMOND
Booth (Booksearch Service), (Geoff), Cheshire... 68
Dolphin Books, Suffolk............................... 226
Fifteenth Century Bookshop (The), E Sussex 104
R. & A. Books, E Sussex............................. 102

- ISHERWOOD, CHRISTOPHER
Booth (Booksearch Service), (Geoff), Cheshire... 68
Criterion Books, London Outer 182
R. & A. Books, E Sussex............................. 102
Tsbbooks, London SW 170

- JACOB, VOILET
Jean Hedger, Berkshire 55

- JAMES, HENRY
Anglo-American Rare Books, Surrey.............. 233
Anthony Neville, Kent 139
Craobh Rua Books, Co. Armagh 260
R. & A. Books, E Sussex............................. 102
Valentine Rare Books, London W 176

- JAMES, M.R.
Bennett & Kerr Books, Oxfordshire 206
Island Books, Devon 85
Trinity Rare Books, Co. Leitrim 766

- JEFFERIES, R.
Chalmers Hallam (E.), Hampshire 125
Coch-y-Bonddu Books, Powys 292
Country Books, Derbyshire 82
Dolphin Books, Suffolk............................... 226
Fifteenth Century Bookshop (The), E Sussex 104
Island Books, Devon 85

- JEWETT, S.O.
Milestone Publications Goss & Crested China,
Hampshire 123

- JOHNS, W.E.
Ardis Books, Hampshire 126
Barely Read Books, Kent 142
Black Cat Bookshop, Leics 147
books2books, Devon.................................. 88
Bookshop on the Heath, The, London SE 164
Chapter Two, London SE............................ 164
Cotswold Internet Books, Glos...................... 113
Cranhurst Books, London 161
D. & M. Books, W Yorks 250
Dormouse Bookshop (The), Norfolk 190
Facet Books, Dorset................................... 91
Fifteenth Century Bookshop (The), E Sussex 104
Harrington (Adrian), London W.................... 173
Intech Books, Northumberland 203
Key Books (Sarah), Cambridgeshire................ 64
Little Stour Books, Kent 137
Lucius Books, N Yorks............................... 199
Schutte (David), Hampshire......................... 124
Stella Books, Monmouthshire 288
TP Children's Bookshop, W Yorks................ 246
Treasure Trove Books, Leics........................ 148
Wright (Norman), Dorset 95

- JOHNSON, SAMUEL
Apocalypse, Surrey 233
Clarke-Hall (J.) Limited, Kent 137
Foster Bookshop (Paul), London SW 168
R. & A. Books, E Sussex............................. 102
Staffs Bookshop (The), Staffordshire 224
Walker Fine Books (Steve), Dorset 92

SPECIALITY INDEX

- JOYCE, JAMES

Apocalypse, Surrey 233
Booth (Booksearch Service), (Geoff), Cheshire... 68
Courtwood Books, Co. Laois....................... 266
Cranhurst Books, London 161
Ellis, Bookseller (Peter), London WC 178
Foster Bookshop (Paul), London SW............. 168
Intech Books, Northumberland 203
Jonkers Rare Books, Oxfordshire 209
Karen Millward, Co. Cork.......................... 263
Norton Books, N Yorks............................. 197
R. & A. Books, E Sussex............................ 102
Trinity Rare Books, Co. Leitrim 266
Williams Rare Books (Nigel), London WC 180

- KEATS, JOHN

Alec-Smith Books (Alex), East Yorkshire 107

- KEEPING, CHARLES

Bookmark (Children's Books), Wiltshire.......... 253
Cameron House Books, Isle of Wight............. 134
Cranhurst Books, London 161
Fifteenth Century Bookshop (The), E Sussex 104
Jean Hedger, Berkshire 55
Key Books (Sarah), Cambridgeshire............... 64

- KENT, ALEXANDER

K Books, Cheshire.................................... 70

- KEROUAC, JACK

Norton Books, N Yorks............................. 197
Roz Hulse, Conwy 286
Sclanders (Beatbooks), (Andrew), London EC... 157
Trinity Rare Books, Co. Leitrim 266

- KERSH, GERALD

R. & A. Books, E Sussex............................ 102

- KING, C. DALY

Trinity Rare Books, Co. Leitrim 266

- KING, STEPHEN

Apocalypse, Surrey 233
Cranhurst Books, London 161
Fantastic Literature, Essex 111
Old Celtic Bookshop (The), Devon 88
R. & A. Books, E Sussex............................ 102
Talisman Books, Cheshire........................... 70

- KIPLING, RUDYARD

Apocalypse, Surrey 233
Armchair Books, Lothian 276
Avonworld Books, Somerset........................ 218
Booth (Booksearch Service), (Geoff), Cheshire... 68
Brock Books, N Yorks 193
Childrens Bookshop, W Yorks 248
Country Books, Derbyshire 82
Cranhurst Books, London 161
Criterion Books, London Outer 182
Daeron's Books, Buckinghamshire................. 62
Faversham Books, Kent 138
Fifteenth Century Bookshop (The), E Sussex 104
Foster Bookshop (Paul), London SW............. 168
Greta Books, Durham 97
Harrington (Adrian), London W................... 173

Jean Hedger, Berkshire 55
Macbuiks, N Yorks 194
Orb's Bookshop, Grampian......................... 274
R. & A. Books, E Sussex............................ 102
Verandah Books, Dorset 95
Wykeham Books, London SW 171

- KOONTZ, DEAN

Cranhurst Books, London 161
Old Celtic Bookshop (The), Devon 88
R. & A. Books, E Sussex............................ 102
Talisman Books, Cheshire........................... 70

- LAITHWAITE, ERIC

K.S.C. Books, Cheshire.............................. 71

- LANG, ANDREW

Bookmark (Children's Books), Wiltshire.......... 253
Booth (Booksearch Service), (Geoff), Cheshire... 68
Cranhurst Books, London 161
Fifteenth Century Bookshop (The), E Sussex 104
Greer (Robin), London SW......................... 168
Greta Books, Durham 97
Hodgkins and Company Limited (Ian), Glos 116
Jean Hedger, Berkshire 55
R. & A. Books, E Sussex............................ 102
Randall (Tom), Somerset............................ 219

- LAWRENCE, D.H.

Apocalypse, Surrey 233
Armchair Books, Lothian 276
Booth (Booksearch Service), (Geoff), Cheshire... 68
Childrens Bookshop, W Yorks 248
Norton Books, N Yorks............................. 197
R. & A. Books, E Sussex............................ 102
Tilston (Stephen E.), London SE................... 166
Trinity Rare Books, Co. Leitrim 266

- LAWRENCE, T.E.

Antique Map and Bookshop (The), Dorset 94
Apocalypse, Surrey 233
Avedikian Rare Books, Somerset 217
Booth (Booksearch Service), (Geoff), Cheshire... 68
Branksome Books, Dorset........................... 94
Coach House Books, Worcestershire 256
Dolphin Books, Suffolk.............................. 226
Fifteenth Century Bookshop (The), E Sussex 104
Jonkers Rare Books, Oxfordshire 209
Joppa Books Ltd., Surrey 231
Lymelight Books & Prints, Dorset..... 93
Moorside Books, Lancashire........................ 144
R. & A. Books, E Sussex............................ 102
Rickaro Books, W Yorks 247
Trinity Rare Books, Co. Leitrim 266
Watkins (R.G.), Somerset 216
Words Etcetera Bookshop, Dorset................. 93

- LE CARRE, JOHN

Apocalypse, Surrey 233
Bookshop on the Heath, The, London SE 164
Booth (Booksearch Service), (Geoff), Cheshire... 68
Cranhurst Books, London 161
R. & A. Books, E Sussex............................ 102
Surprise Books, Glos................................. 113
Trinity Rare Books, Co. Leitrim 266

SPECIALITY INDEX

Wayside Books and Cards, Oxfordshire 207

- LEAR, EDWARD
Bookmark (Children's Books), Wiltshire.......... 253
Fifteenth Century Bookshop (The), E Sussex 104
Jean Hedger, Berkshire 55
R. & A. Books, E Sussex............................ 102

- LEWIS, C.S.
Apocalypse, Surrey 233
Armchair Books, Lothian 276
Booth (Booksearch Service), (Geoff), Cheshire... 68
Cranhurst Books, London 161
Daeron's Books, Buckinghamshire.................. 62
Inner Bookshop (The), Oxfordshire................ 210
Jonkers Rare Books, Oxfordshire 209
Key Books (Sarah), Cambridgeshire............... 64
Lewis First Editions, Kent 138
Lucius Books, N Yorks............................... 199
Oasis Booksearch, Cambridgeshire................. 67
R. & A. Books, E Sussex 102
Rosley Books, Cumbria 81
St Philip's Books, Oxfordshire...................... 210
Trinity Rare Books, Co. Leitrim 266

- LEWIS, SINCLAIR
Booth (Booksearch Service), (Geoff), Cheshire... 68

- LEWIS, WYNDHAM
Booth (Booksearch Service), (Geoff), Cheshire... 68
Dolphin Books, Suffolk............................... 226
Norton Books, N Yorks.............................. 197
Trinity Rare Books, Co. Leitrim 266

- LINDSAY, NORMAN
Norton Books, N Yorks.............................. 197

- LONDON, JACK
Booth (Booksearch Service), (Geoff), Cheshire... 68
R. & A. Books, E Sussex............................ 102
Trinity Rare Books, Co. Leitrim 266

- LORCA, GARCIA
Trinity Rare Books, Co. Leitrim 266

- LOTI, PIERRE
Trinity Rare Books, Co. Leitrim 266

- LOVECRAFT, H.P.
Trinity Rare Books, Co. Leitrim 266
Watkins Books Ltd., London WC.................. 180
Zardoz Books, Wiltshire............................. 254

- LOWRY, MALCOLM
Apocalypse, Surrey 233
Fifteenth Century Bookshop (The), E Sussex 104
Trinity Rare Books, Co. Leitrim 266

- LUCAS, E.V.
Brock Books, N Yorks 193

- MACDONALD, BETTY
Booth (Booksearch Service), (Geoff), Cheshire... 68

- MACDONALD, GEORGE
Bookmark (Children's Books), Wiltshire.......... 253
Booth (Booksearch Service), (Geoff), Cheshire... 68
Daeron's Books, Buckinghamshire 62
Fifteenth Century Bookshop (The), E Sussex 104
Jean Hedger, Berkshire 55
Orb's Bookshop, Grampian......................... 274
Rosley Books, Cumbria 81
Wayside Books and Cards, Oxfordshire 207

- MACHEN, ARTHUR
Apocalypse, Surrey 233
Bass (Ben), Wiltshire 251
Craobh Rua Books, Co. Armagh................... 260
Delectus Books, London WC....................... 177
Trinity Rare Books, Co. Leitrim 266

- MACLEAN, ALISTAIR
Booth (Booksearch Service), (Geoff), Cheshire... 68
R. & A. Books, E Sussex............................ 102
Trinity Rare Books, Co. Leitrim 266

- MADOX FORD, FORD
Meads Book Service (The), E Sussex.............. 104
R. & A. Books, E Sussex............................ 102
Trinity Rare Books, Co. Leitrim 266

- MAILER, NORMAN
Anglo-American Rare Books, Surrey.............. 233
Apocalypse, Surrey 233
Booth (Booksearch Service), (Geoff), Cheshire... 68
Trinity Rare Books, Co. Leitrim 266

- MANNIN, ETHEL
Booth (Booksearch Service), (Geoff), Cheshire... 68
Dolphin Books, Suffolk............................... 226
Trinity Rare Books, Co. Leitrim 266

- MARVELL, ANDREW
Alec-Smith Books (Alex), East Yorkshire 107

- MASEFIELD, JOHN
Apocalypse, Surrey 233
Criterion Books, London Outer 182
Farringdon (J.M.), Swansea......................... 293
Fifteenth Century Bookshop (The), E Sussex 104
Prior (Michael), Lincolnshire 153
R. & A. Books, E Sussex............................ 102
Smith Books (Kelth), Heretfordshire 128
Trinity Rare Books, Co. Leitrim 266

- MASTERS, JOHN
Booth (Booksearch Service), (Geoff), Cheshire... 68
Dolphin Books, Suffolk............................... 226
Fifteenth Century Bookshop (The), E Sussex 104
Orb's Bookshop, Grampian......................... 274
Trinity Rare Books, Co. Leitrim 266

- MAUGHAM, SOMERSET
Booth (Booksearch Service), (Geoff), Cheshire... 68
Greta Books, Durham 97
Orb's Bookshop, Grampian......................... 274
R. & A. Books, E Sussex............................ 102
Roz Hulse, Conwy 286
Trinity Rare Books, Co. Leitrim 266

SPECIALITY INDEX

Wayside Books and Cards, Oxfordshire 207

- MELVILLE, HERMAN
Trinity Rare Books, Co. Leitrim 266

- MENCKEN, H.L.
Trinity Rare Books, Co. Leitrim 266

- MICHAUX, FRANCOIS
Trinity Rare Books, Co. Leitrim 266

- MICHENER, JAMES
Booth (Booksearch Service), (Geoff), Cheshire... 68
Trinity Rare Books, Co. Leitrim 266

- MILLER, HENRY
Apocalypse, Surrey 233
Booth (Booksearch Service), (Geoff), Cheshire... 68
Delectus Books, London WC....................... 177
Norton Books, N Yorks.............................. 197
R. & A. Books, E Sussex............................ 102
Trinity Rare Books, Co. Leitrim 266

- MILLIGAN, SPIKE
Cranhurst Books, London 161
Fifteenth Century Bookshop (The), E Sussex 104
John R. Hoggarth, N Yorks........................ 198
Kineton Nooks, Warwickshire...................... 237
R. & A. Books, E Sussex............................ 102
Trinity Rare Books, Co. Leitrim 266
Wayside Books and Cards, Oxfordshire 207

- MILNE, A.A.
Bookmark (Children's Books), Wiltshire.......... 253
Bookstand, Dorset.................................... 94
Booth (Booksearch Service), (Geoff), Cheshire... 68
Cranhurst Books, London 161
Dolphin Books, Suffolk.............................. 226
Fifteenth Century Bookshop (The), E Sussex 104
Foster Bookshop (Paul), London SW............. 168
Harrington (Adrian), London W................... 173
Jean Hedger, Berkshire 55
Jonkers Rare Books, Oxfordshire 209
R. & A. Books, E Sussex............................ 102
Surprise Books, Glos................................. 113
Tobo Books, Hampshire............................. 123
Trinity Rare Books, Co. Leitrim 266

- MILTON J.
R. & A. Books, E Sussex............................ 102
Trinity Rare Books, Co. Leitrim 266

- MOORE, JOHN
Aucott & Thomas, Leics............................. 147
Cornell Books, Glos.................................. 117
Country Books, Derbyshire 82
Dolphin Books, Suffolk.............................. 226
Elmbury Books, Warwickshire 238
Engaging Gear Ltd., Essex 108
Island Books, Devon 85
Sedgeberrow Books & Framing, Worcestershire. 256
Surprise Books, Glos................................. 113

- MORGAN, CHARLES
Booth (Booksearch Service), (Geoff), Cheshire... 68

Dolphin Books, Suffolk.............................. 226
Trinity Rare Books, Co. Leitrim 266

- MORRIS, JAN
Trinity Rare Books, Co. Leitrim 266

- MORRIS, WILLIAM
Bass (Ben), Wiltshire 251
Brock Books, N Yorks 193
Bruce Holdsworth Books, E Sussex 105
Hodgkins and Company Limited (Ian), Glos 116
R. & A. Books, E Sussex............................ 102
Upper-Room Books, Somerset...................... 218

- MORTON, H.V.
Apocalypse, Surrey 233
Booth (Booksearch Service), (Geoff), Cheshire... 68
Dolphin Books, Suffolk.............................. 226
Fifteenth Century Bookshop (The), E Sussex 104
Fireside Books, Buckinghamshire 62
Island Books, Devon 85
Oasis Booksearch, Cambridgeshire................. 67
Orb's Bookshop, Grampian......................... 274

- MURDOCH, I.
Apocalypse, Surrey 233
Booth (Booksearch Service), (Geoff), Cheshire... 68
Cranhurst Books, London 161
Dolphin Books, Suffolk.............................. 226
Ellis, Bookseller (Peter), London WC 178
R. & A. Books, E Sussex............................ 102
Reaveley Books, Devon 87
Trinity Rare Books, Co. Leitrim 266

- NEEDHAM, V.
Bookmark (Children's Books), Wiltshire.......... 253
Fifteenth Century Bookshop (The), E Sussex 104
Key Books (Sarah), Cambridgeshire............... 64

- NEWMAN, CARDINAL
Cox Rare Books (Charles), Cornwall............... 74
Oasis Booksearch, Cambridgeshire................. 67
St Philip's Books, Oxfordshire...................... 210

- NIALL, IAN
Chalmers Hallam (E.), Hampshire 125
Fifteenth Century Bookshop (The), E Sussex 104
Island Books, Devon 85

- NIN, ANAIS
Apocalypse, Surrey 233
Lucius Books, N Yorks.............................. 199
Norton Books, N Yorks.............................. 197
Trinity Rare Books, Co. Leitrim 266

- NORTON, MARY
Bookmark (Children's Books), Wiltshire.......... 253
Fifteenth Century Bookshop (The), E Sussex 104
John Underwood Antiquarian Books, Norfolk .. 190

- O'BRIAN, PATRICK
Fifteenth Century Bookshop (The), E Sussex 104
Harrington (Adrian), London W................... 173
Intech Books, Northumberland 203
Lucius Books, N Yorks.............................. 199

Orb's Bookshop, Grampian 274
Surprise Books, Glos 113
Trinity Rare Books, Co. Leitrim 266

- OPPENHEIM, E. PHILLIPS
Trinity Rare Books, Co. Leitrim 266

- ORCZY, BARONESS
Brock Books, N Yorks 193
Fifteenth Century Bookshop (The), E Sussex 104
Lucius Books, N Yorks............................... 199
Parrott (Jeremy), London E.......................... 156

- ORWELL, GEORGE
Apocalypse, Surrey 233
Booth (Booksearch Service), (Geoff), Cheshire... 68
Cranhurst Books, London 161
Criterion Books, London Outer 182
Fifteenth Century Bookshop (The), E Sussex 104
Heppa (Christopher), Essex 108
Lucius Books, N Yorks............................... 199
Mandalay Bookshop, London SW 169
R. & A. Books, E Sussex............................. 102
Trinity Rare Books, Co. Leitrim 266

- OSBORNE, JOHN
Apocalypse, Surrey 233
R. & A. Books, E Sussex............................. 102

- OWL, GREY
Bookmark (Children's Books), Wiltshire.......... 253
Booth (Booksearch Service), (Geoff), Cheshire... 68
Fifteenth Century Bookshop (The), E Sussex 104
Greta Books, Durham 97
Trinity Rare Books, Co. Leitrim 266

- OXENHAM, ELSIE
Badger Books, Somerset 220
Bilski (Gill), Buckinghamshire 61
Bookmark (Children's Books), Wiltshire.......... 253
Cranhurst Books, London 161
D. & M. Books, W Yorks 250
Fifteenth Century Bookshop (The), E Sussex 104
Green Meadow Books, Cornwall 74
Intech Books, Northumberland 203
Key Books (Sarah), Cambridgeshire............... 64
Little Stour Books, Kent 137
Lucius Books, N Yorks 199
Mercat Books, Highland 274
R. & A. Books, E Sussex............................. 102
Sims (Sue), Dorset 91
TP Children's Bookshop, W Yorks................ 246
Trinity Rare Books, Co. Leitrim 266

- PALIN, MICHAEL
Apocalypse, Surrey 233
Booth (Booksearch Service), (Geoff), Cheshire... 68
R. & A. Books, E Sussex............................. 102

- PARGETER, EDITH
Baker - Books for the Collector (Colin), Devon . 90

- PASTERNAK, BORIS
Park Gallery & Bookshop (The), Northants 201

- PAUL BOWLES
Riderless Horse Books, Norfolk 187
Trinity Rare Books, Co. Leitrim 266
Tsbbooks, London SW 170

- PEAKE, MERVYN
Cameron House Books, Isle of Wight.............. 134
Criterion Books, London Outer 182
Fifteenth Century Bookshop (The), E Sussex 104
Kemp Booksellers, Lancashire...................... 143
Lucius Books, N Yorks............................... 199
Trinity Rare Books, Co. Leitrim 266

- PENNANT, THOMAS
Atholl Fine Books, Tayside 281

- PEPYS, SAMUEL
Fifteenth Century Bookshop (The), E Sussex 104
Island Books, Devon 85
R. & A. Books, E Sussex............................. 102

- PETER CAREY
R. & A. Books, E Sussex............................. 102
Trinity Rare Books, Co. Leitrim 266

- PETERS, ELLIS
Baker - Books for the Collector (Colin), Devon . 90
Booth (Booksearch Service), (Geoff), Cheshire... 68
Cranhurst Books, London 161
Dolphin Books, Suffolk............................... 226
Fifteenth Century Bookshop (The), E Sussex 104
Surprise Books, Glos 113
Trinity Rare Books, Co. Leitrim 266

- PICASSO, PABLO
Apocalypse, Surrey 233
Brock Books, N Yorks 193
R. & A. Books, E Sussex............................. 102
Trinity Rare Books, Co. Leitrim 266

- PINTER, HAROLD
R. & A. Books, E Sussex............................. 102
Trinity Rare Books, Co. Leitrim 266

- POE, EDGAR ALLAN
R. & A. Books, E Sussex............................. 102

- POPE, A
Calendula Horticultural Books, E Sussex 102
Derek Stirling Bookseller, Kent 142
R. & A. Books, E Sussex............................. 102
Trinity Rare Books, Co. Leitrim 266

- POTTER, BEATRIX
Bookmark (Children's Books), Wiltshire.......... 253
Bookstand, Dorset..................................... 94
Booth (Booksearch Service), (Geoff), Cheshire... 68
Cranhurst Books, London 161
Dolphin Books, Suffolk............................... 226
Fifteenth Century Bookshop (The), E Sussex 104
Hodgkins and Company Limited (Ian), Glos 116
Jean Hedger, Berkshire 55
Jonkers Rare Books, Oxfordshire 209
Key Books (Sarah), Cambridgeshire............... 64
Past & Presents, Cumbria 77

SPECIALITY INDEX

R. & A. Books, E Sussex............................. 102
Treasure Trove Books, Leics......................... 148

- POWELL, ANTHONY
Apocalypse, Surrey 233
Criterion Books, London Outer 182
Fifteenth Century Bookshop (The), E Sussex 104
R. & A. Books, E Sussex............................. 102
Trinity Rare Books, Co. Leitrim 266

- POWYS FAMILY, THE
Berwick Books, Lincolnshire......................... 152
Books Afloat, Dorset.................................. 96
Criterion Books, London Outer 182
Dolphin Books, Suffolk............................... 226
Ferdinando (Steven), Somerset 220
Fifteenth Century Bookshop (The), E Sussex 104
Green Man Books, E Sussex 101
Words Etcetera Bookshop, Dorset.................. 93

- PRATCHETT, TERRY
Allinson (Frank & Stella), Warwickshire 237
Cranhurst Books, London 161
Daeren's Books, Buckinghamshire.................. 62
Fantastic Literature, Essex 111
Fiction First, Cheshire 70
Fifteenth Century Bookshop (The), E Sussex 104
Green Meadow Books, Cornwall 74
Intech Books, Northumberland 203
L.M.S. Books, Herts 132
R. & A. Books, E Sussex............................. 102
Surprise Books, Glos.................................. 113
Talisman Books, Cheshire............................ 70
Trinity Rare Books, Co. Leitrim 266

- PRIESTLEY, J.B.
Booth (Booksearch Service), (Geoff), Cheshire... 68
Cameron House Books, Isle of Wight.............. 134
Criterion Books, London Outer 182
Fifteenth Century Bookshop (The), E Sussex 104
Greta Books, Durham 97
Orb's Bookshop, Grampian.......................... 274

- QUENEAU, RAYMOND
Trinity Rare Books, Co. Leitrim 266

- QUILLER-COUCH, SIR A.T.
Bookends of Fowey, Cornwall 73
Booth (Booksearch Service), (Geoff), Cheshire... 68
Fifteenth Century Bookshop (The), E Sussex 104
Island Books, Devon.................................. 85
R & B Graham Trading, Cornwall 74

- RACKHAM, ARTHUR
Apocalypse, Surrey 233
Bookmark (Children's Books), Wiltshire.......... 253
Bow Windows Book Shop, E Sussex............... 103
Chalmers Hallam (E.), Hampshire 125
Cranhurst Books, London 161
Fifteenth Century Bookshop (The), E Sussex 104
Foster Bookshop (Paul), London SW.............. 168
Harrington (Adrian), London W.................... 173
Jean Hedger, Berkshire 55
Key Books (Sarah), Cambridgeshire................ 64
Little Stour Books, Kent 137

Lucius Books, N Yorks............................... 199
Preston Book Company, Lancashire 145
R. & A. Books, E Sussex............................. 102
Rye Old Books, E Sussex 104
St Mary's Books & Prints, Lincolnshire 154
Stella Books, Monmouthshire 288
Trinity Rare Books, Co. Leitrim 266
World War II Books, Surrey 235

- RAISTRICK, ARTHUR
Anthony Vickers Books, N Yorks 196
Grove Bookshop (The), N Yorks................... 197
Vickers (Anthony), N Yorks......................... 196

- RAND, AYN
Webb Books (John), South Yorkshire.............. 222

- RANKIN, IAN
Apocalypse, Surrey 233
Bookworm, Lothian................................... 277
Cranhurst Books, London 161
Fiction First, Cheshire 70
Intech Books, Northumberland 203
Surprise Books, Glos.................................. 113
Trinity Rare Books, Co. Leitrim.................... 266
Wayside Books and Cards, Oxfordshire 207

- RANSOME, ARTHUR
Bookmark (Children's Books), Wiltshire.......... 253
Bookshop on the Heath, The, London SE 164
Chalmers Hallam (E.), Hampshire 125
Cranhurst Books, London 161
Cygnet Books, East Yorkshire....................... 107
Farringdon (J.M.), Swansea......................... 293
Fifteenth Century Bookshop (The), E Sussex 104
Heppa (Christopher), Essex 108
Key Books (Sarah), Cambridgeshire................ 64
Kirkland Books, Cumbria............................ 79
Past & Presents, Cumbria 77
R. & A. Books, E Sussex............................. 102
Schutte (David), Hampshire......................... 124
Trinity Rare Books, Co. Leitrim 266

- RATCLIFFE, DOROTHY UNA
Brock Books, N Yorks 193
Grove Bookshop (The), N Yorks................... 197
Trinity Rare Books, Co. Leitrim 266

READ, MISS
Annie's Books, South Yorkshire 222
Baker - Books for the Collector (Colin), Devon . 90
Bookmark (Children's Books), Wiltshire.......... 253
Brown-Studies, Strathclyde.......................... 279
Clent Books, Worcestershire 255
Country Books, Derbyshire 82
Cygnet Books, East Yorkshire....................... 107
Fifteenth Century Bookshop (The), E Sussex 104
Intech Books, Northumberland 203
Trinity Rare Books, Co. Leitrim 266

- RICE, ANNE
Fiction First, Cheshire 70
Old Celtic Bookshop (The), Devon 88
Surprise Books, Glos.................................. 113
Trinity Rare Books, Co. Leitrim 266

SPECIALITY INDEX

- RICHARDS, FRANK
Bookmark (Children's Books), Wiltshire.......... 253
Booth (Booksearch Service), (Geoff), Cheshire... 68
Cranhurst Books, London 161
D. & M. Books, W Yorks 250
Fifteenth Century Bookshop (The), E Sussex 104
Heppa (Christopher), Essex 108
Intech Books, Northumberland 203
R. & A. Books, E Sussex............................ 102
Schutte (David), Hampshire........................ 124
Trinity Rare Books, Co. Leitrim 266
Wright (Norman), Dorset 95

- ROBINSON, HEATH W.
Bookmark (Children's Books), Wiltshire.......... 253
Cranhurst Books, London 161
Fifteenth Century Bookshop (The), E Sussex 104
Jean Hedger, Berkshire 55
R. & A. Books, E Sussex............................ 102
Rye Old Books, E Sussex 104

- ROHMER, SAX
Trinity Rare Books, Co. Leitrim 266
Zardoz Books, Wiltshire............................. 254

- ROLFE, F.
Ellis, Bookseller (Peter), London WC 178

- ROLT, L.T.C.
Anthony Vickers Books, N Yorks 196
Baldwin (M. & M.), Worcestershire 255
Bird Books (Nigel), Ceredigion 284
Boox-Box (The), Shropshire 213
Bott, (Bookdealers) Ltd., (Martin), Gr Man 118
Crosby Nethercott Books, London Outer 181
Dales and Lakes Book Centre, Cumbria.......... 80
Henry Wilson Books, Cheshire 69
Liddle (Steve), Bristol 58
Randall (Tom), Somerset............................ 219
Robert Humm & Co, Lincolnshire 154
Trinity Rare Books, Co. Leitrim 266
Vickers (Anthony), N Yorks......................... 196

- ROSSETTI, C.
Cox Rare Books (Charles), Cornwall.............. 74
Dolphin Books, Suffolk.............................. 226
Fifteenth Century Bookshop (The), E Sussex 104
Hodgkins and Company Limited (Ian), Glos 116
R. & A. Books, E Sussex. 102

- ROWLING, J.K.
Apocalypse, Surrey 233
Cranhurst Books, London 161
Fifteenth Century Bookshop (The), E Sussex 104
Harrington (Adrian), London W.................... 173
Intech Books, Northumberland 203
R. & A. Books, E Sussex............................ 102
Saint Mary's Books & Prints, Lincolnshire....... 154
Trinity Rare Books, Co. Leitrim 266

- RUSHDIE, SALMAN
Booth (Booksearch Service), (Geoff), Cheshire... 68
Dolphin Books, Suffolk.............................. 226
Norton Books, N Yorks.............................. 197
R. & A. Books, E Sussex............................ 102

Trinity Rare Books, Co. Leitrim 266

- RUSKIN, JOHN
Apocalypse, Surrey 233
Brock Books, N Yorks 193
Cox Rare Books (Charles), Cornwall.............. 74
Hodgkins and Company Limited (Ian), Glos 116
R. & A. Books, E Sussex............................ 102
Rosley Books, Cumbria 81
Shacklock Books (David), Suffolk 227
Solitaire Books, Somerset........................... 217

- RUSSELL, BERTRAND
R. & A. Books, E Sussex............................ 102

- RUSSELL, W
Karen Millward, Co. Cork........................... 263

- SABATINI, R.
Dusty Books, Powys 292
Fifteenth Century Bookshop (The), E Sussex 104
Greta Books, Durham 97
Lucius Books, N Yorks............................... 199

- SACKVILLE-WEST, VITA
Apocalypse, Surrey 233
Booth (Booksearch Service), (Geoff), Cheshire... 68
Bow Windows Book Shop, E Sussex.............. 103
Ellis, Bookseller (Peter), London WC 178
Evans Books (Paul), W Sussex 243
Fifteenth Century Bookshop (The), E Sussex 104
Island Books, Devon 85
Trinity Rare Books, Co. Leitrim 266

- SASSOON, SIEGFRIED
Anglo-American Rare Books, Surrey.............. 233
Booth (Booksearch Service), (Geoff), Cheshire... 68
Ellis, Bookseller (Peter), London WC 178
Fifteenth Century Bookshop (The), E Sussex 104
Island Books, Devon 85
R. & A. Books, E Sussex............................ 102
Roz Hulse, Conwy 286
Trinity Rare Books, Co. Leitrim 266

- SAVILLE, M.
Ardis Books, Hampshire 126
Bookmark (Children's Books), Wiltshire.......... 253
Bookpassage (The), Shropshire.................... 213
Fifteenth Century Bookshop (The), E Sussex 104
Green Meadow Books, Cornwall 74
Key Books (Sarah), Cambridgeshire............... 64
Lewis First Editions, Kent 138
Little Stour Books, Kent 137
Schutte (David), Hampshire........................ 124
TP Children's Bookshop, W Yorks................ 246

- SAYERS, DOROTHY
Avonworld Books, Somerset........................ 218
Booth (Booksearch Service), (Geoff), Cheshire... 68
Cranhurst Books, London 161
Fifteenth Century Bookshop (The), E Sussex 104
Lucius Books, N Yorks............................... 199
R. & A. Books, E Sussex............................ 102
Trinity Rare Books, Co. Leitrim 266

SPECIALITY INDEX

- SEARLE, RONALD
Allinson (Frank & Stella), Warwickshire 237
Bookmark (Children's Books), Wiltshire.......... 253
Bookshop on the Heath, The, London SE 164
Cranhurst Books, London 161
Facet Books, Dorset................................... 91
Fifteenth Century Bookshop (The), E Sussex 104
Intech Books, Northumberland 203

- SELOUS, FREDERICK
Edmund Pollinger Rare Books, London SW..... 167
Preston Book Company, Lancashire 145

- SENDAK, MAURICE
Bookmark (Children's Books), Wiltshire.......... 253
Cranhurst Books, London 161
Fifteenth Century Bookshop (The), E Sussex 104
Intech Books, Northumberland 203
Jean Hedger, Berkshire 55
R. & A. Books, E Sussex............................. 102

- SERVICE, ROBERT W.
Booth (Booksearch Service), (Geoff), Cheshire... 68
Fifteenth Century Bookshop (The), E Sussex 104

- SEYMOUR, JOHN
Coch-y-Bonddu Books, Powys 292
Dolphin Books, Suffolk............................... 226
Mount's Bay Books, Cornwall 75

- SHAKESPEARE, WILLIAM
Apocalypse, Surrey 233
Bennett & Kerr Books, Oxfordshire 206
Byre Books, Dumfries & Galloway................. 270
Chaucer Head Bookshop, Warwickshire.......... 238
Fifteenth Century Bookshop (The), E Sussex 104
R. & A. Books, E Sussex............................. 102
Trinity Rare Books, Co. Leitrim 266
Uncle Phil's Books, West Midlands 240

- SHAW, GEORGE BERNARD
Apocalypse, Surrey 233
Booth (Booksearch Service), (Geoff), Cheshire... 68
Brock Books, N Yorks 193
Dolphin Books, Suffolk............................... 226
Ellis, Bookseller (Peter), London WC 178
Fifteenth Century Bookshop (The), E Sussex 104
R, & A. Books, E Sussex............................. 102

- SHELLEY, PERCY B
Alec-Smith Books (Alex), East Yorkshire 107

- SHEPARD, E.H.
Bookmark (Children's Books), Wiltshire.......... 253
Booth (Booksearch Service), (Geoff), Cheshire... 68
Fifteenth Century Bookshop (The), E Sussex 104
Jean Hedger, Berkshire 55
Key Books (Sarah), Cambridgeshire............... 64
R. & A. Books, E Sussex............................. 102

- SHUTE, NEVILLE
Booth (Booksearch Service), (Geoff), Cheshire... 68
Dusty Books, Powys 292
Fifteenth Century Bookshop (The), E Sussex 104
Greta Books, Durham 97

Intech Books, Northumberland 203
Lewis First Editions, Kent 138
Lucius Books, N Yorks............................... 199
Orb's Bookshop, Grampian......................... 274
R. & A. Books, E Sussex............................. 102
The Sanctuary Bookshop, Dorset.................. 94
Trinity Rare Books, Co. Leitrim 266
Webb Books (John), South Yorkshire............. 222

- SIMENON, GEORGES
Bass (Ben), Wiltshire 251
Lucius Books, N Yorks............................... 199
Treasure Trove Books, Leics........................ 148
Trinity Rare Books, Co. Leitrim 266
Wayside Books and Cards, Oxfordshire 207
Williams (Bookdealer), (Richard), N Lincs....... 154

- SIMON, ANDRE L.
Roberts Wine Books (John), Bristol................ 59

- SITWELL FAMILY
Apocalypse, Surrey 233
Booth (Booksearch Service), (Geoff), Cheshire... 68
Ellis, Bookseller (Peter), London WC 178
Fifteenth Century Bookshop (The), E Sussex 104
Trinity Rare Books, Co. Leitrim 266

- SMITH, WILBUR
Booth (Booksearch Service), (Geoff), Cheshire... 68
R. & A. Books, E Sussex............................. 102
Surprise Books, Glos................................. 113
Trinity Rare Books, Co. Leitrim 266

- SOLZHENITSYN, ALEXANDER
Apocalypse, Surrey 233
Booth (Booksearch Service), (Geoff), Cheshire... 68
R. & A. Books, E Sussex............................. 102
Trinity Rare Books, Co. Leitrim 266

- SOMERVILLE & ROSS
Booth (Booksearch Service), (Geoff), Cheshire... 68
Darkwood Books, Co. Cork......................... 263
Fifteenth Century Bookshop (The), E Sussex 104
Greta Books, Durham 97
Trinity Rare Books, Co. Leitrim 266

- SPARE, AUSTIN O.
Inner Bookshop (The), Oxfordshire................. 210
Lucius Books, N Yorks............................... 199

- SPARE, AUSTIN OSMAN
Apocalypse, Surrey 233
Atlantis Bookshop, London WC.................... 177
Inner Bookshop (The), Oxfordshire................. 210
Occultique, Northants................................ 200
Trinity Rare Books, Co. Leitrim 266

- SPARK, MURIEL
Booth (Booksearch Service), (Geoff), Cheshire... 68
Brian Troath Books, London E...................... 155
Criterion Books, London Outer..................... 182
Dolphin Books, Suffolk............................... 226
Fifteenth Century Bookshop (The), E Sussex 104
Trinity Rare Books, Co. Leitrim 266

SPECIALITY INDEX

- STEADMAN, RALPH
Barmby (C. & A.J.), Kent............................ 141
Dylans Bookstore, Swansea 294
Fifteenth Century Bookshop (The), E Sussex 104
Lucius Books, N Yorks............................... 199

- STEGNER, WALLACE
Booth (Booksearch Service), (Geoff), Cheshire... 68

- STEIN, GERTRUDE
Norton Books, N Yorks.............................. 197
R. & A. Books, E Sussex............................. 102
Trinity Rare Books, Co. Leitrim 266

- STEINBECK, JOHN
Booth (Booksearch Service), (Geoff), Cheshire... 68
Fifteenth Century Bookshop (The), E Sussex 104
Trinity Rare Books, Co. Leitrim 266

- STEINER, RUDOLF
Anthroposophical Books, Glos 116
Inner Bookshop (The), Oxfordshire................. 210
Trinity Rare Books, Co. Leitrim 266

- STENDHAL
Apocalypse, Surrey 233
Fifteenth Century Bookshop (The), E Sussex 104

- STERNE, L
Spelman (Ken), N Yorks............................. 199

- STEVENSON, ROBERT LOUIS
Apocalypse, Surrey 233
Bookmark (Children's Books), Wiltshire........... 253
Bookshop on the Heath, The, London SE 164
Booth (Booksearch Service), (Geoff), Cheshire... 68
Brock Books, N Yorks 193
Dolphin Books, Suffolk............................... 226
Fifteenth Century Bookshop (The), E Sussex 104
Greta Books, Durham 97
Jean Hedger, Berkshire 55
Jonkers Rare Books, Oxfordshire 209
Olynthiacs, Shropshire 214
Parrott (Jeremy), London E.......................... 156
R. & A. Books, E Sussex............................. 102
Trinity Rare Books, Co. Leitrim 266

- STOKER, B.
R. & A. Books, E Sussex............................. 102
Rider Haggard Society (The), Tyne and Wear... 236
Trinity Rare Books, Co. Leitrim 266

- STRACHEY, LYTTON
Evans Books (Paul), W Sussex 243
Fifteenth Century Bookshop (The), E Sussex 104
R. & A. Books, E Sussex............................. 102

- STRATTON PORTER, GENE
Fifteenth Century Bookshop (The), E Sussex 104
Greta Books, Durham 97

- STREET, A.G.
Baker - Books for the Collector (Colin), Devon. 90
Books for Content, Herefordshire................... 128

Dolphin Books, Suffolk............................... 226
Greta Books, Durham 97

- STRINDBERG, A.
R. & A. Books, E Sussex............................. 102

- SWIFT, J
R. & A. Books, E Sussex............................. 102
Trinity Rare Books, Co. Leitrim 266

- SWINBURNE, A.C.
Cameron House Books, Isle of Wight.............. 134
Cox Rare Books (Charles), Cornwall............... 74
Fifteenth Century Bookshop (The), E Sussex 104
Hodgkins and Company Limited (Ian), Glos 116
R. & A. Books, E Sussex............................. 102

- TANGYE, D.
Annie's Books, South Yorkshire 222
Baker - Books for the Collector (Colin), Devon. 90
Bass (Ben), Wiltshire 231
Bonython Bookshop, Cornwall...................... 6
Bosco Books, Cornwall 73
Emjay Books, Surrey................................. 231
Fifteenth Century Bookshop (The), E Sussex 104
Green Meadow Books, Cornwall 74
Intech Books, Northumberland 203
Island Books, Devon.................................. 85
Just Books, Cornwall 76
R. & A. Books, E Sussex............................. 102

- TENNYSON, LORD ALFRED
Apocalypse, Surrey 233
Brock Books, N Yorks 193
Cameron House Books, Isle of Wight.............. 134
Cox Rare Books (Charles), Cornwall............... 74
Fifteenth Century Bookshop (The), E Sussex 104

- THACKERY, WILLIAM M.
Apocalypse, Surrey 233
Dolphin Books, Suffolk............................... 226
Fifteenth Century Bookshop (The), E Sussex 104
R. & A. Books, E Sussex............................. 102

- THELWELL, N
Bookstand, Dorset..................................... 94
Country Books, Derbyshire 82
Fifteenth Century Bookshop (The), E Sussex ... 104

- THEROUX, P.
Dolphin Books, Suffolk............................... 226
Fifteenth Century Bookshop (The), E Sussex 104
R. & A. Books, E Sussex............................. 102
Trinity Rare Books, Co. Leitrim 266

- THIRKELL, ANGELA
Bookmark (Children's Books), Wiltshire.......... 253
Booth (Booksearch Service), (Geoff), Cheshire... 68
Fifteenth Century Bookshop (The), E Sussex 104

- THOMAS, DYLAN
Cofion Books, Pembrokeshire 288
Criterion Books, London Outer..................... 182
Dylans Bookstore, Swansea.......................... 294
Fifteenth Century Bookshop (The), E Sussex 104

SPECIALITY INDEX

R. & A. Books, E Sussex.............................. 102
Trinity Rare Books, Co. Leitrim 266

- THOMAS, EDWARD
Dylans Bookstore, Swansea 294
Karen Millward, Co. Cork........................... 263
Smith Books (Keith), Herefordshire 128

- THOMPSON-SETON, ERNEST E.
Fifteenth Century Bookshop (The), E Sussex 104
Green Meadow Books, Cornwall 74

- THORNDIKE, RUSSELL
Fifteenth Century Bookshop (The), E Sussex 104
Meads Book Service (The), East Sussex........... 104

- THURBER, JAMES
Fifteenth Century Bookshop (The), East Sussex. 104

- TOKLAS, ALICE B.
Fifteenth Century Bookshop (The), East Sussex. 104
Norton Books, N Yorks.............................. 197

- TOLKIEN, J.R.R.
Barter Books, Northumberland 202
Cranhurst Books, London 161
Daeron's Books, Buckinghamshire.................. 62
Fifteenth Century Bookshop (The), East Sussex. 104
Green Meadow Books, Cornwall 74
Harrington (Adrian), London W.................... 173
Key Books (Sarah), Cambridgeshire................ 64
Lucius Books, N Yorks............................... 199
R. & A. Books, East Sussex 102
Rosley Books, Cumbria 81
Thorntons of Oxford Ltd., Oxfordshire............ 207
Tobo Books, Hampshire.............................. 123
Trinity Rare Books, Co. Leitrim 266

- TOLSTOY, LEO
Fifteenth Century Bookshop (The), East Sussex. 104
R. & A. Books, East Sussex 102

- TOURTEL, M
Bookmark (Children's Books), Wiltshire.......... 253
Cranhurst Books, London 161
Fifteenth Century Bookshop (The), East Sussex. 104
Jean Hedger, Berkshire 55
R. & A. Books, East Sussex 102
Stella Books, Monmouthshire 288

- TROLLOPE, ANTHONY
Ash Rare Books, London SW....................... 167
Bookshop on the Heath, The, London SE 164
Booth (Booksearch Service), (Geoff), Cheshire... 68
Fifteenth Century Bookshop (The), East Sussex. 104
Sen Books, Hampshire................................ 127
Tobo Books, Hampshire.............................. 123
Trinity Rare Books, Co. Leitrim 266

- TUDOR, TASHA
Bookmark (Children's Books), Wiltshire.......... 253
Fifteenth Century Bookshop (The), East Sussex. 104

- TULLY, JIM
Loretta Lay Books, London NW.................... 162

- TWAIN, MARK
Dolphin Books, Suffolk............................... 226
Fifteenth Century Bookshop (The), East Sussex. 104
Harrington (Adrian), London W.................... 173
Parrott (Jeremy), London E......................... 156
R. & A. Books, East Sussex 102
Trinity Rare Books, Co. Leitrim 266

- UPFIELD, ARTHUR
Loretta Lay Books, London NW.................... 162

- UTTLEY, ALISON
Bookmark (Children's Books), Wiltshire.......... 253
Country Books, Derbyshire 82
Fifteenth Century Bookshop (The), East Sussex. 104
Green Meadow Books, Cornwall 74
Jean Hedger, Berkshire 55
R. & A. Books, East Sussex 102
Scarthin Books, Derbyshire 82

- VAN LOON, H.
Booth (Booksearch Service), (Geoff), Cheshire... 68
Dolphin Books, Suffolk............................... 226

- VAN VOGT, A. E.
Orb's Bookshop, Grampian.......................... 274
Trinity Rare Books, Co. Leitrim 266

- VERNE, JULES
Booth (Booksearch Service), (Geoff), Cheshire... 68
Cox, Andrew, Shropshire............................. 215
Fifteenth Century Bookshop (The), East Sussex. 104
Parrott (Jeremy), London E......................... 156
R. & A. Books, East Sussex 102
Trinity Rare Books, Co. Leitrim 266

- VONNEGUT, KURT
Cranhurst Books, London 161
Trinity Rare Books, Co. Leitrim 266

- WAINWRIGHT, ALFRED
Anthony Vickers Books, N Yorks 196
Country Books, Derbyshire 82
Fifteenth Century Bookshop (The), East Sussex. 104
Intech Books, Northumberland 203
Vickers (Anthony), N Yorks......................... 196

- WAINWRIGHT, ARTHUR
Kirkland Books, Cumbria............................ 79
R. & A. Books, East Sussex 102

- WALLACE, EDGAR
Bookshop on the Heath, The, London SE 164
Dolphin Books, Suffolk............................... 226
Fifteenth Century Bookshop (The), East Sussex. 104
Mercat Books, Highland 274
R. & A. Books, East Sussex 102
Trinity Rare Books, Co. Leitrim 266
Williams (Bookdealer), (Richard), N Lincs....... 154
Zardoz Books, Wiltshire.............................. 254

- WALMSLEY, LEO
Fifteenth Century Bookshop (The), East Sussex. 104
Intech Books, Northumberland 203

SPECIALITY INDEX

- WALSH, M.
Darkwood Books, Co. Cork 263
Greta Books, Durham 97

- WATKINS, VERNON
Dylans Bookstore, Swansea 294

- WATKINS-PITCHFORD, DENYS ('B.B.')
Baker - Books for the Collector (Colin), Devon . 90
Bookmark (Children's Books), Wiltshire 253
Bookshop on the Heath, The, London SE 164
Booth (Booksearch Service), (Geoff), Cheshire... 68
Chalmers Hallam (E.), Hampshire 125
Coch-y-Bonddu Books, Powys 292
Country Books, Derbyshire 82
Fifteenth Century Bookshop (The), East Sussex . 104
Heppa (Christopher), Essex 108
Intech Books, Northumberland 203
Island Books, Devon 85
Key Books (Sarah), Cambridgeshire 64
Lucius Books, N Yorks 199
McEwan Fine Books, Grampian 273
St Mary's Books & Prints, Lincolnshire 154
Shakeshaft (Dr. B.), Cheshire 71
Trinity Rare Books, Co. Leitrim 266
Yesterday Tackle & Books, Dorset 92

- WEBB, MARY
R. & A. Books, East Sussex 102
Trinity Rare Books, Co. Leitrim 266
Woodbine Books, W Yorks 246

- WELCH, R.
Fifteenth Century Bookshop (The), East Sussex . 104
Key Books (Sarah), Cambridgeshire 64

- WELLS, H.G.
Antique Map and Bookshop (The), Dorset 94
Brock Books, N Yorks 193
Cox, Andrew, Shropshire 215
Fantastic Literature, Essex 111
Fifteenth Century Bookshop (The), East Sussex . 104
Harrington (Adrian), London W 173
R. & A. Books, East Sussex 102
RGS Books, Surrey 235
Trinity Rare Books, Co. Leitrim 266

- WENDELL HOLMES, OLIVER
Roz Hulse, Conwy 286

- WHARTON, EDITH
Apocalypse, Surrey 233
Meads Book Service (The), East Sussex 104
Norton Books, N Yorks 197

- WHEATLEY, DENNIS
Apocalypse, Surrey 233
Bookstand, Dorset 94
Broadwater Books, Hampshire 125
Cranhurst Books, London 161
Dolphin Books, Suffolk 226
Fifteenth Century Bookshop (The), East Sussex . 104
Heckmondwike Book Shop, W Yorks 249
Lucius Books, N Yorks 199
Orb's Bookshop, Grampian 274

R. & A. Books, East Sussex 102
Surprise Books, Glos 113
Trinity Rare Books, Co. Leitrim 266

- WHITE, GILBERT
Country Books, Derbyshire 82
Fifteenth Century Bookshop (The), East Sussex . 104
Sen Books, Hampshire 127

- WHITE, T.H.
Coch-y-Bonddu Books, Powys 292
Fifteenth Century Bookshop (The), East Sussex . 104
Gildas Books, Cheshire 68
John Underwood Antiquarian Books, Norfolk .. 190
Trinity Rare Books, Co. Leitrim 266

- WHITMAN, W.
R. & A. Books, East Sussex 102
Trinity Rare Books, Co. Leitrim 266

- WILDE, OSCAR
Apocalypse, Surrey 233
Courtwood Books, Co. Laois 266
Cox Rare Books (Charles), Cornwall 74
Fifteenth Century Bookshop (The), East Sussex . 104
Harrington (Adrian), London W 173
Karen Millward, Co. Cork 263
R. & A. Books, East Sussex 102
Trinity Rare Books, Co. Leitrim 266

- WILLIAMS, CHARLES
Booth (Booksearch Service), (Geoff), Cheshire... 68
Rosley Books, Cumbria 81
Trinity Rare Books, Co. Leitrim 266

- WILLIAMS, TENNESSEE
R. & A. Books, East Sussex 102
Trinity Rare Books, Co. Leitrim 266
Tsbbooks, London SW 170

- WILLIAMSON, HENRY
Booth (Booksearch Service), (Geoff), Cheshire... 68
Dolphin Books, Suffolk 226
Fifteenth Century Bookshop (The), East Sussex . 104
Grove Bookshop (The), N Yorks 197
Heppa (Christopher), Essex 108
Island Books, Devon 85
R. & A. Books, East Sussex 102
Tarka Books, Devon 84
Trinity Rare Books, Co. Leitrim 266

- WILSON, COLIN
Apocalypse, Surrey 233
Booth (Booksearch Service), (Geoff), Cheshire... 68
Fifth Element, West Midlands 240
Gildas Books, Cheshire 68
Loretta Lay Books, London NW 162
Star Lord Books, Gr Man 119
Yarwood Rare Books (Edward), Gr Man 118

- WODEHOUSE, P.G.
Bass (Ben), Wiltshire 251
Cranhurst Books, London 161
Fifteenth Century Bookshop (The), East Sussex . 104
Harrington (Adrian), London W 173

SPECIALITY INDEX

Heppa (Christopher), Essex 108
Intech Books, Northumberland 203
Jonkers Rare Books, Oxfordshire 209
Little Stour Books, Kent 137
Lucius Books, N Yorks............................... 199
Mercat Books, Highland 274
N V Books, Warwickshire............................ 237
Not Just Books, Dorset............................... 94
Olynthiacs, Shropshire 214
Orb's Bookshop, Grampian.......................... 274
R. & A. Books, East Sussex 102
Trinity Rare Books, Co. Leitrim 266
Williams Rare Books (Nigel), London WC 180

- WOLFE, THOMAS
Idle Genius Books, London N 159
R. & A. Books, East Sussex 102
Trinity Rare Books, Co. Leitrim 266

- WOODEFORD, PARSON JAMES
Country Books, Derbyshire 82
Fifteenth Century Bookshop (The), East Sussex. 104

- WOOLF, LEONARD
Evans Books (Paul), W Sussex 243
Fifteenth Century Bookshop (The), East Sussex. 104

- WOOLF, VIRGINIA
Bookbox, Glos 116
Booth (Booksearch Service), (Geoff), Cheshire... 68
Bow Windows Book Shop, East Sussex 103
Evans Books (Paul), W Sussex 243
Fifteenth Century Bookshop (The), East Sussex. 104
Foster Bookshop (Paul), London SW 168
Jonkers Rare Books, Oxfordshire 209
Lucius Books, N Yorks............................... 199
Orb's Bookshop, Grampian.......................... 274
R. & A. Books, East Sussex 102
Trinity Rare Books, Co. Leitrim 266
Words Etcetera Bookshop, Dorset.................. 93

- WORDSWORTH, WILLIAM
Alec–Smith Books (Alex), East Yorkshire 107
Apocalypse, Surrey 233
Fifteenth Century Bookshop (The), East Sussex. 104
Island Books, Devon 85
R. & A. Books, East Sussex 102

- YATES, DORNFORD
Book For All Reasons (A.), Suffolk 229
Booth (Booksearch Service), (Geoff), Cheshire... 68
Fifteenth Century Bookshop (The), East Sussex. 104
Heppa (Christopher), Essex 108
Trinity Rare Books, Co. Leitrim 266

- YEATS, W.B.
Apocalypse, Surrey 233
Craobh Rua Books, Co. Armagh 260
Criterion Books, London Outer...................... 182
Read Ireland, Co. Dublin 264
Trinity Rare Books, Co. Leitrim 266

- YEE, CHIANG
Booth (Booksearch Service), (Geoff), Cheshire... 68
Greta Books, Durham 97

- YOUNG, FRANCIS BRETT
Clent Books, Worcestershire 255
Dolphin Books, Suffolk............................... 226
Orb's Bookshop, Grampian.......................... 274
Sedgeberrow Books & Framing, Worcestershire. 256

- ZOLA, EMILE
Apocalypse, Surrey 233
Cranhurst Books, London 161
Trinity Rare Books, Co. Leitrim 266

AUTHORS - AUSTRALIAN
Eggeling Books (John), W Yorks 250

- BRITISH
Booth (Booksearch Service), (Geoff), Cheshire... 68
Cranhurst Books, London 161
Eggeling Books (John), W Yorks 250
Glasheen-Books, Surrey 232
Harvest Books, Lancashire........................... 145
Intech Books, Northumberland 203
R. & A. Books, East Sussex 102
Shakeshaft (Dr. B.), Cheshire 71
Valentine Rare Books, London W.................. 176

- LOCAL
Atholl Fine Books, Tayside 281
Bookpassage (The), Shropshire 213
Colonsay Bookshop, Isle of Colonsay.............. 276
Eggeling Books (John), W Yorks 250
Esoteric Dreams Bookshop, Cumbria 78
Facet Books, Dorset................................... 91
Farquharson, (Hilary), Tayside...................... 281
Fifteenth Century Bookshop (The), East Sussex. 104
hullbooks.com, East Yorkshire 107
Intech Books, Northumberland 203
Joel Segal Books, Devon 86
Just Books, Cornwall 76
MK Book Services, Cambridgeshire 66
The Sanctuary Bookshop, Dorset................... 94

- NATIONAL
Booth (Booksearch Service), (Geoff), Cheshire... 68
Jane Jones Books, Grampian 272
Joel Segal Books, Devon 86

- WOMEN
Al Saqi Books, London W........................... 172
Books & Bygones (Pam Taylor), West Midlands 241
Crawford (Elizabeth), London EC................... 157
dgbbooks, W Sussex 244
Dolphin Books, Suffolk............................... 226
Dylans Bookstore, Swansea 294
Eggeling Books (John), W Yorks 250
Elaine Lonsdale Books, W Yorks................... 248
Esoteric Dreams Bookshop, Cumbria 78
Fifteenth Century Bookshop (The), East Sussex. 104
Hobgoblin Books, Hampshire 125
Intech Books, Northumberland 203
Joel Segal Books, Devon 86
Johnson Rare Book Collections (C.R.),
London NW 162
Kenny's Bookshops and Art Galleries Ltd,
Co. Galway 266
Lane Books (Shirley), Isle of Wight 135

Maghreb Bookshop (The), London WC 178
McCrone (Audrey), Isle of Arran 275
Reading Lasses, Dumfries & Galloway 271
Scrivener's Books & Bookbinding, Derbyshire... 82
Stevens (Joan), Cambridgeshire..................... 65
Susanne Schulz-Falster Rare Books, London N. 160
Symes Books (Naomi), Cheshire 72
Tiger Books, Kent 137
Treasure Trove Books, Leics......................... 148
Tucker (Alan & Joan), Glos 117
Willmott Bookseller (Nicholas), Cardiff........... 283

AUTISM

Westons, Herts 133

AUTOBIOGRAPHY

Abacus Gallery, Staffordshire........................ 224
Addyman Books, Powys.............................. 289
Annie's Books, South Yorkshire 222
Anthony Spranger, Wiltshire......................... 252
Antiques on High, Oxfordshire.................... 209
Archer (Steve), London Outer 181
Bell (Peter), Lothian................................... 276
Beware of the Leopard, Bristol...................... 58
Black Five Books, Shropshire 215
Bob Mallory (Books), Derbyshire................... 83
Book Shelf (The), Devon 87
Bookroom (The), Surrey.............................. 234
Books, Oxfordshire 206
books2books, Devon 88
BOOKS4U, Flintshire................................. 286
Booth (Booksearch Service), (Geoff), Cheshire... 68
Brad Books, Essex..................................... 111
Castleton (Pat), Kent................................. 138
Catalyst Booksearch Services, Devon.............. 87
Chaucer Bookshop, Kent............................. 136
Cheshire Book Centre, Cheshire................ 69
Childrens Bookshop, W Yorks 248
Church Street Books, Norfolk 187
Clements (R.W.), London Outer 182
Clent Books, Worcestershire 255
Cofion Books, Pembrokeshire 288
Cornucopia Books, Lincolnshire 153
Darkwood Books, Co. Cork 263
Discovery Bookshop, Carmarthenshire............ 283
Dolphin Books, Suffolk............................... 226
Ewell Bookshop Ltd, Surrey 232
Family-Favourites, East Yorkshire.................. 106
Fifteenth Century Bookshop (The), East Sussex. 104
firstpagebooks, Norfolk............................... 190
G. C. Books Ltd., Dumfries & Galloway.......... 271
George St. Books, Derbyshire 83
Grahame Thornton, Bookseller, Dorset........... 93
Great Oak Bookshop (The), Powys 292
Hab Books, London W............................... 173
Hurst (Jenny), Kent 138
Jade Mountain Bookshop, Hampshire 126
Joel Segal Books, Devon 86
Karen Millward, Co. Cork 263
Kyrios Books, Nottinghamshire..................... 204
Little Bookshop (The), Gr Man..................... 119
Lyngheath Books, Norfolk........................... 189
Marine and Cannon Books, Cheshire 69
McCrone (Audrey), Isle of Arran 275
MilitaryHistoryBooks.com, Kent................... 138

Moreton Books, Devon............................... 87
Murphy (C.J.), Norfolk............................... 190
Norton Books, N Yorks.............................. 197
Oopalba Books, Cheshire............................ 71
Orb's Bookshop, Grampian......................... 274
Park Gallery & Bookshop (The), Northants 201
Parker Books (Mike), Cambridgeshire 64
Poetry Bookshop (The), Powys..................... 291
Price (R.D.M. & I.M.) (Books), Gr Man......... 120
R. & A. Books, East Sussex 102
Reading Lasses, Dumfries & Galloway 271
Reads, Dorset 95
Richard Thornton Books, London N 160
Roland Books, Kent 139
Rothwell & Dunworth, Somerset 218
Samovar Books, Co. Dublin 264
Sax Books, Suffolk 229
Scrivener's Books & Bookbinding, Derbyshire... 82
SETI Books, Staffordshire........................... 225
Stalagluft Books, Tyne and Wear 236
Sturford Books, Wiltshire 254
Tarka Books, Devon 84
Tiffin (Tony and Gill), Durham 97
Treasure Island (The), Gr Man..................... 119
Trinity Rare Books, Co. Leitrim 266
Uncle Phil's Books, West Midlands 240
Wheen O'Books, Scottish Borders 269
Wiend Books, Lancashire 144
Willmott Bookseller (Nicholas), Cardiff........... 283

AUTOGRAPHS

Baron (H.), London NW 161
Bertram Rota Ltd., London WC 177
Book Business (The), London W 172
Books & Bygones (Pam Taylor), West Midlands 241
Bookshop (The), Norfolk 192
Bookstand, Dorset..................................... 94
Bristow & Garland, Hampshire 122
Chas J. Sawyer, Kent 141
Cox Music (Lisa), Devon............................. 86
Cox Rare Books (Charles), Cornwall............... 74
Davids Ltd., (Roy), Oxfordshire 209
Farahar & Dupre (Clive & Sophie), Wiltshire ... 251
Finch Rare Books Ltd. (Simon), London W..... 173
firstpagebooks, Norfolk............................... 190
Ford (Richard), London W.......................... 173
Franks Booksellers, Gr Man......................... 119
Harrington Antiquarian Bookseller (Peter),
London SW... 169
Ken's Paper Collectables, Buckinghamshire 62
Maggs Brothers Limited, London W 174
Marine & Cannon Books, Cheshire 71
Marine and Cannon Books, Cheshire 69
Modern Firsts Etc, Lancashire 143
Neil Summersgill, Lancashire 143
Rassam (Paul), London NW 162
Silverman (Michael), ... 166
Stevens (Joan), Cambridgeshire..................... 65
Treasure Island (The), Gr Man..................... 119
Trinity Rare Books, Co. Leitrim 266
Wilson (Manuscripts) Ltd., (John), Glos.......... 114

AUTOLITHOGRAPHY

Dolphin Books, Suffolk............................... 226
Temperley (David), West Midlands................. 239

SPECIALITY INDEX

AUTOMATA
Randall (Tom), Somerset 219

AUTOMOBILIA/AUTOMOTIVE
Bob Mallory (Books), Derbyshire 83
Brad Books, Essex 111
Burroughs (Andrew), Lincolnshire 153
Cornucopia Books, Lincolnshire 153
Cowley, Auto-in-Print (John), Essex 108
Falconwood Transport & Military Bookshop,
London Outer 184
Fifteenth Century Bookshop (The), East Sussex. 104
Intech Books, Northumberland 203
J & J Burgess Booksellers, Cambridgeshire 64
Jade Mountain Bookshop, Hampshire 126
Joel Segal Books, Devon 86
McCrone (Audrey), Isle of Arran 275
Morris Secondhand & Antiquarian
Books (Chris), Oxfordshire 210
R. & A. Books, East Sussex 102
Stroh (M.A.), London E 155
Wiend Books, Lancashire 144

AVANT-GARDE
Norton Books, N Yorks 197
R. & A. Books, East Sussex 102
Sclanders (Beatbooks), (Andrew), London EC... 157
Trinity Rare Books, Co. Leitrim 266
Woburn Books, London N 160
Worlds End Bookshop, London SW 171

AVIATION
Addyman Books, Powys 289
All Books, Essex 110
Anchor Books, Lincolnshire 151
Andron (G.W.), London N 158
Anthony Vickers Books, N Yorks 196
Armchair Auctions, Hampshire 121
Askew Books (Vernon), Wiltshire 251
Avedikian Rare Books, Somerset 217
Aviabooks, Glos 114
Aviation Book Supply, Herts 130
Baldwin (M. & M.), Worcestershire 255
Bancroft (David G.), Isle of Wight 134
Barbican Bookshop, N Yorks 198
Barely Read Books, Kent 142
Barnes (Peter), Wiltshire 253
Beware of the Leopard, Bristol 58
Black Five Books, Shropshire 215
Bonner (John), W Yorks 249
Books Afloat, Dorset 96
Books Bought & Sold, Surrey 232
books2books, Devon 88
Bookshelf – Aviation Books, W Sussex 242
Bookshop (The), Norfolk 192
BookShop, The, Dumfries & Galloway 270
Bookworms, Norfolk 187
Booth (Booksearch Service), (Geoff), Cheshire... 68
Bott, (Bookdealers) Ltd., (Martin), Gr Man 118
Brad Books, Essex 111
Brewin Books Ltd., Warwickshire 238
Broadhurst of Southport Ltd., Merseyside 186
Camilla's Bookshop, East Sussex 101
Castle Bookshop, Essex 109
Castleton (Pat), Kent 138

Chelifer Books, Cumbria 81
Cheshire Book Centre, Cheshire 69
Chevin Books, W Yorks 250
Church Street Books, Norfolk 187
Cobbles Books, Somerset 218
Cobweb Books, N Yorks 195
Cocks (Brian), Cambridgeshire 67
Coles (T.V.), Cambridgeshire 67
Cornucopia Books, Lincolnshire 153
Cotswold Internet Books, Glos 113
Coulthurst (Richard), Gr Man 120
Cox (Geoff), Devon 90
D'Arcy Books, Wiltshire 252
Darkwood Books, Co. Cork 263
Duck (William), Hampshire 124
Eastgate Bookshop, East Yorkshire 106
Edwards (London) Limited (Francis),
London WC 177
Ewell Bookshop Ltd, Surrey 232
Falconwood Transport & Military Bookshop,
London Outer 184
Family-Favourites, East Yorkshire 106
Farnborough Gallery, Hampshire 122
Fifteenth Century Bookshop (The), East Sussex. 104
Fine Books Oriental Ltd., London WC 178
Fylde Books, Lancashire 146
Gallimaufry Books, Herts 132
Gaullifmaufry Books, Herts 132
Good for Books, Lincolnshire 151
Grant, Lothian 278
Hall's Bookshop, Kent 141
Harlequin Books, Bristol 59
Harris (George J.), Co. Derry 260
Helion & Company, West Midlands 240
Hornsey's, N Yorks 195
Horsham Rare Books, W Sussex 243
Internet Bookshop UK Ltd., Glos 113
Invicta Bookshop, Berkshire 56
J & J Burgess Booksellers, Cambridgeshire 64
J.B. Books, Berkshire 56
Jade Mountain Bookshop, Hampshire 126
Joel Segal Books, Devon 86
Keegan's Bookshop, Berkshire 56
Keel Row Bookshop, Tyne and Wear 236
Kerr (Norman), Cumbria 78
Lawrence Books, Nottinghamshire 204
Libris (Weston) Books, Somerset 217
Lost Books, Northants 201
Malvern Bookshop (The), Worcestershire 255
Marine & Cannon Books, Cheshire 71
Marine and Cannon Books, Cheshire 69
Meekins Books (Paul), Warwickshire 238
Mercat Books, Highland 274
Milestone Books, Devon 89
Military Parade Bookshop, Wiltshire 252
MilitaryHistoryBooks.com, Kent 138
Morley Case, Hampshire 125
N1 Books, East Sussex 105
Nelson (Elizabeth), Suffolk 227
Phelps (Michael), W Sussex 243
Postings, Surrey 234
Prior (Michael), Lincolnshire 153
R. & A. Books, East Sussex 102
Richmond Books, N Yorks 195
Robert Humm & Co, Lincolnshire 154

SPECIALITY INDEX

Rowan (H. & S.J.), Dorset 91
Scrivener's Books & Bookbinding, Derbyshire... 82
Sedgeberrow Books & Framing, Worcestershire. 256
Smith Maritime Aviation Books (Frank),
Tyne and Wear 236
Soldridge Books Ltd, Hampshire 124
Spooner (John E.), Dorset 91
Stour Bookshop, Dorset 95
Stroh (M.A.), London E 155
Suffolk Rare Books, Suffolk 230
Tarka Books, Devon 84
Thin Read Line, Merseyside 185
Treasure Chest Books, Suffolk 227
Treasure Island (The), Gr Man 119
Vanstone - Aviation Books, (Derek), Suffolk 230
Vickers (Anthony), N Yorks 196
Wadard Books, Kent 138
War & Peace Books, Hampshire 122
Weiner (Graham), London N 160
Westwood Books Ltd, Cumbria 80
Wheen O'Books, Scottish Borders 269
Wiend Books, Lancashire 144
World War Books, Kent 141
Yeoman Books, Lothian 279

AWARD WINNERS

books2books, Devon 88
Bufo Books, Hampshire 125

AYURVEDA

Inner Bookshop (The), Oxfordshire 210
Joel Segal Books, Devon 86

BACTERIOLOGY

Bernard Dixon and Kath Adams, Middlesex 183
Parkinsons Books, Merseyside 186
Phelps (Michael), W Sussex 243
R M Books, Herts 132
Stroh (M.A.), London E 155
Turret House, Norfolk 192
Westons, Herts 133

BAMBOO

Park (Mike), London Outer 183

BANKING & INSURANCE

Abrahams (Mike), Staffordshire 224
Collectables (W.H.), Suffolk 230
Drury Rare Books (John), Essex 110
Prospect House Books, Co. Down 261
Rainford (Sheila), Herts 130
Susanne Schulz-Falster Rare Books, London N. 160

BEAT WRITERS

Addyman Books, Powys 289
Elephant Books, W Yorks 249
Ellis, Bookseller (Peter), London WC 178
Fifth Element, West Midlands 240
Joel Segal Books, Devon 86
Orlando Booksellers, Lincolnshire 152
Poetry Bookshop (The), Powys 291
Price (R.W.), Nottinghamshire 204
Sclanders (Beatbooks), (Andrew), London EC... 157
Trinity Rare Books, Co. Leitrim 266
Woburn Books, London N 160

Words Etcetera Bookshop, Dorset 93
Worlds End Bookshop, London SW 171
Zardoz Books, Wiltshire 254

BEER

Empire Books, N Yorks 198
Joel Segal Books, Devon 86
R. & A. Books, East Sussex 102
Sax Books, Suffolk 229
Stroh (M.A.), London E 155
Thorne (John), Essex 109

BELL-RINGING (CAMPANOLOGY)

Birchden Books, London E 155
Church Green Books, Oxfordshire 211
Country Books, Derbyshire 82
Farringdon (J.M.), Swansea 293
Hadfield (G.K.), Cumbria 80
R. & A. Books, East Sussex 102
Saint Mary's Books & Prints, Lincolnshire 154

BELLE-LETTRES

Apocalypse, Surrey 233
Brian Troath Books, London E 155
Fortune Green Books, London NW 161
Grahame Thornton, Bookseller, Dorset 93
Joel Segal Books, Devon 86
Trinity Rare Books, Co. Leitrim 266

BIBLES

Addyman Books, Powys 289
Ardis Books, Hampshire 126
Barbican Bookshop, N Yorks 198
Bardsley's Books, Suffolk 226
Beckham Books Ltd., Suffolk 230
Bernstein (Nicholas), London W 172
Biblion, London W 172
Bookshop on the Heath, The, London SE 164
Butler Cresswell Rare Books, Buckinghamshire . 61
Chandos Books, Devon 85
Chapter Two, London SE 164
Cobnar Books, Kent 142
Copnal Books, Cheshire 69
Courtenay Bookroom, Oxfordshire 206
Derek Stirling Bookseller, Kent 142
Du Ry Medieval Manuscripts (Marc-Antoine),
London W 173
Fishburn Books, London NW 161
G. C. Books Ltd., Dumfries & Galloway 271
Golden Age Books, Worcestershire 256
Harrington Antiquarian Bookseller (Peter),
London SW 169
Hennessey Bookseller (Ray), East Sussex 100
Hilton (Books) (P.J.), London W 174
Humber Books, Lincolnshire 150
Jade Mountain Bookshop, Hampshire 126
Kirkman Ltd., (Robert), Bedfordshire 54
Oasis Booksearch, Cambridgeshire 67
Paper Moon Books, Glos 116
Pendleburys Bookshop, London N 159
Preston Book Company, Lancashire 145
Prospect House Books, Co. Down 261
R. & A. Books, East Sussex 102
Roscrea Bookshop, Co. Tipperary 267
Rosemary Pugh Books, Wiltshire 253

SPECIALITY INDEX

Rosley Books, Cumbria 81
S.P.C.K., Bristol 60
St Philip's Books, Oxfordshire...................... 210
Samovar Books, Co. Dublin 264
Scrivener's Books & Bookbinding, Derbyshire... 82
Spooner & Co, Somerset 220
Trinity Rare Books, Co. Leitrim 266
Tuft (Patrick), London Outer....................... 182

BIBLICAL STUDIES

Beckham Books Ltd., Suffolk 230
Butler Cresswell Rare Books, Buckinghamshire . 61
Discovery Bookshop, Carmarthenshire............ 283
Dolphin Books, Suffolk............................... 226
Fishburn Books, London NW....................... 161
G. C. Books Ltd., Dumfries & Galloway......... 271
Golden Age Books, Worcestershire 256
Jade Mountain Bookshop, Hampshire 126
Oasis Booksearch, Cambridgeshire................. 67
Parkinsons Books, Merseyside...................... 186
Pendleburys Bookshop, London N 159
PsychoBabel Books & Journals, Oxfordshire..... 206
R. & A. Books, East Sussex 102
S.P.C.K., Bristol 60
St Philip's Books, Oxfordshire...................... 210
Samovar Books, Co. Dublin 264
Spooner & Co, Somerset 220
Walker Fine Books (Steve), Dorset 92

BIBLIOGRAPHY

Alec-Smith Books (Alex), East Yorkshire 107
Andron (G.W.), London N 158
Ash Rare Books, London SW....................... 167
Askew Books (Vernon), Wiltshire.................. 251
Barry McKay Rare Books, Cumbria............... 77
Bettridge (Gordon), Fife............................. 272
Bianco Library, W Sussex........................... 242
Biblion, London W.................................... 172
Bookcase, Cumbria.................................... 78
Brinded (Scott), Kent 139
Broadhurst of Southport Ltd., Merseyside 186
Budd (Richard), Somerset........................... 219
Caledonia Books, Strathclyde....................... 280
Chandos Books, London Outer 183
Chas J. Sawyer, Kent 141
Childrens Bookshop, W Yorks 248
Cooper Hay Rare Books, Strathclyde 280
Cox Old & Rare Books (Claude), Suffolk 228
Dew (Roderick), East Sussex 101
Ford (Richard), London W.......................... 173
Forest Books, Nottinghamshire 205
Fortune Green Books, London NW................ 161
Fotheringham (Alex), Northumberland 202
Grampian Books, Grampian......................... 274
Howes Bookshop, East Sussex 102
Island Books, Devon.................................. 85
Jackson (M.W.), Wiltshire........................... 254
Joel Segal Books, Devon 86
Maggs Brothers Limited, London W.............. 174
Marlborough Rare Books Ltd., London W 174
Mead (P.J.), Shropshire.............................. 214
Mills Rare Books (Adam), Cambridgeshire 64
MK Book Services, Cambridgeshire............... 66
Moorhead Books, W Yorks 246
Mulyan (Don), Merseyside.......................... 186

Muttonchop Manuscripts, W Sussex 244
O'Connor Fine Books, Lancashire................. 145
Parrott (Jeremy), London E......................... 156
Quaritch Ltd., (Bernard), London W.............. 175
Quentin Books Ltd, Essex........................... 109
R. & A. Books, East Sussex 102
RGS Books, Surrey 235
Rivendale Press, Buckinghamshire 62
Seydi Rare Books (Sevin), London NW 162
Smith Books, (Sally), Suffolk 227
Solitaire Books, Somerset............................ 217
Spooner & Co, Somerset 220
Stroh (M.A.), London E 155
Sue Lowell Natural History Books, London W . 176
Susanne Schulz-Falster Rare Books, London N. 160
Taylor & Son (Peter), Herts......................... 133
Taylor Rare Books (Michael), Norfolk 187
The Sanctuary Bookshop, Dorset.................. 94
Thornber (Peter M.), N Yorks 196
Tuft (Patrick), London Outer....................... 182
Unsworth's Booksellers, London WC 163, 180
Unsworths Booksellers, London WC.............. 180
Ventnor Rare Books, Isle of Wight................ 135
Wakeman Books (Frances), Nottinghamshire.... 205
Williams (Bookdealer), (Richard), N Lincs....... 154
Williams (Christopher), Dorset 94
Wykeham Books, London SW 171

BIBLIOPHILY

Budd (Richard), Somerset........................... 219
Cox Old & Rare Books (Claude), Suffolk 228
Ford (Richard), London W.......................... 173
Hilton (Books) (P.J.), London W 174
Jean Hedger, Berkshire 55
Stalagluft Books, Tyne and Wear.................. 236
Stroh (M.A.), London E 155
Thornber (Peter M.), N Yorks 196

BINDINGS

Abacus Gallery, Staffordshire....................... 224
Addyman Annexe (The), Powys.................... 289
Addyman Books, Powys.............................. 289
Allsop (Duncan M.), Warwickshire................ 238
Atholl Fine Books, Tayside 281
Barry McKay Rare Books, Cumbria............... 77
Bates & Hindmarch, W Yorks 249
Baxter (Steve), Surrey 234
Bayntun (George), Somerset 216
Bernstein (Nicholas), London W................... 172
Biblion, London W.................................... 172
Booklore, Leics... 148
Bookshop on the Heath, The, London SE 164
Camilla's Bookshop, East Sussex 101
Chandos Books, Devon............................... 85
Chapter & Verse, Lincolnshire...................... 152
Chas J. Sawyer, Kent 141
Classic Bindings Ltd, London SW 167
Cobnar Books, Kent 142
Cooper Hay Rare Books, Strathclyde............. 280
Courtney & Hoff, N Yorks 198
Cox Old & Rare Books (Claude), Suffolk 228
Cumming Limited (A. & Y.), East Sussex........ 104
David (G.), Cambridgeshire......................... 63
Davis, Antiquarian Books (Guy), Notts 205
de Beaumont (Robin), London SW 167

SPECIALITY INDEX

De Burca Rare Books, Co. Dublin 264
Design Gallery 1850-1950 (The), Kent 142
Eclectica, London SE 165
Edwards (London) Limited (Francis),
London WC 177
Elgar (Raymond), East Sussex...................... 99
Ely Books, Cambridgeshire 65
Eton Antique Bookshop, Berkshire................. 57
Finch Rare Books Ltd. (Simon), London W..... 173
Fine Books at Ilkley, W Yorks..................... 248
Fletcher (H.M.), Herts 132
Forest Books, Notts................................... 205
Foster Bookshop (Paul), London SW............. 168
Fosters Bookshop, London W 173
Frew Limited (Robert), London W................. 173
Garbett Antiquarian Books (Michael), Glos 116
Golden Books Group, Devon 85
Grove Bookshop (The), N Yorks................... 197
Hall's Bookshop, Kent................................ 141
Harrington Antiquarian Bookseller (Peter),
London SW.. 169
Hereward Books, Cambridgeshire.................. 66
Heritage, West Midlands 239
Hodgkins and Company Limited (Ian), Glos 116
Horsham Rare Books, W Sussex................... 243
Howes Bookshop, East Sussex 102
Island Books, Devon.................................. 85
Junk & Spread Eagle, London SE.................. 165
Kay Books, London W............................... 174
Kenny's Bookshops and Art Galleries Ltd, Co.
Galway 266
Kings Bookshop Callander, Central 269
Kirkman Ltd., (Robert), Bedfordshire.............. 54
Liddle (Steve), Bristol 58
Maggs Brothers Limited, London W.............. 174
Mair Wilkes Books, Fife 272
Malvern Bookshop (The), Worcestershire 255
Marlborough Rare Books Ltd., London W...... 174
Maynard & Bradley, Leics 148
McConnell Fine Books, Kent....................... 137
Mead (P.J.), Shropshire.............................. 214
Moore (C.R.), Shropshire 214
Moorhead Books, W Yorks 246
Moorside Books, Lancashire......................... 144
Muttonchop Manuscripts, W Sussex 244
N1 Books, East Sussex 105
Neil Summersgill, Lancashire 143
Offa's Dyke Books, Shropshire..................... 214
Old Town Bookshop (The), Lothian 278
Paper Moon Books, Glos 116
Petworth Antique Market (Bookroom),
W Sussex 244
Poetry Bookshop (The), Powys..................... 291
Pordes Books Ltd., (Henry), London WC........ 179
Quentin Books Ltd, Essex........................... 109
R. & A. Books, East Sussex 102
Red Star Books, Herts................................ 130
Richard Thornton Books, London N.............. 160
Roger Collicott Books, Cornwall 75
Russell (Charles), London SW...................... 170
St Mary's Books & Prints, Lincolnshire 154
Scrivener's Books & Bookbinding, Derbyshire... 82
Seydi Rare Books (Sevin), London NW.......... 162
Sotheran Limited (Henry), London W............ 176
Staniland (Booksellers), Lincolnshire 154

Sterling Books, Somerset 221
Studio (The), Strathclyde 280
Temperley (David), West Midlands................. 239
Thomas (Books) (Leona), Cheshire 71
Thorntons of Oxford Ltd., Oxfordshire 207
Tobo Books, Hampshire.............................. 123
Trinity Rare Books, Co. Leitrim 266
Turton (John), Durham 98
Vandeleur Antiquarian Books, Surrey.............. 232
Ventnor Rare Books, Isle of Wight................. 135
Woodbine Books, W Yorks.......................... 246
Yates Antiquarian Books (Tony), Leics........... 148

BIOCHEMISTRY

Bernard Dixon and Kath Adams, Middlesex 183
Parkinsons Books, Merseyside....................... 186
Phelps (Michael), W Sussex 243
R M Books, Herts..................................... 132
Stroh (M.A.), London E 155
Turret House, Norfolk 192
Westons, Herts 133

BIOGRAPHY

Abacus Gallery, Staffordshire........................ 224
Alexander's Books, Warwickshire................... 238
Anthony Spranger, Wiltshire......................... 252
Antiquary Ltd., (Bar Bookstore), N Yorks....... 196
Antiques on High, Oxfordshire...................... 209
Applin (Malcolm), Berkshire......................... 55
Archer (Steve), London Outer 181
Arden Books & Cosmographia, Warwickshire... 237
Askew Books (Vernon), Wiltshire.................. 251
Aurora Books Ltd, Lothian........................... 276
Baldwin's Scientific Books, Essex 112
Barcombe Services, Essex............................. 108
Bass (Ben), Wiltshire 251
Bell (Peter), Lothian................................... 276
Bianco Library, W Sussex............................ 242
Black Five Books, Shropshire 215
Blythswood Bookshop, Highland 275
Bob Mallory (Books), Derbyshire................... 83
Bonner (John), W Yorks 249
Book Shelf (The), Devon 87
Bookroom (The), Surrey.............................. 234
Books (For All), N Yorks............................. 194
Books Antiques & Collectables, Devon 90
Books For All, N Yorks 194
Books for Writers, Monmouthshire........... 287
books2books, Devon................................... 88
Bookworms, Norfolk................................... 187
Booth (Booksearch Service), (Geoff), Cheshire... 68
Bosco Books, Cornwall................................ 73
Bosorne Books, Cornwall 75
Brad Books, Essex...................................... 111
Brighton Books, East Sussex......................... 99
Brimstones, East Sussex 103
Broadhurst of Southport Ltd., Merseyside 186
Brock Books, N Yorks 193
Caledonia Books, Strathclyde........................ 280
Carnforth Bookshop (The), Lancashire 143
Castleton (Pat), Kent.................................. 138
Catalyst Booksearch Services, Devon.............. 87
Chaucer Bookshop, Kent............................. 136
Childrens Bookshop, W Yorks 248
Church Street Books, Norfolk....................... 187

SPECIALITY INDEX

Classic Bindings Ltd, London SW 167
Clements (R.W.), London Outer 182
Clent Books, Worcestershire 255
Clifford Elmer Books Ltd., Cheshire 68
Cobbles Books, Somerset............................ 218
Cobweb Books, N Yorks............................. 195
Cofion Books, Pembrokeshire 288
Cornucopia Books, Lincolnshire 153
Criterion Books, London Outer 182
Dales & Lakes Book Centre, Cumbria............ 80
Dandy Lion Editions, Surrey 233
Darkwood Books, Co. Cork 263
dgbbooks, W Sussex 244
Discovery Bookshop, Carmarthenshire........... 283
Dolphin Books, Suffolk............................... 226
Doolin Dinghy Books, Co. Clare 262
Eastleach Books, Berkshire........................... 56
Elaine Lonsdale Books, W Yorks.................. 248
Ellis, Bookseller (Peter), London WC 178
Ely Books, Cambridgeshire 65
Esoteric Dreams Bookshop, Cumbria 78
Family-Favourites, East Yorkshire................. 106
Fifteenth Century Bookshop (The), E Sussex 104
Garfi Books, Powys 293
George St. Books, Derbyshire 83
Good for Books, Lincolnshire 151
Graham (John), Dorset 96
Grahame Thornton, Bookseller, Dorset........... 93
Great Hall Bookshop, Buckinghamshire.......... 61
Great Oak Bookshop (The), Powys 292
Green Meadow Books, Cornwall 74
Hab Books, London W............................... 173
Hall's Bookshop, Kent................................ 141
Hawley (C.L.), N Yorks.............................. 197
Heraldry Today, Wiltshire........................... 252
Hilton (Books) (P.J.), London W 174
Hollett and Son (R.F.G.), Cumbria 80
Holmes Books (Harry), East Yorkshire........... 107
Horsham Rare Books, W Sussex................... 243
Hurst (Jenny), Kent 138
Jade Mountain Bookshop, Hampshire 126
Joel Segal Books, Devon 86
Kalligraphia, Isle of Wight 134
Karen Millward, Co. Cork 263
Kingsmere Books, Bedfordshire 53
Little Bookshop (The), Gr Man.................... 119
Little Bookshop (The), Cumbria 81
Lyngheath Books, Norfolk........................... 189
Maggy Browne, Lincolnshire 150
Malvern Bookshop (The), Worcestershire 255
Martin's Books, Powys 292
McCaughtrie (K.A.), N Yorks 194
McCrone (Audrey), Isle of Arran 275
Meads Book Service (The), E Sussex.............. 104
Michael J Carroll, Co. Cork 263
Missing Books, Essex 109
Modlock (Lilian), Dorset............................. 93
Mogul Diamonds, West Midlands.................. 241
Mr. Pickwick of Towcester, Northants............ 201
Murch Booksend, (Herbert), London SE......... 166
Naughton Booksellers, Co. Dublin 265
Nineteenth Century Books, Oxfordshire 211
O'Brien Books & Photo Gallery, Co. Limerick.. 266
O'Donoghue Books, Powys......................... 291
Olynthiacs, Shropshire 214

Oopalba Books, Cheshire............................. 71
Orb's Bookshop, Grampian......................... 274
Paperbacks Plus, Bristol 59
Park Gallery & Bookshop (The), Northants 201
Parrott Books, Oxfordshire 211
Pauline Harries Books, Hampshire 123
Poetry Bookshop (The), Powys.................... 291
Pooks Motor Books, Leics........................... 148
Portobello Books, London W 175
Price (R.D.M. & I.M.) (Books), Gr Man......... 120
Primrose Hill Books, London NW 162
Pringle Booksellers (Andrew), Lothian........... 278
Quentin Books Ltd, Essex........................... 109
R. & A. Books, E Sussex............................. 102
Reading Lasses, Dumfries & Galloway 271
Reads, Dorset 95
Richard Frost Books, Herts.......................... 130
Richmond Books, N Yorks.......................... 195
Rivendale Press, Buckinghamshire................. 62
Roland Books, Kent 139
Roundstone Books, Lancashire..................... 144
Samovar Books, Co. Dublin 264
Saunders (Tom), Caerphilly......................... 283
Shacklock Books (David), Suffolk 227
Shakeshaft (Dr. B.), Cheshire....................... 71
Skoob Russell Square, Suffolk...................... 230
Smith Books, (Sally), Suffolk 227
Stalagluft Books, Tyne and Wear.................. 236
Stern Antiquarian Bookseller (Jeffrey), N Yorks 199
Strathtay Antiquarian - Secondhand Books,
Tayside 282
Stroma Books, Borders 268
Sturford Books, Wiltshire 254
Taylor & Son (Peter), Herts......................... 133
The Sanctuary Bookshop, Dorset.................. 94
Tiffin (Tony and Gill), Durham 97
Tilston (Stephen E.), London SE................... 166
Tombland Bookshop, Norfolk 191
Trevorrow (Edwin), Herts........................... 130
Trinity Rare Books, Co. Leitrim 266
Uncle Phil's Books, West Midlands 240
War & Peace Books, Hampshire................... 122
Wayside Books and Cards, Oxfordshire 207
Whitfield (Ken), Essex 111
Willmott Bookseller (Nicholas), Cardiff........... 283
Words Etcetera Bookshop, Dorset................. 93
Worlds End Bookshop, London SW 171
Yarwood Rare Books (Edward), Gr Man........ 118

BIOLOGY - GENERAL

Alba Books, Grampian 274
Arden, Bookseller (C.), Powys...................... 289
Austwick Hall Books, N Yorks 193
Barcombe Services, Essex............................ 108
Baron - Scientific Book Sales (P.J.), Somerset ... 217
Bernard Dixon and Kath Adams, Middlesex 183
Bracton Books, Cambridgeshire.................... 63
Mogul Diamonds, West Midlands.................. 241
Orb's Bookshop, Grampian......................... 274
Orchid Book Distributors, Co. Clare.............. 262
Parkinsons Books, Merseyside...................... 186
Prospect House Books, Co. Down................. 261
R M Books, Herts..................................... 132
R. & A. Books, E Sussex............................. 102
Smith (David & Lynn), London Outer............ 182

Tarka Books, Devon 84
Transformer, Dumfries & Galloway 271
Turret House, Norfolk 192
Westons, Herts 133
Wyseby House Books, Berkshire 55

- MARINE
Periplus Books, Buckinghamshire 62
Westons, Herts 133

BLACK STUDIES

Afar Books International, West Midlands 239
Black Voices, Merseyside 185
Bookshop (The), Gr Man 118
Empire Books, N Yorks 198
Hylton Booksearch, Merseyside 185
R. & A. Books, E Sussex 102
Reading Lasses, Dumfries & Galloway 271
Spurrier (Nick), Kent 138
Stevens (Joan), Cambridgeshire 65
Woburn Books, London N 160
Yesterday's Books, Dorset 2

BOHEMIANISM

R. & A. Books, E Sussex 102
Trinity Rare Books, Co. Leitrim 266

BOOK ARTS

Alauda Books, Cumbria 78
Barry McKay Rare Books, Cumbria 77
Bertram Rota Ltd., London WC 177
Bruce Holdsworth Books, E Sussex 105
Chalk (Old & Out of Print Books)
(Christine M.), West Midlands 239
Collinge & Clark, London WC 177
Cornucopia Books, Lincolnshire 153
Ford (Richard), London W 173
Jackdaw Books, Norfolk 189
Mannwaring (M.G.), Bristol 59
Naughton Booksellers, Co. Dublin 265
R. & A. Books, E Sussex 102
Solitaire Books, Somerset 217
Stevens (Joan), Cambridgeshire 65
Susanne Schulz-Falster Rare Books, London N. 160
Wykeham Books, London SW 171

BOOK OF HOURS

Addyman Books, Powys 289
Du Ry Medieval Manuscripts (Marc-Antoine),
London W 173
John Underwood Antiquarian Books, Norfolk .. 190
R. & A. Books, E Sussex 102

BOOKBINDING

Alauda Books, Cumbria 78
Andron (G.W.), London N 158
Barry McKay Rare Books, Cumbria 77
Beverley Old Bookshop, East Yorkshire 106
Chandos Books, Devon 85
Chas J. Sawyer, Kent 141
Cheshire Book Centre, Cheshire 69
Coupland (Terry W.), Staffordshire 224
Cox Old & Rare Books (Claude), Suffolk 228
Elgar (Raymond), E Sussex 99
Family-Favourites, East Yorkshire 106

Forest Books, Notts 205
Intech Books, Northumberland 203
Island Books, Devon 85
R. & A. Books, E Sussex 102
Scrivener's Books & Bookbinding, Derbyshire... 82
Spooner & Co, Somerset 220
Stroh (M.A.), London E 155
Sue Lowell Natural History Books, London W. 176
Trinity Rare Books, Co. Leitrim 266
Walker Fine Books (Steve), Dorset 92
Wykeham Books, London SW 171

BOOKS ABOUT BOOKS

Addyman Books, Powys 289
Alec-Smith Books (Alex), East Yorkshire 107
Andron (G.W.), London N 158
Bardsley's Books, Suffolk 226
Bates Books, London Outer 182
Besleys Books, Suffolk 226
Bettridge (Gordon), Fife 272
Biblion, London W 172
Book Palace (The), London SE 164
Bracton Books, Cambridgeshire 63
Brian Troath Books, London E 155
Brinded (Scott), Kent 139
Brock Books, N Yorks 193
Chandos Books, Devon 85
Chapter & Verse, Lincolnshire 152
Collinge & Clark, London WC 177
Cooper Hay Rare Books, Strathclyde 280
Cowley, Bookdealer (K.W.), Somerset 218
Cox Old & Rare Books (Claude), Suffolk 228
Deverell Books, Bristol 59
Eastgate Bookshop, East Yorkshire 106
Family-Favourites, East Yorkshire 106
Ford (Richard), London W 173
Forest Books, Notts 205
Freeman's Corner Shop, Norfolk 190
Glasheen-Books, Surrey 232
Green Meadow Books, Cornwall 74
Hylton Booksearch, Merseyside 185
Island Books, Devon 85
Jean Hedger, Berkshire 55
Joel Segal Books, Devon 86
Malvern Bookshop (The), Worcestershire 255
Mead (P.J.), Shropshire 214
Mills Rare Books (Adam), Cambridgeshire 64
Mr. Pickwick of Towcester, Northants 201
Muttonchop Manuscripts, W Sussex 244
Naughton Booksellers, Co. Dublin 265
Nineteenth Century Books, Oxfordshire 211
Parrott (Jeremy), London E 156
Prospect House Books, Co. Down 261
Quentin Books Ltd, Essex 109
R. & A. Books, E Sussex 102
RGS Books, Surrey 235
Rivendale Press, Buckinghamshire 62
Scott (Peter), E Sussex 104
Seabreeze Books, Lancashire 145
Solitaire Books, Somerset 217
Spooner & Co, Somerset 220
Stroh (M.A.), London E 155
Susanne Schulz-Falster Rare Books, London N. 160
Thomas (Books) (Leona), Cheshire 71
Thornber (Peter M.), N Yorks 196

SPECIALITY INDEX

Trinity Rare Books, Co. Leitrim 266
Unsworth's Booksellers, London WC 163, 180
Updike Rare Books (John), Lothian 279
Wakeman Books (Frances), Notts 205
Walker Fine Books (Steve), Dorset 92
Williams (Bookdealer), (Richard), N Lincs....... 154
Wilson (James), Herts................................. 130
Wykeham Books, London SW 171
Yates Antiquarian Books (Tony), Leics........... 148
Zardoz Books, Wiltshire.............................. 254

BOOKS IN GREEK

Hall's Bookshop, Kent................................ 141
Hellenic Bookservices, London NW............... 162
Joel Segal Books, Devon 86
Kalligraphia, Isle of Wight 134
Seydi Rare Books (Sevin), London NW 162
Thorntons of Oxford Ltd., Oxfordshire........... 207

BOTANY

Alauda Books, Cumbria.............................. 78
Antique Map and Bookshop (The), Dorset 94
Arden, Bookseller (C.), Powys...................... 289
Ashwell Books, Wiltshire............................. 252
Austwick Hall Books, N Yorks...................... 193
Aviabooks, Glos 114
Baldwin's Scientific Books, Essex 112
Baron - Scientific Book Sales (P.J.), Somerset ... 217
Bernard Dixon and Kath Adams, Middlesex 183
Besleys Books, Suffolk 226
Bianco Library, W Sussex............................ 242
Blest (Peter), Kent 139
Brown (Books) (P.R.), Durham..................... 98
Burden Ltd., (Clive A.), Herts...................... 132
Calluna Books, Dorset................................ 95
Camilla's Bookshop, E Sussex...................... 101
Castleton (Pat), Kent................................. 138
Chantrey Books, South Yorkshire 222
Cornucopia Books, Lincolnshire 153
Court Hay Books, West Midlands.................. 240
Dales & Lakes Book Centre, Cumbria............ 80
Dene Barn Books & Prints, Somerset 220
Dolphin Books, Suffolk............................... 226
Goodyer (Nicholas), London N 159
Harrington Antiquarian Bookseller (Peter),
London SW... 169
Hollingshead (Chris), London Outer 183
Inner Bookshop (The), Oxfordshire................ 210
Joel Segal Books, Devon 86
Kalligraphia, Isle of Wight 134
Kennedy (Peter), Surrey 235
Mandalay Bookshop, London SW 169
Mannwaring (M.G.), Bristol 59
Martin's Books, Powys 292
Old Town Bookshop (The), Lothian 278
Orchid Book Distributors, Co. Clare.............. 262
Park (Mike), London Outer.......................... 183
Parkinsons Books, Merseyside...................... 186
Pemberley Books, Buckinghamshire 62
Phelps (Michael), W Sussex 243
Pholiota Books, London WC....................... 179
R. & A. Books, E Sussex............................. 102
Reeves Technical Books, N Yorks.................. 196
Roz Hulse, Conwy 286
Steven Simpson Books, Norfolk 191

Sue Lowell Natural History Books, London W. 176
Summerfield Books Ltd, Cumbria 77
Tant Yn Ellen Books, Powys 293
Thin Read Line, Merseyside 185
Treasure Trove Books, Leics........................ 148
Trinity Rare Books, Co. Leitrim 266
Westons, Herts 133
Woodside Books, Kent 136
Wyseby House Books, Berkshire................... 55

BRAZILIANA

Hodgson (Judith), London W 174
Orssich (Paul), London SW......................... 170

BREWING

Anthony Vickers Books, N Yorks 196
Bernard Dixon and Kath Adams, Middlesex 183
Cornucopia Books, Lincolnshire 153
Country Books, Derbyshire.......................... 82
Joel Segal Books, Devon 86
Lucas (Richard), London NW....................... 162
Past & Present Books, Glos......................... 114
Phelps (Michael), W Sussex 243
R. & A. Books, E Sussex............................. 102
Secondhand Bookshop, The, Kent................. 141
Stroh (M.A.), London E 155
Thorne (John), Essex................................. 109
Vickers (Anthony), N Yorks........................ 196

BRIDGE

Beaver Booksearch, Suffolk 226
Dunstan Books, Dorset............................... 91
Erian Books, London N.............................. 158
Glenbower Books, Co. Dublin 265
Joel Segal Books, Devon 86
R. & A. Books, E Sussex............................. 102
R. S. & P. A. Scowen, Middlesex.................. 182
Reeves Technical Books, N Yorks.................. 196

BRITISH ART & DESIGN

Art Book Company, (The), Suffolk................. 228
Bruce Holdsworth Books, E Sussex 105
Butts Books (Mary), Berkshire 56
Jean Hedger, Berkshire 55
Joel Segal Books, Devon 86
Mannwaring (M.G.), Bristol 59
Nelson (Elizabeth), Suffolk........................... 227
Ouse Valley Books, Bedfordshire 54
Pagan Limited (Hugh), London SW,............... 170
Stevens (Joan), Cambridgeshire.................... 65
Treasure Island (The), Gr Man..................... 119
Trinity Rare Books, Co. Leitrim 266

BRITISH BOOKS

Apocalypse, Surrey 233
Blackwell's Rare Books, Oxfordshire.............. 209
Books at Star Dot Star, West Midlands 241
Burmester (James), Bristol.......................... 59
Cornucopia Books, Lincolnshire 153
Darkwood Books, Co. Cork 263
Gildas Books, Cheshire 68
Joel Segal Books, Devon 86
McCrone (Audrey), Isle of Arran 275
O'Flynn Books, N Yorks............................. 199
Parkinsons Books, Merseyside...................... 186

R. & A. Books, E Sussex............................. 102
Roberts Books, Ayrshire 280
Samovar Books, Co. Dublin......................... 264
Trinity Rare Books, Co. Leitrim 266
Uncle Phil's Books, West Midlands 240
Wheen O'Books, Scottish Borders 269

BROADCASTING

Apocalypse, Surrey 233
Cornucopia Books, Lincolnshire 153
Dolphin Books, Suffolk................................ 226
Empire Books, N Yorks............................... 198
Greenroom Books, W Yorks 248
Joel Segal Books, Devon 86
Kelly Books, Devon.................................... 89
Kent T. G., Surrey 231
Morris Secondhand & Antiquarian
Books (Chris), Oxfordshire........................ 210
R. & A. Books, E Sussex............................. 102
Saintfield Antiques & Fine Books, Co. Down ... 261
Stroh (M.A.), London E 155
Weiner (Graham), London N 160
Wood (Peter), Cambridgeshire...................... 65
Yesterday's News, Conwy............................ 285

BUILDING & CONSTRUCTION

Amwell Book Company, London EC.............. 157
Brown-Studies, Strathclyde.......................... 279
Darkwood Books, Co. Cork 263
Elton Engineering Books, London W 173
Greta Books, Durham 97
Inch's Books, Kent 137
Joel Segal Books, Devon 86
N1 Books, E Sussex.................................... 105
Pagan Limited (Hugh), London SW............... 170
Parkinsons Books, Merseyside...................... 186
Reeves Technical Books, N Yorks.................. 196
Roberts Books, Ayrshire 280
Scrivener's Books & Bookbinding, Derbyshire... 82
Staniland (Booksellers), Lincolnshire 154
Stobart Davies Limited, Carmarthernshire 284
Trinders' Fine Tools, Suffolk 227
Trinity Rare Books, Co. Leitrim 266
Whistler's Books, London SW 170

BULL FIGHTING

Askew Books (Vernon), Wiltshire.................. 251
Books on Spain, London Outer..................... 184
Craobh Rua Books, Co. Armagh................... 260
Orsslch (Paul), London SW.......................... 170
R. & A. Books, E Sussex.............................. 102

BUSES/TRAMS

Addyman Books, Powys.............................. 289
Anvil Books, West Midlands 240
Barbican Bookshop, N Yorks 198
Books at Star Dot Star, West Midlands 241
Booth (Booksearch Service), (Geoff), Cheshire... 68
Bott, (Bookdealers) Ltd., (Martin), Gr Man 118
Broadhurst of Southport Ltd., Merseyside 186
Browse Books, Lancashire 144
Cavern Books, Cheshire 70
Classic Crime Collections, Gr Man................. 119
Coulthurst (Richard), Gr Man 120
Cox (Geoff), Devon 90

Dales & Lakes Book Centre, Cumbria............. 80
Dinnages Transport Publishing, E Sussex 103
Falconwood Transport & Military Bookshop,
London Outer 184
Fifteenth Century Bookshop (The), E Sussex 104
Jade Mountain Bookshop, Hampshire 126
Joel Segal Books, Devon 86
Knowles (John), Norfolk 188
Milestone Books, Devon 89
R. & A. Books, E Sussex.............................. 102
Randall (Tom), Somerset............................. 219
Robert Humm & Co, Lincolnshire 154
Roland Books, Kent 139
Rolling Stock Books, Gr Man....................... 120
Salway Books, Essex 112
Simon Lewis Transport Books, Glos 115
Vintage Motorshop, W Yorks....................... 246
Yesteryear Railwayana, Kent 139

BUSHMEN

Chalmers Hallam (E.), Hampshire 125
Michael Graves-Johnston, London SW 169

BUSINESS STUDIES

Ardis Books, Hampshire 126
Barcombe Services, Essex............................ 108
Boer (Louise), Arthurian Books, Powys 289
Brockwells Booksellers, Lincolnshire 150
Cornucopia Books, Lincolnshire 153
Esoteric Dreams Bookshop, Cumbria 78
Reading Lasses, Dumfries & Galloway 271
Roland Books, Kent 139
Stern Antiquarian Bookseller (Jeffrey), N Yorks 199

BYZANTIUM

Askew Books (Vernon), Wiltshire.................. 251
Bennett & Kerr Books, Oxfordshire................ 206
Caliver Books, Essex 110
Hellenic Bookservices, London NW................ 162
Joel Segal Books, Devon 86
Michael Graves-Johnston, London SW 169
Quest Books, East Yorkshire 107
Samovar Books, Co. Dublin......................... 264
Thorntons of Oxford Ltd., Oxfordshire........... 207
Unsworth's Booksellers, London WC 163, 180
Whitchurch Books Ltd., Cardiff..................... 283

CALLIGRAPHY

Apocalypse, Surrey 233
Barry McKay Rare Books, Cumbria............... 77
Bettridge (Gordon), Fife.............................. 272
Cheshire Book Centre, Cheshire.................... 69
Eastgate Bookshop, East Yorkshire 106
Glacier Books, Tayside 282
Hay Cinema Bookshop Ltd., Powys............... 290
Joel Segal Books, Devon 86
John Underwood Antiquarian Books, Norfolk .. 190
Larkham Books (Patricia), Glos..................... 117
Print Matters, London SE............................ 166
R. & A. Books, E Sussex.............................. 102
Scrivener's Books & Bookbinding, Derbyshire... 82
Susanne Schulz-Falster Rare Books, London N. 160
Taylor Rare Books (Michael), Norfolk 187
Treasure Island (The), Gr Man...................... 119
Whittle, Bookseller (Avril), Cumbria 81

SPECIALITY INDEX

Young (D. & J.), Powys 293

CANADIANA

McEwan Fine Books, Grampian.................... 273
Preston Book Company, Lancashire 145
Whistler (R.A.), E Sussex 99
Yesterday's News, Conwy 285

CANALS/INLAND WATERWAYS

Abrahams (Mike), Staffordshire.................... 224
Addyman Books, Powys.............................. 289
Al Saqi Books, London W........................... 172
Anchor Books, Lincolnshire 151
Anthony Vickers Books, N Yorks 196
Anvil Books, West Midlands 240
Archer (Steve), London Outer...................... 181
Arden Books & Cosmographia, Warwickshire... 237
Baldwin (M. & M.), Worcestershire 255
Barbican Bookshop, N Yorks 198
Bianco Library, W Sussex........................... 242
Bird Books (Nigel), Ceredigion..................... 284
Books Afloat, Dorset................................. 96
BookShop, The, Dumfries & Galloway........... 270
Bott, (Bookdealers) Ltd., (Martin), Gr Man 118
Cavern Books, Cheshire 70
Cheshire Book Centre, Cheshire.................... 69
Classic Crime Collections, Gr Man................ 119
Cornucopia Books, Lincolnshire 153
Cottage Books, Leics................................. 147
Coulthurst (Richard), Gr Man 120
Country Books, Derbyshire 82
Cox (Geoff), Devon 90
Crosby Nethercott Books, London Outer 181
Dales and Lakes Book Centre, Cumbria.......... 80
Duck (William), Hampshire......................... 124
Eastcote Bookshop (The), London Outer......... 181
Fifteenth Century Bookshop (The), E Sussex 104
Fine Books Oriental Ltd., London WC........... 178
Hennessey Bookseller (Ray), E Sussex 100
Henry Wilson Books, Cheshire 69
Island Books, Devon 85
Jade Mountain Bookshop, Hampshire 126
Joel Segal Books, Devon 86
K.S.C. Books, Cheshire.............................. 71
Keith Langford, London E 155
Kerr (Norman), Cumbria 78
Lewcock (John), Cambridgeshire................... 66
Marcet Books, London SE...... 165
Nevis Railway Bookshops (The Antique &
Book Collector), Wiltshire.......................... 252
Nicolas - Antiquarian Booksellers & Art
Dealers, London N 159
R. & A. Books, E Sussex............................ 102
Roadmaster Books, Kent............................ 137
Robert Humm & Co, Lincolnshire 154
Rochdale Book Company, Gr Man 120
Rolling Stock Books, Gr Man...................... 120
Salway Books, Essex 112
Scrivener's Books & Bookbinding, Derbyshire... 82
Skyrack Books, W Yorks 248
Tony Pollastrone Railway Books, Wiltshire...... 251
Trinity Rare Books, Co. Leitrim 266
Vickers (Anthony), N Yorks........................ 196
Winchester Bookshop (The), Hampshire.......... 127

CARICATURE

Apocalypse, Surrey 233
Batterham (David), London W..................... 172
Hogan (F. & J.), London N 159
Joel Segal Books, Devon 86
Keith Langford, London E 155
N1 Books, E Sussex.................................. 105
Tooley, Adams & Co, Oxfordshire 211
Trinity Rare Books, Co. Leitrim 266

CARPETS

Abington Bookshop, Suffolk........................ 228
Apocalypse, Surrey 233
Barmby (C. & A.J.), Kent........................... 141
Byrom Textile Bookroom (Richard), Lancashire 143
Don Kelly Books, London W 172
Heneage Art Books (Thomas), London SW 169
Joel Segal Books, Devon 86
Judith Mansfield, W Yorks 250
Potterton Books, N Yorks 197
Stroh (M.A.), London E 155
Trinders' Fine Tools, Suffolk 227

CARRIAGES & DRIVING

Country Books, Derbyshire 82
Joel Segal Books, Devon 86
Keeble Antiques, Somerset 219
Pennymead Books, N Yorks........................ 194
Phenotype Books, Cumbria 80
R. & A. Books, E Sussex............................ 102
Stroh (M.A.), London E 155

CARTOGRAPHY

Alauda Books, Cumbria.............................. 78
Anthony Vickers Books, N Yorks 196
Archer (David), Powys............................... 292
Bannister (David), Glos.............................. 113
Booth (Booksearch Service), (Geoff), Cheshire... 68
Burden Ltd., (Clive A.), Herts...................... 132
Chas J. Sawyer, Kent 141
Frew Limited (Robert), London W................ 173
Heritage, West Midlands 239
Hogan (F. & J.), London N 159
InterCol London, London N 159
Joel Segal Books, Devon 86
Marcet Books, London SE.......................... 165
O'Flynn Books, N Yorks............................ 199
Paralos Ltd., London WC 178
Shapero Rare Books (Bernard J.), London W... 175
Stalagluft Books, Tyne and Wear.................. 236
Taney Books, Co. Dublin 264
Tooley, Adams & Co, Oxfordshire 211
Vickers (Anthony), N Yorks........................ 196

CARTOONS

Apocalypse, Surrey 233
Book Palace (The), London SE 164
Cheshire Book Centre, Cheshire.................... 69
D. & M. Books, W Yorks 250
Dales & Lakes Book Centre, Cumbria............ 80
Facet Books, Dorset.................................. 91
Fine Books Oriental Ltd., London WC........... 178
Goldman (Paul), Dorset 94
Jade Mountain Bookshop, Hampshire 126
Joel Segal Books, Devon 86

SPECIALITY INDEX

Longden (George), Cheshire 70
N1 Books, E Sussex................................... 105
R. & A. Books, E Sussex............................. 102
Wright (Norman), Dorset 95

CATALOGUES RAISONNÉ

Apocalypse, Surrey 233
Ars Artis, Oxfordshire 209
Art Book Company, (The), Suffolk................. 228
Barlow (Vincent G.), Hampshire.................... 125
Book Palace (The), London SE 164
Facet Books, Dorset................................... 91
Heneage Art Books (Thomas), London SW 169
Old Town Bookshop (The), Lothian 278
Reeves Technical Books, N Yorks.................. 196
Studio Bookshop, E Sussex 100

CATERING & HOTEL MANAGEMENT

Gardener & Cook, London SW..................... 168

CATS

Annie's Books, South Yorkshire 222
Archivist (The), Devon........................... 90
Bookline, Co. Down 261
Brad Books, Essex..................................... 111
Castleton (Pat), Kent.................................. 138
Cat Lit, Somerset 219
Cheshire Book Centre, Cheshire.................... 69
Cornucopia Books, Lincolnshire 153
Dales & Lakes Book Centre, Cumbria............ 80
Fifteenth Century Bookshop (The), E Sussex 104
Green Meadow Books, Cornwall 74
Jade Mountain Bookshop, Hampshire 126
Joel Segal Books, Devon 86
Mayhew (Veronica), Berkshire....................... 57
Ming Books, Dumfries & Galloway................ 271
Old Station Pottery & Bookshop (The), Norfolk 192
R. & A. Books, E Sussex............................. 102
Roland Books, Kent 139
St Swithin's Illustrated & Children's Books, London
W........... 175
Stella Books, Monmouthshire 288
Tarka Books, Devon................................... 4

CATTLEMEN

Americanabooksuk, Cumbria........................ 77
Country Books, Derbyshire 82
Hodgson (Books) (Richard J.), N Yorks 198
Phenotype Books, Cumbria 80

CELTICA

Addyman Books, Powys,. 289
Atlantis Bookshop, London WC.................... 177
Byre Books, Dumfries & Galloway................. 270
Colin Hancock, Ceredigion 284
Colonsay Bookshop, Isle of Colonsay............. 276
Ellwood Editions, Wiltshire 253
Gildas Books, Cheshire 68
Hyland (C.P.), Co. Cork 263
Joel Segal Books, Devon 86
McCrone (Audrey), Isle of Arran 275
Michael J Carroll, Co. Cork 263
Old Celtic Bookshop (The), Devon 88
Orb's Bookshop, Grampian.......................... 274
PsychoBabel Books & Journals, Oxfordshire..... 206

R. & A. Books, E Sussex............................. 102
Trinity Rare Books, Co. Leitrim 266

CEMETERIES

Birchden Books, London E 155
Joel Segal Books, Devon 86
Orb's Bookshop, Grampian.......................... 274
R. & A. Books, E Sussex............................. 102

CENSORSHIP

R. & A. Books, E Sussex............................. 102
Susanne Schulz-Falster Rare Books, London N. 160

CERAMICS

Abacus Gallery, Staffordshire........................ 224
Addyman Books, Powys.............................. 289
Anthony Vickers Books, N Yorks 196
Art Reference Books, Hampshire 125
Aviabooks, Glos 114
Axe Rare & Out of Print Books (Richard),
N Yorks........... 194
Barnby (C. & A.J.), Kent............................ 141
Bookroom (The), Surrey............................. 234
Brad Books, Essex..................................... 111
Bruce Holdsworth Books, E Sussex 105
Clark (Nigel A.), London SE 165
Cornucopia Books, Lincolnshire 153
Cover to Cover, Merseyside.......................... 186
Heneage Art Books (Thomas), London SW 169
Ives Bookseller (John), London Outer 184
Joel Segal Books, Devon 86
McEwan Fine Books, Grampian.................... 273
Milestone Publications Goss & Crested China,
Hampshire 123
Moss Books, London NW 162
Nelson (Elizabeth), Suffolk 227
Potterton Books, N Yorks 197
R. & A. Books, E Sussex............................. 102
Reference Works Ltd., Dorset....................... 95
Silver Trees Books, West Midlands................. 240
Stroh (M.A.), London E 155
Uncle Phil's Books, West Midlands 240

CHARITY

Cornucopia Books, Lincolnshire 153
R. & A. Books, E Sussex............................. 102
Reading Lasses, Dumfries & Galloway 271

CHEMISTRY

Barcombe Services, Essex............................. 108
Baron - Scientific Book Sales (P.J.), Somerset ... 217
Bernard Dixon and Kath Adams, Middlesex 183
Dean Byass, Bristol.................................... 60
Glenbower Books, Co. Dublin 265
Parkinsons Books, Merseyside....................... 186
Phelps (Michael), W Sussex 243
Pickering & Chatto, London W..................... 175
R. & A. Books, E Sussex............................. 102
Stroh (M.A.), London E 155
Transformer, Dumfries & Galloway 271
Turret House, Norfolk................................. 192
Weiner (Graham), London N 160
Westons, Herts 133
Westwood Books Ltd, Cumbria..................... 80

SPECIALITY INDEX

CHESS

Addyman Books, Powys.............................. 289
Barcombe Services, Essex............................ 108
Bowers Chess Suppliers (Francis), Cambs 67
Caissa Books, Surrey.................................. 234
Cheshire Book Centre, Cheshire.................... 69
Glenbower Books, Co. Dublin 265
Joel Segal Books, Devon 86
Peterson (Tony), Essex................................ 111
R. & A. Books, E Sussex............................. 102
R. S. & P. A. Scowen, Middlesex 182
Roger Treglown, Cheshire........................... 70
Saunders (Tom), Caerphilly......................... 283
Scrivener's Books & Bookbinding, Derbyshire... 82
Uncle Phil's Books, West Midlands 240
Westwood Books Ltd, Cumbria..................... 80
Whistler's Books, London SW 170
Yates Antiquarian Books (Tony), Leics........... 148

CHILDREN'S - GENERAL

A. & R. Booksearch, Cornwall...................... 74
AA1 Books, Dumfries & Galloway................. 270
Abrahams (Mike), Staffordshire 224
Addyman Books, Powys.............................. 289
Alexander's Books, Warwickshire.................. 238
Allinson (Frank & Stella), Warwickshire 237
Altshuler (Jean), Cumbria 79
Ampersand Books, Shropshire...................... 213
Andrew Morton (Books), Powys.................... 289
Annie's Books, South Yorkshire 222
Anthony Whittaker, Kent............................ 136
Antiques on High, Oxfordshire..................... 209
Anwoth Books Ltd, Dumfries & Galloway 270
Apocalypse, Surrey.................................... 233
Arden Books & Cosmographia, Warwickshire... 237
Armitage (Booksearch), (Kate), Devon 85
Assinder Books, Essex 110
Aucott & Thomas, Leics.............................. 147
Aurora Books Ltd, Lothian........................... 276
Autolycus, Shropshire................................. 213
Badger Books, Somerset.............................. 220
Baker - Books for the Collector (Colin), Devon. 90
Barely Read Books, Kent 142
Barter Books, Northumberland 202
Bates Books, London Outer 182
Bayntun (George), Somerset 216
Beck (John), E Sussex................................. 103
Beverley Old Bookshop, East Yorkshire.......... 106
Biblion, London W........... 172
Biblipola, London NW 161
Bilski (Gill), Buckinghamshire 61
Black Cat Bookshop, Leics 147
Black Five Books, Shropshire 215
Blacket Books, Lothian................................ 277
Book Business (The), London W 172
Book House (The), Cumbria......................... 77
Book Palace (The), London SE 164
Bookbarrow, Cambs 63
Bookline, Co. Down 261
Bookmark (Children's Books), Wiltshire.......... 253
Bookroom (The), Surrey.............................. 234
Books & Collectables Ltd., Cambs 63
Books (For All), N Yorks............................. 194
Books Antiques & Collectables, Devon........... 90
Books Bought & Sold, Surrey 232

Books For All, N Yorks 194
books2books, Devon.................................. 88
Bookseller (The), Cumbria 80
Bookshop at the Plain, Lincolnshire............... 151
Bookshop on the Heath, The, London SE 164
Bookworm, Essex...................................... 110
Bookworms, Norfolk.................................. 187
Booth Books, Powys 289
Border Bookshop, W Yorks 250
Boris Books, Hampshire.............................. 126
Brazenhead Ltd., Norfolk 189
Bridport Old Books, Dorset 92
Bright (P.G.), Cambs.................................. 65
Brighton Books, E Sussex 99
Broadhurst of Southport Ltd.,
Merseyside 186
Broadleaf Books, Torfaen 294
Browning Books, Torfaen 294
Bryony Books, W Yorks 249
Bufo Books, Hampshire 125
Butts Books (Mary), Berkshire 56
Byre Books, Dumfries & Galloway................. 270
Camilla's Bookshop, E Sussex...................... 101
Canterbury Bookshop (The), Kent 136
Castleton (Pat), Kent.................................. 138
Catalyst Booksearch Services, Devon.............. 87
Chandos Books, Devon............................... 85
Chapter Two, London SE............................ 164
Children's Bookshop (The), Powys 289
Childrens Bookshop, W Yorks...................... 248
Churchgate Books, Suffolk........................... 227
Clear (Mrs. Patricia), Surrey........................ 231
Clements (R.W.), London Outer................... 182
Cobweb Books, N Yorks............................. 195
Collectables (W.H.), Suffolk 230
Copnal Books, Cheshire 69
Cornell Books, Glos................................... 117
Cotswold Internet Books, Glos..................... 113
Countrymans Gallery (The), Leics 147
Coupland (Terry W.), Staffordshire................ 224
Cranhurst Books, London 161
Cygnet Books, East Yorkshire....................... 107
D'Arcy Books, Wiltshire.............................. 252
D. & M. Books, W Yorks 250
Dales & Lakes Book Centre, Cumbria............ 80
Dandy Lion Editions, Surrey 233
David (G.), Cambs 63
David Flint, Hampshire 124
Dean Illustrated Books (Myra), Powys 288
Deverell Books, Bristol 59
Doolin Dinghy Books, Co. Clare 262
Doorbar (P. & D.), Gwynedd........................ 287
Dormouse Bookshop (The), Norfolk 190
Draca Books, W Yorks................................ 249
Drummond Pleasures of Past Times (David),
London WC 177
Eastcote Bookshop (The), London Outer......... 181
Ellis, Bookseller (Peter), London WC 178
Everett (Richard), Norfolk........................... 188
Everett (Richard, at the Southwold
Antiques Centre, Suffolk........................... 229
Ewell Bookshop Ltd, Surrey........................ 232
Facet Books, Dorset................................... 91
Fackley Services, Notts 205
Ferguson (Elizabeth), Grampian 272

SPECIALITY INDEX

Fifteenth Century Bookshop (The), E Sussex 104
Firecatcher Books, Gr Man......................... 118
First State Books, London W 173
firstpagebooks, Norfolk.............................. 190
Firsts in Print, Isle of Wight 134
Ford Books (David), Herts 133
Foster Bookshop (Paul), London SW............. 168
Fosters Bookshop, London W 173
Franks Booksellers, Gr Man........................ 119
Freya Books & Antiques, Norfolk.................. 191
Furneaux Books (Lee), Devon...................... 89
Game Advice, Oxfordshire 210
Gander, (Jacques), Glos 115
Garfi Books, Powys 293
Gemini–Books, Shropshire 215
George St. Books, Derbyshire 83
Gloucester Road Bookshop, London SW 168
Good Books, Shropshire 214
Good for Books, Lincolnshire 151
Grahame Thornton, Bookseller, Dorset........... 93
Grange Old Bookshop, Merseyside............... 185
Green Meadow Books, Cornwall 71
Greer (Robin), London SW......................... 168
Hall's Bookshop, Kent............................... 141
Hambleton Books, N Yorks 197
Hancock (Peter), W Sussex......................... 243
Harrington (Adrian), London W.................... 173
Harrington Antiquarian Bookseller (Peter),
London SW... 169
Harvest Books, Lancashire.......................... 145
Hawley (C.L.), N Yorks............................. 197
HCB Wholesale, Powys.............................. 290
Heppa (Christopher), Essex 108
Heywood Hill Limited (G.), London W 174
Hodgkins and Company Limited (Ian), Glos 116
Hollett and Son (R.F.G.), Cumbria 80
Holtom (Christopher), Cornwall 75
Hornsey's, N Yorks 195
Hurly Burly Books, Wiltshire....................... 254
Hurst (Jenny), Kent 138
Hylton Booksearch, Merseyside................... 185
Innes Books, Shropshire............................. 214
Intech Books, Northumberland 203
Internet Bookshop UK Ltd., Gloucestershire 113
Jackson (M.W.), Wiltshire........................... 254
Jade Mountain Bookshop, Hampshire 126
Jane Badger Books, Northants 200
Jane Jones Books, Grampian 272
JB Books & Collectables, W Sussex 244
Jean Hedger, Berkshire 55
Joel Segal Books, Devon 86
John Underwood Antiquarian Books, Norfolk .. 190
Jolly Good Read (A.), Tayside 281
Jonkers Rare Books, Oxfordshire.................. 209
Junk & Spread Eagle, London SE.................. 165
K Books, Cheshire..................................... 70
Kalligraphia, Isle of Wight 134
Karen Millward, Co. Cork........................... 263
Katnap Arts, Norfolk................................. 191
Keel Row Bookshop, Tyne and Wear 236
Kellow Books, Oxfordshire 207
Keswick Bookshop, Cumbria 79
Kevin S. Ogilvie Modern First Editions,
Grampian 273
Key Books (Sarah), Cambs 64

Kineton Nooks, Warwickshire....................... 237
Kirkpatrick (Robert J.), London W 174
Lake (David), Norfolk 191
Leabeck Books, Oxfordshire........................ 210
Leaf Ends, Northumberland 203
Little Stour Books, Kent 137
Lloyd-Davies (Sue), Carmarthenshire 284
Lucius Books, N Yorks............................... 199
Macbuiks, N Yorks 194
Mainly Fiction, Cheshire 68
Malvern Bookshop (The), Worcestershire 255
March House Books, Dorset 95
Marchpane, London WC............................. 178
Mason (Mary), Oxfordshire......................... 206
McCrone (Audrey), Isle of Arran................... 275
McNaughtan's Bookshop, Lothian 278
Meads Book Service (The), E Sussex.............. 104
Mellon's Books, E Sussex 101
Minster Gate Bookshop, N Yorks.................. 199
Modlock (Lilian), Dorset 93
Moorhead Books, W Yorks 246
Much Ado Books, E Sussex 99
Murphy (C.J.), Norfolk.............................. 190
New Strand Bookshop (The), Herefordshire 128
Old Celtic Bookshop (The), Devon................ 88
Old Hall Bookshop (The), Northants 200
Old Station Pottery & Bookshop (The), Norfolk 192
Old Town Bookshop (The), Lothian 278
Oopalba Books, Cheshire............................ 71
Oxfam Books and Music, Hampshire............. 126
Paperbacks Plus, Bristol 59
Park Gallery & Bookshop (The), Northants 201
Parrott Books, Oxfordshire 211
Peakirk Books, Cambs............................... 67
Peter Lyons Books, Gloucestershire 114
Peter's Bookshop, Norfolk 192
Pickering Bookshop, N Yorks...................... 197
Pomes Penyeach, Staffordshire 224
Porcupine Books, London Outer................... 182
Price (R.W.), Notts................................... 204
Priestpopple Books, Northumberland............. 202
Pyecroft (Ruth), Gloucestershire 117
R. & A. Books, E Sussex............................ 102
Richard Thornton Books, London N 160
Rickaro Books, W Yorks 247
Ripping Yarns, London N 160
River Reads Bookshop, Devon..................... 90
Roberts Fine Books (Julian), Lincolnshire........ 153
Robertson Books, Lothian 278
Rochdale Book Company, Gr Man 120
Roe and Moore, London WC....................... 179
Roland Books, Kent 139
Roscrea Bookshop, Co. Tipperary................. 267
Rose's Books, Powys................................. 291
Ross & Company Ltd., (Louise), Worcestershire 255
Roundstone Books, Lancashire..................... 144
Rowan House Books, Surrey 232
Rye Old Books, E Sussex 104
Ryeland Books, Northants.......................... 200
St Mary's Books & Prints, Lincolnshire 154
St Swithin's Illustrated & Children's Books,
London W 175
Saintfield Antiques & Fine Books, Co. Down ... 261
Saunders (Tom), Caerphilly......................... 283
Savage (Keith A.), Suffolk 229

SPECIALITY INDEX

Schutte (David), Hampshire......................... 124
Scrivener's Books & Bookbinding, Derbyshire... 82
Seabreeze Books, Lancashire........................ 145
Second Edition, Lothian.............................. 278
Sesemann (Julia), Kent............................... 136
Shakeshaft (Dr. B.), Cheshire....................... 71
Sharpe (Mary), Somerset 221
Shelley (E. & J.), Buckinghamshire 61
Sillan Books, Co. Cavan.............................. 262
Silver Trees Books, West Midlands................. 240
Simpson (Dave), Stirlingshire 269
Sims (Sue), Dorset..................................... 91
Sleepy Elephant Books & Artefacts, Cumbria ... 80
Smith Books, (Sally), Suffolk 227
Sotheran Limited (Henry), London W 176
Staffs Bookshop (The), Staffordshire 224
Stansbury (Rosemary), Devon....................... 89
Stella Books, Monmouthshire 288
Stepping Stones Bookshop, N Yorks.............. 194
Stinton (Judith), Dorset.............................. 92
Stothert Old Books, Cheshire........................ 69
Strathtay Antiquarian - Secondhand Books,
Tayside 282
Stroma Books, Borders 268
Surprise Books, Gloucestershire 113
Tant Yn Ellen Books, Powys 293
Tarka Books, Devon 84
The Old Abbey Bookshop, Co. Down 261
The Old Children's Bookshelf, Lothian 278
Tiffin (Tony and Gill), Durham 97
Till's Bookshop, Lothian 279
TP Children's Bookshop, W Yorks................. 246
Trafalgar Bookshop, E Sussex....................... 100
Transformer, Dumfries & Galloway 271
Treasure Trove Books, Leics......................... 148
Trinity Rare Books, Co. Leitrim 266
Tucker (Alan & Joan), Gloucestershire 117
Uncle Phil's Books, West Midlands 240
Updike Rare Books (John), Lothian 279
Wadard Books, Kent 138
Westwood Books Ltd, Cumbria..................... 80
Wheen O'Books, Scottish Borders 269
Wilbraham (J. & S.), London NW 163
Words Etcetera Bookshop, Dorset.................. 93
Wright (Norman), Dorset 95
Wychwood Books, Gloucestershire 116
Xanadu Books, Cleveland 98
Yorkshire Relics, W Yorks........................... 247

- EARLY TITLES

Addyman Books, Powys.............................. 289
Autolycus, Shropshire................................. 213
Barter Books, Northumberland 202
Biblipola, London NW 161
Blackwell's Rare Books, Oxfordshire.............. 209
Bookmark (Children's Books), Wiltshire.......... 253
Books For All, N Yorks 194
Castleton (Pat), Kent.................................. 138
Children's Bookshop (The), Powys 289
Cox Old & Rare Books (Claude), Suffolk 228
Cygnet Books, East Yorkshire....................... 107
David Flint, Hampshire 124
Embleton (Paul), Essex 111
Facet Books, Dorset................................... 91
Ferguson (Elizabeth), Grampian 272

Glenbower Books, Co. Dublin 265
Grange Old Bookshop, Merseyside 185
JB Books & Collectables, W Sussex 244
Jean Hedger, Berkshire 55
Joel Segal Books, Devon 86
Lake (David), Norfolk 191
March House Books, Dorset 95
McCrone (Audrey), Isle of Arran 275
Mercat Books, Highland 274
Minster Gate Bookshop, N Yorks.................. 199
Old Celtic Bookshop (The), Devon 88
Oopalba Books, Cheshire............................. 71
R. & A. Books, E Sussex............................. 102
Roberts Fine Books (Julian), Lincolnshire........ 153
Scrivener's Books & Bookbinding, Derbyshire... 82
Seydi Rare Books (Sevin), London NW 162
Smith Books, (Sally), Suffolk 227
Stella Books, Monmouthshire 288
Talisman Books, Cheshire............................ 70
Tiffin (Tony and Gill), Durham 97
Uncle Phil's Books, West Midlands 240
Wadard Books, Kent 138
Wheen O'Books, Scottish Borders 269
Yates Antiquarian Books (Tony), Leics........... 148

- ILLUSTRATED

A. & R. Booksearch, Cornwall...................... 74
Addyman Books, Powys.............................. 289
Allinson (Frank & Stella), Warwickshire 237
Ampersand Books, Shropshire....................... 213
Amwell Book Company, London EC.............. 157
Apocalypse, Surrey 233
Art Reference Books, Hampshire 125
Autolycus, Shropshire................................. 213
Baker - Books for the Collector (Colin), Devon. 90
Barely Read Books, Kent 142
Barlow (Vincent G.), Hampshire.................... 125
Bates Books, London Outer 182
Bath Old Books, Somerset 216
Bayntun (George), Somerset 216
Biblipola, London NW 161
Birmingham Books, West Midlands 239
Blackwell's Rare Books, Oxfordshire.............. 209
Book Palace (The), London SE 164
Bookmark (Children's Books), Wiltshire.......... 253
Books & Things, London W......................... 172
Books For All, N Yorks 194
books2books, Devon 88
BOOKS4U, Flintshire................................. 286
Bookseller (The), Cumbria 80
Bow Windows Book Shop, E Sussex............... 103
Bridport Old Books, Dorset 92
Brock Books, N Yorks 193
Browning Books, Torfaen 294
Camilla's Bookshop, E Sussex....................... 101
Castleton (Pat), Kent.................................. 138
Chalk (Old & Out of Print Books)
(Christine M.), West Midlands 239
Children's Bookshop (The), Powys 289
Chris Phillips, Wiltshire............................... 251
Cobweb Books, N Yorks.............................. 195
Cooper Hay Rare Books, Strathclyde.............. 280
Cox Old & Rare Books (Claude), Suffolk 228
Cox, Andrew, Shropshire............................. 215
Cygnet Books, East Yorkshire....................... 107

SPECIALITY INDEX

D. & M. Books, W Yorks 250
Dales & Lakes Book Centre, Cumbria............ 80
Dandy Lion Editions, Surrey 233
Deverell Books, Bristol 59
Doorbar (P. & D.), Gwyned........................ 287
Eastwood Books (David), Cornwall 73
Embleton (Paul), Essex 111
Ewell Bookshop Ltd, Surrey........................ 232
Facet Books, Dorset................................... 91
Ferguson (Elizabeth), Grampian 272
Fifteenth Century Bookshop (The), E Sussex 104
Fine Books at Ilkley, W Yorks..................... 248
Firecatcher Books, Gr Man......................... 118
Foster Bookshop (Paul), London SW............. 168
Fosters Bookshop, London W 173
Green Meadow Books, Cornwall 74
Greer (Robin), London SW......................... 168
Hennessey Bookseller (Ray), E Sussex 100
Hurly Burly Books, Wiltshire....................... 254
Ian Briddon, Derbyshire............................. 82
Intech Books, Northumberland 203
Jackson (M.W.), Wiltshire.............. 254
Jane Jones Books, Grampian 272
JB Books & Collectables, W Sussex 244
Jean Hedger, Berkshire 55
Joel Segal Books, Devon 86
John Underwood Antiquarian Books, Norfolk .. 190
Jonkers Rare Books, Oxfordshire.................. 209
Junk & Spread Eagle, London SE................. 165
Kernaghans, Merseyside 186
Kineton Nooks, Warwickshire....................... 237
Lake (David), Norfolk 191
Lloyd-Davies (Sue), Carmarthenshire 284
Lucius Books, N Yorks............................... 199
Lymelight Books & Prints, Dorset................. 93
Macbuiks, N Yorks 194
Mannwaring (M.G.), Bristol 59
March House Books, Dorset 95
McCrone (Audrey), Isle of Arran................... 275
Minster Gate Bookshop, N Yorks.................. 199
N1 Books, E Sussex................................... 105
Old Celtic Bookshop (The), Devon................ 88
Oopalba Books, Cheshire............................ 71
Peakirk Books, Cambs............................... 67
Portobello Books, London W 175
R. & A. Books, E Sussex............................ 102
Rhodes, Bookseller (Peter), Hampshire 126
Roberts Fine Books (Julian), Lincolnshire........ 153
Roscrea Bookshop, Co. Tipperary................. 267
Rose's Books, Powys.... 291
St Swithun's Illustrated & Children's Books,
London W 175
Scrivener's Books & Bookbinding, Derbyshire... 82
Shakeshaft (Dr. B.), Cheshire....................... 71
Stella Books, Monmouthshire 288
Stepping Stones Bookshop, N Yorks.............. 194
Stroma Books, Borders 268
Studio (The), Strathclyde 280
Tant Yn Ellen Books, Powys 293
The Old Children's Bookshelf, Lothian 278
Tiffin (Tony and Gill), Durham 97
TP Children's Bookshop, W Yorks................ 246
Trafalgar Bookshop, E Sussex...................... 100
Treasure Trove Books, Leics........................ 148
Trinity Rare Books, Co. Leitrim 266

Uncle Phil's Books, West Midlands 240
Wadard Books, Kent 138
Wheen O'Books, Scottish Borders 269
Worlds End Bookshop, London SW 171
Xanadu Books, Cleveland 98
Yates Antiquarian Books (Tony), Leics........... 148

CHRISTMAS

Addyman Books, Powys.............................. 289
Castleton (Pat), Kent................................. 138
Childrens Bookshop, W Yorks..................... 248
Cygnet Books, East Yorkshire...................... 107
Dolphin Books, Suffolk............................... 226
Green Meadow Books, Cornwall 74
Joel Segal Books, Devon 86
Nostalgia Unlimited, Merseyside................... 186
Oasis Booksearch, Cambs 67
R. & A. Books, E Sussex............................ 102
Roscrea Bookshop, Co. Tipperary................. 267
St Swithin's Illustrated & Children's Books,
London W 175
Samovai Books, Co. Dublin......................... 264
Tarka Books, Devon 84
Uncle Phil's Books, West Midlands 240

CHURCHILLIANA

Askew Books (Vernon), Wiltshire.................. 251
Barely Read Books, Kent 142
Barn Books, Buckinghamshire...................... 61
Baxter (Steve), Surrey 234
BookShop, The, Dumfries & Galloway........... 270
Cheshire Book Centre, Cheshire.................... 69
Craobh Rua Books, Co. Armagh.................. 260
Dolphin Books, Suffolk............................... 226
Foster Bookshop (Paul), London SW............. 168
Grahame Thornton, Bookseller, Dorset........... 93
Guildmaster Books, Cheshire 70
Harrington (Adrian), London W................... 173
Harrington Antiquarian Bookseller (Peter),
London SW.. 169
Island Books, Devon.................................. 85
Joel Segal Books, Devon 86
Mellon's Books, E Sussex 101
R. & A. Books, E Sussex............................ 102
Seabreeze Books, Lancashire........................ 145
Shacklock Books (David), Suffolk 227
Sotheran Limited (Henry), London W 176
Uncle Phil's Books, West Midlands 240
Updike Rare Books (John), Lothian 279
Wadard Books, Kent 138
Yesterday's News, Conwy........................... 285

CINEMA/FILM

Abbey Books, Cornwall 74
Apocalypse, Surrey 233
Armstrong's Books & Collectables, Leics 147
Bardsley's Books, Suffolk............................ 226
Barn Books, Buckinghamshire...................... 61
Beware of the Leopard, Bristol..................... 58
Bob Mallory (Books), Derbyshire.................. 83
Book Palace (The), London SE 164
Bookroom (The), Surrey............................. 234
Books, Denbighshire 286
Books & Collectables Ltd., Cambs 63
Books For All, N Yorks 194

SPECIALITY INDEX

books2books, Devon 88
Bookshop (The), Norfolk 192
BookShop, The, Dumfries & Galloway 270
Brian Troath Books, London E 155
Brighton Books, E Sussex 99
Byre Books, Dumfries & Galloway 270
Caledonia Books, Strathclyde 280
Camilla's Bookshop, E Sussex 101
Capel Mawr Collectors Centre, Gwynedd 287
Cheshire Book Centre, Cheshire 69
Cover to Cover, Merseyside 186
Cowley, Bookdealer (K.W.), Somerset 218
Dales & Lakes Book Centre, Cumbria 80
Darkwood Books, Co. Cork 263
Decorum Books, London N 158
Delectus Books, London WC 177
Dolphin Books, Suffolk 226
Eastcote Bookshop (The), London Outer 181
Evans (Mark), Lincolnshire 153
Fifteenth Century Bookshop (The), E Sussex 104
firstpagebooks, Norfolk 190
Fitzsimons (Anne), Cumbria 78
Ford Books (David), Herts 133
Fossgate Books, N Yorks 198
Franks Booksellers, Gr Man 119
Greenroom Books, W Yorks 248
Hambleton Books, N Yorks 197
Hancock & Monks, Powys 290
Hay Castle, Powys 290
Hay Cinema Bookshop Ltd., Powys 290
HCB Wholesale, Powys 290
Inprint, Gloucestershire 116
Jade Mountain Bookshop, Hampshire 126
Joel Segal Books, Devon 86
Judd Books, London WC 178
Junk & Spread Eagle, London SE 165
Kelly Books, Devon 89
Kenny's Bookshops and Art Galleries Ltd,
Co. Galway 266
Kent T. G., Surrey 231
Kirkman Ltd., (Robert), Bedfordshire 54
McGee (Terence J.), London Outer 181
Mellon's Books, E Sussex 101
Modlock (Lilian), Dorset 93
Moon's Bookshop (Michael), Cumbria 81
Morris Secondhand & Antiquarian Books
(Chris), Oxfordshire 210
My Back Pages, London SW 169
Nevitsky (Philip), Gr Man 119
O'Brien Books & Photo Gallery, Co. Limerick .. 266
Paramor (C.D.), Suffolk 229
Pickering Bookshop, N Yorks 197
Pordes Books Ltd., (Henry), London WC 179
Portobello Books, London W 175
Prescott - The Bookseller (John), London Outer 184
Priestpopple Books, Northumberland 202
R. & A. Books, E Sussex 102
Reads, Dorset 95
Roland Books, Kent 139
Saintfield Antiques & Fine Books, Co. Down ... 261
Scrivener's Books & Bookbinding, Derbyshire ... 82
Skoob Russell Square, Suffolk 230
Sleepy Elephant Books & Artefacts, Cumbria ... 80
Stroma Books, Borders 268
Tarka Books, Devon 84

Terence Kaye, London NW 162
Theatreshire Books, N Yorks 193
Till's Bookshop, Lothian 279
Trafalgar Bookshop, E Sussex 100
Treasure Chest Books, Suffolk 227
Waxfactor, E Sussex 100
Whittle, Bookseller (Avril), Cumbria 81
Williams (Bookdealer), (Richard), N Lincs 154
Wood (Peter), Cambs 65
Worlds End Bookshop, London SW 171
Wright (Norman), Dorset 95
Yesterday's News, Conwy 285
Zardoz Books, Wiltshire 254

CIRCUS

Addyman Books, Powys 289
Apocalypse, Surrey 233
Cover to Cover, Merseyside 186
Decorum Books, London N 158
Drummond Pleasures of Past Times (David),
London WC 177
Fitzsimons (Anne), Cumbria 78
R. & A. Books, E Sussex 102
St Swithin's Illustrated &
Children's Books, London W 175
Terence Kaye, London NW 162
Webster (D.), Strathclyde 280

CITIES - GENERAL

Amwell Book Company, London EC 157
Duck (William), Hampshire 124
Inch's Books, Kent 137
Joel Segal Books, Devon 86
Keith Langford, London E 155
Marlborough Rare Books Ltd., London W 174
O'Flynn Books, N Yorks 199
R. & A. Books, E Sussex 102

- CITY OF LONDON

Apocalypse, Surrey 233
Ash Rare Books, London SW 167
Bookroom (The), Surrey 234
Camilla's Bookshop, E Sussex 101
Chas J. Sawyer, Kent 141
Dolphin Books, Suffolk 226
Ewell Bookshop Ltd, Surrey 232
Fifteenth Century Bookshop (The), E Sussex 104
Joel Segal Books, Devon 86
Junk & Spread Eagle, London SE 165
Marcet Books, London SE 165
Marlborough Rare Books Ltd., London W 174
Missing Books, Essex 109
Oopalba Books, Cheshire 71
Portobello Books, London W 175
R. & A. Books, E Sussex 102
Roland Books, Kent 139
Uncle Phil's Books, West Midlands 240

- NEW YORK CITY AND BROOKLYN

R. & A. Books, E Sussex 102

CIVIL ENGINEERING

Camden Books, Somerset 216
Cox (Geoff), Devon 90
Duck (William), Hampshire 124

SPECIALITY INDEX

Joel Segal Books, Devon 86
Parkinsons Books, Merseyside...................... 186
Phelps (Michael), W Sussex 243
Reeves Technical Books, N Yorks.................. 196
Stroh (M.A.), London E 155
Vickers (Anthony), N Yorks................. 196
Weiner (Graham), London N 160
Westons, Herts 133
Wheen O'Books, Scottish Borders 269
Winchester Bookshop (The), Hampshire.......... 127

CIVIL RIGHTS

Left on The Shelf, Cumbria.......................... 79
R. & A. Books, E Sussex............................. 102

CLASSICAL STUDIES

Apocalypse, Surrey 233
BookShop, The, Dumfries & Galloway.......... 270
Brian Troath Books, London E...................... 155
Camden Books, Somerset 216
Carnforth Bookshop (The), Lancashire 143
Chthonios Books, E Sussex 102
Classics Bookshop (The), Oxfordshire 207
Cornucopia Books, Lincolnshire 153
Cotswold Internet Books, Gloucestershire 113
Crouch Rare Books, Surrey.......................... 233
Grahame Thornton, Bookseller, Dorset........... 93
Hall's Bookshop, Kent................................ 141
Hellenic Bookservices, London NW 162
Hill (Peter), Hampshire 122
Howes Bookshop, E Sussex.......................... 102
Joel Segal Books, Devon 86
Kings Bookshop Callander, Central 269
Lamb (R.W.), Suffolk................................. 229
O'Flynn Books, N Yorks............................. 199
Olynthiacs, Shropshire 214
Paralos Ltd., London WC 178
Parkinsons Books, Merseyside...................... 186
Poole (William), London W 175
Quest Books, East Yorkshire 107
R. & A. Books, E Sussex............................. 102
Sandpiper Books Ltd., London SW 170
Scrivener's Books & Bookbinding, Derbyshire... 82
Seydi Rare Books (Sevin), London NW 162
Skoob Russell Square, Suffolk...................... 230
Sokol Books Ltd., London W....................... 175
Staniland (Booksellers), Lincolnshire 154
Thorntons of Oxford Ltd., Oxfordshire........... 207
Unsworth's Booksellers, London WC 163, 180
Winchester Bookshop (The), Hampshire.......... 127
Winghale Books, Lincolnshire 153
Wizard Books, Cambs 67

CLASSICS, THE

Addyman Books, Powys.............................. 289
Bayntun (George), Somerset 216
Beware of the Leopard, Bristol...................... 58
Butler Cresswell Rare Books, Buckinghamshire . 61
Cornucopia Books, Lincolnshire 153
Dolphin Books, Suffolk............................... 226
Elstree Books, Herts.................................. 131
Fifteenth Century Bookshop (The), E Sussex 104
Hancock (Peter), W Sussex.......................... 243
Joel Segal Books, Devon 86
Just Books, Cornwall 76

N1 Books, E Sussex................................... 105
O'Flynn Books, N Yorks............................. 199
Print Matters, London SE............................ 166
R. & A. Books, E Sussex...... 102
Staniland (Booksellers), Lincolnshire 154
Tarka Books, Devon 84
Till's Bookshop, Lothian 279
Uncle Phil's Books, West Midlands 240
Winchester Bookshop (The), Hampshire.......... 127

CLIMATOLOGY

Cornucopia Books, Lincolnshire 153
Joel Segal Books, Devon 86
Phelps (Michael), W Sussex 243
R. & A. Books, E Sussex............................. 102
Weiner (Graham), London N 160
Westons, Herts 133

COASTAL DEFENCE

Earth Science Books, Wiltshire 252
MilitaryHistoryBooks.com, Kent................... 138
R, & A. Books, E Sussex............................. 102

COCKFIGHTING

Blest (Peter), Kent 139
Chalmers Hallam (E.), Hampshire................. 125
Coch-y-Bonddu Books, Powys 292
Country Books, Derbyshire 82
Home Farm Books, Warwickshire.................. 237
Kilgour (Sporting Books) (Ian), Leics 149
Phenotype Books, Cumbria 80
R. & A. Books, E Sussex............................. 102
Thomas (Barry), Ceredigion 284

COFFEE

Kenya Books, E Sussex............................... 100
R. & A. Books, E Sussex............................. 102
Stroh (M.A.), London E 155
Susanne Schulz-Falster Rare Books, London N . 160

COLLECTABLES

Apocalypse, Surrey 233
BC Books, Cheshire................................... 70
Book Palace (The), London SE 164
Bookmark (Children's Books), Wiltshire.......... 253
books2books, Devon.................................. 88
Booth (Booksearch Service), (Geoff), Cheshire... 68
Chalk (Old & Out of Print Books)
(Christine M), West Midlands 239
Clark (Nigel A.), London SE........................ 165
Collectors Carbooks, Northants..................... 200
Cornucopia Books, Lincolnshire 153
Cover to Cover, Merseyside......................... 186
Darkwood Books, Co. Cork......................... 263
Don Kelly Books, London W 172
Green Meadow Books, Cornwall 74
Hylton Booksearch, Merseyside 185
Joel Segal Books, Devon 86
Milestone Publications Goss & Crested China,
Hampshire 123
Oxfam Books and Music, Hampshire 126
R. & A. Books, E Sussex............................. 102
Randall (Tom), Somerset............................. 219
Read (C.&J.), Gorleston Books, Norfolk 188
Spink, London WC 179

SPECIALITY INDEX

Tarka Books, Devon 84
Uncle Phil's Books, West Midlands 240
Wiend Books, Lancashire 144

COLLECTING

Abrahams (Mike), Staffordshire 224
Ancient Art Books, London SW 167
Antiques on High, Oxfordshire 209
Apocalypse, Surrey 233
Art Reference Books, Hampshire 125
Barmby (C. & A.J.), Kent 141
Barn Books, Buckinghamshire 61
Bianco Library, W Sussex 242
Books, Kent 137
Booth (Booksearch Service), (Geoff), Cheshire... 68
Browzers, Gr Man 119
Chalk (Old & Out of Print Books)
(Christine M.), West Midlands 239
Clark (Nigel A.), London SE 165
Collectors Corner, Wiltshire 253
Cornucopia Books, Lincolnshire 153
Don Kelly Books, London W 172
Embleton (Paul), Essex 111
Fifteenth Century Bookshop (The), E Sussex 104
Forest Books of Manchester, Cheshire 71
Green Meadow Books, Cornwall 74
Hanshan Tang Books, London SW 168
Heneage Art Books (Thomas), London SW 169
Hollett and Son (R.F.G.), Cumbria 80
Ives Bookseller (John), London Outer 184
Joel Segal Books, Devon 86
John R. Hoggarth, N Yorks 198
Junk & Spread Eagle, London SE 165
Martin (Books and Pictures), (Brian P)., Surrey. 232
Milestone Publications Goss & Crested China,
Hampshire 123
Nostalgia Unlimited, Merseyside 186
R. & A. Books, E Sussex 102
Read (C.&J.), Gorleston Books, Norfolk 188
Restormel Books, Worcestershire 257
Spink, London WC 179
Stella Books, Monmouthshire 288
Thin Read Line, Merseyside 185
Trinders' Fine Tools, Suffolk 227
Uncle Phil's Books, West Midlands 240
Watkins (R.G.), Somerset 216
Westwood Books Ltd, Cumbria 80
Wiend Books, Lancashire 144

COLONIAL

Afar Books International, West Midlands 239
Bickford-Smith (G.), Surrey 233
Caliver Books, Essex 110
Collectables (W.H.), Suffolk 230
Empire Books, N Yorks 198
G. C. Books Ltd., Dumfries & Galloway 271
Kenny's Bookshops and Art Galleries Ltd,
Co. Galway 266
Maghreb Bookshop (The), London WC 178
Mandalay Bookshop, London SW 169
MilitaryHistoryBooks.com, Kent 138
Pennymead Books, N Yorks 194
Price (R.D.M. & I.M.) (Books), Gr Man 120
R. & A. Books, E Sussex 102
Winghale Books, Lincolnshire 153

Woolcott Books, Dorset 92

COLOUR-PLATE

Artco, Notts 204
Aurelian Books, London NW 161
Besleys Books, Suffolk 226
Bianco Library, W Sussex 242
Biblion, London W 172
Black Cat Books, Norfolk 188
Bolton Books, Hampshire 121
Bowden Books, Leics 149
Chas J. Sawyer, Kent 141
Corvus Books, Buckinghamshire 61
Eastcote Bookshop (The), London Outer 181
Fine Art, London SW 168
Frew Limited (Robert), London W 173
Goodyer (Nicholas), London N 159
Grayling (David A.H.), Cumbria 79
Halson Books, Cheshire 71
Harrington (Adrian), London W 173
Harrington Antiquarian Bookseller (Peter),
London SW 169
Hodgkins and Company Limited (Ian),
Gloucestershire 116
Hodgson (Books) (Richard J.), N Yorks 198
Hollett and Son (R.F.G.), Cumbria 80
Joel Segal Books, Devon 86
Lake (David), Norfolk 191
Lymelight Books & Prints, Dorset 93
Mannwaring (M.G.), Bristol 59
Marlborough Rare Books Ltd., London W 174
Marshall Rare Books (Bruce), Gloucestershire... 113
Maynard & Bradley, Leics 148
Moorhead Books, W Yorks 246
Peter M Daly, Hampshire 127
Preston Book Company, Lancashire 145
R. & A. Books, E Sussex 102
Remington (Reg & Philip), Herts 133
Roz Hulse, Conwy 286
Sephton (A.F.), London W 175
Shapero Rare Books (Bernard J.), London W ... 175
Temperley (David), West Midlands 239
Wilson (James), Herts 130

COMEDY

Addyman Books, Powys 289
Books Only, Suffolk 227
Booth (Booksearch Service), (Geoff), Cheshire... 68
Cornucopia Books, Lincolnshire 153
Dales & Lakes Book Centre, Cumbria 80
Facet Books, Dorset 91
firstpagebooks, Norfolk 190
Goldman (Paul), Dorset 94
Greenroom Books, W Yorks 248
Joel Segal Books, Devon 86
McGee (Terence J.), London Outer 181
Price (R.W.), Notts 204
R. & A. Books, E Sussex 102
Sarawak Books, East Yorkshire 106

COMIC BOOKS & ANNUALS

Abrahams (Mike), Staffordshire 224
Bates Books, London Outer 182
Beck (John), E Sussex 103
Black Cat Bookshop, Leics 147

SPECIALITY INDEX

Bookmark (Children's Books), Wiltshire.......... 253
Books & Collectables Ltd., Cambs 63
Booth (Booksearch Service), (Geoff), Cheshire... 68
Border Bookshop, W Yorks 250
Camilla's Bookshop, E Sussex..................... 101
Cheshire Book Centre, Cheshire.................... 69
Cygnet Books, East Yorkshire..................... 107
D. & M. Books, W Yorks 250
Dales & Lakes Book Centre, Cumbria............. 80
Dawlish Books, Devon 86
Facet Books, Dorset................................... 91
Fifteenth Century Bookshop (The), E Sussex 104
firstpagebooks, Norfolk............................... 190
Franks Booksellers, Gr Man........................ 119
Hambleton Books, N Yorks 197
Intech Books, Northumberland 203
Jean Hedger, Berkshire 55
Joel Segal Books, Devon 86
K Books, Cheshire.................................... 70
Key Books (Sarah), Cambs 64
Longden (George), Cheshire 70
Murphy (C.J.), Norfolk.............................. 190
Nostalgia Unlimited, Merseyside 186
Old Celtic Bookshop (The), Devon 88
Pickering Bookshop, N Yorks...................... 197
Pyecroft (Ruth), Gloucestershire 117
R. & A. Books, East Sussex 102
Readers World, West Midlands 239
Savage (Keith A.), Suffolk 229
Scrivener's Books & Bookbinding, Derbyshire... 82
Sesemann (Julia), Kent............................... 136
Stella Books, Monmouthshire 288
Till's Bookshop, Lothian 279
Tilleys Vintage Magazine Shop, Derbyshire...... 82
Tilleys Vintage Magazine Shop, South Yorkshire 223
Towers (Mark), Lancashire 144
Wheen O'Books, Scottish Borders 269
Wright (Norman), Dorset 95
Yesterday's News, Conwy........................... 285
Yorkshire Relics, W Yorks.......................... 247

COMICS

Ardis Books, Hampshire 126
Armstrong's Books & Collectables, Leics 147
Beck (John), East Sussex 103
Black Cat Bookshop, Leics 147
Book Palace (The), London SE 164
Bookbarrow, Cambs 63
Books & Collectables Ltd., Cambs 63
Bookshop (The), Norfolk 192
Border Bookshop, W Yorks 250
Capel Mawr Collectors Centre, Gwynedd 287
Collectables (W.H.), Suffolk 230
Cranhurst Books, London 161
D. & M. Books, W Yorks 250
Facet Books, Dorset................................... 91
Intech Books, Northumberland 203
Ken's Paper Collectables, Buckinghamshire 62
Longden (George), Cheshire 70
McGee (Terence J.), London Outer 181
Nostalgia Unlimited, Merseyside................... 186
Print Matters, London SE........................... 166
Pyecroft (Ruth), Gloucestershire 117
Savage (Keith A.), Suffolk 229
The Old Children's Bookshelf, Lothian 278

Tilleys Vintage Magazine Shop, S Yorks 223
Towers (Mark), Lancashire 144
Tsbbooks, London SW 170
Wiend Books, Lancashire 144
Wright (Norman), Dorset 95
Yesterday's News, Conwy........................... 285
Yorkshire Relics, W Yorks.......................... 247

COMMERCE - GENERAL

Ardis Books, Hampshire 126
Cornucopia Books, Lincolnshire 153
Robert Humm & Co, Lincolnshire 154
Susanne Schulz-Falster Rare Books, London N. 160
Uncle Phil's Books, West Midlands 240

COMMERCIAL VEHICLES

Bott, (Bookdealers) Ltd., (Martin), Gr Man 118
Brad Books, Essex.................................... 111
Cox (Geoff), Devon 90
Fifteenth Century Bookshop (The), E Sussex 104
Joel Segal Books, Devon 86
Kenneth Ball, E Sussex 101
R. & A. Books, E Sussex............................ 102

COMMUNICATION

Apocalypse, Surrey 233
Barcombe Services, Essex........................... 108
Cornucopia Books, Lincolnshire 153
Joel Segal Books, Devon 86
R. & A. Books, E Sussex............................ 102
Weiner (Graham), London N 160

COMMUNISM

G. C. Books Ltd., Dumfries & Galloway......... 271
Hab Books, London W.............................. 173
Hylton Booksearch, Merseyside 185
Joel Segal Books, Devon 86
Left on The Shelf, Cumbria......................... 79
Northern Herald Books, W Yorks.................. 246
Parkinsons Books, Merseyside...................... 186
PsychoBabel Books & Journals, Oxfordshire..... 206
R. & A. Books, E Sussex............................ 102
Reading Lasses, Dumfries & Galloway 271
Red Star Books, Herts............................... 130
Roz Hulse, Conwy 286
Samovar Books, Co. Dublin........................ 264

COMPANY HISTORY

Aardvark Books, Wiltshire.......................... 254
Bell (Peter), Lothian................................. 276
Bott, (Bookdealers) Ltd., (Martin), Gr Man 118
Byrom Textile Bookroom (Richard), Lancashire 143
Cheshire Book Centre, Cheshire.................... 69
Cornucopia Books, Lincolnshire 153
Crosby Nethercott Books, London Outer 181
Delph Books, Gr Man............................... 120
Dolphin Books, Suffolk.............................. 226
Handsworth Books, Essex........................... 112
Joel Segal Books, Devon 86
Kellow Books, Oxfordshire 207
R. & A. Books, E Sussex............................ 102
Randall (Tom), Somerset............................ 219
Roadmaster Books, Kent............................ 137
Robert Humm & Co, Lincolnshire 154
Rochdale Book Company, Gr Man 120

SPECIALITY INDEX

Roland Books, Kent 139
Saintfield Antiques & Fine Books, Co. Down ... 261
Salway Books, Essex 112
Spurrier (Nick), Kent 138
Uncle Phil's Books, West Midlands 240
Whistler's Books, London SW 170

COMPUTING

Apocalypse, Surrey 233
Ardis Books, Hampshire 126
Barcombe Services, Essex............................ 108
Beware of the Leopard, Bristol..................... 58
Cornucopia Books, Lincolnshire 153
Downie Fine Books Ltd., (Robert), Shropshire.. 215
Game Advice, Oxfordshire 210
Jade Mountain Bookshop, Hampshire 126
Old Celtic Bookshop (The), Devon 88
Plurabelle Books, Cambs 64
Print Matters, London SE............................ 166
R. & A. Books, E Sussex............................. 102
Roland Books, Kent 139
Roscrea Bookshop, Co. Tipperary................. 267
Skoob Russell Square, Suffolk...................... 230
Stern Antiquarian Bookseller (Jeffrey), N Yorks 199
Stroh (M.A.), London E 155
Tarka Books, Devon 84
Treasure Island (The), Gr Man..................... 119
Westons, Herts 133
Woodland Books, Devon............................. 84

CONCHOLOGY (SEE MALACOLOGY)

Earth Science Books, Wiltshire 252
Joel Segal Books, Devon 86
Parkinsons Books, Merseyside...................... 186
R. & A. Books, E Sussex............................. 102
Sub Aqua Prints and Books, Hampshire 123

CONSERVATION

Arden, Bookseller (C.), Powys...................... 289
Aurelian Books, London NW 161
Coch-y-Bonddu Books, Powys 292
Colonsay Bookshop, Isle of Colonsay............. 276
Demar Books (Grant), Kent......................... 141
Earth Science Books, Wiltshire 252
Elmbury Books, Warwickshire 238
Heneage Art Books (Thomas), London SW 169
Joel Segal Books, Devon 86
Newgate Books and Translations,
Northumberland 202
R. & A. Books, E Sussex............................. 102
Roadmaster Books, Kent............................. 137
Trinders' Fine Tools, Suffolk 227

CONSPIRACY

Apocalypse, Surrey 233
SETI Books, Staffordshire........................... 225

COOKERY - PROFESSIONAL

Addyman Books, Powys.............................. 289
Bookroom (The), Surrey............................. 234
Books & Bygones, Berkshire......................... 57
Books at Star Dot Star, West Midlands 241
Castleton (Pat), Kent................................. 138
Cover to Cover, Merseyside......................... 186
Dolphin Books, Suffolk............................... 226

Gardener & Cook, London SW..................... 168
Gardner and Cook, London SW.................... 168
Joel Segal Books, Devon 86
Marcet Books, London SE........................... 165
Oopalba Books, Cheshire............................ 71
R & B Graham Trading, Cornwall 74
Uncle Phil's Books, West Midlands 240
Wheen O'Books, Scottish Borders 269

COOKERY/GASTRONOMY

A. & R. Booksearch, Cornwall...................... 74
Abacus Gallery, Staffordshire....................... 224
Abrahams (Mike), Staffordshire.................... 224
Addyman Books, Powys.............................. 289
Al Saqi Books, London W........................... 172
Annie's Books, S Yorks 222
Apocalypse, Surrey 233
Armstrong's Books & Collectables, Leics......... 147
Autumn Leaves, Lincolnshire....................... 152
Axe Rare & Out of Print Books (Richard),
N Yorks... 194
Bacon (Josephine), London WC 177
Black Cat Books, Norfolk............................ 188
Bookbox, Gloucestershire 116
Books, Oxfordshire................................... 206
Books & Bygones, Berkshire......................... 57
Books & Collectables Ltd., Cambs 63
Books (For All), N Yorks............................ 194
Books at Star Dot Star, West Midlands 241
Books For All, N Yorks 194
Books for Content, Herefordshire.................. 128
Books Only, Suffolk.................................. 227
Books Plus, Devon 84
Booth Books, Powys 289
Bosorne Books, Cornwall 75
Brown-Studies, Strathclyde.......................... 279
Burmester (James), Bristol.......................... 59
Capel Mawr Collectors Centre, Gwynedd 287
Carningli Centre, Pembrokeshire................... 288
Chandos Books, Devon............................... 85
Chantrey Books, S Yorks 222
Clarke (Janet), Somerset............................. 216
Cobnar Books, Kent 142
Cooks Books, E Sussex............................... 99
Cotswold Internet Books, Gloucestershire 113
Country Books, Derbyshire 82
Cover to Cover, Merseyside......................... 186
D'Arcy Books, Wiltshire............................. 252
Dales & Lakes Book Centre, Cumbria............ 80
Deeside Books, Grampian........................... 273
Discovery Bookshop, Carmarthenshire............ 283
Dolphin Books, Suffolk.............................. 226
Dusty Books, Powys 292
Elmfield Books, West Midlands.................... 239
Esoteric Dreams Bookshop, Cumbria 78
Fifteenth Century Bookshop (The), E Sussex 104
Fiona Edwards, Notts 204
Fox Books (J. & J.), Kent........................... 140
Gardener & Cook, London SW..................... 168
Gardner and Cook, London SW.................... 168
Garfi Books, Powys 293
Garwood & Voigt, Kent.............................. 140
Good for Books, Lincolnshire 151
Grahame Thornton, Bookseller, Dorset........... 93
Gresham Books, Somerset 218

SPECIALITY INDEX

Hall's Bookshop, Kent................................. 141
Harrington (Adrian), London W................... 173
Hay Cinema Bookshop Ltd., Powys............... 290
HCB Wholesale, Powys............................... 290
Internet Bookshop UK Ltd., Gloucestershire 113
Invicta Bookshop, Berkshire 56
Island Books, Devon 85
Jade Mountain Bookshop, Hampshire 126
Joel Segal Books, Devon 86
Lamb's Tales Books, Devon 87
Lucas (Richard), London NW....................... 162
Maggs Brothers Limited, London W.............. 174
Mannwaring (M.G.), Bristol 59
Maynard & Bradley, Leics 148
McNaughtan's Bookshop, Lothian 278
Mellon's Books, E Sussex 101
Modlock (Lilian), Dorset 93
Moorhead Books, W Yorks 246
Much Ado Books, E Sussex 99
Oopalba Books, Cheshire............................. 71
Parrott Books, Oxfordshire 211
Peter M Daly, Hampshire 127
Pholiota Books, London WC 179
Price (John), London N 159
Quaritch Ltd., (Bernard), London W.............. 175
Queen Victoria PH, Torfaen 294
R & B Graham Trading, Cornwall 74
R. & A. Books, E Sussex............................. 102
Rainford (Sheila), Herts 130
River Reads Bookshop, Devon...................... 90
Roberts Fine Books (Julian), Lincolnshire........ 153
Roland Books, Kent 139
Sax Books, Suffolk 229
Scrivener's Books & Bookbinding, Derbyshire... 82
Seeber (Liz), E Sussex................................ 102
Sleepy Elephant Books & Artefacts, Cumbria ... 80
Smith (Clive), Essex 109
Stroma Books, Borders 268
Susanne Schulz-Falster Rare Books, London N. 160
Talisman Books, Cheshire............................ 70
Tant Yn Ellen Books, Powys 293
Tarka Books, Devon 84
Tilston (Stephen E.), London SE................... 166
Trinity Rare Books, Co. Leitrim 266
Uncle Phil's Books, West Midlands 240
Wadard Books, Kent 138
Wheen O'Books, Scottish Borders 269
Whitchurch Books Ltd., Cardiff.................... 283
Whittle, Bookseller (Avril), Cumbria 81
Williams (Christopher), Dorset 94
Wychwood Books, Gloucestershire 116
Yates Antiquarian Books (Tony), Leics........... 148

COSMOLOGY

Apocalypse, Surrey 233
Inner Bookshop (The), Oxfordshire................ 210
Joel Segal Books, Devon 86
Moorside Books, Lancashire......................... 144
Stroh (M.A.), London E 155
Westons, Herts 133

COUNSELLING

Fifteenth Century Bookshop (The), E Sussex 104
Inner Bookshop (The), Oxfordshire................ 210
Joel Segal Books, Devon 86

Oast Books, Kent...................................... 137
Reading Lasses, Dumfries & Galloway 271

COUNTERCULTURE

Atlas, London N 158
Black Cat Bookshop, Leics 147
Capel Mawr Collectors Centre, Gwynedd 287
Church Street Books, Norfolk....................... 187
Fifth Element, West Midlands...................... 240
Invisible Books, E Sussex............................ 100
McGee (Terence J.), London Outer 181
Poetry Bookshop (The), Powys.................... 291
Sclanders (Beatbooks), (Andrew), London EC... 157

COUNTIES IN ENGLAND

Ambra Books, Bristol................................. 58

COUNTRIES - GENERAL

Aurora Books Ltd, Lothian.... 276
Blackwell's Rare Books, Oxfordshire 209
Biad Books, Essex 111
Cotswold Internet Books, Gloucestershire 113
Dolphin Books, Suffolk............................... 226
Ewell Bookshop Ltd, Surrey........................ 232
Fifteenth Century Bookshop (The), E Sussex 104
Freeman's Corner Shop, Norfolk 190
Glasheen-Books, Surrey 232
Good for Books, Lincolnshire 151
Harrington Antiquarian Bookseller (Peter),
London SW... 169
J & J Burgess Booksellers, Cambs 64
Jade Mountain Bookshop, Hampshire 126
Joel Segal Books, Devon 86
Naughton Booksellers, Co. Dublin 265
O'Flynn Books, N Yorks............................. 199
R. & A. Books, E Sussex............................. 102
Wheen O'Books, Scottish Borders 269
Winchester Bookshop (The), Hampshire.......... 127

- AFGANISTAN

Bates & Hindmarch, W Yorks 249
David Warnes Books, Herefordshire 129
R. & A. Books, E Sussex............................. 102
Remington (Reg & Philip), Herts 133
Traveller's Bookshelf (The), Somerset 217
Verandah Books, Dorset 95

- AFRICA

Afar Books International, West Midlands 239
Allsworth Rare Books Ltd., London SW.......... 167
Apocalypse, Surrey 233
Ayre (Peter J.), Somerset 220
Barn Books, Buckinghamshire....................... 61
Bonham (J. & S.L.), London W 172
Bracton Books, Cambs 63
Chalmers Hallam (E.), Hampshire 125
Chapter Two, London SE............................ 164
Chas J. Sawyer, Kent 141
Coch-y-Bonddu Books, Powys 292
Deeside Books, Grampian............................ 273
Dolphin Books, Suffolk............................... 226
Empire Books, N Yorks.............................. 198
Folios Limited, London SW 168
G. C. Books Ltd., Dumfries & Galloway......... 271
Halewood & Sons, Lancashire....................... 145

SPECIALITY INDEX

Hall, (Anthony C.) Antiquarian Bookseller, London O .... 184 Harrington Antiquarian Bookseller (Peter), London SW .... 169 Heritage Books, Isle of Wight .... 134 J.C. Deyong Books, London SW .... 169 Kenny's Bookshops and Art Galleries Ltd, Co. Galway .... 266 Kenya Books, E Sussex............................... 100 Lawson & Company (E.M.), Oxfordshire .... 208 Marble Hill Books, Middlesex .... 184 Michael Graves-Johnston, London SW .... 169 Oopalba Books, Cheshire............................ 71 Peter M Daly, Hampshire .... 127 Popeley (Frank T.), Cambs .... 67 Post-Horn Books, N Yorks .... 193 Probsthain (Arthur), London WC .... 179 R. & A. Books, E Sussex............................. 102 Remington (Reg & Philip), Herts .... 133 Roland Books, Kent .... 139 Wheen O'Books, Scottish Borders .... 269 Wiend Books, Lancashire .... 144 Woolcott Books, Dorset.............................. 92 Yesterday's Books, Dorset 92

- ALASKA

Cavendish Rare Books, London N .... 158 David Warnes Books, Herefordshire .... 129 R. & A. Books, E Sussex............................. 102 Remington (Reg & Philip), Herts 133

- ALBANIA

de Visser Books, Cambs .... 63 Joppa Books Ltd., Surrey .... 231 Remington (Reg & Philip), Herts .... 133 Traveller's Bookshelf (The), Somerset 217

- ALGERIA

Apocalypse, Surrey .... 233 Empire Books, N Yorks.............................. 198 Remington (Reg & Philip), Herts 133

- AMERICAS, THE

Americanabooksuk, Cumbria .... 77 Bracton Books, Cambs .... 63 Halewood & Sons, Lancashire...................... 145 Lawson & Company (E.M.), Oxfordshire .... 208 R. & A. Books, E Sussex............................. 102 Remington (Reg & Philip), Herts 133

- ANDORRA

Books on Spain, London Outer .... 184 Orssich (Paul), London SW 170

- ANTARCTIC, THE

Bluntisham Books, Cambs .... 63 Cavendish Rare Books, London N .... 158 Chalmers Hallam (E.), Hampshire .... 125 Craobh Rua Books, Co. Armagh .... 260 Empire Books, N Yorks.............................. 198 Fifteenth Century Bookshop (The), E Sussex .... 104 Glacier Books, Tayside .... 282 Harrington Antiquarian Bookseller (Peter), London SW .... 169 Henry Wilson Books, Cheshire 69

Hill (Peter), Hampshire .... 122 Libris (Weston) Books, Somerset .... 217 Marble Hill Books, Middlesex .... 184 McEwan Fine Books, Grampian.................... 273 Peter M Daly, Hampshire .... 127 Prospect House Books, Co. Down................. 261 R. & A. Books, E Sussex............................. 102 Remington (Reg & Philip), Herts 133

- ARABIA

Allsworth Rare Books Ltd., London SW .... 167 Apocalypse, Surrey .... 233 Bonham (J. & S.L.), London W .... 172 David Warnes Books, Herefordshire .... 129 Eastern Traveller (The), Somerset .... 220 Empire Books, N Yorks.............................. 198 Folios Limited, London SW .... 168 J.C. Deyong Books, London SW .... 169 Kenny's Bookshops and Art Galleries Ltd, Co. Galway .... 266 P. and P. Books, Worcestershire .... 256 Peter M Daly, Hampshire .... 127 Quest Books, East Yorkshire .... 107 Remington (Reg & Philip), Herts .... 133 Traveller's Bookshelf (The), Somerset 217

- ARABIAN PENINSULA

J.C. Deyong Books, London SW .... 169 Joppa Books Ltd., Surrey .... 231 Moorside Books, Lancashire........................ 144 P. and P. Books, Worcestershire .... 256 Remington (Reg & Philip), Herts 133

- ARCTIC, THE

Bluntisham Books, Cambs .... 63 Cavendish Rare Books, London N .... 158 Chalmers Hallam (E.), Hampshire .... 125 Craobh Rua Books, Co. Armagh .... 260 Deeside Books, Grampian........................... 273 Empire Books, N Yorks.............................. 198 Fifteenth Century Bookshop (The), E Sussex .... 104 Harrington Antiquarian Bookseller (Peter), London SW .... 169 Hill (Peter), Hampshire .... 122 J & J Burgess Booksellers, Cambs .... 64 McEwan Fine Books, Grampian.................... 273 Peter M Daly, Hampshire .... 127 Prospect House Books, Co. Down................. 261 R. & A. Books, E Sussex............................. 102 Remington (Reg & Philip), Herts .... 133 Roz Hulse, Conwy 286

- ARGENTINA

Empire Books, N Yorks.............................. 198 Hodgson (Judith), London W .... 174 R. & A. Books, E Sussex............................. 102 Remington (Reg & Philip), Herts 133

- ARMENIA

David Warnes Books, Herefordshire .... 129 Joppa Books Ltd., Surrey .... 231 Remington (Reg & Philip), Herts .... 133 Traveller's Bookshelf (The), Somerset 217

SPECIALITY INDEX

- ASCENSION ISLANDS
MK Book Services, Cambs 66

- ASIA
Allsworth Rare Books Ltd., London SW......... 167
Bates & Hindmarch, W Yorks 249
Bonham (J. & S.L.), London W 172
Bracton Books, Cambs 63
Cavendish Rare Books, London N 158
Chapter Two, London SE............................ 164
David Warnes Books, Herefordshire 129
Eastern Traveller (The), Somerset.................. 220
Empire Books, N Yorks.............................. 198
Fine Books Oriental Ltd., London WC........... 178
Grayling (David A.H.), Cumbria 79
Hall, (Anthony C.) Antiquarian Bookseller,
London Outer 184
J.C. Deyong Books, London SW 169
Kenny's Bookshops and Art Galleries Ltd,
Co. Galway... 266
Mandalay Bookshop, London SW 169
Peter M Daly, Hampshire........................... 127
Post-Horn Books, N Yorks 193
Rayner (Hugh Ashley), Somerset 217
Remington (Reg & Philip), Herts 133

- ASIA MINOR
Empire Books, N Yorks.............................. 198
Quest Books, East Yorkshire 107
Remington (Reg & Philip), Herts 133
Seydi Rare Books (Sevin), London NW 162
Traveller's Bookshelf (The), Somerset 217

- ATLANTIC OCEAN
Empire Books, N Yorks.............................. 198

- AUSTRALASIA
Bonham (J. & S.L.), London W 172
Cavendish Rare Books, London N 158
Empire Books, N Yorks.............................. 198
J.C. Deyong Books, London SW 169
Lawson & Company (E.M.), Oxfordshire 208
Preston Book Company, Lancashire 145
R. & A. Books, E Sussex............................ 102
Remington (Reg & Philip), Herts 133
Roz Hulse, Conwy 286

- AUSTRALIA
Bonham (J. & S.L.), London W 172
Empire Books, N Yorks.............................. 198
Halewood & Sons, Lancashire...................... 145
Moore (Peter), Cambs 64
R. & A. Books, E Sussex............................ 102
Remington (Reg & Philip), Herts 133
Roz Hulse, Conwy 286

- AUSTRIA
de Visser Books, Cambs 63
Empire Books, N Yorks.............................. 198
R. & A. Books, E Sussex............................ 102

- AZORES, THE
Empire Books, N Yorks.............................. 198
Hodgson (Judith), London W 174

- BAHAMAS, THE
Empire Books, N Yorks.............................. 198
Pennymead Books, N Yorks........................ 194
Remington (Reg & Philip), Herts 133

- BALKANS, THE
David Warnes Books, Herefordshire 129
de Visser Books, Cambs 63
Empire Books, N Yorks.............................. 198
Kenny's Bookshops and Art Galleries Ltd,
Co. Galway... 266
Marijana Dworski Books, via Hereford........... 290
Peter M Daly, Hampshire........................... 127
Quest Books, East Yorkshire 107
Thorntons of Oxford Ltd., Oxfordshire........... 207
Traveller's Bookshelf (The), Somerset 217

- BALTIC STATES
Baldwin (Jack), Strathclyde 280
de Visser Books, Cambs 63
MK Book Services, Cambs 66

- BALUCHISTAN
Remington (Reg & Philip), Herts 133

- BELGIUM
Empire Books, N Yorks.............................. 198
R. & A. Books, E Sussex............................ 102

- BERMUDA
Empire Books, N Yorks.............................. 198
Leapman Ltd. (G. & R.), Herts 130
Pennymead Books, N Yorks........................ 194
Remington (Reg & Philip), Herts 133

- BHUTAN
Remington (Reg & Philip), Herts 133

- BOLIVIA
Empire Books, N Yorks.............................. 198
Hodgson (Judith), London W 174
Remington (Reg & Philip), Herts 133

- BRAZIL
Empire Books, N Yorks.............................. 198
Hodgson (Judith), London W 174
R. & A. Books, E Sussex............................ 102
Remington (Reg & Philip), Herts 133

- BRITISH NORTH BORNEO
Eastgate Bookshop, East Yorkshire 106
Empire Books, N Yorks.............................. 198
Park (Mike), London Outer......................... 183
Remington (Reg & Philip), Herts 133
Sarawak Books, East Yorkshire.................... 106

- BULGARIA
de Visser Books, Cambs 63
Empire Books, N Yorks.............................. 198
R. & A. Books, E Sussex............................ 102

- BURMA
Empire Books, N Yorks.............................. 198
Mandalay Bookshop, London SW 169

SPECIALITY INDEX

MK Book Services, Cambs 66
Rayner (Hugh Ashley), Somerset 217
Remington (Reg & Philip), Herts 133
Verandah Books, Dorset 95

- CAMBODIA
Empire Books, N Yorks............................. 198

- CANADA
Chalmers Hallam (E.), Hampshire 125
Empire Books, N Yorks............................. 198
Glacier Books, Tayside 282
R. & A. Books, E Sussex............................ 102
Remington (Reg & Philip), Herts 133

- CARIBBEAN, THE
Afar Books International, West Midlands 239
Allsworth Rare Books Ltd., London SW 167
Burton-Garbett (A.), London Outer 183
Craobh Rua Books, Co. Armagh 260
Empire Books, N Yorks............................. 198
Leapman Ltd. (G. & R.), Herts 130
Naughton Booksellers, Co. Dublin 265
Norton Books, N Yorks............................. 197
Pennymead Books, N Yorks........................ 194
Remington (Reg & Philip), Herts 133

- CENTRAL AMERICA
Books on Spain, London Outer 184
Burton-Garbett (A.), London Outer 183
Chalmers Hallam (E.), Hampshire 125
Empire Books, N Yorks............................. 198
Orssich (Paul), London SW......................... 170
Remington (Reg & Philip), Herts 133

- CENTRAL ASIA
Al Saqi Books, London W 172
Allsworth Rare Books Ltd., London SW 167
Bates & Hindmarch, W Yorks 249
Bonham (J. & S.L.), London W 172
Cavendish Rare Books, London N 158
Chalmers Hallam (E.), Hampshire 125
David Warnes Books, Herefordshire 129
Empire Books, N Yorks............................. 198
Hanshan Tang Books, London SW 168
J.C. Deyong Books, London SW 169
Joppa Books Ltd., Surrey 231
Peter M Daly, Hampshire........................... 127
Rayner (Hugh Ashley), Somerset 217
Remington (Reg & Philip), Herts 133
Riddell (Peter), East Yorkshire 106
Traveller's Bookshelf (The), Somerset 217

- CENTRAL EAST EUROPE
de Visser Books, Cambs 63
Hylton Booksearch, Merseyside 185

- CHANNEL ISLANDS
Books and Things, CI................................ 258
Cornucopia Books, Lincolnshire 153
R. & A. Books, E Sussex............................ 102

- CHINA
Allsworth Rare Books Ltd., London SW 167
Bow Windows Book Shop, E Sussex.............. 103

Cavendish Rare Books, London N 158
Empire Books, N Yorks............................. 198
Hanshan Tang Books, London SW 168
Hobgoblin Books, Hampshire 125
J.C. Deyong Books, London SW 169
Kenny's Bookshops and Art Galleries Ltd,
Co. Galway... 266
Mandalay Bookshop, London SW 169
Peter M Daly, Hampshire........................... 127
R. & A. Books, E Sussex............................ 102
Remington (Reg & Philip), Herts 133
Skoob Russell Square, Suffolk...................... 230
Transformer, Dumfries & Galloway................ 271
Traveller's Bookshelf (The), Somerset 217

- CUBA
Books on Spain, London Outer 184
Empire Books, N Yorks............................. 198
Hodgson (Judith), London W 174
Naughton Booksellers, Co. Dublin 265
Pennymead Books, N Yorks........................ 194
Remington (Reg & Philip), Herts 133

- CYPRUS
Antique Prints of the World, London N.......... 158
Askew Books (Vernon), Wiltshire.................. 251
Crouch Rare Books, Surrey......................... 233
Empire Books, N Yorks............................. 198
Hellenic Bookservices, London NW............... 162
Joppa Books Ltd., Surrey 231
Kalligraphia, Isle of Wight 134
Nicolas - Antiquarian Booksellers & Art
Dealers, London N 159
Quest Books, East Yorkshire 107
R. & A. Books, E Sussex............................ 102

- CZECH REPUBLIC
de Visser Books, Cambs 63
Empire Books, N Yorks............................. 198
R. & A. Books, E Sussex............................ 102

- DOMINICAN REPUBLIC
Empire Books, N Yorks............................. 198
Pennymead Books, North Yorkshire 194
Remington (Reg & Philip), Herts 133

- EAST AFRICA
Chalmers Hallam (E.), Hampshire 125
Coch-y-Bonddu Books, Powys 292
Empire Books, North Yorkshire 198
J.C. Deyong Books, London SW 169
Kenya Books, E Sussex.............................. 100
Peter M Daly, Hampshire........................... 127
Preston Book Company, Lancashire 145
Remington (Reg & Philip), Herts 133
Samovar Books, Co. Dublin 264
Yesterday's Books, Dorset 92

- EAST EUROPE
Apocalypse, Surrey 233
de Visser Books, Cambs 63
Dolphin Books, Suffolk.............................. 226
Hab Books, London W.............................. 173
Hall, (Anthony C.) Antiquarian Bookseller,
London Outer 184

SPECIALITY INDEX

Hylton Booksearch, Merseyside 185
Orbis Books (London) Ltd., London W 175
R. & A. Books, E Sussex............................. 102

- EAST MEDITERRANEAN, THE

Seydi Rare Books (Sevin), London NW 162

- EAST TIMOR

Hylton Booksearch, Merseyside 185
Remington (Reg & Philip), Herts 133

- EGYPT

Afar Books International, West Midlands 239
Atlantis Bookshop, London WC.................... 177
Chalmers Hallam (E.), Hampshire 125
Empire Books, North Yorkshire 198
Joppa Books Ltd., Surrey 231
Oasis Booksearch, Cambs 67
Occultique, Northants................................ 200
P. and P. Books, Worcestershire 256
Quest Books, East Yorkshire 107
R & A. Books, E Sussex............................. 102
Remington (Reg & Philip), Herts 133
Samovar Books, Co. Dublin 264
Yesterday's Books, Dorset 92

- ENGLAND

Anthony Vickers Books, North Yorkshire 196
Barn Books, Shropshire............................... 215
Bell (Peter), Lothian 276
Broadwater Books, Hampshire 125
Castleton (Pat), Kent.................................. 138
Chapman (Neville), Lancashire...................... 146
Cornell Books, Gloucestershire 117
Cornucopia Books, Lincolnshire 153
Cox (Geoff), Devon 90
Empire Books, North Yorkshire 198
Grove Bookshop (The), North Yorkshire 197
Island Books, Devon 85
McCrone (Audrey), Isle of Arran 275
Missing Books, Essex 109
Naughton Booksellers, Co. Dublin 265
Park Gallery & Bookshop (The), Northants 201
R. & A. Books, E Sussex............................. 102
Read (C.&J.), Gorleston Books, Norfolk 188
Roberts Books, Ayrshire 280
Samovar Books, Co. Dublin 264
SETI Books, Staffordshire........................... 225
Vickers (Anthony), North Yorkshire 196
Wadard Books, Kent 138
Wheen O'Books, Scottish Borders 269

- ESTONIA

de Visser Books, Cambs 63

- ETHIOPIA

Chalmers Hallam (E.), Hampshire 125
Craobh Rua Books, Co. Armagh 260
Empire Books, North Yorkshire 198
Joppa Books Ltd., Surrey 231
Remington (Reg & Philip), Herts 133
Traveller's Bookshelf (The), Somerset 217
Yesterday's Books, Dorset 92

- EUROPE

Empire Books, North Yorkshire 198
Kenny's Bookshops and Art Galleries Ltd,
Co. Galway.. 266
Naughton Booksellers, Co. Dublin 265
owenbooks65, Conwy................................. 285
Pholiota Books, London WC........................ 179
Prospect House Books, Co. Down.................. 261
R. & A. Books, E Sussex............................. 102
York (Graham), Devon............................... 86

- FALKLANDS, THE

Bluntisham Books, Cambs 63
Craobh Rua Books, Co. Armagh 260
Empire Books, North Yorkshire 198
Miles Apart, Suffolk................................... 229
R. & A. Books, E Sussex............................. 102
Remington (Reg & Philip), Herts 133

- FAR EAST, THE

Cavendish Rare Books, London N 158
Chalmers Hallam (E.), Hampshire 125
Empire Books, North Yorkshire 198
Marble Hill Books, Middlesex....................... 184
Oxley (Laurence), Hampshire....................... 121
Peter M Daly, Hampshire............................ 127
R. & A. Books, E Sussex............................. 102
Remington (Reg & Philip), Herts 133
Robert G Sawers Ltd, London NW................ 162
Traveller's Bookshelf (The), Somerset 217

- FIJI

Empire Books, North Yorkshire 198
Remington (Reg & Philip), Herts 133

- FINLAND

Empire Books, North Yorkshire 198
R. & A. Books, E Sussex............................. 102

- FORMOSA

Empire Books, North Yorkshire 198
Remington (Reg & Philip), Herts 133

- FRANCE

Colwyn Books, Conwy 285
Empire Books, North Yorkshire 198
Glacier Books, Tayside 282
Kenya Books, E Sussex............................... 100
Owen (J.V.), Conwy.................................. 285
owenbooks65, Conwy................................. 285
R. & A. Books, E Sussex............................. 102
Roscrea Bookshop, Co. Tipperary 267
Seydi Rare Books (Sevin), London NW 162

- GERMANY

de Visser Books, Cambs 63
Empire Books, North Yorkshire 198
Helion & Company, West Midlands 240
R. & A. Books, E Sussex............................. 102

- GIBRALTAR

Books on Spain, London Outer 184
Empire Books, North Yorkshire 198
Orssich (Paul), London SW.......................... 170
R. & A. Books, E Sussex............................. 102

SPECIALITY INDEX

- GREAT BRITAIN
Booth (Booksearch Service), (Geoff), Cheshire... 68
Broadwater Books, Hampshire 125
Castleton (Pat), Kent................................. 138
Clarke Books (David), Somerset 219
Dolphin Books, Suffolk............................... 226
Empire Books, North Yorkshire 198
G. C. Books Ltd., Dumfries & Galloway......... 271
Jackdaw Books, Norfolk 189
Joel Segal Books, Devon 86
Kalligraphia, Isle of Wight.......................... 134
Oopalba Books, Cheshire............................ 71
Orb's Bookshop, Grampian......................... 274
Parkinsons Books, Merseyside...................... 186
Peter M Daly, Hampshire........................... 127
R. & A. Books, E Sussex............................. 102
Samovar Books, Co. Dublin 264
Shakeshaft (Dr. B.), Cheshire 71
Vickers (Anthony), North Yorkshire 196

- GREAT LAKES, THE
R. & A. Books, E Sussex............................. 102
Remington (Reg & Philip), Herts 133

- GREECE
Antique Prints of the World, London N.......... 158
Ballantyne–Way (Roger), Suffolk 229
Crouch Rare Books, Surrey......................... 233
Empire Books, North Yorkshire 198
Hellenic Bookservices, London NW............... 162
Kalligraphia, Isle of Wight.......................... 134
Morris Secondhand & Antiquarian Books
(Chris), Oxfordshire 210
Nicolas - Antiquarian Booksellers & Art
Dealers, London N................................... 159
Quest Books, East Yorkshire 107
R. & A. Books, E Sussex............................. 102
Remington (Reg & Philip), Herts 133
Seydi Rare Books (Sevin), London NW 162
Traveller's Bookshelf (The), Somerset 217

- GREENLAND
Bluntisham Books, Cambs 63
Empire Books, North Yorkshire 198
Glacier Books, Tayside 282
Michael Graves-Johnston, London SW 169
R. & A. Books, E Sussex............................. 102

- GUATEMALA
Empire Books, North Yorkshire 198
Orssich (Paul), London SW......................... 170
R. & A. Books, E Sussex............................. 102
Remington (Reg & Philip), Herts 133

- HAITI
Empire Books, North Yorkshire 198
Pennymead Books, North Yorkshire 194
Remington (Reg & Philip), Herts 133

- HAWAII
Empire Books, North Yorkshire 198
R. & A. Books, E Sussex............................. 102
Remington (Reg & Philip), Herts 133

- HIMALAYAS, THE
Chalmers Hallam (E.), Hampshire................. 125
David Warnes Books, Herefordshire 129
Glacier Books, Tayside 282
Hanshan Tang Books, London SW 168
Hunter and Krageloh, Derbyshire 83
Kabristan Archives, Shropshire..................... 215
Peter M Daly, Hampshire........................... 127
R. & A. Books, E Sussex............................. 102
Rayner (Hugh Ashley), Somerset 217
Remington (Reg & Philip), Herts 133
Traveller's Bookshelf (The), Somerset 217
Verandah Books, Dorset 95

- HOLY LAND, THE
P. and P. Books, Worcestershire 256
R. & A. Books, E Sussex............................. 102
Remington (Reg & Philip), Herts 133
Samovar Books, Co. Dublin 264

- HONG KONG
Allsworth Rare Books Ltd., London SW.......... 167
Empire Books, North Yorkshire 198
R. & A. Books, E Sussex............................. 102
Remington (Reg & Philip), Herts 133

- HUNGARY
de Visser Books, Cambs 63
Empire Books, North Yorkshire 198
Parrott (Jeremy), London E......................... 156
R. & A. Books, E Sussex............................. 102
Traveller's Bookshelf (The), Somerset 217

- ICELAND
Bluntisham Books, Cambs 63
Empire Books, North Yorkshire 198
Glacier Books, Tayside 282
R. & A. Books, E Sussex............................. 102

- INDIA
Bates & Hindmarch, W Yorks 249
Chalmers Hallam (E.), Hampshire................. 125
David Warnes Books, Herefordshire 129
Donovan Military Books (Tom), E Sussex 99
Empire Books, North Yorkshire 198
Fine Books Oriental Ltd., London WC........... 178
G. C. Books Ltd., Dumfries & Galloway......... 271
Jackson (M.W.), Wiltshire........................... 254
Kabristan Archives, Shropshire..................... 215
Mandalay Bookshop, London SW 169
My Back Pages, London SW........................ 169
Oxley (Laurence), Hampshire....................... 121
Peter M Daly, Hampshire........................... 127
Rayner (Hugh Ashley), Somerset 217
Remington (Reg & Philip), Hertfordshire......... 133
Rhodes, Bookseller (Peter), Hampshire 126
Roland Books, Kent 139
Traveller's Bookshelf (The), Somerset 217
Verandah Books, Dorset 95
Woolcott Books, Dorset 92

- INDIAN OCEAN, THE
Empire Books, North Yorkshire 198
Kenya Books, E Sussex............................... 100
R. & A. Books, E Sussex............................. 102

SPECIALITY INDEX

Remington (Reg & Philip), Hertfordshire......... 133

- INDONESIA

Empire Books, North Yorkshire 198
Park (Mike), London Outer......................... 183
R. & A. Books, E Sussex............................ 102
Remington (Reg & Philip), Hertfordshire......... 133

- IRAN

Bates & Hindmarch, W Yorks 249
David Warnes Books, Herefordshire 129
Empire Books, North Yorkshire 198
Joppa Books Ltd., Surrey 231
Quest Books, East Yorkshire 107
R. & A. Books, E Sussex............................ 102
Remington (Reg & Philip), Hertfordshire......... 133
Traveller's Bookshelf (The), Somerset 217

- IRAQ

Bates & Hindmarch, W Yorks 249
Empire Books, North Yorkshire 198
Joppa Books Ltd., Surrey 231
R. & A. Books, E Sussex............................ 102
Remington (Reg & Philip), Hertfordshire......... 133

- IRELAND

Abbey Books, Cornwall 74
Apocalypse, Surrey 233
Armchair Books, Lothian 276
Bell Gallery (The), Co. Antrim 260
Celtic Bookshop (The), Co. Limerick 266
Courtwood Books, Co. Laois....................... 266
Darkwood Books, Co. Cork 263
De Burca Rare Books, Co. Dublin 264
Delectus Books, London WC....................... 177
Empire Books, North Yorkshire 198
Foyle Books, Co. Derry 260
Greene's Bookshop Ltd, Co. Dublin 265
Grove Bookshop (The), North Yorkshire 197
Hyland (C.P.), Co. Cork 263
Hylton Booksearch, Merseyside 185
Jackson (M.W.), Wiltshire.......................... 254
Jiri Books, Co. Antrim 260
Kabristan Archives, Shropshire.................... 215
Karen Millward, Co. Cork.......................... 263
Kenny's Bookshops and Art Galleries Ltd,
Co. Galway 266
Kenya Books, E Sussex.............................. 100
Kernaghans, Merseyside 186
Michael J Carroll, Co. Cork 263
Naughton Booksellers, Co. Dublin 265
Oasis Booksearch, Cambs 67
Prospect House Books, Co. Down................. 261
R. & A. Books, E Sussex............................ 102
Read Ireland, Co. Dublin 264
Red Star Books, Hertfordshire 130
Roscrea Bookshop, Co. Tipperary 267
Rowan (P. & B.), Co. Antrim 260
Rye Old Books, E Sussex 104
Schull Books, Co. Cork 263
Skelton (Tony), Kent................................ 141
Taney Books, Co. Dublin 264
Whelan (P. & F.), Kent.............................. 141

- ISLE OF MAN

Craobh Rua Books, Co. Armagh 260
Garretts Antiquarian Books, Isle of Man......... 259
Kernaghans, Merseyside 186
Mulyan (Don), Merseyside 186
R. & A. Books, E Sussex............................ 102

- ISLE OF WIGHT

Apocalypse, Surrey 233
Cameron House Books, Isle of Wight............. 134
Heritage Books, Isle of Wight 134
R. & A. Books, E Sussex............................ 102

- ISLES OF SCILLY

R. & A. Books, E Sussex............................ 102

- ISRAEL

Fishburn Books, London NW....................... 161
Pholiota Books, London WC....................... 179
R. & A. Books, E Sussex............................ 102
Samovar Books, Co Dublin 264

- ITALY

Apocalypse, Surrey 233
Campbell (Fiona), London SE 164
Empire Books, North Yorkshire 198
Glacier Books, Tayside 282
Hava Books, London SE............................ 165
McGee (Terence J.), London Outer 181
R. & A. Books, E Sussex............................ 102
Seydi Rare Books (Sevin), London NW 162
Spelman (Ken), North Yorkshire 199
Susanne Schulz-Falster Rare Books, London N. 160

- JAPAN

Allsworth Rare Books Ltd., London SW......... 167
Bow Windows Book Shop, E Sussex.............. 103
Burebank Books, Norfolk 187
Empire Books, North Yorkshire 198
Fine Books Oriental Ltd., London WC........... 178
Hanshan Tang Books, London SW 168
Hobgoblin Books, Hampshire 125
Orb's Bookshop, Grampian......................... 274
R. & A. Books, E Sussex............................ 102
Remington (Reg & Philip), Hertfordshire......... 133
Robert G Sawers Ltd, London NW................ 162
Roberts Books, Ayrshire 280
Transformer, Dumfries & Galloway................ 271
Traveller's Bookshelf (The), Somerset 217

- KENYA

Ayre (Peter J.), Somerset 220
Bonham (J. & S.L.), London W 172
Chalmers Hallam (E.), Hampshire 125
Empire Books, North Yorkshire 198
Kenya Books, E Sussex.............................. 100
Peter M Daly, Hampshire........................... 127
Popeley (Frank T.), Cambs 67
R. & A. Books, E Sussex............................ 102
Remington (Reg & Philip), Hertfordshire......... 133
Yesterday's Books, Dorset 92

- KOREA

Allsworth Rare Books Ltd., London SW......... 167
Empire Books, North Yorkshire 198

SPECIALITY INDEX

Hanshan Tang Books, London SW 168
R. & A. Books, E Sussex............................ 102
Remington (Reg & Philip), Hertfordshire......... 133
Transformer, Dumfries & Galloway............... 271
Traveller's Bookshelf (The), Somerset 217

- LADAKH
Bates & Hindmarch, W Yorks 249
Chalmers Hallam (E.), Hampshire................. 125
Hunter and Krageloh, Derbyshire 83
Kabristan Archives, Shropshire..................... 215
Rayner (Hugh Ashley), Somerset 217
Remington (Reg & Philip), Hertfordshire......... 133

- LAOS
Empire Books, North Yorkshire 198
Empire Books, North Yorkshire 198
Remington (Reg & Philip), Hertfordshire......... 133
Remington (Reg & Philip), Hertfordshire......... 133

- LAPLAND
R. & A. Books, E Sussex............................ 102

- LATIN AMERICA
Baldwin (Jack), Strathclyde 280
Books on Spain, London Outer..................... 184
Chalmers Hallam (E.), Hampshire................. 125
Delectus Books, London WC....................... 177
Empire Books, North Yorkshire 198
Hodgson (Judith), London W 174
Hünersdorff Rare Books, London SW............ 169
Marble Hill Books, Middlesex...................... 184
R. & A. Books, E Sussex............................ 102
Remington (Reg & Philip), Hertfordshire......... 133

- LATVIA
de Visser Books, Cambs 63
R. & A. Books, E Sussex............................ 102

- LITHUANIA
de Visser Books, Cambs 63
R. & A. Books, E Sussex............................ 102

- MADEIRA
Chas J. Sawyer, Kent 141
Empire Books, North Yorkshire 198
Hodgson (Judith), London W 174
Orssich (Paul), London SW 170
Pennymead Books, North Yorkshire 194
R. & A. Books, E Sussex............................ 102

- MALAYA
Empire Books, North Yorkshire 198
R. & A. Books, E Sussex............................ 102
Remington (Reg & Philip), Hertfordshire......... 133

- MALAYSIA
Beardsley (A.E.), Notts 205
Bonham (J. & S.L.), London W 172
Empire Books, North Yorkshire 198
R. & A. Books, E Sussex............................ 102
Remington (Reg & Philip), Hertfordshire......... 133
Traveller's Bookshelf (The), Somerset 217

- MALTA
Empire Books, North Yorkshire 198
Nicolas - Antiquarian Booksellers &
Art Dealers, London N............................. 159
R. & A. Books, E Sussex............................ 102

- MAURITIUS
Chas J. Sawyer, Kent 141
Empire Books, North Yorkshire 198
R. & A. Books, E Sussex............................ 102
Remington (Reg & Philip), Hertfordshire......... 133

- MELANESIA
Bonham (J. & S.L.), London W 172
Books, Denbighshire 286
Bracton Books, Cambs 63
Broadwater Books, Hampshire..................... 125
Chalmers Hallam (E.), Hampshire................. 125
Empire Books, North Yorkshire 198
Michael Graves-Johnston, London SW........... 169
Modern First Editions, London Outer 183
Remington (Reg & Philip), Hertfordshire......... 133
Wayside Books and Cards, Oxfordshire 207

- MEXICO
Baldwin (Jack), Strathclyde 280
Bardsley's Books, Suffolk............................ 226
Books on Spain, London Outer..................... 184
Booth Books, Powys................................. 289
Burton–Garbett (A.), London Outer 183
Delectus Books, London WC....................... 177
Empire Books, North Yorkshire 198
L.M.S. Books, Hertfordshire........................ 132
Modern First Editions, London Outer 183
Orssich (Paul), London SW 170
R. & A. Books, E Sussex............................ 102
Remington (Reg & Philip), Hertfordshire......... 133

- MIDDLE EAST, THE
Chalmers Hallam (E.), Hampshire................. 125
David Warnes Books, Herefordshire 129
Delectus Books, London WC....................... 177
Empire Books, North Yorkshire 198
Fishburn Books, London NW....................... 161
Hall, (Anthony C.) Antiquarian Bookseller,
London Outer 184
Hylton Booksearch, Merseyside 185
J.C. Deyong Books, London SW 169
Joppa Books Ltd., Surrey 231
Maghrob Bookshop (The), London WC.......... 178
P. and P. Books, Worcestershire 256
Peter M Daly, Hampshire........................... 127
R. & A. Books, E Sussex............................ 102
Remington (Reg & Philip), Hertfordshire......... 133
Ryeland Books, Northants........................... 200
Thorntons of Oxford Ltd., Oxfordshire........... 207
Traveller's Bookshelf (The), Somerset 217
Trotter Books (John), London N 160

- MONGOLIA
Chalmers Hallam (E.), Hampshire................. 125
Empire Books, North Yorkshire 198
R. & A. Books, E Sussex............................ 102
Remington (Reg & Philip), Hertfordshire......... 133
Traveller's Bookshelf (The), Somerset 217

SPECIALITY INDEX

- MONTE CARLO
R. & A. Books, E Sussex............................. 102

- MOROCCO
Books on Spain, London Outer 184
Empire Books, North Yorkshire 198
Orssich (Paul), London SW 170
R. & A. Books, E Sussex.............................. 102
Remington (Reg & Philip), Hertfordshire......... 133
Traveller's Bookshelf (The), Somerset 217
Yesterday's Books, Dorset 92

- NATAL
Chalmers Hallam (E.), Hampshire 125
Empire Books, North Yorkshire 198
R. & A. Books, E Sussex.............................. 102
Remington (Reg & Philip), Hertfordshire......... 133
Yesterday's Books, Dorset 92

- NEAR EAST, THE
Marble Hill Books, Middlesex....................... 184
Peter M Daly, Hampshire............. 127
Quest Books, East Yorkshire 107
R. & A. Books, E Sussex.............................. 102
Remington (Reg & Philip), Hertfordshire......... 133
Seydi Rare Books (Sevin), London NW 162
Thorntons of Oxford Ltd., Oxfordshire 207
Traveller's Bookshelf (The), Somerset 217

- NEPAL
Chalmers Hallam (E.), Hampshire 125
David Warnes Books, Herefordshire 129
Glacier Books, Tayside 282
Hunter and Krageloh, Derbyshire 83
Little Bookshop (The), Cumbria 81
R. & A. Books, E Sussex.............................. 102
Rayner (Hugh Ashley), Somerset 217
Remington (Reg & Philip), Hertfordshire. 133
Traveller's Bookshelf (The), Somerset 217
Verandah Books, Dorset 95

- NETHERLANDS, THE
Empire Books, North Yorkshire 198
R. & A. Books, East Sussex 102

- NEW ZEALAND
Empire Books, North Yorkshire 198
Preston Book Company, Lancashire 145
R. & A. Books, East Sussex 102
Remington (Reg & Philip), Hertfordshire......... 133

- NICARAGUA
Empire Books, North Yorkshire 198
Orssich (Paul), London SW.......................... 170
R. & A. Books, East Sussex 102
Remington (Reg & Philip), Hertfordshire......... 133

- NORTH AFRICA
Chalmers Hallam (E.), Hampshire 125
Empire Books, North Yorkshire 198
Maghreb Bookshop (The), London WC.......... 178
R. & A. Books, East Sussex 102
Remington (Reg & Philip), Hertfordshire......... 133
Samovar Books, Co. Dublin......................... 264
Yesterday's Books, Dorset 92

- NORTH EAST ASIA
Chalmers Hallam (E.), Hampshire 125
R. & A. Books, East Sussex 102
Remington (Reg & Philip), Hertfordshire......... 133

- NORTH WEST FRONTIER PROVINCE
Bonham (J. & S.L.), London W 172
David Warnes Books, Herefordshire 129
Rayner (Hugh Ashley), Somerset 217
Remington (Reg & Philip), Hertfordshire......... 133
Verandah Books, Dorset 95

- NORWAY
Apocalypse, Surrey 233
Empire Books, North Yorkshire 198
Glacier Books, Tayside 282
Mulyan (Don), Merseyside........................... 186
R. & A. Books, East Sussex 107

- ORIENT, THE
J.C. Deyong Books, London SW 169
R. & A. Books, East Sussex 102
Rayner (Hugh Ashley), Somerset 217
Remington (Reg & Philip), Hertfordshire......... 133

- PACIFIC NORTH WEST, THE
Michael Graves-Johnston, London SW 169
Remington (Reg & Philip), Hertfordshire......... 133

- PACIFIC, THE
Chalmers Hallam (E.), Hampshire 125
Empire Books, North Yorkshire 198
Moore (Peter), Cambs 64
R. & A. Books, East Sussex 102
Remington (Reg & Philip), Hertfordshire......... 133

- PAKISTAN
Empire Books, North Yorkshire 198
Glacier Books, Tayside 282
R. & A. Books, East Sussex 102
Rayner (Hugh Ashley), Somerset 217
Remington (Reg & Philip), Hertfordshire......... 133
Traveller's Bookshelf (The), Somerset 217
Verandah Books, Dorset 95

- PALESTINE
Joppa Books Ltd., Surrey 231
R. & A. Books, East Sussex 102
Remington (Reg & Philip), Hertfordshire......... 133
Samovar Books, Co. Dublin 264
Traveller's Bookshelf (The), Somerset 217

- PANAMA CANAL
Pennymead Books, North Yorkshire 194
R. & A. Books, East Sussex 102
Remington (Reg & Philip), Hertfordshire......... 133

- PAPUA NEW GUINEA
Bonham (J. & S.L.), London W 172
Empire Books, North Yorkshire 198
Moore (Peter), Cambs 64
Remington (Reg & Philip), Hertfordshire......... 133
Traveller's Bookshelf (The), Somerset 217

SPECIALITY INDEX

- PHILIPPINES, THE
Empire Books, North Yorkshire 198
Hodgson (Judith), London W 174
Orssich (Paul), London SW 170
R. & A. Books, East Sussex 102
Remington (Reg & Philip), Hertfordshire......... 133
Traveller's Bookshelf (The), Somerset 217

- POLAND
Bardsley's Books, Suffolk............................. 226
Caledonia Books, Strathclyde........................ 280
de Visser Books, Cambs 63
Empire Books, North Yorkshire 198
Orbis Books (London) Ltd., London W 175
R. & A. Books, East Sussex 102

- POLAR
Allinson (Frank & Stella), Warwickshire 237
Bluntisham Books, Cambs 63
Bonham (J. & S.L.), London W 172
Empire Books, North Yorkshire 198
Glacier Books, Tayside 282
J & J Burgess Booksellers, Cambs 64
McEwan Fine Books, Grampian.................... 273
R. & A. Books, East Sussex 102
Remington (Reg & Philip), Hertfordshire......... 133
Riddell (Peter), East Yorkshire 106
Roz Hulse, Conwy 286

- POLYNESIA
Bracton Books, Cambs 63
Chalmers Hallam (E.), Hampshire 125
Empire Books, North Yorkshire 198
Michael Graves-Johnston, London SW 169
R. & A. Books, East Sussex 102
Remington (Reg & Philip), Hertfordshire......... 133

- PORTUGAL
Baldwin (Jack), Strathclyde 280
Books on Spain, London Outer 184
Empire Books, North Yorkshire 198
Hodgson (Judith), London W 174
Orssich (Paul), London SW 170
R. & A. Books, East Sussex 102
York (Graham), Devon............................... 86

- PUERTO RICO
Empire Books, North Yorkshire 198
Orssich (Paul), London SW,......................... 170
Pennymead Books, North Yorkshire 194
R. & A. Books, East Sussex 102
Remington (Reg & Philip), Hertfordshire......... 133

- PUNJAB
R. & A. Books, East Sussex 102
Rayner (Hugh Ashley), Somerset 217
Remington (Reg & Philip), Hertfordshire......... 133

- PYRENEES, THE
Bass (Ben), Wiltshire 251
Glacier Books, Tayside 282
R. & A. Books, East Sussex 102

- RAJASTHAN
Chalmers Hallam (E.), Hampshire 125

R. & A. Books, East Sussex 102
Rayner (Hugh Ashley), Somerset 217
Remington (Reg & Philip), Hertfordshire......... 133

- REUNION
Empire Books, North Yorkshire 198
Remington (Reg & Philip), Hertfordshire......... 133

- ROMANIA
de Visser Books, Cambs 63
Empire Books, North Yorkshire 198
R. & A. Books, East Sussex 102
Traveller's Bookshelf (The), Somerset 217

- RUSSIA
Baldwin (Jack), Strathclyde 280
de Visser Books, Cambs 63
Empire Books, North Yorkshire 198
Hab Books, London W............................... 173
Hall, (Anthony C.) Antiquarian Bookseller,
London Outer 184
Kenny's Bookshops and Art Galleries Ltd, Co.
Galway 266
Left on The Shelf, Cumbria.......................... 79
Orb's Bookshop, Grampian.......................... 274
Orbis Books (London) Ltd., London W 175
R. & A. Books, East Sussex 102
Remington (Reg & Philip), Hertfordshire......... 133
Thorntons of Oxford Ltd., Oxfordshire 207
Traveller's Bookshelf (The), Somerset 217

- SAHARA, THE
Apocalypse, Surrey 233
Chalmers Hallam (E.), Hampshire 125
Empire Books, North Yorkshire 198
R. & A. Books, East Sussex 102
Remington (Reg & Philip), Hertfordshire......... 133
Yesterday's Books, Dorset 92

- SANTO DOMINGO
Empire Books, North Yorkshire 198
Pennymead Books, North Yorkshire 194
Remington (Reg & Philip), Hertfordshire......... 133

- SARAWAK
Eastgate Bookshop, East Yorkshire 106
Empire Books, North Yorkshire 198
R. & A. Books, East Sussex 102
Remington (Reg & Philip), Hertfordshire......... 133
Sarawak Books, East Yorkshire...................... 106
Traveller's Bookshelf (The), Somerset 217

- SCANDINAVIA
Empire Books, North Yorkshire 198
R. & A. Books, East Sussex 102

- SCOTLAND
Alba Books, Grampian 274
Armchair Books, Lothian 276
Atholl Fine Books, Tayside 281
Bell (Peter), Lothian 276
Benny Gillies Books Ltd, Dumfries & Galloway 269
Bookworm, Lothian 277
Border Books, Borders................................ 268
Broadwater Books, Hampshire 125

SPECIALITY INDEX

Byre Books, Dumfries & Galloway 270
Clifford Milne Books, Grampian 272
Colonsay Bookshop, Isle of Colonsay 276
Cooper Hay Rare Books, Strathclyde 280
Cornell Books, Gloucestershire 117
Cornucopia Books, Lincolnshire 153
Creaking Shelves, Inverness-shire 275
David Houston - Bookseller, London E 155
Empire Books, North Yorkshire 198
Farquharson, (Hilary), Tayside 281
Ferguson (Elizabeth), Grampian 272
Freader's Books, Tayside 281
G. C. Books Ltd., Dumfries & Galloway 271
Glacier Books, Tayside 282
Grampian Books, Grampian 274
Greta Books, Durham 97
Holmes Books (Harry), East Yorkshire 107
Hughes Rare Books (Spike), Borders 268
Hutchison (Books) (Larry), Fife 271
Iona Bookshop (The), Isle of Iona 276
Joel Segal Books, Devon 86
Last Century Books, Borders 268
Leakey's Bookshop, Highland 275
Loch Croispol Bookshop & Restaurant,
Highland 275
McCrone (Audrey), Isle of Arran 275
McNaughtan's Bookshop, Lothian 278
Mercat Books, Highland 274
Oopalba Books, Cheshire 71
Orb's Bookshop, Grampian 274
Prospect House Books, Co. Down 261
R. & A. Books, East Sussex 102
Read (C.&J.), Gorleston Books, Norfolk 188
Roberts Books, Ayrshire 280
Samovar Books, Co. Dublin 264
Stroma Books, Borders 268
Wheen O'Books, Scottish Borders 269
Wilson (David), Buckinghamshire 61

- SEYCHELLES, THE
Chas J. Sawyer, Kent 141
Empire Books, North Yorkshire 198
R. & A. Books, East Sussex 102
Remington (Reg & Philip), Hertfordshire 133
Yesterday's Books, Dorset 92

- SIAM
Empire Books, North Yorkshire 198
R. & A. Books, East Sussex 102
Remington (Reg & Philip), Hertfordshire 133
Traveller's Bookshelf (The), Somerset 217

- SIBERIA
Bonham (J. & S.L.), London W 172
Orb's Bookshop, Grampian 274
R. & A. Books, East Sussex 102
Remington (Reg & Philip), Hertfordshire 133

- SINGAPORE
Allsworth Rare Books Ltd., London SW 167
Empire Books, North Yorkshire 198
R. & A. Books, East Sussex 102
Remington (Reg & Philip), Hertfordshire 133

- SOUTH AFRICA
Barn Books, Buckinghamshire 61
Boer War Books, North Yorkshire 198
Bonham (J. & S.L.), London W 172
Chalmers Hallam (E.), Hampshire 125
Chas J. Sawyer, Kent 141
Empire Books, North Yorkshire 198
Kenya Books, East Sussex 100
R. & A. Books, East Sussex 102
Remington (Reg & Philip), Hertfordshire 133
Samovar Books, Co. Dublin 264
Smith (Ray), Hertfordshire 130

- SOUTH AMERICA
Baldwin (Jack), Strathclyde 280
Bonham (J. & S.L.), London W 172
Books on Spain, London Outer 184
Brock Books, North Yorkshire 193
Burton-Garbett (A.), London Outer 183
Chalmers Hallam (E.), Hampshire 125
Empire Books, North Yorkshire 198
Hodgson (Judith), London W 174
Hünersdorff Rare Books, London SW 169
Orssich (Paul), London SW 170
Prescott - The Bookseller (John), London Outer 184
R. & A. Books, East Sussex 102
Remington (Reg & Philip), Hertfordshire 133

- SOUTH ATLANTIC ISLANDS
Empire Books, North Yorkshire 198
Miles Apart, Suffolk 229
MK Book Services, Cambs 66
R. & A. Books, East Sussex 102
Remington (Reg & Philip), Hertfordshire 133

- SOUTH EAST ASIA
Chalmers Hallam (F.), Hampshire 125
David Warnes Books, Herefordshire 129
Eastgate Bookshop, East Yorkshire 106
Empire Books, North Yorkshire 198
Hanshan Tang Books, London SW 168
J.C. Deyong Books, London SW 169
Mandalay Bookshop, London SW 169
Peter M Daly, Hampshire 127
R. & A. Books, East Sussex 102
Remington (Reg & Philip), Hertfordshire 133
Transformer, Dumfries & Galloway 271
Traveller's Bookshelf (The), Somerset 217
Verandah Books, Dorset 95

- SOUTH EAST EUROPE
de Visser Books, Cambs 63
R. & A. Books, East Sussex 102

- SOUTH PACIFIC ISLANDS
Chalmers Hallam (E.), Hampshire 125
Empire Books, North Yorkshire 198
Michael Graves-Johnston, London SW 169
R. & A. Books, East Sussex 102
Remington (Reg & Philip), Hertfordshire 133

- SPAIN
Baldwin (Jack), Strathclyde 280
Bass (Ben), Wiltshire 251
Books on Spain, London Outer 184

SPECIALITY INDEX

Empire Books, North Yorkshire 198
Hodgson (Judith), London W 174
Orssich (Paul), London SW 170
R. & A. Books, East Sussex 102
Studio Bookshop, East Sussex...................... 100
York (Graham), Devon............................... 86

- SRI LANKA
Chalmers Hallam (E.), Hampshire 125
Empire Books, North Yorkshire 198
R. & A. Books, East Sussex 102
Rayner (Hugh Ashley), Somerset 217
Remington (Reg & Philip), Hertfordshire......... 133
Verandah Books, Dorset 95

- STRAITS SETTLEMENTS, THE
Empire Books, North Yorkshire 198
Remington (Reg & Philip), Hertfordshire......... 133
Traveller's Bookshelf (The), Somerset 217

- SUDAN, THE
Bonham (J. & S.L.), London W 172
Chalmers Hallam (E.), Hampshire 125
Empire Books, North Yorkshire 198
Joppa Books Ltd., Surrey 231
Michael Graves-Johnston, London SW 169
P. and P. Books, Worcestershire 256
R. & A. Books, East Sussex 102
Remington (Reg & Philip), Hertfordshire......... 133
Traveller's Bookshelf (The), Somerset 217
Yesterday's Books, Dorset 92

- SURINAM
Empire Books, North Yorkshire 198
Pennymead Books, North Yorkshire 194
Remington (Reg & Philip), Hertfordshire......... 133

- SWEDEN
Empire Books, North Yorkshire 198
R. & A. Books, East Sussex 102

- SWITZERLAND
Cavendish Rare Books, London N 158
Empire Books, North Yorkshire 198
Glacier Books, Tayside 282
Hunter and Krageloh, Derbyshire 83
R. & A. Books, East Sussex 102

- SYRIA
Bonham (J. & S.L.), London W 172
Empire Books, North Yorkshire 198
R. & A. Books, East Sussex 102
Remington (Reg & Philip), Hertfordshire......... 133

- TANZANIA
Ayre (Peter J.), Somerset 220
Chalmers Hallam (E.), Hampshire 125
Empire Books, North Yorkshire 198
Kenya Books, East Sussex 100
Popcley (Frank T.), Cambs 67
R. & A. Books, East Sussex 102
Remington (Reg & Philip), Hertfordshire......... 133
Yesterday's Books, Dorset 92

- TIBET
Bates & Hindmarch, W Yorks 249
Bonham (J. & S.L.), London W 172
Cavendish Rare Books, London N 158
Chalmers Hallam (E.), Hampshire 125
Craobh Rua Books, Co. Armagh................... 260
David Warnes Books, Herefordshire 129
Empire Books, North Yorkshire 198
Glacier Books, Tayside 282
Hanshan Tang Books, London SW 168
Hunter and Krageloh, Derbyshire 83
Inner Bookshop (The), Oxfordshire................ 210
Peter M Daly, Hampshire 127
R. & A. Books, East Sussex 102
Remington (Reg & Philip), Hertfordshire......... 133
Traveller's Bookshelf (The), Somerset 217
Verandah Books, Dorset 95

- TRISTAN DA CUNHA
Empire Books, North Yorkshire 198
Remington (Reg & Philip), Hertfordshire......... 133

- TURKEY
Bonham (J. & S.L.), London W 172
Empire Books, North Yorkshire 198
Joppa Books Ltd., Surrey 231
Nicolas - Antiquarian Booksellers & Art
Dealers, London N 159
Quest Books, East Yorkshire 107
R. & A. Books, East Sussex 102
Remington (Reg & Philip), Hertfordshire......... 133
Seydi Rare Books (Sevin), London NW 162
Traveller's Bookshelf (The), Somerset 217

- U.S.A.
Americanabooksuk, Cumbria 77
Empire Books, North Yorkshire 198
Glacier Books, Tayside 282
Little Stour Books, Kent 137
Marble Hill Books, Middlesex 184
Preston Book Company, Lancashire 145
R. & A. Books, East Sussex 102
Remington (Reg & Philip), Hertfordshire......... 133
Roland Books, Kent 139
Roz Hulse, Conwy 286
Shakeshaft (Dr. B.), Cheshire....................... 71

- UGANDA
Bonham (J. & S.L.), London W 172
Chalmers Hallam (E.), Hampshire 125
Empire Books, North Yorkshire 198
Kenya Books, East Sussex 100
Michael Graves-Johnston, London SW 169
Popeley (Frank T.), Cambs 67
R. & A. Books, East Sussex 102
Remington (Reg & Philip), Hertfordshire......... 133
Yesterday's Books, Dorset 92

- VANUATU
Empire Books, North Yorkshire 198
Remington (Reg & Philip), Hertfordshire......... 133

- VIETNAM
Empire Books, North Yorkshire 198
R. & A. Books, East Sussex 102

SPECIALITY INDEX

Remington (Reg & Philip), Hertfordshire......... 133
Traveller's Bookshelf (The), Somerset 217

- WALES

Browning Books, Torfaen 294
Capital Bookshop, Cardiff 283
Carningli Centre, Pembrokeshire 288
Castle Bookshop, Powys.............................. 292
Colin Hancock, Ceredigion 284
Cornell Books, Gloucestershire 117
Dylans Bookstore, Swansea 294
Empire Books, North Yorkshire 198
Fifteenth Century Bookshop (The), East Sussex. 104
Gildas Books, Cheshire 68
Glacier Books, Tayside 282
Great Oak Bookshop (The), Powys 292
Island Books, Devon 85
Modern Welsh Publications I td., Merseyside 185
R. & A. Books, East Sussex 102
Read (C.&J.), Gorleston Books, Norfolk 188
Siop Lyfrau'r Hen Bost, Gwynedd 287
Stella Books, Monmouthshire 288
Thomas (E. Wyn), Conwy 285
Vickers (Anthony), North Yorkshire 196
Whitchurch Books Ltd., Cardiff..................... 283
Ystwyth Books, Ceredigion 284

- WEST AFRICA

Chalmers Hallam (E.), Hampshire 125
Empire Books, North Yorkshire 198
Kenya Books, East Sussex 100
Michael Graves-Johnston, London SW 169
Oopalba Books, Cheshire............................. 71
Peter M Daly, Hampshire 127
R. & A. Books, East Sussex 102
Remington (Reg & Philip), Hertfordshire......... 133
Yesterday's Books, Dorset 92

- WEST INDIES, THE

Bonham (J. & S.L.), London W 172
Empire Books, North Yorkshire 198
Pennymead Books, North Yorkshire 194
R. & A. Books, East Sussex 102
Remington (Reg & Philip), Hertfordshire......... 133
Roz Hulse, Conwy 286

- WESTERN CAPE

R. & A. Books, East Sussex 102
Yesterday's Books, Dorset 92

- YUKON

Chalmers Hallam (E.), Hampshire 125
Remington (Reg & Philip), Hertfordshire......... 133

- ZULULAND

Chalmers Hallam (E.), Hampshire 125
Empire Books, North Yorkshire 198
R. & A. Books, East Sussex 102
Remington (Reg & Philip), Hertfordshire......... 133
Yesterday's Books, Dorset 92

COUNTRY HOUSES

Apocalypse, Surrey 233
Art Reference Books, Hampshire 125
Cornucopia Books, Lincolnshire 153

Dales & Lakes Book Centre, Cumbria 80
Fifteenth Century Bookshop (The), East Sussex. 104
Lighthouse Books (The), Dorset 92
Mannwaring (M.G.), Bristol 59
Marlborough Rare Books Ltd., London W 174
Old Town Bookshop (The), Lothian 278
R. & A. Books, East Sussex 102
Spenceley Books (David), W Yorks 249
Staniland (Booksellers), Lincolnshire 154
Trinity Rare Books, Co. Leitrim 266

COUNTY - LOCAL

Ambra Books, Bristol 58
Anthony Vickers Books, North Yorkshire 196
Barn Books, Shropshire............................... 215
Barter Books, Northumberland 202
Bath Old Books, Somerset 216
Benny Gillies Books Ltd, Dumfries & Galloway 269
Blackwell's Rare Books, Oxfordshire 209
Bookpassage (The), Shropshire 213
Bosorne Books, Cornwall 75
Bury Bookshop, Suffolk 226
Churchgate Books, Suffolk 227
Clark (Nigel A.), London SE 165
Cobnar Books, Kent 142
Cornucopia Books, Lincolnshire 153
Country Books, Derbyshire 82
Dales & Lakes Book Centre, Cumbria 80
Delph Books, Gr Man 120
Eagle Bookshop (The), Bedfordshire 53
Fifteenth Century Bookshop (The), East Sussex. 104
Glasheen-Books, Surrey 232
Hall's Bookshop, Kent................................ 141
Inner Bookshop (The), Oxfordshire................ 210
Jade Mountain Bookshop, Hampshire 126
MK Book Services, Cambs 66
Post-Horn Books, North Yorkshire 193
R & B Graham Trading, Cornwall 74
Read (C.&J.), Gorleston Books, Norfolk 188
Roger Collicott Books, Cornwall 75
Roundstone Books, Lancashire...................... 144
Sax Books, Suffolk 229
Spooner & Co, Somerset 220
Uncle Phil's Books, West Midlands 240
York (Graham), Devon............................... 86

COURTESY

Black Cat Books, Norfolk............................ 188
Burmester (James), Bristol........................... 59
Weininger Antiquarian Books (Eva M.),
London NW 163

COWBOYS

Americanabooksuk, Cumbria 77
Joel Segal Books, Devon 86
Phenotype Books, Cumbria 80
R. & A. Books, East Sussex 102
Williams (Bookdealer), (Richard), N Lincs 154

CRAFTS

Andrew Morton (Books), Powys.................... 289
Apocalypse, Surrey 233
Arden Books & Cosmographia, Warwickshire... 237
Baldwin (M. & M.), Worcestershire 255
Barn Books, Buckinghamshire....................... 61

SPECIALITY INDEX

Books for Content, Herefordshire.................. 128
Brad Books, Essex..................................... 111
Brock Books, North Yorkshire...................... 193
Browse Books, Lancashire 144
Bruce Holdsworth Books, East Sussex 105
Cavern Books, Cheshire 70
Cheshire Book Centre, Cheshire.................... 69
Cornucopia Books, Lincolnshire 153
Cottage Books, Leics.................................. 147
Country Books, Derbyshire 82
Cover to Cover, Merseyside......................... 186
Crouch Rare Books, Surrey.......................... 233
Dales & Lakes Book Centre, Cumbria............. 80
Design Gallery 1850-1950 (The), Kent 142
Discovery Bookshop, Carmarthenshire............ 283
DPE Books, Devon 87
Dusty Books, Powys 292
Fifteenth Century Bookshop (The), East Sussex. 104
Footrope Knots, Suffolk.............................. 228
Four Shire Bookshops, Gloucestershire 114
Furneaux Books (Lee), Devon....................... 89
George St. Books, Derbyshire 83
Grahame Thornton, Bookseller, Dorset........... 93
Hay Castle, Powys.................................... 290
J & J Burgess Booksellers, Cambs 64
Joel Segal Books, Devon 86
Judith Mansfield, W Yorks 250
Just Books, Cornwall 76
Kalligraphia, Isle of Wight 134
Macbuiks, North Yorkshire.......................... 194
McCrone (Audrey), Isle of Arran 275
N1 Books, East Sussex 105
Priestpopple Books, Northumberland 202
R. & A. Books, East Sussex 102
Reeves Technical Books, North Yorkshire 196
Scrivener's Books & Bookbinding, Derbyshire... 82
Sleepy Elephant Books & Artefacts, Cumbria ... 80
Smith Books (Keith), Herefordshire 128
Smith Books, (Sally), Suffolk 227
Sterling Books, Somerset 221
Stobart Davies Limited, Carmarthernshire 284
Tarka Books, Devon 84
Treasure Island (The), Gr Man..................... 119
Trinders' Fine Tools, Suffolk 227
Upper-Room Books, Somerset...................... 218
Wheen O'Books, Scottish Borders 269
Whittle, Bookseller (Avril), Cumbria 81
Williams (Christopher), Dorset 94

CRIME (TRUE)

Abrahams (Mike), Staffordshire 224
Bolland Books, Bedfordshire......................... 53
Booth (Booksearch Service), (Geoff), Cheshire... 68
Cavern Books, Cheshire 70
Cheshire Book Centre, Cheshire.................... 69
Classic Crime Collections, Gr Man 119
Clifford Elmer Books Ltd., Cheshire 68
Crimes Ink, London E................................ 155
Dunstan Books, Dorset............................... 91
Eastcote Bookshop (The), London Outer......... 181
Eastgate Bookshop, East Yorkshire 106
Fifteenth Century Bookshop (The), East Sussex. 104
ForensicSearch, Hertfordshire 132
Garfi Books, Powys 293
HCB Wholesale, Powys.............................. 290

Hylton Booksearch, Merseyside 185
Intech Books, Northumberland 203
J & J Burgess Booksellers, Cambs 64
Jade Mountain Bookshop, Hampshire 126
Joel Segal Books, Devon 86
John Underwood Antiquarian Books, Norfolk .. 190
Just Books, Cornwall 76
Lawful Occasions, Essex............................. 108
Loretta Lay Books, London NW 162
Maggy Browne, Lincolnshire 150
McCaughtrie (K.A.), North Yorkshire 194
McCrone (Audrey), Isle of Arran 275
Ming Books, Dumfries & Galloway 271
Murder & Mayhem, Powys 291
Porter Bookshop (The), S Yorks................... 222
R M Books, Hertfordshire 132
R. & A. Books, East Sussex 102
Roland Books, Kent 139
Roscrea Bookshop, Co. Tipperary................. 267
Ruebotham (Kirk), Cheshire........................ 71
Rupert Books, Cambs 65
Simply Read Books, East Sussex.................... 101
Star Lord Books, Gr Man 119
Tarka Books, Devon 84
Treasure Trove Books, Leics........................ 148
Undercover Books, Lincolnshire 154
Whitehall Books, East Sussex....................... 103
Wiend Books, Lancashire 144
Williams (Bookdealer), (Richard), N Lincs 154
Yesterday's News, Conwy........................... 285
Zardoz Books, Wiltshire............................. 254

CRIMINAL LAW

Hylton Booksearch, Merseyside 185
R. & A. Books, East Sussex 102
Williams (Bookdealer), (Richard), N Lincs 154

CRIMINOLOGY

Bolland Books, Bedfordshire......................... 53
Chesters (G. & J.), Staffordshire 225
Clifford Elmer Books Ltd., Cheshire 68
Craobh Rua Books, Co. Armagh................... 260
Crimes Ink, London E................................ 155
Delectus Books, London WC........................ 177
Garfi Books, Powys 293
hullbooks.com, East Yorkshire 107
Hylton Booksearch, Merseyside 185
Joel Segal Books, Devon 86
Lawful Occasions, Essex............................. 108
Loretta Lay Books, London NW 162
Murder & Mayhem, Powys 291
R M Books, Hertfordshire 132
R. & A. Books, East Sussex 102
Reading Lasses, Dumfries & Galloway 271
Roscrea Bookshop, Co. Tipperary 267
Transformer, Dumfries & Galloway................ 271
Undercover Books, Lincolnshire 154
Whitehall Books, East Sussex....................... 103
Williams (Bookdealer), (Richard), N Lincs 154

CRITICAL THEORY

Joel Segal Books, Devon 86
Reading Lasses, Dumfries & Galloway 271

SPECIALITY INDEX

CROCHET
Browse Books, Lancashire 144
Byrom Textile Bookroom (Richard), Lancashire 143
Cover to Cover, Merseyside......................... 186
Joel Segal Books, Devon 86
Judith Mansfield, W Yorks 250
R. & A. Books, East Sussex 102
Sleepy Elephant Books & Artefacts, Cumbria ... 80
Whittle, Bookseller (Avril), Cumbria 81

CRUSTACEA
Joel Segal Books, Devon 86
Parkinsons Books, Merseyside...................... 186

CRYPTOGRAPHY
Baldwin (M. & M.), Worcestershire 255
Joel Segal Books, Devon 86
Susanne Schulz-Falster Rare Books, London N. 160

CRYPTOZOOLOGY
Atlantis Bookshop, London WC.................... 177
Gildas Books, Cheshire 68
Inner Bookshop (The), Oxfordshire................ 210
Randall (Tom), Somerset............................ 219
SETI Books, Staffordshire........................... 225
Wizard Books, Cambs 67

CULTS
Inner Bookshop (The), Oxfordshire................ 210
Joel Segal Books, Devon 86
R. & A. Books, East Sussex 102
Samovar Books, Co. Dublin......................... 264

CULTURE - FOREIGN
Books on Spain, London Outer 184
Joel Segal Books, Devon 86
Print Matters, London SE............................ 166
Transformer, Dumfries & Galloway... 271
Wadard Books, Kent 138
Weininger Antiquarian Books (Eva M.),
London NW.. 163

- NATIONAL
Colin Hancock, Ceredigion 284
De Burca Rare Books, Co. Dublin 264
Guildmaster Books, Cheshire 70
Joel Segal Books, Devon 86
Kenny's Bookshops and Art Galleries Ltd, Co.
Galway 266
Leakey's Bookshop, Highland. 275
Orb's Bookshop, Grampian......................... 274
Print Matters, London SE............................ 166
Samovar Books, Co. Dublin......................... 264
Stokes Books, Co. Dublin........................... 265
Weininger Antiquarian Books (Eva M.),
London NW.. 163

- POPULAR
Apocalypse, Surrey 233
Book Palace (The), London SE 164
Bookshop (The), Gr Man 118
Joel Segal Books, Devon 86
Print Matters, London SE............................ 166
Pyecroft (Ruth), Gloucestershire 117
R. & A. Books, East Sussex 102

Reid of Liverpool, Merseyside...................... 185

CUNEIFORM STUDIES
Thorntons of Oxford Ltd., Oxfordshire 207

CURIOSA
Delectus Books, London WC....................... 177
Edmund Pollinger Rare Books, London SW..... 167
R. & A. Books, East Sussex 102
Susanne Schulz-Falster Rare Books, London N. 160

CURIOSITIES
Bernstein (Nicholas), London W................... 172
Don Kelly Books, London W 172
Dylans Bookstore, Swansea......................... 294
N1 Books, East Sussex 105
Philip Hopper, Essex 110
R. & A. Books, East Sussex 102

CURRENT AFFAIRS
R. & A. Books, East Sussex. 102

CUSTOMS & EXCISE
Cox (Geoff), Devon 90

CYBERNETICS
Dylans Bookstore, Swansea......................... 294
Stroh (M.A.), London E 155
Westons, Hertfordshire 133

D.I.Y. (DO IT YOURSELF)
Barcombe Services, Essex........................... 108
Brown-Studies, Strathclyde.......................... 279
Carningli Centre, Pembrokeshire................... 288
Cover to Cover, Merseyside......................... 186
Jade Mountain Bookshop, Hampshire 126
Junk & Spread Eagle, London SE.................. 165
Larkham Books (Patricia), Glos.................... 117
McCrone (Audrey), Isle of Arran 275
R. & A. Books, East Sussex 102
Reeves Technical Books, N Yorkshire 196
Roscrea Bookshop, Co. Tipperary................. 267
Stobart Davies Limited, Carmarthenshire 284
Tarka Books, Devon 84
Trinity Rare Books, Co. Leitrim 266
Uncle Phil's Books, West Midlands 240

DADAISM
Joel Segal Books, Devon 86
R. & A. Books, East Sussex 102

DANCE
Addyman Books, Powys............................. 289
Baxter - Books (Eddie), Somerset 221
Brock Books, North Yorkshire...................... 193
Byre Books, Dumfries & Galloway................ 270
Cornucopia Books, Lincolnshire 153
Cover to Cover, Merseyside......................... 186
Dance Books Ltd, Hampshire 121
Dooley (Rosemary), Cumbria 78
Fifteenth Century Bookshop (The), E Sussex 104
Fitzsimons (Anne), Cumbria 78
Greenroom Books, W Yorks 248
Hylton Booksearch, Merseyside 185
Joel Segal Books, Devon 86

SPECIALITY INDEX

Paramor (C.D.), Suffolk 229
R. & A. Books, East Sussex 102

DEATH & FUNERALS

Inner Bookshop (The), Oxfordshire................. 210
R. & A. Books, East Sussex 102

DECORATIVE ART

Amwell Book Company, London EC 157
Antiques on High, Oxfordshire...................... 209
Apocalypse, Surrey 233
Art Reference Books, Hampshire 125
Ballantyne-Way (Roger), Suffolk 229
Barlow (Vincent G.), Hampshire 125
Barmby (C. & A.J.), Kent............................ 141
Books & Things, London W......................... 172
Bruce Holdsworth Books, East Sussex 105
Butts Books (Mary), Berkshire 56
Chalk (Old & Out of Print Books)
(Christine M.), West Midlands 239
Cornucopia Books, Lincolnshire 153
Cover to Cover, Merseyside.......................... 186
Decorum Books, London N 158
Don Kelly Books, London W 172
Duck (William), Hampshire.......................... 124
Foster (Stephen), London NW 161
Goodyer (Nicholas), London N 159
Heneage Art Books (Thomas), London SW 169
Hodgkins and Company Limited (Ian),
Gloucestershire 116
Jean Hedger, Berkshire 55
Joel Segal Books, Devon 86
Judith Mansfield, W Yorks 250
Junk & Spread Eagle, London SE 165
Keswick Bookshop, Cumbria 79
N1 Books, East Sussex 105
Old Town Bookshop (The), Lothian 278
Pagan Limited (Hugh), London SW................ 170
Phelan Books, Co. Dublin 265
Portobello Books, London W 175
Potterton Books, North Yorkshire.................. 197
R. & A. Books, East Sussex 102
Reference Works Ltd., Dorset 95
St Swithin's Illustrated & Children's Books,
London W 175
Studio (The), Strathclyde 280
Tasburgh Books, Norfolk 191
Temperley (David), West Midlands................. 239
Trinders' Fine Tools, Suffolk 227
Uncle Phil's Books, West Midlands 240
Whittle, Bookseller (Avril), Cumbria 81
Worlds End Bookshop, London SW 171
Wyseby House Books, Berkshire 55

DEEP SEA DIVING

Green Ltd. (G.L.), Hertfordshire.................... 132
Larkham Books (Patricia), Gloucestershire....... 117
Lewcock (John), Cambs 66
Lost Books, Northants................................. 201
Marine and Cannon Books, Cheshire 69
R. & A. Books, East Sussex 102
Rods Books, Devon 88
Stroh (M.A.), London E 155
Sub Aqua Prints and Books, Hampshire 123

DEMOGRAPHY

R. & A. Books, East Sussex 102

DENTISTRY

R. & A. Books, East Sussex 102
Weiner (Graham), London N 160

DESIGN

Amwell Book Company, London EC 157
Apocalypse, Surrey 233
Art Book Company, (The), Suffolk.................. 228
Art Reference Books, Hampshire 125
Ballantyne-Way (Roger), Suffolk 229
Bianco Library, W Sussex............................ 242
Blaenavon Books, Torfaen 294
Broadleaf Books, Torfaen 294
Brock Books, North Yorkshire...................... 193
Bruce Holdsworth Books, East Sussex 105
Cover to Cover, Merseyside.......................... 186
David Flint, Hampshire 124
Decorum Books, London N 158
Don Kelly Books, London W 172
Duck (William), Hampshire.......................... 124
Finch Rare Books Ltd. (Simon), London W..... 173
Greenroom Books, W Yorks 248
Inch's Books, Kent 137
Jean Hedger, Berkshire 55
Joel Segal Books, Devon 86
Malvern Bookshop (The), Worcestershire 255
Martin - Bookseller (Colin), East Yorkshire 107
O'Flynn Books, North Yorkshire 199
R. & A. Books, East Sussex 102
Ray Rare and Out of Print Books (Janette),
N Yorks... 199
Roe and Moore, London WC 179
Sleepy Elephant Books & Artefacts, Cumbria ... 80
Trinders' Fine Tools, Suffolk 227
Uncle Phil's Books, West Midlands 240
Whittle, Bookseller (Avril), Cumbria 81

DIARIES

Country Books, Derbyshire 82
Dolphin Books, Suffolk................................ 226
Fifteenth Century Bookshop (The), E Sussex 104
Handley (Christopher), Tyne and Wear........... 236
Joel Segal Books, Devon 86
Lawrence Books, Notts................................ 204
Piccadilly Rare Books, E Sussex 105
R. & A. Books, E Sussex............................. 102
Wembdon Books, Somerset.......................... 217

DICTIONARIES

Addyman Books, Powys.............................. 289
Alec-Smith Books (Alex), East Yorkshire 107
Apocalypse, Surrey 233
Askew Books (Vernon), Wiltshire................... 251
Bernstein (Nicholas), London W 172
Books & Bygones (Pam Taylor), W Mids........ 241
BOOKS4U, Flintshire................................. 286
Chandos Books, Devon............................... 85
Church Street Books, Norfolk....................... 187
Cornucopia Books, Lincolnshire 153
Courtenay Bookroom, Oxfordshire 206
Delectus Books, London WC........................ 177
Fifteenth Century Bookshop (The), E Sussex 104

SPECIALITY INDEX

Hava Books, London SE.............................. 165
Jade Mountain Bookshop, Hampshire 126
Joel Segal Books, Devon 86
Kenya Books, E Sussex............................... 100
Murphy (C.J.), Norfolk............................... 190
Portobello Books, London W 175
R. & A. Books, E Sussex............................ 102
Sax Books, Suffolk 229
Scrivener's Books & Bookbinding, Derbyshire... 82
Seydi Rare Books (Sevin), London NW 162
Unsworths Booksellers, London WC.............. 163
Yates Antiquarian Books (Tony), Leics........... 148

DINOSAURS

Baldwin's Scientific Books, Essex 112
Joel Segal Books, Devon 86
Kalligraphia, Isle of Wight........................... 134
R. & A. Books, E Sussex............................. 102

DIRECTORIES - GENERAL

Heritage, West Midlands 239
Joel Segal Books, Devon 86
Roger Collicott Books, Cornwall 75
Sparkes (Books) (Ray), Staffordshire 225

- BRITISH

Chapter & Verse, Lincolnshire....................... 152
Craobh Rua Books, Co. Armagh................... 260
Delph Books, Gr Man................................ 120
Facet Books, Dorset................................... 91
Joel Segal Books, Devon 86
Sparkes (Books) (Ray), Staffordshire 225

DISNEYANA

Book Palace (The), London SE 164
Cygnet Books, East Yorkshire....................... 107
Fifteenth Century Bookshop (The), E Sussex 104
Green Meadow Books, Cornwall 74
R. & A. Books, E Sussex 102
Roscrea Bookshop, Co. Tipperary.................. 267
Stroh (M.A.), London E 155

DIVINING

Inner Bookshop (The), Oxfordshire................ 210
Joel Segal Books, Devon 86
Magis Books, Leics.................................... 149
McCrone (Audrey), Isle of Arran 275
Occultique, Northants................................. 200
Wizard Books, Cambs 67

DOCUMENTS - GENERAL

Collectables (W.H.), Suffolk 230
Farahar & Dupre (Clive & Sophie), Wiltshire ... 251
Ford (Richard), London W.......................... 173
Junk & Spread Eagle, London SE 165
Kenny's Bookshops and Art Galleries Ltd,
Co. Galway 266
Silverman (Michael), ... 166
Wilson (Manuscripts) Ltd., (John), Glos.......... 114

DOGS

Annie's Books, S Yorks 222
Apocalypse, Surrey 233
Bookline, Co. Down 261
Castleton (Pat), Kent.................................. 138

Cat Lit, Somerset 219
Chalmers Hallam (E.), Hampshire 125
Coch-y-Bonddu Books, Powys 292
Country Books, Derbyshire 82
Countrymans Gallery (The), Leics 147
Dales & Lakes Book Centre, Cumbria............ 80
Debbage (John), Norfolk............................. 190
Discovery Bookshop, Carmarthenshire............ 283
Dolphin Books, Suffolk............................... 226
Doorbar (P. & D.), Gwyned 287
Evergreen Livres, Oxfordshire 208
Fifteenth Century Bookshop (The), E Sussex 104
Fylde Books, Lancashire 146
Green Meadow Books, Cornwall 74
Halson Books, Cheshire 71
Head (John & Judith), Wiltshire 253
Home Farm Books, Warwickshire.................. 237
Intech Books, Northumberland 203
Jane Jones Books, Grampian 272
Joel Segal Books, Devon 86
Kilgour (Sporting Books) (Ian), Leics 149
London & Sussex Antiquarian Book &
Print Services, E Sussex............................ 101
McInnes (P.F. & J.R.), Dorset 91
Oopalba Books, Cheshire............................. 71
Peel (Valerie), Berkshire 55
Priestpopple Books, Northumberland 202
R. & A. Books, E Sussex............................. 102
Roger Collicott Books, Cornwall 75
Roland Books, Kent 139
Rolfe (John), London SE............................. 166
Sleepy Elephant Books & Artefacts, Cumbria ... 80
Stella Books, Monmouthshire 288
Tarka Books, Devon 84
Treasure Trove Books, Leics......................... 148
Wheen O'Books, Scottish Borders 269
Whittle, Bookseller (Avril), Cumbria 81
Wright Trace Books, West Midlands............... 240

DOLLS & DOLLS' HOUSES

Addyman Books, Powys.............................. 289
Apocalypse, Surrey 233
Art Reference Books, Hampshire 125
BC Books, Cheshire................................... 70
Bookmark (Children's Books), Wiltshire.......... 253
Cover to Cover, Merseyside......................... 186
Discovery Bookshop, Carmarthenshire............ 283
Joel Segal Books, Devon 86
Oopalba Books, Cheshire............................. 71
R. & A. Books, E Sussex............................. 102
Roadmaster Books, Kent............................. 137
St Swithin's Illustrated & Children's Books, London
W... 175
Sleepy Elephant Books & Artefacts, Cumbria ... 80
Staffs Bookshop (The), Staffordshire 224
Stroh (M.A.), London E 155
Twigg (Keith), Staffordshire......................... 224
Whittle, Bookseller (Avril), Cumbria 81

DOMESTICITY

Reading Lasses, Dumfries & Galloway 271
Susan Taylor Books, W Yorks 248
Whittle, Bookseller (Avril), Cumbria 81

SPECIALITY INDEX

DRAMA

Addyman Books, Powys.............................. 289
Apocalypse, Surrey 233
Autumn Leaves, Lincolnshire........................ 152
babelog.books, Herefordshire 128
Bookbox, Glos 116
Brian Troath Books, London E...................... 155
Brighton Books, E Sussex 99
Brock Books, North Yorkshire...................... 193
Byre Books, Dumfries & Galloway................. 270
Caledonia Books, Strathclyde....................... 280
Catalyst Booksearch Services, Devon.............. 87
Chaucer Head Bookshop, Warwickshire.......... 238
Clements (R.W.), London Outer.................... 182
Cox Rare Books (Charles), Cornwall............... 74
Dales & Lakes Book Centre, Cumbria............. 80
Darkwood Books, Co. Cork......................... 263
Fifteenth Century Bookshop (The), E Sussex 104
Forest Books of Manchester, Cheshire............ 71
Greenroom Books, W Yorks 248
Joel Segal Books, Devon 86
Judd Books, London WC 178
Junk & Spread Eagle, London SE.................. 165
Kenny's Bookshops and Art Galleries Ltd,
Co. Galway... 266
Kent T. G., Surrey 231
Mellon's Books, E Sussex 101
Pordes Books Ltd., (Henry), London WC........ 179
R. & A. Books, E Sussex............................ 102
Robert Temple, London N........................... 160
Roundstone Books, Lancashire...................... 144
Skoob Russell Square, Suffolk...................... 230
Terence Kaye, London NW 162
Theatreshire Books, North Yorkshire 193
Till's Bookshop, Lothian 279
Travis & Emery Music Bookshop, London WC 180
Trinity Rare Books, Co. Leitrim 266
Updike Rare Books (John), Lothian 279
Willmott Bookseller (Nicholas), Cardiff........... 283

DRAWING

Apocalypse, Surrey 233
Book Palace (The), London SE 164
Booth (Booksearch Service), (Geoff), Cheshire... 68
Fifteenth Century Bookshop (The), E Sussex 104
Jean Hedger, Berkshire 55
Joel Segal Books, Devon 86
Print Matters, London SE........................... 166
R. & A. Books, E Sussex... 102
Treasure Island (The), Gr Man..................... 119

DRUGS

Bernard Dixon and Kath Adams, Middlesex 183
Delectus Books, London WC....................... 177
Joel Segal Books, Devon 86
Parkinsons Books, Merseyside...................... 186
Weiner (Graham), London N 160

DYES

Cover to Cover, Merseyside......................... 186
Joel Segal Books, Devon 86
Judith Mansfield, W Yorks 250
N1 Books, E Sussex.................................. 105
Parkinsons Books, Merseyside...................... 186
Sleepy Elephant Books & Artefacts, Cumbria ... 80

Weiner (Graham), London N 160

EARLY IMPRINTS

Barry McKay Rare Books, Cumbria............... 77
Blackwell's Rare Books, Oxfordshire.............. 209
Cobnar Books, Kent.................................. 142
David (G.), Cambs 63
Edwards (Christopher), Berkshire.................. 55
Finch Rare Books Ltd. (Simon), London W..... 173
Golden Books Group, Devon 85
House of Figgis Ltd (The), Co. Galway 266
Junk & Spread Eagle, London SE.................. 165
Maggs Brothers Limited, London W.............. 174
Paralos Ltd., London WC 178
Pickering & Chatto, London W.................... 175
Quaritch Ltd., (Bernard), London W.............. 175
Roger Treglown, Cheshire........................... 70
Seydi Rare Books (Sevin), London NW.......... 162
Sokol Books Ltd., London W....................... 175
Susanne Schulz-Falster Rare Books, London N. 160
Unsworth's Booksellers, London WC 180

EARTH MYSTERIES

Abrahams (Mike), Staffordshire.................... 224
Atlantis Bookshop, London WC................... 177
Byre Books, Dumfries & Galloway................. 270
Chthonios Books, E Sussex 102
Country Books, Derbyshire 82
Fifteenth Century Bookshop (The), E Sussex 104
Gildas Books, Cheshire 68
Inner Bookshop (The), Oxfordshire................ 210
J & J Burgess Booksellers, Cambs 64
Joel Segal Books, Devon 86
McCrone (Audrey), Isle of Arran................... 275
Occultique, Northants................................ 200
Philip Hopper, Essex 110
Pyecroft (Ruth), Glos 117
R. & A. Books, E Sussex............................ 102
SETI Books, Staffordshire........................... 225
Star Lord Books, Gr Man 119

EARTH SCIENCES

Baldwin's Scientific Books, Essex 112
Dean Byass, Bristol................................... 60
Hunter–Rare Books (Andrew), London SW 169
Jay Books, Lothian................................... 278
Kalligraphia, Isle of Wight.......................... 134
Orchid Book Distributors, Co. Clare.............. 262
Parkinsons Books, Merseyside...................... 186
R & A. Books, E Sussex............................ 102
Roberts Books, Ayrshire 280
Roger Collicott Books, Cornwall 75
Weiner (Graham), London N 160
Westons, Hertfordshire 133

EASTER

R. & A. Books, E Sussex............................ 102
St Swithin's Illustrated & Children's Books, London
W... 175
Samovar Books, Co. Dublin......................... 264

EASTERN PHILOSOPHY

Art Book Company, (The), Suffolk................. 228
Bookbarrow, Cambs 63
Fifteenth Century Bookshop (The), E Sussex 104

SPECIALITY INDEX

Inner Bookshop (The), Oxfordshire................. 210
Joel Segal Books, Devon 86
Occultique, Northants................................. 200
Orchid Book Distributors, Co. Clare.............. 262
Parkinsons Books, Merseyside...................... 186
Portobello Books, London W 175
PsychoBabel Books & Journals, Oxfordshire..... 206
R. & A. Books, E Sussex............................. 102
Star Lord Books, Gr Man 119
Till's Bookshop, Lothian 279

ECCLESIASTICAL HISTORY & ARCHITECTURE

Apocalypse, Surrey 233
Barbican Bookshop, North Yorkshire............. 198
Bardsley's Books, Suffolk............................. 226
Beckham Books Ltd., Suffolk 230
Bell (Peter), Lothian................................... 276
Bennett & Kerr Books, Oxfordshire............... 206
Berwick Books, Lincolnshire........................ 152
Birchden Books, London E 155
Carter, (Brian), Oxfordshire........................ 211
Cheshire Book Centre, Cheshire.................... 69
Courtney & Hoff, North Yorkshire................. 198
Crouch Rare Books, Surrey.......................... 233
Edwards (Alan & Margaret), Kent 142
Fifteenth Century Bookshop (The), E Sussex 104
Gage Postal Books, Essex............................ 111
Grampian Books, Grampian......................... 274
Hall's Bookshop, Kent................................ 141
Haskell (R.H. & P.), Dorset 94
Hedgerow Books, S Yorks 222
Island Books, Devon................................... 85
Joel Segal Books, Devon 86
Kyrios Books, Notts 204
Mannwaring (M.G.), Bristol 59
Michael J Carroll, Co. Cork 263
Moss Books, London NW 162
Olynthiacs, Shropshire 214
Pagan Limited (Hugh), London SW............... 170
Pendleburys Bookshop, London N 159
PsychoBabel Books & Journals, Oxfordshire..... 206
R. & A. Books, E Sussex............................. 102
Rosemary Pugh Books, Wiltshire 253
S.P.C.K., Bristol 60
St Philip's Books, Oxfordshire...................... 210
Salsus Books, Worcestershire 256
Samovar Books, Co. Dublin 264
Scrivener's Books & Bookbinding, Derbyshire... 82
South Downs Book Service, W Sussex...... 244
Spenceley Books (David), W Yorks 249
Spooner & Co, Somerset 220
Staniland (Booksellers), Lincolnshire 154
Taylor & Son (Peter), Hertfordshire............... 133
Thornber (Peter M.), North Yorkshire............ 196
Turton (John), Durham 98
Turton (John), Durham 98
Uncle Phil's Books, West Midlands 240
Unsworths Booksellers, London WC.............. 163
Whitchurch Books Ltd., Cardiff.................... 283
Winghale Books, Lincolnshire 153

ECOLOGY

Arden, Bookseller (C.), Powys...................... 289
Baron - Scientific Book Sales (P.J.), Somerset ... 217

Bernard Dixon and Kath Adams, Middlesex 183
Brown-Studies, Strathclyde.......................... 279
Cornucopia Books, Lincolnshire 153
Dolphin Books, Suffolk............................... .. 226
Hawley (C.I.), North Yorkshire 197
Inner Bookshop (The), Oxfordshire................ 210
Joel Segal Books, Devon 86
Orb's Bookshop, Grampian......................... 274
Orchid Book Distributors, Co. Clare.............. 262
Parkinsons Books, Merseyside...................... 186
R. & A. Books, E Sussex............................. 102
Rosemary Pugh Books, Wiltshire 253
Shearwater Books, Northumberland............... 202
Wildside Books, Worcestershire 255
Wyseby House Books, Berkshire.................... 55

ECONOMICS

Barcombe Services, Essex............................. 108
Bernstein (Nicholas), London W.. 172
Billing (Brian), Berkshire 57
Bloomsbury Bookshop, London Outer 182
Booth Books, Powys 289
Burmester (James), Bristol........................... 59
Camden Books, Somerset 216
Chesters (G. & J.), Staffordshire 225
Clifton Books, Essex 112
Cornucopia Books, Lincolnshire 153
Darkwood Books, Co. Cork......................... 263
Delectus Books, London WC........................ 177
Drury Rare Books (John), Essex................... 110
Edwards (London) Limited (Francis),
London WC 177
Edwards in Hay-on-Wye (Francis), Powys 290
Empire Books, North Yorkshire 198
Foster Bookshop (Paul), London SW............. 168
Glenbower Books, Co. Dublin 265
Hamish Riley-Smith, Norfolk 192
Harrington Antiquarian Bookseller (Peter),
London SW.. 169
Hay Cinema Bookshop Ltd., Powys............... 290
Herb Tandree Philosophy Books, Glos 116
Jade Mountain Bookshop, Hampshire 126
Jarndyce Antiquarian Booksellers, London WC. 178
Kenny's Bookshops and Art Galleries Ltd,
Co. Galway.. 266
Lawson & Company (E.M.), Oxfordshire 208
Lee Rare Books (Rachel), Bristol 59
Left on The Shelf, Cumbria.......................... 79
Maghreb Bookshop (The), London WC.......... 178
Northern Herald Books, W Yorks.................. 246
Parkinsons Books, Merseyside...................... 186
Pickering & Chatto, London W.................... 175
Pollak (P.M.), Devon 89
PsychoBabel Books & Journals, Oxfordshire..... 206
Quaritch Ltd., (Bernard), London W.............. 175
R. & A. Books, E Sussex............................. 102
Rainford (Sheila), Hertfordshire.................... 130
Reading Lasses, Dumfries & Galloway 271
Rowan (P. & B.), Co. Antrim 260
Skoob Russell Square, Suffolk....................... 230
Spurrier (Nick), Kent 138
Staniland (Booksellers), Lincolnshire 154
Stern Antiquarian Bookseller (Jeffrey), N Yorks 199
Susanne Schulz-Falster Rare Books, London N. 160
Webb Books (John), S Yorks........................ 222

SPECIALITY INDEX

Wetherell (Frances), Cambs 65
Woburn Books, London N 160

EDUCATION & SCHOOL

Alba Books, Grampian 274
Apocalypse, Surrey 233
Barcombe Services, Essex............................ 108
Black Five Books, Shropshire 215
Burmester (James), Bristol........................... 59
Cornucopia Books, Lincolnshire 153
Delph Books, Gr Man................................ 120
Drury Rare Books (John), Essex................... 110
Game Advice, Oxfordshire 210
Holtom (Christopher), Cornwall 75
hullbooks.com, East Yorkshire 107
Jarndyce Antiquarian Booksellers, London WC. 178
Joel Segal Books, Devon 86
Kenny's Bookshops and Art Galleries Ltd,
Co. Galway 266
Kirkpatrick (Robert J.), London W 174
McGee (Terence J.), London Outer 181
Oopalba Books, Cheshire............................. 71
Parkinsons Books, Merseyside...................... 186
Picking & Chatto, London W...................... 175
Priestpopple Books, Northumberland 202
R. & A. Books, E Sussex............................. 102
Reading Lasses, Dumfries & Galloway 271
Roland Books, Kent 139
Rutland Bookshop (The), Rutland 212
Saunders (Tom), Caerphilly 283
The Old Children's Bookshelf, Lothian 278
Tiffin (Tony and Gill), Durham 97
Transformer, Dumfries & Galloway................ 271
Wise (Derek), E Sussex 104
Yates Antiquarian Books (Tony), Leics........... 148

EGYPTOLOGY

Afar Books International, West Midlands 239
Alpha Books, London N 158
Apocalypse, Surrey 233
Atlantis Bookshop, London WC................... 177
Books B.C., London Outer 181
Bookworm, Lothian.................................... 277
Byre Books, Dumfries & Galloway................ 270
Cavern Books, Cheshire 70
Chthonios Books, E Sussex 102
Crouch Rare Books, Surrey.......................... 233
Ewell Bookshop Ltd, Surrey 232
Ford Books (David), Hertfordshire 133
Hylton Booksearch, Merseyside 185
Joel Segal Books, Devon 86
Kenny's Bookshops and Art Galleries Ltd,
Co. Galway 266
Kingswood Books, Dorset 94
Michael Graves-Johnston, London SW 169
My Back Pages, London SW 169
Occultique, Northants................................. 200
P. and P. Books, Worcestershire 256
Parkinsons Books, Merseyside...................... 186
Prospect House Books, Co. Down.................. 261
R. & A. Books, E Sussex............................. 102
Scrivener's Books & Bookbinding, Derbyshire... 82
Sue Lowell Natural History Books, London W . 176
Treasure Island (The), Gr Man..................... 119
Treasure Trove Books, Leics......................... 148

Uncle Phil's Books, West Midlands 240
Unsworths Booksellers, London WC.............. 163
Whitchurch Books Ltd., Cardiff.................... 283
Wiend Books, Lancashire 144
Yesterday's Books, Dorset 92

ELECTRICITY & GAS

Elton Engineering Books, London W 173
Weiner (Graham), London N 160
Westons, Hertfordshire 133

ELECTRONICS

R. & A. Books, E Sussex............................. 102
Skoob Russell Square, Suffolk....................... 230
Westons, Hertfordshire 133
Whistler's Books, London SW 170

EMBLEMATA

John Underwood Antiquarian Books, Norfolk .. 190
Parikian, Rare Books (Diana), London W 175
Seydi Rare Books (Sevin), London NW 162

EMBROIDERY

Addyman Books, Powys.............................. 289
Apocalypse, Surrey 233
Black Cat Books, Norfolk............................ 188
Browse Books, Lancashire 144
Byrom Textile Bookroom (Richard), Lancashire 143
Camilla's Bookshop, E Sussex...................... 101
Cornucopia Books, Lincolnshire 153
Cover to Cover, Merseyside......................... 186
Crouch Rare Books, Surrey.......................... 233
Don Kelly Books, London W 172
DPE Books, Devon 87
Fifteenth Century Bookshop (The), E Sussex 104
Four Shire Bookshops, Glos......................... 114
Hennessey Bookseller (Ray), E Sussex 100
Joel Segal Books, Devon 86
Judith Mansfield, W Yorks 250
Just Books, Cornwall 76
McCrone (Audrey), Isle of Arran 275
Old Bookshop (The), West Midlands 241
Oopalba Books, Cheshire............................. 71
R. & A. Books, E Sussex............................. 102
Reading Lasses, Dumfries & Galloway 271
Scrivener's Books & Bookbinding, Derbyshire... 82
Sleepy Elephant Books & Artefacts, Cumbria ... 80
Smith Books (Keith), Herefordshire 128
Traveller's Bookshelf (The), Somerset 217
Trinders' Fine Tools, Suffolk 227
Uncle Phil's Books, West Midlands 240
Warnes (Felicity J.), London Outer................ 181
Wheen O'Books, Scottish Borders 269
Whittle, Bookseller (Avril), Cumbria 81
Young (D. & J.), Powys.............................. 293

ENAMEL

Cover to Cover, Merseyside......................... 186
Joel Segal Books, Devon 86
R. & A. Books, E Sussex............................. 102

ENCAUSTIC ART

Cover to Cover, Merseyside......................... 186

SPECIALITY INDEX

ENCYCLOPAEDIAS

Apocalypse, Surrey 233
Barter Books, Northumberland 202
Cornucopia Books, Lincolnshire 153
Frew Limited (Robert), London W................. 173
PsychoBabel Books & Journals, Oxfordshire..... 206
R. & A. Books, E Sussex............................. 102
Susanne Schulz-Falster Rare Books, London N . 160

ENERGY - GENERAL

Coulthurst (Richard), Gr Man 120
Parkinsons Books, Merseyside...................... 186
R. & A. Books, E Sussex............................. 102
Westons, Hertfordshire 133

- ALTERNATIVE

Coulthurst (Richard), Gr Man 120
Inner Bookshop (The), Oxfordshire................ 210
R. & A. Books, E Sussex............................. 102
Westons, Hertfordshire 133

- FUELS

Coulthurst (Richard), Gr Man 120
R. & A. Books, E Sussex............................. 102
Stroh (M.A.), London E 155
Westons, Hertfordshire 133

- POWER

Coulthurst (Richard), Gr Man 120
R. & A. Books, E Sussex............................. 102
Westons, Hertfordshire 133

ENGINEERING - GENERAL

Baron - Scientific Book Sales (P.J.), Somerset ... 217
Bianco Library, W Sussex............................ 242
Book House (The), Cumbria......................... 77
BookShop, The, Dumfries & Galloway............ 270
Bott, (Bookdealers) Ltd., (Martin), Gr Man 118
Brockwells Booksellers, Lincolnshire 150
Courtwood Books, Co. Laois........................ 266
Cox (Geoff), Devon 90
Elton Engineering Books, London W 173
Falconwood Transport & Military Bookshop,
London Outer.. 184
Gaskell Rare Books (Roger), Cambs............... 66
Hylton Booksearch, Merseyside 185
Just Books, Cornwall 76
K.S.C. Books, Cheshire.............................. 71
Kerr (Norman), Cumbria 78
Parkinsons Books, Merseyside...................... 186
Phelps (Michael), W Sussex 243
R. & A. Books, E Sussex............................. 102
Robert Humm & Co, Lincolnshire 154
Roberts Books, Ayrshire 280
Salway Books, Essex 112
Skoob Russell Square, Suffolk....................... 230
Stroh (M.A.), London E 155
Theatreshire Books, N Yorks........................ 193
Treasure Island (The), Gr Man...................... 119
Trinders' Fine Tools, Suffolk 227
Vickers (Anthony), N Yorks......................... 196
Weiner (Graham), London N 160
Westons, Hertfordshire 133
Wheen O'Books, Scottish Borders 269
Whistler's Books, London SW 170

- ELECTRICAL

Treasure Island (The), Gr Man...................... 119
Westons, Hertfordshire 133

ENGLISH

Apocalypse, Surrey 233
babelog.books, Herefordshire 128
Brian Troath Books, London E 155
Burmester (James), Bristol........................... 59
Classics Bookshop (The), Oxfordshire............. 207
Cornucopia Books, Lincolnshire 153
Dales & Lakes Book Centre, Cumbria............. 80
Fifteenth Century Bookshop (The), E Sussex 104
Hawley (C.L.), N Yorks.............................. 197
Joel Segal Books, Devon 86
Naughton Booksellers, Co. Dublin 265
Olynthiacs, Shropshire 214
R. & A. Books, E Sussex............................. 102
Wheen O'Books, Scottish Borders 269

ENGRAVING

Apocalypse, Surrey 233
Besleys Books, Suffolk 226
Chapter & Verse, Lincolnshire...................... 152
Collinge & Clark, London WC...................... 177
Heritage, West Midlands 239
Mulyan (Don), Merseyside........................... 186
R. & A. Books, E Sussex............................. 102
Robin Doughty - Fine Books, West Midlands... 239
Stroh (M.A.), London E 155
Waddington Books & Prints (Geraldine),
Northants 200
Webb Books (John), S Yorks........................ 222
Woodbine Books, W Yorks.......................... 246

ENTERTAINMENT - GENERAL

Apocalypse, Surrey 233
Aurora Books Ltd, Lothian........................... 276
Autumn Leaves, Lincolnshire........................ 152
Bookshop (The), Norfolk 192
Byre Books, Dumfries & Galloway................. 270
Cavern Books, Cheshire 70
DaSilva Puppet Books, Dorset 93
Discovery Bookshop, Carmarthenshire............ 283
Dolphin Books, Suffolk............................... 226
Greenroom Books, W Yorks 248
Jade Mountain Bookshop, Hampshire 126
Joel Segal Books, Devon 86
Junk & Spread Eagle, London SE 165
Katnap Arts, Norfolk.................................. 191
Kent T. G., Surrey 231
Nevitsky (Philip), Gr Man 119
Paramor (C.D.), Suffolk 229
Pyecroft (Ruth), Glos 117
R. & A. Books, E Sussex............................. 102
Roland Books, Kent 139
Stroma Books, Borders 268
Terence Kaye, London NW 162
Till's Bookshop, Lothian 279
Whitfield (Ken), Essex 111
Wood (Peter), Cambs 65
Yesterday's News, Conwy............................ 285

ENTOMOLOGY

Arden, Bookseller (C.), Powys...................... 289

SPECIALITY INDEX

Aurelian Books, London NW 161
Aviabooks, Glos 114
Besleys Books, Suffolk 226
Blest (Peter), Kent 139
Calluna Books, Dorset................................ 95
Demar Books (Grant), Kent........................ 141
Edmund Pollinger Rare Books, London SW..... 167
Elmbury Books, Warwickshire 238
Joel Segal Books, Devon 86
Mobbs (A.J.), West Midlands 241
Orb's Bookshop, Grampian......................... 274
Parkinsons Books, Merseyside...................... 186
Pemberley Books, Buckinghamshire 62
Pendleside Books, Lancashire....................... 144
Peter M Daly, Hampshire........................... 127
R M Books, Hertfordshire 132
R. & A. Books, E Sussex............................ 102
Shearwater Books, Northumberland............... 202
Tant Yn Ellen Books, Powys 293
Thin Read Line, Merseyside 185
Weiner (Graham), London N 160
Woodside Books, Kent 136

ENVIRONMENT, THE

Barcombe Services, Essex............................ 108
Country Books, Derbyshire 82
Fifteenth Century Bookshop (The), E Sussex 104
Hylton Booksearch, Merseyside 185
Joel Segal Books, Devon 86
Kenny's Bookshops and Art Galleries Ltd, Co.
Galway 266
Newgate Books and Translations,
Northumberland 202
Parkinsons Books, Merseyside...................... 186
Post-Horn Books, N Yorks 193
R. & A. Books, E Sussex............................ 102
Reading Lasses, Dumfries & Galloway 271
Westons, Hertfordshire 133

EROTICA

Apocalypse, Surrey 233
Delectus Books, London WC....................... 177
Edmund Pollinger Rare Books, London SW..... 167
Eggeling Books (John), W Yorks 250
High Street Books, Devon 86
Hylton Booksearch, Merseyside 185
InterCol London, London N 159
Joel Segal Books, Devon 86
NI Books, E Sussex................................... 105
Occultique, Northants................................ 200
Paper Pleasures, Somerset 219
Price (R.W.), Notts................................... 204
R. & A. Books, E Sussex............................ 102
Tsbbooks, London SW 170
Zardoz Books, Wiltshire............................. 254

ESKIMOS

R. & A. Books, E Sussex............................ 102

ESOTERIC

Alpha Books, London N 158
Armchair Books, Lothian 276
Berwick Books, Lincolnshire........................ 152
Beware of the Leopard, Bristol..................... 58
Bookbarrow, Cambs 63

Books (For All), N Yorks............................ 194
Books For All, N Yorks 194
Caduceus Books, Leics............................... 147
Central Bookshop, Warwickshire 238
Cofion Books, Pembrokeshire 288
Dawlish Books, Devon 86
Eastcote Bookshop (The), London Outer......... 181
Fifteenth Century Bookshop (The), E Sussex 104
Green Man Books, E Sussex 101
Greensleeves, Oxfordshire 207
IKON, Devon.. 89
Inner Bookshop (The), Oxfordshire................ 210
Joel Segal Books, Devon 86
Magis Books, Leics................................... 149
Main Point Books, Lothian.......................... 278
Occultique, Northants................................ 200
Old Aberdeen Bookshop, Grampian 272
Old Station Pottery & Bookshop (The), Norfolk 192
Orchid Book Distributors, Co. Clare.............. 262
Pyecroft (Ruth), Glos 117
R. & A. Books, E Sussex............................ 102
Reid of Liverpool, Merseyside...................... 185
Roger Treglown, Cheshire........................... 70
SETI Books, Staffordshire........................... 225
Skoob Russell Square, Suffolk...................... 230
Star Lord Books, Gr Man 119
Watkins Books Ltd., London WC.................. 180
Waxfactor, E Sussex 100
Worlds End Bookshop, London SW 171

ESPIONAGE

AA1 Books, Dumfries & Galloway................. 270
Baldwin (M. & M.), Worcestershire 255
Bolland Books, Bedfordshire........................ 53
Burroughs (Andrew), Lincolnshire 153
Corfe Books, Surrey.................................. 231
Crimes Ink, London E................................ 155
Dolphin Books, Suffolk.............................. 226
Ewell Bookshop Ltd, Surrey........................ 232
Grahame Thornton, Bookseller, Dorset........... 93
Hylton Booksearch, Merseyside 185
Island Books, Devon................................. 85
Loretta Lay Books, London NW................... 162
Lost Books, Northants............................... 201
MilitaryHistoryBooks.com, Kent................... 138
Ming Books, Dumfries & Galloway................ 271
Murphy (C.J.), Norfolk.............................. 190
Price (R.W.), Notts................................... 204
R. & A. Books, E Sussex............................ 102
Transformer, Dumfries & Galloway............... 271
Trinity Rare Books, Co. Leitrim 266
Undercover Books, Lincolnshire 154
Williams (Bookdealer), (Richard), N Lincs....... 154

ETHICS

Apocalypse, Surrey 233
Hawley (C.L.), N Yorks............................. 197
Joel Segal Books, Devon 86
Parkinsons Books, Merseyside...................... 186
R. & A. Books, E Sussex............................ 102
Reading Lasses, Dumfries & Galloway 271
Samovar Books, Co. Dublin......................... 264
Skoob Russell Square, Suffolk...................... 230

SPECIALITY INDEX

ETHNOBOTANY
Atlantis Bookshop, London WC................... 177
Kenya Books, E Sussex............................... 100
Park (Mike), London Outer.......................... 183
Westons, Hertfordshire 133

ETHNOGRAPHY
Bickford-Smith (G.), Surrey......................... 233
Bracton Books, Cambs 63
Butcher (Pablo), Oxfordshire 207
Campbell Hewson Books (R.), Fife................. 271
Chalmers Hallam (E.), Hampshire 125
Delectus Books, London WC....................... 177
Empire Books, N Yorks.............................. 198
J.C. Deyong Books, London SW 169
Joel Segal Books, Devon 86
Kenya Books, E Sussex............................... 100
Maghreb Bookshop (The), London WC.......... 178
Michael Graves-Johnston, London SW 169
Reading Lasses, Dumfries & Galloway 271
Traveller's Bookshelf (The), Somerset 217
Yesterday's Books, Dorset 92

ETHNOLOGY
Allsworth Rare Books Ltd., London SW......... 167
Anwoth Books Ltd, Dumfries & Galloway 270
Craobh Rua Books, Co. Armagh................... 260
Delectus Books, London WC....................... 177
Empire Books, N Yorks.............................. 198
Inner Bookshop (The), Oxfordshire................ 210
J.C. Deyong Books, London SW 169
Kenya Books, E Sussex............................... 100
Maghreb Bookshop (The), London WC.......... 178
Mandalay Bookshop, London SW 169
Michael Graves-Johnston, London SW 169
Randall (Tom), Somerset............................. 219
Sue Lowell Natural History Books, London W . 176

ETIQUETTE
Apocalypse, Surrey 233
Black Cat Books, Norfolk............................ 188
Lucas (Richard), London NW....................... 162
R. & A. Books, E Sussex............................. 102
Weininger Antiquarian Books (Eva M.),
London NW.. 163

EUROPEAN BOOKS
Baldwin (Jack), Strathclyde 280
Hava Books, London SE............................. 165
Joel Segal Books, Devon 86
PsychoBabel Books & Journals, Oxfordshire..... 206
R. & A. Books, E Sussex............................. 102
Seydi Rare Books (Sevin), London NW 162
Skoob Russell Square, Suffolk...................... 230

EUROPEAN STUDIES
PsychoBabel Books & Journals, Oxfordshire..... 206
R. & A. Books, E Sussex............................. 102
Studio Bookshop, E Sussex 100
Winghale Books, Lincolnshire 153

EVOLUTION
Arden, Bookseller (C.), Powys...................... 289
Austwick Hall Books, N Yorks 193
Baldwin's Scientific Books, Essex 112

Bernard Dixon and Kath Adams, Middlesex 183
Bracton Books, Cambs 63
Earth Science Books, Wiltshire 252
Humanist Book Services, Cornwall 73
Ice House Books, Wiltshire 253
Joel Segal Books, Devon 86
Kalligraphia, Isle of Wight.......................... 134
Parkinsons Books, Merseyside...................... 186
R M Books, Hertfordshire 132
R. & A. Books, E Sussex............................. 102
Turret House, Norfolk................................ 192
Wayside Books and Cards, Oxfordshire 207

EX-LIBRIS
Baldwin's Scientific Books, Essex 112
Cox Old & Rare Books (Claude), Suffolk 228
Darkwood Books, Co. Cork......................... 263
Derek Stirling Bookseller, Kent 142
Heraldry Today, Wiltshire........................... 252
Heritage, West Midlands 239
Hodgson (Books) (Richard J.), N Yorks 198
Joel Segal Books, Devon 86
Murphy (C.J.), Norfolk.............................. 190
Paper Pleasures, Somerset 219
Reeves Technical Books, N Yorks.................. 196
RGS Books, Surrey 235
Stalagluft Books, Tyne and Wear.................. 236
Waddington Books & Prints (Geraldine),
Northants 200

EXAMINATION PAPERS
Apocalypse, Surrey 233

EXHIBITIONS
R. & A. Books, E Sussex............................. 102
Studio Bookshop, E Sussex 100
Weiner (Graham), London N 160

EXOTIC BOOKS
R. & A. Books, E Sussex............................. 102

EXPEDITIONS
Americanabooksuk, Cumbria........................ 77
Brad Books, Essex..................................... 111
Cavendish Rare Books, London N 158
Craobh Rua Books, Co. Armagh................... 260
Dolphin Books, Suffolk............................... 226
Empire Books, N Yorks.............................. 198
Gildas Books, Cheshire............................... 68
Jarvis Books, Derbyshire 83
Joel Segal Books, Devon 86
Kineton Nooks, Warwickshire....................... 237
Mandalay Bookshop, London SW 169
Peter M Daly, Hampshire............................ 127
R. & A. Books, E Sussex............................. 102
Samovar Books, Co. Dublin 264

EXPLORATION
Americanabooksuk, Cumbria........................ 77
Austwick Hall Books, N Yorks 193
BookShop, The, Dumfries & Galloway........... 270
Byre Books, Dumfries & Galloway................. 270
Chalmers Hallam (E.), Hampshire.................. 125
Coch-y-Bonddu Books, Powys 292
Dolphin Books, Suffolk............................... 226

SPECIALITY INDEX

Empire Books, N Yorks............................ 198
Garfi Books, Powys 293
Glacier Books, Tayside 282
Jarvis Books, Derbyshire 83
Joel Segal Books, Devon 86
Just Books, Cornwall 76
Kingswood Books, Dorset 94
Kirkland Books, Cumbria............................ 79
Lost Books, Northants................................ 201
Mandalay Bookshop, London SW 169
Marble Hill Books, Middlesex...................... 184
Mercat Books, Highland 274
Peter M Daly, Hampshire............................ 127
Pinnacle Books, Lothian............................. 278
Preston Book Company, Lancashire 145
R. & A. Books, E Sussex............................ 102
Saintfield Antiques & Fine Books, Co. Down ... 261
Samovar Books, Co. Dublin......................... 264
Wheen O'Books, Scottish Borders 269

EXPLORATION - POLAR REGIONS

Bluntisham Books, Cambs 63
Fifteenth Century Bookshop (The), E Sussex 104
Henry Wilson Books, Cheshire...................... 69
Jarvis Books, Derbyshire 83
Joel Segal Books, Devon 86
Kineton Nooks, Warwickshire...................... 237
Lost Books, Northants................................ 201
R. & A. Books, E Sussex............................ 102
Roz Hulse, Conwy 286

EXPLOSIVES

Stroh (M.A.), London E 155
Weiner (Graham), London N 160

EXPRESSIONISM

R. & A. Books, E Sussex............................ 102

FABLES

Biblion, London W.................................... 172
Byre Books, Dumfries & Galloway................ 270
Country Books, Derbyshire 82
Derek Stirling Bookseller, Kent 142
Eggeling Books (John), West Yorks 250
Fifteenth Century Bookshop (The), E Sussex 104
Gildas Books, Cheshire 68
Holtom (Christopher), Cornwall 75
Jean Hedger, Berkshire 55
Junk & Spread Eagle, London SE 165
Muttonchop Manuscripts, W Sussex 244
Prescott - The Bookseller (John), London O 184
R. & A. Books, E Sussex............................ 102
Williams Rare Books (Nigel), London WC 180

FAIRGROUNDS

Anthony Vickers Books, N Yorks 196
Cottage Books, Leics................................. 147
Country Books, Derbyshire 82
Cover to Cover, Merseyside......................... 186
Decorum Books, London N 158
R. & A. Books, E Sussex............................ 102
Randall (Tom), Somerset............................ 219
Stroh (M.A.), London E 155
Terence Kaye, London NW 162
Vickers (Anthony), N Yorks........................ 196

FAIRY/FOLK TALES

Apocalypse, Surrey 233
Bookmark (Children's Books), Wiltshire.......... 253
Byre Books, Dumfries & Galloway................ 270
Castleton (Pat), Kent................................. 138
Children's Bookshop (The), Powys 289
Cornucopia Books, Lincolnshire 153
Country Books, Derbyshire 82
Cox, Andrew, Shropshire............................ 215
Dales & Lakes Book Centre, Cumbria............ 80
Fifteenth Century Bookshop (The), E Sussex 104
Gildas Books, Cheshire 68
Harvest Books, Lancashire........................... 145
Jean Hedger, Berkshire 55
Joel Segal Books, Devon 86
Just Books, Cornwall 76
McCrone (Audrey), Isle of Arran 275
Orb's Bookshop, Grampian......................... 274
R. & A. Books, E Sussex............................ 102
Randall (Tom), Somerset............................ 219
Seydi Rare Books (Sevin), London NW 162

FAMILY

Gildas Books, Cheshire 68
Reading Lasses, Dumfries & Galloway 271

FAMOUS PEOPLE - GENERAL

Booth (Booksearch Service), (Geoff), Cheshire... 68
Brad Books, Essex.................................... 111
Discovery Bookshop, Carmarthenshire............ 283
Dolphin Books, Suffolk.............................. 226
Ewell Bookshop Ltd, Surrey 232
Fifteenth Century Bookshop (The), E Sussex 104
J & J Burgess Booksellers, Cambs 64
Joel Segal Books, Devon 86
MilitaryHistoryBooks.com, Kent................... 138
R. & A. Books, E Sussex............................ 102

- BADEN POWELL, LORD & LADY R.S.S.

John R. Hoggarth, N Yorks 198
R. & A. Books, E Sussex............................ 102

- BEATLES, THE

firstpagebooks, Norfolk.............................. 190
R. & A. Books, E Sussex............................ 102

- CHURCHILL, SIR WINSTON

Annie's Books, S Yorks 222
Antique Map and Bookshop (The), Dorset 94
Apocalypse, Surrey 233
Booth (Booksearch Service), (Geoff), Cheshire... 68
Dolphin Books, Suffolk.............................. 226
Kineton Nooks, Warwickshire...................... 254
Little Stour Books, Kent 137
Lost Books, Northants................................ 201
McCrone (Audrey), Isle of Arran 275
Mellon's Books, E Sussex 101
Preston Book Company, Lancashire 145
R. & A. Books, E Sussex............................ 102
Sax Books, Suffolk 229
Uncle Phil's Books, West Midlands 240

- CONAN DOYLE, SIR ARTHUR

Preston Book Company, Lancashire 145
R. & A. Books, E Sussex............................ 102

SPECIALITY INDEX

- CONNERY, SEAN
R. & A. Books, E Sussex............................ 102

- ENTERTAINERS
Booth (Booksearch Service), (Geoff), Cheshire... 68
Dolphin Books, Suffolk............................... 226
Hylton Booksearch, Merseyside 185
R. & A. Books, E Sussex............................ 102
SETI Books, Staffordshire........................... 225

- KENNEDY, JOHN F
Bolland Books, Bedfordshire........................ 53
Clifford Elmer Books Ltd., Cheshire 68
R. & A. Books, E Sussex............................ 102
SETI Books, Staffordshire........................... 225

- MONROE, MARILYN
Booth (Booksearch Service), (Geoff), Cheshire... 68
R. & A. Books, E Sussex............................ 102
Simply Read Books, E Sussex 101
Whittle, Bookseller (Avril), Cumbria 81

- NELSON & LADY HAMILTON, LORD
Marine & Cannon Books, Cheshire 71
Marine and Cannon Books, Cheshire 69
Old Station Pottery & Bookshop (The), Norfolk 192
R. & A. Books, E Sussex............................ 102

- PITT, WILLIAM (THE YOUNGER)
R. & A. Books, E Sussex............................ 102

- STANLEY, W.M.
Kenya Books, E Sussex.............................. 100

- WAGNER, RICHARD
R. & A. Books, E Sussex............................ 102

- WORDSWORTH, WILLIAM
Country Books, Derbyshire 82
R. & A. Books, E Sussex............................ 102

FARMING & LIVESTOCK
Barn Books, Shropshire.............................. 215
Besleys Books, Suffolk 226
Books for Content, Herefordshire................... 128
Carningli Centre, Pembrokeshire 288
Castleton (Pat), Kent................................. 138
Cheshire Book Centre, Cheshire.................... 69
Clarke Books (David), Somerset 219
Cornucopia Books, Lincolnshire 153
Country Books, Derbyshire 82
Debbage (John), Norfolk............................ 190
Evergreen Livres, Oxfordshire 208
Farquharson, (Hilary), Tayside..................... 281
Fifteenth Century Bookshop (The), E Sussex 104
Greta Books, Durham 97
Hodgson (Books) (Richard J.), N Yorks 198
Jane Jones Books, Grampian 272
Joel Segal Books, Devon 86
Kilgour (Sporting Books) (Ian), Leics 149
Mayhew (Veronica), Berkshire...................... 57
Muttonchop Manuscripts, W Sussex 244
Old Station Pottery & Bookshop (The), Norfolk 192
Phenotype Books, Cumbria 80
R. & A. Books, East Sussex 102

Rutland Bookshop (The), Rutland 212
Scrivener's Books & Bookbinding, Derbyshire... 82
Stroh (M.A.), London E 155
Thornber (Peter M.), N Yorks 196
Westons, Hertfordshire 133

FARRIERS
Austwick Hall Books, N Yorks 193
Country Books, Derbyshire 82
Jane Jones Books, Grampian 272
Phenotype Books, Cumbria 80
R. & A. Books, East Sussex 102
Rutland Bookshop (The), Rutland 212

FASHION & COSTUME
Abrahams (Mike), Staffordshire.................... 224
Art Reference Books, Hampshire 125
Ballantyne-Way (Roger), Suffolk 229
Barn Books, Buckinghamshire...................... 61
Batterham (David), London W..................... 172
Black Cat Books, Norfolk 188
Bookroom (The), Surrey............................. 234
Byrom Textile Bookroom (Richard), Lancs 143
Caliver Books, Essex 110
Cheshire Book Centre, Cheshire.................... 69
Cornucopia Books, Lincolnshire 153
Duncan & Reid, Lothian 277
Dyson (Anthony), West Midlands 240
Forest Books of Manchester, Cheshire............ 71
Garfi Books, Powys 293
Goodyer (Nicholas), London N..................... 159
Greenroom Books, W Yorks 248
Gresham Books, Somerset 218
Hornsey's, N Yorks 195
Ives Bookseller (John), London Outer 184
Joel Segal Books, Devon 86
Lighthouse Books (The), Dorset 92
Meekins Books (Paul), Warwickshire.............. 238
My Back Pages, London SW 169
N1 Books, East Sussex 105
Photo Books International, London WC 179
Pordes Books Ltd., (Henry), London WC........ 179
Portobello Books, London W 175
R. & A. Books, East Sussex 102
Read (C.&J.), Gorleston Books, Norfolk......... 188
Reading Lasses, Dumfries & Galloway 271
Roland Books, Kent 139
Sleepy Elephant Books & Artefacts,
Cumbria 80
Stroh (M.A.), London E 155
Trinders' Fine Tools, Suffolk 227
Warnes (Felicity J.), London Outer................ 181
Whittle, Bookseller (Avril), Cumbria 81
Worlds End Bookshop, London SW............... 171
Young (D. & J.), Powys............................. 293

FEMINISM
Delectus Books, London WC....................... 177
Dolphin Books, Suffolk............................... 226
Dylans Bookstore, Swansea......................... 294
Fortune Green Books, London NW................ 161
Game Advice, Oxfordshire 210
Hylton Booksearch, Merseyside 185
Joel Segal Books, Devon 86
Judd Books, London WC........................... 178

SPECIALITY INDEX

Kenny's Bookshops and Art Galleries Ltd, Co. Galway .... 266 Lane Books (Shirley), Isle of Wight .... 135 R. & A. Books, East Sussex .... 102 Reading Lasses, Dumfries & Galloway .... 271 Red Star Books, Hertfordshire .... 130 Rosemary Pugh Books, Wiltshire .... 253 Spurrier (Nick), Kent .... 138 Stevens (Joan), Cambs .... 65 Susan Taylor Books, W Yorks .... 248 Symes Books (Naomi), Cheshire .... 72 Till's Bookshop, Lothian .... 279 Treasure Trove Books, Leics......................... 148 Willmott Bookseller (Nicholas), Cardiff........... 283 Yesterday's News, Conwy 285

FICTION - GENERAL

A. & R. Booksearch, Cornwall...................... 74 Abacus Gallery, Staffordshire........................ 224 Abbey Books, Cornwall .... 74 Addyman Books, Powys.............................. 289 ahbooks, Merseyside .... 185 Allinson (Frank & Stella), Warwickshire .... 237 Anglo-American Rare Books, Surrey.............. 233 Annie's Books, S Yorks .... 222 Antiques on High, Oxfordshire...................... 209 Apocalypse, Surrey .... 233 Applin (Malcolm), Berkshire......................... 55 Aurora Books Ltd, Lothian........................... 276 Autumn Leaves, Lincolnshire........................ 152 babelog.books, Herefordshire .... 128 Barter Books, Northumberland .... 202 Bass (Ben), Wiltshire .... 251 Beaton (Richard), East Sussex .... 103 Bernstein (Nicholas), London W .... 172 Berwick Books, Lincolnshire......................... 152 Beware of the Leopard, Bristol...................... 58 Black Cat Bookshop, Leics .... 147 Black Five Books, Shropshire .... 215 Blackwell's Rare Books, Oxfordshire .... 209 Book For All Reasons (A.), Suffolk .... 229 Book House (The), Cumbria......................... 77 Bookcase, Cumbria.................................... 78 Bookpassage (The), Shropshire .... 213 Books & Collectables Ltd., Cambs .... 63 Books Afloat, Dorset.................................. 96 Books Antiques & Collectables, Devon .... 90 Books for Writers, Monmouthshire................. 287 books2books, Devon .... 88 BOOKS4U, Flintshire................................. 286 Bookworm, Lothian................................... 277 Bookworm (The), Lothian .... 277 Booth (Booksearch Service), (Geoff), Cheshire... 68 Boris Books, Hampshire.............................. 126 Bosco Books, Cornwall .... 73 Bowie Books & Collectables, East Yorkshire .... 107 Boz Books, Powys..................................... 289 Brad Books, Essex..................................... 111 Brighton Books, East Sussex......................... 99 Broadhurst of Southport Ltd., Merseyside .... 186 Caledonia Books, Strathclyde........................ 280 Capel Mawr Collectors Centre, Gwynedd .... 287 Carnforth Bookshop (The), Lancashire .... 143 Carningli Centre, Pembrokeshire .... 288 Castleton (Pat), Kent................................. 138

Catalyst Booksearch Services, Devon.............. 87 Cecilia Marsden, Middlesex .... 183 Celtic Bookshop (The), Co. Limerick .... 266 Chalk (Old & Out of Print Books) (Christine M.), West Midlands .... 239 Chaucer Bookshop, Kent............................. 136 Cheshire Book Centre, Cheshire.................... 69 Church Street Books, Norfolk .... 187 Clarke Books (David), Somerset .... 219 Clements (R.W.), London Outer .... 182 Clent Books, Worcestershire .... 255 Cobbles Books, Somerset............................. 218 Cofion Books, Pembrokeshire .... 288 Colwyn Books, Conwy .... 285 Corfe Books, Surrey................................... 231 Cox Rare Books (Charles), Cornwall.............. 74 Crimes Ink, London E .... 155 D'Arcy Books, Wiltshire.............................. 252 Dales & Lakes Book Centre, Cumbria............ 80 Dartmoor Bookshop (The), Devon .... 84 dgbbooks, W Sussex .... 244 Dolphin Books, Suffolk............................... 226 Doolin Dinghy Books, Co. Clare .... 262 Dormouse Bookshop (The), Norfolk .... 190 Eastcote Bookshop (The), London Outer......... 181 Eggeling Books (John), W Yorks .... 250 Elaine Lonsdale Books, W Yorks................... 248 Ellis, Bookseller (Peter), London WC .... 178 Ellwood Editions, Wiltshire .... 253 Fackley Services, Notts .... 205 Fiction First, Cheshire .... 70 Fifteenth Century Bookshop (The), East Sussex. 104 Fireside Bookshop, Cumbria......................... 81 First State Books, London W .... 173 Ford Books (David), Hertfordshire................. 133 Fortune Green Books, London NW................ 161 Fossgate Books, N Yorks .... 198 Freeman's Corner Shop, Norfolk .... 190 Freya Books & Antiques, Norfolk.................. 191 Gemini–Books, Shropshire .... 215 George St. Books, Derbyshire .... 83 Glasheen-Books, Surrey .... 232 Glenbower Books, Co. Dublin .... 265 Gloucester Road Bookshop, London SW .... 168 Great Hall Bookshop, Buckinghamshire.......... 61 Greta Books, Durham .... 97 Grove Bookshop (The), N Yorks................... 197 Hab Books, London W............................... 173 Hall's Bookshop, Kent................................ 141 Hambleton Books, N Yorks .... 197 Hardback Hotel, Lancashire .... 144 Harrington (Adrian), London W.................... 173 Hay Cinema Bookshop Ltd., Powys............... 290 Heckmondwike Book Shop, W Yorks .... 249 Hilton (Books) (P.J.), London W .... 174 Hurst (Jenny), Kent .... 138 Hylton Booksearch, Merseyside .... 185 Ian McKelvie Bookseller, London N.............. 159 Innes Books, Shropshire .... 214 Intech Books, Northumberland .... 203 J & J Burgess Booksellers, Cambs .... 64 Jade Mountain Bookshop, Hampshire .... 126 Jane Jones Books, Grampian .... 272 Joel Segal Books, Devon .... 86 Just Books, Cornwall 76

SPECIALITY INDEX

K Books, Cheshire...................................... 70
Kellow Books, Oxfordshire 207
Kim's Bookshop, W Sussex..............242, 243, 245
L.M.S. Books, Hertfordshire......................... 132
Last Century Books, Borders 268
Lewis (J.T. & P.), Cornwall. 74
Little Bookshop (The), Gr Man.................... 119
Little Stour Books, Kent 137
Maggy Browne, Lincolnshire 150
Main Point Books, Lothian........................... 278
Marble Hill Books, Middlesex....................... 184
Marine Workshop Bookshop, Dorset 93
Martin's Books, Powys 292
Meads Book Service (The), East Sussex........... 104
Modern First Editions, London Outer 183
Moffat Book Exchange, Dumfries & Galloway.. 270
Mr. Pickwick of Towcester, Northants............ 201
Much Ado Books, East Sussex....................... 99
Mundy (David), Hertfordshire....................... 130
Murphy (C.J.), Norfolk............................... 190
Naughton Booksellers, Co. Dublin 265
Neeve (P.), Cambs.................................... 63
Neil's Books, London NW........................... 162
New Strand Bookshop (The), Herefordshire 128
O'Brien Books & Photo Gallery, Co. Limerick.. 266
O'Flynn Books, N Yorks............................. 199
Olynthiacs, Shropshire 214
Oxfam Books and Music, Hampshire 126
Pamona Books, Lancashire 145
Paperbacks Plus, Bristol 59
Park Gallery & Bookshop (The), Northants 201
Parker Books (Mike), Cambs........................ 64
Paton Books, Hertfordshire 132
Peter's Bookshop, Norfolk 192
Pickering Bookshop, N Yorks....................... 197
Poor Richard's Books, Suffolk 227
Portobello Books, London W 175
Prescott - The Bookseller (John), London Outer 181
Price (R.D.M & I.M.) (Books), Gr Man......... 120
Price (R.W.), Notts.................................... 204
Pyecroft (Ruth), Glos 117
Quinto of Charing Cross Road, London WC ... 179
Quinto of Great Russell Street, London WC 179
R. & A. Books, East Sussex 102
Reading Lasses, Dumfries & Galloway 271
Reaveley Books, Devon 87
RGS Books, Surrey 235
Richmond Books, N Yorks........................... 195
Robert (Leslie), London W 175
Robert Temple, London N........... 160
Roberts Fine Books (Julian), Lincolnshire........ 153
Roland Books, Kent 139
Roundstone Books, Lancashire...................... 144
Rutland Bookshop (The), Rutland 212
Rye Old Books, East Sussex 104
Savery Books, East Sussex 99
Sax Books, Suffolk 229
Seabreeze Books, Lancashire......................... 145
Shacklock Books (David), Suffolk 227
Shakeshaft (Dr. B.), Cheshire....................... 71
Simpson (Dave), Stirlingshire 269
Sleepy Elephant Books & Artefacts, Cumbria ... 80
Smith Books, (Sally), Suffolk 227
Sol Books, Devon 84
Spooner & Co, Somerset 220

Strathtay Antiquarian - Secondhand Books,
Tayside 282
Sturford Books, Wiltshire 254
Surprise Books, Glos..................... 113
Tarka Books, Devon................................... 84
Thistle Books, Strathclyde............................ 280
Thomas (E. Wyn), Conwy 285
Till's Bookshop, Lothian 279
Tilston (Stephen E.), London SE.................... 166
Tindley & Chapman, London WC 179
Trevorrow (Edwin), Hertfordshire 130
Trinity Rare Books, Co. Leitrim 266
Ventnor Rare Books, Isle of Wight................. 135
Vokes Books Ltd., N Yorks 195
VOL:II, Essex 108
Wadard Books, Kent 138
Ward (R.F. & C.), Norfolk 188
Warrington Book Loft (The), Cheshire 72
Wealden Books, Kent.......... 139
Wheen O'Books, Scottish Borders 269
Whitfield (Ken), Essex 111
Williams (Bookdealer), (Richard), N Lincs....... 154
Williams Rare Books (Nigel), London WC 180
Willmott Bookseller (Nicholas), Cardiff........... 283
Winchester Bookshop (The), Hampshire.......... 127
Worlds End Bookshop, London SW............... 171
Yarborough House Bookshop, Shropshire 213
Zardoz Books, Wiltshire.............................. 254

- 18TH CENTURY

Barter Books, Northumberland 202
Burmester (James), Bristol........................... 59
Joel Segal Books, Devon 86
Johnson Rare Book Collections (C.R.),
London NW... 162
Seydi Rare Books (Sevin), London NW 162
Tiger Books, Kent 137
Valentine Rare Books, London W.................. 176

- ADVENTURE

Annie's Books, S Yorks 222
Apocalypse, Surrey 233
Bookpassage (The), Shropshire...................... 213
Dolphin Books, Suffolk............................... 226
Hylton Booksearch, Merseyside 185
Joel Segal Books, Devon 86
Onepoundpaperbacks, N Yorks..................... 193
R. & A. Books, East Sussex 102
Roland Books, Kent 139
Simpson (Dave), Stirlingshire 269
Surprise Books, Glos.................................. 113
Tarka Books, Devon................................... 84
Wheen O'Books, Scottish Borders 269
Williams (Bookdealer), (Richard), N Lincs....... 154
Zardoz Books, Wiltshire.............................. 254

- CRIME, DETECTIVE, SPY, THRILLERS

AA1 Books, Dumfries & Galloway................. 270
Abbey Books, Cornwall 74
Annie's Books, S Yorks 222
Apocalypse, Surrey 233
Armstrong's Books & Collectables, Leics......... 147
Aucott & Thomas, Leics.............................. 147
Barter Books, Northumberland 202
Bell (Books) (Mrs. V.S.), Suffolk................... 228

SPECIALITY INDEX

Berwick Books, Lincolnshire 152
Beware of the Leopard, Bristol 58
Biblion, London W 172
Birmingham Books, West Midlands 239
Book Business (The), London W 172
Bookbarrow, Cambs 63
Bookpassage (The), Shropshire 213
Bookshop on the Heath, The, London SE 164
Bookworm (The), Lothian 277
Booth (Booksearch Service), (Geoff), Cheshire... 68
Catalyst Booksearch Services, Devon 87
Cecilia Marsden, Middlesex 183
Classic Crime Collections, Gr Man 119
Cotswold Internet Books, Glos 113
Cowley, Bookdealer (K.W.), Somerset 218
Crimes Ink, London E 155
Dolphin Books, Suffolk 226
Dunstan Books, Dorset 91
Dyson (Anthony), West Midlands 240
Eggeling Books (John), W Yorks 250
Enigma Books, Norfolk 190
Fantastic Literature, Essex 111
Farringdon Books, Essex 109
Fiction First, Cheshire 70
firstpagebooks, Norfolk 190
Firsts in Print, Isle of Wight 134
Garfi Books, Powys 293
George St. Books, Derbyshire 83
Hardback Hotel, Lancashire 144
HCB Wholesale, Powys 290
Heckmondwike Book Shop, W Yorks 249
Heppa (Christopher), Essex 108
Hight (Norman F.), Glamorgan 286
Hill (John S.), Devon 86
Hylton Booksearch, Merseyside 185
Ian McKelvie Bookseller, London N 159
Innes Books, Shropshire 214
J & J Burgess Booksellers, Cambs 64
J. & J. Books, Lincolnshire 151
Jade Mountain Bookshop, Hampshire 126
Joel Segal Books, Devon 86
John Gorton Booksearch, East Sussex 105
Junk & Spread Eagle, London SE 165
Kent (Books) (Mrs. A.), Suffolk 228
Kevin S. Ogilvie Modern First Editions,
Grampian 273
Loretta Lay Books, London NW 162
Lucius Books, N Yorks 199
Mainly Fiction, Cheshire 68
McCaughtrie (K.A.), N Yorks 194
Ming Books, Dumfries & Galloway 271
Murder & Mayhem, Powys 291
New Strand Bookshop (The), Herefordshire 128
Newgate Books and Translations,
Northumberland 202
Old Celtic Bookshop (The), Devon 88
Onepoundpaperbacks, N Yorks 193
Orb's Bookshop, Grampian 274
Oxfam Books and Music, Hampshire 126
Paperbacks Plus, Bristol 59
Porcupine Books, London Outer 182
Post Mortem Books, W Sussex 243
Price (R.W.), Notts 204
Pyecroft (Ruth), Glos 117
R. & A. Books, East Sussex 102

Reading Lasses, Dumfries & Galloway 271
Reaveley Books, Devon 87
Richmond Books, N Yorks 195
Robert (Leslie), London W 175
Robert Temple, London N 160
Roland Books, Kent 139
Roscrea Bookshop, Co. Tipperary 267
Ruebotham (Kirk), Cheshire 71
Savery Books, East Sussex 99
Sax Books, Suffolk 229
Simpson (Dave), Stirlingshire 269
Surprise Books, Glos 113
Sutcliffe (Mark), W Yorks 248
Tarka Books, Devon 84
The Glass Key, W Yorks 247
The Sanctuary Bookshop, Dorset 94
Till's Bookshop, Lothian 279
Tindley & Chapman, London WC 179
TP Children's Bookshop, W Yorks 246
Transformer, Dumfries & Galloway 271
Treasure Trove Books, Leics 148
Uncle Phil's Books, West Midlands 240
Vokes (Jeremiah), Durham 97
Ward (R.F. & C.), Norfolk 188
Wayside Books and Cards, Oxfordshire 207
Wheen O'Books, Scottish Borders 269
Wiend Books, Lancashire 144
Williams (Bookdealer), (Richard), N Lincs 154
Zardoz Books, Wiltshire 254

- FANTASY, HORROR

AA1 Books, Dumfries & Galloway 270
Apocalypse, Surrey 233
Armstrong's Books & Collectables, Leics 147
Barter Books, Northumberland 202
Beware of the Leopard, Bristol 58
Birmingham Books, West Midlands 239
Bookpassage (The), Shropshire 213
Books and Beans, Grampian 272
Books B.C., London Outer 181
Bookworm (The), Lothian 277
Booth (Booksearch Service), (Geoff), Cheshire... 68
Cowley, Bookdealer (K.W.), Somerset 218
Crimes Ink, London E 155
Daeron's Books, Buckinghamshire 62
Dalby (Richard), N Yorks 196
Eggeling Books (John), W Yorks 250
Enigma Books, Norfolk 190
Fantastic Literature, Essex 111
Fantasy Centre, London N 158
Farringdon Books, Essex 109
Fiction First, Cheshire 70
Firsts in Print, Isle of Wight 134
Gildas Books, Cheshire 68
HCB Wholesale, Powys 290
Hight (Norman F.), Glamorgan 286
Hylton Booksearch, Merseyside 185
Interstellar Master Traders, Lancashire 144
Joel Segal Books, Devon 86
Lucius Books, N Yorks 199
Ming Books, Dumfries & Galloway 271
Modern First Editions, London Outer 183
Murder & Mayhem, Powys 291
Occultique, Northants 200
Old Celtic Bookshop (The), Devon 88

SPECIALITY INDEX

Onepoundpaperbacks, N Yorks 193
Orb's Bookshop, Grampian 274
Paperbacks Plus, Bristol 59
Porcupine Books, London Outer 182
Price (R.W.), Notts 204
Pyecroft (Ruth), Glos 117
R. & A. Books, East Sussex 102
Robert Temple, London N 160
Roland Books, Kent 139
Ruebotham (Kirk), Cheshire 71
Sensawunda Books, Cheshire 68
Simpson (Dave), Stirlingshire 269
Solaris Books, East Yorkshire 106
Surprise Books, Glos 113
Tarka Books, Devon 84
The Glass Key, W Yorks 247
Till's Bookshop, Lothian 279
Transformer, Dumfries & Galloway 271
Uncle Phil's Books, West Midlands 240
Williams (Bookdealer), (Richard), N Lincs 154
Zardoz Books, Wiltshire 254

- GAY FICTION

R. & A. Books, East Sussex 102
Tsbbooks, London SW 170

- HISTORICAL

Americanabooksuk, Cumbria 77
Annie's Books, S Yorks 222
Apocalypse, Surrey 233
Black Cat Bookshop, Leics 147
Black Five Books, Shropshire 215
Book For All Reasons (A.), Suffolk 229
Bookpassage (The), Shropshire 213
Boris Books, Hampshire 126
Cox, Andrew, Shropshire 215
Dolphin Books, Suffolk 226
Eggeling Books (John), W Yorks 250
Enscot Books, London SE 165
Fantastic Literature, Essex 111
Heppa (Christopher), Essex 108
Keel Row Bookshop, Tyne and Wear 236
Ming Books, Dumfries & Galloway 271
Naughton Booksellers, Co. Dublin 265
Onepoundpaperbacks, N Yorks 193
Orb's Bookshop, Grampian 274
R. & A. Books, East Sussex 102
Reaveley Books, Devon 87
Robert Temple, London N 160
Roland Books, Kent 139
Simpson (Dave), Stirlingshire 269
Sturford Books, Wiltshire 254
Surprise Books, Glos 113
Tarka Books, Devon 84
Trevorrow (Edwin), Hertfordshire 130
Uncle Phil's Books, West Midlands 240
Wheen O'Books, Scottish Borders 269
Williams (Bookdealer), (Richard), N Lincs 154
Williams Rare Books (Nigel), London WC 180
Zardoz Books, Wiltshire 254

- ROMANTIC

Book For All Reasons (A.), Suffolk 229
Bookpassage (The), Shropshire 213
Eggeling Books (John), W Yorks 250

Mandalay Bookshop, London SW 169
Onepoundpaperbacks, N Yorks 193
Orb's Bookshop, Grampian 274
Price (R.W.), Notts 204
R. & A. Books, East Sussex 102
Tarka Books, Devon 84
Wheen O'Books, Scottish Borders 269
Williams (Bookdealer), (Richard), N Lincs 154

- SCIENCE FICTION

AA1 Books, Dumfries & Galloway 270
Abbey Books, Cornwall 74
Altshuler (Jean), Cumbria 79
Annie's Books, S Yorks 222
Apocalypse, Surrey 233
Armchair Books, Lothian 276
Armstrong's Books & Collectables, Leics 147
Barter Books, Northumberland 202
Beware of the Leopard, Bristol 58
Birmingham Books, West Midlands 239
Black Cat Bookshop, Leics 147
Bookbarrow, Cambs 63
Bookpassage (The), Shropshire 213
Books & Bygones (Pam Taylor), W Mids 241
Books (For All), N Yorks 194
Books B.C., London Outer 181
Bookworm (The), Lothian 277
Booth (Booksearch Service), (Geoff), Cheshire... 68
Booth Books, Powys 289
Carningli Centre, Pembrokeshire 288
Cecilia Marsden, Middlesex 183
Cold Tonnage Books, Surrey 235
Cowley, Bookdealer (K.W.), Somerset 218
Cox, Andrew, Shropshire 215
Crimes Ink, London E 155
Daeron's Books, Buckinghamshire 67
Discovery Bookshop, Carmarthenshire 283
Driffield Bookshop (The), East Yorkshire 106
Eggeling Books (John), W Yorks 250
Fantastic Literature, Essex 111
Fantasy Centre, London N 158
Farringdon Books, Essex 109
Fiction First, Cheshire 70
firstpagebooks, Norfolk 190
Gildas Books, Cheshire 68
Glasheen-Books, Surrey 232
Hardback Hotel, Lancashire 144
Heckmondwike Book Shop, W Yorks 249
Hight (Norman F), Glamorgan 286
Hill (John S.), Devon 86
Idle Genius Books, London N 159
Interstellar Master Traders, Lancashire 144
Joel Segal Books, Devon 86
K Books, Cheshire 70
Lucius Books, N Yorks 199
Ming Books, Dumfries & Galloway 271
Modern First Editions, London Outer 183
New Strand Bookshop (The), Herefordshire 128
Onepoundpaperbacks, N Yorks 193
Orb's Bookshop, Grampian 274
Paperbacks Plus, Bristol 59
Porcupine Books, London Outer 182
Price (R.W.), Notts 204
Pyecroft (Ruth), Glos 117
R. & A. Books, East Sussex 102

SPECIALITY INDEX

Reid of Liverpool, Merseyside...................... 185
Robert Temple, London N.......................... 160
Rods Books, Devon.................................. 88
Roland Books, Kent................................. 139
Ruebotham (Kirk), Cheshire........................ 71
Sensawunda Books, Cheshire....................... 68
Simpson (Dave), Stirlingshire....................... 269
Solaris Books, East Yorkshire...................... 106
Surprise Books, Glos................................ 113
Tarka Books, Devon................................. 84
The Glass Key, W Yorks............................ 247
The Sanctuary Bookshop, Dorset.................. 94
Till's Bookshop, Lothian............................ 279
Transformer, Dumfries & Galloway................ 271
Treasure Trove Books, Leics....................... 148
Trevorrow (Edwin), Hertfordshire.................. 130
Uncle Phil's Books, West Midlands................ 240
Ward (R.F. & C.), Norfolk.......................... 188
Waxfactor, East Sussex............................. 100
Wayside Books and Cards, Oxfordshire.......... 207
Wiend Books, Lancashire........................... 144
Williams (Bookdealer), (Richard), N Lincs....... 154
Zardoz Books, Wiltshire............................ 254

- SUPERNATURAL

Annie's Books, S Yorks............................. 222
Dalby (Richard), N Yorks.......................... 196
Eggeling Books (John), W Yorks.................. 250
Enigma Books, Norfolk............................. 190
Fantastic Literature, Essex......................... 111
Gildas Books, Cheshire............................. 68
J & J Burgess Booksellers, Cambs................ 64
Occultique, Northants............................... 200
Porcupine Books, London Outer................... 182
R. & A. Books, East Sussex........................ 102
Ruebotham (Kirk), Cheshire........................ 71
Skirrid Books, Monmouthshire..................... 287
Surprise Books, Glos................................ 113
Tarka Books, Devon................................. 84
The Glass Key, W Yorks............................ 247
Williams (Bookdealer), (Richard), N Lincs....... 154
Zardoz Books, Wiltshire............................ 254

- WESTERNS

AA1 Books, Dumfries & Galloway................. 270
Americanabooksuk, Cumbria....................... 77
Black Cat Bookshop, Leics......................... 147
Crimes Ink, London E............................... 155
firstpagebooks, Norfolk............................. 190
Ming Books, Dumfries & Galloway................ 271
Onepoundpaperbacks, N Yorks.................... 193
Price (R.W.), Notts.................................. 204
R. & A. Books, East Sussex........................ 102
Rods Books, Devon.................................. 88
Roscrea Bookshop, Co. Tipperary................. 267
Surprise Books, Glos................................ 113
Tarka Books, Devon................................. 84
Ward (R.F. & C.), Norfolk.......................... 188
Williams (Bookdealer), (Richard), N Lincs....... 154
Zardoz Books, Wiltshire............................ 254

- WOMEN

Apocalypse, Surrey.................................. 233
Applin (Malcolm), Berkshire........................ 55
Black Cat Bookshop, Leics......................... 147

Burmester (James), Bristol.......................... 59
Cheshire Book Centre, Cheshire................... 69
Eggeling Books (John), W Yorks.................. 250
Elaine Lonsdale Books, W Yorks.................. 248
Fortune Green Books, London NW................ 161
Joel Segal Books, Devon........................... 86
Paperbacks Plus, Bristol............................ 59
Poor Richard's Books, Suffolk...................... 227
R. & A. Books, East Sussex........................ 102
Reading Lasses, Dumfries & Galloway............ 271
Robert Temple, London N.......................... 160
Stevens (Joan), Cambs.............................. 65
Susan Taylor Books, W Yorks..................... 248
Symes Books (Naomi), Cheshire.................. 72
Tarka Books, Devon................................. 84
Tiger Books, Kent................................... 137
Tindley & Chapman, London WC................. 179
Treasure Trove Books, Leics....................... 148
Wheen O'Books, Scottish Borders................. 269
Williams (Bookdealer), (Richard), N Lincs....... 154
Yesterday's News, Conwy.......................... 285

- YOUNG ADULT MYSTERY & ADVENTURE SERIES

Annie's Books, S Yorks............................. 222
Apocalypse, Surrey.................................. 233
Bookroom (The), Surrey............................ 234
Green Meadow Books, Cornwall................... 74
Porcupine Books, London Outer................... 182
R. & A. Books, East Sussex........................ 102
Reaveley Books, Devon............................. 87
Robert (Leslie), London W......................... 175
Wheen O'Books, Scottish Borders................. 269
Williams (Bookdealer), (Richard), N Lincs....... 154

FICTIONAL CHARACTERS

Apocalypse, Surrey.................................. 233
Fifteenth Century Bookshop (The), East Sussex. 104
R. & A. Books, East Sussex........................ 102

FINANCE - GENERAL

Aurora Books Ltd, Lothian.......................... 276
Barcombe Services, Essex.......................... 108
Beware of the Leopard, Bristol..................... 58
Empire Books, N Yorks............................. 198
Reid of Liverpool, Merseyside...................... 185

FINE & RARE

Allsop (Duncan M.), Warwickshire................ 238
Amwell Book Company, London EC.............. 157
Antique Map and Bookshop (The), Dorset...... 94
Arden, Bookseller (C.), Powys..................... 289
Ardis Books, Hampshire............................ 126
Atholl Fine Books, Tayside......................... 281
Baldwin's Scientific Books, Essex.................. 112
Barry McKay Rare Books, Cumbria............... 77
Baxter (Steve), Surrey.............................. 234
Biblion, London W.................................. 172
Blackwell's Rare Books, Oxfordshire.............. 209
Books at Star Dot Star, West Midlands.......... 241
Books on Spain, London Outer.................... 184
Bookshop on the Heath, The, London SE....... 164
Booth (Booksearch Service), (Geoff), Cheshire... 68
Brian Troath Books, London E..................... 155
Bristow & Garland, Hampshire.................... 122

SPECIALITY INDEX

Broadhurst of Southport Ltd., Merseyside 186
Brock Books, N Yorks 193
Burmester (James), Bristol........................... 59
Byblos Antiquarian & Rare Book, Hampshire .. 121
Camden Books, Somerset 216
Carnforth Bookshop (The), Lancashire 143
Cobnar Books, Kent 142
Cobweb Books, N Yorks............................. 195
Colin Hancock, Ceredigion 284
Cooper Hay Rare Books, Strathclyde 280
Cox Rare Books (Charles), Cornwall............... 74
Dartmoor Bookshop (The), Devon 84
David (G.), Cambs 63
Dean Byass, Bristol................................... 60
Dean Illustrated Books (Myra), Powys 288
Drury Rare Books (John), Essex................... 110
Eastwood Books (David), Cornwall 73
Ellwood Editions, Wiltshire 253
Farquharson, (Hilary), Tayside..................... 281
Fletcher (H.M.), Hertfordshire 132
Foster (Stephen), London NW...................... 161
Fosters Bookshop, London W 171
Gardener & Cook, London SW..................... 168
Golden Books Group, Devon 85
Grahame (Major Iain), Suffolk 226
Grayling (David A.H.), Cumbria 79
Green Man Books, East Sussex 101
Harrington (Adrian), London W.................... 173
Harrington Antiquarian Bookseller (Peter),
London SW.. 169
Hava Books, London SE............................. 165
Heath (A.R.), Bristol.................................. 59
Heritage, West Midlands 239
Hughes Rare Books (Spike), Borders.............. 268
Hutchison (Books) (Larry), Fife.................... 271
Ian Briddon, Derbyshire............................. 82
Ian McKelvie Bookseller, London N............... 159
Island Books, Devon 85
Joel Segal Books, Devon 86
Johnson Rare Book Collections (C.R.),
London NW... 162
Jones (Andrew), Suffolk 228
Kenny's Bookshops and Art Galleries Ltd,
Co. Galway 266
Kernaghans, Merseyside............................. 186
Kerr (Norman), Cumbria 78
Kilgarriff (Raymond), East Sussex................. 105
Kirkman Ltd., (Robert), Bedfordshire............. 54
Lost Books, Northants................................ 201
Lucius Books, N Yorks............................... 199
Mair Wilkes Books, Fife 272
Marble Hill Books, Middlesex 184
Marks Limited (Barrie), London N................. 159
N V Books, Warwickshire............................ 237
Offa's Dyke Books, Shropshire 214
Orlando Booksellers, Lincolnshire 152
Paralos Ltd., London WC 178
Parikian, Rare Books (Diana), London W 175
Parkinsons Books, Merseyside...................... 186
Poetry Bookshop (The), Powys..................... 291
Poole (William), London W 175
R. & A. Books, East Sussex 102
Reeves Technical Books, N Yorks.................. 196
Rochdale Book Company, Gr Man 120
Rosley Books, Cumbria 81

Rowan (P. & B.), Co. Antrim 260
Roz Hulse, Conwy 286
Rutland Bookshop (The), Rutland 212
Rye Old Books, East Sussex 104
Saint Mary's Books & Prints, Lincolnshire....... 154
Saintfield Antiques & Fine Books, Co. Down ... 261
Sokol Books Ltd., London W 175
Solitaire Books, Somerset............................ 217
Stalagluft Books, Tyne and Wear.................. 236
Stern Antiquarian Bookseller (Jeffrey), N Yorks 199
Susanne Schulz-Falster Rare Books, London N. 160
Taylor & Son (Peter), Hertfordshire 133
Temperley (David), West Midlands................ 239
Thorntons of Oxford Ltd., Oxfordshire........... 207
Tobo Books, Hampshire.............................. 123
Trinity Rare Books, Co. Leitrim 266
Unsworth's Booksellers, London WC 180
Updike Rare Books (John), Lothian 279
Valentine Rare Books, London W.................. 176
Venables (Morris & Juliet), Bristol................. 60
Wildside Books, Worcestershire 255
Woodbine Books, W Yorks.......................... 246
Words Etcetera Bookshop, Dorset................. 93
Yates Antiquarian Books (Tony), Leics........... 148
York (Graham), Devon............................... 86

FINE ART

Amwell Book Company, London EC 157
Apocalypse, Surrey 233
Ars Artis, Oxfordshire 209
Art Book Company, (The), Suffolk................. 228
Art Reference Books, Hampshire 125
Besleys Books, Suffolk 226
Book Palace (The), London SE 164
Bookroom (The), Surrey............................. 234
Brock Books, N Yorks 193
Bruce Holdsworth Books, East Sussex 105
Central Bookshop, Warwickshire 238
Chalk (Old & Out of Print Books
(Christine M.), West Midlands 239
Cooper Hay Rare Books, Strathclyde 280
Cornucopia Books, Lincolnshire 153
Cover to Cover, Merseyside......................... 186
Decorum Books, London N 158
Dew (Roderick), East Sussex 101
Dolphin Books, Suffolk............................... 226
Don Kelly Books, London W 172
Farnborough Gallery, Hampshire.................. 122
Grosvenor Prints, London WC..................... 178
Handsworth Books, Essex............................ 112
Heneage Art Books (Thomas), London SW 169
Hollett and Son (R.F.G.), Cumbria 80
Inprint, Glos... 116
Joel Segal Books, Devon 86
Kenny's Bookshops and Art Galleries Ltd,
Co. Galway 266
Mannwaring (M.G.), Bristol 59
Marlborough Rare Books Ltd., London W 174
Nelson (Elizabeth), Suffolk 227
Pagan Limited (Hugh), London SW............... 170
Phelan Books, Co. Dublin 265
Pordes Books Ltd., (Henry), London WC........ 179
Potterton Books, N Yorks 197
Pugh Books (Ian K.), Worcestershire.............. 256
R. & A. Books, East Sussex 102

SPECIALITY INDEX

Ray Rare and Out of Print Books (Janette), N Yorks.. 199
Roe and Moore, London WC...................... 179
Second Edition, Lothian............................. 278
Sleepy Elephant Books & Artefacts, Cumbria ... 80
Spelman (Ken), N Yorks............................ 199
Stroh (M.A.), London E 155
Sykes (Graham), W Yorks.......................... 249
Tasburgh Books, Norfolk 191
Trinders' Fine Tools, Suffolk 227
Webb Books (John), S Yorks...................... 222
Whittle, Bookseller (Avril), Cumbria 81
Wyseby House Books, Berkshire.................... 55

FINE LEATHER BINDINGS (SEE ALSO FINE & RARE)

Antique Map and Bookshop (The), Dorset 94
Atholl Fine Books, Tayside 281
Bayntun (George), Somerset 216
Booklore, Leics.. 148
Eastwood Books (David), Cornwall 73
Ely Books, Cambs..................................... 65
Foster (Stephen), London NW..................... 161
Foster Bookshop (Paul), London SW............ 168
Fosters Bookshop, London W 173
Freeman's Corner Shop, Norfolk 190
Grove Bookshop (The), N Yorks.................. 197
Hava Books, London SE............................. 165
Kirkman Ltd., (Robert), Bedfordshire............. 54
Mercat Books, Highland 274
R. & A. Books, East Sussex 102
Red Star Books, Hertfordshire 130
Staniland (Booksellers), Lincolnshire 154
Winchester Bookshop (The), Hampshire......... 127
Woodbine Books, W Yorks......................... 246

FINE PRINTING

Apocalypse, Surrey 233
Ballantyne–Way (Roger), Suffolk 229
Bardsley's Books, Suffolk........................... 226
Barlow (Vincent G.), Hampshire................... 125
Barnitt (Peter), Wiltshire............................ 254
Barry McKay Rare Books, Cumbria............... 77
Biblion, London W................................... 172
Blackwell's Rare Books, Oxfordshire............. 209
Bookstand, Dorset.................................... 94
Colin Hancock, Ceredigion 284
Collinge & Clark, London WC..................... 177
Cox Old & Rare Books (Claude), Suffolk 228
Dales & Lakes Book Centre, Cumbria............ 80
Dean Illustrated Books (Myra), Powys 288
Ewell Bookshop Ltd, Surrey....................... 232
Maggs Brothers Limited, London W.............. 174
Mills Rare Books (Adam), Cambs................. 64
Pordes Books Ltd., (Henry), London WC....... 179
R. & A. Books, East Sussex 102
Seydi Rare Books (Sevin), London NW 162
Solitaire Books, Somerset........................... 217
Susanne Schulz-Falster Rare Books, London N. 160
Tucker (Alan & Joan), Glos 117
Updike Rare Books (John), Lothian 279
Woodbine Books, W Yorks......................... 246

FIRE & FIRE FIGHTERS

Cox (Geoff), Devon 90

Henry Wilson Books, Cheshire..................... 69
Maggy Browne, Lincolnshire 150
R. & A. Books, East Sussex 102
St Swithin's Illustrated & Children's Books, London W.. 175
Theatreshire Books, N Yorks....................... 193
Vickers (Anthony), N Yorks........................ 196

FIREARMS/GUNS

Americanabooksuk, Cumbria....................... 77
Bookworm, Lothian.................................. 277
Bookworm (The), Lothian 277
Cader Idris Books, Powys........................... 292
Caliver Books, Essex................................. 110
Camilla's Bookshop, East Sussex 101
Chalmers Hallam (E.), Hampshire................. 125
Cornucopia Books, Lincolnshire 153
Duck (William), Hampshire......................... 124
Farnborough Gallery, Hampshire.................. 122
Greta Books, Durham 97
Guildmaster Books, Cheshire....................... 70
Helion & Company, West Midlands 240
Heneage Art Books (Thomas), London SW 169
Home Farm Books, Warwickshire................. 237
Joel Segal Books, Devon 86
Kilgour (Sporting Books) (Ian), Leics............ 149
Lost Books, Northants............................... 201
Meekins Books (Paul), Warwickshire............. 238
MilitaryHistoryBooks.com, Kent................... 138
Muttonchop Manuscripts, W Sussex 244
N1 Books, East Sussex 105
Prospect Books, Conwy 285
R. & A. Books, East Sussex 102
Stroh (M.A.), London E 155
Trinders' Fine Tools, Suffolk 227
Vinovium Books, Durham 97

FIRST EDITIONS

Allinson (Frank & Stella), Warwickshire 237
Amwell Book Company, London EC............. 157
Anthony Sillem, East Sussex........................ 102
Antiques on High, Oxfordshire..................... 209
Apocalypse, Surrey 233
Armchair Books, Lothian 276
Ash Rare Books, London SW...................... 167
Aurora Books Ltd, Lothian.......................... 276
Autolycus, Shropshire............................... 213
Bass (Ben), Wiltshire 251
Bates Books, London Outer 182
Bath Old Books, Somerset 216
Baxter (Steve), Surrey 234
Bayntun (George), Somerset 216
BC Books, Cheshire.................................. 70
Beck (John), East Sussex 103
Bertram Rota Ltd., London WC 177
Berwick Books, Lincolnshire....................... 152
Bibliophile Books, London E 155
Biblipola, London NW 161
Blackwell's Rare Books, Oxfordshire............. 209
Blythswood Bookshop, Highland 275
Book Business (The), London W 172
Book Gallery (The), Cornwall...................... 75
Bookbarrow, Cambs 63
Books & Collectables Ltd., Cambs 63
Books Only, Suffolk.................................. 227

SPECIALITY INDEX

books2books, Devon 88
Bookshop (The), Co. Donegal 263
Bookshop on the Heath, The, London SE 164
Booth (Booksearch Service), (Geoff), Cheshire... 68
Boris Books, Hampshire 126
Bowie Books & Collectables, East Yorkshire 107
Brian Troath Books, London E 155
Brighton Books, East Sussex 99
Budd (Richard), Somerset 219
Carta Regis, Powys 293
Castle Bookshop, Essex 109
Cheshire Book Centre, Cheshire 69
Cobweb Books, N Yorks 195
Cox Rare Books (Charles), Cornwall 74
Craobh Rua Books, Co. Armagh 260
Darkwood Books, Co. Cork 263
Deeside Books, Grampian 273
Dolphin Books, Suffolk 226
Eastcote Bookshop (The), London Outer 181
Eastwood Books (David), Cornwall 73
Elaine Lonsdale Books, W Yorks 248
Ellis, Bookseller (Peter), London WC 178
Ely Books, Cambs 65
English (Toby), Oxfordshire 211
Enigma Books, Norfolk 190
Evergreen Livres, Oxfordshire 208
Family-Favourites, East Yorkshire 106
Farnborough Gallery, Hampshire 122
Fiction First, Cheshire 70
Fifteenth Century Bookshop (The), E Sussex 104
First State Books, London W 173
firstpagebooks, Norfolk 190
Ford Books (David), Hertfordshire 133
Foster (Stephen), London NW 161
Foster Bookshop (Paul), London SW 168
Fosters Bookshop, London W 173
Gekoski (R.A.), London WC 178
Gildas Books, Cheshire 68
Glyn's Books, Shropshire 213
Greta Books, Durham 97
Hambleton Books, N Yorks 197
Hardback Hotel, Lancashire 144
Harrington (Adrian), London W 173
Harrington Antiquarian Bookseller (Peter),
London SW 169
Heppa (Christopher), Essex 108
Hill (John S.), Devon 86
Hylton Booksearch, Merseyside 185
Ian Briddon, Derbyshire 82
Ian McKelvie Bookseller, London N 159
Intech Books, Northumberland 203
Island Books, Devon 85
Jarndyce Antiquarian Booksellers, London WC. 178
Joel Segal Books, Devon 86
John Underwood Antiquarian
Books, Norfolk 190
Junk & Spread Eagle, London SE 165
K Books, Cheshire 70
Katnap Arts, Norfolk 191
Kendall–Carpenter (Tim), Gr Man 119
Kenny's Bookshops and Art Galleries Ltd,
Co. Galway 266
Keswick Bookshop, Cumbria 79
Kevin S. Ogilvie Modern First Editions,
Grampian 273

Kineton Nooks, Warwickshire 237
Kirkman Ltd., (Robert), Bedfordshire 54
L.M.S. Books, Hertfordshire 132
Leabeck Books, Oxfordshire 210
Little Stour Books, Kent 137
Lloyd-Davies (Sue), Carmarthenshire 284
Lucius Books, N Yorks 199
Mainly Fiction, Cheshire 68
Marcet Books, London SE 165
Martin's Books, Powys 292
Mellon's Books, East Sussex 101
Ming Books, Dumfries & Galloway 271
Modern First Editions, London Outer 183
Modern Firsts Etc, Lancashire 143
Murphy (C.J.), Norfolk 190
N V Books, Warwickshire 237
O'Flynn Books, N Yorks 199
Palladour Books, Hampshire 126
Pamona Books, Lancashire 145
Paton Books, Hertfordshire 132
Pickering Bookshop, N Yorks 197
Poetry Bookshop (The), Powys 291
Pomes Penyeach, Staffordshire 224
Prescott - The Bookseller (John), London O 184
Price (R.W.), Notts 204
Primrose Hill Books, London NW 162
R. & A. Books, East Sussex 102
Rassam (Paul), London NW 162
Reading Lasses, Dumfries & Galloway 271
Richard Frost Books, Hertfordshire 130
Riderless Horse Books, Norfolk 187
Robert (Leslie), London W 175
Robert Temple, London N 160
Rowan House Books, Surrey 232
Roz Hulse, Conwy 286
Ruebotham (Kirk), Cheshire 71
Sansovino Books, W Sussex 244
Scrivener's Books & Bookbinding, Derbyshire ... 82
Sensawunda Books, Cheshire 68
Shakeshaft (Dr. B.), Cheshire 71
Shelley (E. & J.), Buckinghamshire 61
Skelton (Tony), Kent 141
Stevens (Joan), Cambs 65
Surprise Books, Glos 113
Sutcliffe (Mark), W Yorks 248
Sykes (Graham), W Yorks 249
The Glass Key, W Yorks 247
Tiffin (Tony and Gill), Durham 97
Till's Bookshop, Lothian 279
Tindley & Chapman, London WC 179
Trevorrow (Edwin), Hertfordshire 130
Trinity Rare Books, Co. Leitrim 266
Updike Rare Books (John), Lothian 279
Ward (R.F. & C.), Norfolk 188
Waterfield's, Oxfordshire 210
Webb Books (John), S Yorks 222
Wheen O'Books, Scottish Borders 269
Williams (Bookdealer), (Richard), N Lincs 154
Williams Rare Books (Nigel), London WC 180
Winchester Bookshop (The), Hampshire 127
Woodbine Books, W Yorks 246

FISHERIES

Chalmers Hallam (E.), Hampshire 125
Coch-y-Bonddu Books, Powys 292

SPECIALITY INDEX

Garfi Books, Powys 293
Head (John & Judith), Wiltshire 253
hullbooks.com, East Yorkshire 107
Joel Segal Books, Devon 86
Parkinsons Books, Merseyside....................... 186

FISHES

Alauda Books, Cumbria 78
Atholl Fine Books, Tayside 281
Chalmers Hallam (E.), Hampshire 125
Coch-y-Bonddu Books, Powys 292
Cornucopia Books, Lincolnshire 153
Edmund Pollinger Rare Books, London SW..... 167
Head (John & Judith), Wiltshire 253
Joel Segal Books, Devon 86
Kalligraphia, Isle of Wight 134
Parkinsons Books, Merseyside....................... 186
R. & A. Books, East Sussex 102
River Reads Bookshop, Devon...................... 90
Steven Simpson Books, Norfolk 191
Sub Aqua Prints and Books, Hampshire 123

FLAGS

Joel Segal Books, Devon 86
Marine & Cannon Books, Cheshire 71
Marine and Cannon Books, Cheshire 69
R. & A. Books, East Sussex 102

FLORA & FAUNA

Alauda Books, Cumbria 78
Antique Map and Bookshop (The), Dorset 94
Baldwin's Scientific Books, Essex 112
Besleys Books, Suffolk 226
Calendula Horticultural Books, East Sussex 102
Carningli Centre, Pembrokeshire 288
Castleton (Pat), Kent.................................. 138
Coch-y-Bonddu Books, Powys 292
Dales & Lakes Book Centre, Cumbria............. 80
Edmund Pollinger Rare Books, London SW..... 167
Ewell Bookshop Ltd, Surrey 232
Fifteenth Century Bookshop (The), East Sussex. 104
Garfi Books, Powys 293
Grahame Thornton, Bookseller, Dorset........... 93
Inner Bookshop (The), Oxfordshire................ 210
J & J Burgess Booksellers, Cambs 64
Jay Books, Lothian..................................... 278
Joel Segal Books, Devon 86
Kalligraphia, Isle of Wight 134
Maudalay Bookshop, London SW 169
Mercat Books, Highland 274
Orb's Bookshop, Grampian.......................... 274
Parkinsons Books, Merseyside....................... 186
Prospect House Books, Co. Down.................. 261
R. & A. Books, East Sussex 102
Roger Collicott Books, Cornwall 75
Shakeshaft (Dr. B.), Cheshire....................... 71
Shearwater Books, Northumberland............... 202
Summerfield Books Ltd, Cumbria 77
Treasure Island (The), Gr Man...................... 119
Westons, Hertfordshire 133

FLOWER ARRANGING

Blest (Peter), Kent 139
Calendula Horticultural Books, East Sussex 102
Court Hay Books, West Midlands.................. 240

Farnborough Gallery, Hampshire................... 122
Joel Segal Books, Devon 86
Park (Mike), London Outer.......................... 183
R. & A. Books, East Sussex 102
Reading Lasses, Dumfries & Galloway 271
Roadmaster Books, Kent............................. 137

FOLIO SOCIETY, THE

Ardis Books, Hampshire 126
Avery (Alan), N Yorks 195
Barbican Bookshop, N Yorks 198
Bath Old Books, Somerset 216
Birmingham Books, West Midlands................ 239
Bookbox, Glos 116
Books For All, N Yorks 194
BOOKS4U, Flintshire................................. 286
Booth (Booksearch Service), (Geoff), Cheshire... 68
Camilla's Bookshop, East Sussex 101
Central Bookshop, Warwickshire 238
Cheshire Book Centre, Cheshire.................... 69
Chevin Books, W Yorks.............................. 250
Coach House Books, Worcestershire 256
Cobbles Books, Somerset............................ 218
Dales & Lakes Book Centre, Cumbria............ 80
Dandy Lion Editions, Surrey 233
Discovery Bookshop, Carmarthenshire............ 283
Dolphin Books, Suffolk............................... 226
Eastgate Bookshop, East Yorkshire 106
Ellwood Editions, Wiltshire 253
Fifteenth Century Bookshop (The), E Sussex 104
Fisher & Sperr, London N........................... 158
Fossgate Books, N Yorks 198
Fosters Bookshop, London W 173
G. C. Books Ltd., Dumfries & Galloway......... 271
Good for Books, Lincolnshire 151
Hab Books, London W............................... 173
JB Books & Collectables, W Sussex 244
Joel Segal Books, Devon 86
Junk & Spread Eagle, London SE.................. 165
Lighthouse Books (The), Dorset 92
My Back Pages, London SW 169
O'Brien Books & Photo Gallery,
Co. Limerick... 266
O'Connor Fine Books, Lancashire.................. 145
Old Station Pottery & Bookshop (The), Norfolk 192
Parrott Books, Oxfordshire 211
Poetry Bookshop (The), Powys..................... 291
Portobello Books, London W 175
Prescott - The Bookseller (John), London O..... 184
R. & A. Books, East Sussex 102
Ross Old Books & Prints, Herefordshire 128
Saintfield Antiques & Fine Books, Co. Down ... 261
Sax Books, Suffolk 229
Scrivener's Books & Bookbinding, Derbyshire... 82
Shacklock Books (David), Suffolk 227
Sleepy Elephant Books & Artefacts, Cumbria ... 80
Tasburgh Books, Norfolk 191
Thomas (Books) (Leona), Cheshire................ 71
Tiffin (Tony and Gill), Durham 97
Treasure Trove Books, Leics........................ 148
Trinity Rare Books, Co. Leitrim 266
Waddington Books & Prints (Geraldine),
Northants 200
Westwood Books (Mark), Powys 291
Westwood Books Ltd, Cumbria..................... 80

SPECIALITY INDEX

Whittle, Bookseller (Avril), Cumbria 81

FOLKLORE

Alpha Books, London N 158
Apocalypse, Surrey 233
Books, Denbighshire 286
Books on Spain, London Outer 184
Bracton Books, Cambs 63
Byre Books, Dumfries & Galloway 270
Cottage Books, Leics 147
Country Books, Derbyshire 82
Daeron's Books, Buckinghamshire 62
Dales & Lakes Book Centre, Cumbria 80
Dancing Goat Bookshop (The), Norfolk 188
Delectus Books, London WC 177
Doolin Dinghy Books, Co. Clare 262
DPE Books, Devon 87
Edwards (London) Limited (Francis),
London WC 177
Edwards in Hay-on-Wye (Francis), Powys 290
Ellwood Editions, Wiltshire 253
Fifteenth Century Bookshop (The), East Sussex. 104
Gilbert (R.A), Bristol.... 59
Gildas Books, Cheshire 68
Grampian Books, Grampian 274
Green Man Books, East Sussex 101
Harvest Books, Lancashire 145
Hobgoblin Books, Hampshire 125
Holtom (Christopher), Cornwall 75
Hutchison (Books) (Larry), Fife 271
Inner Bookshop (The), Oxfordshire 210
Joel Segal Books, Devon 86
Lowe (John), Norfolk 189
Magis Books, Leics 149
Michael J Carroll, Co. Cork 263
Minster Gate Bookshop, N Yorks 199
Occultique, Northants 200
Orb's Bookshop, Grampian 274
Philip Hopper, Essex 110
R. & A. Books, East Sussex 102
Randall (Tom), Somerset 219
Royal Carbery Books Ltd., Co. Cork 262
Thornber (Peter M.), N Yorks 196
Walker Fine Books (Steve), Dorset 92

FOOD & DRINK

Apocalypse, Surrey 233
Arden Books & Cosmographia, Warwickshire... 237
Aurora Books Ltd, Lothian 276
Black Cat Books, Norfolk 188
Books & Bygones, Berkshire 57
Books at Star Dot Star, West Midlands 241
Capel Mawr Collectors Centre, Gwynedd 287
Castleton (Pat), Kent 138
Chantrey Books, S Yorks 222
Clarke (Janet), Somerset 216
Collectable Books, London SE 165
Cooking = The Books, Glos 115
Cooks Books, East Sussex 99
Dales & Lakes Book Centre, Cumbria 80
Dusty Books, Powys 292
Edmund Pollinger Rare Books, London SW 167
Elmfield Books, West Midlands 239
Fifteenth Century Bookshop (The), East Sussex. 104
Foster (Stephen), London NW 161

Gardener & Cook, London SW 168
Garfi Books, Powys 293
Grahame Thornton, Bookseller, Dorset 93
Gresham Books, Somerset 218
Hall's Bookshop, Kent 141
Hurst (Jenny), Kent 138
Ian Briddon, Derbyshire 82
Joel Segal Books, Devon 86
Junk & Spread Eagle, London SE 165
Lucas (Richard), London NW 162
Marcet Books, London SE 165
Much Ado Books, East Sussex 99
N1 Books, East Sussex 105
Parkinsons Books, Merseyside 186
Pholiota Books, London WC 179
R. & A. Books, East Sussex 102
Sleepy Elephant Books & Artefacts, Cumbria ... 80
Stroh (M.A.), London E 155
Susanne Schulz-Falster Rare Books, London N. 160
The Glass Key, W Yorks 247
The Sanctuary Bookshop, Dorset 94
Weiner (Graham), London N 160
Wheen O'Books, Scottish Borders 269
Whittle, Bookseller (Avril), Cumbria 81

FORE-EDGE PAINTINGS

Carta Regis, Powys 293
Chas J. Sawyer, Kent 141
Cox Old & Rare Books (Claude), Suffolk 228
Davis, Antiquarian Books (Guy), Notts 205
Game Advice, Oxfordshire 210
Harrington (Adrian), London W 173
Harrington Antiquarian Bookseller (Peter),
London SW 169
Kirkman Ltd., (Robert), Bedfordshire 54
Poetry Bookshop (The), Powys 291

FOREIGN TEXTS

Anthony Neville, Kent 139
Apocalypse, Surrey 233
Artco, Notts 204
Atlas, London N 158
Baldwin (Jack), Strathclyde 280
Books on Spain, London Outer 184
Classic Bindings Ltd, London SW 167
Colwyn Books, Conwy 285
Crouch Rare Books, Surrey 233
Foyle Books, Co. Derry 260
Hab Books, London W 173
Hellenic Bookservices, London NW 162
Hesketh & Ward Ltd., London SW 169
Joel Segal Books, Devon 86
Naughton Booksellers, Co. Dublin 265
Needham Books, (Russell), Somerset 220
Orbis Books (London) Ltd., London W 175
Owen (J.V.), Conwy 285
owenbooks65, Conwy 285
Parikian, Rare Books (Diana), London W 175
Poetry Bookshop (The), Powys 291
Poole (William), London W 175
Robertshaw (John), Cambs 66
Sturford Books, Wiltshire 254
Thorntons of Oxford Ltd., Oxfordshire 207

SPECIALITY INDEX

FORESTRY
Besleys Books, Suffolk 226
Coch-y-Bonddu Books, Powys 292
Country Books, Derbyshire 82
Court Hay Books, West Midlands.................. 240
Dales & Lakes Book Centre, Cumbria............ 80
Joel Segal Books, Devon 86
Mandalay Bookshop, London SW 169
Park (Mike), London Outer.......................... 183
Parkinsons Books, Merseyside...................... 186
R. & A. Books, East Sussex 102
Stobart Davies Limited, Carmarthernshire 284
Summerfield Books Ltd, Cumbria 77
Westons, Hertfordshire 133

FOSSILS
Baldwin's Scientific Books, Essex 112
Cox, Andrew, Shropshire............................. 215
Inner Bookshop (The), Oxfordshire................ 210
J & J Burgess Booksellers, Cambridgeshire....... 64
Joel Segal Books, Devon 86
Kalligraphia, Isle of Wight 134
Parkinsons Books, Merseyside...................... 186
R. & A. Books, East Sussex 102
Randall (Tom), Somerset............................. 219
Roberts Books, Ayrshire 280
Roger Collicott Books, Cornwall 75
The Sanctuary Bookshop, Dorset................... 94

FOURTH WAY
Inner Bookshop (The), Oxfordshire................ 210
Needham Books, (Russell), Somerset.............. 220

FREE THOUGHT
Church Street Books, Norfolk....................... 187
Forder (R.W.), Hampshire 121
Humanist Book Services, Cornwall 73
Kenny's Bookshops and Art Galleries Ltd, Co.
Galway 266
Left on The Shelf, Cumbria.......................... 79
Northern Herald Books, W Yorks.................. 246
Stevens (Joan), Cambridgeshire..................... 65
Turton (John), Durham 98
Turton (John), Durham 98
Webb Books (John), S Yorks........................ 222

FREEMASONRY & ANTI-MASONRY
Alpha Books, London N 158
Bibliophole (The), S Yorks.......................... 222
Bookworm, Lothian.................................... 277
Chas J. Sawyer, Kent 141
Fun in Books, Surrey 235
Gilbert (R.A.), Bristol................................. 59
Hava Books, London SE.............................. 165
Inner Bookshop (The), Oxfordshire................ 210
InterCol London, London N 159
Occultique, Northants................................. 200
R. & A. Books, East Sussex 102
Samovar Books, Co. Dublin 264
SETI Books, Staffordshire........................... 225
Treasure Island (The), Gr Man...................... 119
Yesterday's News, Conwy............................ 285

FRENCH FOREIGN LEGION, THE
Burroughs (Andrew), Lincolnshire 153

Wiend Books, Lancashire 144

FREUDIANA
Apocalypse, Surrey 233
Barcombe Services, Essex............................ 108
Inner Bookshop (The), Oxfordshire................ 210
Joel Segal Books, Devon 86
Parkinsons Books, Merseyside...................... 186
R M Books, Hertfordshire 132

FRUITARIANISM
Park (Mike), London Outer.......................... 183

FUNGI
Bernard Dixon and Kath Adams, Middlesex 183
Court Hay Books, West Midlands.................. 240
Edmund Pollinger Rare Books, London SW..... 167
Gardener & Cook, London SW..................... 168
Joel Segal Books, Devon 86
Kalligraphia, Isle of Wight.......................... 134
Park (Mike), London Outer.......................... 183
Parkinsons Books, Merseyside...................... 186
Pholiota Books, London WC........................ 179
R. & A. Books, East Sussex 102
Summerfield Books Ltd, Cumbria 77

FUR TRADE
Americanabooksuk, Cumbria........................ 77

FURNITURE
Art Reference Books, Hampshire 125
Brock Books, N Yorks 193
Clark (Nigel A.), London SE 165
Cornucopia Books, Lincolnshire 153
Dales & Lakes Book Centre, Cumbria............ 80
Don Kelly Books, London W 172
Fifteenth Century Bookshop (The), East Sussex. 104
Foster (Stephen), London NW...................... 161
Hadfield (G.K.), Cumbria............................ 80
Heneage Art Books (Thomas), London SW 169
Joel Segal Books, Devon 86
Keith Langford, London E 155
N1 Books, East Sussex 105
Nelson (Elizabeth), Suffolk........................... 227
Phillips of Hitchin (Antiques) Ltd., Hertfordshire 131
R. & A. Books, East Sussex 102
Reeves Technical Books, N Yorks.................. 196
Scrivener's Books & Bookbinding, Derbyshire... 82
Sleepy Elephant Books & Artefacts, Cumbria ... 80
Trinders' Fine Tools, Suffolk 227
Upper-Room Books, Somerset...................... 218
Vickers (Anthony), N Yorks......................... 196
Whittle, Bookseller (Avril), Cumbria 81

GAMBLING
Amos (Denis W.), Hertfordshire 131
Delectus Books, London WC........................ 177
Garwood & Voigt, Kent.............................. 140
InterCol London, London N 159
Joel Segal Books, Devon 86
Junk & Spread Eagle, London SE 165
R. & A. Books, East Sussex 102
Susanne Schulz-Falster Rare Books, London N. 160
Yesterday's News, Conwy............................ 285

SPECIALITY INDEX

GAMES

Annie's Books, S Yorks 222
Baron (Christopher), Gr Man 118
Bookmark (Children's Books), Wiltshire.......... 253
Cheshire Book Centre, Cheshire..................... 69
Cornucopia Books, Lincolnshire 153
Fifteenth Century Bookshop (The), East Sussex. 104
Game Advice, Oxfordshire 210
Garwood & Voigt, Kent.............................. 140
Green Meadow Books, Cornwall 74
InterCol London, London N 159
Joel Segal Books, Devon 86
R. & A. Books, East Sussex 102
R. S. & P. A. Scowen, Middlesex.................. 182
S Swithin's Illustrated & Children's Books,
London W 175
Treasure Island (The), Gr Man..................... 119

GANDHIANA

Empire Books, N Yorks.............................. 198
Inner Bookshop (The), Oxfordshire................ 210

GARDENING - GENERAL

Abacus Gallery, Staffordshire........................ 224
Apocalypse, Surrey 233
Arden Books & Cosmographia, Warwickshire... 237
Arden, Bookseller (C.), Powys...................... 289
Ashwell Books, Wiltshire............................. 252
Barn Books, Shropshire............................... 215
Barnhill Books, Isle of Arran 275
Besleys Books, Suffolk 226
Bianco Library, W Sussex............................ 242
Blest (Peter), Kent 139
Book House (The), Cumbria......................... 77
Bookbox, Glos 116
Bookroom (The), Surrey.............................. 234
Books, Denbighshire 286
Books & Collectables Ltd., Cambridgeshire 63
Books for Content, Herefordshire................... 128
Bosco Books, Cornwall 73
Brighton Books, East Sussex......................... 99
Brown-Studies, Strathclyde........................... 279
Browse Books, Lancashire 144
Calendula Horticultural Books, East Sussex 102
Camilla's Bookshop, East Sussex 101
Castleton (Pat), Kent.................................. 138
Chantrey Books, S Yorks 222
Chaucer Bookshop, Kent............................. 136
Cheshire Book Centre, Cheshire..................... 69
Clark (M.R.), W Yorks............................... 246
Clarke Books (David), Somerset 219
Court Hay Books, West Midlands.................. 240
Cousens (W.C.), Devon............................... 84
D'Arcy Books, Wiltshire............................. 252
Dales & Lakes Book Centre, Cumbria 80
Dartmoor Bookshop (The), Devon 84
Davies Fine Books, Worcestershire 257
Discovery Bookshop, Carmarthenshire............ 283
Dolphin Books, Suffolk............................... 226
Duck (William), Hampshire......................... 124
Dusty Books, Powys 292
Ellis, Bookseller (Peter), London WC 178
Esoteric Dreams Bookshop, Cumbria 78
Evergreen Livres, Oxfordshire 208
Fifteenth Century Bookshop (The), East Sussex. 104

Ford Books (David), Hertfordshire................. 133
Furneaux Books (Lee), Devon....................... 89
Gardener & Cook, London SW..................... 168
Gardner and Cook, London SW.................... 168
Garfi Books, Powys 293
George St. Books, Derbyshire 83
GfB: the Colchester Bookshop, Essex 109
Glasheen-Books, Surrey 232
Good for Books, Lincolnshire 151
Goodyer (Nicholas), London N 159
HCB Wholesale, Powys.............................. 290
Hennessey Bookseller (Ray), East Sussex......... 100
Hollett and Son (R.F.G.), Cumbria 80
Hollingshead (Chris), London Outer 183
Hünersdorff Rare Books, London SW............ 169
Inprint, Glos.. 116
Internet Bookshop UK Ltd., Glos.................. 113
Jade Mountain Bookshop, Hampshire 126
Joel Segal Books, Devon 86
Junk & Spread Eagle, London SE.................. 165
Just Books, Cornwall 76
Macbuiks, N Yorks 194
Mannwaring (M.G.), Bristol 59
Marble Hill Books, Middlesex...................... 184
McCrone (Audrey), Isle of Arran 275
My Back Pages, London SW 169
Optimus Books Ltd, W Sussex 245
Paper Moon Books, Glos 116
Park (Mike), London Outer.......................... 183
Park Gallery & Bookshop (The), Northants 201
Parrott Books, Oxfordshire 211
Peter M Daly, Hampshire............................ 127
Portobello Books, London W 175
Potterton Books, N Yorks 197
Queen Victoria PH, Torfaen 294
R. & A. Books, East Sussex 102
Rare & Racy, S Yorks................................ 222
River Reads Bookshop, Devon...................... 90
Roland Books, Kent 139
Rutland Bookshop (The), Rutland 212
Seeber (Liz), East Sussex 102
Silver Trees Books, West Midlands................ 240
Staniland (Booksellers), Lincolnshire 154
Sue Lowell Natural History Books, London W . 176
Summerfield Books Ltd, Cumbria 77
Tant Yn Ellen Books, Powys 293
Tarka Books, Devon 84
Thin Read Line, Merseyside 185
Trinders Fine Tools, Suffolk 227
Vokes Books Ltd., N Yorks 195
Wadard Books, Kent 138
Westwood Books Ltd, Cumbria..................... 80
Winchester Bookshop (The), Hampshire.......... 127
Wyseby House Books, Berkshire.................... 55

- ORGANIC

Court Hay Books, West Midlands.................. 240
Fifteenth Century Bookshop (The), East Sussex. 104
Gardner and Cook, London SW.................... 168
Inner Bookshop (The), Oxfordshire................ 210
Joel Segal Books, Devon 86
R. & A. Books, East Sussex 102
Saracen Books, Derbyshire........................... 83
Wheen O'Books, Scottish Borders 269

SPECIALITY INDEX

GEMMOLOGY

Baldwin's Scientific Books, Essex 112
Barmby (C. & A.J.), Kent............................ 141
Don Kelly Books, London W 172
Hadfield (G.K.), Cumbria 80
J.G. Natural History Books, Surrey 234
Joel Segal Books, Devon 86
Mandalay Bookshop, London SW 169
Nibris Books, London SW........................... 170
Phelps (Michael), W Sussex 243
R. & A. Books, East Sussex 102
Saintfield Antiques & Fine Books, Co. Down ... 261
Trinders' Fine Tools, Suffolk 227

GENDER STUDIES

Hylton Booksearch, Merseyside 185
Joel Segal Books, Devon 86
PsychoBabel Books & Journals, Oxfordshire..... 206
R. & A. Books, East Sussex 102
Reading Lasses, Dumfries & Galloway 271
Tsbbooks, London SW 170

GENEALOGY

Aitchison (Lesley), Bristol 58
Ambra Books, Bristol................................. 58
Bell (Peter), Lothian.................................. 276
Booth Books, Powys 289
Brewin Books Ltd., Warwickshire 238
Cofion Books, Pembrokeshire 288
De Burca Rare Books, Co. Dublin 264
Delph Books, Gr Man................................ 120
Farquharson, (Hilary), Tayside..................... 281
Grampian Books, Grampian......................... 274
Hawes Books, Norfolk................................ 191
Hay Cinema Bookshop Ltd., Powys............... 290
Heraldry Today, Wiltshire........................... 252
Heritage, West Midlands 239
Herne Bay Books, Kent 139
Hill Books (Alan), S Yorks 222
Hutchison (Books) (Larry), Fife.................... 271
Idle Booksellers (The), W Yorks 246
Island Books, Devon.................................. 85
Joel Segal Books, Devon 86
Kabristan Archives, Shropshire..................... 215
Kent T. G., Surrey 231
Kingswood Books, Dorset 94
Moore (C.R.), Shropshire 214
Saintfield Antiques & Fine Books, Co. Down ... 261
Spooner & Co, Somerset 220
Thornber (Peter M.), N Yorks 196
Titford (John), Derbyshire 82
Townsend (John), Berkshire 57
Turton (John), Durham 98
Tyger Press, London N............................... 160
Williams (Bookdealer), (Richard), N Lincs....... 154

GENETICS

Baldwin's Scientific Books, Essex 112
Bernard Dixon and Kath Adams, Middlesex 183
Parkinsons Books, Merseyside...................... 186
R M Books, Hertfordshire 132
Stroh (M.A.), London E 155
Turret House, Norfolk................................ 192
Westons, Hertfordshire 133

GEOGRAPHY

Altea Antique Maps & Books, London W 172
Archer (David), Powys............................... 292
Barcombe Services, Essex............................ 108
Chesters (G. & J.), Staffordshire 225
Cornucopia Books, Lincolnshire 153
Empire Books, N Yorks.............................. 198
George St. Books, Derbyshire 83
Harrington Antiquarian Bookseller (Peter),
London SW... 169
Joel Segal Books, Devon 86
Kabristan Archives, Shropshire..................... 215
Kalligraphia, Isle of Wight 134
Maghreb Bookshop (The), London WC.......... 178
R. & A. Books, East Sussex 102
Roadmaster Books, Kent............................. 137
Sparrow Books, W Yorks............................ 246
Taney Books, Co. Dublin 264
Tooley, Adams & Co, Oxfordshire 211

GEOLOGY

Archer (David), Powys............................... 292
Austwick Hall Books, N Yorks 193
Baldwin's Scientific Books, Essex 112
Bernard Dixon and Kath Adams, Middlesex 183
Bow Windows Book Shop, East Sussex 103
Cheshire Book Centre, Cheshire.................... 69
Chesters (G. & J.), Staffordshire 225
Clevedon Books, Somerset 218
Cornucopia Books, Lincolnshire 153
Cox (Geoff), Devon 90
Cox, Andrew, Shropshire............................. 215
Duck (William), Hampshire......................... 124
Earth Science Books, Wiltshire 252
Esoteric Dreams Bookshop, Cumbria 78
Geophysical Books, Kent............................. 140
Henly (John), W Sussex 245
Hollett and Son (R.F.G.), Cumbria 80
Joel Segal Books, Devon 86
K.S.C. Books, Cheshire.............................. 71
Kalligraphia, Isle of Wight 134
Little Bookshop (The), Cumbria 81
Lymelight Books & Prints, Dorset................. 93
Maggs Brothers Limited, London W.............. 174
Park (Mike), London Outer......................... 183
Parkinsons Books, Merseyside...................... 186
Pauline Harries Books, Hampshire 123
Periplus Books, Buckinghamshire.................. 62
Peter M Daly, Hampshire........................... 127
Phelps (Michael), W Sussex 243
R. & A. Books, E Sussex............................ 102
Randall (Tom), Somerset............................ 219
Reads, Dorset 95
Roadmaster Books, Kent............................. 137
Roger Collicott Books, Cornwall 75
Sparrow Books, W Yorks............................ 246
Stalagluft Books, Tyne and Wear.................. 236
Vickers (Anthony), N Yorks........................ 196
Weiner (Graham), London N 160
Westwood Books Ltd, Cumbria..................... 80
Whitchurch Books Ltd., Cardiff.................... 283
Wiend Books, Lancashire 144

GEOPHYSICS

Earth Science Books, Wiltshire 252

SPECIALITY INDEX

Geophysical Books, Kent................................. 140
Parkinsons Books, Merseyside...................... 186
Westons, Hertfordshire 133

GHOSTS

AA1 Books, Dumfries & Galloway................. 270
Apocalypse, Surrey 233
Cornucopia Books, Lincolnshire 153
Country Books, Derbyshire 82
Cowley, Bookdealer (K.W.), Somerset 218
Dalby (Richard), N Yorks 196
Enigma Books, Norfolk 190
Esoteric Dreams Bookshop, Cumbria 78
Gildas Books, Cheshire 68
Inner Bookshop (The), Oxfordshire................. 210
Loretta Lay Books, London NW 162
Magis Books, Leics..................................... 149
Meads Book Service (The), East Sussex........... 104
Occultique, Northants................................. 200
R. & A. Books, East Sussex 102
Roger Collicott Books, Cornwall 75
Sax Books, Suffolk 229
SETI Books, Staffordshire............................ 225
Wizard Books, Cambridgeshire...................... 67

GLAMOUR

Book Palace (The), London SE 164
Fun in Books, Surrey 235
Muttonchop Manuscripts, W Sussex 244
N1 Books, East Sussex 105
Paper Pleasures, Somerset 219
Print Matters, London SE............................ 166
R. & A. Books, East Sussex 102
Tilleys Vintage Magazine Shop, Derbyshire...... 82
Yesterday's News, Conwy 285
Zardoz Books, Wiltshire.............................. 254

GLASS

Ancient Art Books, London SW 167
Art Reference Books, Hampshire 125
Barmby (C. & A.J.), Kent............................ 141
Booth (Booksearch Service), (Geoff), Cheshire... 68
Clark (Nigel A.), London SE 165
Fifteenth Century Bookshop (The), East Sussex. 104
Heneage Art Books (Thomas), London SW 169
Joel Segal Books, Devon 86
R. & A. Books, East Sussex 102
Stained Glass Books, Kent........................... 140
Stroh (M.A.), London E 155
Trinders' Fine Tools, Suffolk 227

GNOSTICS / GNOSTICISM

Chthonios Books, East Sussex....................... 102
Gilbert (R.A.), Bristol................................. 59
Hava Books, London SE.............................. 165
IKON, Devon.. 89
J & J Burgess Booksellers, Cambridgeshire....... 64
Joel Segal Books, Devon 86
Occultique, Northants................................. 200
Rosemary Pugh Books, Wiltshire 253
S.P.C.K., Bristol 60

GOLD RUSH

Americanabooksuk, Cumbria........................ 77
Apocalypse, Surrey 233

R. & A. Books, East Sussex 102

GOLDSMITHS

Don Kelly Books, London W 172
Joel Segal Books, Devon 86
R. & A. Books, East Sussex 102

GOTHIC REVIVAL

Design Gallery 1850-1950 (The), Kent 142
Don Kelly Books, London W........................ 172
Haskell (R.H. & P.), Dorset 94
R. & A. Books, East Sussex 102

GRAND CANYON & COLORADO RIVER, THE

Americanabooksuk, Cumbria........................ 77

GRAPHIC NOVELS

Book Palace (The), London SE 164
Print Matters, London SE............................ 166

GRAPHICS

Amwell Book Company, London EC 157
Barlow (Vincent G.), Hampshire 125
Book Palace (The), London SE 164
Burden (Derek), Surrey 233
Cornucopia Books, Lincolnshire 153
Joel Segal Books, Devon 86
Print Matters, London SE............................ 166
Whittle, Bookseller (Avril), Cumbria 8 1

GRAPHOLOGY

Inner Bookshop (The), Oxfordshire................ 210
Joel Segal Books, Devon 86
Magis Books, Leics..................................... 149
R. & A. Books, East Sussex 102

GRAVEYARDS

Kabristan Archives, Shropshire..................... 215
R. & A. Books, East Sussex 102

GUIDE BOOKS

Abrahams (Mike), Staffordshire.................... 224
Apocalypse, Surrey 233
Arden Books & Cosmographia, Warwickshire... 237
Baedekers & Murray Guides, S Yorks 222
Brad Books, Essex...................................... 111
Cavern Books, Cheshire 70
Church Street Books, Norfolk....................... 187
Collectables (W.H.), Suffolk 230
Cornucopia Books, Lincolnshire 153
Cox (Geoff), Devon.................................... 90
Dales & Lakes Book Centre, Cumbria............ 80
Fifteenth Century Bookshop (The), East Sussex. 104
Hellenic Bookservices, London NW................ 162
Hodgson (Books) (Richard J.), N Yorks 198
Island Books, Devon................................... 85
Jarvis Books, Derbyshire 83
Joel Segal Books, Devon 86
Mandalay Bookshop, London SW 169
Michael J Carroll, Co. Cork 263
Prospect House Books, Co. Down.................. 261
R. & A. Books, East Sussex 102
Roger Collicott Books, Cornwall 75
Royal Carbery Books Ltd., Co. Cork.............. 262

SPECIALITY INDEX

Shacklock Books (David), Suffolk 227
Shapero Rare Books (Bernard J.), London W... 175
Trinders' Fine Tools, Suffolk 227
Trinity Rare Books, Co. Leitrim 266
Tyger Press, London N............................... 160

GYNAECOLOGY

Alba Books, Grampian 274
Parkinsons Books, Merseyside...................... 186
R M Books, Hertfordshire 132
Reading Lasses, Dumfries & Galloway 271

GYPSIES

A Holmes Books, Notts 204
Abrahams (Mike), Staffordshire.................... 224
Coch-y-Bonddu Books, Powys 292
Cottage Books, Leics................................. 147
Country Books, Derbyshire 82
Cover to Cover, Merseyside......................... 186
Dales & Lakes Book Centre, Cumbria 80
Delectus Books, London WC....................... 177
Doorbar (P. & D.), Gwyned......................... 287
Joel Segal Books, Devon 86
John Underwood Antiquarian Books, Norfolk.. 190
Just Books, Cornwall 76
Philip Hopper, Essex 110
R. & A. Books, East Sussex 102
Winchester Bookshop (The), Hampshire.......... 127
York (Graham), Devon............................... 86

HAIRDRESSING

Black Cat Books, Norfolk............................ 188
Judith Mansfield, W Yorks 250
R. & A. Books, East Sussex 102

HALLOWEEN

Inner Bookshop (The), Oxfordshire................ 210
Occultique, Northants................................ 200
R. & A. Books, East Sussex 102

HAND BOOKBINDING

Barry McKay Rare Books, Cumbria............... 77
John Underwood Antiquarian Books, Norfolk.. 190
Shearwater Books, Northumberland............... 202

HANDWRITING

Barry McKay Rare Books, Cumbria 77
Joel Segal Books, Devon 86

HANDWRITTEN BOOKS

Apocalypse, Surrey 233
John Underwood Antiquarian Books, Norfolk.. 190
O'Flynn Books, N Yorks............................. 199

HEALTH

Autumn Leaves, Lincolnshire....................... 152
Cheshire Book Centre, Cheshire.................... 69
Collectable Books, London SE 165
Country Books, Derbyshire 82
Empire Books, N Yorks.............................. 198
Greensleeves, Oxfordshire 207
Hurst (Jenny), Kent 138
IKON, Devon 89
Inner Bookshop (The), Oxfordshire................ 210
Joel Segal Books, Devon 86

Orchid Book Distributors, Co. Clare.............. 262
Oxfam Books and Music, Hampshire 126
Pickering & Chatto, London W.................... 175
Prescott - The Bookseller (John), London Outer 184
R M Books, Hertfordshire 132
Reading Lasses, Dumfries & Galloway 271
River Reads Bookshop, Devon..................... 90
Roland Books, Kent 139
Roundstone Books, Lancashire..................... 144
Till's Bookshop, Lothian 279
Woburn Books, London N 160

HEBRAICA

Beckham Books Ltd., Suffolk 230
Joel Segal Books, Devon 86
Samovar Books, Co. Dublin......................... 264
Thorntons of Oxford Ltd., Oxfordshire........... 207

HERALDRY

Aardvark Books, Wiltshire.......................... 254
Bookshop on the Heath, The, London SE 164
Heraldry Today, Wiltshire........................... 252
Heritage, West Midlands 239
Joel Segal Books, Devon 86
Marcet Books, London SE.......................... 165
McEwan Fine Books, Grampian................... 273
Moore (C.R.), Shropshire 214
N1 Books, East Sussex 105
R. & A. Books, East Sussex 102
RGS Books, Surrey 235
Sax Books, Suffolk 229
Scrivener's Books & Bookbinding, Derbyshire... 82
Spooner & Co, Somerset 220
Taylor & Son (Peter), Hertfordshire............... 133
Titford (John), Derbyshire 82
Townsend (John), Berkshire 57
Turton (John), Durham 98

HERBALISM

Blest (Peter), Kent.................................... 139
Broadhurst of Southport Ltd., Merseyside 186
Brown-Studies, Strathclyde.......................... 279
Calendula Horticultural Books, East Sussex 102
Chantrey Books, S Yorks 222
Dolphin Books, Suffolk............................... 226
Edmund Pollinger Rare Books, London SW..... 167
Fifteenth Century Bookshop (The), East Sussex. 104
Gardener & Cook, London SW.................... 168
Greensleeves, Oxfordshire 207
Guildmaster Books, Cheshire....................... 70
Hollingshead (Chris), London Outer 183
IKON, Devon.. 89
Inner Bookshop (The), Oxfordshire................ 210
Joel Segal Books, Devon 86
Lucas (Richard), London NW...................... 162
Occultique, Northants................................ 200
Orchid Book Distributors, Co. Clare.............. 262
Park (Mike), London Outer......................... 183
Phelps (Michael), W Sussex 243
R. & A. Books, East Sussex 102
Wadard Books, Kent 138

HEREDITY

Joel Segal Books, Devon 86
Parkinsons Books, Merseyside...................... 186

SPECIALITY INDEX

R M Books, Hertfordshire 132
R. & A. Books, East Sussex 102

HERITAGE

Cornucopia Books, Lincolnshire 153
Dolphin Books, Suffolk............................... 226
G. C. Books Ltd., Dumfries & Galloway......... 271
Joel Segal Books, Devon 86
R. & A. Books, East Sussex 102
Winchester Bookshop (The), Hampshire.......... 127

HERMETICISM

Alpha Books, London N 158
Chthonios Books, East Sussex...................... 102
IKON, Devon.. 89
Inner Bookshop (The), Oxfordshire................ 210
Magis Books, Leics................................... 149
Occultique, Northants................................ 200
Star Lord Books, Gr Man 119

HERPETOLOGY

Blest (Peter), Kent 139
J.G. Natural History Books, Surrey 234
Kenya Books, East Sussex 100
Mobbs (A.J.), West Midlands 241
Parkinsons Books, Merseyside...................... 186
Pemberley Books, Buckinghamshire 62
Steven Simpson Books, Norfolk 191
Westons, Hertfordshire 133

HIMALAYAN KINGDOMS

Cavendish Rare Books, London N 158
David Warnes Books, Herefordshire 129
Jarvis Books, Derbyshire 83
Kabristan Archives, Shropshire..................... 215
Rayner (Hugh Ashley), Somerset 217
Verandah Books, Dorset 95
Winchester Bookshop (The), Hampshire.......... 127

HISPANICA

Baldwin (Jack), Strathclyde 280
Hodgson (Judith), London W 174
York (Graham), Devon............................... 86

HISTORY - GENERAL

A. & H. Peasgood, Cambridgeshire 67
AA1 Books, Dumfries & Galloway................. 270
Abacus Gallery, Staffordshire....................... 224
Abbey Books, Cornwall 74
Addyman Books, Powys............................. 289
Alexander's Books, Warwickshire.................. 238
All Books, Essex 110
Allinson (Frank & Stella), Warwickshire 237
Anchor Books, Lincolnshire 151
Andrew Morton (Books), Powys.................... 289
Anthony Vickers Books, N Yorks 196
Antiquary Ltd., (Bar Bookstore), N Yorks....... 196
Antique Map and Bookshop (The), Dorset 94
Antiques on High, Oxfordshire..................... 209
Apocalypse, Surrey 233
Arden Books & Cosmographia,
Warwickshire 237
Askew Books (Vernon), Wiltshire.................. 251
Aurora Books Ltd, Lothian.......................... 276
Autumn Leaves, Lincolnshire....................... 152

Axe Rare & Out of Print Books (Richard),
N Yorks... 194
Baker Limited (A.P. & R.), D. & Galloway...... 270
Barbican Bookshop, N Yorks 198
Barcombe Services, Essex........................... 108
Bardsley's Books, Suffolk............................ 226
Barn Books, Buckinghamshire...................... 61
Barnes (Peter), Wiltshire............................ 253
Bath Old Books, Somerset 216
Baxter (Steve), Surrey 234
Beardsell Books, W Yorks 247
Bell (Peter), Lothian.................................. 276
Bennett & Kerr Books, Oxfordshire............... 206
Beware of the Leopard, Bristol..................... 58
Black Five Books, Shropshire 215
Bookbox, Glos 116
Bookroom (The), Surrey............................. 234
Books, Denbighshire 286
Books & Bygones (Pam Taylor), W Mids........ 241
Books & Collectables Ltd., Cambridgeshire...... 63
Books (For All), N Yorks 194
Books Antiques & Collectables, Devon........... 90
Books at Star Dot Star, West Midlands 241
Books Bought & Sold, Surrey...................... 232
Books For All, N Yorks 194
books2books, Devon................................. 88
Bookshop (The), Gr Man 118
Bookshop (The), W Sussex.......................... 243
Bookshop at the Plain, Lincolnshire............... 151
Bookworm, Lothian................................... 277
Bookworm (The), Lothian 277
Bookworms, Norfolk.................................. 187
Bookworms of Evesham, Worcestershire 257
Booth Books, Powys................................. 289
Bosorne Books, Cornwall 75
Bracton Books, Cambridgeshire.................... 63
Brad Books, Essex.................................... 111
Brimstones, East Sussex 103
Broadhurst of Southport Ltd., Merseyside 186
Broadwater Books, Hampshire..................... 125
Brockwells Booksellers, Lincolnshire 150
Browsers Bookshop, Cornwall...................... 73
Caledonia Books, Strathclyde....................... 280
Caliver Books, Essex 110
Carnforth Bookshop (The), Lancashire 143
Carningli Centre, Pembrokeshire................... 288
Castle Hill Books, Herefordshire................... 128
Castleton (Pat), Kent................................. 138
Catalyst Booksearch Services, Devon.............. 87
Celtic Bookshop (The), Co. Limerick 266
Central Bookshop, Warwickshire 238
CI Galleries Limited, CI............................. 258
Chaucer Bookshop, Kent............................ 136
Cheshire Book Centre, Cheshire.................... 69
Chesters (G. & J.), Staffordshire 225
Clarendon Books, Leics.............................. 147
Classic Bindings Ltd, London SW 167
Clements (R.W.), London Outer................... 182
Clent Books, Worcestershire 255
Cobbles Books, Somerset............................ 218
Cobweb Books, N Yorks............................. 195
Coombes (A.J.), Surrey 231
Corfe Books, Surrey.................................. 231
Courtenay Bookroom, Oxfordshire................ 206
Cox Old & Rare Books (Claude), Suffolk 228

SPECIALITY INDEX

Crouch Rare Books, Surrey.......................... 233
D'Arcy Books, Wiltshire............................. 252
Dales & Lakes Book Centre, Cumbria............ 80
Dandy Lion Editions, Surrey 233
Darkwood Books, Co. Cork......................... 263
Davids Ltd., (Roy), Oxfordshire 209
Debbage (John), Norfolk............................. 190
Deeside Books, Grampian............................ 273
Derek Stirling Bookseller, Kent 142
Dolphin Books, Suffolk............................... 226
Dormouse Bookshop (The), Norfolk.............. 190
Driffield Bookshop (The), East Yorkshire 106
Eagle Bookshop (The), Bedfordshire 53
Eastern Traveller (The), Somerset.................. 220
Eastleach Books, Berkshire........................... 56
Edwards (Christopher), Berkshire.................. 55
Edwards (London) Limited (Francis),
London WC 177
Edwards in Hay-on-Wye (Francis), Powys 290
Elaine Lonsdale Books, W Yorks................... 248
Ellis, Bookseller (Peter), London WC 178
Empire Books, N Yorks............................... 198
Esoteric Dreams Bookshop, Cumbria 78
Eton Antique Bookshop, Berkshire................ 57
Ewell Bookshop Ltd, Surrey........................ 232
Farnborough Gallery, Hampshire.................. 122
Fifteenth Century Bookshop (The), East Sussex. 104
Fireside Books, Buckinghamshire 62
Fireside Bookshop, Cumbria........................ 81
Ford Books (David), Hertfordshire................ 133
Fossgate Books, N Yorks 198
Foster (Stephen), London NW 161
Freeman's Corner Shop, Norfolk 190
Frew Limited (Robert), London W................ 173
Furneaux Books (Lee), Devon...................... 89
G. C. Books Ltd., Dumfries & Galloway......... 271
Garfi Books, Powys 293
George St. Books, Derbyshire 83
Gildas Books, Cheshire 68
Glasheen-Books, Surrey 232
Glenbower Books, Co. Dublin 265
Gloucester Road Bookshop, London SW 168
Glyn's Books, Shropshire............................ 213
Golden Books Group, Devon 85
Good for Books, Lincolnshire 151
Graham (John), Dorset............................... 96
Grahame Thornton, Bookseller, Dorset.......... 93
Great Hall Bookshop, Buckinghamshire.......... 61
Greta Books, Durham 97
Hall's Bookshop, Kent................................ 141
Hambleton Books, N Yorks 197
Handsworth Books, Essex............................ 112
Hawley (C.L.), N Yorks.............................. 197
Hay Cinema Bookshop Ltd., Powys............... 290
HCB Wholesale, Powys.............................. 290
Helion & Company, West Midlands 240
Heraldry Today, Wiltshire........................... 252
Heywood Hill Limited (G.), London W 174
Hornsey's, N Yorks 195
Horsham Rare Books, W Sussex................... 243
Howes Bookshop, East Sussex 102
Hughes Rare Books (Spike), Borders.............. 268
hullbooks.com, East Yorkshire 107
Hurst (Jenny), Kent 138
Hutchison (Books) (Larry), Fife.................... 271

Ice House Books, Wiltshire 253
J & J Burgess Booksellers, Cambridgeshire....... 64
Jade Mountain Bookshop, Hampshire 126
JB Books & Collectables, W Sussex 244
Joel Segal Books, Devon 86
Jones (Andrew), Suffolk 228
Judd Books, London WC............................ 178
Junk & Spread Eagle, London SE.................. 165
Just Books, Cornwall 76
Kalligraphia, Isle of Wight.......................... 134
Karen Millward, Co. Cork........................... 263
Katnap Arts, Norfolk................................. 191
Keel Row Bookshop, Tyne and Wear 236
Keith Langford, London E 155
Kelsall (George), Gr Man............................ 118
Kemp Booksellers, Lancashire...................... 143
Kilgarriff (Raymond), East Sussex................. 105
Kim's Bookshop, W Sussex...............242, 243, 245
Lawrence Books, Notts............................... 204
Leabeck Books, Oxfordshire........................ 210
Lewis (J.T. & P.), Cornwall......................... 74
Libris (Weston) Books, Somerset 217
Little Bookshop (The), Gr Man.................... 119
Lost Books, Northants................................ 201
Maggy Browne, Lincolnshire 150
Mannwaring (M.G.), Bristol 59
Marble Hill Books, Middlesex...................... 184
Marcet Books, London SE........................... 165
Marijana Dworski Books, via Hereford........... 290
McCrone (Audrey), Isle of Arran 275
McNaughtan's Bookshop, Lothian 278
Meekins Books (Paul), Warwickshire.............. 238
Mellon's Books, East Sussex........................ 101
MilitaryHistoryBooks.com, Kent................... 138
Ming Books, Dumfries & Galloway................ 271
Modern Welsh Publications Ltd., Merseyside.... 185
Morgan (H.J.), Bedfordshire 54
Mundy (David), Hertfordshire...................... 130
Mundy (David), Buckinghamshire 61
Murphy (C.J.), Norfolk.............................. 190
My Back Pages, London SW 169
N1 Books, East Sussex 105
Naughton Booksellers, Co. Dublin 265
Neeve (P.), Cambridgeshire 63
Nicolas - Antiquarian Booksellers &
Art Dealers, London N............................. 159
Nineteenth Century Books, Oxfordshire 211
Nonsuch Books, Surrey............................... 234
O'Brien Books & Photo Gallery, Co. Limerick.. 266
O'Flynn Books, N Yorks............................. 199
Oasis Booksearch, Cambridgeshire................ 67
Old Bookshop (The), West Midlands 241
Old Town Bookshop (The), Lothian 278
Olynthiacs, Shropshire 214
Oxfam Books and Music, Hampshire.............. 126
Parker Books (Mike), Cambridgeshire 64
Parkinsons Books, Merseyside...................... 186
Parrott Books, Oxfordshire 211
Paton Books, Hertfordshire.......................... 132
Pauline Harries Books, Hampshire 123
Peter Lyons Books, Glos............................. 114
Pickering Bookshop, N Yorks...................... 197
Polmorla Books, Cornwall 76
Pomes Penyeach, Staffordshire 224
Pordes Books Ltd., (Henry), London WC........ 179

SPECIALITY INDEX

Portobello Books, London W 175
PsychoBabel Books & Journals, Oxfordshire..... 206
Quentin Books Ltd, Essex........................... 109
Quinto of Charing Cross Road, London WC ... 179
Quinto of Great Russell Street, London WC 179
Read (C.&J.), Gorleston Books, Norfolk 188
Reading Lasses, Dumfries & Galloway 271
RGS Books, Surrey 235
Richard Frost Books, Hertfordshire............... 130
Richard Thornton Books, London N 160
Richmond Books, N Yorks......................... 195
Rods Books, Devon 88
Roland Books, Kent 139
Rothwell & Dunworth, Somerset 218
Roundstone Books, Lancashire..................... 144
Rowan (P. & B.), Co. Antrim 260
Royal Carbery Books Ltd., Co. Cork.............. 262
St Philip's Books, Oxfordshire...................... 210
Saintfield Antiques & Fine Books, Co. Down ... 261
Samovar Books, Co. Dublin 264
Saracen Books, Derbyshire.......................... 83
Sax Books, Suffolk 229
Scott (Peter), East Sussex........................... 104
Scrivener's Books & Bookbinding, Derbyshire... 82
Shacklock Books (David), Suffolk 227
Sillan Books, Co. Cavan............................. 262
Silverman (Michael), ... 166
Singleton (Anthony), S Yorks 222
Skoob Russell Square, Suffolk...................... 230
Smith Books (Keith), Herefordshire 128
Spelman (Ken), N Yorks............................ 199
Spurrier (Nick), Kent 138
Staffs Bookshop (The), Staffordshire 224
Stalagluft Books, Tyne and Wear.................. 236
Staniland (Booksellers), Lincolnshire 154
Star Lord Books, Gr Man 119
Sterling Books, Somerset 221
Stern Antiquarian Bookseller (Jeffrey), N Yorks 199
Stothert Old Books, Cheshire....................... 69
Sturford Books, Wiltshire 254
Sykes (Graham), W Yorks.......................... 249
Symes Books (Naomi), Cheshire 72
Tarka Books, Devon 84
The Glass Key, W Yorks............................ 247
Thistle Books, Strathclyde........................... 280
Thomas (Books) (Leona), Cheshire................ 71
Thomas (E. Wyn), Conwy 285
Till's Bookshop, Lothian 279
Tilston (Stephen E.), London SE................... 166
Titford (John), Derbyshire 82
Townsend (John), Berkshire 57
Treasure Trove Books, Leics........................ 148
Tuft (Patrick), London Outer....................... 182
Tyger Press, London N 160
Uncle Phil's Books, West Midlands 240
Unsworth's Booksellers, London WC 163, 180
Village Books, Norfolk 187
Water Lane Bookshop, Wiltshire 253
Waterfield's, Oxfordshire 210
Watkins (R.G.), Somerset 216
Waxfactor, East Sussex 100
Westcountry Old Books, Cornwall................. 76
Westwood Books (Mark), Powys 291
Westwood Books Ltd, Cumbria.................... 80
Whig Books Ltd., Leics.............................. 149

Whitchurch Books Ltd., Cardiff.................... 283
Whitfield (Ken), Essex 111
Williams (Bookdealer), (Richard), N Lincs....... 154
Willmott Bookseller (Nicholas), Cardiff......... 283
Words Etcetera Bookshop, Dorset................. 93
Worlds End Bookshop, London SW 171
Yesterday's Books, Dorset 92
Yewtree Books, Cumbria............................ 79

- 19TH CENTURY

Aitchison (Lesley), Bristol 58
Americanabooksuk, Cumbria........................ 77
Apocalypse, Surrey 233
Bell (Peter), Lothian.................................. 276
Castleton (Pat), Kent................................. 138
Cox Rare Books (Charles), Cornwall.............. 74
Darkwood Books, Co. Cork......................... 263
Debbage (John), Norfolk............................. 190
Derek Stirling Bookseller, Kent 142
Dolphin Books, Suffolk............................... 226
Empire Books, N Yorks........... 198
Fifteenth Century Bookshop (The), East Sussex. 104
Hall's Bookshop, Kent............................... 141
Handsworth Books, Essex............................ 112
Helion & Company, West Midlands 240
hullbooks.com, East Yorkshire 107
J & J Burgess Booksellers, Cambridgeshire....... 64
Jackdaw Books, Norfolk 189
Joel Segal Books, Devon 86
Junk & Spread Eagle, London SE 165
Karen Millward, Co. Cork 263
Kenny's Bookshops and Art Galleries Ltd,
Co. Galway 266
Lost Books, Northants................................ 201
MilitaryHistoryBooks.com, Kent................... 138
N1 Books, East Sussex 105
R. & A. Books, East Sussex 102
Symes Books (Naomi), Cheshire 72
Wheen O'Books, Scottish Borders 269
Whitchurch Books Ltd., Cardiff.................... 283

- 20TH CENTURY

Browsers Bookshop, Cornwall...................... 73
Burroughs (Andrew), Lincolnshire 153
Darkwood Books, Co. Cork......................... 263
Debbage (John), Norfolk............................. 190
Dolphin Books, Suffolk............................... 226
Empire Books, N Yorks.............................. 198
Fifteenth Century Bookshop (The), East Sussex. 104
Handsworth Books, Essex............................ 112
hullbooks.com, East Yorkshire 107
IKON, Devon 89
Joel Segal Books, Devon 86
Kineton Nooks, Warwickshire....................... 237
MilitaryHistoryBooks.com, Kent................... 138
Old Bookshop (The), West Midlands 241
Old Station Pottery & Bookshop (The), Norfolk 192
PsychoBabel Books & Journals, Oxfordshire..... 206
R. & A. Books, East Sussex 102
Rods Books, Devon 88
SETI Books, Staffordshire........................... 225
Stella Books, Monmouthshire 288
War & Peace Books, Hampshire................... 122
Winghale Books, Lincolnshire 153
York Modern Books, N Yorks...................... 197

SPECIALITY INDEX

- AMERICAN

Americanabooksuk, Cumbria 77
Darkwood Books, Co. Cork 263
Dolphin Books, Suffolk 226
Fifteenth Century Bookshop (The), East Sussex. 104
Helion & Company, West Midlands 240
Joel Segal Books, Devon 86
Kenny's Bookshops and Art Galleries Ltd, Co.
Galway 266
Quentin Books Ltd, Essex 109
Winghale Books, Lincolnshire 153

- AMERICAN REVOLUTION

Americanabooksuk, Cumbria 77
Fifteenth Century Bookshop (The), East Sussex. 104

- ANARCHISM

Delectus Books, London WC 177
Helion & Company, West Midlands 240
Northern Herald Books, W Yorks 246
Red Star Books, Hertfordshire 130
Star Lord Books, Gr Man 119

- ANCIENT

Aviabooks, Glos 114
BC Books, Cheshire 70
Black Five Books, Shropshire 215
Bloomsbury Bookshop, London Outer 182
Books B.C., London Outer 181
Byre Books, Dumfries & Galloway 270
Classics Bookshop (The), Oxfordshire 207
Crouch Rare Books, Surrey 233
Fifteenth Century Bookshop (The), E Sussex 104
Ford Books (David), Hertfordshire 133
GfB: the Colchester Bookshop, Essex 109
Gildas Books, Cheshire 68
Golden Age Books, Worcestershire 256
Handsworth Books, Essex 112
Helion & Company, West Midlands 240
Joel Segal Books, Devon 86
Junk & Spread Eagle, London SE 165
Kingswood Books, Dorset 94
Meekins Books (Paul), Warwickshire 238
Michael Graves-Johnston, London SW 169
N1 Books, East Sussex 105
P. and P. Books, Worcestershire 256
Parkinsons Books, Merseyside 186
R. & A. Books, East Sussex 102
Rods Books, Devon 88
Rosanda Books, Leics 148
SETI Books, Staffordshire 225
Stalagluft Books, Tyne and Wear 236
Thorntons of Oxford Ltd., Oxfordshire 207
Trotter Books (John), London N 160
Uncle Phil's Books, West Midlands 240
Unsworth's Booksellers, London WC 163, 180
Walker Fine Books (Steve), Dorset 92
Whitchurch Books Ltd., Cardiff 283
Winghale Books, Lincolnshire 153

- ARGENTINA

Baldwin (Jack), Strathclyde 280
Hodgson (Judith), London W 174
Orssich (Paul), London SW 170

- AUSTRALIAN

Empire Books, N Yorks 198
Fifteenth Century Bookshop (The), East Sussex. 104
Joel Segal Books, Devon 86

- BERMUDAN

Pennymead Books, N Yorks 194

- BRAZIL

Baldwin (Jack), Strathclyde 280
Hodgson (Judith), London W 174
Orssich (Paul), London SW 170

- BRITISH

Aardvark Books, Wiltshire 254
Anthony Spranger, Wiltshire 252
Apocalypse, Surrey 233
Ardis Books, Hampshire 126
Aviabooks, Glos 114
Barbican Bookshop, N Yorks 198
BC Books, Cheshire 70
Bell (Peter), Lothian 276
Black Five Books, Shropshire 215
BookShop, The, Dumfries & Galloway 270
Brad Books, Essex 111
Burmester (James), Bristol 59
Clarke Books (David), Somerset 219
Clifton Books, Essex 112
Cobbles Books, Somerset 218
Coombes (A.J.), Surrey 231
Corder (Mark W.), Kent 140
Country Books, Derbyshire 82
Darkwood Books, Co. Cork 263
Dolphin Books, Suffolk 226
Ellis, Bookseller (Peter), London WC 178
Fifteenth Century Bookshop (The), East Sussex. 104
Garfi Books, Powys 293
GfB: the Colchester Bookshop, Essex 109
Gildas Books, Cheshire 68
Guildmaster Books, Cheshire 70
Hall's Bookshop, Kent 141
Handsworth Books, Essex 112
Hawley (C.L.), N Yorks 197
Helion & Company, West Midlands 240
hullbooks.com, East Yorkshire 107
Island Books, Devon 85
JB Books & Collectables, W Sussex 244
Joel Segal Books, Devon 86
Junk & Spread Eagle, London SE 165
K.S.C. Books, Cheshire 71
Lost Books, Northants 201
Lowe (John), Norfolk 189
Marine and Cannon Books, Cheshire 69
Meekins Books (Paul), Warwickshire 238
Minster Gate Bookshop, N Yorks 199
N1 Books, East Sussex 105
Naughton Booksellers, Co. Dublin 265
Niner (Marcus), Isle of Wight 134
Orb's Bookshop, Grampian 274
Ouse Valley Books, Bedfordshire 54
Prospect House Books, Co. Down 261
R. & A. Books, East Sussex 102
Rods Books, Devon 88
Roland Books, Kent 139
Rosanda Books, Leics 148

SPECIALITY INDEX

St Philip's Books,Oxfordshire........................ 210
Samovar Books, Co. Dublin......................... 264
Saracen Books, Derbyshire........................... 83
Sax Books, Suffolk 229
Shakeshaft (Dr. B.), Cheshire........................ 71
Skoob Russell Square, Suffolk......... 230
Spenceley Books (David), W Yorks 249
Stalagluft Books, Tyne and Wear................... 236
Stella Books, Monmouthshire 288
Studio Bookshop, East Sussex....................... 100
Symes Books (Naomi), Cheshire 72
Taylor & Son (Peter), Hertfordshire................ 133
Uncle Phil's Books, West Midlands 240
Unsworth's Booksellers, London WC 163, 180
Wheen O'Books, Scottish Borders 269
Whitchurch Books Ltd., Cardiff..................... 283
Wiend Books, Lancashire 144
York Modern Books, N Yorks....................... 197

- BRITISH EMPIRE, THE

Apocalypse, Surrey 233
Burroughs (Andrew), Lincolnshire.................. 153
Caliver Books, Essex 110
Dolphin Books, Suffolk................................ 226
Empire Books, N Yorks............................... 198
Fifteenth Century Bookshop (The), East Sussex. 104
G. C. Books Ltd., Dumfries & Galloway......... 271
Joel Segal Books, Devon 86
Kenya Books, East Sussex 100
Lost Books, Northants................................. 201
Marine and Cannon Books, Cheshire 69
N1 Books, East Sussex 105
Pennymead Books, N Yorks......................... 194
Peter M Daly, Hampshire............................ 127
R. & A. Books, East Sussex 102
Saracen Books, Derbyshire........................... 83
SETI Books, Staffordshire............................ 225
Uncle Phil's Books, West Midlands 240
Wheen O'Books, Scottish Borders 269
Winghale Books, Lincolnshire 153

- BYZANTINE

Bennett & Kerr Books, Oxfordshire................ 206
Camden Books, Somerset 216
Helion & Company, West Midlands 240
Kingswood Books, Dorset 94
Olynthiacs, Shropshire 214
St Philip's Books, Oxfordshire....................... 210
Samovar Books, Co. Dublin......................... 264
Unsworth's Booksellers, London WC ......, 163, 180

- CANADIAN

Empire Books, N Yorks............................... 198

- COLONIAL

Burroughs (Andrew), Lincolnshire.................. 153
Caliver Books, Essex.................................. 110
Dolphin Books, Suffolk................................ 226
Fifteenth Century Bookshop (The), E Sussex.... 104
Joel Segal Books, Devon 86
Kabristan Archives, Shropshire...................... 215
Lost Books, Northants................................. 201
N1 Books, East Sussex 105
Pennymead Books, N Yorks......................... 194
Winghale Books, Lincolnshire 153

- CARIBBEAN

Empire Books, N Yorks............................... 198
Pennymead Books, N Yorks......................... 194

- DESIGN

Art Reference Books, Hampshire................... 125
Ballantyne-Way (Roger), Suffolk 229
Black Cat Books, Norfolk............................. 188
Don Kelly Books, London W 172
Inch's Books, Kent.................................... 137
Joel Segal Books, Devon 86
Judith Mansfield, W Yorks 250
R. & A. Books, East Sussex 102
Sleepy Elephant Books & Artefacts, Cumbria ... 80

- DEVELOPMENT OF TRANS-MISSISSIPPI WEST

Americanabooksuk, Cumbria........................ 77

- DUTCH EAST INDIA COMPANY

Drury Rare Books (John), Essex.................... 110

- ECONOMIC THOUGHT

Drury Rare Books (John), Essex.................... 110
Empire Books, N Yorks............................... 198
Hamish Riley-Smith, Norfolk........................ 192
Northern Herald Books, W Yorks.................. 246
Parkinsons Books, Merseyside....................... 186
Susanne Schulz-Falster Rare Books, London N. 160
Winghale Books, Lincolnshire 153

- EUROPEAN

Apocalypse, Surrey 233
Bloomsbury Bookshop, London Outer............. 182
Books on Spain, London Outer..................... 184
Broadwater Books, Hampshire...................... 125
de Visser Books, Cambridgeshire.................... 63
Empire Books, N Yorks............................... 198
Fifteenth Century Bookshop (The), E Sussex.... 104
Helion & Company, West Midlands 240
IKON, Devon... 89
Joel Segal Books, Devon 86
medievalbookshop, Hertfordshire 133
Naughton Booksellers, Co. Dublin 265
Parkinsons Books, Merseyside....................... 186
Roland Books, Kent 139
Rosanda Books, Leics 148
St Philip's Books, Oxfordshire....................... 210
Seydi Rare Books (Sevin), London NW 162
Stella Books, Monmouthshire 288
Symes Books (Naomi), Cheshire 72
Unsworth's Booksellers, London WC 163, 180
Winghale Books, Lincolnshire 153
York (Graham), Devon................................ 86

- FAMILY

Aitchison (Lesley), Bristol 58
Atholl Fine Books, Tayside.......................... 281
Country Books, Derbyshire 82
Delph Books, Gr Man................................. 120
Fifteenth Century Bookshop (The), E Sussex.... 104
Joel Segal Books, Devon 86
McEwan Fine Books, Grampian.................... 273
Symes Books (Naomi), Cheshire 72
Thornber (Peter M.), N Yorks 196

SPECIALITY INDEX

Turton (John), Durham 98
Tyger Press, London N............................... 160

- GUILDS & LIVERY COMPANIES

Chas J. Sawyer, Kent 141
Joel Segal Books, Devon 86

- INDUSTRIAL

Anvil Books, W Mids................................. 240
Baldwin (M. & M.), Worcestershire 255
Barbican Bookshop, N Yorks 198
Blanchfield (John), W Yorks........................ 249
Book House (The), Cumbria......................... 77
Books & Bygones (Pam Taylor), W Mids 241
Bott, (Bookdealers) Ltd., (Martin), Gr Man 118
Clevedon Books, Somerset 218
Coulthurst (Richard), Gr Man 120
Cox (Geoff), Devon 90
Crosby Nethercott Books, London Outer 181
Dales and Lakes Book Centre, Cumbria.......... 80
Delph Books, Gr Man................................ 120
Graham (John), Dorset............................... 96
Hall, (Anthony C.) Antiquarian Bookseller,
London Outer 184
Hedgerow Books, S Yorks 222
Helion & Company, W Mids........................ 240
Henry Wilson Books, Cheshire...................... 69
Hutchison (Books) (Larry), Fife.................... 271
Joel Segal Books, Devon 86
John L Capes (Books Maps & Prints), Cleveland 197
Kelsall (George), Gr Man 118
Kenny's Bookshops and Art Galleries Ltd,
Co. Galway 266
N1 Books, E Sussex 105
Parkinsons Books, Merseyside...................... 186
Phelps (Michael), W Sussex 243
R. & A. Books, E Sussex.............................. 102
Rainford (Sheila), Hertfordshire.................... 130
Randall (Tom), Somerset............................. 219
Robert Humm & Co, Lincolnshire 154
Rochdale Book Company, Gr Man 120
Rolling Stock Books, Gr Man....................... 120
Salway Books, Essex 112
Scarthin Books, Derbyshire 82
Skyrack Books, W Yorks 248
Stroh (M.A.), London E 155
Symes Books (Naomi), Cheshire 72
Tony Pollastrone Railway Books, Wiltshire 251
Trinders' Fine Tools, Suffolk 227
Tyger Press, London N............................... 160
Vickers (Anthony), N Yorks......................... 196
Whitchurch Books Ltd., Cardiff.................... 283
Winghale Books, Lincolnshire 153
Wizard Books, Cambridgeshire..................... 67
Ystwyth Books, Ceredigion 284

- IRISH

Abbey Books, Cornwall 74
Ann & Mike Conry, Worcestershire................ 257
Apocalypse, Surrey 233
Armchair Books, Lothian 276
Bloomsbury Bookshop, London Outer............ 182
Book Business (The), London W 172
Bookline, Co. Down 261
Celtic Bookshop (The), Co. Limerick 266

Colonsay Bookshop, Isle of Colonsay............. 276
Craobh Rua Books, Co. Armagh................... 260
Darkwood Books, Co. Cork......................... 263
Delectus Books, London WC........................ 177
Fifteenth Century Bookshop (The), E Sussex 104
Gildas Books, Cheshire............................... 68
Grove Bookshop (The), N Yorks 197
Helion & Company, W Mids........................ 240
Joel Segal Books, Devon 86
Kabristan Archives, Shropshire..................... 215
Karen Millward, Co. Cork........................... 263
Kenny's Bookshops and Art Galleries Ltd,
Co. Galway 266
Kenya Books, E Sussex............................... 100
Naughton Booksellers, Co. Dublin 265
Prospect House Books, Co. Down.................. 261
R. & A. Books, E Sussex.............................. 102
Read Ireland, Co. Dublin 264
Roscrea Bookshop, Co. Tipperary.................. 267
Rowan (P. & B.), Co. Antrim 260
Saintfield Antiques & Fine Books, Co. Down ... 261
Schull Books, Co. Cork 263
Stokes Books, Co. Dublin............................ 265
Taylor & Son (Peter), Hertfordshire............... 133

- LABOUR/ RADICAL MOVEMENTS

Berwick Books, Lincolnshire........................ 152
Bloomsbury Bookshop, London Outer............ 182
Cox Rare Books (Charles), Cornwall............... 74
Delectus Books, London WC........................ 177
Drury Rare Books (John), Essex.................... 110
Fifteenth Century Bookshop (The), E Sussex 104
Helion & Company, W Mids........................ 240
Joel Segal Books, Devon 86
Left on The Shelf, Cumbria.......................... 79
Northern Herald Books, W Yorks.................. 246
R. & A. Books, E Sussex.............................. 102
Reading Lasses, Dumfries & Galloway 271
Red Star Books, Hertfordshire 130
Symes Books (Naomi), Cheshire 72
Woburn Books, London N 160

- LOCAL

Abrahams (Mike), Staffordshire.................... 224
Ambra Books, Bristol................................. 58
Arden Books & Cosmographia, Warwickshire... 237
Atholl Fine Books, Tayside 281
Barbican Bookshop, N Yorks 198
Barn Books, Shropshire............................... 215
Bear Island Books, Cardiff........................... 283
Beardsell Books, W Yorks 247
Beckham Books Ltd., Suffolk 230
Beverley Old Bookshop, East Yorkshire 106
Black Five Books, Shropshire 215
Blore's Bookshop (Geoffrey), Notts 204
Bonython Bookshop, Cornwall...................... 76
Book For All Reasons (A.), Suffolk 229
Bookshop (The), Co. Donegal...................... 263
Border Books, Borders................................ 268
Brazenhead Ltd., Norfolk 189
Brown (Books) (P.R.), Durham 98
Browning Books, Torfaen 294
Browsers Bookshop, Cornwall....................... 73
Burebank Books, Norfolk............................. 187
Bury Bookshop, Suffolk 226

SPECIALITY INDEX

Carlton Books, Norfolk 190
Carnforth Bookshop (The), Lancashire 143
Castle Bookshop, Essex............................... 109
Castle Hill Books, Herefordshire 128
Castleton (Pat), Kent.................................. 138
Chapman (Neville), Lancashire 146
Chaucer Bookshop, Kent................ 136
Clarendon Books, Leics............................... 147
Clark (Nigel A.), London SE 165
Colin Hancock, Ceredigion 284
Colonsay Bookshop, Isle of Colonsay.............. 276
Compass Books, Devon 85
Coombes (A.J.), Surrey 231
Cornucopia Books, Lincolnshire 153
Cottage Books, Leics.................................. 147
Country Books, Derbyshire 82
Courtwood Books, Co. Laois........................ 266
Cox (Geoff), Devon 90
Daeron's Books, Buckinghamshire.................. 62
Dinnages Transport Publishing, E Sussex 103
Dobson (Bob), Lancashire 143
Dormouse Bookshop (The), Norfolk 190
Eastgate Bookshop, East Yorkshire 106
Elaine Lonsdale Books, W Yorks... 248
Ellis, Bookseller (Peter), London WC 178
Empire Books, N Yorks.............................. 198
Fackley Services, Notts 205
Fifteenth Century Bookshop (The), E Sussex 104
Forest Books of Manchester, Cheshire............ 71
Fosters Bookshop, London W 173
Foyle Books, Co. Derry 260
Freeman's Corner Shop, Norfolk 190
G. C. Books Ltd., Dumfries & Galloway......... 271
Garretts Antiquarian Books, Isle of Man.......... 259
Gildas Books, Cheshire 68
Glenwood Books, Surrey............................. 235
Godmanchester Books, Cambridgeshire 66
Good for Books, Lincolnshire 151
Graham (John), Dorset............................... 96
Handsworth Books, Essex....... 112
Hawes Books, Norfolk................................ 191
Hawley (C.L.), N Yorks.............................. 197
Helion & Company, W Mids........................ 240
Hicks (Ronald C.), Cornwall 73
Horsham Rare Books, W Sussex.................... 243
Hughes Rare Books (Spike), Borders.............. 268
hullbooks.com, East Yorkshire 107
Iona Bookshop (The), Isle of Iona................. 276
J C Books, Devon 87
Jackdaw Books, Norfolk 189
Joel Segal Books, Devon 86
John Barton, Hampshire 126
Just Books, Cornwall 76
Karen Millward, Co. Cork 263
Kingsgate Books & Prints, Hampshire 126
Letterbox Books, Notts............................... 204
Liddle (Steve), Bristol 58
Logie Steading Bookshop, Grampian 274
Michael J Carroll, Co. Cork 263
Missing Books, Essex 109
MK Book Services, Cambridgeshire............... 66
Mogul Diamonds, W Mids 241
Moon's Bookshop (Michael), Cumbria 81
Old Bookshelf (The), Strathclyde.................. 279
Old Bookshop (The), W Mids...................... 241

Orb's Bookshop, Grampian.......................... 274
Paton Books, Hertfordshire 132
Peter White, Hampshire 121
Polmorla Books, Cornwall 76
R. & A. Books, F Sussex............................. 102
Randall (1om), Somerset............................. 219
Rare & Racy, S Yorks................................ 222
Richard Thornton Books, London N 160
Rickaro Books, W Yorks 247
Roberts Books, Ayrshire 280
Rods Books, Devon.................................... 88
Rose Books, Gr Man 119
Ross Old Books & Prints, Herefordshire 128
Roundstone Books, Lancashire...................... 144
Royal Carbery Books Ltd., Co. Cork.............. 262
Salway Books, Essex 112
Samovar Books, Co. Dublin 264
Scarthin Books, Derbyshire 82
Sedgeberrow Books & Framing, Worcestershire. 256
SETI Books, Staffordshire........................... 225
Siop Lyfrau'r Hen Bost, Gwynedd 287
Skyrack Books, W Yorks 248
Smith Books (Keith), Herefordshire 128
Spooner & Co, Somerset 220
Stacpoole (George), Co. Limerick.................. 266
Studio (The), Strathclyde 280
Suffolk Rare Books, Suffolk 230
Symes Books (Naomi), Cheshire 72
Taylor & Son (Peter), Hertfordshire............... 133
Turton (John), Durham 98
Tyger Press, London N............................... 160
Vickers (Anthony), N Yorks......................... 196
Wealden Books, Kent................................. 139
Yates Antiquarian Books (Tony), Leics........... 148

- MAFEKING

Empire Books, N Yorks....... 198

- MIDDLE AGES

Bennett & Kerr Books, Oxfordshire 206
Bloomsbury Bookshop, London Outer............ 182
Bookshop at the Plain, Lincolnshire............... 151
Caliver Books, Essex 110
Camden Books, Somerset 216
Dolphin Books, Suffolk............................... 226
Fifteenth Century Bookshop (The), E Sussex 104
Handsworth Books, Essex............................ 112
Helion & Company, W Mids........................ 240
Jackdaw Books, Norfolk 189
Joel Segal Books, Devon 86
Kingswood Books, Dorset............................ 94
medievalbookshop, Hertfordshire 133
Meekins Books (Paul), Warwickshire.............. 238
Michael J Carroll, Co. Cork 263
N1 Books, E Sussex................................... 105
Rosanda Books, Leics 148
Spenceley Books (David), W Yorks 249
Thorntons of Oxford Ltd., Oxfordshire........... 207
Uncle Phil's Books, W Mids......................... 240
Unsworth's Booksellers, London WC 163, 180
Winghale Books, Lincolnshire 153
Wizard Books, Cambridgeshire..................... 67

- MODERN

Barcombe Services, Essex............................. 108

SPECIALITY INDEX

Bloomsbury Bookshop, London Outer............ 182
Bookshop at the Plain, Lincolnshire............... 151
Fifteenth Century Bookshop (The), E Sussex 104
Joel Segal Books, Devon 86
Michael J Carroll, Co. Cork 263
Naughton Booksellers, Co. Dublin 265
SETI Books, Staffordshire........................... 225
Symes Books (Naomi), Cheshire 72
Unsworth's Booksellers, London WC 180
Wizard Books, Cambridgeshire..................... 67

- NAPOLEONIC
Apocalypse, Surrey 233
Fifteenth Century Bookshop (The), E Sussex 104
Green Ltd. (G.L.), Hertfordshire................... 132
Marine & Cannon Books, Cheshire 71
Marine and Cannon Books, Cheshire 69
N1 Books, E Sussex.................................. 105
Solaris Books, East Yorkshire 106
Trotman (Ken), Cambridgeshire 66
Wizard Books, Cambridgeshire..................... 67

- NATIONAL
Apocalypse, Surrey 233
Bloomsbury Bookshop, London Outer............ 182
Carnforth Bookshop (The), Lancashire 143
Cox (Geoff), Devon 90
Craobh Rua Books, Co. Armagh................... 260
Davidson Books, Co. Down 261
De Burca Rare Books, Co. Dublin 264
Doolin Dinghy Books, Co. Clare 262
Fifteenth Century Bookshop (The), E Sussex 104
Foyle Books, Co. Derry 260
Fuchsia Books, Co. Wexford 267
Graham (John), Dorset 96
Hawes Books, Norfolk............................... 191
Helion & Company, W Mids....................... 240
Hughes Rare Books (Spike), Borders.............. 268
Joel Segal Books, Devon 86
Joppa Books Ltd., Surrey 231
Kingswood Books, Dorset 94
Pringle Booksellers (Andrew), Lothian 278
Siop y Morfa, Denbighshire 286
Thistle Books, Strathclyde.......................... 280
Whelan (P. & F.), Kent.............................. 141
Winghale Books, Lincolnshire 153
Wizard Books, Cambridgeshire..................... 67
Woolcott Books, Dorset............................. 92

- OTTOMAN EMPIRE
Empire Books, N Yorks............................. 198
Joppa Books Ltd., Surrey 231
Seydi Rare Books (Sevin), London NW 162

- PHOTOGRAPHY
Ballantyne-Way (Roger), Suffolk 229
Dally Books & Collectables, Powys................ 292
Joel Segal Books, Devon 86
R. & A. Books, E Sussex............................ 102
Stroh (M.A.), London E 155

- POSTAL
Apocalypse, Surrey 233
Joel Segal Books, Devon 86
Pennymead Books, N Yorks........................ 194

Postings, Surrey 234
R. & A. Books, E Sussex............................ 102

- PUERTO RICO
Pennymead Books, N Yorks........................ 194

- REFORMATION
Apocalypse, Surrey 233
Bloomsbury Bookshop, London Outer............ 182
Dolphin Books, Suffolk.............................. 226
Fifteenth Century Bookshop (The), E Sussex 104
Handsworth Books, Essex........................... 112
Joel Segal Books, Devon 86
medievalbookshop, Hertfordshire 133
Pendleburys Bookshop, London N 159
St Philip's Books, Oxfordshire..................... 210
Samovar Books, Co. Dublin........................ 264
Unsworth's Booksellers, London WC 180
Wizard Books, Cambridgeshire..................... 67

- RENAISSANCE, THE
All Books, Essex 110
Apocalypse, Surrey 233
Art Reference Books, Hampshire 125
Bennett & Kerr Books, Oxfordshire 206
Caliver Books, Essex 110
Dolphin Books, Suffolk.............................. 226
Fifteenth Century Bookshop (The), E Sussex 104
Handsworth Books, Essex........................... 112
Helion & Company, W Mids....................... 240
Joel Segal Books, Devon 86
medievalbookshop, Hertfordshire 133
R. & A. Books, E Sussex............................ 102
Seydi Rare Books (Sevin), London NW 162
Spenceley Books (David), W Yorks 249
Unsworth's Booksellers, London WC 163, 180
Winghale Books, Lincolnshire 153

- ROMAN
Apocalypse, Surrey 233
Aviabooks, Glos 114
Brock Books, N Yorks 193
Caliver Books, Essex 110
Fifteenth Century Bookshop (The), E Sussex 104
Handsworth Books, Essex........................... 112
Helion & Company, W Mids....................... 240
Joel Segal Books, Devon 86
N1 Books, E Sussex.................................. 105
R. & A. Books, E Sussex............................ 102
Stalagluft Books, Tyne and Wear.................. 236
Unsworth's Booksellers, London WC 163, 180

- RUSSIAN IMPERIAL
Caliver Books, Essex 110
Cox (Geoff), Devon 90
Darkwood Books, Co. Cork........................ 263
de Visser Books, Cambridgeshire................... 63
Dolphin Books, Suffolk.............................. 226
Marijana Dworski Books, via Hereford........... 290
R. & A. Books, E Sussex............................ 102
Wizard Books, Cambridgeshire..................... 67

- SCIENCE
Barcombe Services, Essex........................... 108
Bernard Dixon and Kath Adams, Middlesex 183

SPECIALITY INDEX

Dean Byass, Bristol................................... 60
Empire Books, N Yorks............................. 198
Handsworth Books, Essex........................... 112
Joel Segal Books, Devon 86
Kingswood Books, Dorset 94
Orb's Bookshop, Grampian..... 274
Park (Mike), London Outer......................... 183
Parkinsons Books, Merseyside...................... 186
Polczynski (Udo K.H.), Powys 291
Roberts Books, Ayrshire 280
Seydi Rare Books (Sevin), London NW 162
Turret House, Norfolk................................ 192
Weiner (Graham), London N 160
Westons, Hertfordshire 133

- SCOTTISH

Atholl Fine Books, Tayside 281
Bell (Peter), Lothian............................ ... 276
Bloomsbury Bookshop, London Outer............ 182
Byre Books, Dumfries & Galloway................. 270
Caliver Books, Essex 110
Colonsay Bookshop, Isle of Colonsay............. 276
Cooper Hay Rare Books, Strathclyde............. 280
Darkwood Books, Co. Cork......................... 263
Dolphin Books, Suffolk............................... 226
Farquharson, (Hilary), Tayside..................... 281
Fifteenth Century Bookshop (The), E Sussex 104
Grampian Books, Grampian......................... 274
Greta Books, Durham 97
Handsworth Books, Essex............................ 112
Jane Jones Books, Grampian 272
Joel Segal Books, Devon 86
Loch Croispol Bookshop & Restaurant,
Highland 275
McCrone (Audrey), Isle of Arran 275
Mercat Books, Highland 274
Orb's Bookshop, Grampian......................... 274
R. & A. Books, E Sussex............................. 102
Samovar Books, Co. Dublin 264
Stalagluft Books, Tyne and Wear.................. 236
Thistle Books, Strathclyde........................... 280
Till's Bookshop, Lothian 279
Wheen O'Books, Scottish Borders 269

- SOUTH AFRICA

Barn Books, Buckinghamshire....................... 61
Caliver Books, Essex 110
Chalmers Hallam (E.), Hampshire................. 125
Hawley (C.L.), N Yorks.............................. 197
Yesterday's Books, Dorset 92

- SPANISH CIVIL WAR

Baldwin (Jack), Strathclyde 280
Bass (Ben), Wiltshire 251
Fifteenth Century Bookshop (The), E Sussex 104
Left on The Shelf, Cumbria.......................... 79
Meekins Books (Paul), Warwickshire.............. 238
Orssich (Paul), London SW.......................... 170
Red Star Books, Hertfordshire 130

- SPORTS

Bermondsey Basement Bookstore, London SE .. 164
Collectors Carbooks, Northants..................... 200
Joel Segal Books, Devon 86
Old Bookshop (The), W Mids...................... 241

- TROTSKYISM

Left on The Shelf, Cumbria.......................... 79
Northern Herald Books, W Yorks.................. 246
R. & A. Books, E Sussex................... 102
Red Star Books, Hertfordshire 130

- WOMEN

Burmester (James), Bristol........................... 59
Dolphin Books, Suffolk............................... 226
Drury Rare Books (John), Essex................... 110
Elaine Lonsdale Books, West Yorkshire 248
Fifteenth Century Bookshop (The), E Sussex 104
Northern Herald Books, West Yorkshire.......... 246
Reading Lasses, Dumfries & Galloway 271
Scorpio Books, Suffolk 226
Spenceley Books (David), West Yorkshire........ 249
Symes Books (Naomi), Cheshire 72

HISTORY OF CIVILISATION

Apocalypse, Surrey 233
Camden Books, Somerset 216
Crouch Rare Books, Surrey......................... 233
Fifteenth Century Bookshop (The), E Sussex 104
Helion & Company, W Mids........................ 240
Michael Graves-Johnston, London SW 169
N1 Books, E Sussex................................... 105
R. & A. Books, E Sussex............................. 102
Star Lord Books, Gr Man 119
Taylor & Son (Peter), Hertfordshire............... 133
Treadwell's Books, London WC 180

HISTORY OF IDEAS

Apocalypse, Surrey 233
Bernard Dixon and Kath Adams, Middlesex 183
Bernstein (Nicholas), London W................... 172
Clevedon Books, Somerset 218
Dean Byass, Bristol................................... 60
Drury Rare Books (John), Essex................... 110
Eagle Bookshop (The), Bedfordshire 53
Fifteenth Century Bookshop (The), E Sussex 104
Game Advice, Oxfordshire 210
Gildas Books, Cheshire 68
Helion & Company, W Mids........................ 240
Herb Tandree Philosophy Books, Glos 116
IKON, Devon... 89
Kenny's Bookshops and Art Galleries Ltd,
Co. Galway... 266
Lee Rare Books (Rachel), Bristol 59
Mair Wilkes Books, Fife 272
Parkinsons Books, Merseyside...................... 186
Pendleburys Bookshop, London N 159
Phillips (Nigel), Hampshire.......................... 122
Price (John), London N 159
St Philip's Books, Oxfordshire...................... 210
Seydi Rare Books (Sevin), London NW 162
Sokol Books Ltd., London W....................... 175
Taylor & Son (Peter), Hertfordshire............... 133
Treadwell's Books, London WC 180
Unsworths Booksellers, London WC.............. 163
Weininger Antiquarian Books (Eva M.),
London NW.. 163
Westwood Books Ltd, Cumbria..................... 80

HOBBIES

Books For All, N Yorks 194

SPECIALITY INDEX

Cheshire Book Centre, Cheshire.................... 69
Cornucopia Books, Lincolnshire 153
Cover to Cover, Merseyside......................... 186
Dales & Lakes Book Centre, Cumbria............ 80
DPE Books, Devon 87
Esoteric Dreams Bookshop, Cumbria 78
Fifteenth Century Bookshop (The), E Sussex 104
Joel Segal Books, Devon 86
McCrone (Audrey), Isle of Arran 275
R. & A. Books, E Sussex............................ 102
Reeves Technical Books, N Yorks................. 196
River Reads Bookshop, Devon..................... 90
Treasure Island (The), Gr Man..................... 119
Wheen O'Books, Scottish Borders 269

HOLOCAUST

Bookshop (The), Gr Man 118
Booth (Booksearch Service), (Geoff), Cheshire... 68
Fishburn Books, London NW....................... 161
Helion & Company, W Mids....................... 240
IKON, Devon.. 89
Island Books, Devon 85
Joel Segal Books, Devon 86
MilitaryHistoryBooks.com, Kent................... 138
Rosemary Pugh Books, Wiltshire 253
Samovar Books, Co. Dublin 264
SETI Books, Staffordshire........................... 225
World War Books, Kent 141

HOME IMPROVEMENTS

Uncle Phil's Books, W Mids........................ 240

HOMEOPATHY

Dales & Lakes Book Centre, Cumbria............ 80
Edmund Pollinger Rare Books, London SW..... 167
Esoteric Dreams Bookshop, Cumbria 78
Fifteenth Century Bookshop (The), E Sussex 104
Greensleeves, Oxfordshire 207
Hinchliffe Books, Bristol............................. 59
IKON, Devon.. 89
Inner Bookshop (The), Oxfordshire................ 210
Joel Segal Books, Devon 86
Magis Books, Leicestershire......................... 149
Occultique, Northants................................ 200
Orchid Book Distributors, Co. Clare.............. 262
Phelps (Michael), W Sussex......................... 243
R. & A Books, E Sussex............................. 102
Scrivener's Books & Bookbinding, Derbyshire 82
Till's Bookshop, Lothian 279

HOMOSEXUALITY & LESBIANISM

Bookshop (The), Gr Man 118
Delectus Books, London WC....................... 177
Esoteric Dreams Bookshop, Cumbria 78
Gay's The Word, London WC...................... 178
Ian Briddon, Derbyshire............................. 82
Joel Segal Books, Devon 86
Judd Books, London WC............................ 178
Paper Pleasures, Somerset 219
R. & A. Books, E Sussex............................ 102
Reading Lasses, Dumfries & Galloway 271
Till's Bookshop, Lothian 279
Tsbbooks, London SW 170

HORIZON WRITERS

Criterion Books, London Outer..................... 182

HOROLOGY

Anthony Vickers Books, N Yorks 196
Barmby (C. & A.J.), Kent........................... 141
Baron (Christopher), Gr Man 118
Cheshire Book Centre, Cheshire.................... 69
Clark (Nigel A.), London SE 165
Cornucopia Books, Lincolnshire 153
Delph Books, Gr Man................................ 120
Engaging Gear Ltd., Essex 108
Formby Antiques (Jeffrey), Glos 115
Hadfield (G.K.), Cumbria 80
Joel Segal Books, Devon 86
Nibris Books, London SW........................... 170
Rogers Turner Books, London SE.................. 166
Scrivener's Books & Bookbinding, Derbyshire... 82
Sue Lowell Natural History Books, London W . 176
Trinders' Fine Tools, Suffolk 227
Vickers (Anthony), N Yorks........................ 196

HORSES (SEE ALSO UNDER SPORT)

Bob Mallory (Books), Derbyshire.................. 83
Browzers, Gr Man.................................... 119
Castleton (Pat), Kent................................. 138
Cornucopia Books, Lincolnshire 153
Country Books, Derbyshire 82
Dales & Lakes Book Centre, Cumbria............ 80
Darkwood Books, Co. Cork......................... 263
Discovery Bookshop, Carmarthenshire............ 283
Fifteenth Century Bookshop (The), E Sussex 104
Garfi Books, Powys 293
Grove Bookshop (The), N Yorks................... 197
Hünersdorff Rare Books, London SW............ 169
Jane Badger Books, Northants 200
Jane Jones Books, Grampian 272
Joel Segal Books, Devon 86
Karen Millward, Co. Cork........................... 263
Kennedy & Farley, E Sussex........................ 104
Phenotype Books, Cumbria 80
R. & A. Books, E Sussex............................ 102

HORTICULTURE

Barn Books, Shropshire.............................. 215
Besleys Books, Suffolk 226
Black Five Books, Shropshire 215
Blest (Peter), Kent 139
Books (For All), N Yorks............................ 194
Books for Content, Herefordshire.................. 128
Burmester (James), Bristol.......................... 59
Calendula Horticultural Books, E Sussex......... 102
Clarke Books (David), Somerset 219
Coach House Books, Worcestershire 256
Court Hay Books, W Mids.......................... 240
Dales & Lakes Book Centre, Cumbria............ 80
Dolphin Books, Suffolk.............................. 226
Eastcote Bookshop (The), London Outer......... 181
Evergreen Livres, Oxfordshire 208
Fifteenth Century Bookshop (The), E Sussex 104
Gardener & Cook, London SW..................... 168
Garfi Books, Powys 293
Hollingshead (Chris), London Outer 183
Hünersdorff Rare Books, London SW............ 169
Joel Segal Books, Devon 86

SPECIALITY INDEX

Mobbs (A.J.), W Mids................................. 241
Orb's Bookshop, Grampian.......................... 274
Park (Mike), London Outer.......................... 183
Parkinsons Books, Merseyside...................... 186
Peter M Daly, Hampshire............................ 127
Phelps (Michael), W Sussex......................... 243
Pugh Books (Ian K.), Worcestershire.............. 256
R. & A. Books, E Sussex............................. 102
Spelman (Ken), N Yorks............................. 199
Summerfield Books Ltd, Cumbria.................. 77
Thin Read Line, Merseyside........................ 185
Uncle Phil's Books, W Mids......................... 240
Vokes Books Ltd., N Yorks.......................... 195
Westons, Hertfordshire............................... 133

HOSPITALS

Bernard Dixon and Kath Adams, Middlesex 183
Empire Books, N Yorks............................... 198
J & J Burgess Booksellers, Cambridgeshire....... 64
R. & A. Books, E Sussex............................. 102
Westons, Hertfordshire............................... 133

HOUSEKEEPING

Black Cat Books, Norfolk............................ 188
Country Books, Derbyshire.......................... 82
DPE Books, Devon.................................... 87
Fifteenth Century Bookshop (The), E Sussex 104
HCB Wholesale, Powys.............................. 290
R. & A. Books, E Sussex............................. 102
Sleepy Elephant Books & Artefacts, Cumbria ... 80
Susan Taylor Books, West Yorkshire 248

HUDSON BAY COMPANY

Americanabooksuk, Cumbria........................ 77

HUMANISM

Books Only, Suffolk................................... 227
Chthonios Books, E Sussex.......................... 102
Forder (R.W.), Hampshire........................... 121
Humanist Book Services, Cornwall................. 73
Northern Herald Books, West Yorkshire......... 246
Parkinsons Books, Merseyside...................... 186
Poole (William), London W......................... 175
R. & A. Books, E Sussex............................. 102
Unsworth's Booksellers, London WC 163, 180

HUMANITIES

Aurora Books Ltd, Lothian........................... 276
Bristol Books, Bristol................................. 60
Chandos Books, London Outer..................... 183
Crouch Rare Books, Surrey.......................... 233
Drury Rare Books (John), Essex.................... 110
Fireside Bookshop, Cumbria........................ 81
Forest Books of Manchester, Cheshire............ 71
Hawley (C.L.), N Yorks.............................. 197
hullbooks.com, East Yorkshire...................... 107
Joel Segal Books, Devon............................. 86
Lee Rare Books (Rachel), Bristol.................. 9
Maghreb Bookshop (The), London WC.......... 178
Naughton Booksellers, Co. Dublin................. 265
Parkinsons Books, Merseyside...................... 186
Pickering & Chatto, London W..................... 175
Plurabelle Books, Cambridgeshire.................. 64
Porter Bookshop (The), S Yorks.................... 222
Reading Lasses, Dumfries & Galloway............ 271

Samovar Books, Co. Dublin......................... 264
Till's Bookshop, Lothian............................. 279
Unsworth's Booksellers, London WC 163, 180
Waterfield's, Oxfordshire............................ 210

HUMOUR

Apocalypse, Surrey.................................... 233
Autumn Leaves, Lincolnshire....................... 152
BC Books, Cheshire................................... 70
Black Five Books, Shropshire....................... 215
Bob Mallory (Books), Derbyshire.................. 83
Book Palace (The), London SE..................... 164
Books Only, Suffolk................................... 227
Bookstand, Dorset..................................... 94
Browse Books, Lancashire........................... 144
Carningli Centre, Pembrokeshire................... 288
Chapter & Verse, Lincolnshire...................... 152
Cheshire Book Centre, Cheshire.................... 69
Cornucopia Books, Lincolnshire................... 153
Dales & Lakes Book Centre, Cumbria............ 80
Dolphin Books, Suffolk............................... 226
Eastcote Bookshop (The), London Outer........ 181
Fifteenth Century Bookshop (The), E Sussex 104
Fun in Books, Surrey................................. 235
Goldman (Paul), Dorset.............................. 94
Grahame Thornton, Bookseller, Dorset........... 93
Hay Castle, Powys.................................... 290
Ian Briddon, Derbyshire............................. 82
Jade Mountain Bookshop, Hampshire............ 126
Joel Segal Books, Devon............................. 86
Poetry Bookshop (The), Powys..................... 291
Print Matters, London SE............................ 166
Scrivener's Books & Bookbinding, Derbyshire... 82
Uncle Phil's Books, W Mids......................... 240
Wayside Books and Cards, Oxfordshire.......... 207
Willmott Bookseller (Nicholas), Cardiff.......... 283
Yesterday's News, Conwy........................... 285

HYDROGRAPHY

Earth Science Books, Wiltshire..................... 252
Phelps (Michael), W Sussex......................... 243

HYMNOLOGY

Humber Books, Lincolnshire........................ 150
Oasis Booksearch, Cambridgeshire................ 67
Parkinsons Books, Merseyside...................... 186
Rosemary Pugh Books, Wiltshire.................. 253
Samovar Books, Co. Dublin......................... 264
Spooner & Co, Somerset............................. 220
Stalagluft Books, Tyne and Wear.................. 236
Travis & Emery Music Bookshop, London WC 180

HYPNOTISM

Magis Books, Leicestershire......................... 149
Occultique, Northants................................ 200
Phelps (Michael), W Sussex......................... 243
R. & A. Books, E Sussex............................. 102

I-CHING

Atlantis Bookshop, London WC.................... 177
Inner Bookshop (The), Oxfordshire................ 210
Joel Segal Books, Devon............................. 86

ICHTHYOLOGY

Chalmers Hallam (E.), Hampshire.................. 125

SPECIALITY INDEX

Parkinsons Books, Merseyside...................... 186
Sub Aqua Prints and Books, Hampshire 123

ICONOGRAPHY

Bardsley's Books, Suffolk............................ 226
Baron (H.), London NW............................. 161
Bennett & Kerr Books, Oxfordshire 206
Foster (Stephen), London NW 161
Parikian, Rare Books (Diana), London W 175
Print Matters, London SE............................ 166
Rosemary Pugh Books, Wiltshire 253

ILLUMINATED MANUSCRIPTS

Bardsley's Books, Suffolk............................ 226
Bennett & Kerr Books, Oxfordshire 206
Birchden Books, London E 155
Bookstand, Dorset..................................... 94
Collectables (W.H.), Suffolk 230
Cox Old & Rare Books (Claude), Suffolk 228
Derek Stirling Bookseller, Kent 142
Du Ry Medieval Manuscripts (Marc-Antoine),
London W 173
John Underwood Antiquarian Books, Norfolk .. 190
Maggs Brothers Limited, London W 174
Taylor & Son (Peter), Hertfordshire 133

ILLUSTRATED - GENERAL

Alastor Rare Books, Hampshire 124
Alexander's Books, Warwickshire 238
Anthony Neville, Kent 139
Anthony Whittaker, Kent 136
Antique Map and Bookshop (The), Dorset 94
Antiques on High, Oxfordshire..................... 209
Art Reference Books, Hampshire 125
Artco, Notts 204
Assinder Books, Essex 110
Autolycus, Shropshire................................ 213
Baker - Books for the Collector (Colin), Devon. 90
Ballantyne-Way (Roger), Suffolk 229
Barlow (Vincent G.), Hampshire 125
Barry McKay Rare Books, Cumbria 77
Bates Books, London Outer 182
Batterham (David), London W..................... 172
Bayntun (George), Somerset 216
Beck (John), E Sussex................................ 103
Bermondsey Basement Bookstore, London SE .. 164
Besleys Books, Suffolk 226
Bettridge (Gordon), Fife............................. 272
Beverley Old Bookshop, East Yorkshire.......... 106
Biblion, London W................................... 172
Bolton Books, Hampshire........................... 121
Book Palace (The), London SE 164
Book Shelf (The), Devon 87
Bookline, Co. Down 261
Bookmark (Children's Books), Wiltshire.......... 253
Books & Things, London W........................ 172
Books Bought & Sold, Surrey 232
books2books, Devon 88
Bookstand, Dorset.................................... 94
Boris Books, Hampshire............................. 126
Boxwood Books & Prints, Somerset............... 220
Bright (P.G.), Cambridgeshire 65
Brighton Books, E Sussex........................... 99
Burden (Derek), Surrey 233
Burden Ltd., (Clive A.), Hertfordshire 132

Butts Books (Mary), Berkshire 56
Bygone Books, Orkney 276
Cameron House Books, Isle of Wight............. 134
Camilla's Bookshop, E Sussex...................... 101
Canterbury Bookshop (The), Kent 136
Castleton (Pat), Kent................................. 138
Chalk (Old & Out of Print Books)
(Christine M.), W Mids........................... 239
Chantrey Books, S Yorks 222
Chris Phillips, Wiltshire............................. 251
Cobweb Books, N Yorks............................ 195
Coupland (Terry W.), Staffordshire................ 224
Cox Old & Rare Books (Claude), Suffolk 228
Criterion Books, London Outer 182
Cumming Limited (A. & Y.), E Sussex 104
D'Arcy Books, Wiltshire............................ 252
David (G.), Cambridgeshire........................ 63
Davies Fine Books, Worcestershire 257
de Beaumont (Robin), London SW 167
Dean Illustrated Books (Myra), Powys 288
Derek Stirling Bookseller, Kent 142
Deverell Books, Bristol 59
Doorbar (P. & D.), Gwyned 287
DPE Books, Devon 87
Drummond Pleasures of Past Times (David),
London WC 177
Eastcote Bookshop (The), London Outer......... 181
Eastwood Books (David), Cornwall 73
Eclectica, London SE 165
Elmfield Books, W Mids 239
Elstree Books, Hertfordshire 131
Ely Books, Cambridgeshire 65
Embleton (Paul), Essex 111
Erian Books, London N 158
Everett (Richard), Norfolk 188
Ferdinando (Steven), Somerset 220
Ferguson (Elizabeth), Grampian 272
Fifteenth Century Bookshop (The), E Sussex 104
Firecatcher Books, Gr Man......................... 118
Fletcher (H.M.), Hertfordshire 132
Fosters Bookshop, London W 173
Frew Limited (Robert), London W................ 173
Golden Goose Books, Lincolnshire................ 152
Goldman (Paul), Dorset 94
Goodyer (Nicholas), London N 159
Green Meadow Books, Cornwall 74
Grove Bookshop (The), N Yorks.................. 197
Hanborough Books, Oxfordshire................... 210
Harrington (Adrian), London W................... 173
Harrington Antiquarian Bookseller (Peter),
London SW 169
Harvest Books, Lancashire.......................... 145
Harwich Old Books, Essex 110
Hatchard & Daughters, West Yorkshire.......... 247
Hava Books, London SE............................ 165
Hennessey Bookseller (Ray), E Sussex 100
Heppa (Christopher), Essex 108
Hereward Books, Cambridgeshire.................. 66
Heywood Hill Limited (G.), London W 174
Hodgkins and Company Limited (Ian), Glos 116
Hodgson (Books) (Richard J.), N Yorks 198
Hummingbird Books, Herefordshire............... 128
Hurly Burly Books, Wiltshire...................... 254
Innes Books, Shropshire............................. 214
Island Books, Devon................................. 85

SPECIALITY INDEX

Jane Jones Books, Grampian 272
JB Books & Collectables, W Sussex 244
Jean Hedger, Berkshire 55
Jermy & Westerman, Notts 205
Joel Segal Books, Devon 86
Junk & Spread Eagle, London SE 165
Katharine House Gallery, Wiltshire 252
Kennedy (Peter), Surrey 235
Kerr (Norman), Cumbria 78
Keswick Bookshop, Cumbria 79
Key Books (Sarah), Cambridgeshire................ 64
Kineton Nooks, Warwickshire....................... 237
Leabeck Books, Oxfordshire 210
Leigh Gallery Books, Essex 110
Lenton (Alfred), Leicestershire...................... 147
Little Stour Books, Kent 137
Lloyd-Davies (Sue), Carmarthenshire 284
Lucius Books, N Yorks............................... 199
Lymelight Books & Prints, Dorset 93
March House Books, Dorset 95
Marchpane, London WC............................. 178
Marks Limited (Barrie), London N.................. 159
Marlborough Rare Books Ltd., London W 174
Martin Bookshop & Gallery (Richard), Hants... 123
Mason (Mary), Oxfordshire.......................... 206
Maynard & Bradley, Leicestershire 148
McCrone (Audrey), Isle of Arran 275
Mereside Books, Cheshire 70
Mills Rare Books (Adam), Cambridgeshire 64
Minster Gate Bookshop, N Yorks.................. 199
Modlock (Lilian), Dorset 93
Nonsuch Books, Surrey............................... 234
O'Flynn Books, N Yorks............................. 199
O'Kill (John), Kent................................... 138
Old Town Bookshop (The), Lothian 278
Poetry Bookshop (The), Powys..................... 291
Print Matters, London SE............................ 166
Pugh Books (Ian K.), Worcestershire.............. 256
R. & A. Books, E Sussex............................. 102
Rees & O'Neill Rare Books, London WC........ 179
Ripping Yarns, London N 160
Rising Tide Books, Fife............................... 271
Robin Doughty - Fine Books, W Mids 239
Rochdale Book Company, Gr Man 120
Roe and Moore, London WC 179
Rose's Books, Powys.................................. 291
Ross & Company Ltd., (Louise), Worcs 255
Rowan House Books, Surrey 232
Roz Hulse, Conwy 286
Rye Old Books, E Sussex 104
Sabin (Printed Works) (P.R. & V.), Kent........ 136
Saint Mary's Books & Prints, Lincolnshire....... 154
Scrivener's Books & Bookbinding, Derbyshire... 82
Second Edition, Lothian.............................. 278
Sephton (A.F.), London W 175
Sesemann (Julia), Kent............................... 136
Seydi Rare Books (Sevin), London NW 162
Shakeshaft (Dr. B.), Cheshire 71
Sharpe (Mary), Somerset 221
Shelley (E. & J.), Buckinghamshire 61
Sillan Books, Co. Cavan.............................. 262
Sims Reed Limited, London SW.................... 170
Sotheran Limited (Henry), London W 176
Stella Books, Monmouthshire 288
Stevens (Joan), Cambridgeshire..................... 65

Stothert Old Books, Cheshire........................ 69
Taylor Rare Books (Michael), Norfolk 187
Temperley (David), W Mids 239
Ulysses, London WC.................................. 180
Updike Rare Books (John), Lothian 279
Waddington Books & Prints (Geraldine),
Northants 200
Wheen O'Books, Scottish Borders 269
Whitehall Books, E Sussex 103
Whittle, Bookseller (Avril), Cumbria 81
Woodbine Books, West Yorkshire.................. 246
Words Etcetera Bookshop, Dorset.................. 93
Xanadu Books, Cleveland............................ 98
Yates Antiquarian Books (Tony), Leicestershire. 148
York Modern Books, N Yorks...................... 197

- 19TH & 20TH CENTURY

Antique Map and Bookshop (The), Dorset 94
Ballantyne-Way (Roger), Suffolk 229
Barlow (Vincent G.), Hants.......................... 125
Blackwell's Rare Books, Oxfordshire.............. 209
Cornucopia Books, Lincolnshire 153
Courtwood Books, Co. Laois........................ 266
Ellis, Bookseller (Peter), London WC 178
Fifteenth Century Bookshop (The), E Sussex 104
Foster Bookshop (Paul), London SW 168
Goldman (Paul), Dorset 94
Greer (Robin), London SW.......................... 168
Hava Books, London SE.............................. 165
Jean Hedger, Berkshire 55
Joel Segal Books, Devon 86
Liddle (Steve), Bristol 58
R. & A. Books, E Sussex............................. 102
Robin Doughty - Fine Books, W Mids 239
Wheen O'Books, Scottish Borders 269

ILLUSTRATORS

Barlow (Vincent G.), Hants.......................... 125
books2books, Devon 88
Brown-Studies, Strathclyde 279
Cornucopia Books, Lincolnshire 153
Fifteenth Century Bookshop (The), E Sussex 104
Greer (Robin), London SW.......................... 168
Jean Hedger, Berkshire 55
Mannwaring (M.G.), Bristol 59
Woodbine Books, West Yorkshire.................. 246

IMAGINARY VOYAGES

Susanne Schulz-Falster Rare Books, London N. 160

IMMIGRATION

Empire Books, N Yorks.............................. 198
Fishburn Books, London NW....................... 161

IMMUNOLOGY

Bernard Dixon and Kath Adams, Middlesex 183
Parkinsons Books, Merseyside....................... 186
R M Books, Hertfordshire 132
Westons, Hertfordshire 133

IMPRINTS

Seydi Rare Books (Sevin), London NW 162

INCUNABULA

Butler Cresswell Rare Books, Buckinghamshire . 61

SPECIALITY INDEX

De Burca Rare Books, Co. Dublin 264
Fletcher (H.M.), Hertfordshire 132
Hunter-Rare Books (Andrew), London SW 169
Pickering & Chatto, London W 175
Quaritch Ltd., (Bernard), London W.............. 175
Seydi Rare Books (Sevin), London NW 162
Sokol Books Ltd., London W....................... 175
Unsworth's Booksellers, London WC 180

INDUSTRIAL DESIGN

Ballantyne-Way (Roger), Suffolk 229
Cornucopia Books, Lincolnshire 153
Joel Segal Books, Devon 86
N1 Books, E Sussex................................... 105
Westons, Hertfordshire 133

INDUSTRY

Anvil Books, W Mids................................. 240
Blanchfield (John), West Yorkshire................ 249
Book House (The), Cumbria........................ 77
Bott, (Bookdealers) Ltd., (Martin), Gr Man 118
Byrom Textile Bookroom (Richard), Lancashire 143
Cheshire Book Centre, Cheshire.................... 69
Cornucopia Books, Lincolnshire 153
Country Books, Derbyshire 82
Cox (Geoff), Devon 90
Duck (William), Hants............................... 124
Elton Engineering Books, London W 173
Empire Books, N Yorks.............................. 198
Hinchliffe Books, Bristol............................. 59
Keel Row Bookshop, Tyne and Wear 236
Parkinsons Books, Merseyside...................... 186
Past & Present Books, Glos......................... 114
PsychoBabel Books & Journals, Oxfordshire..... 206
Rainford (Sheila), Hertfordshire.................... 130
Robert Humm & Co, Lincolnshire 154
Rochdale Book Company, Gr Man 120
Stroh (M.A.), London E 155
Westons, Hertfordshire 133
Whistler's Books, London SW 170
Wiend Books, Lancashire 144

INSTITUTIONS

G. C. Books Ltd., Dumfries & Galloway......... 271
Joel Segal Books, Devon 86

INTERIOR DESIGN

Ballantyne-Way (Roger), Suffolk 229
Barlow (Vincent G.), Hants......................... 125
Black Cat Books, Norfolk............................ 188
Cornucopia Books, Lincolnshire 153
Don Kelly Books, London W 172
Foster (Stephen), London NW 161
Haskell (R.H. & P.), Dorset 94
Heneage Art Books (Thomas), London SW 169
Joel Segal Books, Devon 86
Judd Books, London WC............................ 178
Judith Mansfield, West Yorkshire.................. 250
Keswick Bookshop, Cumbria........................ 79
Martin - Bookseller (Colin), East Yorkshire 107
N1 Books, E Sussex................................... 105
Pagan Limited (Hugh), London SW................ 170
Phillips of Hitchin (Antiques) Ltd., Herts......... 131
Portobello Books, London W 175
Potterton Books, N Yorks 197

Ray Rare and Out of Print Books (Janette),
N Yorks... 199
Sleepy Elephant Books & Artefacts, Cumbria ... 80
Staniland (Booksellers), Lincolnshire 154
Trinders' Fine Tools, Suffolk 227
Uncle Phil's Books, W Mids......................... 240
Whittle, Bookseller (Avril), Cumbria 81

INTERNATIONAL AFFAIRS

Al Saqi Books, London W........................... 172
Bickford-Smith (G.), Surrey......................... 233
Brimstones, E Sussex................................. 103
Empire Books, N Yorks.............................. 198
Game Advice, Oxfordshire 210
Melvin Tenner, London W........................... 174

INVENTORS & INVENTIONS

Bernard Dixon and Kath Adams, Middlesex 183
Elton Engineering Books, London W............. 173
Gildas Books, Cheshire.............................. 68
Joel Segal Books, Devon 86
McGee (Terence J.), London Outer 181
N1 Books, E Sussex................................... 105
Stroh (M.A.), London E 155
Westons, Herts 133

INVESTMENTS

Barcombe Services, Essex............................ 108

IRIDOLOGY

Inner Bookshop (The), Oxfordshire................ 210
Orchid Book Distributors, Co. Clare.............. 262

IRISH INTEREST

Anglo-American Rare Books, Surrey.............. 233
Ann & Mike Conry, Worcs.......................... 257
Barcombe Services, Essex............................ 108
Bath Old Books, Somerset 216
Bell Gallery (The), Co. Antrim..................... 260
Books Ulster, Co. Down 261
Bookshop (The), Co. Donegal...................... 263
Bookshop (The), Gr Man 118
Bott, (Bookdealers) Ltd., (Martin), Gr Man 118
Byre Books, Dumfries & Galloway................ 270
Caledonia Books, Strathclyde....................... 280
Camilla's Bookshop, E Sussex...................... 101
Carraig Books Ltd., Co. Dublin 264
Cecilia Marsden, Middlesex......................... 183
Chapter Two, London SE............................ 164
Clements (R.W.), London Outer................... 182
Country Books, Derbyshire 82
Courtwood Books, Co. Laois....................... 266
Craobh Rua Books, Co. Armagh.................. 260
Darkwood Books, Co. Cork......................... 263
Davidson Books, Co. Down 261
De Burca Rare Books, Co. Dublin 264
Drury Rare Books (John), Essex................... 110
Dublin Bookbrowsers, Co. Dublin................. 265
Ferdinando (Steven), Somerset 220
Foyle Books, Co. Derry 260
Fuchsia Books, Co. Wexford 267
G. C. Books Ltd., Dumfries & Galloway......... 271
Glenbower Books, Co. Dublin 265
Greene's Bookshop Ltd, Co. Dublin 265
Grove Bookshop (The), N Yorks.................. 197

SPECIALITY INDEX

Harris (George J.), Co. Derry 260
House of Figgis Ltd (The), Co. Galway 266
Hyland (C.P.), Co. Cork 263
Jackdaw Books, Norfolk 189
Jackson (M.W.), Wiltshire........................... 254
Jiri Books, Co. Antrim 260
Joel Segal Books, Devon 86
Karen Millward, Co. Cork........................... 263
Kenny's Bookshops and Art Galleries Ltd,
Co. Galway 266
Kenya Books, E Sussex.............................. 100
Kernaghans, Merseyside 186
Lighthouse Books (The), Dorset 92
My Back Pages, London SW 169
Naughton Booksellers, Co. Dublin 265
O'Brien Books & Photo Gallery, Co. Limerick .. 266
Poetry Bookshop (The), Powys..................... 291
R. & A. Books, E Sussex............................ 102
Read Ireland, Co. Dublin 264
Roscrea Bookshop, Co. Tipperary 267
Rowan (P. & B.), Co. Antrim 260
Royal Carbery Books Ltd., Co. Cork 262
Rye Old Books, E Sussex 104
Saintfield Antiques & Fine Books, Co. Down ... 261
Samovar Books, Co. Dublin 264
Schull Books, Co. Cork 263
Sillan Books, Co. Cavan............................. 262
Stokes Books, Co. Dublin........................... 265
The Old Abbey Bookshop, Co. Down 261
Trinity Rare Books, Co. Leitrim 266
Updike Rare Books (John), Lothian 279
Whelan (P. & F.), Kent.............................. 141

ISLANDS

Miles Apart, Suffolk.................................. 229

JEWELLERY

Art Reference Books, Hants 125
Barmby (C. & A.J.), Kent........................... 141
Cover to Cover, Merseyside......................... 186
Design Gallery 1850-1950 (The), Kent 142
Don Kelly Books, London W 172
Edmund Pollinger Rare Books, London SW..... 167
Heneage Art Books (Thomas), London SW 169
Ives Bookseller (John), London Outer 184
Joel Segal Books, Devon 86
Judith Mansfield, West Yorkshire.................. 250
Nelson (Elizabeth), Suffolk 227
Nibris Books, London SW 170
Orchid Book Distributors, Co. Clare.............. 262
Potterton Books, N Yorks 197
R. & A. Books, E Sussex............................ 102
Sleepy Elephant Books & Artefacts, Cumbria ... 80
Trinders' Fine Tools, Suffolk 227
Warnes (Felicity J.), London Outer................ 181
Whittle, Bookseller (Avril), Cumbria 81

JOURNALISM

Archivist (The), Devon............................... 90
Barcombe Services, Essex............................ 108
Bob Mallory (Books), Derbyshire................... 83
Books at Star Dot Star, W Mids................... 241
Cornucopia Books, Lincolnshire 153
Kelly Books, Devon 89
Pastmasters, Derbyshire.............................. 83

Uncle Phil's Books, W Mids........................ 240
Williams (Bookdealer), (Richard), N Lincs....... 154

JOURNALS - GENERAL

Baldwin's Scientific Books, Essex 112
Batterham (David), London W..................... 172
Bettridge (Gordon), Fife............................. 272
Border Books, Borders............................... 268
Derek Stirling Bookseller, Kent 142
Fifteenth Century Bookshop (The), E Sussex 104
Handley (Christopher), Tyne and Wear........... 236
Joel Segal Books, Devon 86
Kenneth Ball, E Sussex 101
PsychoBabel Books & Journals, Oxfordshire..... 206
Robert Temple, London N.......................... 160
Siop Lyfrau'r Hen Bost, Gwynedd 287
Stroh (M.A.), London E 155
Turton (John), Durham 98
Wayside Books and Cards, Oxfordshire 207
Williams (Bookdealer), (Richard), N Lincs....... 154

- MARITIME

Joel Segal Books, Devon 86

JUDAICA

Bacon (Josephine), London WC 177
Biblion, London W................................... 172
de Visser Books, Cambridgeshire................... 63
Delectus Books, London WC....................... 177
Fishburn Books, London NW....................... 161
Golden Age Books, Worcs........................... 256
Inner Bookshop (The), Oxfordshire................ 210
Joel Segal Books, Devon 86
Kenny's Bookshops and Art Galleries Ltd,
Co. Galway 266
Nautical Antique Centre (The), Dorset 96
Occultique, Northants................... 200
Pordes Books Ltd., (Henry), London WC........ 179
Rosemary Pugh Books, Wiltshire 253
St Swithin's Illustrated & Children's Books,
London W 175
Samovar Books, Co. Dublin 264
Skoob Russell Square, Suffolk...................... 230
Yesterday's News, Conwy 285

JUNGIANA

Apocalypse, Surrey 233
Inner Bookshop (The), Oxfordshire................ 210
Joel Segal Books, Devon 86

JUVENILE

Barry McKay Rare Books, Cumbria 77
Beck (John), E Sussex................................ 103
Blackwell's Rare Books, Oxfordshire.............. 209
Bookmark (Children's Books), Wiltshire.......... 253
Canterbury Bookshop (The), Kent 136
Castleton (Pat), Kent................................. 138
Childrens Bookshop, West Yorkshire 248
Cooper Hay Rare Books, Strathclyde.............. 280
Coupland (Terry W.), Staffordshire................ 224
Demetzy Books, Oxfordshire 208
Fifteenth Century Bookshop (The), E Sussex 104
Foster Bookshop (Paul), London SW.............. 168
Freya Books & Antiques, Norfolk 191
Game Advice, Oxfordshire 210

SPECIALITY INDEX

Holtom (Christopher), Cornwall 75
Jean Hedger, Berkshire 55
Joel Segal Books, Devon 86
John R. Hoggarth, N Yorks......................... 198
K Books, Cheshire...................................... 70
Kirkpatrick (Robert J.), London W 174
Korn (M. Eric), London N 159
Mason (Mary), Oxfordshire.......................... 206
Mead (P.J.), Shropshire............................... 214
Peakirk Books, Cambridgeshire 67
R. & A. Books, E Sussex............................. 102
Robert Temple, London N............................ 160
Roe and Moore, London WC....................... 179
Roscrea Bookshop, Co. Tipperary................. 267
St Swithin's Illustrated & Children's Books,
London W 175
Sesemann (Julia), Kent................................ 136
Shacklock Books (David), Suffolk 227
Smith Books, (Sally), Suffolk 227
Stella Books, Monmouthshire 288
Stour Bookshop, Dorset.............................. 95
The Old Children's Bookshelf, Lothian 278
Wheen O'Books, Scottish Borders 269

KABBALAH/CABBALA/CABALA

Atlantis Bookshop, London WC................... 177
Book Business (The), London W 172
Bygone Books, Orkney 276
Chthonios Books, E Sussex 102
Inner Bookshop (The), Oxfordshire................ 210
Magis Books, Leicestershire......................... 149
Occultique, Northants................................. 200
Star Lord Books, Gr Man 119

KNITTING

Apocalypse, Surrey 233
Autumn Leaves, Lincolnshire....................... 152
Black Cat Books, Norfolk............................ 188
Brown-Studies, Strathclyde.......................... 279
Browse Books, Lancashire 144
Byrom Textile Bookroom (Richard), Lancashire 143
Cover to Cover, Merseyside......................... 186
DPE Books, Devon 87
Fifteenth Century Bookshop (The), E Sussex 104
Joel Segal Books, Devon 6
Judith Mansfield, West Yorkshire.................. 250
Reading Lasses, Dumfries & Galloway 271
Sleepy Elephant Books & Artefacts, Cumbria ... 80
Treasure Island (The), Gr Man..................... 119
Warnes (Felicity J.), London Outer................ 181
Wheen O'Books, Scottish Borders 269
Whittle, Bookseller (Avril), Cumbria 81
Young (D. & J.), Powys.............................. 293

KU KLUX KLAN

Loretta Lay Books, London NW 162

LACE

Black Cat Books, Norfolk............................ 188
Byrom Textile Bookroom (Richard), Lancashire 143
Cover to Cover, Merseyside......................... 186
Crouch Rare Books, Surrey.......................... 233
Ely Books, Cambridgeshire 65
Fifteenth Century Bookshop (The), E Sussex 104
Heneage Art Books (Thomas), London SW 169

Hennessey Bookseller (Ray), E Sussex 100
Joel Segal Books, Devon 86
Judith Mansfield, West Yorkshire.................. 250
Reading Lasses, Dumfries & Galloway 271
Sleepy Elephant Books & Artefacts, Cumbria ... 80
Warnes (Felicity J.), London Outer................ 181
Whittle, Bookseller (Avril), Cumbria 81
Williams (Christopher), Dorset 94
York (Graham), Devon................................ 86
Young (D. & J.), Powys.............................. 293

LANDSCAPE

Apocalypse, Surrey 233
Arden, Bookseller (C.), Powys...................... 289
Burebank Books, Norfolk 187
Calendula Horticultural Books, E Sussex......... 102
Castleton (Pat), Kent.................................. 138
Cornucopia Books, Lincolnshire 153
Cottage Books, Leicestershire....................... 147
Duck (William), Hants................................ 124
Haskell (R.H. & P.), Dorset 94
Hollingshead (Chris), London Outer 183
Hünersdorff Rare Books, London SW............ 169
Inch's Books, Kent.................................... 137
Joel Segal Books, Devon 86
Marlborough Rare Books Ltd., London W...... 174
Modlock (Lilian), Dorset............................. 93
Park (Mike), London Outer.......................... 183
R. & A. Books, E Sussex............................. 102
Ray Rare and Out of Print Books (Janette),
N Yorks.. 199
Spelman (Ken), N Yorks............................. 199

LANGUAGES - AFRICAN

J.C. Deyong Books, London SW 169
Kenya Books, E Sussex............................... 100
Marijana Dworski Books, via Hereford........... 290
owenbooks65, Conwy................................. 285
Yesterday's Books, Dorset 92

- ANCIENT

Blackwell's Rare Books, Oxfordshire.............. 209
Hava Books, London SE............................. 165
Marijana Dworski Books, via Hereford........... 290
Parkinsons Books, Merseyside...................... 186
Samovar Books, Co. Dublin 264
Seydi Rare Books (Sevin), London NW 162
Unsworth's Booksellers, London WC 180

- FOREIGN

Al Saqi Books, London W........................... 172
Autumn Leaves, Lincolnshire....................... 152
Bacon (Josephine), London WC 177
Baldwin (Jack), Strathclyde 280
Book House (The), Cumbria........................ 77
Bookcase, Cumbria.................................... 78
Books on Spain, London Outer..................... 184
Booth Books, Powys.................................. 289
Carnforth Bookshop (The), Lancashire 143
Crouch Rare Books, Surrey.......................... 233
Fifteenth Century Bookshop (The), E Sussex 104
George St. Books, Derbyshire 83
Hab Books, London W............................... 173
Hava Books, London SE............................. 165
Hodgson (Judith), London W 174

SPECIALITY INDEX

Hünersdorff Rare Books, London SW 169
Joel Segal Books, Devon 86
Korn (M. Eric), London N 159
Mandalay Bookshop, London SW 169
Marijana Dworski Books, via Hereford........... 290
Midnight Oil Books, Fife...... 272
Oupalba Books, Cheshire............................ 71
Owen (J.V.), Conwy.................................. 285
owenbooks65, Conwy................................. 285
Parkinsons Books, Merseyside...................... 186
Pholiota Books, London WC....................... 179
Priestpopple Books, Northumberland 202
Robertshaw (John), Cambridgeshire............... 66
Roundstone Books, Lancashire..................... 144
Scrivener's Books & Bookbinding, Derbyshire... 82
Stokes Books, Co. Dublin........................... 265
Tarka Books, Devon.................................. 84
Thorntons of Oxford Ltd., Oxfordshire........... 207
Transformer, Dumfries & Galloway............... 271

- NATIONAL

Book House (The), Cumbria......................... 77
BOOKS4U, Flintshire 286
Browning Books, Torfaen 294
Colin Hancock, Ceredigion 284
Derek Stirling Bookseller, Kent 142
Doolin Dinghy Books, Co. Clare 262
Hünersdorff Rare Books, London SW............ 169
Hyland (C.P.), Co. Cork 263
Joel Segal Books, Devon 86
Kenya Books, E Sussex............................... 100
Marijana Dworski Books, via Hereford........... 290
owenbooks65, Conwy................................. 285
Spenceley Books (David), West Yorkshire........ 249
Treasure Island (The), Gr Man..................... 119
Walker Fine Books (Steve), Dorset 92

- PIDGIN AND CREOLE

Joel Segal Books, Devon 86
Kenya Books, E Sussex............................... 100
Marijana Dworski Books, via Hereford........... 290
Yesterday's Books, Dorset 92

LAW - GENERAL

Armstrong's Books & Collectables, Leics 147
Aurora Books Ltd, Lothian.......................... 276
Booth Books, Powys 289
Crimes Ink, London E................................ 155
Dean Byass, Bristol................................... 60
Drury Rare Books (John), Essex,... 110
Edwards (London) Limited (Francis),
London WC 177
Edwards in Hay–on–Wye (Francis), Powys 290
PsychoBabel Books & Journals, Oxfordshire..... 206
Roscrea Bookshop, Co. Tipperary................. 267
Skoob Russell Square, Suffolk...................... 230
Susanne Schulz-Falster Rare Books, London N. 160
Thornber (Peter M.), N Yorks 196
Undercover Books, Lincolnshire 154
Unsworth's Booksellers, London WC 180
Wayside Books and Cards, Oxfordshire 207
Webb Books (John), S Yorks....................... 222
Westfield Books, N Yorks........................... 199
Wheen O'Books, Scottish Borders 269
Wildy & Sons Ltd, London WC 180

- CONSTITUTIONAL

Wildy & Sons Ltd, London WC 180

LEGAL PAPERWORK

John Underwood Antiquarian Books, Norfolk .. 190
Thornber (Peter M.), N Yorks 196

LENINISM

Northern Herald Books, West Yorkshire.......... 246
Reading Lasses, Dumfries & Galloway 271

LEPIDOPTEROLOGY

Aurelian Books, London NW 161
Aviabooks, Glos 114
Edmund Pollinger Rare Books, London SW..... 167
Joel Segal Books, Devon 86
Moss Books, London NW 162
Park (Mike), London Outer......................... 183
Pemberley Books, Buckinghamshire 62
Sue Lowell Natural History Books, London W. 176

LETTERING

Joel Segal Books, Devon 86
N1 Books, E Sussex................................... 105
Woodbine Books, West Yorkshire.................. 246

LETTERPRESS BROADSIDES

Burmester (James), Bristol.......................... 59

LETTERS

Baron (H.), London NW............................ 161
Davids Ltd., (Roy), Oxfordshire 209
Farahar & Dupre (Clive & Sophie), Wiltshire ... 251
Fifteenth Century Bookshop (The), E Sussex 104
Gekoski (R.A.), London WC....................... 178
Hodgkins and Company Limited (Ian), Glos 116
James Fergusson Books & Manuscripts,
London W 174
Joel Segal Books, Devon 86
Just Books, Cornwall 76
Lawrence Books, Notts............................... 204
Maggs Brothers Limited, London W.............. 174
Marine & Cannon Books, Cheshire 71
Marine and Cannon Books, Cheshire 69
Neil Summersgill, Lancashire 143
Poetry Bookshop (The), Powys.................... 291
Reading Lasses, Dumfries & Galloway 271
Robert Temple, London N.......................... 160
Scrivener's Books & Bookbinding, Derbyshire... 82
Silverman (Michael), ... 166

LIBERTARIANISM

Joel Segal Books, Devon 86

LIBRARIES - EVERYMAN'S

Fifteenth Century Bookshop (The), E Sussex 104
Hava Books, London SE............................. 165
Joel Segal Books, Devon 86
Just Books, Cornwall 76
Williams (Bookdealer), (Richard), N Lincs 154

LIBRARY SCIENCE

Skoob Russell Square, Suffolk...................... 230
Smith Books, (Sally), Suffolk 227
Westons, Herts 133

SPECIALITY INDEX

LIMITED EDITIONS - GENERAL

Apocalypse, Surrey 233
Artco, Notts 204
Ballantyne–Way (Roger), Suffolk 229
Barlow (Vincent G.), Hants.......................... 125
Besleys Books, Suffolk 226
Biblion, London W.................................... 172
Blackwell's Rare Books, Oxfordshire 209
BOOKS4U, Flintshire................................. 286
Brian Troath Books, London E...................... 155
Budd (Richard), Somerset 219
Chapter & Verse, Lincolnshire...................... 152
Coach House Books, Worcs 256
Collinge & Clark, London WC...................... 177
Cox Old & Rare Books (Claude), Suffolk 228
Dean Illustrated Books (Myra), Powys 288
Eastwood (David), Cornwall 73
Ellis, Bookseller (Peter), London WC 178
Fiction First, Cheshire 70
Hanborough Books, Oxfordshire.................... 210
Harwich Old Books, Essex 110
Hava Books, London SE............................. 165
Hollett and Son (R.F.G.), Cumbria 80
JB Books & Collectables, W Sussex 244
Kirkman Ltd., (Robert), Bedfordshire.............. 54
Lucius Books, N Yorks............................... 199
Mannwaring (M.G.), Bristol 59
Marks Limited (Barrie), London N................. 159
Mills Rare Books (Adam), Cambridgeshire 64
Modern First Editions, London Outer 183
N V Books, Warwickshire........................... 237
Reaveley Books, Devon 87
Robert Temple, London N........................... 160
Roz Hulse, Conwy 286
Rye Old Books, E Sussex 104
Sabin (Printed Works) (P.R. & V.), Kent......... 136
Scrivener's Books & Bookbinding, Derbyshire... 82
Seabreeze Books, Lancashire........................ 145
Stevens (Joan), Cambridgeshire..................... 65
Talisman Books, Cheshire............................ 70
Tucker (Alan & Joan), Glos 117
Updike Rare Books (John), Lothian 279
Woodbine Books, West Yorkshire.................. 246
Words Etcetera Bookshop, Dorset.................. 93

- CLUB BOOKS

Dean Illustrated Books (Myra), Powys 288

LINGUISTICS

Baldwin (Jack), Strathclyde 280
Barcombe Services, Essex............................. 108
Bates Books, London Outer 182
Chesters (G. & J.), Staffordshire 225
Derek Stirling Bookseller, Kent 142
Game Advice, Oxfordshire 210
Hava Books, London SE............................. 165
Joel Segal Books, Devon 86
Judd Books, London WC 178
Kenya Books, E Sussex................................ 100
Mandalay Bookshop, London SW 169
Michael Graves-Johnston, London SW 169
Midnight Oil Books, Fife............................. 272
Olynthiacs, Shropshire 214
Oopalba Books, Cheshire............................. 71
Parkinsons Books, Merseyside....................... 186

Plurabelle Books, Cambridgeshire.................. 64
PsychoBabel Books & Journals, Oxfordshire..... 206
Reading Lasses, Dumfries & Galloway 271
Skoob Russell Square, Suffolk....................... 230
Staniland (Booksellers), Lincolnshire 154
Unsworths Booksellers, London WC............... 163
York (Graham), Devon............................... 86

LITERACY

Calendula Horticultural Books, E Sussex 102
Oopalba Books, Cheshire............................. 71

LITERARY CRITICISM

Alec-Smith Books (Alex), East Yorkshire 107
Ann & Mike Conry, Worcs.......................... 257
Apocalypse, Surrey 233
Applin (Malcolm), Berkshire......................... 55
Autumn Leaves, Lincolnshire........................ 152
Axe Rare & Out of Print Books (Richard),
N Yorks... 194
Bennett & Kerr Books, Oxfordshire 206
Boer (Louise), Arthurian Books, Powys 289
Bookcase, Cumbria.................................... 78
Books, Denbighshire 286
Books For All, N Yorks 194
BOOKS4U, Flintshire................................. 286
Bracton Books, Cambridgeshire..................... 63
Brian Troath Books, London E...................... 155
Broadhurst of Southport Ltd., Merseyside 186
Budd (Richard), Somerset 219
Caledonia Books, Strathclyde........................ 280
Carta Regis, Powys.................................... 293
Chaucer Bookshop, Kent............................. 136
Chesters (G. & J.), Staffordshire 225
Clarendon Books, Leics............................... 147
Cobbles Books, Somerset............................. 218
Darkwood Books, Co. Cork.......................... 263
Delectus Books, London WC........................ 177
Dolphin Books, Suffolk............................... 226
Dyson (Anthony), W Mids........................... 240
Elaine Lonsdale Books, West Yorkshire 248
Ellis, Bookseller (Peter), London WC 178
Ellwood Editions, Wiltshire 253
Fifteenth Century Bookshop (The), E Sussex 104
Fisher & Sperr, London N........................... 158
Fortune Green Books, London NW................. 161
Freeman's Corner Shop, Norfolk 190
George St. Books, Derbyshire 83
GfB: the Colchester Bookshop, Essex 109
Handsworth Books, Essex............................. 112
Hawkes (James), London SE 165
Hawley (C.L.), N Yorks.............................. 197
Hellenic Bookservices, London NW................ 162
Ian McKelvie Bookseller, London N............... 159
Innes Books, Shropshire.............................. 214
Island Books, Devon 85
Joel Segal Books, Devon 86
Kingsgate Books & Prints, Hants................... 126
Marcet Books, London SE............................ 165
Naughton Booksellers, Co. Dublin 265
Nineteenth Century Books, Oxfordshire 211
Oopalba Books, Cheshire............................. 71
Oxfam Books and Music, Hants 126
Parkinsons Books, Merseyside....................... 186
Parrott (Jeremy), London E.......................... 156

SPECIALITY INDEX

Parrott Books, Oxfordshire 211
Poetry Bookshop (The), Powys...................... 291
Polmorla Books, Cornwall 76
Pomes Penyeach, Staffordshire 224
Pordes Books Ltd., (Henry), London WC........ 179
PsychoBabel Books & Journals, Oxfordshire..... 206
R. & A. Books, E Sussex............................. 102
Reading Lasses, Dumfries & Galloway 271
Red Star Books, Herts................................ 130
Richard Frost Books, Herts.......................... 130
Riderless Horse Books, Norfolk.................... 187
Robert Temple, London N........................... 160
Rosley Books, Cumbria 81
Roundstone Books, Lancashire...................... 144
Rutland Bookshop (The), Rutland 212
Rye Old Books, E Sussex 104
Samovar Books, Co. Dublin 264
Scrivener's Books & Bookbinding, Derbyshire... 82
Skoob Russell Square, Suffolk...................... 230
Staniland (Booksellers), Lincolnshire 154
Stevens (Joan), Cambridgeshire.............. 65
Studio Bookshop, East Sussex...................... 100
Symes Books (Naomi), Cheshire 72
The Glass Key, West Yorkshire.................... 247
Tombland Bookshop, Norfolk 191
Tucker (Alan & Joan), Glos 117
Uncle Phil's Books, W Mids......................... 240
Unsworths Booksellers, London WC.............. 163
Venables (Morris & Juliet), Bristol.................. 60
Waterfield's, Oxfordshire 210
Whitehall Books, East Sussex....................... 103
Yesterday's News, Conwy........................... 285

LITERARY TRAVEL

Al Saqi Books, London W........................... 172
Amwell Book Company, London EC.............. 157
Ann & Mike Conry, Worcs.......................... 257
Anthony Sillem, East Sussex 102
Archer (Steve), London Outer 181
Askew Books (Vernon), Wiltshire.................. 251
Books on Spain, London Outer.................... 184
Cobbles Books, Somerset............................ 218
Collectables (W.H.), Suffolk 230
Cox Rare Books (Charles), Cornwall.............. 74
Criterion Books, London Outer.................... 182
Ellis, Bookseller (Peter), London WC 178
Fifteenth Century Bookshop (The), East Sussex. 104
Hodgkins and Company Limited (Ian), Glos 116
Ian McKelvie Bookseller, London N.............. 159
Joel Segal Books, Devon 86
Keith Langford, London E 155
Nineteenth Century Books, Oxfordshire 211
Orb's Bookshop, Grampian......................... 274
R. & A. Books, East Sussex 102
Rayner (Hugh Ashley), Somerset 217
Robert Temple, London N.......................... 160
Royal Carbery Books Ltd., Co. Cork.............. 262
The Glass Key, West Yorkshire.................... 247
Tiger Books, Kent 137
Trinity Rare Books, Co. Leitrim 266
Tucker (Alan & Joan), Glos 117
War & Peace Books, Hants.......................... 122
Yesterday's Books, Dorset 92
York (Graham), Devon............................... 86
York Modern Books, N Yorks...................... 197

LITERATURE - GENERAL

A. & H. Peasgood, Cambridgeshire 67
Abbey Books, Cornwall 74
Addyman Annexe (The), Powys.................... 289
Addyman Books, Powys............................. 289
Alba Books, Grampian 274
Alexander's Books, Warwickshire.................. 238
Allinson (Frank & Stella), Warwickshire 237
Andrew Morton (Books), Powys................... 289
Anglo-American Rare Books, Surrey.............. 233
Ann & Mike Conry, Worcs.......................... 257
Anthony Sillem, East Sussex........................ 102
Antiquary Ltd., (Bar Bookstore), N Yorks....... 196
Antique Map and Bookshop (The), Dorset 94
Apocalypse, Surrey 233
Archer (Steve), London Outer...................... 181
Archivist (The), Devon............................... 90
Armchair Books, Lothian 276
Artco, Notts 204
Aurora Books Ltd, Lothian.......................... 276
Autolycus, Shropshire 213
Autumn Leaves, Lincolnshire....................... 152
Avonworld Books, Somerset........................ 218
Axe Rare & Out of Print Books (Richard),
N Yorks.. 194
babelog.books, Herefordshire 128
Barbican Bookshop, N Yorks 198
Bass (Ben), Wiltshire 251
Bath Old Books, Somerset 216
Baxter (Steve), Surrey................................ 234
Bayntun (George), Somerset 216
BC Books, Cheshire 70
Bernstein (Nicholas), London W................... 172
Bertram Rota Ltd., London WC 177
Beware of the Leopard, Bristol..................... 58
Black Five Books, Shropshire 215
Blackwell's Rare Books, Oxfordshire.............. 209
Book Business (The), London W 172
Books & Collectables Ltd., Cambridgeshire...... 63
Books (For All), N Yorks............................ 194
Books For All, N Yorks 194
Books on Spain, London Outer.................... 184
books2books, Devon 88
BOOKS4U, Flintshire................................ 286
Bookshop (The), Norfolk 192
Bookshop at the Plain, Lincolnshire.............. 151
Bookworm, Lothian................................... 277
Bookworms, Norfolk.................................. 187
Bookworms of Evesham, Worcs 257
Booth (Booksearch Service), (Geoff), Cheshire... 68
Booth Books, Powys 289
Boris Books, Hants................................... 126
Bow Windows Book Shop, East Sussex 103
Bowie Books & Collectables, East Yorkshire 107
Boz Books, Powys.................................... 289
Bracton Books, Cambridgeshire.................... 63
Brian Troath Books, London E..................... 155
Bright (P.G.), Cambridgeshire 65
Brinded (Scott), Kent 139
Bristol Books, Bristol 60
Broadhurst of Southport Ltd., Merseyside 186
Brock Books, N Yorks 193
Budd (Richard), Somerset........................... 219
Burmester (James), Bristol.......................... 59
Butts Books (Mary), Berkshire 56

SPECIALITY INDEX

Caledonia Books, Strathclyde........................ 280
Camden Books, Somerset 216
Carnforth Bookshop (The), Lancashire 143
Carta Regis, Powys.................................... 293
Chaucer Bookshop, Kent............................. 136
Cheshire Book Centre, Cheshire..................... 69
Chevin Books, West Yorkshire...................... 250
Chris Phillips, Wiltshire.............................. 251
Church Street Books, Norfolk....................... 187
Clarendon Books, Leics............................... 147
Clements (R.W.), London Outer.................... 182
Cobbles Books, Somerset............................. 218
Cobweb Books, N Yorks............................. 195
Cofion Books, Pembrokeshire 288
Cox Old & Rare Books (Claude), Suffolk 228
Cox Rare Books (Charles), Cornwall............... 74
Craobh Rua Books, Co. Armagh................... 260
Criterion Books, London Outer..................... 182
Crouch Rare Books, Surrey.......................... 233
Cumming Limited (A. & Y.), East Sussex........ 104
D'Arcy Books, Wiltshire.............................. 252
Dalby (Richard), N Yorks 196
Dales & Lakes Book Centre, Cumbria............ 80
Darkwood Books, Co. Cork......................... 263
David (G.), Cambridgeshire.......................... 63
Davidson Books, Co. Down 261
De Burca Rare Books, Co. Dublin 264
Dean Byass, Bristol.................................... 60
Derek Stirling Bookseller, Kent 142
Dolphin Books, Suffolk............................... 226
Doolin Dinghy Books, Co. Clare 262
Driffield Bookshop (The), East Yorkshire 106
Duncan & Reid, Lothian 277
Dyson (Anthony), W Mids.......................... 240
Eastwood Books (David), Cornwall................ 73
Edrich (I.D.), London E.............................. 155
Edwards (Christopher), Berkshire.................. 55
Edwards (London) Limited (Francis),
London WC 177
Edwards in Hay-on-Wye (Francis), Powys 290
Elaine Lonsdale Books, West Yorkshire.......... 248
Elephant Books, West Yorkshire.................... 249
Ellis, Bookseller (Peter), London WC 178
Esoteric Dreams Bookshop, Cumbria 78
Eton Antique Bookshop, Berkshire................. 57
Ewell Bookshop Ltd, Surrey........................ 232
Farahar & Dupre (Clive & Sophie), Wiltshire ... 251
Ferdinando (Steven), Somerset 220
Fifteenth Century Bookshop (The), East Sussex. 104
Finch Rare Books Ltd. (Simon), London W. 173
Firsts in Print, Isle of Wight 134
Fortune Green Books, London NW................ 161
Fossgate Books, N Yorks 198
Foster (Stephen), London NW 161
Foster Bookshop (Paul), London SW............. 168
Fotheringham (Alex), Northumberland 202
Frew Limited (Robert), London W................. 173
Furneaux Books (Lee), Devon....................... 89
G. C. Books Ltd., Dumfries & Galloway......... 271
GfB: the Colchester Bookshop, Essex 109
Gibbs Books, (Jonathan), Worcs.................... 256
Gilbert and Son (H.M.), Hants...................... 126
Glenbower Books, Co. Dublin 265
Gloucester Road Bookshop, London SW 168
Glyn's Books, Shropshire............................. 213

Goldman (Paul), Dorset 94
Good for Books, Lincolnshire 151
Grahame Thornton, Bookseller, Dorset........... 93
Gregory (George), Somerset 216
Grove Bookshop (The), N Yorks................... 197
Hall's Bookshop, Kent................................ 141
Harrington (Adrian), London W.................... 173
Harrington Antiquarian Bookseller (Peter),
London SW... 169
Hart (John), Norfolk 187
Harvest Books, Lancashire........................... 145
Harwich Old Books, Essex........................... 110
Hava Books, London SE.............................. 165
Hawkes (James), London SE 165
Hennessey Bookseller (Ray), East Sussex......... 100
Heppa (Christopher), Essex 108
Heywood Hill Limited (G.), London W 174
Hollett and Son (R.F.G.), Cumbria 80
Holmes Books (Harry), East Yorkshire............ 107
House of Figgis Ltd (The), Co. Galway.......... 266
Howes Bookshop, East Sussex 102
Hünersdorff Rare Books, London SW............ 169
Hughes Rare Books (Spike), Borders.............. 268
Hunter-Rare Books (Andrew), London SW 169
Hurst (Jenny), Kent 138
Hutchison (Books) (Larry), Fife.................... 271
Ian McKelvie Bookseller, London N............... 159
Idle Genius Books, London N 159
Innes Books, Shropshire.............................. 214
Jackson (M.W.), Wiltshire............................ 254
Jane Jones Books, Grampian 272
Jarndyce Antiquarian Booksellers, London WC. 178
JB Books & Collectables, W Sussex 244
Jermy & Westerman, Notts 205
Jiri Books, Co. Antrim 260
Joel Segal Books, Devon 86
Johnson Rare Book Collections (C.R.),
London NW.. 162
Jonkers Rare Books, Oxfordshire................... 209
Judd Books, London WC 178
Just Books, Cornwall 76
Kalligraphia, Isle of Wight........................... 134
Karen Millward, Co. Cork........................... 263
Katnap Arts, Norfolk................................. 191
Kilgarriff (Raymond), East Sussex.................. 105
Killeen (John), N Yorks 194
Kingsgate Books & Prints, Hants................... 126
Kirkman Ltd., (Robert), Bedfordshire............. 54
L.M.S. Books, Herts 132
Lawson & Company (E.M.), Oxfordshire 208
Leabeck Books, Oxfordshire 210
Leigh Gallery Books, Essex 110
Lenton (Alfred), Leics................................. 147
Liddle (Steve), Bristol 58
Lloyd-Davies (Sue), Carmarthenshire 284
Lymelight Books & Prints, Dorset 93
Maggs Brothers Limited, London W............... 174
Maghreb Bookshop (The), London WC.......... 178
Main Point Books, Lothian........................... 278
Malvern Bookshop (The), Worcs 255
Mannwaring (M.G.), Bristol 59
Marks Limited (Barrie), London N................. 159
Marlborough Rare Books Ltd., London W...... 174
McCarty, Bookseller (M.E.),
Dumfries & Galloway.............................. 271

SPECIALITY INDEX

McCarty, Bookseller (M.E.), Western Isles 276
McCrone (Audrey), Isle of Arran 275
McNaughtan's Bookshop, Lothian 278
Mermaid Books (Burlingham), Norfolk........... 192
Mills Rare Books (Adam), Cambridgeshire 64
Minster Gate Bookshop, N Yorks.................. 199
Moreton Books, Devon............... 87
Morgan (H.J.), Bedfordshire 54
Mr. Pickwick of Towcester, Northants............ 201
Murch Booksend, (Herbert), London SE 166
Murphy (C.J.), Norfolk............................... 190
Naughton Booksellers, Co. Dublin 265
Needham Books, (Russell), Somerset.............. 220
Neeve (P.), Cambridgeshire 63
Niner (Marcus), Isle of Wight 134
Nineteenth Century Books, Oxfordshire 211
Nonsuch Books, Surrey............................... 234
Norton Books, N Yorks............................... 197
O'Brien Books & Photo Gallery, Co. Limerick.. 266
Offa's Dyke Books, Shropshire..................... 214
Old Aberdeen Bookshop, Grampian 277
Old Bookshop (The), W Mids.. 241
Old Town Bookshop (The), Lothian 278
Oopalba Books, Cheshire.. 71
Orangeberry Books, Oxfordshire 209
Orlando Booksellers, Lincolnshire 152
Over-Sands Books, Cumbria......................... 78
Oxfam Books and Music, Hants 126
Palladour Books, Hants 126
Paper Moon Books, Glos 116
Paper Pleasures, Somerset 219
Parker Books (Mike), Cambridgeshire 64
Parrott (Jeremy), London E......................... 156
Peter's Bookshop, Norfolk 192
Pickering & Chatto, London W..................... 175
Plurabelle Books, Cambridgeshire.................. 64
Polmorla Books, Cornwall 76
Pomes Penyeach, Staffordshire 224
Poor Richard's Books, Suffolk 227
Porter Bookshop (The), S Yorks................... 222
Price (John), London N 159
Pringle Booksellers (Andrew), Lothian 278
PsychoBabel Books & Journals, Oxfordshire..... 206
Quaritch Ltd., (Bernard), London W.............. 175
Quinto of Charing Cross Road, London WC ... 179
Quinto of Great Russell Street, London WC 179
R. & A. Books, East Sussex 102
Rainford (Sheila), Herts 130
Rassam (Paul), London NW 162
Reaveley Books, Devon 87
Rees & O'Neill Rare Books, London WC., ... 179
Richard Thornton Books, London N 160
Richmond Books, N Yorks........................... 195
Riderless Horse Books, Norfolk..................... 187
Ripping Yarns, London N 160
Robert Temple, London N........................... 160
Roberts Fine Books (Julian), Lincolnshire........ 153
Robin Doughty - Fine Books, W Mids 239
Rosley Books, Cumbria 81
Ross & Company Ltd., (Louise), Worcs.......... 255
Roundstone Books, Lancashire...................... 144
Rowan (P. & B.), Co. Antrim 260
Rye Old Books, East Sussex 104
St Philip's Books, Oxfordshire...................... 210
Saintfield Antiques & Fine Books, Co. Down ... 261

Samovar Books, Co. Dublin......................... 264
Sansovino Books, W Sussex 244
Scott (Peter), East Sussex............................ 104
Scrivener's Books & Bookbinding, Derbyshire... 82
Second Edition, Lothian.............................. 278
Shakespeare Books (Colin), Staffordshire......... 224
Sharpe (Mary), Somerset 221
Shelley (E. & J.), Buckinghamshire 61
Silverman (Michael), ... 166
Simpson (Dave), Stirlingshire 269
Siop Lyfrau'r Hen Bost, Gwynedd 287
Siop y Morfa, Denbighshire 286
Skelton (Tony), Kent.................................. 141
Skoob Russell Square, Suffolk...................... 230
Sokol Books Ltd., London W 175
Sotheran Limited (Henry), London W............ 176
Spelman (Ken), N Yorks............................. 199
Staffs Bookshop (The), Staffordshire 224
Staniland (Booksellers), Lincolnshire 154
Stern Antiquarian Bookseller (Jeffrey), N Yorks 199
Stevens (Joan), Cambridgeshire..................... 65
Stinton (Judith), Dorset.............................. 92
Stokes Books, Co. Dublin............................ 265
Stone Trough Books, N Yorks...................... 199
Sturford Books, Wiltshire 254
Surprise Books, Glos.................................. 113
Symes Books (Naomi), Cheshire 72
Talisman Books, Cheshire............................ 70
Tiffin (Tony and Gill), Durham 97
Tiger Books, Kent 137
Till's Bookshop, Lothian 279
Tindley & Chapman, London WC 179
Trafalgar Bookshop, East Sussex 100
Treasure Trove Books, Leics......................... 148
Trevorrow (Edwin), Herts 130
Trinity Rare Books, Co. Leitrim 266
Tucker (Alan & Joan), Glos 117
Uncle Phil's Books, W Mids......................... 240
Unsworth's Booksellers, London WC 180
Updike Rare Books (John), Lothian 279
Valentine Rare Books, London W.................. 176
Venables (Morris & Juliet), Bristol.................. 60
Ventnor Rare Books, Isle of Wight................. 135
Walden Books, London NW 163
Walker Fine Books (Steve), Dorset 92
War & Peace Books, Hants.......................... 122
Waterfield's, Oxfordshire 210
Waxfactor, East Sussex 100
Westcountry Old Books, Cornwall.................. 76
Westcountry Oldbooks, Devon...................... 90
Wetherell (Frances), Cambridgeshire 65
Wheen O'Books, Scottish Borders 269
Whig Books Ltd., Leics............................... 149
Whitehall Books, East Sussex........................ 103
Wilbraham (J. & S.), London NW 163
Williams Rare Books (Nigel), London WC 180
Willmott Bookseller (Nicholas), Cardiff........... 283
Wise (Derek), E Sussex 104
Wizard Books, Cambridgeshire...................... 67
Worlds End Bookshop, London SW 171
Wychwood Books, Glos............................... 116
Yates Antiquarian Books (Tony), Leics........... 148
Yesterday's Books, Dorset 92
Yesterday's News, Conwy 285

SPECIALITY INDEX

- 17TH CENTURY

Bennett & Kerr Books, Oxfordshire 206
Burmester (James), Bristol........................... 59
Cobnar Books, Kent 142
Dean Byass, Bristol................................... 60
Derek Stirling Bookseller, Kent 142
Fifteenth Century Bookshop (The), E Sussex 104
Joel Segal Books, Devon 86
Seydi Rare Books (Sevin), London NW 162
Stevens (Joan), Cambridgeshire..................... 65

- 19TH CENTURY

Alec-Smith Books (Alex), East Yorkshire 107
Atholl Fine Books, Tayside 281
babelog.books, Herefordshire 128
Book Business (The), London W 172
Boz Books, Powys.................................... 289
Budd (Richard), Somerset 219
Burmester (James), Bristol........................... 59
Cox Rare Books (Charles), Cornwall............... 74
Derek Stirling Bookseller, Kent 142
Dolphin Books, Suffolk............................... 226
Elaine Lonsdale Books, West Yorkshire 248
Ellis, Bookseller (Peter), London WC 178
Fifteenth Century Bookshop (The), E Sussex 104
Fortune Green Books, London NW................ 161
Foster Bookshop (Paul), London SW 168
Glenwood Books, Surrey 235
JB Books & Collectables, W Sussex 244
Joel Segal Books, Devon 86
Keith Langford, London E 155
Marble Hill Books, Middlesex 184
R. & A. Books, E Sussex............................. 102
Seydi Rare Books (Sevin), London NW 162
Sillan Books, Co. Cavan............................. 262
The Glass Key, West Yorkshire..................... 247
Valentine Rare Books, London W 176
Walden Books, London NW 163
Wheen O'Books, Scottish Borders 269
Wizard Books, Cambridgeshire..................... 67

- AFRICAN

Hawley (C.L.), N Yorks.............................. 197
Joel Segal Books, Devon 86
Kenya Books, E Sussex............................... 100
Stevens (Joan), Cambridgeshire..................... 65

- AFRICAN-AMERICAN

Black Voices, Merseyside 185
Chalmers Hallam (E.), Hants 125
Joel Segal Books, Devon 86
Stevens (Joan), Cambridgeshire..................... 65

- CANADIAN

Fifteenth Century Bookshop (The), E Sussex 104
Joel Segal Books, Devon 86
Stevens (Joan), Cambridgeshire..................... 65

- FRENCH

Anthony Sillem, E Sussex 102
Baldwin (Jack), Strathclyde 280
Budd (Richard), Somerset 219
Fifteenth Century Bookshop (The), E Sussex 104
Foyle Books, Co. Derry 260
Joel Segal Books, Devon 86

Seydi Rare Books (Sevin), London NW 162
Thorntons of Oxford Ltd., Oxfordshire 207

- GERMAN

IKON, Devon.. 89
Joel Segal Books, Devon 86
PsychoBabel Books & Journals, Oxfordshire..... 206
Seydi Rare Books (Sevin), London NW 162
Thorntons of Oxford Ltd., Oxfordshire 207

- IRISH

Ann & Mike Conry, Worcs.......................... 257
Budd (Richard), Somerset 219
Celtic Bookshop (The), Co. Limerick 266
Ellis, Bookseller (Peter), London WC 178
Fifteenth Century Bookshop (The), E Sussex 104
Foster Bookshop (Paul), London SW 168
Glenbower Books, Co. Dublin 265
Ian McKelvie Bookseller, London N 159
Jackson (M.W.), Wiltshire........................... 254
Joel Segal Books, Devon 86
Karen Millward, Co. Cork 263
Naughton Booksellers, Co. Dublin 265
Rowan (P. & B.), Co. Antrim 260
Skelton (Tony), Kent................................. 141
Stokes Books, Co. Dublin........................... 265

- NEW ZEALAND

Joel Segal Books, Devon 86

- PROLETARIAN

Left on The Shelf, Cumbria......................... 79
Northern Herald Books, West Yorkshire 246

- SCOTTISH

Armchair Books, Lothian 276
Atholl Fine Books, Tayside 281
Byre Books, Dumfries & Galloway 270
Cheshire Book Centre, Cheshire.................... 69
Cox Rare Books (Charles), Cornwall............... 74
David Houston - Bookseller, London E 155
Dolphin Books, Suffolk............................... 226
Fifteenth Century Bookshop (The), E Sussex 104
Grampian Books, Grampian......................... 274
Greta Books, Durham 97
Hutchison (Books) (Larry), Fife.................... 271
Ian McKelvie Bookseller, London N 159
Jane Jones Books, Grampian 272
Joel Segal Books, Devon 86
Loch Croispol Bookshop & Restaurant,
Highland 275
McCrone (Audrey), Isle of Arran 275
Orb's Bookshop, Grampian.................. 274
R. & A. Books, E Sussex............................. 102
Roberts Books, Ayrshire 280
Stroma Books, Borders 268
Thistle Books, Strathclyde........................... 280
Till's Bookshop, Lothian 279
Wheen O'Books, Scottish Borders 269

- SOUTH AFRICAN

Black Voices, Merseyside 185
Chalmers Hallam (E.), Hants....................... 125
Criterion Books, London Outer 182
Stevens (Joan), Cambridgeshire..................... 65

SPECIALITY INDEX

Yesterday's Books, Dorset 92

- SPANISH

Baldwin (Jack), Strathclyde 280
Hodgson (Judith), London W 174
Joel Segal Books, Devon 86
Orssich (Paul), London SW 170
Sturford Books, Wiltshire 254
York (Graham), Devon............................... 86

- VICTORIAN

Antique Map and Bookshop (The), Dorset 94
Apocalypse, Surrey 233
Beaton (Richard), E Sussex 103
Bell (Peter), Lothian 276
Brock Books, N Yorks 193
Burmester (James), Bristol.......................... 59
Cox Rare Books (Charles), Cornwall.............. 74
Derek Stirling Bookseller, Kent 142
Dolphin Books, Suffolk............................... 226
Ely Books, Cambridgeshire 65
Enigma Books, Norfolk 190
Fifteenth Century Bookshop (The), E Sussex 104
Jannlyce Antiquarian Booksellers, London WC. 178
Joel Segal Books, Devon 86
Parrott (Jeremy), London E......................... 156
Quest Booksearch, Cambridgeshire 65
R. & A. Books, E Sussex............................ 102
Robert Temple, London N........................... 160
Rosley Books, Cumbria 81
Seabreeze Books, Lancashire........................ 145
Smith Books, (Sally), Suffolk 227
South Downs Book Service, W Sussex 244
Symes Books (Naomi), Cheshire 72
Tiger Books, Kent 137
Tobo Books, Hants 123
Valentine Rare Books, London W 176
Wheen O'Books, Scottish Borders 269

- WESTERN AMERICAN

Americanabooksuk, Cumbria 77
Budd (Richard), Somerset 219
Fifteenth Century Bookshop (The), E Sussex 104
Stevens (Joan), Cambridgeshire..................... 65

LITERATURE IN TRANSLATION

AA1 Books, Dumfries & Galloway................. 270
Atlas, London N....................................... 158
babelog.books, Herefordshire 128
Books on Spain, London Outer 184
Burmester (James), Bristol.......................... 59
Chthonios Books, E Sussex 102
Fifteenth Century Bookshop (The), E Sussex 104
Hab Books, London W............................... 173
Hava Books, London SE............................. 165
Ian McKelvie Bookseller, London N 159
Joel Segal Books, Devon 86
Modern Welsh Publications Ltd., Merseyside.... 185
Naughton Booksellers, Co. Dublin 265
Parrott (Jeremy), London E......................... 156
Pholiota Books, London WC 179
Riderless Horse Books, Norfolk..................... 187
Robert Temple, London N........................... 160
Rosley Books, Cumbria 81
Stevens (Joan), Cambridgeshire..................... 65

Tiger Books, Kent 137
Tucker (Alan & Joan), Glos 117
Updike Rare Books (John), Lothian 279
Liturgics
Beckham Books Ltd., Suffolk 230
Bennett & Kerr Books, Oxfordshire 206
St Philip's Books, Oxfordshire...................... 210

LOCAL STUDIES - SUSSEX

Fifteenth Century Bookshop (The), E Sussex 104
Joel Segal Books, Devon 86
Mellon's Books, E Sussex 101
Muttonchop Manuscripts, W Sussex 244
R. & A. Books, E Sussex............................ 102

LOCKS & LOCKSMITHS

Baron (Christopher), Gr Man 118
Stroh (M.A.), London E 155

LOGGING/LUMBERING

Reeves Technical Books, N Yorks 196

LOGIC

Barcombe Services, Essex............................ 108
Joel Segal Books, Devon 86
Parkinsons Books, Merseyside...................... 186

LOST CIVILISATIONS

Apocalypse, Surrey 233
Byre Books, Dumfries & Galloway 270
Fifteenth Century Bookshop (The), E Sussex 104
R. & A. Books, E Sussex............................ 102

MAFIA

Bolland Books, Bedfordshire........................ 53
Booth (Booksearch Service), (Geoff), Cheshire... 68
Clifford Elmer Books Ltd., Cheshire 68
Loretta Lay Books, London NW 162

MAGAZINES & PERIODICALS - GENERAL

Anglo-American Rare Books, Surrey............... 233
Apocalypse, Surrey 233
Art Reference Books, Hants 125
Barnes (Peter), Wiltshire 253
Bianco Library, W Sussex 242
Black Cat Bookshop, Leics 147
Book Palace (The), London SE 164
Books & Collectables Ltd., Cambridgeshire 63
Books & Things, London W......................... 172
Border Bookshop, West Yorkshire 250
Bracton Books, Cambridgeshire 63
Brian Troath Books, London E 155
Derek Stirling Bookseller, Kent 142
Downie Fine Books Ltd., (Robert), Shropshire.. 215
Eggeling Books (John), West Yorkshire 250
Fosters Bookshop, London W 173
Franks Booksellers, Gr Man......................... 119
Green Meadow Books, Cornwall 74
Ken's Paper Collectables, Buckinghamshire 62
Mr. Pickwick of Towcester, Northants............ 201
Mulyan (Don), Merseyside 186
Naughton Booksellers, Co. Dublin 265
Norton Books, N Yorks.............................. 197
Nostalgia Unlimited, Merseyside 186

SPECIALITY INDEX

Palladour Books, Hants 126
Paper Pleasures, Somerset 219
Peter Lyons Books, Glos 114
Phenotype Books, Cumbria 80
Poetry Bookshop (The), Powys...................... 291
Reading Lasses, Dumfries & Galloway 271
Riderless Horse Books, Norfolk..................... 187
Robert Temple, London N........................... 160
Saintfield Antiques & Fine Books, Co. Down ... 261
Tennis Collectables, Cheshire 68
Tiger Books, Kent 137
Tilleys Vintage Magazine Shop, S Yorks 223
Tilleys Vintage Magazine Shop, Derbyshire 82
Tony Hutchinson, Surrey............................. 234
Updike Rare Books (John), Lothian 279
Williams (Bookdealer), (Richard), N Lincs....... 154
Williams Rare Books (Nigel), London WC 180
Words Etcetera Bookshop, Dorset.................. 93
Yesterday's News, Conwy 285
Yorkshire Relics, West Yorkshire................... 247

MAGAZINES - WOMEN'S

Black Cat Books, Norfolk............................ 188
Green Meadow Books, Cornwall 74
Judith Mansfield, West Yorkshire................... 250
Tilleys Vintage Magazine Shop, Derbyshire 82

MAGIC & CONJURING

Abrahams (Mike), Staffordshire 224
Books & Bygones (Pam Taylor), W Mids 241
Booth (Booksearch Service), (Geoff), Cheshire... 68
Cheshire Book Centre, Cheshire.................... 69
Drummond Pleasures of Past Times (David),
London WC 177
Edmund Pollinger Rare Books, London SW..... 167
Elgar (Raymond), E Sussex 99
Elmbury Books, Warwickshire 238
Fitzsimons (Anne), Cumbria 78
Franks Booksellers, Gr Man......................... 119
Game Advice, Oxfordshire 210
Harrington (Adrian), London W.................... 173
Joel Segal Books, Devon 86
N1 Books, E Sussex 105
St Swithin's Illustrated & Children's Books,
London W 175
Scrivener's Books & Bookbinding, Derbyshire... 82
Treasure Island (The), Gr Man...................... 119
Wiend Books, Lancashire 144
Wizard Books, Cambridgeshire..................... 67

MAGIC LANTERNS

R. & A. Books, E Sussex............................. 102
Stroh (M.A.), London E 155

MAGICK

Atlantis Bookshop, London WC................... 177
Bygone Books, Orkney 276
Inner Bookshop (The), Oxfordshire................ 210
Just Books, Cornwall 76
Old Celtic Bookshop (The), Devon 88
Star Lord Books, Gr Man 119
Treasure Island (The), Gr Man..................... 119

MAGNETICISM

Magis Books, Leics................................... 149

R. & A. Books, E Sussex............................. 102
Stroh (M.A.), London E 155
Weiner (Graham), London N 160

MALACOLOGY

Earth Science Books, Wiltshire 252
Parkinsons Books, Merseyside...................... 186

MAMMALS

Austwick Hall Books, N Yorks 193
Dales & Lakes Book Centre, Cumbria 80
Fifteenth Century Bookshop (The), E Sussex 104
Joel Segal Books, Devon 86
Kalligraphia, Isle of Wight 134
Mobbs (A.J.), W Mids............................... 241
Parkinsons Books, Merseyside...................... 186
Peter M Daly, Hants................................. 127
R. & A. Books, E Sussex............................. 102
Westons, Herts 133

MANAGEMENT

Bob Mallory (Books), Derbyshire.................. 83
Cornucopia Books, Lincolnshire 153
Northern Herald Books, West Yorkshire.......... 246
Reading Lasses, Dumfries & Galloway 271

MANUALS

Cornucopia Books, Lincolnshire 153
Elmbury Books, Warwickshire 238
MilitaryHistoryBooks.com, Kent................... 138

MANUALS - SEAMANSHIP (SEE ALSO UNDER SEAMANSHIP)

Cheshire Book Centre, Cheshire.................... 69
Elmbury Books, Warwickshire 238
Footrope Knots, Suffolk............................. 228
Greta Books, Durham 97
Joel Segal Books, Devon 86
Lewcock (John), Cambridgeshire................... 66
Marine & Cannon Books, Cheshire 71
Marine and Cannon Books, Cheshire 69
McLaren Books, Strathclyde........................ 280
Milestone Books, Devon 89
Nautical Antique Centre (The), Dorset 96

MANUFACTURING

Parkinsons Books, Merseyside...................... 186
Susanne Schulz-Falster Rare Books, London N. 160

MANUSCRIPTS

Aitchison (Lesley), Bristol 58
Apocalypse, Surrey 233
Bertram Rota Ltd., London WC 177
Biblion, London W................................... 172
Bookstand, Dorset.................................... 94
Bristow & Garland, Hants 122
Cox Music (Lisa), Devon............................ 86
Cox Rare Books (Charles), Cornwall.............. 74
Davids Ltd., (Roy), Oxfordshire 209
De Burca Rare Books, Co. Dublin 264
Dean Byass, Bristol................................... 60
Drury Rare Books (John), Essex................... 110
Elmbury Books, Warwickshire 238
Farahar & Dupre (Clive & Sophie), Wiltshire ... 251
Finch Rare Books Ltd. (Simon), London W..... 173

SPECIALITY INDEX

Fogg Rare Books & Manuscripts (Sam), London W .... 173 Ford (Richard), London W .... 173 Gekoski (R.A.), London WC .... 178 Golden Books Group, Devon .... 85 Heath (A.R.), Bristol .... 59 Hodgson (Judith), London W .... 174 Humber Books, Lincolnshire .... 150 Hunter–Rare Books (Andrew), London SW ..... 169 James Fergusson Books & Manuscripts, London W .... 174 Jarndyce Antiquarian Booksellers, London WC. 178 John Underwood Antiquarian Books, Norfolk .. 190 Ken's Paper Collectables, Buckinghamshire ...... 62 Kenny's Bookshops and Art Galleries Ltd, Co. Galway .... 266 Kunkler Books (Paul), Cambridgeshire .... 64 Lucius Books, N Yorks............................... 199 Maggs Brothers Limited, London W............... 174 Marine & Cannon Books, Cheshire .... 71 Marine and Cannon Books, Cheshire .... 69 Neil Summersgill, Lancashire .... 113 Pickering & Chatto, London W .... 175 Quaritch Ltd., (Bernard), London W............... 175 Rassam (Paul), London NW .... 162 Rowan (P. & B.), Co. Antrim .... 260 Seydi Rare Books (Sevin), London NW .... 162 Silverman (Michael), ... 166 Spelman (Ken), N Yorks .... 199 Taylor & Son (Peter), Herts......................... 133 Townsend (John), Berkshire .... 57 Tyger Press, London N .... 160 Williams Rare Books (Nigel), London WC ...... 180 Wilson (Manuscripts) Ltd., (John), Glos.......... 114

MAORI

Empire Books, N Yorks.............................. 198

MAPS & MAPMAKING

Altea Antique Maps & Books, London W .... 172 Anthony Vickers Books, N Yorks .... 196 Arthur Hook, Bristol.................................. 58 Baynton–Williams Gallery, W Sussex .... 242 Bookshop on the Heath, The, London SE .... 164 Chas J. Sawyer, Kent .... 141 Chris Phillips, Wiltshire .... 251 Colin Hancock, Ceredigion .... 284 Cornell Books, Glos................................... 117 Empire Books, N Yorks.............................. 198 Fifteenth Century Bookshop (The), E Sussex .... 104 Frew Limited (Robert), London W................. 173 Garwood & Voigt, Kent.............................. 140 Grahame Thornton, Bookseller, Dorset........... 93 Grove Bookshop (The), N Yorks .... 197 Harlequin Gallery, Lincolnshire .... 152 Just Books, Cornwall .... 76 Kalligraphia, Isle of Wight .... 134 Moorside Books, Lancashire........................ 144 Mulyan (Don), Merseyside .... 186 R. & A. Books, E Sussex............................ 102 Robin Doughty - Fine Books, W Mids .... 239 Roz Hulse, Conwy .... 286 Stalagluft Books, Tyne and Wear .... 236 Vickers (Anthony), N Yorks......................... 196

MARINE SCIENCES

Arden, Bookseller (C.), Powys...................... 289 Baldwin's Scientific Books, Essex .... 112 Cheshire Book Centre, Cheshire.................... 69 Elmbury Books, Warwickshire .... 238 Kalligraphia, Isle of Wight .... 134 Parkinsons Books, Merseyside...................... 186 R. & A. Books, E Sussex............................ 102 Sub Aqua Prints and Books, Hants 123

MARITIME/NAUTICAL

Alba Books, Grampian .... 274 All Books, Essex .... 110 Altea Antique Maps & Books, London W .... 172 Anchor Books, Lincolnshire .... 151 Andron (G.W.), London N .... 158 Anthony Vickers Books, N Yorks .... 196 Anvil Books, W Mids................................. 240 Arden Books & Cosmographia, Warwickshire... 237 Argent (Alan), Isle of Wight .... 135 Armitage (Booksearch), (Kate), Devon .... 85 Aviabooks, Glos .... 114 Axe Rare & Out of Print Books (Richard), N Yorks .... 194 Baldwin (M. & M.), Worcs .... 255 Barbican Bookshop, N Yorks .... 198 Barmby (C. & A.J.), Kent........................... 141 Books Afloat, Dorset.................................. 96 Bookworm, Lothian................................... 277 Bosorne Books, Cornwall .... 75 Bott, (Bookdealers) Ltd., (Martin), Gr Man ..... 118 Broadhurst of Southport Ltd., Merseyside .... 186 Browsers Bookshop, Cornwall...................... 73 Burebank Books, Norfolk .... 187 Burroughs (Andrew), Lincolnshire .... 153 Butterworth (Robert F.), Lancashire .... 145 Cavendish Rare Books, London N .... 158 Cheshire Book Centre, Cheshire.................... 69 Cofion Books, Pembrokeshire .... 288 Collectables (W.H.), Suffolk .... 230 Collectors Carbooks, Northants..................... 200 Colonsay Bookshop, Isle of Colonsay............. 276 Compass Books, Devon .... 85 Cornucopia Books, Lincolnshire .... 153 Cox (Geoff), Devon .... 90 Crouch Rare Books, Surrey......................... 233 Curtle Mead Books, Isle of Wight .... 134 D'Arcy Books, Wiltshire............................. 252 Dartmoor Bookshop (The), Devon .... 84 Discovery Bookshop, Carmarthenshire............ 283 Dolphin Books, Suffolk .... 226 Duck (William), Hants............................... 124 Elmbury Books, Warwickshire .... 238 Elton Engineering Books, London W.............. 173 Embleton (Paul), Essex .... 111 Ewell Bookshop Ltd, Surrey .... 232 Falconwood Transport & Military Bookshop, London Outer .... 184 Fifteenth Century Bookshop (The), E Sussex .... 104 Fireside Bookshop, Cumbria........................ 81 Fisher Nautical, E Sussex .... 100 Footrope Knots, Suffolk............................. 228 Fox Books (J. & J.), Kent........................... 140 G. C. Books Ltd., Dumfries & Galloway......... 271 George St. Books, Derbyshire 83

SPECIALITY INDEX

Gerald Lee Maritime Books, E Sussex............ 105
Green Ltd. (G.L.), Herts 132
Greta Books, Durham 97
Guildmaster Books, Cheshire 70
Hall's Bookshop, Kent................................ 141
Harlequin Books, Bristol 59
Harrington Antiquarian Bookseller (Peter),
London SW.. 169
Hay Cinema Bookshop Ltd., Powys............... 290
Helion & Company, W Mids........................ 240
Henry Wilson Books, Cheshire 69
High Street Books, Devon 86
Holdenhurst Books, Dorset 91
Island Books, Devon.................................. 85
J & J Burgess Booksellers, Cambridgeshire....... 64
Joel Segal Books, Devon 86
Just Books, Cornwall 76
Kalligraphia, Isle of Wight.......................... 134
Keegan's Bookshop, Berkshire 56
Kellow Books, Oxfordshire 207
Kerr (Norman), Cumbria 78
Kirkman Ltd., (Robert), Bedfordshire............. 54
Lamb's Tales Books, Devon 87
Larkham Books (Patricia), Glos.................... 117
Lawrence Books, Notts............................... 204
Lewcock (John), Cambridgeshire................... 66
Lost Books, Northants................................ 201
Marcet Books, London SE........................... 165
Marine & Cannon Books, Cheshire 69, 71
Marine Workshop Bookshop, Dorset 93
Martin Bookshop & Gallery (Richard), Hants... 123
McCarty, Bookseller (M.E.),
Dumfries & Galloway.............................. 271
McCarty, Bookseller (M.E.), Western Isles....... 276
McConnell Fine Books, Kent........................ 137
McCrone (Audrey), Isle of Arran................... 275
McLaren Books, Strathclyde........................ 280
Michael J Carroll, Co. Cork 263
Milestone Books, Devon 89
Military Parade Bookshop, Wiltshire.............. 252
Mothergoose Bookshop, Isle of Wight 135
Mulyan (Don), Merseyside.......................... 186
My Back Pages, London SW 169
Nautical Antique Centre (The), Dorset 96
Nelson (Elizabeth), Suffolk.......................... 227
Oasis Booksearch, Cambridgeshire................. 67
Parrott Books, Oxfordshire 211
Paton Books, Herts................................... 132
Peter M Daly, Hants................................. 127
Portus Books, Hants 122
Prior (Michael), Lincolnshire 153
Quentin Books Ltd, Essex........................... 109
R. & A. Books, E Sussex............................ 102
Read (C.&J.), Gorleston Books, Norfolk 188
Richmond Books, North Yorkshire 195
Roadmaster Books, Kent............................ 137
Rods Books, Devon................................... 88
Roz Hulse, Conwy 286
Saintfield Antiques & Fine Books, Co. Down ... 261
Sansovino Books, W Sussex 244
Sea Chest Nautical Bookshop (The), Devon 88
Simmonds (Anthony J.), London SE............... 166
Smith Maritime Aviation Books (Frank),
Tyne and Wear...................................... 236
Stella Books, Monmouthshire 288

Stroma Books, Borders 268
Sub Aqua Prints and Books, Hants 123
Suffolk Rare Books, Suffolk 230
Taylor & Son (Peter), Herts......................... 133
Tilston (Stephen E.), London SE................... 166
Treasure Island (The), Gr Man..................... 119
Trinders' Fine Tools, Suffolk 227
Vanstone - Aviation Books, (Derek), Suffolk 230
Vickers (Anthony), North Yorkshire 196
War & Peace Books, Hants......................... 122
Warsash Nautical Bookshop, Hants............... 126
Wiend Books, Lancashire 144
Wise (Derek), E Sussex 104
World War Books, Kent 141

MARITIME/NAUTICAL - HISTORY

Aardvark Books, Wiltshire.......................... 254
Anchor Books, Lincolnshire 151
Baynton–Williams Gallery, W Sussex 242
books2books, Devon.................................. 88
Bookworm, Lothian................................... 277
Bott, (Bookdealers) Ltd., (Martin), Gr Man 118
Browsers Bookshop, Cornwall...................... 73
Cornucopia Books, Lincolnshire 153
Cox (Geoff), Devon 90
Deeside Books, Grampian........................... 273
Ewell Bookshop Ltd, Surrey........................ 232
Falconwood Transport & Military Bookshop,
London Outer.. 184
Fifteenth Century Bookshop (The), E Sussex 104
Gerald Lee Maritime Books, E Sussex............ 105
Handsworth Books, Essex........................... 112
Joel Segal Books, Devon 86
Keel Row Bookshop, Tyne and Wear 236
Lost Books, Northants............................... 201
Marine & Cannon Books, Cheshire 71
Marine and Cannon Books, Cheshire 69
Martin Bookshop & Gallery (Richard), Hants... 123
Michael J Carroll, Co. Cork 263
MilitaryHistoryBooks.com, Kent................... 138
Oasis Booksearch, Cambridgeshire................. 67
R. & A. Books, E Sussex............................ 102
Read (C.&J.), Gorleston Books, Norfolk 188
Robert Humm & Co, Lincolnshire 154
Rods Books, Devon................................... 88
Sax Books, Suffolk 229
Sub Aqua Prints and Books, Hants 123
Wadard Books, Kent 138

MARITIME/NAUTICAL - LOG BOOKS

Aardvark Books, Wiltshire.......................... 254
Anchor Books, Lincolnshire 151
Gerald Lee Maritime Books, E Sussex............ 105
Hicks (Ronald C.), Cornwall 73
Marine & Cannon Books, Cheshire 71
Marine and Cannon Books, Cheshire 69
Martin Bookshop & Gallery (Richard), Hants... 123
McLaren Books, Strathclyde........................ 280
Nautical Antique Centre (The), Dorset 96
Stroh (M.A.), London E 155
Tyger Press, London N.............................. 160
Warsash Nautical Bookshop, Hants............... 126

MARQUE HISTORIES (SEE ALSO MOTORING)

Burroughs (Andrew), Lincolnshire 153
Collectors Carbooks, Northants..................... 200
Falconwood Transport & Military Bookshop,
London Outer 184
Fylde Books, Lancashire 146
Joel Segal Books, Devon 86
Kenneth Ball, E Sussex 101
Knowles (John), Norfolk 188
Pooks Motor Books, Leics 148
Roadmaster Books, Kent............................. 137

MARXISM

Books Only, Suffolk 227
Delectus Books, London WC........................ 177
Hab Books, London W............................... 173
Joel Segal Books, Devon 86
Killeen (John), North Yorkshire 194
Left on The Shelf, Cumbria............. 79
Northern Herald Books, West Yorkshire 246
Parkinsons Books, Merseyside............ 186
Reading Lasses, Dumfries & Galloway 271
Red Star Books, Herts................................ 130
Spurrier (Nick), Kent 138
Susanne Schulz-Falster Rare Books, London N. 160
Treasure Trove Books, Leics........................ 148
Woburn Books, London N 160

MATHEMATICS

Barcombe Services, Essex............................ 108
Baron - Scientific Book Sales (P.J.), Somerset ... 217
Camden Books, Somerset 216
Chesters (G. & J.), Staffordshire 225
Eagle Bookshop (The), Bedfordshire 53
Ely Books, Cambridgeshire 65
Esplin (David), Hants................................. 124
Game Advice, Oxfordshire 210
GtB: the Colchester Bookshop, Essex 109
Glenbower Books, Co. Dublin 265
Hadfield (G.K.), Cumbria 80
Hinchliffe Books, Bristol.............................. 59
Holtom (Christopher), Cornwall 75
Hunter–Rare Books (Andrew), London SW 169
Hurst (Jenny), Kent 138
Joel Segal Books, Devon 86
John Gorton Booksearch, E Sussex 105
Moorside Books, Lancashire......................... 144
Parkinsons Books, Merseyside.................. 186
Phelps (Michael), West Sussex...................... 243
Pickering & Chatto, London W..................... 175
Roberts Books, Ayrshire 280
Skoob Russell Square, Suffolk...................... 230
Stroh (M.A.), London E 155
Susanne Schulz-Falster Rare Books, London N. 160
Taylor & Son (Peter), Herts.......................... 133
Transformer, Dumfries & Galloway................ 271
Treasure Trove Books, Leics........................ 148
Turret House, Norfolk................................ 192
Wayside Books and Cards, Oxfordshire 207
Westons, Herts 133
Westwood Books (Mark), Powys 291
Westwood Books Ltd, Cumbria..................... 80
Whistler's Books, London SW 170

MAYFLOWER VOYAGE OF 1620

R. & A. Books, E Sussex............................. 102

MECHANICAL ENGINEERING

Brad Books, Essex 111
Elton Engineering Books, London W 173
N1 Books, E Sussex................................... 105
Parkinsons Books, Merseyside....................... 186
Phelps (Michael), West Sussex...................... 243
Robert Humm & Co, Lincolnshire 154
Stroh (M.A.), London E 155
Treasure Island (The), Gr Man...................... 119
Westons, Herts 133

MEDIA

Aurora Books Ltd, Lothian........................... 276
Barcombe Services, Essex............................ 108
Cornucopia Books, Lincolnshire 153
Greenroom Books, West Yorkshire 248
Joel Segal Books, Devon 86
Judd Books, London WC 178
Kelly Books, Devon................................... 89
Morris Secondhand & Antiquarian Books
(Chris), Oxfordshire 210
Murch Booksend, (Herbert), London SE 166
My Back Pages, London SW 169
Reading Lasses, Dumfries & Galloway 271

MEDICINE

Alba Books, Grampian 274
Axe Rare & Out of Print Books (Richard),
North Yorkshire 194
Barcombe Services, Essex............................ 108
Baron - Scientific Book Sales (P.J.), Somerset ... 217
Bernard Dixon and Kath Adams, Middlesex 183
Beware of the Leopard, Bristol...................... 58
Bibliophile (The), S Yorks..... 222
Bookshop (The), Co. Donegal...................... 263
Bracton Books, Cambridgeshire..................... 63
Carta Regis, Powys................................... 293
Cheshire Book Centre, Cheshire.................... 69
Childrens Bookshop, West Yorkshire 248
Collectable Books, London SE 165
Dean Byass, Bristol................................... 60
Dunstan Books, Dorset............................... 91
Edwards (London) Limited (Francis),
London WC 177
Edwards in Hay–on–Wye (Francis), Powys 290
Erian Books, London N 158
Flnch Rare Books Ltd. (Simon), London W..... 173
Game Advice, Oxfordshire 210
Gaskell Rare Books (Roger), Cambridgeshire ... 66
Glenbower Books, Co. Dublin 265
Grahame Thornton, Bookseller, Dorset........... 93
Hay Cinema Bookshop Ltd., Powys............... 290
Hünersdorff Rare Books, London SW............ 169
Hunter–Rare Books (Andrew), London SW 169
Kalligraphia, Isle of Wight.......................... 134
Lawson & Company (E.M.), Oxfordshire 208
Macfarlane (Mr. H.), Essex 112
Orchid Book Distributors, Co. Clare.............. 262
Outcast Books, Powys 291
Parkinsons Books, Merseyside...................... 186
Phelps (Michael), West Sussex...................... 243
Phillips (Nigel), Hants................................ 122

SPECIALITY INDEX

Pickering & Chatto, London W.................... 175
Pollak (P.M.), Devon 89
Portobello Books, London W 175
Pratt (B.A. & C.W.M.), Herefordshire 128
Prospect House Books, Co. Down.................. 261
PsychoBabel Books & Journals, Oxfordshire..... 206
Quaritch Ltd., (Bernard), London W............... 175
Quinto of Charing Cross Road, London WC ... 179
Quinto of Great Russell Street, London WC 179
R M Books, Herts..................................... 132
Scrivener's Books & Bookbinding, Derbyshire... 82
Second Edition, Lothian.............................. 278
Smith (Clive), Essex 109
Smith (David & Lynn), London Outer............. 182
Stern Antiquarian Bookseller (Jeffrey), N Yorks 199
Stroh (M.A.), London E 155
Treasure Island (The), Gr Man..................... 119
Turret House, Norfolk................................ 192
Village Books, Norfolk 187
Weiner (Graham), London N 160
Westons, Herts 133
Westwood Books (Mark), Powys 291
Westwood Books Ltd, Cumbria..................... 80
Wheen O'Books, Scottish Borders 269
White (David), Cambridgeshire..................... 65
Worcester Rare Books, Worcs....................... 257

MEDICINE - HISTORY OF

Alba Books, Grampian 274
Baldwin's Scientific Books, Essex 112
Barcombe Services, Essex............................ 108
Bernard Dixon and Kath Adams, Middlesex 183
Biblion, London W.................................... 172
Cheshire Book Centre, Cheshire.................... 69
Chesters (G. & J.), Staffordshire 225
Childrens Bookshop, West Yorkshire 248
Dean Byass, Bristol................................... 60
Empire Books, North Yorkshire 198
Erian Books, London N.............................. 158
Esplin (David), Hants................................ 124
Fireside Bookshop, Cumbria........................ 81
Game Advice, Oxfordshire 210
Hunter-Rare Books (Andrew), London SW 169
Joel Segal Books, Devon 86
Kingswood Books, Dorset 94
London & Sussex Antiquarian Book
& Print Services, E Sussex......................... 101
Maggs Brothers Limited, London W............... 174
Mair Wilkes Books, Fife 272
Meekins Books (Paul), Warwickshire.............. 238
Parkinsons Books, Merseyside...................... 186
Phelps (Michael), West Sussex...................... 243
Pordes Books Ltd., (Henry), London WC........ 179
PsychoBabel Books & Journals, Oxfordshire..... 206
R M Books, Herts..................................... 132
R. & A. Books, E Sussex............................. 102
Rowan (P. & B.), Co. Antrim 260
Smith (David & Lynn), London Outer............. 182
Stroh (M.A.), London E 155
Sue Lowell Natural History Books, London W . 176
Taylor & Son (Peter), Herts......................... 133
Westons, Herts 133
Westwood Books (Mark), Powys 291
White (David), Cambridgeshire..................... 65

MEDIEVAL

Alexander's Books, Warwickshire................... 238
Bennett & Kerr Books, Oxfordshire................ 206
Byre Books, Dumfries & Galloway................. 270
Camden Books, Somerset 216
Crouch Rare Books, Surrey......................... 233
Du Ry Medieval Manuscripts (Marc-Antoine),
London W.. 173
Fifteenth Century Bookshop (The), E Sussex.... 104
Gildas Books, Cheshire 68
Grampian Books, Grampian......................... 274
Hobgoblin Books, Hants 125
Jackdaw Books, Norfolk 189
Joel Segal Books, Devon 86
John Underwood Antiquarian Books, Norfolk.. 190
Kingswood Books, Dorset 94
Lost Books, Northants................................ 201
medievalbookshop, Herts............................ 133
Meekins Books (Paul), Warwickshire.............. 238
Michael J Carroll, Co. Cork 263
MilitaryHistoryBooks.com, Kent................... 138
N1 Books, E Sussex................................... 105
Priestpopple Books, Northumberland 202
St Philip's Books, Oxfordshire...................... 210
Samovar Books, Co. Dublin......................... 264
Sandpiper Books Ltd., London SW 170
Spenceley Books (David), West Yorkshire........ 249
Taylor & Son (Peter), Herts......................... 133
Unsworth's Booksellers, London WC 163, 180
Winghale Books, Lincolnshire 153

MEMOIRS

Bell (Peter), Lothian.................................. 276
Brimstones, E Sussex................................. 103
Cornucopia Books, Lincolnshire 153
Darkwood Books, Co. Cork......................... 263
Discovery Bookshop, Carmarthenshire............ 283
Dolphin Books, Suffolk............................... 226
Fifteenth Century Bookshop (The), E Sussex 104
Hab Books, London W............................... 173
Jackdaw Books, Norfolk 189
Joel Segal Books, Devon 86
Kirkpatrick (Robert J.), London W 174
Marine & Cannon Books, Cheshire 71
Marine and Cannon Books, Cheshire 69
Mr. Pickwick of Towcester, Northants............ 201
N V Books, Warwickshire............................ 237
Samovar Books, Co. Dublin......................... 264

MEMORABILIA

Art Reference Books, Hants 125
Collectors Carbooks, Northants..................... 200
Dally Books & Collectables, Powys................ 292
Embleton (Paul), Essex 111
firstpagebooks, Norfolk.............................. 190
Kent T. G., Surrey 231
Morris Secondhand & Antiquarian Books
(Chris), Oxfordshire 210
R. & A. Books, E Sussex............................. 102
Tyger Press, London N............................... 160

METAPHYSICS

Alpha Books, London N 158
Barcombe Services, Essex............................ 108
Chthonios Books, E Sussex 102

SPECIALITY INDEX

Greensleeves, Oxfordshire 207
Inner Bookshop (The), Oxfordshire................ 210
Old Celtic Bookshop (The), Devon 88
R. & A. Books, E Sussex............................. 102
SETI Books, Staffordshire............................ 225
Star Lord Books, Gr Man 119
Trinity Rare Books, Co. Leitrim 266

METEOROLOGY

Joel Segal Books, Devon 86
Parkinsons Books, Merseyside...................... 186
Periplus Books, Buckinghamshire................... 62

MEXICANA

Baldwin (Jack), Strathclyde 280
Hodgson (Judith), London W 174
Orssich (Paul), London SW 170

MICROSCOPY

Baron (Christopher), Gr Man 118
Bernard Dixon and Kath Adams, Middlesex 183
Hadfield (G.K.), Cumbria............................ 80
Phelps (Michael), West Sussex...................... 243
R M Books, Herts..................................... 132
Stroh (M.A.), London E 155
Turret House, Norfolk................................ 192
Westons, Herts 133

MILITARY - GENERAL

Aardvark Books, Wiltshire........................... 254
Abacus Gallery, Staffordshire....................... 224
Addyman Annexe (The), Powys.................... 289
Addyman Books, Powys.............................. 289
Alauda Books, Cumbria.............................. 78
Albion Books, W Mids............................... 239
Allinson (Frank & Stella), Warwickshire 237
Anchor Books, Lincolnshire 151
Andrew Morton (Books), Powys.................... 289
Andron (G.W.), London N 158
Anglo-American Rare Books, Surrey.............. 233
Antiquary Ltd., (Bar Bookstore), N Yorks....... 196
Antique Map and Bookshop (The), Dorset 94
Apocalypse, Surrey 233
Ardis Books, Hants 126
Armchair Auctions, Hants 121
Austen (Phillip), Lincolnshire 153
Aviabooks, Glos 114
Axe Rare & Out of Print Books (Richard),
North Yorkshire 194
B D McManmon, Lancashire 145
Baldwin (M. & M.), Worcs 255
Barbican Bookshop, North Yorkshire............. 198
Barn Books, Buckinghamshire...................... 61
Barnes (Peter), Wiltshire 253
Bath Old Books, Somerset 216
Big Bairn Books, Tayside 281
Blacket Books, Lothian............................... 277
Boer War Books, North Yorkshire 198
Bonner (John), West Yorkshire 249
Book Business (The), London W 172
Books, Denbighshire 286
Books & Collectables Ltd., Cambridgeshire...... 63
Books Bought & Sold, Surrey 232
Books Plus, Devon 84
Bookworm, Lothian................................... 277

Bookworm, Essex...................................... 110
Bookworm (The), Lothian 277
Bookworms of Evesham, Worcs 257
Booth (Booksearch Service), (Geoff), Cheshire... 68
Booth Books, Powys 289
Border Books, Borders............................... 268
Bosco Books, Cornwall............................... 73
Brazenhead Ltd., Norfolk 189
Broadhurst of Southport Ltd., Merseyside 186
Browsers Bookshop, Cornwall...................... 73
Bufo Books, Hants.................................... 125
Burroughs (Andrew), Lincolnshire 153
Cader Idris Books, Powys........................... 292
Caliver Books, Essex 110
Camilla's Bookshop, E Sussex...................... 101
Cassidy (Bookseller) (P.), Lincolnshire 153
Castleton (Pat), Kent................................. 138
Cavern Books, Cheshire 70
Central Bookshop, Warwickshire 238
Chaucer Bookshop, Kent............................ 136
Chelifer Books, Cumbria 81
Cheshire Book Centre, Cheshire.................... 69
Chevin Books, West Yorkshire...................... 250
Clent Books, Worcs 255
Coach House Books, Worcs 256
Cobweb Books, North Yorkshire 195
Cofion Books, Pembrokeshire 288
Coles (T.V.), Cambridgeshire 67
Collectors Corner, Wiltshire......................... 253
Cornucopia Books, Lincolnshire 153
Cotswold Internet Books, Glos..................... 113
Cox (Geoff), Devon 90
D'Arcy Books, Wiltshire............................. 252
Dally Books & Collectables, Powys................ 292
Dartmoor Bookshop (The), Devon 84
Deeside Books, Grampian........................... 273
Devanha Military Books, Tayside 281
Discovery Bookshop, Carmarthenshire........... 283
Donovan Military Books (Tom), E Sussex 99
Eastern Traveller (The), Somerset.................. 220
Eastgate Bookshop, East Yorkshire 106
Edwards (London) Limited (Francis),
London WC 177
Edwards in Hay-on-Wye (Francis), Powys 290
Embleton (Paul), Essex 111
Empire Books, North Yorkshire 198
Eton Antique Bookshop, Berkshire................ 57
Fackley Services, Notts 205
Falconwood Transport & Military Bookshop,
London Outer..................................... 184
Farnborough Gallery, Hants........................ 122
Fifteenth Century Bookshop (The), E Sussex 104
Fireside Bookshop, Cumbria........................ 81
Ford Books (David), Herts 133
Fox Books (J. & J.), Kent............................ 140
Freeman's Corner Shop, Norfolk 190
G. C. Books Ltd., Dumfries & Galloway......... 271
Gallimaufry Books, Herts 132
Gaullifmaufry Books, Herts......................... 132
Grahame Thornton, Bookseller, Dorset........... 93
Grove Bookshop (The), North Yorkshire 197
Hall's Bookshop, Kent............................... 141
Hancock (Peter), West Sussex 243
Harlequin Books, Bristol 59
Harris (George J.), Co. Derry 260

SPECIALITY INDEX

Heartland Old Books, Devon........................ 89
Helion & Company, W Mids....................... 240
High Street Books, Devon 86
Hill (John S.), Devon 86
Holdenhurst Books, Dorset 91
Hünersdorff Rare Books, London SW............ 169
hullbooks.com, East Yorkshire 107
Hurst (Jenny), Kent 138
Hutchison (Books) (Larry), Fife.................... 271
Internet Bookshop UK Ltd., Glos.................. 113
Invicta Bookshop, Berkshire 56
Island Books, Devon.................................. 85
Joel Segal Books, Devon 86
Joppa Books Ltd., Surrey 231
Just Books, Cornwall 76
Keegan's Bookshop, Berkshire 56
Keel Row Bookshop, Tyne and Wear 236
Kenya Books, E Sussex............................... 100
Lamb's Tales Books, Devon 87
Last Century Books, Borders....................... 268
Lawrence Books, Notts 204
Lost Books, Northants................................ 201
Malvern Bookshop (The), Worcs 255
Mandalay Bookshop, London SW 169
Marcet Books, London SE........................... 165
Marine & Cannon Books, Cheshire 71
Marine and Cannon Books, Cheshire 69
McCrone (Audrey), Isle of Arran 275
Meads Book Service (The), E Sussex.............. 104
Meekins Books (Paul), Warwickshire............. 238
Military Bookworm, London SE.................... 165
MilitaryHistoryBooks.com, Kent................... 138
Morley Case, Hants 125
Mothergoose Bookshop, Isle of Wight............ 135
Mundy (David), Herts 130
My Back Pages, London SW 169
N1 Books, E Sussex................................... 105
Nelson (Elizabeth), Suffolk 227
Old Aberdeen Bookshop, Grampian 272
Palladour Books, Hants 126
Park Gallery & Bookshop (The), Northants 201
Parker Books (Mike), Cambridgeshire 64
Parlour Bookshop (The), Oxfordshire............. 207
Paton Books, Herts................................... 132
Pedlar's Pack Books, Devon 84
Prior (Michael), Lincolnshire 153
Queen Victoria PH, Torfaen 294
Quinto of Great Russell Street, London WC 179
R. & A Books, E Sussex............................. 102
Read (C.&J.), Gorleston Books, Norfolk......... 188
Readers World, W Mids............................. 239
Richard Thornton Books, London N 160
Rickaro Books, West Yorkshire..................... 247
Rods Books, Devon................................... 88
Royal Carbery Books Ltd., Co. Cork.............. 262
St Swithin's Illustrated & Children's
Books, London W 175
Saintfield Antiques & Fine Books, Co. Down ... 261
Samovar Books, Co. Dublin 264
Sansovino Books, West Sussex 244
Saracen Books, Derbyshire.......................... 83
Savery Books, E Sussex.............................. 99
Scrivener's Books & Bookbinding, Derbyshire... 82
Seabreeze Books, Lancashire........................ 145
Sedgeberrow Books & Framing, Worcs........... 256

Shacklock Books (David), Suffolk 227
Shakeshaft (Dr. B.), Cheshire....................... 71
Sidey, Bookdealer (Philip), Kent 140
Silver Trees Books, W Mids 240
Skoob Russell Square, Suffolk...................... 230
Smith (Clive), Essex 109
Smith Books (Keith), Herefordshire 128
Spink, London WC 179
Spooner (John E.), Dorset 91
Stella Books, Monmouthshire 288
Stroma Books, Borders 268
Suffolk Rare Books, Suffolk 230
Sutcliffe (Victor), Norfolk 188
Tarka Books, Devon.................................. 84
The Sanctuary Bookshop, Dorset.................. 94
Tiffin (Tony and Gill), Durham..................... 97
Tilston (Stephen E.), London SE................... 166
Tombland Bookshop, Norfolk 191
Trotman (Ken), Cambridgeshire 66
Tyger Press, London N 160
Vanstone - Aviation Books, (Derek), Suffolk 230
Vickers (Anthony), North Yorkshire 196
Wadard Books, Kent 138
War & Peace Books, Hants......................... 122
Warnes (Felicity J.), London Outer................ 181
Wembdon Books, Somerset......................... 217
Westwood Books Ltd, Cumbria..................... 80
Wheen O'Books, Scottish Borders 269
Wiend Books, Lancashire 144
Wise (Derek), E Sussex 104
Wizard Books, Cambridgeshire..................... 67
Woolcott Books, Dorset.............................. 92
World War Books, Kent 141
Xanadu Books, Cleveland........................... 98
Yeoman Books, Lothian 279
Yesterday's News, Conwy........................... 285

– HISTORY

Aardvark Books, Wiltshire.......................... 254
Albion Books, W Mids............................... 239
Americanabooksuk, Cumbria....................... 77
Anchor Books, Lincolnshire 151
Andron (G.W.), London N 158
Antiques on High, Oxfordshire..................... 209
Apocalypse, Surrey 233
Armchair Books, Lothian 276
Armitage (Booksearch), (Kate), Devon 85
Askew Books (Vernon), Wiltshire.................. 251
Avedikian Rare Books, Somerset 217
Baldwin (M. & M.) Worcs 255
Barbican Bookshop, North Yorkshire............. 198
Barn Books, Buckinghamshire...................... 61
Barnes (Peter), Wiltshire 253
Biblion, London W................................... 172
Black Five Books, Shropshire 215
Books Afloat, Dorset................................. 96
Books on Spain, London Outer.................... 184
Bookshop on the Heath, The, London SE 164
Bookworm, Lothian................................... 277
Bookworm (The), Lothian 277
Bosorne Books, Cornwall 75
Brockwells Booksellers, Lincolnshire 150
Burroughs (Andrew), Lincolnshire 153
Caliver Books, Essex 110
Carnforth Bookshop (The), Lancashire 143

SPECIALITY INDEX

Cassidy (Bookseller) (P.), Lincolnshire 153
Castle Bookshop, Essex............................... 109
Cavern Books, Cheshire 70
Central Bookshop, Warwickshire 238
Chaucer Bookshop, Kent............................. 136
Chelifer Books, Cumbria 81
Cheshire Book Centre, Cheshire..................... 69
Chevin Books, West Yorkshire 250
Churchgate Books, Suffolk........................... 227
Cobbles Books, Somerset............................. 218
Coles (T.V.), Cambridgeshire 67
Corfe Books, Surrey................................... 231
Cornucopia Books, Lincolnshire 153
Cotswold Internet Books, Glos...................... 113
Cox (Geoff), Devon 90
Dally Books & Collectables, Powys................. 292
Dandy Lion Editions, Surrey 233
Darkwood Books, Co. Cork.......................... 263
Dartmoor Bookshop (The), Devon 84
David Warnes Books, Herefordshire 129
Debbage (John), Norfolk 190
Deeside Books, Grampian............................ 273
Delph Books, Gr Man........ 120
Devanha Military Books, Tayside 281
Dolphin Books, Suffolk............................... 226
Donovan Military Books (Tom), E Sussex 99
Dormouse Bookshop (The), Norfolk 190
Driffield Bookshop (The), East Yorkshire 106
Eastern Traveller (The), Somerset.................. 220
Fackley Services, Notts 205
Falconwood Transport & Military Bookshop,
London Outer 184
Farnborough Gallery, Hants......................... 122
Fifteenth Century Bookshop (The), E Sussex 104
firstpagebooks, Norfolk............................... 190
G. C. Books Ltd., Dumfries & Galloway.......... 271
Garfi Books, Powys 293
Gaullifmaufry Books, Herts......................... 132
George St. Books, Derbyshire 83
Grant, Lothian 278
Guildmaster Books, Cheshire 70
Handsworth Books, Essex............................ 112
Harlequin Books, Bristol 59
Harris (George J.), Co. Derry 260
Hay Cinema Bookshop Ltd., Powys................ 290
Helion & Company, W Mids 240
Heppa (Christopher), Essex 108
Hornsey's, North Yorkshire.......................... 195
Hummingbird Books, Herefordshire................ 128
Island Books, Devon 85
Jackson (M.W.), Wiltshire........................... 254
Joel Segal Books, Devon 86
Keegan's Bookshop, Berkshire 56
Keel Row Bookshop, Tyne and Wear 236
Kellow Books, Oxfordshire 207
Kenny's Bookshops and Art Galleries Ltd,
Co. Galway 266
Fackley Services, Notts 205
Lost Books, Northants................................ 201
Maggs Brothers Limited, London W............... 174
Mandalay Bookshop, London SW 169
Marble Hill Books, Middlesex 184
Marcet Books, London SE........................... 165
Marine & Cannon Books, Cheshire 71
Marine and Cannon Books, Cheshire 69

McCrone (Audrey), Isle of Arran 275
Meads Book Service (The), E Sussex.............. 104
Meekins Books (Paul), Warwickshire.............. 238
Military Bookworm, London SE.................... 165
Military Parade Bookshop, Wiltshire.............. 252
MilitaryHistoryBooks.com, Kent.................... 138
Morten (Booksellers) (E.J.), Gr Man 119
My Back Pages, London SW 169
N1 Books, E Sussex................................... 105
Not Just Books, Dorset............................... 94
O'Brien Books & Photo Gallery, Co. Limerick .. 266
Orssich (Paul), London SW 170
Oxfam Books and Music, Hants 126
Paperbacks Plus, Bristol 59
Parrott Books, Oxfordshire 211
Peter M Daly, Hants.................................. 127
Pordes Books Ltd., (Henry), London WC......... 179
Prescott - The Bookseller (John), London Outer 184
Priestpopple Books, Northumberland 202
Prior (Michael), Lincolnshire 153
Queen Victoria PH, Torfaen 294
Quinto of Charing Cross Road, London WC ... 179
R. & A. Books, E Sussex............................. 102
Richard Thornton Books, London N 160
Richmond Books, North Yorkshire 195
Robert Humm & Co, Lincolnshire 154
Rochdale Book Company, Gr Man 120
Rods Books, Devon.................................... 88
Roland Books, Kent 139
Sax Books, Suffolk 229
Schull Books, Co. Cork 263
Scorpio Books, Suffolk 226
Second Edition, Lothian.............................. 278
Solaris Books, East Yorkshire 106
Sutcliffe (Victor), Norfolk 188
Taylor & Son (Peter), Herts......................... 133
Thin Read Line, Merseyside 185
Tiffin (Tony and Gill), Durham..................... 97
Tilston (Stephen E.), London SE................... 166
Tombland Bookshop, Norfolk 191
Trotman (Ken), Cambridgeshire 66
Turton (John), Durham 98
Tyger Press, London N 160
Ventnor Rare Books, Isle of Wight................. 135
Village Books, Norfolk 187
Vokes Books Ltd., North Yorkshire................ 195
Wadard Books, Kent 138
War & Peace Books, Hants.......................... 122
Water Lane Bookshop, Wiltshire 253
Wheen O'Books, Scottish Borders 269
Wise (Derek), E Sussex 104
Wizard Books, Cambridgeshire...................... 67
Words Etcetera Bookshop, Dorset.................. 93
World War II Books, Surrey 235
Worlds End Bookshop, London SW 171
Yeoman Books, Lothian 279
Yesterday's News, Conwy 285
Zardoz Books, Wiltshire.............................. 254

– MODELLING

Aardvark Books, Wiltshire........................... 254
Barn Books, Buckinghamshire....................... 61
Bookworm, Lothian.................................... 277
Burroughs (Andrew), Lincolnshire 153
Chelifer Books, Cumbria 81

SPECIALITY INDEX

Falconwood Transport & Military Bookshop, London Outer....................................... 184 Gallimaufry Books, Herts .... 132 Joel Segal Books, Devon .... 86 Marine & Cannon Books, Cheshire .... 71 Marine and Cannon Books, Cheshire .... 69 Meekins Books (Paul), Warwickshire.............. 238 MilitaryHistoryBooks.com, Kent.................... 138 Rods Books, Devon .... 88 Trotman (Ken), Cambridgeshire .... 66 World War Books, Kent 141

– UNIFORMS

Aardvark Books, Wiltshire .... 254 Bookworm, Lothian................................... 277 Burroughs (Andrew), Lincolnshire .... 153 Caliver Books, Essex .... 110 Chelifer Books, Cumbria .... 81 Debbage (John), Norfolk .... 190 Fifteenth Century Bookshop (The), E Sussex .... 104 Joel Segal Books, Devon .... 86 Lost Books, Northants................................ 201 Marine & Cannon Books, Cheshire .... 71 Marine and Cannon Books, Cheshire .... 69 Meekins Books (Paul), Warwickshire.............. 238 MilitaryHistoryBooks.com, Kent.................... 138 N1 Books, E Sussex .... 105 R. & A. Books, E Sussex............................. 102 Thin Read Line, Merseyside .... 185 Trotman (Ken), Cambridgeshire 66

MIND, BODY & SPIRIT

Abbey Books, Cornwall .... 74 Annie's Books, S Yorks .... 222 Atlantis Bookshop, London WC.................... 177 Chthonios Books, E Sussex .... 102 Cornucopia Books, Lincolnshire .... 153 Dales & Lakes Book Centre, Cumbria............. 80 Dandy Lion Editions, Surrey .... 233 Discovery Bookshop, Carmarthenshire............ 283 DPE Books, Devon .... 87 Esoteric Dreams Bookshop, Cumbria .... 78 Fifteenth Century Bookshop (The), E Sussex .... 104 Furneaux Books (Lee), Devon...................... 89 J & J Burgess Booksellers, Cambridgeshire....... 64 Joel Segal Books, Devon .... 86 Just Books, Cornwall .... 76 Neeve (P.), Cambridgeshire .... 63 Oasis Booksearch, Cambridgeshire.... .... 67 Occultique, Northants................................ 200 Old Celtic Bookshop (The), Devon .... 88 Orchid Book Distributors, Co. Clare............... 262 Philip Hopper, Essex .... 110 Reading Lasses, Dumfries & Galloway .... 271 Roosterbooks, Northants............................. 200 Sedgeberrow Books & Framing, Worcs........... 256 SETI Books, Staffordshire............................ 225 Star Lord Books, Gr Man .... 119 Tarka Books, Devon .... 84 Till's Bookshop, Lothian .... 279 Trafalgar Bookshop, E Sussex .... 100 Treasure Trove Books, Leics......................... 148 Trinity Rare Books, Co. Leitrim .... 266 Watkins Books Ltd., London WC.................. 180

MINERALOGY

Baldwin's Scientific Books, Essex .... 112 Cox (Geoff), Devon .... 90 Earth Science Books, Wiltshire .... 252 Henly (John), West Sussex .... 245 Joel Segal Books, Devon .... 86 Nibris Books, London SW .... 170 Parkinsons Books, Merseyside...................... 186 Phelps (Michael), West Sussex...................... 243 R. & A. Books, E Sussex............................. 102 Westons, Herts 133

MINIATURE BOOKS

Apocalypse, Surrey .... 233 Bernstein (Nicholas), London W................... 172 Demetzy Books, Oxfordshire .... 208 G. C. Books Ltd., Dumfries & Galloway......... 271 Garbett Antiquarian Books (Michael), Glos ..... 116 Hennessey Bookseller (Ray), E Sussex .... 100 Mead (P.J.), Shropshire.............................. 214 Moorhead Books, West Yorkshire.................. 246 R. & A. Books, E Sussex............................. 102 RGS Books, Surrey .... 235 Roscrea Bookshop, Co. Tipperary.................. 267 Scrivener's Books & Bookbinding, Derbyshire... 82 Temperley (David), W Mids 239

MINING

Anthony Vickers Books, North Yorkshire .... 196 Book House (The), Cumbria......................... 77 Bott, (Bookdealers) Ltd., (Martin), Gr Man ..... 118 Browning Books, Torfaen .... 294 Browsers Bookshop, Cornwall....................... 73 Collectables (W.H.), Suffolk .... 230 Cox (Geoff), Devon .... 90 Duck (William), Hants................................ 124 Empire Books, North Yorkshire .... 198 G. C. Books Ltd., Dumfries & Galloway......... 271 Joel Segal Books, Devon .... 86 Just Books, Cornwall .... 76 Past & Present Books, Glos......................... 114 Phelps (Michael), West Sussex...................... 243 Randall (Tom), Somerset............................. 219 Turton (John), Durham .... 98 Vickers (Anthony), North Yorkshire .... 196 Vinovium Books, Durham .... 97 Westons, Herts .... 133 Whitchurch Books Ltd., Cardiff.................... 283

MINORITY STUDIES

Al Saqi Books, London W .... 177 Left on The Shelf, Cumbria.......................... 79 Reading Lasses, Dumfries & Galloway .... 271 Samovar Books, Co. Dublin 264

MISSIONARIES & MISSIONS

G. C. Books Ltd., Dumfries & Galloway......... 271 Kenya Books, E Sussex............................... 100 Oasis Booksearch, Cambridgeshire................. 67 Pendleburys Bookshop, London N .... 159 St Philip's Books, Oxfordshire...................... 210 Samovar Books, Co. Dublin 264

MODEL ENGINEERING

Bott, (Bookdealers) Ltd., (Martin), Gr Man 118

SPECIALITY INDEX

Cornucopia Books, Lincolnshire 153
Cover to Cover, Merseyside......................... 186
Robert Humm & Co, Lincolnshire 154
Stroh (M.A.), London E 155
Yesteryear Railwayana, Kent........................ 139

MODEL RAILWAYS

Bianco Library, West Sussex......................... 242
Bott, (Bookdealers) Ltd., (Martin), Gr Man 118
Cornucopia Books, Lincolnshire 153
Cover to Cover, Merseyside......................... 186
Cox (Geoff), Devon 90
Dales and Lakes Book Centre, Cumbria........... 80
Deeside Books, Grampian............................ 273
Falconwood Transport & Military Bookshop,
London Outer 184
Fifteenth Century Bookshop (The), E Sussex 104
Henry Wilson Books, Cheshire...................... 69
Joel Segal Books, Devon 86
Milestone Books, Devon 89
R. & A. Books, E Sussex............................ 102
Roadmaster Books, Kent............................. 137
Robert Humm & Co, Lincolnshire 154
Yesteryear Railwayana, Kent........................ 139

MODEL THEATRE

Cover to Cover, Merseyside......................... 186
R. & A. Books, E Sussex............................ 102

MODERN

Joel Segal Books, Devon 86
Surprise Books, Glos................................. 113
Wheen O'Books, Scottish Borders 269

MODERN ART

Ballantyne-Way (Roger), Suffolk 229
Booth (Booksearch Service), (Geoff), Cheshire... 68
Bruce Holdsworth Books, E Sussex 105
Cornucopia Books, Lincolnshire 153
Cover to Cover, Merseyside......................... 186
Fifteenth Century Bookshop (The), E Sussex 104
Joel Segal Books, Devon 86
Just Books, Cornwall 76
Lucius Books, North Yorkshire..................... 199
R. & A. Books, E Sussex............................ 102
Worlds End Bookshop, London SW................ 171

MODERN FIRST EDITIONS

Addyman Annexe (The), Powys..................... 289
Addyman Books, Powys.............................. 289
ahbooks, Merseyside 185
Allinson (Frank & Stella), Warwickshire 237
Amwell Book Company, London EC............... 157
Anglo-American Rare Books, Surrey............... 233
Ann & Mike Conry, Worcs.......................... 257
Antique Map and Bookshop (The), Dorset 94
Apocalypse, Surrey 233
Archer (Steve), London Outer...................... 181
Armitage (Booksearch), (Kate), Devon 85
Askew Books (Vernon), Wiltshire.................. 251
Autolycus, Shropshire................................ 213
Avonworld Books, Somerset......................... 218
babelog.books, Herefordshire........................ 128
Bass (Ben), Wiltshire 251
BC Books, Cheshire.................................. 70

Bertram Rota Ltd., London WC 177
Biblion, London W................................... 172
Biblipola, London NW............................... 161
Blackwell's Rare Books, Oxfordshire.............. 209
Book Business (The), London W 172
Book Shelf (The), Devon............................ 87
Bookcase, Cumbria................................... 78
Books, Oxfordshire................................... 206
Books & Things, London W......................... 172
Books Only, Suffolk.................................. 227
BOOKS4U, Flintshire................................ 286
Bookshop on the Heath, The, London SE 164
Bookstand, Dorset.................................... 94
Booth (Booksearch Service), (Geoff), Cheshire... 68
Bow Windows Book Shop, E Sussex............... 103
Bowie Books & Collectables, East Yorkshire 107
Broadhurst of Southport Ltd., Merseyside 186
Budd (Richard), Somerset........................... 219
Caledonia Books, Strathclyde....................... 280
Cameron House Books, Isle of Wight.............. 134
Camilla's Bookshop, E Sussex...................... 101
Carta Regis, Powys.. 293
Castle Bookshop, Essex.............................. 109
Central Bookshop, Warwickshire 238
Childrens Bookshop, West Yorkshire 248
Chris Adam Smith Modern First Editions,
West Sussex... 244
Chris Phillips, Wiltshire............................. 251
Church Street Books, Norfolk....................... 187
Clifford Milne Books, Grampian................... 272
Corfe Books, Surrey.................................. 231
Cornucopia Books, Lincolnshire 153
Criterion Books, London Outer..................... 182
Dales & Lakes Book Centre, Cumbria............ 80
Dolphin Books, Suffolk.............................. 226
Dormouse Bookshop (The), Norfolk............... 190
Driffield Bookshop (The), East Yorkshire 106
Ellis, Bookseller (Peter), London WC 178
Ellwood Editions, Wiltshire......................... 253
Enscot Books, London SE 165
Fifteenth Century Bookshop (The), E Sussex 104
Finch Rare Books Ltd. (Simon), London W..... 173
First State Books, London W 173
firstpagebooks, Norfolk.............................. 190
Firsts in Print, Isle of Wight........................ 134
Foster Bookshop (Paul), London SW.............. 168
Gander, (Jacques), Glos 115
Gildas Books, Cheshire 68
Good for Books, Lincolnshire 151
Heppa (Christopher), Essex 108
Hight (Norman F.), Glamorgan..................... 286
Hollett and Son (R.F.G.), Cumbria 80
House of Figgis Ltd (The), Co. Galway 266
Hylton Booksearch, Merseyside.................... 185
Ian McKelvie Bookseller, London N............... 159
Idle Genius Books, London N 159
Innes Books, Shropshire............................. 214
Intech Books, Northumberland 203
Island Books, Devon.................................. 85
Jackson (M.W.), Wiltshire.......................... 254
Joel Segal Books, Devon 86
Jonkers Rare Books, Oxfordshire 209
K Books, Cheshire.................................... 70
Katharine House Gallery, Wiltshire 252
Kendall-Carpenter (Tim), Gr Man 119

SPECIALITY INDEX

Kennedy & Farley, E Sussex........................ 104
Kestrel Books, Hereford............................. 290
Kevin S. Ogilvie Modern First Editions,
Grampian... 273
L.M.S. Books, Herts................................. 132
Lewis (J.T. & P.), Cornwall......................... 74
Lewis First Editions, Kent.......................... 138
Little Stour Books, Kent............................. 137
Lucius Books, North Yorkshire.................... 199
Mainly Fiction, Cheshire............................. 68
Mair Wilkes Books, Fife............................. 272
Mannwaring (M.G.), Bristol........................ 59
McCrone (Audrey), Isle of Arran.................. 275
Ming Books, Dumfries & Galloway............... 271
Modern First Editions, London Outer........... 183
Moore (Sue), Cornwall............................... 73
Moreton Books, Devon............................... 87
Murphy (C.J.), Norfolk.............................. 190
N V Books, Warwickshire........................... 237
Needham Books, (Russell), Somerset............. 220
Neil's Books, London NW........................... 162
Norton Books, North Yorkshire.................... 197
O'Flynn Books, North Yorkshire.................. 199
Orlando Booksellers, Lincolnshire................ 152
Parker Books (Mike), Cambridgeshire........... 64
Parrott (Jeremy), London E......................... 156
Peter Lyons Books, Glos............................. 114
Peter White, Hants.................................... 121
Poetry Bookshop (The), Powys.................... 291
Pomes Penyeach, Staffordshire.................... 224
Pordes Books Ltd., (Henry), London WC....... 179
Portus Books, Hants.................................. 122
Price (R.W.), Notts................................... 204
Pringle Booksellers (Andrew), Lothian.......... 278
R. & A. Books, E Sussex............................ 102
Reading Lasses, Dumfries & Galloway.......... 271
Reaveley Books, Devon.............................. 87
Rees & O'Neill Rare Books, London WC....... 179
Richard Thornton Books, London N............. 160
Rising Tide Books, Fife.............................. 271
Robert (Leslie), London W......................... 175
Robert Temple, London N.......................... 160
Roberts Fine Books (Julian), Lincolnshire....... 153
Rye Old Books, E Sussex............................ 104
Seabreeze Books, Lancashire....................... 145
Second Edition, Lothian............................. 278
Shakeshaft (Dr. B.), Cheshire...................... 71
Shapero Rare Books (Bernard J.),
London W.. 175
Sillan Books, Co. Cavan............................. 262
Silver Trees Books, W Mids........................ 240
Simply Read Books, E Sussex...................... 101
Simpson (Dave), Stirlingshire...................... 269
Skelton (Tony), Kent................................. 141
Solaris Books, East Yorkshire...................... 106
Strathtay Antiquarian - Secondhand Books,
Tayside... 282
Stroma Books, Borders.............................. 268
Surprise Books, Glos................................. 113
Talisman Books, Cheshire........................... 70
Thistle Books, Strathclyde.......................... 280
Thornber (Peter M.), North Yorkshire........... 196
Till's Bookshop, Lothian............................ 279
Trevorrow (Edwin), Herts.......................... 130
Trinity Rare Books, Co. Leitrim................... 266

Ulysses, London WC................................. 180
Walden Books, London NW........................ 163
Warrender (Andrew), West Yorkshire............ 250
Webb Books (John), S Yorks....................... 222
Wiend Books, Lancashire........................... 144
Williams (Bookdealer), (Richard), N Lincs....... 154
Willmott Bookseller (Nicholas), Cardiff.......... 283
Words Etcetera Bookshop, Dorset................. 93
Wright Trace Books, W Mids...................... 240
Wychwood Books, Glos.............................. 116
York Modern Books, North Yorkshire........... 197

MONOGRAPHS

Barlow (Vincent G.), Hants......................... 125
Campbell Art Books (Marcus), London SE...... 164
Coch-y-Bonddu Books, Powys..................... 292
Heneage Art Books (Thomas), London SW..... 169
Parkinsons Books, Merseyside..................... 186
Taylor & Son (Peter), Herts......................... 133
Trinders' Fine Tools, Suffolk....................... 227
Walden Books, London NW........................ 163

MOTORBIKES / MOTORCYCLES

Chaters Motoring Booksellers, London Outer... 182
Cheshire Book Centre, Cheshire................... 69
Collectors Carbooks, Northants.................... 200
Cox (Geoff), Devon................................... 90
Dales & Lakes Book Centre, Cumbria........... 80
Falconwood Transport & Military Bookshop,
London Outer....................................... 184
Holdenhurst Books, Dorset......................... 91
Joel Segal Books, Devon............................ 86
Kenneth Ball, E Sussex.............................. 101
Knowles (John), Norfolk............................ 188
Main-Smith & Co. Ltd. (Bruce), Leics........... 148
Merlin Books, West Sussex......................... 243
Peake (Robin), Lincolnshire........................ 153
Pooks Motor Books, Leics.......................... 148
R. & A. Books, E Sussex............................ 102
Roadmaster Books, Kent............................ 137
Simon Lewis Transport Books, Glos.............. 115
Stroh (M.A.), London E............................. 155
Uncle Phil's Books, W Mids........................ 240
Vintage Motorshop, West Yorkshire.............. 246
Yeoman Books, Lothian............................. 279

MOTORING

Abrahams (Mike), Staffordshire................... 224
Allinson (Frank & Stella), Warwickshire......... 237
Baldwin (M. & M.), Worcs......................... 255
Books & Collectables Ltd., Cambridgeshire...... 63
Books Bought & Sold, Surrey...................... 232
books2books, Devon................................. 88
Brewin Books Ltd., Warwickshire................. 238
Browse Books, Lancashire.......................... 144
Chandos Books, Devon.............................. 85
Chaters Motoring Booksellers, London Outer... 182
Cheshire Book Centre, Cheshire................... 69
Chevin Books, West Yorkshire..................... 250
Cobweb Books, North Yorkshire.................. 195
Collectors Carbooks, Northants.................... 200
Corfe Books, Surrey.................................. 231
Cornucopia Books, Lincolnshire................... 153
Cowley, Auto-in-Print (John), Essex.............. 108
Cox (Geoff), Devon................................... 90

SPECIALITY INDEX

Discovery Bookshop, Carmarthenshire............. 283
Eastcote Bookshop (The), London Outer......... 181
Emjay Books, Surrey................................. 231
Falconwood Transport & Military Bookshop,
London Outer.. 184
Fifteenth Century Bookshop (The), E Sussex ... 104
Fylde Books, Lancashire 146
Hames (Peter), Devon................................ 85
Harlequin Books, Bristol 59
Holdenhurst Books, Dorset.......................... 91
Hornsey's, North Yorkshire......................... 195
Horsham Rare Books, West Sussex 243
Janus Books, W Mids................................. 240
Joel Segal Books, Devon 86
Kenneth Ball, E Sussex 101
Kerr (Norman), Cumbria 78
Knowles (John), Norfolk 188
McGlynn (John), Lancashire........................ 143
Morris Secondhand & Antiquarian Books
(Chris), Oxfordshire 210
Peake (Robin), Lincolnshire.......... 153
Pooks Motor Books, Leics........................... 148
R. & A. Books, E Sussex.... 102
Richard Thornton Books, London N 160
Roadmaster Books, Kent............................. 137
Roberts (Booksellers), (Ray), Staffordshire 224
Rochdale Book Company, Gr Man 120
Roland Books, Kent 139
Saint Mary's Books & Prints, Lincolnshire....... 154
St Paul's Street Bookshop, Lincolnshire 154
Sax Books, Suffolk 229
Scrivener's Books & Bookbinding, Derbyshire... 82
Simon Lewis Transport Books, Glos 115
Smith Maritime Aviation Books (Frank),
Tyne and Wear....................................... 236
Stella Books, Monmouthshire 288
Stour Bookshop, Dorset.............................. 95
Stroh (M.A.), London E 155
Vintage Motorshop, West Yorkshire 246
Volumes of Motoring, Glos.......................... 113
Yeoman Books, Lothian 279

MOUNTAIN MEN

Americanabooksuk, Cumbria........................ 77
Gildas Books, Cheshire 68
Glacier Books, Tayside 282
Jarvis Books, Derbyshire 83
Mercat Books, Highland 274
Pinnacle Books, Lothian.............................. 278
Roz Hulse, Conwy 286

MOUNTAINS

Allinson (Frank & Stella), Warwickshire 237
Bonham (J. & S.L.), London W 172
Cavendish Rare Books, London N 158
Chalmers Hallam (E.), Hants........................ 125
Craobh Rua Books, Co. Armagh................... 260
Creaking Shelves, Inverness-shire................... 275
Dales & Lakes Book Centre, Cumbria............. 80
David Warnes Books, Herefordshire 129
Deeside Books, Grampian............................ 273
Earth Science Books, Wiltshire 252
Gildas Books, Cheshire 68
Glacier Books, Tayside 282
Hunter and Krageloh, Derbyshire 83

Jarvis Books, Derbyshire 83
Joel Segal Books, Devon 86
Kalligraphia, Isle of Wight........................... 134
Marcet Books, London SE........................... 165
McCrone (Audrey), Isle of Arran................... 275
Mercat Books, Highland 274
Page (David), Lothian 278
Pinnacle Books, Lothian.............................. 278
R. & A. Books, E Sussex............................. 102

MOVEABLE & 3D

Fifteenth Century Bookshop (The), E Sussex 104

MOVIE & TELEVISION SCRIPTS

Apocalypse, Surrey 233
Byre Books, Dumfries & Galloway................. 270
Greenroom Books, West Yorkshire 248
Joel Segal Books, Devon 86

MUSIC - GENERAL

AA1 Books, Dumfries & Galloway................. 270
Abacus Gallery, Staffordshire....................... 224
Alba Secondhand Music, Strathclyde.............. 279
Anthony Spranger, Wiltshire........................ 252
Antiquary Ltd., (Bar Bookstore), N Yorks....... 196
Antiques on High, Oxfordshire..................... 209
Apocalypse, Surrey.................................... 233
Armstrong's Books & Collectables, Leics......... 147
Aurora Books Ltd, Lothian........................... 276
Autumn Leaves, Lincolnshire....................... 152
Axe Rare & Out of Print Books (Richard),
N Yorks... 194
Bardsley's Books, Suffolk............................. 226
Baron (H.), London NW............................. 161
Baxter - Books (Eddie), Somerset 221
Beware of the Leopard, Bristol...................... 58
Blackwell's Music Shop, Oxfordshire.............. 209
Bookcase, Cumbria.................................... 78
Books, Denbighshire 286
Books & Collectables Ltd., Cambridgeshire...... 63
Books (For All), N Yorks............................. 194
Books For All, N Yorks 194
Books Plus, Devon..................................... 84
books2books, Devon 88
Bookshop (The), Norfolk 192
Bookshop on the Heath, The, London SE 164
Bookworms, Norfolk.................................. 187
Booth (Booksearch Service), (Geoff), Cheshire... 68
Boris Books, Hants.... 126
Bosorne Books, Cornwall 75
Browne (Christopher I.), West Yorkshire......... 247
Byre Books, Dumfries & Galloway................. 270
Calendula Horticultural Books, E Sussex......... 102
Carnforth Bookshop (The), Lancashire 143
Carningli Centre, Pembrokeshire................... 288
Carta Regis, Powys.................................... 293
Chaucer Bookshop, Kent............................. 136
Cheshire Book Centre, Cheshire.................... 69
Clapham (M. & B.), Hants........................... 124
Clements (R.W.), London Outer 182
Colin Hancock, Ceredigion 284
Dales & Lakes Book Centre, Cumbria............. 80
Darkwood Books, Co. Cork......................... 263
Davids Ltd., (Roy), Oxfordshire 209
Decorum Books, London N 158

SPECIALITY INDEX

Discovery Bookshop, Carmarthenshire............ 283
Dolphin Books, Suffolk............................... 226
Dooley (Rosemary), Cumbria 78
East Riding Books, East Yorkshire................ 107
Elgar (Raymond), E Sussex 99
Esoteric Dreams Bookshop, Cumbria 78
Evans (Mark), Lincolnshire 153
Ewell Bookshop Ltd, Surrey........................ 232
Fifteenth Century Bookshop (The), E Sussex 104
Fiona Edwards, Notts 204
Fitzsimons (Anne), Cumbria........................ 78
Forest Books of Manchester, Cheshire............ 71
Freeman's Corner Shop, Norfolk 190
George St. Books, Derbyshire 83
Gibbs Books, (Jonathan), Worcs................... 256
Gloucester Road Bookshop, London SW 168
Good for Books, Lincolnshire 151
Goodden (Peter), Somerset.......................... 216
Hancock & Monks, Powys........................... 290
Handsworth Books, Essex........................... 112
Hay Cinema Bookshop Ltd., Powys............... 290
HCB Wholesale, Powys.............................. 290
Hurst (Jenny), Kent 138
Internet Bookshop UK Ltd., Glos.................. 113
Jade Mountain Bookshop, Hants................... 126
Joel Segal Books, Devon 86
Judd Books, London WC 178
Just Books, Cornwall 76
Kalligraphia, Isle of Wight.......................... 134
Kenny's Bookshops and Art Galleries Ltd,
Co. Galway.. 266
Kent T. G., Surrey 231
Kim's Bookshop, W Sussex..............242, 243, 245
Malvern Bookshop (The), Worcs 255
Marcet Books, London SE........................... 165
Martin Music Books (Philip), N Yorks 199
McGee (Terence J.), London Outer 181
Mogul Diamonds, W Mids 241
Music By The Score, Cornwall...................... 73
Neeve (P.), Cambridgeshire 63
Newgate Books and Translations,
Northumberland 202
Paramor (C.D.), Suffolk 229
Parrott Books, Oxfordshire 211
Pastmasters, Derbyshire.............................. 83
Portobello Books, London W 175
Price (R.W.), Notts................................... 204
Priestpopple Books, Northumberland 202
Quinto of Charing Cross Road, London WC ... 179
Quinto of Great Russell Street, London WC 179
Roland Books, Kent 139
Saint Mary's Books & Prints, Lincolnshire....... 154
Sax Books, Suffolk 229
Scarthin Books, Derbyshire 82
Sheet Music Warehouse (The), Devon 88
Sherlaw-Johnson (Austin), Oxfordshire 210
Skoob Russell Square, Suffolk...................... 230
Staniland (Booksellers), Lincolnshire 154
Stern Antiquarian Bookseller (Jeffrey), N Yorks 199
Stevens (Joan), Cambridgeshire..................... 65
Tarka Books, Devon.................................. 84
The Sanctuary Bookshop, Dorset................... 94
Till's Bookshop, Lothian 279
Travis & Emery Music Bookshop, London WC 180
Uncle Phil's Books, W Mids........................ 240

Venables (Morris & Juliet), Bristol.................. 60
Wiend Books, Lancashire 144
Willmott Bookseller (Nicholas), Cardiff........... 283
Wood (Peter), Cambridgeshire...................... 65
Woodlands Books, West Yorkshire................. 249
Worlds End Bookshop, London SW............... 171

- CHART HISTORIES & RESEARCH

Decorum Books, London N 158
Morris Secondhand & Antiquarian Books
(Chris), Oxfordshire 210
Sheet Music Warehouse (The), Devon 88
Travis & Emery Music Bookshop, London WC 180

- CLASSICAL

Alba Secondhand Music, Strathclyde.............. 279
Barnes - Books (Lyndon), Shropshire 214
Bermondsey Basement Bookstore, London SE .. 164
Biblion, London W................................... 172
Blackwell's Music Shop, Oxfordshire.............. 209
Browne (Christopher I.), West Yorkshire......... 247
Chesters (G. & J.), Staffordshire 225
Decorum Books, London N 158
Dolphin Books, Suffolk.............................. 226
Dooley (Rosemary), Cumbria 78
East Riding Books, East Yorkshire................. 107
Ely Books, Cambridgeshire 65
Ewell Bookshop Ltd, Surrey........................ 232
Fifteenth Century Bookshop (The), East Sussex. 104
Gibbs Books, (Jonathan), Worcs................... 256
Goodden (Peter), Somerset.......................... 216
Grahame Thornton, Bookseller, Dorset........... 93
Hancock & Monks, Powys.......................... 290
Handsworth Books, Essex........................... 112
Joel Segal Books, Devon 86
John R. Hoggarth, N Yorks......................... 198
Marcan, Bookseller (Peter), London SE 165
Mogul Diamonds, W Mids 241
Music By The Score, Cornwall...................... 73
Musicalania, Norfolk................................. 189
Newgate Books and Translations,
Northumberland 202
Pordes Books Ltd., (Henry), London WC........ 179
Prescott - The Bookseller (John), London Outer 184
Reads, Dorset 95
Scrivener's Books & Bookbinding, Derbyshire... 82
Sheet Music Warehouse (The), Devon 88
Sherlaw-Johnson (Austin), Oxfordshire 210
Staniland (Booksellers), Lincolnshire 154
Travis & Emery Music Bookshop, London WC 180
Uncle Phil's Books, W Mids........................ 240
Venables (Morris & Juliet), Bristol.................. 60
Willmott Bookseller (Nicholas), Cardiff........... 283

- COMPOSERS

Alba Secondhand Music, Strathclyde.............. 279
Bath Old Books, Somerset 216
Blackwell's Music Shop, Oxfordshire.............. 209
Boris Books, Hants................................... 126
Browne (Christopher I.), West Yorkshire......... 247
Dales & Lakes Book Centre, Cumbria............ 80
Decorum Books, London N 158
Dolphin Books, Suffolk.............................. 226
Dooley (Rosemary), Cumbria 8
East Riding Books, East Yorkshire................. 107

SPECIALITY INDEX

Fifteenth Century Bookshop (The), East Sussex. 104
Glenbower Books, Co. Dublin 265
Goodden (Peter), Somerset.......................... 216
Hancock & Monks, Powys........................... 290
Handsworth Books, Essex............................ 112
Joel Segal Books, Devon 86
Marcet Books, London SE........................... 165
Martin Music Books (Philip), N Yorks 199
Mogul Diamonds, W Mids 241
Music By The Score, Cornwall 73
Musicalania, Norfolk.................................. 189
Price (John), London N 159
R. & A. Books, East Sussex 102
Sheet Music Warehouse (The), Devon 88
Sherlaw-Johnson (Austin), Oxfordshire 210
Staniland (Booksellers), Lincolnshire 154
Travis & Emery Music Bookshop, London WC 180
Venables (Morris & Juliet), Bristol.................. 60
Whistler's Books, London SW 170
Willmott Bookseller (Nicholas), Cardiff........... 283

- COUNTRY & WESTERN

A. & R. Booksearch, Cornwall 74
Barnes - Books (Lyndon), Shropshire 214
Decorum Books, London N 158
Fifteenth Century Bookshop (The), East Sussex. 104
Joel Segal Books, Devon 86
Sheet Music Warehouse (The), Devon 88
Travis & Emery Music Bookshop, London WC 180

- FOLK & IRISH FOLK

Alba Secondhand Music, Strathclyde.............. 279
Aucott & Thomas, Leics.............................. 147
Bookshop (The), Norfolk 192
Church Green Books, Oxfordshire.................. 211
Country Books, Derbyshire 82
Dancing Goat Bookshop (The), Norfolk 188
Dooley (Rosemary), Cumbria 78
Fifteenth Century Bookshop (The), East Sussex. 104
Green Man Books, East Sussex 101
Handsworth Books, Essex............................. 112
Joel Segal Books, Devon 86
K.S.C. Books, Cheshire............................... 71
Music By The Score, Cornwall 73
Naughton Booksellers, Co. Dublin 265
R. & A. Books, East Sussex 102
Randall (Tom), Somerset 219
Royal Carbery Books Ltd., Co. Cork 262
Sheet Music Warehouse (The), Devon 88
Sherlaw-Johnson (Austin), Oxfordshire 210
Travis & Emery Music Bookshop, London WC 180

- GILBERT & SULLIVAN

Alba Secondhand Music, Strathclyde.............. 279
Brock Books, N Yorks 193
Browne (Christopher I.), West Yorkshire......... 247
Decorum Books, London N 158
Fifteenth Century Bookshop (The), E Sussex 104
Goodden (Peter), Somerset........................... 216
Greenroom Books, West Yorkshire 248
Hancock & Monks, Powys........................... 290
Joel Segal Books, Devon 86
Martin Music Books (Philip), N Yorks 199
Musicalania, Norfolk................................... 189
R. & A. Books, E Sussex............................. 102

Sherlaw-Johnson (Austin), Oxfordshire 210
Theatreshire Books, N Yorks........................ 193
Travis & Emery Music Bookshop, London WC 180

- GREGORIAN CHANTS

Alba Secondhand Music, Strathclyde.............. 279
Birchden Books, London E 155
Browne (Christopher I.), West Yorkshire......... 247
Decorum Books, London N 158
Dooley (Rosemary), Cumbria 78
Goodden (Peter), Somerset........................... 216
Hancock & Monks, Powys........................... 290
Sheet Music Warehouse (The), Devon 88
Sherlaw-Johnson (Austin), Oxfordshire 210
Travis & Emery Music Bookshop, London WC 180

- ILLUSTRATED SHEET MUSIC

Alba Secondhand Music, Strathclyde.............. 279
Browne (Christopher I.), West Yorkshire......... 247
Decorum Books, London N 158
Ferguson (Elizabeth), Grampian 272
Gibbs Books, (Jonathan), Worcs.................... 256
Hancock & Monks, Powys........................... 290
McGee (Terence J.), London Outer 181
Music By The Score, Cornwall 73
Sheet Music Warehouse (The), Devon 88
Sherlaw-Johnson (Austin), Oxfordshire 210
The Old Music Master, Bristol 60
Travis & Emery Music Bookshop, London WC 180

- JAZZ & BLUES

A. & R. Booksearch, Cornwall...................... 74
Barnes - Books (Lyndon), Shropshire 214
Baxter - Books (Eddie), Somerset 221
Bookroom (The), Surrey.............................. 234
Bosorne Books, Cornwall 75
Courtyard Books, Glos 113
Decorum Books, London N 158
East Riding Books, East Yorkshire................. 107
Fifteenth Century Bookshop (The), E Sussex 104
Fossgate Books, N Yorks 198
Hames (Peter), Devon................................. 85
Hancock & Monks, Powys........................... 290
Handsworth Books, Essex............................. 112
Joel Segal Books, Devon 86
Martin Music Books (Philip), N Yorks 199
My Back Pages, London SW 169
R. & A. Books, E Sussex............................. 102
Scorpio Books, Suffolk 226
Sheet Music Warehouse (The), Devon 88
Sherlaw-Johnson (Austin), Oxfordshire 210
Travis & Emery Music Bookshop, London WC 180

- MUSIC HALL

Browne (Christopher I.), West Yorkshire......... 247
Decorum Books, London N 158
Fitzsimons (Anne), Cumbria 78
Greenroom Books, West Yorkshire 248
Hancock & Monks, Powys........................... 290
Joel Segal Books, Devon 86
McGee (Terence J.), London Outer 181
Music By The Score, Cornwall 73
Paramor (C.D.), Suffolk 229
R. & A. Books, E Sussex............................. 102
Sheet Music Warehouse (The), Devon 88

SPECIALITY INDEX

Sherlaw-Johnson (Austin), Oxfordshire 210
Terence Kaye, London NW 162
Travis & Emery Music Bookshop, London WC 180

- MUSICIANS

Alba Secondhand Music, Strathclyde.............. 279
Bath Old Books, Somerset 216
Blackwell's Music Shop, Oxfordshire.............. 209
Browne (Christopher I.), West Yorkshire......... 247
Decorum Books, London N 158
Dooley (Rosemary), Cumbria 78
East Riding Books, East Yorkshire................. 107
Fifteenth Century Bookshop (The), E Sussex 104
Goodden (Peter), Somerset.......................... 216
Hancock & Monks, Powys........................... 290
Handsworth Books, Essex............................ 112
Joel Segal Books, Devon 86
Price (John), London N 159
R. & A. Books, E Sussex............................ 102
Sheet Music Warehouse (The), Devon 88
Sherlaw-Johnson (Austin), Oxfordshire 210
Travis & Emery Music Bookshop, London WC 180
Willmott Bookseller (Nicholas), Cardiff........... 283
Woodlands Books, West Yorkshire................. 249

- OPERA

Alba Secondhand Music, Strathclyde.............. 279
Blackwell's Music Shop, Oxfordshire.............. 209
Browne (Christopher I.), West Yorkshire......... 247
Dales & Lakes Book Centre, Cumbria............ 80
Decorum Books, London N 158
Dooley (Rosemary), Cumbria 78
East Riding Books, East Yorkshire................. 107
Fifteenth Century Bookshop (The), E Sussex 104
Fitzsimons (Anne), Cumbria........................ 78
Garwood & Voigt, Kent.............................. 140
Greenroom Books, West Yorkshire 248
Hancock & Monks, Powys........................... 290
Handsworth Books, Essex............................ 112
Hodgkins and Company Limited (Ian), Glos 116
Joel Segal Books, Devon 86
Marcet Books, London SE........................... 165
Martin Music Books (Philip), N Yorks............ 199
Music By The Score, Cornwall 73
Musicalania, Norfolk.................................. 189
Price (John), London N 159
R. & A. Books, E Sussex............................ 102
Sheet Music Warehouse (The), Devon 88
Sherlaw Johnson (Austin), Oxfordshire 210
Staniland (Booksellers), Lincolnshire 154
Travis & Emery Music Bookshop, London WC 180
Whistler's Books, London SW 170
Willmott Bookseller (Nicholas), Cardiff........... 283

- ORCHESTRAL

Alba Secondhand Music, Strathclyde.............. 279
Browne (Christopher I.), West Yorkshire......... 247
Decorum Books, London N 158
Fifteenth Century Bookshop (The), E Sussex 104
Hancock & Monks, Powys........................... 290
Handsworth Books, Essex............................ 112
Joel Segal Books, Devon 86
Music By The Score, Cornwall 73
R. & A. Books, E Sussex............................ 102
Sheet Music Warehouse (The), Devon 88

Sherlaw-Johnson (Austin), Oxfordshire 210
Staniland (Booksellers), Lincolnshire 154
Travis & Emery Music Bookshop, London WC 180

- POLITICAL SONGS & BALLADS

Barry McKay Rare Books, Cumbria............... 77
Browne (Christopher I.), West Yorkshire......... 247
Decorum Books, London N 158
Left on The Shelf, Cumbria......................... 79
Music By The Score, Cornwall 73
Randall (Tom), Somerset............................ 219
Sheet Music Warehouse (The), Devon 88
Sherlaw-Johnson (Austin), Oxfordshire 210
Travis & Emery Music Bookshop, London WC 180

- POPULAR

A. & R. Booksearch, Cornwall..................... 74
Apocalypse, Surrey 233
Barnes - Books (Lyndon), Shropshire 214
Black Cat Bookshop, Leics 147
Browne (Christopher I.), West Yorkshire......... 247
Dancing Goat Bookshop (The), Norfolk 188
Decorum Books, London N 158
Fifteenth Century Bookshop (The), E Sussex 104
firstpagebooks, Norfolk.............................. 190
Furneaux Books (Lee), Devon...................... 89
Inprint, Glos... 116
Joel Segal Books, Devon 86
John R. Hoggarth, N Yorks......................... 198
Kent T. G., Surrey 231
Morris Secondhand & Antiquarian Books (Chris), Oxfordshire 210
Music By The Score, Cornwall..................... 73
Musicalania, Norfolk.................................. 189
Nevitsky (Philip), Gr Man 119
Pordes Books Ltd., (Henry), London WC........ 179
Pyecroft (Ruth), Glos 117
R. & A. Books, E Sussex............................ 102
Sheet Music Warehouse (The), Devon 88
Sherlaw-Johnson (Austin), Oxfordshire 210
Travis & Emery Music Bookshop, London WC 180
Uncle Phil's Books, W Mids........................ 240
Whistler's Books, London SW 170
Willmott Bookseller (Nicholas), Cardiff........... 283
Yorkshire Relics, West Yorkshire................... 247

- PRINTED, SHEET MUSIC & SCORES

Alba Secondhand Music, Strathclyde.............. 279
Browne (Christopher I.), West Yorkshire......... 247
Carningli Centre, Pembrokeshire................... 288
Cornucopia Books, Lincolnshire 153
Cox Music (Lisa), Devon............................ 86
Decorum Books, London N 158
Gibbs Books, (Jonathan), Worcs................... 256
Hab Books, London W............................... 173
Hancock & Monks, Powys........................... 290
Jade Mountain Bookshop, Hants................... 126
Joel Segal Books, Devon 86
Just Books, Cornwall 76
Martin Music Books (Philip), N Yorks............ 199
Music By The Score, Cornwall..................... 73
Musicalania, Norfolk.................................. 189
Paramor (C.D.), Suffolk 229
Sheet Music Warehouse (The), Devon 88
Sherlaw-Johnson (Austin), Oxfordshire 210

SPECIALITY INDEX

The Old Music Master, Bristol 60
The Sanctuary Bookshop, Dorset 94
Travis & Emery Music Bookshop, London WC 180
Willmott Bookseller (Nicholas), Cardiff........... 283

- ROCK & ROLL

A. & R. Booksearch, Cornwall 74
Aucott & Thomas, Leics............................. 147
Barnes - Books (Lyndon), Shropshire 214
Bookpassage (The), Shropshire..................... 213
Bookshop (The), Norfolk 192
Dancing Goat Bookshop (The), Norfolk 188
Decorum Books, London N 158
firstpagebooks, Norfolk............................... 190
Furneaux Books (Lee), Devon...................... 89
Gravity Books, Lincolnshire 151
Joel Segal Books, Devon 86
McGee (Terence J.), London Outer 181
Morris Secondhand & Antiquarian Books
(Chris), Oxfordshire 210
Music By The Score, Cornwall...................... 73
R. & A. Books, E Sussex..... 102
Roland Books, Kent 139
Sclanders (Beatbooks), (Andrew), London EC... 157
Sheet Music Warehouse (The), Devon 88
Sherlaw-Johnson (Austin), Oxfordshire 210
Till's Bookshop, Lothian 279
Travis & Emery Music Bookshop, London WC 180
Yorkshire Relics, West Yorkshire................... 247

- SHEET MUSIC

Alba Secondhand Music, Strathclyde.............. 279
Apocalypse, Surrey 233
Bookshop (The), Norfolk 192
Browne (Christopher I.), West Yorkshire......... 247
Carningli Centre, Pembrokeshire................... 288
Cornucopia Books, Lincolnshire 153
Decorum Books, London N 158
Esoteric Dreams Bookshop, Cumbria 78
Ferguson (Elizabeth), Grampian 272
Forest Books, Rutland................................ 212
Good Book Shop, The, Devon...................... 90
Hab Books, London W............................... 173
Hancock & Monks, Powys.......................... 290
Joel Segal Books, Devon 86
McGee (Terence J.), London Outer 181
Mogul Diamonds, W Mids 241
Music By The Score, Cornwall...................... 73
Sheet Music Warehouse (The), Devon 88
Sherlaw-Johnson (Austin), Oxfordshire 210
Travis & Emery Music Bookshop, London WC 180
Willmott Bookseller (Nicholas), Cardiff........... 283

- SONGS & BALLADS

Alba Secondhand Music, Strathclyde.............. 279
Browne (Christopher I.), West Yorkshire......... 247
Decorum Books, London N 158
Fifteenth Century Bookshop (The), E Sussex 104
Hancock & Monks, Powys.......................... 290
Joel Segal Books, Devon 86
McGee (Terence J.), London Outer 181
Music By The Score, Cornwall...................... 73
Musicalania, Norfolk.................................. 189
Paramor (C.D.), Suffolk 229
Randall (Tom), Somerset............................ 219

Sheet Music Warehouse (The), Devon 88
Sherlaw-Johnson (Austin), Oxfordshire 210
Travis & Emery Music Bookshop, London WC 180

- THEORY

Alba Secondhand Music, Strathclyde.............. 279
Bath Old Books, Somerset 216
Browne (Christopher I.), West Yorkshire......... 247
Calendula Horticultural Books, E Sussex......... 102
Decorum Books, London N 158
Dooley (Rosemary), Cumbria 78
East Riding Books, East Yorkshire................. 107
Fifteenth Century Bookshop (The), E Sussex 104
Goodden (Peter), Somerset.......................... 216
Hancock & Monks, Powys.......................... 290
Joel Segal Books, Devon 86
Music By The Score, Cornwall...................... 73
Price (John), London N 159
Sheet Music Warehouse (The), Devon 88
Sherlaw-Johnson (Austin), Oxfordshire 210
Travis & Emery Music Bookshop, London WC 180

- WESTERNS

Decorum Books, London N 158
Sheet Music Warehouse (The), Devon 88
Sherlaw-Johnson (Austin), Oxfordshire 210
Travis & Emery Music Bookshop, London WC 180

MUSICAL INSTRUMENTS

Alba Secondhand Music, Strathclyde.............. 279
Barmby (C. & A.J.), Kent........................... 141
Bath Old Books, Somerset 216
Decorum Books, London N 158
Dooley (Rosemary), Cumbria 78
East Riding Books, East Yorkshire................. 107
Elgar (Raymond), E Sussex 99
Fifteenth Century Bookshop (The), E Sussex 104
Goodden (Peter), Somerset.......................... 216
Hancock & Monks, Powys.......................... 290
Handsworth Books, Essex........................... 112
Joel Segal Books, Devon 86
K.S.C. Books, Cheshire.............................. 71
Kitley (A.J.), Bristol.................................. 59
Martin Music Books (Philip), N Yorks 199
Orchid Book Distributors, Co. Clare............... 262
Sherlaw-Johnson (Austin), Oxfordshire 210
Travis & Emery Music Bookshop, London WC 180
Trinders' Fine Tools, Suffolk 227

MUSICAL INSTRUMENTS - GUITARS

Bookpassage (The), Shropshire..................... 213
Decorum Books, London N 158
Fifteenth Century Bookshop (The), E Sussex 104
K.S.C. Books, Cheshire.............................. 71
Sherlaw-Johnson (Austin), Oxfordshire 210
Travis & Emery Music Bookshop, London WC 180

MUSICIANS

Alba Secondhand Music, Strathclyde.............. 279
Bath Old Books, Somerset 216
Browne (Christopher I.), West Yorkshire......... 247
Dolphin Books, Suffolk............................... 226
Dooley (Rosemary), Cumbria 78
Fifteenth Century Bookshop (The), E Sussex 104
Goodden (Peter), Somerset.......................... 216

SPECIALITY INDEX

Hancock & Monks, Powys.......................... 290
Joel Segal Books, Devon 86
Martin Music Books (Philip), N Yorks 199
R. & A. Books, E Sussex............................ 102
Sheet Music Warehouse (The), Devon 88
Sherlaw-Johnson (Austin), Oxfordshire 210
Travis & Emery Music Bookshop, London WC 180
Willmott Bookseller (Nicholas), Cardiff........... 283

MYCOLOGY

Bernard Dixon and Kath Adams, Middlesex 183
Coch-y-Bonddu Books, Powys 292
Hollingshead (Chris), London Outer 183
Joel Segal Books, Devon 86
Park (Mike), London Outer.......................... 183
Parkinsons Books, Merseyside...................... 186
Pendleside Books, Lancashire....................... 144
R M Books, Herts..................................... 132

MYSTERIES

Apocalypse, Surrey 233
Furneaux Books (Lee), Devon...................... 89
Gildas Books, Cheshire 68
Inner Bookshop (The), Oxfordshire................ 210
Joel Segal Books, Devon 86
L.M.S. Books, Herts 132
Ming Books, Dumfries & Galloway................ 271
Mostly Mysteries Bookstore, Lincolnshire........ 152
Occultique, Northants................................. 200
Philip Hopper, Essex 110
R. & A. Books, E Sussex............................ 102
Robert Temple, London N........................... 160
Seabreeze Books, Lancashire........................ 145
Wheen O'Books, Scottish Borders 269
Wizard Books, Cambridgeshire..................... 67

MYSTICISM

Bardsley's Books, Suffolk............................ 226
Beckham Books Ltd., Suffolk 230
Bookbarrow, Cambridgeshire........................ 63
Bygone Books, Orkney 276
Cavern Books, Cheshire 70
Esoteric Dreams Bookshop, Cumbria 78
Facet Books, Dorset................................... 91
Fifteenth Century Bookshop (The), E Sussex 104
Greensleeves, Oxfordshire 207
Hancock (Peter), West Sussex 243
Hava Books, London SE............................. 165
Inner Bookshop (The), Oxfordshire................ 210
Joel Segal Books, Devon 86
Magis Books, Leics.................................... 149
Needham Books, (Russell), Somerset.............. 220
Occultique, Northants................................. 200
Pendleburys Bookshop, London N 159
Philip Hopper, Essex 110
R. & A. Books, E Sussex............................ 102
Reid of Liverpool, Merseyside...................... 185
Rosemary Pugh Books, Wiltshire 253
Samovar Books, Co. Dublin 264
Star Lord Books, Gr Man 119
Wizard Books, Cambridgeshire..................... 67

MYTHOLOGY

Alpha Books, London N 158
Apocalypse, Surrey 233

Atlantis Bookshop, London WC.................... 177
Brad Books, Essex..................................... 111
Brighton Books, E Sussex 99
Byre Books, Dumfries & Galloway................ 270
Cheshire Book Centre, Cheshire.................... 69
Daeron's Books, Buckinghamshire................. 62
Esoteric Dreams Bookshop, Cumbria 78
Fifteenth Century Bookshop (The), E Sussex 104
Galloway & Porter Limited, Cambridgeshire..... 64
Gildas Books, Cheshire 68
Green Man Books, E Sussex 101
Greensleeves, Oxfordshire 207
Inner Bookshop (The), Oxfordshire................ 210
Joel Segal Books, Devon 86
Karen Millward, Co. Cork........................... 263
Magis Books, Leics.................................... 149
Occultique, Northants................................. 200
R. & A. Books, E Sussex............................ 102
Randall (Tom), Somerset............................ 219
SETI Books, Staffordshire........................... 225
Seydi Rare Books (Sevin), London NW 162
Treadwell's Books, London WC 180
Watkins Books Ltd., London WC.................. 180
Wizard Books, Cambridgeshire..................... 67

NATIONAL GEOGRAPHIC

G. C. Books Ltd., Dumfries & Galloway......... 271
Hab Books, London W............................... 173
Naughton Booksellers, Co. Dublin 265
Orb's Bookshop, Grampian......................... 274
The Sanctuary Bookshop, Dorset.................. 94

NATIONAL PARKS

R. & A. Books, E Sussex............................ 102

NATIVE AMERICAN

Americanabooksuk, Cumbria........................ 77
Bookbarrow, Cambridgeshire........................ 63
Byre Books, Dumfries & Galloway................ 270
Fifteenth Century Bookshop (The), E Sussex 104
Inner Bookshop (The), Oxfordshire................ 210
Joel Segal Books, Devon 86
Magis Books, Leics.................................... 149
Occultique, Northants................................. 200
Optimus Books Ltd, West Sussex.................. 245
Orchid Book Distributors, Co. Clare.............. 262

NATIVE CANADIAN

Americanabooksuk, Cumbria........................ 77
Joel Segal Books, Devon 86

NATURAL HEALTH

Cheshire Book Centre, Cheshire.................... 69
Fifteenth Century Bookshop (The), E Sussex 104
Greensleeves, Oxfordshire 207
Hay Cinema Bookshop Ltd., Powys............... 290
IKON, Devon... 89
Joel Segal Books, Devon 86
Just Books, Cornwall 76
Occultique, Northants................................. 200
R. & A. Books, E Sussex............................ 102

NATURAL HISTORY

Abacus Books, Cheshire.............................. 68
Abacus Gallery, Staffordshire....................... 224

SPECIALITY INDEX

Alauda Books, Cumbria 78
Allhalland Books, Devon............................ 85
Allinson (Frank & Stella), Warwickshire 237
Andron (G.W.), London N 158
Anthony Whittaker, Kent 136
Antique Map and Bookshop (The), Dorset 94
Antiques on High, Oxfordshire......... 209
Arden Books & Cosmographia, Warwickshire... 237
Arden, Bookseller (C.), Powys...................... 289
Armstrong's Books & Collectables, Leics 147
Aurelian Books, London NW 161
Austwick Hall Books, N Yorks 193
Autumn Leaves, Lincolnshire 152
Aviabooks, Glos 114
Axe Rare & Out of Print Books (Richard),
N Yorks.. 194
Ayre (Peter J.), Somerset 220
Baldwin's Scientific Books, Essex 112
Barn Books, Buckinghamshire..................... 61
Barnhill Books, Isle of Arran 275
Baron (Christopher), Gr Man 118
Baron - Scientific Book Sales (P.J.), Somerset ... 217
Bath Old Books, Somerset 216
Bernard Dixon and Kath Adams, Middlesex 183
Besleys Books, Suffolk 226
Biblion, London W.................................... 172
Biblipola, London NW 161
Billing (Brian), Berkshire 57
Birdnet Optics Ltd., Derbyshire 82
Blest (Peter), Kent 139
Book Business (The), London W 172
Bookcase, Cumbria.................................... 78
Books & Collectables Ltd., Cambridgeshire 63
Books (For All), N Yorks............................ 194
Books and Things, CI................................. 258
Books For All, N Yorks 194
Bookworms, Norfolk.................................. 187
Booth Books, Powys 289
Bosorne Books, Cornwall 75
Bow Windows Book Shop, E Sussex.............. 103
Broadhurst of Southport Ltd., Merseyside 186
Broadleaf Books, Torfaen 294
Brock Books, N Yorks 193
Brookes (Gerard), Devon............................ 87
Burden Ltd., (Clive A.), Herts...................... 132
Calluna Books, Dorset................................ 95
Carlton Books, Norfolk 190
Carnforth Bookshop (The), Lancashire 143
Carningli Centre, Pembrokeshire................... 288
Castle Hill Books, Herefordshire................... 128
Castleton (Pat), Kent................................. 138
Chalmers Hallam (E.), Hants....................... 125
Chandos Books, Devon............................... 85
Channel Islands Galleries Limited, CI............. 258
Cheshire Book Centre, Cheshire.................... 69
Chevin Books, West Yorkshire 250
Chris Phillips, Wiltshire.............................. 251
Clark (M.R.), West Yorkshire...................... 246
Clarke Books (David), Somerset 219
Clent Books, Worcs 255
Cobbles Books, Somerset............................ 218
Coch-y-Bonddu Books, Powys 292
Collectable Books, London SE 165
Colonsay Bookshop, Isle of Colonsay............. 276
Corvus Books, Buckinghamshire................... 61

Country Books, Derbyshire 82
Cox Old & Rare Books (Claude), Suffolk 228
Creaking Shelves, Inverness-shire................... 275
Cumming Limited (A. & Y.), E Sussex 104
Curtle Mead Books, Isle of Wight 134
D'Arcy Books, Wiltshire............................. 252
Dales & Lakes Book Centre, Cumbria 80
Dandy Lion Editions, Surrey 233
Dartmoor Bookshop (The), Devon 84
David (G.), Cambridgeshire......................... 63
Davies Fine Books, Worcs 257
Demar Books (Grant), Kent 141
Dene Barn Books & Prints, Somerset 220
Dolphin Books, Suffolk............................... 226
Earth Science Books, Wiltshire 252
Eastcote Bookshop (The), London Outer......... 181
Edmund Pollinger Rare Books, London SW..... 167
Edwards (London) Limited (Francis),
London WC 177
Edwards in Hay-on-Wye (Francis), Powys 290
Elmbury Books, Warwickshire 238
Elmfield Books, W Mills 239
Evergreen Livres, Oxfordshire 208
Fifteenth Century Bookshop (The), E Sussex 104
Fine Art, London SW 168
Fine Books at Ilkley, West Yorkshire 248
Fireside Bookshop, Cumbria........................ 81
firstpagebooks, Norfolk............................... 190
Ford Books (David), Herts 133
Freader's Books, Tayside............................. 281
Freeman's Corner Shop, Norfolk 190
Garfi Books, Powys 293
Gaullifmaufry Books, Herts......................... 132
GfB: the Colchester Bookshop, Essex 109
Gibbard (A. & T.), E Sussex........................ 101
Gillmark Gallery, Herts............................... 131
Glenbower Books, Co. Dublin 265
Gloucester Road Bookshop, London SW 168
Goodyer (Nicholas), London N 159
Goodyer, Natural History Books (Eric), Leics... 148
Grahame (Major Iain), Suffolk 226
Grayling (David A.H.), Cumbria 79
Hall's Bookshop, Kent................................ 141
Halson Books, Cheshire 71
Harrington (Adrian), London W................... 173
Hawkridge Books, Derbyshire...................... 82
Hay Cinema Bookshop Ltd., Powys............... 290
Henly (John), West Sussex 245
Hereward Books, Cambridgeshire 66
Heywood Hill Limited (G.), London W 174
Hodgson (Books) (Richard J.), N Yorks 198
Hollett and Son (R.F.G.), Cumbria 80
Hollingshead (Chris), London Outer 183
Home Farm Books, Warwickshire.................. 237
Hünersdorff Rare Books, London SW 169
Ice House Books, Wiltshire 253
Inner Bookshop (The), Oxfordshire................ 210
Island Books, Devon.................................. 85
J. & J. Books, Lincolnshire 151
Jackson (M.W.), Wiltshire........................... 254
Jane Jones Books, Grampian 272
Jay Books, Lothian.................................... 278
JB Books & Collectables, West Sussex 244
Joel Segal Books, Devon 86
Just Books, Cornwall 76

SPECIALITY INDEX

Kalligraphia, Isle of Wight.......................... 134
Katnap Arts, Norfolk................................. 191
Keeble Antiques, Somerset.......................... 219
Keel Row Bookshop, Tyne and Wear 236
Kellow Books, Oxfordshire 207
Kennedy (Peter), Surrey 235
Kernaghans, Merseyside 186
Kim's Bookshop, West Sussex...........242, 243, 245
Kingsgate Books & Prints, Hants................... 126
Kingshead Books, Wales 293
Kingsmere Books, Bedfordshire 53
Kirkman Ltd., (Robert), Bedfordshire............. 54
Knapton Bookbarn, N Yorks 198
Korn (M. Eric), London N 159
Larkham Books (Patricia), Glos.................... 117
Lenton (Alfred), Leics................................. 147
Lymelight Books & Prints, Dorset................. 93
Maggs Brothers Limited, London W.............. 174
Malvern Bookshop (The), Worcs 255
Mannwaring (M.G.), Bristol 59
Marshall Rare Books (Bruce), Glos 113
Martin (Books and Pictures), (Brian P)., Surrey. 232
Martin's Books, Powys 292
McCrone (Audrey), Isle of Arran................... 275
McEwan Fine Books, Grampian.................... 273
McNaughtan's Bookshop, Lothian 278
Meads Book Service (The), E Sussex.............. 104
Mobbs (A.J.), W Mids................................ 241
Moorhead Books, West Yorkshire.................. 246
Moreton Books, Devon............................... 87
Muse Bookshop (The), Gwynedd 287
Neil Summersgill, Lancashire 143
New Strand Bookshop (The), Herefordshire 128
Nineteenth Century Books, Oxfordshire 211
O'Flynn Books, N Yorks............................. 199
Old Station Pottery & Bookshop (The), Norfolk 192
Old Town Bookshop (The), Lothian 278
Orb's Bookshop, Grampian......................... 274
Oxfam Books and Music, Hants 126
Page (David), Lothian 278
Pandion Books, N Yorks............................. 195
Paralos Ltd., London WC 178
Park (Mike), London Outer.......................... 183
Parrott Books, Oxfordshire 211
Pemberley Books, Buckinghamshire 62
Peregrine Books (Leeds), West Yorkshire......... 249
Peter M Daly, Hants.................................. 127
Phelps (Michael), West Sussex...................... 243
Pordes Booke I td., (Henry), London WC........ 179
Priestpopple Books, Northumberland 202
Quentin Books Ltd, Essex........................... 109
Quinto of Great Russell Street, London WC 179
R. & A. Books, E Sussex............................. 102
R.E. & G.B. Way, Suffolk 229
Read (C.&J.), Gorleston Books, Norfolk 188
Richard Thornton Books, London N 160
River Reads Bookshop, Devon...................... 90
Roland Books, Kent 139
Roz Hulse, Conwy 286
Russell (Charles), London SW....................... 170
Rutland Bookshop (The), Rutland 212
Rye Old Books, E Sussex 104
Ryeland Books, Northants........................... 200
St Ann's Books, Worcs............................... 255
Saintfield Antiques & Fine Books, Co. Down ... 261

Saracen Books, Derbyshire.......................... 83
Second Edition, Lothian.............................. 278
Shakeshaft (Dr. B.), Cheshire....................... 71
Shearwater Books, Northumberland............... 202
Smith (Clive), Essex 109
Smith Books, (Sally), Suffolk 227
Sotheran Limited (Henry), London W 176
Stella Books, Monmouthshire 288
Stone, (G.& R.), Borders............................ 268
Stroma Books, Borders 268
Sue Lowell Natural History Books, London W . 176
Sykes (Graham), West Yorkshire 249
Tant Yn Ellen Books, Powys 293
Tarka Books, Devon.................................. 84
Temperley (David), W Mids 239
The Old Abbey Bookshop, Co. Down 261
Thomas (E. Wyn), Conwy 285
Trinity Rare Books, Co. Leitrim 266
Uncle Phil's Books, W Mids........................ 240
Vickers (Anthony), N Yorks........................ 196
Vinovium Books, Durham 97
Vokes Books Ltd., N Yorks 195
Wadard Books, Kent 138
Westons, Herts 133
Westwood Books Ltd, Cumbria.................... 80
Wheen O'Books, Scottish Borders 269
Whistler (R.A.), E Sussex 99
Wildside Books, Worcs 255
Wilson (David), Buckinghamshire 61
Wise (Derek), E Sussex 104
Wizard Books, Cambridgeshire..................... 67
Woodbine Books, West Yorkshire.................. 246
Woodside Books, Kent 136
Words Etcetera Bookshop, Dorset................. 93
Wychwood Books, Glos.............................. 116
Wyseby House Books, Berkshire................... 55

NATURAL SCIENCES

Alauda Books, Cumbria.............................. 78
Austwick Hall Books, N Yorks 193
Barcombe Services, Essex............................ 108
Bernard Dixon and Kath Adams, Middlesex 183
Cheshire Book Centre, Cheshire.................... 69
Cornucopia Books, Lincolnshire 153
Demetzy Books, Oxfordshire 208
Earth Science Books, Wiltshire 252
Esplin (David), Hants................................ 124
Fifteenth Century Bookshop (The), E Sussex 104
J & J Burgess Booksellers, Cambridgeshire....... 64
Jackdaw Books, Norfolk 189
Joel Segal Books, Devon 86
Kalligraphia, Isle of Wight 134
Lymelight Books & Prints, Dorset............ ,, 93
Mannwaring (M.G.), Bristol 59
Mercat Books, Highland 274
Mobbs (A.J.), W Mids................................ 241
Moorside Books, Lancashire........................ 144
Parkinsons Books, Merseyside...................... 186
Phelps (Michael), West Sussex...................... 243
Pollak (P.M.), Devon 89
R M Books, Herts..................................... 132
Summerfield Books Ltd, Cumbria 77
Turret House, Norfolk................................ 192
Westons, Herts 133
Wildside Books, Worcs 255

SPECIALITY INDEX

Wyseby House Books, Berkshire 55

NATURE

Alauda Books, Cumbria 78
Castleton (Pat), Kent 138
Coch-y-Bonddu Books, Powys 292
Cornucopia Books, Lincolnshire 153
Dales & Lakes Book Centre, Cumbria 80
Demar Books (Grant), Kent 141
Dolphin Books, Suffolk 226
Fifteenth Century Bookshop (The), E Sussex 104
Inner Bookshop (The), Oxfordshire................. 210
Joel Segal Books, Devon 86
Kineton Nooks, Warwickshire........................ 237
Mercat Books, Highland 274
Mobbs (A.J.), W Mids................................ 241
Peter M Daly, Hants 127
R. & A. Books, E Sussex............................. 102
Summerfield Books Ltd, Cumbria 77
Wheen O'Books, Scottish Borders 269

NATURISM

Green (Paul), Cambridgeshire 67
R. & A Books, E Sussex.............................. 102

NAVAL

AA1 Books, Dumfries & Galloway.................. 270
Alauda Books, Cumbria............................... 78
Anchor Books, Lincolnshire 151
Andron (G.W.), London N 158
Armchair Auctions, Hants 121
Aviabooks, Glos 114
Barnes (Peter), Wiltshire 253
Baynton–Williams Gallery, West Sussex 242
Book For All Reasons (A.), Suffolk 229
Bookends of Fowey, Cornwall 73
books2books, Devon 88
Bookworm, Lothian 277
Bookworm (The), Lothian 277
Bott, (Bookdealers) Ltd., (Martin), Gr Man 118
Broadhurst of Southport Ltd., Merseyside 186
Burroughs (Andrew), Lincolnshire 153
Camilla's Bookshop, E Sussex 101
Cavern Books, Cheshire 70
Cheshire Book Centre, Cheshire..................... 69
Cofion Books, Pembrokeshire 288
Coles (T.V.), Cambridgeshire 67
Corfe Books, Surrey................................... 231
Cornucopia Books, Lincolnshire 153
Cotswold Internet Books, Glos...................... 113
Cox (Geoff), Devon 90
Curtle Mead Books, Isle of Wight 134
Dormouse Bookshop (The), Norfolk 190
Edwards (London) Limited (Francis),
London WC 177
Edwards in Hay-on-Wye (Francis), Powys 290
Elton Engineering Books, London W 173
Empire Books, N Yorks............................... 198
Fifteenth Century Bookshop (The), E Sussex 104
Gallimaufry Books, Herts 132
Gaullifmaufry Books, Herts.......................... 132
George St. Books, Derbyshire 83
Gerald Lee Maritime Books, E Sussex 105
Good for Books, Lincolnshire 151
Green Ltd. (G.L.), Herts 132

Handsworth Books, Essex............................ 112
Harris (George J.), Co. Derry 260
Helion & Company, W Mids........................ 240
Internet Bookshop UK Ltd., Glos.................. 113
J & J Burgess Booksellers, Cambridgeshire....... 64
Jade Mountain Bookshop, Hants 126
Joel Segal Books, Devon 86
Keegan's Bookshop, Berkshire 56
Lewcock (John), Cambridgeshire.................... 66
Lost Books, Northants................................. 201
Marcet Books, London SE............................ 165
Marine & Cannon Books, Cheshire 71
Marine and Cannon Books, Cheshire 69
Martin Bookshop & Gallery (Richard), Hants... 123
McCrone (Audrey), Isle of Arran 275
McLaren Books, Strathclyde......................... 280
Meekins Books (Paul), Warwickshire.............. 238
Milestone Books, Devon 89
MilitaryHistoryBooks.com, Kent.................... 138
N1 Books, E Sussex 105
Nautical Antique Centre (The), Dorset 96
Not Just Books, Dorset 94
Prior (Michael), Lincolnshire 153
R. & A. Books, E Sussex............................. 102
Robert Humm & Co, Lincolnshire 154
Rods Books, Devon 88
Second Edition, Lothian............................... 278
Simmonds (Anthony J.), London SE............... 166
Spooner (John E.), Dorset 91
Sub Aqua Prints and Books, Hants 123
Surprise Books, Glos.................................. 113
Thin Read Line, Merseyside 185
Tilston (Stephen E.), London SE.................... 166
Wadard Books, Kent 138
War & Peace Books, Hants.......................... 122
Warwick Leadley Gallery, London SE............. 166
Webb Books (John), S Yorks.................. 222
Wheen O'Books, Scottish Borders 269
Wise (Derek), E Sussex 104
World War Books, Kent 141
World War II Books, Surrey 235
Yesterday's News, Conwy 285

NAVIGATION

Anvil Books, W Mids................................. 240
Books Afloat, Dorset.................................. 96
Cornucopia Books, Lincolnshire 153
Curtle Mead Books, Isle of Wight 134
Jade Mountain Bookshop, Hants 126
Joel Segal Books, Devon 86
Keith Langford, London E 155
Lewcock (John), Cambridgeshire.................... 66
Marcet Books, London SE............................ 165
Marine & Cannon Books, Cheshire 71
Marine and Cannon Books, Cheshire 69
McLaren Books, Strathclyde......................... 280
Milestone Books, Devon 89
Nautical Antique Centre (The), Dorset 96
R. & A. Books, E Sussex............................. 102
Rods Books, Devon.................................... 88
Sea Chest Nautical Bookshop (The), Devon 88
Warsash Nautical Bookshop, Hants................ 126

NAVY, THE

Aardvark Books, Wiltshire........................... 254

SPECIALITY INDEX

Bath Old Books, Somerset 216
Empire Books, N Yorks.............................. 198
Falconwood Transport & Military Bookshop,
London Outer 184
Fifteenth Century Bookshop (The), E Sussex 104
Gerald Lee Maritime Books, E Sussex 105
Green Ltd. (G.L.), Herts 132
Jade Mountain Bookshop, Hants 126
Joel Segal Books, Devon 86
Keith Langford, London E 155
Marcet Books, London SE........................... 165
Marine and Cannon Books, Cheshire 69
Martin Bookshop & Gallery (Richard), Hants... 123
Milestone Books, Devon 89
N1 Books, E Sussex 105
R. & A. Books, E Sussex............................. 102
Robert Humm & Co, Lincolnshire 154
Rods Books, Devon 88
War & Peace Books, Hants.......................... 122
Wheen O'Books, Scottish Borders 269
World War II Books, Surrey 235

NEEDLEWORK

Apocalypse, Surrey 233
Arden Books & Cosmographia, Warwickshire... 237
Axe Rare & Out of Print Books (Richard),
N Yorks... 194
Birchden Books, London E 155
Black Cat Books, Norfolk............................ 188
Brock Books, N Yorks 193
Brown-Studies, Strathclyde.......................... 279
Byrom Textile Bookroom (Richard), Lancashire 143
Chevin Books, West Yorkshire 250
Cover to Cover, Merseyside......................... 186
Don Kelly Books, London W 172
DPE Books, Devon 87
Fifteenth Century Bookshop (The), E Sussex 104
Four Shire Bookshops, Glos......................... 114
Good for Books, Lincolnshire 151
Gresham Books, Somerset 218
Heneage Art Books (Thomas), London SW 169
Hennessey Bookseller (Ray), E Sussex 100
Ives Bookseller (John), London Outer 184
Joel Segal Books, Devon 86
Judith Mansfield, West Yorkshire.................. 250
McNaughtan's Bookshop, Lothian 278
Old Bookshop (The), W Mids...................... 241
R. & A. Books, E Sussex............................. 102
Reading Lasses, Dumfries & Galloway 271
Scrivener's Books & Bookbinding, Derbyshire .. 82
Sleepy Elephant Books & Artefacts, Cumbria ... 80
Smith Books (Keith), Herefordshire 128
Trinders' Fine Tools, Suffolk 227
Wheen O'Books, Scottish Borders 269
Whittle, Bookseller (Avril), Cumbria 81

NEUROLOGY

Alba Books, Grampian 274
Barcombe Services, Essex............................ 108
Bernard Dixon and Kath Adams, Middlesex 183
Erian Books, London N.............................. 158
Game Advice, Oxfordshire 210
Mair Wilkes Books, Fife 272
Parkinsons Books, Merseyside...................... 186
Phelps (Michael), West Sussex...................... 243

R M Books, Herts..................................... 132
R. & A. Books, E Sussex............................. 102
Turret House, Norfolk 192
Westons, Herts 133

NEW AGE

2 Ravens, Cumbria 79
Abacus Gallery, Staffordshire....................... 224
Books For All, N Yorks 194
Chthonios Books, E Sussex 102
Dawlish Books, Devon 86
DPE Books, Devon 87
Esoteric Dreams Bookshop, Cumbria 78
Greensleeves, Oxfordshire 207
IKON, Devon.. 89
Inner Bookshop (The), Oxfordshire................ 210
Innes Books, Shropshire 214
Invisible Books, E Sussex............................ 100
Joel Segal Books, Devon 86
Keel Row Bookshop, Tyne and Wear 236
Magis Books, Leics................................... 149
Occultique, Northants................................ 200
Orchid Book Distributors, Co. Clare............... 262
R. & A. Books, E Sussex............................. 102
SETI Books, Staffordshire........................... 225
Till's Bookshop, Lothian 279
Trinity Rare Books, Co. Leitrim 266
Words Etcetera Bookshop, Dorset................. 93
Worlds End Bookshop, London SW............... 171

NEW NATURALIST

Alauda Books, Cumbria 78
Antique Map and Bookshop (The), Dorset 94
Birdnet Optics Ltd., Derbyshire 82
Blest (Peter), Kent 139
Books and Things, Channel Islands 258
BOOKS4U, Flintshire................................ 286
BookShop, The, Dumfries & Galloway........... 270
Broadhurst of Southport Ltd., Merseyside 186
Calluna Books, Dorset................................ 95
Chalmers Hallam (E.), Hants....................... 125
Cheshire Book Centre, Cheshire.................... 69
Coch-y-Bonddu Books, Powys 292
Creaking Shelves, Inverness-shire.................. 275
Dales & Lakes Book Centre, Cumbria............ 80
Demar Books (Grant), Kent 141
Fifteenth Century Bookshop (The), E Sussex 104
Ford Books (David), Herts 133
Hollett and Son (R.F.G.), Cumbria 80
J & J Burgess Booksellers, Cambridgeshire....... 64
J. & J. Books, Lincolnshire 151
Jackdaw Books, Norfolk 189
Jay Books, Lothian................................... 278
Joel Segal Books, Devon 86
Just Books, Cornwall 76
Muse Bookshop (The), Gwynedd 287
Park (Mike), London Outer......................... 183
Pemberley Books, Buckinghamshire 62
Peter M Daly, Hants................................. 127
Polmorla Books, Cornwall 76
Poor Richard's Books, Suffolk 227
R. & A. Books, E Sussex............................. 102
Roger Collicott Books, Cornwall 75
St Ann's Books, Worcs 255
Scrivener's Books & Bookbinding, Derbyshire... 82

SPECIALITY INDEX

Shakeshaft (Dr. B.), Cheshire 71
Shearwater Books, Northumberland 202
Sue Lowell Natural History Books, London W . 176
Summerfield Books Ltd, Cumbria 77
Vickers (Anthony), N Yorks 196
Westwood Books (Mark), Powys 291
Westwood Books Ltd, Cumbria 80
Wildside Books, Worcs 255

NEW WORLD

Joel Segal Books, Devon 86

NEWBERY & CALDECOTT AWARD-WINNERS

Bufo Books, Hants 125
Fifteenth Century Bookshop (The), E Sussex 104

NEWSPAPERS

Derek Stirling Bookseller, Kent 142
John Underwood Antiquarian Books, Norfolk .. 190
Ken's Paper Collectables, Buckinghamshire 62
Mr. Pickwick ot Towcester, Northants 201
Mulyan (Don), Merseyside 186
Nostalgia Unlimited, Merseyside 186
Tilleys Vintage Magazine Shop, Derbyshire 82
Yesterday's News, Conwy 285

NON-FICTION

Abbey Books, Cornwall 74
Apocalypse, Surrey 233
Barcombe Services, Essex 108
Bath Old Books, Somerset 216
books2books, Devon 88
Booth (Booksearch Service), (Geoff), Cheshire... 68
Carningli Centre, Pembrokeshire 288
Castleton (Pat), Kent 138
Catmax Books, Norfolk 187
Clent Books, Worcs 255
Dolphin Books, Suffolk 226
Fackley Services, Notts 205
Fifteenth Century Bookshop (The), E Sussex 104
Foster Bookshop (Paul), London SW 168
George St. Books, Derbyshire 83
HCB Wholesale, Powys 290
Joel Segal Books, Devon 86
Loretta Lay Books, London NW 162
Marble Hill Books, Middlesex 184
MilitaryHistoryBooks.com, Kent 138
Mobbs (A.J.), W Mids 241
Morris Secondhand & Antiquarian Books (Chris),
Oxfordshire 210
Mount's Bay Books, Cornwall 75
Muttonchop Manuscripts, West Sussex 244
Naughton Booksellers, Co. Dublin 265
Orb's Bookshop, Grampian 274
R. & A. Books, E Sussex 102
Reading Lasses, Dumfries & Galloway 271
Sax Books, Suffolk 229
SETI Books, Staffordshire 225
Shakeshaft (Dr. B.), Cheshire 71
Skoob Russell Square, Suffolk 230
Star Lord Books, Gr Man 119
Wheen O'Books, Scottish Borders 269
Williams (Bookdealer), (Richard), N Lincs 154

NOSTALGIA

Border Bookshop, West Yorkshire 250
Fifteenth Century Bookshop (The), E Sussex 104
McGee (Terence J.), London Outer 181
Nostalgia Unlimited, Merseyside 186
Prior (Michael), Lincolnshire 153
Till's Bookshop, Lothian 279
Yesterday's News, Conwy 285

NOVELTY

Fifteenth Century Bookshop (The), E Sussex 104
Green Meadow Books, Cornwall 74

NUCLEAR ISSUES

Westons, Herts 133

NUMEROLOGY

Inner Bookshop (The), Oxfordshire 210
Magis Books, Leics 149

NUMISMATICS

Clark (Nigel A.), London SE 165
Heneage Art Books (Thomas), London SW 169
InterCol London, London N 159
Joel Segal Books, Devon 86
Parkinsons Books, Merseyside 186
Spink, London WC 179
Taylor & Son (Peter), Herts 133

NURSERY RHYMES

Castleton (Pat), Kent 138
Country Books, Derbyshire 82
Fifteenth Century Bookshop (The), E Sussex 104
Green Meadow Books, Cornwall 74
JB Books & Collectables, West Sussex 244
Jean Hedger, Berkshire 55
Joel Segal Books, Devon 86
Lake (David), Norfolk 191
R. & A. Books, E Sussex 102
Travis & Emery Music Bookshop, London WC 180

NURSES/DOCTORS

Game Advice, Oxfordshire 210
R M Books, Herts 132
Reading Lasses, Dumfries & Galloway 271

OCCULT

Alpha Books, London N 158
Annie's Books, S Yorks 222
Anthroposophical Books, Glos 116
Apocalypse, Surrey 233
Atlantis Bookshop, London WC 177
Berwick Books, Lincolnshire 152
Bookbarrow, Cambridgeshire 63
Books, Denbighshire 286
Bygone Books, Orkney 276
Byre Books, Dumfries & Galloway 270
Caduceus Books, Leics 147
Cavern Books, Cheshire 70
Central Bookshop, Warwickshire 238
Cheshire Book Centre, Cheshire 69
Chthonios Books, E Sussex 102
Clegg (David), Staffordshire 224
Dartmoor Bookshop (The), Devon 84
Dawlish Books, Devon 86

SPECIALITY INDEX

Delectus Books, London WC...................... 177
Enigma Books, Norfolk 190
Esoteric Dreams Bookshop, Cumbria 78
Gilbert (R.A.), Bristol................................ 59
Gildas Books, Cheshire 68
Green Man Books, E Sussex 101
Greensleeves, Oxfordshire 207
Hava Books, London SE............................ 165
Hay Cinema Bookshop Ltd., Powys............... 290
Inner Bookshop (The), Oxfordshire................ 210
J & J Burgess Booksellers, Cambridgeshire....... 64
Joel Segal Books, Devon 86
Loretta Lay Books, London NW................... 162
Lucius Books, N Yorks.............................. 199
Magis Books, Leics................................... 149
Needham Books, (Russell), Somerset.............. 220
Occultique, Northants................................ 200
Old Celtic Bookshop (The), Devon 88
Philip Hopper, Essex................................. 110
R. & A. Books, E Sussex............................ 102
SETI Books, Staffordshire........................... 225
Till's Bookshop, Lothian 279
Treadwell's Books, London WC 180
Treasure Chest Books, Suffolk 227
Victoria Bookshop (The), Devon................... 84
Walker Fine Books (Steve), Dorset 92
Watkins Books Ltd., London WC.................. 180
Waxfactor, E Sussex 100
Wizard Books, Cambridgeshire..................... 67
Worlds End Bookshop, London SW............... 171

OCEAN LINERS

Chas J. Sawyer, Kent 141
Cox (Geoff), Devon 90
Dales and Lakes Book Centre, Cumbria.......... 80
Fifteenth Century Bookshop (The), E Sussex 104
Gerald Lee Maritime Books, E Sussex 105
Joel Segal Books, Devon 86
Marine & Cannon Books, Cheshire 71
Marine and Cannon Books, Cheshire 69
Milestone Books, Devon 89
Robert Humm & Co, Lincolnshire 154

OCEANOGRAPHY

Baldwin's Scientific Books, Essex 112
Parkinsons Books, Merseyside...................... 186
Periplus Books, Buckinghamshire.................. 62
Weiner (Graham), London N 160

ODD & UNUSUAL

Book Business (The), London W 172
Delectus Books, London WC....................... 177
Esoteric Dreams Bookshop, Cumbria 78
Facet Books, Dorset.................................. 91
Game Advice, Oxfordshire 210
Gildas Books, Cheshire 68
Glenbower Books, Co. Dublin 265
Good for Books, Lincolnshire 151
Hurst (Jenny), Kent 138
Just Books, Cornwall 76
Lewis (J.T. & P.), Cornwall 74
Lighthouse Books (The), Dorset 92
Moss Books, London NW........................... 162
Muttonchop Manuscripts, West Sussex 244
Occultique, Northants................................ 200

Old Station Pottery & Bookshop (The), Norfolk 192
Parkinsons Books, Merseyside...................... 186
Reid of Liverpool, Merseyside...................... 185
Roger Treglown, Cheshire........................... 70
Rutland Bookshop (The), Rutland 212
Williams (Bookdealer), (Richard), N Lincs....... 154

OIL INDUSTRY

Joel Segal Books, Devon 86
Mandalay Bookshop, London SW 169
Weiner (Graham), London N 160

OIL LAMPS

Don Kelly Books, London W....................... 172
Weiner (Graham), London N 160

OLD WEST

Americanabooksuk, Cumbria 77
Fifteenth Century Bookshop (The), E Sussex 104
Joel Segal Books, Devon 86
Keel Row Bookshop, Tyne and Wear 236

OPHTHALMOLOGY

Parkinsons Books, Merseyside...................... 186
R M Books, Herts.................................... 132
Weiner (Graham), London N 160
Westons, Herts 133

OPTICAL

Parkinsons Books, Merseyside...................... 186
Stroh (M.A.), London E 155
Weiner (Graham), London N 160
Westons, Herts 133

ORDERS, DECORATIONS & MEDALS

Clark (Nigel A.), London SE 165
Joel Segal Books, Devon 86
MilitaryHistoryBooks.com, Kent................... 138

ORGANS

Birchden Books, London E 155
Joel Segal Books, Devon 86
Martin Music Books (Philip), N Yorks 199
Travis & Emery Music Bookshop, London WC 180

ORIENTAL

Art Reference Books, Hants 125
Books, Denbighshire 286
Canon Gate Books, West Sussex................... 244
Hosains Books, London NW 162
Joel Segal Books, Devon 86
Joppa Books Ltd., Surrey 231
Mandalay Bookshop, London SW 169
Probsthain (Arthur), London WC 179
R. & A. Books, E Sussex............................ 102

ORNITHOLOGY

Alauda Books, Cumbria.............................. 78
Anwoth Books Ltd, Dumfries & Galloway 270
Arden, Bookseller (C.), Powys..................... 289
Aviabooks, Glos 114
Barnhill Books, Isle of Arran 275
Besleys Books, Suffolk 226
Birdnet Optics Ltd., Derbyshire 82
Blest (Peter), Kent 139

SPECIALITY INDEX

Bosco Books, Cornwall 73
Brad Books, Essex 111
Brock Books, N Yorks 193
Brown (Books) (P.R.), Durham 98
Calendula Horticultural Books, E Sussex 102
Calluna Books, Dorset 95
Carlton Books, Norfolk 190
Coach House Books, Worcs 256
Coch-y-Bonddu Books, Powys 292
Cornucopia Books, Lincolnshire 153
Countrymans Gallery (The), Leics 147
Curtle Mead Books, Isle of Wight 134
Dancing Goat Bookshop (The), Norfolk 188
Demar Books (Grant), Kent 141
Dolphin Books, Suffolk 226
Edmund Pollinger Rare Books, London SW 167
Fifteenth Century Bookshop (The), E Sussex 104
Goodyer (Nicholas), London N 159
Hawkridge Books, Derbyshire 82
Inner Bookshop (The), Oxfordshire 210
Internet Bookshop UK Ltd., Glos 113
Jay Books, Lothian 278
Joel Segal Books, Devon 86
Kellow Books, Oxfordshire 207
Kirkman Ltd., (Robert), Bedfordshire 54
Mandalay Bookshop, London SW 169
Martin (Books and Pictures), (Brian P)., Surrey . 232
Martin's Books, Powys 292
Mayhew (Veronica), Berkshire 57
McEwan Fine Books, Grampian 273
Mobbs (A.J.), W Mids 241
Moss Books, London NW 162
Pandion Books, N Yorks 195
Park (Mike), London Outer 183
Parkinsons Books, Merseyside 186
Pauline Harries Books, Hants 123
Pemberley Books, Buckinghamshire 62
Peter M Daly, Hants 127
Poor Richard's Books, Suffolk 227
Prospect House Books, Co. Down 261
R. & A. Books, E Sussex 102
Richard Thornton Books, London N 160
Rutland Bookshop (The), Rutland 212
St Ann's Books, Worcs 255
Saintfield Antiques & Fine Books, Co. Down ... 261
Shearwater Books, Northumberland 202
Staniland (Booksellers), Lincolnshire 154
Stella Books, Monmouthshire 288
Sue Lowell Natural History Books, London W . 176
Uncle Phil's Books, W Mids 240
Wensum Books, Norfolk 191
Westons, Herts 133
Wildside Books, Worcs 255
Woodside Books, Kent 136
Wyseby House Books, Berkshire 55

OSTEOPATHY

Inner Bookshop (The), Oxfordshire 210
Phelps (Michael), West Sussex 243

OTTOMAN EMPIRE

Collectables (W.H.), Suffolk 230
Empire Books, N Yorks 198
Hosains Books, London NW 162
Joppa Books Ltd., Surrey 231

Seydi Rare Books (Sevin), London NW 162

OUT-OF-PRINT

Apocalypse, Surrey 233
Aurora Books Ltd., Lothian 276
Black Cat Books, Norfolk 188
Black Cat Bookshop, Leics 147
Book Business (The), London W 172
Book Mad, Lancashire 143
Book Palace (The), London SE 164
Brad Books, Essex 111
Central Bookshop, Warwickshire 238
Chelifer Books, Cumbria 81
Clifford Elmer Books Ltd., Cheshire 68
Coch-y-Bonddu Books, Powys 292
Cornucopia Books, Lincolnshire 153
Cotswold Internet Books, Glos 113
Country Books, Derbyshire 82
Dales & Lakes Book Centre, Cumbria 80
Dolphin Books, Suffolk 226
Fackley Services, Notts 205
Fifteenth Century Bookshop (The), E Sussex 104
Foster (Stephen), London NW 161
Foster Bookshop (Paul), London SW 168
Fosters Bookshop, London W 173
Glasheen-Books, Surrey 232
Glenbower Books, Co. Dublin 265
Good for Books, Lincolnshire 151
Hava Books, London SE 165
Inner Bookshop (The), Oxfordshire 210
J & J Burgess Booksellers, Cambridgeshire 64
Joel Segal Books, Devon 86
Just Books, Cornwall 76
Marine and Cannon Books, Cheshire 69
Naughton Booksellers, Co. Dublin 265
Orb's Bookshop, Grampian 274
Parkinsons Books, Merseyside 186
Print Matters, London SE 166
Reading Lasses, Dumfries & Galloway 271
Samovar Books, Co. Dublin 264
Sax Books, Suffolk 229
Shakeshaft (Dr. B.), Cheshire 71
Skoob Russell Square, Suffolk 230
Sol Books, Devon 84
Uncle Phil's Books, W Mids 240
Volume Three, Clackmannanshire 269
Wheen O'Books, Scottish Borders 269

OUTDOORS

Castleton (Pat), Kent 138
Dales & Lakes Book Centre, Cumbria 80
Fifteenth Century Bookshop (The), E Sussex 104
Greta Books, Durham 97
John R. Hoggarth, N Yorks 198

OUTLAWS

Americanabooksuk, Cumbria 77
Loretta Lay Books, London NW 162

OXFORD MOVEMENT

Beckham Books Ltd., Suffolk 230
Carter, (Brian), Oxfordshire 211
Dolphin Books, Suffolk 226
Morris Secondhand & Antiquarian Books (Chris),
Oxfordshire 210

SPECIALITY INDEX

R. & A. Books, E Sussex............................ 102
Rosemary Pugh Books, Wiltshire 253
S.P.C.K., Bristol 60
Samovar Books, Co. Dublin 264

PACIFISM

Books Only, Suffolk................................... 227
Larkham Books (Patricia), Glos.................... 117
Left on The Shelf, Cumbria.......................... 79
Moss Books, London NW 162
Spurrier (Nick), Kent 138
Woburn Books, London N 160
Yesterday's Books, Dorset 92
Yesterday's News, Conwy............................ 285

PADDLE BOATS

Bott, (Bookdealers) Ltd., (Martin), Gr Man 118
Cox (Geoff), Devon 90
Fifteenth Century Bookshop (The), E Sussex 104
Marine & Cannon Books, Cheshire 71
Marine and Cannon Books, Cheshire 69
Robert Humm & Co, Lincolnshire 154
Yesteryear Railwayana, Kent........................ 139

PAGANISM

Atlantis Bookshop, London WC.................... 177
Bygone Books, Orkney 276
Chthonios Books, E Sussex 102
Inner Bookshop (The), Oxfordshire................. 210
Joel Segal Books, Devon 86
Occultique, Northants................................. 200
R. & A. Books, E Sussex............................. 102
Treasure Trove Books, Leics......................... 148

PAINTING

Apocalypse, Surrey 233
Art Reference Books, Hants 125
Booth (Booksearch Service), (Geoff), Cheshire... 68
Butts Books (Mary), Berkshire 56
Cheshire Book Centre, Cheshire..................... 69
Don Kelly Books, London W 172
Fifteenth Century Bookshop (The), E Sussex 104
Grosvenor Prints, London WC...................... 178
Heneage Art Books (Thomas), London SW 169
Joel Segal Books, Devon 86
McCrone (Audrey), Isle of Arran................... 275
Modern Firsts Etc, Lancashire 143
Polmorla Books, Cornwall 76
Print Matters, London SE............................ 166
R. & A. Books, E Sussex............................. 102
Treasure Island (The), Gr Man...................... 119
Trinity Rare Books, Co. Leitrim 266

PALAEOGRAPHY

Bennett & Kerr Books, Oxfordshire 206
Brinded (Scott), Kent 139
Earth Science Books, Wiltshire 252
Gildas Books, Cheshire 68
Island Books, Devon................................... 85
Leeds Bookseller, West Yorkshire 249
Taylor & Son (Peter), Herts.......................... 133

PALAEONTOLOGY

Baldwin's Scientific Books, Essex 112
Cox, Andrew, Shropshire............................. 215

Earth Science Books, Wiltshire 252
Esoteric Dreams Bookshop, Cumbria 78
Henly (John), West Sussex 245
Kalligraphia, Isle of Wight........................... 134
Kenya Books, E Sussex............................... 100
Kingswood Books, Dorset 94
Little Bookshop (The), Cumbria 81
Lymelight Books & Prints, Dorset.................. 93
Parkinsons Books, Merseyside....................... 186
Pemberley Books, Buckinghamshire 62
Sykes (Graham), West Yorkshire 249
The Sanctuary Bookshop, Dorset................... 94
Webb Books (John), S Yorks........................ 222
Weiner (Graham), London N 160

PALMISTRY & FORTUNE-TELLING

Alpha Books, London N 158
Cavern Books, Cheshire 70
Fifteenth Century Bookshop (The), E Sussex 104
Inner Bookshop (The), Oxfordshire................. 210
Joel Segal Books, Devon 86
Magis Books, Leics.................................... 149
Occultique, Northants................................. 200
R. & A. Books, E Sussex............................. 102
Treasure Island (The), Gr Man...................... 119

PANTOMIME

R. & A. Books, E Sussex............................. 102

PAPER COLLECTABLES

Book Palace (The), London SE 164
Embleton (Paul), Essex 111
Green Meadow Books, Cornwall 74
Joel Segal Books, Devon 86
John Underwood Antiquarian Books, Norfolk .. 190
Ken's Paper Collectables, Buckinghamshire 62
Murphy (C.J.), Norfolk............................... 190
Print Matters, London SE............................ 166
Stalagluft Books, Tyne and Wear................... 236
Wiend Books, Lancashire 144
Williams (Bookdealer), (Richard), N Lincs....... 154

PAPERMAKING

Barry McKay Rare Books, Cumbria................ 77
Bettridge (Gordon), Fife.............................. 272
Brinded (Scott), Kent 139
Coupland (Terry W.), Staffordshire................. 224
Cox Old & Rare Books (Claude), Suffolk 228
Forest Books, Notts................................... 205
Joel Segal Books, Devon 86
R. & A. Books, E Sussex............................. 102
Stroh (M.A.), London E 155
Wakeman Books (Frances), Notts 205

PARAPSYCHOLOGY

Atlantis Bookshop, London WC.................... 177
Cavern Books, Cheshire 70
Esoteric Dreams Bookshop, Cumbria.............. 78
Greensleeves, Oxfordshire 207
Inner Bookshop (The), Oxfordshire................. 210
Joel Segal Books, Devon 86
Occultique, Northamptonshire....................... 200
SETI Books, Staffordshire............................ 225

SPECIALITY INDEX

PARISH REGISTERS

Grampian Books, Grampian........................ 274
Island Books, Devon................................. 85
Taylor & Son (Peter), Herts........................ 133
Townsend (John), Berkshire 57
Turton (John), Durham 98
Turton (John), Durham 98
Williams (Bookdealer), (Richard), N Lincs....... 154

PARKS AND GARDENS

Bermondsey Basement Bookstore, London SE .. 164
Besleys Books, Suffolk 226
Fifteenth Century Bookshop (The), E Sussex 104
Joel Segal Books, Devon 86
Park (Mike), London Outer......................... 183

PASSENGER LINERS

Bott, (Bookdealers) Ltd., (Martin), Gr Man 118
Cox (Geoff), Devon 90
Falconwood Transport & Military Bookshop,
London Outer 184
Fifteenth Century Bookshop (The), E Sussex 104
Green Ltd. (G.L.), Herts 132
Henry Wilson Books, Cheshire...................... 69
Joel Segal Books, Devon 86
Marine & Cannon Books, Cheshire 71
Marine and Cannon Books, Cheshire 69
R. & A. Books, E Sussex............................ 102
Robert Humm & Co, Lincolnshire 154
Rods Books, Devon................................... 88

PATENTS

Stroh (M.A.), London E 155

PATHOLOGY

Parkinsons Books, Merseyside...................... 186
Phelps (Michael), West Sussex...................... 243
R M Books, Herts.................................... 132
Westons, Herts 133

PERFORMING ARTS

Anthony Spranger, Wiltshire........................ 252
Book Palace (The), London SE 164
Books & Bygones (Pam Taylor), W Mids 241
Booth Books, Powys 289
Brian Troath Books, London E 155
Brock Books, N Yorks 193
Browne (Christopher I.), West Yorkshire......... 247
Catalyst Booksearch Services, Devon.............. 87
Chaucer Bookshop, Kent............................ 136
Cornucopia Books, Lincolnshire 153
Cover to Cover, Merseyside......................... 186
Cox Rare Books (Charles), Cornwall.............. 74
D'Arcy Books, Wiltshire............................. 252
DaSilva Puppet Books, Dorset 93
Dolphin Books, Suffolk.............................. 226
Drummond Pleasures of Past Times (David),
London WC 177
Fifteenth Century Bookshop (The), East Sussex. 104
Fitzsimons (Anne), Cumbria 78
Fossgate Books, N Yorks............................ 198
Franks Booksellers, Gr Man........................ 119
Garwood & Voigt, Kent............................. 140
Gibbs Books, (Jonathan), Worcs................... 256
Gloucester Road Bookshop, London SW 168

Greenroom Books, West Yorkshire 248
Hancock & Monks, Powys.......................... 290
Inprint, Glos.. 116
Jarndyce Antiquarian Booksellers, London WC. 178
Joel Segal Books, Devon 86
Kent T. G., Surrey 231
Libris (Weston) Books, Somerset 217
Malvern Bookshop (The), Worcs 255
Martin Music Books (Philip), N Yorks 199
McCrone (Audrey), Isle of Arran 275
McGee (Terence J.), London Outer 181
N1 Books, East Sussex 105
Paramor (C.D.), Suffolk............................. 229
Poor Richard's Books, Suffolk 227
Price (John), London N 159
R. & A. Books, East Sussex 102
Reads, Dorset 95
Scorpio Books, Suffolk 226
Scrivener's Books & Bookbinding, Derbyshire... 82
Skoob Russell Square, Suffolk...................... 230
Terence Kaye, London NW 162
Theatreshire Books, N Yorks....................... 193
Till's Bookshop, Lothian 279
Treasure Trove Books, Leics........................ 148
Uncle Phil's Books, W Mids........................ 240
Willmott Bookseller (Nicholas), Cardiff........... 283
Wood (Peter), Cambridgeshire...................... 65

PETROLEUM GEOLOGY

Earth Science Books, Wiltshire 252
Geophysical Books, Kent............................ 140
Joel Segal Books, Devon 86
Parkinsons Books, Merseyside...................... 186
Weiner (Graham), London N 160
Westons, Herts 133

PETROLEUM TECHNOLOGY

Earth Science Books, Wiltshire 252
Geophysical Books, Kent............................ 140
Parkinsons Books, Merseyside...................... 186
Westons, Herts 133

PHARMACY/PHARMACOLOGY

Alba Books, Grampian 274
Baldwin's Scientific Books, Essex 112
Bernard Dixon and Kath Adams, Middlesex 183
Empire Books, N Yorks............................. 198
Hunter-Rare Books (Andrew), London SW 169
Orchid Book Distributors, Co. Clare.............. 262
Parkinsons Books, Merseyside...................... 186
Phelps (Michael), West Sussex...................... 243
Pickering & Chatto, London W.................... 175
R M Books, Herts.................................... 132
Smith (David & Lynn), London Outer............ 182
Westons, Herts 133
White (David), Cambridgeshire.................... 65

PHENOMENA

Joel Segal Books, Devon 86
SETI Books, Staffordshire........................... 225

PHILATELY

32 Seconds, East Sussex 104
Clark (Nigel A.), London SE 165
Hodgson (Books) (Richard J.), N Yorks 198

SPECIALITY INDEX

Joel Segal Books, Devon 86
Pennymead Books, N Yorks........................ 194
Postings, Surrey 234
R. & A. Books, East Sussex 102
Richard Frost Books, Herts......................... 130
Spooner & Co, Somerset 220
Treasure Island (The), Gr Man..................... 119

PHILOLOGY

Baldwin (Jack), Strathclyde 280
Bennett & Kerr Books, Oxfordshire 206
Derek Stirling Bookseller, Kent 142
Ice House Books, Wiltshire 253
Joel Segal Books, Devon 86
Kenya Books, East Sussex 100
Midnight Oil Books, Fife............................. 272
Nineteenth Century Books, Oxfordshire 211
Olynthiacs, Shropshire 214
Parkinsons Books, Merseyside...................... 186
Polczynski (Udo K.H.), Powys 291
Price (John), London N 159
Seydi Rare Books (Sevin), London NW 162
Susanne Schulz-Falster Rare Books, London N. 160
Unsworth's Booksellers, London WC 163, 180

PHILOSOPHY

Abbey Books, Cornwall 74
Anthroposophical Books, Glos 116
Apocalypse, Surrey 233
Armchair Books, Lothian 276
Barcombe Services, Essex............................ 108
Bath Old Books, Somerset 216
Bell (Peter), Lothian 276
Bloomsbury Bookshop, London Outer............ 182
Books, Denbighshire 286
Books Antiques & Collectables, Devon 90
Books For All, N Yorks 194
Bookshop (The), Gr Man 118
Bookshop (The), Co. Donegal....................... 263
Booth Books, Powys 289
Brimstones, East Sussex 103
Caledonia Books, Strathclyde....................... 280
Camden Books, Somerset 216
Carter, (Brian), Oxfordshire......................... 211
Cheshire Book Centre, Cheshire.................... 69
Chesters (G. & J.), Staffordshire 225
Chthonios Books, East Sussex...................... 102
Darkwood Books, Co. Cork 263
Dead Mons Minds on uk, Powys 292
Dean Byass, Bristol.................................... 60
Dolphin Books, Suffolk............................... 226
Drury Rare Books (John), Essex 110
Edwards (London) Limited (Francis),
London WC 177
Edwards in Hay-on-Wye (Francis), Powys 290
Elephant Books, West Yorkshire................... 249
Fifteenth Century Bookshop (The), East Sussex. 104
Fisher & Sperr, London N........................... 158
Fossgate Books, N Yorks 198
Game Advice, Oxfordshire 210
GfB: the Colchester Bookshop, Essex 109
Gloucester Road Bookshop, London SW 168
Hamish Riley-Smith, Norfolk........................ 192
Handsworth Books, Essex............................ 112
Herb Tandree Philosophy Books, Glos 116

Hughes Rare Books (Spike), Borders.............. 268
Humanist Book Services, Cornwall 73
Joel Segal Books, Devon 86
John Gorton Booksearch, East Sussex 105
Judd Books, London WC 178
Kenny's Bookshops and Art Galleries Ltd,
Co. Galway 266
Killeen (John), N Yorks 194
Kyrios Books, Notts 204
Lee Rare Books (Rachel), Bristol 59
My Back Pages, London SW 169
O'Donoghue Books, Powys......................... 291
Occultique, Northamptonshire...................... 200
Orb's Bookshop, Grampian......................... 274
Parkinsons Books, Merseyside...................... 186
Pendleburys Bookshop, London N 159
Pickering & Chatto, London W 175
Plurabelle Books, Cambridgeshire.................. 64
Polczynski (Udo K.H.), Powys 291
Pomes Penyeach, Staffordshire 224
Pordes Books Ltd., (Henry), London WC........ 179
Portobello Books, London W 175
Price (John), London N 159
Quaritch Ltd., (Bernard), London W.............. 175
Quinto of Charing Cross Road, London WC ... 179
R. & A. Books, East Sussex 102
Readers World, W Mids............................. 239
Reading Lasses, Dumfries & Galloway 271
Reads, Dorset 95
Roland Books, Kent 139
Roosterbooks, Northamptonshire.................. 200
Rosemary Pugh Books, Wiltshire 253
Rowan (P. & B.), Co. Antrim 260
St Philip's Books, Oxfordshire...................... 210
Samovar Books, Co. Dublin 264
Savery Books, East Sussex 99
Scrivener's Books & Bookbinding, Derbyshire... 82
Second Edition, Lothian.............................. 278
Seydi Rare Books (Sevin), London NW 162
Skoob Russell Square, Suffolk...................... 230
Spurrier (Nick), Kent 138
Staniland (Booksellers), Lincolnshire 154
Stokes Books, Co. Dublin............................ 265
Susanne Schulz-Falster Rare Books, London N. 160
Tarka Books, Devon 84
Thorntons of Oxford Ltd., Oxfordshire........... 207
Till's Bookshop, Lothian 279
Trafalgar Bookshop, East Sussex 100
Transformer, Dumfries & Galloway 271
Trinity Rare Books, Co. Leitrim 266
Uncle Phil's Books, W Mids......................... 240
Unsworths Booksellers, London WC.............. 163
Walden Books, London NW 163
Waterfield's, Oxfordshire 210
Webb Books (John), S Yorks........................ 222
Westwood Books (Mark), Powys 291
Wiend Books, Lancashire 144
Winchester Bookshop (The), Hants................ 127
Winghale Books, Lincolnshire 153
Woburn Books, London N 160
Worcester Rare Books, Worcs...................... 257
Worlds End Bookshop, London SW 171
Yarwood Rare Books (Edward), Gr Man 118

SPECIALITY INDEX

PHONOLOGY

Kenya Books, East Sussex 100

PHOTOGRAPHY

Abacus Gallery, Staffordshire........................ 224
Allsworth Rare Books Ltd., London SW......... 167
Amwell Book Company, London EC............. 157
Apocalypse, Surrey.................................... 233
Ars Artis, Oxfordshire 209
Aviabooks, Glos 114
Bermondsey Basement Bookstore, London SE .. 164
Biblion, London W.................................... 172
Blaenavon Books, Torfaen 294
Books, Denbighshire 286
Books & Collectables Ltd., Cambridgeshire...... 63
Books & Things, London W......................... 172
Books For All, N Yorks 194
Books Only, Suffolk................................... 227
Brighton Books, East Sussex......................... 99
Broadleaf Books, Torfaen 294
Bruce Holdsworth Books, East Sussex 105
Butcher (Pablo), Oxfordshire 207
Cameron House Books, Isle of Wight............. 134
Cavern Books, Cheshire 70
Cofion Books, Pembrokeshire 288
Collectables (W.H.), Suffolk 230
Dally Books & Collectables, Powys................ 292
Derek Stirling Bookseller, Kent 142
Farahar & Dupre (Clive & Sophie), Wiltshire ... 251
Fifteenth Century Bookshop (The), East Sussex. 104
Finch Rare Books Ltd. (Simon), London W..... 173
Grays of Westminster, London SW 168
Hay Castle, Powys..................................... 290
Hill House Books, Devon 88
Holleyman (J.F.), East Sussex 103
Intech Books, Northumberland 203
Jill Howell, Kent....................................... 102
Joel Segal Books, Devon 86
Judd Books, London WC............................ 178
Keswick Bookshop, Cumbria........................ 79
McGee (Terence J.), London Outer 181
N1 Books, East Sussex 105
O'Brien Books & Photo Gallery, Co. Limerick.. 266
Orlando Booksellers, Lincolnshire 152
Paper Pleasures, Somerset........................... 219
Peter Lyons Books, Glos 114
Photo Books International, London WC 179
Phototitles.com, Essex................................ 109
Pollak (P.M.), Devon 89
Prescott - The Bookseller (John), London Outer 184
Print Matters, London SE............................ 166
Quaritch Ltd., (Bernard), London W.............. 175
Ray Rare and Out of Print Books (Janette),
N Yorks... 199
Rayner (Hugh Ashley), Somerset 217
Rhodes, Bookseller (Peter), Hants 126
Solaris Books, East Yorkshire 106
Soldridge Books Ltd, Hants 124
Stroh (M.A.), London E 155
Sykes (Graham), West Yorkshire 249
Tarka Books, Devon................................... 84
Treasure Island (The), Gr Man...................... 119
Uncle Phil's Books, W Mids......................... 240
Weiner (Graham), London N 160
Wiend Books, Lancashire 144

Woburn Books, London N 160

PHRENOLOGY

Atlantis Bookshop, London WC.................... 177
Occultique, Northamptonshire...................... 200
Phelps (Michael), West Sussex...................... 243

PHYSICAL CULTURE

Combat Arts Archive, Durham 97
Webster (D.), Strathclyde............................ 280

PHYSICS

Barcombe Services, Essex............................. 108
Camden Books, Somerset 216
Eagle Bookshop (The), Bedfordshire 53
Ely Books, Cambridgeshire 65
Esplin (David), Hants 124
Treader's Books, Tayside............................. 281
Hinchliffe Books, Bristol.............................. 59
Moorside Books, Lancashire......................... 144
Parkinsons Books, Merseyside............. 186
Phelps (Michael), West Sussex...................... 243
The Sanctuary Bookshop, Dorset.................. 94
Transformer, Dumfries & Galloway................ 271
Turret House, Norfolk................................ 192
Wayside Books and Cards, Oxfordshire 207
Weiner (Graham), London N 160
Westons, Herts 133
Whistler's Books, London SW 170

PHYSIOLOGY

Barcombe Services, Essex............................. 108
Bernard Dixon and Kath Adams, Middlesex 183
Parkinsons Books, Merseyside...................... 186
Phelps (Michael), West Sussex...................... 243
R M Books, Herts..................................... 132
R. & A. Books, East Sussex 102
Weiner (Graham), London N 160
Westons, Herts 133

PIGS

Hodgson (Books) (Richard J.), N Yorks 198
Joel Segal Books, Devon 86
Phenotype Books, Cumbria.......................... 80

PILGRIMS

Joel Segal Books, Devon 86
R. & A. Books, East Sussex 102

PIONEERS

Americanabooksuk, Cumbria........................ 77
Joel Segal Books, Devon 86

PIRATES

Book Palace (The), London SE 164
Cox (Geoff), Devon 90
Fifteenth Century Bookshop (The), East Sussex. 104
Joel Segal Books, Devon 86
Loretta Lay Books, London NW................... 162
Marine & Cannon Books, Cheshire 71
Marine and Cannon Books, Cheshire 69
Print Matters, London SE............................ 166
R. & A. Books, East Sussex 102
Treasure Island (The), Gr Man...................... 119

SPECIALITY INDEX

PLANNING - CITY

Haskell (R.H. & P.), Dorset	94
Joel Segal Books, Devon	86

PLANT HUNTING

Abacus Books, Cheshire	68
Alauda Books, Cumbria	78
Anne Harris Books & Bags Booksearch, Devon	88
Arden, Bookseller (C.), Powys	289
Barnhill Books, Isle of Arran	275
Bernard Dixon and Kath Adams, Middlesex	183
Besleys Books, Suffolk	226
Blest (Peter), Kent	139
Calendula Horticultural Books, East Sussex	102
Chantrey Books, S Yorks	222
Dales & Lakes Book Centre, Cumbria	80
Edmund Pollinger Rare Books, London SW	167
Fifteenth Century Bookshop (The), East Sussex.	104
Hollett and Son (R.F.G.), Cumbria	80
Hollingshead (Chris), London Outer	183
Hunter and Krageloh, Derbyshire	83
Joel Segal Books, Devon	86
Mandalay Bookshop, London SW	169
McEwan Fine Books, Grampian	273
Page (David), Lothian	278
Park (Mike), London Outer	183
Peter M Daly, Hants	127
R. & A. Books, East Sussex	102
Summerfield Books Ltd, Cumbria	77
Traveller's Bookshelf (The), Somerset	217
Trinity Rare Books, Co. Leitrim	266
Westons, Herts	133

PLATO

Joel Segal Books, Devon	86
R. & A. Books, East Sussex	102
Seydi Rare Books (Sevin), London NW	162

PLAYS

Abbey Books, Cornwall	74
Amwell Book Company, London EC	157
Apocalypse, Surrey	233
babelog.books, Herefordshire	128
Books Antiques & Collectables, Devon	90
Bosorne Books, Cornwall	75
Brock Books, N Yorks	193
Byre Books, Dumfries & Galloway	270
Catalyst Booksearch Services, Devon	87
Cheshire Book Centre, Cheshire	69
Church Street Books, Norfolk	187
Cox Rare Books (Charles), Cornwall	74
Derek Stirling Bookseller, Kent	142
Ewell Bookshop Ltd, Surrey	232
Fifteenth Century Bookshop (The), East Sussex.	104
G. C. Books Ltd., Dumfries & Galloway	271
Greenroom Books, West Yorkshire	248
Ian McKelvie Bookseller, London N	159
Jade Mountain Bookshop, Hants	126
Jarndyce Antiquarian Booksellers, London WC.	178
Joel Segal Books, Devon	86
Just Books, Cornwall	76
Pastmasters, Derbyshire	83
R. & A. Books, East Sussex	102
Reading Lasses, Dumfries & Galloway	271
Scrivener's Books & Bookbinding, Derbyshire...	82

Skelton (Tony), Kent	141
Stalagluft Books, Tyne and Wear	236
Surprise Books, Glos	113
The Sanctuary Bookshop, Dorset	94
Till's Bookshop, Lothian	279
Willmott Bookseller (Nicholas), Cardiff	283

POETRY

Abacus Gallery, Staffordshire	224
Addyman Books, Powys	289
Amwell Book Company, London EC	157
Anglo-American Rare Books, Surrey	233
Antiques on High, Oxfordshire	209
Anwoth Books Ltd, Dumfries & Galloway	270
Apocalypse, Surrey	233
Applin (Malcolm), Berkshire	55
Arden Books & Cosmographia, Warwickshire...	237
Armchair Books, Lothian	276
Ash Rare Books, London SW	167
babelog.books, Herefordshire	128
Barnby (C. & A.J.), Kent	141
Bayntun (George), Somerset	216
Big Bairn Books, Tayside	281
Book Shelf (The), Devon	87
Bookroom (The), Surrey	234
Books, Oxfordshire	206
Books, Denbighshire	286
Books & Bygones (Pam Taylor), W Mids	241
Books Antiques & Collectables, Devon	90
Bookstand, Dorset	94
Bosorne Books, Cornwall	75
Bracton Books, Cambridgeshire	63
Brad Books, Essex	111
Brian Troath Books, London E	155
Bridge Books, Cumbria	81
Brighton Books, East Sussex	99
Browse Books, Lancashire	144
Budd (Richard), Somerset	219
Byre Books, Dumfries & Galloway	270
Calendula Horticultural Books, East Sussex	102
Cameron House Books, Isle of Wight	134
Carningli Centre, Pembrokeshire	288
Castleton (Pat), Kent	138
Catalyst Booksearch Services, Devon	87
Cheshire Book Centre, Cheshire	69
Church Street Books, Norfolk	187
Classic Bindings Ltd, London SW	167
Clements (R.W.), London Outer	182
Clent Books, Worcs	255
Cofion Books, Pembrokeshire	288
Cox Rare Books (Charles), Cornwall	74
Criterion Books, London Outer	182
D'Arcy Books, Wiltshire	252
Dales & Lakes Book Centre, Cumbria	80
Dancing Goat Bookshop (The), Norfolk	188
Dandy Lion Editions, Surrey	233
Derek Stirling Bookseller, Kent	142
Dolphin Books, Suffolk	226
Eastcote Bookshop (The), London Outer	181
Edrich (I.D.), London E	155
Elaine Lonsdale Books, West Yorkshire	248
Ellis, Bookseller (Peter), London WC	178
Ellwood Editions, Wiltshire	253
Erian Books, London N	158
Eton Antique Bookshop, Berkshire	57

SPECIALITY INDEX

Ewell Bookshop Ltd, Surrey 232
Fifteenth Century Bookshop (The), East Sussex. 104
Ford Books (David), Herts 133
Foster Bookshop (Paul), London SW 168
GfB: the Colchester Bookshop, Essex 109
Gloucester Road Bookshop, London SW 168
Good for Books, Lincolnshire 151
Green (Paul), Cambridgeshire 67
Hall's Bookshop, Kent................................ 141
Hancock (Peter), West Sussex 243
Hava Books, London SE............................. 165
Hellenic Bookservices, London NW 162
Hennessey Bookseller (Ray), East Sussex......... 100
Hurst (Jenny), Kent 138
Ian McKelvie Bookseller, London N 159
Innes Books, Shropshire 214
Jackdaw Books, Norfolk 189
Jane Jones Books, Grampian 272
JB Books & Collectables, West Sussex 244
Jiri Books, Co. Antrim 260
Joel Segal Books, Devon 86
Just Books, Cornwall 76
Karen Millward, Co. Cork........................... 263
Kendall-Carpenter (Tim), Gr Man 119
Kineton Nooks, Warwickshire....................... 237
Kings Bookshop Callander, Central 269
Kingsgate Books & Prints, Hants 126
Kingsmere Books, Bedfordshire 53
Lawrence Books, Notts 204
Libris (Weston) Books, Somerset 217
Little Bookshop (The), Gr Man..................... 119
Loch Croispol Bookshop & Restaurant,
Highland 275
Lymelight Books & Prints, Dorset 93
Main Point Books, Lothian 278
Malvern Bookshop (The), Worcs 255
Marine Workshop Bookshop, Dorset 93
Martin's Books, Powys 292
McCrone (Audrey), Isle of Arran 275
Mermaid Books (Burlingham), Norfolk........... 192
Modlock (Lilian), Dorset 93
Moreton Books, Devon............................... 87
Naughton Booksellers, Co. Dublin 265
Nineteenth Century Books, Oxfordshire 211
Orangeberry Books, Oxfordshire 209
Orlando Booksellers, Lincolnshire 152
Palladour Books, Hants 126
Paper Moon Books, Glos 116
Peter Lyons Books, Glos 114
Poetry Bookshop (The), Powys 291
Polmorla Books, Cornwall 76
Pomes Penyeach, Staffordshire 224
Poor Richard's Books, Suffolk 227
Prescott - The Bookseller (John), London Outer 184
Price (John), London N 159
Primrose Hill Books, London NW 162
Quest Booksearch, Cambridgeshire 65
R & B Graham Trading, Cornwall 74
R. & A. Books, East Sussex 102
Reading Lasses, Dumfries & Galloway 271
Richmond Books, N Yorks 195
Riderless Horse Books, Norfolk..................... 187
Rivendale Press, Buckinghamshire 62
Robert Temple, London N........................... 160
Roundstone Books, Lancashire...................... 144

Rutland Bookshop (The), Rutland 212
Samovar Books, Co. Dublin 264
Scrivener's Books & Bookbinding, Derbyshire... 82
Seabreeze Books, Lancashire........................ 145
Shelley (E. & J.), Buckinghamshire 61
Skelton (Tony), Kent................................. 141
Skoob Russell Square, Suffolk 230
Smith Books (Keith), Herefordshire 128
Staniland (Booksellers), Lincolnshire 154
Stevens (Joan), Cambridgeshire..................... 65
Stone, (G.& R.), Borders 268
Stroma Books, Borders 268
Sturford Books, Wiltshire 254
Tant Yn Ellen Books, Powys 293
The Old Abbey Bookshop, Co. Down 261
Thomas (Books) (Leona), Cheshire 71
Tiffin (Tony and Gill), Durham 97
Till's Bookshop, Lothian 279
Tilston (Stephen E.), London SE................... 166
Tindley & Chapman, London WC 179
Tucker (Alan & Joan), Glos 117
Updike Rare Books (John), Lothian 279
Venables (Morris & Juliet), Bristol................. 60
War & Peace Books, Hants......................... 122
Wheen O'Books, Scottish Borders 269
Whittle, Bookseller (Avril), Cumbria 81
Willmott Bookseller (Nicholas), Cardiff........... 283
Woburn Books, London N 160
Woodbine Books, West Yorkshire 246
Words Etcetera Bookshop, Dorset................. 93
Yesterday's News, Conwy 285

POLICE FORCE HISTORIES

Anthony Vickers Books, N Yorks 196
Bolland Books, Bedfordshire......................... 53
Clifford Elmer Books Ltd., Cheshire 68
Crimes Ink, London E................................ 155
Delph Books, Gr Man................................ 120
Joel Segal Books, Devon 86
Kenya Books, East Sussex 100
Lawful Occasions, Essex 108
Maggy Browne, Lincolnshire 150
R. & A. Books, East Sussex 102
Roscrea Bookshop, Co. Tipperary 267
Undercover Books, Lincolnshire 154

POLITICAL HISTORY

Apocalypse, Surrey 233
Berwick Books, Lincolnshire........................ 152
Books at Star Dot Star, W Mids................... 241
Brimstones, East Sussex 103
Cornucopia Books, Lincolnshire 153
Dolphin Books, Suffolk............................... 226
Drury Rare Books (John), Essex 110
Fifteenth Century Bookshop (The), E Sussex 104
G. C. Books Ltd., Dumfries & Galloway......... 271
Joel Segal Books, Devon 86
Left on The Shelf, Cumbria......................... 79
Northern Herald Books, West Yorkshire......... 246
R. & A. Books, E Sussex............................ 102
Reading Lasses, Dumfries & Galloway 271
Star Lord Books, Gr Man 119

POLITICS

Al Saqi Books, London W........................... 172

SPECIALITY INDEX

Ann & Mike Conry, Worcs........................ 257
Apocalypse, Surrey................................... 233
Barcombe Services, Essex............................ 108
Barn Books, Buckinghamshire...................... 61
Berwick Books, Lincolnshire........................ 152
Books, Denbighshire.................................. 286
Books at Star Dot Star, W Mids.................... 241
Bookshop (The), Gr Man............................ 118
Booth Books, Powys.................................. 289
Brimstones, E Sussex................................. 103
Brockwells Booksellers, Lincolnshire 150
Catalyst Booksearch Services, Devon.............. 87
Chas J. Sawyer, Kent................................ 141
Chesters (G. & J.), Staffordshire 225
Chichester Bookshop (The), West Sussex......... 242
Church Street Books, Norfolk....................... 187
Cornucopia Books, Lincolnshire 153
Delectus Books, London WC........................ 177
Dolphin Books, Suffolk............................... 226
Drury Rare Books (John), Essex................... 110
Dunstan Books, Dorset............................... 91
Fifteenth Century Bookshop (The), E Sussex.... 104
firstpagebooks, Norfolk.............................. 190
G. C. Books Ltd., Dumfries & Galloway......... 271
Garfi Books, Powys................................... 293
Hab Books, London W............................... 173
Hambleton Books, N Yorks......................... 197
Hurst (Jenny), Kent.................................. 138
Ice House Books, Wiltshire 253
Innes Books, Shropshire............................. 214
Internet Bookshop UK Ltd., Glos.................. 113
Jarndyce Antiquarian Booksellers, London WC. 178
Judd Books, London WC............................ 178
Just Books, Cornwall................................. 76
Kelsall (George), Gr Man........................... 118
Left on The Shelf, Cumbria......................... 79
Maggy Browne, Lincolnshire 150
Modern Welsh Publications Ltd., Merseyside.... 185
My Back Pages, London SW........................ 169
Northern Herald Books, West Yorkshire......... 246
O'Donoghue Books, Powys......................... 291
Parkinsons Books, Merseyside...................... 186
Price (John), London N.............................. 159
R. & A. Books, E Sussex............................ 102
Reading Lasses, Dumfries & Galloway 271
Reads, Dorset.. 95
Red Star Books, Herts............................... 130
Roland Books, Kent.................................. 139
Rosemary Pugh Books, Wiltshire 253
Samovar Books, Co. Dublin......................... 264
Saracen Books, Derbyshire.......................... 83
Saunders (Tom), Caerphilly......................... 283
Skoob Russell Square, Suffolk...................... 230
Sparrow Books, West Yorkshire 246
Spurrier (Nick), Kent................................ 138
Staniland (Booksellers), Lincolnshire 154
Star Lord Books, Gr Man........................... 119
Stroma Books, Borders.............................. 268
Till's Bookshop, Lothian............................ 279
Tilston (Stephen E.), London SE................... 166
Uncle Phil's Books, W Mids........................ 240
War & Peace Books, Hants......................... 122
Webb Books (John), S Yorks....................... 222
Winghale Books, Lincolnshire 153
Woburn Books, London N 160

POMOLOGY

Edmund Pollinger Rare Books, London SW..... 167
Hava Books, London SE............................. 165
Joel Segal Books, Devon 86
Park (Mike), London Outer......................... 183

POP-UP, MOVABLE & CUT OUT

Ampersand Books, Shropshire...................... 213
Biblipola, London NW............................... 161
Bookmark (Children's Books), Wiltshire......... 253
Castleton (Pat), Kent................................. 138
Cheshire Book Centre, Cheshire.................... 69
Ferguson (Elizabeth), Grampian 272
Fifteenth Century Bookshop (The), E Sussex.... 104
Hava Books, London SE............................. 165
Intech Books, Northumberland 203
Jean Hedger, Berkshire.............................. 55
Joel Segal Books, Devon 86
Kernaghans, Merseyside............................. 186
Print Matters, London SE........................... 166
R. & A. Books, E Sussex............................ 102
Roe and Moore, London WC....................... 179
St Swithin's Illustrated & Children's Books,
London W.. 175
Scrivener's Books & Bookbinding, Derbyshire... 82
Seabreeze Books, Lancashire........................ 145
Temperley (David), W Mids........................ 239
The Old Children's Bookshelf, Lothian 278

PORNOGRAPHY

Apocalypse, Surrey................................... 233
Delectus Books, London WC........................ 177
R. & A. Books, E Sussex............................ 102

POTTERY & GLASS

Abacus Books, Cheshire............................. 68
Ancient Art Books, London SW.................... 167
Apocalypse, Surrey................................... 233
Bruce Holdsworth Books, E Sussex 105
Clark (Nigel A.), London SE........................ 165
Cornucopia Books, Lincolnshire 153
Cover to Cover, Merseyside......................... 186
Don Kelly Books, London W....................... 172
Fifteenth Century Bookshop (The), E Sussex.... 104
Joel Segal Books, Devon 86
Mannwaring (M.G.), Bristol........................ 59
Nelson (Elizabeth), Suffolk.......................... 227
Orchid Book Distributors, Co. Clare.............. 262
R. & A. Books, E Sussex............................ 102

POULTRY

Blest (Peter), Kent................................... 139
Cheshire Book Centre, Cheshire.................... 69
Countrymans Gallery (The), Leics 147
Edmund Pollinger Rare Books, London SW..... 167
Hodgson (Books) (Richard J.), N Yorks 198
Joel Segal Books, Devon 86
Keith Langford, London E 155
Phenotype Books, Cumbria......................... 80
R. & A. Books, E Sussex............................ 102
Thomas (Barry), Ceredigion 284

PRAYER BOOKS

Barbican Bookshop, N Yorks...................... 198
Beckham Books Ltd., Suffolk 230

SPECIALITY INDEX

Fifteenth Century Bookshop (The), E Sussex 104
Hilton (Books) (P.J.), London W 174
Jade Mountain Bookshop, Hants 126
Kyrios Books, Notts 204
Oasis Booksearch, Cambridgeshire.................. 67
Paper Moon Books, Glos 116
Pendleburys Bookshop, London N 159
R. & A. Books, E Sussex............................. 102
Roscrea Bookshop, Co. Tipperary.................. 267
Rosemary Pugh Books, Wiltshire 253
S.P.C.K., Bristol 60
Samovar Books, Co. Dublin......................... 264
Stalagluft Books, Tyne and Wear 236
Staniland (Booksellers), Lincolnshire 154

PRE-RAPHAELITES

Ballantyne-Way (Roger), Suffolk 229
Joel Segal Books, Devon 86
R. & A. Books, E Sussex............................. 102

PRECIOUS METALS - SILVER

Art Reference Books, Hants 125
Cox (Geoff), Devon 90
Don Kelly Books, London W 172
Joel Segal Books, Devon 86
Nibris Books, London SW 170
R. & A. Books, E Sussex............................. 102
Trinders' Fine Tools, Suffolk 227

PREHISTORY

Barcombe Services, Essex............................. 108
Fifteenth Century Bookshop (The), E Sussex 104
Joel Segal Books, Devon 86
Parkinsons Books, Merseyside....................... 186
SETI Books, Staffordshire............................ 225

PRESIDENTIAL

Dolphin Books, Suffolk............................... 226

PRINTED TEXTILES

Don Kelly Books, London W 172
Joel Segal Books, Devon 86
Judith Mansfield, West Yorkshire................... 250
N1 Books, E Sussex................................... 105
R. & A. Books, E Sussex............................. 102
Stroh (M.A.), London E 155
Weiner (Graham), London N 160

PRINTING - GENERAL

Andron (G.W.), London N 158
Atholl Fine Books, Tayside 281
Ballantyne-Way (Roger), Suffolk 229
Baynton-Williams Gallery, West Sussex 242
Bettridge (Gordon), Fife.............................. 272
Bibliophile (The), S Yorks........................... 222
Boxwood Books & Prints, Somerset................ 220
Brinded (Scott), Kent 139
Collinge & Clark, London WC...................... 177
Coupland (Terry W.), Staffordshire................. 224
Cox Old & Rare Books (Claude), Suffolk 228
Dean Illustrated Books (Myra), Powys 288
Finch Rare Books Ltd. (Simon), London W..... 173
Forest Books, Notts................................... 205
Goldman (Paul), Dorset 94
Grosvenor Prints, London WC...................... 178

Joel Segal Books, Devon 86
Judd Books, London WC 178
Macfarlane (Mr. H.), Essex 112
Mannwaring (M.G.), Bristol 59
Moore (C.R.), Shropshire 214
Naughton Booksellers, Co. Dublin 265
O'Connor Fine Books, Lancashire.................. 145
R. & A. Books, E Sussex............................. 102
Robin Doughty - Fine Books, W Mids........... 239
Solitaire Books, Somerset............................ 217
Susanne Schulz-Falster Rare Books, London N. 160
Wakeman Books (Frances), Notts 205

- NORTH OF ENGLAND PROVINCIAL

Barry McKay Rare Books, Cumbria 77
Keel Row Bookshop, Tyne and Wear 236

PRINTING AND MIND OF MAN

Dean Byass, Bristol.................................... 60
Foster Bookshop (Paul), London SW.............. 168
Hamish Riley-Smith, Norfolk........................ 192
Seydi Rare Books (Sevin), London NW 162
Susanne Schulz-Falster Rare Books, London N. 160

PRIVATE PRESS

Anthony Neville, Kent................................ 139
Artco, Notts 204
Askew Books (Vernon), Wiltshire................... 251
Ballantyne-Way (Roger), Suffolk 229
Barlow (Vincent G.), Hants.......................... 125
Barnitt (Peter), Wiltshire............................. 254
Barry McKay Rare Books, Cumbria............... 77
Bertram Rota Ltd., London WC 177
Besleys Books, Suffolk 226
Bettridge (Gordon), Fife.............................. 272
Biblion, London W.................................... 172
Blackwell's Rare Books, Oxfordshire.............. 209
Bookline, Co. Down 261
Books & Things, London W......................... 172
Bookstand, Dorset..................................... 94
Bow Windows Book Shop, E Sussex............... 103
Boxwood Books & Prints, Somerset................ 220
Brian Troath Books, London E..................... 155
Broadhurst of Southport Ltd., Merseyside 186
Bruce Holdsworth Books, E Sussex 105
Collinge & Clark, London WC...................... 177
Coupland (Terry W.), Staffordshire................. 224
Cox Old & Rare Books (Claude), Suffolk 228
Dean Illustrated Books (Myra), Powys 288
Dylans Bookstore, Swansea 294
Eastcote Bookshop (The), London Outer......... 181
Ellis, Bookseller (Peter), London WC 178
Elstree Books, Herts.................................. 131
Emjay Books, Surrey.................................. 231
English (Toby), Oxfordshire.......................... 211
Franks Booksellers, Gr Man......................... 119
Good Books, Shropshire 214
Hanborough Books, Oxfordshire.................... 210
Heritage, W Mids...................................... 239
Hodgkins and Company Limited (Ian), Glos 116
Hollett and Son (R.F.G.), Cumbria 80
Keeble Antiques, Somerset 219
Macfarlane (Mr. H.), Essex 112
Mannwaring (M.G.), Bristol 59
Marks Limited (Barrie), London N................. 159

SPECIALITY INDEX

Martin's Books, Powys 292
Maynard & Bradley, Leics 148
Mills Rare Books (Adam), Cambridgeshire 64
Poetry Bookshop (The), Powys..................... 291
R.E. & G.B. Way, Suffolk 229
Rivendale Press, Buckinghamshire 62
Robert Temple, London N........................... 160
Robin Doughty - Fine Books, W Mids 239
Roz Hulse, Conwy 286
Sabin (Printed Works) (P.R. & V.), Kent......... 136
Sansovino Books, West Sussex 244
Solitaire Books, Somerset............................ 217
Sotheran Limited (Henry), London W 176
Staniland (Booksellers), Lincolnshire 154
Sue Lowell Natural History Books, London W . 176
Taylor Rare Books (Michael), Norfolk 187
Updike Rare Books (John), Lothian 279
Waddington Books & Prints (Geraldine),
Northamptonshire 200
Wakeman Books (Frances), Notts 205
Williams Rare Books (Nigel), London WC 180
Woodbine Books, West Yorkshire.................. 246
Words Etcetera Bookshop, Dorset................. 93
York Modern Books, N Yorks...................... 197

PROOF COPIES

Brian Troath Books, London E..................... 155
Broadhurst of Southport Ltd., Merseyside 186
Firsts in Print, Isle of Wight 134
G. C. Books Ltd., Dumfries & Galloway......... 271
Hab Books, London W............................... 173
Hylton Booksearch, Merseyside 185
Kendall-Carpenter (Tim), Gr Man 119
Marble Hill Books, Middlesex...................... 184
Richard Thornton Books, London N 160
Robert Temple, London N.......................... 160
Scrivener's Books & Bookbinding, Derbyshire... 82
Williams Rare Books (Nigel), London WC 180

PROSTITUTION

Delectus Books, London WC....................... 177

PROVINCES OF CANADA - BRITISH COLUMBIA

Empire Books, N Yorks.............................. 198
Preston Book Company, Lancashire 145

- LABRADOR

Empire Books, N Yorks.............................. 198

- NEWFOUNDLAND

Empire Books, N Yorks.............................. 198
Preston Book Company, Lancashire 145

- NOVA SCOTIA

Empire Books, N Yorks.............................. 198
Grampian Books, Grampian......................... 274

- ST. PIERRE ET MIQUELON

MK Book Services, Cambridgeshire 66

PSYCHIC

Alpha Books, London N 158
Byre Books, Dumfries & Galloway 270
Cavern Books, Cheshire 70

Chthonios Books, E Sussex 102
Dawlish Books, Devon 86
Discovery Bookshop, Carmarthenshire........... 283
Facet Books, Dorset................................... 91
Fifteenth Century Bookshop (The), E Sussex 104
Fine Books Oriental Ltd., London WC........... 178
Gilbert (R.A.), Bristol................................ 59
Greensleeves, Oxfordshire 207
Hurst (Jenny), Kent 138
Inner Bookshop (The), Oxfordshire................ 210
Joel Segal Books, Devon 86
Magis Books, Leics.................................... 149
Occultique, Northamptonshire...................... 200
R. & A. Books, E Sussex............................. 102
SETI Books, Staffordshire........................... 225
Trafalgar Bookshop, E Sussex...................... 100
Wizard Books, Cambridgeshire..................... 67

PSYCHIC SURGERY

Magis Books, Leics.................................... 149

PSYCHOANALYSIS

Alba Books, Grampian 274
Barcombe Services, Essex............................ 108
Delectus Books, London WC....................... 177
Fifteenth Century Bookshop (The), E Sussex 104
Game Advice, Oxfordshire 210
Inner Bookshop (The), Oxfordshire................ 210
Joel Segal Books, Devon 86
Magis Books, Leics.................................... 149
Oast Books, Kent...................................... 137
Outcast Books, Powys 291
Parkinsons Books, Merseyside...................... 186
PsychoBabel Books & Journals, Oxfordshire..... 206
Quentin Books Ltd, Essex........................... 109
Reading Lasses, Dumfries & Galloway 271
Rosemary Pugh Books, Wiltshire 253
Savery Books, E Sussex.............................. 99
Treasure Trove Books, Leics........................ 148
Trinity Rare Books, Co. Leitrim 266
Westons, Herts 133

PSYCHOKINESIS

Atlantis Bookshop, London WC................... 177
Inner Bookshop (The), Oxfordshire................ 210
Magis Books, Leics.................................... 149

PSYCHOLOGY/PSYCHIATRY

Abbey Books, Cornwall 74
Alba Books, Grampian 274
Barcombe Services, Essex 108
Bath Old Books, Somerset 216
Beckham Books Ltd., Suffolk 230
Bernard Dixon and Kath Adams, Middlesex 183
Bracton Books, Cambridgeshire.................... 63
Brimstones, E Sussex................................. 103
Cheshire Book Centre, Cheshire.................... 69
Chesters (G. & J.), Staffordshire 225
Delectus Books, London WC....................... 177
Discovery Bookshop, Carmarthenshire........... 283
Elephant Books, West Yorkshire.................... 249
Erian Books, London N.............................. 158
Fireside Bookshop, Cumbria........................ 81
Game Advice, Oxfordshire 210
GfB: the Colchester Bookshop, Essex 109

SPECIALITY INDEX

Greensleeves, Oxfordshire 207
Hawley (C.L.), N Yorks.............................. 197
Hurst (Jenny), Kent 138
Jade Mountain Bookshop, Hants 126
Joel Segal Books, Devon 86
Judd Books, London WC 178
Mair Wilkes Books, Fife 272
Marathon Books, Gr Man 118
Marine Workshop Bookshop, Dorset 93
O'Donoghue Books, Powys 291
Oast Books, Kent...................................... 137
Occultique, Northamptonshire...................... 200
Orchid Book Distributors, Co. Clare.............. 262
Outcast Books, Powys 291
Parkinsons Books, Merseyside...................... 186
Phelps (Michael), West Sussex..................... 243
Pomes Penyeach, Staffordshire 224
PsychoBabel Books & Journals, Oxfordshire..... 206
Quentin Books Ltd, Essex,... 109
R M Books, Herts..................................... 132
Reading Lasses, Dumfries & Galloway 271
Reid of Liverpool, Merseyside...................... 185
Rosemary Pugh Books, Wiltshire 253
Savery Books, E Sussex.............................. 99
Scrivener's Books & Bookbinding, Derbyshire... 82
Skoob Russell Square, Suffolk 230
Spurrier (Nick), Kent 138
Transformer, Dumfries & Galloway............... 271
Treasure Trove Books, Leics........................ 148
Victoria Bookshop (The), Devon.................. 84
Waxfactor, E Sussex 100
Westons, Herts 133
Westwood Books (Mark), Powys 291
Westwood Books Ltd, Cumbria.................... 80
Wizard Books, Cambridgeshire.................... 67
Worlds End Bookshop, London SW 171

PSYCHOTHERAPY

Alba Books, Grampian 274
Barcombe Services, Essex........................... 108
Delectus Books, London WC....................... 177
Dunstan Books, Dorset.............................. 91
Fifteenth Century Bookshop (The), E Sussex 104
Game Advice, Oxfordshire 210
Greensleeves, Oxfordshire 207
Inner Bookshop (The), Oxfordshire............... 210
Joel Segal Books, Devon 86
Oast Books, Kent...................................... 137
Orchid Book Distributors, Co. Clare.............. 262
Outcast Books, Powys 291
Parkinsons Books, Merseyside...................... 186
PsychoBabel Books & Journals, Oxfordshire..... 206
Quentin Books Ltd, Essex........................... 109
Reading Lasses, Dumfries & Galloway'........... 271
Rosemary Pugh Books, Wiltshire 253
Savery Books, E Sussex.............................. 99
Treasure Trove Books, Leics........................ 148
Westons, Herts 133

PUBLIC ADMINISTRATION

Reading Lasses, Dumfries & Galloway 271

PUBLIC HEALTH

Bernard Dixon and Kath Adams, Middlesex 183
Joel Segal Books, Devon 86

Phelps (Michael), West Sussex..................... 243
R M Books, Herts..................................... 132
Reading Lasses, Dumfries & Galloway 271
Susanne Schulz-Falster Rare Books, London N. 160
Westons, Herts 133
Wheen O'Books, Scottish Borders 269

PUBLIC HOUSES

Anthony Vickers Books, N Yorks 196
Joel Segal Books, Devon 86
Lucas (Richard), London NW...................... 162
Thornber (Peter M.), N Yorks 196
Thorne (John), Essex................................. 109

PUBLIC SCHOOLS

Delph Books, Gr Man................................ 120
Joel Segal Books, Devon 86
Kirkpatrick (Robert J.), London W 174
Oopalba Books, Cheshire............................ 71
Reading Lasses, Dumfries & Galloway 271
Rutland Bookshop (The), Rutland 212
Thornber (Peter M.), N Yorks 196
Tiffin (Tony and Gill), Durham 97
Westwood Books Ltd, Cumbria.................... 80
Wise (Derek), E Sussex 104

PUBLIC TRANSPORT

Bath Old Books, Somerset 216
Bott, (Bookdealers) Ltd., (Martin), Gr Man 118
Falconwood Transport & Military Bookshop,
London Outer 184
Jade Mountain Bookshop, Hants 126
Joel Segal Books, Devon 86
Roadmaster Books, Kent............................ 137
Robert Humm & Co, Lincolnshire 154
Salway Books, Essex 112
Tony Pollastrone Railway Books, Wiltshire...... 251
Yesteryear Railwayana, Kent 139

PUBLISHERS - GENERAL

Adrem Books, Herts 131
Apocalypse, Surrey 233
Aurora Books Ltd, Lothian.......................... 276
books2books, Devon.................................. 88
Dinnages Transport Publishing, E Sussex 103
Fifteenth Century Bookshop (The), E Sussex 104
Ford (Richard), London W 173
G. C. Books Ltd., Dumfries & Galloway......... 271
HCB Wholesale, Powys............................. 290
Joel Segal Books, Devon 86
Poole (William), London W 175
Robert Temple, London N.......................... 160
Smith Books, (Sally), Suffolk 227
Wheen O'Books, Scottish Borders 269
Zardoz Books, Wiltshire............................. 254

- ARABIS BOOKS

Al Saqi Books, London W.......................... 172
Art Book Company, (The), Suffolk................. 228

- BATSFORD

Fifteenth Century Bookshop (The), E Sussex 104
Hennessey Bookseller (Ray), E Sussex 100
Island Books, Devon.................................. 85
Joel Segal Books, Devon 86

SPECIALITY INDEX

Roland Books, Kent 139
Samovar Books, Co. Dublin 264

- BISON BOOKS (UNIVERSITY OF NEBRASKA)
Americanabooksuk, Cumbria 77

- BLACK, A. & C.
Bolton Books, Hampshire 121
Bowden Books, Leics 149
Chapter Two, London SE 164
Fifteenth Century Bookshop (The), E Sussex 104
Intech Books, Northumberland 203
Joel Segal Books, Devon 86
Missing Books, Essex 109
Paul Hoare, Cornwall 75
Wheen O'Books, Scottish Borders 269

- BLACKIE
Bookmark (Children's Books), Wiltshire 253
Fifteenth Century Bookshop (The), E Sussex 104
Grampian Books, Grampian 274
Green Meadow Books, Cornwall 74
Jean Hedger, Berkshire 55
Joel Segal Books, Devon 86
Studio (The), Strathclyde 280
Wheen O'Books, Scottish Borders 269

- CHAMBERS
Maggy Browne, Lincolnshire 150
Wheen O'Books, Scottish Borders 269

- COLLINS (CRIME CLB, THE)
Lucius Books, N Yorks 199
Ming Books, Dumfries & Galloway 271
Roland Books, Kent 139
Shearwater Books, Northumberland 202
Sutcliffe (Mark), West Yorkshire 248
Wheen O'Books, Scottish Borders 269
Williams (Bookdealer), (Richard), N Lincs 154

- CONWAY
Henry Wilson Books, Cheshire 69

- CUNDALL, JOSEPH
Jean Hedger, Berkshire 55

- DAVID & CHARLES
Ardis Books, Hampshire 126
Bott, (Bookdealers) Ltd., (Martin), Gr Man 118
Cox (Geoff), Devon 90
HCB Wholesale, Powys 290
Henry Wilson Books, Cheshire 69
Joel Segal Books, Devon 86
Roadmaster Books, Kent 137
Robert Humm & Co, Lincolnshire 154

- EDINBURGH UNIVERSITY
Bell (Peter), Lothian 276
Joel Segal Books, Devon 86

- FOULIS, T.N.
Bolton Books, Hampshire 121
Cameron House Books, Isle of Wight 134
Fifteenth Century Bookshop (The), E Sussex 104

Grampian Books, Grampian 274
Wheen O'Books, Scottish Borders 269

- GHOST STORY PRESS
Fantastic Literature, Essex 111

- GOLLANCZ
Books Only, Suffolk 227
Joel Segal Books, Devon 86
Samovar Books, Co. Dublin 264
Williams (Bookdealer), (Richard), N Lincs 154

- GUINNESS
Maggy Browne, Lincolnshire 150

- HACKER ART BOOKS
Art Book Company, (The), Suffolk 228

- HAKLUYT SOCIETY, THE
Joel Segal Books, Devon 86

- HARDING, PETER A
Dinnages Transport Publishing, E Sussex 103

- HAYNES PUBLISHING
Colwyn Books, Conwy 285
Joel Segal Books, Devon 86
Roland Books, Kent 139

- HOGARTH PRESS
Eastwood Books (David), Cornwall 73
Ellis, Bookseller (Peter), London WC 178
Evans Books (Paul), West Sussex 243
Fifteenth Century Bookshop (The), E Sussex 104
Ian McKelvie Bookseller, London N 159
Orlando Booksellers, Lincolnshire 152
Roz Hulse, Conwy 286

- JANE'S MILITARY
Joel Segal Books, Devon 86
Robert Humm & Co, Lincolnshire 154

- JOSEPH LTD., MICHAEL
Archivist (The), Devon 90
Joel Segal Books, Devon 86
Samovar Books, Co. Dublin 264
Wheen O'Books, Scottish Borders 269

- KNOPF, A.A.
Wheen O'Books, Scottish Borders 269

- LADYBIRD BOOKS
Annie's Books, S Yorks 222
Armchair Books, Lothian 276
Chapter Two, London SE 164
Dormouse Bookshop (The), Norfolk 190
Fifteenth Century Bookshop (The), E Sussex 104
Green Meadow Books, Cornwall 74
Hawley (C.L.), N Yorks 197
Intech Books, Northumberland 203
Joel Segal Books, Devon 86
Kineton Nooks, Warwickshire 237
Oasis Booksearch, Cambridgeshire 67
Rose's Books, Powys 291
Shakeshaft (Dr. B.), Cheshire 71

SPECIALITY INDEX

Shearwater Books, Northumberland............... 202
Stella Books, Monmouthshire 288
Treasure Trove Books, Leics........................ 148
Wiend Books, Lancashire 144
Williams (Bookdealer), (Richard), N Lincs 154

- LAKESIDE CLASSICS
Americanabooksuk, Cumbria 77

- NISTER
Fifteenth Century Bookshop (The), E Sussex 104
Jean Hedger, Berkshire 55
Lake (David), Norfolk 191

- OAKWOOD PRESS
Bott, (Bookdealers) Ltd., (Martin), Gr Man 118
Coulthurst (Richard), Gr Man 120
Henry Wilson Books, Cheshire...................... 69
Robert Humm & Co, Lincolnshire 154

- OBSERVERS BOOKS
Black Cat Bookshop, Leics 147
Fifteenth Century Bookshop (The), E Sussex 104
Intech Books, Northumberland 203
Jade Mountain Bookshop, Hampshire 126
Joel Segal Books, Devon 86
Stella Books, Monmouthshire 288
Williams (Bookdealer), (Richard), N Lincs 154

- OXFORD UNIVERSITY PRESS
BOOKS4U, Flintshire................................. 286
Joel Segal Books, Devon 86
Solitaire Books, Somerset........................... 217
Wheen O'Books, Scottish Borders 269

- PAN
Bookbarrow, Cambridgeshire....................... 63
Castleton (Pat), Kent................................. 138
Hab Books, London W............................... 173
Heckmondwike Book Shop, West Yorkshire 249
Joel Segal Books, Devon 86
Ming Books, Dumfries & Galloway 271
Orlando Booksellers, Lincolnshire 152
Williams (Bookdealer), (Richard), N Lincs 154
Zardoz Books, Wiltshire............................. 254

- PELICAN
Bass (Ben), Wiltshire 251
Fifteenth Century Bookshop (The), E Sussex 104
Joel Segal Books, Devon 86
Orb's Bookshop, Grampian......................... 274
Samovar Books, Co. Dublin 264
Wayside Books and Cards, Oxfordshire 207
Williams (Bookdealer), (Richard), N Lincs 154
Willmott Bookseller (Nicholas), Cardiff........... 283

- PENGUIN
Arcadia, Oxfordshire 209
Armstrong's Books & Collectables, Leics 147
Bell (Peter), Lothian 276
Bettridge (Gordon), Fife............................. 272
Black Cat Bookshop, Leics 147
Bookbarrow, Cambridgeshire....................... 63
Books at the Warehouse, N Yorks 195
Carningli Centre, Pembrokeshire 288

Fifteenth Century Bookshop (The), E Sussex 104
Grahame Thornton, Bookseller, Dorset........... 93
Hab Books, London W............................... 173
Heckmondwike Book Shop, West Yorkshire 249
J. & J. Books, Lincolnshire 151
Jade Mountain Bookshop, Hampshire 126
Joel Segal Books, Devon 86
Ming Books, Dumfries & Galloway 271
Orb's Bookshop, Grampian......................... 274
Orlando Booksellers, Lincolnshire 152
Price (R.W.), Notts................................... 204
Richmond Books, N Yorks.......................... 195
Shearwater Books, Northumberland............... 202
Skelton (Tony), Kent................................. 141
The Sanctuary Bookshop, Dorset 94
Wayside Books and Cards, Oxfordshire 207
Williams (Bookdealer), (Richard), N Lincs 154
Willmott Bookseller (Nicholas), Cardiff........... 283
Zardoz Books, Wiltshire............................. 254

- PICKERING, WILLIAM
Cox Old & Rare Books (Claude), Suffolk 228

- POYSERS
Birdnet Optics Ltd., Derbyshire 82
Joel Segal Books, Devon 86
Shearwater Books, Northumberland............... 202

- PUFFIN
Books at the Warehouse, N Yorks 195
Castleton (Pat), Kent................................. 138
Fifteenth Century Bookshop (The), E Sussex 104
Heckmondwike Book Shop, West Yorkshire 249
Jean Hedger, Berkshire 55
Joel Segal Books, Devon 86
Shearwater Books, Northumberland............... 202
Treasure Trove Books, Leics........................ 148
Williams (Bookdealer), (Richard), N Lincs 154
Willmott Bookseller (Nicholas), Cardiff........... 283

- ROUNDWOOD PRESS
Meekins Books (Paul), Warwickshire.............. 238

- SHELL GUIDES
J. & J. Books, Lincolnshire 151

- SKOOB
Skoob Russell Square, Suffolk...................... 230

- SMALL PRESS
Samovar Books, Co. Dublin 264

- SOUTHDOWN CLUB
Dinnages Transport Publishing, E Sussex 103

- STUDIO, THE
Books & Things, London W......................... 172
Eastwood Books (David), Cornwall 73
Joel Segal Books, Devon 86

- TAUCHNITZ
Beaton (Richard), E Sussex 103
Williams (Bookdealer), (Richard), N Lincs 154

SPECIALITY INDEX

- THAMES & HUDSON

Ardis Books, Hampshire	126
Joel Segal Books, Devon	86

- WARNES

Everett (Richard), Norfolk	188
Everett (Richard, at the Southwold	
Antiques Centre, Suffolk	229
Hine (Anne), Somerset	218
Intech Books, Northumberland	203
Jean Hedger, Berkshire	55
Joel Segal Books, Devon	86
Shearwater Books, Northumberland	202
Wheen O'Books, Scottish Borders	269

- WISDENS

Coach House Books, Worcs	256
Fifteenth Century Bookshop (The), E Sussex	104
Jade Mountain Bookshop, Hampshire	126
Joel Segal Books, Devon	86
Saint Mary's Books & Prints, Lincolnshire	154

PUBLISHING

Bettridge (Gordon), Fife	272
Coupland (Terry W.), Staffordshire	224
Ford (Richard), London W	173
Kabristan Archives, Shropshire	215
R. & A. Books, E Sussex	102
Roadmaster Books, Kent	137
Smith Books, (Sally), Suffolk	227
Wakeman Books (Frances), Notts	205

PULPS

Askew Books (Vernon), Wiltshire	251
Book Palace (The), London SE	164
Bristol Books, Bristol	60
Cowley, Bookdealer (K.W.), Somerset	218
Delectus Books, London WC	177
Trinity Rare Books, Co. Leitrim	266
Williams (Bookdealer), (Richard), N Lincs	154
Zardoz Books, Wiltshire	254

PUNK FANZINES

Marchpane, London WC	178

PUPPETS & MARIONETTES

Cover to Cover, Merseyside	186
DaSilva Puppet Books, Dorset	93
Fitzsimons (Anne), Cumbria	78
R. & A. Books, E Sussex	102
St Swithin's Illustrated & Children's Books,	
London W	175
Westwood Books Ltd, Cumbria	80

PUZZLES

Ænigma Designs (Books), Devon	86
Adrem Books, Herts	131
Jean Hedger, Berkshire	55
St Swithin's Illustrated & Children's Books, London	
W	175

QUAKERS, THE

Beckham Books Ltd., Suffolk	230
Bookseeker, Tayside	282
Broadhurst of Southport Ltd., Merseyside	186

Dales & Lakes Book Centre, Cumbria	80
Hollett and Son (R.F.G.), Cumbria	80
Joel Segal Books, Devon	86
R. & A. Books, E Sussex	102
Rosemary Pugh Books, Wiltshire	253

RADAR

Aardvark Books, Wiltshire	254
R. & A. Books, E Sussex	102
Stroh (M.A.), London E	155
Westons, Herts	133

RADICAL ISSUES

Forder (R.W.), Hampshire	121
G. C. Books Ltd., Dumfries & Galloway	271
Kenny's Bookshops and Art Galleries Ltd,	
Co. Galway	266
Left on The Shelf, Cumbria	79
Northern Herald Books, West Yorkshire	246
Reading Lasses, Dumfries & Galloway	271
Red Star Books, Herts	130
Spurrier (Nick), Kent	138
Tobo Books, Hampshire	123

RADIO/WIRELESS

Bernard Dixon and Kath Adams, Middlesex	183
Brad Books, Essex	111
Cover to Cover, Merseyside	186
Dormouse Bookshop (The), Norfolk	190
Fifteenth Century Bookshop (The), E Sussex	104
Greenroom Books, West Yorkshire	248
Hambleton Books, N Yorks	197
Joel Segal Books, Devon	86
Kelly Books, Devon	89
Maggy Browne, Lincolnshire	150
McGee (Terence J.), London Outer	181
Orb's Bookshop, Grampian	274
R. & A. Books, E Sussex	102
Roland Books, Kent	139
Stroh (M.A.), London E	155
Transformer, Dumfries & Galloway	271
Weiner (Graham), London N	160
Whistler's Books, London SW	170

RADIOLOGY

Bernard Dixon and Kath Adams, Middlesex	183
Parkinsons Books, Merseyside	186
R M Books, Herts	132
R. & A. Books, E Sussex	102
Weiner (Graham), London N	160
Westons, Herts	133

RAILWAYS & RAILROADS

Abacus Gallery, Staffordshire	224
Adrem Books, Herts	131
Anthony Vickers Books, N Yorks	196
Anvil Books, W Mids	240
Apocalypse, Surrey	233
Arden Books & Cosmographia, Warwickshire	237
Axe Rare & Out of Print Books (Richard),	
N Yorks	194
Baker (Gerald), Bristol	60
Baldwin (M. & M.), Worcs	255
Barbican Bookshop, N Yorks	198
Barter Books, Northumberland	202

SPECIALITY INDEX

Bath Old Books, Somerset 216
Bianco Library, W Sussex........................... 242
Bird Books (Nigel), Ceredigion 284
Black Five Books, Shropshire 215
Book House (The), Cumbria......................... 77
Books & Collectables Ltd., Cambridgeshire 63
Books Afloat, Dorset.................................. 96
Books Bought & Sold, Surrey 232
Books Plus, Devon 84
BookShop, The, Dumfries & Galloway........... 270
Bott, (Bookdealers) Ltd., (Martin), Gr Man 118
Brad Books, Essex..................................... 111
Brewin Books Ltd., Warwickshire 238
Broadhurst of Southport Ltd., Merseyside 186
Browning Books, Torfaen 294
Carningli Centre, Pembrokeshire 288
Cavern Books, Cheshire 70
Cheshire Book Centre, Cheshire.................... 69
Chevin Books, West Yorkshire 250
Clarke Books (David), Somerset 219
Classic Crime Collections, Gr Man 119
Cobbles Books, Somerset............................ 218
Cobweb Books, N Yorks............................. 195
Cofion Books, Pembrokeshire 288
Collectables (W.H.), Suffolk 230
Collectors Corner, Wiltshire......................... 253
Corfe Books, Surrey................................... 231
Cornucopia Books, Lincolnshire 153
Coulthurst (Richard), Gr Man 120
Cox (Geoff), Devon 90
Crosby Nethercott Books, London Outer 181
Dales & Lakes Book Centre, Cumbria............ 80
Deeside Books, Grampian........................... 273
Dinnages Transport Publishing, E Sussex 103
Duck (William), Hampshire......................... 124
Eastcote Bookshop (The), London Outer......... 181
Elton Engineering Books, London W 173
Empire Books, N Yorks.............................. 198
Esoteric Dreams Bookshop, Cumbria 78
Ewell Bookshop Ltd, Surrey 232
Falconwood Transport & Military Bookshop,
London Outer 184
Farnborough Gallery, Hampshire................... 122
Fifteenth Century Bookshop (The), E Sussex 104
Garfi Books, Powys 293
Good Books, Shropshire 214
Hambleton Books, N Yorks......................... 197
Harlequin Books, Bristol 59
Hatchard & Daughters, West Yorkshire 247
Hay Castle, Powys.................................... 290
Henry Wilson Books, Cheshire 69
Howard Loftus Rail Books, S Yorks............... 222
Internet Bookshop UK Ltd., Glos 113
Island Books, Devon 85
J C Books, Devon 87
Jade Mountain Bookshop, Hampshire 126
Joel Segal Books, Devon 86
Jones (Barry), West Sussex 243
Junk & Spread Eagle, London SE 165
Just Books, Cornwall 76
Keegan's Bookshop, Berkshire 56
Kerr (Norman), Cumbria 78
Kirkland Books, Cumbria............................ 79
Milestone Books, Devon 89
Moreton Books, Devon............................... 87

My Back Pages, London SW 169
Nevis Railway Books, Oxfordshire 209
Nevis Railway Bookshops (The Antique &
Book Collector), Wiltshire......................... 252
Newband (D M), Powys 293
Old Celtic Bookshop (The), Devon 88
Old Station Pottery & Bookshop (The), Norfolk 192
Over-Sands Books, Cumbria........................ 78
Park Gallery & Bookshop (The), Northants 201
Parlour Bookshop (The), Oxfordshire............. 207
Paton Books, Herts.................................... 132
Peter White, Hampshire 121
Postings, Surrey 234
R. & A. Books, E Sussex............................ 102
Railway Book and Magazine Search, Berks...... 56
Railway Shop (The), Torfaen 294
recollectionsbookshop.co.uk, Cornwall........... 74
Roadmaster Books, Kent............................. 137
Robert Humm & Co, Lincolnshire 154
Rochdale Book Company, Gr Man 120
Roland Books, Kent 139
Rolling Stock Books, Gr Man....................... 120
Roz Hulse, Conwy 286
St Swithin's Illustrated & Children's Books,
London W 175
Salway Books, Essex 112
Sax Books, Suffolk 229
Scrivener's Books & Bookbinding,
Derbyshire 82
Sedgeberrow Books & Framing, Worcs........... 256
Simon Lewis Transport Books, Glos 115
Skyrack Books, W Yorkshire........................ 248
Soccor Books Limited, Lincolnshire............... 150
Staffs Bookshop (The), Staffordshire 224
Stella Books, Monmouthshire 288
Stroh (M.A.), London E 155
Suffolk Rare Books, Suffolk 230
Tony Pollastrone Railway Books, Wiltshire...... 251
Tozer Railway Books (Nick), W Yorkshire 248
Treasure Island (The), Gr Man...................... 119
Trinders' Fine Tools, Suffolk 227
Uncle Phil's Books, W Mids........................ 240
Vailima Books, Dumfries & Galloway 270
Vickers (Anthony), N Yorks........................ 196
Weiner (Graham), London N 160
Winchester Bookshop (The), Hampshire.......... 127
Wizard Books, Cambridgeshire..................... 67
Yesteryear Railwayana, Kent 139
Yewtree Books, Cumbria 79

RATIONALISM

Forder (R.W.), Hampshire 121
Joel Segal Books, Devon 86
Northern Herald Books, W Yorkshire 246

REFERENCE

Adrem Books, Herts 131
Archivist (The), Devon............................... 90
Art Reference Books, Hampshire 125
Axe Rare & Out of Print Books (Richard),
N Yorks.. 194
Bannister (David), Glos.............................. 113
Books, Denbighshire 286
Books for Writers, Monmouthshire................ 287
Corder (Mark W.), Kent 140

SPECIALITY INDEX

Cornucopia Books, Lincolnshire 153
Downie Fine Books Ltd., (Robert), Shropshire.. 215
Emjay Books, Surrey.................................. 231
Fifteenth Century Bookshop (The), E Sussex 104
G. C. Books Ltd., Dumfries & Galloway......... 271
Hurst (Jenny), Kent 138
Joel Segal Books, Devon 86
Naughton Booksellers, Co. Dublin 265
R. & A. Books, E Sussex............................. 102
Sax Books, Suffolk 229
Shacklock Books (David), Suffolk 227
Worlds End Bookshop, London SW 171

REGISTERS

Brad Books, Essex..................................... 111
Delph Books, Gr Man................................. 120
Joel Segal Books, Devon 86
Thornber (Peter M.), N Yorks 196

RELIGION - GENERAL

Adrem Books, Herts 131
Armchair Books, Lothian 276
Aurora Books Ltd, Lothian........................... 276
Axe Rare & Out of Print Books (Richard),
N Yorks.. 194
Barcombe Services, Essex............................ 108
Bardsley's Books, Suffolk............................ 226
Bath Old Books, Somerset 216
Beckham Books Ltd., Suffolk 230
Beware of the Leopard, Bristol...................... 58
Blackwell's Rare Books, Oxfordshire.............. 209
Blythswood Bookshop, Highland 275
Books, Denbighshire 286
Books (For All), N Yorks............................ 194
Bookshop at the Plain, Lincolnshire............... 151
Bosorne Books, Cornwall 75
Bowie Books & Collectables, East Yorkshire 107
Brimstones, E Sussex................................. 103
Broadwater Books, Hampshire...................... 125
Bunyan Books, Bedfordshire......................... 53
Camilla's Bookshop, E Sussex...................... 101
Canon Gate Books, West Sussex.................... 244
Carningli Centre, Pembrokeshire................... 288
Carta Regis, Powys................................... 293
Cheshire Book Centre, Cheshire.................... 69
Church Street Books, Norfolk....................... 187
Clegg (David), Staffordshire......................... 224
Cobweb Books, N Yorks............................. 195
Cofion Books, Pembrokeshire 288
Collectable Books, London SE 165
Colwyn Books, Conwy 285
D'Arcy Books, Wiltshire............................. 252
Ely Books, Cambridgeshire 65
Fifteenth Century Bookshop (The), E Sussex 104
G. C. Books Ltd., Dumfries & Galloway......... 271
Gage Postal Books, Essex 111
Garfi Books, Powys 293
Geneva Books, London SW 168
Gilbert (R.A.), Bristol................................. 59
Glenbower Books, Co. Dublin 265
Golden Age Books, Worcs........................... 256
Good for Books, Lincolnshire....................... 151
Hall's Bookshop, Kent............................... 141
Handsworth Books, Essex........................... 112
Hava Books, London SE............................. 165

Hawley (C.L.), N Yorks............................. 197
Hay Cinema Bookshop Ltd., Powys............... 290
HCB Wholesale, Powys.............................. 290
Herb Tandree Philosophy Books, Glos 116
Joel Segal Books, Devon 86
Just Books, Cornwall 76
Kalligraphia, Isle of Wight.......................... 134
Kenny's Bookshops and Art Galleries Ltd,
Co. Galway.. 266
Kyrios Books, Notts 204
Last Century Books, Borders........................ 268
Lewis (J.T. & P.), Cornwall......................... 74
Little Bookshop (The), Gr Man.................... 119
Maggy Browne, Lincolnshire 150
medievalbookshop, Herts............................ 133
Moss Books, London NW 162
Murphy (C.J.), Norfolk.............................. 190
Naughton Booksellers, Co. Dublin 265
Needham Books, (Russell), Somerset.............. 220
Old Bookshop (The), W Mids...................... 241
Old Station Pottery & Bookshop (The), Norfolk 192
Oxfam Books and Music, Hampshire 126
Parkinsons Books, Merseyside...................... 186
Parrott Books, Oxfordshire 211
Paton Books, Herts................................... 132
Pendleburys Bookshop, London N 159
Portobello Books, London W 175
Priestpopple Books, Northumberland 202
Prospect House Books, Co. Down................. 261
PsychoBabel Books & Journals, Oxfordshire..... 206
Pyecroft (Ruth), Glos 117
Quinto of Great Russell Street, London WC 179
R. & A. Books, E Sussex............................ 102
Reading Lasses, Dumfries & Galloway 271
Robin Doughty - Fine Books, W Mids........... 239
Roland Books, Kent 139
Roscrea Bookshop, Co. Tipperary................. 267
Rosemary Pugh Books, Wiltshire.................. 253
Rye Old Books, E Sussex 104
St Philip's Books, Oxfordshire...................... 210
Saintfield Antiques & Fine Books, Co. Down ... 261
Salsus Books, Worcs 256
Saunders (Tom), Caerphilly......................... 283
Scott (Peter), E Sussex 104
Scrivener's Books & Bookbinding, Derbyshire... 82
Sillan Books, Co. Cavan............................. 262
Skoob Russell Square, Suffolk...................... 230
Star Lord Books, Gr Man 119
Stroma Books, Borders 268
Tarka Books, Devon.................................. 84
The Sanctuary Bookshop, Dorset.................. 94
Tobo Books, Hampshire............................. 123
Treasure Trove Books, Leics........................ 148
Trinity Rare Books, Co. Leitrim 266
Uncle Phil's Books, W Mids........................ 240
Walker Fine Books (Steve), Dorset 92
Wayside Books and Cards, Oxfordshire 207
Westwood Books Ltd, Cumbria.................... 80
Wheen O'Books, Scottish Borders 269
Wiend Books, Lancashire 144
Wizard Books, Cambridgeshire..................... 67
Worcester Rare Books, Worcs...................... 257

- ARAMAIC CHRISTIANITY

Collectable Books, London SE 165

SPECIALITY INDEX

Thorntons of Oxford Ltd., Oxfordshire 207

- BUDDHISM

Bookbarrow, Cambridgeshire 63
Inner Bookshop (The), Oxfordshire................. 210
Joel Segal Books, Devon 86
Mandalay Bookshop, London SW 169
Occultique, Northants................................ 200
Parrott (Jeremy), London E......................... 156
Pendleburys Bookshop, London N 159
Trinity Rare Books, Co. Leitrim 266
Waxfactor, E Sussex 100

- CATHOLIC

Beckham Books Ltd., Suffolk 230
Bell (Peter), Lothian.................................. 276
Britons Catholic Library, Co. Wexford 267
Carraig Books Ltd., Co. Dublin 264
Collectable Books, London SE 165
Craobh Rua Books, Co. Armagh................... 260
Dolphin Books, Suffolk............................... 226
Hilton (Books) (P.J.), London W 174
Joel Segal Books, Devon 86
Karen Millward, Co. Cork........................... 263
Killeen (John), N Yorks.............................. 194
Naughton Booksellers, Co. Dublin 265
Oasis Booksearch, Cambridgeshire................. 67
Parkinsons Books, Merseyside...................... 186
Pendleburys Bookshop, London N 159
Prospect House Books, Co. Down.................. 261
Roscrea Bookshop, Co. Tipperary................. 267
Rye Old Books, E Sussex 104
S.P.C.K., Bristol 60
St Philip's Books, Oxfordshire...................... 210
Samovar Books, Co. Dublin......................... 264
Sims (Sue), Dorset..................................... 91

- CHRISTIAN

Barbican Bookshop, N Yorks 198
Beckham Books Ltd., Suffolk 230
Bennett & Kerr Books, Oxfordshire................ 206
Berwick Books, Lincolnshire........................ 152
Bevan (John), Wiltshire.............................. 252
Black Five Books, Shropshire 215
Blythswood Bookshop, Highland 275
Bookshop (The), Co. Donegal...................... 263
Bookshop at the Plain, Lincolnshire............... 151
Bookworm Alley, Devon 89
Butler Cresswell Rare Books, Buckinghamshire . 61
Canon Gate Books, West Sussex................... 244
Carnforth Bookshop (The), Lancashire 143
Chapter Two, London SE............................ 164
Chthonios Books, E Sussex 102
Classic Bindings Ltd, London SW 167
Copnal Books, Cheshire 69
Crouch Rare Books, Surrey......................... 233
Dolphin Books, Suffolk............................... 226
Facet Books, Dorset................................... 91
Fifteenth Century Bookshop (The), E Sussex 104
Foyle Books, Co. Derry 260
Golden Age Books, Worcs........................... 256
Greensleeves, Oxfordshire 207
Hab Books, London W............................... 173
Hava Books, London SE............................. 165
Hilton (Books) (P.J.), London W 174

Holmes Books (Harry), East Yorkshire........... 107
Humber Books, Lincolnshire 150
Inner Bookshop (The), Oxfordshire................ 210
Joel Segal Books, Devon 86
Kernaghans, Merseyside............................. 186
Kyrios Books, Notts 204
Naughton Booksellers, Co. Dublin 265
Oasis Booksearch, Cambridgeshire................. 67
Orb's Bookshop, Grampian......................... 274
Parkinsons Books, Merseyside...................... 186
Pendleburys Bookshop, London N 159
Price (John), London N 159
Roscrea Bookshop, Co. Tipperary................. 267
Rose Books, Gr Man 119
S.P.C.K., Bristol 60
S.P.C.K., Hampshire................................. 127
St Philip's Books, Oxfordshire...................... 210
Salsus Books, Worcs 256
Samovar Books, Co. Dublin......................... 264
Shacklock Books (David), Suffolk 227
Spooner & Co, Somerset 220
Stalagluft Books, Tyne and Wear.................. 236
Staniland (Booksellers), Lincolnshire 154
Thornber (Peter M.), N Yorks 196
Thorntons of Oxford Ltd., Oxfordshire........... 207
Trinity Rare Books, Co. Leitrim 266
Tuft (Patrick), London Outer....................... 182
Victoria Bookshop (The), Devon................... 84
Wayside Books and Cards, Oxfordshire 207
Wheen O'Books, Scottish Borders 269
Williams (Bookdealer), (Richard), N Lincs....... 154

- CHRISTIAN SPIRITISM

Stalagluft Books, Tyne and Wear.................. 236
Trinity Rare Books, Co. Leitrim 266

- CHRISTIANITY, SYRIAN ORTHODOX

Samovar Books, Co. Dublin......................... 264
Trinity Rare Books, Co. Leitrim 266
Winghale Books, Lincolnshire 153

- CHURCH OF ENGLAND

Beckham Books Ltd., Suffolk 230
Bell (Peter), Lothian.................................. 276
Collectable Books, London SE 165
Dolphin Books, Suffolk............................... 226
Hilton (Books) (P.J.), London W 174
Joel Segal Books, Devon 86
Oasis Booksearch, Cambridgeshire 67
Olynthiacs, Shropshire 214
Parkinsons Books, Merseyside...................... 186
Pendleburys Bookshop, London N 159
Rye Old Books, E Sussex 104
S.P.C.K., Bristol 60
Stalagluft Books, Tyne and Wear.................. 236
Williams (Bookdealer), (Richard), N Lincs....... 154

- COPTIC

P. and P. Books, Worcs 256

- HEBRAICA

Beckham Books Ltd., Suffolk 230
Chthonios Books, E Sussex 102
Fishburn Books, London NW....................... 161
Golden Age Books, Worcs........................... 256

SPECIALITY INDEX

Hava Books, London SE............................ 165
Joel Segal Books, Devon 86
Pendleburys Bookshop, London N 159
Samovar Books, Co. Dublin 264
Thorntons of Oxford Ltd., Oxfordshire 207
Trinity Rare Books, Co. Leitrim 266

- HINDI
Collectable Books, London SE 165
Inner Bookshop (The), Oxfordshire................ 210

- HINDU
Bookbarrow, Cambridgeshire....................... 63
Inner Bookshop (The), Oxfordshire................ 210
Pendleburys Bookshop, London N 159

- ISLAM
Al Saqi Books, London W.......................... 172
Beckham Books Ltd., Suffolk 230
Books on Spain, London Outer 184
Delectus Books, London WC....................... 177
Folios Limited, London SW 168
Inner Bookshop (The), Oxfordshire................ 210
Joppa Books Ltd., Surrey 231
Kingswood Books, Dorset 94
Occultique, Northants................................ 200
Pendleburys Bookshop, London N 159
Quaritch Ltd., (Bernard), London W............... 175
Samovar Books, Co. Dublin 264
Thorntons of Oxford Ltd., Oxfordshire 207
Trinity Rare Books, Co. Leitrim 266

- JAINISM
Collectable Books, London SE 165

- JEHOVAH'S WITNESSES
Golden Age Books, Worcs 256

- JESUITS, THE
Hodgson (Judith), London W 174
Pendleburys Bookshop, London N 159
St Philip's Books, Oxfordshire...................... 210
Samovar Books, Co. Dublin 264
Trinity Rare Books, Co. Leitrim 266

- JEWISH
Beckham Books Ltd., Suffolk 230
Books on Spain, London Outer 184
Collectable Books, London SE 165
Crouch Rare Books, Surrey......................... 233
Delectus Books, London WC....................... 177
Fishburn Books, London NW....................... 161
Golden Age Books, Worcs 256
Inner Bookshop (The), Oxfordshire................ 210
Joel Segal Books, Devon 86
Occultique, Northants................................ 200
Pendleburys Bookshop, London N 159
Samovar Books, Co. Dublin 264
Thorntons of Oxford Ltd., Oxfordshire 207
Trotter Books (John), London N 160

- METHODISM
Barbican Bookshop, N Yorks 198
Beckham Books Ltd., Suffolk 230
Bookshop at the Plain, Lincolnshire............... 151

Humber Books, Lincolnshire 150
Joel Segal Books, Devon 86
MK Book Services, Cambridgeshire 66
Oasis Booksearch, Cambridgeshire................. 67
Parkinsons Books, Merseyside...................... 186
Pendleburys Bookshop, London N 159
Price (John), London N 159
Rosley Books, Cumbria 81
S.P.C.K., Bristol 60
Samovar Books, Co. Dublin 264

- MORMONISM
Trinity Rare Books, Co. Leitrim 266

- MUSLIM
Al Saqi Books, London W.......................... 172
Collectable Books, London SE 165
Occultique, Northants................................ 200
Salsus Books, Worcs 256

- NON CONFORMITY
Beckham Books Ltd., Suffolk 230
Humber Books, Lincolnshire 150
Joel Segal Books, Devon 86
Oasis Booksearch, Cambridgeshire................. 67
Parkinsons Books, Merseyside...................... 186
Pendleburys Bookshop, London N 159
Richard Thornton Books, London N 160
S.P.C.K., Bristol 60
Samovar Books, Co. Dublin 264
Stalagluft Books, Tyne and Wear.................. 236

- ORIENTAL
Chthonios Books, E Sussex 102
Fine Books Oriental Ltd., London WC............ 178
Greensleeves, Oxfordshire 207
Inner Bookshop (The), Oxfordshire................ 210
Joel Segal Books, Devon 86
Occultique, Northants................................ 200
Trinity Rare Books, Co. Leitrim 266

- PARSEEISM
Collectable Books, London SE 165

- PRE-VATICAN II CATHOLICISM
Parkinsons Books, Merseyside...................... 186
S.P.C.K., Bristol 60
St Philip's Books, Oxfordshire...................... 210
Samovar Books, Co. Dublin 264
Stalagluft Books, Tyne and Wear 236

- PRESBYTERIAN
Beckham Books Ltd., Suffolk 230
Bell (Peter), Lothian 276
Pendleburys Bookshop, London N 159
Prospect House Books, Co. Down.................. 261
S.P.C.K., Bristol 60
Samovar Books, Co. Dublin 264
Trinity Rare Books, Co. Leitrim 266
Wheen O'Books, Scottish Borders 269

- PROTESTANTISM
Beckham Books Ltd., Suffolk 230
Collectable Books, London SE 165
Hilton (Books) (P.J.), London W 174

SPECIALITY INDEX

Humber Books, Lincolnshire 150
Joel Segal Books, Devon 86
Parkinsons Books, Merseyside...................... 186
Pendleburys Bookshop, London N 159
Prospect House Books, Co. Down................. 261
S.P.C.K., Bristol 60
Samovar Books, Co. Dublin 264
Spooner & Co, Somerset 220

- PURITANISM

Beckham Books Ltd., Suffolk 230
Humber Books, Lincolnshire 150
Parkinsons Books, Merseyside...................... 186
S.P.C.K., Bristol 60
Samovar Books, Co. Dublin 264
Spooner & Co, Somerset 220

- QUAKERS

Barbican Bookshop, N Yorks 198
Beckham Books Ltd., Suffolk 230
Bookseeker, Tayside................................... 282
Dales & Lakes Book Centre, Cumbria......... 80
Joel Segal Books, Devon 86
Post-Horn Books, N Yorks 193
Prospect House Books, Co. Down................. 261
Robin Doughty - Fine Books, W Mids 239
Rosley Books, Cumbria 81
S.P.C.K., Bristol 60
Samovar Books, Co. Dublin 264
Trinity Rare Books, Co. Leitrim 266

- SALVATION ARMY

Bookworm Alley, Devon 89
Collectable Books, London SE 165
Dolphin Books, Suffolk............................... 226
Prospect House Books, Co. Down................. 261
Samovar Books, Co. Dublin 264

- SIKH

Trinity Rare Books, Co. Leitrim 266

- TAOISM

Chthonios Books, E Sussex 102
Collectable Books, London SE 165
Inner Bookshop (The), Oxfordshire................ 210
Joel Segal Books, Devon 86
Occultique, Northants................................. 200

RELIGIOUS TEXTS

Apocalypse, Surrey 233
Beckham Books Ltd., Suffolk 230
Brimstones, E Sussex.................................. 103
Chthonios Books, E Sussex 102
Fifteenth Century Bookshop (The), E Sussex 104
Foster Bookshop (Paul), London SW 168
Golden Age Books, Worcs 256
Magis Books, Leics..................................... 149
Parkinsons Books, Merseyside...................... 186
Pendleburys Bookshop, London N 159
Rosemary Pugh Books, Wiltshire 253
Samovar Books, Co. Dublin 264

REVOLUTIONS

Left on The Shelf, Cumbria.......................... 79

RHETORIC

Price (John), London N 159

RHODESIANA

Chalmers Hallam (E.), Hampshire 125
Kenya Books, E Sussex............................... 100

RIVER BOATS & RIVER MEN

Baldwin (M. & M.), Worcs 255
Cox (Geoff), Devon 90
Fifteenth Century Bookshop (The), E Sussex 104
Joel Segal Books, Devon 86
Marine & Cannon Books, Cheshire 71
Marine and Cannon Books, Cheshire 69

RIVER THAMES

Apocalypse, Surrey 233
Baldwin (M. & M.), Worcs 255
Cornucopia Books, Lincolnshire 153
Empire Books, N Yorks............................... 198
Fifteenth Century Bookshop (The), E Sussex 104
Marine and Cannon Books, Cheshire 69
R. & A. Books, E Sussex............................. 102
Salway Books, Essex 112
Tooley, Adams & Co, Oxfordshire 211

ROCK ART

Book Palace (The), London SE 164
Print Matters, London SE............................ 166
R. & A. Books, E Sussex............................. 102

ROMANCE

Apocalypse, Surrey 233
Wheen O'Books, Scottish Borders 269

ROMANTICISM

Hawley (C.L.), N Yorks.............................. 197
Joel Segal Books, Devon 86
R. & A. Books, E Sussex............................. 102

ROPEMAKING & KNOTS

Footrope Knots, Suffolk.............................. 228
Marine and Cannon Books, Cheshire 69
Mercat Books, Highland 274

ROSICRUCIANISM

Gildas Books, Cheshire 68
Inner Bookshop (The), Oxfordshire................ 210
Magis Books, Leics..................................... 149
Occultique, Northants................................. 200

ROYALTY - GENERAL

Barn Books, Buckinghamshire....................... 61
Books & Collectables Ltd., Cambridgeshire 63
Dally Books & Collectables, Powys................ 292
Dolphin Books, Suffolk............................... 226
Farahar & Dupre (Clive & Sophie), Wiltshire ... 251
Fifteenth Century Bookshop (The), E Sussex 104
Hay Cinema Bookshop Ltd., Powys............... 290
Heraldry Today, Wiltshire........................... 252
Heritage, W Mids...................................... 239
Jade Mountain Bookshop, Hampshire 126
Lost Books, Northants................................. 201
Piccadilly Rare Books, E Sussex 105
R. & A. Books, E Sussex............................. 102

SPECIALITY INDEX

St Swithin's Illustrated & Children's Books, London W.. 175 Sax Books, Suffolk .... 229 Shacklock Books (David), Suffolk .... 227 Ventnor Rare Books, Isle of Wight................. 135 Wheen O'Books, Scottish Borders .... 269 Yesterday's News, Conwy............................ 285

- EUROPEAN

Dolphin Books, Suffolk............................... 226 Fackley Services, Notts .... 205 Henry Wilson Books, Cheshire...................... 69 Orb's Bookshop, Grampian.......................... 274 Piccadilly Rare Books, E Sussex .... 105 Saintfield Antiques & Fine Books, Co. Down ... 261

ROYCROFT

Atholl Fine Books, Tayside 281

RUBAIYAT OF OMAR KHAYYAM

Cornucopia Books, Lincolnshire .... 153 Fifteenth Century Bookshop (The), E Sussex .... 104 Inner Bookshop (The), Oxfordshire................ 210 N1 Books, E Sussex................................... 105 R. & A. Books, E Sussex............................. 102

RUGS

Apocalypse, Surrey .... 233 Byrom Textile Bookroom (Richard), Lancashire 143 Cover to Cover, Merseyside.......................... 186 Don Kelly Books, London W .... 172 Judith Mansfield, W Yorkshire..................... 250 Reading Lasses, Dumfries & Galloway .... 271 Sleepy Elephant Books & Artefacts, Cumbria ... 80 Smith Books (Keith), Herefordshire .... 128 Thornber (Peter M.), N Yorks .... 196 Trinders' Fine Tools, Suffolk .... 227 Whittle, Bookseller (Avril), Cumbria 81

RUPERT BEAR

Dales & Lakes Book Centre, Cumbria............ 80 Fifteenth Century Bookshop (The), E Sussex .... 104 Joel Segal Books, Devon .... 86 R. & A. Books, E Sussex............................. 102 Stella Books, Monmouthshire 288

RURAL LIFE

2 Ravens, Cumbria .... 79 Anwoth Books Ltd, Dumfries & Galloway ...... 270 Arden Books & Cosmographia, Warwickshire... 237 Arnold (Roy), Suffolk................................. 228 Barn Books, Shropshire............................... 215 Blest (Peter), Kent .... 139 Books for Content, Herefordshire.................. 128 Brad Books, Essex..................................... 111 Campbell Hewson Books (R.), Fife................ 271 Carningli Centre, Pembrokeshire................... 288 Castleton (Pat), Kent.................................. 138 Chalmers Hallam (E.), Hampshire .... 125 Chantrey Books, S Yorks .... 222 Church Green Books, Oxfordshire................. 211 Clarke Books (David), Somerset .... 219 Cobbles Books, Somerset............................ 218 Coch-y-Bonddu Books, Powys .... 292 Colonsay Bookshop, Isle of Colonsay............. 276

Cornucopia Books, Lincolnshire .... 153 Cottage Books, Leics.................................. 147 Country Books, Derbyshire .... 82 Cover to Cover, Merseyside......................... 186 Cox (Geoff), Devon .... 90 Dales & Lakes Book Centre, Cumbria............ 80 Dolphin Books, Suffolk............................... 226 Doorbar (P. & D.), Gwyned........................ 287 Dusty Books, Powys .... 292 Fackley Services, Notts .... 205 Fifteenth Century Bookshop (The), E Sussex .... 104 Fireside Books, Buckinghamshire .... 62 Fireside Bookshop, Cumbria........................ 81 Furneaux Books (Lee), Devon....................... 89 Greta Books, Durham .... 97 Grove Bookshop (The), N Yorks................... 197 Harvest Books, Lancashire........................... 145 Home Farm Books, Warwickshire.................. 237 J & J Burgess Booksellers, Cambridgeshire...... 64 Joel Segal Books, Devon .... 86 Keeble Antiques, Somerset.......................... 219 Kilgour (Sporting Books) (Ian), Leics .... 149 Martin (Books and Pictures), (Brian P)., Surrey. 232 McCrone (Audrey), Isle of Arran................... 275 Mercat Books, Highland .... 274 Missing Books, Essex .... 109 Moss End Bookshop, Berks .... 57 Mount's Bay Books, Cornwall .... 75 Murphy (C.J.), Norfolk............................... 190 Orb's Bookshop, Grampian......................... 274 Park (Mike), London Outer.......................... 183 Periwinkle Press, Kent .... 139 Petworth Antique Market (Bookroom), W Sussex .... 244 Phenotype Books, Cumbria .... 80 Randall (Tom), Somerset............................. 219 Read (C.&J.), Gorleston Books, Norfolk .... 188 Roadmaster Books, Kent............................. 137 Rods Books, Devon................................... 88 Rutland Bookshop (The), Rutland .... 212 Shacklock Books (David), Suffolk .... 227 Singleton (Anthony), S Yorks .... 222 Uncle Phil's Books, W Mids........................ 240 Vickers (Anthony), N Yorks......................... 196 Wheen O'Books, Scottish Borders .... 269 Wildside Books, Worcs .... 255 Woodbine Books, W Yorkshire..................... 246

RUSSIAN HISTORY - IMPERIAL RUSSIA

Cox (Geoff), Devon .... 90 Dolphin Books, Suffolk............................... 226 Joel Segal Books, Devon .... 86 Marijana Dworski Books, via Hereford........... 290

SALVATION ARMY

Hollett and Son (R.F.G.), Cumbria .... 80 R. & A. Books, East Sussex .... 102 Roscrea Bookshop, Co. Tipperary................. 267 Samovar Books, Co. Dublin......................... 264

SATIRE

Adrem Books, Herts .... 131 Burmester (James), Bristol........................... 59 Cornucopia Books, Lincolnshire .... 153 Fifteenth Century Bookshop (The), East Sussex. 104

SPECIALITY INDEX

Print Matters, London SE........................... 166
Yesterday's News, Conwy........................... 285

SCHOOL REGISTERS ROLLS OF HONOUR

Camilla's Bookshop, East Sussex 101
Coach House Books, Worcs 256
Delph Books, Gr Man............................... 120
Heraldry Today, Wiltshire........................... 252
Joel Segal Books, Devon 86
Military Bookworm, London SE................... 165
Palladour Books, Hampshire 126
Tiffin (Tony and Gill), Durham.................... 97
Townsend (John), Berks 57
Turton (John), Durham 98
Turton (John), Durham 98
Williams (Bookdealer), (Richard), N Lincs....... 154
Wise (Derek), East Sussex.......................... 104
World War Books, Kent 141

SCHOOLS - GENERAL

Barcombe Services, Essex........................... 108
Empire Books, North Yorkshire 198
Kirkpatrick (Robert J.), London W 174
Williams (Bookdealer), (Richard), N Lincs....... 154

SCIENCE - GENERAL

Alba Books, Grampian 274
Aurora Books Ltd, Lothian.......................... 276
Baldwin's Scientific Books, Essex 112
Barcombe Services, Essex........................... 108
Baron (Christopher), Gr Man 118
Baron - Scientific Book Sales (P.J.), Somerset ... 217
Bernard Dixon and Kath Adams, Middlesex 183
Beware of the Leopard, Bristol..................... 58
Book Annex (The), Essex 109
Bookcase, Cumbria.................................. 78
Books & Collectables Ltd., Cambridgeshire...... 63
Bookshop (The), Co. Donegal...................... 263
Booth Books, Powys 289
Camden Books, Somerset 216
Carningli Centre, Pembrokeshire................... 288
Carta Regis, Powys.................................. 293
Cheshire Book Centre, Cheshire.................... 69
Eagle Bookshop (The), Bedfordshire 53
Finch Rare Books Ltd. (Simon), London W..... 173
Gaskell Rare Books (Roger), Cambridgeshire ... 66
GfB: the Colchester Bookshop, Essex 109
Glenbower Books, Co. Dublin 265
Good for Books, Lincolnshire...................... 151
Hay Cinema Bookshop Ltd., Powys............... 290
Hinchliffe Books, Bristol............................ 59
Hollett and Son (R.F.G.), Cumbria 80
Hünersdorff Rare Books, London SW 169
Hunter–Rare Books (Andrew), London SW 169
Hurst (Jenny), Kent 138
Ice House Books, Wiltshire 253
Innes Books, Shropshire............................ 214
J C Books, Devon 87
Jay Books, Lothian.................................. 278
Just Books, Cornwall 76
Lawson & Company (E.M.), Oxfordshire 208
Lenton (Alfred), Leics............................... 147
Lewis (J.T. & P.), Cornwall........................ 74
Little Stour Books, Kent 137

Lymelight Books & Prints, Dorset................. 93
Macfarlane (Mr. H.), Essex 112
McCrone (Audrey), Isle of Arran.................. 275
McGee (Terence J.), London Outer 181
Mogul Diamonds, W Mids 241
Mollie's Loft, Swansea.............................. 294
Moorside Books, Lancashire........................ 144
Orangeberry Books, Oxfordshire................... 209
Parkinsons Books, Merseyside...................... 186
Pauline Harries Books, Hampshire 123
Phillips (Nigel), Hampshire......................... 122
Pickering & Chatto, London W.................... 175
Plurabelle Books, Cambridgeshire................. 64
Pollak (P.M.), Devon 89
Pomes Penyeach, Staffordshire 224
Prospect House Books, Co. Down................. 261
PsychoBabel Books & Journals, Oxfordshire..... 206
Quaritch Ltd., (Bernard), London W.............. 175
Quinto of Charing Cross Road, London WC :.. 179
Quinto of Great Russell Street, London WC 179
R M Books, Herts................................... 132
Roberts Books, Ayrshire 280
Rogers Turner Books, London SE................. 166
Scrivener's Books & Bookbinding, Derbyshire... 82
Skoob Russell Square, Suffolk...................... 230
Smith (David & Lynn), London Outer............ 182
Staniland (Booksellers), Lincolnshire 154
Stern Antiquarian Bookseller (Jeffrey), N Yorks 199
Stroh (M.A.), London E 155
The Sanctuary Bookshop, Dorset.................. 94
Tony Hutchinson, Surrey........................... 234
Transformer, Dumfries & Galloway............... 271
Turret House, Norfolk............................... 192
Wayside Books and Cards, Oxfordshire 207
Weiner (Graham), London N 160
Westons, Herts 133
Westwood Books Ltd, Cumbria.................... 80
Wheen O'Books, Scottish Borders 269
Whistler's Books, London SW 170
Worcester Rare Books, Worcs...................... 257

- FOOD

Bernard Dixon and Kath Adams, Middlesex 183
Parkinsons Books, Merseyside...................... 186
Westons, Hertfordshire 133

- FORENSIC

Bernard Dixon and Kath Adams, Middlesex 183
Bolland Books, Bedfordshire....................... 53
Cheshire Book Centre, Cheshire.................... 69
ForensicSearch, Hertfordshire 132
Lawful Occasions, Essex............................ 108
Wayside Books and Cards, Oxfordshire 207

- HISTORY OF

Axe Rare & Out of Print Books (Richard),
North Yorkshire 194
Baldwin's Scientific Books, Essex 112
Barcombe Services, Essex........................... 108
Baron (Christopher), Gr Man 118
Bernard Dixon and Kath Adams, Middlesex 183
Camden Books, Somerset 216
Cheshire Book Centre, Cheshire.................... 69
Chesters (G. & J.), Staffordshire 225
Clevedon Books, Somerset 218

SPECIALITY INDEX

Dean Byass, Bristol................................... 60
Earth Science Books, Wiltshire 252
Erian Books, London N.............................. 158
Esplin (David), Hampshire.......................... 124
Fireside Bookshop, Cumbria........................ 81
Hamish Riley-Smith, Norfolk....................... 192
Jay Books, Lothian................................... 278
Joel Segal Books, Devon 86
Judd Books, London WC 178
Kingswood Books, Dorset 94
Mair Wilkes Books, Fife 272
McGee (Terence J.), London Outer 181
Moorside Books, Lancashire........................ 144
N1 Books, E Sussex.................................. 105
Orb's Bookshop, Grampian......................... 274
Park (Mike), London Outer......................... 183
Parkinsons Books, Merseyside...................... 186
Phelps (Michael), West Sussex...................... 243
Phillips (Nigel), Hampshire......................... 122
Plurabelle Books, Cambridgeshire.................. 64
Pollak (P.M.), Devon 89
Pordes Books Ltd., (Henry), London WC........ 179
Price (John), London N 159
R M Books, Hertfordshire 132
Roberts Books, Ayrshire 280
Roger Collicott Books, Cornwall 75
Rogers Turner Books, London SE.................. 166
Rowan (P. & B.), Co. Antrim 260
Skoob Russell Square, Suffolk...................... 230
Smith (David & Lynn), London Outer............ 182
Sokol Books Ltd., London W 175
Stalagluft Books, Tyne and Wear.................. 236
Sue Lowell Natural History Books, London W. 176
Susanne Schulz-Falster Rare Books, London N. 160
Turret House, Norfolk............................... 192
Wayside Books and Cards, Oxfordshire 207
Weiner (Graham), London N 160
Westwood Books (Mark), Powys 291
Westwood Books Ltd, Cumbria.................... 80
Worcester Rare Books, Worcs...................... 257
Wyseby House Books, Berks 55

- PURE & APPLIED

Baldwin's Scientific Books, Essex 112
Barcombe Services, Essex............................ 108
Bernard Dixon and Kath Adams, Middlesex 183
Book Annex (The), Essex 109
Glenbower Books, Co. Dublin 265
Hunter–Rare Books (Andrew), London SW 169
Parkinsons Books, Merseyside...................... 186
R M Books, Hertfordshire 132
Roberts Books, Ayrshire 280
The Sanctuary Bookshop, Dorset.................. 94
Transformer, Dumfries & Galloway............... 271
Westons, Hertfordshire 133

SCIENTIFIC INSTRUMENTS

Arnold (Roy), Suffolk................................ 228
Baron (Christopher), Gr Man 118
Bernard Dixon and Kath Adams, Middlesex 183
Formby Antiques (Jeffrey), Glos 115
Hadfield (G.K.), Cumbria 80
Hunter–Rare Books (Andrew), London SW 169
Parkinsons Books, Merseyside...................... 186
Phelps (Michael), West Sussex...................... 243

Pollak (P.M.), Devon 89
Rogers Turner Books, London SE.................. 166
Smith (David & Lynn), London Outer............ 182
Tony Hutchinson, Surrey............................ 234
Trinders' Fine Tools, Suffolk 227
Turret House, Norfolk............................... 192
Westons, Hertfordshire 133

SCIENTISTS

Baldwin's Scientific Books, Essex 112
Barcombe Services, Essex............................ 108
Bernard Dixon and Kath Adams, Middlesex 183
Earth Science Books, Wiltshire 252
Joel Segal Books, Devon 86
K.S.C. Books, Cheshire.............................. 71
Kalligraphia, Isle of Wight.......................... 134
Parkinsons Books, Merseyside...................... 186
R M Books, Hertfordshire 132
Wayside Books and Cards, Oxfordshire 207

SCOTTISH ENLIGHTENMENT

Atholl Fine Books, Tayside 281
Grampian Books, Grampian........................ 274
Hamish Riley-Smith, Norfolk....................... 192
Leakey's Bookshop, Highland...................... 275
Loch Croispol Bookshop & Restaurant,
Highland 275
Mercat Books, Highland 274
Orb's Bookshop, Grampian......................... 274
Susanne Schulz-Falster Rare Books, London N. 160

SCOTTISH INTEREST

Adrem Books, Hertfordshire........................ 131
Alba Books, Grampian 274
Anwoth Books Ltd, Dumfries & Galloway 270
Armchair Books, Lothian 276
Atholl Browse, Perthshire 281
Atholl Fine Books, Tayside 281
Aurora Books Ltd, Lothian.......................... 276
Axe Rare & Out of Print Books (Richard),
N Yorks.. 194
Bell (Peter), Lothian................................. 276
Benny Gillies Books Ltd, Dumfries & Galloway 269
Big Bairn Books, Tayside 281
Blacket Books, Lothian.............................. 277
BookShop, The, Dumfries & Galloway........... 270
Bookworm, Lothian.................................. 277
Bookworm (The), Lothian 277
Bouquiniste Bookshop, Fife......................... 272
Byre Books, Dumfries & Galloway................ 270
Caledonia Books, Strathclyde...................... 280
Cheshire Book Centre, Cheshire.................... 69
Chesters (G. & J.), Staffordshire 225
Coleman (Tom), Highland 274
Colonsay Bookshop, Isle of Colonsay............. 276
Cooper Hay Rare Books, Strathclyde............. 280
Cornucopia Books, Lincolnshire 153
Cottage Books, Leics................................. 147
Craobh Rua Books, Co. Armagh.................. 260
Darkwood Books, Co. Cork......................... 263
Duncan & Reid, Lothian............................ 277
Farquharson, (Hilary), Tayside..................... 281
Ferguson (Elizabeth), Grampian 272
Fifteenth Century Bookshop (The), E Sussex 104
Freader's Books, Tayside............................ 281

SPECIALITY INDEX

G. C. Books Ltd., Dumfries & Galloway......... 271
Glacier Books, Tayside 282
Grampian Books, Grampian......................... 274
Grayling (David A.H.), Cumbria 79
Greta Books, Durham 97
Hunter-Rare Books (Andrew), London SW 169
Jane Jones Books, Grampian 272
Kings Bookshop Callander, Central 269
Leakey's Bookshop, Highland 275
Loch Croispol Bookshop & Restaurant,
Highland 275
Mactaggart (Caroline), Dorset...................... 92
Main Point Books, Lothian 278
Mair Wilkes Books, Fife 272
McCrone (Audrey), Isle of Arran 275
McNaughtan's Bookshop, Lothian 278
Mercat Books, Highland 274
Ming Books, Dumfries & Galloway 271
O'Flynn Books, N Yorks............................. 199
Old Bookshelf (The), Strathclyde.................. 279
Old Town Bookshop (The), Lothian 278
Oopalba Books, Cheshire............................. 71
Orb's Bookshop, Grampian.. 271
Pinnacle Books, Lothian.............................. 278
Poetry Bookshop (The), Powys..................... 291
Price (John), London N 159
Pringle Booksellers (Andrew), Lothian 278
Reading Lasses, Dumfries & Galloway 271
Rising Tide Books, Fife............................... 271
Robert Temple, London N........................... 160
Roberts Books, Ayrshire 280
Saintfield Antiques & Fine Books, Co. Down ... 261
Second Edition, Lothian.............................. 278
Strathtay Antiquarian - Secondhand Books,
Tayside 282
Stroma Books, Borders 268
Thistle Books, Strathclyde........................... 280
Updike Rare Books (John), Lothian 279
Wheen O'Books, Scottish Borders 269

SCOUTS & GUIDES

Adrem Books, Hertfordshire........................ 131
Askew Books (Vernon), Wiltshire.................. 251
Books & Bygones (Pam Taylor), W Mids........ 241
Collectables (W.H.), Suffolk 230
Fifteenth Century Bookshop (The), E Sussex 104
Greta Books, Durham 97
Jean Hedger, Berks.................................... 55
Joel Segal Books, Devon 86
John R. Hoggarth, N Yorks......................... 198
Old Station Pottery & Bookshop (The), Norfolk 192
R. & A. Books, E Sussex............................. 102
The Old Children's Bookshelf, Lothian 278
Wheen O'Books, Scottish Borders 269
Yesterday's News, Conwy............................ 285

SCRIMSHAW

Don Kelly Books, London W 172

SCULPTURE

Birchden Books, London E 155
Bruce Holdsworth Books, E Sussex 105
Cornucopia Books, Lincolnshire 153
Cover to Cover, Merseyside......................... 186
Don Kelly Books, London W 172

Fifteenth Century Bookshop (The), E Sussex 104
Heneage Art Books (Thomas), London SW 169
Joel Segal Books, Devon 86
Lighthouse Books (The), Dorset 92
Madalyn S. Jones, W Yorkshire 217
Martin - Bookseller (Colin), East Yorkshire 107
Trinders' Fine Tools, Suffolk 227

SEAFARING & SHIPPING

Browsers Bookshop, Cornwall...................... 73
Burroughs (Andrew), Lincolnshire................. 153
Canringli Centre, Pembrokeshire 288
Cavendish Rare Books, London N 158
Cox (Geoff), Devon 90
Fifteenth Century Bookshop (The), E Sussex 104
Greta Books, Durham 97
Jade Mountain Bookshop, Hampshire 126
Joel Segal Books, Devon 86
Loch Croispol Bookshop & Restaurant,
Highland 275
Marine & Cannon Books, Cheshire 71
Marine and Cannon Books, Cheshire 69
Mercat Books, Highland 274
Milestone Books, Devon 89
Robert Humm & Co, Lincolnshire 154
Sea Chest Nautical Bookshop (The), Devon 88
Wheen O'Books, Scottish Borders 269
Wizard Books, Cambridgeshire..................... 67

SEAMANSHIP

Argent (Alan), Isle of Wight 135
Cornucopia Books, Lincolnshire 153
Fifteenth Century Bookshop (The), E Sussex 104
Footrope Knots, Suffolk.............................. 228
Greta Books, Durham 97
Jade Mountain Bookshop, Hampshire 126
Joel Segal Books, Devon 86
Marine & Cannon Books, Cheshire 71
Marine and Cannon Books, Cheshire 69

SECRET SOCIETIES

Apocalypse, Surrey 233
Inner Bookshop (The), Oxfordshire................ 210
Joel Segal Books, Devon 86
Occultique, Northants................................. 200
SETI Books, Staffordshire........................... 225

SEEDS

Park (Mike), London Outer.......................... 183

SELF-HELP

Annie's Books, S Yorks 222
Discovery Bookshop, Carmarthenshire............ 283
Fifteenth Century Bookshop (The), E Sussex 104
HCB Wholesale, Powys.............................. 290
Inner Bookshop (The), Oxfordshire................ 210
Joel Segal Books, Devon 86
Just Books, Cornwall 76
Occultique, Northants................................. 200
Reading Lasses, Dumfries & Galloway 271

SELF-IMPROVEMENT

Cornucopia Books, Lincolnshire 153
Esoteric Dreams Bookshop, Cumbria 78
Fifteenth Century Bookshop (The), E Sussex 104

SPECIALITY INDEX

Inner Bookshop (The), Oxfordshire................. 210
Joel Segal Books, Devon 86
Occultique, Northants................................ 200
Reading Lasses, Dumfries & Galloway 271

SELF-SUFFICIENCY

Coch-y-Bonddu Books, Powys 292
Colonsay Bookshop, Isle of Colonsay............. 276
Cornucopia Books, Lincolnshire 153
Country Books, Derbyshire 82
Fifteenth Century Bookshop (The), E Sussex 104
Greta Books, Durham 97
Inner Bookshop (The), Oxfordshire................ 210
Joel Segal Books, Devon 86
Mount's Bay Books, Cornwall 75
Reading Lasses, Dumfries & Galloway 271

SETS OF BOOKS

Apocalypse, Surrey 233
Baxter (Steve), Surrey 234
Bernstein (Nicholas), London W 172
Bow Windows Book Shop, E Sussex.............. 103
Browse Books, Lancashire 144
Cheshire Book Centre, Cheshire.................... 69
Crouch Rare Books, Surrey......................... 233
Dales & Lakes Book Centre, Cumbria 80
Ely Books, Cambridgeshire 65
Eton Antique Bookshop, Berks 57
Fisher & Sperr, London N........................... 158
Foster (Stephen), London NW 161
Foster Bookshop (Paul), London SW 168
Fosters Bookshop, London W 173
Frew Limited (Robert), London W................. 173
Golden Books Group, Devon 85
Grove Bookshop (The), N Yorks 197
Harrington (Adrian), London W.................... 173
Harrington Antiquarian Bookseller (Peter),
London SW.. 169
Hava Books, London SE............................. 165
Joel Segal Books, Devon 86
Kirkman Ltd., (Robert), Bedfordshire.............. 54
Old Town Bookshop (The), Lothian 278
Poetry Bookshop (The), Powys..................... 291
R. & A. Books, E Sussex............................ 102
Sotheran Limited (Henry), London W 176
Staniland (Booksellers), Lincolnshire 154
Treasure Trove Books, Leics........................ 148
Williams (Bookdealer), (Richard), N Lincs 154

SETTE OF ODD VOLUMES

Cox Old & Rare Books (Claude), Suffolk 228
N1 Books, E Sussex 105

SEXOLOGY

Apocalypse, Surrey 233
Delectus Books, London WC....................... 177
Inner Bookshop (The), Oxfordshire................ 210
Paper Pleasures, Somerset 219
Reading Lasses, Dumfries & Galloway 271

SHEEP/SHEPHERDING

Byrom Textile Bookroom (Richard), Lancashire 143
Fifteenth Century Bookshop (The), E Sussex 104
Greta Books, Durham 97
Hodgson (Books) (Richard J.), N Yorks 198

Joel Segal Books, Devon 86
Phenotype Books, Cumbria 80
Thornber (Peter M.), N Yorks 196

SHELL COUNTY GUIDES

Baker - Books for the Collector (Colin), Devon . 90
Chris Phillips, Wiltshire.............................. 251
Joel Segal Books, Devon 86
Staniland (Booksellers), Lincolnshire 154
World War II Books, Surrey 235

SHERLOCKIANA

Askew Books (Vernon), Wiltshire.................. 251
Black Cat Bookshop, Leics 147
Ming Books, Dumfries & Galloway................ 271
Murder & Mayhem, Powys......................... 291
Post Mortem Books, West Sussex 243
Preston Book Company, Lancashire 145
Randall (Tom), Somerset............................ 219
Rupert Books, Cambridgeshire..................... 65
Scrivener's Books & Bookbinding, Derbyshire... 82
Trinity Rare Books, Co. Leitrim 266
Vokes (Jeremiah), Durham.......................... 97
Williams Rare Books (Nigel), London WC 180
Yesterday's News, Conwy........................... 285

SHIP MODELLING

Aviabooks, Glos 114
Cover to Cover, Merseyside......................... 186
Curtle Mead Books, Isle of Wight 134
Fifteenth Century Bookshop (The), E Sussex 104
Henry Wilson Books, Cheshire..................... 69
Joel Segal Books, Devon 86
Marine & Cannon Books, Cheshire 71
Marine and Cannon Books, Cheshire 69
McLaren Books, Strathclyde........................ 280
Milestone Books, Devon 89
Prior (Michael), Lincolnshire 153
Trinders' Fine Tools, Suffolk 227

SHIPBUILDING AND SHIPPING

Aardvark Books, Wiltshire.......................... 254
Anthony Vickers Books, N Yorks 196
Anvil Books, W Mids................................ 240
Bott, (Bookdealers) Ltd., (Martin), Gr Man 118
Burroughs (Andrew), Lincolnshire 153
Cheshire Book Centre, Cheshire.................... 69
Cox (Geoff), Devon 90
Curtle Mead Books, Isle of Wight 134
Empire Books, N Yorks.............................. 198
Fifteenth Century Bookshop (The), F Sussex 104
G. C. Books Ltd., Dumfries & Galloway......... 271
Green Ltd. (G.L.), Hertfordshire................... 132
Henry Wilson Books, Cheshire..................... 69
Joel Segal Books, Devon 86
Kerr (Norman), Cumbria 78
Lewcock (John), Cambridgeshire................... 66
Marine & Cannon Books, Cheshire 71
Marine and Cannon Books, Cheshire 69
McLaren Books, Strathclyde........................ 280
Milestone Books, Devon 89
Mulyan (Don), Merseyside.......................... 186
N1 Books, E Sussex 105
Nautical Antique Centre (The), Dorset 96
Phelps (Michael), West Sussex..................... 243

SPECIALITY INDEX

Prior (Michael), Lincolnshire 153
Railway Shop (The), Torfaen 294
Roadmaster Books, Kent............................. 137
Rods Books, Devon 88
Roz Hulse, Conwy 286
Salway Books, Essex 112
Smith Maritime Aviation Books (Frank),
Tyne and Wear....................................... 236
Stalagluft Books, Tyne and Wear 236
Stroh (M.A.), London E 155
Trinders' Fine Tools, Suffolk 227
Vickers (Anthony), N Yorks......................... 196

SHIPWRECKS

Aardvark Books, Wiltshire.......................... 254
Cornucopia Books, Lincolnshire 153
Cox (Geoff), Devon 90
Henry Wilson Books, Cheshire...................... 69
Joel Segal Books, Devon 86
Marine & Cannon Books, Cheshire 71
Marine and Cannon Books, Cheshire 69
R. & A. Books, E Sussex............................. 102

SHORTHAND

Ainslie Books, Strathclyde........................... 279
Naughton Booksellers, Co. Dublin 265

SIGILLOGRAPHY

Taylor & Son (Peter), Hertfordshire 133

SIGNED EDITIONS

Adrem Books, Hertfordshire......................... 131
Ann & Mike Conry, Worcs.......................... 257
Apocalypse, Surrey 233
Bibliophile Books, London E 155
Black Cat Bookshop, Leics 147
Bookbarrow, Cambridgeshire....................... 63
BOOKS4U, Flintshire................................ 286
Bookstand, Dorset....... 94
Corfe Books, Surrey.................................. 231
Dales & Lakes Book Centre, Cumbria 80
Eastwood Books (David), Cornwall 73
Ellis, Bookseller (Peter), London WC 178
Ellwood Editions, Wiltshire 253
Ely Books, Cambridgeshire 65
Farahar & Dupre (Clive & Sophie), Wiltshire ... 251
Fifteenth Century Bookshop (The), E Sussex 104
firstpagebooks, Norfolk.............................. 190
Firsts in Print, Isle of Wight 134
Foster Bookshop (Paul), London SW 168
Fosters Bookshop, London W 173
Green Meadow Books, Cornwall 74
Greta Books, Durham 97
Harrington Antiquarian Bookseller (Peter),
London SW... 169
Heppa (Christopher), Essex 108
Hylton Booksearch, Merseyside 185
Ian Briddon, Derbyshire.............................. 82
Ian McKelvie Bookseller, London N............... 159
Jean Hedger, Berks................................... 55
Kevin S. Ogilvie Modern First Editions,
Grampian 273
Kirkman Ltd., (Robert), Bedfordshire.............. 54
L.M.S. Books, Hertfordshire........................ 132
Little Stour Books, Kent 137

Marine and Cannon Books, Cheshire 69
N V Books, Warwickshire........................... 237
Parker Books (Mike), Cambridgeshire 64
Poetry Bookshop (The), Powys..................... 291
Portobello Books, London W 175
Richard Thornton Books, London N 160
Robert Temple, London N........................... 160
Scrivener's Books & Bookbinding, Derbyshire... 82
Sensawunda Books, Cheshire 68
Shacklock Books (David), Suffolk 227
Shakeshaft (Dr. B.), Cheshire....................... 71
Simpson (Dave), Stirlingshire 269
Till's Bookshop, Lothian 279
Trinity Rare Books, Co. Leitrim 266
Updike Rare Books (John), Lothian 279
Williams Rare Books (Nigel), London WC 180
Woodbine Books, W Yorkshire 246
Words Etcetera Bookshop, Dorset.................. 93

SILVERSMITHS

Don Kelly Books, London W 172
Nibris Books, London SW 170
R. & A. Books, E Sussex............................. 102

SIXTIES, THE

Cornucopia Books, Lincolnshire 153
Joel Segal Books, Devon 86

SLAVERY

Alec–Smith Books (Alex), East Yorkshire 107
Drury Rare Books (John), Essex.................... 110
Kenny's Bookshops and Art Galleries Ltd, Co.
Galway 266
N1 Books, E Sussex.................................. 105
Pennymead Books, N Yorks......................... 194
Reading Lasses, Dumfries & Galloway 271
Seydi Rare Books (Sevin), London NW 162
Star Lord Books, Gr Man 119

SMALL PRESS PUBLISHED BOOKS

Ballantyne–Way (Roger), Suffolk 229
Blackwell's Rare Books, Oxfordshire 209
Samovar Books, Co. Dublin 264

SOCIAL ECONOMICS

Adrem Books, Hertfordshire......................... 131
Drury Rare Books (John), Essex.................... 110
Hamish Riley-Smith, Norfolk........................ 192
Johnson Rare Book Collections (C.R.),
London NW 162
Left on The Shelf, Cumbria......................... 79
Parkinsons Books, Merseyside...................... 186
PsychoBabel Books & Journals, Oxfordshire..... 206
Reading Lasses, Dumfries & Galloway 271

SOCIAL HISTORY

Adrem Books, Hertfordshire......................... 131
Apocalypse, Surrey 233
Barcombe Services, Essex............................ 108
Bell (Peter), Lothian.................................. 276
Bermondsey Basement Bookstore, London SE .. 164
Bibliophile Books, London E 155
Black Cat Books, Norfolk............................ 188
Brimstones, E Sussex................................. 103
Byrom Textile Bookroom (Richard), Lancashire 143

SPECIALITY INDEX

Castleton (Pat), Kent................................. 138
Chesters (G. & J.), Staffordshire 225
Clifton Books, Essex 112
Cottage Books, Leics................................. 147
Country Books, Derbyshire 82
Cox (Geoff), Devon 90
Debbage (John), Norfolk............................. 190
Delectus Books, London WC........................ 177
Dolphin Books, Suffolk............................... 226
Drury Rare Books (John), Essex.................... 110
Duck (William), Hampshire.......................... 124
Eggle (Mavis), Hertfordshire........................ 131
Elaine Lonsdale Books, W Yorkshire 248
Fifteenth Century Bookshop (The), E Sussex 104
Fireside Bookshop, Cumbria........................ 81
Forest Books of Manchester, Cheshire............ 71
Gardener & Cook, London SW..................... 168
Graham (John), Dorset.............................. 96
Harvest Books, Lancashire.......................... 145
Helion & Company, W Mids........................ 240
Hughes Rare Books (Spike), Borders............... 268
Jarndyce Antiquarian Booksellers, London WC. 178
Joel Segal Books, Devon 86
Judd Books, London WC............................ 178
Kelsall (George), Gr Man............................ 118
Left on The Shelf, Cumbria......................... 79
Maggy Browne, Lincolnshire 150
Maghreb Bookshop (The), London WC.......... 178
Marcan, Bookseller (Peter), London SE 165
Meekins Books (Paul), Warwickshire.............. 238
Murphy (C.J.), Norfolk.............................. 190
N1 Books, E Sussex................................... 105
Naughton Booksellers, Co. Dublin 265
Northern Herald Books, W Yorkshire............ 246
Parkinsons Books, Merseyside...................... 186
Pollak (P.M.), Devon 89
R. & A. Books, E Sussex............................. 102
Reading Lasses, Dumfries & Galloway 271
Red Star Books, Hertfordshire 130
Roadmaster Books, Kent............................ 137
Russell (Charles), London SW...................... 170
Scrivener's Books & Bookbinding, Derbyshire... 82
Sephton (A.F.), London W 175
South Downs Book Service, West Sussex......... 244
Stalagluft Books, Tyne and Wear.................. 236
Stern Antiquarian Bookseller (Jeffrey), N Yorks 199
Stevens (Joan), Cambridgeshire.................... 65
Symes Books (Naomi), Cheshire 72
Unsworths Booksellers, London WC.............. 163
Warnes (Felicity J.), London Outer................ 181
Weininger Antiquarian Books (Eva M.),
London NW.. 163
Westwood Books Ltd, Cumbria..................... 80
Wetherell (Frances), Cambridgeshire 65
Whitchurch Books Ltd., Cardiff.................... 283
Whittle, Bookseller (Avril), Cumbria 81
Woburn Books, London N 160

SOCIAL SCIENCES

Adrem Books, Hertfordshire........................ 131
Barcombe Services, Essex........................... 108
Bernard Dixon and Kath Adams, Middlesex 183
Bracton Books, Cambridgeshire.................... 63
Brimstones, E Sussex................................. 103
Cheshire Book Centre, Cheshire.................... 69

Chesters (G. & J.), Staffordshire 225
Dandy Lion Editions, Surrey 233
Delectus Books, London WC....................... 177
Drury Rare Books (John), Essex.................... 110
Hamish Riley-Smith, Norfolk....................... 192
hullbooks.com, East Yorkshire..................... 107
Ice House Books, Wiltshire 253
Judd Books, London WC 178
Left on The Shelf, Cumbria......................... 79
Northern Herald Books, W Yorkshire............ 246
O'Donoghue Books, Powys 291
Orb's Bookshop, Grampian......................... 274
Outcast Books, Powys 291
Parkinsons Books, Merseyside...................... 186
PsychoBabel Books & Journals, Oxfordshire..... 206
Reading Lasses, Dumfries & Galloway 271
Reid of Liverpool, Merseyside...................... 185
Scott (Peter), E Sussex 104
Susanne Schulz-Falster Rare Books, London N. 160
Westwood Books Ltd, Cumbria.................... 80
Woburn Books, London N 160

SOCIALISM

Adrem Books, Hertfordshire........................ 131
Berwick Books, Lincolnshire........................ 152
Dolphin Books, Suffolk............................... 226
Drury Rare Books (John), Essex.................... 110
Hylton Booksearch, Merseyside 185
Left on The Shelf, Cumbria......................... 79
Naughton Booksellers, Co. Dublin 265
Northern Herald Books, W Yorkshire............ 246
Parkinsons Books, Merseyside...................... 186
Reading Lasses, Dumfries & Galloway 271
Red Star Books, Hertfordshire 130
Spurrier (Nick), Kent 138
Star Lord Books, Gr Man 119
Symes Books (Naomi), Cheshire 72
Trinity Rare Books, Co. Leitrim 266
Woburn Books, London N 160

SOCIOLOGY

Apocalypse, Surrey 233
Barcombe Services, Essex........................... 108
Bracton Books, Cambridgeshire.................... 63
Brimstones, E Sussex................................. 103
Chesters (G. & J.), Staffordshire 225
hullbooks.com, East Yorkshire..................... 107
Hylton Booksearch, Merseyside 185
Left on The Shelf, Cumbria......................... 79
Northern Herald Books, W Yorkshire............ 246
O'Donoghue Books, Powys......................... 291
Parkinsons Books, Merseyside...................... 186
PsychoBabel Books & Journals, Oxfordshire..... 206
Reading Lasses, Dumfries & Galloway 271
Red Star Books, Hertfordshire 130
Stalagluft Books, Tyne and Wear.................. 236
Tarka Books, Devon.................................. 84
Trinity Rare Books, Co. Leitrim 266

SOUTH AUSTRALIANA

Empire Books, N Yorks.............................. 198

SOUTH SEAS

Adrem Books, Hertfordshire........................ 131
Empire Books, N Yorks.............................. 198

SPECIALITY INDEX

Marine and Cannon Books, Cheshire 69

SOUTHERN AMERICANA

PsychoBabel Books & Journals, Oxfordshire..... 206

SPACE

Adrem Books, Hertfordshire........................ 131
K Books, Cheshire.................................... 70

SPANISH LITERATURE

Baldwin (Jack), Strathclyde 280
Hodgson (Judith), London W 174
Joel Segal Books, Devon 86
Orssich (Paul), London SW......................... 170
York (Graham), Devon............................... 86

SPECIAL COLLECTIONS

Downie Fine Books Ltd., (Robert), Shropshire.. 215
Kohler (C.C.), Surrey 231
Murphy (C.J.), Norfolk.............................. 190
Price (John), London N 159
Robert Temple, London N.......................... 160
Stalagluft Books, Tyne and Wear.................. 236

SPIRITISM

Occultique, Northants................................ 200

SPIRITUAL

Beckham Books Ltd., Suffolk 230
Bookbarrow, Cambridgeshire....................... 63
Inner Bookshop (The), Oxfordshire................ 210
Joel Segal Books, Devon 86
Just Books, Cornwall 76
Occultique, Northants................................ 200
Parkinsons Books, Merseyside...................... 186
S.P.C.K., Bristol 60
Susan Taylor Books, W Yorkshire 248

SPIRITUALISM

Atlantis Bookshop, London WC.................... 177
Cavern Books, Cheshire 70
Chthonios Books, E Sussex 102
Craobh Rua Books, Co. Armagh................... 260
Dawlish Books, Devon 86
Esoteric Dreams Bookshop, Cumbria 78
Facet Books, Dorset.................................. 91
Fine Books Oriental Ltd., London WC........... 178
Forest Books of Manchester, Cheshire............ 71
Greensleeves, Oxfordshire 207
Holmes Books (Harry), East Yorkshire............ 107
Hurst (Jenny), Kent 138
Loretta Lay Books, London NW 162
Magis Books, Leics................................... 149
Minster Gate Bookshop, N Yorks.................. 199
Needham Books, (Russell), Somerset.............. 220
Occultique, Northants................................ 200
Orchid Book Distributors, Co. Clare.............. 262
Preston Book Company, Lancashire 145
PsychoBabel Books & Journals, Oxfordshire..... 206
R. & A. Books, E Sussex............................ 102
Reading Lasses, Dumfries & Galloway 271
St Swithin's Illustrated & Children's Books,
London W 175
SETI Books, Staffordshire........................... 225
Tilleys Vintage Magazine Shop, S Yorks 223

Waxfactor, E Sussex 100
Wizard Books, Cambridgeshire..................... 67

SPORT - GENERAL

Abacus Gallery, Staffordshire....................... 224
Adrem Books, Hertfordshire........................ 131
Allinson (Frank & Stella), Warwickshire 237
Amos (Denis W.), Hertfordshire 131
Ann & Mike Conry, Worcs.......................... 257
Annie's Books, S Yorks 222
Antique Map and Bookshop (The), Dorset 94
Archways Sports Books, Lothian 276
Armstrong's Books & Collectables, Leics......... 147
Aurora Books Ltd, Lothian.......................... 276
Autumn Leaves, Lincolnshire....................... 152
Axe Rare & Out of Print Books (Richard),
N Yorks.. 194
Bath Old Books, Somerset 216
Bob Mallory (Books), Derbyshire.................. 83
Bodyline Books, Surrey.............................. 233
Bookcase, Cumbria.................................. 78
Books Plus, Devon 84
books2books, Devon................................. 88
Bookworms, Norfolk................................. 187
Bookzone, Berks...................................... 55
Capel Mawr Collectors Centre, Gwynedd 287
Carningli Centre, Pembrokeshire................... 288
Carta Regis, Powys.................................. 293
Chandos Books, Devon.............................. 85
Chaucer Bookshop, Kent............................ 136
Chris Phillips, Wiltshire............................. 251
Clements (R.W.), London Outer 182
Cobweb Books, N Yorks............................ 195
Cofion Books, Pembrokeshire 288
Cotswold Internet Books, Glos..................... 113
Dublin Bookbrowsers, Co. Dublin................. 265
Eastcote Bookshop (The), London Outer....... 181
Elmo Books, E Sussex 99
Esoteric Dreams Bookshop, Cumbria 78
Eton Antique Bookshop, Berks 57
Evans (Mark), Lincolnshire 153
Ewell Bookshop Ltd, Surrey........................ 232
Fackley Services, Notts 205
Fifteenth Century Bookshop (The), E Sussex 104
Fiona Edwards, Notts 204
Ford Books (David), Hertfordshire................. 133
Freeman's Corner Shop, Norfolk 190
Garfi Books, Powys 293
Garwood & Voigt, Kent............................. 140
Gathern (D.), Conwy 285
George St. Books, Derbyshire 83
Good for Books, Lincolnshire...................... 151
Gravity Books, Lincolnshire 151
Handsworth Books, Essex........................... 112
Hatchard & Daughters, W Yorkshire 247
Hay Cinema Bookshop Ltd., Powys............... 290
HCB Wholesale, Powys............................. 290
Hollett and Son (R.F.G.), Cumbria 80
Hornsey's, N Yorks 195
Hummingbird Books, Herefordshire............... 128
Hurst (Jenny), Kent 138
Innes Books, Shropshire 214
J & J Burgess Booksellers, Cambridgeshire....... 64
Jackson (M.W.), Wiltshire.......................... 254
Jade Mountain Bookshop, Hampshire 126

SPECIALITY INDEX

Joel Segal Books, Devon 86
Lyngheath Books, Norfolk.......................... 189
Malvern Bookshop (The), Worcs 255
Marble Hill Books, Middlesex....................... 184
McCrone (Audrey), Isle of Arran 275
Mead (P.J.), Shropshire............................... 214
Mellon's Books, E Sussex 101
Moore (C.R.), Shropshire 214
Morten (Booksellers) (E.J.), Gr Man 119
Mr. Pickwick of Towcester, Northants............ 201
Mundy (David), Hertfordshire....................... 130
Murphy (C.J.), Norfolk............................... 190
Old Station Pottery & Bookshop (The), Norfolk 192
Oopalba Books, Cheshire............................. 71
Oxfam Books and Music, Hampshire 126
Parker Books (Mike), Cambridgeshire 64
Portobello Books, London W 175
Price (R.W.), Notts.................................... 204
Priestpopple Books, Northumberland 202
Quinto of Charing Cross Road, London WC ... 179
Quinto of Great Russell Street, London WC 179
R. & A. Books, E Sussex............................. 102
Richard Thornton Books, London N 160
Roberts Fine Books (Julian), Lincolnshire........ 153
Roland Books, Kent 139
Rutland Bookshop (The), Rutland 212
Saintfield Antiques & Fine Books, Co. Down ... 261
Scrivener's Books & Bookbinding, Derbyshire... 82
Stothert Old Books, Cheshire........................ 69
Stroma Books, Borders 268
Tarka Books, Devon 84
Tiffin (Tony and Gill), Durham 97
Trafalgar Bookshop, E Sussex....................... 100
Treasure Trove Books, Leics......................... 148
Wadard Books, Kent 138
Wheen O'Books, Scottish Borders 269
Wiend Books, Lancashire 144
Yewtree Books, Cumbria............................. 79

- AMERICAN FOOTBALL

Archways Sports Books, Lothian 276
Bodyline Books, Surrey............................... 233
Saunders (Tom), Caerphilly.......................... 283

- ANGLING/FISHING

Atholl Fine Books, Tayside 281
Aucott & Thomas, Leics.............................. 147
Baron (Christopher), Gr Man 118
Biblion, London W.................................... 172
Big Bairn Books, Tayside 281
Blest (Peter), Kent 139
Bodyline Books, Surrey............................... 233
Branksome Books, Dorset............................ 94
Chalmers Hallam (E.), Hampshire 125
Chevin Books, W Yorkshire 250
Classics Bookshop (The), Oxfordshire............. 207
Coch-y-Bonddu Books, Powys 292
Cornucopia Books, Lincolnshire 153
Countrymans Gallery (The), Leics 147
Darkwood Books, Co. Cork......................... 263
Deeside Books, Grampian............................ 273
Dusty Books, Powys 292
Edmund Pollinger Rare Books, London SW..... 167
Eggle (Mavis), Hertfordshire......................... 131
Fifteenth Century Bookshop (The), E Sussex 104

Fylde Books, Lancashire 146
Garfi Books, Powys 293
Good Books, Shropshire 214
Grayling (David A.H.), Cumbria 79
Grove Bookshop (The), N Yorks................... 197
Head (John & Judith), Wiltshire 253
Hereward Books, Cambridgeshire................... 66
Home Farm Books, Warwickshire.................. 237
Intech Books, Northumberland 203
Internet Bookshop UK Ltd., Glos.................. 113
Jane Jones Books, Grampian 272
Joel Segal Books, Devon 86
Just Books, Cornwall 76
Keith Langford, London E 155
Kilgour (Sporting Books) (Ian), Leics 149
Lion Books, Worcs.................................... 256
McEwan Fine Books, Grampian.................... 273
Murphy (C.J.), Norfolk............................... 190
Not Just Books, Dorset............................... 94
Pauline Harries Books, Hampshire 123
Peter M Daly, Hampshire............................ 127
Petersfield Bookshop (The), Hampshire........... 124
Petworth Antique Market (Bookroom),
W Sussex.. 244
Rare Books & Berry, Somerset...................... 219
Richard Thornton Books, London N 160
River Reads Bookshop, Devon...................... 90
Rothwell & Dunworth, Somerset 218
Saint Mary's Books & Prints, Lincolnshire....... 154
Sax Books, Suffolk 229
Stella Books, Monmouthshire 288
Stroh (M.A.), London E 155
Treasure Island (The), Gr Man...................... 119
Vinovium Books, Durham 97
Worlds End Bookshop, London SW 171
Yesterday Tackle & Books, Dorset 92

- ARCHERY

Bodyline Books, Surrey............................... 233
Cader Idris Books, Powys............................ 292
Chalmers Hallam (E.), Hampshire 125
Coch-y-Bonddu Books, Powys 292
Head (John & Judith), Wiltshire 253
Joel Segal Books, Devon 86
Lake (Fred), Surrey 235
Meekins Books (Paul), Warwickshire.............. 238

- ATHLETICS

Archways Sports Books, Lothian 276
Bob Mallory (Books), Derbyshire................... 83
Bodyline Books, Surrey............................... 233
Bookzone, Berks....................................... 55
Marathon Books, Gr Man............................ 118
Rugby Relics, West Glamorgan 294
Stroh (M.A.), London E 155

- BADMINTON

Bodyline Books, Surrey............................... 233
Pennymead Books, N Yorks......................... 194

- BALLOONING

Bodyline Books, Surrey............................... 233
J.B. Books, Berks...................................... 56
Just Books, Cornwall 76
Postings, Surrey.. 234

SPECIALITY INDEX

Stroh (M.A.), London E 155

- BASEBALL

Bodyline Books, Surrey.............................. 233
Gathern (D.), Conwy 285

- BASKETBALL

Adrem Books, Hertfordshire........................ 131
Archways Sports Books, Lothian 276
Bodyline Books, Surrey.............................. 233

- BIG GAME HUNTING

Allsworth Rare Books Ltd., London SW......... 167
Ayre (Peter J.), Somerset 220
Barnhill Books, Isle of Arran 275
Bates & Hindmarch, W Yorkshire................. 249
Bodyline Books, Surrey.............................. 233
Campbell Hewson Books (R.), Fife................ 271
Chalmers Hallam (E.), Hampshire................. 125
Coch-y-Bonddu Books, Powys 292
Countryman Books, East Yorkshire............... 106
Deeside Books, Grampian........................... 273
Edmund Pullinger Rare Books, London SW..... 167
Empire Books, N Yorks.............................. 198
Farahar & Dupre (Clive & Sophie), Wiltshire ... 251
Grayling (David A.H.), Cumbria 79
Head (John & Judith), Wiltshire 253
Home Farm Books, Warwickshire.................. 237
Joel Segal Books, Devon 86
Kenya Books, E Sussex............................... 100
Kilgour (Sporting Books) (Ian), Leics 149
McEwan Fine Books, Grampian.................... 273
Peter M Daly, Hampshire............................ 127
Popeley (Frank T.), Cambridgeshire............... 67
R.E. & G.B. Way, Suffolk 229
Vandeleur Antiquarian Books, Surrey............. 232

- BILLIARDS/SNOOKER/POOL

Ben–Nathan (Jack), London Outer 181
Bodyline Books, Surrey.............................. 233
Craobh Rua Books, Co. Armagh................... 260
R. S. & P. A. Scowen, Middlesex.................. 182
Richard Thornton Books, London N 160
Stroh (M.A.), London E 155

- BOWLS

Bodyline Books, Surrey.............................. 233
Cornucopia Books, Lincolnshire 153

- BOXING

Allinson (Frank & Stella), Warwickshire 237
Archways Sports Books, Lothian 276
Askew Books (Vernon), Wiltshire.................. 251
Bodyline Books, Surrey.............................. 233
Bookzone, Berks 55
Burmester (James), Bristol.......................... 59
Combat Arts Archive, Durham 97
Derek Stirling Bookseller, Kent 142
Dublin Bookbrowsers, Co. Dublin................. 265
Franks Booksellers, Gr Man........................ 119
Hedgerow Books, S Yorks 222
Joel Segal Books, Devon 86
McInnes (P.F. & J.R.), Dorset 91
Roland Books, Kent 139
Rugby Relics, West Glamorgan 294

- CANOEING/KAYAKS

Baldwin (M. & M.), Worcs 255
Bodyline Books, Surrey.............................. 233
Craobh Rua Books, Co. Armagh................... 260
McLaren Books, Strathclyde........................ 280

- CAVING (SPELAEOLOGY)

Bodyline Books, Surrey.............................. 233
Dales & Lakes Book Centre 80
Grove Bookshop (The), N Yorks................... 197
Jarvis Books, Derbyshire 83
Letterbox Books, Notts.............................. 204
Post–Horn Books, N Yorks 193

- CLIMBING & TREKKING

Allinson (Frank & Stella), Warwickshire 237
Bodyline Books, Surrey.............................. 233
Booth (Booksearch Service), (Geoff), Cheshire... 68
Craobh Rua Books, Co. Armagh................... 260
Dales & Lakes Book Centre 80
George St. Books, Derbyshire 83
Gildas Books, Cheshire.............................. 68
Glacier Books, Tayside 282
Hunter and Krageloh, Derbyshire 83
Jarvis Books, Derbyshire 83
Joel Segal Books, Devon 86
Little Bookshop (The), Cumbria 81
Main Point Books, Lothian.......................... 278
O'Reilly - Mountain Books (John), Derbyshire.. 83

- COURSING

Bodyline Books, Surrey.............................. 233
Chalmers Hallam (E.), Hampshire................. 125
Coch-y-Bonddu Books, Powys 292
Head (John & Judith), Wiltshire 253
Kilgour (Sporting Books) (Ian), Leics............ 149
Wychwood Books, Glos............................. 116

- CRICKET

Aardvark Books, Lincolnshire...................... 152
Acumen Books, Staffordshire....................... 225
Archways Sports Books, Lothian 276
Baker - Books for the Collector (Colin), Devon. 90
Barbican Bookshop, N Yorks 198
Bardsley's Books, Suffolk............................ 226
Barmby (C. & A.J.), Kent........................... 141
Beighton (Brian), Norfolk 187
Black Cat Bookshop, Leics 147
Black Five Books, Shropshire 215
Bob Mallory (Books), Derbyshire.................. 83
Bodyline Books, Surrey.............................. 233
Bookzone, Berks 55
Booth (Booksearch Service), (Geoff), Cheshire... 68
Border Bookshop, W Yorkshire.................... 250
Brad Books, Essex.................................... 111
Bright (P.G.), Cambridgeshire 65
Chas J. Sawyer, Kent 141
Chevin Books, W Yorkshire 250
Christopher Saunders (Orchard Books), Glos.... 115
Classic Crime Collections, Gr Man................ 119
Coach House Books, Worcs 256
Cobbles Books, Somerset............................ 218
Dales & Lakes Book Centre, Cumbria............ 80
David Summerfield Books, E Sussex 99
Derek Stirling Bookseller, Kent 142

SPECIALITY INDEX

Esoteric Dreams Bookshop, Cumbria 78
Fifteenth Century Bookshop (The), E Sussex 104
firstpagebooks, Norfolk 190
Gathern (D.), Conwy 285
GS Cricket Books / The Old Book Shop,
W Mids... 241
Hambleton Books, N Yorks 197
Internet Bookshop UK Ltd., Glos 113
Invicta Bookshop, Berks.............................. 56
Jackson (M.W.), Wiltshire............................ 254
Joel Segal Books, Devon 86
Just Books, Cornwall 76
Keith Langford, London E 155
Lion Books, Worcs 256
Maynard & Bradley, Leics 148
McCrone (Audrey), Isle of Arran 275
McEwan Fine Books, Grampian.................... 273
McKenzie (J.W.), Surrey 232
Mellon's Books, E Sussex 101
My Back Pages, London SW 169
Old Bookshop (The), W Mids....................... 241
Poor Richard's Books, Suffolk 227
Prescott - The Bookseller (John), London Outer 184
Red Rose Books, Lancashire 145
Roberts Fine Books (Julian), Lincolnshire........ 153
Roland Books, Kent 139
Rugby Relics, West Glamorgan 294
Saint Mary's Books & Prints, Lincolnshire....... 154
Sax Books, Suffolk 229
Tiffin (Tony and Gill), Durham 97
Treasure Island (The), Gr Man...................... 119
Treasure Trove Books, Leics......................... 148
William H. Roberts, W Yorkshire 248
Wood Cricket Books (Martin), Kent............... 140
Yesterday's News, Conwy............................ 285

- CROQUET
Bodyline Books, Surrey............................... 233
Edmund Pollinger Rare Books, London SW..... 167

- CYCLING
Archways Sports Books, Lothian 276
Bodyline Books, Surrey............................... 233
Dales & Lakes Book Centre, Cumbria 80
Engaging Gear Ltd., Essex........................... 108
Larkham Books (Patricia), Glos..................... 117
Ouse Valley Books, Bedfordshire 54
Rugby Relics, West Glamorgan 294
Stroh (M.A.), London E 155
Weiner (Graham), London N 160

- DIVING/SUB-AQUA
Bodyline Books, Surrey............................... 233
Cornucopia Books, Lincolnshire 153
Internet Bookshop UK Ltd., Glos.................. 113
Sidey, Bookdealer (Philip), Kent 140
Stroh (M.A.), London E 155
Underwater Books, E Sussex 103

- DUELLING
Bodyline Books, Surrey............................... 233
Combat Arts Archive, Durham 97

- FALCONRY
Barnhill Books, Isle of Arran 275

Blest (Peter), Kent 139
Bodyline Books, Surrey............................... 233
Chalmers Hallam (E.), Hampshire 125
Coch-y-Bonddu Books, Powys 292
Countryman Books, East Yorkshire................ 106
Fifteenth Century Bookshop (The), E Sussex 104
Grove Bookshop (The), N Yorks 197
Head (John & Judith), Wiltshire 253
Hereward Books, Cambridgeshire.................. 66
Home Farm Books, Warwickshire.................. 237
Kilgour (Sporting Books) (Ian), Leics 149
Walker (Adrian), Bedfordshire 54
Wildside Books, Worcs 255
Winchester Bookshop (The), Hampshire.......... 127

- FENCING
Bodyline Books, Surrey............................... 233
Chalmers Hallam (E.), Hampshire 125
Combat Arts Archive, Durham 97
Joel Segal Books, Devon 86

- FIELD SPORTS
Barnhill Books, Isle of Arran 275
Blest (Peter), Kent 139
Bodyline Books, Surrey............................... 233
Bookbox, Glos 116
Bookline, Co. Down 261
Border Books, Borders................................ 268
Cat Lit, Somerset 219
Chalmers Hallam (E.), Hampshire 125
Coch-y-Bonddu Books, Powys 292
Cornucopia Books, Lincolnshire 153
Countrymans Gallery (The), Leics 147
Dales & Lakes Book Centre, Cumbria 80
Discovery Bookshop, Carmarthenshire............ 283
Edmund Pollinger Rare Books, London SW..... 167
Fifteenth Century Bookshop (The), E Sussex 104
Fylde Books, Lancashire 146
Garfi Books, Powys 293
Good Books, Shropshire 214
Grahame (Major Iain), Suffolk...................... 226
Grayling (David A.H.), Cumbria 79
Grove Bookshop (The), N Yorks................... 197
Head (John & Judith), Wiltshire 253
Heartland Old Books, Devon........................ 89
Hereward Books, Cambridgeshire.................. 66
Hollett and Son (R.F.G.), Cumbria 80
Home Farm Books, Warwickshire.................. 237
Jane Jones Books, Grampian 272
Joel Segal Books, Devon 86
Karen Millward, Co. Cork........................... 263
Kerr (Norman), Cumbria 78
Kilgour (Sporting Books) (Ian), Leics 149
Maynard & Bradley, Leics 148
McEwan Fine Books, Grampian.................... 273
Moss End Bookshop, Berks 57
Neil Summersgill, Lancashire 143
Peter M Daly, Hampshire............................ 127
Petworth Antique Market (Bookroom),
W Sussex... 244
R.E. & G.B. Way, Suffolk 229
Stacpoole (George), Co. Limerick.................. 266
Strathtay Antiquarian - Secondhand Books,
Tayside 282
Vinovium Books, Durham 97

SPECIALITY INDEX

Winchester Bookshop (The), Hampshire.......... 127
Wychwood Books, Glos 116

- FOOTBALL (AMERICAN)

Bodyline Books, Surrey............................... 233
Hambleton Books, N Yorks 197

- FOOTBALL (SOCCER)

Allinson (Frank & Stella), Warwickshire 237
Amos (Denis W.), Hertfordshire 131
Ann & Mike Conry, Worcs.......................... 257
Annie's Books, S Yorks 222
Archways Sports Books, Lothian 276
Big Bairn Books, Tayside 281
Black Cat Bookshop, Leics 147
Bob Mallory (Books), Derbyshire.................. 83
Bodyline Books, Surrey............................... 233
BOOKS4U, Flintshire.................. 286
Bookshop on the Heath, The, London SE 164
Bookzone, Berks 55
Booth (Booksearch Service), (Geoff), Cheshire... 68
Border Bookshop, W Yorkshire.................... 250
Chevin Books, W Yorkshire 250
Elmo Books, E Sussex 99
Esoteric Dreams Bookshop, Cumbria 78
firstpagebooks, Norfolk............................... 190
Footballana, Berks 56
Franks Booksellers, Gr Man......................... 119
Gathern (D.), Conwy 285
Green Meadow Books, Cornwall 74
Hedgerow Books, S Yorks 222
Joel Segal Books, Devon 86
Lion Books, Worcs.................................... 256
McCrone (Audrey), Isle of Arran 275
Moore (C.R.), Shropshire 214
Peter White, Hampshire 121
Richard Thornton Books, London N 160
Roland Books, Kent 139
Rugby Relics, West Glamorgan 294
Soccor Books Limited, Lincolnshire 150
Stroh (M.A.), London E 155
Treasure Trove Books, Leics........................ 148
Wiend Books, Lancashire 144
Yesterday's News, Conwy 285

- GOLF

Abrahams (Mike), Staffordshire 224
Archways Sports Books, Lothian 276
Big Bairn Books, Tayside 281
Bob Mallory (Books), Derbyshire.................. 83
Bodyline Books, Surrey............................... 233
Bookzone, Berks 55
Classic Crime Collections, Gr Man 119
Clifford Milne Books, Grampian................... 272
Coupland (Terry W.), Staffordshire................ 224
Dublin Bookbrowsers, Co. Dublin................. 265
Dunstan Books, Dorset............................... 91
Esoteric Dreams Bookshop, Cumbria 78
Fifteenth Century Bookshop (The), E Sussex 104
Garfi Books, Powys 293
Gathern (D.), Conwy 285
Grant Books, Worcs 255
Gresham Books, Somerset 218
Hennessey Bookseller (Ray), E Sussex 100
Joel Segal Books, Devon 86

Little Stour Books, Kent 137
McEwan Golf Books (Rhod), Grampian 273
Morley Case, Hampshire 125
Murphy (C.J.), Norfolk............................... 190
Poor Richard's Books, Suffolk 227
Roland Books, Kent 139
Rugby Relics, West Glamorgan 294
Schofield Golf Books (Steve), W Yorkshire 250
Seabreeze Books, Lancashire........................ 145
Strathtay Antiquarian - Secondhand Books,
Tayside 282
Stroh (M.A.), London E 155
Trinity Rare Books, Co. Leitrim 266

- GREYHOUND RACING

Bodyline Books, Surrey............................... 233
Coch-y-Bonddu Books, Powys 292

- GYMNASTICS

Archways Sports Books, Lothian 276
Bodyline Books, Surrey............................... 233

- HIGHLAND GAMES

Archways Sports Books, Lothian 276
Bodyline Books, Surrey............................... 233
Grampian Books, Grampian......................... 274
Webster (D.), Strathclyde............................ 280

- HOCKEY

Archways Sports Books, Lothian 276
Bodyline Books, Surrey............................... 233
Pennymead Books, N Yorks......................... 194
Yesterday's Books, Dorset 92

- HORSE RACING (INC. RIDING/ BREEDING/EQUESTRIAN)

Allinson (Frank & Stella), Warwickshire 237
Amos (Denis W.), Hertfordshire 131
Archways Sports Books, Lothian 276
Askew Books (Vernon), Wiltshire.................. 251
Aucott & Thomas, Leics............................. 147
Bob Mallory (Books), Derbyshire.................. 83
Bodyline Books, Surrey............................... 233
Bookzone, Berks 55
Brown (Books) (Steve), Staffordshire 224
Browzers, Gr Man..................................... 119
Carters (Janet), Suffolk 226
Castleton (Pat), Kent................................. 138
Cobbles Books, Somerset............................ 218
Cornucopia Books, Lincolnshire 153
Dales & Lakes Book Centre, Cumbria............ 80
Fifteenth Century Bookshop (The), E Sussex 104
Garfi Books, Powys 293
Gibbs Books, (Jonathan), Worcs................... 256
Grayling (David A.H.), Cumbria 79
Grove Bookshop (The), N Yorks 197
Hambleton Books, N Yorks 197
J.H. Day, Hampshire 124
Jane Badger Books, Northants 200
Jane Jones Books, Grampian 272
Joel Segal Books, Devon 86
Karen Millward, Co. Cork 263
Kennedy & Farley, E Sussex........................ 104
Kirkman Ltd., (Robert), Bedfordshire............. 54
Leeper (Romilly), London SW 169

SPECIALITY INDEX

MK Book Services, Cambridgeshire............... 66
Richard Thornton Books, London N............. 160
Roland Books, Kent.................................. 139
Treasure Island (The), Gr Man..................... 119
Winchester Bookshop (The), Hampshire.......... 127
Wychwood Books, Glos.............................. 116

- HUNTING

Baynton–Williams Gallery, W Sussex............. 242
Bodyline Books, Surrey.............................. 233
Bonham (J. & S.L.), London W................... 172
Booth (Booksearch Service), (Geoff), Cheshire... 68
Cobbles Books, Somerset............................ 218
Coch-y-Bonddu Books, Powys..................... 292
Cornucopia Books, Lincolnshire................... 153
Countryman Books, East Yorkshire............... 106
Countrymans Gallery (The), Leics................ 147
Darkwood Books, Co. Cork........................ 263
Deeside Books, Grampian........................... 273
Edmund Pollinger Rare Books, London SW..... 167
Farquharson, (Hilary), Tayside.................... 281
Fifteenth Century Bookshop (The), E Sussex.... 104
Garfi Books, Powys.................................. 293
Grove Bookshop (The), N Yorks.................. 197
Hancock (Peter), W Sussex......................... 243
Head (John & Judith), Wiltshire.................. 253
Jane Badger Books, Northants..................... 200
Jane Jones Books, Grampian....................... 272
Joel Segal Books, Devon............................ 86
Kennedy & Farley, E Sussex........................ 104
Kilgour (Sporting Books) (Ian), Leics............ 149
Kirkman Ltd., (Robert), Bedfordshire............ 54
Peter M Daly, Hampshire........................... 127
Rare Books & Berry, Somerset..................... 219
Saint Mary's Books & Prints, Lincolnshire....... 154
Saintfield Antiques & Fine Books, Co. Down... 261
Vinovium Books, Durham.......................... 97
Wychwood Books, Glos............................. 116

- ICE HOCKEY

Archways Sports Books, Lothian.................. 276
Bodyline Books, Surrey.............................. 233

- ICE-SKATING

Archways Sports Books, Lothian.................. 276
Bodyline Books, Surrey.............................. 233
Joel Segal Books, Devon............................ 86

- MARTIAL ARTS

Archways Sports Books, Lothian.................. 276
Bodyline Books, Surrey.............................. 233
Books Bought & Sold, Surrey...................... 232
Combat Arts Archive, Durham..................... 97
Joel Segal Books, Devon............................ 86

- MOTOR RACING

Archways Sports Books, Lothian.................. 276
Bob Mallory (Books), Derbyshire.................. 83
Bodyline Books, Surrey.............................. 233
books2books, Devon.................................. 88
Booth (Booksearch Service), (Geoff), Cheshire... 68
Burroughs (Andrew), Lincolnshire................ 153
Collectors Carbooks, Northants.................... 200
Elmo Books, E Sussex............................... 99
Falconwood Transport & Military Bookshop,

London Outer.. 184
Heritage, West Midlands............................ 239
Joel Segal Books, Devon............................ 86
Kerr (Norman), Cumbria........................... 78
Knowles (John), Norfolk............................ 188
Lion Books, Worcs................................... 256
Morris Secondhand & Antiquarian Books
(Chris), Oxfordshire................................. 210
Richard Thornton Books, London N............. 160
St Paul's Street Bookshop, Lincolnshire.......... 154
Simon Lewis Transport Books, Glos.............. 115
Vintage Motorshop, W Yorkshire................. 246
Volumes of Motoring, Glos......................... 113

- OLYMPIC GAMES, THE

Archways Sports Books, Lothian.................. 276
Bob Mallory (Books), Derbyshire.................. 83
Bodyline Books, Surrey.............................. 233
Dolphin Books, Suffolk.............................. 226

- PIG-STICKING

Bodyline Books, Surrey.............................. 233
Chalmers Hallam (E.), Hampshire................ 125
Coch-y-Bonddu Books, Powys..................... 292
Edmund Pollinger Rare Books, London SW..... 167

- POLO

Askew Books (Vernon), Wiltshire.................. 251
Blacklock's, Surrey................................... 232
Bodyline Books, Surrey.............................. 233
Countryman Books, East Yorkshire............... 106

- POTHOLING

Bodyline Books, Surrey.............................. 233
Glacier Books, Tayside.............................. 282
Hunter and Krageloh, Derbyshire................. 83
Jarvis Books, Derbyshire............................ 83
Letterbox Books, Notts.............................. 204

- RACING

Bob Mallory (Books), Derbyshire.................. 83
Bodyline Books, Surrey.............................. 233
Bookzone, Berks...................................... 55
Browzers, Gr Man.................................... 119
Fifteenth Century Bookshop (The), E Sussex.... 104
Grove Bookshop (The), N Yorks.................. 197
Head (John & Judith), Wiltshire.................. 253
Karen Millward, Co. Cork.......................... 263

- RACKET SPORTS

Bodyline Books, Surrey.............................. 233
Joel Segal Books, Devon............................ 86
Stroh (M.A.), London E............................ 155

- REAL TENNIS

Bodyline Books, Surrey.............................. 233
Edmund Pollinger Rare Books, London SW..... 167
Marlborough Rare Books Ltd., London W...... 174

- ROWING

Archways Sports Books, Lothian.................. 276
Bodyline Books, Surrey.............................. 233
McLaren Books, Strathclyde....................... 280
Vandeleur Antiquarian Books, Surrey............ 232

SPECIALITY INDEX

- RUGBY

Archways Sports Books, Lothian 276
Bodyline Books, Surrey 233
Bookzone, Berks 55
Chas J. Sawyer, Kent 141
Dylans Bookstore, Swansea 294
Franks Booksellers, Gr Man......................... 119
Joel Segal Books, Devon 86
Just Books, Cornwall 76
Lion Books, Worcs 256
Poor Richard's Books, Suffolk 227
Roland Books, Kent 139
Rugby Relics, West Glamorgan 294
Saunders (Tom), Caerphilly 283
Treasure Island (The), Gr Man...................... 119
Wiend Books, Lancashire 144

- RUNNING

Archways Sports Books, Lothian 276
Bodyline Books, Surrey 233
Bookzone, Berks 55

- SAILING

Argent (Alan), Isle of Wight 135
Bodyline Books, Surrey 233
Fifteenth Century Bookshop (The), E Sussex 104
Greta Books, Durham 97
Joel Segal Books, Devon 86
Just Books, Cornwall 76
Kalligraphia, Isle of Wight 134
Lewcock (John), Cambridgeshire................... 66
Portus Books, Hampshire 122
Sea Chest Nautical Bookshop (The), Devon 88

- SHOOTING

Atholl Fine Books, Tayside 281
Blest (Peter), Kent 139
Bodyline Books, Surrey 233
Chalmers Hallam (E.), Hampshire 125
Coch-y-Bonddu Books, Powys 292
Countryman Books, East Yorkshire................ 106
Countrymans Gallery (The), Leics 147
Darkwood Books, Co. Cork 263
Edmund Pollinger Rare Books, London SW 167
Fifteenth Century Bookshop (The), E Sussex 104
Fylde Books, Lancashire 146
Garfi Books, Powys 293
Grayling (David A.H.), Cumbria 79
Greta Books, Durham 97
Head (John & Judith), Wiltshire 253
Joel Segal Books, Devon 86
Karen Millward, Co. Cork 263
Kilgour (Sporting Books) (Ian), Leics 149
Roland Books, Kent 139
Vinovium Books, Durham 97
Winchester Bookshop (The), Hampshire.......... 127
Wychwood Books, Glos 116

- SKIING

Archways Sports Books, Lothian 276
Bodyline Books, Surrey 233
Frew Limited (Robert), London W 173
Glacier Books, Tayside 282
Hunter and Krageloh, Derbyshire 83
Jarvis Books, Derbyshire 83

Joel Segal Books, Devon 86
Pinnacle Books, Lothian............................. 278

- SQUASH

Bodyline Books, Surrey 233
Joel Segal Books, Devon 86

- SUMO

Bodyline Books, Surrey 233
Combat Arts Archive, Durham 97

- SURFING

Bodyline Books, Surrey 233

- SWIMMING

Bodyline Books, Surrey 233
Joel Segal Books, Devon 86
Rugby Relics, West Glamorgan 294

- TENNIS

Amos (Denis W.), Herts 131
Archways Sports Books, Lothian 276
Bodyline Books, Surrey 233
Bookzone, Berks 55
Dolphin Books, Suffolk 226
Joel Segal Books, Devon 86
Stroh (M.A.), London E 155
Tennis Collectables, Cheshire 68

- WATERSPORTS

Archways Sports Books, Lothian 276
Bodyline Books, Surrey 233
Joel Segal Books, Devon 86

- WEIGHTLIFTING/BODYBUILDING

Archways Sports Books, Lothian 276
Bodyline Books, Surrey 233
Combat Arts Archive, Durham 97
Webster (D.), Strathclyde 280

- WRESTLING

Bodyline Books, Surrey 233
Combat Arts Archive, Durham 97
Webster (D.), Strathclyde 280

- YACHTING

Baldwin (M. & M.), Worcs 255
Bodyline Books, Surrey 233
Bookends of Fowey, Cornwall 73
Books Afloat, Dorset 96
Clapham (M. & B.), Hampshire.................... 124
Cornucopia Books, Lincolnshire 153
Crouch Rare Books, Surrey 233
Curtle Mead Books, Isle of Wight 134
Fifteenth Century Bookshop (The), E Sussex 104
Footrope Knots, Suffolk 228
G Collins Bookdealers, Herts 131
Greta Books, Durham 97
Internet Bookshop UK Ltd., Glos 113
Joel Segal Books, Devon 86
Lewcock (John), Cambridgeshire................... 66
McLaren Books, Strathclyde 280
Milestone Books, Devon 89
Prior (Michael), Lincolnshire 153
Roland Books, Kent 139

SPECIALITY INDEX

Saintfield Antiques & Fine Books, Co. Down ... 261
Sea Chest Nautical Bookshop (The), Devon 88
Smith Maritime Aviation Books (Frank),
Tyne and Wear...................................... 236

STAGE

Brock Books, N Yorks 193
Dolphin Books, Suffolk............................... 226
Fifteenth Century Bookshop (The), E Sussex 104
Greenroom Books, W Yorkshire.................... 248
Joel Segal Books, Devon 86
Morris Secondhand & Antiquarian
Books (Chris), Oxfordshire........................ 210
Richard Thornton Books, London N 160
Whittle, Bookseller (Avril), Cumbria 81

STAINED GLASS

Barnby (C. & A.J.), Kent............................ 141
Bennett & Kerr Books, Oxfordshire 206
Birchden Books, London E 155
Don Kelly Books, London W 172
Heneage Art Books (Thomas), London SW 169
Joel Segal Books, Devon 86
Stained Glass Books, Kent.......................... 140
Staniland (Booksellers), Lincolnshire 154
Taylor & Son (Peter), Herts......................... 133
Trinders' Fine Tools, Suffolk 227
Venables (Morris & Juliet), Bristol.................. 60
Whittle, Bookseller (Avril), Cumbria 81

STATES OF AMERICA - LOUISIANA

Apocalypse, Surrey 233

STATES OF AUSTRALIA - NEW SOUTH WALES

Roz Hulse, Conwy 286

- QUEENSLAND

Roz Hulse, Conwy 286

- TASMANIA

Roz Hulse, Conwy 286

STATISTICS

Adrem Books, Herts 131
Barcombe Services, Essex............................ 108
Susanne Schulz-Falster Rare Books, London N . 160
Transformer, Dumfries & Galloway................ 271

STEAM ENGINES

Abrahams (Mike), Staffordshire 224
All Books, Essex 110
Anthony Vickers Books, N Yorks 196
Biblion, London W.................................... 172
Boox-Box (The), Shropshire 213
Bott, (Bookdealers) Ltd., (Martin), Gr Man 118
Brewin Books Ltd., Warwickshire 238
Browning Books, Torfaen 294
Cornucopia Books, Lincolnshire 153
Coulthurst (Richard), Gr Man 120
Cox (Geoff), Devon 90
Dales and Lakes Book Centre, Cumbria.......... 80
Duck (William), Hampshire......................... 124
Empire Books, N Yorks.............................. 198
Henry Wilson Books, Cheshire 69

J & J Burgess Booksellers, Cambridgeshire....... 64
Joel Segal Books, Devon 86
Kenneth Ball, E Sussex 101
Kerr (Norman), Cumbria 78
Marine & Cannon Books, Cheshire 71
Marine and Cannon Books, Cheshire 69
N1 Books, E Sussex................................... 105
Nautical Antique Centre (The), Dorset 96
Newband (D.M.), Powys 293
Randall (Tom), Somerset............................ 219
Roadmaster Books, Kent............................. 137
Robert Humm & Co, Lincolnshire 154
Roland Books, Kent 139
Roz Hulse, Conwy 286
Uncle Phil's Books, West Midlands 240
Vickers (Anthony), N Yorks......................... 196
Vintage Motorshop, W Yorkshire 246
Wiend Books, Lancashire 144
Yesteryear Railwayana, Kent 139

STONE MASONRY

Courtney & Hoff, N Yorks 198

STUDENT ACTIVISM

Left on The Shelf, Cumbria.......................... 79

SUFFRAGETTES

Delectus Books, London WC........................ 177
Dolphin Books, Suffolk............................... 226
Elaine Lonsdale Books, W Yorkshire 248
Joel Segal Books, Devon 86
R. & A. Books, E Sussex............................. 102
Reading Lasses, Dumfries & Galloway 271

SUFISM

Bookbarrow, Cambridgeshire........................ 63
Fifteenth Century Bookshop (The), E Sussex 104
Inner Bookshop (The), Oxfordshire................ 210
Joel Segal Books, Devon 86
Occultique, Northants................................. 200
Portobello Books, London W 175
The Sanctuary Bookshop, Dorset................... 94

SUNDIALS

Country Books, Derbyshire 82
Hadfield (G.K.), Cumbria............................ 80

SUPERNATURAL

Adrem Books, Herts 131
Caduceus Books, Leics................................ 147
Country Books, Derbyshire 82
Cowley, Bookdealer (K.W.), Somerset 218
Enigma Books, Norfolk 190
Facet Books, Dorset................................... 91
Gildas Books, Cheshire 68
Inner Bookshop (The), Oxfordshire................ 210
Joel Segal Books, Devon 86
Loretta Lay Books, London NW 162
Occultique, Northants................................. 200
R. & A. Books, E Sussex............................. 102
Robert Temple, London N........................... 160
SETI Books, Staffordshire............................ 225
Zardoz Books, Wiltshire.............................. 254

SPECIALITY INDEX

SURGERY

Bernard Dixon and Kath Adams, Middlesex 183
Demetzy Books, Oxfordshire 208
G. C. Books Ltd., Dumfries & Galloway......... 271
Parkinsons Books, Merseyside....................... 186
Phelps (Michael), W Sussex 243
R M Books, Herts..................................... 132
Weiner (Graham), London N 160
Westons, Herts 133

SURREALISM

Atlas, London N....................................... 158
Decorum Books, London N 158
Delectus Books, London WC........................ 177
Ellis, Bookseller (Peter), London WC 178
Joel Segal Books, Devon 86
Print Matters, London SE............................ 166
Trinity Rare Books, Co. Leitrim 266

SURVEYING

Stroh (M A.), London E 155

SURVIVAL

Coch-y-Bonddu Books, Powys 292
Greta Books, Durham 97

SYMBOLISM

Apocalypse, Surrey 233
Delectus Books, London WC........................ 177
Inner Bookshop (The), Oxfordshire................. 210
Joel Segal Books, Devon 86
Occultique, Northants................................. 200

TAPESTRY

Abington Bookshop, Suffolk......................... 228
Art Reference Books, Hampshire 125
Bennett & Kerr Books, Oxfordshire 206
Books, Oxfordshire 206
Byrom Textile Bookroom (Richard), Lancashire 143
Don Kelly Books, London W 172
Fifteenth Century Bookshop (The), E Sussex 104
Heneage Art Books (Thomas), London SW 169
Hennessey Bookseller (Ray), E Sussex 100
Joel Segal Books, Devon 86
Judith Mansfield, W Yorkshire...................... 250
R. & A. Books, E Sussex............................. 102
Sleepy Elephant Books & Artefacts, Cumbria ... 80
Trinders' Fine Tools, Suffolk 227
Whittle, Bookseller (Avril), Cumbria 81

TAXATION

Empire Books, N Yorks.............................. 198
Wayside Books and Cards, Oxfordshire 207

TAXIDERMY

Blest (Peter), Kent 139
Chalmers Hallam (E.), Hampshire 125
Coch-y-Bonddu Books, Powys 292
Dead Mens Minds.co.uk, Powys 292
Home Farm Books, Warwickshire.................. 237

TEA

Gardener & Cook, London SW..................... 168
Joel Segal Books, Devon 86

TEACHING

Barcombe Services, Essex............................. 108
Cornucopia Books, Lincolnshire 153
Ice House Books, Wiltshire 253
Joel Segal Books, Devon 86
Reading Lasses, Dumfries & Galloway 271

TECHNICAL

Adrem Books, Herts 131
Barcombe Services, Essex............................. 108
Bernard Dixon and Kath Adams, Middlesex 183
Brimstones, E Sussex.................................. 103
Cotswold Internet Books, Glos...................... 113
Duck (William), Hampshire.......................... 124
Fine Books at Ilkley, W Yorkshire 248
Fylde Books, Lancashire 146
Moorhead Books, W Yorkshire...................... 246
Parkinsons Books, Merseyside....................... 186
Roberts Books, Ayrshire 280
Stroh (M.A.), London E 155
Westons, Herts 133
Yesteryear Railwayana, Kent 139

TECHNOLOGY

Barcombe Services, Essex............................. 108
Baron (Christopher), Gr Man 118
Batterham (David), London W...................... 172
Bernard Dixon and Kath Adams, Middlesex 183
Book House (The), Cumbria......................... 77
Booth Books, Powys 289
Bott, (Bookdealers) Ltd., (Martin), Gr Man 118
Chris Phillips, Wiltshire.............................. 251
Eagle Bookshop (The), Bedfordshire 53
Eggle (Mavis), Herts 131
Esplin (David), Hampshire........................... 124
Gaskell Rare Books (Roger), Cambridgeshire ... 66
Hinchliffe Books, Bristol.............................. 59
K.S.C. Books, Cheshire............................... 71
Mollie's Loft, Swansea................................ 294
Orangeberry Books, Oxfordshire 209
Parkinsons Books, Merseyside....................... 186
Phelps (Michael), W Sussex 243
Phillips (Nigel), Hampshire.......................... 122
Pollak (P.M.), Devon 89
Roberts Books, Ayrshire 280
Rogers Turner Books, London SE.................. 166
Skoob Russell Square, Suffolk....................... 230
Stroh (M.A.), London E 155
Susanne Schulz-Falster Rare Books, London N. 160
Trinders' Fine Tools, Suffolk 227
Weiner (Graham), London N 160
Westons, Herts 133
Westwood Books (Mark), Powys 291
Whistler's Books, London SW 170
Ystwyth Books, Ceredigion 284

TEDDY BEARS

Bookmark (Children's Books), Wiltshire.......... 253
DPE Books, Devon 87
Green Meadow Books, Cornwall 74
Jean Hedger, Berks.................................... 55
Joel Segal Books, Devon 86
R. & A. Books, E Sussex............................. 102
St Swithin's Illustrated & Children's Books,
London W 175

SPECIALITY INDEX

TELEGRAPH

Chris Phillips, Wiltshire	251
Elton Engineering Books, London W	173
Roz Hulse, Conwy	286
Stroh (M.A.), London E	155
Yesteryear Railwayana, Kent	139

TELEVISION

Byre Books, Dumfries & Galloway	270
Cover to Cover, Merseyside	186
Decorum Books, London N	158
Evans (Mark), Lincolnshire	153
firstpagebooks, Norfolk	190
Fitzsimons (Anne), Cumbria	78
Greenroom Books, W Yorkshire	248
Hambleton Books, N Yorks	197
Joel Segal Books, Devon	86
Kelly Books, Devon	89
Maggy Browne, Lincolnshire	150
McGee (Terence J.), London Outer	181
Morris Secondhand & Antiquarian	
Books (Chris), Oxfordshire	210
Mr. Pickwick of Towcester, Northants	201
Paramor (C.D.), Suffolk	229
Pyecroft (Ruth), Glos	117
Stroh (M.A.), London E	155
Terence Kaye, London NW	162
Wiend Books, Lancashire	144
Williams (Bookdealer), (Richard), N Lincs	154
Wright (Norman), Dorset	95
Yesterday's News, Conwy	285
Zardoz Books, Wiltshire	254

TERRORISM/GUERRILLA WARFARE

Delectus Books, London WC	177
Left on The Shelf, Cumbria	79
MilitaryHistoryBooks.com, Kent	138
Red Star Books, Herts	130

TEUTONIC HISTORY & CULTURE

Joel Segal Books, Devon	86
MilitaryHistoryBooks.com, Kent	138

TEXANA

Americanabooksuk, Cumbria	77

TEXTBOOKS

Barcombe Services, Essex	108
Cornucopia Books, Lincolnshire	153
Oopalba Books, Cheshire	71
Parkinsons Books, Merseyside	186
Stalagluft Books, Tyne and Wear	236
The Sanctuary Bookshop, Dorset	94

TEXTILES

Abington Bookshop, Suffolk	228
Anthony Vickers Books, N Yorks	196
Art Reference Books, Hampshire	125
Black Cat Books, Norfolk	188
Brock Books, N Yorks	193
Byrom Textile Bookroom (Richard), Lancashire	143
Cover to Cover, Merseyside	186
Crouch Rare Books, Surrey	233
Decorum Books, London N	158
Delph Books, Gr Man	120

Don Kelly Books, London W	172
Forest Books of Manchester, Cheshire	71
Gallimaufry Books, Herts	132
Heneage Art Books (Thomas), London SW	169
Hennessey Bookseller (Ray), E Sussex	100
Ives Bookseller (John), London Outer	184
Joel Segal Books, Devon	86
Judith Mansfield, W Yorkshire	250
Meekins Books (Paul), Warwickshire	238
Potterton Books, N Yorks	197
R. & A. Books, E Sussex	102
Reading Lasses, Dumfries & Galloway	271
Sleepy Elephant Books & Artefacts, Cumbria	80
Stroh (M.A.), London E	155
Susan Taylor Books, W Yorkshire	248
Trinders' Fine Tools, Suffolk	227
Vickers (Anthony), N Yorks	196
Warnes (Felicity J.), London Outer	181
Whittle, Bookseller (Avril), Cumbria	81
Young (D. & J.), Powys	293

THEATRE

Addyman Books, Powys	289
Brian Troath Books, London E	155
Brock Books, N Yorks	193
Byre Books, Dumfries & Galloway	270
Carta Regis, Powys	293
Clark (Nigel A.), London SE	165
Cobbles Books, Somerset	218
Cover to Cover, Merseyside	186
Cox Rare Books (Charles), Cornwall	74
DaSilva Puppet Books, Dorset	93
Decorum Books, London N	158
Dolphin Books, Suffolk	226
Ely Books, Cambridgeshire	65
Evans (Mark), Lincolnshire	153
Fifteenth Century Bookshop (The), E Sussex	104
Fitzsimons (Anne), Cumbria	78
Forest Books of Manchester, Cheshire	71
Greenroom Books, W Yorkshire	248
Hancock & Monks, Powys	290
Ian McKelvie Bookseller, London N	159
J.C. Books, Norfolk	192
Jarndyce Antiquarian Booksellers, London WC	178
Joel Segal Books, Devon	86
Junk & Spread Eagle, London SE	165
Just Books, Cornwall	76
McGee (Terence J.), London Outer	181
medievalbookshop, Herts	133
Morris Secondhand & Antiquarian	
Books (Chris), Oxfordshire	210
My Back Pages, London SW	169
Oopalba Books, Cheshire	71
Paramor (C.D.), Suffolk	229
Pastmasters, Derbyshire	83
Pordes Books Ltd., (Henry), London WC	179
Portobello Books, London W	175
Prescott - The Bookseller (John), London Outer	184
Primrose Hill Books, London NW	162
PsychoBabel Books & Journals, Oxfordshire	206
R. & A. Books, E Sussex	102
Readers World, West Midlands	239
Reading Lasses, Dumfries & Galloway	271
Reads, Dorset	95
Rhodes, Bookseller (Peter), Hampshire	126

SPECIALITY INDEX

Richard Thornton Books, London N 160
Robert Temple, London N.......................... 160
St Swithin's Illustrated & Children's Books, London W.. 175
Scrivener's Books & Bookbinding, Derbyshire... 82
Sleepy Elephant Books & Artefacts, Cumbria ... 80
Terence Kaye, London NW 162
Theatreshire Books, N Yorks....................... 193
Travis & Emery Music Bookshop, London WC 180
Whittle, Bookseller (Avril), Cumbria 81
Willmott Bookseller (Nicholas), Cardiff........... 283
Wood (Peter), Cambridgeshire....................... 65
Yesterday's News, Conwy........................... 285

THEOLOGY

Addyman Books, Powys.............................. 289
Andrews Books & Collectables, Cheshire......... 69
Apocalypse, Surrey.................................... 233
Axe Rare & Out of Print Books (Richard), N Yorks.. 194
Barbican Bookshop, N Yorks 198
Barcombe Services, Essex............................ 108
Bardsley's Books, Suffolk.................. 226
Beckham Books Ltd., Suffolk 230
Bell (Peter), Lothian.................................. 276
Berwick Books, Lincolnshire........................ 152
Beware of the Leopard, Bristol...................... 58
Big Bairn Books, Tayside 281
Blythswood Bookshop, Highland 275
Book Aid, Durham.................................... 97
Bookcase, Cumbria.................................... 78
Bookshop (The), Co. Donegal...................... 263
Bookshop at the Plain, Lincolnshire............... 151
Booth Books, Powys.................................. 289
Brimstones, E Sussex................................. 103
Broadwater Books, Hampshire 125
Butler Cresswell Rare Books, Buckinghamshire . 61
Capel Mawr Collectors Centre, Gwynedd 287
Carta Regis, Powys.. 293
Carter, (Brian), Oxfordshire......................... 211
Chesters (G. & J.), Staffordshire 225
Cobnar Books, Kent.................................. 142
Colwyn Books, Conwy 285
Copnal Books, Cheshire.............................. 69
Corder (Mark W.), Kent 140
Courtenay Bookroom, Oxfordshire 206
Crouch Rare Books, Surrey.......................... 233
Dead Mens Minds.co.uk, Powys................... 292
Edwards (Alan & Margaret), Kent 142
Edwards (London) Limited (Francis), London WC 177
Edwards in Hay-on-Wye (Francis), Powys 290
Fotheringham (Alex), Northumberland 202
Foyle Books, Co. Derry 260
G. C. Books Ltd., Dumfries & Galloway......... 271
Gage Postal Books, Essex 111
Gilbert (R.A.), Bristol................................ 59
Golden Age Books, Worcs........................... 256
Hab Books, London W............................... 173
Hellenic Bookservices, London NW................ 162
Heritage Books, Isle of Wight 134
Howes Bookshop, E Sussex......................... 102
Humber Books, Lincolnshire 150
Kernaghans, Merseyside 186
Kyrios Books, Notts 204

Lewis (J.T. & P.), Cornwall......................... 74
Magis Books, Leics................................... 149
Main Point Books, Lothian.......................... 278
Martin's Books, Powys 292
Mercat Books, Highland 274
Modern Welsh Publications Ltd., Merseyside.... 185
Moss Books, London NW 162
Oasis Booksearch, Cambridgeshire................. 67
Old Aberdeen Bookshop, Grampian 272
Old Bookshop (The), West Midlands 241
Olynthiacs, Shropshire 214
Parkinsons Books, Merseyside...................... 186
Pendleburys Bookshop, London N 159
Price (John), London N 159
PsychoBabel Books & Journals, Oxfordshire..... 206
Quinto of Charing Cross Road, London WC ... 179
Rose Books, Gr Man 119
Rosemary Pugh Books, Wiltshire 253
Rosley Books, Cumbria.............................. 81
Rutland Bookshop (The), Rutland 212
S.P.C.K., Hampshire 127
S P.C.K., Bristol 60
St Philip's Books, Oxfordshire...................... 210
Saintfield Antiques & Fine Books, Co. Down ... 261
Salsus Books, Worcs 256
Samovar Books, Co. Dublin 264
Scott (Peter), E Sussex 104
Singleton (Anthony), S Yorks 222
Spooner & Co, Somerset 220
Staffs Bookshop (The), Staffordshire 224
Stalagluft Books, Tyne and Wear.................. 236
Staniland (Booksellers), Lincolnshire 154
Sterling Books, Somerset 221
Stokes Books, Co. Dublin........................... 265
Thornber (Peter M.), N Yorks 196
Thorntons of Oxford Ltd., Oxfordshire 207
Westwood Books (Mark), Powys 291
Winchester Bookshop (The), Hampshire.......... 127

THEOSOPHY

Alpha Books, London N 158
Bookcase, Cumbria................................... 78
Bookshop on the Heath, The, London SE 164
Inner Bookshop (The), Oxfordshire................ 210
Joel Segal Books, Devon 86
Occultique, Northants................................ 200
Rosemary Pugh Books, Wiltshire 253
Star Lord Books, Gr Man 119
The Sanctuary Bookshop, Dorset 94

THERAPY - MARITAL & FAMILY

Joel Segal Books, Devon 86
Reading Lasses, Dumfries & Galloway 271

TIMBER TECHNOLOGY

Joel Segal Books, Devon 86
Parkinsons Books, Merseyside...................... 186
Reeves Technical Books, N Yorks.................. 196

TOBACCO

Game Advice, Oxfordshire 210
Joel Segal Books, Devon 86
Stroh (M.A.), London E 155

SPECIALITY INDEX

TOPOGRAPHY - GENERAL

A. & H. Peasgood, Cambridgeshire 67
Abacus Gallery, Staffordshire....................... 224
Addyman Books, Powys.............................. 289
Adrem Books, Herts 131
Alexander's Books, Warwickshire................... 238
Allhalland Books, Devon............................ 85
Altea Antique Maps & Books, London W....... 172
Andrews Books & Collectables, Cheshire......... 69
Andron (G.W.), London N 158
Anthony Spranger, Wiltshire........................ 252
Anthony Vickers Books, N Yorks 196
Antiquary Ltd., (Bar Bookstore), N Yorks....... 196
Antique Map and Bookshop (The), Dorset 94
Antiques on High, Oxfordshire..................... 209
Anvil Books, West Midlands 240
Arden Books & Cosmographia, Warwickshire... 237
Arthur Hook, Bristol.................................. 58
Arts & Antiques Centre (The), Cheshire 69
Atholl Fine Books, Tayside 281
Autolycus, Shropshire................................ 213
Baker - Books for the Collector (Colin), Devon. 90
Bardsley's Books, Suffolk............................ 226
Barnes (Peter), Wiltshire 253
Bath Old Books, Somerset 216
Beardsley (A.E.), Notts 205
Bermondsey Basement Bookstore, London SE .. 164
Bolton Books, Hampshire........................... 121
Bonham (J. & S.L.), London W 172
Bookbox, Glos 116
Books, Denbighshire 286
Books & Collectables Ltd., Cambridgeshire 63
Books (For All), N Yorks........................... 194
Books Afloat, Dorset................................. 96
Books For All, N Yorks 194
books2books, Devon.................................. 88
BOOKS4U, Flintshire................................ 286
Bookshop (The), Norfolk 192
Bookworms, Norfolk................................. 187
Booth Books, Powys 289
Bowden Books, Leics 149
Brinded (Scott), Kent 139
Broadhurst of Southport Ltd., Merseyside 186
Brock Books, N Yorks 193
Burden Ltd., (Clive A.), Herts 132
Carnforth Bookshop (The), Lancashire 143
Carta Regis, Powys................................... 293
Castle Bookshop, Essex.............................. 109
Castle Hill Books, Herefordshire 128
Castleton (Pat), Kent................................. 138
Cavern Books, Cheshire 70
Channel Islands Galleries Limited, CI............. 258
Chapter & Verse, Lincolnshire...................... 152
Chaucer Bookshop, Kent............................ 136
Cheshire Book Centre, Cheshire.................... 69
Chevin Books, W Yorkshire 250
Clarke (J.&D), Norfolk 190
Clarke Books (David), Somerset 219
Classic Bindings Ltd, London SW 167
Clent Books, Worcs 255
Coach House Books, Worcs 256
Cobnar Books, Kent 142
Cobweb Books, N Yorks............................. 195
Cofion Books, Pembrokeshire 288
Coles (T.V.), Cambridgeshire 67
Coombes (A.J.), Surrey 231
Cornucopia Books, Lincolnshire 153
Cotswold Internet Books, Glos..................... 113
Country Books, Derbyshire 82
Craobh Rua Books, Co. Armagh................... 260
Cumming Limited (A. & Y.), E Sussex 104
D'Arcy Books, Wiltshire............................. 252
Dales & Lakes Book Centre, Cumbria............ 80
Dandy Lion Editions, Surrey 233
Dartmoor Bookshop (The), Devon 84
De Burca Rare Books, Co. Dublin 264
Debbage (John), Norfolk............................ 190
Delph Books, Gr Man................................ 120
Edwards (Alan & Margaret), Kent 142
Elaine Lonsdale Books, W Yorkshire 248
Ellwood Editions, Wiltshire......................... 253
Elmfield Books, West Midlands 239
Elstree Books, Herts.................................. 131
Eton Antique Bookshop, Berks 57
Farquharson, (Hilary), Tayside..................... 281
Fifteenth Century Bookshop (The), E Sussex 104
Fine Art, London SW 168
Fireside Books, Buckinghamshire 62
Fisher & Sperr, London N.......................... 158
Ford Books (David), Herts 133
Freader's Books, Tayside............................ 281
G. C. Books Ltd., Dumfries & Galloway......... 271
Garfi Books, Powys 293
Gilbert and Son (H.M.), Hampshire............... 126
Gillmark Gallery, Herts.............................. 131
Glenbower Books, Co. Dublin 265
Good for Books, Lincolnshire...................... 151
Goodyer (Nicholas), London N 159
Green (Mrs. D.M.), Surrey.......................... 235
Grove Bookshop (The), N Yorks 197
Guildmaster Books, Cheshire 70
Hall's Bookshop, Kent............................... 141
Handsworth Books, Essex........................... 112
Harrington Antiquarian Bookseller (Peter),
London SW... 169
Hawes Books, Norfolk................................ 191
Hay Cinema Bookshop Ltd., Powys............... 290
High Street Books, Devon 86
Hinchcliffe Books, Bristol............................ 59
Hollett and Son (R.F.G.), Cumbria 80
Hornsey's, N Yorks 195
Hummingbird Books, Herefordshire............... 128
Intech Books, Northumberland 203
InterCol London, London N 159
Jackson (M.W.), Wiltshire........................... 254
Jade Mountain Bookshop, Hampshire 126
Janus Books, West Midlands 240
Joel Segal Books, Devon 86
John L Capes (Books Maps & Prints), Cleveland 197
Junk & Spread Eagle, London SE 165
Just Books, Cornwall 76
Kalligraphia, Isle of Wight.......................... 134
Kay Books, London W............................... 174
Keegan's Bookshop, Berks 56
Kellow Books, Oxfordshire 207
Kemp Booksellers, Lancashire...................... 143
Kim's Bookshop, W Sussex 242, 243, 245
Kingsmere Books, Bedfordshire 53
Kingswood Books, Dorset 94
Knapton Bookbarn, N Yorks 198

SPECIALITY INDEX

Letterbox Books, Notts.............................. 204
Lewis (J.T. & P.), Cornwall.......................... 74
Libris (Weston) Books, Somerset 217
Liddle (Steve), Bristol 58
Lowe (John), Norfolk................................. 189
Malvern Bookshop (The), Worcs 255
Marcari, Bookseller (Peter), London SE 165
Marlborough Rare Books Ltd., London W...... 174
Martin (Books and Pictures), (Brian P.), Surrey. 232
Martin Bookshop & Gallery (Richard), Hants... 123
Maynard & Bradley, Leics 148
McCrone (Audrey), Isle of Arran.................. 275
Missing Books, Essex 109
Modlock (Lilian), Dorset............................. 93
Mundy (David), Buckinghamshire................. 61
Mundy (David), Herts 130
Murphy (C.J.), Norfolk............................... 190
Naughton Booksellers, Co. Dublin 265
Newlyn & New Street Books, Cornwall 75
Nicolas - Antiquarian Booksellers & Art Dealers,
London N.. 159
Nineteenth Century Books, Oxfordshire 211
O'Flynn Books, N Yorks............................. 199
Old Station Pottery & Bookshop (The), Norfolk 192
Oopalba Books, Cheshire............................. 71
Ouse Valley Books, Bedfordshire 54
Over-Sands Books, Cumbria......................... 78
Oxfam Books and Music, Hampshire............. 126
Oxley (Laurence), Hampshire....................... 121
Paper Moon Books, Glos 116
Paralos Ltd., London WC 178
Park Gallery & Bookshop (The), Northants 201
Parlour Bookshop (The), Oxfordshire............. 207
Parrott Books, Oxfordshire 211
Past & Present Books, Glos......................... 114
Peter Lyons Books, Glos............................. 114
Peter M Daly, Hampshire............................ 127
Peter White, Hampshire 121
Poor Richard's Books, Suffolk 227
Pordes Books Ltd., (Henry), London WC........ 179
Prescott - The Bookseller (John), London Outer 184
Quentin Books Ltd, Essex........................... 109
Quinto of Charing Cross Road, London WC ... 179
Quinto of Great Russell Street, London WC 179
R. & A. Books, E Sussex............................. 102
Read (C.&J.), Gorleston Books, Norfolk 188
Reads, Dorset 95
Richard Frost Books, Herts.......................... 130
Richard Thornton Books, London N 160
Robin Doughty - Fine Books, West Midlands... 239
Roger Collicott Books, Cornwall 75
Roland Books, Kent 139
Ross Old Books & Prints, Herefordshire 128
Royal Carbery Books Ltd., Co. Cork.............. 262
Saint Mary's Books & Prints, Lincolnshire....... 154
Samovar Books, Co. Dublin......................... 264
Saunders (Tom), Caerphilly 283
Sax Books, Suffolk 229
Sedgeberrow Books & Framing, Worcs........... 256
Shacklock Books (David), Suffolk 227
Shakeshaft (Dr. B.), Cheshire....................... 71
Shakespeare Books (Colin), Staffordshire......... 224
Sharpe (Mary), Somerset 221
Singleton (Anthony), S Yorks 222
Smith (Clive), Essex 109

Sparrow Books, W Yorkshire 246
Stalagluft Books, Tyne and Wear................... 236
Stella Books, Monmouthshire 288
Sterling Books, Somerset 221
Stothert Old Books, Cheshire....................... 69
Suffolk Rare Books, Suffolk 230
Sykes (Graham), W Yorkshire 249
Temperley (David), West Midlands................ 239
Thornber (Peter M.), N Yorks 196
Thorntons of Oxford Ltd., Oxfordshire........... 207
Tilston (Stephen E.), London SE................... 166
Titford (John), Derbyshire 82
Townsend (John), Berks 57
Treasure Trove Books, Leics........................ 148
Trinders' Fine Tools, Suffolk 227
Turton (John), Durham 98
Tyger Press, London N............................... 160
Unsworth's Booksellers, London WC........ 163, 180
Ventnor Rare Books, Isle of Wight................ 135
Vokes Books Ltd., N Yorks 195
Wadard Books, Kent 138
Water Lane Bookshop, Wiltshire 253
Wealden Books, Kent................................. 139
Westcountry Oldbooks, Devon...................... 90
Whitfield (Ken), Essex 111
Williams (Bookdealer), (Richard), N Lincs....... 154
Winchester Bookshop (The), Hampshire.......... 127
Yewtree Books, Cumbria............................. 79

- LOCAL

2 Ravens, Cumbria.................................... 79
Abacus Gallery, Staffordshire....................... 224
Abrahams (Mike), Staffordshire.................... 224
Aitchison (Lesley), Bristol 58
Alec–Smith Books (Alex), East Yorkshire........ 107
Altea Antique Maps & Books, London W....... 172
Ambra Books, Bristol................................. 58
Andrews Books & Collectables, Cheshire......... 69
Andron (G.W.), London N.......................... 158
Anthony Spranger, Wiltshire........................ 252
Anthony Vickers Books, N Yorks 196
Anthony Whittaker, Kent............................ 136
Antiquary Ltd., (Bar Bookstore), N Yorks....... 196
Antique & Book Shop, Powys...................... 293
Anvil Books, West Midlands 240
Arden Books & Cosmographia, Warwickshire... 237
Atholl Fine Books, Tayside 281
Axe Rare & Out of Print Books (Richard),
N Yorks.. 194
Baker - Books for the Collector (Colin), Devon. 90
Barbican Bookshop, N Yorks 198
Barnby (C. & A.J.), Kent............................ 141
Barn Books, Shropshire.............................. 215
Barnes (Peter), Wiltshire............................. 253
Bath Old Books, Somerset 216
Bear Island Books, Cardiff 283
Benny Gillies Books Ltd, Dumfries & Galloway 269
Bermondsey Basement Bookstore, London SE .. 164
Beware of the Leopard, Bristol..................... 58
Birchden Books, London E 155
Bird (Tony), Powys................................... 293
Black Cat Bookshop, Leics 147
Blore's Bookshop (Geoffrey), Notts 204
Bonython Bookshop, Cornwall...................... 76
Book Business (The), London W 172

SPECIALITY INDEX

Book For All Reasons (A.), Suffolk 229
Book Gallery (The), Cornwall 75
Book House (The), Cumbria........................ 77
Bookbarrow, Cambridgeshire....................... 63
Bookbox, Glos 116
Bookcase, Cumbria.................................... 78
Bookends of Fowey, Cornwall 73
Books & Collectables Ltd., Cambridgeshire...... 63
Books Afloat, Dorset.................................. 96
Books Bought & Sold, Surrey 232
Books Only, Suffolk................................... 227
BOOKS4U, Flintshire................................. 286
Bookshop (The), Co. Donegal...................... 263
Bookshop on the Heath, The, London SE 164
BookShop, The, Dumfries & Galloway........... 270
Bookworms of Evesham, Worcs 257
Border Books, Borders................................ 268
Bott, (Bookdealers) Ltd., (Martin), Gr Man 118
Bowdon Books, Lancashire 144
Brewin Books Ltd., Warwickshire 238
Bridge Books, Cumbria............................... 81
Burden Ltd., (Clive A.), Herts...................... 132
Bury Bookshop, Suffolk 226
Carlton Books, Norfolk 190
Carnforth Bookshop (The), Lancashire 143
Cassidy (Bookseller) (P.), Lincolnshire 153
Castle Bookshop, Essex.............................. 109
Castle Hill Books, Herefordshire................... 128
Castleton (Pat), Kent................................. 138
Cavern Books, Cheshire 70
Chandos Books, Devon............................... 85
Channel Islands Galleries Limited, CI............. 258
Chapman (Neville), Lancashire..................... 146
Chapter & Verse, Lincolnshire...................... 152
Chaucer Bookshop, Kent............................ 136
Chaucer Head Bookshop, Warwickshire.......... 238
Cheshire Book Centre, Cheshire.................... 69
Chevin Books, W Yorkshire 250
Chichester Bookshop (The), W Sussex 242
Church Green Books, Oxfordshire................. 211
Clarke (J.&D), Norfolk 190
Clarke Books (David), Somerset 219
Classic Bindings Ltd, London SW 167
Classic Crime Collections, Gr Man 119
Coach House Books, Worcs 256
Cobbles Books, Somerset............................ 218
Cofion Books, Pembrokeshire 288
Collectors Corner, Wiltshire......................... 253
Colonsay Bookshop, Isle of Colonsay............. 276
Compass Books, Devon 85
Coombes (A.J.), Surrey 231
Copnal Books, Cheshire 69
Corder (Mark W.), Kent 140
Cornucopia Books, Lincolnshire 153
Cotswold Internet Books, Glos..................... 113
Country Books, Derbyshire 82
Courtwood Books, Co. Laois....................... 266
Cousens (W.C.), Devon.............................. 84
Cox Old & Rare Books (Claude), Suffolk 228
Cox, Andrew, Shropshire............................ 215
Creaking Shelves, Inverness-shire.................. 275
Curtle Mead Books, Isle of Wight 134
D'Arcy Books, Wiltshire............................. 252
Dales & Lakes Book Centre, Cumbria 80
Dandy Lion Editions, Surrey 233

Dartmoor Bookshop (The), Devon 84
Davidson Books, Co. Down 261
Debbage (John), Norfolk 190
Delph Books, Gr Man................................ 120
Dene Barn Books & Prints, Somerset 220
Dobson (Bob), Lancashire 143
Dolphin Books, Suffolk............................... 226
Eastgate Bookshop, East Yorkshire 106
Elaine Lonsdale Books, W Yorkshire 248
Ellwood Editions, Wiltshire 253
Elmfield Books, West Midlands.................... 239
Elstree Books, Herts.................................. 131
English (Toby), Oxfordshire......................... 211
Everett (Richard), Norfolk 188
Everett (Richard, at the Southwold Antiques Centre, Suffolk........................... 229
Exeter Rare Books, Devon........................... 86
Farquharson, (Hilary), Tayside..................... 281
Ferdinando (Steven), Somerset 220
Fifteenth Century Bookshop (The), E Sussex 104
Fine Art, London SW 168
Fireside Books, Buckinghamshire 62
Ford Books (David), Herts 133
Foyle Books, Co. Derry.............................. 260
Freader's Books, Tayside............................ 281
Furneaux Books (Lee), Devon...................... 89
Fylde Books, Lancashire 146
G Collins Bookdealers, Herts....................... 131
G. C. Books Ltd., Dumfries & Galloway......... 271
Garretts Antiquarian Books, Isle of Man......... 259
GfB: the Colchester Bookshop, Essex 109
Gibbard (A. & T.), E Sussex........................ 101
Gilbert and Son (H.M.), Hampshire............... 126
Gildas Books, Cheshire 68
Gillmark Gallery, Herts.............................. 131
Godmanchester Books, Cambridgeshire 66
Good for Books, Lincolnshire 151
Greta Books, Durham 97
Grove Bookshop (The), N Yorks 197
Hames (Peter), Devon................................ 85
Harlequin Books, Bristol 59
Helmsley Antiquarian & Secondhand Books, N Yorks... 194
Helston Bookworm, The, Cornwall................ 74
Hennessey Bookseller (Ray), E Sussex 100
Heritage, West Midlands 239
High Street Books, Devon 86
Hill (Peter), Hampshire 122
Hill Books (Alan), S Yorks 222
Hollett and Son (R.F.G.), Cumbria 80
Holmes Books (Harry), East Yorkshire......... 107
Hornsey's, N Yorks 195
Horsham Rare Books, W Sussex................... 243
Howes Bookshop, E Sussex......................... 102
Hutchison (Books) (Larry), Fife.................... 271
Idle Booksellers (The), W Yorkshire.............. 246
Idle Genius Books, London N 159
Intech Books, Northumberland 203
Invicta Bookshop, Berks............................. 56
Iona Bookshop (The), Isle of Iona................. 276
J C Books, Devon 87
J. & J. Books, Lincolnshire 151
Jade Mountain Bookshop, Hampshire 126
Jane Jones Books, Grampian 272
Janus Books, West Midlands 240

SPECIALITY INDEX

Jermy & Westerman, Notts 205
Jiri Books, Co. Antrim 260
Joel Segal Books, Devon 86
John Barton, Hampshire 126
John L Capes (Books Maps & Prints), Cleveland197
Junk & Spread Eagle, London SE 165
Just Books, Cornwall 76
Keeble Antiques, Somerset 219
Keegan's Bookshop, Berks 56
Kellow Books, Oxfordshire 207
Kelsall (George), Gr Man 118
Kemp Booksellers, Lancashire 143
Kernaghans, Merseyside 186
Kerr (Norman), Cumbria 78
Key Books (Sarah), Cambridgeshire 64
Killeen (John), N Yorks 194
Kim's Bookshop, W Sussex 242, 243, 245
Kirkland Books, Cumbria 79
Lake (David), Norfolk 191
Lawrence Books, Notts 204
Leakey's Bookshop, Highland 275
Leigh Gallery Books, Essex 110
Letterbox Books, Notts 204
Little Bookshop (The), Cumbria 81
Lymelight Books & Prints, Dorset 93
M. & D. Books, Worcs 255
Mair Wilkes Books, Fife 272
Malvern Bookshop (The), Worcs 255
Marcan, Bookseller (Peter), London SE 165
Marrin's Bookshop, Kent 138
Martin (Books and Pictures), (Brian P)., Surrey. 232
McCrone (Audrey), Isle of Arran 275
Meads Book Service (The), E Sussex 104
Missing Books, Essex 109
Modlock (Lilian), Dorset 93
Mogul Diamonds, West Midlands 241
Moon's Bookshop (Michael), Cumbria 81
Moore (C.R.), Shropshire 214
Moorhead Books, W Yorkshire 246
Moreton Books, Devon 87
Mount's Bay Books, Cornwall 75
Mulyan (Don), Merseyside 186
Mundy (David), Herts 130
Muttonchop Manuscripts, W Sussex 244
Naughton Booksellers, Co. Dublin 265
Newlyn & New Street Books, Cornwall 75
Niner (Marcus), Isle of Wight 134
Oakwood Books, Glos 115
Old Bookshelf (The), Strathclyde 279
Old Bookshop (The), West Midlands 241
Old Hall Bookshop (The), Northants 200
Old Station Pottery & Bookshop (The), Norfolk 192
Old Town Bookshop (The), Lothian 278
Orb's Bookshop, Grampian 274
Ouse Valley Books, Bedfordshire 54
Over-Sands Books, Cumbria 78
Oxley (Laurence), Hampshire 121
Park Gallery & Bookshop (The), Northants 201
Past & Present Books, Glos 114
Peakirk Books, Cambridgeshire 67
Pendleside Books, Lancashire 144
Periwinkle Press, Kent 139
Peter M Daly, Hampshire 127
Poor Richard's Books, Suffolk 227
Post-Horn Books, N Yorks 193

Postings, Surrey 234
Randall (Tom), Somerset 219
Rare & Racy, S Yorks 222
Rare Books & Berry, Somerset 219
Reads, Dorset 95
recollectionsbookshop.co.uk, Cornwall 74
Restormel Books, Worcs 257
Richard Thornton Books, London N 160
Richmond Books, N Yorks 195
Roadmaster Books, Kent 137
Robin Doughty - Fine Books, West Midlands... 239
Rochdale Book Company, Gr Man 120
Roger Collicott Books, Cornwall 75
Rowan (H. & S.J.), Dorset 91
Rutland Bookshop (The), Rutland 212
St Paul's Street Bookshop, Lincolnshire 154
Salway Books, Essex 112
Scarthin Books, Derbyshire 82
Second Edition, Lothian 278
Sedgeberrow Books & Framing, Worcs 256
Sillan Books, Co. Cavan 267
Skyrack Books, W Yorkshire 248
Sleepy Elephant Books & Artefacts, Cumbria ... 80
Smith (Clive), Essex 109
Smith Books (Keith), Herefordshire 128
Sparrow Books, W Yorkshire 246
Spooner & Co, Somerset 220
Staffs Bookshop (The), Staffordshire 224
Staniland (Booksellers), Lincolnshire 154
Stella Books, Monmouthshire 288
Stinton (Judith), Dorset 92
Stothert Old Books, Cheshire 69
Sue Lowell Natural History Books, London W. 176
Suffolk Rare Books, Suffolk 230
Summerfield Books Ltd, Cumbria 77
Taylor & Son (Peter), Herts 133
Temperley (David), West Midlands 239
Thomas (Books) (Lcona), Cheshire 71
Thomas (E. Wyn), Conwy 285
Thornber (Peter M.), N Yorks 196
Tiffin (Tony and Gill), Durham 97
Tombland Bookshop, Norfolk 191
Townsend (John), Berks 57
Trafalgar Bookshop, E Sussex 100
Treasure Chest Books, Suffolk 227
Treasure Trove Books, Leics 148
Tucker (Alan & Joan), Glos 117
Turton (John), Durham 98
Tyger Press, London N 160
Unsworth's Booksellers, London WC 163, 180
Ventnor Rare Books, Isle of Wight 135
Vickers (Anthony), N Yorks 196
Victoria Bookshop (The), Devon 84
Wadard Books, Kent 138
Water Lane Bookshop, Wiltshire 253
Wealden Books, Kent 139
Wembdon Books, Somerset 217
Whitchurch Books Ltd., Cardiff 283
Williams (Bookdealer), (Richard), N Lincs 154
Williams (Christopher), Dorset 94
Wilson (David), Buckinghamshire 61
Winchester Bookshop (The), Hampshire 127
Words Etcetera Bookshop, Dorset 93
Wychwood Books, Glos 116
Yates Antiquarian Books (Tony), Leics 148

SPECIALITY INDEX

Yewtree Books, Cumbria.............................. 79
Ystwyth Books, Ceredigion 284

TOPOLOGY

Debbage (John), Norfolk.............................. 190
Eagle Bookshop (The), Bedfordshire 53
Trinity Rare Books, Co. Leitrim 266

TOWN PLANNING

Bookroom (The), Surrey.............................. 234
Duck (William), Hampshire.......................... 124
Haskell (R.H. & P.), Dorset 94
Inch's Books, Kent.................................... 137
Joel Segal Books, Devon 86
Reads, Dorset 95

TOWN PLANS

Burden Ltd., (Clive A.), Herts 132
Debbage (John), Norfolk............................. 190
Empire Books, N Yorks.............................. 198
Joel Segal Books, Devon 86
O'Flynn Books, N Yorks............................. 199

TOYS

Addyman Books, Powys.............................. 289
Adrem Books, Herts 131
Barmby (C. & A.J.), Kent........................... 141
Bianco Library, W Sussex............................ 242
Bookmark (Children's Books), Wiltshire.......... 253
Falconwood Transport & Military Bookshop,
London Outer.. 184
Game Advice, Oxfordshire 210
Green Meadow Books, Cornwall 74
Jean Hedger, Berks................................... 55
Joel Segal Books, Devon 86
R. & A. Books, E Sussex............................. 102
St Swithin's Illustrated & Children's Books,
London W 175
Twigg (Keith), Staffordshire......................... 224
Whittle, Bookseller (Avril), Cumbria 81

TRACTION ENGINES

Anvil Books, West Midlands 240
Bott, (Bookdealers) Ltd., (Martin), Gr Man 118
Cottage Books, Leics.................................. 147
Country Books, Derbyshire 82
Cox (Geoff), Devon 90
Dales and Lakes Book Centre, Cumbria.......... 80
Empire Books, N Yorks.............................. 198
Falconwood Transport & Military Bookshop,
London Outer.. 184
Fifteenth Century Bookshop (The), E Sussex 104
Henry Wilson Books, Cheshire...................... 69
Joel Segal Books, Devon 86
Jones (Barry), W Sussex 243
Kerr (Norman), Cumbria 78
N1 Books, E Sussex................................... 105
Phenotype Books, Cumbria 80
Randall (Tom), Somerset............................. 219
Roadmaster Books, Kent............................. 137
Roberts (Booksellers), (Ray), Staffordshire 224
Salway Books, Essex 112
Simon Lewis Transport Books, Glos............... 115
Stella Books, Monmouthshire 288
Stroh (M.A.), London E 155

Vickers (Anthony), N Yorks......................... 196
Vintage Motorshop, W Yorkshire 246
Winchester Bookshop (The), Hampshire.......... 127
Yesteryear Railwayana, Kent........................ 139

TRADE CATALOGUES

Black Cat Books, Norfolk............................. 188
Don Kelly Books, London W 172
G. C. Books Ltd., Dumfries & Galloway......... 271
Marlborough Rare Books Ltd., London W...... 174
Reeves Technical Books, N Yorks.................. 196
Weiner (Graham), London N 160

TRADE UNIONS

Adrem Books, Herts 131
Berwick Books, Lincolnshire......................... 152
Byrom Textile Bookroom (Richard), Lancashire 143
Clifton Books, Essex 112
Delectus Books, London WC........................ 177
Dolphin Books, Suffolk............................... 226
Empire Books, N Yorks.............................. 198
Joel Segal Books, Devon 86
Left on The Shelf, Cumbria.......................... 79
Northern Herald Books, W Yorkshire 246
R. & A. Books, E Sussex............................. 102
Reading Lasses, Dumfries & Galloway 271
Red Star Books, Herts................................ 130
Spurrier (Nick), Kent 138
Symes Books (Naomi), Cheshire 72
Woburn Books, London N 160

TRADES & PROFESSIONS

Adrem Books, Herts 131
Garwood & Voigt, Kent.............................. 140
Joel Segal Books, Devon 86
N1 Books, E Sussex................................... 105
Susanne Schulz-Falster Rare Books, London N. 160

TRADITIONAL CHINESE MEDICINE

Inner Bookshop (The), Oxfordshire................ 210
Joel Segal Books, Devon 86
Orchid Book Distributors, Co. Clare............... 262

TRADITIONS

Country Books, Derbyshire 82
Gildas Books, Cheshire............................... 68
Joel Segal Books, Devon 86
Philip Hopper, Essex.................................. 110
Randall (Tom), Somerset............................. 219

TRANSPORT

Addyman Books, Powys.............................. 289
Adrem Books, Herts 131
Allinson (Frank & Stella), Warwickshire 237
Anthony Vickers Books, N Yorks 196
Anvil Books, West Midlands 240
Archer (David), Powys............................... 292
Arden Books & Cosmographia, Warwickshire... 237
Armstrong's Books & Collectables, Leics......... 147
Aurora Books Ltd, Lothian........................... 276
Autumn Leaves, Lincolnshire........................ 152
Baker (Gerald), Bristol................................ 60
Baldwin (M. & M.), Worcs 255
Barbican Bookshop, N Yorks 198
Barter Books, Northumberland 202

SPECIALITY INDEX

Bath Old Books, Somerset 216
Bianco Library, W Sussex........................... 242
Bird Books (Nigel), Ceredigion.................... 284
Black Five Books, Shropshire 215
Book House (The), Cumbria......................... 77
Bookcase, Cumbria................................... 78
Books, Kent 137
Books, Denbighshire 286
Books & Bygones (Pam Taylor), West Midlands 241
Books Afloat, Dorset................................. 96
Books at Star Dot Star, West Midlands 241
Books For All, N Yorks 194
Bookworms, Norfolk................................. 187
Bookworms of Evesham, Worcs 257
Border Books, Borders............................... 268
Bosco Books, Cornwall 73
Bott, (Bookdealers) Ltd., (Martin), Gr Man 118
Brad Books, Essex.................................... 111
Brewin Books Ltd., Warwickshire 238
Browning Books, Torfaen 294
Browse Books, Lancashire 144
Castle Bookshop, Essex.............................. 109
Cavern Books, Cheshire 70
Chaucer Bookshop, Kent............................ 136
Cheshire Book Centre, Cheshire.................... 69
Chevin Books, W Yorkshire 250
Classic Crime Collections, Gr Man 119
Clements (R.W.), London Outer 182
Clevedon Books, Somerset 218
Clifton Books, Essex 112
Cobweb Books, N Yorks............................. 195
Collectables (W.H.), Suffolk 230
Collectors Carbooks, Northants..................... 200
Collectors Corner, Wiltshire......................... 253
Cornucopia Books, Lincolnshire 153
Coulthurst (Richard), Gr Man 120
Crosby Nethercott Books, London Outer 181
Dales & Lakes Book Centre, Cumbria 80
Dales and Lakes Book Centre, Cumbria.......... 80
Dandy Lion Editions, Surrey 233
Deeside Books, Grampian........................... 273
Dinnages Transport Publishing, E Sussex 103
Duck (William), Hampshire......................... 124
Elton Engineering Books, London W 173
Falconwood Transport & Military Bookshop,
London Outer 184
Fifteenth Century Bookshop (The), E Sussex 104
Fireside Bookshop, Cumbria........................ 81
George St. Books, Derbyshire 83
Green Ltd. (G.L.), Herts 132
Hall's Bookshop, Kent............................... 141
Hay Castle, Powys.................................... 290
Henry Wilson Books, Cheshire 69
J C Books, Devon 87
J.B. Books, Berks 56
Joel Segal Books, Devon 86
Jones (Barry), W Sussex 243
Kelsall (George), Gr Man 118
Kerr (Norman), Cumbria 78
Kim's Bookshop, W Sussex...............242, 243, 245
Kirkland Books, Cumbria............................ 79
Knowles (John), Norfolk 188
Malvern Bookshop (The), Worcs 255
Marine & Cannon Books, Cheshire 71
Marine and Cannon Books, Cheshire 69

McGlynn (John), Lancashire........................ 143
Milestone Books, Devon 89
Muttonchop Manuscripts, W Sussex 244
My Back Pages, London SW 169
Newband (D.M.), Powys 293
Over-Sands Books, Cumbria........................ 78
Paton Books, Herts................................... 132
Pauline Harries Books, Hampshire 123
Periwinkle Press, Kent 139
Peter White, Hampshire 121
Pooks Motor Books, Leics........................... 148
Postings, Surrey....................................... 234
Prior (Michael), Lincolnshire 153
Railway Shop (The), Torfaen....................... 294
Randall (Tom), Somerset............................ 219
Read (C.&J.), Gorleston Books, Norfolk 188
Reid of Liverpool, Merseyside...................... 185
Richard Thornton Books, London N 160
Roadmaster Books, Kent............................. 137
Robert Humm & Co, Lincolnshire 154
Rochdale Book Company, Gr Man 120
Rods Books, Devon................................... 88
Roland Books, Kent 139
Rolling Stock Books, Gr Man....................... 120
Saintfield Antiques & Fine Books, Co. Down ... 261
Salway Books, Essex 112
Simon Lewis Transport Books, Glos 115
Stothert Old Books, Cheshire....................... 69
Suffolk Rare Books, Suffolk 230
The Glass Key, W Yorkshire 247
Treasure Chest Books, Suffolk 227
Trinity Rare Books, Co. Leitrim 266
Vailima Books, Dumfries & Galloway 270
Ventnor Rare Books, Isle of Wight................ 135
Vickers (Anthony), N Yorks......................... 196
Vintage Motorshop, W Yorkshire 246
Weiner (Graham), London N 160
Westwood Books Ltd, Cumbria..................... 80
Whitfield (Ken), Essex 111
Yesteryear Railwayana, Kent 139

TRAVEL - GENERAL

A. & H. Peasgood, Cambridgeshire 67
Abacus Gallery, Staffordshire....................... 224
Addyman Books, Powys.............................. 289
Adrem Books, Herts 131
Allsworth Rare Books Ltd., London SW.......... 167
Altea Antique Maps & Books, London W 172
Andron (G.W.), London N 158
Ann & Mike Conry, Worcs.......................... 257
Anne Harris Books & Bags Booksearch, Devon 88
Antique Map and Bookshop (The), Dorset 94
Antiques on High, Oxfordshire..................... 209
Arden Books & Cosmographia, Warwickshire... 237
Armstrong's Books & Collectables, Leics......... 147
Askew Books (Vernon), Wiltshire.................. 251
Aurora Books Ltd, Lothian.......................... 276
Autolycus, Shropshire................................ 213
Autumn Leaves, Lincolnshire....................... 152
Aviabooks, Glos 114
B D McManmon, Lancashire 145
Baedekers & Murray Guides, S Yorks 222
Barnhill Books, Isle of Arran 275
Bath Old Books, Somerset 216
Baynton–Williams Gallery, W Sussex 242

SPECIALITY INDEX

Beardsley (A.E.), Notts 205
Bianco Library, W Sussex........................... 242
Biblion, London W.................................... 172
Billing (Brian), Berks................................. 57
Black Five Books, Shropshire 215
Blackwell's Rare Books, Oxfordshire.............. 209
Bonham (J. & S.L.), London W 172
Book Business (The), London W 172
Book Shelf (The), Devon............................ 87
Bookcase, Cumbria.................................... 78
Bookpassage (The), Shropshire..................... 213
Books & Collectables Ltd., Cambridgeshire...... 63
Books Afloat, Dorset.................................. 96
Books in Cardigan, Ceredigion...................... 284
books2books, Devon.................................. 88
Bookshop (The), Co. Donegal...................... 263
Bookshop at the Plain, Lincolnshire............... 151
Bookshop on the Heath, The, London SE 164
Bookworms, Norfolk.................................. 187
Bookworms of Evesham, Worcs 257
Booth (Booksearch Service), (Geoff), Cheshire... 68
Booth Books, Powys.................................. 289
Border Books, Borders................................ 268
Bosorne Books, Cornwall 75
Bowden Books, Leics 149
Bracton Books, Cambridgeshire.................... 63
Brad Books, Essex..................................... 111
Broadhurst of Southport Ltd., Merseyside 186
Broadwater Books, Hampshire...................... 125
Brock Books, N Yorks............................... 193
Brockwells Booksellers, Lincolnshire 150
Burden Ltd., (Clive A.), Herts...................... 132
Byre Books, Dumfries & Galloway................. 270
Campbell (Fiona), London SE 164
Carnforth Bookshop (The), Lancashire 143
Carningli Centre, Pembrokeshire................... 288
Castleton (Pat), Kent................................. 138
Catalyst Booksearch Services, Devon.............. 87
Chalmers Hallam (E.), Hampshire................. 125
Chandos Books, Devon............................... 85
Chaucer Bookshop, Kent............................ 136
Cheshire Book Centre, Cheshire.................... 69
Chris Phillips, Wiltshire.............................. 251
Church Street Books, Norfolk...................... 187
Clegg (David), Staffordshire......................... 224
Clements (R.W.), London Outer................... 182
Clent Books, Worcs................................... 255
Clevedon Books, Somerset.......................... 218
Collectable Books, London SE...................... 165
Collectables (W.H.), Suffolk 230
Cornucopia Books, Lincolnshire 153
Corvus Books, Buckinghamshire................... 61
Cotswold Internet Books, Glos..................... 113
Cox (Geoff), Devon................................... 90
Cox Old & Rare Books (Claude), Suffolk 228
Craobh Rua Books, Co. Armagh................... 260
Cumming Limited (A. & Y.), E Sussex 104
D'Arcy Books, Wiltshire............................. 252
D.C. Books, Lincolnshire............................ 151
Dales & Lakes Book Centre, Cumbria............ 80
Dandy Lion Editions, Surrey 233
Darkwood Books, Co. Cork......................... 263
Dartmoor Bookshop (The), Devon 84
David (G.), Cambridgeshire......................... 63
David Warnes Books, Herefordshire 129

Davies Fine Books, Worcestershire 257
Deeside Books, Grampian............................ 273
Demetzy Books, Oxfordshire 208
Dolphin Books, Suffolk............................... 226
Driffield Bookshop (The), East Yorkshire 106
Eastern Traveller (The), Somerset.................. 220
Edwards in Hay-on-Wye (Francis), Powys 290
Ellis, Bookseller (Peter), London WC 178
Ely Books, Cambridgeshire 65
Empire Books, N Yorks.............................. 198
Esoteric Dreams Bookshop, Cumbria............. 78
Ewell Bookshop Ltd, Surrey........................ 232
Farahar & Dupre (Clive & Sophie), Wiltshire ... 251
Ferdinando (Steven), Somerset 220
Fifteenth Century Bookshop (The), E Sussex.... 104
Fireside Books, Buckinghamshire.................. 62
Ford Books (David), Herts 133
Fossgate Books, N Yorks............................ 198
Fosters Bookshop, London W 173
Freeman's Corner Shop, Norfolk................... 190
Frew Limited (Robert), London W................. 173
Furneaux Books (Lee), Devon...................... 89
Garfi Books, Powys................................... 293
Garwood & Voigt, Kent.............................. 140
Gibbard (A. & T.), E Sussex........................ 101
Glacier Books, Tayside 282
Glasheen-Books, Surrey 232
Glenbower Books, Co. Dublin 265
Gloucester Road Bookshop, London SW 168
Goodyer (Nicholas), London N..................... 159
Grahame Thornton, Bookseller, Dorset........... 93
Great Hall Bookshop, Buckinghamshire.......... 61
Hall's Bookshop, Kent................................ 141
Hancock (Peter), W Sussex.......................... 243
Handsworth Books, Essex............................ 112
Harrington (Adrian), London W.................... 173
Harrington Antiquarian Bookseller (Peter),
London SW... 169
Hay Cinema Bookshop Ltd., Powys............... 290
HCB Wholesale, Powys.............................. 290
Heartland Old Books, Devon........................ 89
Hereward Books, Cambridgeshire.................. 66
High Street Books, Devon 86
Hill (Peter), Hampshire 122
Hodgson (Books) (Richard J.), N Yorks 198
Hollett and Son (R.F.G.), Cumbria 80
Howes Bookshop, E Sussex......................... 102
Hurst (Jenny), Kent 138
Hylton Booksearch, Merseyside 185
Innes Books, Shropshire.............................. 214
Internet Bookshop UK Ltd., Glos.................. 113
Jackson (M.W.), Wiltshire........................... 254
Jade Mountain Bookshop, Hampshire............ 126
Jay Books, Lothian.................................... 278
Jiri Books, Co. Antrim 260
Joel Segal Books, Devon 86
Junk & Spread Eagle, London SE.................. 165
Kalligraphia, Isle of Wight.......................... 134
Karen Millward, Co. Cork........................... 263
Kay Books, London W............................... 174
Keeble Antiques, Somerset.......................... 219
Kenny's Bookshops and Art Galleries Ltd,
Co. Galway... 266
Kenya Books, E Sussex............................... 100
Kernaghans, Merseyside............................. 186

SPECIALITY INDEX

Killeen (John), N Yorks.............................. 194
Kingswood Books, Dorset 94
Knapton Bookbarn, N Yorks 198
Larkham Books (Patricia), Glos.................... 117
Leabeck Books, Oxfordshire 210
Lewis (J.T. & P.), Cornwall......................... 74
Liddle (Steve), Bristol 58
Lighthouse Books (The), Dorset 92
Little Bookshop (The), Gr Man.................... 119
Lloyd-Davies (Sue), Carmarthenshire 284
Lost Books, Northants................................ 201
Lucas (Richard), London NW...................... 162
Lymelight Books & Prints, Dorset................. 93
Maggs Brothers Limited, London W............... 174
Malvern Bookshop (The), Worcestershire 255
Marble Hill Books, Middlesex...................... 184
Marcet Books, London SE........................... 165
Marco Polo Travel & Adventure Books, Dorset 92
Marijana Dworski Books, via Hereford........... 290
Marlborough Rare Books Ltd., London W...... 174
Marshall Rare Books (Bruce), Glos 113
Martin Bookshop & Gallery (Richard), Hants... 123
McCarty, Bookseller (M.E.),
Dumfries & Galloway............................... 271
McCarty, Bookseller (M.E.), Western Isles....... 276
McNaughtan's Bookshop, Lothian 278
Miles Apart, Suffolk................................... 229
Modlock (Lilian), Dorset 93
Moreton Books, Devon............................... 87
Morgan (H.J.), Bedfordshire 54
Morten (Booksellers) (E.J.), Gr Man.............. 119
Mulyan (Don), Merseyside.......................... 186
Mundy (David), Buckinghamshire 61
Murphy (C.J.), Norfolk.............................. 190
Muse Bookshop (The), Gwynedd 287
My Back Pages, London SW 169
Naughton Booksellers, Co. Dublin 265
Neil Summersgill, Lancashire 143
Nicolas - Antiquarian Booksellers &
Art Dealers, London N............................. 159
Niner (Marcus), Isle of Wight 134
O'Flynn Books, N Yorks............................. 199
Old Hall Bookshop (The), Northants 200
Old Station Pottery & Bookshop (The), Norfolk 192
Oopalba Books, Cheshire............................ 71
Orangeberry Books, Oxfordshire 209
Oxfam Books and Music, Hants 126
Page (David), Lothian 278
Parker Books (Mike), Cambridgeshire 64
Parrott Books, Oxfordshire 211
Paton Books, Herts................................... 132
Peregrine Books (Leeds), W Yorkshire............ 249
Petersfield Bookshop (The), Hants................ 124
Pordes Books Ltd., (Henry), London WC........ 179
Portobello Books, London W 175
Portus Books, Hants 122
Prescott - The Bookseller (John), London Outer 184
Preston Book Company, Lancashire 145
Price (R.W.), Notts................................... 204
Prospect House Books, Co. Down................. 261
Quaritch Ltd., (Bernard), London W.............. 175
Quest Books, East Yorkshire 107
Quinto of Charing Cross Road, London WC ... 179
R. & A. Books, E Sussex............................ 102
Reading Lasses, Dumfries & Galloway 271

Richard Frost Books, Herts......................... 130
Richard Thornton Books, London N 160
Richmond Books, N Yorks.......................... 195
Robert Temple, London N.......................... 160
Roberts (Booksellers), (Ray), Staffordshire 224
Roberts Fine Books (Julian), Lincolnshire........ 153
Rochdale Book Company, Gr Man 120
Roland Books, Kent 139
Roundstone Books, Lancashire..................... 144
Rowan (P. & B.), Co. Antrim 260
Roz Hulse, Conwy 286
Russell (Charles), London SW...................... 170
Saintfield Antiques & Fine Books, Co. Down ... 261
Samovar Books, Co. Dublin........................ 264
Sax Books, Suffolk 229
Second Edition, Lothian............................. 278
Shacklock Books (David), Suffolk 227
Shapero Rare Books (Bernard J.), London W... 175
Simply Read Books, E Sussex 101
Singleton (Anthony), S Yorks 222
Smith (Clive), Essex 109
Smith Books, (Sally), Suffolk 227
Sokol Books Ltd., London W...................... 175
Sotheran Limited (Henry), London W............ 176
Spearman Books, E Sussex.......................... 104
Sterling Books, Somerset 221
Stothert Old Books, Cheshire....................... 69
Strathtay Antiquarian - Secondhand Books,
Tayside 282
Stroma Books, Borders 268
Sturford Books, Wiltshire 254
Sue Lowell Natural History Books, London W. 176
Sykes (Graham), W Yorkshire 249
Temperley (David), West Midlands................ 239
The Glass Key, W Yorkshire 247
Thorntons of Oxford Ltd., Oxfordshire........... 207
Till's Bookshop, Lothian 279
Tilston (Stephen F), London SE................... 166
Travel Bookshop (The), London W 176
Treadwell's Books, London WC 180
Treasure Island (The), Gr Man..................... 119
Treasure Trove Books, Leics........................ 148
Trinity Rare Books, Co. Leitrim 266
Uncle Phil's Books, West Midlands 240
Vokes Books Ltd., N Yorks 195
Wembdon Books, Somerset......................... 217
Westwood Books Ltd, Cumbria.................... 80
Wheen O'Books, Scottish Borders 269
Whitfield (Ken), Essex 111
Words Etcetera Bookshop, Dorset................. 93
Worlds End Bookshop, London SW 171
Yesterday's Books, Dorset 92
Yesterday's News, Conwy........................... 285
Yewtree Books, Cumbria............................ 79

- AFRICA

Ayre (Peter J.), Somerset 220
Bickford-Smith (G.), Surrey......................... 233
Bonham (J. & S.L.), London W 172
Bow Windows Book Shop, E Sussex.............. 103
Butcher (Pablo), Oxfordshire 207
Campbell Hewson Books (R.), Fife................ 271
Chalmers Hallam (E.), Hants....................... 125
Chandos Books, Devon.............................. 85
Coch-y-Bonddu Books, Powys 292

SPECIALITY INDEX

Dartmoor Bookshop (The), Devon 84
Deeside Books, Grampian............................ 273
Dolphin Books, Suffolk............................... 226
Eastern Traveller (The), Somerset................... 220
Edmund Pollinger Rare Books, London SW..... 167
Empire Books, N Yorks............................... 198
Farahar & Dupre (Clive & Sophie), Wiltshire ... 251
Fine Books at Ilkley, W Yorkshire 248
Glacier Books, Tayside 282
Grayling (David A.H.), Cumbria 79
Hall, (Anthony C.) Antiquarian
Bookseller, London Outer.......................... 184
Hosains Books, London NW 162
J.C. Deyong Books, London SW 169
Joel Segal Books, Devon 86
Keith Langford, London E 155
Kenya Books, E Sussex............................... 100
Lloyd-Davies (Sue), Carmarthenshire 284
Maghreb Bookshop (The), London WC.......... 178
Michael Graves-Johnston, London SW 169
Page (David), Lothian 278
Peter M Daly, Hants.................................. 127
Remington (Reg & Philip), Herts 133
Roz Hulse, Conwy 286
Samovar Books, Co. Dublin 264
Shapero Rare Books (Bernard J.), London W ... 175
Smith (Ray), Herts 130
Stokes Books, Co. Dublin............................ 265
Trinity Rare Books, Co. Leitrim 266
Vandeleur Antiquarian Books, Surrey............. 232
White (C.R.), London W 176
Woolcott Books, Dorset.............................. 92
Yesterday's Books, Dorset 92

- AMERICAS

Americanabooksuk, Cumbria........................ 77
Bonham (J. & S.L.), London W 172
Books on Spain, London Outer..................... 184
Burden Ltd., (Clive A.), Herts...................... 132
Butcher (Pablo), Oxfordshire 207
Chalmers Hallam (E.), Hants....................... 125
Dartmoor Bookshop (The), Devon 84
Empire Books, N Yorks.............................. 198
Farahar & Dupre (Clive & Sophie), Wiltshire ... 251
Fine Books at Ilkley, W Yorkshire 248
Glacier Books, Tayside 282
Grayling (David A.H.), Cumbria 79
Joel Segal Books, Devon 86
Leapman Ltd. (G. & R.), Herts.................... 130
Orssich (Paul), London SW 170
Pinnacle Books, Lothian............................. 278
Remington (Reg & Philip), Herts 133
Trinity Rare Books, Co. Leitrim 266
Vandeleur Antiquarian Books, Surrey............. 232

- ASIA

Abington Bookshop, Suffolk........................ 228
Alpha Books, London N 158
Bates & Hindmarch, W Yorkshire................. 249
Bickford-Smith (G.), Surrey......................... 233
Bonham (J. & S.L.), London W 172
Bow Windows Book Shop, E Sussex.............. 103
Cavendish Rare Books, London N 158
Chalmers Hallam (E.), Hants....................... 125
Coch-y-Bonddu Books, Powys 292

Craobh Rua Books, Co. Armagh................... 260
Dartmoor Bookshop (The), Devon 84
David Warnes Books, Herefordshire 129
Dolphin Books, Suffolk............................... 226
Eastern Traveller (The), Somerset.................. 220
Eastgate Bookshop, East Yorkshire 106
Empire Books, N Yorks.............................. 198
Farahar & Dupre (Clive & Sophie), Wiltshire ... 251
Fine Books Oriental Ltd., London WC........... 178
Glacier Books, Tayside 282
Grayling (David A.H.), Cumbria 79
Hall, (Anthony C.) Antiquarian Bookseller,
London Outer 184
Hunter and Krageloh, Derbyshire 83
J.C. Deyong Books, London SW 169
Jarvis Books, Derbyshire 83
Joel Segal Books, Devon 86
Lloyd-Davies (Sue), Carmarthenshire 284
Mannwaring (M.G.), Bristol 59
Moorside Books, Lancashire........................ 144
O'Reilly - Mountain Books (John), Derbyshire.. 83
Page (David), Lothian 278
Parrott (Jeremy), London E......................... 156
Peter M Daly, Hants.................................. 127
Pinnacle Books, Lothian............................. 278
Rayner (Hugh Ashley), Somerset 217
Remington (Reg & Philip), Herts 133
Smith (Clive), Essex 109
Traveller's Bookshelf (The), Somerset 217
Trinity Rare Books, Co. Leitrim 266
Vandeleur Antiquarian Books, Surrey............. 232
Verandah Books, Dorset 95
Woolcott Books, Dorset.............................. 92

- ASIA, SOUTH EAST

Butcher (Pablo), Oxfordshire 207
Chalmers Hallam (E.), Hants....................... 125
David Warnes Books, Herefordshire 129
Dolphin Books, Suffolk............................... 226
Farahar & Dupre (Clive & Sophie), Wiltshire ... 251
Fine Books at Ilkley, W Yorkshire 248
J.C. Deyong Books, London SW 169
Jarvis Books, Derbyshire 83
Joel Segal Books, Devon 86
Keith Langford, London E 155
Leeper (Romilly), London SW 169
Mandalay Bookshop, London SW 169
Michael Graves-Johnston, London SW 169
Pholiota Books, London WC....................... 179
Traveller's Bookshelf (The), Somerset 217
Trinity Rare Books, Co Leitrim 266

- AUSTRALASIA/AUSTRALIA

Bonham (J. & S.L.), London W 172
Burden Ltd., (Clive A.), Herts...................... 132
Catalyst Booksearch Services, Devon.............. 87
Cavendish Rare Books, London N 158
Chalmers Hallam (E.), Hants....................... 125
Dartmoor Bookshop (The), Devon 84
Empire Books, N Yorks.............................. 198
Farahar & Dupre (Clive & Sophie), Wiltshire ... 251
Joel Segal Books, Devon 86
Michael Graves-Johnston, London SW 169
Moore (Peter), Cambridgeshire..................... 64
Pinnacle Books, Lothian............................. 278

SPECIALITY INDEX

Remington (Reg & Philip), Herts 133
Trinity Rare Books, Co. Leitrim 266

- BALKANS

Bickford-Smith (G.) (formerly Snowden Smith Books), Surrey 233
Craobh Rua Books, Co. Armagh 260
Dolphin Books, Suffolk............................... 226
J.C. Deyong Books, London SW 169
Joppa Books Ltd., Surrey 231
Marijana Dworski Books, via Hereford........... 290
Traveller's Bookshelf (The), Somerset 217
Trinity Rare Books, Co. Leitrim 266

- BURMA

Chalmers Hallam (E.), Hants....................... 125
Dolphin Books, Suffolk............................... 226
Jackdaw Books, Norfolk 189
Mandalay Bookshop, London SW 169
Pinnacle Books, Lothian.............................. 278
Kayner (Hugh Ashley), Somerset 217
Trinity Rare Books, Co. Leitrim 266
Verandah Books, Dorset 95

- CARIBBEAN

Joel Segal Books, Devon 86
Pennymead Books, N Yorks......................... 194

- CHINA

Cavendish Rare Books, London N 158
Craobh Rua Books, Co. Armagh................... 260
Fine Books at Ilkley, W Yorkshire 248
Joel Segal Books, Devon 86
Lloyd-Davies (Sue), Carmarthenshire 284
Mandalay Bookshop, London SW 169
Traveller's Bookshelf (The), Somerset 217
Trinity Rare Books, Co. Leitrim 266

- EARLY

Altea Antique Maps & Books, London W....... 172
Coch-y-Bonddu Books, Powys 292
Joel Segal Books, Devon 86
Trinity Rare Books, Co. Leitrim 266

- EUROPE

Bonham (J. & S.L.), London W 172
Books on Spain, London Outer..................... 184
Campbell (Fiona), London SE 164
Dartmoor Bookshop (The), Devon 84
de Visser Books, Cambridgeshire................... 63
Dolphin Books, Suffolk.................. 226
Doolin Dinghy Books, Co. Clare 262
Empire Books, N Yorks.............................. 198
Fifteenth Century Bookshop (The), E Sussex 104
Fine Books at Ilkley, W Yorkshire 248
Glacier Books, Tayside 282
Hall, (Anthony C.) Antiquarian Bookseller, London Outer 184
Jarvis Books, Derbyshire 83
Keith Langford, London E 155
McGee (Terence J.), London Outer 181
Naughton Booksellers, Co. Dublin 265
Orssich (Paul), London SW......................... 170
Peter M Daly, Hants.................................. 127
Samovar Books, Co. Dublin......................... 264

Spelman (Ken), N Yorks............................. 199
Sturford Books, Wiltshire 254
Trinity Rare Books, Co. Leitrim 266
Undercover Books, Lincolnshire 154
Vandeleur Antiquarian Books, Surrey............. 232
York (Graham), Devon............................... 86

- FAR EAST

Cavendish Rare Books, London N 158
Fine Books at Ilkley, W Yorkshire 248
Joel Segal Books, Devon 86
Lloyd-Davies (Sue), Carmarthenshire 284
Transformer, Dumfries & Galloway................ 271
Traveller's Bookshelf (The), Somerset 217
Trinity Rare Books, Co. Leitrim 266

- GREECE

Frew Limited (Robert), London W................. 173
Hellenic Bookservices, London NW............... 162
Joel Segal Books, Devon 86
Seydi Rare Books (Sevin), London NW 162
Trinity Rare Books, Co. Leitrim 266

- INDIA

BookShop, The, Dumfries & Galloway........... 270
Butcher (Pablo), Oxfordshire 207
Catalyst Booksearch Services, Devon.............. 87
Chalmers Hallam (E.), Hants....................... 125
Fine Books at Ilkley, W Yorkshire 248
Glacier Books, Tayside 282
Joel Segal Books, Devon 86
Keith Langford, London E 155
Mandalay Bookshop, London SW 169
N1 Books, E Sussex................................... 105
Naughton Booksellers, Co. Dublin 265
Rayner (Hugh Ashley), Somerset 217
Trinity Rare Books, Co. Leitrim 266
Verandah Books, Dorset 95

- ISLAMIC WORLD

Al Saqi Books, London W........................... 172
Bickford-Smith (G.), Surrey......................... 233
Butcher (Pablo), Oxfordshire 207
Clarke Books (David), Somerset 219
David Warnes Books, Herefordshire 129
J.C. Deyong Books, London SW 169
Joppa Books Ltd., Surrey 231
Kingswood Books, Dorset 94
Traveller's Bookshelf (The), Somerset 217
Trinity Rare Books, Co. Leitrim 266
Verandah Books, Dorset 95

- JAPAN

Fine Books at Ilkley, W Yorkshire 248
Joel Segal Books, Devon 86
Lloyd-Davies (Sue), Carmarthenshire 284
Murphy (C.J.), Norfolk............................... 190
Trinity Rare Books, Co. Leitrim 266

- MEXICO

Fine Books at Ilkley, W Yorkshire 248
Hodgson (Judith), London W 174
Orssich (Paul), London SW......................... 170
Sturford Books, Wiltshire 254
Trinity Rare Books, Co. Leitrim 266

SPECIALITY INDEX

- MIDDLE EAST

Al Saqi Books, London W........................... 172
Bickford-Smith (G.), Surrey......................... 233
Bonham (J. & S.L.), London W 172
Bookshop at the Plain, Lincolnshire............... 151
Chalmers Hallam (E.), Hants....................... 125
Clarke Books (David), Somerset 219
Craobh Rua Books, Co. Armagh................... 260
Dartmoor Bookshop (The), Devon................. 84
David Warnes Books, Herefordshire 129
Eastern Traveller (The), Somerset.................. 220
Empire Books, North Yorkshire 198
Farahar & Dupre (Clive & Sophie), Wiltshire ... 251
Fine Books at Ilkley, W Yorkshire 248
Fine Books Oriental Ltd., London WC............ 178
Hall, (Anthony C.) Antiquarian Bookseller,
London Outer...................................... 184
J.C. Deyong Books, London SW................... 169
Joel Segal Books, Devon 86
Joppa Books Ltd., Surrey 231
Kingswood Books, Dorset 94
Maghreb Bookshop (The), London WC.......... 178
Michael Graves-Johnston, London SW........... 169
Moorside Books, Lancashire........................ 144
P. and P. Books, Worcestershire 256
Page (David), Lothian 278
Pholiota Books, London WC....................... 179
Quest Books, East Yorkshire 107
Remington (Reg & Philip), Herts 133
Traveller's Bookshelf (The), Somerset 217
Trinity Rare Books, Co. Leitrim 266
Trotter Books (John), London N 160
Woolcott Books, Dorset............................. 92
Worlds End Bookshop, London SW.............. 171

- POLAR

Bluntisham Books, Cambridgeshire................ 63
Bonham (J. & S.L.), London W 172
Cavendish Rare Books, London N 158
Chalmers Hallam (E.), Hants....................... 125
Dartmoor Bookshop (The), Devon................. 84
David Warnes Books, Herefordshire 129
Deeside Books, Grampian........................... 273
Empire Books, North Yorkshire 198
Farahar & Dupre (Clive & Sophie), Wiltshire ... 251
Fifteenth Century Bookshop (The), E Sussex.... 104
Fine Books at Ilkley, W Yorkshire 248
Glacier Books, Tayside 282
Holmes Books (Harry), East Yorkshire........... 107
Hunter and Krageloh, Derbyshire 83
Internet Bookshop UK Ltd., Glos.................. 113
Jarvis Books, Derbyshire 83
Joel Segal Books, Devon 86
Miles Apart, Suffolk.................................. 229
O'Reilly - Mountain Books (John), Derbyshire.. 83
Page (David), Lothian 278
Pinnacle Books, Lothian............................. 278
Remington (Reg & Philip), Herts 133
Roz Hulse, Conwy 286
Vandeleur Antiquarian Books, Surrey............. 232
Walcot (Patrick), West Midlands................... 241
White (C.R.), London W............................ 176

- REGIONAL

Bookshop at the Plain, Lincolnshire............... 151

Fifteenth Century Bookshop (The), E Sussex.... 104
Joel Segal Books, Devon 86
Samovar Books, Co. Dublin........................ 264

- THAILAND

Apocalypse, Surrey 233
Mandalay Bookshop, London SW 169
Trinity Rare Books, Co. Leitrim 266

TRIALS

Bolland Books, Bedfordshire........................ 53
Clifford Elmer Books Ltd., Cheshire 68
Loretta Lay Books, London NW................... 162

TRIBAL

Bickford-Smith (G.) ,Surrey......................... 233
Bracton Books, Cambridgeshire.................... 63
David Warnes Books, Herefordshire 129
J.C. Deyong Books, London SW................... 169
Joel Segal Books, Devon 86
Kenya Books, E Sussex.............................. 100
Michael Graves-Johnston, London SW........... 169
Popeley (Frank T.), Cambridgeshire............... 67
Traveller's Bookshelf (The), Somerset 217
Yesterday's Books, Dorset 92

TROPICAL FISH

Joel Segal Books, Devon 86

TROTSKYISM

Left on The Shelf, Cumbria......................... 79
Northern Herald Books, W Yorkshire............ 246
Reading Lasses, Dumfries & Galloway 271
Red Star Books, Herts............................... 130

TYPOGRAPHY

Andron (G.W.), London N 158
Ballantyne-Way (Roger), Suffolk 229
Batterham (David), London W..................... 172
Bettridge (Gordon), Fife............................. 272
Blackwell's Rare Books, Oxfordshire.............. 209
BOOKS4U, Flintshire................................ 286
Brinded (Scott), Kent 139
Canterbury Bookshop (The), Kent 136
Collinge & Clark, London WC..................... 177
Cox Old & Rare Books (Claude), Suffolk........ 228
English (Toby), Oxfordshire........................ 211
Forest Books, Notts.................................. 205
Fox Books (J. & J.), Kent........................... 140
Hanborough Books, Oxfordshire................... 210
Joel Segal Books, Devon 86
Katnap Arts, Norfolk..................... 191
Keel Row Bookshop, Tyne and Wear 236
Mills Rare Books (Adam), Cambridgeshire 64
Naughton Booksellers, Co. Dublin 265
Robin Doughty - Fine Books, West Midlands... 239
Solitaire Books, Somerset........................... 217
Taylor Rare Books (Michael), Norfolk 187
Wakeman Books (Frances), Notts 205

U-BOATS

Baldwin (M. & M.), Worcestershire 255
Burroughs (Andrew), Lincolnshire 153
Fifteenth Century Bookshop (The), E Sussex.... 104
Green Ltd. (G.L.), Herts 132

SPECIALITY INDEX

Marine & Cannon Books, Cheshire 71
Marine and Cannon Books, Cheshire 69
Meekins Books (Paul), Warwickshire.............. 238

U.F.O.S

Alpha Books, London N 158
Bookbarrow, Cambridgeshire....................... 63
Cavern Books, Cheshire 70
Dawlish Books, Devon 86
Facet Books, Dorset.................................. 91
Gildas Books, Cheshire 68
Greensleeves, Oxfordshire 207
Inner Bookshop (The), Oxfordshire................ 210
Joel Segal Books, Devon 86
Occultique, Northants................................ 200
Parker Books (Mike), Cambridgeshire 64
SETI Books, Staffordshire........................... 225
Star Lord Books, Gr Man 119
Wizard Books, Cambridgeshire..................... 67

U.S. PRESIDENTS

Dolphin Books, Suffolk............................... 226
Hab Books, London W 173
Shakeshaft (Dr. B.), Cheshire....................... 71

UMBRELLAS/PARASOLS

Adrem Books, Herts 131
Judith Mansfield, W Yorkshire..................... 250

UNEXPLAINED, THE

Dawlish Books, Devon 86
Esoteric Dreams Bookshop, Cumbria 78
Fantastic Literature, Essex 111
Fifteenth Century Bookshop (The), E Sussex 104
Gildas Books, Cheshire 68
Inner Bookshop (The), Oxfordshire................ 210
Joel Segal Books, Devon 86
Occultique, Northants................................ 200
Old Celtic Bookshop (The), Devon 88
Parker Books (Mike), Cambridgeshire 64
SETI Books, Staffordshire........................... 225
Till's Bookshop, Lothian 279

UNIVERSITY HISTORIES

Bernard Dixon and Kath Adams, Middlesex 183
G. C. Books Ltd., Dumfries & Galloway......... 271

UNIVERSITY PRESS

Adrem Books, Herts 131
Barcombe Services, Essex........................... 108
Book Annex (The), Essex 109
G. C. Books Ltd., Dumfries & Galloway......... 271
Joel Segal Books, Devon 86
Stalagluft Books, Tyne and Wear.................. 236

UNIVERSITY TEXTS

Barcombe Services, Essex........................... 108
Book Annex (The), Essex 109
Cornucopia Books, Lincolnshire 153
Downie Fine Books Ltd., (Robert), Shropshire.. 215
G. C. Books Ltd., Dumfries & Galloway......... 271
Hurst (Jenny), Kent 138
Murphy (C.J.), Norfolk.............................. 190
Pomes Penyeach, Staffordshire 224
Scrivener's Books & Bookbinding, Derbyshire... 82

Stalagluft Books, Tyne and Wear.................. 236
Warrington Book Loft (The), Cheshire 72

URBAN HISTORY

Cornucopia Books, Lincolnshire 153
Inch's Books, Kent 137
Joel Segal Books, Devon 86
Northern Herald Books, W Yorkshire 246
Reading Lasses, Dumfries & Galloway 271
Stern Antiquarian Bookseller (Jeffrey), North
Yorkshire.. 199
Symes Books (Naomi), Cheshire 72

UTOPIAS

Seydi Rare Books (Sevin), London NW 162
Star Lord Books, Gr Man 119
Susanne Schulz-Falster Rare Books, London N. 160

VATICAN AND PAPAL HISTORY, THE

Adrem Books, Herts 131
Dolphin Books, Suffolk............................... 226
R. & A. Books, E Sussex 102
Samovar Books, Co. Dublin 264
Scrivener's Books & Bookbinding, Derbyshire... 82
Taylor & Son (Peter), Herts......................... 133
Tuft (Patrick), London Outer....................... 182

VEGETARIANISM

Annie's Books, S Yorks 222
Books Only, Suffolk................................... 227
Gardener & Cook, London SW.................... 168
Inner Bookshop (The), Oxfordshire................ 210
Occultique, Northants................................ 200

VENTRILOQUISM

DaSilva Puppet Books, Dorset 93

VETERINARY

Alba Books, Grampian 274
Grahame Thornton, Bookseller, Dorset........... 93
Jane Jones Books, Grampian 272
Parkinsons Books, Merseyside...................... 186
Phenotype Books, Cumbria 80
R. & A. Books, E Sussex............................ 102
Westons, Herts 133

VICTORIAN MULTI-DECKERS

Beaton (Richard), E Sussex 103
Burmester (James), Bristol.......................... 59
Enigma Books, Norfolk 190
Valentine Rare Books, London W.................. 176

VICTORIANA

Art Reference Books, Hants 125
Beaton (Richard), E Sussex 103
Bell (Peter), Lothian.................................. 276
Book Shelf (The), Devon............................ 87
Books at Star Dot Star, West Midlands 241
Bosco Books, Cornwall............................... 73
Castleton (Pat), Kent................................. 138
Cornucopia Books, Lincolnshire 153
de Beaumont (Robin), London SW 167
Don Kelly Books, London W....................... 172
Embleton (Paul), Essex 111
Fifteenth Century Bookshop (The), E Sussex 104

SPECIALITY INDEX

Goldman (Paul), Dorset 94
Joel Segal Books, Devon 86
Kenny's Bookshops and Art Galleries Ltd,
Co. Galway 266
N1 Books, E Sussex 105
R. & A. Books, E Sussex............................. 102
St Swithin's Illustrated & Children's Books, London
W.. 175
Shacklock Books (David), Suffolk 227
Symes Books (Naomi), Cheshire 72
Trinity Rare Books, Co. Leitrim 266
Yesterday's News, Conwy........................... 285

VINTAGE CARS

Baldwin (M. & M.), Worcestershire 255
Camilla's Bookshop, E Sussex 101
Collectors Carbooks, Northants..................... 200
Cornucopia Books, Lincolnshire 153
Cox (Geoff), Devon 90
Falconwood Transport & Military Bookshop,
London Outer 184
Fifteenth Century Bookshop (The), E Sussex 104
Henry Wilson Books, Cheshire 69
Joel Segal Books, Devon 86
Kenneth Ball, E Sussex 101
Knowles (John), Norfolk 188
Peake (Robin), Lincolnshire......................... 153
Pooks Motor Books, Leics........................... 148
R. & A. Books, E Sussex............................. 102
Roadmaster Books, Kent............................. 137
Roberts (Booksellers), (Ray), Staffordshire 224
Simon Lewis Transport Books, Glos 115
Stour Bookshop, Dorset............................. 95
Stroh (M.A.), London E 155
Vintage Motorshop, W Yorkshire 246
Weiner (Graham), London N 160

VINTAGE PAPERBACKS

Black Cat Bookshop, Leics 147
Castleton (Pat), Kent................................. 138
Cowley, Bookdealer (K.W.), Somerset 218
Dancing Goat Bookshop (The), Norfolk 188
Eggeling Books (John), W Yorkshire............... 250
Esoteric Dreams Bookshop, Cumbria 78
Fifteenth Century Bookshop (The), E Sussex 104
Gildas Books, Cheshire 68
Heckmondwike Book Shop, W Yorkshire........ 249
J. & J. Books, Lincolnshire 151
Joel Segal Books, Devon 86
Katnap Arts, Norfolk................................. 191
Morris Secondhand & Antiquarian
Books (Chris), Oxfordshire......................... 210
Murphy (C.J.), Norfolk............................... 190
Old Station Pottery & Bookshop (The), Norfolk 192
Onepoundpaperbacks, North Yorkshire 193
Readers World, West Midlands 239
Roscrea Bookshop, Co. Tipperary.................. 267
Ruebotham (Kirk), Cheshire......................... 71
Scrivener's Books & Bookbinding, Derbyshire... 82
Trevorrow (Edwin), Herts 130
Yorkshire Relics, W Yorkshire 247
Zardoz Books, Wiltshire............................. 254

VIROLOGY

Bernard Dixon and Kath Adams, Middlesex 183

Parkinsons Books, Merseyside....................... 186
R M Books, Herts..................................... 132
Westons, Herts 133

VISUAL

Joel Segal Books, Devon 86

VITICULTURE

Joel Segal Books, Devon 86
Keel Row Bookshop, Tyne and Wear 236
Lucas (Richard), London NW....................... 162
Roberts Wine Books (John), Bristol................ 59
Thorne (John), Essex................................. 109

VOYAGES & DISCOVERY

Adrem Books, Herts 131
Afar Books International, West Midlands........ 239
Allsworth Rare Books Ltd., London SW.......... 167
Altea Antique Maps & Books, London W....... 172
Americanabooksuk, Cumbria........................ 77
Avedikian Rare Books, Somerset 217
Barn Books, Buckinghamshire....................... 61
Books on Spain, London Outer..................... 184
BookShop, The, Dumfries & Galloway........... 270
Bookworm, Lothian................................... 277
Brockwells Booksellers, Lincolnshire 150
Campbell Hewson Books (R.), Fife................. 271
Castleton (Pat), Kent................................. 138
Cornucopia Books, Lincolnshire 153
Cox (Geoff), Devon 90
Dartmoor Bookshop (The), Devon 84
Dolphin Books, Suffolk............................... 226
Eastern Traveller (The), Somerset.................. 220
Edwards (London) Limited (Francis),
London WC 177
Edwards in Hay-on-Wye (Francis), Powys 290
Ely Books, Cambridgeshire 65
Farahar & Dupre (Clive & Sophie), Wiltshire ... 251
Fifteenth Century Bookshop (The), E Sussex 104
Glacier Books, Tayside 282
Harrington (Adrian), London W.................... 173
Harrington Antiquarian Bookseller (Peter),
London SW... 169
Holmes Books (Harry), East Yorkshire............ 107
Hosains Books, London NW........................ 162
Joel Segal Books, Devon 86
Lawson & Company (E.M.), Oxfordshire 208
Lewcock (John), Cambridgeshire................... 66
Mandalay Bookshop, London SW 169
Marine & Cannon Books, Cheshire 71
Marine and Cannon Books, Cheshire 69
McEwan Fine Books, Grampian.................... 273
N1 Books, E Sussex 105
Nicholson of Chester (Richard), Cheshire 68
O'Reilly - Mountain Books (John), Derbyshire.. 83
Page (David), Lothian 278
Preston Book Company, Lancashire 145
Prior (Michael), Lincolnshire 153
Quinto of Charing Cross Road, London WC ... 179
Quinto of Great Russell Street, London WC 179
R. & A. Books, E Sussex............................. 102
Remington (Reg & Philip), Herts 133
Richard Thornton Books, London N 160
Rowan (P. & B.), Co. Antrim 260
Roz Hulse, Conwy 286

SPECIALITY INDEX

St Mary's Books & Prints, Lincolnshire 154
St Swithin's Illustrated & Children's Books,
London W 175
Shapero Rare Books (Bernard J.), London W ... 175
Smith (Clive), Essex 109
Vandeleur Antiquarian Books, Surrey............. 232
Wheen O'Books, Scottish Borders 269

WAR - GENERAL

Adrem Books, Herts 131
Albion Books, West Midlands....................... 239
Andron (G.W.), London N 158
Anthony Vickers Books, North Yorkshire 196
Armstrong's Books & Collectables, Leics......... 147
Aurora Books Ltd, Lothian........................... 276
Barbican Bookshop, North Yorkshire............. 198
Barn Books, Buckinghamshire....................... 61
Barnes (Peter), Wiltshire 253
Bath Old Books, Somerset 216
Beware of the Leopard, Bristol...................... 58
Bookcase, Cumbria..................... 78
Books at Star Dot Star, West Midlands 241
books2books, Devon 88
BookShop, The, Dumfries & Galloway 270
Bookworm, Lothian................................... 277
Bookworm (The), Lothian 277
Bookworms, Norfolk.................................. 187
Bowland Bookfinders, Lancashire.................. 143
Brad Books, Essex..................................... 111
Broadhurst of Southport Ltd., Merseyside 186
Browsers Bookshop, Cornwall....................... 73
Bufo Books, Hants 125
Caliver Books, Essex 110
Cavern Books, Cheshire 70
Chelifer Books, Cumbria 81
Chris Phillips, Wiltshire.............................. 251
Cofion Books, Pembrokeshire 288
Criterion Books, London Outer 182
Dally Books & Collectables, Powys................ 292
Dartmoor Bookshop (The), Devon 84
Eastcote Bookshop (The), London Outer......... 181
Embleton (Paul), Essex 111
Esoteric Dreams Bookshop, Cumbria 78
Ewell Bookshop Ltd, Surrey 232
Fackley Services, Notts 205
Fifteenth Century Bookshop (The), E Sussex 104
G. C. Books Ltd., Dumfries & Galloway......... 271
Gallimaufry Books, Herts 132
Good for Books, Lincolnshire 151
Grahame Thornton, Bookseller, Dorset........... 93
Hambleton Books, North Yorkshire 197
Handsworth Books, Essex............................ 112
Harlequin Books, Bristol 59
Harrington Antiquarian Bookseller (Peter),
London SW.. 169
Harris (George J.), Co. Derry 260
Hay Cinema Bookshop Ltd., Powys............... 290
HCB Wholesale, Powys............................... 290
Hurst (Jenny), Kent 138
Jackdaw Books, Norfolk 189
Jackson (M.W.), Wiltshire........................... 254
Jade Mountain Bookshop, Hants 126
Janus Books, West Midlands 240
Joel Segal Books, Devon 86
Just Books, Cornwall 76

Lewis (J.T. & P.), Cornwall 74
Lost Books, Northants................................ 201
Marine & Cannon Books, Cheshire 71
Marine and Cannon Books, Cheshire 69
McCrone (Audrey), Isle of Arran 275
Meekins Books (Paul), Warwickshire.............. 238
MilitaryHistoryBooks.com, Kent................... 138
Murphy (C.J.), Norfolk............................... 190
N1 Books, E Sussex.................................... 105
Nelson (Elizabeth), Suffolk........................... 227
Old Station Pottery & Bookshop (The), Norfolk 192
Oxfam Books and Music, Hants 126
Palladour Books, Hants 126
Parker Books (Mike), Cambridgeshire 64
Poetry Bookshop (The), Powys..................... 291
Priestpopple Books, Northumberland 202
Prior (Michael), Lincolnshire 153
Quinto of Charing Cross Road, London WC ... 179
Quinto of Great Russell Street, London WC ... 179
R. & A. Books, E Sussex............................. 102
Richard Thornton Books, London N 160
Rods Books, Devon 88
Roland Books, Kent 139
Scrivener's Books & Bookbinding, Derbyshire... 82
Smith Books, (Sally), Suffolk 227
Spurrier (Nick), Kent 138
Stevens (Joan), Cambridgeshire..................... 65
Stothert Old Books, Cheshire 69
The Sanctuary Bookshop, Dorset 94
Thin Read Line, Merseyside 185
Tiffin (Tony and Gill), Durham 97
Treasure Trove Books, Leicestershire.............. 148
Uncle Phil's Books, West Midlands 240
Wadard Books, Kent 138
War & Peace Books, Hants.......................... 122
Ward (R.F. & C.), Norfolk 188
Wheen O'Books, Scottish Borders 269
Wiend Books, Lancashire 144
Williams (Bookdealer), (Richard), N Lincs....... 154
World War Books, Kent 141
Yeoman Books, Lothian 279
Yesterday's News, Conwy 285
Zardoz Books, Wiltshire.............................. 254

- AMERICAN CIVIL

Adrem Books, Herts 131
Americanabooksuk, Cumbria........................ 77
Bookworm, Lothian................................... 277
Broadhurst of Southport Ltd., Merseyside 186
Caliver Books, Essex 110
Chelifer Books, Cumbria 81
Farnborough Gallery, Hants......................... 122
Helion & Company, West Midlands 240
Joel Segal Books, Devon 86
Marble Hill Books, Middlesex....................... 184
Meekins Books (Paul), Warwickshire.............. 238
MilitaryHistoryBooks.com, Kent................... 138
Rods Books, Devon 88
Shakeshaft (Dr. B.), Cheshire 71
Trinity Rare Books, Co. Leitrim 266
Wadard Books, Kent 138
Wiend Books, Lancashire 144

- AUSTRALIAN

Meekins Books (Paul), Warwickshire.............. 238

SPECIALITY INDEX

MilitaryHistoryBooks.com, Kent.................... 138
World War II Books, Surrey 235

- BOER, THE

Boer War Books, North Yorkshire 198
Bookworm, Lothian.................................. 277
Chalmers Hallam (E.), Hants....................... 125
Chelifer Books, Cumbria 81
Dolphin Books, Suffolk............................... 226
Empire Books, North Yorkshire 198
Fifteenth Century Bookshop (The), E Sussex 104
Helion & Company, West Midlands 240
Kenya Books, E Sussex............................... 100
Marine & Cannon Books, Cheshire 71
Marine and Cannon Books, Cheshire 69
Meekins Books (Paul), Warwickshire.............. 238
MilitaryHistoryBooks.com, Kent.................... 138
N1 Books, E Sussex.................................. 105
Preston Book Company, Lancashire 145
Thin Read Line, Merseyside 185
Wheen O'Books, Scottish Borders 269

- BUSH WARS

Al Saqi Books, London W........................... 172
MilitaryHistoryBooks.com, Kent.................... 138

- CIVIL, & ENGLISH CIVIL WARS

Bookworm, Lothian................................... 277
Caliver Books, Essex 110
Chelifer Books, Cumbria 81
Clifford Elmer Books Ltd., Cheshire 68
Dolphin Books, Suffolk............................... 226
Helion & Company, West Midlands 240
Joel Segal Books, Devon 86
John Underwood Antiquarian Books, Norfolk .. 190
Meekins Books (Paul), Warwickshire.............. 238
MilitaryHistoryBooks.com, Kent.................... 138
N1 Books, E Sussex.................................. 105
Roger Collicott Books, Cornwall 75
Shakeshaft (Dr. B.), Cheshire....................... 71
Spenceley Books (David), W Yorkshire........... 249
Taylor & Son (Peter), Herts......................... 133
Thomas (Books) (Leona), Cheshire 71
Trinity Rare Books, Co. Leitrim 266
Wiend Books, Lancashire 144

- MEXICAN WAR

MilitaryHistoryBooks.com, Kent.................... 138

- NAPOLEONIC

Adrem Books, Herts 131
Armchair Books, Lothian 276
Books on Spain, London Outer..................... 184
Bookworm, Lothian................................... 277
Caliver Books, Essex 110
Chelifer Books, Cumbria 81
Donovan Military Books (Tom), E Sussex 99
Falconwood Transport & Military Bookshop,
London Outer 184
Green Ltd. (G.L.), Herts 132
Helion & Company, West Midlands 240
Joel Segal Books, Devon 86
Lost Books, Northants................................ 201
Marine & Cannon Books, Cheshire 71
Marine and Cannon Books, Cheshire 69

Meekins Books (Paul), Warwickshire.............. 238
Miles Apart, Suffolk.................................. 229
MilitaryHistoryBooks.com, Kent.................... 138
N1 Books, E Sussex.................................. 105
Orssich (Paul), London SW......................... 170
Prior (Michael), Lincolnshire 153
R. & A. Books, E Sussex............................ 102
Thin Read Line, Merseyside 185
Vickers (Anthony), North Yorkshire 196
Wadard Books, Kent 138

- REVOLUTIONARY

Bookworm, Lothian................................... 277
Caliver Books, Essex 110
Chelifer Books, Cumbria 81
Left on The Shelf, Cumbria......................... 79
MilitaryHistoryBooks.com, Kent.................... 138

- SPANISH CIVIL WAR

Bass (Ben), Wiltshire 251
Books on Spain, London Outer..................... 184
Caliver Books, Essex 110
Chelifer Books, Cumbria 81
Helion & Company, West Midlands 240
Left on The Shelf, Cumbria......................... 79
Little Stour Books, Kent 137
Meekins Books (Paul), Warwickshire.............. 238
MilitaryHistoryBooks.com, Kent.................... 138
Orssich (Paul), London SW......................... 170
Red Star Books, Herts................................ 130
York (Graham), Devon............................... 86

- VIETNAM

Anglo-American Rare Books, Surrey.............. 233
Caliver Books, Essex 110
Chelifer Books, Cumbria 81
Falconwood Transport & Military Bookshop,
London Outer 184
Helion & Company, West Midlands 240
Meekins Books (Paul), Warwickshire.............. 238
MilitaryHistoryBooks.com, Kent.................... 138

- WORLD WAR I

Aardvark Books, Wiltshire 254
Albion Books, West Midlands....................... 239
Anglo-American Rare Books, Surrey.............. 233
Armchair Auctions, Hants 121
Arthur Hook, Bristol.................................. 58
Avedikian Rare Books, Somerset 217
Aviabooks, Glos 114
Ballantyne-Way (Roger), Suffolk 229
Barbican Bookshop, North Yorkshire............. 198
Bookworm, Lothian................................... 277
Browsers Bookshop, Cornwall....................... 73
Burroughs (Andrew), Lincolnshire 153
Caliver Books, Essex 110
Chelifer Books, Cumbria 81
Cocks (Brian), Cambridgeshire 67
Cornucopia Books, Lincolnshire 153
Cox (Geoff), Devon 90
Dally Books & Collectables, Powys................ 292
Delph Books, Gr Man................................ 120
Dolphin Books, Suffolk............................... 226
Dormouse Bookshop (The), Norfolk............... 190
Ellis, Bookseller (Peter), London WC 178

SPECIALITY INDEX

Ewell Bookshop Ltd, Surrey 232
Falconwood Transport & Military Bookshop,
London Outer 184
Farnborough Gallery, Hants......................... 122
Fifteenth Century Bookshop (The), E Sussex 104
Garfi Books, Powys 293
Gaullifmaufiy Books, Herts......................... 132
Good for Books, Lincolnshire 151
Green Ltd. (G.L.), Herts 132
Helion & Company, West Midlands 240
Heppa (Christopher), Essex 108
Joel Segal Books, Devon 86
Joppa Books Ltd., Surrey 231
Lost Books, Northants................................ 201
Marine & Cannon Books, Cheshire 71
Marine and Cannon Books, Cheshire 69
Meekins Books (Paul), Warwickshire............... 238
MilitaryHistoryBooks.com, Kent.................... 138
Ming Books, Dumfries & Galloway 271
My Back Pages, London SW 169
N1 Books, E Sussex 105
Palladour Books, Hants 126
Peter M Daly, Hants 127
Prior (Michael), Lincolnshire 153
R. & A. Books, E Sussex............................. 102
Robert Humm & Co, Lincolnshire 154
Rods Books, Devon 88
SETI Books, Staffordshire........................... 225
Smith Books (Keith), Herefordshire 128
Symes Books (Naomi), Cheshire 72
Thin Read Line, Merseyside 185
Tiffin (Tony and Gill), Durham 97
Tilston (Stephen E.), London SE.................... 166
Trinity Rare Books, Co. Leitrim 266
Tyger Press, London N 160
Updike Rare Books (John), Lothian 279
Wadard Books, Kent 138
War & Peace Books, Hants.......................... 122
Wheen O'Books, Scottish Borders 269
Wiend Books, Lancashire 144
Wizard Books, Cambridgeshire...................... 67

- WORLD WAR II

Aardvark Books, Wiltshire 254
Armchair Auctions, Hants 121
Arthur Hook, Bristol.................................. 58
Aviabooks, Glos 114
Baldwin (M. & M.), Worcestershire 255
Barbican Bookshop, North Yorkshire.............. 198
Book For All Reasons (A.), Suffolk 229
Bookworm, Lothian................................... 277
Bosorne Books, Cornwall 75
Browsers Bookshop, Cornwall....................... 73
Burroughs (Andrew), Lincolnshire 153
Caliver Books, Essex 110
Chaucer Bookshop, Kent............................. 136
Chelifer Books, Cumbria 81
Cocks (Brian), Cambridgeshire 67
Cornucopia Books, Lincolnshire 153
Dally Books & Collectables, Powys................. 292
Dolphin Books, Suffolk............................... 226
Donovan Military Books (Tom), E Sussex 99
Dormouse Bookshop (The), Norfolk 190
Ellis, Bookseller (Peter), London WC 178
English (Toby), Oxfordshire.......................... 211

Ewell Bookshop Ltd, Surrey 232
Falconwood Transport & Military Bookshop,
London Outer 184
Farnborough Gallery, Hants......................... 122
Fifteenth Century Bookshop (The), E Sussex 104
Foster Bookshop (Paul), London SW 168
Garfi Books, Powys 293
Gaullifmaufry Books, Herts......................... 132
Good for Books, Lincolnshire 151
Green Ltd. (G.L.), Herts 132
Hab Books, London W............................... 173
Helion & Company, West Midlands 240
Joel Segal Books, Devon 86
Lost Books, Northants................................ 201
Mandalay Bookshop, London SW 169
Marine & Cannon Books, Cheshire 71
Marine and Cannon Books, Cheshire 69
Meekins Books (Paul), Warwickshire............... 238
MilitaryHistoryBooks.com, Kent.................... 138
Ming Books, Dumfries & Galloway 271
My Back Pages, London SW 169
Palladour Books, Hants 126
Prior (Michael), Lincolnshire 153
R. & A. Books, E Sussex............................. 102
Richard Thornton Books, London N 160
Robert Humm & Co, Lincolnshire 154
Rods Books, Devon 88
Roland Books, Kent 139
Samovar Books, Co. Dublin 264
Stalagluft Books, Tyne and Wear 236
Symes Books (Naomi), Cheshire 72
Thin Read Line, Merseyside 185
Tilston (Stephen E.), London SE.................... 166
Trinity Rare Books, Co. Leitrim 266
Tyger Press, London N 160
Uncle Phil's Books, West Midlands 240
Updike Rare Books (John), Lothian 279
Wadard Books, Kent 138
War & Peace Books, Hants.......................... 122
Wembdon Books, Somerset.......................... 217
Wheen O'Books, Scottish Borders 269
Wiend Books, Lancashire 144
Wizard Books, Cambridgeshire..................... 67
World War II Books, Surrey 235

- WWII HOME FRONT UK (1939-45)

Baldwin (M. & M.), Worcestershire 255
Browsers Bookshop, Cornwall....................... 73
Burroughs (Andrew), Lincolnshire 153
Chelifer Books, Cumbria 81
Falconwood Transport & Military Bookshop,
London Outer 184
Farnborough Gallery, Hants......................... 122
Fifteenth Century Bookshop (The), E Sussex 104
Joel Segal Books, Devon 86
Marchpane, London WC............................. 178
Marine & Cannon Books, Cheshire 71
Marine and Cannon Books, Cheshire 69
MilitaryHistoryBooks.com, Kent.................... 138
R. & A. Books, E Sussex............................. 102
Read (C.&J.), Gorleston Books, Norfolk 188
Richard Thornton Books, London N 160
Stella Books, Monmouthshire 288
Symes Books (Naomi), Cheshire 72
Uncle Phil's Books, West Midlands 240

SPECIALITY INDEX

Wheen O'Books, Scottish Borders 269
Wiend Books, Lancashire 144

- ZULU

Aardvark Books, Wiltshire 254
Bookworm, Lothian 277
Caliver Books, Essex 110
Chalmers Hallam (E.), Hants 125
Chelifer Books, Cumbria 81
Dolphin Books, Suffolk 226
Marine & Cannon Books, Cheshire 71
Marine and Cannon Books, Cheshire 69
Meekins Books (Paul), Warwickshire.............. 238
MilitaryHistoryBooks.com, Kent................... 138
R. & A. Books, E Sussex............................. 102
Thin Read Line, Merseyside 185
Wadard Books, Kent 138

WARGAMES

Bardsley's Books, Suffolk............................ 226
Barnes (Peter), Wiltshire 253
Bookworm (The), Lothian 277
Caliver Books, Essex 110
Chelifer Books, Cumbria 81
Helion & Company, West Midlands 240
Meekins Books (Paul), Warwickshire.............. 238
MilitaryHistoryBooks.com, Kent................... 138

WASHING

Judith Mansfield, W Yorkshire..................... 250
Stroh (M.A.), London E 155

WATERCOLOURS

Abacus Books, Cheshire 68
Booth (Booksearch Service), (Geoff), Cheshire... 68
Bruce Holdsworth Books, E Sussex 105
Chalk (Old & Out of Print Books) (Christine M.),
West Midlands 239
Clark (Nigel A.), London SE 165
Don Kelly Books, London W 172
Fifteenth Century Bookshop (The), E Sussex 104
Joel Segal Books, Devon 86
R. & A. Books, E Sussex............................. 102
Trinity Rare Books, Co. Leitrim 266

WAYSIDE AND WOODLAND

Cornucopia Books, Lincolnshire 153
Dales & Lakes Book Centre, Cumbria............ 80

WEAPONS

Coch-y-Bonddu Books, Powys 292
Prospect Books, Conwy 285

WEIRD & WONDERFUL

Adrem Books, Herts 131
Delectus Books, London WC....................... 177
Gildas Books, Cheshire 68
Inner Bookshop (The), Oxfordshire................ 210
Joel Segal Books, Devon 86
Morris Secondhand & Antiquarian Books (Chris),
Oxfordshire 210
N1 Books, E Sussex 105
R. & A. Books, E Sussex............................. 102
Stalagluft Books, Tyne and Wear.................. 236
Star Lord Books, Gr Man 119

Trinity Rare Books, Co. Leitrim 266

WELSH INTEREST

Adrem Books, Herts 131
Bear Island Books, Cardiff 283
Books in Cardigan, Ceredigion 284
BOOKS4U, Flintshire................................ 286
Brock Books, North Yorkshire..................... 193
Browning Books, Torfaen 294
Cader Idris Books, Powys........................... 292
Carta Regis, Powys................................... 293
Castle Bookshop, Powys............................. 292
Chapter Two, London SE........................... 164
Cheshire Book Centre, Cheshire.................... 69
Coch-y-Bonddu Books, Powys 292
Cofion Books, Pembrokeshire 288
Colin Hancock, Ceredigion 284
Country Books, Derbyshire 82
Dally Books & Collectables, Powys................ 292
Doorbar (P. & D.), Gwyned 287
Dusty Books, Powys 292
Fifteenth Century Bookshop (The), E Sussex 104
Gildas Books, Cheshire 68
Great Oak Bookshop (The), Powys 292
Joel Segal Books, Devon 86
Kingshead Books, Wales 293
Lighthouse Books (The), Dorset 92
Lloyd-Davies (Sue), Carmarthenshire 284
Mollie's Loft, Swansea 294
Naughton Booksellers, Co. Dublin 265
Oopalba Books, Cheshire............................ 71
Poetry Bookshop (The), Powys.................... 291
Rhos Point Books, Conwy 285
Siop Lyfrau'r Hen Bost, Gwynedd 287
Siop y Morfa, Denbighshire 286
Stella Books, Monmouthshire 288
Stothert Old Books, Cheshire....................... 69
Willmott Bookseller (Nicholas), Cardiff........... 283

WESTERN AMERICANA

Adrem Books, Herts 131
Americanabooksuk, Cumbria....................... 77
Clifford Elmer Books Ltd., Cheshire 68
Joel Segal Books, Devon 86

WESTERNS

Adrem Books, Herts 131
Americanabooksuk, Cumbria....................... 77
Bookworm, Lothian 277
Esoteric Dreams Bookshop, Cumbria 78
firstpagebooks, Norfolk.............................. 190
Ming Books, Dumfries & Galloway 271
Williams (Bookdealer), (Richard), N Lincs 154

WHALING

Bluntisham Books, Cambridgeshire................ 63
Glacier Books, Tayside 282
Marine & Cannon Books, Cheshire 71
Marine and Cannon Books, Cheshire 69
McEwan Fine Books, Grampian.................... 273
McLaren Books, Strathclyde........................ 280
Preston Book Company, Lancashire 145
Prior (Michael), Lincolnshire 153
Stroh (M.A.), London E 155

SPECIALITY INDEX

WHISKY

Anthony Vickers Books, North Yorkshire 196
Edmund Pollinger Rare Books, London SW..... 167
Joel Segal Books, Devon 86
Lucas (Richard), London NW...................... 162
McEwan Fine Books, Grampian................... 273
R. & A. Books, E Sussex............................ 102
Roberts Wine Books (John), Bristol 59
Sleepy Elephant Books & Artefacts, Cumbria ... 80
Strathtay Antiquarian - Secondhand Books,
Tayside 282
Thorne (John), Essex................................. 109
Vickers (Anthony), North Yorkshire 196

WINDMILLS & WATERMILLS

Abacus Books, Cheshire 68
Arnold (Roy), Suffolk................................. 228
Cornucopia Books, Lincolnshire 153
Cottage Books, Leicestershire....................... 147
Country Books, Derbyshire 82
Cox (Geoff), Devon 90
Fifteenth Century Bookshop (The), E Sussex 104
Island Books, Devon.................................. 85
Joel Segal Books, Devon 86
R. & A. Books, E Sussex............................ 102
Randall (Tom), Somerset............................ 219
Reads, Dorset 95
Robert Humm & Co, Lincolnshire 154
Salway Books, Essex 112
Stroh (M.A.), London E 155
Vickers (Anthony), North Yorkshire 196
Winchester Bookshop (The), Hants................ 127

WINE - GENERAL

Apocalypse, Surrey 233
Clarke (Janet), Somerset 216
Collectable Books, London SE 165
Cornucopia Books, Lincolnshire 153
Dusty Books, Powys 292
Fifteenth Century Bookshop (The), E Sussex 104
Gresham Books, Somerset 218
Joel Segal Books, Devon 86
Lucas (Richard), London NW...................... 162
Macbuiks, North Yorkshire.......................... 194
Moorhead Books, W Yorkshire..................... 246
Pholiota Books, London WC....................... 179
R. & A. Books, E Sussex............................ 102
Roberts Wine Books (John), Bristol 59
Thorne (John), Essex................................. 109
Uncle Phil's Books, West Midlands 240

- BURGUNDY

Thorne (John), Essex................................. 109

WITCHCRAFT

Adrem Books, Herts 131
Alpha Books, London N 158
Annie's Books, S Yorks 222
Atlantis Bookshop, London WC................... 177
Bookbarrow, Cambridgeshire....................... 63
Caduceus Books, Leicestershire..................... 147
Chthonios Books, E Sussex 102
Cornucopia Books, Lincolnshire 153
Country Books, Derbyshire 82
Edmund Pollinger Rare Books, London SW..... 167

Esoteric Dreams Bookshop, Cumbria 78
Gilbert (R.A.), Bristol................................ 59
Gildas Books, Cheshire 68
Inner Bookshop (The), Oxfordshire................ 210
Joel Segal Books, Devon 86
Occultique, Northants................................ 200
Old Celtic Bookshop (The), Devon................ 88
Philip Hopper, Essex 110
R. & A. Books, E Sussex............................ 102
SETI Books, Staffordshire........................... 225
Star Lord Books, Gr Man 119
Trinity Rare Books, Co. Leitrim 266
Walker Fine Books (Steve), Dorset 92
Waxfactor, E Sussex 100
Wizard Books, Cambridgeshire..................... 67

WOMEN

Adrem Books, Herts 131
Black Cat Books, Norfolk............................ 188
Book Annex (The), Essex 109
Books & Bygones (Pam Taylor), West Midlands 241
Chesters (G & J.), Staffordshire 225
Crawtord (Elizabeth), London EC.................. 157
Dolphin Books, Suffolk............................... 226
Drury Rare Books (John), Essex................... 110
Dylans Bookstore, Swansea 294
Elaine Lonsdale Books, W Yorkshire 248
Fortune Green Books, London NW................ 161
Harvest Books, Lancashire.......................... 145
Hobgoblin Books, Hants 125
Jarndyce Antiquarian Booksellers, London WC. 178
Joel Segal Books, Devon 86
Lane Books (Shirley), Isle of Wight 135
Left on The Shelf, Cumbria......................... 79
Northern Herald Books, W Yorkshire 246
Orlando Booksellers, Lincolnshire 152
Pickering & Chatto, London W.................... 175
Polmorla Books, Cornwall 76
Price (John), London N 159
Reading Lasses, Dumfries & Galloway 271
Scorpio Books, Suffolk 226
Spurrier (Nick), Kent 138
Stevens (Joan), Cambridgeshire.................... 65
Stone, (G.& R.), Borders 268
Susan Taylor Books, W Yorkshire 248
Symes Books (Naomi), Cheshire 72
Willmott Bookseller (Nicholas), Cardiff.......... 283
Woburn Books, London N 160

WOODCUT NOVELS

Elstree Books, Herts.................................. 131
Joel Segal Books, Devon 86
R. & A. Books, E Sussex............................ 102
Roz Hulse, Conwy 286

WOODLAND CRAFTS

Abacus Books, Cheshire.............................. 68
Adrem Books, Herts 131
Cornucopia Books, Lincolnshire 153
Fifteenth Century Bookshop (The), E Sussex 104
Joel Segal Books, Devon 86

WOODWORK

Abacus Books, Cheshire.............................. 68
Adrem Books, Herts 131

SPECIALITY INDEX

Arnold (Roy), Suffolk................................. 228
Birchden Books, London E 155
Brown-Studies, Strathclyde.......................... 279
Camilla's Bookshop, E Sussex...................... 101
Cavern Books, Cheshire 70
Cheshire Book Centre, Cheshire.................... 69
Cornucopia Books, Lincolnshire 153
Fifteenth Century Bookshop (The), E Sussex 104
Joel Segal Books, Devon 86
N1 Books, E Sussex................................... 105
Phillips of Hitchin (Antiques) Ltd., Herts......... 131
Stobart Davies Limited, Carmarthenshire 284
Trinders' Fine Tools, Suffolk 227
Trinity Rare Books, Co. Leitrim 266
Upper–Room Books, Somerset...................... 218
Whittle, Bookseller (Avril), Cumbria 81

WORLD FAIRS & EXHIBITIONS

Don Kelly Books, London W 172
Weiner (Graham), London N 160

WRISTWATCHES

Delph Books, Gr Man................................ 120
R. & A. Books, E Sussex............................. 102

WRITING & WRITING EQUIPMENT

Adrem Books, Herts 131
Apocalypse, Surrey 233
Barcombe Services, Essex............................ 108
Byre Books, Dumfries & Galloway 270
Cornucopia Books, Lincolnshire 153
Joel Segal Books, Devon 86
R. & A. Books, E Sussex............................. 102

X-RAY

Bernard Dixon and Kath Adams, Middlesex 183
Phelps (Michael), W Sussex 243
Westons, Herts 133

YEARBOOKS

Adrem Books, Herts 131
Collectors Carbooks, Northants.................... 200
McGee (Terence J.), London Outer 181

YOGA

Bookbarrow, Cambridgeshire....................... 63
Combat Arts Archive, Durham 97
Dales & Lakes Book Centre, Cumbria 80
Greensleeves, Oxfordshire 207
Inner Bookshop (The), Oxfordshire................ 210
Joel Segal Books, Devon 86
Magis Books, Leicestershire......................... 149
Occultique, Northants................................ 200
Orchid Book Distributors, Co. Clare 262
Portobello Books, London W 175
R. & A. Books, E Sussex............................. 102
Till's Bookshop, Lothian 279
Trinity Rare Books, Co. Leitrim 266

YOUTH MOVEMENTS

MilitaryHistoryBooks.com, Kent................... 138
R. & A. Books, E Sussex............................. 102
Reading Lasses, Dumfries & Galloway 271

ZOOLOGY

Adrem Books, Herts 131
Alba Books, Grampian 274
Arden, Bookseller (C.), Powys...................... 289
Baldwin's Scientific Books, Essex 112
Baron - Scientific Book Sales (P.J.), Somerset ... 217
Blest (Peter), Kent 139
Demar Books (Grant), Kent......................... 141
Grayling (David A.H.), Cumbria 79
Harrington Antiquarian Bookseller (Peter),
London SW... 169
Joel Segal Books, Devon 86
Orb's Bookshop, Grampian......................... 274
Parkinsons Books, Merseyside...................... 186
Pemberley Books, Buckinghamshire 62
Peter M Daly, Hants.................................. 127
Phelps (Michael), W Sussex 243
R. & A. Books, E Sussex............................. 102
St Ann's Books, Worcestershire 255
Steven Simpson Books, Norfolk 191
Sue Lowell Natural History Books, London W . 176
Westons, Herts 133
Wildside Books, Worcestershire 255
Wyseby House Books, Berks 55

ZOOS

Adrem Books, Herts 131
Glenbower Books, Co. Dublin 265
Joel Segal Books, Devon 86
R. & A. Books, E Sussex............................. 102

BOOKSEARCH SERVICE
Index of dealers who offer a booksearch service

A. & R. Booksearch, Cornwall..................... 74
Adrem Books, Herts 131
Afar Books International, West Midlands........ 239
Ainslie Books, Strathclyde........................... 279
Albion Books, West Midlands....................... 239
Alexander's Books, Warwickshire................... 238
Alton Secondhand Books, Hants 121
Americanabooksuk, Cumbria........................ 77
Annie's Books, S Yorks 222
Antiquary Ltd., (Bar Bookstore), North Yorkshire ..
196
Anvil Books, West Midlands 240
Archer (Steve), London Outer....................... 181
Armchair Auctions, Hants 121
Arnold (Roy), Suffolk................................. 228
Askew Books (Vernon), Wiltshire................... 251
Autolycus, Shropshire 213
Ayre (Peter J.), Somerset 220
Baggins Book Bazaar Ltd., Kent.................... 140
Ballantyne-Way (Roger), Suffolk 229
Bardsley's Books, Suffolk............................. 226
Barn Books, Buckinghamshire....................... 61
Bass (Ben), Wiltshire 251
Bath Book Exchange, Somerset 216
Baxter (Steve), Surrey 234
Baxter - Books (Eddie), Somerset.................. 221
Beardsley (A.E.), Notts 205
Beaver Booksearch, Suffolk 226
Bell (Books) (Mrs. V.S.), Suffolk.................... 228
Ben-Nathan (Jack), London Outer................. 181
Bertram Rota Ltd., London WC 177
Bilski (Gill), Buckinghamshire 61
Birmingham Books, West Midlands................ 239
Black Cat Bookshop, Leicestershire 147
Black Voices, Merseyside 185
Blue Penguin (The), Glos............................. 116
Blythswood Bookshop, Highland 275
Bonython Bookshop, Cornwall...................... 76
Book Depot (The), London NW.................... 161
Book House (The), Cumbria......................... 77
Bookcase, Cumbria.................................... 78
Bookends, Hants....................................... 122
Bookline, Co. Down 261
Bookmark (Children's Books), Wiltshire.......... 253
Bookquest, Devon 84
Books Bought & Sold, Surrey 232
Books For Content..................................... 128
Books for Writers, Monmouthshire................. 287
books2books, Devon................................... 88
Bookseeker, Tayside................................... 282
Bookshelf – Aviation Books, W Sussex........... 242
Bookshop (The), Co. Donegal....................... 263
Bookshop (The), Gr Man 118
Bookshop (The), W Sussex........................... 243
Booktrace International, Devon 86
Bookworld, Shropshire................................ 214
Booth (Booksearch Service), (Geoff), Cheshire... 68
Border Books, Borders................................ 268
Bott, (Bookdealers) Ltd., (Martin), Gr Man 118

Bowland Bookfinders, Lancashire.................. 143
Broadhurst of Southport Ltd., Merseyside 186
Butts Books (Mary), Berks........................... 56
Byblos Antiquarian & Rare Book, Hants 121
Caliver Books, Essex 110
Candle Lane Books, Shropshire..................... 215
Canon Gate Books, W Sussex....................... 244
Capital Bookshop, Cardiff 283
Carningli Centre, Pembrokeshire................... 288
Carta Regis, Powys.................................... 293
Catalyst Booksearch Services, Devon.............. 87
Chandos Books, Devon............................... 85
Chapter House Books, Dorset....................... 95
Chapter Two, London SE............................. 164
Chapters Bookstore, Co. Dublin 264
Chaters Motoring Booksellers, London Outer... 182
Cheshire Book Centre, Cheshire.................... 69
Children's Bookshop (The), Powys 289
Christine's Book Cabin, Leicestershire 149
Chthonios Books, E Sussex 102
Church Green Books, Oxfordshire.................. 211
Church Street Books, Norfolk 187
Clark (M.R.), W Yorkshire 246
Clark (Nigel A.), London SE 165
Clarke Books (David), Somerset 219
Classic Crime Collections, Gr Man................ 119
Coach House Books, Worcestershire 256
Coch-y-Bonddu Books, Powys 292
Collectors Carbooks, Northants..................... 200
Colwyn Books, Conwy 285
Corfe Books, Surrey................................... 231
Coulthurst (Richard), Gr Man 120
Cousens (W.C.), Devon............................... 84
Cowley, Auto-in-Print (John), Essex.............. 108
Craobh Rua Books, Co. Armagh................... 260
Curtle Mead Books, Isle of Wight.................. 134
D Robertson (Booksellers & Booksearch Services),
Lothian 277
D'Arcy Books, Wiltshire.............................. 252
D. & M. Books, W Yorkshire....................... 250
D.C. Books, Lincolnshire............................. 151
Dales and Lakes Book Centre, Cumbria.......... 80
Debbage (John), Norfolk............................. 190
Dolphin Books, Suffolk................................ 226
Dusty Books, Powys 292
Eastern Books of London, London SW 167
Eastgate Bookshop, East Yorkshire 106
Elmbury Books, Warwickshire 238
Elstree Books, Herts................................... 131
Embleton (Paul), Essex 111
Emjay Books, Surrey.................................. 231
English (Toby), Oxfordshire......................... 211
Erian Books, London N............................... 158
Eton Antique Bookshop, Berks 57
Evans (Mark), Lincolnshire 153
Facet Books, Dorset................................... 91
Fackley Services, Notts 205
Fantastic Literature, Essex 111
Farquharson, (Hilary), Tayside..................... 281

Farringdon (J.M.), Swansea......................... 293
Ferguson (Elizabeth), Grampian 272
Find That Book, W Yorkshire 249
Fiona Edwards, Notts 204
Fireside Books, Buckinghamshire 62
Fisher Nautical, E Sussex 100
ForensicSearch, Herts................................ 132
Forest Books, Rutland................................ 212
Foster (Stephen), London NW..................... 161
Fosters Bookshop, London W 173
Four Shire Bookshops, Glos........................ 114
Foyle Books, Co. Derry 260
Freeman's Corner Shop, Norfolk 190
Freya Books & Antiques, Norfolk................. 191
Fuchsia Books, Co. Wexford 267
Fullerton's Booksearch, Norfolk 189
G. C. Books Ltd., Dumfries & Galloway......... 271
Game Advice, Oxfordshire 210
Gardener & Cook, London SW.................... 168
Gaullifmaufry Books, Herts........................ 132
Gillmark Gallery, Herts.............................. 131
Gloucester Road Bookshop, London SW 168
Glyn's Books, Shropshire........................... 213
Godmanchester Books, Cambridgeshire 66
Goldsworth Books, Surrey 235
Graham (John), Dorset 96
Grahame (Major Iain), Suffolk..................... 226
Green (Paul), Cambridgeshire 67
Greensleeves, Oxfordshire 207
Hadfield (G.K.), Cumbria 80
Halewood & Sons, Lancashire...................... 145
Harlequin Books, Bristol 59
Hawley (C.L.), N Yorks............................. 197
Helion & Company, West Midlands 240
Hencotes Books & Prints, Northumberland...... 202
Heneage Art Books (Thomas), London SW 169
Heppa (Christopher), Essex 108
Heraldry Today, Wiltshire........................... 252
Heywood Hill Limited (G.), London W 174
Hicks (Ronald C.), Cornwall 73
Hill (John S.), Devon 86
Hollingshead (Chris), London Outer 183
Holmes Books (Harry), East Yorkshire........... 107
Home Farm Books, Warwickshire................. 237
Hoovey's Books, E Sussex 102
HP Bookfinders, Central 269
Hutchison (Books) (Larry), Fife................... 271
Hylton Booksearch, Merseyside 185
Idler (The), Suffolk 228
Intech Books, Northumberland 203
J. & J. Books, Lincolnshire 151
Jean Hedger, Berks................................... 55
Jobson (N.W.), Oxfordshire......................... 208
Joel Segal Books, Devon 86
Just Books, Cornwall 76
Kalligraphia (formerly Charmouth Bounty Books),
Isle of Wight.. 134
Katnap Arts, Norfolk................................. 191
Keeble Antiques, Somerset 219
Kenny's Bookshops and Art Galleries Ltd, Co.
Galway 266
Kent (Books) (Mrs. A.), Suffolk 228
Kent T. G., Surrey 231
Kerr (Norman), Cumbria 78
Lawful Occasions, Essex............................. 108

Leapman Ltd. (G. & R.), Herts 130
Lee Rare Books (Rachel), Bristol 59
Letterbox Books, Notts.............................. 204
Little Bookshop (The), Gr Man.................... 119
Lloyd-Davies (Sue), Carmarthenshire 284
Lost Books, Northants................................ 201
Lymelight Books & Prints, Dorset................. 93
Madalyn S. Jones, W Yorkshire 247
Maggy Browne, Lincolnshire 150
Maghreb Bookshop (The), London WC.......... 178
Malvern Bookshop (The), Worcestershire 255
Marine & Cannon Books, Cheshire 71
Marine and Cannon Books, Cheshire 69
Martin (Books and Pictures), (Brian P)., Surrey. 232
Maynard & Bradley, Leicestershire 148
Meadowcroft Books, W Sussex 242
Meads Book Service (The), E Sussex.............. 104
Meekins Books (Paul), Warwickshire.............. 238
Mellon's Books, E Sussex 101
Melvin Tenner, London W.......................... 174
Merlin Books, W Sussex............................. 243
Minster Gate Bookshop, N Yorks.................. 199
MK Book Services, Cambridgeshire............... 66
Modlock (Lilian), Dorset............................ 93
Monmouth House Books, Monmouthshire 288
Moon's Bookshop (Michael), Cumbria 81
Moore (Sue), Cornwall 73
Morris Secondhand & Antiquarian Books (Chris),
Oxfordshire 210
Mr. Pickwick of Towcester, Northants............ 201
Murphy (C.J.), Norfolk.............................. 190
Newband (D.M.), Powys 293
Nineteenth Century Books, Oxfordshire 211
Occultique, Northants................................ 200
Orbis Books (London) Ltd., London W.......... 175
Over-Sands Books, Cumbria........................ 78
Oxfam Books and Music, Hants 126
Palladour Books, Hants 126
Paramor (C.D.), Suffolk 229
Park (Mike), London Outer......................... 183
Park Gallery & Bookshop (The), Northants 201
Pedlar's Pack Books, Devon 84
Peel (Valerie), Berks................................. 55
Petersfield Bookshop (The), Hants................. 124
Phelan Books, Co. Dublin 265
Phillips of Hitchin (Antiques) Ltd., Herts......... 131
Pimpernel Booksearch, London SW............... 170
Poetry Bookshop (The), Powys..................... 291
Pomes Penyeach, Staffordshire 224
Potterton Books, N Yorks 197
Price (R.D.M. & I.M.) (Books), Gr Man......... 120
Quest Books, East Yorkshire 107
Raftery Books (Michael D.), Leicestershire....... 149
Randall (Tom), Somerset............................ 219
Readers World, West Midlands 239
Rider Haggard Society (The), Tyne and Wear... 236
Roadmaster Books, Kent............................ 137
Rods Books, Devon 88
Rolling Stock Books, Gr Man....................... 120
Rosemary Pugh Books, Wiltshire 253
Roundstone Books, Lancashire..................... 144
Rowan (H. & S.J.), Dorset.......................... 91
Ruskin Books, Kent.................................. 136
S.P.C.K., Hants 127
St Mary's Books & Prints, Lincolnshire 154

BOOKSEARCH SERVICE

Saltburn Bookshop, N Yorks....................... 195
Sansovino Books, W Sussex 244
Sax Books, Suffolk 229
Scarthin Books, Derbyshire 82
Schull Books, Co. Cork 263
Scrivener's Books & Bookbinding, Derbyshire .. 82
Sea Chest Nautical Bookshop (The), Devon 88
Seeber (Liz), E Sussex................................ 102
Sen Books, Hants..................................... 127
Shacklock Books (David), Suffolk 227
Simmonds (Anthony J.), London SE.............. 166
Simply Read Books, E Sussex 101
Sims (Sue), Dorset 91
Skelton (Tony), Kent................................. 141
Skyrack Books, W Yorkshire....................... 248
Solaris Books, East Yorkshire 106
Sparrow Books, W Yorkshire 246
Spelman (Ken), N Yorks............................ 199
Spenceley Books (David), W Yorkshire.......... 249
Spooner & Co, Somerset 220
Spurrier (Nick), Kent 138
Stacpoole (George), Co. Limerick................. 266
Sterling Books, Somerset 221
Sturtord Books, Wiltshire 254
Symes Books (Naomi), Cheshire 72
Tarka Books, Devon.................................. 84
Temperley (David), West Midlands................ 239
Terence Kaye, London NW 162
The Sanctuary Bookshop, Dorset 94
Thorntons of Oxford Ltd., Oxfordshire 207
Tiger Books, Kent 137
Titford (John), Derbyshire 82
Tozer Railway Books (Nick), W Yorkshire 248
TP Children's Bookshop, W Yorkshire 246
Trevorrow (Edwin), Herts........................... 130
Trinity Rare Books, Co. Leitrim 266
Trotter Books (John), London N 160
Tsbbooks, London SW 170
Twiggers Booksearch, Bedfordshire 53
Undercover Books, Lincolnshire 154
Vokes (Jeremiah), Durham.......................... 97
Vokes Books Ltd., N Yorks 195
Warsash Nautical Bookshop, Hants............... 126
Watkins (R.G.), Somerset 216
Webster (D.), Strathclyde........................... 280
Wells (Mary), London SW.......................... 170
Wembdon Books, Somerset......................... 217
Wetherell (Frances), Cambridgeshire 65
Whistler's Books, London SW 170
Whitchurch Books Ltd., Cardiff.................... 283
Woolcott Books, Dorset 92
Worrallo (J. & M.A.), W Mid...................... 241
Wright Trace Books, W Mid 240
Yesterday's News, Conwy........................... 285

LARGE PRINT
Dealers who stock books in large print

Apocalypse, Surrey	233
Arden Books & Cosmographia, Warwickshire...	237
Family Favorites, E Yorkshire	106
Oxfam Books and Music, Hants	126
Peter's Bookshop, Norfolk	192

BOOK SEARCH

TRIED ABEBOOKS, ALIBRIS, BIBLIOPHILE, ET AL?

IF YOUR SEARCHES SHOW NO RESULTS
IT'S NOT THEIR FAULT

WHEN THIS HAPPENS – TRY A NEW METHOD
FOR BOOKSEARCH

Most book dealers do not have the time, or resources, to create records of all their current stock to show on Internet search engines. So although dealers may specialise in specific subjects, a substantial number of titles in those subjects will not be available to your searches.

When your search fails, Sheppard's World offers you a quick method of locating dealers who specialise in the subject of the book you seek, and provides a platform to enable you to rapidly send numerous and individual e-mail requests.

It is as easy a writing the original, then copying and pasting it. Best of all, you can chose which dealers to write to with your request.

For more information Visit Sheppard's World on

www.sheppardsworld.co.uk

Index of Advertisers

Abrams – Books, Harvey	52
Adrian Harrington	Bookmark
atlanticweb.co.uk	43
Book Collector	27
Bookdealer	31
Game Advice	208
Humber Books	150
P.B.F.A.	21, 28
Project Portmanteaux	206
The Old Town Bookshop	277
Rare Book Review	44
Rhod McEwan Golf	273
Ripping Yarns	160
Stella Books	288
Temple Bookbinders	Bookmark
Thurbans Publishing Services	30
TL Dallas (City) Ltd	35